A Textbook
on
Media Law

JOURNALISM

A Textbook
on
Media Law

Marie McGonagle
B.A. (QUB), LL.M. (NUI)

Gill & Macmillan

Gill & Macmillan Ltd
Goldenbridge
Dublin 8

with associated companies throughout the world
© Marie McGonagle 1996
0 7171 2312 X

Index compiled by Juliltta Clancy
Print origination by Typeform Repro Ltd, Dublin

Printed by ColourBooks Ltd, Dublin

A catalogue record is available for this book from the British Library.

1   3   5   4   2

Contents

Chapter 2   Media Rights

Chapter 3   The Historical Development of the Media and the Law

Chapter 4   Defamation

Chapter 5   Privacy

Chapter 6   The Principle of Open Justice: The Media and the Courts

Chapter 7   Reporting the Courts, Parliament and Local Government

Contents

Preface

This is not a traditional law book because Media Law is not a traditional law subject. It is only in recent years that it has been offered in University Law Schools in Ireland. Media Law is not confined to law schools of course; it is becoming an important component of the many established and emerging communications and journalism programmes offered at third level and postgraduate level. The fact that it is a new area of study has certain advantages. First, the approach to the subject is not constrained by any set format or long-standing wisdom in the way that Contract Law, for example, has been until recently. Second, courses in Media Law can be designed to take account of the rapid changes occurring in media technology and can examine the relevant law from both an historical and practical perspective.

At a period in our history when law has become all-pervasive in our daily lives, and information a highly-prized commodity in society, it is perhaps fitting to develop a multi- or inter-disciplinary approach to the study of a subject like Media Law. The nature of communications and journalism courses positively invites such an approach. The present text, therefore, aims to facilitate a broad, exploratory study of the subject by adopting a flexible approach to each of the topics covered. It is hoped to give students an understanding of the nature and role of the media in a modern democratic society, to introduce them to the legal framework of the various media (broadcast, print, film, video), and to invite consideration of the content, purpose, scope and impact of legal rules and restrictions on both the day-to-day operations and the development—actual and potential—of the media.

The material in this book has been tried and tested over several years on law students and applied communications students. The aim has been to keep the text itself as simple as possible, but to annotate it to an extent that will provide a starting-point for students wishing to do further research. It is hoped that the text will also be of interest to practising journalists, lawyers and teachers of a variety of media and law related subjects. While it cannot answer all the questions or address all the issues that arise in a media context, it endeavours to point out some of those that have arisen to date and, where appropriate, to indicate proposals for reform.

Reference to cases and materials is necessarily selective. In this field, very many cases are not reported in the official law reports. Some are Circuit Court decisions and there is no written judgment. Others are jury decisions in the High Court, and juries do not have to give reasons for their decision. Reliance is placed, therefore, on accounts of cases published in newspapers, particularly *The Irish Times*, to a lesser extent, the *Sunday Tribune*, *Irish Independent*, and *Irish Press*. In some chapters, for example Chapter 6 which deals with contempt of court and injunctions, numerous cases are mentioned. The purpose is to give an indication of how legal rules and principles apply in practice and the frequency with which those rules and principles are invoked against the media. It is not that the Irish media are irresponsible, quite the opposite, but rather that rules and principles devised in an earlier period of media development may not take sufficient account of the realities of modern media practice.

The subject-matter of the text is primarily the news and information aspects of the media role, since that is where the law is most developed. The entertainment aspect is touched upon where appropriate, and will, it is hoped, be given greater weight in any future edition. The concept of artistic expression, the developing law on concentration of ownership, changes in copyright law, the nature of publishing, recording, film and retransmission rights will no doubt in the future provide material for extended coverage. In the meantime, this book is offered as a first step in documenting and analysing media law as it pertains in Ireland but within an increasingly globalised context.

At the time of writing a number of important cases are in progress but not yet decided and legislation in certain key areas is in preparation. In particular, the European Court of Human Rights judgment in *Goodwin v UK*, concerning protection of journalists' sources, is eagerly awaited, as is the Irish government's promised legislation on freedom of information. Unfortunately discussion of these will have to wait till another day.

Dóibh siúd atá ag freastal ar chúrsaí faoi dhlí na meán cumarsáide trí Ghaeilge, tá liosta téarmaí ag deireadh an leabhair. Téarmaí oifigiúla dlí atá iontu, chomh maith le leagan Gaeilge de na hailt sin den Bhunreacht a bhaineann leis na meáin chumarsáide.

This book would never have been written were it not for the help and support of so many people, in particular my family, my colleagues in the Law Faculty UCG, especially Liam O'Malley, who as Dean of the Faculty facilitated my research, Tom O'Malley, Denny Driscoll and Gerard Quinn who passed on materials and information and Michael O'Neill and Donncha O'Connell who read proofs of some of the chapters. Law librarian Maeve Doyle answered all my queries, and research students Fiona Fitzpatrick and Niamh Nic Shuibhne painstakingly checked out the references for me. I am grateful also to the staff and research fellows of the Institute for Information Law, University of Amsterdam, where I carried out some of the research and to Professor Bruno de Witte of the Law Faculty, University of Limburg in Maastricht who gave me the opportunity to teach on a comparative media law course there. The National Newspapers of Ireland (NNI), Provincial Newspapers Association of Ireland, National Union of Journalists, Irish Book Publishers Association and many individual publishers, editors and journalists in the print and audio-visual media both in Ireland and abroad have been of great assistance over the years. My thanks are due to all of these but especially to Kevin Boyle, formerly professor of law at UCG, who first suggested Media Law to me as an area of research and who has been very supportive of that research ever since. My work has benefited enormously from his breadth of knowledge and international experience in promoting freedom of expression and human rights generally. Finally, Finola O'Sullivan of Gill & Macmillan and her colleague Deirdre Greenan have been very understanding and helpful throughout.

Mo bhuíochas fosta do Ghearóid O Casaide, Rannóg an Aistriúcháin, Teach Laighean as diosca ríomhaire de na téarmaí dlí a sholáthar dom.

Marie McGonagle
Law Faculty
University College Galway

December 1995

List of Abbreviations

Standard abbreviations are used in the case of mainstream law journals. Readers may not be familiar with the following:

JMLP — Journal of Media Law and Practice (Tolley Publishing, UK)

ENT LR — Entertainment Law Review (Sweet and Maxwell, UK)

C&L — Communications and the Law (US)

FCLJ — Federal Communications Law Journal

JQ — Journalism Quarterly

Harv CR-CL Rev — Harvard Civil Rights-Civil Liberties Law Review

Hastings Comm/Ent LJ — Hastings Communications and Entertainment Law Journal (US)

ITLR — Irish Times Law Reports

Table of Cases

Table of Statutes – Irish/UK

Rules of Court

Table of Statutory Instruments/International Conventions/EC Legislation

Table of Articles of the Constitution

Legal Terms in Irish
Tearmaí Dlíthilúa Gaeilge

ACCUSE, I: cúisím

ACCUSED (n.): cúisí (g. id., f.)

ACCUSED (adj.): cúisithe

ADMISSIBLE (AS EVIDENCE): inghlactha

ADMIT, I (AS EVIDENCE): glacaim

ADMIT, I (A FACT, ETC.) : géillim (do)

AFFIDAVIT: mionnscríbhinn

ALLEGATION: líomhain (g.-e, b.)

ALLEGE, I: líomhnaím

AMBIGUITY: athbhrí

AMBIGUOUS: athbhríoch

AMEND, I: leasaím

AMENDMENT: leasú

AMENDS, OFFER OF: tairiscint shásaimh

APOLOGY: apalacht (g.-a, b.)

APPEAL, I: achomharcaim

APPEAL (n.): achomharc

  GROUND OF APPEAL: foras achomhairc

  LEAVE TO APPEAL: cead achomhairc

APPELLANT: achomharcóir

APPELLATE JURISDICTION: dlínse achomhairc

APPLICANT: iarratasóir (g.-óra, f.)

APPLICATION: iarratas

  APPLICATION EX PARTE: iarratas ex parte

APPLY, I: déanaim iarratas

  APPLY FOR, I: déanaim iarratas ar

ARREST, I: gabhaim

ARREST (n.): gabháil

ATTACH, I (for contempt, etc.): astaím

ATTORNEY-GENERAL: Ard-Aighne

BARRISTER: abhcóide

BEHAVIOUR: iompar

  OF GOOD BEHAVIOUR: dea-iomprach

BILL: bille

BLASPHEMOUS: diamhaslach

BLASPHEMY: diamhasla

BREACH (n.): sárú

BREACH OF THE PEACE: briseadh síochána

BURDEN OF PROOF, THE: an dualgas cruthúnais

BYE-LAW: fodhlí

CAMERA, HEARING IN: éisteacht i gcúirt iata

CAPTION: teideal

CHARGE, I (WITH A CRIME, ETC.): cúisím

CHARGE (n.) (I.E. CRIMINAL): cúiseamh (g. -simh, f.)

  CHARGE SHEET: duilleog na gcúiseamh

CHIEF JUSTICE, THE: an Príomh Bhreitheamh

CIVIL: sibhialta

CIVIL PROCEEDINGS: imeachtaí sibhialta

CLAIM, I: éilím

CLAIM (n.): éileamh

CLAIMANT: éilitheoir

COMMENT, FAIR: imchaint dhlisteanach

COMMISSIONER, PEACE: feidhmeannach síochána

COMMIT, I (AN OFFENCE): déanaim

COMMIT, I (TO PRISON): cimím

COMMITTAL (TO PRISON): cimiú (i.e. OF A WITNESS)

COMMITTAL ORDER: ordú cimithe

COMMON GOOD, THE: an mhaitheas phoiblí

COMMON LAW: dlí coiteann

COMPENSATE, I: cúitím

COMPENSATION: cúiteamh

COMPLAIN, I: gearánaim

COMPLAINANT: gearánach

COMPLAINT: gearán

CONTEMPT OF COURT: díspeagadh
Cúirte
CONVICT, I: ciontaím
COPYRIGHT: cóipcheart
CORONER: cróinéir
CORPORATE, BODY: comhlacht
corpraithe
CORPORATION (I.E. ARTIFICIAL PERSON):
corparáid (g. -e, b.)
CORRESPONDENT: comhfhreagróir (g. -
óra, f.)
COSTS: costais
COUNSEL: abhcóide
COURT: cúirt
CENTRAL CRIMINAL COURT: an
Phríomh-Chúirt Choiriúil
CHILDREN'S COURT: an Chúirt Leanaí
CIRCUIT COURT, THE: an Chúirt
Chuarda
COURT MARTIAL: armchúirt
COURT OF CRIMINAL APPEAL, THE: an
Chúirt Achomhairc Choiriúil
COURT OF FINAL APPEAL: cúirt
achomhairc dheiridh
COURT OF FIRST INSTANCE: cúirt
chéadchéime
COURT OF JUSTICE: Cúirt
Bhreithiúnais
DISTRICT COURT, THE: an Chúirt
Dúiche
*EUROPEAN COURT OF HUMAN RIGHTS:
an Chúirt Eorpach um
Chearta an Duine
HEARING IN OPEN COURT: éisteacht i
gcúirt oscailte
HIGH COURT, THE: an Ard-Chúirt
HIGH COURT ON CIRCUIT, THE: an Ard-
Chúirt ar Cuaird
INFERIOR COURT: íoschúirt
MASTER OF THE HIGH COURT, THE:
Máistir na hArd-Chúirte
RULE OF COURT: riail Chúirte
SPECIAL CRIMINAL COURT, THE: an
Chúirt Choiriúil Speisialta
SUPERIOR COURT: uaschúirt
SUPREME COURT, THE: an Chúirt
Uachtarach

WARD OF COURT: Coimircí Cúirte
COVENANT (n.): cúnant (g. -aint, f.)
CRIME: coir
CRIMINAL (n.): coirpeach
CRIMINAL (adj.): coiriúil

DAMAGE: damáiste
DAMAGE, SPECIAL: damáiste speisialta
DAMAGES: damáistí
*AGGRAVATED DAMAGES: damáistí
forthromaithe
EXEMPLARY DAMAGES: damáistí
eiseamláireacha
MEASURE OF DAMAGES: tomhas na
ndamáistí
MITIGATION OF DAMAGES: maolú
damáistí
NOMINAL DAMAGES: miondamáistí
PUNITIVE DAMAGES: damáistí
pionósacha
DECIDE, I: breithním
DECISION: breith
DECLARATION: dearbhú
DECLARATORY ORDER: ordú dearbhaithe
Declare, I: dearbhaím
DEFAMATION: clúmhilleadh
DEFAMATORY: clúmhillteach
DEFAME, I: clúmhillim
DEFENCE: cosaint
SELF-DEFENCE: féinchosaint
DEFEND, I: cosnaím
DEFENDANT: cosantóir
DENY, I: séanaim
DISCLAIMER: séanadh
DISCLOSE, I: nochtaim
DISCOVERY (I.E. OF DOCUMENTS, ETC.):
follasú
DISCRETION, judicial: rogha
bhreithiúnach
DISCRETIONARY POWER: cumhacht
lánroghnach
DOCUMENT: doiciméad (g. -éid, f.)
DUTY: dualgas

ENACT, I: achtaím
EQUITABLE: cothromasach
EQUITY: cothromas

EVIDENCE: fianaise
  CONCLUSIVE EVIDENCE: fianaise dhochloíte
  CONFLICT OF EVIDENCE: easaontacht fhianaise
  EXPERT EVIDENCE: fianaise shaineolach
  HEARSAY EVIDENCE: fianaise chlostráchta
  I ADDUCE EVIDENCE: tugaim fianaise ar aird
  ORAL EVIDENCE: fianaise béil
EXAMINATION (I.E. OF DEBTOR, WITNESS): ceistiú
  CROSS-EXAMINATION: croscheistiú
EXAMINE, I (i.e. a debtor, witness): ceistím
  I CROSS-EXAMINE: croscheistím
EXAMINE, I (DOCUMENTS, ETC.): scrúdaím
EXAMINER (IN CHAMBERS): scrúdaitheoir
EXCEPTION: eisceacht
EXCLUSIVE RIGHT: ceart eisiatach
EXECUTION, STAY OF: bac ar fhorghníomhú
EX PARTE APPLICATION: iarratas ex parte

FACT: fíoras (*g.* -ais, *f.*)
FAIR COMMENT: imchaint dhlisteanach
FINDING (OF FACT, ETC.): cinneadh
FINE, I: fíneálaim
FINE (*n.*): fíneáil
  I INCUR A F.: téim faoi fhíneáil
FORCE, IN: i bhfeidhm

GUILT: ciontacht
GUILTY: ciontach
  I PLEAD GUILTY: pléadálaim ciontach

HEAR, I: éistim
HEARING: éisteacht
  HEARING IN CAMERA: éisteacht i gcúirt iata
  HEARING IN OPEN COURT: éisteacht i gcúirt oscailte
HEARSAY (*n.*): clostrácht
  HEARSAY EVIDENCE: fianaise chlostráchta
IMPARTIAL: neamhchlaon
IMPARTIALITY: neamhchlaontacht

IMPRISON, I: príosúnaím
IMPRISONMENT: príosúnacht
INCEST: ciorrú coil
INCITE, I: gríosaím
INCITEMENT: gríosú
INDECENT: mígheanasach
INDEMNIFY, I: slánaím
INDEMNITY: slánaíocht (*g.* -a *b.*)
  CONTRACT OF INDEMNITY: conradh slánaíochta
INFORMANT, source: faisnéiseoir
INJUNCTION: urghaire (*g. id., b.*)
  INTERIM INJUNCTION: urghaire eatramhach
  INTERLOCUTORY INJUNCTION: urghaire idirbhreitheach
  MANDATORY INJUNCTION: urghaire shainordaitheach
  PERPETUAL INJUNCTION: urghaire shuthain
INNOCENCE: neamhchiontacht
INNOCENT: neamhchiontach
INNUENDO: claontagairt
INQUEST: ionchoisne (*g. id., f.*)
INQUIRE, I: fiosraím
INQUIRY: fiosrúchán
INTERNATIONAL LAW: dlí idirnáisiúnta
INVESTIGATE, I: imscrúdaím
IRRELEVANT: neamhábhartha

JUDGE (*n.*): breitheamh
JUDGMENT: breithiúnas
  DISSENTING JUDGMENT: breithiúnas easaontach
JURISDICTION: dlínse
JUROR: giúróir (*g.* -óra, *f.*)
JURY: giúiré (*g. id., f.*)
JUSTIFICATION (I.E. OF DEFAMATORY STATEMENT): fírinniú
LAW: dlí
  COMMON LAW: dlí coiteann
  CONSTITUTIONAL LAW: dlí bunreachtúil
  INTERNATIONAL LAW: dlí idirnáisiúnta
  PRESUMPTION OF LAW: toimhde dlí
  QUESTION OF LAW: ceist dlí
LAWFUL: dleathach
LEGAL: dlíthiúil
  LEGAL ARGUMENT: argóint dhlíthiúil

LEGALITY: dlíthiúlacht
LEGISLATIVE: reachtach
LEGISLATURE: reachtas
LEGISLATURE, the: an tOireachtas
LIABILITY: dliteanas (*g.* -ais, *f.*)
LIABLE, I AM: dlitear díom
LIABLE TO BE FINED, I AM: dlitear fíneáil
a chur orm
LIBEL, I: leabhlaím
LIBEL (*n.*): leabhal (*g.* -ail, *f.*)
LICENCE: ceadúnas
LICENSE, I: ceadúnaím
LICENSEE: ceadúnaí
LIMIT, I: teorannaím
LIMIT (*n.*): teorainn
LIMITATIONS: cinnteachtaí
LIMITATIONS, STATUTE OF: Reacht na
dTréimhsí
LITIGANT: dlíthí (*g. id.*, *f.*)
LITIGATION: dlíthíocht
LITIGIOUS: dlíthíoch
LODGE, I (DOCUMENTS, ETC.): taiscim
LODGMENT (OF DOCUMENTS, ETC.):
taisceadh
*LODGMENT IN COURT: taisceadh
airgid sa chúirt
LOSS: caillteanas

MALICE: mailís
MALICIOUS: mailíseach
MISTAKE: dearmad
MITIGATE, I: maolaím
MITIGATION: maolú
IN MITIGATION OF: de mhaolú ar
MITIGATION OF DAMAGES: maolú
damáistí

NEGLIGENCE: faillí
NOTICE (*n.*): fógra

OBSCENE: graosta
ONUS OF PROOF, THE: an dualgas
cruthúnais
OPINION: tuairim
ORDER (*n.*): ordú
DECLARATORY ORDER: ordú
dearbhaithe

PENDING (*adj.*): ar feitheamh
PLAINTIFF: gearánaí

PLEA: pléadáil (*g.* -ála, *b.*)
THE ROLLED-UP PLEA: an phléadáil
chonlaithe
PLEAD, I: pléadálaim
I PLEAD GUILTY: pléadálaim ciontach
PLEADINGS: pléadálacha
PRESUMPTION: toimhde (*g.* -an, *b.*)
*PRESUMPTION OF FALSITY: toimhde
bréige
REBUTTABLE PRESUMPTION: toimhde
infhrisnéise
PRIVILEGE (*n.*): pribhléid
ABSOLUTE PRIVILEGE: pribhléid iomlán
QUALIFIED PRIVILEGE: pribhléid
shrianta
PRIVILEGED: faoi phribhléid
PROCEDURE: nós imeachta
PROCEEDINGS: imeachtaí
CIVIL PROCEEDINGS: imeachtaí
sibhialta
I BRING PROCEEDINGS: tionscnaím
imeachtaí
INSTITUTION OF PROCEEDINGS:
tionscnamh imeachtaí
PROOF: cruthúnas
PROSECUTE, I (A PERSON): ionchúisím
PROSECUTE, I (APPEAL, PROCEEDINGS, ETC.):
tugaim ar aghaidh
PROSECUTION (OF A PERSON):
ionchúiseamh (*g.* -simh, *f.*)
PUBLIC AUTHORITY: údarás poiblí
PUBLIC BODY: comhlacht poiblí
PUBLICATION: foilsiú
PUBLISH, I: foilsím
PURGE, I (*i.e.* CONTEMPT): déanaim
leorghníomh i

QUESTION (*n.*): ceist
QUESTION OF FACT: ceist fíorais
QUESTION OF LAW: ceist dlí

RATIFICATION: daingniú
RATIFY, I: daingním
RECKLESS: meargánta
RECKLESSNESS: meargántacht
RECTIFICATION: ceartú
RECTIFY, I: ceartaím
REFUSAL: diúltú

REFUSE, I: diúltaím
REGULATION: rialachán
REMEDY, I: leigheasaim
REMEDY (*n*.): leigheas
REPORT, I (I.E. A CASE): tuairiscím
REPORT (I.E. OF A CASE): tuairisc
REPUBLISH, I: athfhoilsím
REPUTATION: clú
RESPONSIBILITY: freagracht
RESPONSIBLE: freagrach
RE-TRIAL: atriail
REVIEW, I: athbhreithním
REVIEW (*n*.): athbhreithniú
  *JUDICIAL REVIEW: athbhreithniú
    breithiúnach
RIGHT (*n*.) : ceart
  *RIGHT OF REPLY: ceart freagra
  *HUMAN RIGHT: ceart daonna
  *PERFORMING RIGHTS: cearta
    taibhiúcháin
ROYALTY: ríchíos
RULE, I: rialaím
RULE (*n*.): riail
  RULE OF COURT: riail Chúirte
RULING: rialú

SCHEDULE (*n*.): sceideal (*g*. -dil, *f*.)
SCRIPT: scríbhinn
SEDITION: ceannairc (*g*. -e, *b*.)
SEDITIOUS: ceannairceach
SENTENCE, I: cuirim pianbhreith ar
SENTENCE (*n*.): pianbhreith
SETTLE, I: socraím
SETTLEMENT: socraíocht (*g*. -a, *b*.)
SLANDER, I: déanaim béadchaint (ar)
SLANDER (*n*.): béadchaint
SOLICITOR: aturnae
STATE, THE: an Stát
STATEMENT: ráiteas
STATUTE: reacht
STATUTORY: reachtúil
STAY, I (E.G. PROCEEDINGS): bacaim
STAY (*n*.) (E.G. OF PROCEEDINGS): bac
STRIKE OUT, I: scriosaim amach
SUBJECT-MATTER (I.E. OF CONTRACT):
    ábhar
SUE, I: agraím
SUMMARILY: go hachomair

SUMMARY (*adj*.): achomair
  COURT OF SUMMARY JURISDICTION: cúirt
    dlínse achomaire
  SUMMARY JURISDICTION: dlínse
    achomair
  SUMMARY OFFENCE: cion achomair

THIRD PARTY: an tríú páirtí
THREAT (*n*.): bagairt
TITLE: teideal
TRESPASS, I: foghlaim
TRESPASS (*n*.): foghail
  TRESPASS TO GOODS: foghail ar earraí
  TRESPASS TO LANDS: foghail ar
    thalamh
  TRESPASS TO THE PERSON: foghail ar
    an bpearsa
TRIAL: triail
  I SET DOWN FOR TRIAL: cuirim síos i
    gcomhair trialach
  NOTICE OF TRIAL: fógra trialach
TRIBUNAL: binse
TRY, I (I.E. A CASE): trialaim

UNDERTAKE, I (TO APPEAR, ETC.): geallaim
UNDERTAKING (*n*.) (TO APPEAR, ETC.):
    gealltanas
  I GIVE AN UNDERTAKING THAT: geallaim
    go

VERIFY, I: fíoraím
VIOLENCE: foréigean
VIOLENT: foréigneach
VULGAR ABUSE: díbliú

WITHDRAW, I: tarraingím siar
WITHDRAWAL: tarraingt siar
WITNESS (*n*.): finné
WRONG (*n*.): éagóir
WRONGFUL: éagórach
  WRONGFUL DISMISSAL: dífhostú
    éagórach
WRONGFULLY: go héagórach

[Tiomsaíodh an foclóirín seo as na
hOrduithe a rinneadh faoin Acht
Téarmaí Dlithiúla Gaeilge ach amháin
i gcás na dtéarmaí úd a bhfuil * leo.]

Bunreacht Na hÉireann

| Airteagal 40.3.1 | Ráthaíonn an Stát gan cur isteach lena dhlíthe ar chearta pearsanta aon saoránaigh, agus ráthaíonn fós na cearta sin a chosaint is a shuíomh lena dhlithe sa mhéid gur féidir é. |

40.3.2   Déanfaidh an Stát, go sonrach, lena dhlíthe, beatha agus pearsa agus dea-chlú agus maoinchearta an uile shaoránaigh a chosaint ar ionsaí éagórach chomh fada lena chumas, agus iad a shuíomh i gcás éagóra.

Airteagal 40.6.1   Ráthaíonn an Stát saoirse chun na cearta seo a leanas a oibriú ach sin a bheith faoi réir oird is moráltachta poiblí:-

i. Ceart na saoránach chun a ndeimhní is a dtuairimí a nochtadh gan bac.
Ach toisc oiliúint aigne an phobail a bheith chomh tábhachtach sin do leas an phobail, féachfaidh an Stát lena chur in áirithe nach ndéanfaidh orgain aigne an phobail, mar shampla, an raidió is an preas is an cineama, a úsáid chun an t-ord nó an mhoráltacht phoiblí nó údarás an Stáit a bhonn-bhriseadh. San am chéanna coimeádfaidh na horgain sin an saoirse is dleacht dóibh chun tuairimí a nochtadh agus orthu sin tuairimí léirmheasa ar bheartas an Rialtais.
Aon ní diamhaslach nó ceannairceach nó graosta a fhoilsiú nó a aithris is cion inphionóis é de réir dlí.

CHAPTER ONE

The Media and Media Law

To define and understand the subject matter of this textbook, three basic sets of questions are posed at the outset.

1. What are the media, their content and their role?
2. What is law and how is it implemented?
3. What is media law and how does it operate in practice?

This chapter attempts to answer these questions. Students taking communications or journalism courses involving detailed study of the sociology of the media may already be familiar with the first section of this chapter, 'What are the media?' Law students and those who have studied the basic principles of law may be familiar with the second section, 'What is law?'

What Are the Media?

The first question that arises is what is meant by 'the media'. The term itself comes from the Latin *medium* which in the singular form signifies a means, method or way of doing something. The plural form, *media*, in a modern context, signifies ways or means of *communicating*. In this text the term refers to methods or means of communicating with mass audiences and includes the various forms of mass communication in operation today:

- broadcasting media—radio, television, cable and satellite
- the press or print media—newspapers, magazines, books
- audio-visual media—film, audio cassette and video.

Historically, the first of these forms was the print media which began to take shape as early as the sixteenth century, following the invention of the printing-press. By the middle of the nineteenth century, newspapers had begun to circulate in very large numbers. Increased literacy had augmented the potential readership, while advances in technology had improved printing capacity and reduced the unit cost so that mass circulation became possible. In other words, newspapers could be produced quickly in large numbers, and the public was able to read them and could afford to buy them.

As a result, the term 'mass media' was first applied to the print media and only later to broadcasting once it could reach large audiences who were able to pay for the receiving equipment. Today the term serves two purposes: it distinguishes those media that reach the masses (mass media) from both the older interpersonal media (post, telephone) and the newer interactive media that are developing towards the end of the present century as a result of computer technology, some of which have already become a reality. Others like digital compression, are operating on pilot schemes and only awaiting trade agreements to allow them to be implemented. Artistic expression in the form of drama, painting, sculpture and, indeed, computer-aided programmes is largely outside the scope of the present work but will be touched upon where relevant.

What Is the Media's Content?

1. News and Information

The essence of the media's role is communication. Because this role has greatly expanded in modern society, the media now serve as a source of news and information, opinion, advertising and entertainment.

Traditionally the media communicated news and information. It was for this purpose that news-sheets and later newspapers were first introduced. Advertising of local and national products formed a large part of the content, for commercial reasons and also because of the paucity of news and difficulty of obtaining it. News-gathering used to be a long, slow process because of poor transport. In the days before the setting up of a national postal service, newspapers had to await the arrival of steamers carrying the mail packets by sea, and then their transfer over land by horseback or stage coach. Even when a postal service was established, newspapers could appear only when the news had been received by sea and delivered by post.

Nowadays, in contrast, modern technology has made it possible to have almost instantaneous news, not only within a particular landmass, but virtually globally. The *International Herald Tribune*, for example, is published simultaneously in cities across the world on a daily basis. Likewise, technology has made it possible for us to watch and hear events as they unfold around the world, where formerly only printed reports or still photographs would have been available some considerable time after the event. One network, CNN, broadcasts news reports and analysis on an up-to-the-minute basis around the clock.

The Gulf War was probably the starkest example of instantaneous audio-visual reporting in recent times.

However, it is not only news as it unfolds that is available to us through the media but also a whole range of information that can shape and affect our lives. We have access to information across the spectrum: information on medical and scientific research; business and commercial life; education and lifestyles; health and leisure; environment and weather; news and information on local, national, regional and global developments that impinge on our lives.

What is the value of the news and information content of the media? It can be said that it leads to a more informed public, to a greater awareness on the part of the readership or audience of the world around them and the major issues of the day. It stirs the public consciousness and allows individuals and groups to react to and have an input into matters that have an impact on their lives. In that sense it encourages and advances participatory democracy. For example, in western democracies the media serve as the main sources of news and information about the world for the vast majority of people. The broadcasting media give up-to-the-minute coverage, visual images and sound; serious newspapers give extended background information, context and detail. Both offer some degree of analysis and discussion of the major events of the day and of issues arising in a variety of political and social spheres. Both broadcasting and print media have become indispensable to today's citizen. Each has a function and they should be seen as complementary not as alternatives.

In addition to reporting events, keeping the public informed and reflecting society, the media also have a capacity to shape events and determine the issues of the day. The desirability of that function is often criticised on the grounds that the media are not a democratically elected body. That in itself would not be a problem as long as a variety of sources of information existed. Increasingly, however, the media are becoming privatised and power is concentrated in the hands of a few media moguls whose work ethic is profit rather than public spiritedness. At a time when eastern Europe is emerging from a situation of no-choice, state-run media, the western world, at national and European Union levels, is becoming increasingly concerned about the risks that privatisation and overconcentration pose to pluralism.[1]

In Australia, for example, the group owned by Rupert Murdoch, controls approximately seventy-five per cent of the print media and has extensive interests in other media at home and abroad. In Ireland, Independent Newspapers now controls or has a significant interest in nine of the fourteen national newspapers (if one includes the virtually defunct *Irish Press* titles) and at least ten of the provincials and has a stake in a number of commercial radio stations. It also lent money to the ailing Press Group (see Chapter 11). In addition it has media interests in the UK, Australia, New Zealand and South Africa.

The implications of concentration of ownership, including cross-ownership in the electronic media, are a cause for concern throughout the world. The risk to diversity in news coverage and views is one of the main reasons put forward to support the introduction of restrictions on ownership of the press. However, the mere fact of multiple ownership does not necessarily mean proprietorial influence over editorial decisions, but as long as the opportunity for influence is there the possibility cannot be ruled out.[2] Much depends on the internal structures; it is possible to ensure a plurality of views within newspapers through freedom from proprietorial influence. That is where editors and journalists have a role to play. Additionally, in a democracy media organisations themselves must be both responsible in their internal operations and accountable to their public.

2. Comment — The Expression of Views and Opinions

In the early days of newspapers and broadcasting there was little evidence of comment, analysis or criticism. The function of newspapers was regarded as that of straight reporting. In newspaper parlance reporting consisted of the five 'w's: who, what, where, when, why. Criticism was left to the pamphleteers. In time newspapers came to be prized mainly for their political content. In contrast the function of radio and television broadcasting in its early days was seen primarily as entertainment, with a cultural or educational dimension. Current affairs programming, with its emphasis on discussion and expert analysis, came much later. Opinion pieces and diary, gossip and social columns in newspapers were the result of intense competition for sales in a mass market economy earlier this century.

The essence of media comment and analysis is that it *interprets* the news and information being disseminated to the public. What is the value of such interpretation? It lies in the expression of a variety of viewpoints and possible interpretations that stimulate public discussion and debate. One may agree or disagree with a particular analysis. Such is the essence of discussion and debate in the formation of public and individual opinion.

There are perceived dangers, however, in this aspect of media content. Depending on the particular forum in which they appear, opinions may actually be dictating public sympathies or reactions rather than eliciting others and prompting discussion. Also the range of opinions expressed in the media may be very limited or one-sided and an opportunity may not exist to air others. In Ireland, there is constant tension between the so-called 'Dublin 4' mentality, reflected in many of the opinion pieces of the purportedly national media, and the more conservative and traditional views that prevail in the rest of the country. This tension may be more apparent than real. At any rate, some degree of tension and airing of differing viewpoints is healthy. It has been said that a good newspaper is a nation talking to itself. There would be a greater problem if there were no diversity in the media and therefore no forum for competing ideas and opinions. It is also unlikely that people would react and form their own opinions to the extent that they do if the media merely reported the news and did not comment or attempt to interpret that news and offer viewpoints on its implications.

The role of the newspaper and private broadcaster is somewhat different in this regard to that of the public service broadcaster. As long as a diversity of sources remains, the former can adopt a particular stance or bias; the public know to expect that and if they do not like it, they can always change to another newspaper or broadcast channel. On the other hand, public service or state broadcasting was perceived differently. When broadcasting was still a new and uncertain medium and frequencies on the electromagnetic spectrum were limited, states endeavoured to keep broadcasting as a monopoly within their control and to ensure its operation as a public service. At a time when no alternative audio or audio-visual source was available, radio and television reporting had to be objective and balanced; broadcasters were not to express their own views. Both sides of an issue had to be addressed in a programme, and programmers had to have regard for cultural and other values of the community (Broadcasting Authority Act 1960, section 18). This remains the case even with the advent of the commercial broadcasting stations (Radio and Television Act 1988, section 9).

3. Advertising

Advertising, the main economic base of the Irish media,[3] may be regarded as a form of consumer information, although the techniques used and the requirement that it be differentiated from news and information programming or reporting tend to put it into the entertainment category. The nature and impact of advertising are such that a vast array of legal regulations govern it, particularly in the broadcast and audio-visual media, which are regarded as having a greater immediacy than the print media.[4] Sponsorship, a form of indirect funding, which has become an important source of finance for programme makers, is also regulated.[5]

4. Entertainment

All media now have an entertainment role. They serve to divert people by providing material for leisure. Media entertainment is a form of communication through the arts; literary, scientific and artistic presentations, stories, drama and music all play a part. Newspaper cartoons, crosswords, bridge columns and prize games have an appeal of their own and have come to be relied on by people as part of their daily lives. The entertainment value of radio and television broadcasting, with music, quiz programmes, films and soap operas, is firmly established. The role of the law in this sphere is very limited and confined to requirements not to offend against public decency, to defame others or to offend against the State.[6]

The value of the entertainment content of the media lies in part in its role in extending the imagination. In German constitutional law, for example, the protection afforded the media extends to its entertainment function, which is regarded as relating to developments in social life.[7]

One might ask if all media content has a value. The content and sensationalist approach adopted in tabloid journalism are frequently criticised, yet people continue to buy tabloid newspapers in very large numbers. Whether they are bought for content, entertainment, curiosity or for more salacious reasons is another matter. The large amounts of damages awarded against them by juries in defamation cases are open to interpretation but it is noteworthy that the highest awards made in Ireland have been against the *Sunday News* and *Daily Mirror*. (For further discussion on defamation issues, see Chapter 4.)

What Is the Media's Role?

The importance of a free press or free media is said to lie in its function as a watchdog on government and authority. As a conduit of information, communicating news, views, ideas and analysis, the press offers a safeguard against abuse of power by ensuring accountability. It does so by keeping public opinion informed and by providing a forum for open debate. As John Stuart Mill expressed it in his essay on the liberty of the press:

The importance of free discussion . . . concerns equally every member of the community. It is of equal value to good government, because without it good government cannot exist. Once remove it, and not only are all existing abuses perpetuated, but all which, in the course of successive ages it has overthrown, revive in a moment, along with that ignorance and imbecility, against which it is the only safeguard.[8]

In a reflection equally applicable today, Francis Holt, in a treatise on the law of libel, published in Dublin in 1812, and a standard work in its time, asked:

It was from the press that originated . . . the main distinction of the ancient and modern world, public opinion . . . is it possible that a Nero or Tiberius would be suffered to live or reign?[9]

Whatever the answer may be to this question, there can be no doubt but that independent media are the first guarantor of freedom of expression. They have become the main vehicle for the dissemination and exchange of information and ideas, particularly for public discussion and debate of governmental and social policy. As Anthony Lewis, distinguished columnist of the *New York Times*, put it:

We value the freedom in part because of its liberating spirit . . . but more and more we are concerned with the social function of free speech: to assure that in a political system intended to be responsive to the public will, public opinion is informed. In a word, the purpose is accountability. Government must be accountable for what it does, and there can be no accountability in the dark.

The press and the citizen critic of government need freedom to speak not only as a negative check to prevent corruption or abuse of power. We believe affirmatively that better policy will emerge where there is a choice among possibilities. Wisdom is more likely to come from open debate.[10]

The European Court of Human Rights has repeatedly spoken of the watchdog role of the media. In a recent media case, *Jersild v Denmark*,[11] involving a broadcast interview with a group of youths known as the 'Greenjackets', who made racist remarks carried in the programme, the Court once again emphasised the important role of the media:

Not only does the press have the task of imparting such information and ideas [i.e. of public interest], the public also has a right to receive them. Were it otherwise, the press would be unable to play its vital role of 'public watchdog'. Although formulated primarily with regard to the print media, these principles doubtless apply also to the audio-visual media.[12]

Indeed the Court went further and declared that the methods of objective and balanced reporting may vary according to the particular medium and other factors, and that it is not, therefore, for the courts to substitute their own views for those of the press as to what technique of reporting should be adopted by journalists. For instance:

> News reporting based on interviews, whether edited or not, constitutes one of the most important means whereby the press is able to play its vital role of public watchdog.

These are important and real functions of the media, and the European Court of Human Rights has adopted a positive and practical attitude to them.

For media critics, however, the reality is that lofty ideals do not always triumph in practice.[13] 'How free should the press be?', ran an advertisement in *Times Mirror* in the US a few years ago, 'Is it [the press] Frankenstein's monster in disguise—a well-meaning but socially disruptive force?'[14] Whatever the answer it is true that technological capabilities and market forces in the shape of commercial pressures, the profit ethic, competition, the resultant concentration of ownership and the emergence of the press barons and media moguls have all played a part in redefining the media role. The function of the media nowadays is still communication, but it is communication that includes entertainment, not just information.[15]

Whatever the relative strengths and weaknesses in the structure and operations of the media, today can properly be dubbed a 'media or communications age'. This arises from the extent of technological development and advance, which continue to augment the range and capabilities of mass communication, as well as the technical quality, if not the content. Technological development and the resulting globalisation have brought with them the need for forward planning to cope with the new problems and situations that will arise. The movement away from independence to the interdependence of states, brought about in no small part by media technology, will involve some form of transnational regulation of the media, which in turn will involve the operation of law. The imbalance in world communications, identified by the United Nations in the 1970s has had to be addressed.[16] The concept of state sovereignty over information and the media has been overtaken by the potentialities of transnational satellite communication. The opportunity and power to regulate and control content have diminished as satellite transmissions transcend national boundaries. Technological development, therefore, offers new possibilities, and presents new challenges, but it also necessitates a reappraisal of existing structures, regulations and, consequently, laws.

What Is Law?

Law is essentially a body of rules and principles that authorise, guide, dictate, limit or prohibit behaviour in support of certain values or objectives in society. These rules come from a variety of sources, national and international. In Ireland, Bunreacht na hEireann, the Constitution of 1937, is the fundamental law of the land and other national laws must conform with it. These include statutes (also called legislation or acts of parliament, for example, the Broadcasting Acts), which are written law in fixed format passed by the legislature or law-making body of the State (in Ireland's case, the Oireachtas), and judge-made law, which comprises rules and principles devised by judges in actual court cases and subsequently relied upon and developed by other courts to meet new situations as they arise. For example, the neighbour principle formulated by Lord Atkin in the case of *Donoghue v Stevenson*[17] which held the manufacturer liable for a faulty product that caused harm to the consumer was relied on in later cases to impose liability also on suppliers, providers of services, doctors, lawyers, accountants and other professionals whose skill and advice their clients depended on, clients who suffered if that skill or advice was given negligently. The law of defamation (causing harm to a person's reputation or good name), for example, which affects the media, is made up mostly of judge-made rules derived from court cases and legislation, in particular the Defamation Act 1961.

In addition to the Constitution, legislation and judge-made law, European Community law has become an important source of law in recent decades, initially in the area of commerce but gradually expanding as the European Union developed to encompass many other areas of the relations and activities of citizens of member states. The EEC Treaty, which formed the framework of the Community, is put into effect through legislation, usually in the form of Regulations or Directives: Regulations are automatically applicable rules made in accordance with the Treaty and Directives are rules that Member States are required to introduce into their domestic law within a period of two years or so. Questions or disputes regarding the Treaty and its implementation are referred to the European Court of Justice in Luxembourg.

International human rights instruments have an impact on national laws too. For instance, Ireland has signed and ratified the European Convention on Human Rights and the United Nations Covenant on Civil and Political Rights. As a result, Ireland has obligations to protect human rights. Those rights include rights to freedom of expression, privacy and fair trial, all of which have implications for the media. (For further discussion, see Chapter 2.)

When all of these sources of law are taken into account, it is clear that the law covers the broad spectrum of everyday activities, from road traffic regulations and accidents to shopping and consumer contracts, from health and safety at work to what can or cannot be shown on television. In addition, it is an instrument to determine the structures and functioning of states and governments and to determine agreements and conflicts among nations and the rights of their citizens. Law is therefore wide ranging and difficult to define with any degree of precision. It can, however, be categorised according to its social function, sphere of application or historical origins.

Divisions of Law

1. *Common-Law and Civil-Law Traditions*

First, there are the distinct traditions or families of law, principally the common-law and civil-law systems. The common law, which is the system of developing legal rules by following judicial decisions, is native to Britain but has spread to the Commonwealth and most of the English-speaking world. Ireland, as Britain's immediate neighbour, inherited the common-law system, with the Anglo-Norman invasion of the twelfth century. Common law is variously known as 'case law' or 'judge-made law' because it emanates from judgments delivered in actual court cases.

The rules and principles formulated in the context of judgments in court cases act as precedents that judges hearing later cases rely on to reach their decision. Precedents may be binding or persuasive. The core principle(s) of a case, such as the neighbour principle in *Donoghue v Stevenson* mentioned previously, which is formulated and handed down by a higher court to a lower court in the courts system and which is relevant to the new case at hearing, is binding, whereas decisions of lower courts in the system or foreign national courts are not binding but may be of persuasive value, to be relied on by judges in subsequent court cases if helpful to them in reaching a verdict. The laws of the European Community are binding as a condition of membership. The Irish Constitution was amended to provide accordingly (Article 29.4.5). Otherwise, international treaties, sometimes called conventions or covenants, and in essence agreements between nations, are not binding as part of domestic law unless specifically declared to be binding by the Oireachtas in accordance with Article 29.6 of the Irish Constitution.

The other principal family of law is the civil-law tradition, which has its origins in the law of ancient Rome, preserved in codes (written lists of rules) and expounded in the universities of medieval Europe. This is the tradition prevalent in continental Europe today. The codes, which are updated at intervals, remain the central source of legal rules. Decisions in court cases are less important as a source. Ireland, like the countries of mainland Europe and the United States, has a written constitution, setting out the state structures (government, legislature, court system) and guarantees of the fundamental rights of the citizen.

2. Common Law and Equity

Further distinctions are made within the common-law system between common law and equity. The rules of equity, which came to supplement the common law, grew out of appeals to the fairness (i.e. 'equity') of the situation addressed to the Lord Chancellor, the official known as the keeper of the king's conscience, when the common-law courts failed to provide a remedy. In the early days of its operation, the common law was very rigid. It was based on a writ system, that is, the right to bring a case before the common-law courts depended on a person being able to obtain a writ or order issued in the name of the king, obliging the defendant to appear in court to answer the allegations against him. If the facts of the case did not fit within the terms of an existing writ, one was left without a remedy. In time, new types of writs were made available and the system began to develop and become less rigid. However, to bridge the gaps left in the common-law system, equity developed into a separate area of law with its own remedies and procedures, administered in the Court of Chancery (called after the Lord Chancellor). In the nineteenth century, in a restructuring of the court system under the Judicature Acts, equity merged with the common law but remained the source of remedies such as injunctions. (For a fuller discussion of injunctions, see Chapter 6.)

3. Public and Private Law

Areas of law that impinge on the community at large and in which the community or public has an interest are known collectively as 'public law'. These include constitutional law, the administration of government and criminal law, where the public interest lies in the detection and punishment of crime, the deterrence of criminals and the protection of the community. Private law, on the other hand, refers mainly to relations, agreements and disputes between individuals in which the state or community has no interest beyond that of the individual.

4. Civil and Criminal Law

The word 'civil' is also used to describe private law, in particular to differentiate between civil and criminal law, and the different court procedures that apply. Civil law encompasses torts (civil wrongs between individuals) such as trespass, negligence and, of particular interest in media terms, defamation. Criminal law involves the commission of offences, which are provided for in statute law or common law, which also set out penalties. The main remedy for breach of the civil law is compensation or damages (which are synonymous), while fines and imprisonment are the main sanctions imposed by the criminal law. A journalist found to be in contempt of court for publishing material deemed prejudicial to a court case might be subjected to a fine. Refusal to reveal sources or breach of the Official Secrets Act or Offences against the State Act might result in a fine or imprisonment.

How Is the Law Implemented?

1. The Courts System

In Ireland there is a hierarchical courts system. At the bottom is the District Court, presided over by a single judge, no jury, which deals with minor cases, both civil and criminal. The District Court can award compensation up to a maximum of £5,000 in civil cases and impose fines of up to £1,000 along with, or instead of, prison sentences of up to one year in criminal cases. Appeals from decisions of the District Court in minor matters lie to the Circuit Court. More serious cases can begin in the Circuit Court, which also hears both civil and criminal cases. In civil cases heard in the Circuit Court there is no jury, but in criminal cases a jury of twelve people drawn at random from the electoral register can bring in a verdict of guilty or not guilty on a majority 11 to 1 or 10 to 2 basis. When the Circuit Court is hearing criminal cases, it is known as the Circuit Criminal Court. In civil cases the Circuit Court can award compensation up to £30,000, while in criminal cases, the upper limit for fines and imprisonment is usually laid down in statute by the Oireachtas. Appeals from decisions of the Circuit Court lie to the High Court.

The most serious cases, both civil and criminal, can go directly to the High Court. In civil cases there is no jury, except in a few tort cases such as defamation, and there is no limit on the amount of compensation that can be awarded. Juries were removed from personal injuries cases by the Courts Act 1988 as a result of intense lobbying by the insurance industry. They were retained in defamation cases in the belief that twelve ordinary people from the real world are better equipped to determine whether words are defamatory than is a single judge. Where there is a jury in civil cases, its function is to answer questions of fact, while questions of law fall to the judge. When engaged in hearing criminal cases, the High Court is known as the Central Criminal Court and a jury is present. The function of a jury in a criminal case is to decide innocence or guilt on the basis of the evidence presented in court. It is the function of the judge to sentence the guilty. Appeals from the decision of the High Court in civil cases are taken directly to the Supreme Court. In criminal cases appeals at present lie to the Court of Criminal Appeal and sometimes also to the Supreme Court if there is a particularly important point of law at issue.

The Supreme Court is the highest court in the land and the court of final appeal. It has power to affirm, vary or reverse decisions of the lower courts and can vary the amount of compensation payable.

Challenges to statute law or administrative decisions on constitutional grounds are brought in the High Court and, if necessary, to the Supreme Court on appeal. These courts have the power to strike down legislation as unconstitutional. When they do so they create a void that they cannot fill. The courts cannot substitute their own wording for the wording they have found to be unconstitutional. This is because of the doctrine of separation of powers stated in the Constitution. Under that doctrine, power is divided among the three branches of government—the legislature, executive and judiciary—so as to prevent any of them having excessive power.

The High Court also has the power of judicial review, that is, the power to examine and, if necessary, vary or quash decisions of administrative officers, bodies and tribunals. Orders of certiorari (to quash a decision), mandamus (ordering a lower body to carry out some obligation it has failed to fulfil), prohibition (ordering it not to do something) and habeas corpus (an order to produce a person being held in detention so that the court can ascertain whether his/her detention is lawful) can be issued. These orders can be directed at government ministers or local authorities with statutory powers or tribunals, such as employment or planning tribunals, which have a judicial, quasi-judicial or administrative function. A decision of RTÉ, the IRTC or the Broadcasting Complaints Commission, for example, could be judicially reviewed.[18]

2. Procedure

In civil cases, which involve individuals, the 'plaintiff' is the person who sues, that is who brings the court action. The person against whom the action is brought is called the 'defendant'. The plaintiff carries the burden of proving his/her case on the balance of probabilities, i.e. that it is more probable than not that the defendant was at fault or committed the wrong of which the plaintiff complained. The usual remedy sought is compensation, but injunctions can also be useful in many situations.

In criminal cases, the person charged with a criminal offence is prosecuted in the name of the people by the State's Director of Public Prosecutions. The prosecution carries the onus of proving the accused person guilty. Because a guilty verdict results in punishment, which in some cases involves deprivation of liberty, the burden of proof is higher in criminal cases than in civil, where the penalty is only payment of money as compensation for the harm done. In criminal cases, guilt must be proven beyond all reasonable doubt.

What Is Media Law?

Where does media law fit into this overall picture? Media law is not a distinct division of law in the sense that the law of contract or torts is. It derives in part from all of the sources listed above: Constitution, statute, judicial decisions, European Community law and international conventions and covenants. It does not belong exclusively to the realm of either public law or private law. Instead it comprises elements of both. Similarly, some aspects are dealt with by the criminal law and others by the civil law. In short, media law is that myriad of laws that relate to the media and affect media activities.

1. The Constitution

The Constitution guarantees media rights and freedoms (Article 40.6.1) but indicates that they are not absolute and therefore authorises their restriction in support of other rights. Thus, the right of the media to convey information and ideas can be restricted in the interests of the good name of the individual (Article 40.3.2), the proper administration of justice (Article 34), public order and morality (Article 40.6.1.i), the authority of the state (Article 40.6.1.i) and so on. There are other rights that are protected by the Constitution but not spelled out in it. These are known as 'unspecified rights' and are left to the courts to articulate. The source of unspecified rights in the Constitution is Article 40.3.2. There it is stated that the state shall protect and vindicate 'in particular' the life, person, good name, and property rights of every citizen. Use of the words 'in particular' signals that other rights are protected in addition to those actually listed. Among the unspecified rights recognised by the courts to date as entitled to constitutional protection are the right to a passport, to travel, to earn a living and to marital privacy.

2. Statute Law

The Constitution impinges on all areas of law. Statute law, passed in conformity with the Constitution, provides the framework for broadcasting, the setting up of the RTÉ Authority and Independent Radio and Television Commission (IRTC), for example, and the Broadcasting Complaints Commission. Statute law sets out the roles and procedures to be adopted by these bodies and the regulations and guiding principles for broadcasting. Other statutes like the Official Secrets Act 1963 and Offences against the State Acts 1939–72 are not aimed directly at the media but can affect media operations, for example, by leading to the prosecution of journalists for the publication of information or broadcast of material thought injurious to state security.

3. Judge-Made Laws

Judges interpret the Constitution and legislation. It is judges in court cases who determine ultimately the scope of the constitutional guarantees and the application of statutory provisions. When the telephones of two journalists were tapped by order of the Minister for

Justice, the journalists took a High Court case to determine that the Constitution protected the right to privacy and that their right to privacy in their telephone conversations had been infringed.[19] When Sinn Féin was refused airtime to make a party political broadcast before the general election of 1982 it brought a High Court case alleging that Section 31 of the Broadcasting Authority Act 1960 as amended by the Broadcasting Authority (Amendment) Act of 1976 was unconstitutional.[20] The Supreme Court on appeal held that the section was constitutional.

Judge-made law is an important source of media law, particularly in those areas that are not governed by statute. For instance, the law on contempt of court is wholly judge made; there is no contempt of court legislation in Ireland. Defamation is also largely the result of judicial decisions down through the centuries, although there is also an act, the Defamation Act 1961, which incorporates and modifies slightly some of the common-law or judge-made rules.

4. European Community Law

European Community law impinges on the business activities of the media, and European competition rules apply to media organisations as to other industries. Article 86 of the EEC Treaty prohibits the abuse of a dominant position and applied in the Magill TV listings case (discussed in Chapter 11). National governments and broadcasting organisations may not restrict the access of actual or potential competitors to the market such as in the Flemish television case 1991 and the EBU Eurosport case, 1991 (also discussed in Chapter 11).

Specifically, the EC Directive on Transfrontier Broadcasting 1989 regards broadcasting as a service within the meaning of the EEC Treaty and lays down minimum rules to guarantee freedom of transmission and reception in broadcasting between Member States. The Directive applies only to television but includes transmission by wire, over the air or by satellite, in unencoded or encoded form (Article 1). A majority proportion of transmission time is to be devoted to European works (Article 4); advertising and sponsorship are regulated (Articles 10–18); Member States are to take appropriate measures to ensure that minors are protected from programmes that might seriously impair their physical, mental or moral development; incitement to hatred is specifically prohibited; a right of reply must be provided by all broadcasters in Member States.[21] In accordance with the Directive, provision for a right of reply was made in the Irish Broadcasting Act

1990. Problems concerning the application of the provisions of the Directive, and EC law generally, are dealt with by the European Court of Justice.

5. International Conventions and Covenants

Unlike many of the continental European states, Ireland has not incorporated the European Convention on Human Rights into the national law. The Convention, therefore, retains the status of guiding principle that our courts ought to follow but are not obliged to unless the European Court of Human Rights in Strasbourg decides in a given case that a particular aspect or provision of Irish law is in breach of the Convention. In the *Norris* case,[22] for instance, the court found that the criminalisation of homosexual activities between consenting adults in private was a breach of Article 8 of the Convention, which guarantees respect for private and family life, home and correspondence. The Oireachtas was then obliged to bring in amending legislation to give effect to the Court's decision. In *Open Door Counselling v Ireland*,[23] the European Court of Human Rights found that a ban on the provision of abortion information was in breach of the Convention and Ireland was obliged to give effect to that decision. Indeed, it was a decision of that Court also in a case brought by the Sunday Times newspaper that led to the passing of the Contempt of Court Act 1981 in Britain.[24] Other decisions of the Court have had major implications for the development of media law and will be discussed in the chapters that follow.

How Does Media Law Operate in Practice?

Media law is implemented through the courts system, in either the civil or criminal courts, depending on the particular subject matter and type of case. Defamation cases are an exception to the general rule that minor cases are heard in the District Court. The option for the defamation plaintiff is to have his/her case heard by a judge sitting alone in the Circuit Court with power to award up to £30,000 damages or to go for a High Court hearing in which a jury is entrusted to assess damages with no upper limit imposed. One of the relevant factors is, of course, legal costs, which are much higher in the High Court. Also the time factor is a consideration. Circuit Court cases take on average one year to come to trial, whereas High Court cases take on average three years (see Chapter 4).

The common-law system administered by judges in court cases has traditionally been plaintiff orientated. Individual rights, including that to good name, have tended to take precedence over press or media rights to freedom of expression. That tendency may well be reflected in the fact that of every one hundred defamation cases, eighty are settled out of court, often with some level of compensation, and, of the remaining twenty that go to court, the media win only four or five (see Chapter 4). Similarly, the courts are very protective of themselves and of their important function of administering justice on behalf of the public. As a result, inaccuracies in media reports of court cases lead to journalists and editors being summoned to court on a regular basis to show cause why they should not be held in contempt of court (see Chapter 6).

Legal rules and their implementation seek to achieve a balance between important competing rights: media rights on the one hand and those of individuals or the public at large on the other. However, it must be understood that the media perform a very valuable role on behalf of the public—they are the eyes and ears of the public and are therefore an essential component of a modern democratic society, as repeatedly underscored by the European Court of Human Rights. The technological capabilities of the media and the centrality of their role make them a very different force today than in the last century or early part of the present century when many of the legal rules were drawn up. Some legal rules devised in the formative years of the print media (e.g. defamation, contempt of court) continue to be applied with little or no modification to the markedly different modern print media and to the audio-visual and electronic media, which were not even envisaged at the time. It is possible therefore that some of those rules have been overtaken by events and become anachronistic or worse, over-restrictive of one of the most vibrant forces in modern society. On the other side of the coin, it could be argued that some of the old rules, which suited a different era, are insufficiently strict and inadequate to deal with 'Frankenstein's monster in disguise'.

Such arguments prompt the questions: What should the role of the law be? What are its objectives? In answer it is safe to assume that the role of the law should not be confined to a negative role of curtailment but should have a positive function in promoting fundamental values. A positive regulatory framework for broadcasting, for example, can ensure that a variety of opinions is aired, that minority interests are catered for and so on. If one looks at the purpose of the various laws that affect the media, one sees a number of distinct objectives, which include:

1. to provide a constitution or framework to facilitate media activity, e.g. broadcasting
2. to regulate media activities and content in order to protect other rights, e.g. a person's reputation or privacy
3. to restrict the zone and nature of activity (time and place regulation) in order to safeguard particular values, e.g. the amount of advertising can be restricted so as not to interfere with the integrity of a programme
4. to punish, e.g. for prejudicing a person's right to a fair trial and
5. to remedy grievances, e.g. where there is a breach of contract or dispute as to copyright.

It is important therefore to assess to what extent these objectives are met in practice.

The chapters that follow begin by addressing the nature and scope of media rights and then sketching in the historical development of media and law: how the media evolved and the response of law to the media. The historical dimension contextualises and helps to explain the rationale of particular legal rules that have survived into the modern media era. It is then possible to begin to assess whether that rationale is still valid today and whether the means used to achieve it are still effective or whether law reform is necessary.

Further Reading

Article 19, International Centre Against Censorship, *Press Law and Practice: A Comparative Study of Press Freedom in Euopean and Other Democracies*, London, 1993.

Byrne, Raymond, and McCutcheon, Paul, *The Irish Legal System*, Dublin: Butterworths, 1989.

Euromedia Research Group, *The Media in Western Europe*, London: Sage Publications, 1992.

Notes

1 European Union plans to introduce a directive on pluralism have been delayed because of the sensitivity of the subject (*Irish Independent*, 23 September 1994). Part of the problem for the EU was the Berlusconi media empire and the Italian legislation that allowed for the retention of the status quo (*The Irish Times*, 29 October 1994, 13 June 1995).
2 Owen M. Fiss, 'Why the State?' in Judith Lichtenberg, ed., *Democracy and the Mass Media*, Cambridge University Press, 1990.
3 RTÉ receives its income partly from advertising and partly from licence fees. Advertising was always allowed on RTÉ television, although it was prohibited in broadcasting in

some European countries until quite recently. See generally, Euromedia Research Group, *The Media in Western Europe*, London: Sage Publications, 1992; Article 19, *Information, Freedom and Censorship—World Report* 1991, London: Library Association Publishing, 1991.

4 Apart from legislation governing advertising, RTÉ and the Advertising Standards Authority for Ireland (ASAI) operate voluntary codes. Along with similar bodies in other countries, the ASAI is involved in voluntary regulation on a European-wide basis (see annual reports of ASAI). In the US, it is estimated that sixty per cent of total newspaper content is taken up by advertising. Newspapers there are as dependent on advertising as are television stations: Jeffrey B. Abrahamson, 'Four Criticisms of Press Ethics', in Lichtenberg n. 2 pp 229, 259.

5 Broadcasting Authority Act 1960, s. 20(8) and Television Broadcasting without Frontiers 1989, Article 17 89/552/EEC. See also RTÉ, 'Sponsorship' *Broadcasting Guidelines for RTÉ Personnel'* Dublin: RTÉ, 1989, at p. 109. Sponsored programmes were a feature of radio broadcasting in Ireland from an early date.

6 In the US approximately thirty-six per cent of total newspaper content is made up of sales boosters such as comics, TV listings, horoscopes, sports' results, and only four per cent is national and international news: Abrahamson, n. 4.

7 Wolfgang Hoffmann-Riem, 'Freedom of Information and New Technological Developments in the Federal Republic of Germany: A Case Law Analysis' in Antonio Cassesse and Andrew Clapham, eds., *Transfrontier Television in Europe: The Human Rights Dimension*, Baden-Baden: Nomos Verlagsgesellschaft, 1990, p. 49, at p. 58.

8 John Stuart Mill, 'Law of Libel and Liberty of the Press' in John M. Robson, ed., *Essays on Equality, Law and Education*, Toronto University Press, 1980, p. 3, at p. 34.

9 Francis Holt, *The Law of Libel*, London: Reed; Dublin: Phelan, 1812, 1st edn., pp 39–40, cited in n. 8, at p. 18.

10 Anthony Lewis, John Foster Memorial Lecture 1987, 9 *London Review of Books*, no. 21, 26 (November 1987). See also Anthony Lewis, *Make No Law*, New York: Vintage Books, 1992.

11 Series A, No. 298; (1995) 19 EHRR 1.

12 *Jersild*, at pp 25–6.

13 See the remarks about the shortcomings of the press by Watergate journalist, Carl Bernstein, *Let in the Light*, Dingle: Brandon Books, 1993, at p. 17.

14 Times Mirror, *We're Interested in What you Think*, The Times Mirror Co., Los Angeles, 1987, p. 4. See also *The People of the Press*, Times Mirror, Los Angeles, 1986.

15 See n. 7, Hoffmann-Riem.

16 The MacBride Report, *Many Voices, One World*, New York: UNESCO, 1980. 'Issues of Common Concern', p. 105 at 113ff; 'Communication Tomorrow', p. 191, at p. 195ff.

17 *Donoghue v Stevenson* [1932] AC 562.

18 For example, the decision of RTÉ and the IRTC not to allow Gerry Adams's book of short stories, *The Street*, to be advertised on radio or television was judicially reviewed in 1993. *Brandon Book Publishers Ltd v RTÉ* [1993] ILRM 806; *Brandon Book Publishers Ltd v IRTC*, unreported, High Court, 29 October 1993.

19 *Kennedy and Arnold v Ireland* [1987] IR 587, [1988] ILRM 472.

20 *State (Lynch) v Cooney* [1982] IR 337, [1983] ILRM 89. See further ch. 10.

21 In comparison see the European Convention on Transfrontier Television, Council of Europe, 1989.

22 *Norris v Ireland*, Series A, No. 142; (1991) 13 EHRR 186.

23 Series A, No. 246; (1993) 15 EHRR 244.

24 *The Sunday Times v UK*, Series A, No. 30; (1980) 2 EHRR 245.

CHAPTER TWO

Media Rights

As discussed in Chapter 1, the role of law in relation to the media is not wholly negative. The media have positive rights that are recognised and protected by law. They are essentially rights that all individuals have by reason of their humanity but certain of them become particularised to journalists, whether print, broadcast or audiovisual, because of the nature of their work and the function they perform in a democracy on behalf of the citizenry. It is the very essence of human rights that they are universal, although their implementation may be on a national, regional or global basis. In Ireland, for instance, human rights are protected nationally by the Constitution of 1937, regionally by the European Convention on Human Rights 1950 and globally by the United Nations Declaration of Human Rights 1948 and Covenants on Civil and Political Rights and Social and Economic Rights 1966.

Rights Protected by the Irish Constitution

1. Freedom of Expression

Article 40.6.1 of the Irish Constitution guarantees freedom to express opinions and convictions, subject to considerations of public order and morality: The State guarantees liberty for the exercise of the following rights, subject to public order and morality:

(i)   The right of the citizens to express freely their convictions and opinions.

The education of public opinion being, however, a matter of such grave import to the common good, the State shall endeavour to ensure that organs of public opinion, such as the radio, the press, the cinema, while preserving their rightful liberty of expression, including criticism of Government policy, shall not be used to undermine public order or morality or the authority of the State.

The publication or utterance of blasphemous, seditious, or indecent matter is an offence which shall be punishable in accordance with law.

The formulation of this Article (40.6.1.i) is problematic on a number of fronts. To begin, the right of the citizens is said to be to express 'freely' their convictions and opinions, yet how can they be entitled to express them 'freely' if the right is subject to public order and morality, as stated at the very beginning of the Article?[1] Also, if public order and morality are the only overriding interests expressly mentioned, is it intended that the expression of convictions and opinions should be unrestricted except when they endanger public order or morality? In that case, what about opinions based on erroneous information that tend to injure a person's good name or invade his/her privacy or prejudice his/her right to a fair trial, for example? As we shall see, this right to express 'freely' one's convictions and opinions is in fact subject to a number of restrictions and considerations. It is a qualified right, not an absolute right.

That said, there is a positive, though limited, right at the core of Article 40.6.1.i, which all citizens have, to express freely their thoughts, beliefs and views. It is a freedom to comment. Does it include the freedom to express facts, to impart factual information? Because beliefs and views are formed on the basis of information, is it a natural corollary of freedom of expression that freedom to impart factual information is also included in the guarantee? The German Constitutional Court has answered a similar question in the affirmative, as has Carroll J., in effect, in AG *for England and Wales v Brandon Book Publishers Ltd*.[2] However, some of the Irish courts have taken the opposite view and have looked elsewhere in the Constitution for protection for factual information. The appropriate source of protection they have identified as the unspecified right to communicate in Article 40.3.2.[3] There are therefore conflicting High Court decisions and a definitive ruling of the Supreme Court is required.[4]

Whatever its scope, the guarantee in Article 40.6.1.i is at best a tentative and qualified one.[5] The emphasis is on the limitations rather than the right itself. Freedom of the press is acknowledged, albeit in a type of parenthesis, in an instruction to the State to ensure that its own authority or public order or morality is not undermined by the press or other media. The 'rightful liberty' of the press, which includes criticism of government policy, we are told, has to be preserved, but so important is the 'education of public opinion' that the onus is on the State to ensure that the organs of public opinion are not used to undermine the important values of public order, morality and the authority of the State. In that formulation the burden is on the State not so much to safeguard the liberty of the press but rather to regulate its use in support of other specified interests. This formulation is unfortunate and does little to secure media freedoms. The result has been that the courts have not paid much attention to the guarantee of freedom of expression, particularly in the media context. Other rights have been allowed to take precedence over it. Long-standing common-law rules, such as defamation and contempt of court, have been allowed to continue to operate unabated.

There have been relatively few instances of the courts invoking Article 40.6.1.i in support of media freedom. In X *v* RTÉ[6] McCarthy J. invoked the guarantee of freedom of expression to refuse an injunction against RTÉ broadcasting a programme on the Birmingham bombings of 1974. Other examples include the High Court's refusal of an injunction to the Attorney General for England and Wales to prevent distribution of a book, *One Girl's War*, about the wartime activities of the British Secret Service, MI5.[7] In *Cullen v Toibin*[8] the Supreme Court took the view that a magazine article based on an interview with a witness in a murder case may have been in bad taste but that:

> There is, however, the matter of the freedom of the press and of communication which is guaranteed by the Constitution and which cannot be lightly curtailed. Such can only be curtailed or restricted by the courts . . . where such action is necessary for the administration of justice.

2. Right to Good Name

While several areas of restriction on freedom of expression or of the press are specified in Article 40.6.1.i, not specified is the right to good name, which is protected by Article 40.3.2 of the Constitution and operates in practice as the principal restriction on the day-to-day workings of the media:

> The State shall, in particular, by its laws protect as best it may from unjust attack and, in the case of injustice done, vindicate the . . . good name . . . of every citizen.

3. Right to Fair Trial

Not expressly mentioned either is the restriction of the media in the interests of the administration of justice, which O'Hanlon J. in *Desmond v Glackin No. 1*[9] considered came within the scope of the phrase 'public order and morality' in Article 40.6.1.i, or which otherwise is governed by Article 34.1:

> Justice shall be administered in courts established by law ... and, save in such special and limited cases as may be prescribed by law, shall be administered in public.

Those 'special and limited cases' may authorise the exclusion of the press, as representatives of the public or may restrict what they may report in relation to court cases. (For further discussion see Chapters 6 and 7.)

4. *Balancing Conflicting Rights*

Normally, when constitutionally protected rights come into conflict, attempts must be made to harmonise them. However, the restrictions specified in Article 40.6.1.i are presented in such a way as to suggest that they take precedence over the central right. The core value has thus been undermined and the restrictions have been invoked to curtail freedom of expression and media activities without due consideration as to their justification. The same has applied in relation to good name, although the Supreme Court has recently indicated in *Burke v Central Television*,[10] a case concerning information used to make a television programme about the IRA, that good name is not a trump card that must prevail over other rights. The court was faced with a choice:

> The very unusual situation with which the court is faced in this case of choosing between a plausible risk to the lives of persons asserted on the basis that the plaintiffs if given a sight of documents might inform terrorists who would injure the parties identified in the documents on the one hand and the diminution of the capacity of the plaintiffs to protect and vindicate their good names on the other . . .[11]

The Court's decision was that the right to life and bodily integrity took precedence over the rights to good name and access to documents:

> . . . [I]t is more important to preserve life . . . [I]f the right to life is under threat that is a more sacred right than the right of full and untramelled resort to the courts.[12]

One aspect of the problem is that the Irish Constitution does not provide any mechanism for reconciling competing rights. In its formulation of the rights to good name and freedom of the press, it appears to mirror the long-standing British tradition that attached great importance to good name and relegated freedom of the press to the status of a residual right, to be considered only when all other rights and interests had been accounted for and to be protected only to the extent that the law did not restrict it. If that is the case in relation to freedom of expression, can any greater solace be derived from the constitutional protection of the right to communicate?

5. The Right to Communicate

Communication is so central to our very existence and well-being as humans that it has been recognised as a basic human right. In Ireland, it has been recognised by the courts as one of the unspecified personal rights guaranteed protection by the Constitution in Article 40.3. It was first enunciated by Costello J. in AG v *Paperlink*[13] and reaffirmed by him in *Kearney v Ireland*.[14] In *Paperlink*, a case which concerned the state monopoly on postal communications under the Post Office Act 1908, Costello J. held:

> that the act of communication is the exercise of such a basic human faculty that the right to communicate must inhere in the citizen by virtue of his human personality and must be guaranteed by the Constitution . . . The exercise of the right to communicate can take many forms . . . I conclude that the very general and basic right to communicate which I am considering must be one of those personal unspecified rights of the citizen protected by Article 40.3.1.[15]

Such a right, however, is not absolute:

> But the right to communicate is obviously not an absolute one. Laws may restrict the nature of the matter communicated (for example, by prohibiting the communication of confidential information or treasonable, blasphemous, obscene or defamatory matter) and laws may also restrict the mode of communication (for example, by prohibiting communication by advertisement contrary to the planning code or by radio contrary to wireless telegraphy regulations). It follows, therefore, that it is not correct, and indeed, can be misleading, to suggest that the defendants enjoy a right to communicate 'freely'. Along with other citizens they enjoy a right to communicate.[16]

Therefore, there is a right to communicate, but it is not a right to communicate freely. The right in whatever form—freedom of expression, freedom to receive and impart information, freedom of the press—is not absolute and can legitimately be curtailed by law in order to protect other interests. The right to form and *hold* opinions and ideas is absolute,[17] but the communication of information and ideas to others is subject to consideration of other prevailing rights, such as the right to good name or fair trial.

There may be a case, however, for distinguishing between private communication and public communication.[18] Private communication occurs where people want to get things off their mind by telling them to others, confiding in them, or by seeking advice from them, and where it is not their wish to spread their opinion widely around. Such communication or expression, according to one leading commentator, requires the highest degree of protection.[19] Public communication, on the other hand, involves the desire to spread ideas or opinions, and includes professional communication by the media, advertisers and so on.

The Irish Constitution does not appear to distinguish between private and public communication as such, although it does recognise the need to protect certain communications such as reports and publications of the Oireachtas and utterances made in either House thereof in the interests of parliamentary debate (Article 15.12). The Supreme Court has also pronounced in favour of Cabinet confidentiality in the interests of internal discussions within government.[20] Cabinet decisions, however, are not protected. Private communications, such as private telephone conversations, are also protected as part of the general unspecified right to privacy in Article 40.3.2.

Rights Protected by International Human Rights Instruments

One of our concerns in the chapters that follow will be the level of recognition and protection afforded these values in the Irish Constitution and to what extent they are reflected in legal rules and practice. How strong or effective are the constitutional guarantees and to what extent have they been litigated? How do they compare with the protection provided by the international human rights instruments, the European Convention on Human Rights, the Universal Declaration on Human Rights and the United Nations Covenant on Civil and Political Rights? Is there a similar balance or system for reconciling conflicting rights in these instruments? One thing is clear from the international human rights instruments: the media have certain defined rights but they are far from absolute. They are subject to restrictions that are wide ranging but narrowly prescribed.

1. The European Convention on Human Rights

The European Convention on Human Rights, which Ireland has ratified and agreed to be bound by, affects Irish law in a number of ways. It is not part of the domestic law and therefore is not directly applicable in Irish courts in the way that European Community law is, yet it may be referred to in the Irish courts and may be relied on by judges for guiding principle. In *Desmond v Glackin No. 1*,[21] for example, which concerned contempt of court, O'Hanlon J. relied on the Convention and its application in *Sunday Times v UK*,[22] a case which challenged the granting of a court injunction to prevent the applicant newspaper publishing articles on the thalidomide drug tragedy and the quest of the victims for compensation. In this way, the Convention operates as a yardstick to measure existing protection for human rights in national laws and to determine an appropriate level of protection where national laws are undeveloped. Secondly, it operates as a kind of outer layer of protection for Irish citizens who feel aggrieved that their human rights are being infringed and who cannot obtain appropriate redress in the national courts. If they have exhausted their domestic remedies, they can take their complaint to Strasbourg, to the Commission of Human Rights, alleging a breach of the provisions of the Convention.

The article of the Convention that protects media rights is Article 10, which states:

1. Everyone has the right to freedom of expression. This right shall include freedom to hold opinions and to receive and impart information and ideas without interference by public authority and regardless of frontiers. This Article shall not prevent States from requiring the licensing of broadcasting, television or cinema enterprises.

2. The exercise of these freedoms, since it carries with it duties and responsibilities, may be subject to such formalities, conditions, restrictions or penalties as are prescribed by law and are necessary in a democratic society, in the interests of national security, territorial integrity or public safety, for the prevention of disorder or crime, for the protection of health or morals, for the protection of the reputation or rights of others, for preventing the disclosure of information received in confidence, or for maintaining the authority and impartiality of the judiciary.

The formulation of the right to freedom of expression in the Convention contrasts starkly with that of the Irish Constitution. In the Convention, the right is stated boldly and positively in paragraph 1, unencumbered by any mention of restrictions, other than the power to license particular forms of media. The ambit of the right is clearly set out: it includes factual information as well as opinions and the right to receive and impart information. The reference to broadcasting, television and cinema makes it evident that the media are contemplated as coming within the scope of the guarantee and can rely on it for protection, as has been borne out by the case-law of the Court of Human Rights, which applies the Convention.

Not all cases involving the media have been decided in their favour. Much depends on the subject matter of the complaint and the circumstances of the interference. In relation to moral issues, for example, the Commission and Court appear to accord states a wider margin of appreciation and are less likely to interfere with their decisions. Several cases illustrating the point will be discussed in later chapters.[23] The same has been true of restrictions invoked in support of state security. The European Court has tended to take the view that states themselves are in the best position to decide the degree of protection they require. *Purcell v Ireland*,[24] concerning section 31 of the Broadcasting Act, was declared inadmissible by the Commission on that basis and so did not go forward to the Court for decision. However, in *Spycatcher* (*The Observer and Guardian v* UK),[25] the Court for the first time indicated that in certain circumstances government restrictions invoking state security could fall foul of the necessity test in Article 10. *Spycatcher* therefore breaks new ground but still indicates a minimalist approach on the part of the Court. (For further discussion see Chapter 10.)

However, the strength of the media protection can be gauged from cases such as *Handyside v* UK, where the Court acknowledged that the national legislatures and courts are the first arbiter and enjoy a margin of appreciation as regards both the framing of the national law and its implementation but went on to emphasise its own supervisory role:

> The Court's supervisory functions oblige it to pay the utmost attention to the principles characterising a 'democratic society'. Freedom of expression constitutes one of the essential foundations of such a society, one of the basic conditions for its progress and for the development of every man. Subject to Article 10.2 it is applicable not only to 'information' or 'ideas' that are favourably received or regarded as inoffensive or as a matter of indifference, but also to those that offend, shock or disturb the State or any sector of the population. Such are the demands of that pluralism, tolerance and broadmindedness without which there is no 'democratic society'.[26]

The direct application of this approach to the media can be seen in a line of cases from *Handyside* to *Jersild v Denmark*.[27] Further decisions on media issues are expected shortly.[28] The only Irish case involving the media that has gone to Strasbourg is *Purcell v Ireland*,[29] the case that challenged section 31, the broadcasting ban. This case was declared inadmissible by the Commission and therefore did not benefit from a Court ruling. Another Irish case involving freedom of expression in a non-media situation, namely the provision of abortion information, *Open Door Counselling v Ireland*,[30] has been decided by the Court. The injunction imposed on the applicant clinics by the Irish courts was held to amount to a breach of Article 10.

The essence of Article 10 is that freedom of expression is the rule— the key value—and limitations on it are the exception. The Court has said that in evaluating a particular restriction it is faced 'not with a choice between two conflicting principles but with a principle of freedom of expression that is subject to a number of exceptions which must be narrowly interpreted'.[31] The areas of limitation specified in paragraph 2 cover a wide range of competing interests but their application is constrained by the requirements that:

- they be prescribed by law
- they be necessary in a democratic society,
- they have a legitimate aim, i.e. in support of one of the specified interests.

It is for the Member State invoking a restriction to justify it by reference to these criteria.

Prescribed by Law

In *Sunday Times*[32] the Court interpreted the phrase 'prescribed by law' to mean that the law authorising the restriction, whether written or unwritten, needed to be sufficiently clear and accessible and the penalty reasonably foreseeable; it must be formulated with sufficient precision, the Court said, to enable the citizen to regulate his/her conduct.

Necessary in a Democratic Society

To be 'necessary' in a democratic society, a restriction or limitation on freedom of expression or of the press must correspond to a pressing social need. It is not enough that the restriction is desirable or reasonable, the necessity of the restriction must be convincingly established. By the same token, it does not have to be imperative or indispensable. In deciding if the interference is necessary, the Court will have regard to the facts· and circumstances prevailing in the particular case before it. Thus in *Handyside*,[33] the fact that the book in question was aimed at children and adolescents weighed heavily with the Court. Similarly, the fact that the book *Spycatcher* had already been published in the United States with the result that the information it contained was already in the public domain led to the Court's decision that an injunction at that stage was a breach of Article 10.[34] National security was not at risk and the right of the press and public to the information outweighed the State's interest in protecting the reputation of its security services.[35] However, in *Purcell v Ireland*, the Commission found that the Section 31 restriction on the broadcasting of interviews with spokespersons for Sinn Féin was 'necessary in a democratic society', given 'the limited scope of the restrictions imposed . . . and the overriding interests they were designed to protect'.[36]

Legitimate Aim

In addition to being prescribed by law and necessary in a democratic society, the measure to be invoked to restrict press freedom must have a legitimate aim and be proportionate to that aim. A measure will be regarded as having a legitimate aim if it is clearly invoked in support of one of those interests specified in Article 10.2. It must not be overly broad. The Court will consider whether the reasons put forward by the national authorities to justify the restriction are relevant and sufficient. In doing so, it will look at the case as a whole. In *Lingens v Austria*,[37] for example, the Court found that Austrian law, which subjected journalists to criminal penalties for defamation without the benefit of a fair comment defence, was excessively strict. The interference with the applicant's freedom of expression under Article 10 was held unanimously, therefore, to be disproportionate to the legitimate aim pursued. Whereas Article 10 protects both factual information and comment, the Court expressed its view that 'a careful distinction needs to be made between facts and value-judgments'.38 To penalise value-judgments made in good faith was liable to deter journalists from contributing to public discussion, particularly, as in *Lingens*, on political issues.

Two recurring themes in the Court's jurisprudence on media issues are the recognition of the 'pre-eminent role of the press' in a democratic society and the public's right to receive information:

> [I]t is incumbent on [the press] to impart information and ideas on political issues just as those in other areas of public interest. Not only does the press have the task of imparting such information and ideas; the public also has a right to receive them.[39]

This is particularly so in the realm of political debate:

> Freedom of the press affords the public one of the best means of discovering and forming an opinion of the ideas and attitudes of their political leaders. In particular, it gives politicians the opportunity to

reflect and comment on the preoccupations of public opinion; it thus enables everyone to participate in the free political debate which is at the very core of the concept of a democratic society.[40]

In fact, as the President of the Court, Judge Ryssdal, has observed, the Court has 'adopted clearly an activist stand in matters of public criticism of governments and politicians' but 'taken a more nuanced attitude in cases relating to contempt of court, trial by newspaper, and similar issues'.[41]

The clear distinction made by the Court between politicians and private citizens is reminiscent of the stance taken by the United States Supreme Court. In the United States the absolutist nature of the press guarantee lies in the First Amendment to the Constitution: 'Congress shall make no law . . . abridging the freedom of speech, or of the press . . . .' Based on its understanding of the intentions of the founding fathers in formalising this common-law right, the Court has distinguished between public and private persons in defamation law[42] and substantially relaxed contempt of court laws. Because there are no restrictions on the press specified in the Constitution, the courts have been able to take a bold stand in striking down state restrictions on media activities. The European Court of Human Rights is more confined as a result of the restrictions specified in Article 10.2 but nevertheless has been gradually pushing back the boundaries. It is up to the media to present cases to the Court that will allow it to continue in this vein.

2. United Nations Declaration and Covenants

The rights of the Irish media are also protected at a global level by other international human rights documents containing statements declaratory of various aspects of freedom of expression (or of the right to communicate) and setting out areas of restriction.

The United Nations Universal Declaration of Human Rights at Article 19 refers to the right of everyone to freedom of opinion and expression:

> Everyone has the right to freedom of opinion and expression; this right includes freedom to hold opinions without interference and to seek, receive and impart information and ideas through any media and regardless of frontiers.

The Declaration itself makes no reference to areas of restriction; that is left to be elaborated in the International Covenant on Civil and Political Rights at Article 19:

1.   Everyone shall have the right to hold opinions without interference.

2.   Everyone shall have the right to freedom of expression; this right
      shall include freedom to seek, receive and impart information and
      ideas of all kinds, regardless of frontiers, either orally, in writing or in
      print, in the form of art, or through any other media of his choice.

3.   The exercise of the rights provided for in paragraph 2 of this Article
      carries with it special duties and responsibilities. It may therefore be
      subject to certain restrictions, but these shall only be such as are
      provided by law and are necessary:

      (a) For respect of the rights or reputations of others;

      (b) For the protection of national security or of public order (ordre
      public), or of public health or morals.

The areas of restriction detailed in paragraph 3 appear to be less
extensive than those specified in the European Convention on Human
Rights at Article 10.2. The latter are also more specific. A further
difference between the two documents relates to the right itself. The
guarantee in the Covenant extends to seeking, receiving and imparting
information and ideas of all kinds, while the European Convention
makes no mention of 'seeking' information or 'of all kinds'. However,
the European Commission considers the seeking of information
implicit in the Article since 'the right to receive information . . .
envisages first of all access to general sources of information'.[43] The
Committee of Ministers has since included the right to seek
information in Articles 5 and 8 of its Declaration on the Freedom of
Expression and Information.[44] On the second point, the Court has
interpreted Article 10 to extend to information and ideas 'of all
kinds'.[45]

The case-law of the United Nations Human Rights Committee, which
applies the Covenant on Civil and Political Rights, is also instructive.
The decision in *Ballantyne and Davidson v Canada*,[46] for example,
suggests a much greater and decisive protection for commercial
information and advertising than has yet emerged from the European
Court of Human Rights.[47]

Ireland ratified the Covenant on Civil and Political Rights in 1989. It
was then obliged under Article 40 to submit a report to the Human
Rights Committee in 1993 on the protection of human rights in this
country. With respect to freedom of expression and the right of access
to information, the Committee noted with concern

> that the exercise of those rights is unduly restricted under present laws
> concerning censorship, blasphemy and information on abortion. The
> prohibition on interviews with certain groups outside the borders by the

broadcast media infringes upon the freedom to receive and impart information under Article 19, paragraph 2, of the Covenant.[48]

The Committee recommended that

> the State party take the necessary measures to ensure the enjoyment of the freedom of expression as set out in Article 19 of the Covenant. In this regard . . . steps should be taken to repeal strict laws on censorship and ensure judicial review of decisions taken by the Censorship on [sic] Publications Board.[49]

Since the Committee reported in 1993, the ministerial order invoking Section 31 of the Broadcasting Authority Act 1960 (as amended) has not been renewed, and freedom of information legislation is contemplated. Moreover, as the Covenant enshrines the right to 'seek' information, one can speculate that the provisions of the Tribunals of Inquiry (Evidence) (Amendment) Act 1979, under which journalist Susan O'Keeffe was prosecuted in January 1995 for refusing to disclose her sources to the Beef Tribunal, would require amendment to satisfy the requirements of the Covenant.[50]

The Covenant, therefore, while not part of the domestic law of this State, may operate at arm's length to bring about changes in national laws to the benefit of the media. The Committee in its report on Ireland further emphasised that the 'need to comply with the international obligations should be taken fully into account by the judiciary'.[51] Individual petitions are also possible under the Covenant machinery.

In summary, it is important to appreciate the fact that there is a positive guarantee of media rights in all of these documents and a commitment to those rights built into the enforcement systems. Despite the extensive range of possible restrictions, it is permissible to invoke a restriction to curtail the exercise of the rights concerned only when the restriction is prescribed by law and is necessary in a democratic society. The restriction must be in support of one of the interests listed and the means used must be proportionate to the given aim. It is not clear that the Irish Constitution has any such built-in system for prioritising and reconciling competing rights. The international documents and the jurisprudence, in particular that of the European Court of Human Rights, therefore provide a useful yardstick for assessing the legitimacy, reach and efficacy of Irish law in relation to the media and expression.

The United Nations Declaration, Covenant and European Convention all make specific reference to information, while Article 40.6.1.i of the Irish Constitution refers only to convictions and opinions. On the other hand, the Irish Constitution specifically mentions the press, albeit in parenthesis, but other international instruments do not. In their case, the media come under the general guarantee of freedom of information. Nevertheless their freedom is of central importance, as borne out by the jurisprudence of the European Court and the findings of the United Nations Human Rights Committee.

Towards a Reappraisal of Media Rights and Freedoms

On a different level, the emergence of new media and the maturing of the older, longer-established media invite a redefinition of related rights and freedoms. The original concept, apparent in the first wave of national constitutions in the nineteenth century, of freedom of expression as the freedom to speak, write and print has become too simple a formulation. The 'free communication of thoughts and ideas' of the Declaration of the Rights of Man of the French revolutionaries has taken on a new meaning in the late twentieth century. State monopolies and traditional perceptions of the media have been overtaken by technological developments, which have extended the capacity and capabilities for transmitting print, sound and visual images around the world.

New forms of media have focused attention on the fact that freedom of expression envisages not only the emission of thoughts and ideas but also the freedom to receive them and, therefore, access to the means to receive them. Access, so long limited by states on the basis of the limitations of the electromagnetic spectrum, has now been opened by advances in cable and satellite technology and precipitated by computer and digitalisation. The European Court of Human Rights has responded to the challenge. In *Groppera Radio v Switzerland*[52] in 1989, the effect of the phrase in Article 10.1 that 'this article shall not prevent States from requiring the licensing of broadcasting, television or cinema enterprises' has been declared to be mainly technical and confined to ensuring the orderly control of broadcasting. Licensing must be for technical purposes, the Court said, not content-based purposes, to which Article 10.2 applies.

A reappraisal of media rights and freedoms is underway. Media rights have come to be classified according to the nature and role of the media as institutional and instrumental freedoms;[53] old characterisations and assumptions are being questioned;[54] the relationship between the right to communicate and freedom of expression is still being explored.[55]

As Costello J. stated in *Paperlink*,[56] the right to communicate is viewed as part of, or one form of, a wider right to freedom of expression. The concept involves not only the expression of thoughts, ideas and information but also their reception. Its exercise implies the use of a means of diffusion, a medium of communication. It also implies a choice of medium and in that sense is wider than the traditional concept of freedom of the press, but capable of being realised through the element of choice inherent in the new interactive media. Communication concerns the diffusion of material, not the content or outcome.[57]

Technology and commercial pressures are conspiring to push for deregulation and a minimisation of restrictions on access to the media. As restrictions are no longer demanded by the limitations of the technology, they must henceforth be justified on the grounds of the activity itself: the extent to which it may encroach on other freedoms.[58] In the past, the focus has been on the limitations rather than the right itself, for example, the formulation in the Irish Constitution. The freedom was a negative freedom, a freedom from, rather than freedom for; a freedom from interference once all other rights had been protected as opposed to a positive freedom to carry out its functions of informing the public, subject to limitation only in a narrow context and to the minimum extent necessary, where clearly defined interests required it. A new understanding of the media role is emerging but one which takes cognisance of the entertainment function and profit ethic of the media, as well as their democratic functions:

> Media freedom is not something that belongs or is of concern only to the press; it is a public freedom in which all have an interest . . . . [There is still] a tendency to consider the media as wholly a private and commercial special interest. Undoubtedly it is the case that newspapers, publishers and broadcasters have to make profits otherwise they would fail. But there is more to the media than simply a business and it is that public function which needs to be fostered and recognised in a society concerned to strengthen democracy.[59]

The dangers of manipulation by the media and lack of diversity as a result of concentration of ownership and the profit ethic are very real. One measure to minimise the effects is to ensure that there is an educated and critical public. Technology may find its own solutions in terms of the range of media, number of broadcasting channels available, access to international and global media, for example. Positive action through law to ensure plurality of sources has proved impractical[60] and is vulnerable to challenge on rights' grounds.

However, the need for openness and accountability in the media, for codes of ethics and for avenues of redress for individual complaints is an important counterbalance.[61]

Further Reading

Article 19, The *Article* 19 *Freedom of Expression Manual, International and Comparative Law, Standards and Procedures*, London, 1993.

Barendt, Eric, *Freedom of Speech*, 2nd ed., Oxford: Clarendon Press, 1989.

Barendt, Eric, ed., *Media Law*, New York: Dartmouth Press, 1993.

Cohen, Jeremy, and Gleason, Timothy, *Social Research in Communication and Law*, London: Sage Publications, 1990.

Errera, Roger, 'The Freedom of the Press: The United States, France and Other European Countries' in Henkin and Rosenthal, eds., *Constitutionalism and Rights*, New York: Columbia Univ. Press, 1990, p.63.

Heffernan, Liz, ed. *Human Rights: A European Perspective*, Dublin: The Round Hall Press, 1994.

Keane, John, *The Media and Democracy*, Cambridge: Polity Press, 1991.

Kelly, J. M. *The Irish Constitution*, 3rd ed., Gerard Hogan and Gerry Whyte, eds., Dublin: Butterworths, 1994.

Notes

1 See Costello J. in AG *v Paperlink* [1984] ILRM 373.
2 [1986] IR 597, [1987] ILRM 135.
3 See n. 1, *per* Costello J. at pp 381–2; Keane J. in *Oblique Financial Services Ltd v The Promise Production Co. Ltd*, High Court 24 February 1993, [1994] 1 ILRM 74; but see Eoin O'Dell, 'Does Defamation Value Free Expression?' (1990) 12 DULJ 50 and Marc McDonald, 'Defamation Report—A Response to the Law Reform Commission Report' (1992) 10 ILT 270.
4 Geoghegan J., in *Goodman International v Hamilton* (No. 2), High Court, 18 February 1993, [1993] 3 IR 307; *Burke v Central Television* [1994] 2 ILRM 161.
5 'The text of Article 40.6.1 includes enough qualifications to leave in some doubt the commitment of the Constitution to full, democratic, freedom of thought and freedom of speech.' Desmond Clarke, 'Section 31 and Censorship: A Philosophical Perspective' (1994) 12 ILT 53.
6 Supreme Court, 27 March 1990 *ex tempore, The Irish Times*, 28 March 1990. See also Raymond Byrne and William Binchy, *Annual Review of Irish Law*, Dublin: The Round Hall Press, 1990, p. 534.
7 See n. 2, at p. 602; 137–8.
8 [1984] ILRM 577, *per* O'Higgins C.J. at p. 582.
9 [1993] 3 IR 1, [1992] ILRM 490.
10 [1994] 2 ILRM 161.

11 *Per* Finlay C.J. ibid., at p. 177.
12 *Per* O'Flaherty J. ibid., at p. 185.
13 *Per* Costello J. in n. 1 at pp 381–2.
14 *Per* Costello J. in *Kearney v. Ireland* [1986] IR 116, at pp 118–19.
15 *Per* Costello J. in n. 1, at p. 381
16 See n. 1 at p. 382.
17 See Article 9 ECHR re freedom of thought: '1. Everyone has the right of freedom of thought, conscience and religion; this right includes freedom to change his religion or belief, and freedom, either alone or in a community with others and in public or private, to manifest his religion or belief, in worship, teaching, practice and observance. 2. Freedom to manifest one's religion or beliefs shall be subject only to such limitations as are prescribed by law and are necessary in a democratic society in the interests of public safety, for the protection of public order, health or morals, or for the protection of the rights and freedoms of others.'
18 See Henry G. Schermers, 'Freedom of Expression' in Liz Heffernan, ed., *Human Rights: A European Perspective*, Dublin: The Round Hall Press, 1994, p. 201. One illustration of such a distinction in our law is that between slander and libel in defamation law (see Chapter 4) and also to some extent the common-law qualified privilege as a defence to a defamation action. Thus, communications between husband and wife, employer and employee or secretary are privileged. The distinction between private and public communication is apparent if, as the courts seem to suggest, the qualified privilege defence is available only to limited communication and does not extend to media communication to the world at large.
19 Ibid., at pp 203–5.
20 *AG v Hamilton* (*No.* 1) [1993] 2 IR 250, [1993] ILRM 81.
21 See n. 9 at pp 26–9.
22 Series A, No 30; [1980] 2 EHRR 245, paras 6–7.
23 See *Gay News Ltd. and Lemon v* UK (1983) 5 EHRR 123; *Choudhury v* UK, App. No. 17439/90 (both declared inadmissible by the Commission) *Handyside v* UK, Series A, No. 24; (1979) 1 EHRR 737; *Müller v Switzerland*, Series A No. 133; (1991) 13 EHRR 212; *Otto Preminger Institut v Austria* Judgment of 20 September 1994, Series A, No. 295–A; (1995) 19 EHRR 34.
24 (1991) 12 HRLJ 254.
25 (1992) 14 EHRR 153.
26 *Handyside v* UK (1979) 1 EHRR 737, at para. 49.
27 App. No. 15890/89; decision of Commission, 8 September 1992, decision of Court 24 September 1994. Series A, No. 298; (1995) 19 EHRR 1.
28 *Goodwin v* UK App. No. 17488/90, declared admissible 7 September 1993, Court heard final submissions 24 April 1995; *Tolstoy v* UK, *The Irish Times*, 1 December 1989, 14 HRLJ 377 (1993); judgment 13 July 1995.
29 See n. 24.
30 Series A, No. 246; (1993) 15 EHRR 244.
31 *Sunday Times v* UK, Series A, No. 30; (1980) 2 EHRR 245, at para. 65.
32 Ibid., at paras 47–50.
33 (1979) 1 EHRR 737, at pp 755–7.
34 See n. 25, at pp 242–3.
35 In contrast consider *Weber v Switzerland* (1990) 12 EHRR 508, a case concerning a press conference held by Mr Weber to complain about how a judge had dealt with a defamation action. The European Court of Human Rights held that the conviction of Mr Weber for disclosing confidential information was an interference with his freedom of expression under Article 10, which was not necessary because the interest in maintaining the confidentiality of a judicial investigation no longer existed at the time of the press conference when the applicant revealed the facts.
36 See n. 24, at p. 260.
37 (1986) 8 EHRR 407.
38 Ibid., at p. 420.
39 Ibid., at para. 41.

40 Castells v Spain (1992) 14 EHRR 445 at para. 43.
41 'Freedom of Expression under the European Convention on Human Rights', lecture given by Rolv Ryssdal, President of the European Court of Human Rights, at the Faculty of Law, University College Galway, 11 April 1994.
42 New York Times v Sullivan 376 US 255 (1964), and the following line of cases.
43 Eur. Comm. H.R. (1980) 17 Decisions and Reports 227. No. 8383/78.
44 Declaration of 29 April 1982.
45 See, for example, n. 26, at p. 754.
46 Comm. No. 359/1989 and McIntyre v Canada Comm. No. 385/1989, (1993) 14 HRLJ 171.
47 See Markt Intern v Germany (1990) 12 EHRR 161, where the Court accepted that Article 10 extended to commercial speech.
48 Comments of the Human Rights Committee 28 July 1993, at para. 15.
49 Ibid., at para. 21.
50 A private member's bill to amend the defamation laws and give protection for journalists' sources was introduced in February 1995. The government put a stay of nine months on it, with a view to bringing in its own proposals.
51 See n. 48, at para. 18.
52 (1990) 12 EHRR 321 at para. 61, p. 339.
53 Barendt, 'Press and Broadcasting Freedom: Does Anyone Have Any Right to Free Speech?', 44 CLP 63 (1991).
54 Geoffrey Marshall, 'Press Freedom and Free Speech Theory', in Public Law 1992, p. 40.
55 See, for example, UNESCO, Many Voices, One World; Francis Balle, Médias et Sociétés, 4th edn., Paris: Monchrestien, 1988, p. 217.
56 See n. 1, at p. 381.
57 See n. 55, F. Balle, p. 219.
58 See n. 55 above, F. Balle, p. 223.
59 Kevin Boyle, 'Freedom of Expression and Democracy' in Liz Heffernan, ed., Human Rights: A European Perspective, Dublin: The Round Hall Press, 1994, at p. 217.
60 EC attempts to bring in a Directive have been unsuccessful. See also, Thomas Gibbons, 'Freedom of the Press: Ownership and Editorial Values', in Eric Barendt, ed., Public Law 1992, p. 279; Eric Barendt, Broadcasting Law, Oxford: Clarendon Press, 1993, pp 122–4.
61 See Kevin Boyle and Marie McGonagle, Media Accountability: the Readers' Representative in Irish Newspapers, Dublin: NNI, 1995.

CHAPTER THREE

The Historical Development of the Media and the Law

The Times is one of the greatest powers in the world; in fact, I don't know anything which has more power, except perhaps the Mississippi. Abraham Lincoln[1]

The need to communicate is inherent in all civilisations. The posting of news on walls of buildings was practised by the early Romans. Paper was invented in China at the beginning of the Christian era and the first book was assembled there in the ninth century. Later, handwritten news circulated in Italy from the commercial centre of Venice in the thirteenth century, but already ecclesiastical censorship (Papal Orders) and official censorship thwarted the authors. It was not until the invention of the printing press by Gutenberg in the fifteenth century that book publishing in the western world began, with the release of the Gutenberg Bible in 1455. With the development of the postal service around the same time,[2] the news media began to emerge.

The Development of Newspapers

Initially printing was reserved for important events, but by the beginning of the seventeenth century, papers had begun to appear regularly right across Europe. The first periodical in the world to appear on a regular basis was *Die Niewe Tidjingler* (*Les Nouvelles d'Angers*) (1605), the official chronicle of the French court. A Strasbourg almanac, *Le Mercure Francais* (1611), began to be published annually but gradually developed into a monthly, then a weekly and finally a daily, which lasted until the present century. *Le Journal des Savants* (1665) paved the way for literary and scientific journalism. *Le Mercure Galant* published in Paris (1672) was the world's first literary periodical. Book form, however, remained the choice of the philosophers, and pamphlets the choice of the political commentator and critic.[3] All were subject to official censorship, in the form of authorisation, licensing or bans.[4]

The first printing-press in England was set up at Westminster by Claxton in 1476, but it was quite some time before its potential was realised. The main stumbling-block was the requirement of a government licence to print, with the result that newsletters compiled in London and sent to the provinces were usually handwritten, just as they had been in Italy.[5] It was not until the early part of the seventeenth century that the first printed newspapers began to appear in England, and it was to be another century once the licensing laws had lapsed[6] before the first daily, *The Daily Courant*, began publication in 1702. The first ever daily paper had appeared in Germany in 1660 (the *Leipziger Zeitung*), whereas in most other countries, dailies were unknown until the eighteenth century and not a significant force until the nineteenth. In the United States, for example, regular publications emerged at the end of the seventeenth century, but the first daily, the *Pennsylvania Pocket*, only began in 1784. The forerunners of the modern British newspapers, the *Daily Telegraph* and *The Times*, appeared in 1772 and 1785, respectively. The oldest Sunday paper, the *Observer*, was established in 1791.[7]

In Ireland newspaper publishing may be said to have begun in the mid-seventeenth century with the publication by the Cromwellians of Cork of *The Irish Monthly Mercury*, followed by a short-lived Dublin weekly. The demand for news was fuelled by tension and war. The Irish postal service began in 1635 and was well established by the end of the century when a real newspaper press began to emerge. Even then, however, except in times of hostilities, it consisted mainly of news brought from England, with some scant local news and advertisements. Publication depended on the arrival in Irish ports of packet boats bringing foreign letters and dispatches of news. Coffee houses and ale houses, the social meeting places of the day, played an important part in circulation, by providing newspapers as an integral part of their service for their patrons. A regular distribution system, based on the postal services, was later developed. It was well into the eighteenth century, however, before provincial papers took off and before the generic term 'newspaper' began to be used to describe the myriad of newssheets and newsletters that had developed.[8] The newspapers at that time were the products of individuals who were printer–stationers or bookseller–printers.

1. Newspaper Content

Early newspapers in England had been licensed until 1695, with the result that their factual content was rather limited; investigative journalism, criticism or comment were virtually unknown; advertisements and notices predominated. Indirect controls by way of taxes and stamp duties, imposed from 1696 on, immediately after the official licensing system was lifted, continued to be used for almost two centuries. Governments sponsored their own newspapers, while threats and inducements to others augmented the state's arsenal against the press.

Developments in Ireland tended to lag behind and mirror those in Britain. Most of the early newspapers were very dull by today's standards, badly produced, containing little apart from news copied from the London papers of the previous weeks or days, with the addition of a few local advertisements and snippets.[9] As in England, however, fear of the power of the press resulted in even greater government control:

> Hand in hand with the growth and development of the press, both in England and Ireland, was the continuous effort by those in authority to restrict and control this new and dangerous medium.[10]

At first the papers were single sheets, later expanded to four pages. They contained only a minimal amount of home news and no political reporting or comment — that was left to the pamphleteers. In this way they stayed clear of the wrath of the administration.

The early papers were essentially commercial enterprises undertaken and run by individual stationers. They were one-man operations; the editor had not yet been identified as a distinct functionary bearing legal responsibility; the journalist, if he existed, remained shielded by the printer. William Carey, who produced the *National Evening Star*, described his task in 1792:

> To preserve my interest with my old advertising friends and to obtain news I had a daily round of visitation to make through the principal street of business. To collect in money due for advertisements, I had also a number of calls out in the day. As I had neither editor nor writer, all the literary labour devolved on me. Besides essays to write I had also to run over the London, Dublin and country Irish papers, to digest the packets, to make extracts, and furnish articles of domestic intelligence and of general observation. I had also to run to the coffee houses to pick up the news of the day, to attend the theatre in the season to give an account of the performance and the parliament house to take down debate... . When I add [that] I had to correct the proofs, to write letters to country correspondents and to act as my own clerk ... it will appear my hands were pretty full.[11]

Unfortunately, his paper did not last very long, not because his task became too much for him but because of his prosecution for seditious libel (see Chapter 10).

It was only from the beginning of the eighteenth century that the first long-lived newspapers began to appear in Dublin and Belfast. They were in the English language, a factor which restricted circulation to the English-speaking Protestant population. The *Newsletter* in Belfast, for example, began publication in 1737 and continues to the present day. Early Irish newspapers were prized mainly for their advertisements, which were also the profitable part of the paper and the basis for subscription and therefore competition.

2. Political Comment

During the eighteenth century, as newspaper advertising caught the imagination of the public and became an important source of revenue, the Irish newspaper changed from a part-time effort to a highly-organised undertaking employing full-time workers.[12] Newspapers became part of the daily life of the English-speaking population and as the readership grew with the spread of literacy, so too did the scope of newspaper content, embracing literature, entertainment and educational material. The informational and educative role of the press was established and the scene was set for the introduction of political comment during the political turmoil at the end of the century:

> Political polemics and public controversy were always dangerous subjects for the press, particularly for the periodic press, while private controversy, to avoid personal implication and even the remote chance of a libel action, was relegated to the advertisement columns.[13]

No outspoken or pro-Catholic press existed until the nineteenth century.[14]

In the first half of the eighteenth century at least one hundred and sixty newspapers were published in Dublin, although most of them did not last very long.[15] There were also a few provincial papers. By the middle of the century Irish politics were hotting up and the newspapers were beginning to respond with political comment. The government did not like it and reacted by punishing for contempt of parliament. This response of government was not peculiar to Ireland. In Britain and the United States, as in some European countries, the printing-press was tightly controlled; debate and dissent were not tolerated. In the United States, as in Britain and Ireland, parliament was not even open to the public before 1766 and the publication of proceedings was prohibited. Apart from taxes and stamp duties, bribes and threats, the main weapons used against the press were contempt of parliament, contempt of court, and prosecutions for seditious or defamatory libel.

3. Strict Censorship

Until 1774 Irish newspapers had been free of stamp duties but not immune from prosecutions. If publishers published anything that might be deemed obscene, blasphemous or seditious, they would be answerable for it in a court of law or before parliament. Such laws were used to 'harass and curtail the press with what amounted to a strict censorship'.[16] The most adverse effects of such laws were the fear they engendered, the heavy fees payable and the long periods of time for which publishers could be held pending trial, with consequent disruption of their publication.[17] Newspaper offices could be searched and equipment seized and destroyed.

Press offences occupied a regular and prominent slot in parliamentary proceedings. Not only criticism but even the reporting of parliamentary proceedings or of anything relating to them was treated as a breach of privilege and prosecuted until 1772.[18] Once they came to be tolerated by the authorities, reports of parliamentary debates were to form a significant part of many Irish newspapers.

The measure of legislative independence granted to the Irish parliament in 1782 led to a new concentration on home news and politics. The greatest influence of the period, however, was the rise of the Volunteer movement, which brought about a rapid increase in the number of newspapers being published and also in their content. The same had happened with the Revolution in France and the Civil War in America, which were followed, respectively, by the Declaration of the Rights of Man and the United States Constitution, which gave new recognition and status to the press. The first press law in France was enacted in 1791 but censorship, heavy duties and subventions to the loyal press continued unabated until 1830. In Ireland, some of the papers became antagonistic towards government, even scurrilous in their attacks, as when the Volunteers' *Journal* described the House of Commons as a 'den of thieves', a 'Gomorrah of iniquity'.[19] The government retaliated with prosecutions or threats of prosecutions for seditious libel. Criticism and vehemence were equated with sedition. On the other hand, by the 1820s up to £20,000 a year was being spent on subsidies, proclamations and notices, in a measure designed to keep the press under control.[20] Papers that offered allegiance got more proclamations, those that offered criticism and opposition got little or none.

The judiciary, dependent on the administration for job security and advancement, facilitated repression. Juries could be circumvented altogether or 'packed'.[21] Sentences imposed were often harsh and out of all proportion to the offence charged. Fines of up to £500 and periods of two years' imprisonment were not unknown. Newspaper proprietors could be attached or held on informations for many months awaiting trial and other publications could not comment on the case lest they be held to be in contempt of court.[22] Some papers went under as a result, but those that survived had become livelier and more varied—the tone and character of Irish newspapers had been changed unalterably.

Nineteenth-century England saw some attempts to liberalise press laws. Pressure from newspapers themselves resulted in some limited reform of the libel laws. The Libel Acts 1843–88 and the Newspaper Libel and Registration Act 1881 provided for defences for newspapers, ranging from apologies to privilege for parliamentary and court reports. Liberalisation of German laws relating to the press began in 1874. In France, the long struggle for press freedom was finally realised with the Press Law of 1881.[23]

4. Mass Circulation Becomes a Reality

The first news agency had been established in Paris in 1832, followed by Berlin in 1849 and London (Reuters) in 1851. During that period the press began to reap the benefits of the invention of the telegraph. Improvements in transportation, particularly railways, meant that news was not so stale. As a result, sales which had averaged two to three thousand in the mid-eighteenth century now climbed so rapidly that combined sales of the Dublin dailies in 1871 was over thirteen thousand.[24] In the same year, the London *Daily Telegraph* was able to claim the highest circulation in the world: over two hundred and forty thousand copies daily.[25] Competition and low sale prices contributed to the process. In England, the popularity among working-class people of the illegal but cheaper, unstamped press led to the abandonment of stamp duties in 1855 (1870 in France), and mass circulation became a reality, beckoning the heyday of the press and the arrival of the first press barons. In Ireland, as elsewhere, technological developments and improvements in literacy brought about by the introduction of formal primary-level schooling paved the way for mass circulation in the middle of the nineteenth century.[26]

Meanwhile in Ireland, *The Nation*, first published in 1842, with Charles Gavin Duffy as editor, sold more copies than any other newspaper in

Ireland before it (selling out its initial print-run of twelve thousand) and was distributed through reading-rooms and from hand to hand and read aloud, as had been common practice in an age of low levels of literacy.[27] It was sixteen pages long and had no illustrations. It was suppressed in July 1848 but resumed in 1849.[28] *The Cork Examiner* first appeared in 1841; Belfast's *Irish News* in 1855; *The Irish Times* in 1859. Of the provincials still in operation, the oldest appears to be the *Limerick Chronicle* (1766), followed by the *Leinster Express* (1831); the *Sligo Champion* (1836); the *Herald and Western Advertiser* (1837). Elsewhere, the *London Times* had been in operation from 1785 and already become a powerful force when the *New York Times* was established in 1851. By 1866, the French *Le Figaro* had become a daily. By 1887 the *New York Herald Tribune* was producing a European edition.

It was the rapid technological advances of the twentieth century that were to bring about the greatest changes in the media landscape, with the advent of illustrated and then colour magazines, the invention of new audio-visual media and later computer, satellite and multimedia developments. However, at the turn of the century, the era of popularisation in which the British *Daily Express* and *Daily Mirror* were founded, Irish newspapers were still rather dull, with endless columns of print and not much analysis or punch. The news items of the *Daily Independent*, however, were of the titbit variety taken mostly from English papers, with headlines such as 'The King on dancing', 'Lady injured by bull', 'Madman in Church', 'Headless vicar suicide'— definitely the sort of stuff to make one part with the halfpenny cover price.[29] As the visual and content quality improved and circulations increased, the papers became important sources of all kinds of information and political comment. The demand for them and the degree to which people identified with them in their daily lives made them less amenable to control. However, the pattern of censorship and attempts at suppression continued in times of war or strife. The early twentieth century saw military censorship in the aftermath of the 1916 rising and in the Black and Tans era.

The Development of Book Publishing

The book trade in Ireland was also slow to develop. Up to the beginning of the eighteenth century there was only one printer in Dublin producing books on a regular basis, yet in the eighteenth century both the newspaper and book publishing industries flourished.[30] The reasons for the delay in making full use of the printing press are both legal and political. The King's printer had a complete monopoly over the printing and sale of books in Ireland. In other words book printing was confined by law, through the grant of a patent, to the printing of official matter: books of statutes, grammars, almanacs, proclamations, bibles and such others as the law provided 'may or ought to be exposed for sale . . . so long as the same are not contrary, repugnant or scandalous to the laws or government or state'.[31] It was an offence for anyone other than the King's printer to engage in the publishing of books, with a penalty of ten shillings per copy and rights of seizure.[32] In this way, book publishing was subject to a system of official censorship from its very inception, although it would appear that there was some degree of unauthorised printing going on. For instance, in 1618, when the Company of Stationers took over the patents, they were authorised to seize 'all Popish and prohibited books'.[33]

The Star Chamber, which was to be the author of many of the legal rules governing the print media to this day, was established in 1488 to monitor and suppress criticism of church and state. For almost two centuries until its abolition in 1641, it concerned itself with seditious and blasphemous libel, and, in order to suppress duelling, defamatory libel. Its concern was with the breach of the peace aspect of libel rather than with reputation as such.[34]

Public peace was also invoked to impose another form of prior censorship in the latter half of the seventeenth century when copy had to be submitted to the Council of State which was to vet it for anything 'tending to the prejudice of the commonwealth or the public peace and welfare'.[35] By this time regional printing had begun in Cork, Waterford, Kilkenny and other major cities, but the King's printer as licensor remained responsible to the government for preventing the publication of seditious or scandalous matter throughout Ireland.[36] The struggle to end the King's printer's monopoly continued into the final decades of the seventeenth century, but, despite some degree of success, it was a further one hundred years until 1794 when the Lord Chancellor, Viscount Fitzgibbon, asked: 'Has the validity of this patent ever been established at law?—I do not know that the Crown has a right to erect a monopoly of that kind.'[37]

The Development of Radio Broadcasting

Wireless telephones were developed rapidly for military purposes during the First World War, and a short-range broadcast during the

Easter Rising in Dublin in 1916 heralded the introduction of radio broadcasting in Ireland.[38] Radio was then immediately subjected to control through licensing, in Ireland as elsewhere, partly because of the security situation that pertained at the time but more as a matter of course, following the model of the telegraph established in 1851.[39]

The potential of radio was not really appreciated but governments ensured they kept control because of the public nature of the airwaves and the limited spectrum. Receivers were expensive and therefore their use confined. The public service character of radio was recognised but radio developed initially as an entertainment medium rather than an information medium, as programme schedules in the early years show.[40]

In Britain in 1922, all the companies interested in acquiring a broadcasting licence were brought together to form a separate company, which was to have a monopoly of broadcasting: the British Broadcasting Company. Four years later when the State bought back the company, it became the British Broadcasting Corporation, the BBC, which was later to become the model for public service broadcasting in many countries. In Ireland, a similar move was considered but rejected.[41] The Irish authorities, like their French and German counterparts, decided to keep radio broadcasting within the control of the Department for Posts and Telegraphs.[42]

After the Civil War, when it came to be realised that radio could play a major role in commercial and cultural progress, a special Dáil committee recommended that broadcasting should be a state service, solely in the hands of the postal ministry. Despite the expressed fears of the radio association, broadcasting began from the Dublin station, 2RN, in January 1926, under the control of the government department. Broadcasting had already begun in Belfast in 1924 under the BBC but the aftermath of the Civil War caused the delay in Dublin.[43]

The legislative structure for radio broadcasting was provided for in the Wireless Telegraphy Act 1926, which *inter alia* made it an offence for anyone else to broadcast or possess broadcasting equipment without a licence. For over six decades no such licence was forthcoming.

2RN began with what would nowadays be called 'wall-to-wall' music but from small groups of instrumentalists, solo traditional musicians, singers and amateur choirs, the Army Number 1 Band and the Garda Band. There were some language programmes, talks on poultry keeping and horticulture but very little news.[44] Radio therefore presented a very minimal threat to the authorities at that time, although some government interference did take place: the Secretary of the Gaelic League was banned from taking part in heritage programmes because he had criticised the Minister for allowing 'jazz' and 'alien' music on air.[45] Much more severe control was exercised over content, however, by means of the purse strings, leading to indirect censorship. The printed press, on the other hand, was still subject to direct censorship.

Media Censorship

1. From Military Censorship to Moral Censorship

Article 9 of the 1922 Constitution of SaorStát Eireann guaranteed the 'right of free expression of opinion . . . for purposes not opposed to public morality', but despite the guarantee, the media, particularly the print media, suffered in turbulent times. Military censorship was introduced for a period during the Civil War 1922–3; government advertising continued to be withheld in response to criticism; newspapers supporting the irregulars were banned; editors were called in by the government's Director of Publicity to account for their misdeeds.[46] The period of turmoil in 1927 following the killing of the Minister for Justice saw the introduction of the Public Safety Act 1927, which prohibited publications, including newspapers, connected with illegal organisations (section 9) and allowed for ministerial suppression of seditious publications (section 10). The Act was a temporary measure and was repealed at the end of 1928.

Attention then turned to public morals. For some decades there had been pressure for censorship on moral grounds.[47] Film censorship had already been introduced in 1923 as one of the first pieces of legislation of the new State (Censorship of Films Act 1923). Public opinion not only in Ireland but in most of Europe favoured censorship of publications also. The Geneva Convention for the Suppression of the Circulation and Traffic in Obscene Publications in 1923 had set the scene but legislative action in Ireland awaited the report of the Committee on Evil Literature, established by the Minister for Justice in 1926. The resulting Bill in 1928 implemented some of the Committee's recommendations but did not heed its warnings about attempting to include books: the target should be the unsavoury periodicals and newspapers circulating from abroad, the Committee said, not books, which at any rate were the preserve of the educated. At the time Ireland was regarded as a newspaper-reading public, not a book-reading public. In any event, the Censorship of Publications Act 1929, which was to blight the Irish literary scene for many decades, was passed. Among its more notorious features were the permanent nature of the bans, the lack of appeal (which is particularly surprising, given that the Censorship of Films Act 1923 did provide for an appeal) and the restrictions on court reporting, still applicable today (see Chapter 9).

Although concern with morality endured, political events again came to dominate. The Constitution (Amendment No. 17) Act 1931 established a military tribunal whose wide-ranging powers included the power to declare any publication seditious and impose unlimited sentences. It was not amenable to the courts and there was no appeal from its decisions. The Act was used to prosecute Frank Gallagher, the editor of the newly founded *Irish Press*, for seditious libel arising out of a series of articles alleging police brutality towards Republican sympathisers.[48] The Act remained in operation until the new Constitution came into force in 1937.

2. At War with the Censors

The Second World War brought with it additional censorship, and press and radio, as well as postal and telephone services, were very strictly controlled. Even Old Moore's Almanac was seized because of its wartime predictions. Weather reports could be censored because information on the weather was 'sensitive' in terms of foreign intelligence. The Emergency Power Order prohibited any material 'which could cause offence to the people of a friendly nation'.[49]

A distinction was made between publications that reflected adversely on Ireland's neutrality and publications that threatened public morality. The Censorship of Publications Act 1929 was regarded as the appropriate mechanism for dealing with the latter, not the emergency legislation under which wartime censorship operated.[50]

The censors had the power to silence offending journalists by cutting off their telephones and banning their telegraphed reports, which had to be submitted to the censors in advance of publication.[51] Irish people were not allowed to publish any views on the war; the censors would not allow this sort of controversy to be carried on in the public press. Even school annuals were to be warned to submit proofs before publication because of announcements in the *Clongownian* 1944 about past pupils killed when serving with British forces.[52] The *Sunday Times* was among the newspapers temporarily banned, but the only Irish paper seized was the *Enniscorthy Echo* in 1940 because of a report on the bombing of a local creamery.[53] The censors could not legally require newspapers to print anything; they could only order them not to print something, but requests to do so were usually complied with. Photographs, bishops' pastorals and films all came under scrutiny.[54]

The censors had no direct control over radio: it was left to the Director of the Government Information Bureau to see to it that the station was supplied with its material for news. In 1941, after a news bulletin carried remarks made in the Dáil opposing trade union legislation, the minister intervened and ordered that the radio newsroom read over to the censor any doubtful item to seek approval for broadcasting.[55]

Even in neutral Ireland the requirements of war overshadowed the guarantee of press freedom enshrined in the new Constitution of 1937. Anyway, the guarantee of freedom to express convictions and opinions contained only an oblique reference to 'organs of public opinion such as the radio, the press, the cinema . . .'. Moreover, it was too hedged in by conditions and restrictions to prove an effective bulwark for the media even in times of stability. (The constitutional text is examined in detail in Chapter 2.)

The Dawn of Television

The postwar period witnessed a greater degree of tolerance than ever before in the history of the press, but the sheer scale of media operations and the emergence of new and more pervasive media brought new challenges and new attempts at control. Such was the level of technical progress, much of it in the US, that by the 1930s regular, though limited, television broadcasting services were already in operation in some countries. By the 1950s a trans-American service had been developed. The coronation of Queen Elizabeth was televised; major sports events could be seen across Europe; and plans were being made to introduce television broadcasting into Ireland. Television was 'the most powerful and pervasive medium of mass-communication yet devised', as Minister Hilliard said at the time. 'Its potentialities are indeed incalculable: already it has altered in many respects the pattern of living in those countries where it has most developed. The television set has even become a modern household god.'[56] By 1969 the world could watch the first steps taken by Neil Armstrong on the moon.

Following the report of a television commission, the legislature enacted the Broadcasting Authority Act 1960, which invested in a semi-state body, the RTÉ Authority, the sole right to operate broadcasting services. The Act established the structures for television broadcasting and provided for the regulation of programming in terms of both operation and content. It imposed requirements of fairness and impartiality, regard for privacy and cultural aims and gave the minister the right to direct the authority to refrain from broadcasting certain matter (section 31). The government was given the power to appoint the authority and to dismiss it. The 1960 Act thus combined statutory autonomy with government control. The ministerial and governmental powers were later curtailed by amending legislation in 1976 (Broadcasting Authority (Amendment) Act 1976).

The 1960 Act provided a new framework for radio as well as television and gave RTÉ a monopoly over both forms of broadcasting (see Chapter 11). Nonetheless, illegal pirate radio stations continued to flourish, with up to eighty or more operating up to 1988 when the Broadcasting and Wireless Telegraphy Act finally forced them off the air, if they were to be eligible to apply for the new commercial licences. Over the decades there had been repeated attempts to use the Wireless Telegraphy Act 1926 against the pirate stations but without success. Constitutional challenges in the High Court by two of the stations did not succeed in having the 1926 legislation set aside as unconstitutional.[57] (See also Chapter 11 for further discussion.)

Private Commercial Broadcasting

Just as in other countries, the monopoly enjoyed by RTÉ began to be dismantled by legislation in 1988 and continued with legislation in 1990 and 1993. Private commercial broadcasting was sanctioned by the Radio and Television Act 1988, which established the Independent Radio and Television Commission (IRTC) with power to grant licences and monitor the operation and programme content of the new stations. The principles of objective and impartial reporting of news and treatment of current affairs imposed on RTÉ by the Broadcasting Authority Acts 1960–76 were imposed also on the commercial stations by the Radio and Television Act 1988, as were obligations not to broadcast anything that might 'reasonably be regarded as offending against good taste or decency, or as being likely to promote, or incite to, crime or as tending to undermine the authority of the State', and to ensure that 'the privacy of any individual is not unreasonably encroached upon' (Section 9).

As the new stations struggled financially to establish themselves, measures were introduced to cap the advertising revenue earned by RTÉ (Broadcasting Act 1990). The concern was that in a small country with a limited advertising cake, the portions would be very small indeed and the commercial stations would find it very difficult to survive.[58] However, the measures adopted proved unworkable and were abolished (Broadcasting Authority (Amendment) Act 1993). Since then, some of the commercial stations appear to be weathering the market and the IRTC has begun to grant licences for community broadcasting. A government green paper on the future of broadcasting was published in 1995 (see Chapter 11).

The Future of Broadcasting

The fact that both public service and private commercial broadcasting are regulated by law and the print media are not remains an anomaly. The difference in approach is difficult to justify now that the core argument—the limits of the electromagnetic spectrum—which allowed governments to keep control of broadcasting and operate a monopoly, no longer holds up. The divergent approach is also difficult to implement in practice as the two forms of media coalesce. We now have the computerised newspaper, teletext services on television and newspapers using electronic means to distribute copy to printing plants. The practical aspect of the problem tends to suggest deregulation as the answer, as has happened in the United States, for example. The other possibility, which would be difficult to justify either in terms of principle or practice, would be to regulate the print media as well. That would spell the death knell for the most prized freedom of the press.

However, such is the pace of technological development of the media that market forces on a global scale threaten the continued existence of the smaller and more traditional media. Large newspaper and multimedia groups are swallowing up small newspapers and broadcasting stations across the world, leading to problems of concentration of ownership and cross-ownership and fears of lack of diversity in media content. The future of public service broadcasting is now in the balance because of commercial and satellite capabilities.

The European Commission has made a number of abortive attempts to regulate media ownership but has been hampered by a lack of will and by the status quo—the dominance of the Italian market by the Berlusconi empire, for example. Meanwhile, the EC Directive on Transfrontier Television 1989 governs certain aspects of television broadcasting as between member states (see Chapter 1), but the EU remains fearful of the giant American multinational media conglomerates that continue to saturate the market.

The ability of the law to meet the problems perceived in existing and potential media technology may be rather limited. Legal rules would be difficult to enforce with respect to satellite broadcasting, for example, even if there were agreement as to what the objectives of those legal rules should be. Be that as it may, one thing is certain: legal restrictions, dating from previous centuries or decades which still apply in Ireland but which have not kept pace with, or taken account of, the dramatic changes occurring in the media environment, are unlikely to prove helpful and may indeed pose a constant and unnecessary threat to the media. The provisions of the Emergency Powers Acts, Offences against the State Acts, Official Secrets Act and many common-law rules may not be invoked very often but do cast a shadow over press activities and are in urgent need of reform.

Further Reading

Adams, Michael, *Censorship: The Irish Experience*, Alabama: The University of Alabama Press, 1968.

Hall, Eamon, *The Electronic Age: Telecommunication in Ireland*, Dublin: Oak Tree Press, 1993.

Inglis, Brian, *Freedom of the Press in Ireland 1784–1841*, London: Faber and Faber, 1954.

Munter, Robert, *The History of the Irish Newspaper 1685–1760*, Cambridge: Cambridge University Press, 1967.

Notes

1 In 1861, cited in Central Office of Information, *The British Press*, London 1958, at p. 3.
2 The postal service was developed in France in 1464, in England in 1478, in Germany 1502, in Ireland 1635; see Jean-Marie Auby and Robert Ducos-Ader, *Droit de l'Information*, 2nd edn., Paris: Dalloz, 1982; Robert Munter, *The History of the Irish Newspaper 1685–1760*, Cambridge: Cambridge University Press, 1967, at p. 72.
3 See n. 2, Auby and Ducos-Ader, at pp 23–4; Francis Balle, *Médias et Sociétés*, 4th edn., Paris: Monchrestien, 1988, at pp 76–7.
4 See n. 2, Auby and Ducos-Ader, at pp 23–4 on the appointment of official censors in France and the banning of a political monthly 1689–91.
5 See n. 1 at p. 2.
6 The licensing laws were renewed in 1693 for two years and then finally allowed to lapse in 1695.
7 See n. 1 at p. 3.
8 Robert Munter, *A Handlist of Irish Newspapers*, London: Bowes and Bowes, 1960, at p. vii.
9 Compare the early papers in France, where one page consisted of French news (court and town, literature, snippets) and the remainder was made up of foreign news; see n. 2, Auby and Ducos-Ader, at p. 25.

10 See n. 2, Munter, at p. 9; Brian Inglis, *Freedom of the Press in Ireland: 1784–1841*, London: Faber & Faber, 1954, pp 19ff.

11 R B McDowell, 'Irish Newspapers in the Eighteenth Century', in *Media and Popular Culture, The Crane Bag*, vol. 8, no. 2, 1984, p. 40.

12 Munter, n. 2, at p. 66.

13 Ibid., at p. 100.

14 Ibid., at p. 69.

15 See n. 11, at p. 40.

16 Munter, n. 2 at pp 100–1.

17 For example, see n. 2, Munter, at pp 148–9: 'It appears that Harding was imprisoned for about six months, for there is a break in the production of his DINL from 6 August 1723 to 18 February 1723/4'.

18 See n. 2, Munter, at pp 144–156; n. 11, at p. 42; n. 10, Inglis, at p. 38.

19 Inglis, n. 10, at p. 23.

20 Kevin B Nowlan in Brian Farrell, ed., *Communications and Community in Ireland*, Dublin and Cork: Mercier Press, 1984, p. 7, at p. 12.

21 In France, there was no jury in press cases until well into the nineteenth century see n. 2, Auby and Ducos-Ader, at p. 29. In Germany, prior restraint was abolished in 1874 and the competence of the jury re-established, but otherwise strict control of the press continued; ibid., at p. 45.

22 See n. 10, Inglis, at p. 46ff.

23 See n. 2, Auby and Ducos-Ader, at p. 415ff.

24 Circulated through Smith's Dublin office; see L M Cullen, 'Establishing a Communications System: News, Post and Transport' in Brian Farrell, ed., *Communications and Community in Ireland*, Dublin and Cork: Mercier Press, 1984, p. 25.

25 See n. 1 at p. 40. In France, the circulation of one paper had risen from twelve hundred in the seventeenth century to twelve thousand in the eighteenth, while sales of the daily Paris press increased to one million; see n. 2, Auby and Ducos-Ader, at p. 29. The most rapid expansion, however, was in the US; ibid., at p. 45.

26 Up to 1847 fifty-three per cent of the population was still illiterate; by 1901 the figure had fallen to fourteen per cent and newspapers themselves had undoubtedly played a part in bringing about that reduction. See D McCartney, 'William Martin Murphy: An Irish Press Baron and the Rise of the Popular Press' in Brian Farrell, ed., n. 24, p. 30.

27 See *The Irish Times* 14 October 1992, article by Brendan O Cathaoir for further information on the nationalist and campaigning aspects of the paper.

28 Op. cit.

29 McCartney, n. 26, at p. 34.

30 See M Pollard, 'Control of the Press in Ireland through the King's Printer's Patent 1600–1800' in 1978–80 *Irish Booklore*, Belfast: Blackstaff Press, vol. 4, at p. 79.

31 Ibid., at p. 80.

32 Ibid., at p. 81.

33 Ibid., at p. 82.

34 The category of obscene libel was not recognised until 1727 in *Curl's Case* (1727) 2 Stra. 788, 93 ER 899. The only intention required for criminal libel, whether defamatory, obscene or seditious, was the intention to publish, the reason being that the jury would then have only a minimal say. This was altered by the 1792 Libel Act. The Great Reform Act of 1832 marked the beginning of a more liberal political climate. See the Law Reform Commission *Consultation Paper on The Crime of Libel*, 1991, ch. 1, p. 4, at p. 7.

35 See n. 30, Pollard, at p. 84.

36 See n. 30, Pollard, at p. 89.

37 See n. 30, Pollard, at p. 93.

38 In Russia in 1917, radio was used to send messages regarding the resistance, just hours after the presses of two bolshevik newspapers had been destroyed. In the US the 1920 Presidential election campaign was covered by radio; see n. 3, Balle, at pp 115, 116.

39 Cf. France, law of 1923. See n. 2, Auby and Ducos-Ader, at p. 320.

40　See P Mulryan, *Radio, Radio,* Dublin: Borderline Publications, 1988; R Cathcart, 'Broadcasting—the Early Decades' in Brian Farrell, ed., *Communications and Community in Ireland,* Dublin and Cork: Mercier Press, 1984, p. 39.

41　Several companies including Marconi and Lord Beaverbrook had offered to set up radio stations in Dublin; see 'RTÉ Radio: Sixtieth Anniversary'—Special Report, *The Irish Times,* 28/29 March 1986.

42　See n. 3, at p. 117.

43　See n. 41.

44　See n. 40, Cathcart, at p. 42.

45　Ibid., at p. 43.

46　John Horgan, 'State Policy and the Press', in *Media and Popular Culture, The Crane Bag,* vol. 8, no. 2, 1984, p. 51.

47　This pressure existed despite the fact that there were already a number of nineteenth-century statutes penalising obscene publications: the Obscene Publications Act 1857 and Indecent Advertisements Act 1889, for example. See Michael Adams, *Censorship: The Irish Experience,* Alabama: The University of Alabama Press, 1968, ch.1.

48　See n. 46, at p. 52.

49　*The Irish Times,* 10 August 1993. Ireland's neutral image was paramount. See the series of articles by Joe Carroll in *The Irish Times* 7–13 August 1993.

50　*The Irish Times,* 11 August 1993.

51　*The Irish Times,* 7 August 1993.

52　*The Irish Times,* 9 August 1993.

53　*The Irish Times,* 12 August 1993.

54　*The Irish Times,* 12–13 August 1993.

55　*The Irish Times,* 12 August 1993.

56　Minister for Posts and Telegraphs, 52 *Seanad Debates,* cols 11, 13. See also Muiris Mac Conghail, 'The Creation of RTÉ and the Impact of Television' in Brian Farrell, ed., *Communications and Community in Ireland,* Dublin and Cork: Mercier Press, 1984, p. 64.

57　*Nova Media Services Ltd v Minister for Posts and Telegraphs* [1984] ILRM 161 and *Sunshine Radio Productions Ltd v Minister for Posts and Telegraphs* [1984] ILRM 170.

58　For statistics on the Irish market, see the publications of the National Newspapers of Ireland (NNI), periodic market surveys published in the national newspapers and *The Irish Times,* 13 March 1993, where media correspondent Michael Foley pointed out that in a relatively small media market in Ireland, the existence of diversity depends on a delicate balance. Most of the media depend to a greater or lesser extent on advertising for funding. The fragility of the media here is evident, he says, in the number of organisations that are struggling: of the national newspapers only the Independent are making profits. One third of local radio stations are suffering losses and another third are carrying heavy debts from their first two years of operation.

CHAPTER FOUR

Defamation

> To deny any advantage to censure . . . is to give an undue preponderance
> to praise . . .[1]

A person's good name is priceless. Irrespective of possessions, land,
money or social status, a person can have his/her good name among
friends, neighbours, colleagues, clients and community. Also priceless,
however, is freedom of expression: the freedom to communicate our
thoughts, opinions and criticisms; to receive and impart information;
to engage in dialogue, and in public and private debate. The modern
media play an important role in that information and communication
process.

The first questions that arise are how to protect both good name and
freedom of expression and what is to happen if these two priceless
values come into conflict? What happens if public debate reflects
adversely on the good name of an individual or company? Must public
debate give way to the concerns of that individual or company, or
should good name take second place to the interests of society in open
public debate? The problem boils down to one of how to reconcile two
conflicting values. How a society resolves this conflict sheds a great
deal of light on the national character.

A second series of questions in the media context is to what extent
existing laws take account of, regulate or underpin the important role
and function of the media in today's society. In the common-law world
the tool devised to protect good name or reputation (the esteem in
which others hold us) is the civil law of defamation and, in particularly
serious cases, the law of criminal libel. This chapter concerns the civil
law as it affects the media; criminal libel will be dealt with in Chapters
8 (prosecutions for defamatory libel), 9 (obscene and blasphemous
libel) and 10 (political and seditious libel).[2]

What Is Defamation?

'Defamation' is the generic term for two torts or civil wrongs, libel and
slander. 'Libel' refers to publication in any lasting or permanent form,
and 'slander' refers to publication in a passing or transient form,

usually the spoken word. The distinction is purely historical and serves no useful purpose today.[3] In the media context, therefore, the terms 'defamation' and 'libel' tend to be used interchangeably, and 'slander' for the most part does not apply except, for example, where a journalist says something defamatory in interviewing someone for a story or in a personal capacity, in which case it is not a media issue. The Defamation Act 1961, section 15, specifies that defamation occurring in broadcasting is to be treated as publication in permanent form, that is, as libel rather than slander.

Libel can also be prosecuted in some circumstances as a crime (see Chapter 8). Prosecutions nowadays are rare, while civil actions for damages are frequent and becoming increasingly so.[4] Civil actions, or suits, may be taken in the Circuit Court or High Court, seeking compensation (damages) or possibly an injunction. In the Circuit Court there is no jury and the upper limit on compensation at present is £30,000; in the High Court there is still a jury in defamation cases and no upper limit; damages are said to be 'at large'.[5]

Historical Development

In the seventeenth century when the tort of defamation was developed, the usual course of conduct if someone insulted you or said something to injure your good name was to resort to violence or challenge him to a duel. A more peaceable solution had to be found in the interests of public order. Initially the Star Chamber offered the possibility of prosecuting and punishing the offender, as an alternative to duelling, but, in time, private prosecutions in the courts became so popular and numerous, often dealing with trivial matters, that they had to be discouraged. Because truth was not a defence to a criminal prosecution, those with something to hide preferred to prosecute rather than run the risk of a civil action in which the defence of truth might succeed against them. Besides, damages were less important to the rich and powerful than a successful prosecution and consequent punishment of the perpetrator of the libel. It was not money they wanted but rather the satisfaction of having the offender fined or imprisoned.

From 1697 on, prosecutions could only be brought for written defamation, and from 1888 the Newspaper Libel and Registration Act made it more difficult to prosecute newspaper proprietors, publishers and editors by requiring the leave of a judge in chambers to do so. Since 1835, a more liberal regime existed and state prosecutions for political or seditious libels had been discontinued. However, the crown law officers were still willing to take up criminal libel actions started by individuals against newspapers and were even willing to intervene in civil actions brought by individuals in order to ensure a fine and prison sentence.[6]

Criminal prosecutions in Britain and Ireland eventually gave way in the present century[7] to civil actions for damages, in contrast to other European countries, like France and Germany, where criminal prosecutions, though rare by comparison, are the norm. That is so for a variety of reasons, including the fact that in Germany, in particular, money damages are not regarded as an appropriate remedy for injury to good name or reputation.[8] It is thought to be demeaning to reduce a person's reputation to money terms.

During the nineteenth century, cases of civil defamation usually involved private individuals rather than the press. For example, there were the notorious cases of a Father O'Keeffe who sued the cardinal for punishing him under canon law. He was punished, he said, because he had remained faithful to his oath of allegiance to the crown and had refused to recognise the temporal supremacy of the pope. A few years prior to that, Fr O'Keeffe had also sued the bishop for slander, for which he had been suspended, so he sued the vicar general of the diocese for libel and slander in suspending him. At one stage he was awarded one farthing but that verdict was set aside and the case never came before the courts again.[9] It was not unknown either for newspaper proprietors to settle their differences, which often spilled over into their papers, by means of civil actions for defamation. The most notorious civil actions for libel during that period, however, were taken by Orangemen against the *Evening Mail* and the *Evening Post*, which had expressed disgust at the selection of one of them as subsheriff of Monaghan. A jury in each case awarded what for the time were heavy damages (£250, £300).[10]

1. Rules Laid Down by Statute

The rules governing the tort of defamation were formulated over a long period by judges in the common-law courts, but some of these rules were then modified or clarified by statutes dating from 1792 to 1888. Nineteenth-century England saw the introduction of a number of measures designed to ease the situation for the press. These legislative measures came about as a result of intense lobbying by the newspapers themselves, aided by the fact that a number of newspaper proprietors were then in parliament.

obtained from the European Convention on Human Rights, Article 10, which prioritises freedom of expression. Freedom of expression is the core value and it can only be restricted to the extent necessary in a democratic society to protect other specified rights and interests. Among those interests is reputation, or good name.

In Ireland the constitutional statement on freedom of the press has always been considered too weak to have any real impact on the common-law approach to defamation. In direct contrast, the United States Constitution, with its strong First Amendment commitment to freedom of the press, has dominated and reshaped the tort of defamation in that country. In Ireland, as a consequence of following developments in Britain, which has no such guarantee, the tort of defamation has continued to operate along common-law lines as if the Constitution did not exist. It is arguable that at least some of those common-law rules and how they affect the media could be challenged successfully under Article 10 of the European Convention of Human Rights, although no defamation case has yet been taken to Strasbourg from Ireland,[12] and the common-law position has been adhered to in practice. Good name has been protected strongly against attack from the media and generously compensated, without much reference to competing values. The constitutional argument based on freedom of the press has not often been advanced, and when it has, it has not been embraced with any great enthusiasm by the courts. Judges have shown a reluctance to introduce constitutional jurisprudence into an area that for centuries has been wholly common law, with only minor statutory modifications, and when they do address the constitutional dimension, they tend to refer only to Article 40.3—the right to good name.[13] The underlying assumption is that the common law of defamation, partly codified in the Defamation Act, has got the balance right. 'The law of defamation has two basic purposes: to enable the individual to protect his reputation, and to preserve the right of free speech. These two purposes necessarily conflict. The law of defamation is sound if it preserves a proper balance between them.'[14] But does it? Is the law of defamation sound?

Given Ireland's history of dispossession and poverty in the material sense, it is understandable that human dignity, and with it good name, should occupy a special place in the value system. This may go some way to explaining why a jury made up of twelve citizens will sometimes award higher damages for reputation than they would for physical injuries. It is also a fact of life that the higher a person's material wealth and standing in the community, the higher the amount of damages likely to be awarded. The more ordinary the person, the lower the damages—if the person can afford to bring an action in the first place, because free legal aid is not available in defamation cases.[15] It is incongruous that good name should be so highly valued and yet no legal aid provided to enable less well-off individuals access to the courts to seek a remedy for attacks made on their good name.

The Irish Constitution speaks of protection for, and vindication of, good name. The protection provided for good name by defamation law lies partly in the availability, in limited circumstances, of injunctions but mainly in the threat of high awards of damages. Although the case should not be overstated, the threat of damages awards to the very survival of the indigenous media is so acute that some stories are simply not being published, reports are being so watered down as to be almost unrecognisable and cases that ought to be fought in the courts are being settled out of court for sizeable sums of money. Research has shown that of every one hundred cases against the media, approximately eighty are settled out of court or during the hearing, in most instances with some monetary payment. Of the remaining twenty, approximately fifteen are won by the plaintiffs and five by the media.[16] Some newspapers and books are read from cover to cover by lawyers before publication to try to detect possible libels.

The Constitution puts the onus on the State to vindicate the good name of every citizen. The question that inevitably arises is whether an award of damages when a case finally comes to court some three years after publication actually vindicates a person's good name. Perhaps more immediate remedies would be appropriate in many circumstances. Furthermore, if the remedy is court based, it remains questionable whether every citizen's good name can be vindicated in the absence of legal aid. There is an inequity also in the fact that there is no legal aid available to defend reputation and yet the State pays the costs of civil servants and other State employees who sue for defamation in respect of their official role. If they win, they keep their damages; if they lose, the State pays their costs.[17] All of these issues and more have been addressed by the Law Reform Commission in its *Consultation Paper* and *Report on the Civil Law of Defamation* in 1991 but to date its recommendations have not been acted upon, although a private member's bill based on them was introduced in 1995. The courts[18] have intimated, also, that, in respect to constitutional rights, good name is not a 'trump' card that takes precedence over all other rights. This may be the first step towards a new balance or constitutionalising of the tort of defamation. For the present, it is necessary to examine the existing rules, with the constitutional requirements in mind.

Key Elements in Proving Defamation

There is no statutory definition of defamation and therefore it is necessary to fall back on judicial dicta to formulate one. A working definition based on such dicta, is:

> Defamation consists of the wrongful publication of a false statement about a person, which tends to lower that person in the eyes of right-thinking members of society or tends to hold that person up to hatred, ridicule or contempt, or causes that person to be shunned or avoided by right-thinking members of society.[19]

While such a definition is not rigid and must not be parsed and analysed with the precision due to a statutory definition, nevertheless it does pinpoint elements of the tort and offer a structure in which to discuss and analyse the rules. Each of the main elements of that definition will be discussed in turn.

1. Wrongful Publication

For present purposes the word 'wrongful' indicates publication of a kind, or of matter, prohibited by law. 'Publication' refers to the making or communicating of a statement about a person to a third party, that is, someone other than the person himself/herself. Because the essence of defamation is the harm done to the esteem in which a person is held by others, the defamatory remarks must have been made to others, even one other, but not just the person they concern:

> If a plaintiff loses the respect for his reputation of some or even one right-thinking person he suffers some injury. [20]

In a media setting, publication is always present, in that it is part of the media's function that information and comment be communicated to others, whether in the pages of a newspaper, on radio or television, on video, film or other medium. Where the defendant is a part of the media, it is unlikely therefore that there will be any difficulty proving that there was publication and that publication was by the defendant. Furthermore, publication by the media takes the form of libel[21] and can be in the form of words, visual images, gestures and other methods of signifying meaning.[22] Thus print, photographs, drawings, cartoons, film, music, satire can all give rise to libel actions. There are, however, two aspects of publication that are of particular significance for the media.

(a) Who Is Liable?

Firstly, because publication refers to the making or communicating of defamatory matter, everyone in the publication process is technically liable and can be pursued for damages. That may include the reporter, subeditor, editor, proprietor, publisher, printer and distributor, and in appropriate circumstances the letter writer, advertiser, or public relations firm, even the caller to a radio talk show. No one is immune, although employees (reporter, subeditor and printer, for example) may be indemnified by the publisher in the case of a newspaper or by the broadcasting company in the case of a radio or television programme. In other cases the individual might not have enough money to be worth pursuing. While there is a limited common-law defence available to distributors, it is not available to printers, and in this and other respects, the law is outdated and fails to take account of modern technology.

It is quite common in Ireland for plaintiffs to sue some or all of the people involved in the publication process, depending on their relative ability to pay. For instance, in the case of a small book publisher or the publisher of a small-circulation magazine, it might be felt that the distributor would be a better mark financially. It is open to a plaintiff to sue one publication for offending matter and not sue others who carried the same material. Moreover, it is also possible to have a number of actions arising from the same defamatory matter, either because more than one individual is affected or because there is republication, a new edition of a book, for example, or the rebroadcasting of a programme. Likewise, various media may be sued by the same person arising out of the same story.[23] At the time of his death Robert Maxwell had taken out numerous writs for libel. It should be remembered also that libel actions can be commenced at any time up to six years after publication.[24] Because repetition of defamatory matter is itself actionable, it is possible to sue for something that was unchallenged in the past when repeated at a later date; for example, the inclusion of news items or snippets from the past, if persons concerned are still alive.

(b) Repeating a Libel

Secondly, because repetition of a libel is itself a libel, to publish defamatory remarks made by someone else can incur liability. Both the original speaker and those involved in the publication process of the offending matter can be pursued.[25] Sometimes the plaintiff will decide to ignore the original speaker and simply go after the media, e.g. remarks made by a politician outside the Dáil or Seanad and by officials at private meetings as well as extracts from press releases have given rise to actions against the media.[26] Stories 'lifted' in whole or in part, from other sources, facts published elsewhere and reprinted have also resulted in actions by aggrieved plaintiffs.[27]

In this regard it is no defence to say that the remarks were made by someone else, whether named or not.[28] Neither is it a defence in itself to preface the remarks with such phrases as 'it is believed that', 'it is widely rumoured that', or 'it has been alleged that'. Even for the journalist to state that the allegations are strongly refuted or not believed will not necessarily provide a defence if sued. It is the act of publishing, of passing on the defamatory matter to others, even one other, that incurs liability. Because publication need only be to one other or a small number of people, circulation or audience figures are largely irrelevant, although they may influence the size of damages awarded. Circulation figures did not seem to have any effect in 1991 when an award of £75,000 was made against the Dundalk *Argus*, a local newspaper with a circulation of about eight thousand copies. The paper, in reference to late-night trouble and vandalism in the mall in the town, had published a report that 'Garda want "killing fields" closed down', along with a picture of 'the offending chip vans'. The owners of the chip vans sued and were awarded £25,000 each for defamation.[29]

The use of quotation marks will not provide protection either. Indeed, use of quotation marks carries a dual responsibility:

(i) to publish the words verbatim, as any deviation or inaccuracy could lead to a defamatory meaning and leave one open to suit by the speaker and

(ii) to ensure that the words quoted are not defamatory of another identifiable person because that person could sue both the speaker and the media who carried them.

Take for example, the following headline that appeared over a court report:

Peace Commissioner 'refused to honour £700 bet'.

The part of the headline in quotation marks suggests that it is a direct quote from a person or document. However, in the court report that followed this particular headline, there was no such statement. Moreover, the amount of money referred to in the report was £500 not £700. In addition the evidence given in court and referred to in the report was that the bookmaker had refused to 'accept' the bet, which is very different from refusing to 'honour' the bet. The inaccuracy in the headline led to a defamation action. Incidentally, it was true that the bookmaker concerned happened to be a peace commissioner.[30]

2. Of a False Statement

Theoretically, it is only the publication of *false* statements that is actionable. As it is the reputation of or the esteem in which a person is held by others that the law of defamation is designed to protect, it follows that there should be no protection against the publication of true statements about a person. His/her reputation is entitled to be assessèd on the basis of the truth and there is no entitlement to protection for a good reputation not warranted by truth. Truth, therefore, is a complete defence to an action for defamation (see the section 'Defences' later in this chapter) but it is not as simple as that in practice. On the contrary, the defence is rather a double-edged sword. If truth can be proved to the satisfaction of the court, then the plaintiff will have no remedy no matter how hurtful or harmful the publication may have been to him/her, morally, financially or otherwise. This is so no matter how private the details given or how long ago the events recounted occurred. It is so even if there is no public interest involved in publication. In one sense this is how it should be in that it should not be a function of defamation law to protect privacy. There should be separate protection for one's private life and family. In the absence of such privacy protection, however, it seems harsh that a person harmed by the publication of true but harmful details should have no legal remedy. (Privacy will be considered in Chapter 5.)

(a) The Presumption of Falsity

In practice, however, it may not be that difficult for the plaintiff to succeed in an action for defamation. This is so because Irish law retains the old common-law presumption of falsity.[31] What this means is that when a plaintiff goes to court alleging defamation, the court proceeds on the basis that what was published about him/her was false and it is then up to the (media) defendant to prove that it was in fact true. The plaintiff does not have to satisfy the court that what was published concerning him/her was false, only that it was defamatory. Indeed, the issue of truth or falsity will not even arise unless the defendant seeks to rely on the defence of truth, called 'justification'. (See the section 'Defences' later in this chapter.)

The reality for the media is that every statement published in whatever form is potentially actionable. Every statement challenged is in law false unless or until proven otherwise. The onus of proof is on the defendant, in contrast to all other torts, where the onus is on the plaintiff to prove the elements of the tort. In the tort of negligence, for example, if the plaintiff alleges negligent driving or negligent medical care, he/she must first establish that the defendant owed him/her a duty of care, that the defendant had breached that duty, and that as a consequence of the breach the plaintiff suffered damage. In defamation, on the other hand, it is only necessary for the plaintiff to establish that the matter was published by the defendant, that it referred to the plaintiff and that it had a defamatory effect. Damage is presumed; fault is not in issue. Defamation is a strict liability tort, so the degree of care taken by the journalist or media organisation and the reason or motive for publishing is irrelevant.[32]

Like all presumptions, the presumption of falsity can be rebutted, in this case by a showing of truth on the part of the defence. In practice, that can prove exceedingly difficult for a media defendant because of the journalistic practice of promising confidentiality to those who provide information—usually referred to as journalists' sources. Sources, even if not promised anonymity or confidentiality, may be unwilling to appear in court to testify against a plaintiff. It is often easier for plaintiffs to get friends and associates to come into court to testify on their behalf than it is for the media to get witnesses to come into court to testify against a plaintiff as to truth. In a case against the *Phoenix* magazine in 1986, for instance, an accountant accused of being a 'hatchet-man' and 'Captain Bligh' because of his alleged cost-cutting of 'luxuries such as functioning typewriters . . . even toilet rolls that the pampered staff had become accustomed to' was able to get his wife and a friend to give evidence in court. His wife gave evidence of the distress and hurt involved and that when her husband was late for an after-work drink, someone had remarked that he must have stayed back in the office to count the sheets of toilet paper.[33]

It is not so easy for the media defendant to get people to come into court to say that someone was a hatchet-man or similar statements. However, witnesses do need to be produced in court, as other evidence such as journalists' notes and out-of-court statements are likely to be inadmissible. In legal terms notes may amount only to 'hearsay' but are nonetheless useful and should be retained by journalists. For instance, when an allegation of defamation is made against a newspaper, it is important that journalists' notes be available to check out how the remarks complained of came to be published. Similarly outcuts or footage from television programmes should be retained. The information they provide may be crucial to the newspaper, broadcaster or the lawyers in deciding whether to defend an action or settle out of court. Difficulties in the past have led some newspapers to take the precaution of getting sworn affidavits from witnesses before they decide to publish.[34]

If the defendants fail in their defence of truth (justification), aggravated damages may be awarded against them. As a result, plaintiffs may sometimes succeed in defamation cases even though the matter complained of was true, simply because the media could not, for one or more of the above reasons, rely on the defence of truth. Alternatively, the media may be reluctant to plead the defence because of the consequences if they should fail to establish it to the satisfaction of the court. The degree of proof required is proof on the balance of probabilities, i.e. that it is more likely than not that the matter was true. This may not appear a very exacting standard but it can be in practice. In other cases the defence may simply not be open because what was published was inaccurate or untrue.

(b) Inaccuracy and Error

However, it is not every false publication that will lead to an action for defamation. To incur liability, the publication must also refer to the complainant and be defamatory, in the sense of adversely affecting his/her reputation. Some inaccuracies may be inconvenient, embarrassing or hurtful but not defamatory and, therefore, are more appropriately handled by a correction or retraction system, such as is operated by the Readers' Representative in Irish newspapers or by the Broadcasting Complaints Commission.[35] Other inaccuracies, though apparently trivial, can be defamatory and can found a successful action.

Mistakes resulting from human error, even though understandable, can also result in sizeable damages. For example, a transcription error which resulted in a reference to 'the Clarke family' rather than 'Mrs Clarke's family' led to an award of £47,500 in *Clarke v Independent Newspapers*,[36] and a typesetting error in which it was stated that a solicitor might 'willingly' rather than 'unwittingly' give information to an illegal organisation led to substantial undisclosed damages in *Rice v Irish Times*.[37] John Browne, spelt with an 'e' carried a price tag of £75,000 in *Browne v Independent Newspapers*, even though the piece in question carried a disclaimer to the effect that the names used were fictitious and not intended to refer to any living person.[38] The report, about corruption and bribery in the building trade, used the fictitious names of Black, White and Browne. There was only one builder named 'Browne' in the area at the time and he sued.

In another case, a photograph of two men was to be used by the *Evening Press* to show the defendant in a court case. The picture was cut in half to eliminate the second person but the wrong half was published. It resulted in an award of £50,000.[39] The positioning of an unrelated photograph beside a story on the maltreatment of horses led to a £20,000 settlement by *The Star*.[40] The question of damages is discussed further at the end of this chapter.

It may be argued that an individual's good name must be protected against inadvertent error as well as deliberate error or error arising from negligence. After all, the effect on the individual's reputation is the same regardless of how the error arose. Indeed, that is the rationale behind the strict liability nature of the tort of defamation. On the other hand, the media role in modern society in providing information, in reflecting public opinion and in stimulating debate is so important that, it could be argued, some allowance should be made for the time pressures under which the media operate in the almost instantaneous reporting of news. Both arguments can be accommodated by making provision for remedies of correction, clarification and declaration, in addition to what is as present virtually the sole remedy of damages.

To what extent the present law engenders caution and promotes accuracy is open to question. There is no doubt that it penalises inaccuracy and that one of the few self-help options open to the media under the present law is to take steps to ensure the highest possible degree of accuracy; and in the event of inaccuracy, to be prepared to correct or clarify at the earliest possible opportunity. If the individual concerned still proceeds to court, the fact that a correction or clarification was published should be seen as mitigating damage.

On the question of accuracy, particular attention needs to be paid to the spelling of people's names, as in the *Browne* case,[41] and to their title or rank. Research has confirmed that people are very sensitive about how they are portrayed in the media and can be upset and angered by inaccuracies concerning them.[42] The greatest percentage of defamation actions relate to factual inaccuracies, as do the greatest percentage of complaints to the Readers' Representatives of the national newspapers, for example.[43] Of major concern to people is their business or professional reputation (involved in fifty per cent of actions) because of what they see as possible consequences to their livelihood.

Journalists are so familiar with media coverage and their own input into it that they can become blasé about how they portray others. They too, however, are sensitive about their own reputations when editors want to publish apologies about their work[44] or when they become the subject matter of someone else's story—a fact borne out by statistics on defamation actions against the media, which show journalists themselves as five per cent of plaintiffs.[45] As regards the exercise of their own profession, it is important for journalists to realise that getting facts about identifiable people right is essential. In the first place it is essential for avoiding libel; it is also essential if they are sued and want to be able to rely on the defences of justification or fair comment (which will be discussed later in this chapter). The answer is careful checking of factual details about identifiable people, their activities, business or professional undertakings. If the journalist or reporter preparing the story does not assume responsibility for that, then the chances of someone further down the line in the sub-editing or publication process being able to do so, when not in possession of the facts that were at the journalist's disposal, will be greatly lessened.

(c) Fact or Comment

The definition of defamation given at the outset speaks of a false *statement*. Normally, therefore, at issue will be a statement of fact or facts about a person. That is not to say that all comment, i.e. expression of opinions as opposed to facts, is free and immune from suit. One measure of the law's regard, or lack of regard, for freedom of expression is the amount of latitude accorded to comment. As indicated in Chapter 2, the freedom to *hold* opinions is absolute and cannot be restricted. The right to comment, i.e. to *express* opinions, one would imagine, should also be largely untramelled. The law of defamation does attempt to effect a balance between the protection of reputation and freedom of expression in this regard. Unlike the European Convention on Human Rights, however, it does not provide that all comment is free except to the extent that it encroaches on reputation, but rather provides a defence of fair comment, which will be discussed later in this chapter. The distinction between fact and comment is more developed in the United States. In relation to facts, the presumption of falsity has been removed and public plaintiffs must prove malice, i.e. that the defendant knew or ought to have known that the matter was false or was reckless as to whether it was or not.[46] Private plaintiffs have to prove negligence, i.e. that the defendant was careless as to whether the matter was true or false.[47]

3. About a Person

Defamation concerns the wrongful publication of a false statement about a person. The fact that the person is not actually named is not necessarily a bar to taking an action. A person may just as easily be identified by description, reference to locality or other information. If, however, a person cannot show that the statement concerned him/her, then he/she will not be able to sue successfully on it. There are several issues involved here.

(a) Individuals and 'Legal' Persons

First of all, a 'person' is any individual human being (including infants, bankrupts, lunatics, foreigners, convicted prisoners)[48] or any 'legal person'; a 'legal person' being a company or other incorporated body, or a body such as a local authority. These are creatures of the law and have a legal status of their own, which allows them to sue or be sued. Thus a company could sue for defamation in its own right, separately from the rights of its directors or members. Companies are the plaintiffs in approximately seven and a half per cent of defamation cases in Ireland. If the defamatory imputations are likely to have financial implications for the company, the amount of damages awarded may be greater than in the case of an individual. Recently, a court in England awarded £1 million sterling to a company engaged in yacht design as a result of an unfavourable criticism of one of its designs. The company director and his wife received separate awards, bringing the total to £1.45 million.[49] The size of the award to the company would appear to reflect the plaintiff director's contention that the criticism in the yachting magazine was designed to put the company out of business. In an earlier case in England, *Derbyshire County Council v Times Newspapers*,[50] the court decided that a local authority could no longer sue for defamation in respect of its collective or official reputation. The position in Ireland regarding local authorities remains unchanged, although cases taken by them are rare. Trade unions can also sue in Ireland.[51]

(b) Living Persons

It is a truism to say that only the living can sue for defamation. If a person dies, the action dies with him/her. Since reputation is a personal right, it is deemed to die with the person, so that no right of action accrues to the next of kin. This position has been upheld under the Constitution in *Hilliard v Penfield Enterprises*,[52] an application to bring a prosecution for criminal libel (see Chapter 8). Similarly, relatives or associates cannot sue in respect of defamatory publication concerning a person who is already dead. Otherwise history could never be written. If, however, the relatives or associates of the deceased are themselves defamed by the remarks about the deceased, a cause of action will lie.[53]

While Irish law seems clear, it is not universally accepted that one's reputation, i.e. the esteem in which one is held by others, dies with one.[54] It is true that a deceased person will not feel the hurt or shame and will not be affected personally or financially, although the business or estate may well be. To allow claims by the next of kin or relatives of a deceased person would place a heavy burden on historians and on the media. However, the memory in which the deceased is held endures and may be worthy of protection. Some reform bodies have recommended a period of three to five years following the death during which close relatives could sue.[55] Damages would not be available; only a declaratory order would be or, where appropriate, an injunction to prevent repetition of the defamation.

(c) Groups

There is no group action as such for libel or defamation. However, the key factor is identification. Therefore, if the group mentioned is relatively small, individual members may be able to succeed by showing that they are personally identifiable. There is no magic number for the size of the group.[56] In D*ineen v Irish Press*,[57] the newspaper had published details of a letter critical of the expenses incurred by officers of the Irish Medical Organisation, and referring to a meal and drinks on a particular occasion. The plaintiff, who was one of only three such officers and who was not present on the occasion mentioned, was awarded £72,000 damages by a High Court jury.

(d) Identification

In the case of any defamation plaintiff, the key question is identification. The plaintiff must prove that the defamatory reference complained of would be taken by others to refer to him/her. If the person is named, there is usually no problem, except where there is more than one person of the same name (see next subsection for further discussion) or confusion of similar names as in M*errill v Sunday Newspapers Ltd*.[58] If the person is not named, it is still possible that he/she is sufficiently identified by details of location, by description or by use of photographs, images or other information given in the publication, as in C*usack v RTÉ*,[59] in which no names were given during a radio interview but the locality was mentioned. The woman interviewed on the 'Liveline' programme about her husband's suicide referred to the fact that he had received letters from the revenue sheriff before his death. There were only three revenue sheriffs in the locality mentioned and one of them sued successfully and was awarded £40,000. Similarly, in M*oore and Byrne v Irish Press*,[60] the plaintiffs were not named in the publication complained of but the article at various points revealed that the subjects were two senior executives in the construction division of AnCo (the semi-state employment training authority at the time) based in Dublin. Two men who met the description sued and were awarded £23,000 each. Likewise, a report on the hustings in an election referred to two brothers who were fuel merchants in a named town and who had close links with a particular political party. The description was so specific that the plaintiffs, though not named, would have had little difficulty meeting the burden of proof. The case was settled without going to court.[61] In *Cooney v Sunday World*,[62] identification was by photograph. In *Fullam v Associated Newspapers Ltd*,[63] there was evidence of jeering by the crowd at a football match to indicate that the plaintiff was identified as the person referred to in a sports report in the newspaper as only being able to kick with one foot.

The test is whether reasonable people would take the reference to be to the plaintiff. If no name is given and only vague details, then it is unlikely that anyone will be able to prove that others took the reference to be to him/her. On the other hand it is possible that more than one person could sue if the details given were sufficiently imprecise to lead people to think they referred to a second or other persons not intended by the reporter or publisher. That is so even if the publication was intended to be fictitious and the details were different in some respects, as in *Sinclair v Gogarty*.[64] Gogarty was sued for a reference to two Jews in his book, *As I Was Going Down Sackville Street*, even though the occupation and street of business of the plaintiffs differed from those of the two Jews in the book. It should be noted that there is no defence in defamation law for fiction as such. If the plaintiff is able to satisfy the court that the reference would be taken to be to him/her, that is sufficient, even if a disclaimer has been published.

The burden of proof on the plaintiff is not very exacting. It is usually sufficient to bring in friends or acquaintances as witnesses to say that they took the reference to be to the plaintiff.[65] For example, in *Sinclair v Gogarty*, Samuel Beckett, who swore an affidavit, admitted in cross-examination that his aunt was married to the plaintiff's brother, who, it was also claimed, was referred to in the book and was the subject of the verse:

> But Willie spent the sesterces
> And brought on strange disasters
> Because he sought new mistresses
> More keenly than old Masters.

This verse had appeared only in the American edition[66] and anyway by the time of the court case, Willie was dead and could not sue. The other witnesses in the case were also relatives, employees or acquaintances who had only read the book when prompted to do so by the plaintiff. The award against Gogarty in 1937 was £900 plus costs. The total came to £2,000 and sales of the book were also affected.[67]

4. Which Tends to Lower That Person

(a) Tends to

Libel is actionable per se. Except in cases where special damage is claimed, proof of actual harm arising from a defamatory publication is not required. Harm to reputation is presumed, and all that it is necessary to show is that the matter complained of would tend to make people think less of the plaintiff. It is sufficient for witnesses to say that they thought less of the plaintiff as a result of the publication or broadcast, and it is not permissible for witnesses to be asked their interpretation of the matter complained of. That becomes a question for the jury in the High Court or judge in the Circuit Court. The judge decides whether the matter is capable of being defamatory and it is for the jury then to decide whether it was defamatory in fact. The standard is an objective one: the effect on 'right-thinking' members of society. However, such a standard is problematic since community viewpoints can vary widely and be sharply divided.[68]

One problem that arises from the fact that harm is presumed and that actual harm need not be shown is that plaintiffs may sometimes receive compensation even though they suffered no injury to their reputation. Put another way, the media may have to pay compensation even though the publication has not actually harmed the plaintiff. This is a serious concern because large awards of compensation are crippling some of the smaller Irish media organisations. Small book or magazine publishers, local newspapers or radio stations and even some of the national newspapers could be put out of business.[69] Should the plaintiff be obliged, therefore, to prove actual harm to his/her reputation? In reality, most plaintiffs do offer some indication of harm: snide remarks made by others, crowds booing a footballer, a fall-off in trade, etc. However, to require all plaintiffs to prove actual harm to the satisfaction of the court might be unfair because injury to reputation could be very difficult to assess or prove in some cases.

(b) Lower that Person

Matter is defamatory if it tends to lower the person in the eyes of right-thinking members of society, to hold the person up to ridicule, odium or contempt or to cause the person to be shunned by right-thinking members of society. However, social values and attitudes are peculiar to particular cultures and subject to change, with the result that what is regarded as defamatory varies with time, place and circumstance. For instance, to call someone a landgrabber or an informer might have had connotations in Ireland at particular periods of our history that they would not have now or elsewhere.[70] The significance of words like 'gay', 'rebel' or 'fenian' would depend very much on time and circumstance. Decided cases, particularly older ones or those from other jurisdictions, are, consequently, of limited value in indicating what will be regarded as defamatory. Also, very few defamation cases are included in official law reports, unless they are appealed to the Supreme Court, because there are no written judgments given in the Circuit Court and juries in the High Court do not give reasons for their decisions. Thus the only source for details of the pleadings, evidence, and decision is newspaper reports of cases at the time of the hearings. An added problem is that approximately eighty per cent of defamation cases are settled out of court and accordingly only scant details, if any, are reported in the media.

In *Barrett v Independent Newspapers*,[71] one of the few defamation cases to go to the Supreme Court in recent years, an allegation that an elected representative had pulled at a journalist's beard and made a triumphalist remark about the outcome of a party leadership crisis was accepted as defamatory. Counsel for the plaintiff contended that it amounted to a very serious allegation that the TD had assaulted the journalist, but the Supreme Court advised that the jury should have been told to consider where the allegation would fall on the scale of seriousness of allegations that might be levelled at a politician. The jury award of £65,000 was considered excessive by the Supreme Court and a new trial was ordered. In *McDonagh v Newsgroup Newspapers*,[72] however, seven years later, the Supreme Court held that a jury award of £90,000 was at the top end of the scale but not excessive. In that case, the *Sun* newspaper had alleged that an unnamed representative of the Irish government at the Gibraltar inquest into the death of three IRA volunteers was *inter alia* 'a lefty spy'.

In *Prior v Irish Press*,[73] where the allegation was that the plaintiff, a local farmer, was involved in a kidnapping, the Supreme Court upheld an award of £30,000. The farmer had been arrested but later released. The newspaper published an apology as soon as his release became known. In *Egan v BBC*[74] a character in a television play uttered words to the effect that the plaintiff garda had tortured local suspects. The fact that the words were uttered in a play or docudrama did not negate their defamatory effect and damages were awarded. In *Lynch v Irish Press*[75] it was held to be defamatory to say that an actor (Joe Lynch, alias 'Dinny Byrne' of the television series 'Glenroe') had left the punters in the lurch when he failed to turn up for a cabaret booking of which he said he had no knowledge. A High Court jury awarded him £25,000 compensation. The earlier case of *Fullam v Associated Newspapers*[76] had decided that a remark to the effect that a professional footballer did not use his left foot because he could not was defamatory; likewise in *Quigley v Creation Ltd*[77] a remark that a well-known actor had left the country not to further his art but to fill his pockets was held to be defamatory. A Northern Ireland court in *Doyle v The Economist*[78] awarded £50,000 to Judge Doyle when *The Economist* suggested he had been appointed to the bench solely because he was a Catholic. A similar sum each was awarded to a prominent Northern politician and barrister when the *Sunday World* reported that the two had had words about which of them had been first to see the last chocolate eclairs in a baker's shop.[79]

Decided cases show that it is enough that the plaintiff was held up to ridicule and made to look a fool or a laughing stock . That was the complaint in *Madigan v Irish Press*,[80] which involved an allegation in a light-hearted column that the plaintiff, a local councillor, had bought a map of an island owned by his party leader, believing it to be an original. The jury award of £30,000 was upheld on appeal. In *Agnew v Independent Newspapers*[81] a report of the plaintiff's wedding elicited a similar complaint, while an error which resulted in the wrong T.D. being named in a local newspaper report of a television programme on betting taxes was also held to be defamatory.[82]

The issue involved is the tendency to make one look ridiculous to others, not the embarrassment caused to oneself or the hurt to one's feelings, although a perusal of defamation cases and, in particular, the apologies often read in court following settlements suggest otherwise. The essence of good name or reputation is the esteem in which others hold one and not self-esteem.[83] In defamation law it is the defamatory effect that is important, not the intention of the speaker.[84] Vulgar abuse is not regarded as defamatory. This is particularly so with regard to verbal abuse uttered in the heat of the moment. In the case of written abuse, which is more considered, less hasty and more lasting, it is less likely that remarks would be dismissed as mere vulgar abuse.[85]

By Innuendo

A statement can be defamatory on its face or by innuendo. It can be defamatory in its ordinary and natural sense or it can be defamatory because of some secondary or hidden meaning. Some imputations are obviously capable of being defamatory in their ordinary everyday sense. For example, to say wrongly that a person has unlawfully evaded tax liability and is a fugitive from justice would be defamatory.[86] Likewise it would be defamatory in the ordinary sense to say that someone was involved in drugs or with the IRA, was racist, accepted bribes or that a nurse would not attend bomb victims because she was sympathetic to the bombers.[87] As a good example of the complexity of defamation law, however, one can point to the fact that there are two kinds of innuendo, confusingly called: (a) false or popular innuendo and (b) true or legal innuendo.

False or Popular Innuendo

By false or popular innuendo is meant a secondary meaning that derives from the words themselves, a case of 'reading between the lines'. For example, in *Campbell v Irish Press*,[88] a review of a snooker exhibition complained that 'the table told lies'. The plaintiff pleaded an innuendo that this meant he was incompetent in organising the exhibition. Other examples include *Kavanagh v The Leader*[89]; *Fisher v The Nation*[90]; *Kenny v The Freeman's Journal*.[91] In *Kennan v Irish Press*,[92] a statement made, in the course of a long interview, by the new incumbent of the office of Director of Restrictive Practices that he might have acted differently from his predecessor, might not appear defamatory on its face but could imply that his predecessor in office had not acted in an appropriate manner.

True or Legal Innuendo

By true or legal innuendo is meant a secondary meaning of the words complained of, not drawn from the words themselves, but from extrinsic facts. Such an innuendo must be pleaded specifically. Examples include *Bell v Northern Constitution*,[93] in 1943, in which a bogus birth announcement was telephoned through to a newspaper. The two people mentioned in it as the parents, who knew each other but were not married, pleaded an innuendo to the effect that they were immoral and were having sexual relations with each other outside of marriage.[94] In 1994 *The Irish Times* published an apology to the family of a deceased woman because a death notice, which should have read 'beloved of James her late husband', had contained the word 'and' after 'James'.[95] Where justification, or truth, is pleaded in defence, it must meet the innuendo.[96] The situation regarding innuendos and the pleading of innuendos is unduly complex and begs the question as to whether there is any need to retain the distinction between the two types and distinct rules regarding pleading or whether a simpler procedure might not be found.[97]

5. In the Eyes of Right-thinking Members of Society

Who or what are 'right-thinking' members of society and how or what do they think? The phrase is used to indicate that not all persons or groups will be regarded as an acceptable barometer of defamatory meaning or effect. To say that someone is a police informer, for example, may lower his/her reputation in the eyes of wrongdoers, criminals and terrorists yet not be regarded as defamatory in law because the law is not concerned with the esteem or lack of it in which those elements of society view an individual. There are thus moral connotations and a censorious note to the phrase 'right-thinking members of society' that are not present in the normal legal standard of the 'reasonable person'. It would appear that the standard of the reasonable person is perfectly adequate in defamation, as in other torts, and that there is nothing to be gained from applying a different standard. Indeed, in modern defamation practice the standard adopted appears to be that of the reasonable person, particularised as the reasonable reader, listener or viewer.[98] The concept of reasonableness can accommodate different community values and viewpoints.

Practical Issues Regarding Defamation

1. Who Sues?

In practical terms, the more important question is often not who can sue but who is likely to sue.[99] A study of High Court cases reveals that the majority of libel plaintiffs are male, and are businessmen or professionals, whose primary concern is for their business or professional reputation and for possible financial harm rather than personal reputation. The next largest category of libel plaintiff is that of State employees, followed by lawyers and politicians. Women represent only ten to fifteen percent of plaintiffs, although that marks an increase over the previous five-year period studied.[100] Interestingly, women who sue usually do so jointly with a spouse or male colleague; they rarely do so on their own.[101] Women are much more likely to use the Readers' Representative or voluntary complaints system on their own initiative.[102] This may be because procedures are so much simpler under the latter system. If so, that might strengthen the argument in favour of simpler procedures and remedies for defamation also. Journalists themselves make up five percent of plaintiffs who sue the media.[103]

2. Why Do They Sue?

The reason so many people sue for defamation may be related to the very high value put on reputation in our society. On the other hand, it may be just a reflection of the general climate of litigiousness that characterises society today. The media are seen as wealthy, as a source of easy money. A study of defamation plaintiffs suing the media in the US[104] found that people sued to get even with the media or because there was no other remedy available. The study made the case for simpler, more immediate remedies; for the creation of a climate of correction and clarification. This is already part of the culture of other EU countries, which provide rights of rectification and reply to aggrieved readers. The EC Directive on Television Broadcasting 1989 led to the introduction of a right of reply in this country also but only in relation to television. Newspapers operate a voluntary system of correction through the Readers' Representatives scheme introduced in 1989.

3. Who Is Sued?

Technically, any individual, legal person or anyone involved in the publication process can be sued. In the print media that means anyone from the reporter, editor and proprietor through to the printer, distributor and even, possibly, the seller. In the broadcast media it means everyone from presenter, editor, producer to broadcasting authority. The reason for including printers and distributors, in particular, is twofold. First, there is the concern to ensure that someone will be able to meet an award of damages. If the publisher is a small and relatively impecunious outfit, or a fly-by-night operator, or a person or persons unknown, the defamed plaintiff should not have to suffer the consequences. However, the inability to pay of those directly responsible would not of itself seem sufficient grounds to impose liability on others whose involvement is removed from the harmful act.

The key issue, therefore, would seem to be control. When the laws were devised, media operations were essentially one-man commercial operations, run by printer/stationers. Thus the printer fulfilled all of the obligations now shared by reporter, editor, proprietor, printer and distributor/seller. Accordingly, he had complete control over content at every stage of the process and could therefore be held legally responsible for any libel arising from his publications. Over time, as media operations developed and separate roles of reporter, editor and subeditor emerged, the common law conceded the diminished responsibility of distributors, who had now begun to handle large numbers of publications from various printing houses. A defence of reasonable care was introduced, whereby a distributor, who did not know, and who had no way of knowing, that a particular publication contained a libel, would not be liable for it, provided his lack of knowledge did not stem from an absence of reasonable care. Nowadays, with distributors handling enormous numbers of publications and with an increased use of technology, control over content is minimal. Checking for libel is unduly burdensome, if not impossible, and, therefore, even the requirement of reasonable care is problematic. What constitutes reasonable care in the case of a distributor handling in excess of half a million titles per year?

A defence of reasonable care was not recognised in the case of printers, who were deemed still to have control and to be a good financial mark. Nowadays, the picture is quite different. Direct input by computer means that usually the printer has no control whatsoever over content. Often, the printer no longer sets up the type or corrects proofs marked for correction by the publisher. For these reasons, reform bodies have recommended a defence for printers.[105] In the case of broadcasters also, the guiding principle for reform of the law should be control. In that way, account could be taken of the impact of technology on the roles of those involved in the various stages of programme production and broadcasting.

It is not surprising that the media are sued in eighty percent of defamation cases. In recent years the number of cases taken against the media in Ireland has increased. The largest increase, however, has been against the British media circulating or transmitted in Ireland: eleven and a half per cent of all libel cases against the media in the period 1986–90, as opposed to four per cent for the previous five years. Cases against national newspapers make up sixty-one per cent, those against the provincial papers and broadcasting each make up just over nine per cent, with periodicals at five per cent and books at four per cent.[106]

Defamatory matter can occur in any section of a newspaper (birth or death notices, advertisements, business to sports pages), in any type of broadcast programme (not only news or current affairs but documentaries, docudramas, drama, film—including those that are foreign-produced, satirical programmes, advertisements), in any book, whether factual or fiction and any other media. As a result everyone in the business needs to be on his/her guard. Also, since the repetition of defamatory remarks is actionable, particular care must be taken with press releases,[107] open letters,[108] extracts from other publications, reports of what politicians and others have said outside of the Dáil or Seanad; even editorial comment.[109]

4. *Public/Private Plaintiff Distinction*

At present the Irish law of defamation makes no distinction between public and private plaintiffs. The traditional view taken by the common-law courts was expressed by Raymond L.C.J., in his speech in the trial of Thomas Woolston in 1729:

> Even a private man's character is not to be . . . scandalized . . . And much less is a magistrate, minister of state, or other public person's character to be stained, either directly or indirectly. And the law reckons it a greater offence when the libel is pointed at persons in a public capacity, as it is a reproach to the government to have corrupt magistrates, etc. substituted by his majesty, and tends to sow sedition, and disturb the peace of the kingdom.[110]

With the dawn of democracy, attitudes to public persons changed. Public persons have come to be regarded as public property, as fair game for criticism: 'Anyone who throws a hat into a public arena must be prepared to have it mercilessly, though not maliciously, trampled upon.'[111] Public discussion and criticism must not be stifled. The doctrine that the governed must not criticise their governors is now obsolete. In *New York Times v Sullivan*,[112] the United States Supreme Court went further.[113] There must be free debate and a breathing-space for error, the Court said, because error is inevitable in free debate. Inadvertent error should not be penalised. The media in fulfilling their central and fundamental role in society should not have to compensate a public official because of an error they did not make deliberately or recklessly. In other words, in order to succeed in a defamation action against the media, a public person must prove malice, i.e. that the offending remarks were published knowingly or recklessly, without regard to their truth or falsity.

The *New York Times* decision was regarded as a major breakthrough for freedom of speech, but its practical effect was somewhat negated in the years that followed by a relaxation of standards on the part of the press no longer threatened by the likely success of multimillion dollar suits from public officials and also by further court cases seeking to refine and develop the *New York Times* decision. That decision should extend not only to public officials but to public figures, said the courts, because both

(a) have significantly greater access to the channels of communication and therefore a better chance of correcting or counteracting false statements about them than have private individuals and

(b) have voluntarily sought the public gaze by assuming roles of power and influence in society and must, as a consequence, accept the increased risk of criticism.

Private persons have not done so and therefore require greater protection, it is argued. However, as inadvertent error must be tolerated, the private individual must at least prove negligence on the part of a media defendant. In Ireland there is no such hurdle as malice or negligence for public or private plaintiff and even a typesetter's error or a wrong caption on a photograph, or two stories transposed, can result in sizeable awards of damages. The *New York Times* decision has not solved all the problems. It has not solved basic problems of high awards and costs but it has lessened the chilling effect of libel actions for the media.[114] There is now a huge volume of pre-trial proceedings in the US, so much so that some plaintiffs, particularly public plaintiffs, cannot get to a defamation hearing at all. To place the hurdle so high might well amount to a denial of the plaintiff's right of access to the courts.

The European Court of Human Rights in *Lingens v Austria*[115] also recognised the distinction between public and private plaintiffs. The case arose out of the publication by a journalist of criticism of the attitude of the Austrian Federal Chancellor to National Socialism and the participation of Nazis in the governance of the country. The Court emphasised the importance of a free press in that it affords the public one of the best means of discovering and forming an opinion of the ideas and attitudes of political leaders, and freedom of political debate is at the very core of the concept of a democratic society. It follows, therefore, that the limits of acceptable criticism are wider as regards a politician as such, the Court said, than as regards a private individual. The politician inevitably and knowingly lays himself open to close scrutiny of his every word and deed by both journalists and the public at large, and he must consequently display a greater degree of tolerance. Everyone is entitled to have his reputation protected, including politicians, but in their case that protection has to be weighed in relation to the interests in open discussion of political issues. To fine a journalist for political comment was a censure likely to deter journalists from contributing to public discussion of issues affecting the life of the country and to hamper the press in its role as purveyor of information and public watchdog.[116]

The European Court has maintained and elaborated the public/private distinction in subsequent defamation cases.[117] The Court's approach is likely to influence our law either directly, through cases being brought against Ireland, or indirectly, insofar as there is a presumption that our law is in conformity with the Convention, which operates as a yardstick in relation to our domestic law. The public/private distinction should therefore not be ignored, even though the Law Reform Commission did not recommend its introduction.

Defences

There are a number of defences specific to defamation, in addition to those available in tort cases generally. The defences specific to defamation are: justification, fair comment and privilege, both absolute and qualified. If established, they are complete defences to defamation. The offer of amends for unintentional defamation can serve as a bar to an action if accepted or as a defence if offered in accordance with the conditions laid down in the Defamation Act 1961, section 21, but not accepted. An apology on its own is not a complete defence but may be pleaded in mitigation.

1. General Tort Defences

The general tort defences include the defences of consent and self-defence. Consent in the defamation context means consent to publication, where a person volunteers a statement for publication or broadcast, enters into a publishing contract or expressly waives his/her rights to sue. The consent must relate to the actual libel published, not just to agreement to appear on a programme or be interviewed.[118] Self-defence is a general defence to tort actions and applies equally to defamation. A person whose reputation is attacked is entitled to respond to defend and protect it. However, just as a person who is physically attacked may not use more force than is necessary in self-defence, so in defamation the response must be proportionate in the extent of its content and in the medium used. Thus, a person responding to a defamatory allegation must not introduce irrelevancies that would defame others and must confine his/her response to those to whom the original remarks were addressed. (These two conditions, that there not be excess of content or excess of publication, will be discussed further in Section 4–Privilege.)

In relation to defamation, self-defence is part of the defence of privilege. Self-protection affords a ground for the plea of privilege, as illustrated by the case of *Willis v Irish Press*.[119] In *Willis*, the paper was threatened with a libel action in relation to a journalist's articles on sporting events, which had appeared in the paper. In response to the threat, it published an apology. The journalist then sued for defamation of his reputation, but the publication of the apology was held by the Supreme Court to be privileged and the apology itself a privileged communication. The question of malice was then a matter for the jury. The decision was based both on the duty element of qualified privilege (see later discussion) and on the ground of 'reasonable purpose of self-protection', following the English Court of Appeal decision in *Adam v Ward*.[120] The *Willis* decision should be noted by journalists, some of whom have sued their papers in the past for publishing apologies concerning their work. The apologies, they claim, undermine their professional reputation as journalists. Apologies or corrections should, therefore, be published in consultation with the journalist concerned. Furthermore, journalists concerned about the form of a proposed apology reflecting on their work should probably obtain independent legal advice.

Does the self-defence privilege extend to the protection of others or to the protection of property? The English case *Bowen-Rowlands v Argus Press Ltd*,[121] cited in *Willis*, is instructive. There it was held that a letter, written by the daughter of a deceased, complaining of a story about him quoted in a book review in the newspaper, was privileged. However, it is not clear whether the privilege stemmed from self-protection on the part of the daughter, whose feelings the story was 'clearly calculated to injure', or from protection of the memory of the father. At any rate, it was held that the publication of the letter in the newspaper which had published the book review was privileged. The form of apology printed in *Willis*, accepting that the statements published contained 'accusations and imputations of dishonourable and unprofessional conduct . . . wholly unfounded', though agreed at the time by the parties' solicitors and settled by counsel, would probably not be countenanced by lawyers today. The court held that the newspaper had a duty to put right the injury caused by the published articles and that there were no other means open to it to do so than by publishing the apology.

2. Justification

John Stuart Mill has said:

> . . . if there are cases in which a truth unpleasant to individuals is of no advantage to the public, there are others in which it is of the greatest; and that the truths which it most imports to the public to know, are precisely those which give most annoyance to individuals, whose vices and follies they expose.[122]

Justification is the old term used to signify the defence of truth. It stems from the belief that if the allegations were true their publication was justified in the sense that a person is entitled only to his true reputation, not to a good reputation that is false and therefore undeserved. Truth is a complete defence to an action for defamation.[123] To rely on it the defendant must be able to prove substantial truth, enough to take the sting out of the defamation. At common law, the defendant had at one time to prove the precise truth of the allegation and, where there were two or more distinct allegations, that each and every allegation complained of was substantially true. The Defamation Act 1961 modified the old rule. It provides that where there is more than one allegation, it is not necessary to prove the truth of every single one, provided that any words not proven true do not materially injure the plaintiff's reputation, given the truth of the others:

> In an action for libel or slander in respect of words containing two or more distinct charges against the plaintiff, a defence of justification shall not fail by reason only that the truth of every charge is not proved, if the words not proved to be true do not materially injure the plaintiff's reputation having regard to the truth of the remaining charges. (Defamation Act, section 22)

Section 22 also has the effect of modifying the old common-law rule on partial justification.[124] Even with this mitigation of the old common-law rules, the defence is a difficult one to sustain in practice and is pleaded on its own in only five per cent of cases. A high standard of truth is required by the courts and the position in this country is still a very far cry from the American case *Lakian v Boston Globe*,[125] in which the jury found that five paragraphs of a newspaper story were false and defamatory but the gist of it true and awarded no damages.

Truth must be proven on the balance of probabilities: that the words complained of are more probably true than not. That degree of proof may not appear very high or onerous; yet the defence is difficult to set up in practice, particularly for media defendants who often rely for their information on sources to whom they promise confidentiality or witnesses who may be unwilling to appear in court. The allegations must be proved true in any reasonable sense contended by the plaintiff. Where an innuendo is pleaded, the words must be proven true according to the sense arising out of the innuendo. Doubts remain as to whether evidence of previous convictions can be used to justify imputations of criminal activities.[126]

One of the difficulties for the media defendant lies in the fact that aggravated damages may be awarded if justification is pleaded but fails. Such an award of aggravated damages signals that the conduct of the defendant has added to the harm. The rationale behind an award of aggravated damages where a plea of justification fails is that the defendant, in standing over the story and asserting that it was true, has 'persisted in a lie'. Not only has he/she impugned the plaintiff's reputation in the first instance but has maintained throughout the pre-trial and trial stages that the allegations were true, thus adding to the harm to the plaintiff's reputation. The defence is therefore a dangerous one. The possibility of an award of aggravated damages acts as a deterrent to defendants to rely on the defence.[127]

The primary task of juries in assessing damages is to compensate the injured party for the harm done, not to punish the defendant. Nevertheless, the Supreme Court in *McIntyre v Lewis*[128] supported the retention of punitive damages in certain circumstances in defamation cases. This decision has, however, clarified the issue and laid down criteria to apply.[129] Where punitive damages are awarded, they tend to be much greater than the compensatory award. For instance, in the English case of *Elton John v Sunday Mirror*,[130] £75,000 was awarded as compensation and £275,000 as punitive or exemplary damages.[131] In Scotland, where juries are seldom used in defamation cases and compensation levels are low, punitive damages are not part of the law.[132]

The defence of justification is therefore problematic on a number of fronts. However, it relates only to facts, as only facts can be proved true or false. There is a separate defence for comment. In practical terms, journalists who want to stand over what they have reported, need to be satisfied not only that they have got their facts right and that what they have said was true but also that they would be able to prove it in court. Journalists need to be careful when describing or commenting on a single incident not to give the impression that it is a habitual occurrence, in which case the defence of truth may not be satisfied. They need to be careful not to ascribe motives or reasons for behaviour, unless they are sure those motives or reasons can also be proven true in court. For instance, to say that a solicitor did not raise the matter of diplomatic immunity in court because he had forgotten to bring the documentation with him resulted in an award of £30,000 in the Circuit Court against two newspapers. It was true that the solicitor did not raise the matter of immunity but he was able to satisfy the court that his decision not to do so was a deliberate one and not the result of forgetting the documents.[133]

It can be dangerous also to draw inferences from facts. In *Prior v Irish Press*,[134] for example, a local farmer had been arrested during a search for kidnappers, and the inference was drawn that he was one of the kidnappers. In fact, he merely happened to be passing and was in the wrong place at the wrong time. Such an inference brings the allegation into the realm of fact. The formulation in *Campbell v Spottiswoode*[135] of the law regarding imputations of dishonourable motives is somewhat unclear, and there do not appear to be any Irish authorities on the subject except *Black v Northern Whig*[136] and *Foley v Independent Newspapers*,[137] in which Geoghegan J. in the High Court was satisfied that *Campbell v Spottiswoode* was still good law in this jurisdiction.

In order to avail of the defence of justification, journalists need to have evidence that would stand up in court. They need to be able to rely in part on witnesses who would be willing to testify. Journalists depend on confidential sources and therefore have no alternative in some cases but to settle or forego their defence. Even when sources have not been promised confidentiality they may not be willing to appear, and the availability of witnesses who are willing to testify is often a difficulty for the media in defending a case.[138] Journalists also rely on their own detailed notes of the story and of the checks they ran. Their notes and tape-recordings have a value. They are useful to lawyers in determining whether a case should be fought or settled. Where they record events first-hand, they may also have an evidential value in court. To that end, journalists should be encouraged or required by their employers to date notes as they make them and keep them for a reasonable period of time.[139] Where they merely record what others said, journalists' notes might not be admissible in evidence in court on the grounds that they amount to 'hearsay'. The same applies to tape-recordings and video evidence. It is for the courts to decide on admissibility in accordance with the law of evidence.

Most important, for all aspects of the media, is the creation or promotion of a climate of carefulness and checking. This will remain the key to avoiding defamation even if law reform along the lines proposed by the Law Reform Commission becomes a reality. If the Commission's proposals are acted upon, negligence or absence of reasonable care will be the test applied in claims for general damages. The media will no longer be liable to pay damages in all cases of defamation but only in those where it is established that there was a failure to take reasonable care. In this respect, our law would be brought more into line with that of the United States (malice and negligence standards) and most European countries (*bonne foi* in France, for example). The idea behind a defence of reasonable care is to allow some latitude to the media, a breathing-space for error, as the United States Supreme Court put it in NY *Times v Sullivan*,[140] while at the same time encouraging careful research in journalism. It may be argued that promotion of standards or of media accountability is not, and should not be, the purpose of defamation law. Nonetheless, reasonable care is the standard demanded by tort law of all other professions; negligence is the test of their liability and is preferable to the strict liability situation under current defamation law.[141]

3. Fair Comment

Fair comment is the defence most often relied on by the media, with limited success. It is pleaded in over forty per cent of the defamation cases against the media that go to court but is successful in only five per cent. To establish the defence of fair comment, the defendant must show:

(a) that the words complained of were comment, as opposed to fact,
(b) that the comment was fair, in the sense of being honestly held, and
(c) that the comment was made on a matter of public interest.

(a) Comment as opposed to fact

The greatest difficulty with the defence of fair comment lies in distinguishing between fact and comment. 'Comment' is the expression of opinion, whereas 'fact' is the statement of verifiable information.[142] In practice, however, it can be difficult to separate the two, which are often intertwined. For instance, if a restaurant review states that 'the sausages were swimming in grease' or that 'the peas were frozen on the plate', is that fact or comment?[143] If the words are prefaced by phrases such as 'in my opinion' or 'it seems to me that', does that necessarily signal that what follows is comment as opposed to fact? If that were so, journalists and publishers would have very great scope indeed and could use the device to cover all kinds of insinuations and inferences. Would that necessarily be a bad thing? After all, the other two requirements of the defence, honest opinion and public interest ((b) and (c) above), would still apply as 'brakes'. The legal position is that the use of such phrases will normally signal comment,[144] but it is open to the court to decide if that is so in the particular case. However, it might be inimical to good journalism to use such phrases because of the impact they have on the authoritativeness or readability of the material being presented.[145] Who would want to read or listen to a story or review peppered with 'in my opinion'? The reader or listener knows when he/she reads an editorial that it is the expression of the views of the newspaper. The reader knows that a review is only the reviewer's opinion and assessment. How much weight readers or listeners place on editorials or reviews depends largely on what the newspaper is or who the particular reviewer is.

Newspaper editorials are normally accepted as comment but can be sued upon successfully, as seen in *Donoghue v Irish Press*.[146] In that case, editorial comment referred to a so-called 'passports for sale' case, in which an official at the Irish Embassy in London, who had been accused of 'selling' Irish passports, was allowed to go free. The editorial stated that the 'slip-up over diplomatic immunity' was difficult to understand and that 'if the case had been properly handled in the first place . . . no embarrassing second attempt would be needed'. A lawyer from the Chief State Solicitor's Office, who was in charge of the case, sued successfully, although he had not been named. An editorial is by its very nature a comment, but, in the eyes of the law, to say that there had been a 'slip-up' is verifiable, and therefore more in the realm of fact than comment. To reduce the analysis of the language used to this degree of particularity is, however, artificial and can distract from the overall impression of the piece.[147] At any rate, while the comment in *Donoghue* was on a matter of public interest, the Circuit Court judge did not accept that it was fair comment.

In the same way, opinion pieces in the 'op. ed.' pages, diary pieces, book, theatre and restaurant reviews are normally expected to be comment pieces but can be sued upon. A diary piece on army evidence in a case in which a soldier had been convicted of child sexual abuse gave rise to an action in *Foley v Irish Times*.[148] A Circuit Court award of £5,000, which is low by defamation standards, reflected the fact that a prompt apology was published in the diary. W*ard and Ní Fhlatharta v Independent Newspapers*[149] arose out of a column piece which commented on the voting on an abortion motion by delegates to an NUJ conference. The High Court jury found that the facts were substantially true but that the comment was not fair comment. In *Harkin and Kendricks v Irish Times*,[150] the Circuit Court awarded £15,000 to the plaintiffs based on a restaurant review. The judge was persuaded by the not inconsiderable influence and propensity to cause harm that critics have, most notably the theatre critic of the *New York Times*. Nonetheless, the judge's view that a restaurant critic should visit a restaurant on at least two separate occasions before writing about it is simply not practical. The High Court, on appeal, found part of the review inaccurate but not defamatory and reversed the decision. Costs, nonetheless, were awarded to the plaintiffs, which meant that in financial terms at least it was a hollow victory for the newspaper.

Letters to the editor, a mechanism to allow readers to express opinions or to react to coverage, are also vulnerable and require particular scrutiny, although, if they can be shown to be written in self-defence or if absence of malice can be proved, then they may not incur liability in certain circumstances.[151] Headlines are even more problematic. They will seldom be treated as fair comment, which precludes the use of that defence. Equally they are unlikely to be regarded as 'reporting' to come within the protection of the defence of privilege, which the Defamation Act 1961 provides for fair and accurate reports. The only possible defence in respect of headlines, therefore, is justification.[152]

It can be so difficult to distinguish between fact and comment or to predict how a court will distinguish between them, especially in the early stages of an action, that the practice has developed of lawyers pleading the 'rolled-up' plea:

> Insofar as the words complained of consist of allegations of fact, they are true in substance and in fact, and insofar as they consist of opinion they are fair comments made in good faith and without malice upon the said facts, which are matters of public interest.

The only advantage of this plea is that it allows defence lawyers to buy time. In order to keep their options open in case the court will find that the words contain facts rather than, or in addition to, comments, defence lawyers must further plead justification. This must be pleaded separately because the rolled-up plea relates to the defence of fair comment only. Confusion arose in *Campbell v Irish Press*,[153] the case about the snooker exhibition and the remark that 'the table told lies'. Despite evidence that the plaintiff had lost money on subsequent exhibitions, the jury assessed damages at 'nil', for which the Supreme Court substituted £1 since a finding of libel carries a right to at least nominal damages. The defendants, who had published an apology withdrawing their remarks, later tried to stand over them in court. They pleaded the 'rolled-up plea', but the trial judge was of the opinion that the article complained of contained no comment, only facts. Therefore, the defence of fair comment was not open to them. As a result the rolled-up plea, which covers only facts on which comment is based, for the purposes of the defence of fair comment, was not available to them. They should have pleaded justification as well. It is an element of the defence of fair comment that, even when the words complained of are established as comment rather than fact, the comment must be shown to be based on true facts, either expressly stated or readily accessible to the reader, listener or viewer, as the case may be. The truth of every fact need not be proven, just sufficient facts to support the comment:

> In an action for libel or slander in respect of words consisting partly of allegations of fact and partly of expression of opinion, a defence of fair comment shall not fail by reason only that the truth of every allegation of fact is not proved, if the expression of opinion is fair comment having regard to such of the facts alleged or referred to in the words complained of as are proved. (Defamation Act, section 23)

If the supporting facts are not shown to be true, it is possible that aggravated damages could be awarded.[154] The rule in *Mangena v Wright*[155] established that the defence will still be available even if the supporting facts are untrue but were spoken on an occasion of privilege. This is an exception to the general rule and the extent of its application is unclear.[156]

Despite the fact that the right to comment, to express one's opinions and convictions, is expressly protected by Article 40.6.1.i of the Constitution, Irish courts appear to take a very narrow and static approach to the defence of fair comment. The courts have not shown any willingness to develop the defence or to allow it to expand to accommodate the role of the media in commenting on and criticising standards in society generally. Book, cinema, theatre, even restaurant, reviews are a valid part of media content and should be given a wide latitude. They have a potential to cause harm and therefore should be answerable in law where they are actuated by spite or other wrongful motive. However, the present distinction between fact and comment becomes totally artificial in practice (as shown by the previous examples) and means that the defence is rarely successful. An easier and more meaningful test would be to ask: was the remark an expression of the journalist's opinion? Otherwise, it is possible that reviews will cease to be part of media content and will be replaced by an uncritical litany of praise, courtesy of the public relations industry. That industry has a very valid role but it should not become a substitute for criticism and analysis in the media. The European Court of Human Rights in Lingens[157] and following cases has made a clear distinction between fact and opinion and has held that the requirement (of Austrian law) that the defendant prove the truth of an allegedly defamatory opinion infringed his/her right to impart ideas as well as the public's right to receive ideas under Article 10 of the Convention:

> [A] careful distinction needs to be made between facts and value-judgments. The existence of facts can be demonstrated, whereas the truth of value-judgments is not susceptible of proof . . . As regards value-judgments, this requirement [to prove truth] is impossible of fulfilment and it infringes freedom of opinion itself . . . .[158]

(b) An Opinion Honestly Held

To establish the defence of fair comment it must be shown that the comment was fair in the sense of being an opinion honestly held. The test is not a subjective one,[159] but rather an objective one as to whether a commentator, however biased or irrational, however exaggerated or extreme the language used, could honestly have held such an opinion given the truth of the facts on which it was based.

Confusion arises, however, because malice is also relevant to the defence of fair comment and the test of malice is a subjective one, although the question of malice is only relevant if the elements of the defence have been established. This and other distinctions and nuances that have developed in relation to the defence make it very confusing for juries, in particular.

The essence of the defence of fair comment is the factual basis for the comment. The expression of the opinion need not be fair; intemperate, exaggerated or vehement language may be used since the defence protects 'the honest views of the crank and the eccentric', as much as those of any other, but not when they are based on dishonest statements of fact.[160] As Mill said, ridicule and invective should be tolerated: 'They may stimulate partizans, but they are not calculated to make converts.'[161]

In theory, the trenchancy or irrational nature of the comment, or the vehemence of the language used, will not destroy the defence. Only a finding of malice will do so. Malice here means some wrongful motive: spite, ill will, personal vendetta or want of good faith. The onus is on the plaintiff alleging it to establish malice. Evidence of a concerted campaign against the plaintiff may be sufficient to establish malice. A failure to retract a statement or apologise for it will not usually be taken as proof of malice, but it depends on the circumstances. As the Supreme Court said in *Barrett v Independent Newspapers*,[162] the conduct of the media from publication right through the trial process can be taken into account. Repetition of the comment or publication of an inadequate or damaging apology may be taken as evidence of malice. A particular difficulty arises where the matter complained of has come unsolicited, for example, in a letter to the editor. What if the author was actuated by malice, unknown to the editor or publisher? The law is not altogether clear, but it seems that the malice of the author will not deprive the publisher of the defence.[163]

While the language used is not fatal to the defence, it should be noted that, unlike other jurisdictions, there is no defence in Irish law for criticism as such, whether in the form of literary criticism, humour, satire, irony or hyperbole. These are merely factors to be considered in deciding whether the words complained of are defamatory or whether any of the defences, such as fair comment, are established. To penalise them would make for very dull copy in an area where readers or audiences expect opinion and, indeed, originality or individuality on the part of the reviewer. Reviewers need latitude to 'gild the lily', even if it means that the publisher of the work ultimately loses sales as a result.[164] As the United States Supreme Court asserted, ideas and opinions should be corrected not by judges and juries but by the competition of other ideas.[165]

(c) Public Interest

The question of the public interest is a matter for the judge to decide. Judges have consistently stated that the public interest is not the same as the interest of the public. Other than that, they have not given any detailed guidance as to what constitutes the public interest or any great support for media appeals to the public interest. It is therefore a nebulous concept of uncertain scope.[166] In the context of the fair comment defence, however, comment on a wide range of public as opposed to private matters is envisaged, from arts and restaurant reviews to comments on national and local issues.

In *Thorgeirson v Iceland*[167] the European Court of Human Rights held that media reporting and comment on matters of public interest are entitled to the same degree of protection as political discussion. The case concerned two articles on police brutality for which the journalist had been fined in the Icelandic courts. Individual police officers were not named in the articles, but there were references to 'brutes in uniform' and allegations of serious assault. The issue was a matter of public concern, the Court of Human Rights held, and the articles had the legitimate purpose of promoting reform of the system for investigating complaints against the police. The articles were based on public opinion following the recent conviction of a police officer for brutality. In those circumstances, although the articles relied heavily on rumours, stories and the statements of others, they related to an important matter of public interest and the journalist should not be required to prove the factual basis for those statements. It would seem therefore that where media comment is based on public opinion on an important matter of public interest it will be given wide protection in the same way as political criticism and comment.[168]

A recent Irish case might well have come under the *Thorgeirson* rubric. An *Irish Times* diary piece commenting on the prosecution of a brothel keeper criticised the witnesses who had given evidence against her, referring to them as 'ticks' and suggesting that giving evidence against her was 'ten times more odious than using her house'.[169] A garda who had given evidence in the case claimed that he had been defamed, but the opening sentence of the diary column had intimated that the gardaí were only doing their job. The Circuit Court judge found that there was no defamation involved. It would appear also from the circumstances of the case that a defence of fair comment could have succeeded.[170]

4. Privilege

There are two forms of privilege applicable to defamation: absolute privilege and qualified privilege. The former stems from the Constitution and from statute, while the second has its roots in the common law and statute.

(a) Absolute privilege

The Constitution speaks only of privilege, the adjective 'absolute' is not used, but the privilege is nonetheless regarded as absolute, i.e. it is not destroyed by malice. Under Article 13.8.1 of the Constitution the

President of Ireland has absolute privilege in respect of the exercise and performance of the powers and functions of his/her office. Article 15.12 of the Constitution accords privilege to all official reports and publications of the Oireachtas or of either House thereof and to utterances made in either House wherever published:

> All official reports and publications of the Oireachtas or of either House thereof and utterances made in either House wherever published shall be privileged.

The Irish language version 'táid saor ar chúrsa; dlí cibé áit a bhfoilsítear' makes clear the absolute nature of the privilege. The privilege has been extended to committees of the Oireachtas by the Committees of the Houses of the Oireachtas (Privilege and Procedure) Act 1976 section 2. Doubts as to whether it extended to witnesses appearing before committees were put to rest,[171] partly by the passing of legislation at the end of 1994 and by further legislation introduced in 1995.[172]

By virtue of the Defamation Act 1961, section 18, absolute privilege attaches to fair and accurate reports of court proceedings published contemporaneously:

> A fair and accurate report published in any newspaper or broadcast by means of wireless telegraphy as part of any programme or service provided by means of a broadcasting station within the State or in Northern Ireland of proceedings publicly heard before any court established by law and exercising judicial authority within the State or Northern Ireland shall, if published or broadcast contemporaneously with such proceedings, be privileged. (section 18(1))

The requirement of contemporaneity means that only reports published during the hearing or immediately after the hearing are privileged. That means that rebroadcasts or republication at a later date may not have the benefit of the privilege. Moreover, the privilege is confined to the more immediate news media; it attaches only to newspaper and broadcast reports, not to film, video or book publishing.[173] The reason for confining the privilege to contemporaneous reports is that matter given in evidence in court, whether by way of charge or countercharge, may subsequently be refuted or proven groundless. If such charges can later be repeated at will under the protection of privilege, the person concerned may suffer undue harm. Nonetheless, it may be argued that the requirement of contemporaneity is not necessary as the need to ensure that a report is fair and accurate will of itself provide adequate protection for the parties. It follows that for a court report to be considered fair and accurate if published some weeks, months or years later, both sides of the evidence would have to be given and the outcome of the case, if completed. Besides, only reports of cases are covered by privilege; comments on cases are not covered, although it may be possible to rely on the defence of fair comment instead.

It also appears to be something of an anachronism to exclude 'any blasphemous or obscene matter' from the privilege, if that is the intended effect of section 18.2:

> Nothing in subsection (1) of this section shall authorise the publication of any blasphemous or obscene matter.[174]

While tabloid journalism, with its emphasis on the unseemly and the sensational, is not to be encouraged, it is at least arguable that to deliberately exclude any blasphemous or obscene matter from a court report could render the report unfair or inaccurate and cause it to lose the privilege altogether. How could cases such as *Whitehouse v Lemon*[175] (poem depicting Christ as a homosexual), *R v Bow Street Magistrates' Court ex parte Choudhury*[176] (regarding Salman Rushdie's *Satanic Verses*) or *DPP v Fleming*[177] (a criminal libel case about obscene remarks on telephone boxes) ever be reported, if the inclusion of the allegedly blasphemous or obscene remarks would not attract privilege and would leave the reporter open to charges? The privilege for reporting court cases here or in Northern Ireland (Defamation Act 1961, section 18) is regarded as absolute privilege and will not be defeated by a showing of malice. Reports of cases heard in foreign courts, however, are governed by qualified privilege only (Defamation Act 1961, section 24 and Schedule), as discussed in the next section.

(b) Qualified privilege

Qualified privilege arises on occasions when:
  (i) the speaker has a duty, whether legal, moral or social[178] to publish the information complained of and
  (ii) the person to whom the information is addressed has a reciprocal duty or interest in receiving it.

The privilege rests on this notion of duty or common interest. The purpose behind the privilege is to allow business and commerce and the activities of daily life to operate without the constant threat of libel actions. The privilege is conferred where communication takes place for honest purposes and is therefore destroyed by malice or any wrongful motive. It does not matter if the allegations made on a privileged occasion turn out to be unfounded as long as they are made honestly and without malice.

The privilege can be lost if there is excess of publication, if the statement contains irrelevant allegations, for example, or if it is addressed to someone who has no interest in receiving it. An example would be a complaint made to the wrong body, as in *Hynes-O'Sullivan v O'Driscoll*,[179] where a solicitor, unhappy with the behaviour and fees charged by a doctor for attendance in court, complained to the wrong medical body.[180] To attract the privilege the communication must be confined to the particular matter in which the parties have a legitimate common interest, i.e. it must not be excessive in terms of either content or circulation. In *Doyle v The Economist*[181] the court held that there was no such interest involved in the publication of the opinion of unnamed barristers that the plaintiff judge had been appointed to the bench for reasons other than merit. Where the only effective mode of discharging the duty or protecting the interest which gives rise to the privilege is to insert a notice or advertisement in a newspaper, surely such notice or advertisement will attract the privilege so as to protect the advertiser and the paper. In *O'Connor v The Kerryman*[182] solicitors representing fishermen who had allegedly been attacked in a sermon at Mass issued an open letter on their behalf. Was there excess of publication in that case? If Mass is an open forum, it is arguable that the open letter was privileged also, provided its content did not go beyond what was necessary to defend the clients. On that argument, the media that carried the letter would then have privilege too, at least if it had been published verbatim without comment. Where the matter is of general public interest and it is the duty of the defendants to publish it, privilege will apply.

To date, however, the courts have been reluctant to acknowledge the availability of the common-law qualified privilege defence to the media. They have been unwilling to recognise a general media duty to inform or a general public right to be informed. It might be easier to establish such a duty and right in a specialised newspaper, periodical or broadcast, or on a local level where circulation is limited. It is very difficult for a national newspaper or broadcaster to establish the privilege. In their case it might be necessary to establish, in addition to a duty and right to be informed, that the media publication was the only option available. Beyond that, the best that can be said is that the courts are reluctant to recognise a media qualified privilege but that the application of the duty/interest formula could be argued for depending on the particular circumstances of the case.

The defence of qualified privilege with its insistence on duty or common interest is wide enough to encompass self-protection. If the initial attack was made in a newspaper or broadcast, use of the same medium to counteract the attack entitles both the respondent and the newspaper or broadcast which carries the response to privilege.[183] In *Nevin v Roddy and Carty*,[184] the Supreme Court said:

> . . . a man who appeals to the public through the medium of the press cannot complain if those whom he has attacked reply to him through the same public medium.[185]

The Court went on to state that:

> where a party publishes in a public newspaper statements reflecting upon the conduct or character of another, the aggrieved party is entitled to have recourse to the public press for his defence and vindication . . . .[186]

In *O'Brien v The Freeman's Journal Ltd*,[187] it was held that, to establish legitimate self-defence, it must be shown that the alleged libels were published to refute attacks and charges publicly made and that there was an intimate connection between them. The key is vindication: the defendants, said the Court, are entitled to vindicate themselves against false aspersions on them by the plaintiff:

> Their privilege was to defend themselves against an attack made upon them by the plaintiff, not to make an independent attack upon the plaintiff unconnected with and irrelevant to the attack made by the plaintiff upon them.[188]

Sufficient facts must therefore be shown in the plea to establish the necessary connection and relevance and to show that the charges being refuted were defamatory or false, as there would be no privilege if they were true.[189] Privilege is a method of defence, not of attack and, therefore, enables defendants to meet the charges brought against them, not to bring further accusations.[190] The privilege is to defend a character already aspersed, not to assume the initiative in attack.[191] It is a 'right of reply privilege'[192] and, insofar as it enables a reputation to be vindicated is in keeping with the constitutional guarantees expressed in Article 40.3. It is for the judge to decide whether the occasion is privileged. It is then for the jury to decide whether the defendant abused the privilege and exceeded its due limits. The privilege extends only so far as to enable a person to repel the charges made against him/her, not to bring fresh accusations.[193] Once an occasion is shown to be privileged, it is for the plaintiff to prove malice in order to destroy the privilege. Proof of lack of belief that the matter is true may be regarded as malice, unless the speaker was under a duty to pass on the information and did not endorse it.[194]

Statutory Qualified Privilege

There is also a specific media qualified privilege provided by statute. It is contained in section 24 of the Defamation Act 1961 and elaborated in the second schedule to the Act. Unlike the privilege for court reporting contained in section 18 of the Act, the section 24 privilege is a qualified privilege only and will be lost if there is a showing of malice. It is a privilege that attaches firstly to fair and accurate reports of the proceedings in public of foreign legislatures, international organisations of which Ireland is a member or at which Ireland is represented, the International Court of Justice, foreign courts, extracts from public registers, notices, etc.[195] Secondly, provision is made for a privilege that is 'subject to explanation or contradiction'. In this case, the privilege is lost if the publisher is requested by the plaintiff to publish a reasonable statement by way of explanation or contradiction and refuses or neglects to do so or does so in a manner not adequate or not reasonable having regard to all the circumstances (section 24(2)). This type of privilege extends to fair and accurate reports of the findings or decision of certain stated types of bodies and associations in the State or Northern Ireland, the proceedings at public meetings bona fide and lawfully held on matters of public concern, whether admission is general or restricted, meetings of local authorities, statutory commissions and tribunals, reports or summaries of official notices issued for the information of the public by government, local authority or gardai, and their counterparts in Northern Ireland.[196] In all cases, the privilege protects only matter that:

- is not prohibited by law
- is of public concern and
- the publication of which is for the public benefit (section 24(3)).

The case of *Ahern v Cork Evening Echo*[197] is a good example of this kind of privilege and of the limited circumstances in which the law accepts a media duty to inform the public. The case concerned the publication of a warning issued by gardaí about the activities of bogus charity collectors. The plaintiff, a bona fide collector, claimed that the reference would be taken to be to him. The newspaper published a clarification. In court it was accepted that the newspaper had qualified privilege. It had acted on information received in good faith and had taken the necessary steps to safeguard the plaintiff's reputation. There was no liability.

The privilege, while useful to the media, is limited in a number of ways. It applies, rather incongruously, to newspapers and broadcasting only, thus creating a difficulty for book publishers and other media defendants who are not included. It does not extend to coverage of press conferences, which are a major forum nowadays for making information available to the public.[198]

Remedies

1. Damages

The principal remedy for defamation is damages. Damages are a sum of money intended to compensate the plaintiff. Compensation can be claimed for damage to reputation, and special damages for pecuniary or material loss that is quantifiable can also be claimed. In certain circumstances aggravated or punitive damages may be awarded.[199]

One of the difficulties with damages is that jury awards tend to be unpredictable. Juries are given no guidance on how to assess damages, although the Supreme Court in *Barrett v Independent Newspapers*[200] has said that they should. The plaintiff was entitled to be compensated for the damage to his reputation and also for the hurt, anxiety and distress, the Chief Justice said.[201] The judges offered specific guidelines as to how a jury might arrive at a suitable figure: in the context of *Barrett*, by taking into account that the plaintiff was a full-time politician[202] and the effect on him in the particular circumstances of the case and by fitting the allegation into its appropriate place on the scale of defamatory remarks to which the plaintiff as a politician might have been subjected.[203] Damages should be compensatory and should therefore be reasonable, fair and bear a due correspondence with the injury suffered.[204] The Court also said that juries should take into account such matters as the plaintiff's position and standing in the community, the nature of the libel, the absence or refusal of any retraction or apology, any social disadvantages that may result or be thought likely to result from the wrong done to the plaintiff, the injury to his feelings, i.e. the natural distress he may have felt at having been spoken or written of in defamatory terms, the whole conduct of the defendants from the time of publication down to the moment of their verdict and the conduct and attitude of the plaintiff himself.[205]

Some judges in England have been rather more colourful, telling juries in assessing damages not to think of football pools or telephone numbers but to think of a figure somewhere between the price of a house and a clapped-out Volvo;[206] or to award the plaintiff either the price of a night out at his favourite night club where a bottle of champagne costs £55, or the price of a car, or the price of a house.[207]

Because of the unpredictability of juries and the prospects of high damages and even higher costs, media defendants might be inclined to settle cases at an early stage, but if they do so, they come to be recognised as 'an easy touch', which in itself encourages more claims and perpetuates the problem. If they hold out and go to court, their chances of winning are very small and there is the possibility of high jury awards, factors that encourage plaintiffs not to settle unless an offer of a considerable sum of money is made.

If the media go to court, the plaintiff has nothing to lose, because of present rules regarding payment into court. Payment into court, whereby a defendant will not have to pay plaintiff's costs if the damages awarded are less than the sum offered and lodged with the court, is not available to the defendant under Irish rules of court (in contrast to the UK where a similar rule was abolished in 1933–4) unless the defendant first admits liability, in which case, the only matter to be resolved is the level of damages to be awarded. The defendant who has admitted liability will not then be able to rely on a defence. Legal costs are also very high, often much higher than the damages awarded, with the result that small publishers are invariably advised to settle cases for a fixed sum rather than face the uncertainty of a court case with the possibility of a large award of damages and costs that could destroy the company. Book publishers and smaller and newer periodical and newspaper publishers usually have no insurance, either because it is not available or because the premiums are too high.

The highest sum ever awarded in Ireland for defamation was £275,000 in *Denny v Sunday News*.[208] In that case, the plaintiff, a County Monaghan soldier, was named in an article with a huge headline: 'British "spy" was Irish Soldier'. An army investigation after publication of the story cleared the soldier of any involvement. The paper did not contest the case and the only issue in court was the amount of damages. In 1986[209] the Supreme Court clarified its position in relation to substituting its own award of damages in an appeal for those of a lower court or jury. However, in the defamation cases that have come before it since then the Court has upheld the jury award.[210] In *Barrett*, which pre-dated the 1986 decision, the Court ordered a retrial and the parties settled. In England the Court of Appeal has exercised its right to substitute its own award rather than order a new trial. In *Rantzen v Mirror Group Newspapers*[211] the Court reduced the award from £250,000 to £110,000. Recently the European Court of Human Rights in *Tolstoy v UK*[212] has held that an award of £1.5 million was so disproportionately large as to constitute a violation of the plaintiff's right to freedom of expression under Article 10 of the Convention.[213]

It is difficult to gauge the part played by emotional distress in jury cases. It may be that who the particular defendant is becomes a factor in determining the size of the award. It appears that awards against tabloid newspapers, which publish emotional and sensational stories, are likely to be significantly higher than those against the non-tabloid newspaper or public service broadcaster. There may be some significance in the fact that the highest awards in Ireland were against the *Sunday News* (a Northern Ireland paper) and the *Daily Mirror* and *Sun*,[214] or were they totally attributable to the seriousness of the allegations of IRA links which all three cases concerned?

The greatest obstacle to reform of defamation law is the reliance on the damages remedy. As long as damages remain the central remedy, there is little incentive to try other remedies and little room for reform. The provision of simpler, swifter remedies as alternatives to damages was one of the key proposals of the Law Reform Commission. Retractions, corrections, clarifications, declaratory proceedings and judgments should be made available to those who want to vindicate their good name, quickly and effectively, rather than having to go through a court case to obtain damages some three years after publication of the harmful matter.[215]

2. Mitigation

Certain factors may be taken in mitigation of damages.[216] The most common is the publication of an apology (Defamation Act, section 17), but factors such as circulation figures, the conduct of the plaintiff and evidence of previous bad reputation[217] are also relevant. It is less clear whether the defendant's state of mind will be taken in mitigation.[218] The LRC points out that a defendant can mitigate damages by showing that he repeated material from another source *and* disclosed that source in the publication.[219]

The apology provided for in section 17 of the Defamation Act is intended as a means of mitigating damage. The apology must be made or offered to the plaintiff before the commencement of the action or as soon afterwards as he/she has an opportunity of doing so. To avail of the section, it is necessary to give prior notice in writing of an intention to do so. An apology is not therefore a complete defence to a libel action but, if accepted as wholehearted and fulsome by the court, can mitigate damage and lead to a reduction in the amount of compensation payable. See, for example, *Bowman v Connaught Telegraph*,[220] where the judge acknowledged that the defamatory remark was the result of a typesetting error and took account of the fact that an apology had been published. He awarded £1,000. Likewise in *Foley v Irish Times*,[221] allowance was made for the publication of an apology and £5,000 awarded. On the other hand, if the apology is regarded as half-hearted, it may only compound the original injury, as was claimed in *McSharry v Waterford Post*,[222] and could conceivably lead to a higher award of damages.

Another difficulty with apologies is that they are often taken to be an admission of liability. If that happens, then the defendant may find that he/she cannot rely on any of the defences to defamation and is totally at the mercy of the jury. It becomes simply a matter of how much money the jury will award. The media, therefore, are cautious about publishing apologies. In addition, it happens in practice that solicitors for the plaintiff try to exact a form of apology which is so abject and a negation of the defendant's right to defend the action as to make agreement impossible. In those circumstances, capital is made of the fact that the media refused to publish an apology. The position of broadcasters is different only to the extent that the Broadcasting Act 1990 now requires them to afford a complainant a right of reply (see further discussion in Chapter 11).

Unintentional Defamation and the Offer of Amends

Many defamatory publications are unintentional but that does not mean that they will not attract liability. Defamation is a strict liability tort, that is, once the elements of the tort are proved (i.e. publication by the defendant, reference to the plaintiff, defamatory nature), the publisher is liable, regardless of motives or intent unless he/she can establish one of the defences provided for in the Defamation Act 1961 or at common law. The only remedy provided in the case of unintentional defamation is the offer of amends in section 21 of the Defamation Act 1961. This was devised by parliament as a remedy for the harshness of the situation encountered in Britain in cases such as *Hulton v Jones*[223] and *Newstead v London Express*.[224] In the former, it turned out that there was a barrister of the same name as a fictitious church warden referred to in a light-hearted sketch about sober Englishmen living it up on the other side of the Channel. In the second, an accurate court report was sued upon by the plaintiff who happened to have the same name and come from the same locality as a man convicted of bigamy. The remedy devised by parliament was intended to provide a form of right of reply, a method of setting the record straight. The aim was admirable, because the most sensible way to clear up confusion is to publish a clarification, rather than proceeding to court for damages. A clarification published immediately or soon after the event can undo any possible damage in a way that an award of money some years later can not. In fact, it is quite common nowadays for newspapers and broadcasting stations to publish clarifications in such circumstances and the people concerned are usually satisfied.[225] In some cases at least a clarification is better vindication of reputation, as required by the Irish Constitution, Article 40.3, than damages.

In that sense, the offer of amends should provide a remedy for fiction and many other areas of unintentional defamation. However, the offer of amends in section 21 of the Defamation Act 1961 applies only to a very limited category of unintentional defamation. It applies only where a person who has published words alleged to be defamatory of another person claims that 'the words were published by him innocently in relation to that other person'. Even then, it can be availed of only if the publisher

(a)   did not intend to publish them about that other person and did not know of circumstances by which they might be understood to refer to him; or

(b)   the words were not defamatory on their face and the publisher did not know of circumstances by virtue of which they might be understood to be defamatory of that other person,

and, in either case, the publisher 'exercised all reasonable care in relation to the publication' (section 21(5)). 'Publisher' in this instance includes any servant or agent concerned with the contents of the publication.

If the publisher meets these conditions, he/she may offer to publish a suitable correction of the words complained of and a sufficient apology. He/she must also take such steps as are reasonably practicable to notify persons to whom copies have been distributed that the words are alleged to be defamatory of the party aggrieved (section 21(3)). If the offer is accepted and duly performed, the publisher will incur no further liability. Any question arising, following acceptance, will be determined by the High Court (section 21(4)). If the offer is not accepted, it may be possible for the publisher to rely on the making of the offer as a defence (section 21(1)(b)). However, a number of difficulties arise. The defence will not be available if the party aggrieved proves that he/she has suffered special damage, usually financial damage (section 21(6)). Nor will it be available to a publisher who is not the author of the offending words unless he/she proves that the words were written by the author without malice (section 21(7)). Moreover, there are practical difficulties involved in setting up the defence. The offer must have been expressed to have been made for the purpose of the section (that is, section 21 of the Act); it must have been made as soon as practicable after the defendant received notice of the alleged defamation; it must not have been withdrawn (section 21(1)(b)); it must be accompanied by an affidavit specifying the facts relied upon to show that the words were published innocently of the plaintiff (section 21(2)); and no evidence other than evidence of facts specified in the affidavit shall be admissible on behalf of the publisher to prove that the words were so published (section 21(2)).

The section relating to the offer of amends has seven subsections, four of which are further subdivided into paragraphs (a) and (b); it spans two and a half pages of print. While there is some evidence to suggest that it can dispose of defamation cases if accepted,[226] it has proved totally impractical as a defence. Two of the difficulties encountered with the offer of amends are the requirement of reasonable case and the requirement of an affidavit.

One stumbling block to the use of the offer of amends in either guise, as a complete remedy or as a defence, is the requirement of reasonable care. What constitutes, in journalistic terms, reasonable care? While the concept of reasonable care in relation to manufacturers, professionals, local authorities and other such bodies is well developed in tort law, its application to journalists and media has never been litigated. That is so because defamation in our law is a strict liability tort, not a tort of negligence, and the issue of reasonable care does not arise except in relation to the offer of amends and the common-law defence for distributors (see discussion later in this chapter). A case such as the previously cited *Browne v Independent Newspapers*[227] might have been the kind of case where one would expect the offer of amends to provide a remedy. It may be that the requirement of reasonable care would not have been met since a perusal of the relevant telephone directory would presumably have provided the information that a builder of that name operated in the locality. The problem was further compounded by the fact that unlike the other 'colour' surnames used—Green, White, Black—Browne was spelt with an 'e'. The publisher may have felt that the publication of a disclaimer and categorisation of the names used in the article as fictitious would prevent liability. However, a jury awarded the plaintiff £75,000.

In the case of the media, reasonable care must necessitate at least the checking of sources and facts. In the English case of *Ross v*

Hopkinson[228] the requirement was not met as the name chosen for the fictitious actress was the same as that of a leading West End actress. An indication of what might constitute reasonable care in journalistic terms can be gleaned from the standard imposed on the private plaintiff in the United States to show negligence and from the French concept of *bonne foi*. In the US public plaintiffs, such as politicians and public figures, must show malice on the part of the media, whereas private plaintiffs must show negligence.[229] The steps taken by the journalist and media organisation in the pre-publication stages come under scrutiny. The state of the defendant's mind becomes relevant. In *Herbert v Lando*,[230] the Supreme Court held that the plaintiff was entitled to enquire into the editorial process and even to rummage through journalists' research notes, paperwork and unused film, in order to gauge their state of mind at the time of publication. The effect of the decision was to encourage the creation of a paper trail: to stop issuing critical internal memos and issue positive statements approving and commending the journalists' work instead.

In France it is possible for journalists to plead *bonne foi*, i.e. that they acted in good faith. The court will then look to see if certain criteria are met: was there a legitimate purpose in publishing the story? an absence of personal animosity? serious and objective investigation? prudent expression? For instance, in 1993 the Cour de Cassation (equivalent of our Supreme Court) decided that an allegation that a doctor was profiting from AIDS by offering illusory treatment for financial gain was capable of being defamatory. However, it found that the purpose in publishing the article was to inform the reader on a matter of public interest and that the journalist had researched the story thoroughly, contacting doctors and experts with opposing views, so that *bonne foi* was established and there was no liability.[231] In contrast, the BBC in 1983 settled a case taken by a Harley Street slimming expert against the 'That's Life' programme, which he said portrayed him as 'a profiteering, unscrupulous quack'. The case, *Gee v BBC*,[232] had been running in the High Court in London for eighty-nine days when the BBC agreed to pay £75,000 damages, plus the doctor's share of the total legal bill, estimated at £1.2 million. The trial began with a jury but they were later discharged when the hearing, which was largely taken up with detailed medical evidence, became too complex for them.

The second stumbling block to the use of the offer of amends is the requirement of an affidavit. The most obvious difficulty with this requirement stems from the conditions attaching to it by virtue of section 21(1)(b) and section 21(2). An offer of amends must be made as soon as practicable, must be accompanied by an affidavit and only the facts set out in the affidavit can then be relied on if the case goes to court. The problem, therefore, is that if the media delay in making the offer of amends in order to check out the facts thoroughly, they run the risk that the offer will not be considered to have been made as soon as practicable.[233] On the other hand, if they make the offer 'as soon as practicable', there is a danger of overlooking facts that would be important for their defence but that could not then be raised in court because only facts contained in the affidavit are admissible. The usefulness of the section is further reduced by the fact that it does not apply in cases where special damage is proved. It is also exceedingly burdensome to expect the publisher of letters to the editor, works of fiction and so on to prove absence of malice on the part of the author in order to be able to rely on the offer of amends. In sum, the statutory remedy envisaged by section 21 is good in theory but virtually impossible to avail of in practice. Reform bodies in a number of countries have recommended overhauling it or replacing it entirely.[234]

Law Reform

Even with the refinements and improvements carried over into the Defamation Act 1961, defamation law in Ireland has proved less than satisfactory. The Act has not stood the test of time, it does not take account of modern technological realities in the media field and needs to be replaced with an updated law. Libel law at present is unduly complex, a 'mad jumble', as one commentator has called it,[235] and many would argue that it manages to achieve the worst of two worlds: it does little to protect reputation and it does much to deter speech and hinder the media. As the Law Reform Commission said, current defamation law fails to serve either the plaintiff, defendant or public.[236] It fails to give due respect to the constitutional provisions. Many of the problems stem from lack of clarity and lack of certainty.[237] Consequently, the Commission made a number of substantive recommendations to be included in a new defamation act.[238] A private member's bill, based on the LRC's recommendations was introduced in 1995, and the government in response announced its intention to bring in its own proposals.

If the government implements the Law Reform Commission's proposals, many of the difficulties experienced with current defamation law, as outlined above, will be lessened or removed. The focus will no longer be on damages alone, and there will be an incentive to try other means, such as correction or declaratory orders, to vindicate reputation. The proposed defence of reasonable care, if implemented, will give the media the incentive to maintain high standards of care and accuracy in the preparation and presentation of stories. With that in mind, the following 'checklist' is offered to journalism students as a practical guide to avoiding libel.[239] However, it is only a checklist, not a substitute for being familiar with the rules of libel law, discussed in this chapter.

Checklist for Journalists

In preparing your story:
1. Have you named, or otherwise identified, any individual(s) or company? Could anything you have said point to, or reasonably be taken to refer to, any group small enough that its individual members might be identifiable?
2. Have you checked out and stated accurately all the facts about them that you intend to include in the publication? Have you sought the other side of the story?
3. Can you prove all those facts through witnesses, documents that will stand up in court and notes of the checks that you have made?
4. Is anything you have said capable of being regarded as defamatory, either in its ordinary sense or by virtue of an innuendo?
5. Will you have a defence?

Further Reading

Bezanson, Randall P., Cranberg, Gilbert and Soloski, John, *Libel Law and the Press: Myth and Reality*, New York: The Free Press, a Division of Macmillan Inc., 1987.

Boyle, Kevin, and McGonagle, Marie, *Press Freedom and Libel*, Dublin: National Newspapers of Ireland, 1988.

Law Reform Commission, *Consultation Paper on the Civil Law of Defamation*, 1991, and *Report on the Civil Law of Defamation* (LRC 38–1991) Dublin: 1991.

McDonald, Marc, *Irish Law of Defamation*, 2nd ed., Dublin: The Round Hall Press, 1989.

Robertson, Geoffrey, and Nicol, Andrew, *Media Law*, 3rd ed., London: Penguin Books, 1992.

Soloski, John, and Bezanson, Randall P., *Reforming Libel Law*, New York: The Guilford Press, 1992.

Notes

1 John Stuart Mill, 'Law of Libel and Liberty of the Press' in John M. Robson, ed., *Essays on Equality, Law and Education*, University of Toronto Press, 1980, p. 3 at p. 16.
2 For a fuller treatment of defamation, see Marc McDonald, *Irish Law of Defamation*, 2nd ed., Dublin: The Round Hall Press, 1989; Sir Brian Neill and Richard Rampton, *Duncan and Neill on Defamation*, London: Butterworths, 1983; Peter Frederick Carter-Ruck et al., *Carter-Ruck on Libel and Slander*, 4th edn., London: Butterworths, 1991.
3 All the reform bodies have recommended its abolition. See, for example, Irish Law Reform Commission, *Report on the Civil Law of Defamation* 1991, (LRC 38–1991) at p. 5; Australian Law Reform Commission, *Unfair Publication: Defamation and Privacy*, 1979, at para. 76; Faulks Committee *Report of the Committee on Defamation*, London, 1975, cmnd 5909, ch. 2.
4 An examination of High Court records in defamation cases revealed that the total number of cases set down for hearing in the five-year period 1986–90 was more than double that of 1981–85. The number for 1990 alone was more than double that for 1986 and more than four times that for 1980. See Kevin Boyle and Marie McGonagle, A *Report on Press Freedom and Libel*, Dublin: NNI, 1988, and 'Reform of Defamation Law' in Marie McGonagle, ed., *Essays on Law and Media*, Dublin: The Round Hall Press, forthcoming. Statistics, where quoted and not otherwise attributed, are from these two sources.
5 The Law Reform Commission has, however, put forward proposals for change (see n. 3), and a private member's bill, incorporating most of those changes was introduced in the Oireachtas in February 1995. The government put a stay of nine months on it, with a view to bringing in its own proposals.
6 For example, see Brian Inglis, *The Freedom of the Press in Ireland: 1784–1841*, London: Faber and Faber, 1954, at p. 225 (the Attorney General intervened in a civil suit to procure the publisher of *The Pilot* a three-month prison sentence and fine, even though the libels complained of were not particularly offensive).
7 This occurred from the time of the Second World War in Britain see J.R. Spencer, 'Criminal Libel—A Skeleton in the Cupboard', Parts 1 and 2; [1977] Crim LR 383, 465, at p. 389.
8 See Professor Werner Lorenz, 'Privacy and the Press—A German Experience', *Butterworth's Lectures*, 1989–90, London: Butterworths, 1990.
9 The Archbishop of Dublin, 'The O'Keeffe Cases', 1 Ir Eccles Rec 1913, pp 113–31.
10 See n. 6, Inglis. at p. 225: *Gray v Evening Post* (£250); *Jones v Evening Mail* (£300).
11 See n. 3; also reform has been urged by the Neill Committee in Britain: Supreme Court Procedure Committee, *Report on Practice and Procedure in Defamation* 1991. Amending legislation was brought in in New Zealand, Defamation Act 1992.
12 See *Lingens v Austria*, Series A, no. 103; [1986] 8 EHRR 407, *Oberschlick v Austria*, Series A, no. 204; [1995] 19 EHRR 389, *Schwabe v Austria*, Series A, no. 242–B, 19 , 20. In *Tolstoy v UK* the European Court of Human Rights has held that a jury award of £1.5 million constitutes an unwarranted infringement of the defendant's right to freedom of expression and amounts to a breach of Article 10 of the Convention. See *The Irish Times* 1 December 1989; case 8/1994/455/536, judgment 13 July 1995.
13 Academic commentators over the last decade or so, McDonald, O'Dell, Boyle and McGonagle and others, have advocated a new approach based on the Constitution; see notes 2 McDonald, 4 and 238; also ch. 2, n. 3, O'Dell.
14 Faulks Committee, *Report of the Committee on Defamation*, cmnd 5909, London, 1975, at para. 19.
15 This is despite the recommendations of the Pringle Committee in 1977: *Report of the Committee on Civil Legal Aid and Advice*, Dublin: Government Publications, 1977, Prl. 6862.

16 Kevin Boyle and Marie McGonagle, n. 4. The problem is particularly acute for small publications and book publishers. See, for example, *Sunday Tribune*, 23 October 1988 and *The Irish Times*, 11 November 1989. (Gill & Macmillan, for example, had paid out well over £100,000 in out-of-court settlements and costs in the previous eighteen months and had to discontinue libel insurance as it could not afford the premiums demanded.) Libel cases are believed to have led to the demise of the *Irish Statesman* in 1928 (*Clandillon v Irish Statesman*, unreported, High Court, 14 November 1928, a case that arose out of a review of a book of folk songs *Lon Dubh a' Chairn*); *The Leader* in 1955 (*Kavanagh v The Leader*, unreported, Supreme Court, 4 March 1955; a reference in a literary article to poet Patrick Kavanagh); the Irish language newspaper *Amárach* in 1983 (*Lindsay v Amárach*, *The Irish Times*, 15 February 1983, a reference to how a government minister was allocating state money). More recently, libel actions were reported to have caused the sale of the *Cavan Leader* (*Sunday Tribune*, 17 November 1991).

17 See, for example, the discussion of cases like *Cole v RTÉ*, *The Irish Times*, 3–11 May 1989, 13 May 1989; *Holloway v Business and Finance* [1987] ILRM 790, [1988] IR 494, *The Irish Times*, 1 December 1990. In the latter case, the articles complained of were published in 1985 but the case was not disposed of until 1990. State employees constitute the third largest group of people suing for libel. Business and professionals constitute the largest; see n. 16, Boyle and McGonagle, at para. 6.14.

18 *Goodman v Hamilton* (No.2) [1993] 3 IR 307; *Burke v Central Television* [1994] 2 ILRM 161.

19 Bryan McMahon and William Binchy, *Irish Law of Torts*, 2nd edn., Dublin: Butterworths, 1991, p. 609; see also *Quigley v Creation Ltd* [1971] IR 269; *Berry v The Irish Times* [1973] IR 368.

20 Per McLoughlin J. in n. 19, *Berry*.

21 Defamation Act 1961, s. 15, includes broadcasting as libel. The reference is only to civil libel; broadcasting is not included in Part 1 of the Act dealing with criminal libel.

22 Defamation Act 1961, s. 14.2.

23 See n. 2, McDonald, at p. 75 (multiple publication), at p. 267 (on joinder of parties); *Duffy v Newsgroup Newspapers* [1992] 2 IR 369; [1992] ILRM 855, re consolidation of actions.

24 Statute of Limitations 1957, s. 11. Contrast other jurisdictions, e.g. UK, where the period was reduced to three years on the recommendation of the Faulks Committee (Limitation Act 1980, section 4A) and where the Neill Committee, n. 11, recommended a further reduction to one year. The period was reduced to two years in New Zealand: Defamation Act 1992, No. 105, s. 55. The LRC here has recommended a three-year period: Law Reform Commission, *Report on the Civil Law of Defamation* (LRC 38–1991), para. 13.1. See also discussion in LRC, *Consultation Paper on the Civil Law of Defamation*, 1991, para. 524.

25 See, for example, DPP v *Woods and Independent Newspapers*, *The Irish Times*, 10 July 1986.

26 See, for example, reports headed 'Deputy accuses teacher unions' and 'Keating condemns teacher strikes' in *The Irish Times*, 27 November 1985, which led to a defamation action: *Mulvey v IT, IP and Keating*, *The Irish Times*, 15 July 1986. The case was compromised on the basis of an acknowledgment by the defendants that the plaintiff had always acted in a proper and professional manner. Further proceedings were stayed. The matter complained of in *Ryan v IT*, *The Irish Times*, 11 June 1993, came from a press release, that the journalist had taken steps to verify.

27 For example, *The Irish Times* was jointly sued with the BBC when it republished extracts from *The Listener* in 1983. The case resulted in a settlement: *Sloan v IT and BBC*, *The Irish Times*, 24 Octobr 1985.

28 See, for example, *Doyle v The Economist* [1981] NI 171.

29 *Morgan v Argus*, *The Irish Times*, 22, 27, 28 February 1991.

30 See *Irish Independent*, 9 January 1986. The defamation case was later dismissed on the application of the plaintiff (*Doran v Independent Newspapers*, *The Irish Times*, 10–11 February 1989). Inaccurate headlines over court reports can also lead to contempt of court proceedings (see Chapter 6).

31 The presumption of falsity has been abandoned in the US in *Philadelphia Newspapers Inc. v Hepps* 475 US 767 (1986). The Irish LRC was divided on the issue of removing the presumption but by a majority recommended its abolition; n. 3, LRC, at paras 7.28–7.35.

32 The presumption of falsity is therefore a separate issue from fault but has the effect of putting the onus on the defendant to prove the truth of the allegations. See n. 24, *Paper,* at p. 46 and *Report,* at p. 55.

33 *Kavanagh v The Phoenix, The Irish Times,* 5 November 1986, arising out of an article published in *The Phoenix,* 11 April 1986.

34 An example is the *Sunday Tribune,* 4 December 1994, when the paper decided to name the swimming coach alleged to have sexually abused some of the children under his care.

35 See recommendations of the LRC in this regard: n. 24, *Report,* ch. 9; Kevin Boyle and Marie McGonagle, *Media Accountability: The Readers' Representative in Irish Newspapers,* Dublin: NNI, 1995

36 *The Irish Times,* 1 February 1991.

37 *The Irish Times,* 6 December 1991.

38 *The Irish Times,* 19 November 1991.

39 *O'Kelly v Evening Press, The Irish Times,* 23–28 May 1992. Cf. *Doyle v Irish Press, The Irish Times,* 6 December 1984, cited in n. 2, McDonald, at p. 22.

40 *Glennon v The Star, The Irish Times,* 1 July 1992. However, in *de Valera v Independent Newspapers, The Irish Times,* 14 December 1984, the plaintiff failed to show that the placing of her photograph alongside an unrelated story was defamatory.

41 See n. 38. Cf. *Merrill v Sunday Newspapers Ltd, The Irish Times,* 9–10 June 1989, in which the *Sunday World* confused the very similar names of two Americans prominent in the art world and living in Ireland around the same time. Publication of a photograph of the wrong man in relation to a conviction for theft resulted in a jury award of £35,000.

42 See n. 35, Boyle and McGonagle, at p. 24.

43 Ibid., at pp 24–5. See also Australian Press Council Review of Complaints 1988–1993, APC News 1994 Sydney (self-published).

44 There have been cases in England and elsewhere in which journalists have sued their papers because of apologies published concerning their work (see, for instance, UK *Press Gazette* 19 October 1991). However, where the paper is threatened with a libel action arising out of what the journalist has written, a published apology should be covered by the privilege for self-defence; see *Willis v IP* (1938) 72 ILTR 238.

45 Boyle and McGonagle, n. 4.

46 *NY Times v Sullivan* 376 US 254 (1964), *Gertz v Robert Welch Inc.* 418 US 323 (1974).

47 *Philadelphia Inquirer v Hepps* 475 US 767 (1986). The European Court of Human Rights has also drawn a clear distinction between facts which are susceptible to proof and value judgments which are not: see *Lingens,* n. 12.

48 See n. 2, McDonald, ch. 12. Two men convicted of receiving stolen cigarettes successfully sued in 1986 when newspaper reports stated that they had been charged with having arms with intent to endanger life. They had been charged with robbery but the robbery charge had been dropped. They were awarded £2,000 each: *Latham and Byrne v Independent Newspapers and Irish Press, The Irish Times,* 9 May 1986. Re foreigners, see the decision of the European Court of Justice in *Shevill v Presse Alliance, The Times,* 6 April 1995.

49 *Walker v Yachting World.* The size of the awards was due to be appealed ; see *The Irish Times,* 9 July 1994. An out-of-court settlement of £160,000 was later reached. *The Irish Times,* 23 August 1995.

50 [1993] 2 WLR 449 HL 1993. See, Eric Barendt, 'Libel and Freedom of Speech in English Law', *Public Law* 1993, p. 449.

51 Trade unions cannot sue in the UK; see Geoffrey Robertson and Andrew Nicol, *Media Law,* 3rd edn., London: Penguin Books, 1993, at p. 56. In Ireland, they can do so; see n. 2, McDonald, at pp 57, 278–80: they have 'pseudo-corporate status . . . by virtue of statutory control'. See, for example, *ATGWU v Cork Examiner, The Irish Times,* 7 November 1987. Trade unions, however, are immune from liability in tort in certain circumstances by virtue of s. 4 of the Trade Disputes Act 1906 and the Industrial Relations Act 1990 (see *The Irish Times,* 23 November 1994). See LRC, *Paper,* n. 24, at p. 411. Cases involving other bodies include: *Royal College of Surgeons v Sunday World, The Irish Times,* 8 February 1989.

52 [1990] 1 IR 138.
53 Ibid; see also n. 2, McDonald, at pp 281–4; n. 24, *Paper*, at p. 401; n. 24, *Report*, at p. 83.
54 The personality right in Article 2 of the German Constitution expires on death but the dignity right in Article 1 endures. The law protects the dignity of the deceased for at least ten years. Gregory Thwaite and Wolfgang Brehm, 'German Privacy and Defamation Law' [1994] 8 EIPR 336. See also Richard P. Mandel and Renee Hobbs, 'The Right to a Reputation after Death', (1991) 13 C & L p. 25 (US).
55 The LRC recommended a period of three years; see n. 24, *Report*, at p. 92.
56 In *O'Brien v Eason and Son* (1913) 47 ILTR 266, a member of the Ancient Order of Hibernians sued, but as the matter complained of did not concern him personally over and above the other members and as the Order had about 100,000 members, the action failed; see n. 2, McDonald, at p. 57. Cf. *Gallagher and Shatter v Independent Newspapers*, *The Irish Times*, 10 May 1980, where the solicitors were held not to be personally identifiable. In another case, *Black v Northern Whig* (1942) 77 ILTR 5, concerning a government report on 'grave scandals' in a Northern Ireland hospital, ten members of the fifteen-member statutory committee that ran the hospital sued, and the court held that each was so closely identified with the board as to be personally associated with the offending remarks. Each was awarded £50, plus costs; see n. 2, McDonald, at pp 57–8 also cites a case in 1975 when the High Court held that twenty-four companies had each shown a prima facie claim against Independent Newspapers. An article had suggested that a number of companies in the beef processing industry were falsifying returns in order to claim EC intervention money. For individual members of a group to succeed, the defamatory statement must reflect on them in a personal way and not just on the group or organisation. The decision was appealed on other grounds.
57 *The Irish Times*, 30 June 1989.
58 *The Irish Times*, 9–10 June 1989 and n. 41, *Merrill*.
59 *The Irish Times*, 15–16 November 1989.
60 *The Irish Times*, 4 December 1986.
61 *Ryan v Irish Times*, *The Irish Times*, 11 June 1993.
62 *The Irish Times*, 8 November 1978, cited in n. 2, McDonald, at p. 40.
63 [1953–4] Ir Jur Rep 79; [1955–6] Ir Jur Rep 45.
64 [1937] IR 377.
65 See n. 33.
66 Ulick O'Connor, *Oliver St. John Gogarty*, London: Mandarin Paperbacks, 1990, at p. 278.
67 See n. 66, pp 284–5.
68 See n. 24, *Report*, at pp 6–7.
69 See n. 16.
70 See O Dálaigh C.J. in *Berry v The Irish Times* [1973] IR 368, where he held that the label 'Twentieth-century Felon Setter' was not defamatory but that if the word 'informer' had been used instead, it might have been. The law of defamation reflects certain community values, a certain ethos, which varies widely between cultures and tells us a lot about them; but defamation is about more than community values, abstract ideas or rights. It is about real people, injury to their reputations and the anger, hurt, frustration and embarrassment that often accompany it.
71 [1986] IR 13, [1986] ILRM 601.
72 ITLR, 27 December 1993.
73 *The Irish Times*, 25–26 February 1987; *The Irish Times*, 24 October 1989.
74 *The Irish Times*, 12 December 1980.
75 *The Irish Times*, 8–11 February 1989.
76 See n. 63.
77 [1971] IR 269.
78 [1981] NI 171.
79 *Boal and McCartney v Sunday World*, *The Irish Times*, 14–19 October 1988.
80 *The Irish Times*, 19–20 November 1987.
81 *The Irish Times*, 29 June 1985.
82 *McSharry v Waterford Post*, *The Irish Times*, 1 May 1985.

83 Per Gannon J. in *Hilliard* [1990] 1 IR 138. That is one of the reasons why the courts have been reluctant to allow the tort of intentional infliction of emotional suffering to spill over into the realm of defamation law; see the US case of *Hustler Magazine Inc. v Falwell* 485 US 46 (1988) and the Irish case *Thomas v Independent Newspapers, The Irish Times*, 26 July 1988, where a twelve-year-old boy, suing through his parents, claimed that publication of his name as a witness to an armed robbery amounted to the intentional infliction of emotional suffering. The claim was rejected.

84 See n. 24, LRC, *Paper*, at pp 10–11.

85 Ibid., at p. 11.

86 *Boland v RTÉ, The Irish Times*, 1 July 1989.

87 *Corrigan v The Cork Examiner, The Irish Times*, 30 June 1989.

88 (1955) 90 ILTR 105.

89 Unreported, Supreme Court, 4 March 1955.

90 [1901] 2 IR 465.

91 (1892) 27 ILTR 8. See n. 24, *Paper*, at p. 16, re innuendo and ordinary meaning. To say that an actor failed to turn up for an engagement and left the patrons in the lurch suggests that he is unreliable (n. 75, *Lynch v Irish Press*). To say that a man who had committed suicide had been sent letters by the revenue sheriff suggested, according to plaintiff's counsel, that the sheriff had abused his powers, was unfit to hold public office, had murdered the deceased, was guilty of dishonourable, cruel and inhumane tactics and conduct in the discharge of his duties and that his inhumane actions caused or contributed to the man's death by terrorising him to the extent that he committed suicide (n. 59, *Cusack v RTÉ*).

92 *The Irish Times*, 3 February 1984.

93 [1943] NI 108.

94 Cf. *Cassidy v Daily Mirror* [1929] 2 KB 331.

95 See *The Irish Times*, 25 June 1994, 29 June 1994.

96 See n. 24, *Paper*, at pp 46–7.

97 The LRC makes some recommendations in this regard; see n. 24, *Report*, at pp 9–10.

98 See, for example, Griffin J. in *Barrett*, n. 71 at p. 30: 'typical readers of reasonable intelligence', and Geoghegan J. in *Foley*, n. 137 at p. 65: 'any ordinary reader'. On the role of the jury see *Barrett* and on the question of striking out a case see *Conlon v Times Newspapers Ltd* [1995] 2 ILRM 76.

99 See n. 51, Robertson and Nicol at pp 54–60 and the pragmatic approach adopted by British newspapers and broadcasting companies detailed in Russell L. Weaver and Geoffrey Bennett, 'New York Times Co. v Sullivan: The "Actual Malice" Standard and Editorial Decision-Making', (1993) 14 JMLP 2.

100 See Boyle and McGonagle, n. 4.

101 Exceptions include *Campbell-Sharpe v Magill, The Irish Times*, 29 June 1985; *Agnew v Independent Newspapers, The Irish Times*, 29 June 1985; *Ní Chiaráin v Evening Herald*, 25 June 1986; *McAleese v Independent Newspapers, The Irish Times*, 18 November 1988; *Corrigan v Cork Examiner, The Irish Times*, 30 June 1989; *Dineen v IP, The Irish Times*, 30 June 1989; *Flanagan v The Star, The Irish Times*, 3 March 1990.

102 See n. 35, Boyle and McGonagle, at p. 18.

103 For example, see *Devine v Magill, Sunday Tribune*, 2 February 1986; *Ward and Ní Fhlatharta v Independent Newspapers, The Irish Times*, 29 June–7 July 1989; *O'Rourke v Independent Newspapers, The Irish Times*, 3 May 1995.

104 The Iowa study. See under 'Further Reading' above, Bezanson et al., at pp 79–94.

105 See n. 24, *Paper*, at p. 417; *Report*, at p. 87.

106 See n. 100.

107 For example, in *Ryan v Irish Times, The Irish Times*, 11 June 1993, the information about fuel merchants allegedly giving money and fuel in exchange for votes had come from a press release.

108 In *O'Connor v The Kerryman, The Irish Times*, 22 February 1991, fishermen, who had allegedly been verbally attacked from the altar by a priest, responded through an open letter from their solicitors and a paper that published it was sued.

109 Donoghue v Irish Press and Sunday Tribune, The Irish Times, 20–22 October 1990, concerned, respectively, remarks in an editorial about the handling of a court case ar ' remarks made by the defence solicitor to a journalist outside the court.

110 94 ER 113; Holt, The Law of Libel, London: Reed, Dublin: Phelan, 1812 1st edn; p. 55, cited in n. 1, at p. 29.

111 See n. 51, Robertson and Nicol, at p. 85. See also Lord Lester, 'Defaming Politicians and Public Officials', Public Law 1995, p. 1.

112 See n. 46.

113 For a detailed analysis of New York Times v Sullivan, see Anthony Lewis, Make No Law, New York: Vintage Books 1992.

114 See, for example, n. 99, Weaver and Bennett, at p. 9, on how few threats of libel actions the media in the US receive in comparison with the media in the UK.

115 See n. 12.

116 Ibid., Lingens, at pp 419–20.

117 Ibid. Also Thorgeirson v Iceland, Series A, no. 239; (1992) 14 EHRR 843; Castells v Spain, Series A, no. 236; (1992) 14 EHRR 445.

118 Under the Civil Liability Act 1961, as interpreted by the Supreme Court in O'Hanlon v ESB [1969] IR 75, consent is not established by contract alone; it must be expressly communicated.

119 (1938) 72 ILTR 238. See also n. 2, McDonald, at p. 146.

120 [1917] AC 309; see also discussion in Section 4(b) Qualified privilege.

121 The Times, 10 February 1926, 26 March 1926.

122 See n. 1, at p. 15.

123 Subject, in the UK, to the limitation of Rehabilitation of Offenders Act 1974.

124 See n. 24, Paper, at p. 48; n. 2, McDonald, at pp 100–10.

125 Lakian v Boston Globe, Time, 19 August 1985.

126 See n. 24, Paper, at pp 52–4.

127 CLÉ, the Irish Book Publishers Association, in its submission on defamation to the Law Reform Commission in 1991, argued that the defendant should not be penalised for exercising his/her right to plead justification. Far from the original injury being repeated and increased by it, failure of the plea effectively and in a very full manner repudiates and lays to rest the defamatory statement, providing the plaintiff with the fullest vindication of reputation, CLE argued.

128 [1991] 1 IR 121.

129 Ibid. per McCarthy J. at p. 138, O'Flaherty J. at pp 139–41.

130 Elton John v Sunday Mirror, The Guardian, 5 November 1993

131 Reduced on appeal: John v MGN Ltd, The Times, 14 December 1995. For an explanation of the terms 'exemplary' and 'punitive' damages, see n. 129, at pp 133–5, 139–41.

132 See Jean McFadden, '£350,000 libel damages for Elton John—why it could not happen in Scotland', 1994 JMLP 15 (1), p. 13. The highest damages award in Scotland for defamation in a non-jury trial was £7,500. There has been only one jury trial in the last forty years, and it resulted in an award of £50,000. Unless economic loss results to a business, e.g. Capital Life v Scottish Daily Record and Sunday Mail, The Times, 19 November 1978, in which £302,000 was awarded, damages are low.

133 See n. 109.

134 The Irish Times, 25–26 February 1987.

135 (1863) 3 B&S 769.

136 (1942) 77 ILTR 5; see also n. 24, Paper, at pp 68–71.

137 [1994] 2 ILRM 61. The defence plea was fair comment.

138 The absence of witnesses was a problem for the defendants in Ryan v Irish Times (n. 107) and O'Connor v The Kerryman (n. 108), for example.

139 Technically, a libel action in this country can be brought up to six years after publication, but in reality the vast majority of cases are commenced within the first month or two.

140 376 US 254 (1964). See also Úna Ní Raifeartaigh, 'Fault Issues and Libel Law—A Comparison between Irish, English and United States Law', (1991) 40 ICLQ, 763.

141 There is a move away from the negligence standard towards strict liability in the case of products liability, but in the media situation, a negligence standard or its use as in a defence of reasonable care or *bonne foi* would achieve a better balance of respective rights.

142 Since the fairness of the comment is not really a factor in the defence, the word 'fair' in the title of the defence is inappropriate. The Law Reform Commission and other reform bodies have recommended renaming the defence simply as 'comment' or 'comment based on fact'. See n. 24, *Report*, recommendation 14.3.

143 The LRC has put forward criteria for distinguishing fact and comment; see n. 24, *Paper*, at pp 281–4; *Report*, at pp 40–43. Duncan and Neill, 2nd edn., 1983, para. 12.13, pp 61–3. See, generally, Úna Ní Raifeartaigh, 'Defences in Irish Defamation Law', (1991) 13 DULJ 76.

144 They are indicative, not decisive, see LRC, n. 143.

145 See n. 2, McDonald, at p. 211.

146 The *Irish Times*, 20–24 October 1990. The editorial in the *Irish Press* had appeared on 3 October 1987.

147 This is the kind of situation in which a right of reply or rectification would seem appropriate. That is the remedy available to public officials in other European countries such as France, Germany, Belgium, Greece. See n. 24, *Paper*, paras 470–71; n. 100, Boyle and McGonagle.

148 The *Irish Times*, 13 November 1991. The case arose from a piece in 'An Irishman's Diary' in the paper on 17 January 1990.

149 The *Irish Times*, 29 June 1989–7 July 1989.

150 The *Irish Times*, 1 April 1993–2 April 1993.

151 For the position in US law, see Kyu Ho Youm, 'Letters to the Editor and US Libel Law', (1992) 13 JMLP 220.

152 See D. McLean, 'Libel Consequences of Headlines (1989) 66 JQ 924'; *Charleston v News Group Newspapers Ltd* [1995] 2 WLR 450 (H.L.).

153 (1955) 90 ILTR 105. See also *Burke v Central Television* [1994] 2 ILRM 161; where disclosure of documents used to make a television programme about the IRA was refused because of the risk to life. The court found that the statements complained of were facts, not comments. The rolled-up plea had been pleaded but it is a plea of fair comment, not justification. In the circumstances, the defendants were given liberty to deliver an amended defence.

154 See *Campbell v Irish Press* (1955) 90 ILTR 105; *McIntyre* [1991] 1 IR 121.

155 [1909] 2 KB 958.

156 See n. 24, *Paper*, at p. 265; n. 24, *Report*, at p. 37; n. 2, McDonald, at pp 215; n. 51, Robertson and Nicol, at p. 83.

157 Series A, no. 103; [1986] 8 EHRR 407.

158 Ibid., at para. 46, n. 12.

159 See discussion in n. 2, McDonald, at p. 209; the dangers of a subjective test can be seen in *Herbert v Lando* 441 US 153 (1979).

160 See n. 51, Robertson and Nicol, at p. 82.

161 See n. 1, John Stuart Mill, at p. 15.

162 [1986] IR 13; [1986] ILRM 601.

163 See n. 51, Robertson and Nicol, at p. 85; *Telnikoff v Matusevitch* [1990] 3 All ER 865, [1991] 4 All ER 817 (HL).

164 This point was made by book publishers themselves in the CLÉ (Irish Book Publishers Association) submission on the law of defamation to the LRC in 1991.

165 Holmes J. in *Abrams v US* 250 US 616 (1919).

166 *Gatley on Libel and Slander*, 8th edn., pp 315–24, paras 732–46 lists topics of public interest, which are quoted in LRC *Paper*, n. 24, at pp 71–2. In German law, opinions except malicious insults are free, whether reasonable or not, unless abusive. If fact and opinion are mixed, the test is whether it refers to concrete events which can be proven/disproven or contains primarily opinion; generally the courts prefer to treat remarks as opinion, and a high level of protection is given to matters of public interest, see n. 54, Thwaite and Brehm, 'German Privacy and Defamation Law' [1994] 8 EIPR 336 at 344.

167 Series A, no. 239; (1992) 14 EHRR 84.
168 Ibid., at para. 64. See also *The Article 19 Freedom of Expression Manual*, London, 1993 at pp 149–50.
169 *Fields v Irish Times*, *The Irish Times*, 26 January 1995.
170 The newspaper report of the case does not disclose whether the defence of fair comment was pleaded, n. 169.
171 See n. 24, *Paper*, at para. 97, p. 76; n. 24, *Report*, at para. 14.10 (4).
172 Select Committee on Legislation and Security of Dáil Eireann (Privilege and Immunity) Act 1994; the Committees of the Houses of the Oireachtas (Compellability, Privileges and Immunities of Witnesses) Bill (No 45 of 1995).
173 The other media therefore have to fall back on common-law qualified privilege; see n. 24, *Paper*, at pp 250–253.
174 'Seditious' matter, which is usually included with blasphemous and obscene matter, in Art. 40.6.1 for example, is not mentioned in s. 18.2.; cf. s. 3 Libel Amendment Act 1888.
175 (1978) 67 Crim App 70. See also the discussion in Chapter 9.
176 [1991] 1 All ER 306.
177 *The Irish Times*, 23 November 1989. Cf. restrictions on court reporting in Censorship of Publications Act 1929. See also the discussion in Chapter 8.
178 See *Willis v Irish Press* (1938) 72 ILTR 238, H. Ct.
179 [1988] IR 436, [1989] ILRM 349.
180 See discussion of *Adam v Ward* in Robertson and Nicol, n. 51 at p. 91, stating that the privilege is one of general application.
181 See n. 78. See also *Lindsay v Maher*, *The Irish Times*, 4 February 1984 (the defendant was an elected representative of the farming community and therefore had a duty to defend farmers. When they were attacked in open court, he also had a right to use an 'open' forum and was entitled to choose a newspaper interview).
182 See n. 108. The case was settled out of court. The argument advanced here is therefore a general one and not intended to reflect on the merits of the particular case.
183 See n. 119, *Willis v Irish Press*. Bryan McMahon and William Binchy, *Irish Law of Torts*, 2nd edn., Dublin: Butterworths 1991, pp 652–3, say that publication to the world at large may be justified . . . where the defendant is merely responding to an accusation through the same medium in which the initial attack was made.
184 [1935] IR 397. Fitzgibbon J. in the Supreme Court in *Nevin* took the view that if 'the writer of the letter [answering the original allegations published in the paper] had lawful justification and excuse for writing and publishing it, it is difficult to see any ground for holding that the innocent proprietor of the newspaper to which it was sent for publication is liable for damages.' (at p. 422) 'But if a man is protected in law in making an appeal to the public through the columns of the public press I can see no ground for holding that the printer and publisher of the paper in which his appeal appears . . . is liable in damages for the publication, at least until it is proved to the satisfaction of a jury that the publisher or printer, as the case may be, was himself actuated by express malice . . . .' (at p. 423).
185 Ibid., at p. 410.
186 Ibid., at p. 414, quoting *O'Donoghue v Hussey* IR 5 CL 124. It may be noted that in *Lindsay* (n. 181) and *O'Connor* (n. 108), the plaintiffs did not publish their original *criticisms* in a newspaper, therefore those cases can be distinguished from *O'Donoghue*.
187 (1907) 41 ILTR 35.
188 Ibid., at p. 37 per Andrews J.
189 Ibid., at p. 38.
190 Ibid., at p. 38, *per Wright* J.
191 *Magrath v Finn* IR (1877) 11 CL 152.
192 See n. 51, Robertson and Nicol, at p. 90.
193 'The privilege is in fact a shield of defence, not a weapon of attack.' *per* May J. in *O'Donoghue v Hussey*, (n. 186) cited in *Nevin*, (n. 184), at p. 418.
194 See n. 24, *Paper*, at p. 101.
195 For more detail see Defamation Act 1961, Part 1, Second Schedule.
196 For more detail see Defamation Act 1961, Part 2, Second Schedule.

197 The Irish Times, 2 March 1989.
198 The LRC has recommended widening the privilege: see n. 24, Paper, at pp 242–5; n. 24, Report, at pp 28–35. See also New Zealand Defamation Act 1992.
199 See notes 128 and 131. See also Kennedy and Arnold v Ireland [1987] IR 587; [1988] ILRM 472 (damages were awarded in addition to a declaration that the plaintiffs' consititutional rights to privacy had been infringed).
200 See n. 71, at p. 23.
201 Ibid., at p. 19.
202 Ibid., at p. 20, per Finlay C.J.
203 Ibid., at p. 23–4, per Henchy J.
204 Ibid., at p. 24, per Henchy J.
205 Ibid., at p. 30, per Griffin J.
206 Sunday Times, 1 April 1990.
207 Sunday Tribune, 4 February 1990. Now in UK see John v MGN, n. 130.
208 The Irish Times, 14 November 1992. Prior to that, the largest award by an Irish court had been £135,000, plus costs in McNamee v Mirror Group Newspapers, The Irish Times, 30 November 1989, 2 December 1989. In a report of the trial on terrorist charges of the plaintiff's brother, the Daily Mirror had mistakenly included the words 'of his' in a reference to two brothers involved in IRA activities, thus associating the plaintiff with the IRA. An apology had been published but the judge considered it unsatisfactory. In N.I. after a 25 day hearing, a jury awarded £450,000: Eastwood v McGuigan, The Irish Times, 11 February–10 March 1992. On the question of the size of awards, it may be noted that the award of £65,000 in Barrett was five times the average industrial wage and that circulations in Ireland are small.
209 Holohan v Donoghue [1986] ILRM 250.
210 Prior v Irish Press, The Irish Times 24 October 1989 (an award of £30,000), Madigan v Irish Press, The Irish Times 4 March 1989 (an award of £30,000); McDonagh v News Group Newspapers ITLR, 27 December 1993 (an award of £90,000).
211 The Times, 6 April 1993.
212 8/1994/455/53, judgment 13 July 1995.
213 Ibid., at para. 51.
214 Denny, McNamee, n. 208.
215 See n. 24, Paper, at pp 365–83. The new US Uniform Corrections Act would give both sides a strong incentive to avoid legal action and instead focus on corrections and retractions. Under its provisions, a plaintiff cannot sue for damages without first seeking a retraction. If the publisher retracts, the plaintiff's claim is limited to actual economic loss. Only where there is no retraction can there be a claim for punitive damages. In Australia, the High Court found an implied guarantee of political communication in the Constitution; see APC News. vol. 6, no. 3, August 1994. In Germany, a right of reply must be sought within two weeks of publication from a newspaper, three months from a magazine. A reply and/or retraction are regarded as primary remedies; damages are only secondary. They are available only after a full hearing and are low. Punitive damages are unknown. The focus of the law is on the rectification of error, not money. The criminal law is reserved for the unusual or flagrant case. See n. 54 Thwaite and Brehm, at p. 350.
216 See n. 24, Paper, at p. 117.
217 The rule in Scott v Sampson (1882) 8 QBD 491 and the exceptions to the rule. The circumstances of the publication or character of the plaintiff cannot be pleaded in mitigation unless notice is given 7 days in advance O. 36 R. 36 RSC (1986). For discussion of the rule, see McDonald, n. 2, at pp 248–50.
218 Lynch v Irish Press, The Irish Times, 8 February 1989–11 February 1989, would suggest not; see also Dinneen v Irish Press, The Irish Times, 22 June 1989–30 June 1989; Boal and McCartney v Sunday World, The Irish Times 14 October 1988–18 October 1988. But contrast France where a finding of good faith on the part of the journalist can relieve him/her of liability altogether.
219 See n. 24, Paper, at p. 126 para. 132. However, it does not elaborate on it or cite any cases in support.

220 *The Irish Times*, 16 May 1986.

221 *The Irish Times*, 13 November 1991.

222 *The Irish Times*, 1 May 1985. Cf. *Campbell-Sharp v Magill*, *The Irish Times*, 29 June 1985; *McConville v Kennelly*, *The Irish Times*, 27 January 1984; *Agnew v Independent Newspapers*, *The Irish Times*, 29 June 1985, n. 51, Robertson and Nicol, at p. 95, point out that an apology is the only means of mitigating damage in the case of an indefensible libel. The authors recommend that when the media agree to publish an apology, they should seek a disclaimer of further legal action as a condition of publishing the apology.

223 [1910] AC 20.

224 [1940] 1KB 377.

225 See n. 35, Boyle and McGonagle, at pp 25–7

226 Lawyers for the *Cork Examiner* report that they have used the offer of amends successfully in one case.

227 See n. 38.

228 *The Times*, 17 October 1956; see n. 51, Robertson and Nicol, at p. 94. See also s. 2 Libel Act 1843 and cases thereon in n. 2, McDonald, at pp 230–31.

229 *Gertz v Robert Welch Inc*. 418 US 323 (1974). See also Randall P. Bezanson et al., *Libel Law and the Press*, New York: The Free Press, A Division of Macmillan Inc., 1987, pp 122–7 passim; John Soloski and Randall P. Bezanson, eds., *Reforming Libel Law*, New York: The Guilford Press, 1992, pp 8–10, 333–4; Frederick Schauer, 'Reflections on the Value of Truth', reproduced in Raymond Wacks, ed., *Privacy*, Aldershot, Hants.: Dartmouth, 1993, at p. 407.

230 441 US 153 (1979).

231 Cour de Cassation, 17 March 1993. Cf. German law: Section 193 of the German Criminal Code recognises that pressure of time or lack of resources leaves the press without adequate means to verify the truth of a statement before publication, therefore, there will be no liability if there is a legitimate interest involved and either reliable sources were referred to or the information received and the person supplying it were thoroughly checked. (*Kant v Der Spiegel* 1990); n. 54 Thwaite and Brehmn, at p. 346.

232 *The Irish Times*, 24 April 1985, 20 October 1986. See also (1986) 136 NLJ 515.

233 See, for example, *Ross v Hopkinson*, *The Times*, 17 October 1956, cited in n. 51, Robertson and Nicol, at p. 94, where a period of seven weeks after publication did not meet the requirement.

234 Faulks Committee, n. 3, at pp 76–8; n. 11, Supreme Court Procedure Committee (Neill Committee) 1991; n. 24, *Paper*, at pp 327–35.

235 Marcel Berlins, cited in Marie McGonagle, 'Practical Aspects of Defamation Law', *Dlí—The Western Law Gazette*, Spring 1991, at p. 17.

236 See n. 24, *Paper*, at p. 194.

237 Ibid.

238 For responses to the LRC, see O'Dell, 'Reflections on a Revolution in Libel' (1991) ILT 181, 214; Marc McDonald, 'Defamation Refor—A Response to the LRC Report' (1992) ILT 270.

239 This checklist, devised by the author, formed part of a training programme initiated by *The Irish Times* and has been published in an *Irish Times* staff booklet. The author is grateful to *The Irish Times* for the opportuntiy to deal directly with journalists and for permission to reproduce the checklist.

CHAPTER FIVE

Privacy

In *Martin Chuzzlewit* Dickens had the newsboys in New York shouting:

> The *New York Sewer*. Here's the Sewer's exposure of the Washington gang and the Sewer's exclusive account of a flagrant act of dishonesty committed by the Secretary of State when he was eight years old, now communicated, at a great expense, by his own nurse.[1]

Dickens was alluding to the capacity of some elements of the press to intrude on personal privacy without any recognisable public value. He calls into question the boundaries of media reporting but in doing so points up some of the uncertainties that still bedevil this area of law.

While there is widespread acceptance of the need to protect privacy, there is some doubt as to what should be protected and how. For instance the right to privacy is protected in the legal systems of continental Europe in some instances by their constitutions or by the incorporation into their law of the European Convention on Human Rights (Article 8) and given effect by their civil and criminal codes. In contrast, the common-law jurisdictions have never seen privacy as a central value to be protected in any systematic or comprehensive way by law. There is no specific tort of invasion of privacy, and only certain aspects of the wider right are criminalised.

Why Protect Privacy?

Awareness of the need for effective protection of the private lives of individuals against intrusion by state authorities grew out of the atrocities of Nazism and the Second World War. The need for protection specifically aimed at intrusion by the media has been fuelled by the capabilities of modern technology and the growth of the 'yellow' or tabloid press, with its appeal to prurience and its spotlight on intimate details and events of people's lives. Throughout the common-law world there have been movements in recent decades to put in place specific privacy laws to curb media intrusion into people's private lives.

In the UK, for example, the Younger Committee on Privacy in its 1972[2] report recommended against a blanket declaration of a right to privacy on the grounds that it would introduce uncertainties into the law and affect freedom of information. In the media field the Committee's recommendations were confined to improvements in the structure and operation of the Press Council and Broadcasting Complaints Commission. The Committee did, however, favour the introduction of a generally applicable tort of disclosure or other use of information unlawfully acquired.[3] In the meantime a number of private members' bills were introduced in parliament but without success. Almost twenty years after the Younger Report, the case of *Kaye v Robertson*[4] (1990) confirmed that in English law there was no right to privacy as such and accordingly no right of action for breach of a person's privacy. The case arose from the intended publication of a *Sunday Sport* article and photographs of well-known actor Gordon Kaye in his hospital bed, seriously ill after a car crash. It prompted the British government to establish the Calcutt Committee,[5] which reported in 1990 and recommended against the introduction of a tort of invasion of privacy (paragraph 12.5) but in favour of the creation of specific criminal offences of entering or placing surveillance on private property and of taking photographs of or recording the voice of an individual who is on private property without consent and with intent to obtain personal information with a view to publication (paragraph 6.33). The press was to be given one final chance to make self-regulation work. The Press Council was abolished and replaced by a Press Complaints Commission with a narrower remit to implement a Code of Practice drawn up by newspaper editors. Calcutt reviewed the situation in 1993 and concluded that the operation of the Press Complaints Commission was not satisfactory and that a statutory regime was needed and should not await the introduction of a statutory tort of privacy.[6]

There is a growing concern in Ireland, too, that media organisations are pushing back the boundaries of privacy and offensiveness. If this is true it may be in response to competition, primarily from the British press which is now making serious inroads into the Irish market, setting up offices in this country and publishing Irish editions. It was the activities of the tabloid press in Britain that led to calls for the introduction of privacy legislation there. Indeed, it was the excesses of the American yellow press that prompted jurists Warren and Brandeis[7] to try to formulate a right to privacy over a century ago.

What to Protect?

It is relatively easy to identify specific facets of a right to privacy but extremely difficult to define the scope and contours of the right. The problem of definition has occupied jurists for decades. The Warren and Brandeis concept of the 'right to be let alone'[8] captures the idea of a zone of privacy but is perhaps too broad and simplistic to aid definition. As members of a community network, people cannot be completely isolated, yet the more intrusive the network and media spotlight become, the greater the need for a recognised retreat or zone of privacy in people's lives. A more modern approach to the problem is encapsulated, therefore, in the concept of the 'right to freedom from unwarranted intrusion . . .'.[9] The use of the word 'unwarranted' takes account of the realities of a complex information society, where some degree of intrusion is inevitable, and of advances in the technology of communication, where the opportunities for intrusion are endless. For example, in the telephone tapping case, *Kennedy and Arnold v Ireland*,[10] the President of the High Court upheld the journalists' constitutional right to privacy in respect of their telephone conversations but pointed out that inadvertent interference from time to time had to be endured as an inevitable incidence of telephonic technology.[11]

In an age when a Chinese student could be identified from US satellite television pictures of Tianamnen Square, even though the pictures had not been shown on American television and must therefore have been intercepted en route, absolute privacy cannot be guaranteed by law and a precise legal definition of privacy is exceedingly difficult to achieve. Attempts to date have tended to focus on either the *methods* used to obtain information on people's private lives—deception, eavesdropping, 'bugging' and the use of technological devices—or on the *form* of intrusion—publishing embarrassing private facts or pictures, causing unnecessary grief and benefitting commercially from using a person's public attributes or persona.

In the US for example, Professor Prosser[12] disagreed with Warren and Brandeis about the existence of a general right to privacy in American law and instead identified four separate privacy-based torts which he said the law protected:

(i) intrusion into another's seclusion
(ii) appropriation of another's image or person for trade or commercial purposes
(iii) portrayal of another in a false light (knowingly or recklessly) and
(iv) publication of private facts.

However his analysis, too, is problematic. The first two of these torts are concerned with property or financial interests and are not aimed particularly at the media. The third, false light, involves portraying someone as a different kind of person than he/she is. It may be to ascribe to the person a characteristic or view that he/she does not hold and finds offensive. False light is closely linked to defamation but goes beyond it in encompassing false but nondefamatory statements as well as false and defamatory statements. By encompassing statements that are not defamatory, it imposes a heavy burden on the media in terms of detecting the problem. The fourth tort, insofar as it protects true facts lawfully obtained, is susceptible to attack on constitutional grounds, given the strong commitment to freedom of the press in the First Amendment. In fact, the case-law has narrowed considerably the scope of the tort and only state interests of the highest order will warrant imposing liability on the media.[13]

In Britain the former Press Council, a self-regulatory, non-statutory body, established in 1953, attempted to delimit privacy in its Declaration of Principle on Privacy 1976[14] and in its Code of Practice 1990. The basis of the Declaration was the Council's 'determination to uphold the right of individuals to be protected against unwarranted intrusion into their private lives or affairs'. The Declaration pointed out that entry into public life does not disqualify an individual from his right to privacy about his private affairs, save when the circumstances relating to the private life of an individual occupying a public position may be likely to affect the performance of his duties or public confidence in him or his office.[15] Of the sixteen-point Press Council Code of 1990, only one point was headed 'privacy' but at least seven others were privacy-related. Under the heading 'Privacy' the Code stated:

> Publishing material or making inquiries about the private lives of individuals is not acceptable unless these are in the public interest, overriding the right to privacy. The Press Council's Declaration of Principle on Privacy should be observed.[16]

The other related sections concern subterfuge; intrusion into grief; the need to exercise care and discretion before deciding to identify innocent relatives; interviewing children under sixteen; identifying children as victims, witnesses or defendants in sexual abuse cases; identifying rape victims; and refraining from publishing pictures that needlessly exacerbate grief or cause distress.

Towards a Legal Definition of Privacy

It is generally accepted that there is a core and penumbra of privacy, but there has been little consensus on actual content, how to determine that content, what objectives to follow and indeed the value or values to be protected. Should concern lie with the effects of the intrusion on the individual concerned or on the readership or audience? Is it the embarrassment and hurt to the victim or the sense of outrage and offensiveness felt by the audience that is to be addressed?[17] Are privacy and public decency separate issues or are they aspects of the same sense of moral values? For instance, experience in Ireland has shown that complaints of invasion of privacy against the media are few and do not come from the victim. Occasionally they come from family relations and friends but most often they come from unconnected third parties.[18] These third parties express rage and outrage at what they perceive to be the consequences of the publication or broadcast for the individual concerned. They speak of falling standards in Irish journalism and bemoan the way the media portray aspects of Irish life by covering subjects that they, the readers or viewers, believe should not be aired in public. Is it possible then that what is talked about under the umbrella of privacy is in fact two separate issues: (i) the right to individual privacy and (ii) the preservation of public morals and ethical standards. The two are related but separate issues. Privacy considerations in this chapter will therefore be confined to the effect on the individual, that is individual privacy. (The public morals aspect will be discussed in Chapter 9.)

The Right to Individual Privacy

When speaking of individual privacy, further questions need to be addressed. For instance, should a distinction be made between the *neutral* concept of privacy (i.e. that the publication of private facts is wrong whether they are true or false, bad or good; it is the very publication of them that is wrong, not their character) and the *moral* concept of personal dignity (i.e. that only those facts that adversely affect a person's dignity are worthy of protection)? If the moral concept is to be adopted, is the appropriate test a subjective or objective one?

In the search for a theoretical basis for privacy, many theses and analyses have been advanced.[19] Some focus on the functions of privacy and the interests it protects. From these, it can be said that the core of privacy is intimacy,[20] the intimate nature of certain details, activities, ideas or emotions that people generally do not want to share with others or only with close family members or friends. Such a core of intimacy would embrace family life, home, correspondence, telephone conversations, sexual relations. In this context, the reporting of intimate details in family law cases could be restricted, for example.

Other facets of the intimacy element of privacy would fall to the courts to determine in accordance with contemporary norms and standards, in an approach similar to that adopted by the European Court of Human Rights (to be discussed later in this chapter). A defence of public interest could apply,[21] and the public/private divide that has found favour with the US Supreme Court and European Court of Human Rights could also be accommodated—that is, a public person would still be entitled to protection against publication of the intimate details of family life that did not impinge on his/her public functions. Following Professor Gerety's analysis, intimacy is the core of the right to privacy but at least two other functions of privacy are also deserving of protection: first, autonomy—keeping control of one's destiny—and second, identity—allowing a person to develop his/her own potential as an individual. This is where false light, copyright, etc. fit into the overall concept of privacy, even though they are closely related to property rights.

The concept of privacy is gradually becoming clearer but the problem of legal definition remains unresolved. However, that should not operate as a barrier to effective protection of privacy. After all, defamation has not been defined either; there is no statutory definition of defamation, only the dicta of individual judges in court cases. A second problem with privacy, however, is to find an appropriate remedy for invasion of privacy. Damages can only compensate after the event when the harm has already been done. Retractions and corrections are likely to be of little help. They can minimise the harm done in defamation cases where the offending statement is shown or admitted to be false; but in privacy cases, the details are likely to be true, otherwise the defamation remedy would be available. Injunctions are of limited value. They pose dangers to the freedom of the press from prior restraint and can only be sought when it is known that the private facts are to be published. Non-legal bodies such as press councils have proven largely ineffective in protecting or defending privacy. There are no sanctions that they can apply, apart from censuring the publication concerned and having that censure carried in the media.

What Is the Legal Basis for the Right?

1. The Constitution

In Ireland it has been accepted by the courts that the Constitution does recognise the right to privacy, even though that right is not spelled out in the text. It remains, therefore, for the courts to identify the right and particular aspects of it, as they did in the McGee case[22] in respect of marital privacy and in *Kennedy and Arnold v Ireland*[23] in respect of telephone conversations. In *Kennedy* the private telephones of two journalists working as political correspondents with two national newspapers were tapped by order of the Minister for Justice. The Court declared the right to privacy to be one of the personal unspecified rights contained in Article 40.3 of the Constitution. It is not an absolute right and can be restricted in the interests of public order, morality and the common good:

> The nature of the right to privacy must be such as to ensure the dignity and freedom of the individual in the type of society envisaged by the Constitution, namely, a sovereign independent and democratic society.[24]

In an earlier case, AG v Norris,[25] which concerned the rights of homosexuals not to have their private behaviour criminalised, Henchy J. identified the right to privacy that 'inheres in each citizen by virtue of his human personality'. The right to privacy, he said, is

> a complex of rights, varying in nature, purpose and range, each necessarily a facet of the citizen's core of individuality within the constitutional order. . . . [O]ther aspects of the right . . . [have] yet to be given judicial recognition. . . . It is sufficient to say that they would all appear to fall within a secluded area of activity or non-activity which may be claimed as necessary for the expression of an individual personality, for purposes not always moral or commendable, but meriting recognition in circumstances which do not endanger considerations such as state security, public order or morality, or other essential components of the common good.[26]

There have been few cases as yet in this jurisdiction in respect of privacy as a restriction on media reporting,[27] other than in the context of court reporting (see discussion in Chapter 7). The freedom of expression clause, Article 40.6.1.i, does not specifically mention privacy as a restriction on the freedom of the press. That is not to say that such a restriction does not exist, but it does point to the need to preserve freedom of the press and not undermine it by according undue weight and scope to the restrictions on it.

This issue arose in *Maguire v Drury*,[28] where a woman sought an injunction to prevent further publication concerning her alleged affair with a Catholic priest, on the grounds that such publication would infringe her constitutional right to privacy. O'Hanlon J. in the High Court decided *inter alia*: (i) that the case did not concern the intimacies of married life or marital communications but rather the husband's allegations of an extra-marital affair, (ii) that other remedies, such as libel, were available in appropriate circumstances to deal with such a situation and (iii) that freedom of the press should not be curtailed merely to avoid the distress caused by publication of matters which show up a parent in a sordid or unfavourable light.[29] In any event, maximum publicity had already been given to the husband's version of events, and the ultimate decision was likely to be that it was quite lawful to publish, in which case, an injunction, if granted, would encroach in a significant manner on the freedom of the press.

2. The European Convention on Human Rights

Article 8 of the European Convention on Human Rights states:

1. Everyone has the right to respect for his private and family life, his home and his correspondence.

2.   There shall be no interference by a public authority with the exercise of this right except such as is in accordance with the law and is necessary in a democratic society in the interests of national security, public safety or the economic well-being of the country, for the prevention of disorder or crime, for the protection of health or morals, or for the protection of the rights and freedoms of others.

The Convention protects both freedom of expression (Article 10) and privacy (Article 8). Within their respective articles, freedom of expression and privacy are the core values, which may only be restricted to the extent necessary in a democracy in support of certain specified interests. However, it is not altogether clear which right would prevail if, for example, an individual complained that legislation or a court decision giving priority to freedom of expression breached his/her right to privacy under the Convention. To date, no case has arisen where a conflict between the two has been contested. It should be noted, however, that Article 8.2 covers interference by a 'public authority' only. It does not mention the media. Article 10.2 does not expressly mention privacy as a ground for restricting freedom of the press, although it does refer to 'the rights of others' and to the disclosure of information received in confidence. States like the Netherlands which have incorporated the Convention into their domestic law tend to give priority to freedom of the press over the right to privacy, in accordance with the jurisprudence of the European Court of Human Rights, which has consistently underscored the value of a free press in a democratic society. French law, however, seems, at least in practice, to favour privacy over freedom of expression, while in Germany the two rights have equal constitutional status under Articles 2.1 and 5, respectively, of the Basic Law.[30] Most countries that protect privacy allow a public interest defence, so that if it can be shown that there was a public interest involved in revealing the private information, there will be no liability in law.[31]

What Protection Is There at Present?

1. Person and Property

In Ireland little or no attempt has been made to define privacy, particularly as concerns the media. It is accepted that the Constitution protects it as a right but the common law is characterised by its fragmented approach and little in the way of systematic privacy protection. Tort law could be said at best to offer incidental or haphazard protection and is notable for its gaps, particularly the lack of a specific tort of breach of privacy.[32] Incidental protection may be offered in certain situations by the torts of trespass to person, land or goods and the tort of nuisance. They can provide a remedy, for example, in the case of unwanted telephone calls, persistent harassment or use of surveillance equipment. For instance, Jeremiah Locke, the man at the centre of the Kerry Babies case in 1985,[33] took an action against two ITN reporters who, he claimed, had been harassing him, calling at his home, telephoning him incessantly, shouting through the letter-box. His tort action for trespass and nuisance yielded damages of £100. He also obtained an injunction restraining the journalists from entering his property and watching or besetting him. In *Thomas v Independent Newspapers*,[34] the plaintiff (a young boy), whose name and address were published in the newspaper as a witness to a bank robbery, sued unsuccessfully for the tort of intentional infliction of emotional suffering. This is a tort that the courts created in order to address a particular situation[35] and have been very reluctant to develop to meet what are in effect defamation or privacy situations.[36]

2. Confidentiality

The Courts of Equity in Britain developed an action for breach of confidence to fill a gap in the common-law protection. However, its use is confined mostly to commercial or national security situations. It has been relied upon in *Spycatcher*,[37] in an attempt to restrain a former member of the Secret Service from revealing in his memoirs details of the Service's operations. The action is more in the nature of a disciplinary measure. The concern in *Spycatcher*, for example, was to discourage civil servants from breaching their contract of employment with the government which required them to be bound by the Official Secrets Act. At stake in such cases is not the right to personal or individual privacy but rather state secrecy *versus* the public interest in disclosure.

Protection of confidentiality has arisen in a number of spheres. For example, in AG *for England and Wales v Brandon Book Publishers Ltd*,[38] an injunction was refused by Carroll J. in the High Court. The material contained in the book *One Girl's War*, about the activities of MI5 some forty years earlier, did not pose any threat to the authority of the Irish State, which under our Constitution was the only justifiable reason for restricting freedom of expression in such a case. In 1992, however, the Supreme Court, by a majority, held in favour of Cabinet confidentiality, by analogy with the constitutional immunity from suit for any statement made in either House of the Oireachtas:

> [Cabinet confidentiality] extends to discussions and to their contents but . . . not . . . to the decisions made and the documentary evidence of them. . . . It is a constitutional right . . . which goes to the fundamental machinery of government, and is, therefore, not capable of being waived by any individual member of a government, nor . . . are the details and contents of discussions at meetings of the government capable of being made public . . . by a decision of any succeeding government.[39]

In a dissenting judgment, McCarthy J. expressed the view that freedom of discussion did not require an absolute constitutional right of confidentiality and that any defamatory statements made in the course of discussion would attract qualified privilege unless they were made maliciously, in which case they should be actionable.[40] The Supreme Court's decision, however, has provoked alarm. It is expected to become the subject of a referendum to amend the Constitution, rather than being examined by the Commission established by the government in 1995 to review the Constitution.

In ACC *v Irish Business*[41] an injunction was granted to prevent publication on the basis of breach of confidence and copyright. Likewise, in *The Council of the Bar of Ireland v Sunday Business Post*,[42] a temporary injunction was granted on grounds of breach of confidence to prevent publication of a letter and statement submitted to the Council's inquiry into the conduct of a barrister. The documents were said to contain information of a sensitive and private nature. The presiding judge accepted that publication could lead to irreparable damage to the Council and its system of investigation of professional misconduct. He was protecting the system, therefore, rather than individual privacy as such. The disciplinary inquiry had been held *in camera* and a rule of the Professional Practices Committee required absolute confidentiality.[43] However, absolute rules of that nature may be open to scrutiny on constitutional grounds. Keane J. in *Oblique Financial Services Ltd v The Promise Production Co. Ltd*[44] based his argument on the Constitution and held that the guarantee of freedom of expression in Article 40.6.1 did not apply to factual information and therefore the right to communicate in Article 40.3 had to be read subject to the plaintiff's right to confidentiality.

Thus, confidentiality in some contexts will be protected by law but not the confidentiality promised by journalists to their sources. The problem for journalists is double-edged. If they refuse to identify a source in court, they may be in contempt of court. If they reveal a source, others will be disinclined to give them information in future. The disclosure in a newspaper in the United States of the identity of a source who had been promised confidentiality by a journalist led to the source taking an action under the law of contract in *Cohen v Cowles Media*.[45] The US Supreme Court upheld his right to sue for breach of promise on the basis of promissory estoppel.

3. Copyright

The law of copyright is not primarily concerned with privacy but rather with property rights in one's creative work. It can, however, operate incidentally to protect privacy or provide a remedy for its breach. It can, for example, protect against the unauthorised use of a photograph.[46] In the Irish courts, Carroll J. accepted in *Brandon Book Publishers*[47] that freedom of expression could be restricted in the interests of copyright or confidential information, although there was no breach of either in the particular case.

4. Legislative Protection

Legislation protects privacy in a number of areas. It imposes restrictions on court reporting in the interests of privacy. These range from family law cases being held *in camera*, to the names of victims of rape and sexual assault being withheld. (For further discussion see

Chapter 6.) Section 18 of the Broadcasting Authority Act 1960, as amended by section 3(1a) of the Broadcasting Authority (Amendment) Act 1976 and incorporated in the Radio and Television Act 1988, section 9(1)(e), requires broadcasters to ensure that the privacy of the individual is not unreasonably encroached upon. The 1976 Act established the Broadcasting Complaints Commission, with power to handle complaints concerning *inter alia* invasion of privacy. An examination of the Commission's decisions, however, indicates that most complaints concern bias, lack of fairness or impartiality and not privacy. One complaint that did concern privacy was that brought by a consultant child psychologist in relation to a programme on child sexual abuse. The objection was to the fact that the children were clearly identifiable and their names given. The decision to uphold the complaint was unanimous.[48] A right of reply for those whose legitimate interests, in particular reputation and good name, have been damaged by incorrect facts, was included in the Broadcasting Act 1990.

The Data Protection Act 1988 gives individuals a right of access to personal information concerning them, where the information is held by agencies on automated systems. They are entitled to have data corrected or erased. The Act also imposes certain obligations on the holders of personal data, including the obligation to register with the Data Protection Commissioner but it applies to automated systems only, not to manual systems. The Act provides for general protection of personal data held on computer and is not specifically aimed at the media.[49]

Other legislation has made it an offence to intercept telephone conversations or correspondence, except in specified circumstances.[50] In 1993 a number of print and radio journalists were fined under the Postal and Telecommunications Services Act 1983 for disclosing or using a telephone conversation between prominent politicians that was intercepted illegally by means of a scanning device. Publication had caused the politicians 'embarrassment', the judge said.[51] Embarrassment is not necessarily the same as invasion of privacy; the real issue is the right to hold telephone conversations in private.

5. Privacy versus Defamation

The embarrassment and hurt that a person suffers on the exposure of private personal facts results from the divergence it causes from the image he/she wants to project of himself/herself.[52] It is this divergence that is the essence of the injury, and therefore it can be caused by the publication of true facts just as readily as by false statements.

Because the publication of true facts can be just as damaging to a person's privacy as the publication of false facts to his/her reputation, truth is not a defence to a breach of privacy. As Barendt[53] put it: 'The whole point of protecting privacy is to keep some information away from public exposure, even if it is true.' Nonetheless, there is an overlap and the boundaries between libel and privacy are uncertain. There is a paradox in common law in that defamation is heavily and systematically protected, while privacy is only accorded incidental protection.[54] In addition, current defamation laws apply to both print and broadcast media, while the obligation to respect privacy is a feature of broadcasting legislation (Broadcasting Authority Act 1960, section 18) but has no direct application to the print media. As far as the print media are concerned, privacy is protected only indirectly and incidentally by tort law but is also a feature of journalists' codes of ethics.[55]

The European Convention on Human Rights speaks of the right of everyone to respect for his private and family life, home and correspondence (Article 8), while the UN Covenant on Civil and Political Rights states that no one shall be subjected to arbitrary or unlawful interference with his privacy, family, home or correspondence, nor to unlawful attacks on his honour and reputation (Article 17). In other words, the Covenant links the rights to privacy and reputation, much as the German Constitution does in its concept of a right to one's dignity and personality (*das Personlichkeitsrecht*) of which the private sphere or zone (*Privatsphare*) is just one component.[56]

6. Self-Regulation

Forms of self-regulation, such as press councils and media ombudsmen, have been adopted in many countries, usually as a result of pressure and threats of intervention from government. Press councils, financed by the industry, have existed since the early part of the century (Sweden 1916, Norway 1928, Britain 1953), but many have since disappeared or been replaced. The British Press Council, for example, came under a great deal of criticism, being regarded as having no teeth and being spurned by tabloid editors. It was replaced in 1991 by the Press Complaints Commission, designed to implement a Code of Practice drawn up by a committee of editors.

There is no press council as such in Ireland but all the national newspapers have had readers' representatives since 1986. It is their task to receive complaints from readers and provide an appropriate avenue of redress. In the case of complaints of inaccuracy or misleading reporting, corrections or clarifications are published. Complaints of invasion of privacy are few, and when they do occur they are brought to the attention of the editor or relevant department. In *Maguire v Drury*[57] the evidence showed that once the editor was aware that photographs of the children of the family had been taken by deception, he gave an assurance that the photographs would not be used. Provincial newspapers, because they are at the heart of the community, can usually handle complaints at a personal level. Their reliance on the community is the best guarantor of protection for privacy. In the case of the broadcast media, the Broadcasting Complaints Commission hears complaints and if it upholds them, its findings must be carried by the broadcaster under the right of reply requirement of the Broadcasting Act 1990, in accordance with the EC Directive on Transfrontier Broadcasting.

A Statutory Regime?

Although invasion of privacy by the media has not been a problem in Ireland, the difficulty in introducing any statutory privacy regime is to decide not only what is to be protected but also how to build in a deterrent element that will be effective and yet not undermine the freedom of the press. Looking at France, where privacy protection is most developed, the French Code Civil and Article 35 of the Press Law of 1881 protect privacy: 'Everyone has the right to respect for his private life'. It is a criminal offence to listen to, record or transmit by means of any machine words spoken by a person in a private place without the consent of that person or to fix or transmit by means of any machine a picture of a person in a private place without the person's consent.[58] The protection offered includes references to a person's love life, family life, disclosure of the private address or telephone number of a public figure or an individual's salary. However, in France there are a large number of actions for breach of privacy. Therefore the deterrent value of the law is slight. The primary remedy is damages but the amount awarded is moderate compared with defamation damages in common-law jurisdictions. In 1985 Marlene Dietrich was awarded about £1,000 when forty lines of the forward to a book were found to contain references to her relationships with several people. More recently, Brigitte Bardot received damages of one franc when she complained about a photograph showing her in her underwear.[59]

In Germany, Articles 1 and 2 of the Basic Law (*Grundgesetz*) together recognise a 'personality right', protecting the dignity, freedom and self-determination of the individual. Privacy and defamation are aspects of that general right and are shaped by it although given separate recognition in the Codes. Privacy is protected under both the civil and criminal law. The public/private distinction is applied. Indeed, the public category contains a further distinction between public persons who have voluntarily entered the public arena on a permanent basis and those who have become involved in particular issues.[60] The degree of protection varies, but as far as family and home are concerned, all categories enjoy a high degree of protection. Article 5, which protects freedom of the press, provides a defence to a breach of privacy, if the breach discloses information of significant interest to the public.[61]

By comparison with other European countries, therefore, Irish law cannot be said to protect privacy in a systematic way. There is quite considerable protection in Irish law for various aspects of privacy but it adds up to something of a patchwork. The theoretical basis and justification for protection have not been addressed in a comprehensive manner. If a right to privacy is to be developed, then in Ireland's case it ought to be developed in a systematic way in accordance with the Constitution and with the guidance of the international human rights instruments.

Further Reading

Lorenz, Professor Werner, 'Privacy and the Press—a German Experience', *Butterworths Lectures* 1989–90, London: Butterworths, 1990.

Markesinis, Basil S., 'Our Patchy Law of Privacy—Time to Do Something about It' (1990) 53 MLR 802.

Markesinis, Basil S., 'The Right to Be Let Alone versus Freedom of Speech' (1986) *Public Law* 67.

Ó hAnnracháin, Fachtna, 'Privacy and Broadcasting' (1971) 105 ILT 225, 231, 241, 247, 257, 267.

Reid, Cheryl, 'Press Censorship into the 1990s: The Calcutt Report and the Protection of Individual Privacy' (1992) 43 NILQ 99.

Notes

1 Cited in Anthony Lewis, John Foster Memorial Lecture, 1987 9 *London Review of Books* No. 21, 26 (November 1987).
2 Kenneth Younger, Chairman, Committee of Privacy, *Report of the Committee on Privacy*, cmnd. 5012, London: HMSO 1972.
3 Ibid., at para. 632.
4 [1991] FSR 62, CA.
5 Sir David Calcutt, Calcutt Report, *Report of the Committee on Privacy and Related Matters*, cmnd. 1102, London: HMSO, 1990.
6 Sir David Calcutt, *Review of Press Self-Regulation*, cmnd. 2135, London: HMSO, 1993.
7 Warren and Brandeis, 'The Right to Privacy', 4 Harv LR 193 (1890).
8 Ibid.
9 See *Broadcasting Guidelines for* RTÉ *Personnel*, Dublin: RTÉ, 1989.
10 [1987] IR 587, [1988] ILRM 472.
11 Cf. the argument advanced by Hall that 'Constitutional guarantees should not be shackled on mere technological grounds.' Eamonn Hall, *The Electronic Age: Telecommunication in Ireland*, Dublin: Oak Tree Press, 1993, at p. 429.
12 Dean Prosser, 'Privacy', 45 Calif. LRev 383 (1960), discussed in Diane Zimmerman, 'Requiem for a Heavyweight: A Farewell to Warren and Brandeis's Privacy Tort', 68 Corn LR 291, in Raymond Wacks, *Privacy*, vol. 2, Dartmouth, 1993.
13 See Harvey L. Zuckman, 'The American Torts of Invasion of Privacy' (1990) 5 ENT LR 173.
14 See Noel Paul, *Principles for the Press*, London: The Press Council, 1985, at p. 183. Code of Practice 15 March 1990; see News Section (1990) 2 ENT LR, E–30.
15 Paul n. 14; The Press Council, *The Press and the People*, London 1984, ch. 7, p. 290, at p. 291.
16 The Declaration stressed that the public interest involved must be a 'legitimate and proper public interest and not only a prurient or morbid curiosity'.
17 The Australian television code for commercial stations (FACTS 1991) treats the issue solely from the perspective of causing distress to viewers and, unlike the Australian Broadcasting Corporation Code (ABC Code 1990), is totally silent on the rights of those portrayed; see Putnis, Peter, 'Television and Privacy: Australian Perspective' (1991) 12 JMLP 83.
18 See Kevin Boyle and Marie McGonagle, *Media Accountability: The Readers' Representative in Irish Newspapers*, Dublin: NNI, 1995, at p. 27.
19 See Thomas I. Emerson, 'The Right of Privacy and Freedom of the Press' (1979) 14 *Harv CR–CL Rev* 329; Frederick F. Schauer, 'Reflections on the Value of Truth', in Raymond Wacks, ed., *Privacy*, vol. 2, Dartmouth, 1993, at p. 407; Eoin O'Dell, 'When Two Tribes Go to War: Privacy Interests and Media Speech', in McGonagle, ed., *Essays on Law and Media*, Dublin: Round Hall Press (forthcoming).
20 See Tom Gerety, 'Redefining Privacy' (1977) 12 *Harv CR–CL Rev* 233, cited in n. 19, Emerson at p. 338.
21 Most European jurisdictions have a public interest defence, the notable exception being France; see Article 19, *Press Law and Practice*, London, 1993, at p. 67.
22 [1974] IR 284.
23 [1987] IR 587, [1988] ILRM 472.
24 Ibid at p. 477, per Hamilton, P.
25 [1984] IR 36.
26 Ibid., at pp 71–72 (Henchy J. dissenting).
27 Research has shown that very few complaints of invasion of privacy are made against the Irish media; see n. 18 and annual reports of the Broadcasting Complaints Commission.
28 [1995] ILRM 108.
29 Ibid., at pp 113–15.
30 See, for example, *Louis van Gasteren v Het Parol*, summarised in [1995] 3 ENT LR News section E-64–5. See also the case law of the European Court of Human Rights on the right to privacy, including *Malone v UK* (1984) 7 EHRR 14, *Klaas v Germany* (1980) 2 EHRR

214, *Schwabe v Austria*, series A, no. 242B (1992). For the protection of privacy in other countries, see Article 19, *Press Law and Practice*, London, 1993, and *The Article 19 Freedom of Expression Handbook*, London, 1993, pp 162–4; *Report of the Committee on Privacy and Related Matters* (Calcutt Report), cmnd. 1102, London: HMSO, 1990, ch. 5.

31 It has been argued that the freedom to express ideas and opinions in Article 10 must also include the freedom to withhold ideas and opinions and the right to decide when and if to impart them; see Keith Schilling, 'Privacy and the Press: Breach of Confidence—the Nemesis of the Tabloids?' (1991) 6 ENT LR 169. What the significance of that argument might be for the media remains to be seen.

32 See Bryan McMahon and William Binchy, *Irish Law of Torts*, 2nd edn., Dublin: Butterworths, 1989.

33 *The Irish Times*, 31 October 1985.

34 *The Irish Times*, 26 July 1988.

35 *Wilkinson v Downton* [1897] 2 QB 57.

36 See *Hustler Magazine Inc. v Falwell* 485 US 46 (1988), a case concerning a cartoon that depicted a politician in a very unfavourable light.

37 *The Observer and the Guardian v UK* (1992) 14 EHRR 153.

38 [1986] IR 597; [1987] ILRM 135.

39 *AG v Hamilton (No.1)* [1993] 2 IR 250, [1993] ILRM 81, *per* Finlay C.J. at p. 100.

40 Ibid., *per* McCarthy J. at pp 275–92; 103–117.

41 *The Irish Times*, 9 August 1985.

42 Unreported, High Court, 30 March 1993.

43 *The Irish Times*, 6 March 1993.

44 [1994] 1 ILRM 74.

45 501 US 663 (1991).

46 See, for example, n. 5, ch. 9.

47 See n. 38, at p. 602, 137.

48 Broadcasting Complaints Commission, Ninth Annual Report, 1987; and Eamonn Hall, *The Electronic Age*, ch. 22, p. 299, Dublin: Oak Tree Press, 1993.

49 See Robert Clark, *Data Protection Law in Ireland*, Dublin: The Round Hall Press, 1990.

50 Postal and Telecommunications Services Act 1983 and Interception of Postal Packets and Telecommunications Messages (Regulation) Act 1993, for example.

51 *The Irish Times*, 29 July 1993. A Consultation Paper on Privacy, dealing primarily with surveillance and the interception of communications is to be published by the Law Reform Commission early in 1996.

52 See n. 12, Zimmerman.

53 Eric Barendt, *Freedom of Speech*, Oxford: Clarendon Press, 1989, at p. 190.

54 The reverse is true in France, where photographs taken without consent and the publication of an article about a divorce and liaison were regarded as an invasion of privacy and resulted in an award of 60,000FF and an order to publish the court's findings (unreported, 5 July 1993, CA Paris). The French courts will not restrain publication, however, on the basis of a perceived danger of invasion of privacy (Tribunal de Grande Instance de Paris, 26 October 1992). See also Sir Louis Blom-Cooper, 'The Right to Be Let Alone' (1989) 10 JMLP 53 at p. 57: 'The first thing to do is to acknowledge the imbalance in the one (that is the law of defamation) and then to address the omission in the other (a law of privacy).'

55 The NUJ Code of Conduct, for example.

56 The UN Declaration on Human Rights of 1948 said: 'No one shall be subjected to arbitrary interference with his privacy, family, home or correspondence, nor to attacks upon his honour and reputation. Everyone has the right to the protection of the law against such interference or attacks.' (Article 12)

57 See n. 28.

58 Cf. Recommendations of Calcutt Report, n. 5, para. 6.35.

59 *The Irish Times*, 20 June 1985, 15 April 1986. See also *Bardot v Daily Express* JCP 1966 II 14 521.

60 See Gregory Thwaite and Wolfgang Brehm, 'German Privacy and Defamation Law' [1994] 8 EIPR 336.

61 Ibid., at p. 340.

CHAPTER SIX

The Principle of Open Justice: The Media and the Courts

The relationship between the media and the courts can be difficult. The courts are concerned with safeguarding the administration of justice and the right to a fair trial. They do not regard the media as an integral part of the process and sometimes treat journalists as an intrusion, particularly when inaccurate or misleading reporting is seen to obstruct the administration of justice or prejudice a fair trial. Nonetheless, the Irish Constitution (Article 34) provides for a system of open justice. Justice is administered on behalf of the public and the public has a right to attend. The media, by extension, have a right to report on court proceedings. 'The actual presence of the public is never necessary', according to Walsh J. in In re R,[1] 'but the administration of justice does require that the doors of the courts must be open so that members of the general public may come and see for themselves that justice is done.' Referring to the preconstitutional position, Walsh J. said:

> The primary object of the courts is to see that justice is done and it was only when the presence of the public or public knowledge of the proceedings would defeat that object that the judges had any discretion to hear cases other than in public. It had to be shown that a public hearing was likely to lead to a denial of justice. . . [2]

This principle was made part of the fundamental law of the State by Article 34 of the Constitution. As the Supreme Court held in *Beamish and Crawford Ltd v Crowley*,[3] apart from the exceptions permitted by law, publicity is inseparable from the administration of justice. Indeed, now, a quarter of a century later, the case could be put more strongly. The media have become such a central part of people's lives that their role in court reporting has taken on a greater importance. It is from the media that most people get their knowledge of the court system and court proceedings. Most people do not read official law reports written in technical legal language by barristers. They read their newspaper for the lay person's (journalist's) account of what is happening or they hear or watch the news clips on radio and television. The value of the journalist's account, therefore, should not be underestimated, but it should be remembered that journalists cannot be expected to report with the precision and level of technical detail that characterises official law reports.

Because they perform a vital public function, court reporters should be viewed as a positive rather than negative force. Courts should be keen to ensure accuracy in reporting, in their own interest, as well as that of the public, and be prepared to facilitate reporters to that end. The court system, personnel, litigants and the administration of justice itself would be the beneficiaries. However, the reality is quite different. Reporters are often viewed as a necessary evil and are only facilitated, if at all, on a personal or informal basis. Although this must be seen in the context of the overall problem of courts that are understaffed and lacking even basic resources and support structures,[4] nonetheless the fundamental attitude to the press has tended to be negative. The courts, rightly scrupulous in their protection of the administration of justice and the right to fair trial, have tended to turn to the law to punish inaccurate or misleading reporting rather than taking positive steps to encourage understanding and a high level of accuracy. One of the principal measures adopted and invoked by the courts to that purpose has been the law of contempt of court.

Contempt of Court

1. Constitutional and Common-Law Origins

The Irish Constitution guarantees freedom of expression and of the press in Article 40.6.1. It also specifies a number of areas of limitation or restriction on that freedom: public order and morality and the authority of the State. It does not specifically mention protection of the courts or the administration of justice as a limitation, yet, in practice, the freedom of the press to report or comment on court proceedings is restricted in a number of ways.

The basis for these restrictions in the interests of the administration of justice is thought to stem, therefore, from Article 34 of the Constitution, which provides *inter alia* for open justice, due process and fair trial. In a recent incest case, DPP *v* W.M.,[5] Carney J. in the High Court appeared to accept Article 34 as the constitutional basis for these restrictions, while O'Hanlon J. in *Desmond v Glackin* (No. 1)[6] considered that the phrase 'public order or morality or the authority of the State' in Article 40.6.1 was 'sufficiently wide to comprehend a restriction on the right to freedom of expression so far as may be necessary for maintaining the authority and impartiality of the judiciary, corresponding to that in Article 10(2) of the European Convention on Human Rights'.[7]

Whatever their formal basis, restrictions, in practice, take two main forms:

(i) denying or limiting access to the courts and

(ii) imposing restrictions on the content of reports of court proceedings.

Both are provided for by statute and will be discussed in Chapter 7. More far-reaching, however, is the common law of contempt of court. In recent years most of the top Irish broadcasters, including Gay Byrne, Pat Kenny and Gerry Ryan, have had to appear in court in relation to contempt. In fact, Gerry Ryan and RTÉ were fined as a result of a radio interview with an alleged rape victim when the case against the accused was pending.[8] The concern of the courts was for the accused's right to a fair trial, i.e. that the trial should not be prejudiced by media coverage. It is a regular occurrence for the national media, newspapers and broadcasters to be summoned before the courts because of the risk to fair trial occasioned by inaccurate headlines, background or colour pieces on cases that have not been finally disposed of or mistakes in relation to evidence. In 1992 alone, there were at least seventeen such instances, mostly attributable to misunderstanding, inadvertent mistakes or human error. In most of these the court was satisfied with an apology, but in some instances, the decision was taken to put back for hearing to the next court term the trial that was believed prejudiced and for the media to pay the costs involved.

Contempt law, which empowers courts to impose fines and imprisonment or the sequestration of assets in response to prejudice or interference with the judicial process, enables the courts to maintain a high level of protection around the courts themselves and the administration of justice. Whether the courts need such a high level of protection today is open to question, as are the long-held assumptions that the media have the capacity to cause serious prejudice to court cases or that juries, in particular, are susceptible to influence by the media. There is an argument to be made that the public, including juries, are media-wise, having grown up in a media environment, and that the courts should reflect that in their handling of, and response to, media reporting.[9] It is true that, historically, the emerging press was viewed with apprehension. The courts feared its potential and its effect on public confidence in the justice system, so resorted to contempt of court as a control mechanism. In the early days, criticism in the press of any of the state institutions was not tolerated and was often equated with sedition. Respect for the courts had to be maintained. Criticism, it was believed, would promote disrespect and cause people to lose confidence in the courts. It had to be quelled. For instance, the editor of the *Dublin Evening Post* in 1785 used his paper to criticise the manner in which he had been treated by the courts in a libel action against him and was duly sentenced to one month's imprisonment for contempt of court, fined £5 and ordered to enter into securities to keep the peace.[10] In 1798 he was jailed again, this time for six months, for criticising the Court of King's Bench.[11] The purpose of contempt of court was disciplinary, to uphold the authority of the courts—the King's courts. Initially it was aimed at court officers, parties and witnesses appearing in court, but with the emergence of the printed press, the jurisdiction was extended to prevent criticism and interference from outside the court.

2. Other Jurisdictions

Contempt of court law is unique to common-law jurisdictions. It is unknown in civil-law countries, where specific criminal offences set out in the penal codes protect the independence and impartiality of the judiciary and the administration of justice. There the system in criminal cases is inquisitorial rather than adversarial, and it may be argued that proceedings in court, because they are not so dependent on oral testimony, do not need the same degree of protection from media reporting as do our courts. Nonetheless, there is something to be said for the clear and defined scope of a statutory offence, as opposed to the imprecise scope of the contempt power.[12]

All the major international human rights instruments proclaim the right to a fair trial but none of them include protection of the administration of justice among the legitimate areas of restriction on freedom of expression. The European Convention on Human Rights does, however, include 'maintaining the authority and impartiality of the judiciary' as an area of restriction in Article 10.2. This was included in response to pressure from the United Kingdom in support of its contempt laws. It was under the heading of 'maintaining the authority and impartiality of the judiciary' that the European Court of Human Rights considered contempt of court law in *Sunday Times v UK*,[13] the thalidomide drug case, although the court concluded that the common law of contempt was much wider than the restriction in Article 10.2.

As with defamation and privacy, the problem arises as to how to reconcile conflicting rights. The approach of the common law has been to give precedence to protection of the courts and the right to fair trial over freedom of reporting and information. Indeed, it could be said that in this respect the common-law approach is at odds with, if not diametrically opposed to, that espoused by the European Convention on Human Rights. There the question is not one of 'a choice between two conflicting principles, but with a principle of freedom of expression that is subject to a number of exceptions which must be narrowly interpreted'.[14] The court in *Sunday Times v UK* recognised that the administration of justice 'requires the co-operation of an enlightened public':

> There is general recognition of the fact that the courts cannot operate in a vacuum. Whilst they are the forum for the settlement of disputes, this does not mean that there can be no prior discussion of disputes elsewhere, be it in specialised journals, in the general press or amongst the public at large. Furthermore, whilst the mass media must not overstep the bounds imposed in the interests of the proper administration of justice, it is incumbent on them to impart information and ideas concerning matters that come before the courts just as in other areas of public interest. Not only have the media the task of imparting such information and ideas; the public also has a right to receive them.[15]

Article 6 of the Convention, which provides for the right to a fair and public hearing, stipulates that the press may be excluded from the courts in the interests of morals, public order and certain other specified interests or when the court considers it 'strictly necessary' in special circumstances where publicity would prejudice the interests of justice.[16] It does not refer to reporting restrictions, however; it is Article 10 that does so. How then would the European Court of Human Rights decide a case, taken under Article 6, alleging that a trial had been unfair because of extensive and prejudicial media coverage? In *Sunday Times v UK* the court emphasised that the expression 'authority and impartiality of the judiciary' had to be understood 'within the meaning of the Convention'. For this purpose, the court said, 'account must be taken of the central position occupied in this context by Article 6, which reflects the fundamental principle of the rule of law'.[17]

The test applied by the Irish Supreme Court in Z *v* DPP[18] was one of a 'real or serious risk' of an unfair trial. It was on the basis of that test that the court allowed the trial of the man accused of offences against the girl in the X case to proceed, despite the fact that there had been extensive media coverage in 1992 when a court injunction was obtained to prevent the fourteen-year-old girl going to Britain for an abortion.

In an unprecedented development in the UK in 1994, two sisters cleared of murder were given leave by the High Court, overturning a decision of the Attorney General, to bring contempt proceedings against a number of newspapers for 'sensational and biased' reporting of their trial. The Appeal Court had allowed their appeal against conviction, in part because of the 'unremitting, extensive, sensational, inaccurate and misleading' reporting of their trial. They had already served eleven months in prison.[19]

In Britain, following recommendations of the Phillimore Committee in 1974[20] and especially the decision of the European Court of Human Rights in *Sunday Times v* UK, the law of contempt is now governed by statute: the Contempt of Court Act 1981. In Ireland contempt remains wholly common law; legislation merely provides for its extension to certain tribunals. As in other jurisdictions, particularly Canada and Australia, there has been dissatisfaction with the uncertainty of the common law and the Law Reform Commission has published proposals for reform. Before addressing questions of reform, however, it is necessary to understand the ground rules.

3. Forms of Contempt

The term 'contempt of court' is somewhat antiquated and inaccurate in so far as it suggests conduct that brings the courts into disrepute or holds them up to ridicule. It does cover such conduct but it also covers much more. There are two principal forms of contempt: (a) Civil contempt and (b) Criminal contempt, although the distinction between them has become more and more blurred in recent decades, particularly with the emergence of a number of 'hybrid' cases (to be discussed later).

(a) Civil Contempt

Civil contempt, according to Ó Dálaigh C.J. in *Keegan v de Búrca*,[21]

> usually arises where there is a disobedience to an order of the court by a party to the proceedings and in which the court generally has no interest to interfere unless moved by the party for whose benefit the order was made.

'Civil' contempt is so-called, therefore, because it involves breach of an order issued as part of the civil side of the court's jurisdiction, not because it relates solely to civil cases or because it gives rise to a civil action. In fact, it is in many respects criminal. For instance, breach of a court order can result in imprisonment. The purpose of civil contempt is coercive rather than punitive, that is, it aims to persuade the person to obey the order, and that seemingly is the justification for the indefinite terms of imprisonment, i.e. *sine die*,[22] which may result. A court may sentence defaulters to imprisonment *sine die*, i.e. for an unspecified period, until such time as they purge their contempt, by agreeing to or taking steps to obey the order. The object of civil contempt is, therefore, to prompt compliance with court orders and in that way to preserve the authority and dignity of the courts. The Law Reform Commission has recommended retaining the *sine die* sanction but looking at the feasibility of accruing, or *per diem* (daily), fines as in the United States, Netherlands and Norway, as an alternative. The Commission did not favour substituting definite terms of imprisonment for *sine die*.[23]

Civil contempt does not have any major implications for the media. From time to time, individual journalists may be restrained by court injunction from entering certain premises, hounding someone for a story or publishing certain information. Breach of such an injunction would constitute civil contempt. More often, media cases are either exclusively criminal contempt or 'hybrid' versions, i.e. where breach of the court order restraining publication is civil contempt but the fact of publishing the story the order concerns is criminal contempt. In a case involving the *Irish Press*,[24] publication of extracts from a report which was subject to a court order amounted to civil contempt. An order had been made under the Companies Acts prohibiting publication of the report to anyone other than the government minister who had commissioned it. The court accepted that there had been a misunderstanding as to the legal position and no intention on the part of the journalist or editor to commit contempt and, therefore, accepted their apology. In this particular case, as breach of the order had already occurred and was unlikely to recur, the *sine die* punishment would not have been appropriate. Nonetheless, counsel argued that breach of the order clearly constituted civil contempt and that the publication of the information was bordering on criminal contempt also. However, Costello J. in the High Court did not make an order against the journalist and editor for contempt, nor did he require them to identify their sources, but he did require them to hand up notes of the extracts from the report.[25]

In 1985 RTÉ was found guilty of contempt in stating the fact of a bankruptcy in a 'Today Tonight' programme on friendly societies and fringe banks.[26] An order prohibiting publication of the bankruptcy had been made a few months earlier. The President of the High Court accepted that RTÉ was not aware of the prohibition but found that this fact did not excuse them. It was RTÉ's responsibility to make all reasonable inquiries, he said.[27] Nonetheless, he accepted an apology. Publication in breach of the court order constituted civil contempt and it was feared also that it would jeopardise the man's chances of making an arrangement with his creditors inside the bankruptcy.

(b) Criminal Contempt

Of much greater consequence for the media is criminal contempt, which Ó Dálaigh C.J. said in *Keegan v de Búrca*:[28]

> consists in behaviour calculated to prejudice the due course of justice, such as contempt in *facie curiae*, words written or spoken or acts calculated to prejudice the due course of justice or disobedience to a writ of habeas corpus by the person to whom it is directed—to give but some examples of this class of contempt . . . . Criminal contempt is a common law misdemeanour and, as such, is punishable by both imprisonment and fine at discretion, that is to say without statutory limit, its object is punitive. . . .

Each of the types of prejudicial behaviour identified by Ó Dálaigh C.J. can be considered in turn.

(i) Contempt in *Facie Curiae* (in the face of the court)

Contempt in *facie curiae*, according to O'Higgins C.J. in the *State* (DPP) *v Walsh and Conneely*:[29]

> consists of conduct which is obstructive or prejudicial to the course of justice, and which is committed during court proceedings.

While this form of contempt can occur in a variety of ways, such as courtroom demonstrations, insulting court personnel, impeding access to the courtroom and so on, its most important aspect from the media point of view concerns the refusal of journalists to disclose their sources of information when called to give evidence in court. If a journalist refuses to answer a relevant question put to him/her, he/she is in contempt of court. There has been no recognition of journalists' privilege, and newspaper proprietors, editors and journalists have gone to jail on occasion rather than disclose their sources.[30] In *O'Brennan v Tully*,[31] the editor of the *Roscommon Herald* was fined £25 on the spot for refusing to identify the author of a letter to the paper, which criticised the plaintiff, a local County Councillor and member of Dáil Eireann. The editor's offence was to refuse to answer a 'relevant' question.[32]

The leading case is In *re Kevin O'Kelly*.[33] Kevin O'Kelly was an RTÉ journalist called as a witness in the trial of Seán Mac Stiofáin for membership of the IRA. O'Kelly refused to identify the voice on a tape-recording as that of Mac Stiofáin and was sentenced to three months imprisonment by the Special Criminal Court. He appealed to the Court of Criminal Appeal, where his prison sentence was quashed and a fine of £250 imposed instead. O'Kelly considered that to answer the question would be a breach of confidence between himself and his client which would not only put his own position as a journalist in jeopardy but would also make it difficult for other journalists to promote the public good by fostering the free exchange of public opinion. Walsh J. who delivered judgment in the appeal, sympathised with the role of journalists but said that

> . . . journalists or reporters are not any more constitutionally or legally immune than other citizens from disclosing information received in confidence . . .
>
> [and the fact that] a communication was made under terms of expressed confidence or implied confidence does not create a privilege against disclosure.[34]

It is interesting to note that Walsh J. did not expressly inquire into the relevance of the particular question put to O'Kelly or the necessity for answering it. He made a passing remark that the obligation to give 'relevant' testimony did not constitute harassment of journalists, and proceeded to quash the prison sentence on the grounds, *inter alia*, that O'Kelly's refusal to answer the question

> while perhaps adding some little extra difficulty to the case, did not effectively impede the presentation of the prosecution's case.[35]

In other words, O'Kelly's answer was not necessary, yet a fine was imposed. The offence is, therefore, primarily disciplinary, to maintain the authority of the courts and, as such, is a strict liability offence.

A few years prior to *O'Kelly*, however, Lord Denning in an English case, AG *v Mulholland and Foster*,[36] had held that a judge should require a journalist to answer only when the question was relevant, proper and necessary in the course of justice to be put and answered. The Contempt of Court Act 1981 in Britain has further narrowed and refined the test, so that a person will not be in contempt of court for refusing to disclose his/her sources of information

> unless it is established to the satisfaction of the court that disclosure is necessary in the interests of justice or national security or for the prevention of disorder or crime. (section 10)

The Act was introduced in Britain to give effect to the decision of the European Court of Human Rights in *Sunday Times v UK*,[37] which found aspects of the common law of contempt to be in breach of the Convention.

The improved protection for journalists (and others) envisaged in the Act has, however, not proved very effective in practice. Despite a promising decision in *AG v Lundin*,[38] when a journalist was held not to be in contempt for refusing to answer because his answers were not necessary 'in the interests of justice', the courts appear to have reverted to the old common-law position. The phrase 'the interests of justice' has been widely interpreted in later cases, e.g. *British Steel Corporation v Granada Television*,[39] *Re Goodwin*.[40] The latter case concerned a journalist, Bill Goodwin, who received information that a leading private company was experiencing financial difficulties. When he contacted the company to check the information, the company sought a court injunction to prevent him publishing the information and an order seeking disclosure of the identity of the source of his information. Goodwin refused to identify his source and was fined £5,000 for contempt. His subsequent complaint to the European Commission of Human Rights under Article 10 of the Convention was declared admissible in September 1993 and a decision of the Court of Human Rights is awaited.[41] In 1992 Channel Four and independent programme makers, Box Productions, were fined £75,000 for contempt for refusing to reveal their sources for a programme on loyalist death squads in Northern Ireland. The powers conferred by the Prevention of Terrorism Act 1989 were invoked to require them to hand over files, documents and other material relating to the programme.[42] The North's emergency legislation and the Criminal Law Act 1976 have been used to seize footage from television companies, including RTÉ, following the killing of two British army corporals in Belfast.[43]

There is no legislation in Ireland equivalent to the British Contempt of Court Act 1981, although a bill was introduced in 1995 and a private member's bill to amend the defamation laws, on which the government has put a nine-month stay, also contains provisions to protect journalists' sources.[44] The latter provisions in the bill were included in response to the case of *DPP v O'Keeffe*,[45] in which a Granada Television journalist was prosecuted for, in effect, contempt of a tribunal of inquiry. A programme on irregularities in the beef processing industry in Ireland had prompted the government to establish a Tribunal of Inquiry. Journalist Susan O'Keeffe was asked by the Tribunal to identify her sources and hand over documentation used in the preparation of the programme. She refused. The Chairman of the Tribunal, under the terms of the Tribunals of Inquiry (Evidence) Acts 1921–79 sent a file to the DPP with a view to prosecuting her for refusing to 'produce any documents . . . in [her] power or control legally required by the Tribunal . . . or to answer any question to which the tribunal may legally require an answer' (section 1(2)(b), as amended). There is no defence provided in the Act, although it was open to her to prove that the documents sought by the Tribunal were not in her 'power or control', belonging as they did to Granada Television. She could also have argued the case as to whether the Tribunal, not being a court of law, could 'legally require' an answer to the question put to her.[46] The case eventually collapsed due to lack of evidence.[47]

In another case arising out of the Beef Tribunal, *Kiberd and Carey v Tribunal of Inquiry into the Beef Industry*,[48] the High Court upheld the right of the Tribunal to make an order pursuant to section 4 of the 1979 Act obliging two journalists to appear before it to tell the Tribunal the source of the information on which two articles published in the *Sunday Business Post* were based and the identity of the person or persons from whom the information had been obtained.[49] The articles concerned matters due to come before the Tribunal. They were based on material given to the Tribunal in confidence, and the Chairman feared that, if the matter were not inquired into, other witnesses might not come forward and documents might be witheld. The High Court held that, apart from this, the order was necessary in the circumstances because the Tribunal had to take steps to ensure that no further articles would be published based on material submitted in confidence to it. Although the right to make the order was upheld, no charges were brought against the journalists for refusing to divulge their sources.[50]

In the United States, a majority of states have now introduced 'shield laws', providing journalists and their sources with varying degrees of protection. Under these laws journalists are usually only required to answer questions or provide documentation if the information is vital to the trial of a serious offence and is not available from any other source. In an interesting development in 1991, the US Supreme Court held in *Cohen v Cowles Media* that a source who had been promised confidentiality by a newspaper journalist but whose name had been revealed in the paper could sue the newspaper for breach of contract on the basis of the promissory estoppel principle, that is, the newspaper would be stopped from going back on the promise given by the journalist.[51] The source, who was the campaign manager for a candidate, had planted damaging information about an opponent in the run-up to an election. The newspaper editor took the decision, in those circumstances, to name the source.

The situation in *Cohen* is not akin, of course, to identifying a source in a court of law. A journalist who did so could hardly be sued for conforming to a legal requirement. However, the practical effect would be the same. The journalist would lose the confidence of other potential sources and the flow of information to him/her and to other journalists would dry up.

If it is accepted that all sources are not wrongdoers and do not act out of personal spite or rancour, the need to identify them becomes secondary to the need to preserve the free flow of information. In Britain there has been a long and deep obsession with identifying 'moles' and singling them out for punishment, regardless of their motivation or the value of the information they passed on. In contrast, countries like Sweden treat the free flow of information as a priority and make it an offence for a journalist to reveal a source.[52] The protection is seen as belonging to the source and as a safety-valve that makes it possible in many a case for necessary facts to be disclosed. Other countries attempt to balance the two interests by giving some protection to journalists. In Finland, Austria and Germany, journalists are not obliged to reveal their sources. The German Constitutional Court regards such protection as indispensable, believing that the press cannot function without such private communications.[53] Denmark has recently strengthened its protection for journalists,[54] so that it is only in serious criminal cases that a journalist in that country can be required to reveal a source and, even then, only if the identity of the source is vital to the outcome of the case and more important than protecting the source.[55]

A journalist's ability to inform the public depends on the maintenance of confidential relationships, yet Irish law refuses to recognise any right to protect confidential sources.[56] No one would argue that the courts do not require some power to secure the important right to a fair trial and the public interest in the effective administration of justice. However, the scope of the contempt power is a source of concern, especially where journalists are liable to be punished if they refuse to answer any question that the court considers relevant. A test of necessity, however framed, would seem preferable.

(ii) Contempt by Scandalising the Court

The second form of criminal contempt indicated by Ó Dálaigh C.J. was 'words written or spoken . . . calculated to prejudice . . . justice'.[57] The form of 'words written or spoken' could otherwise be described as 'constructive' contempt, i.e. contempt committed outside the court, and can be further broken down into two categories: words that amount to scandalising the court, for example criticism of a judge or court if the criticism imputes partiality or corruption, and those that are likely to prejudice a fair trial, for example reference to other offences or past convictions, publication of matter deliberately kept from the jury or publication of photographs where identification is in issue. Again the distinctions have become less marked in recent years but are a convenient vehicle for analysing the nature and range of activities which can amount to criminal contempt.

On the question of scandalising, O'Higgins C.J. in *State* (DPP) *v Walsh and Conneely*[58] has stated:

> Contempt by scandalising the court is committed where what is said or done is of such a nature as to be calculated to endanger public confidence in the court . . . It is not committed by mere criticisms of judges as judges, or by the expression of disagreement—even emphatic disagreement—with what has been decided by a court . . . Such contempt occurs where wild and baseless allegations of corruption or malpractice are made against a court. The right of citizens to express fairly, subject to public order, convictions and opinions is wide enough to comprehend such criticism or expressed disagreement. Such contempt occurs where wild and baseless allegations of corruption or malpractice are made against a court so as to hold the judges ' . . . to the odium of the people as actors playing a sinister part in a caricature of justice'.[59]

To constitute contempt by scandalising, therefore, the attack must be on a court or on a judge acting in his or her judicial capacity and must amount to more than mere criticism. However, tolerance and what is regarded as 'mere criticism' may vary from one era or culture to another, or even from one court to another,[60] although, in fairness, it must be said that Irish judges do take account of freedom of expression and the right to criticise.

Many of the cases that have arisen in Ireland have concerned criticism of the operations of the Special Criminal Court. To accuse it of 'conducting a mock trial' was regarded as contempt,[61] as were two letters imputing improper and base motives and bias to the judges of that Court,[62] while criticism of the establishment of the Court or the retention of the death penalty or the provisions of the Offences against the State Act under which the Court is set up would not be contempt because they are matters that can validly be debated in public.[63]

In the case of In *re Kennedy and McCann*,[64] the journalist reported on a child custody case and implied that justice could not be obtained in an Irish court in our 'sick' and 'hypocritical' society. The report, said the courts, contained a gross misstatement of how the court had dealt with the case, which had been held *in camera*. The journalist and editor apologised and were heavily fined. The judge told them that if they had not apologised, they would have received a substantial prison sentence. The case also raised issues of privacy and the right to report (see further discussion in Chapter 7).

The classic case on scandalising the court was *State* (DPP) *v Walsh and Conneely*,[65] involving once again an attack on the Special Criminal Court. Following the conviction and sentence of two people for capital murder, *The Irish Times* published a statement issued on behalf of the Association for Legal Justice condemning the sentences meted out by a court 'composed of government-appointed judges having no judicial independence which sat without a jury and which so abused the rules of evidence as to make the court akin to a sentencing tribunal'.[66] The case raised questions as to the boundaries of fair criticism, the role of the courts themselves in deciding whether a court has been scandalised and, in particular, the use of summary trial (i.e. without a jury) in contempt cases.

For some time in Britain, although not in Canada, contempt by scandalising has fallen into disuse. In Ireland, it still emerges from time to time, but judges nowadays are more tolerant, more accustomed to media criticism and comment and, therefore, less likely to punish for scandalising. In *Desmond v Glackin* (No.1),[67] which involved media statements by a government minister and the inspector he had appointed to inquire into a property acquisition that had been the subject of considerable public controversy, O'Hanlon J. in the High Court relied on the context of the statements in finding that they did not exceed the bounds of fair and permissible criticism.[68] A statement made by the Minister that the High Court 'certainly facilitated Mr Desmond in blocking the enquiry', was the kind of statement that might once have been regarded as scandalising. However, it was taken in the context of the interview in this case to refer to the expedition with which the application had been processed by the High Court and which had resulted in the inquiry being halted, which the Minister deplored. This approach, it is submitted, is a reasonable and common-sense one, especially as the remarks were made in a radio interview and followed the issuing of a press release on behalf of Mr Desmond by a public relations firm.[69]

The decision in *Desmond v Glackin* continued a trend in recent years of courts no longer feeling threatened by the media but accepting that the media have a legitimate role in commenting on and criticising the operation of the courts. This development is to be expected as the media and public mature together. It is not that the courts have abandoned the notion of contempt or are any less zealous in protecting their authority but rather that they allow more latitude and are less inclined to punish. Relying on the dicta in In *re Kennedy and McCann*, Carroll J. in *Weeland v RTÉ*[70] said:

> I do not see why a judgment cannot be criticised, provided it is not done in a manner calculated to bring the court or the judge into contempt. If that element is not present there is no reason why judgments should not be criticised. Nor does the criticism have to be confined to scholarly articles in legal journals. The mass media are entitled to have their say as well. The public take a great interest in court cases and it is only natural that discussion should concentrate on the result of cases. So criticism which does not subvert justice should be allowed.

Further evidence of that trend can be seen in *McCann v An Taoiseach*.[71] RTÉ admitted that their reporting of the case, which had sought to prevent a broadcast by the Taoiseach in advance of a referendum on the Maastricht Treaty,[72] was careless and inaccurate, imputing remarks to the judge that he had not made. This was a serious contempt, the judge said, but no action was required because it was not intentional or malicious and was immediately and fully repaired.[73] Where the contempt is unintentional, as studies show it almost invariably is,[74] then, as Carney J. recognised, the most effective remedy is rectification or retraction.[75] This was recognised also in a manslaughter case in which inaccurate reports were published by two newspapers and a radio station. Budd J. accepted the explanation that the inaccuracy was due to a transmission error and recommended that no action be taken as corrections had been published and broadcast promptly.[76] The Law Reform Commission[77] has recommended that a court should be empowered to order the publication of an apology and/or a correction in cases of scandalising, similar to the orders recommended in their *Report on the Civil Law of Defamation*.

It is possible to take this view a step further and ask whether, in this day and age, there is any need for this form of contempt at all. It is true that judges cannot readily defend themselves in the media but is there any reason, other than an organisational or economic one, why the courts should not, like other institutions of state, become part of the media age, and establish their own press office or media relations officer to explain procedures, summarise judgments and generally enhance accuracy in reporting and public knowledge? Courts in other jurisdictions have done so, most notably in Canada and Australia.[78]

However, it must be pointed out that the Law Reform Commission[79] did not recommend abolishing contempt by scandalising completely.

They recommended retaining it for imputing corrupt conduct to a judge or court and for publishing to the public a false account of legal proceedings, but only on proof of intention or recklessness and where there is a substantial risk of the administration of justice or the judiciary or any particular judge(s) being brought into serious disrepute. Truth would be a defence. The onus of proving corruption would rest with the defence, that of proving the falsity of an account of legal proceedings, with the prosecution.

(iii) Contempt by Prejudicing a Fair Trial

Contempt by prejudicing a fair trial is the form that most affects the media. It consists of the publication of matter calculated to prejudice ongoing or pending cases, criminal or civil. The perceived danger is of influencing the jury, where there is one. Judges have usually contended that because of their experience and training, they would not be susceptible to media comment or pressure and do not need protection. It could entail a reflection on an accused person so as to jeopardise his chances of a fair trial[80] or it could relate to a civil action, negligence or defamation, for example, and adversely affect the position of one of the parties. In *Desmond v Glackin*,[81] for example, the alleged contempt related to judicial review proceedings. Indeed, as *Desmond* shows, there can be an overlap between the various forms of contempt and one set of facts can give rise to contempt by scandalising and contempt by prejudicing a trial.[82] Other examples from the case-law include newspaper criticism of the Special Criminal Court while it was conducting a murder trial;[83] a letter to a newspaper criticising the Special Criminal Court while an appeal in the case was pending;[84] an article revealing details of *in camera* hearings;[85] an article proclaiming that an accused's statements had not been made voluntarily;[86] a newspaper report on organised crime in Dublin referring to a Mr Daly, who, it turned out, was due before the courts the next day on armed robbery charges.[87] In the last-mentioned case, the jury was discharged and the trial put back to the next court term because of the risk that the jury could be influenced by the report.

The jury was discharged also when a lead story in an evening newspaper risked causing prejudice by mentioning the family relationship between the accused in an ongoing drugs trial and a convicted drugs dealer with the same surname.[88] A case against Gay Byrne in 1989 over remarks he had made in a newspaper article about a case he was taking against a number of accountants was eventually dismissed in 1992.[89] It was always unlikely that there would be a jury involved, and in any event, the case was subsequently withdrawn, so that to pursue the contempt issue was purely academic, 'an exercise in futility', as Carroll J. said in the High Court.[90] Gerry Ryan and RTÉ were fined £200 and £500, respectively, in 1990 following a radio interview with the alleged victim of a rape while the accused's trial was pending before the courts.[91] Other forms of publication can be seen as contempt as well. The publication of photographs can constitute contempt where identification is an issue,[92] as can inaccurate headlines, even when the text of the report or article itself is accurate.[93] Reference to previous convictions[94] has led to a finding of contempt, as, for example, has a song by Christy Moore about the Stardust tragedy.[95]

Criminal investigations undertaken by the media run the greatest risk of being in contempt of court. So-called investigative journalism can lead to what is frequently denounced as 'trial by the media', which was identified by Lord Diplock in the *Sunday Times* case as one of three main forms of prejudice in that the media usurp the functions of courts of law without the safeguards of legal rules of evidence regarding admissibility and override the presumption of innocence.[96] The argument has taken on a new dimension with the televising of 'celebrity' trials in the United States: the Kennedy-Smith, Bobbitt and O.J. Simpson trials. There has been widespread comment and speculation on the likely effects of television on these cases, but the real impact has yet to be assessed (see further discussion in Chapter 7). The counter-argument to the 'trial by media' assertion is that the media do not 'try' anyone in the sense that no sanction is imposed except through the courts. The televised cases in the US, a modern form of 'live show' trials, have no direct counterpart in this jurisdiction, where cameras are not allowed in court. Thus concern here has been mainly with inaccurate or misleading reporting in the media after the day's hearing in court.

(iv) Acts Calculated to Prejudice the Course of Justice

Included in this final category of forms of contempt would be acts aimed at influencing juries, interfering with witnesses or abusing the parties to a case. Checkbook journalism runs a high risk of falling within such a category. The Supreme Court has ruled also that jury deliberations should always be regarded as completely confidential and should not be published after a trial.[97] In Britain the 1981 Act makes it an offence to solicit or disclose jury deliberations. One author describes this as an extraordinarily wide provision, which applies in all cases and does not take account of the particular circumstances of the individual case; that this interferes with bona fide research into jury deliberations and may seriously impede public discussion of the merits of the jury system.[98]

Arguments for and against jury disclosures are set out in the Law Reform Commission's *Consultation Paper on Contempt of Court*.[99] In its final recommendations in 1994, the Commission concluded 'that it is beyond argument that there could be no absolute rule of secrecy' and instead recommended a 'considerable range of secrecy'.[100] Bona fide research would be permitted subject to prior approval and such conditions as may be specified by the Chief Justice or President of the High Court or Circuit Court, as appropriate.[101] Were it to be otherwise, research could not be carried out even to test the assumption that juries are likely to be prejudiced by media reports.

(v) Disobedience to a Writ of Habeas Corpus

Ó Dálaigh C.J. included disobedience to a writ of habeas corpus as an example of criminal contempt. Others have argued, however, that since it involves disobedience to a court order it should be classified as civil contempt. There are clearly borderline cases and cases in which an overlap between civil and criminal contempt occurs. Disobedience to a writ of habeas corpus is therefore discussed in that broader context in section (c) below.

(c) 'Hybrid' Cases: Civil and Criminal Contempt

To the categories of civil and criminal contempt outlined above, a third could be added: mixed or 'hybrid' cases of contempt. Civil contempt, as we have seen, is committed by disobedience to a court order, whereas criminal contempt can be committed in a variety of ways that cause interference with, or prejudice to, the administration of justice in court hearings. A 'hybrid' case involves both civil and criminal contempt. In the media context it could involve breach of a court order not to publish certain information, which amounts to civil contempt, while the fact of publishing it could constitute interference with, or prejudice to, a court hearing and therefore amount to criminal contempt.

The principal distinctions between the two forms historically were, firstly, that in the case of civil contempt the court moved at the instance of the party whose rights had been infringed (i.e. the party who was suffering harm as a result of the breach of the court order) not of its own volition, and secondly, that the indefinite term of imprisonment for civil contempt could not be commuted or remitted in the way that a definite term in a criminal matter could (see Article 13.6 of the Constitution). Both distinctions have been eroded. In *In re*

MacArthur,[102] for instance, a criminal case, an *ex parte* application was made in respect of criminal contempt, although Costello J. thought it undesirable, at least in the circumstances of the particular case. Problems have also arisen with indefinite terms of imprisonment and intervention is often necessary.

The Phillimore Committee[103] in Britain recommended fixed terms in all cases of contempt, and the Contempt of Court Act 1981 in Britain now reflects that recommendation. It may also be noted that since proceedings for civil contempt can result in imprisonment, the degree of proof required is proof beyond reasonable doubt, the standard in a criminal case, and a person charged with civil contempt cannot be compelled to incriminate himself.[104] As a result, there has been some confusion. In *Keegan v de Búrca*,[105] for instance, Ó Dálaigh C.J. listed disobedience to a writ of *habeas corpus* as a criminal contempt, whereas Henchy J. in *State (DPP) v Walsh and Conneely*[106] thought that perhaps this was only a civil contempt now. *Keegan* was an extraordinary case in that, at the hearing of a motion seeking an order for attachment for breach of an injunction (civil contempt), the defendant refused to answer a question put to her (criminal contempt). After allowing counsel an opportunity to explain the position to his client, the President of the High Court made an order committing her to prison *sine die*, i.e. he treated it as civil contempt. The Supreme Court, on appeal, held that the contempt was in fact criminal and therefore should be punished by a definite term of imprisonment. McLoughlin J. [107] in his dissenting judgment, acknowledged that

> Contempts have been classified as criminal contempts and civil contempts, but there does not seem to be any clear dividing line.

Another hybrid case arose during the course of the Beef Tribunal in 1991, when *Sunday Business Post* editor, Damian Kiberd, was called upon to reveal his sources. He refused to do so, which could have been punished as an offence under the Tribunals of Inquiry (Evidence) (Amendment) Act 1979 or as contempt in the face of the tribunal. In addition, as the Chairman pointed out, the editor's remark to him 'you are trawling for information' might itself be punishable there and then as in *facie* contempt.[108]

In *State (Commins) v McRann*,[109] Finlay P. was invited by counsel effectively to abolish whatever distinction remained between civil and criminal contempt. However, he declined to do so, holding himself bound by, and in agreement with, the definition given by Ó Dálaigh C.J. in *Keegan*.[110] It is submitted, nevertheless, that by upholding the summary process (trial by judge alone, without a jury), Finlay P. in effect eroded the distinctions even further. More recently, however, the Law Reform Commission recommended against abolishing the distinction.[111] The Phillimore Committee in Britain in 1994 found the distinction 'more apparent than real' and recommended abolishing the few remaining vestiges of distinction.[112] In the case of the media, the distinction is largely irrelevant. Because breach of an injunction or other court order by the media will normally entail publication, it is likely to constitute both civil and criminal contempt and to be punished, if at all, as criminal rather than civil contempt.

4. Elements of Contempt

After considering the various types of contempt, questions arise as to the elements necessary to constitute contempt.

(a) Degree of Prejudice

The first question is: what degree of prejudice is required to amount to contempt? Kenny J. in R v Dolan[113] put forward a two-fold test: was the publication calculated to prejudice the fair trial of the accused and, if so, was the contempt of so serious a character as to call for the intervention of the court. Madden J. in the same case pointed out that the danger to the administration of justice must be a real one and not an imaginary one.[114] It is not necessary, however, that actual prejudice be proved, just that the publication was calculated to cause prejudice. Gavan Duffy J. in AG v Connolly[115] also recognised that there are two limbs to the test, namely the question of whether the matter was calculated to produce a public mischief and, if so, whether that mischief was a grave one. The question has been decided in Britain in the Contempt of Court Act 1981, section 2.2:

> a publication which creates a substantial risk that the course of justice in the proceedings in question will be seriously impeded or prejudiced.

Thus the degree of risk is qualified, as is the degree of prejudice. It is not enough that the publication presents a slight risk, though of serious damage, or, for that matter, a high risk of marginal damage. In practice, however, the English courts appear to interpret the word 'substantial' in the Act to mean a risk other than a remote one. This is a low threshold, and one that has not proved very helpful to the media.[116]

One advantage of the British formulation is that it eliminates the notion of 'calculated', which is problematic, in that it is imprecise and difficult to define. Does it mean simply that the publication is likely to cause prejudice or is of a kind that would cause prejudice, or does it suggest deliberation or premeditation? Morris J. in a High Court case in 1993 said that it had to be established to his satisfaction beyond all reasonable doubt that the contents of the radio interview in question 'were calculated, in the sense that it would tend to' prejudice the impartiality of potential jurors in the action.[117] As noted above, the test now applied by the Irish Supreme Court in Z v DPP[118] is one of a 'real or serious risk' of an unfair trial. The question of intention is a separate element.

(b) Mens Rea

The question of intention is a vexing one. In the past, Irish courts have accepted the definition of constructive contempt (i.e. contempt out of court) put forward by Lord Eldon in Ex parte Jones,[119] as contempt 'depending upon the inference of an intention to obstruct the course of justice'. Thus, if the publication met the requirement of being 'calculated' to interfere with the proceedings, an intention to interfere was imputed by the courts. In AG v Cooke,[120] however, Sullivan P. separated the two limbs of the test and held that the article in question was not intended to interfere with the court's decision in pending criminal proceedings and was not calculated to do so. It is not clear how he would have resolved the matter had he found the article calculated to interfere but not intended to. In AG v Connolly,[121] Gavan Duffy J. appeared to favour the strict liability rule, i.e. liability regardless of intention. He held that the offending article was calculated to produce a grave public mischief and that it was no defence in law to say that the defendant intended nothing wrong.[122]

It would appear, therefore, that it is the effect of the publication that is important, and that the question of intention or motive only arises in relation to sentencing. According to Finlay P. in State (DPP) v Irish Press,[123] the test is an objective one, i.e. whether the publication is likely to interfere with the due and fair trial of pending proceedings:

> the motive or intention or the mens rea of the party or parties responsible for the making of the publication is not relevant. A man may therefore publish what does in law constitute contempt of court in this category inadvertently but that does not mean . . . that he is liable if it was caused by inadvertence to be punished for it.

In Daly, for example, when a prejudicial article appeared in the Sunday Tribune, there was no intention to cause prejudice but the paper was still held to be in contempt.[124] The jury was discharged; the trial was put back to obviate any possible prejudice, and an apology was accepted. Costello J. in *MacArthur*[125] seemed to sum up the view of the courts today when he said that if

> the words were spoken inadvertently . . . and . . . immediate steps were taken to avoid any possible prejudice that the words might give rise to and if it can be shown . . . that any possible prejudice can be obviated by the direction which the trial judge can give to the jury, then it seems to me to be highly unlikely that the court would exercise its extraordinary punitive powers and punish such a person for contempt. . . .

The approach of Morris J.,[126] in an application brought by six gardaí following a Gay Byrne radio interview with Osgur Breathnach on the subject of the Salins mail robbery and its aftermath, was refreshing. Not only did he show a media awareness, he, himself, also credited the Irish public with the same degree of maturity and a healthy, even sceptical, attitude to what they see and hear. He considered the interview in context, as a human interest piece, and recognised that even views expressed by Gay Byrne would not necessarily find universal support. Many would be unaffected by those views and ignore them; some might even oppose them simply because they were Gay Byrne's.[127] Fortunately, more judges nowadays are inclined to accept an apology and not pursue the matter, but still the threat remains. Over the last few years there have also been a number of instances where the court has accepted an apology but ordered the media to pay a sum of money towards the costs of the trial. In the introduction to a case report on a radio programme, an inadvertent error in confusing the evidence against two accused led to the trial being halted and RTÉ being ordered to pay £5,000 towards the costs of the trial.[128] Since this form of contempt is a criminal offence, the notion of strict liability sits uneasily with the safeguards of the criminal law.[129]

(c) Restricted Comments and the *Sub Judice* Rule

When proceedings are ongoing or pending they are said to be *sub judice* and therefore comment on them is restricted. The question that arises is when are proceedings to be regarded as 'pending'? The current position is that proceedings are pending from the issue of a writ in civil cases and the laying of charges in a criminal case.[130] Comment is then restricted, but not absolutely prohibited, as is widely believed. However, as the risk of prejudice is high, the media must exercise the utmost caution. The rule has been open to abuse by those wishing to stifle comment. It has happened, for instance, that a politician or public official, finding himself or herself in hot water, has taken out a writ and informed the media that he/she has done so, in order to silence them. This process of issuing 'gagging-writs' was helped by the long time-lag from the issue of a writ to the actual court hearing (in the case of the High Court a period, on average, of three years). The case could be dropped by the politician at any stage, but the media would have been silenced until the danger was over. It was possible for the media also to hide behind the *sub judice* rule and not publish anything on the grounds that the matter was *sub judice*. The rule can even be used to stifle comment on important matters of public interest.

(i) *Sub Judice* in the Dáil

Dáil debates on an issue are sometimes refused because the matter is *sub judice*. Under the doctrine of separation of powers in the Constitution, the Dáil must not encroach on the courts. In 1986, for example, a government minister issued a writ for libel against M*agill* magazine over allegations about his business interests. The *Sunday Tribune* sought clarification of the scope and application of the *sub judice* rule and was able to publish an editorial and article on the effects of the rule on press freedom.[131] The Minister was subsequently asked to resign by the Taoiseach and questions were tabled in the Dáil. They were refused on the grounds that the matter was *sub judice*. There is a Dáil convention, as there is in England, to avoid debate that could constitute parliamentary interference with judicial decisions, but it is generally accepted that its scope is too wide. The Committee on Dáil Procedures has examined its operation with a view to reform. In a bizarre incident in 1991, the clerk of the Seanad was subpoenaed to appear as a witness at the trial of a defamation action taken by the Cathaoirleach of the Seanad, Sean Doherty, against the *Sunday Times*. A motion had to be passed to permit this to happen but no debate was allowed because the matter was *sub judice*.[132]

(ii) The *Sunday Times* Case

The question of the operation of the *sub judice* rule arose in Britain in the *Sunday Times* case, which went to the European Court of Human Rights.[133] In that case the perceived prejudice arose from a deliberate attempt on the part of the newspaper to influence the settlement of pending proceedings by bringing pressure to bear on a party to the case, Distillers Ltd, the manufacturers of the thalidomide drug, which when taken by pregnant women had caused their babies to be born with abnormalities. Publication of an article had been restrained by injunction on the grounds that it would amount to contempt of court because its purpose was to enlist public opinion to exert pressure on Distillers to make a more generous settlement to the victims. The Court of Appeal discharged the injunction on the grounds *inter alia* that the public interest in discussion outweighed the potential prejudice to a fair trial or settlement of the action.[134] The House of Lords, however, reinstated the injunction holding that the proposed article would pre-judge the issues and amount to trial by newspaper.[135] Subsequently the European Court of Human Rights, in a majority decision, decided that the injunction was not justified under Article 10.2 of the Convention.[136] Although it was prescribed by law and imposed for a legitimate purpose (maintaining the authority of the judiciary), the restriction was not justified by a pressing social need and could not therefore be regarded as 'necessary' within the meaning of Article 10.2. As a result of the Strasbourg decision, the legislature in Britain intervened and passed the Contempt of Court Act 1981.

(iii) Time Limits and the Rule

One of the purposes of the 1981 Act was to impose time limits on the operation of the *sub judice* rule. Henceforth, applicable proceedings would be classed as 'active' (section 12). Civil proceedings would be 'active' not from the issue of the writ but from the date of setting-down for trial or when a date for the hearing was fixed (section 13). Proceedings would remain active until disposed of, discontinued or withdrawn. Criminal proceedings would be active from the relevant initial step, whether arrest, the issue of a summons to appear, the service of an indictment or other document specifying the charge or the making of an oral charge (section 4). They would remain active until concluded by acquittal, sentence, discontinuance or other final verdict (section 5). Appellate proceedings would also be considered active (section 15).

The advantages of the legislative changes in Britain are two-fold: they impose precise, if arbitrary, time limits and they reduce the time span in which the media can be silenced. While it can take three years in Ireland from the date of issue of a writ for a civil case to come to court, it is usually only a matter of months from the date of setting-down. A similar change in Irish law would be beneficial. In relation to criminal proceedings, the Phillimore Committee in Britain,[137] whose recommendations formed the basis of the new legislation, had suggested the date of charge as the appropriate time for the *sub judice* rule to begin to run. However, while the new legislation was in preparation, the Yorkshire Ripper was finally caught by police. The nature and extent of media coverage of his apprehension and arrest prompted the government to change its mind with regard to the appropriate time to curtail media comment in a criminal case. The date of arrest rather than charge was adopted.

Another aspect of the British legislative changes that might be questioned is whether it is necessary for the *sub judice* rule to apply during appellate proceedings, where there will not be a jury involved. This need has been discounted by the Supreme Court in *Cullen v Toibin*.[138] In that case the plaintiff had been convicted in the Central Criminal Court of murder and malicious damage. His appeal to the Court of Criminal Appeal was based on the insufficiency of evidence of an accomplice, which was the only evidence against him. While his appeal was pending, *Magill* magazine entered into a contract with the accomplice to publish her version of the story. The plaintiff applied for an injunction to prevent publication. The injunction was granted by Barrington J. in the High Court,[139] but the Supreme Court lifted it,[140] stating firstly, that the courts should only interfere with freedom of expression and of communication guaranteed by the Constitution in Article 40.6 where it was necessary for the administration of justice, and secondly, the Court of Criminal Appeal could not be prejudiced by publication because it would be dealing with pure issues of law. Also, the Court noted that the plaintiff could always sue for defamation afterwards. In the High Court, Barrington J. had acknowledged that it was a serious piece of investigative journalism but added that if it had been published before the trial in the Central Criminal Court, it would clearly have been contempt of court.[141] The Supreme Court suggested that it was in bad taste but that freedom of the press should prevail.[142]

In Ireland, the issue of time limits in relation to the *sub judice* rule has also arisen. In *State (DPP) v Independent Newspapers*[143] the High Court adopted the date of charge as the appropriate starting time in criminal cases. In that case the *Evening Herald* had published a story that the DPP intended bringing indecency charges against a local Councillor. The story referred to the political party to which the Councillor belonged but did not name him or the local authority. At the time the story was published, no charges had been brought, although they were brought two days later. Did the publication constitute contempt of court? O'Hanlon J. took the view that if publication had taken place after the preliminary examination of the case against the accused in the District Court, the Criminal Procedure Act 1967 (section 17) would have applied to restrict reporting. However, as no-one had actually been charged in the case and no court actually had seisin of it, the DPP's application for an order of attachment for contempt must be refused. The countervailing importance of freedom of expression would not allow such an extension of the law of contempt, the judge said, and it was undesirable from the point of view of the accused that proceedings for contempt with the attendant publicity should be in progress at the very time when the criminal prosecution against him would be coming on for hearing.[144]

Despite the clarity of that decision, confusion surrounded RTÉ's proposed 'Today Tonight' programme in 1989 on the Dublin property developer Patrick Gallagher, who had earlier pleaded guilty to false accounting and company theft charges in Belfast. RTÉ received conflicting legal advice as to whether the programme could go ahead, even though at the time no charges had been brought against Gallagher in the State.[145]

The position as to whether the *sub judice* rule applies between conviction and sentence awaits clarification from the Supreme Court. In the *Kelly* case, known colloquially as 'the case of all the Kellys', because applicant, judge, barrister and reporter were all called Kelly, the Circuit Court fined the editor of *The Irish Times* and a reporter £5,000.[146] After a three-week trial by jury, Eamonn Kelly had been convicted of possession of £500,000 worth of cocaine for supply and remanded for sentence. Before sentence was passed *The Irish Times* published an article, described by counsel for Kelly as false and irrelevant. The contempt issue was to be referred to the Supreme Court on two points: (i) following the decision of the Supreme Court in *Cullen v Tóibín*, was there any such thing as a contempt of court when the only person who could be affected was the trial judge who was considering the sentence (the trial judge had said his concern was for the expert witnesses who had still to appear before him), and (ii) given the constitutional right to freedom of speech and freedom of expression, did there remain any room for the offence of contempt of court in this case?[147]

Incidentally, Kelly was jailed for fourteen years but appealed the sentence. His conviction was quashed by the Court of Criminal Appeal and a retrial ordered because of reports in the *Star* and *Sunday World* during the trial. The former had named Kelly in a reference to 'cocaine kingpins'; the latter had published a photograph of him and referred to another man who had absconded as an 'arms dealer'. This amounted to prejudicial content, the Court said, and therefore the trial judge should have acceded to applications to discharge the jury.[148]

(iv)   The Scope of the Rule

The cases of *Desmond v Glackin No 1*[149] and *Wong v Minister for Defence*[150] raise further questions about the scope and application of the *sub judice* rule. O'Hanlon J. in *Desmond* said that quite apart from any effect of media comment on judge or jury, the law of contempt is concerned with the potentially harmful effects that may flow from unbridled comments made in a public manner concerning the subject matter of legal proceedings pending before the court or the parties involved in such proceedings.[151] On the facts of the case, however, he found that the *sub judice* rule had not been breached. The remarks of the second defendant, Des O'Malley had been 'injudicious and indiscreet', but he was entitled to a right of reply in the circumstances as his remarks had been 'a response to serious allegations made against him by Mr Desmond which had already been well-publicised'.[152] The balance had to be struck in favour of freedom of expression. Nonetheless, the uncertainty that surrounds the scope of the rule is unsatisfactory for the media; the legislature should intervene to clarify it. Denham J. in *Wong* said that, while the trial judge would be unlikely to be prejudiced, the linking of the plaintiff to the Chinese Triad underworld was prejudicial to the administration of justice 'as a result of a litigant in mid-trial being held up to such public obloquy'[153] and thus constituted a contempt, purged by an apology.[154] Her fear was the effect of the allegations on how her decision would be viewed. If her decision was favourable to the plaintiff, people who had read the allegations might think the judgment perverse, thus undermining public confidence in the justice system. In that respect, the form of contempt involved in the case is closer to contempt by scandalising the court.[155]

5. Defences

The question of appropriate defences to charges of contempt of court has been addressed in a number of jurisdictions. The Contempt of Court Act 1981 in Britain provided for a number of defences, in addition to any that might already be available at common law.[156] The new defences included innocent publication or distribution (section 3) and discussion of public affairs if the risk of impediment or prejudice to particular proceedings is merely incidental to the discussion (section 5). The Australian Law Reform Commission also favoured a defence of innocent publication and a public interest defence.[157] The Irish Commission has proposed a defence of reasonable necessity to publish[158] but not a public interest defence. The fact that a publication involves a matter of public interest cannot, the Commission says, justify prejudicing legal proceedings.[159] In relation to proceedings of the Oireachtas, there should, the Commission said, be an express statutory defence for fair and accurate reports published contemporaneously or within a reasonable time after the proceedings.[160]

6. Persons Legally Responsible for Publication

In the decided cases, it has sometimes been the reporter and editor who have been pursued for contempt, sometimes the editor and proprietor, occasionally the author or company alone. As to who should be legally responsible for the publication of prejudicial matter, the Law Reform Commission[161] has suggested a test centering on three separate (though at times overlapping) criteria: authorship, control and proprietorship. It therefore concludes that:

* the author of material which offends against the *sub judice* rule should in general be liable where the material appears in the publication unamended
* in cases where the offending material was derived from information supplied by a person, whether a journalist or otherwise, such person should be capable of being held responsible for *sub judice* contempt if he or she, in all the circumstances, ought reasonably to have anticipated the publication of the information without correction
* a person may be found guilty of *sub judice* contempt even though what was published represents an amalgamation or cumulation of contemptuous material contributed by himself or herself and another person if, in isolation, the contemptuous material for which he or she is responsible would constitute *sub judice* contempt
* those in control of newspapers and other media, such as editors, should be capable of being criminally responsible for *sub judice* contempt to the extent that, by the exercise of that control, they ought to have prevented the publication of the offending material
* the proprietors of newspapers should be vicariously liable for *sub judice* contempts published in their newspapers. Only fines should be imposed on proprietors by way of punishment.[162]

7. Extensions of the Contempt Power

From time to time new situations present themselves for which the contempt power is pressed into action. Its use can be justified in some cases by reference to the overall objectives of contempt; in others it marks a departure from the norm and an extension of the power.

(a) The Beef Tribunal and Contempt

An example might be the 'misreporting' of the first day of the Beef Tribunal, when a list of allegations, authorised to be read out by the Tribunal, was presented in the media 'as though they were accusations made under oath from the witness box, as though they had been stated as matters of fact'.[163] Counsel's fear was for the client's good name, not fear of prejudice, as the Chairman of the Tribunal had asserted that he would not be influenced in any way by what was said by the press or anyone else. Because the Tribunal was obviously going to last for a very long time, the argument put forward in *Wong v Minister for Defence*[164] (as to the impact on the administration of justice in general) could hardly be said to apply. The first day's reporting in 1991 would long since be forgotten by the time the Tribunal ended and its report was published in 1994. Besides, this was a tribunal, not a court of law. Indeed, it was a public tribunal, a *public* inquiry, so that truth could be ascertained in the public interest. In those circumstances and given that the primary source of danger was the decision of the Tribunal itself to allow the re-reading of the list of allegations, it would seem inappropriate to invoke the contempt power against three national newspapers and RTÉ. The Chairman ruled some three months later that they had not been in contempt.[165] The justification offered by Casey,[166] that the individual's constitutional right of access to the courts must not unlawfully be obstructed, would be applicable in *Wong* (and *Desmond v Glackin*, which Casey points to) but not in the case of the Beef Tribunal, which was not a court, even if it did have certain statutory powers akin to those of the High Court.

(b) Statutory Contempt

There are several statutes that provide for contempt-like powers, and their effect is open to question. For instance, section 4 of the Offences against the State Act 1972 states that

> any public statement made orally, in writing or otherwise . . . that constitutes an interference with the course of justice [or] if it is intended, or is of such a character as to be likely, directly or indirectly, to influence any court . . . [is punishable by fine and/or imprisonment. However,] nothing in this section shall affect the law as to contempt of court.

This apparently leaves intact common-law contempt but creates a supplementary statutory offence of much wider application, as there is no requirement that the interference be a serious one and it envisages punishment even where the interference is unintentional or indirect. Casey[167] believes that the section has never been invoked and hopes that it would be applied in accordance with the European Convention on Human Rights rather than in a way that would imperil legitimate freedom of expression. Its overreach makes it suspect as being disproportionate to its apparent aim. The only thing that might save it is the need to show actual interference and the intention to, or likelihood of, influencing a court.

Other statutes provide for offences punishable 'in like manner' as contempt of court. These offences are statutory forms of contempt, to be punished as in the case of contempt with unlimited fines and/or imprisonment. In so providing, the statutes are declining to set maximum limits. This would seem to be a retrograde step, when one would expect that statute law would seek to replace the unlimited punishment aspect of common-law contempt with fixed sentences, as the British Act of 1981 did. Statutes that have such provisions include the Criminal Procedure Act 1967 at section 17(2).

Some statutes have extended the contempt power beyond the courts to a variety of tribunals.[168] The Defence (Amendment) Act 1987, section 12, creates an offence of contempt of a courtmartial. The Law Reform Commission instanced several other statutes with 'deemed contempt' provisions.[169] The Commission[170] took the following view:

> The generic criminalisation of conduct in relation to tribunals by reference to contempt of the High Court must surely be unconstitutional in view of the arbitrary imposition of criminal responsibility which it necessarily involves.

Support for this view is to be found in the striking down of the Committee of Public Accounts of Dáil Eireann (Privilege and Procedure) Act 1970, section 3(4), by the Supreme Court in In re Haughey.[171] The Companies Act 1990, section 10(5), went even further and was found by the Supreme Court in Desmond v Glackin (No. 2)[172] to be unconstitutional.[173] The Act dealt with the appointment by the Minister for Industry and Commerce of inspectors to investigate the affairs of a company. The section empowered the inspector to certify the refusal of a witness to attend or answer questions to the High Court to be dealt with as if he/she were guilty of contempt of court.

(c) 'Contempt of the Courts'

In Quinn v Ryan,[174] an extradition case, the court held that the plan of the gardaí to whisk Quinn out of the jurisdiction into Northern Ireland was 'contempt of the courts', because its object was to circumvent the courts:

> to eliminate the courts and to defeat the rule of law . . . Anyone who sets

himself such a course is guilty of contempt of the courts and is punishable accordingly.[175]

The gardaí explained their conduct and the matter was not pursued. For that reason it remains unclear whether Ó Dálaigh C.J. intended that such conduct be brought within the existing sphere of common-law contempt or whether in using the form of words 'contempt of the courts' rather than 'contempt of court', he sought to distinguish this conduct from that covered by the common-law of contempt or sought to widen the scope of the latter.

8. Procedure

The procedure to be followed in contempt cases is set out in the Rules of the Superior Courts 1986. Order 44 deals with attachment and committal. An order of attachment directs that the person be brought before the court to answer the contempt in respect of which the order is issued (O.44, R.1). An order of committal directs that the person be lodged in prison until he/she purges the contempt (O. 44, R. 2). With the exception of contempt in the face of the court, an order for attachment or committal can only be issued by leave of the court, following an application on notice to the person against whom the order is to be directed (O. 44, R. 3). Many of the cases referred to in the discussion of contempt in this chapter were more concerned with appropriate procedures than with other aspects of contempt. The long-time practice has been to try cases of contempt summarily, that is, without a jury, but still it causes considerable disquiet. There is the issue of the role of the court as party, judge, witness and jury in its own case in determining whether the Court itself has been brought into contempt. There is the matter also of Article 38 of the Constitution, which asserts a right to trial by jury in all criminal cases except minor ones. Contempt, with its unlimited fines and imprisonment, is avowedly not minor.

The summary power was originally confined to cases of civil contempt and contempt in *facie curiae*. The current practice of dealing summarily with cases of constructive contempt (i.e. contempt committed outside of court, for example in the media) dates from the end of the eighteenth century. It has been challenged on constitutional grounds in this jurisdiction but upheld. All the judges in AG *v* O'Kelly[176] agreed that the High Court had jurisdiction to deal summarily with contempt, although Hanna J. stated that this power was discretionary: the matter could be sent to a jury, but where 'for any good reason' the court thought it should determine the matter itself, it had the power to do so.[177] Summary proceedings were convenient but could never be endorsed just because their rapidity and simplicity might make them attractive to the Executive.[178] The summary procedure could be justified only by the urgent and imperative need of a prophylactic order from the High Court.[179]

Ó Dálaigh C.J. in *Keegan v de Búrca*[180] left open the question of jury trial, while Finlay P. in *State (Commins) v McRann*[181] held that even if the contempt issue involved the trial of a criminal charge to which Article 38.5 of the Constitution *prima facie* applied, the terms of Article 34 constituted a qualification on the provisions of Article 38.5 and authorised the courts to adjudicate the issue of contempt in a summary manner.[182] Finlay P. presented a further argument in support of the summary power, an argument based on the tripartite division of power in the Constitution: if the person charged with contempt were to be entitled to trial by jury, then the court would have to wait for the Attorney General or Director of Prosecutions, i.e. a servant of the Executive, to present an indictment. It would thus be possible for the Executive, by a refusal to present an indictment, to paralyse the capacity of the courts to impose their will.[183]

O'Higgins C.J. endorsed Finlay P.'s argument in *State (DPP) v Walsh and Conneely*.[184] Here the central argument was that the Court did not have a summary jurisdiction in respect of contempt by scandalising, where speed or urgency were not factors. The Court held unanimously, but for different reasons, that the Court did have summary jurisdiction, at least in a case such as this where no issues of fact arose. The independence of the judiciary as proclaimed by Article 35.2 of the Constitution and the protection of judicial proceedings required it. Henchy J. took the view that *O'Kelly* and *Connolly* were right but for the wrong reasons. Having established that there was a *prima facie* right to trial by jury by virtue of Article 38.5 of the Constitution for contempt which is a criminal offence, he concluded[185] that where there were live and real issues of fact to go to the jury, then there was an entitlement to trial by jury:[186]

> it would not seem to be compatible with the constitutional requirement of fundamental fairness of procedures, or with the equality before the law guaranteed by Article 40, s. 1, if contempt of court, which carries with it the risk of a fixed but unlimited term of imprisonment or an unlimited fine, were the only major offence which is exempt from the requirement of a determination by a jury of the controverted facts.

This approach has certain attractions, but what are its practical implications? In the case of the media, it is difficult to envisage many situations where the facts will be in issue, as it is the fact of publication that constitutes the offence and the only issue is the tendency to obstruct, scandalise or prejudice. Nevertheless, it would seem that the summary procedure for criminal contempt is now so firmly entrenched in our law that, despite its unhealthy origins and irregular development, it is now seen as an inherent and necessary power and exercised as the norm but with a consciousness that it must be used with care and restraint. The arguments against it will not easily displace it.[187]

9. Conclusions on Contempt

The whole area of contempt of court is fraught with difficulty. Its uncertain scope, the unlimited fines and terms of imprisonment that it can attract, the potential for arbitrary use by the courts, the strict liability element, all make it suspect on constitutional grounds. Contempt operates without the constitutional safeguards accorded to free speech and fair trial. It is treated as a criminal offence, yet it lacks many of the safeguards of the criminal law, such as a mens rea requirement and right to jury trial. As the Canadian Law Reform Commission remarked, the end result is often a triumph of technicality over logic and clarity.[188] Many of the cases that arise are dealt with *instanter*, that is, on the spot, and are not reported except in the media. There are few written judgments and because judges nowadays often accept an apology rather than imposing fines or imprisonment, few cases are appealed. The result is a lack of jurisprudence and an absence of any clear principles that can be referred to and built on. A codification of specific, narrowly drawn offences, in clear and precise terms, as in other European countries, would seem preferable. The summary procedure should be reserved for cases requiring immediate action only. Aspects of the common law of contempt have already been found to be in breach of the European Convention of Human Rights in the *Sunday Times* case.[189] The tests of necessity and proportionality applicable under the Convention would not be met by current Irish contempt law. Contempt dates from a pre-media age and has never been fully squared with the role of the media in a modern democracy, which the European Court of Human Rights has consistently defended. In this regard, the rather cautious recommendations of the Irish Law Reform Commission, it is submitted, do not go far enough.

Injunctions

Another area of the relationship between the courts and the media is the use of court injunctions to prevent the media from publishing information, whether to safeguard the right to a fair trial or other rights of a private or commercial nature. Injunctions are orders sought from the courts to direct someone to do something (*mandatory injunction*) or to refrain from doing something (*prohibitory injunction*). An *interim* (or temporary) *injunction*, usually lasting for a few days, may be sought at short notice and *ex parte*, i.e. without notice to the party against whom it is being sought. It simply puts the situation on hold for a few days until the matter can be given a preliminary hearing in court. An *interlocutory injunction* may be sought for a longer period, pending a full hearing of the case. However, notice must be given to the other party and a stateable case must be made out, i.e. the applicant must persuade the court that he/she has a reasonable chance of succeeding in the eventual hearing. The court then applies the 'balance of convenience' test: what the effect of granting an injunction would be if the applicant were eventually to succeed or fail and whether, on balance, it would be better to grant it or not. Very infrequently a *perpetual injunction* will be granted at the full hearing, such as the perpetual injunction preventing two Dublin clinics from giving abortion assistance in SPUC *v Open Door Counselling Ltd*.[190] In addition, a *quia timet* injunction may sometimes be required to prevent repetition of a harmful act or to prevent the occurrence of an event that it is feared will happen.

Injunctions Restraining Publication

In the media context an injunction could be sought to restrain publication of information that might damage reputation, privacy or commercial interests, for example, or endanger the right to a fair trial. In 1994 an interim injunction was granted to four priests to prevent publication of a book, *Bless Me Father*, about what transpired between the author and the priests when the author went into the confessional box and pretended to confess as a hoax.[191] An interim injunction was also granted to the girl in the X case and her mother to prevent five newspapers publishing details of the X case, other than matters that could lawfully be disclosed during the criminal prosecution of the man accused of sexual offences against the girl.[192]

The previous year a financial company involved in the Irish film industry succeeded in getting an interlocutory injunction against a magazine on the grounds of confidentiality.[193] In another case the owners of the copyright and serialisation rights of a book about Bishop Casey were granted an interim injunction to stop a number of newspapers publishing extracts from the book.[194] An interlocutory injunction was not granted. Instead certain conditions were imposed in relation to publication, but these respected the newspapers' rights to 'fair dealing' under the Copyright Act 1963 section 12, for example their right to carry reviews of the book.[195] In another case the Bar Council, which was handling a complaint against a barrister, obtained an interlocutory injunction restraining a newspaper from publishing confidential information contained in a letter to the Chairman of its Professional Practices Committee until the hearing of the action.[196] The British tabloid newspaper, the *Sun*, its editor and a journalist were fined for publishing extracts from the letter in breach of the injunction.[197] Some weeks earlier, in a more far-reaching development, the *Sunday Business Post*, which was being sued for libel by Aer Rianta over allegations it had published concerning the State-owned authority's securing of overseas contracts, consented, on legal advice, to the making permanent of two interim orders, restraining it from repeating or publishing any further allegations about the company.[198]

Injunctions are sometimes sought on the grounds that publication would prejudice a fair trial. Thus injunctions have been granted to restrain publication of a magazine article and photographs while a criminal appeal was pending.[199] An application against RTÉ made in 1985 by two people awaiting trial in the Circuit Court resulted not in an injunction but in a three-minute interview being removed from a 'Today Tonight' programme dealing with attacks on elderly people in the West.[200] In a worrying development, a programme on the death in unusual circumstances of a priest was severely curtailed on the grounds that major segments of it could prejudice any possible court hearing in the case.[201] No charges had yet been preferred.

Injunctions as Prior Restraint

Injunctions are, therefore, sought and granted quite regularly to prevent publication or broadcasting. As a prepublication restraint they can have more serious implications for the media than a fine or an award of damages after the event. If the media cannot publish the information, the public cannot receive it. Even if the effect of the injunction is only to delay publication, the delay may mean that the information loses its newsworthiness or is overtaken by events. Depending on the scope of the injunction, it may be that the subsequent events may not be reported either, thus imposing a grave restraint on the media.

Breach of an injunction is liable to be punished as contempt of court. As a form of prior restraint, however, injunctions to prevent publication will not, and should not, be issued lightly. It was argued in the *Spycatcher*[202] case that the appropriate test for granting an injunction affecting freedom of expression is necessity and not the balance of convenience test outlined above and applied by the English courts on *American Cyanamid* principles.[203] The European Court of Human Rights in *Spycatcher* refused to review the *American Cyanamid* principles *in abstracto* and confined itself to determining whether the interference resulting from their application 'was necessary having regard to the facts and circumstances prevailing in the specific case before it'. While Article 10, of the European Convention on Human Rights does not prohibit the imposition of prior restraints as such,

> the dangers inherent in prior restraints are such that they call for the most careful scrutiny on the part of the court. This is especially so as far as the press is concerned, for news is a perishable commodity and to delay its publication, even for a short period, may well deprive it of all its value and interest.[204]

In the US the Supreme Court in the *Pentagon Papers* case[205] stressed the heavy presumption against the constitutional validity of any form of prior restraint, a presumption not reduced by the temporary nature of the restraint because today's news is tomorrow's history.[206] Only in *CNN v Noriega*[207] did the Court entertain a temporary injunction on the broadcasting of tapes of conversations between Noriega and his lawyers. The test applied by the US courts is one of a 'clear threat' of 'immediate and irreparable damage', in this case to the accused's right to a fair trial.[208]

In Ireland Finlay C.J. in SPUC v *Grogan*[209] said that 'where an injunction is sought to protect a constitutional right that the only matter which could properly be capable of being weighed in the balance against the granting of such protection would be another competing constitutional right'. This, in the Chief Justice's view, replaces the ordinary concept of *status quo ante* arising in interlocutory injunction cases. Thus, as the Irish Law Reform Commission has pointed out,[210] injunctions against allegedly defamatory publications are hard to obtain and are subject to constitutional restrictions. In such cases, injunctions will be refused if the defendant newspaper or broadcaster demonstrates an intention and ability to plead any of the defences available, i.e. justification, fair comment or qualified privilege.[211] For example, an application was made to prevent RTÉ transmitting certain allegedly defamatory material in a programme that was to name the real Birmingham bombers. The Supreme Court, upholding the decision of Costello J. in the High Court, refused the injunction. There must be very exceptional circumstances for the courts to intervene by means of an injunction to stop a threatened publication that is defamatory, Costello J. said.[212] An injunction imposed by the British courts against Channel 4 broadcasting a dramatic reconstruction of the appeal in the Birmingham Six case was lifted after the judgment in the appeal had been handed down.[213]

In practice, most judges tend to be pragmatic, and there have been many cases where injunctions against the media have been refused.[214] Nevertheless, journalists need to be familiar with the law and vigilant in order to challenge any attempt to expand the use and scope of court orders granting injunctions to prevent or curtail media reporting. On occasion the need for an injunction will be obviated by an undertaking by the media to remove the offending material and then the remainder of the programme or publication can go ahead.[215]

Nonetheless, even this lesser remedy is still an intrusion on press freedom and should have to be justified on specific grounds, such as privacy or fair trial. Even the threat of an injunction can have repercussions for the media or at least a chilling effect. An application for a High Court injunction in Northern Ireland by one political party candidate caused Ulster Television to cancel a series of EEC election broadcasts, in accordance with the provisions of the Representation of the People Acts, even though similar applications in connection with election broadcasts had previously been refused.[216] An injunction might not be granted to stop the broadcasts, but the fact that one party would not participate meant that there would not be proportionate representation from all lawful parties to meet the requirements of the Act.

Notice of Injunction

Once an injunction has been granted, proper notice must be given to the person or persons to whom it is directed. The court order may state the terms to apply to 'the defendants, their servants or agents' (e.g. the High Court order in SPUC v Open Counselling and the Dublin Well-Woman Centre[217]), or it may be addressed to all those having notice of the order. Thus, when an injunction was granted against the Sunday Business Post and 'any person with notice of the order', the British tabloid newspaper the Sun was fined for contempt for breaching the order. That was so even though the paper argued that it had not been served with the order; it was still bound.[218] Concern was voiced in *Spycatcher* and in the Scottish *Inside Intelligence* case[219] about the fact that an injunction granted against one publication was taken to apply to all publications within the jurisdiction.[220]

The case of *Agricultural Credit Corporation* (ACC) *v Irish Business*[221] involved an application for an injunction on the grounds of libel and the leaking of documents belonging to the ACC, on which it owned the copyright. The High Court order restrained the defendants, their servants and agents and 'any person with notice' of the making of the order. The judge also gave liberty to the plaintiffs to notify any third party who would then be bound by it. Notice was served on all the national newspapers and RTÉ. It stated that the hearing was by order of the judge held *in camera* and accordingly the making of the order could not be published.[222] Such a position was untenable in law and the ban was quickly lifted. There was no legal basis for it.[223] The order was later amended to remove the prohibition on publicity.[224] Nonetheless, while that prohibition remained, it led to caution on the part of all the media. The *Cork Examiner*, which had not received notice in time, published the whole story, but apart from that there was very little reporting of the fact of the hearing, only a short news item on RTÉ and a small piece in *The Irish Times* which had heard independently that the hearing was to be held and had sent a journalist and photographer. A report on the ACC in the *Sunday Tribune* had to be withdrawn at the insistence of the printers and distributors, even though it had been cleared by the paper's own lawyers.[225]

In the subsequent application for an interlocutory injunction, the interests of open justice prevailed. An *in camera* hearing had again been sought, but this time was refused. This was not an urgent hearing like the first one and, therefore, the provision of section 45(1) permitting as an exception a private hearing in applications of an 'urgent nature' for an injunction did not apply.[226]

The ACC case, it seems, was not an isolated incident, and the *Sunday Tribune* in an editorial,[227] for example, informed readers that an injunction had been granted against it nine days previously 'on a matter of considerable public interest', the basis of which the paper claimed was 'now known to be without foundation', yet 'the law' prevented the paper telling readers what it was about. It was reported also that a term of the injunction granted to four priests against publication of a book about what transpired in confessionals was that there should be no publication of the injunction.[228] One issue that this raises is how contempt of court could apply in the case where a newspaper, for example, publishes extracts from such a book, if the fact that the injunction had been granted was not known because the very fact of its existence was not to be published. In such circumstances there would be a technical contempt, but it would be unjust to punish the publisher. In the confessionals case, however, the ban on publication was lifted following an application by the National Newspapers of Ireland (NNI) and a promise by them that they would not invade the privacy of the priests and would only comment on the case in a fair and proper manner without revealing any confidential matter.[229]

In the X case in 1992, when an injunction was sought to restrain a fourteen-year-old pregnant girl from leaving the jurisdiction to have an abortion, the press and public were excluded from the court hearing. They were excluded also from the appeal. The newspapers and RTÉ sought permission to attend, giving assurances of confidentiality in their reporting, but were refused a hearing on the grounds that they had no standing (*locus standi*).[230] In 1988 the *Irish Press* supported by the *Irish Independent* applied to the High Court to have reporting restrictions lifted in proceedings taken by a former Ryanair executive against the company. The application was refused by Costello J. on the grounds that the applicants had no *locus standi* to make it. Only the written judgment would be made available to them; affidavits, exhibits, the petition and any pleadings would be covered by the *in camera* order.[231]

In some cases there is no public interest involved; the information is of a private nature and an injunction is clearly warranted. In others, however, it is imperative that the media receive notice of the application for the injunction, an opportunity to oppose it, and a swift and effective avenue of appeal if an injunction is granted.

Further Reading

Allan, T., 'Disclosure of Journalists' Sources, Civil Disobedience and the Rule of Law' (1991) (50(1) CLJ 131–162.

Korthals Altes, William F., 'The Journalistic Privilege: A Dutch Proposal for Legislation' (1992) *Public Law* 73.

McCormack, Gerard, 'Corrupting the Criminal Process' (1985) 1 ILT 6.
McCormack, Gerard, 'The Right to Jury Trial in Cases of Contempt', (1983) GILSI 177 and 209.

O'Dell, Eoin, 'Speech in a Cold Climate: The 'Chilling Effect' of the Contempt Jurisdiction', in Liz Heffernan, ed., *Human Rights—A European Perspective*, Dublin: Round Hall Press 1994, p. 219.

Palmer, Stephanie, 'Protecting Journalists' Sources: Section 10, Contempt of Court Act 1981' (1992) *Public Law* 61.

Walker, Sally, 'Freedom of Speech and Contempt of Court: the English and Australian Approaches Compared' (1991) 40 ICLQ 583.

For articles on protection of sources in the US, see Monica Langley and Lee Levine, 'Broken Promises', 1988 *Columbia Journalism Review* 21; Kathryn Kase, 'When a Promise Is Not a Promise: The Legal Consequences for Journalists who Break Promises of Confidentiality to Sources', (1990) 12 *Hastings Communications and Entertainment Law Journal* 565; Eileen F. Tanielian, 'Battle of the Privileges; First Amendment vs Sixth Amendment', (1990) 10 *Loyola Entertainment Law Journal* 215; Jill S. Linhardt, 'The California Supreme Court Sets the Stage for Destruction of the Newsperson's Shield Law in *Delaney v Superior Court* [789 P. 2d 934 (Cal)]' (1991) 11 *Loyola Entertainment Law Journal* 181; Jack Colldeweiht and Samuel Pleasants, 'Confidential Sources—The Reporter's Privilege Muddle' (1991) 13 *Communications and the Law* 3; J.H. Youm and H.W. Stonecipher, 'The Legal Bounds of Confidentiality Promises: Promissory Estoppel and the First Amendment' (1992) 45 *Fed. Commun. L.J.* 63; M.J. Parrell, 'Press/Confidential Source Relations: Protecting Sources and the First Amendment' (1993) 15 *Communications and the Law* No. 1 47 and Alexander, 'Enforcing Promises Between Journalists and Sources' (1993) 15 *Communications and the Law* No. 1.

Notes

1   [1989] IR 126, at p. 134.
2   Ibid., at p. 135.
3   [1969] IR 142.
4   See the remarks of Denham J., speaking extra-judicially: *The Irish Times*, 6 May 1995.
5   1 February 1995, ITLR 13 March 1995.
6   [1992] ILRM 490; [1993] 3 IR 1.
7   Ibid., at p. 513.
8   *The Irish Times*, 3 April 1990.
9   See, for example, the arguments raised in Geoffrey Marshall, 'Press Freedom and Free Press Theory', (1992) PL 40; Robert Martin, 'Contempt of Court: The Effect of the Charter', in Anisman and Linden, eds, *The Media, The Courts and The Charter*, Toronto, Carswell 1986, pp 208–210; Robert Martin and G. Stuart Adam, *A Sourcebook of Canadian Media Law*, Ottawa: Carleton Univ. Press, 1989, pp 277–8.
10 Brian Inglis, *The Freedom of the Press in Ireland*, 1784–1841, London: Faber & Faber, 1954, at p. 32.
11 Ibid., at p. 77.
12 In Canada, for example, the Law Reform Commission, *Working Paper No. 20*, 1977, p. 48, recommended that the whole field of offences against the administration of justice, particularly the rules of contempt, become part of the criminal code. However, contempt was to remain largely uncodified, the criminal code mainly authorising its continuance, providing for an appeal and the operation of the *sub judice* rule in respect of certain specified offences. See generally, n. 9, Martin and Adam.

13 (1980) 2 EHRR 245.
14 Ibid., at para. 65.
15 Ibid.
16 Cf. Article 14.1 of the UN Covenant on Civil and Political Rights.
17 See n. 13, at para. 55.
18 [1994] 2 ILRM 481, Supreme Court, 16 March 1994; see Gordon Duffy, 'Pre-trial Publicity; Prejudice and the Right to a Fair Trial' (1994) 4 ICLJ 113 and 141.
19 R v Taylor, The Times, 15 June 1993, The Irish Times, 7 December 1994; Cf. R v Cullen, The Times, 1 May 1990 (the case in which the convictions of the Winchester Three were quashed because of remarks made by Lord Denning and Secretary of State for Northern Ireland, Tom King, about the right to silence); cf. also R v Glennon (1992) 66 ALJR 344, (1992) 173 CLR 592 and C.J. Miller, 'Contempt, Unsafe Convictions and Bias' (1993) 109 LQR 39. There have also been cases in Ireland where extradition to Britain has been refused because of media coverage in that country: Magee v O'Dea [1994] ILRM 540, and the decision of the Attorney General in the Fr Patrick Ryan case, 1989.
20 Report of the Committee on Contempt of Court, cmnd. 5794, London: HMSO, 1974.
21 [1973] IR 223, at p. 227.
22 A Latin term meaning 'without naming the day'.
23 See Law Reform Commission, Consultation Paper on Contempt of Court, 1991, pp 380–88; Report on Contempt of Court, (LRC 47–1994) 1994, at pp 52–3, 72–3.
24 See The Irish Times, 25 October 1991–26 October 1991.
25 Ibid.
26 The Irish Times, 16 March 1985.
27 Ibid.
28 See n. 21.
29 [1981] IR 412 at 421.
30 For example, see n. 10, at p. 143.
31 (1933) 69 ILTR 116.
32 In 1934 the political correspondent of the Irish Press was sent to prison for one month by the military tribunal for refusing to reveal his sources for an article on the banning of the Young Ireland Association (the Blueshirts); see John Horgan, 'Case Made History for Journalism', The Irish Times, 24 April 1992.
33 (1974) 108 ILTR 97.
34 Ibid., at p. 101.
35 Ibid., at p. 102.
36 [1963] 2 WLR 658, [1963] 1 All ER 767.
37 See n. 13.
38 (1982) 75 Cr App R 90, [1982] Crim LR 296, DC.
39 [1982] AC 1096.
40 [1990] 1 All ER 608 Ch D, arising out of X v Morgan Grampian Publishers Ltd and Others [1990] 2 All ER 1.
41 The Commission took the view that compelling disclosure of the source was not necessary in a democratic society, that protection of confidential sources was an 'essential means of enabling the press to perform its important function of public watchdog' and should not be interfered with unless in 'exceptional circumstances where vital public or individual interests are at stake', Report of the Commission, Applic. No. 17488/91, 1 March 1994 at paras 69, 64. See also Robert D. Sack, 'Goodwin v United Kingdom: An American View of Protection for Journalists' Confidential Sources under UK and European Law', (1995) 16 JMLP 86; Bina Cunningham, 'Journalists' privilege from a European perspective', [1995] 1 ENT LR 25.
42 [1993] 2 All ER 577; The Irish Times, 30 April 1992, 28 July 1992
43 The Irish Times, 25 March 1988. The Irish government has since announced an end to the state of emergency (The Irish Times, 7 February 1995). In 1995 a NI court ordered the BBC, UTV and RTÉ to hand over unbroadcast TV film of a stand-off in Portadown between police and Orangemen. The application was brought by the RUC under the 1989 Police and Criminal Evidence Order, The Irish Times, 30 August 1995.

44 Defamation Bill (No. 5 of 1995), ss 43–5. What the new Bill seeks to do is to is to incorporate the provision of s. 10 of the Contempt of Court Act 1981 in Britain, to the effect that contempt will arise only where disclosure of sources is necessary in the interests of justice, national security or for the prevention of disorder or crime. The onus of proving necessity in support of any of these interests shall rest on the prosecution (s. 43(2)). The provision will be extended to Tribunals of Inquiry by s. 44. A separate Contempt of Court Bill (No. 2 of 1995) was also introduced to protect journalists' sources.

45 *The Irish Times*, 28 January 1995. The issue also arose in *Burke v Central Television* [1994] 2 ILRM 161, in which discovery of documents relating to IRA activities, used to make a television programme, 'The Cook Report', was refused because of the risk to life involved.

46 On this and related problems, see n. 23, *Paper*, chs 9 and 17.

47 *The Irish Times*, 28 January 1995.

48 [1992] ILRM 574.

49 The Chairman did not use the power given by the Act to treat the contempt as if it had been contempt of the High Court and punish the journalists himself. This power has been questioned on constitutional grounds by the *Paper*; see n. 23, at p. 422.

50 *The Irish Times*, 15 October 1994. In the case of the *Irish Press* publishing extracts from a report, in breach of a court order (see text for n. 24), Costello J. in the High Court recognised that a free and fearless press with access to sources was important for society to function properly and did not think that it was necessary for the sources to be revealed in the particular case before him (*The Irish Times*, 26 October 1991).

51 *Cohen v Cowles Media*, 501 US 663 (1991). See Jens B. Koepke, 'Reporter Privilege: Shield or Sword? Applying a Modified Breach of Contract Standard When a Newspaper "Burns" a Confidential Source' (1990) 42 FCLJ 277.

52 Freedom of the Press Act 1949, ch. 3, arts 1, 4–5.

53 Applying s. 53 of the Code of Criminal Procedure.

54 Danish Media Law, 1 January 1992.

55 See, generally, Article 19, *Press Law and Practice*, London, 1993. Some countries, like Canada, offer only a very weak pre-trial protection, while Australia offers no protection at all and there have been numerous cases of journalists being fined or imprisoned for refusing to disclose their sources (*The Irish Times*, 9 September 1993). Belgium and France do not cite journalists for contempt but have been known to charge them with the theft or receipt of stolen documents—see recent case in France *of Le Canard Enchaîné* Cour de Cassation, 3 April 1995 (reported in *Le Monde*, 4 April 1995), concerning an article referring to pay rises of 45.9 per cent to Jacques Calvet, head of the Peugeot company, published at a time when the workforce was on strike in a demand for a 2 per cent rise. The paper was found guilty of receiving stolen documents involving a professional secret. The case is expected to go to Strasbourg.

56 In Irish law there is, therefore, no privilege for journalists and their sources, although a qualified privilege has been recognized in other relationships: priests-penitents (*Cook v Carroll* [1945] IR 515); lawyers-clients (See Nuala Jackson and Thomas Courtney, 'Without Prejudice or without Effect?' (March, April 1991) GILSI 49 and 119); police-informers (Paul A. O'Connor, 'The Privilege of Non-Disclosure and Informers' (1980) 15 IR Jur 111); Marc McDonald, 'Some Aspects of the Law on Disclosure of Information' (1979) Vol. 14, Ir Jur 229; and, possibly, doctors-patients (Henchy J. in *Hynes v Garvey* [1978] IR 174, at p. 187).

57 See n. 21.

58 [1981] IR 412, at p. 421.

59 Quoting Gavan Duffy P. in *AG v Connolly* [1947] IR 213.

60 Compare, for example, *AG v O'Kelly* [1928] IR 308, *AG v Connolly* [1947] IR 213, *AG v O'Ryan and Boyd* [1946] IR 70 with the other cases cited in the text. For examples of earlier cases when newspaper proprietors were fined and imprisoned for 'reflections on the court', 'false accounts of the proceedings', and so on, see Inglis, n. 10, at pp 77, 80, 103.

61 *AG v Connolly* [1947] IR 213.

62 In re Hibernia National Review [1976] IR 388.
63 Ibid., per Kenny J. at p. 391.
64 [1976] IR 382.
65 [1981] IR 412.
66 Ibid., at p. 420.
67 See n. 6.
68 See n. 6, at p. 17.
69 The role and influence of public relations firms are a new phenomenon, requiring scrutiny. They were a significant factor in the handling and coverage of the Beef Tribunal, for example.
70 [1987] IR 662, at p. 666 referring to O'Higgins C.J. in n. 64, at p. 386.
71 High Court, 22 June 1992, Carney J., The Irish Times, 23 June 1992.
72 The government intended to use s. 31(2) of the Broadcasting Authority Act 1960 to allow the Taoiseach to make the broadcast.
73 See n. 71.
74 See Kevin Boyle and Marie McGonagle, 'Reform of Contempt of Court Law' in Marie McGonagle, ed., Essays on Law and Media, Dublin: The Round Hall Press, forthcoming.
75 See n. 71.
76 The Irish Times, 6 December 1994.
77 See n. 23, Report, at p. 32.
78 See Robert J. Sharpe, 'The Role of a Media Spokesperson for the Courts—The Supreme Court of Canada Experience' (1990) 1 Media Comm L Rev 271; Australian Law Reform Commission, Discussion Paper No. 26, 1986, referring to the establishment of a media liaison bureau in Victoria.
79 See n. 23 at ch. 5.
80 See Cullen v Tóibín [1984] ILRM 577, at p. 581 (Supreme Court per O'Higgins C.J.); Weeland v RTÉ [1987] IR 662, at p. 666 (High Court per Carroll J.), Wong v Minister for Defence (High Court per Denham J.) 30 July 1992.
81 See n. 67.
82 Both were rejected in Desmond.
83 AG v Connolly [1947] IR 213.
84 State (DPP) v Walsh and Conneely [1981] IR 412.
85 In re Kennedy and McCann [1976] IR 382.
86 State (DPP) v Irish Press Ltd, unreported, High Court, 15 December 1976.
87 See The Irish Times, 1 March 1988, 15 March 1988, Sunday Tribune, 6 March 1988, where an apology was also published. In Britain there is a 'warned list' which alerts the media to cases that are coming on for hearing, so that the risk of inadvertently prejudicing pending cases is lessened.
88 DPP v Dunne, Evening Herald 10 July 1986; The Irish Times, 12 July 1986.
89 The Irish Times, 26 March 1992.
90 Ibid.
91 The Irish Times, 3 April 1990.
92 In re MacArthur [1983] ILRM 355.
93 The Irish Times, 11 Decemberr 1992, referring to an Irish Independent headline 'Girl (13) sexually assaulted by man (55)' which implied the guilt of the accused. The editor was later granted leave to seek an order prohibiting the Circuit Court judge proceeding with a trial for contempt for want of jurisdiction to hold a summary trial (The Irish Times, 19 December 1992). See also The Irish Times, 22 October 1994, referring to a headline in the Star; the editor was given leave to challenge the order fining him £10,000 for contempt (The Irish Times, 8 November 1994). In another case difficulties arose over the use of the word 'drugs' in headlines in several newspapers, when the evidence in court was to 'substances'(The Irish Times, 27 October 1994).
94 A good example is the Australian case Hinch v AG (1987) 164 CLR 15, concerning a programme broadcast in Australia about a priest charged with child molesting.
95 See The Irish Times, 28 August 1985.
96 AG v Times Newspapers [1973] 3 All ER 54 (HL) at pp 72–3.
97 People (DPP) v O'Callaghan, unreported, High Court, 25 February 1993.

98 Eric Barendt, *Freedom of Speech*, Oxford: Clarendon Press, 1989, at p. 216; cf. Paul Robertshaw, 'Leaking the Secrets of the Jury Room' (1993) 12 JMLP 114. Both the Lord Chancellor and the Royal Commission for Criminal Justice believe the law should be changed to enable research to be carried out into how juries reach their verdicts; see *The Times*, 1 May 1995.
99 See n. 23, at pp 364–74.
100 Ibid., at para. 7. 15.
101 Ibid., at paras 7. 14–19.
102 [1983] ILRM 355.
103 See n. 20.
104 *State (DPP) v Irish Press Ltd*, unreported, High Court, 15 December 1976. *In re Mac Arthur* [1983] ILRM 355.
105 [1973] IR 223.
106 [1981] IR 412.
107 See n. 105, at p. 235.
108 *The Irish Times*, 26 February 1992.
109 [1977] IR 78.
110 See n. 105.
111 See n. 23, at paras 2.7 and 8.1.
112 See n. 20, paras 170–76.
113 [1907] 2 IR 260, at p. 268.
114 Ibid., at p. 275.
115 See n. 83, at p. 221
116 For example, see AG v *English* [1983] 1 AC 116, at pp 141–2 per Lord Diplock; AG v *News Group Newspapers* [1986] 2 All ER 833, at p. 841, *per* Donaldson, M.R.
117 *The Irish Times*, 26 June 1993.
118 See n. 18.
119 Cited by Meredith J. in AG v *O'Kelly* [1928] IR 308, at p. 324.
120 (1924) 58 ILTR 157.
121 See n. 61, at p. 219.
122 Ibid., at p. 221. In Britain the 1981 Act provides for a strict liability offence but creates certain defences (ss 3–5). It continues common law (s. 6). An intention to prejudice or subvert the course of justice is not required.
123 See n. 86 at p. 2 of the typescript (as case unreported).
124 See n. 87.
125 See n. 92, at p. 356. It has been pointed out, however, that, if tried and convicted, a conviction will still stand and could have repercussions at a later stage if the publisher were to be charged again; see Sally Walker, 'Freedom of Speech and Contempt of Court: The English and Australian Approaches Compared', (1991) 40 ICLQ 583, at p. 589.
126 *The Irish Times*, 26 June 1993.
127 Ibid.
128 *The Irish Times*, 13 October 1992. See also *The Irish Times*, 30 July 1992.
129 The Law Reform Commission suggests a test of negligence in relation to 'active' proceedings; see n. 23, *Report*, at para. 6.10.
130 See n. 23, *Paper*, at pp 86–7 re relevance of R v *Beaverbrook & Associated Newspapers Ltd* [1962] NI 15 to the question of 'imminent' proceedings.
131 *Sunday Tribune*, 7 September 1986.
132 *Doherty v Sunday Times*, *The Irish Times*, 15 February 1991. A Dáil motion was passed on 8 April 1993 to relax the *sub judice* rule. See n. 23, *Report*, at p. 43.
133 See n. 13.
134 AG v *Times Newspapers* [1974] AC 273, [1973] 1 All ER 815 CA. Cf. *Hinch v AG* (1987) 164 CLR 15, an Australian case in which a balancing test was proposed: if the publisher sought to serve, and did serve, a public interest that outweighs the prejudicial effect of the publication, the publisher is not guilty of contempt of court.
135 See n. 96.
136 See n. 13.

137 See n. 20.
138 See n. 80.
139 Ibid., at pp 578–81.
140 See n. 80, at p. 582.
141 Ibid., at p. 579.
142 Ibid., at p. 581. The Australian Law Reform Commission in its *Discussion Paper* No. 26 (1986) recommended that no restrictions should apply between the jury verdict and an order for a retrial. The Irish Commission departed from its provisional recommendation of 1991 and decided that it 'would be unduly restrictive to extend the operation of the sub judice rule to appellate proceedings, which are invariably decided by non-jury courts' (*Report*, n. 23, at para. 6.14).
143 Unreported, 28 May 1984, HC.
144 Ibid. at p. 5 of typescript.
145 *The Irish Times*, 30 November 1989. Doubts have been cast on O'Hanlon J.'s decision in the *State* (DPP) *v Independent Newspapers*, n. 143, however, by the Law Reform Commission, n. 23, *Paper*, at p. 86–7, where it avers to the fact that O'Hanlon J. did not refer to R *v Beaverbrook & Associated Newspapers Ltd* [1962] NI 15 in his judgment.
146 *The Irish Times*, 23 November 1993, 10 February 1994, 8 March 1994.
147 Ibid.
148 *The Irish Times*, 10 February 1994.
149 See n. 6.
150 Unreported, High Court, 30 July 1992.
151 See n. 6, at p. 20.
152 Ibid., at pp 33–4.
153 See n. 150 at p. 22 of typescript.
154 Cf. *Lovell and Christmas v O'Shaughnessy* (1934) 69 ILTR 34.
155 See n. 23, *Paper*, at pp 310–313; n. 23, *Report*, at para. 6.23.
156 The position regarding common-law defences is not clear; see Current Law Statutes Annotated, vol. 1, 1981, no. 49.
157 See n. 142.
158 See n. 23, *Report*, at para. 6.24.
159 Ibid., at para. 6.25.
160 Ibid., at paras 6.26–32.
161 See n. 23, *Paper*, at p. 336, *Report*, at p. 44, paras 6.33–6.36.
162 See n. 23, *Report*, rec. 32–6.
163 *The Irish Times*, 11 October 1991–13 October 1991.
164 See n. 150. *Wong* itself may represent an extension of the contempt power.
165 *The Irish Times*, 15 January 1992.
166 J.P. Casey, *Constitutional Law in Ireland*, 2nd edn., London: Sweet and Maxwell, 1992, at p. 444.
167 Ibid., at p. 445.
168 There is a worrying development of journalists being subpoenaed to appear before tribunals, disciplinary bodies, etc. For example, a freelance journalist was subpoenaed to appear before the Medical Council to reveal sources in relation to an article published in the *Sunday Independent*, *The Irish Times*, 7 May 1992.
169 See n. 23, *Paper*, at ch. 9.
170 Ibid., at p. 422.
171 [1971] IR 217. See J.M. Kelly *The Irish Constitution*, 3rd edn., Gerard Hogan and Gerry Whyte, eds, Dublin: Butterworths, 1994, at p. 369.
172 [1993] 3 IR 67.
173 See n. 23, *Report*, at p. 59.
174 [1965] IR 70.
175 Ibid., at p. 122.
176 [1928] IR 308.
177 Ibid., at p. 332.
178 Per Gavan Duffy P., n. 83, at p. 218.
179 Ibid.

180 See n. 105.
181 See n. 109.
182 Ibid., at p. 87.
183 Ibid., at p. 88.
184 See n. 65.
185 Ibid., at p. 439.
186 The respective roles of judge and jury are: for the judge to decide questions of law and the jury to decide questions of fact.
187 See n. 23, *Paper*, at chs 7, 8; *Report*, at ch. 3, which concludes that it should be left to the Supreme Court in an appropriate case to clarify the problems left unsolved by *Conneely*.
188 See n. 12, *Working Paper No. 20*, at p. 11.
189 See n. 13.
190 [1988] IR 593.
191 *The Irish Times*, 10 May 1994.
192 *The Irish Times*, 17 May 1994.
193 *The Irish Times*, 11 February 1993, 25 February 1993.
194 *The Irish Times*, 20 March 1993.
195 Ibid.
196 *The Irish Times*, 23 March 1993.
197 *The Irish Time*, 31 March 1993.
198 *The Irish Times*, 5 December 1992, 12 January 1993.
199 *The Irish Times*, 30 November 1993, re *Cullen v Tóibín*, n. 80.
200 *The Irish Times*, 31 May 1985; cf. *The Irish Times*, 4 December 1986.
201 *The Irish Times*, 22 August 1985. See also Gallagher case, n. 145.
202 *The Observer and Guardian v UK* (*Spycatcher case*), European Court of Human Rights, Series A, no. 216; 26 November 1991.
203 [1975] AC 396, where Lord Diplock, at p. 407, held that the court must be satisfied that the claim is not frivolous or vexatious, that there is a serious question to be tried. O'Higgins C.J. in *Campus Oil v Minister for Industry and Energy* (*No. 2*) [1983] IR 88, at p. 107, agreed, saying that the test to be applied is whether a fair bona fide question has been raised.
204 See n. 202, at para. 63. 60.
205 403 US 713 (1971).
206 *Nebraska v Stuart* 427 US 539, 559 (1976).
207 111 Sup. Ct. 451 (1990).
208 Ibid. See also Stephanie Izen, 'Prior Restraints Revisited: Have the Courts Finally Shackled the Press?' (1992) 12 Loyola Ent LJ 535.
209 [1989] IR 753, 765; [1990] ILRM 350, 357.
210 See n. 23, *Paper*, at p. 273; see also discussion in LRC *Consultation Paper on the Civil Law of Defamation* 1991, at paras 136–9.
211 See Marc McDonald, *Irish Law of Defamation*, Dublin: The Round Hall Press, 1987, 2nd edn. 1989 ch. 11; *X v RTÉ*, *The Irish Times*, 28 March 1990.
212 *The Irish Times*, 29 March 1990.
213 *The Irish Times*, 4 December 1987, 30 January 1988. RTÉ had already shown it in part. See also *Hodgson v UK* (1988) 10 EHRR 503, concerning *R v Ponting* (official secrets: discussed in chapter 10). A postponement order had been made under s. 4(2) of the Contempt of Court Act 1981. The Commission rejected the complaint because the order only affected the manner in which the trial could be reported and the judge's evaluation of the risk of prejudice was reasonable in the circumstances. See Glatt, 'Trial by Docudrama', (1990) 9 Cardozo Arts and Ent LJ 201–30.
214 See, for example, applications against RTÉ. *The Irish Times*, 6 February 1985, 14 September 1985.
215 See, for example, *The Irish Times*, 29 March 1985, 4 December 1986.
216 *The Irish Times*, 6 June 1984.
217 See n. 190. [1987] ILRM 477.
218 *The Irish Times*, 31 March 1993.

219 [1989] SLT 705 (HL).
220 See Andrew Halpin, 'Child's Play in the Lords' (1991) NLJ at pp 173–4, Neil Walker, 'Spycatcher's Scottish Sequel' (1990) PL 345–71.
221 (1985). See notes 222–25 .
222 *Sunday Tribune*, 4 August 1985.
223 See n. 210, *Paper on Defamation*, at pp 133 and 365; Adrian Hardiman, 'How ACC Halted Magazine Articles', *The Irish Times*, 10 September 1985.
224 *Sunday Independent*, 4 August 1985.
225 *The Irish Times*, 5 August 1985.
226 Note that disclosure of the identity of the source who gave the documents to the magazine was also sought. *The Irish Times*, 11 September 1985.
227 *Sunday Tribune*, 26 July 1987, also editorial 18 September 1988.
228 *The Irish Times*, 7 May 1994, 10 May 1994; *Irish Independent*, 7 May 1994.
229 *The Irish Times*, 7 May 1994.
230 *The Irish Times*, 25 February 1992. The request was made on the grounds of the public interest and the media undertook to comply with all directions of the court if reporting were allowed. Finlay C.J. stated that they had no right of audience.
231 *The Irish Times*, 15 October 1988.

CHAPTER SEVEN

Reporting the Courts, Parliament and Local Government

Reporting the Courts

The starting point for consideration of the privileges and restrictions that apply to court reporting is Article 34.1 of the Irish Constitution:

> Justice shall be administered in courts established by law . . . and save in such special and limited cases as may be prescribed by law, shall be administered in public.

As we have already seen in the last chapter, Article 34 provides for a system of open justice, with both the media and the public free to attend, and the media entitled to report. That is the norm.[1] The only exceptions are the 'special and limited cases . . . prescribed by law' to which the Constitution refers. The fact that the limitations must be prescribed by law excludes the possibility of judicial discretion, which was a feature of pre-Constitution cases.[2] There is, however, an element of discretion built into some of the statutes that provide for restrictions on media reporting. Also, despite the fact that Article 34 refers to 'special and limited cases' as an exception to the general rule of open justice, in reality statute law provides for quite a number of situations where the media and public can be excluded from the court altogether, or restrictions imposed on what may be reported.

1. Exclusion of the Media from the Court

The Courts (Supplemental Provisions) Act 1961 provides the basis for the exclusion of the public, though not necessarily the media, from the court. Each of the areas of restriction provided for will be considered in turn, to the extent that they affect the media. Section 45 (1) of the 1961 Act states:

> Justice may be administered otherwise than in public in any of the following cases:

(a) applications of an urgent nature for relief by way of habeas corpus, bail, prohibition or injunction;

(b) matrimonial causes and matters;

(c) lunacy and minor matters;

(d) proceedings involving the disclosure of a secret manufacturing process.

Section 45(2) provides that these areas of restriction are in addition to any other cases prescribed by any act of the Oireachtas. Section 45(3) has the effect of resurrecting to 'full force and effect' any earlier statute that provided for the administration of justice otherwise than in public and that 'is not in force solely by reason of its being inconsistent with the provisions of the Constitution . . .'. While the latter provision is peculiar, it does, as Carney J. pointed out in a recent case concerning provisions of the Punishment of Incest Act 1908,[3] enjoy a presumption of constitutionality, the validity of which was not and could not be challenged in the particular proceedings before him. To the extent, however, that section 5 of the 1908 Act provided that all proceedings were to be held in private, it appeared to be incompatible with the Constitution (see below).

(a) Injunctions

The nature and scope of injunctions has already been explained in Chapter 6. The only aspect to be dealt with here, therefore, is the effect on the press when an injunction, usually an interim one, is sought as a matter of urgency. In that case the injunction can be applied for at any time of the day or night and, if outside court hours, may be heard in the judge's own home. Application is generally made on an *ex parte* basis because there is no time to alert the other side or because it is more convenient not to. However, the application is treated as an *ex parte* hearing and even if the other side is present, it seems that there is no opportunity given for that side of the case to be heard at the interim stage.[4] Apart from the time constraints, it is difficult to see why not.

In Chapter 6 we were concerned mainly with injunctions granted against media organisations to prevent publication or broadcasting of particular matter, whereas in this chapter we consider the impact of injunctions granted to others in a situation in which the media are not allowed to attend or report. The media may be excluded either because they do not know that an application for an injunction is to be made at short notice or because the proceeding is to be heard *in camera*, that is, in private. An application might be held *in camera* because of the confidential nature of the subject-matter, for example.

Otherwise, reporters would have to be admitted. The refusal to hear the application for an interlocutory injunction *in camera* in ACC *v Irish Business*[5] is a good example, as is *Maguire v Drury*.[6]

In that respect, it is disappointing that the courts denied the media a right to be heard when they applied to be allowed to report the Supreme Court argument in the appeal against the High Court injunction in the X case.[7] The hearing of the appeal was to be *in camera* with the press and the public excluded. The national newspapers and RTÉ requested permission to attend and gave assurances that they would respect the privacy of the parties and the directions of the Court in their reporting. The Court refused their request and rejected any notion of a public representative function on the part of the media.

The position regarding *locus standi* generally was considered by Walsh J. in SPUC *v Coogan*:[8]

> . . . the Court will, where the circumstances warrant it, permit a person whose personal interest is not directly or indirectly presently or in the future threatened to maintain proceedings if the circumstances are such that the public interest warrant[s] it. In this context the public interest must be taken in the widest sense. . . .

> In the last analysis it is a question reserved exclusively to the Courts to decide. . . .

Walsh J. is referring to the possibility of an 'outsider' being able to maintain an action. If the courts are prepared to contemplate that possibility, then there would seem to be no reason to refuse the media the right to be heard as to why they should be allowed to attend and report on proceedings.[9]

A worrying feature, as pointed out in Chapter 6, is the scope of injunctions. A ban on the very fact of the granting of an injunction is an affront to the public. An injunction addressed to all the media has major implications for freedom of information and the public's right to know. Even injunctions not directly addressed to the media can wreak havoc. In the case of AG (SPUC) *v Open Door Counselling*,[10] for example, a perpetual injunction was granted by the courts restraining two clinics, their servants and agents, from assisting pregnant women in procuring abortions. RTÉ found itself answering a formal complaint to the Broadcasting Complaints Commission arising out of live transmission of an interview with representatives of the clinics in the wake of the decision against them. RTÉ was not guilty of bias, according to the Commission but was in breach of section 18 of the Broadcasting Authority Act 1960, insofar as remarks made by the interviewees could be construed as 'being likely to promote or incite to crime'. RTÉ was advised that there should be no discussion of abortion on live broadcasts and only discussion of the general merits of the law in recorded programmes. There was also a danger that contempt of court law would be invoked against the media while the Supreme Court appeal was pending. Protest marches against the High Court's ruling were either not covered at all or marchers were asked to remove banners displaying the telephone numbers of abortion clinics in Britain. Such was the level of confusion that it was believed the showing of such pictures might constitute defiance of the injunction and amount to civil contempt.[11]

(b) Matrimonial Causes and Matters

In matrimonial causes and matters, proceedings may be held otherwise than in public. In addition, specific statutes provide that family law matters be held *in camera*. Reporting, likewise, is strictly curtailed in the interests of the privacy of the parties and family unit, which the Constitution expressly protects (Article 41). However, the terminology among the various acts is not consistent and can make it difficult for journalists to know what their entitlements are.[12] The Family Law (Maintenance of Spouses and Children) Act 1976, section 25(1) and Family Home Protection Act 1976, section 10(6), provide that cases 'shall' be heard 'otherwise than in public' and, in the High Court and Circuit Court, shall be heard 'in chambers' (section 25(2) and section 10(7), respectively). The Family Law (Protection of Spouses and Children) Act 1981 also contains a mandatory provision: section 14(1) states that 'Proceedings . . . shall be heard otherwise than in public'. In the Circuit Court or High Court on appeal, proceedings 'may be heard in chambers'. The Married Women's Status Act 1957, section 12(4), is discretionary rather than mandatory: 'if either party so requests, the court may hear the application in private'. Cases under the Marriages Act 1972 'may be heard and determined in private' (section 1(3)(c) and section 7(3)(c)). The Adoption Acts 1952–76 provide for the hearing of cases *in camera* (section 20(2) of the 1952 Act regarding cases stated to the High Court).

Where statutes contain a mandatory provision, as in the Judicial Separation Act 1989, section 34, which directs that all proceedings must be heard *in camera*, the judge has no choice but to exclude the media, and the media have to obey.[13] There is more scope for the media where the statutory provision is discretionary rather than mandatory. Representations can be made to the judge to hold the hearing in public in the public interest. In the constitutional challenge to the Judicial Separation Act in F *v* F, *Ireland and* AG,[14] for example, a submission to be allowed to report in the public interest was made by the National Newspapers of Ireland (NNI). Murphy J. relied on the mandatory provision of section 34 of the Act to exclude the media from part of the case in order 'to protect the privacy and confidentiality of the husband and wife in relation to the facts concerning the marriage and the family law matters'.[15] The remainder of the case, which dealt with the constitutionality issue, he heard in public. He acknowledged the public interest in the constitutional issue but asked that the names of the parties not be reported.

When a hearing is conducted in private, publication of any material from it can be restrained by injunction or may be punished as contempt. In *Maguire v Drury*,[16] concerning a case between a man and his wife, which was expected to be followed by an action by the man for damages against the Catholic Church on the grounds that the wife's alleged affair with a priest had caused the breakdown of the marriage in question, publication of any material taken from the *in camera* judicial separation proceedings was restrained by interim injunction. The order was limited to the *in camera* matter and did not prevent publication of the man's account of the proceedings he intended to bring against the Church. However, neither the woman nor the children were to be referred to by name, and no pictures of them were to be published. An interlocutory injunction was later refused on the grounds that the case did not concern the intimacies of married life or the marital communications between husband and wife but rather allegations by the husband of an extramarital liaison entered into by his wife which he wanted to publicise in order to give vent to his anger, and perhaps to make money. The courts are reluctant to intervene in such cases 'in a manner which would entrench on the freedom of expression enjoyed by the press and by the media generally, merely to avoid the distress caused by publication of matters which show up a parent or parents in a sordid or unfavourable light'.[17]

The purpose of these restrictions is overtly to protect the privacy of the parties and, in some cases, the privacy and identity of any children of the marriage. An important dimension is the status and protection accorded to the family and marriage in the Constitution.[18] However, the *in camera* nature of family law proceedings has its drawbacks in terms of public knowledge and in terms of public appreciation of the extent and nature of family law problems in the State. It also hampers the formation of precedent and guidance as to appropriate remedies. People do not know how family cases are handled away from the spotlight of media attention. Practitioners themselves have suggested that improvements in the standard of presentation, in the degree of interest taken and in the general approach to family law cases would result from media reporting. The Law Reform Commission, in its *Consultation Paper on Family Courts* 1994,[19] accepted the dangers but regarded family law cases as:

> a class different from other cases in that they frequently involve detailed discussion of personal and usually private relationships at a time when the parties concerned may be feeling hurt and vulnerable. It is rightly felt that family members should as far as possible be protected from the further stress which may be occasioned by publicity and by exposure of their personal lives to those having only a prurient interest. Even more so, where children are involved, there is a strong desire to maintain what O'Higgins C.J. described in Re *McCann v Kennedy* [sic] as 'a decent privacy', this being regarded as necessary to prevent harm or distress to the child.[20]

The Commission, therefore, provisionally recommended against any change with regard to allowing access by the public or press.[21]

(c) Minors

The media are generally excluded from hearings involving the care and custody of minors. In other cases, involving the prosecution of a minor, for example, the media may be admitted but reporting restrictions will be applied to preserve the anonymity of the minor concerned. Under the Children Act 1908 (section 111(4), as amended by the same of 1941, section 29), only specified persons directly concerned in the case 'shall, except by leave of the court, be allowed to attend' but 'bona fide representatives of a newspaper or news agency shall not be excluded'. The Punishment of Incest Act 1908, section 5, is absolute: 'all proceedings are to be held in camera'. It may appear strange that two acts of the same year should have different provisions in this regard. There are undoubtedly considerable differences in the scope of the two acts: incest may not involve children, although it does involve family members or blood relations, whereas the Children Act concerns a variety of proceedings involving children that are not necessarily criminal. Nonetheless, the different stipulations regarding attendance at the hearings must reflect how incest was viewed at the time. The incest issue will be discussed later in this chapter.

The Illegitimate Children (Affiliation Orders) Act 1930, section 3(5), as amended by the Family Law (Maintenance of Spouses and Children) Act 1976, section 28(i)(d), and later repealed by the Status of Children Act 1987, section 25(1), provided that all proceedings were to be held 'otherwise than in public'. Now, under the Status of Children Act 1987, section 36(4), the court may direct that the whole or any part of the proceedings for a declaration of parentage shall be heard otherwise than in public and that an 'application for a direction . . . shall be so heard unless the Court otherwise directs'. In practice, the courts do exclude the public from such cases.[22] Care proceedings under the Child Care Act 1991, section 29, will be heard in private. Proceedings under the Succession Act 1965, sections 56(ii), 119, 122, and Legitimacy Declarations (Ireland) Act 1868, as amended, 'shall be held in chambers'.

The Guardianship of Infants Act 1964 makes no mention of excluding the media or holding proceedings in private, but because it relates to minors, it would automatically come within the additional categories provided for by section 45(1) of the Courts (Supplemental Provisions) Act 1961. The same is true in relation to wardship proceedings.[23] At any rate provision is made in the Rules of Court[24] for applications under the Guardianship of Infants Act and certain other acts to be heard in private. In *In re Kennedy and McCann*[25] the editor and a journalist with the *Sunday World* newspaper were fined for publishing details of a hearing held *in camera* under the Guardianship of Infants Act. The report was found to be in contempt of court as it was inaccurate in a number of respects, the names of the parties were revealed and it was accompanied by pictures of the mother and children. The Adoption Acts 1952–76 also provide for *in camera* hearings, subject to rules of court (section 20(2), 1952 Act), and for the privacy of records (section 8, 1976 Act) unless in the best interests of the child concerned.

The fact that a hearing is held *in camera* does not of itself mean that nothing can be reported in relation to the hearing, but anything that is reported runs the risk of being in contempt of court if inaccurate or otherwise prejudicial. In 1993 the High Court held that the *Sunday Tribune* had committed no offence in publishing a report relating to an *in camera* hearing. The court accepted the evidence given by the editor and journalist that they did not know that the case had been held *in camera* and accepted an apology.[26]

(d) Disclosure of Secret Manufacturing Process

Provision is made in the Companies Acts for *in camera* hearings. In *In re R* in 1989,[27] the applicant company sought an order under section 205(7) of the Companies Act 1963:

> If in the opinion of the court, the hearing of proceedings under this section would involve the disclosure of information the publication of which would be seriously prejudicial to the legitimate interests of the company, the court may order that the hearing of the proceedings or any part thereof shall be in camera.

The *Irish Press* and *Independent Newspapers* made a submission that proceedings be in public and that they be allowed to attend on the grounds of public interest and freedom of speech. The court refused their request.[28] Then, in response to the application of the plaintiff himself, the Supreme Court directed that the proceedings be held in public on the grounds:

(i) that it was essential to the administration of justice that it be in public unless that requirement by itself operated to deny justice in a particular case and

(ii) the company had failed to show that a public hearing would by itself so impede the doing of justice as between the parties that the judge ought in the exercise of his discretion to order that the proceedings be heard in camera.[29]

A similar decision was reached by the Supreme Court with regard to the hearing of the dispute between Irish Press plc and Ingersoll Irish Publications Ltd. Because much of the information was already in the public arena and there had been no reference to identifiable or particular documents likely to cause specific and identifiable damage of a serious kind such as would seriously prejudice the legitimate interests of the companies, the proceedings should be held in public. The fundamental constitutional right vested in the public, namely the administration of justice in public, must be considered and section 205(7) of the Companies Act 1963 should be strictly construed.[30]

The Companies (Amendment) Act 1990, section 31, also provides that:

> The whole or part of any proceedings under this Act may be heard otherwise than in public if the court, in the interests of justice, considers that the interests of the company concerned or of its creditors as a whole so require.

Under this provision an application by the examiner of Goodman International and related companies was heard *in camera* on the grounds that the disclosure of certain matters mentioned in an affidavit would be seriously prejudicial to the legitimate interests of the companies that were under the protection of the courts.[31] More recently, the High Court, In *the matter of Countyglen plc*,[32] had to consider whether the application for an order by an inspector appointed under section 7(4) of the Companies Act 1990 to investigate the affairs of Countyglen plc could be heard in private. The decision hinged on whether the application was an *administrative* one only and therefore did not come within the requirements of Article 34(1) of the Constitution, which states that *justice* shall be administered in public.

While some of the directions sought by the inspector 'were highly confidential and disclosure of the application would have been likely to prejudice the sensitive enquiries which he was then seeking to pursue, it was clear', Murphy J. said, 'that the 1990 Act did not confer on the court any statutory power to hear the application otherwise than in public'.[33] However, the particular direction sought and given was held not to constitute the administration of justice and accordingly 'was not required under the Constitution to be dealt with in public'.[34]

This case may mark a worrying development for the media. The argument on which it is based could be used to effectively bypass the constitutional requirement of openness in certain circumstances. Surely the hearing of an application for a court order is judicial by nature rather than administrative, regardless of the content of the order or the type of power it confers. Equally, the granting of an order through the court, one would have thought, must constitute a judicial function. In *Countyglen*, however, a distinction was made between an order and a mere direction to the inspector with a view to ensuring that his investigation was carried out as quickly and inexpensively as possible. Furthermore, there was significant precedent to support the contention that the fact that an order was to be made by a court did not, of itself, determine that it constituted the administration of justice. It may be desirable to dispose of adminstrative matters informally but the consequences for media reporting should not be lost sight of.

(e) Other Statutory Provisions

There are several statutes that provide for *in camera* proceedings in certain specified circumstances. These formerly included income tax matters by virtue of the Finance Act 1949, section 30, and the Income Tax Act 1967, section 416(10), whereby appeals reheard before 'the Circuit Court 'shall be held *in camera*' and every hearing by the High Court or Supreme Court of a case stated shall 'if the person . . . so desires, be held *in camera*'. However, following the enactment of the Finance Act 1983, section 9(b), which deleted the latter provision of section 416(10) of the 1967 Act, the High Court refused an application to have proceedings arising out of a judge's tax appeal heard *in camera*. According to the court the intention of the legislature was that any case stated after the 1983 enactment should be heard in public.[35]

In another instance, section 12 of the Official Secrets Act 1963 allows the prosecution to apply to have part of the hearing held in private on the basis that it would otherwise prejudice the safety or preservation of the State. If the prosecution applies, 'the court shall make an order to that effect'. The court does not have a discretion in the matter, which seems to fly in the face of the whole principle of open justice and the role of the courts in that regard. However, the verdict and sentence, if any, shall be pronounced in public. Similarly courtsmartial are open to the public but an order can be made by the convening authority or president of the courtmartial under the Defence Act 1954, section 194, excluding the public where it is deemed 'expedient in the interests of public safety, defence or public morals' for the whole or part of the trial. A mandatory provision occurs in the Defamation Act, section 8, in relation to applications for an order to bring a criminal prosecution for libel against a newspaper. An order must be obtained from a High Court judge sitting *in camera*. The constitutionality of the section has been questioned.[36]

In relation to criminal investigations and trials, there are certain restrictions that can be invoked in support of the right to a fair trial. For a period, the Criminal Justice Act 1951, section 20(1), allowed the court to exclude the public from the preliminary examination of an indictable offence 'if satisfied that it is expedient for the purpose of ensuring that the accused will not be prejudiced in his trial'. That is no longer the case except in relation to any proceedings of an indecent or obscene nature (section 20(3)). Preliminary examinations are now governed by the Criminal Procedure Act 1967, which provides that they shall be in open court except 'where the court is satisfied because of the nature or circumstances of the case or otherwise in the interests of justice' that it is desirable to exclude the public, though not the press (section 16(2)). The extent of the information that can be given in media reports is, however, strictly curtailed (section 17 discussed further later in this chapter). It may be noted also that under section 45 of the Courts (Supplemental Provisions) Act 1961, applications of an urgent nature for relief by way of bail can be heard in private. In practice, reporters often have difficulty distinguishing between bail applications and preliminary examinations.[37]

It may also happen from time to time that the media are admitted to court but asked to leave at some point during the hearing. In a High Court application for an *in camera* hearing in 1993, the media were asked to leave and not report on the proceedings in any form and to treat the matter as an *in camera* hearing, although reporting was allowed on what had been stated in court up until that point. The request was made in 'highly unusual circumstances',[38] and by reference to the Supreme Court's decision in AG *v* X.[39] However, since the instant case involved an application for an *in camera* hearing and related to an alleged offence covered by rape legislation, the question must be asked as to whether the circumstances were so exceptional that the ordinary precautions for preserving the anonymity of the parties under the terms of the Rape Acts did not suffice. It may be significant that the presiding judge declined to make an order of prohibition or injunction, which counsel sought. At any rate, the media can be excluded only where statutory law so provides. Therefore, unless the present case concerned a minor, such an order, if granted, would have been open to challenge.

The question of the admission of reporters to incest trials was raised by Carney J. in DPP *v* WM.[40] The provision of section 5 of the Punishment of Incest Act 1908 appeared mandatory and left no scope for judicial discretion: 'All proceedings under this Act are to be held in camera'.

This contrasted with the provision made for other sexual offences under the Criminal Law (Rape) (Amendment) Act 1990, which allows the judge to exclude from the court all persons 'except . . . bona fide representatives of the press' (section 11). Why should incest be treated differently from all other sexual offences? Is it particularly reprehensible? the parties particularly deserving of privacy? the facts destabilising of marriage and the family as protected by the Irish Constitution? or is it that in the interests of public morality the public should not be entitled to know any details of the case? It is difficult to see how a distinction could be justified on any such grounds, and it is tempting to attribute it to an accident of history and how the offence of incest was viewed at the turn of the century when the 1908 Act was passed. Whatever the reason, how does it stand now, constitutionally and in comparison to rape and sexual assault cases which the media are allowed to attend and report, although with certain restrictions? It is obvious, as Carney J. pointed out,[41] that total secrecy, so that the community at large would not even be entitled to know of the happening of the case or the sentence imposed, would be unacceptable and would not be in conformity with the constitutional scheme for the administration of justice. Neither would this be in conformity with the European Convention on Human Rights, which, at Article 6, states that there is a right to a fair and public hearing of 'any' criminal charge and that:

> . . . Judgment shall be pronounced publicly but the press and public may be excluded from all or part of the trial in the interest of morals, public order or national security in a democratic society, where the interests of juveniles or the protection of the private life of the parties so require, or to the extent strictly necessary in the opinion of the court in special circumstances where publicity would prejudice the interests of justice.

Many jurisdictions[42] accept that some degree of privacy and confidentiality is necessary, particularly in family law cases, but that privacy should not be confused with total secrecy. Secondly, it is privacy that should be protected rather than fear of exposure or embarrassment. As the nature of judicial separation cases changes from fault-based criteria, it may be argued that the same degree of protection is no longer needed and that much would be gained from allowing reporters access and imposing restrictions on the reporting of the names of the parties instead. The Judicial Separation Act 1989 makes provision for property adjustments and other ancillary orders, which also could be determined in public and reported, while preserving the anonymity of the parties. As the Law Reform Commission noted in its *Consultation Paper on Contempt*[43]: 'If the principle of open justice is to be given full effect it should not be subject to limitations unless they are essential in the interests of justice.'

2. Reporting Restrictions

A number of statutes impose reporting restrictions on the media. The Defamation Act 1961, section 18, on the other hand, confers a privilege in respect of fair and accurate reports of court proceedings held in public, provided the reports are published contemporaneously, i.e. while the court hearing is taking place or immediately after its completion. The privilege is therefore a useful one for newspapers and broadcasters but, because of the requirement of contemporaneity, is of little benefit to book publishers, video or film makers or other media.[44] Moreover, the privilege does not extend to the publication or broadcasting of any 'blasphemous or obscene matter' (section 18(2)), the concern being to protect public morals.

This concern for the protection of public morals even in the context of court reporting can be seen, in particular, in the Censorship of Publications Act 1929. Part III of that Act is headed 'Reports of Judicial Proceedings' and provides at section 14:

1. It shall not be lawful to print or publish or cause or procure to be printed or published in relation to any judicial proceedings—

   (a) any indecent matter the publication of which would be calculated to injure public morals, or

   (b) any indecent medical, surgical or physiological details the publication of which would be calculated to injure public morals.

Subsection 2 makes it unlawful to print or publish or cause or procure to be printed or published any report, statement, commentary or other matter of or in relation to any judicial proceedings for divorce, nullity of marriage or judicial separation, other than the names and addresses of the parties and witnesses, names of court, judge and lawyers, a concise statement of the charges, defences, points of law raised and outcome. The section does not apply to the reporting of cases in the official law reports or legal or medical publications (section 14(3)).[45] This section may reflect the moral standards of its time but it is now outdated and largely academic because the courts usually exclude the press from this type of proceeding anyway, thus making it impossible for them to report even to the very limited extent envisaged in the section.[46] Nonetheless, breach of the section, if it should occur, is an offence. It applies to the proprietor, editor, publisher or printer of any book or periodical and can lead to a maximum fine of £500 or six month's imprisonment or both. It does not apply to broadcasts. A prosecution must be brought by the DPP but there appears to have been only one prosecution under the section, that being in 1971 when six national newspapers were fined a total of over £23,000 for publishing details of a 'divorce *a mensa et thoro*' case (literally, divorce from bed and board, i.e. separation).[47]

Several statutes contain provisions preventing publication of any material that would identify the parties. The Criminal Law (Rape) Acts 1981–90 prohibit the publication of any matter likely to lead members of the public to identify the victim or accused, unless or until convicted, or under direction of the court. Even on conviction, the person may not be named if to do so would identify the victim (1990 Act, section 8(2)). As anonymity must be maintained, photographs may not be published. With regard to criminal proceedings, the Criminal Procedure Act 1967, section 17(2), provides that:

> No person shall publish or cause to be published any information as to any particular preliminary examination other than a statement of fact that such examination in relation to a named person on a specified charge has been held and of the decision thereon,

unless the judge permits it at the request of the accused. The purpose of the restriction is undoubtedly to protect the accused and ensure his/her right to a fair trial. However, it could be argued that it is phrased in very broad terms and is overly restrictive in its reach. In practice, the section is constantly breached, not necessarily in a prejudicial manner but certainly in a technical sense.[48] The Law Reform Commission, however, has recommended no change.[49] Whatever the legal restrictions, the key in both cases is not to cause prejudice to the accused's right to a fair trial. The answer to this and other reporting problems is for the courts to facilitate journalists, by clarifying the nature of the proceedings and giving them access to charge sheets, for example, as recommended by the Law Reform Commission.[50]

It may be noted that the Special Criminal Court, as a special court, is governed by Article 38 of the Constitution, not Article 34, as is the case with the regular courts. Its rules provide that it shall be an open court 'subject to such conditions as the court may from time to time impose', but that the court may impose restrictions on reporting in order to protect witnesses.[51]

Difficulties for reporters can also arise when there is a 'trial within a trial', that is, when the jury is asked to leave the court while counsel argue a particular issue. The press may be excluded also or may be allowed to remain in court but ordered not to report. This can lead to practical difficulties for them, because there is generally a pool or rota of court reporters, as it would be too expensive for each organisation to have its own reporters in court every day. A case may be adjourned during the argument in the absence of the jury and a reporter on duty on the next occasion the court is sitting may not realise that he/she is not entitled to report. Again, an acknowledgment of the presence of reporters and an appreciation of their function and the courts' interest in the accuracy of reports would suggest that the nature of the proceedings should be made clear.

3. Access to Evidence

Court reporters are usually known to court officials and are often facilitated in an informal way with regard to information concerning cases. However, there is no formal recognition of the reporter's role and no specific right of access to court documents. In *Home Office v Harmon*[52] a solicitor was held to be in contempt of court for showing documents to a reporter after they had been read in open court. The House of Lords held, by a majority, that the journalist could not be assisted by direct access to the documents themselves. A complaint was lodged with the European Commission on Human Rights in Strasbourg, which found a *prima facie* breach of Article 10 of the Convention, which protects freedom of expression.[53] A friendly settlement was reached with the UK government and now Rules of Court except documents read or referred to in open court. They do not, however, recognise any positive rights of journalists.

In Ireland it has been recommended, by the Law Reform Commission, as previously noted, that reporters should have access to charge sheets. The position regarding other documents is less clear. It has been held by the Supreme Court in *In re* R[54] that a stipulation that 'proceedings' be held *in camera* includes the pleadings, affidavits, exhibits, as well as oral testimony and the judgment in the case. It is also the case that, unlike the UK, there is no 'warned list' here, alerting the media to the fact that particular cases have been referred to the court and are coming up for hearing. In some jurisdictions, as already noted, the solution has been to appoint a media liaison officer to take media enquiries and provide necessary information on the workings of the courts (see discussion in Chapter 6).

4. *Forms of Reporting*

At present cameras are not permitted in court, although the Law Reform Commission has recommended that the possibility be considered.[55] Cameras were allowed into the Supreme Court for the first time for the opening of the argument on the abortion information bill 1995.[56]

The use of tape recorders, video recorders, television cameras or the taking of photographs in court is not regulated by statute in this jurisdiction. The practice has been to allow reporters to take notes and designated artists to sketch, but the courts have not been prepared to allow anything more than that[57] although, as the Law Reform Commission[58] says, the courts have inherent jurisdiction to regulate their own procedure. Considerations include whether use of recorders or cameras would cause interference with court proceedings, whether they would intimidate witnesses, invade their privacy or be used out of court for other purposes, such as to coach future witnesses. It may be argued that all of these evils can be regulated. Reporters at present are not entitled to report everything that is said. In some cases, as we have seen, they are excluded from the court altogether, in others limitations are imposed on what they can report. Journalists and broadcasters maintain that there is no difference between editing on paper and editing on film.[59]

In support of audio or visual recordings, it can be said that they would enhance accuracy in reporting and reduce the potential for disputes as to whether proceedings were accurately reported.[60] It is also likely, as the technology develops and the public becomes more of a participant in the media, that many of the fears expressed at present, such as the fear of the effects on witnesses, will disappear. Many of the misgivings felt by members of the Dáil and Seanad about the televising of proceedings in the Houses of the Oireachtas have proven unfounded. It is probable that the tight restrictions imposed at present will gradually be relaxed as members and viewers become more accustomed to the coverage.

In England, the Contempt of Court Act 1981, section 9, forbids the use of tape recorders except by leave of the court. Practice Directions have indicated that there is no objection to the use of tape recorders in court in principle and that use by the media should be given sympathetic consideration.[61] The tape cannot, however, be broadcast (section 9(1)(b)). Unauthorised use can result in contempt of court and forfeiture of machine and tapes (section 9(3)). Televising the courts is effectively precluded by the Criminal Justice Act 1925, section 41, but the General Council of the Bar is in favour of television broadcasting.[62] Nevertheless, fears have been expressed in various quarters that only notorious criminal trials would be broadcast and that editing would result in sensationalism and distortion. However, as Robertson and Nicol[63] point out, 'present television news reporting, in sixty-second "slots" with breathless presenters pictured outside court quoting snatches of evidence, sometimes over inaccurate "artists" impressions' of the courtroom is of minimal value'.

Dramatic reconstructions of courtroom scenes and docudramas are not covered by legislation but may be suspect on contempt grounds if transmitted during the proceedings. It is difficult to envisage what kind of prejudice could result when the programme obviously involves actors and dramatic techniques. As audiences can clearly differentiate between news and documentaries on the one hand and pure entertainment or dramatic portrayal on the other, it would seem appropriate to assess any possible threat to the courts in the context of the particular medium or programme format.[64] Contrary to popular belief, experience of televising court cases in the United States has not been all negative. Bar associations, initially hostile to the whole idea, report that lawyers are better prepared, judges better behaved and the public better informed as a result of cameras in court.[65]

Reporting Tribunals

Tribunals established by statute are open to the public but may be authorised by statute to hold sittings or part of sittings in private. The Industrial Relations Act 1946, which established the Labour Court, provides that the court 'may hold any sitting or part of a sitting in private' (section 20(7)). The 1969 Act is more confined: an investigation of a trade dispute shall be conducted in private unless otherwise requested by a party to the dispute (section 8(1)), in which case any part of the investigation dealing with the matter that should, in the interests of a party to the dispute be treated as confidential, may be conducted in private (section 8(2)). An investigation by a rights commissioner shall be conducted in private (section 13(8)), as shall an appeal to the court from the commissioner's decision (section 13(9)). The provision for private hearings under the Industrial Relations Acts is therefore very wide.

Tribunals of Inquiry are open to the public unless the Tribunal itself is of the opinion that it is in the public interest to exclude them because of the subject matter of the inquiry or the nature of the evidence (Tribunals of Inquiry (Evidence) Act 1921, section 2). It appears somewhat incongruous to think of a public tribunal of inquiry excluding the public, but it is conceivable in an inquiry such as the Cleveland Child Sex Abuse Inquiry or Kerry Babies Tribunal that the public could be excluded on the grounds of individual privacy. Whether individual privacy would equate with the public interest, which is the only ground in the Act for exclusion, is another matter.

Inquests, which are carried out in accordance with the Coroners Act 1962, are limited in terms of what they can do and the verdict they can bring in. Questions of civil or criminal liability cannot be considered or investigated; the inquest is confined to ascertaining the identity of the person, and how, when and where death occurred (section 30), although the Coroners (Amendment) Bill (No. 12 of 1995), if enacted, will allow a verdict of suicide to be brought in. There must be no note of censure or exoneration, although recommendations of a general character may be made where designed to prevent further fatalities (section 31). The Act does, however, give the coroner very wide discretionary powers in conducting inquests. He/she can decide to sit with or without a jury 'as he thinks proper', unless the manner of death brings it within certain specified categories, for example, murder, infanticide, manslaughter (section 39). There is a right of access to documents but it only accrues after the inquest (section 29(3)), whereas it would be much more useful to all concerned to have information before the inquest as to witnesses to be called, evidence to be given and so forth.

The Defamation Act 1961 (section 24 and Second Schedule) confers a qualified privilege on fair and accurate reports of tribunals of inquiry in foreign states or of any judicial or arbitral tribunal deciding matters in dispute between States. Fair and accurate reports of proceedings at any public meeting or sitting of judicial authorities, other than courts, and of any commission, tribunal, committee, or statutory inquiry, within the State or Northern Ireland are privileged, subject to explanation or contradiction. (For further discussion, see Chapter 4.)

Reporting Parliament

The right to report parliament was hard won but, once established, became an important part of the media apparatus (see Chapter 3). Parliamentary reports became a significant feature of newspaper content. It was in respect of parliament that the principle of free speech was first recognised and members given immunity for what they said there.[66] The right of journalists to be present and report on what was said and done took longer to be recognised. However, both parliamentary privilege and the right to report are enshrined in Article 15.12 of the Irish Constitution:

> All official reports and publications of the Oireachtas or of either House thereof and utterances made in either House wherever published shall be privileged.

The Article does not declare a right to report as such but does establish that all official reports and publications wherever published shall be privileged, as will any utterances made in either House. The Irish language version makes clear that publications and utterances each attract a privilege: 'Gach tuarascáil agus foilseachán oifigiúil . . . maille le caint ar bith dá ndéantar', i.e. all official reports and publications . . . as well as 'any' utterances. They are privileged wherever published, including in the mass media, and there may not be a suit or prosecution for publishing them ('táid saor ar chúrsa' dl''). The privilege may, therefore, be wider than had previously been believed and may offer more scope to the media. For instance, the privilege is wide enough to extend to book publishers, as there is no requirement of contemporaneity such as there is in the case of court reports (Defamation Act, section 18). The Law Reform Commission however, regarded the law as uncertain and recommended that there be an express statutory defence for fair and accurate reports published contemporaneously or within a reasonable time after the proceedings.[67] The Commission also pointed out that the reference to 'utterances' would seem to exclude written statements, which are not actually read out.[68] Additionally, the Constitution does not distinguish between absolute and qualified privilege. It is to be assumed, therefore, that the privilege in Article 15.12 is absolute, given that the Defamation Act, section 24 and Schedule 2, Part 1, make provision for a qualified privilege in respect of fair and accurate reports of the proceedings of foreign legislatures. The Constitution further provides that sittings of both houses shall be in public (Article 15.8.1), except in cases of special emergency, with the assent of two-thirds of the members present (Article 15.8.2).

Utterances made in parliamentary committees are also privileged by virtue of the Committees of the Houses of the Oireachtas (Privilege and Procedure) Act 1976, section 2, which confers privilege on members of either house in respect of any utterance made in or before a committee, as well as documents of the committee or its members, all official reports and publications of the committee and utterances made in committee by members, advisers, officials and agents of the committee, wherever published. A doubt as to whether the privilege extended to witnesses was removed in relation to one committee in 1994 by the Select Committee on Legislation and Security of Dáil Eireann (Privilege and Immunity) Act 1994 and further legislation is expected.[69]

The televising of the Dáil was agreed in principle in 1988,[70] after a successful period of radio broadcasting and shortly after a similar decision in Britain to televise the House of Commons.[71] The rules governing the televising of the Dáil were drawn up by an all-party committee and approved by the Dáil itself. The rules included a ban on showing close-ups of official documents and a 'recommendation' against showing wide shots of the chamber when it was relatively empty. They also included a requirement to focus on the Ceann Comhairle when he was speaking and whenever there were scenes 'of disorder or unparliamentary behaviour'.[72]

In New Zealand, the government in 1991 floated a proposal to charge the media for their accommodation in the press gallery from where they report parliament. In so doing, the government was signalling that use of the parliamentary galleries was not a right but a service for which payment could be demanded and ultimately denied altogether. Representations were made by the media and the proposal was abandoned.[73]

Reporting Local Government

The right of the media to attend and report on meetings of local authorities is more recent than that of parliament. It is governed by the

Local Government (Ireland) Act 1902, section 15.[74] Section 15 of the 1902 Act states:

> No resolution of any council, board or commissioners to exclude from its meetings representatives of the press shall be valid unless sanctioned by the Local Government Board in pursuance of by-laws which the Local Government Board are hereby empowered to frame, regulating the admission of the representatives of the press to such meetings.

This was followed in 1903 by an Order of the Local Government Board which merely provided for the admission of members of the press on production of a document signed by the newspaper proprietor or editor (now a press card), stating that the person seeking admission was a representative of the press. It also reiterated that any decision of a council, board or commissioners to exclude the press would, if sanctioned by the Local Government Board (now the Minister for the Environment), be valid, although it did not stipulate on what basis such exclusion might be sanctioned.[75]

The most effective way for a local authority to exclude the press in practice is by deciding to go into committee (Local Government Act 1955, section 60). The Minister for the Environment has the power to regulate meetings and procedures, but the power does not seem to have been used (section 61(1)). Local authorities can make their own standing orders; most have done so and revise them from time to time (section 62). They can do so unless there are special procedures laid down by statute. There is not thought to be any great impediment to journalists in reporting local authority meetings but if a decision is taken to go into committee and exclude the press, without any apparent justification, journalists present should ask to be allowed to stay or to know what interest it is sought to protect in excluding them. It is not satisfactory to be excluded without good reason and to have to rely on set pieces or what individual councillors may be willing to disclose afterwards. In Britain, under the Public Bodies (Admission to Meetings) Act 1960, the public has to be admitted to committee meetings in so far as is practicable and must not be deliberately excluded by the physical size of the room being used or other such devices. When certain defined categories of confidential information are involved, committees may sit in private.

There is no general right to inspect documents of local authorities, only limited rights under specific statutes. For example, the Local Government (Planning and Development) Act 1963, section 8, obliges a planning authority to keep a register and make it available for inspection during office hours. Certain particulars as to information that must be included in the register are set out in the Act (section 37(8),(9), section 38(4), section 41, sections 44–7). It is further stipulated that regulations may be made to provide for the public to purchase printed copies of development plans (section 19(8)). For example, the Local Government (Sanitary Services) Act 1964, section 3(8)(c), obliges a sanitary authority to keep and make available for inspection at all reasonable times a register containing particulars of all orders made. Notice of intention to enter into a water agreement must be published in a newspaper circulating in the district (section 4(6)). The Local Government (Application of Enactments) Order 1898 conferred a limited right on persons on the electoral register to inspect the books of audits under the control of their local authority.

The Environmental Protection Agency Act 1992, section 110, provides that the Minister for the Environment shall, following consultation with any other government minister concerned, make regulations for public authorities to make available to any person on request specified information relating to the environment. The EC (Environmental Impact Assessment) Regulations 1989, section 7, which amend section 25 of the 1963 Act, make provision for the availability for purchase of copies of environmental impact statements. The cost involved can be prohibitive for local environmental groups and therefore a negation of the openness principle. In order to give effect to EC Directive 90/313, the Minister made regulations in 1993.[76] However, access to information is limited, and the exceptions whereby information can be withheld extensive.[77]

Freedom of Information Legislation

The hopes of environmental groups and journalists alike rest with the prospect of freedom of information legislation being enacted in the near future. A bill is in preparation and is intended to be introduced in the Oireachtas early in 1996.[78] The bill is expected to draw on the experience in Australia and New Zealand, where freedom of information legislation was introduced in 1982. Key factors in the bill will be the range of official information covered, the extent of the exceptions, the right of access, including time and cost, and a review process.[79]

In Britain there is no Freedom of Information Act but there is specific legislation such as the Local Government (Access to Information) Act 1985. Also in Britain a not inconsiderable threat to journalists has been removed by the court decision in *Times v Derbyshire County Council*,[80] which established that a local authority can no longer sue for libel in respect of its governmental and administrative functions. In Ireland the situation is uncertain, but because the number of actions taken by local authorities and such bodies is few, the Law Reform Commission doubted if there was any need for law reform. For the avoidance of doubt, the Commission said, there should be a statutory provision that all corporate bodies have a cause of action.[81] It is to be hoped that in the light of the *Derbyshire case*, the Commission's proposal will not be enacted.

It should be noted that the Defamation Act 1961, section 24 and Schedule 2, make provision for a qualified privilege for a fair and accurate copy of or extract from any register kept in pursuance of any law which is open to inspection by the public or of any other document which is required by law to be open to inspection by the public. A similar privilege, subject to explanation or contradiction, attaches to a fair and accurate report or summary of any notice or other matter issued for the information of the public by, or on behalf of, any government department, local authority or the Commissioner of the Garda Síochána, or their counterparts in Northern Ireland.

Further Reading

Michael, James, 'Open Justice: Publicity and the Judicial Process' (1993) 46 CLP 190.

Notes

1 See Walsh J. in *In re* R [1989] IR 126, at p. 134.
2 See Carney J. in DPP *v* WM, unreported, High Court, 1 February 1995.
3 Ibid.
4 See ACC *v* *Irish Business*, *The Irish Times*, 10 September 1985.
5 Ibid.
6 [1995] ILRM 108. The Supreme Court also rejected an application for an *in camera* hearing, because of the momentous issues of great public concern involved, in a case of withdrawal of a life-support system from a woman in a near-vegetative state, *The Irish Times*, 15 June 1995.
7 *The Irish Times*, 25 February 1992.
8 [1990] ILRM 70, at pp 78–9.
9 The media also made a submission in connection with *In re* R to have the hearing held in open court but were refused. More recently, the interventions in *Maguire v Drury* (the case of the man who was threatening to sue the Catholic Church over an alleged relationship between his wife and a priest) and in the case of the book *Bless Me Father* were more successful. (See the discussion later in this chapter and chapter 6.)
10 [1987] ILRM 477.
11 See Marie McGonagle, 'Freedom of Expression and Information' *Irish Human Rights Yearbook*, Dublin: Roundhall Sweet and Maxwell, 1995, p. 31.

12 For a discussion of the terminology used, see J.M. Kelly, *The Irish Constitution*, 3rd edn., Gerard Hogan and Gerry Whyte, eds, Dublin: Butterworths, 1994, at p. 403 and Tom O'Malley, The Criminal Law (Incest Proceedings) Act 1995, *Irish Law Statutes Annotated*, Dublin: Sweet and Maxwell, 1995.

13 The only other option open to them would seem to be to take a High Court action challenging the constitutionality of the legislative provision. *Locus standi* would be required, and there is also a presumption of constitutionality that applies to all post-1937 legislation passed by the Oireachtas, so the task would be an uphill one.

14 *The Irish Times*, 8 July 1994.

15 *The Irish Times*, 7 July 1994

16 *The Irish Times*, 2 June 1994.

17 [1995] ILRM 108, at pp 114–15.

18 See J.P. Casey, *Constitutional Law in Ireland*, 2nd edn., London: Sweet and Maxwell, 1992, at p. 225.

19 Law Reform Commission, *Consultation Paper on Family Courts*, 1994, at para. 7.44.

20 Ibid., at para. 7.43.

21 Ibid., at para. 7.45.

22 See William Duncan and Paula Scully, *Marriage Breakdown in Ireland: Law and Practice*, Dublin: Butterworths, 1990, at para. 18.024.

23 See Alan Shatter, *Family Law in the Republic of Ireland*, 3rd edn., Dublin: Wolfhound Press, 1986, at p. 51; *The Irish Times*, 4 July 1994.

24 Rule 17 of the Circuit Court Rules, No. 6, 1982.

25 [1976] IR 382.

26 *Irish Press*, 22 January 1992.

27 [1989] IR 126.

28 *The Irish Times*, 15 October 1988.

29 Ibid.

30 *The Irish Times*, 15 June 1993, [1993] ILRM 747, *per* Finlay C.J. at 754.

31 *The Irish Times*, 19 September 1990.

32 [1995] 1 ILRM 213.

33 Ibid., at p. 215.

34 Ibid., at p. 217. See also *Brennan v Minister for Justice* (unreported, High Court, 28 April 1995, Geoghegan J., pp 19–20 of typescript). Note also that the Defamation Act 1961, section 18(1), provides a privilege for fair and accurate reports of court proceedings where the court is exercising 'judicial authority'.

35 *The Irish Times*, 7 December 1987.

36 See Kelly, n. 12, at footnote 32, p. 403.

37 For a discussion of publicity of judicial proceedings, see Law Reform Commission, *Consultation Paper on Contempt*, 1991, at pp 343–50.

38 *The Irish Times*, 28 May 1993.

39 [1992] 1 IR 1; [1992] ILRM 401.

40 ITLR 13 March 1995.

41 Ibid.

42 For example, n. 19, re: Canada, at para. 4.74.

43 See n. 37 at p. 248.

44 The Defamation Act, section 2, defines 'newspaper' as 'any paper containing public news or observations thereon, or consisting wholly or mainly of advertisements, which is printed for sale and is published in the State or in Northern Ireland whether periodically or in parts or numbers at intervals not exceeding thirty-six days.

45 Cf. Judicial Proceedings (Regulation of Reports) Act 1926, s. 1(1)(b), which is the corresponding British legislation.

46 See n. 22, at para. 18.026.

47 See n. 23 at p. 54.

48 This section is rarely invoked against the media.

49 See the discussion in n. 37, *Paper*, at pp 343–7, and *Report on Contempt of Court* (LRC 47–1994) at para. 6.37.

50 Law Reform Commission *Consultation Paper on the Civil Law of Defamation*, 1991, at para. 256.
51 Cf. Criminal Law (Jurisdiction) Act 1976, ss 7(3), and 17(1).
52 [1982] 1 All ER 532 HL.
53 *Harman v UK*, Eur Comm HR (1984) 38 Decisions and Reports 53.
54. [1989] IR 126, *per* Finlay C.J. at p. 131 and Walsh J., at p. 136.
55 See n. 49 *Report*, at paras 4. 45–49.
56 *The Irish Times*, 5 April 1995, The President, under the power conferred on her by Article 26 of the Constitution, referred the Bill to the Supreme Court to test its constitutionality. The Regulation of Information (Services outside the State for Termination of Pregnancies) Bill 1995 was found to be constitutional. *In the matter of Article 26 of the Constitution and in the matter of the reference to the court of the Regulation of Information (Services Outside the State for Termination of Pregnancies) Bill 1995* [1995] 2 ILRM 81.
57 Compare the situation in the UK where the Criminal Justice Act 1925, s. 41, prohibits the taking of photographs or the making with a view to publication of a sketch in the court or its precincts.
58 See n. 37 at pp 8–9.
59 Coverage can be subject to rules and supervision; see Geoffrey Robertson, *Freedom, the Individual and the Law*, 7th edn., London: Penguin Books, 1993, 347.
60 See n. 37 at p. 248–55.
61 See Geoffrey Robertson and Andrew Nicol, *Media Law*, 3rd edn., London: Penguin Books, 1992, at p. 352.
62 See Public Affairs Committee of the General Council of the Bar, *Televising the Courts* 1989; Brian McConnell, 'Cameras in Court' (1990) 140 NLJ 1622. Cameras have been permitted in certain of the Scottish courts since 1993.
63 See n. 61, at p. 362.
64 See Cunningham, 'The Maxwell Musical: a Contempt of Court or the Mere Exercise of the Right to Free Speech' [1994] 2 ENT LR 65; see also chapter 6.
65 See n. 59, at 346; n. 62, Public Affairs Committee, at para. 4.1.
66 For an historical analysis, see *Dillon v Balfour* (1887) 20 LR Ir 600. For a recent examination of the scope of that privilege, see *Goodman International v Hamilton (No.1)* [1992] 2 IR 542, [1992] ILRM 145; *(No.2)* [1993] 3 IR 307; *(No.3)* [1993] 3 IR 320.
67 See n. 49, *Report*, at para. 6.26.
68 See n. 50, at para. 96
69 In the investigation by the Committee on Legislation and Security in 1994 into delays in processing sexual abuse cases involving a priest and into what the Taoiseach and government ministers had told the Dáil about the matter, the Attorney General, Eoin Fitzsimons, required privilege before testifying. A bill to clarify privilege before Committees of the Oireachtas was introduced in the Dáil in November 1995: the Committees of the Houses of the Oireachtas (Compellability, Privileges and Immunities of Witnesses) Bill (No. 45 of 1995).
70 *The Irish Times*, 18 May 1988.
71 Television broadcasts of the Commons began as an experiment in November 1989, just a couple of months before the Dáil. *The Irish Times*, 21 November 1989.
72 See *The Irish Times*, 22 October 1990, 26 January 1991.
73 Karl du Fresne, *Free Press, Free Society*, Newspaper Publishers Association of New Zealand, 1994.
74 There is no equivalent in Ireland of the British Local Authorities (Admission of the Press to Meetings) Act 1908, Public Bodies (Admission to Meetings) Act 1960 or subsequent acts such as the Local Government Act 1972, Local Government (Access to Information) Act 1985, Health Service Joint Consultative Committees (Access to Information) Act 1986, Community Health Councils (Access to Information) Act 1988.
75 See, generally, Richard Woulfe, 'Local Authorities and the Press', *The Media and the Law*, Incorporated Law Society seminar, Dublin, 1985.
76 The EC Directive No. 90/313/EEC (O.J. No. L158/56, 23 June 1990) came into force on 1 January 1993, and the Minister made regulations, Access to Information on the

Environment Regulations 1993 (No. 133 of 1993), bringing it into effect. *The Irish Times,* 21 May 1993, 31 May 1993.

77 See *The Irish Times,* 13 December 1994. Information may be refused if it affects international relations, national security, if the matter is *sub judice* or the subject of an inquiry or investigation. It may be refused also if it involves the confidentiality of the deliberations or proceedings of public authorities, or commercial and industrial confidentiality. Most far-reaching is the right to refuse information where a study or report is incomplete or in preliminary or draft form (No. 133 of 1993, s. 6(1)). New regulations are expected. Re EU, see *Carvel v Council of* EU case 7-194/94 ECJ, 19 October 1995.

78 The heads of the Bill were approved by Cabinet on 5 December 1995. See *The Irish Times,* 7 December 1995 and 12 December 1995.

79 See further Ronan Brady, 'As Transparent as Glass?' in Marie McGonagle, ed., *Essays on Law and Media,* Dublin: The Round Hall Press (forthcoming).

80 [1993] 2 WLR 449.

81 See n. 50, at paras 12.19 – 20.

CHAPTER EIGHT

Public Order and Morality

The Constitution and International Instruments

The primary concerns of Article 40.6.1.i of the Irish Constitution are public order and morality. The central value guaranteed by the Article may well be freedom of expression but the emphasis is very much on the importance of maintaining and safeguarding public order and morality. Even before the right itself is mentioned, there is a warning that it will only be available subject to public order and morality:

> The State guarantees . . . subject to public order and morality . . .

Then in the reference to the 'rightful liberty of expression' of the organs of public opinion (the media), the State is required to ensure that:

> . . . organs of public opinion . . . shall not be used to undermine public order or morality . . .

In addition, a tailpiece to Article 40.6.1.i specifies that certain types of publication constitute an offence:

> The publication or utterance of blasphemous, seditious or indecent matter is an offence which shall be punishable in accordance with law.

While the formulation of the Article is clumsy and repetitive, there is no doubt but that it gives prominence to public order and morality.[1] In fact it treats them almost as a unit, and there are indeed various areas of overlap. Historically, when the burning concern was to prevent criticism of State institutions, including the established church, public order and morality were often interwoven. So, too, was the area of sedition and seditious publications. In fact, the tailpiece to Article 40.6.1.i of the Constitution represents the historical position.

It is also the case that there is a considerable overlap between public order, sedition and 'the authority of the State', which is an additional area of restriction on the freedom of the press and organs of public opinion, specified in Article 40.6.1.i of the Constitution. 'The authority of the State' will be the subject of discussion in Chapter 10. Chapter 9 will deal with morality. The present chapter concentrates on restrictions imposed on the media in the interests of public order and may, therefore, be taken in conjunction with both Chapters 9 and 10.

The maintenance of public order is seen as a legitimate reason for limiting freedom of expression, not only in Ireland but in the international human rights instruments also. For example, Article 10.2 of the European Convention specifically includes 'the prevention of disorder or crime' among the areas of restriction. Under the Convention, however, only those measures that are prescribed by law and necessary in a democratic society may be invoked to restrict the central right which is freedom of expression. Public order is also recognised as a legitimate basis for restriction in Article 19 of the Covenant on Civil and Political Rights. The expression 'public order' (*ordre public*) as used in the Covenant may be defined as

> the sum of rules which ensure the functioning of society or the set of fundamental principles on which society is founded. Respect for human rights is part of public order (*ordre public*).[2]

It is therefore very broad and could be said to be the source of legitimacy for a variety of restrictions imposed on the media, including those imposed in the interests of reputation by defamation law.[3] That is the case in other European countries where defamation is part of the criminal law because of its public order element, in the broad sense.[4] In the international human rights instruments, however, protection of the reputation and rights of others is usually given separate recognition. In the Irish Constitution, Article 40.6.1.i does not specifically mention reputation but the fact that Article 40.3.2 mentions good name has generally been relied on as the source of the right and the constitutional basis for defamation law. Since defamation law is almost exclusively part of the civil law in Ireland, it was dealt with separately in Chapter 4. The residual aspect of defamation, which still forms part of the criminal law, will be discussed below.

Restrictions in the Interests of Public Order

In Ireland the restrictions imposed on the media in the interests of public order, in the narrower sense of the phrase, of preventing disorder, may be divided into three main categories: general criminal-law sanctions, statutory restrictions and specific media-oriented restrictions.

The first category, general sanctions of the criminal law, comprises such crimes as those relating to libel, incitement, conspiracy and unlawful assembly. These are not specifically directed at the media but may apply to the media as to anyone else.

The second category consists of restrictions imposed by statute. For example, a number of statutes like the Offences against the Person Act 1861 and Malicious Damage Act 1861 contain provisions that make it an offence to send letters threatening murder and malicious damage, respectively. Again these are of general application and are not directly or necessarily media-related. Similarly, the Prohibition of Forcible Entry and Occupation Act 1971, section 4, was intended to prevent the encouragement of squatting and although it is generally applicable, it was specifically aimed at the activities of a newspaper at the time. The Criminal Law Act 1976 made it an offence to join or take part in, support or assist the activities of an unlawful organisation.[5]

A more recent example is the Prohibition of Incitement to Hatred Act 1989, which makes it an offence to publish or distribute written material or show or play a recording of visual images or sounds that are threatening, abusive or insulting and are intended, or likely, to stir up hatred. The Criminal Damage Act 1991, section 3, makes it an offence in certain circumstances to threaten to damage property and the Criminal Justice (Public Order) Act 1994, sections 6 and 7, deals with threatening, abusive or insulting behaviour with intent or recklessness to provoke a breach of the peace and the distribution or display in public of threatening, abusive, insulting or obscene material.[6]

The third category consists of those restrictions directly aimed at the media, for example, public order provisions in the Wireless Telegraphy Act 1926, section 11, and in the Broadcasting Authority Acts 1960 - 93. The former makes it an offence to transmit any message or communication subversive of public order. The latter prohibit the broadcasting of anything likely to promote or incite to crime and require the broadcasting authority to be mindful of the need for understanding and peace in the whole island.[7]

Of the generally applicable laws, the one that had most implications for the media historically but less so today is the common-law offence of criminal libel, which has been given statutory recognition and been somewhat modified in relation to the media by Part II of the Defamation Act 1961.[8] Part II of the Act contains specific references to newspapers but makes no reference to broadcasting. In fact Part II is not made to apply to broadcasting at all. Whether this was deliberate policy on the part of the legislators or simply an oversight is not clear.[9] In any event, the statutory provisions and safeguards for newspapers do not apply to broadcasting, which would, therefore, it seems be governed by common-law rules. There does not appear to be any plausible reason for differentiating between broadcasting and the print media in this way.[10] However, because the situation has become so rare, it is no longer considered a threat by the media.

Originally intended to protect the government of the day from harmful criticism, criminal libel developed to take several different forms: blasphemous libel, seditious libel, obscene libel and, finally, defamatory libel, where there was the threat or likelihood of a breach of the peace. Prosecutions for criminal libel in this last form became an effective deterrent to duelling to protect one's honour. It was introduced by the Star Chamber as a measure to suppress duelling and to promote public peace and order.[11] It also became an effective weapon for curtailing the excesses of the press.

Prosecutions for criminal libel in any of its forms are very rare nowadays.[12] In recent years there have been only two applications to prosecute newspapers and both have failed. The first in 1976 was brought against the *Irish Independent* by Eddie Gallagher, jailed for his part in the Dr Herrema kidnapping.[13] The second in 1990 arose out of a piece in the *Phoenix* magazine, in which it was alleged that the Rev. Stephen Hilliard, a Church of Ireland Rector who had been killed by an intruder in his home, had been involved many years earlier in IRA activities.[14] The judgment of Gannon J. in the High Court was instructive. His analysis of the common-law rules, the statutory provisions and the anomalies they contain present a challenge to the legislature to repeal the provisions of the 1961 Act or introduce amending legislation.[15] In the first case of criminal libel in Northern Ireland in 1993, *Monteith v McPhilemy and Others*, an application to prosecute the producer of a controversial television programme which alleged collusion between RUC officers and loyalist death squads was also refused.[16]

The Law Reform Commission in its *Consultation Paper on the Crime of Libel* (as they preferred to call criminal libel to avoid confusion in the public mind) concluded that the offence in its present condition is highly unacceptable:

> It runs contrary to many modern principles of criminal liability and fair trial, and threatens freedom of speech to a high degree, in theory if not in practice, so long as it continues to exist in its present state.[17]

The Commission did not, however, recommend abolishing the offence altogether. Its use in a recent case, the Commission argued, demonstrated that 'its abolition would deprive the criminal law of a valuable weapon'. It was felt that this form of criminal procedure might still have a useful, although limited, function.[18] The Commission's argument does not take account, however, of the various statutory measures available. Those measures have since been augmented by the Criminal Justice (Public Order) Act 1994, sections 6 and 7. The case to which the Commission referred, DPP *v Fleming*,[19] in which Fleming was convicted for writing graffiti about a woman on telephone boxes all around Ireland, could probably now be prosecuted under the 1994 Act. The Act extends to the distribution or display in public of threatening, abusive, insulting or obscene material, with an intention (or recklessness) to cause a breach of the peace.[20]

From the point of view of the media, the recent case of *Hilliard v Penfield Enterprises*[21] illustrates all the elements of the crime, the difficulties and anomalies. *The Phoenix* magazine published what purported to be an account of the funeral of the Rev. Stephen Hilliard, a former *Irish Times* journalist, who had become a Church of Ireland Rector and been killed by an intruder in his home in January 1990. *The Phoenix* made a number of allegations about the deceased's having been involved in criminal activities of a subversive nature many years previously. Gannon J.[22] described it thus:

> It is difficult to believe that . . . the . . . respondents [i.e. the editor, proprietor and publisher of *The Phoenix*] could stoop so low as to present or adopt such a mean, spiteful and wounding attack upon a deceased under the guise of a commentary on his funeral. . . . It would be impossible to describe a libel which accuses a person of having been twenty years ago an intelligence officer for the IRA and of providing contacts to lead to massive bank robberies, or of setting fire to houses and cars on behalf of the IRA as being of a trivial character . . . it can only be described as most serious . . . .

Mrs Hilliard, the wife of the deceased, applied to the High Court, pursuant to section 8 of the Defamation Act, for an order to bring a prosecution against *The Phoenix*. Section 8 states:

> No criminal prosecution shall be commenced against any proprietor, publisher, editor or any person responsible for the publication of a newspaper for any libel published therein without the order of a Judge of the High Court sitting *in camera* being first had and obtained, and every application for such order shall be made on notice to the person accused, who shall have an opportunity of being heard against the application.

The Phoenix qualified as a newspaper under the definition given in the Defamation Act 1961. Gannon J. considered the application on the basis of principles laid down by Wien J. in *Goldsmith v Pressdram*,[23] which had been approved by Finlay P. in the 1978 application of Eddie Gallagher (not circulated). Those principles are:

(i)   there must be a clear *prima facie* case
(ii) the libel must be a serious one, so serious that it is proper for the criminal law to be invoked
(iii) a likelihood of a breach of the peace is not necessary, though it may be relevant[24]
(iv) the judge must ask himself whether the public interest *requires* the institution of criminal proceedings.

In H*illiard*, Gannon J. found that a *prima facie* case could be made out. On the question of seriousness, the test is the likely effect of the publication on a significant section of law-abiding citizens. Furthermore, it is the damage to the good name and repute of the vilified party in the esteem of other people that is important and not self-esteem.[25] A tendency to cause a breach of the peace would signal the seriousness of the libel but proof of the existence of such a tendency is no longer necessary. If such a tendency does exist, it may be relevant. If it does not, it is of no great significance.[26] Because a clear *prima facie* case could be made out in H*illiard* and the matter was a serious one, the remaining question to be considered was whether the public interest required a prosecution. That entailed consideration of the public interest in having crime properly investigated and bringing criminals to justice. The nature and circumstances of the libel had to be considered in that light and not obscured by the right of a party who has been wronged to a remedy.

A further issue that arose was the question of libel of the dead. Historically, there had been some instances of prosecutions being brought in respect of libel of the dead, and some evidence to suggest that if the libel were intended to injure the victim's posterity, it would be indictable.[27] Gannon J., however, came down on the side of R v E*nsor*[28] to the effect that libel of the dead was not part of our law. If the law was to be extended to accommodate it, that was a matter for the legislature. As there was no offence of libelling the dead, then Gannon J. felt he was restricted to considering the gravity of the defamation of the widow and daughter of the deceased, which he concluded did not have the gravity in law to require prosecution for a criminal offence.[29]

The anomalies in the law identified by Gannon J. centre on the following. Under Part II of the Defamation Act 1961, a newspaper cannot be prosecuted for criminal libel unless by order of a judge of the High Court sitting *in camera* (section 8). This procedure was intended to protect the press and prevent frivolous actions being taken against them. However, it is limited to any 'proprietor, publisher, editor or any person responsible for the publication of a newspaper'. In other words, it does not protect journalists, book publishers or indeed broadcasters. Under the definition of 'newspaper' in the Act, magazines appearing on a weekly, fortnightly or monthly basis would all come within the provision. This was so in the case of the *The Phoenix*. A media-wide protection *might* be defensible on account of their democratic role, but one that applies only to newspapers would be difficult to defend on any grounds. The reason for such a confined rule was that by the late nineteenth century the press in England had become a strong lobby, with some of its proprietors elected to the House of Commons and therefore well positioned to secure legislative reform in favour of newspapers, which had become mass-circulations but were hampered by earlier laws designed to keep them in submission.

The question must also be asked as to whether it is appropriate that a judge make the decision on the institution of a prosecution. That is normally the function of the Director of Public Prosecutions. The reason that the legislature decided in 1961 to entrust it to a judge is purely historical: at one time in Britain the Director of Public Prosecutions was perceived to be allowing too many actions, and not just the most serious. Whether such a measure is required in Ireland today is open to question.

Section 9 of the Act gives added protection, again to newspapers only, by allowing a district justice (now district judge) to hear evidence as to truth and public benefit by way of defence. The district judge can dismiss the case if he/she is of the opinion after hearing such evidence that there is a strong or probable presumption that a jury would acquit. He/she can also deal summarily with cases of trivial libels against a newspaper. In such a case the maximum fine is £50. Truth by itself is not a defence to a criminal libel. It is necessary to show not only truth but also publication for the public benefit (section 6), although public benefit is not defined in the Act. The European Court of Human Rights in *Lingens*,[30] *Oberschlick*[31] and *Schwabe*[32] has criticised the requirement of Austrian law that the accused in a criminal prosecution must prove the truth of an allegedly defamatory opinion or value judgment. As long as the facts are reasonably accurate and told in good faith and the value judgment is not meant to imply a falsehood, it should not be considered defamatory.[33]

The Section 9 procedures provoke two questions: is it appropriate that the onus of proof in a criminal case lie with the accused, which is the effect of a district court hearing. Secondly, is the criminal law the appropriate vehicle for dealing with trivial libels against the media? Is there any benefit to be derived from such procedures, either as a preliminary filter or for dismissing trivial cases? The Law Reform Commission has recommended that these provisions be repealed.[34]

A much more fundamental question is whether we need an offence of criminal libel at all. Reform bodies in Australia, New Zealand and the United States have recommended its abolition, while others such as the Faulks Committee and Law Commission in England and some Australian jurisdictions[35] have recommended replacing criminal libel with a narrower offence designed to catch intentional libels. In England the courts, too, have called for radical reform of the law of criminal libel. Lord Diplock, for instance, in *Gleaves v Deakin*,[36] pointed out that it could not be reconciled with Article 10 of the European Convention:

> No onus lies on the prosecution to show that the defamatory matter was of a kind that it is necessary in a democratic society to suppress or penalise in order to protect the public interest. On the contrary, even though no public interest can be shown to be injuriously affected by seriously discreditable conduct of an individual, the publisher of the information must be convicted unless he himself can prove to the satisfaction of the jury that the publication of it was for the public benefit.
>
> This is to turn Article 10 of the Convention on its head. . . .

Criminal libel has been called an 'anti-democratic vestige of British colonial rule'[37] and an unnecessary relic of the past.[38]

Further Reading

Spencer, J.R., 'Criminal Libel—A Skeleton in the Cupboard', [1977] Crim L Rev 383 and 465.

Barendt, Eric, *Freedom of Speech*, Oxford: Clarendon Press, 1989, Ch. vii.

Notes

1 See J.M. Kelly, *The Irish Constitution*, 3rd edn., Gerard Hogan and Gerry Whyte, eds., Dublin: Butterworths, 1994, at pp 921–5 for the significance of the phrase, its interpretation by the Supreme Court as a control mechanism in *State (Lynch) v Cooney* [1982] IR 337, [1983] ILRM 89, and its limitation to public order in this State only in by the High Court in *AG for England and Wales v Brandon Book Publishers Ltd* [1986] IR 597, [1987] ILRM 135.

2 Syracusa Principles No. 22, 7 HRQ 1, 1985.

3 See James P. Casey, *Constitutional Law in Ireland*, 2nd edn., London: Sweet and Maxwell, 1992, at p. 461.

4 European countries also have an integrated approach to privacy and personal rights as seen in their civil codes and in the development of a personality right as, for example, in the German Constitution (*Grundgesetz*), Articles 1–2.

5 A Sinn Féin Councillor was jailed for five years for inciting people to join the IRA. The maximum sentence under the Act was ten years; see *The Irish Times*, 30 July 1989. Another case of a Sinn Féin activist selling pro-IRA t-shirts in Galway was dealt with at District Court level under the Casual Trading Act. He was fined £1,000; *The Sentinel*, 16 September 1990, *The Irish Times*, 19 September 1990. The Criminal Law Act 1976 was part of the emergency legislation resulting from the period of violence in Northern Ireland. The government ended the state of emergency in 1995. See further discussion in Chapter 10.

6 A number of nineteenth-century acts, such as the Dublin Police Act 1842, s. 14, contained similar provisions. It has been suggested in Kelly, n. 1, at p. 932 that statutory provisions that criminalise the use of abusive or insulting language are unconstitutional unless justified by the need to prevent a breach of the peace. The Law Reform Commission in its *Report on Offences under the Dublin Police Acts and Related Offences* (LRC 14–1985) had recommended that the old provisions be replaced by a new offence requiring intent or likelihood to cause a breach of the peace (paras 7.7–7.10).

7 For a discussion of ss 18 and 31 of the Broadcasting Authority Act 1960, as amended, see Chapter 10.

8 It was carried over from the Law of Libel Amendment Act 1888, s. 8.

9 The Dáil Debates on the Defamation Bill reveal that existing statutory provisions were carried over in what was seen merely as a 'tidying-up' exercise; 188 Dáil Debates, col. 1644. See also Marie McGonagle, 'Criminal Libel' (1990) 12 DULJ 138.

10 Geoffrey Robertson and Andrew Nicol, *Media Law*, 3rd edn., London: Penguin, 1992, at p. 101, say that the same tests should be satisfied in relation to libels that have appeared other than in a newspaper or periodical.

11 See J.R. Spencer, 'Criminal Libel—A Skeleton in the Cupboard (1)' [1977] Crim L Rev 383. See also J.R. Spencer, 'Criminal Libel—A Skeleton in the Cupboard (2)' [1977] Crim L Rev 465; Law Reform Commission, *Consultation Paper on the Crime of Libel*, 1991, at ch. 1 'Historical Development of the Crime of Libel'.

12 The non-media case of DPP v Fleming (*The Irish Times*, 23 November 1989), involving indecent phone calls and graffiti, will be discussed briefly in Chapter 9.

13 Unreported, High Court, 3 July 1978, Finlay P.

14 *Hilliard v Penfield Enterprises Ltd* [1990] 1 IR 138.

15 Ibid., at p. 147.

16 *The Irish Times*, 8 January 1993, 31 March 1993.

17 *Paper*, n. 11, at para. 178.

18 *Report on the Crime of Libel* (LRC 41–1991), 1991, at ch. 2. The Commission recommended retention of the offence in a more confined form.

19 See n. 12.

20 The argument that statute law adequately dealt with the type of situation covered by criminal libel was one of the considerations that led the New Zealand Committee on Defamation in its 1977 report to recommend abolition of the common-law offence. The most compelling reason was the adequacy of the civil action for defamation. See discussion in n. 11, *Paper*, at pp 142–3.

21 See n. 14.

22 Ibid., at p. 141.

23 [1976] 3 WLR 191, [1977] 2 All ER 557; n. 14, at p. 142.

24 As held by the Court of Appeal in R v Wicks [1936] 1 All ER 384. In Gleaves v Deakin [1979] 2 All ER 497, at pp 508–9 Lord Scarman said that it is the gravity of the libel that matters; it must be such as to provoke anger or cause resentment, and breach of the peace is but one factor that contributes to the gravity of the libel.

25 See n. 14, at p. 143. Historically, when the emphasis was very much on the tendency to cause a breach of the peace, publication to a third party was not necessary. See n. 9, McGonagle, at p. 143.

26 See n. 14, at p. 143.

27 See n. 11, Spencer, at pp 385, 466 (footnote) which cites the case of the successful prosecution of John Hunt for defamatory libel on the dead King George III, allegedly

contained in a poem by Byron, a lampoon on an official eulogy, which Hunt had published, and for which he was imprisoned.

28 (1887) 3 TLR 366, quoting from the judgment of Lord Kenyan in R v *Topham* (1791) 4 Tem Rep 126, 100 ER 931.

29 The NUJ conducted an inquiry and two journalists working with *The Phoenix* were censured for breaching the Union's Code of Conduct dealing with fairness and accuracy and the elimination of distortion. The magazine article was found to be one-sided and lacking in balance; *The Irish Times*, 6 March 1991. The two journalists appealed and their appeal was upheld.

30 (1986) 8 EHRR 407.

31 Series A, no. 204; (1995) 19 EHRR 389.

32 Series A, no. 242 B, decision 28 August 1992.

33 Ibid., at para. 34.

34 See n. 18, at chs 2 and 4.

35 See n. 18, at pp 140–46.

36 [1979] 2 All ER 497, at p. 499.

37 See n. 10, at p. 102.

38 Article 19, *Manual on Freedom of Expression*, at para. 6.2.

CHAPTER NINE

Moral Censorship of the Media

As we have already seen, the Constitution in Article 40.6.1 lays considerable emphasis on public order and morality, repeating the phrase in its specific reference to the press and adding a tailpiece indicating that the publication or utterance of blasphemous, seditious or indecent matter is an offence, punishable in accordance with law. The Article does not create an offence; it merely acknowledges that such publication or utterance is an offence which is capable of being punished ('punishable') by law. Existing offences at the time the Constitution came into force were common law; there was no statutory offence.

Public morality is still regarded today as a legitimate reason for restricting freedom of expression, although perceptions of what will offend against public morals have undoubtedly changed since 1937. All the international human rights documents recognise the protection of public morals as a legitimate restriction, but the respective courts accept that the concept of morality changes over time and from one culture to another, so states must be entitled to some latitude, a 'margin of appreciation', in deciding their own standards and requirements. Nonetheless, a state that invokes public morality as a ground for restricting freedom of expression bears the onus of demonstrating that the restriction in question is essential to the maintenance of respect for the fundamental values of the community.[1] The European Court of Human Rights has emphasised repeatedly that the domestic margin of appreciation is not unlimited and goes hand in hand with a European supervision of both the aim of the measure, as adopted and applied, and its necessity.[2]

Offences against Public Morality

In assessing the extent of restrictions in Ireland in the interests of public morality, consideration must be given first to the offences referred to in the tailpiece to Article 40.6.1.i of the Constitution. Blasphemy and indecent matter will be discussed here and seditious matter will be covered in Chapter 10.

1. Blasphemy

Blasphemy has both a public order dimension and a moral dimension. Indeed, blasphemy at one time could be equated with sedition, when the Church was regarded as an institution of the State, which was not to be subjected to criticism. Equally, any criticism of the Church or Christian doctrine was regarded as blasphemous, even if put forward in good faith and all seriousness in temperate language. Even the author of a book entitled A *Humble Inquiry into the Scripture Account of Jesus Christ*, published in Dublin in 1702, was prosecuted, not for blasphemy but for sedition.[3] His inquiry was later described as 'candid', and it was decided that he had not spoken with irreverence of Christ, so he could not be convicted on that ground. Punishment was severe—in this case a fine of £1,000, a colossal amount of money at the time, and a year's imprisonment, as well as security for good behaviour for life. The law merely reflected prevailing attitudes and values. Students might be interested to know that an undergraduate at Trinity College Dublin was expelled in 1794 'for expressing heretical and blasphemous opinions to the effect that Christ was not the son of God, that the mode of creation described in Genesis was unreasonable, and that Hell did not answer his conception of a future state'.[4] Fortunately moral principles and values change.

(a) Definitions

In relation to blasphemy, the Constitution seems to contemplate two offences: publication and utterance. Common law, in addition, contemplated blasphemous acts, such as burning the Bible. Statute law, on the other hand, appears more concerned with publication,[5] although a number of nineteenth-century acts penalise the singing of profane songs in public and the use of profane language. However, it is not clear whether they mean blasphemous language or merely language that is offensive.[6] The Criminal Justice (Public Order) Act 1994, for instance, is concerned with offensive language and conduct (sections 5–7).

One advantage that statute law has over common law is that it provides for limits on penalties whereas common law treated all blasphemy as an indictable misdemeanour subject to imprisonment for a fixed but unlimited period. There is, however, no statutory definition of blasphemy and little by way of enlightenment from the courts.[7] In fact, the English Law Commission[8] has acknowledged that there is no single, comprehensive definition of the crime of blasphemy, and the Irish Commission has concluded that there is no certainty as to its precise scope and essential ingredients.[9] A definition offered by Smith and Hogan[10] is that a publication is blasphemous 'if it is couched in indecent or offensive terms likely to shock and outrage the feelings of the general body of Christian believers in the community'. The offence in English law, therefore, relates only to the feelings of Christians and intention or motive is not relevant; it is enough that the publication is 'likely to' cause shock and outrage. In the Irish context, Ó Síocháin[11] has offered the following definition:

> to speak or write offensively about God or religion as to deny the existence of God, or to bring God or religion into contempt, ridicule or disbelief.

Such a definition must be treated with caution,[12] but if representative of Irish law, it would not appear to encompass religions other than Christianity, just as has been decided in respect of English law in the *Gay News* case in 1979[13] and reflected in Smith and Hogan's definition above. Alternatively, it may protect religions in the Judaeo-Christian tradition.[14]

(b) Applicability

The *Gay News* case, which first addressed the problems of blasphemy law in a modern-day context, concerned a poem in a journal for homosexuals, depicting Christ as a homosexual in explicit detail. The poem was accompanied by a drawing illustrating its subject matter. A private prosecution was brought by Mrs Mary Whitehouse, a veteran campaigner for high moral standards in the media.[15] Leave to commence a criminal prosecution had been granted by a judge pursuant to section 8 of the Libel Act 1888, the equivalent of section 8 of the Defamation Act 1961 in Ireland, but the Director of Public Prosecutions declined to take over the prosecution. The charge was that the *Gay News* had 'unlawfully and wickedly published or caused to be published a blasphemous libel concerning the Christian religion, namely an obscene poem and illustration vilifying Christ in his life and crucifixion'.[16] The last such case to be tried in Britain had been in 1921–2.[17]

In *Gay News* the court was taken up with questions of intention. The trial judge ruled that 'intention to publish' was all that was required.[18] The publisher was accordingly fined £1,000 and sentenced to nine months' imprisonment, suspended for eighteen months. The editor was fined £500. The Court of Appeal rejected the appeal and the case went to the House of Lords on a point of law only: the question of intention. There it was decided by a majority that an intention to blaspheme was not necessary, just an intention to publish.[19] In other words, blasphemous libel was a strict liability offence, and once the matter was published, motives—good, bad or indifferent—were irrelevant. At the same time, reasoned argument or a mere denial of the existence of God was insufficient, the Court said, as the offence encompasses 'any contemptuous, reviling, scurrilous or ludicrous matter relating to God, Jesus Christ, or the Bible, or the formularies of the Church of England'.[20] As with other forms of criminal libel, it is no longer necessary to prove a tendency to cause a breach of the peace. The Law Lords did agree, however, that the law of blasphemous libel was unclear.[21]

When the case went to the European Commission on Human Rights,[22] the UK government invoked three separate grounds of justification for the restriction on freedom of expression imposed by the prosecution for blasphemous libel, namely the prevention of disorder, protection of morals, and the rights of others. The Commission found that there had been no violation of Article 10 of the Convention and that the restriction imposed had the legitimate purpose of protecting the rights of citizens not to be offended in their religious feelings by publications.[23] Offensiveness, therefore, was the key and the justification for the restriction on freedom of expression, although the Commission did not elaborate on this point.[24] Provided the principle of proportionality inherent in Article 10(2) was respected, it was a matter for the state concerned how it wished to define the offence. The common-law offence of blasphemous libel did not seem disproportionate to the Commission despite the fact that it was a strict liability offence and did not take account of the intended audience.[25] Nor was there any defence for literary or artistic merit.

(c) Blasphemous Libel

The decision in *Gay News* had major repercussions several years later when Salman Rushdie's book *The Satanic Verses* was published and provoked a Muslim backlash. The Muslim community wanted Rushdie prosecuted for blasphemy but as the common-law offence of blasphemous libel had been held to apply only to Christian religions, the court action failed.[26] The case raised questions not only about the scope of the common-law offence of blasphemous libel but also about the desirability of a blasphemy law and its implications for freedom of speech. If Mr Rushdie's right to freedom of expression was to prevail and the Muslim community was not entitled to protection under the law, then the same standards would have to apply to the rights of the Muslims to freedom of expression. Thus the question of banning a film that depicted Rushdie as a demon could not be entertained. How could one insist on freedom to publish T*he Satanic Verses* and then advocate the banning of a film demonising the author? To do so would smack of double standards and the wish of western Christianity to impose its values on the Muslim community. When the question of a new paperback edition of T*he Satanic Verses* was drawing further ire from the Muslims in Britain and elsewhere, the Muslim community in Ireland was quoted as saying that they would prefer if the publisher did not go ahead with the paperback edition because they would see it as an insult to Muslim 'feelings' rather than as the upholding of free speech.[27] It is arguable, therefore, that the essence of the offence of blasphemy is offensiveness and hurt to religious feelings rather than an attack on God or religion as such.

These developments in England have prompted questions as to whether blasphemous libel should be abolished altogether or extended to protect the feelings of people of other religions. Blasphemous libel is a form of criminal libel and contains all the same uncertainties and anomalies as the other forms (defamatory, obscene and seditious libel). That being so, it is arguable that there is nothing to be gained from retaining it in any shape or form, and if it is already problematic, there can be no value in extending it to other religions.

In Ireland, the Law Reform Commission has concluded that there is no place for an offence of blasphemous libel in a society that respects freedom of speech.[28] However, the Commission does not think it is possible to abolish blasphemous libel without a referendum because of the constitutional requirement in the tailpiece to Article 40.6.1.i.[29] As a referendum on this issue alone would be impractical, the appropriate forum for deleting the reference should be the constitutional review committee recently set up by the government. At any rate, prosecutions for blasphemous libel are now virtually unknown, although occasionally attempts are made or threats issued. In a recent case,[30] the High Court was told that a series of posters carrying messages like 'Kill God', which had been displayed on billboards around Dublin, had been removed so no injunctive relief was granted. The applicant had complained that display of the posters constituted the offence of blasphemy, as well as blasphemous libel.[31]

(d) Statute Law

Existing statutes that make reference to blasphemy include the Censorship of Films Act 1923. The film censor can refuse a certificate for a film on the grounds *inter alia* that it is blasphemous (section 7), but the Act does not define what is meant by blasphemous, nor does it set out criteria for the censor to apply. The censor has exercised this power in relation to a number of films, such as Monty Python's 'Life of Brian', which was banned in 1979 on grounds of blasphemy, but later released following resubmission to the censor.[32] Some films, like Jean-Luc Godard's 'Hail Mary', are not even submitted to the censor because of the expectation that they will not receive a certificate.[33]

It is perhaps surprising that there is no reference to blasphemy in the Wireless Telegraphy Act 1926[34] or in the Censorship of Publications Acts 1929–67 a ground for banning books or periodicals. It is even more surprising that blasphemy should have been included in the Censorship of Films Act 1923 and not a few years later in the Censorship of Publications Act 1929,[35] although it has to be said that there are other surprising differences between the two Acts. For instance, provision was made in the former for an appeal from the film censor's decision, whereas in the latter, no provision for appeal was made until an amending Act was brought in in 1946.

The Defamation Act 1961 makes it an indictable offence to compose, print or publish any blasphemous libel (section 13), an offence punishable by a maximum fine of £500 and/or two years' imprisonment, or seven years' penal servitude. It also makes provision for seizure by the Gardaí of all copies of the libel. The severity of these penalties provided for in the Act indicates the seriousness with which the offence was viewed at one time.[36] The fact that a person who 'composes' a libel can be guilty of the offence in the same way as anyone who prints or publishes a libel suggests that publication to a third party is not a necessary element of the offence.[37]

All of Part II of the Act which deals with 'criminal proceedings for libel' applies to blasphemous libel, as a form of criminal libel, except where the section specifically deals with defamatory libel only, for example, sections 6, 11 and 12. An order of a judge of the High Court is needed, therefore, for the prosecution of a newspaper (section 8).[38] It should be remembered that Part II does not apply to broadcasting. Nor do the Broadcasting Acts make any reference to blasphemy, even though the Broadcasting Authority Act 1960 was passed just one year before the Defamation Act. It may also be noted that the privilege that attaches to fair and accurate reports of court proceedings in section 18(1) does not extend to the publication of any blasphemous matter that might arise therein. The subsection does not prevent the publication of blasphemous matter, but it is at least conceivable that a reporter who omitted such matter from a report could lose the privilege on the grounds that the report was not then fair and accurate.[39]

There is no mention of blasphemy, as such, in the Video Recordings Act 1989, section 3, which allows the censor to refuse a certificate if the video would, among other things, be likely to stir up hatred against a group of persons on account of their religion. This reflects a more modern interpretation of the essence of blasphemy and the type of harm the law seeks to prevent. In 1989 the first video to be banned in England for blasphemy by the British Board of Film Classification (BBFC) was 'Visions of Ecstacy', a short film containing images of St Teresa of Avila having sex with Jesus on the cross.[40] At that time the Irish Video Recordings Act had not yet come into force.

The Prohibition on Incitement to Hatred Act 1989 defines hatred as including hatred against a group of persons in the State or elsewhere on account of their religion (section 1). The Act is wide enough to cover words and images in both print and audio-visual media which 'are threatening, abusive, or insulting and are intended or, having regard to all the circumstances, are likely to stir up hatred' (section 2(1)). The Public Order (Northern Ireland) Act 1987, section 8, also incorporates religious hatred.

As mentioned at the start of this discussion, the Constitution says that the publication or utterance of blasphemous matter is an offence punishable by law. Depending on how one defines the essence of blasphemous matter, it could be argued that the common-law offence of blasphemous libel could be abolished because existing statutory provisions meet the requirements to protect against religious discrimination and speech that is threatening, abusive or insulting and intended to, or likely to, stir up hatred. If necessary, the statutory provisions could be strengthened, or recast, to protect from outrage the feelings of religious groups, if that is seen as an appropriate aim and a justifiable reason for curtailing free speech. However, it is arguable that the real harm to be guarded against is not so much injury to feelings as the stirring up of religious hatred, with its implications for public order. Injury to feelings may be a rather tenuous and anomalous basis on which to restrict freedom of expression.[41]

Of the international instruments, the Convention on the Elimination of All Forms of Racial Discrimination (CERD) 1969 does not define 'racial discrimination' to include religious hatred (Article 1). The European Convention on Transfrontier Television 1989 requires respect for human dignity and the fundamental rights of others in programme services and specifically mentions racial hatred, though not religious hatred (Article 7). Article 20(2) of the Covenant on Civil and Political Rights, on the other hand, declares that 'Any advocacy of national, racial or religious hatred that constitutes incitement to discrimination, hostility or violence shall be prohibited by law'. The EC Directive on Transfrontier Television 1989, Article 22, requires Member States to ensure that broadcasts do not contain any incitement to hatred on grounds of race, sex, religion or nationality. There would appear to be adequate protection, therefore, in both national and international law, without the need to retain blasphemous libel, 'an offence which originated in a period of religious intolerance and was governed by different conceptions of the role of the Church in State matters . . . [and so] would be totally incompatible with modern conditions'.[42]

(e) European Court of Human Rights

The views of the European Court of Human Rights in *Jersild v Denmark*[43] are instructive in this regard. The Court upheld the right of the journalist to broadcast an interview with a racist group as part of the information role of the media. The remarks might well have been offensive to many but the journalist's aim and the effect of the programme were not to promote those ideas or to stir up hatred but merely to inform the viewing public of an ill that existed in their society. The real difficulty lies in trying to square the decision in *Jersild*, which concerned racist speech, with that in *Otto-Preminger v Austria*, which concerned blasphemy.[44] The case involved a film, based on a play written in 1894, which portrayed God the Father as old, infirm and ineffective, Jesus Christ as a 'mummy's boy' of low intelligence and Mary, who is obviously in charge, as an unprincipled wanton. The story line was their decision to punish mankind for its immorality by causing men and women to infect each other with a sexually transmitted disease—a punishment suggested by the devil—but to leave the possibility of redemption. The film was to be shown in the applicant's cinema in Innsbruck to members of the public over seventeen years of age. An application for the seizure of the film and later for its forfeiture was granted by the Austrian courts.[45] The European Court of Human Rights found that the authorities had not violated Article 10 when they seized the film.[46] The fact that the film was to be shown in a predominantly Roman Catholic area meant that the authorities had acted to ensure religious peace in the region. The national authorities were in a better position to assess the need for such a measure in the circumstances than an international court. In other words, the Court continued its stance in allowing States a wide margin of appreciation in cases involving issues of public morals. Three dissenting judges accepted that the showing of the film might have offended people but felt that, as the nature of the showing had been announced in advance and admission was confined to over-seventeens, the seizure and forfeiture of the film was not proportionate to the legitimate aim pursued.[47]

The key difference between *Jersild* and *Otto-Preminger*, it would seem, from the judgment of the Court, is that whereas the interview with the racist group in *Jersild* was part of a serious news programme and contributed information to the public, the film in *Otto-Preminger* was 'gratuitously offensive' and did not 'contribute to any form of public debate capable of furthering progress in human affairs'.[48] As there was no discernible consensus throughout Europe as to the significance of religion in society, States must have a margin of appreciation, the Court said, but because of the importance of the freedoms involved and the necessity for any restriction to be convincingly established, the Court's supervision of that margin must be strict.[49] However, the Court accepted the arguments of the Austrian government that it needed to preserve the peace and prevent people feeling that their religion was the subject of unwarranted attacks, and that it had taken account of the 'freedom of artistic expression' guaranteed by Article 10.[50] It may be surmised, therefore, that the Court places more weight on the information role of the media than it does on artistic expression. Most complaints involving restrictions in the interests of public morals that have been sent to Strasbourg have been found not to violate Article 10. A notable exception was *Open Door Counselling v Ireland*,[51] which, unlike *Jersild* did not concern the media, but which did, like *Jersild*, concern information, in that case, abortion information.

While the distinction drawn by the Court is interesting, the reality is that there are few prosecutions for blasphemy nowadays. Nonetheless, the threat remains and material is sometimes withheld or excised, particularly from plays and films for television viewing, rather than run the risk of prosecution. That is to say that the continued existence of the offence in its uncertain state leads to a degree of self-censorship. It is possible also that the Christian principles underlying blasphemy have been internalised to such an extent that 'blasphemous' matter will be suppressed, consciously or otherwise, even on grounds of good taste.[52]

To the extent that blasphemy in its modern context appears to target offensiveness and outrage rather than doctrinal matters, the best form of protection seems to lie in the Prohibition of Incitement to Hatred Act 1989. The Act is wide enough to protect minority religions and ethnic groups. It also requires intention to incite, which incorporates the *mens rea* principle of criminal law, and respects the need for a threshold for freedom of expression: speech that falls short of incitement will not be restricted. As the dissenting judges in *Otto-Preminger* said:

The need for repressive action amounting to complete prevention of the exercise of freedom of expression can only be accepted if the behaviour concerned reaches so high a level of abuse, and comes so close to a denial of the freedom of religion of others, as to forfeit for itself the right to be tolerated by society.[53]

Supporting the proposal of the New South Wales Law Reform Commission to abolish blasphemy, the Australian Press Council has said:

Blasphemy is an anachronistic and uncertain offence which is more likely to cause problems between groups than to prevent them.[54]

2. Indecent Matter and Obscenity

The poem in the *Gay News* case was also described in the charge as obscene. The Irish Constitution refers to indecent matter; there is no mention of obscenity. The Censorship of Publications Act 1929 refers to both but defines only the word 'indecent' which:

shall be construed as including suggestive of or inciting to sexual immorality or unnatural vice or likely in any other similar way to corrupt or deprave. (section 2)

Cockburn J. in R *v Hicklin*[55], in 1868, put forward the following test for obscentiy:

I think that the test of obscenity is this, whether the tendency of the matter charged as obscenity is to deprave or corrupt those whose minds are open to such immoral influences and into whose hands a publication of this sort may fall.

This test focused on the effect on the most vulnerable members of society. It was rejected in the United States in 1934 in favour of a standard focusing on the effect on the average person of the dominant theme of the work as a whole.[56] The test in *Hicklin* was later supplanted by a statutory definition in Canada and in the UK. The Canadian definition focuses on the 'undue exploitation' of sex or sex combined with violence:

Any publication, a dominant characteristic of which is the undue exploitation of sex, or of sex and any one of the following subjects, namely, crime, horror, cruelty and violence, shall be deemed to be obscene.[57]

The British legislation is the 1959 Obscene Publications Act. In that Act 'indecent' means offensive, shocking, disgusting or revolting, whereas 'obscene' means matter whose effect if taken as a whole is such as to tend to deprave and corrupt persons who are likely, in all the circumstances, to read, see or hear the matter contained or embodied in it. (section 1)

The Irish definition of 'indecent' is therefore closer to the English definition of 'obscene'. Indeed, the two terms are used rather indiscriminately in Irish law.

The *Hicklin* test was examined in Ireland in 1959 in AG *v Simpson*,[58] where the District Justice quoted heavily from the English and American authorities, particularly *Roth v US*, [59] in which Brennan J. found that the *Hicklin* test was 'unconstitutionally restrictive' of the freedoms of speech and press. In *Simpson* Dublin theatre producer Alan Simpson was prosecuted for having produced for gain Tennessee Williams' play 'The Rose Tattoo', the objection being that the performance was indecent, profane and obscene. The District Justice found that no *prima facie* case had been made out and Simpson was discharged.

(a) Obscene Libel

Obscene libel is a common-law offence, a form of criminal libel, and all that has previously been said about criminal libel in any of its forms applies. In fact, the Defamation Act treats blasphemous libel and obscene libel almost identically. In Ireland, there has been no case-law on obscene libel since 1929, because obscene publications have been dealt with under the Censorship of Publications Act of that year. Obscenity in the audio-visual media is also governed by statute.[60] The only prosecutions for obscene libel in recent years have been in the non-media sphere. In DPP *v Fleming*,[61] for example, a farmer charged on two separate occasions with writing graffiti about neighbours (giving their telephone number and suggesting that sex was available) in public toilets, on road signs and in telephone boxes around the country was sentenced to imprisonment of nine months and twenty-one months (of which fourteen months were suspended), respectively. Obscene libel is therefore, in practice, redundant,[62] as are a number of other common-law offences, which surface only occasionally but nonetheless pose a threat to the media. For instance, the offence of conspiracy to corrupt public morals surfaced fleetingly in AG (SPUC) *v Open Door Counselling*,[63] while in the 1959 case of AG *v Simpson*,[64] the prosecution contended that a play being staged in Dublin, 'The Rose Tattoo', outraged the public interest, was contrary to public morals and was obscene. The charge was of showing for gain an indecent and profane performance.[65]

A case that was to raise and help clarify certain aspects of the legal regulation of speech for the protection of public morals was *Handyside v UK*.[66] Controversy arose over the *The Little Red Schoolbook*, translated from Danish and published by the plaintiff in the UK and, after translation, in about twenty other countries. Some English newspapers published accounts of the book's contents and a number of complaints were received. The DPP asked the police to investigate. They got a warrant to search and seize copies but somehow missed 18,800 copies of the 20,000 print run. In a subsequent court action, the publisher was fined £50 and ordered to pay £110 costs. An order was made also for the destruction of the books. The appeal failed. The book cost thirty pence, contained 208 pages and had an introduction entitled 'All grown-ups are paper tigers'. It had chapters on education, learning, teachers, pupils and 'the system'. The chapter on pupils, however, contained a twenty-six page section on sex, which included subsections on everything from masturbation to menstruation, from 'dirty old men' to pornography, from VD to methods of abortion. Marriage was largely ignored. The book was intended as a reference book for schoolchildren from the age of twelve upwards. It contained passages like the following:

> Porn is a harmless pleasure if it isn't taken seriously and believed to be real life. Anybody who mistakes it for reality will be greatly disappointed.

> But it's quite possible that you may get some good ideas from it and you may find something which looks interesting and that you haven't tried before.[67]

Because the book was for twelve-year-olds upwards and the year was 1976, it is not surprising that the Court concluded that, looked at as a whole, the book would tend to deprave and corrupt a significant proportion of the children likely to read it.

The European Court of Human Rights found that the conviction of Mr Handyside was a justifiable interference with his right to freedom of expression and that there had been no breach of Article 10 of the Convention. As it is not possible to find in the domestic law of the various contracting states a uniform European conception of morals, the Court said, Article 10.2 leaves to the contracting states a margin of appreciation.[68] That domestic margin of appreciation goes hand in hand with a European supervision. That is to say that because the concept of morals varies from state to state, the European Court of Human Rights will be less inclined to second-guess a national authority. The Court was at pains to point out that freedom of expression, however, applies not only to 'information' or 'ideas' that are favourably received or regarded as inoffensive, but also to those that offend, shock, or disturb the State or any section of the population. Such are the demands of that pluralism, tolerance and broadmindedness without which there is no 'democratic society'. This means, among other things, that every 'formality', 'condition', 'restriction' or 'penalty' imposed in this sphere must be proportionate to the legitimate aim pursued.[69]

In the particular circumstances of *Handyside*, however, the restriction was justifiable in that the book was intended for children. However, the Court's decision should not be taken to mean that the appropriate test is what would tend to deprave or corrupt children or adolescents. Whereas such a test was justified in *Handyside* because the intended readership was children and adolescents, that test should not be applied generally to the whole population, to publications intended for an adult readership, which is what happened in Ireland with the operation of the censorship machinery. Repeatedly, in the Dáil and elsewhere, concern was expressed with the need to protect the youth and 'ordinary' people of the country from the unwholesome literature that was flooding into the country mainly from the US and the UK. Although the censorship exercised by the Censorship of Publications Board has been less contentious in recent years, the Board does continue to operate. In 1990 a book intended for six to eight-year-olds, *Jenny Lives with Eric and Martin*, published in London and the cause of protests and controversy in Britain, was banned by the Board.[70]

(b) Statute Law

A number of nineteenth-century statutes contained provisions restricting or prohibiting the publication of indecent or obscene matter, including songs, representations and advertisements. They penalised the sale and distribution or exhibition in public of indecent or obscene publications,[71] their importation,[72] as well as indecent or obscene speech or acts.[73] The Obscene Publications Act 1857, which was aimed at preventing the sale of obscene publications, permitted seizure and destruction of such matter but did not define obscenity.[74]

(i) Censorship of Films

In addition to the nineteenth-century acts, a number of measures were introduced shortly after the emergence of the new State, beginning with the Censorship of Films Act 1923. The censor could refuse a certificate on the grounds that the film or part of it was indecent, obscene or blasphemous or would tend to inculcate principles contrary to public morality or would otherwise be subversive of public morality (section 7(2)). Films that have been banned in this way include 'Whore', 'Working Girls' and 'Personal Services', all dealing with prostitution.[75] The ban on 'Personal Services' was later lifted by the Appeal Board.[76] Violence is not specifically mentioned in section 7(2)[77] but was the predominant reason for the censor's decision in October 1994 not to grant a certificate to Oliver Stone's 'Natural Born Killers', which was passed uncut and granted an over-eighteens certificate in Britain. A planned showing of the film at the Irish Film Centre was abandoned when it appeared that an injunction was to be sought to prevent it.[78] An injunction had been granted by Cork Circuit Court in 1994 to prevent the screening and distribution of a David Puttnam film, 'War of the Buttons', when the parents of one of the children in the film complained that he had been filmed in the nude, contrary to their moral and religious beliefs.[79]

The Censorship of Films Act 1923 was followed by the Wireless Telegraphy Act 1926, which made it an offence to send any message of an indecent, obscene or offensive character or subversive of public order (section 11). Later statutes include the Defamation Act 1961, which contains provisions on obscene libel (Part II), the Radio and Television Act 1988 (section 9(1)(d)), which requires broadcasters to ensure that nothing is broadcast 'which may reasonably be regarded as offending against good taste or decency'; the Video Recordings Act, section 3(1), which allows the censor to refuse a certificate if the viewing of the video would be likely to stir up hatred or would tend, by the inclusion of obscene or indecent matter, to deprave or corrupt. The Act also provides for classification according to suitability for persons generally or of certain ages: under twelves accompanied, over fifteens, over eighteens (section 4), and for a labelling system indicating contents (section 12). An appeal from a refusal of a certificate by the censor or in respect of the classification granted can be made within three months to the Censorship of Films Appeal Board (section 10). The most far-reaching measures, however, were contained in the Censorship of Publications Act 1929 as amended.

(ii) Censorship of Publications

There was obviously a great deal of concern with public morals in the early part of the century but no clear legal regime for dealing with it, no clear standards or tests to apply. The common-law approach was confusing and the nineteenth-century legislation in force was mainly concerned with the sale or public exhibition of indecent or obscene publications. From 1911 there had been a movement in favour of censorship, the Irish Vigilance Association. This Association was supported by religious groups and given impetus in 1923 by the Geneva Convention for the Suppression of the Circulation and Traffic in Obscene Publications, held under the auspices of the League of Nations. Three years later a Committee on Evil Literature was established by the Minister for Justice. The Committee examined existing legislation in other countries and the obligations under the Geneva Convention, to which Ireland had acceded in 1924. It heard representations from all interested parties within the State and reported to the Minister at the end of 1926.[80] The Committee found that the ordinary law for dealing with indecent publications had broken down and that the few criminal charges being laid each year were making no impact on the flow of objectionable matter into the country. Many of the Committee's recommendations were included in the Censorship of Publications Bill, which was introduced in 1928.

The political and moral climate at the time was conducive to censorship and the zeal with which censorship was espoused was not wholly attributable to the desires of the newly formed State to shake off the legacy of the past and the harmful influences from outside. There was nothing exceptional about the enactment of censorship legislation at the time. Many European countries, including Britain, were worried about the effects of the spread of objectionable literature and had introduced legislation. However, the scheme adopted by the Irish legislature was to become notorious because of the manner in which it was applied. It was used as authorisation for widespread prior restraint in a paternalistic exercise designed to protect the morals of both the 'youth' and 'ordinary people' of the country and to insulate them from 'unwholesome' external influences.[81]

One of the difficulties with the law prior to the 1929 Act was that, as most authors and publishers were outside the jurisdiction, the only possibility was to prosecute booksellers and distributors. Such a course of action was not desirable in itself, the law was uncertain and, as was argued in the Dáil, the nature of 'indecent' matter was so wide and variable as to make it virtually impossible in many cases for a bookseller or distributor to know whether the handling of particular books or periodicals would constitute an offence.[82] The only real alternative, therefore, it was thought, was to prevent the material from coming into the country in the first place. There were already facilities for doing that under the Customs Consolidation Act 1876 and the Post Office Act 1908. In practice, however, the respective officials were dealing with such a vast range and quantity of matter coming into the country that it would have been impossible for them to concentrate to any significant extent on indecent books or periodicals. Besides, there were no statutory criteria that they could apply, with the result that forfeiture was entirely arbitrary and a matter of chance.[83] Instead of recommending a strengthening of the existing law, the Committee on Evil Literature had recommended a new system of prevention rather than prosecution. Hence, the purpose of the Censorship of Publications Act 1929, as set out in the long title, was to provide for

> the prohibition of the sale and distribution of unwholesome literature and for that purpose to provide for the establishment of a censorship of books and periodical publications, and to restrict the publication of reports of certain classes of judicial proceedings . . . .[84]

The way the Act was applied in practice, to the detriment of works of literature, has been well documented elsewhere,[85] and so the present study will concentrate instead on the substantive law—its aims and its failings.

The Act, which as a bill had been the subject of prolonged debate and was not lightly passed, envisaged a type of prior restraint, in the form of interference with the channels of distribution. It established a censorship board, which was to receive complaints from the public, 'examine' (not necessarily 'read') the publication complained of and report to the Minister.[86] The Board was to have regard to the literary, artistic, scientific or historic merit of the particular publication, its language and general tenor, the nature and extent of publication, the class of reader addressed and any other matter it considered relevant. If the Board reported that a particular publication was in its general tendency indecent, obscene or unduly devoted to crime in the case of a periodical, the Minister could make an order prohibiting its sale and distribution within the State. All of these provisions, contained in Part II of the 1929 Act, were repealed and replaced by the Censorship of Publications Act 1946.

There were various problems with 1929 Act. First, it failed to make provision for an appeal, which was remedied by the 1946 Act (section 3). It also enabled books, though not periodicals, to be banned forever, a defect that was not remedied until a further act of 1967, which imposed a twelve-year limit. Until 1979, when the Health (Family Planning) Act was passed, books and periodicals could be banned on the basis that they advocated contraception, and the printer, publisher, seller or distributor could be prosecuted.[87] As late as 1989 a prosecution was brought against the Irish Family Planning Association for unlawfully selling condoms at the Virgin Megastore in Dublin, contrary to section 4(1)(4) of the Health (Family Planning) Act 1979 as amended by section 2 of the Health (Family Planning) (Amendment)

Act 1985. A fine of £400 was imposed.[88] The legislation, a liberalising measure at the time, imposed an age limit of eighteen and abolished the need for a prescription for contraceptives, which could lawfully be sold by chemists and health boards only. The Misuse of Drugs Act 1984 made it an offence to publish, sell or distribute books, periodicals or other publications which advocate or encourage, or include advertisements for, the use of any controlled drug (section 5).

The censorship of publications that advocate abortion remains unchanged. The ban on the advocacy of abortion in the Censorship Acts 1929–67 caused problems in the period following the right-to-life amendment to the Constitution in 1983 (Article 40.3.3) and the court cases that ensued. The Censorship Board gave the British magazine *Cosmopolitan* an ultimatum in September 1989 to withdraw its advertisements for abortion clinics within six months or face being banned in Ireland. The magazine complied. In February 1990 another British magazine, *Company*, removed a supplement on abortion from copies distributed in Ireland. FÁS, the national employment training authority, removed references to abortion from its guide for young people emigrating to Britain. Two books on women's health were removed from the shelves of public libraries in Dublin following complaints.[89]

The difficulties with the legislation and its application are legendary. Control was exercised on the basis of standards that were vague and imprecise; the terminology was tentative and often inconsistent. Even the definition of 'indecent', which one would have thought was central to the Act, was inserted only at a late stage, when the bill was recommitted to the Dáil. The scope of the Act was so wide and uncertain that how it would operate depended entirely on the personnel, the five part-time, anonymous, ministerial-appointed, upright citizens, meeting in secret, who would comprise the Board. Most of the publishers affected by the decisions were outside the country, sales in Ireland were meagre anyway. Besides, to be banned often gave an added sales boost. In England, *Lady Chatterly's Lover* is said to have sold three million copies in the three months following its prosecution in 1961.[90]

For these reasons, the operation of the Board and its decisions were not subjected to scrutiny for fifty years. It would have been open to an individual author, publisher or reader personally affected by a decision to take a constitutional challenge, but this did not happen. The only case that resulted was *Irish Family Planning Association v Ryan*,[91] which involved the banning by the Board of an information booklet on birth control. The case was decided on natural justice principles rather than freedom of expression. The Supreme Court said that the Board ought to have exercised their discretion to communicate with the publisher, as the publisher was readily contactable, and the book was purely factual, not advocating any course of conduct and not obscene.[92]

After a further flurry of activity in 1987 in which the board banned Dr Alex Comfort's *The Joy of Sex* and *The Erotic Art of India*, a title in Thames and Hudson's acclaimed art series which had already been out of print for two years and which the publishers had no plans to reissue, the Board became less visible and contentious.[93] The ban on *The Joy of Sex* was lifted by the Appeal Board.[94] In 1988, in response to a complaint intended to show how ludicrous the system was, the Board refused to ban the *Bible*.[95] Nonetheless the legitimacy of the Board's continued existence is no less open to question. The Law Reform Commission has recommended that the legislation on obscene and indecent matter and the various schemes of censorship be reviewed to determine whether they are consistent with the requirements of the Constitution as to freedom of speech; to determine whether they are appropriate in modern conditions; and to formulate, if necessary, changes to the existing law.[96]

(iii) Other Aspects of the Censorship Acts

As noted in Chapter 7, the Censorship of Publications Act 1929 also restricts reporting of judicial proceedings in the interests of morals (section 14). The provisions were taken over from the British Judicial Proceedings (Regulation of Reports) Act 1926, section 1, which was aimed at controlling detailed reports of divorce proceedings. The provisions were accepted without challenge in the Dáil. The test in each case is whether the matter would be calculated to injure public morals.

(c) Pornography

The difficulty with the Censorship of Publications Acts in this country is not that they fail to filter out pornography but rather that they are so flexible as to filter out important works of literature as well. The main difficulty is that sufficiently precise standards are not easy to formulate. There is ample evidence of a thriving pornography industry but little consensus on what constitutes pornography of a kind that requires regulation. The problem is accentuated by developments in technology, which mean that pornographic material can appear in all media from print to video to computer. Pornographic material in film and video can be refused a certificate by the censor in accordance with the Censorship of Films Acts and the Video Recordings Acts. The problem is how to define pornography. The film 'The Bad Lieutenant' is reported to have been refused a certificate because it was demeaning to women, and the Madonna film, 'Dangerous Game', because of a violent scene of anal rape.[97] The question is whether either conforms to our idea of pornography? Is matter that is demeaning to women or that contains sexual violence sufficient to constitute pornography, or is something more required? Must both degradation and sexual violence occur to take a film out of the category of simply bad taste or indecency and place it in the category of pornography?

Much has been written about pornography and whether it should be considered outside the constitutional guarantee of free speech on the grounds that it does not constitute speech or whether it should be outlawed on the basis of the avoidance of identifiable harm. A causal relationship has always been difficult to establish. It is not the portrayal of sex as such that is objectionable in today's world but the violence, objectification, degradation and subordination that may accompany it and the effect that the combination may have on attitudes to and treatment of the 'victims', who are usually women and children. Conservative, liberal and feminist theories have prevailed at different times but the essence of the problem remains elusive. Should pornography be curtailed and, if so, on what theory, what test? Is it offensiveness, as has been canvassed in the case of blasphemy, that is the key to objections, or is it the stirring up of hatred and other negative responses to the women and children it objectivises?[98] If so, it might be argued that incitement-to-hatred legislation could provide an adequate model for response. If not, is the appropriate test or standard that of community tolerance, i.e. the moral standards of the community? It may be that standards developed in the context of sex discrimination could be applied. Another possibility is that it could be encompassed within the theory of human dignity, protected by national constitutions. In a broad framework, pornography can be viewed as a denial of human dignity. Article 7 of the European Convention on Transfrontier Broadcasting, for example, requires respect for human dignity and specifically mentions pornography:

1.   All items of programme services, as concerns their presentation and content, shall respect the dignity of the human being and the fundamental rights of others.

     In particular, they shall not:

     (a) be indecent and in particular contain pornography;

(b) give undue prominence to violence or be likely to incite to racial hatred.

The Video Recordings Act 1989 does not specifically mention pornography as such but allows the censor to refuse a certificate if the viewing of the video:

(a) (iii) would tend, by reason of the inclusion in it of obscene or indecent matter, to deprave or corrupt persons who might view it, [or]

(b) it depicts acts of gross violence or cruelty (including mutilation and torture) towards humans or animals. (section 3)

The association representing most of the international video companies operating in Ireland before the Act was passed said that the industry was threatened by two major problems: piracy and pornography.[99]

European Community law also has relevance to this issue. The 1989 EC Directive, 'Television without Frontiers', obliges Member States *inter alia* to ensure freedom of reception for programmes 'retransmitted' from other Member States (Article 2), unless such a programme seriously and gravely infringes Article 22, which is designed to protect minors, particularly from 'pornography or gratuitous violence'. If that is the case, the Member State may 'provisionally suspend retransmissions' (Article 2). The application of the Directive to the retransmission of satellite services was tested in the Red Hot Dutch case, R v *Continental Television*[104] in 1992. Red Hot Dutch was to transmit encrypted films of a pornographic nature into the UK, uplinked from the Netherlands. The relevant domestic law in the UK is the Broadcasting Act 1990, which imposes obligations on broadcasters to exclude matters that offend against good taste and to observe a code on the portrayal of sex and nudity. The Act allows the Secretary of State to make an order proscribing a foreign satellite service that fails to comply with the provisions of the Act. In March 1993 the UK government announced its intention to make such an order. The Dutch company sought judicial review of the decision. The argument centred firstly on the meaning of 'retransmission' in the Directive and the contention that it could not be said to cover a satellite service originating in another member state; and secondly on the scope of Article 22 and its reference to steps taken to ensure that minors will not normally hear or see the broadcasts. The Red Hot Dutch films were to be transmitted between the hours of 11 p.m. and 4 a.m. each Saturday night. The views of the European Court of Justice are not yet known, although the Directive itself is under review.[100]

Advertising

Advertising in the media, whether print,[101] broadcasting,[102] film,[103] video,[104] on billboards or in public places,[105] is restricted in the interests of public morals. In addition to the specific legal requirements, the Advertising Standards Authority of Ireland (ASAI), a self-regulatory body, operates a Code of Standards with which members are required to comply. RTÉ operates a Code of Standards, which gives effect to the provisions relating to privacy, good taste and decency in the Broadcasting Authority Act 1960, section 18. The Independent Radio and Television Commission, likewise, is obliged by the Radio and Television Act 1988 to draw up from time to time a code of standards. Under its code, RTÉ was not prepared to accept advertisements for contraceptives and, as a result, was unwilling for quite some time to accept advertisements for the use of condoms as part of the Health Education Bureau's campaign to combat AIDS.[106] The regulations concerning the advertising of medicines and treatments are extensive. Advertising aimed at children is particularly circumscribed.[107] The Broadcasting Complaints Commission has power to hear any complaint that an advertisement contravened the Code of Standards.[108]

Further Reading

Adams, Michael, Censorship—The Irish Experience, University of Alabama Press, 1968.

Boyle, Kevin, and McGonagle, Marie, 'Censorship of Publications—Irish Style' (1989) 10 JMLP 87.

Carlson, Julia, ed., Banned in Ireland, London: Routledge, 1990.

Colliver, Sandra, ed., Striking a Balance: Hate Speech, Freedom of Expression and Non-discrimination, Article 19, London: International Centre Against Censorship, 1992.

Mahony, Kathleen E., 'Obscenity, Morals and the Law: Challenging Basic Assumptions', in Rosalie Abella and Melvin L. Rothman, eds., Justice beyond Orwell, Montreal, 1985.

John A. Murphy, 'Censorship and the Moral Community', in Farrell, Brian, ed., Community and Communications in Ireland, Dublin and Cork: Mercier Press, 1984, p. 51.

Notes

1 Syracusa Principles No. 27, 7 HRQ 1, 1985.
2 *Handyside v* UK (1979) 1 EHRR 737, at para. 49.
3 See Paul O'Higgins, 'Blasphemy in Irish law', (1960) 23 MLR 151, at 159.
4 Ibid., at p. 160 citing R.B. McDowell, *Irish Public Opinion* 1750–1800, London 1944.
5 See, for example, the Defamation Act 1961, ss 13 and 18, which confer a privilege for court reporting that does not extend to the publication of blasphemous matter.
6 For example, Dublin Police Act 1842; Indecent Advertisements Act 1889; Towns Improvement (Ireland) Act 1854.
7 See, for example, n. 3, at pp 163–4.
8 *Report on Offences against Religion and Public Worship* (No. 145, 1985)
9 Law Reform Commission, *Report on the Crime of Libel* (LRC 41–1991) 1991, at p. 11.
10 J.C. Smith and B. Hogan, *Criminal Law*, 6th edn., Dublin: Butterworths, 1988, at p. 738.
11 *The Criminal Law of Ireland*, 7th edn., Dublin: Foilseacháin Dlí, 1981, at p. 307.
12 It is regarded by O'Higgins, n. 3, at pp 165–6 as 'not very helpful', 'circular and not of much value'.
13 R *v Lemon* [1979] 2 WLR 281.
14 See Law Reform Commission, *Consultation Paper on the Crime of Libel*, 1991, at p. 169.
15 The case was, therefore, known in the first instance as *Whitehouse v Lemon* and variously as R *v Lemon* or R *v Gay News* [1979] AC 617; [1978] 68 Cr App R 381.
16 Ibid., at p. 620.
17 (1982) 5 EHRR 124.
18 See n. 15, at p. 620.
19 Ibid., at p. 665.
20 Per Lord Scarman, quoting Article 214 of Stephens' *Digest of the Criminal Law*, 9th edn., 1950.
21 Ibid., at p. 633 and p. 657.
22 *Gay News and Lemon v* UK (1983) 5 EHRR 123.
23 Ibid., at p. 130.
24 Ibid.
25 Ibid.
26 R. *v Bow Street Magistrate's Court ex parte Choudhury* [1991] 1 All ER 306. *Choudhury* was declared inadmissible by the European Commission, just as *Gay News* had been.
27 *The Irish Times*, 20 January 1990.
28 See n. 9, at p. 11.
29 Ibid.
30 *O'Mahony v Levine* (unreported, High Court, 17 October 1994.)
31 A small percentage of complaints to newspapers from time to time allege blasphemy, but the term is used in a very broad sense by complainants to cover anything critical of the Church or religious beliefs or devotions. See generally on newspaper complaints, Kevin Boyle and Marie McGonagle, *Media Accountability: The Readers' Representative in Irish Newspapers*, Dublin: National Newspapers of Ireland, 1995.
32 *Sunday Tribune*, 16 August 1987. A ban lasts for seven years under the Censorship of Films (Amendment) Act 1970.
33 *The Irish Times*, 22 February 1987.
34 The omission may be due to how radio was viewed and controlled at the time as a state 'service', i.e. a cultural and educational medium, rather than an entertainment medium.
35 Apparently a reference to blasphemy was dropped from the original Censorship of Publications Bill because of the fear of anti-Protestant or anti-Semitic crusades; see *The Irish Times*, 9 February 1985. It is unlikely that it was intended that blasphemy should come under the general rubric of material that was indecent or obscene.
36 The Defamation Act 1961 was intended primarily as a consolidating act, carrying over provisions of various nineteenth-century acts.
37 The House of Lords in R *v Gay News* (n. 19) found that an intention to publish was required.
38 As to the criteria that apply, see Chapter 8 regarding *Hilliard v Penfield Enterprises*.

39 It is not clear what the subsection actually achieves. It attempts to discourage reporters from including blasphemous or obscene matter in court reports.
40 *The Irish Times*, 13 December 1989.
41 See n. 14, at p. 170.
42 App. No. 15890/89, decision of Commission, 8 September 1992, decision of Court, 24 September 1994.
43 [1994] 19 EHRR 34. See also Eamonn Hall, 'Blasphemy' (Dec 94) GILSI 361.
44 The restraint in the former was held to constitute a breach of Article 10, while the latter did not.
45 See n. 43, at p. 60.
46 Ibid., at p. 62
47 Ibid., at para. 49. The dissenting judges rejected this argument, as such a decision was bound to be tainted by the authorities' idea of 'progress'.
48 Ibid., at para. 50.
49 The dissenting judges pointed out that such a right was not expressly guaranteed by the Convention but 'may' be a legitimate ground for restriction if necessary in a democratic society; ibid., at pp 61–2.
50 Ibid., at para. 56. Cf. *Müller v Switzerland*, Series A, no. 1333; (1991) 13 EHRR 212. See also David Pannick, 'Religious Feelings and the European Court', (1995) *Public Law* 7.
51 Series A, no. 246; (1993) 15 EHRR 244.
52 See, generally, Richard Webster, A *Brief History of Blasphemy*, The Orwell Press, 1990.
53 See n. 43, at p. 62.
54 Australian Press Council Submission to the Law Reform Commission of New South Wales on Blasphemy, 14 April 1992, APC *News*, May 1992.
55 (1868) LR 3 QB 360.
56 See US *v One Book called 'Ulysses'* 5 F.Supp. 182 (1934); *Roth v* US 354 US 476 (1957).
57 An Act to Amend the Criminal Code, S.C. 1959, c.40 s. 11
58 (1959) 93 ILTR 33.
59 See n. 56, *Roth*, at p. 489.
60 The Censorship of Films Acts, Broadcasting Acts and Video Recordings Act.
61 *The Irish Times*, 18 November 1986, 23 November 1989, 6 November 1990.
62 See n. 9, *Report*, at p. 13, says that obscene libel is virtually obsolete and should be abolished.
63 [1988] IR 593, [1987] ILRM 477. Cf. In England, *Shaw v DPP* [1962] AC 220, [1961] 2 WLR 897.
64 See n. 58.
65 Ibid. See further, n. 14, at paras 129–32.
66 See n. 2.
67 Ibid., para. 32, at pp 747–8.
68 See n. 2. at para. 59, p. 760.
69 Ibid., at para. 49, pp 754–5.
70 *The Irish Times*, 30 July 1990. The book was about a little girl living with a homosexual couple.
71 Dublin Police Act 1842; Indecent Advertisements Act 1889.
72 Customs Consolidation Act 1876.
73 Dublin Police Act 1842; Towns Improvement (Ireland) Act 1854.
74 This Act is still in use in Northern Ireland, rather than the Obscene Publications Act 1959 which applies in England and Wales. This latter Act is also problematic. See, for example, N.J. Reville, 'Obscenity, Blasphemy and the Law' (1990) 11 JMLP 42: '. . . English obscenity law is illogical in theory, uncertain in scope and unworkable in practice'.
75 *The Irish Times*, 11 October 1991; *Sunday Tribune*, 29 March 1987.
76 *The Irish Times*, 14 May 1987.
77 *The Irish Times*, 27 October 1994.
78 *The Irish Times*, 24 February 1995, 1 April 1995.
79 *The Irish Times*, 2 July 1994. On the censorship of films generally, see Ciaran Carty, *Confessions of a Sewer Rat*, Dublin: New Island Books, 1995.

80 Adams, Michael, *Censorship—The Irish Experience*, University of Alabama Press, 1968, at p. 34.
81 Both groups are constantly referred to throughout the Dáil Debates on the Censorship of Publications Bill 1928, vols 26, 28.
82 28 *Dáil Debates*, cols 273, 699; 12 *Seanad Debates*, cols 112–13.
83 For example, in the US the customs law was amended in 1930 to specifically except classics and works of literary merit and to build in procedural safeguards, including the requirement of a court order for seizure. Tariff Act of 1930, 19 USC, s. 1305 (a).
84 Books were included even though the Committee on Evil Literature had warned of the dangers. Besides, the Irish people at the time were a 'newspaper-reading people', not a book-reading people; 26 *Dáil Debates*, col. 630.
85 See, for example, n. 82; Kieran Woodman, *Media Control in Ireland*, Galway University Press, 1985; Julia Carlson, *Banned in Ireland*, London: Routledge, 1990; *The Bell*, passim, vol. 9, 1945.
86 The role of the customs under the 1929 Act just happened, but it was affirmed and developed by s. 5 of the 1946 Act.
87 In 1929 when the Act became law, contraception was viewed as race-suicide. See, for example, 12 *Seanad Debates*, col. 123.
88 *The Irish Times*, 9 September 1989, 16 May 1990.
89 *The Irish Times*, 1 October 1991, 16 October 1991.
90 Geoffrey Robertson and Andrew Nicol, *Media Law*, 3rd edn., London: Penguin Books, 1992, at p. 107.
91 [1979] IR 295. On the question of the constitutionality of the Board, see James P. Casey, *Constitutional Law in Ireland*, 2nd edn., London: Sweet and Maxwell, 1992, at pp 458–9.
92 Ibid., at pp 314–5, *per* O'Higgins C.J.
93 It emerged from subsequent interviews with the judge who chaired the Board that the concern of the Board was for the protection of children, so that a juvenile standard was being imposed on the whole community; the *Sunday Tribune*, 15 February 1987.
94 *The Irish Times*, 27 September 1989. The ban on 'Playboy' magazine imposed in 1959 was lifted by the Appeal Board in September 1995, *The Irish Times*, 29 September 1995, *The Sunday Tribune*, 1 October 1995.
95 *The Irish Times*, 8 March 1988.
96 See n. 14, at ch. 9; n. 9, at para. 22.
97 *The Irish Times*, 23 November 1994.
98 It has been argued that offensiveness is only a secondary element and not the real root of the problem, which is the influence of pornography on people who use it and the resulting harm to women and children; see Catherine Itzin, ed., *Pornography: Women, Violence and Civil Liberties*, Oxford: OUP, 1992, and Catherine Itzen, 'Pornography, Harm and Human Rights—the European Context', (1995) 16 JMLP 107.
99 *The Irish Times*, 24 April 1986.
100 [1993] 2 CMLR 333, C–327/93. Phillip Dann, 'The Red Hot Channel: Pornography without Frontiers' (1993) 6 ENT LR 191. See Stuart Dowis, 'Still Red-Hot: Pornography; Freedoms and Morality', [1995] 5 ENT LR 201.
101 The Censorship of Publications Act 1929 (s. 17) includes advertisements that relate or refer to any sexual disease, complaint or infirmity or to the prevention or removal of irregularities in menstruation or abortifacients. A reference to contraceptives was removed from the Health (Family Planning) Act 1979 (s. 12(2)).
102 Broadcasting Authority Act 1960, Radio and Television Act 1988 (Pt III) (s. 10), prohibiting the carrying of advertisements directed towards any religious end.
103 Censorship of Films (Amendment) Act 1925, applying the provisions of s. 7(2) of the principal Act of 1923 regarding indecent, obscene or blasphemous matter or matter tending to inculcate principles contrary to public morality to advertising by extract.
104 The Video Recordings Act 1989 is mainly concerned with the supply and importation of video recordings. It exempts works that, taken as a whole, are designed to inform, educate or instruct; that are concerned with religion, music or sport; or are video games. Videos used in broadcasting are governed by the Broadcasting Acts.

105 Indecent Advertisements Act 1889. It is also an offence under the Misuse of Drugs Act 1984 to publish, sell or distribute printed matter which includes advertisements for any controlled drug (s. 5).
106 *The Irish Times*, 14 May 1993.
107 See, generally, RTÉ, *Broadcasting Guidelines for RTÉ Personnel*, 1989.
108 Broadcasting Authority (Amendment) Act 1976 (s. 4(e)(a)).

CHAPTER TEN

The Authority of the State

In 1927 Brandeis J. in the United States Supreme Court[1] wrote that 'public discussion is a political duty', that 'the greatest menace to freedom is an inert people'. At that time, his was still a minority view, but by 1971, Harlan J. was to write for the Court:

> The constitutional right to free expression is powerful medicine . . . It is designed to remove governmental restraints from the arena of public discussion . . . in the hope that use of such freedom will ultimately produce a more capable citizenry and more perfect polity. [In this sense it is] not a sign of weakness but of strength.[2]

Harlan J. regarded freedom of expression as a sign of a self-confident society and a powerful protection against the growing power and intrusiveness of the State.

In the United States that freedom has led to a press that exposes *real* official wrongs, a press that helped force a president from office, candidates from presidential campaigns, nominees from appointment to the Bench of the Supreme Court itself. That is the kind of press that arouses resentment, particularly from politicians who feel victimised, but also from the public who fear that the press is too powerful, arrogant and intrusive. Why should a self-appointed group of people, engaged in a commercial enterprise with a profit ethic, have the power to select its victims, to expose wrongdoing and goings-on in the corridors of power? In answer to that question, Anthony Lewis,[3] celebrated columnist with the *New York Times*, cites three cases:

1. *New York Times v Sullivan*,[4] where an attempt was made to use the law of libel for a new purpose, a political purpose, to frighten news organisations from covering the racial struggle in the South. If that had been allowed to happen, it would have made a great difference to that struggle, because most Americans were not aware of the cruel reality of racism until the news reports of the 1950s and 1960s confronted them with it. The impact of television was particularly powerful and a major player in the quest for new equal rights laws and social change. The US Supreme Court held that the First Amendment to the Constitution allowed robust and uninhibited speech about public life. As politicians have

parliamentary privilege for what they say in the course of their duties, there must be a corollary public privilege to criticise, to assert meaningful control over the political process, and the means to effect that control is through the media.

2. *Near v Minnesota*,[5] which concerned a newspaper that made crude attacks on public officials, accusing them of corrupt alliances with gangsters. The paper was also viciously anti-Semitic. The Minnesota legislature introduced a law to close down newspapers that were a public nuisance, but the US Supreme Court by a five to four majority found that the legislation violated the First Amendment. Open public discussion was necessary to prevent abuse of official power; therefore, there should be no prior restraint.

3. *New York Times v US*,[6] the 'Pentagon Papers' case in which the *New York Times* and *Washington Post* published excerpts from a secret official history of the Vietnam war while the war was still going on. The government sought an injunction against further publication, on the grounds of the threat it posed for national security. The injunction was refused. The government had shown no threat of vital breaches in security, only the possibility of embarrassment. The federal judge sympathised with the government but said:

> a cantankerous press, an obstinate press, a ubiquitous press must be suffered by those in authority in order to preserve the even greater values of freedom of expression and the right of the people to know.[7]

Cases in Britain and in Ireland have raised similar issues but not all, as we shall see, with similar results.

The Irish Constitution

In the United States the constitutional development of freedom of the press has been clear, although not untroubled. In Ireland the constitutional formulation does not appear as positive or forthright. The absolutist nature of the former—'Congress shall make no law abridging . . . the freedom of the press'—can be contrasted with the very tentative nature of Article 40.6.1.i, where freedom of the press could be said to be conceded rather than declared:

> . . . the State shall endeavour to ensure that organs of public opinion, such as the radio, the press, the cinema, while preserving their rightful liberty of expression, including criticism of Government policy, shall not be used to undermine . . . the authority of the State.

In the US the state must not interfere with freedom of the press, while in Ireland the constitutional mandate is the reverse: the State has a duty to ensure that the press will not overstep the mark. The only saving grace is the fact that Article 40.6.1.i talks of actually undermining the authority of the State rather than 'tending to' undermine it, but in case there was any doubt, the tailpiece reminds us that the publication or utterance of seditious matter is an offence punishable by law.

Another issue that arises in this formulation is the meaning of the term the 'rightful liberty' of the press. Mr de Valera wished to prevent 'liberty degenerating into licence'.[8] There was no room, he said, for anarchy or anarchical principles.[9] Freedom of the press was freedom within the bounds of the common good and, in particular, within the requirements of the preservation of the State. The press clause attracted a lot of attention in the Dáil during the debate on the draft constitution, where views ranged from a belief that it was harmless and therefore should not be there at all, to a belief that it completely negated the right the article purported to guarantee. However, the inclusion of the phrase 'including criticism of government policy' was the only concession Mr de Valera was prepared to make. While it is inconceivable in a democracy that the freedom of the press should not extend to criticism of government policy, nonetheless the phrase could be of considerable significance in qualifying and restricting the scope of the mandate on the State not to let the media be used to undermine the 'authority of the State'. The concept of the 'authority of the State' is so wide that, if it were not reined in this way, it could be used to suppress or punish mere expressions of dissent or criticism of State institutions and officials. The 'authority of the State' certainly appears broader than the security or preservation of the State.

The Constitution has not often been invoked in this regard, an exception being AG *for England and Wales v Brandon Book Publishers*.[10] Also in *State (Lynch) v Cooney*[11] the Court was concerned with the 'duty of the State' under Article 40.6.1.i to intervene to prevent broadcasts on radio or television which would endanger the authority of the State. However, the Court recognised that:

> These . . . are objective determinations and obviously the fundamental rights of citizens to express freely their opinions and convictions cannot be curtailed or prevented on any irrational or capricious ground. It must be presumed that when the Oireachtas conferred these powers on the Minister it intended that they be exercised only in conformity with the Constitution.[12]

In setting out Article 40.6.1.i a tailpiece was added that made the 'publication or utterance of blasphemous, seditious, or indecent matter' a punishable offence. Blashphemous and indecent matter were discussed in Chapter 9, leaving seditious matter to be discussed here.

Seditious Matter

Since the sixteenth century there has been concern to prevent the publication of seditious matter, which in reality often meant any matter critical of the government or the institutions of the State. The main weapon used against the press was the common-law offence of seditious libel. Prosecutions and threatened prosecutions were very frequent especially from the end of the eighteenth century when the growth of the Volunteer Movement brought the press into conflict with the administration.[13] The offence of seditious libel was originally intended to protect the government and prevent loss of confidence in it. In the early days even trivial criticisms could be punished and the threat of prosecution proved an effective deterrent. It seems that, unlike blasphemous and other forms of criminal libel, intention—in this case an intention to subvert public order or government—was required.[14] Otherwise, the statutory provisions of Part II of the Defamation Act 1961 apply to seditious libel as to the other forms of criminal libel.

The editor of the *Irish Press* was prosecuted and fined for seditious libel under the Constitution (Amendment No. 17) Act 1931 arising out of a series of articles alleging police brutality towards Republican sympathisers.[15] Otherwise the common-law offence has hardly been used in modern times. One could thus conclude that the common-law offence of seditious libel is no longer necessary in Irish law. Firstly, the original rationale of the offence, namely to protect government from criticism, is no longer a valid aspiration. It belonged to a predemocratic age. Now, with the constitutional recognition of the press's right to criticise government policy, an offence of seditious libel can ultimately play only a residual role, if any, in protecting the State from such criticism as is calculated or intended to undermine the authority of the State but not the authority of the government of the day. Secondly, the common-law offence is rendered unnecessary by the existence of statutory provisions governing a variety of forms of sedition.[16]

1. Statute Law

A number of statutes, especially in the 1920s and 1930s, contained provisions relating to seditious libel. The Public Safety Act 1927, for example, provided for the suppression of and prohibition of the importation of periodicals containing seditious libel (sections 10, 11(1)).[17] The Constitution (Amendment No. 17) Act 1931 removed the requirement of the leave of a High Court judge for the prosecution of a newspaper for seditious libel.[18] The Emergency Powers Act 1939 empowered the government to make orders prohibiting the publication or dissemination of subversive statements and propaganda (section 2(2)(i)). All of these Acts should be seen as emergency legislation, occasioned, if not necessitated, by the unsettled period following the foundation of the State.

The Censorship of Films Act 1923, which was not emergency legislation and which is still in force with slight amendments, did not contain any reference to seditious matter. The Wireless Telegraphy Act in 1926, the Act that provided the foundation for radio broadcasting, authorised ministerial control of wireless telegraphy in time of national emergency (section 10). The short-lived Public Safety Act 1927 contained provisions relating to newspapers, which were to be picked up again in the Constitution (Amendment No.17) Act 1931 and the Offences against the State Act in 1939. The offences provided for included possession of documents relating to unlawful organisations[19] and the publication by newspapers of statements by or on behalf of or emanating from an unlawful organisation.[20]

Indeed, military censorship in the first years of the new State,[21] during which even the *Irish Independent* and *Evening Herald* were temporarily banned because of their support for the irregulars,[22] gave way to wartime censorship. The Emergency Powers Act 1939 was a temporary wartime measure which was renewed annually and expired in 1946. It allowed the government to make emergency orders to

> authorise and provide for the censorship, control, or partial or complete suspension of communication . . . (section 2(2)(h)),

[and to]

> make provision for preserving and safeguarding the secrecy of official documents and information and for controlling the publication of official information and for prohibiting the publication or spreading of subversive statements and propaganda, and authorise and provide for the control and censorship of newspapers and periodicals. (section 2(2)(i))

Wartime censorship was vigorously enforced.[23] All copy had to be submitted to the official censor who was authorised to delete paragraphs and to suggest amendments.[24] The neutrality of the State had to be safeguarded, but media censorship went well beyond that. (See full discussion in Chapter 1.) Weather reports were censored, as were reports of parliamentary debates;[25] a number of newspapers were banned and radio reports were tightly controlled. In addition, import duties were levied on all foreign publications as a budgetary measure in 1933 and maintained until 1971.

(a) Offences against the State Act 1939

The Offences against the State Act 1939, which is still in force, contains provisions in relation to unlawful associations, seditious matter and seditious documents. The Act makes it an offence to set up in type, print or publish any seditious document (section 10(1)), which is defined in the Act as including one containing matter calculated or tending to undermine public order or the authority of the State; or which alleges, implies or suggests that the government in power under the Constitution is not the lawful government; or that the military forces maintained under the Constitution are not the lawful military forces of the State; or a document in which words, abbreviations or symbols, referable to a military body are used in referring to an unlawful organisation (section 2).

It is an offence under the Act to send or contribute seditious matter to any newspaper or periodical and for the proprietor to publish any letter, article or communication which is sent or contributed by, or on behalf of, an unlawful organisation (section 10(2)). The scope of the section is very broad. Punishment includes fines and imprisonment, as well as forfeiture of every copy and of printing machinery (section 10(3)). The forfeiture of printing machinery was always the greatest deterrent because it had the potential of depriving a person of his or her livelihood. It is an offence also to refuse to hand up such a document or publication if requested to do so by a Garda (section 10(4)). In the case of seditious matter printed outside the State, the Minister can authorise the Gardaí to seize and destroy all copies or can prohibit its importation (section 11(1)). Even to have a treasonable, seditious or incriminating document in one's possession, without printing it, is an offence under the Act, regardless of one's purpose (section 12(1)). In that case, it is a good defence for a newspaper proprietor, editor or 'chief officer' to destroy the document within twenty-four hours of receipt without making any copy of it (section 12(5)). The emphasis, therefore, is on suppression of such a document rather than evaluation or consideration of its content or the underlying problem. The definition of 'incriminating' document in the Act is extremely broad,[26] and it is arguable that the present peace process could have been seriously hampered if such provisions had been invoked. Contributions at various points in time from the UDA and IRA might not have been published. In practice, of course, many of these provisions have simply been ignored. Unlawful organisations were denied access to broadcasting but their statements were fully reported and analysed in the print media.

One provision of the Offences against the State Act that is of general application and unrelated to sedition is the requirement that the printer's name and address be on *all* documents—not just seditious documents—printed and intended for the public, with the exception of newspapers printed on their own premises (sections 13 and 14). The latter is not an unusual provision.[27] Other countries, such as France, have similar provisions in their law. Such a provision may have made sense at a time when the printer had control over what he printed. With modern technology that is no longer the case. Nowadays many books, periodicals and newspapers are printed outside the State and there can be little argument for requiring the printer to put his/her name and address on them without requiring the author, editor or publisher to do so, as they are the people who have control over content. In this and other respects, the Offences against the State Act goes far beyond what is necessary for the protection of the State in a modern democracy and could be open to challenge on constitutional grounds.[28] The UN Human Rights Committee has expressed concern about aspects of the Acts and has recommended in particular that the need for the Special Criminal Court be examined for its conformity to the International Covenant on Civil and Political Rights be ensured. The Law Reform Commission has also urged reform.[29] The decision of the Dáil to rescind the state of emergency[30] does not affect these aspects of the Offences against the State Acts, which are part of the ordinary law rather than emergency law.[31]

The Offences against the State (Amendment) Act 1972 contains a provision making it an offence to issue a public statement, orally, in writing or otherwise, that constitutes an interference with the course of justice (section 4). Other statutes make it an offence to advocate the commission of the offence of forcible entry,[32] to recruit, incite or invite others to join, support or assist an unlawful organisation,[33] to incite hatred on grounds of race, colour, nationality, origins, membership of the travelling community or sexual orientation.[34]

The Broadcasting Authority (Amendment) Act 1976 prohibits the broadcasting of matter likely or tending to undermine the authority of the State (section 3(1a)). The ministerial order required to implement the ban on interviews with spokespersons or representatives of certain listed organisations, resulting from section 31 of the Broadcasting Authority Act 1960, as amended by section 16 of the 1976 Act, has not been renewed since January 1994. Discussion of the section 31 ban is therefore largely academic but because it is only the ministerial order that has not been renewed and the statutory provision remains in place and capable of being used again, some explanation of its history and failings is appropriate.

(b) The Broadcasting Bans

The Broadcasting Authority Act 1960, which heralded the advent of television broadcasting, contained a provision at section 31:

> The Minister may direct the Authority in writing to refrain from broadcasting any particular matter of any particular class and the Authority shall comply with the direction.

This section, which was originally intended as a fall-back measure, i.e. a reserve power for use in emergency situations, went unnoticed for over a decade until 1971. In that year the first ministerial directive was issued in accordance with section 31, in response to a '7 Days' current affairs programme on RTÉ which included interviews with members of an illegal organisation, the IRA. In the previous years there had been government interference with programming on a number of occasions,[35] and in 1966 Taoiseach Seán Lemass had said in a Dáil speech:

> . . . the Government reject[s] the view that Radio Teilifís Éireann should be, either generally or in regard to its current affairs and news programmes, completely independent of Government supervision. As a public institution supported by public funds and operating under statute it has the duty . . . to sustain public respect for the institutions of Government . . . The Government will take such action by way of making representations or otherwise as may be necessary to ensure that RTÉ does not deviate from the due performance of this duty.[36]

Section 31 was to become a central feature of Irish broadcasting as ministerial orders invoking it were renewed annually from 1976 on. The scope of the provision was narrowed by the Broadcasting Authority (Amendment) Act 1976, section 16, which states:

> Where the Minister is of the opinion that the broadcasting of a particular matter or any matter of a particular class would be likely to promote, or

incite to, crime or would tend to undermine the authority of the State, he may by order direct the Authority to refrain from broadcasting the matter or any matter of the particular class, and the Authority shall comply with the order. (section 16(1))

An order under the section was to remain in force for up to twelve months and could be extended by further orders of similar duration (section 16(1A)). An order could be annulled by either house of the Oireachtas (section 16(1B)) but this never happened. One of the safeguards pointed to when the amending legislation was being introduced was the provision for regular parliamentary scrutiny. In fact, that never happened. There was no parliamentary debate and very few parliamentary questions about section 31. Those that were asked drew very little response.

The intended effect of the section 31 orders was to deny airtime to the IRA and other organisations banned in the State and in Northern Ireland—to deprive them of the oxygen of publicity and the air of legitimacy that it was believed appearing on the broadcast media would accord them. Sinn Féin, which was not a banned organisation, was later added to the list and, although it was to become a legally registered political party in the State, was prohibited from making a party political broadcast in the run-up to the general election of 1982, in which it was fielding candidates. The Supreme Court in *State (Lynch) v Cooney*,[37] in which Sinn Féin challenged the section 31 order, applied the presumption of constitutionality, i.e. all statutes passed by the Oireachtas since the coming into force of the Constitution in 1937 are presumed to be in conformity with the Constitution:

> The basis for any attempt at control must be, according to the Constitution [Article 40.6.1], the overriding considerations of public order and public morality. The constitutional provision in question refers to organs of public opinion and these must be held to include television as well as radio. It places upon the State the obligation to ensure that these organs of public opinion shall not be used to undermine public order or public morality or the authority of the State. It follows that the use of such organs of public opinion for the purpose of securing or advocating support for organisations which seek by violence to overthrow the State or its institutions is a use which is prohibited by the Constitution. Therefore it is clearly the duty of the State to intervene to prevent broadcasts on radio or television which are aimed at such a result or which in any way would be likely to have the effect of promoting or inciting to crime or endangering the authority of the State. These, however, are objective determinations and obviously the fundamental rights of citizens to express freely their convictions and opinions cannot

be curtailed or prevented on any irrational or capricious ground. It must be presumed that when the Oireachtas conferred these powers on the Minister [i.e. to make orders invoking section 31] it intended that they be exercised only in conformity with the Constitution.[38]

Section 31, therefore, was not unconstitutional. That did not necessarily mean that the State was obliged to keep it in force, but merely that the Constitution did not prevent such a measure. Needless to say, the State took the Court's decision as the green light to continue the ban. This occurred despite the fact that the ban was impractical, given that the British channels, which were not affected by the ban, could be received in Ireland. The ban also created a climate of repression and self-censorship within RTÉ. The tendency was always to err on the safe side, and it was easier not to make programmes that might cause problems. Besides, the Supreme Court had said *inter alia* in *Cooney* that the fact that the text of the broadcast might be innocuous was not relevant to the issues before the Court.[39] This led to some confusion and a tendency to interpret the ban more widely than was ultimately decided to be necessary. RTÉ excluded from the airwaves anyone who was a member of Sinn Féin, regardless of the topic on which he/she was to speak. Mushroom-growing, local water schemes, trade union matters, a strike in a factory were all excluded because the intended interviewees were members of Sinn Féin. The orders invoking section 31 referred only to spokespersons for, or representatives of, Sinn Féin. It would later be held in *O'Toole v RTÉ*[40] that RTÉ had interpreted the ban too broadly, and that the order did not prevent ordinary members of Sinn Féin speaking on an innocuous subject on the airwaves. The Broadcasting Complaints Commission rejected a complaint about section 31 in 1988. The Commission did not give any reasons but in effect upheld the extension of section 31 to ordinary members of Sinn Féin speaking on innocuous subjects.[41]

Meanwhile, election coverage was also affected. When Gerry Adams won his seat at Westminster, he could be interviewed on broadcast stations all over the world. On RTÉ only the losing candidate could be interviewed. By 1984 Sinn Féin had won over one hundred thousand votes in the North and about thirty local council seats in the Republic, yet the electorate was not allowed to hear them interviewed on RTÉ. Voters could not have their views or grievances expressed on radio or television by their elected representatives. The right of the public to information on a whole host of issues, including the political situation in the North, was denied in this way. This effect was at its most poignant during the Hume-Adams talks, which were crucial to the development of the present peace process. However, Adams could not be interviewed about these talks nor about his defeat in the Westminster elections of 1992.

Section 31 continued to operate, therefore, until January 1994, despite the fact that the Broadcasting Authority Act 1976 already offered a viable alternative in section 18(1A):

> The Authority is hereby prohibited from including in any of its broadcasts or in any matter referred to in paragraph (c) of subsection (1) [i.e. news, current affairs] of this section anything which may reasonably be regarded as being likely to promote, or incite to, crime or as tending to undermine the authority of the State.

This section had been relied on to prevent interviews with Martin Galvin of Noraid in 1984[42] and with journalist Nell McCafferty in 1987.[43] It also caused transmission of a programme 'Irish America Report' to be deferred. An edited version of the programme, which reported on the activities of Irish-American groups in relation to Northern Ireland, was later transmitted.[44]

It seems peculiar that an act would have two separate sections dealing with the same problem. Section 31, as amended, requires a ministerial order of limited duration to implement it, while section 18(1A) is permanent and automatic. The same remedy attaches to both: a complaint that either section has been breached can be made to the Broadcasting Complaints Commission. One advantage that section 18(1A) has over section 31 is that it incorporates a standard of reasonableness: the authority is prohibited from broadcasting any matter which 'may reasonably be regarded' as likely to promote or incite to crime or as tending to undermine the authority of the State. The ministerial orders implementing section 31, on the other hand, were directed at specified organisations and confined mainly to interviews or reports of interviews with representatives of, or spokespersons for, them. It is true that the original section 31 of the 1960 Act was of broader scope and could have been invoked by a minister to prevent the broadcasting of totally unrelated matter, but since the amendment in the 1976 Act that is no longer the case. Since then, section 31 and section 18 cover the same ground.

Section 31, as amended, was extended to the local radio stations by the Radio and Television Act 1988 (section 12). In the same year Jenny McGeever, a journalist with RTÉ who breached section 31, lost her job. She had included a few words from Martin McGuinness, a leading member of Sinn Féin, in her report for the 'Morning Ireland' radio programme on the funeral of three alleged IRA members killed in the

Gibraltar shooting.[45] Some months later, in October, the British government announced its decision to introduce a similar, though less restrictive, ban. The British ban did not extend to elected representatives, election campaigns or parliamentary proceedings. Only words spoken by a person appearing on a programme were covered; therefore films or stills with voice-overs were permitted.[46] Both bans became the subject of (separate) complaints to Strasbourg.

2. European Commission on Human Rights

(i) Purcell v Ireland

The European Commission on Human Rights in *Purcell v Ireland*[47] accepted that section 31 constituted an interference with the journalists' right under Article 10.1 of the Convention to receive and impart information and ideas but was satisfied that the restrictions were prescribed by law and that the aim pursued was legitimate. The applicants had not disputed the seriousness of the terrorist threat in Ireland, and section 31 did not prohibit the reporting of the activities of the listed organisations, only interviews with their spokespeople:

> It thus prohibits the use of the broadcast media for the purpose of advocating support for organisations which seek to undermine by violence and other illegal means, the constitutional order and the fundamental rights and freedoms it guarantees.[48]

The restriction was necessary in a democratic society, the Commission said, as there was evidence of a pressing social need. Besides, states have a margin of appreciation in assessing whether such a need exists. It was not the Commission's role to determine whether other measures were more appropriate nor to assess the expediency and efficiency of the measures taken. The Commission's role was rather to determine:

(i) whether the reasons adduced for the section 31 restrictions were relevant and sufficient under Article 10(2) and

(ii) whether the Minister had convincing reasons for assuming the existence of a pressing social need.[49]

In a situation where politically motivated violence was a constant threat to the lives and security of the population and where the advocates of this violence seek access to the mass media for publicity purposes, it is particularly difficult to strike a fair balance, the Commission said.[50] The Commission was satisfied that section 31 was designed to deny the possibility of using the broadcast media as a platform for advocating an organisation's cause, encouraging support and conveying the impression of their legitimacy. The restrictions might cause the broadcasters 'inconvenience' but were not incompatible with Article 10.2.

The decision was a disappointing one for a number of reasons. The Commission seemed to be swayed by the level of violence, the particular impact of television and the fact that the complainants did not reject the government's argument that Sinn Féin was closely linked to the IRA. It is a pity that the case did not clear the first hurdle and go to the Court, especially in light of the Court's subsequent decision in *Jersild v Denmark*.[51] In *Jersild*, the Court emphasised again the important role of the print and broadcast media. It was for journalists, not courts, to decide what techniques of reporting should be adopted. Furthermore:

> News reporting based on interviews, whether edited or not, constitutes one of the most important means whereby the press is able to play its vital role . . . The punishment of a journalist for assisting in the dissemination of statements made by another person in an interview would seriously hamper the contribution of the press to discussion of matters of public interest and should not be envisaged unless there are particularly strong reasons for doing so.[52]

It is possible that the scale of the problem in Northern Ireland at the time would have constituted a 'particularly strong' reason. One telling difference between the presentation of the case before the Court in *Jersild*, compared with that in *Purcell*, was that in the former it was possible to show the court footage of the programme containing the interviews with the racist Greenjackets. In the case of *Purcell*, on the other hand, it was not as easy to do so because the section 31 ban, as a form of prior restraint, had prevented the broadcasting of interviews.

(ii) Developments after *Purcell*

Following the Commission's decision that *Purcell* was manifestly ill-founded, it was perhaps inevitable that the *Brind*[53] case on the British ban would also be declared inadmissible.[54] Nonetheless, *Brind* was useful, at least for lawyers, in the sense that it provided the opportunity to fight the case in the Court of Appeal and House of Lords with reference to the European Convention on Human Rights and the principles and standards it enshrines. *Purcell* was also useful in that it focused attention on section 31 and demanded, for the first time in its contentious history, that its use be justified by the authorities. The victory for the government was a hollow one and the first step in the dismantling process of section 31. As one of the lawyers involved in the case said:

> This decision [*Purcell*] . . . seemed to effectively reverse the special status of political speech acknowledged in earlier decisions of the Commission and Court. But there is the basis of a jurisprudence which can be built on that recognises the role of the media which Irish and British courts ought to be encouraged to follow.[55]

Meanwhile in 1990, when the *Purcell* case was still pending before the European Commission on Human Rights, Larry O'Toole, the chairman of a strike committee at the Gateaux bakery in Dublin, had been interviewed on a number of occasions by RTÉ about the strike. The first interview was broadcast but the remainder were not, because it had emerged that Mr O'Toole was a member of Sinn Féin. In the High Court action that followed,[56] it was found that RTÉ was wrong on three counts in its interpretation of the ministerial order invoking section 31:

(i)   RTÉ had misinterpreted the Ministerial order by applying it to ordinary members of Sinn Féin, when it was clearly confined to representatives of, and spokespersons for, Sinn Féin[57]

(ii)   the obligations of fairness and impartiality in respect of news and current affairs imposed on RTÉ by the Broadcasting Authority Acts were infringed by the refusal on arbitrary grounds to allow the views of the workers in a major industrial dispute which was arousing widespread public attention, to be put forward on their behalf by the person they had appointed to be their spokesman.[58]

(iii)   while access to broadcasting was not a right, a decision to single out a particular person or group and impose a blanket prohibition against his or their views on any topic whatever, expressed in their personal capacity and not as spokesman for or as representing any organisation, would have to be justified on very substantial grounds.[59]

The High Court's decision was appealed to the Supreme Court by RTÉ, apparently for purposes of clarification, and was upheld. The section 31 order only applied to spokespersons for, and representatives of, Sinn Féin and not to ordinary members speaking on an innocuous subject, who 'should be treated equally with others when [their] views do not transgress either the Constitution or the law'.[60]

The Irish government in the *Purcell* case had argued that allowing airtime to Sinn Féin would lend validity and respectability to their cause and activities. It may be argued that accessibility itself does not necessarily lend credibility. However, a similar argument prevailed in the application by Brandon Book Publishers for judicial review of the decision by RTÉ and the IRTC not to permit the broadcasting of pre-recorded advertisements for Gerry Adams's book, *The Street and Other Stories*.[61] The independent radio stations had already interviewed Gerry Adams about his book and the ban on it.[62] Carney J. in the IRTC case accepted that there was evidence to support the broadcasters' view that:

> ... Mr Adams could not be separated from his office as President of Sinn Féin and that any broadcast by him on any topic would have the de facto effect of advocating support for Sinn Féin.[63]

Their decision not to permit the advertisement could only be interfered with if it were perverse, irrational or malicious, the judge said, and none of those considerations arose.[64] It may be noted that Lord Diplock in GCHQ[65] identified illegality, irrationality and procedural impropriety as grounds for judicial review and suggested that the European test of proportionality (deriving from administrative law and applied in such cases as *Sunday Times v* UK) might be added as a fourth ground in due course. The Court of Appeal was invited to adopt proportionality as a ground in *Brind*, the British broadcasting ban case[66] but refused to accept it as anything more than a criterion for assessing one of the three grounds identified in GCHQ. The House of Lords concurred but left open the possibility of future development.[66]

A somewhat unexpected boost to the fight against section 31 came from the UN Human Rights Committee in 1993. Ireland had ratified the Covenant on Civil and Political Rights in November 1989 and was required to submit a report to the Committee concerning the implementation of the Covenant in Ireland. In response to that report, the Committee stated that the section 31 ban infringed the freedom to receive and impart information under Article 19, paragraph 2 of the Covenant[68] and that the State should take the necessary measures to ensure that Article 19 was complied with.[69] Incidentally, Ireland has also ratified the Optional Protocol to the International Covenant under which individual complaints can be taken to the Committee in a similar way as to the European Commission and Court. Ireland is required to submit a further report in March 1996 and at three-year intervals after that.

In January 1994 the Irish government decided not to renew the order implementing section 31.[70] The section itself remains, however, which means that it could be reactivated. The British ban was lifted shortly after the Irish one, as the peace process developed and the cessation of violence came to be accepted as genuine. However, before the British ban had been lifted, an interview with Gerry Adams on CNN in the United States caused some controversy, not because of its content, but because it was dubbed, not only for broadcast in Britain, but for the rest of Europe as well, as the signal was uplifted to CNN's satellite from Britain.[71]

3. European Court of Human Rights

The question of political violence and terrorism has been considered by the European Court of Human Rights in a number of cases. It arose in *Castells v Spain*,[72] where the threat came from the Basque separatists, whom Castells represented as a senator. In a magazine article he accused the government of not investigating crimes carried out by armed groups on Basque citizens. In fact, he went so far as to accuse the government of instigating the attacks. The article was published during a particularly violent period and Mr Castells was sentenced to imprisonment and disqualification from public office for one year. Nevertheless, the European Court of Human Rights made clear that governments must tolerate criticism and scrutiny, even more so than politicians, and that it is only in the most exceptional circumstances that a government may resort to the criminal law to punish criticism of itself:

> In a democratic system the actions or omissions of the Government must be subject to the close scrutiny . . . of the press and public opinion.[73]

In *Thorgeirson v Iceland*,[74] in which a journalist alleged that the incidence of police brutality was increasing, the Court found that the journalist's main purpose had been to promote reform and because the conduct of the police was a legitimate matter of public concern, he consequently deserved a higher level of protection.

The Court also considered the question of official secrets and breach of confidence in the *Spycatcher* case.[75] The intended publication in Australia in 1985 of the memoirs of Peter Wright, a former member of the British Secret Service (MI5), triggered a series of actions against publication of the book itself and against newspaper articles about the book, serialising it or containing information from it. Among the allegations made by Mr Wright were that MI5 had conducted unlawful activities calculated to undermine the Labour government in the 1970s, had burgled and 'bugged' the embassies of allied and hostile countries and had planned and participated in other unlawful and covert activities at home and abroad.[76] In 1987 the book was published in the United States.

The case eventually made its way to the European Court of Human Rights, which found that there had been a violation of Article 10 during the period when the injunctions against publication were continued by the English courts after the information had been published in the United States. During the earlier period the injunctions were found to be justified for two reasons: firstly, because of the need to maintain the authority of the judiciary during the period up to the hearing of the claim for permanent injunctions; and, secondly, to protect national security, in the sense of the integrity of the Security Service.[77] Indeed, the protection of national security is a widely recognised area of restriction on media activities. In Ireland the most far-reaching protection is contained in the Official Secrets Act 1963.

Official Secrets

1. Official Secrets Act 1963

The Official Secrets Act 1963 was passed as part of the government's plan to consolidate laws and pass indigenous laws to replace those of earlier legislatures, in this case the British Official Secrets Acts of 1911 and 1920. Several deputies asked why it was necessary to do so in this case and the explanation they were given was that examination papers had been leaked by an apprentice printer and therefore legislation was necessary to deal with such leaks.[78] The remedy, if it was a remedy, was to pass a full-scale official secrets act.

The reality of the times, however, suggests that the IRA campaign of the 1950s may have been a more significant factor in the decision. In any event, it was pointed out in the Dáil that it was unsatisfactory to have to rely on British legislation, especially when, as in this case, it was unsuitable and defective. The British Act of 1911 had been rushed through as emergency legislation and had passed all stages in a single day.[79] However, when one considers that there had been only one prosecution brought in Ireland under the British acts and that it had been in 1933 and unsuccessful,[80] it is still difficult to explain why the new Act was passed in 1963 and especially in the form in which it was passed.

By way of analysis, the Act is extremely wide in its application, protecting virtually every document connected with the running of the country. Official information, for instance, is defined in section 2 as:

any secret official code word or password, and any sketch, plan, model, article, note, document or information which is secret or confidential or is expressed to be either and which is or has been in the possession, custody or control of a holder of public office, or to which he has or had access by virtue of his office, and includes information recorded by film or magnetic tape or by any other recording medium.

The term 'public office' is defined in the Act and is again very broad. It extends to 'appointment to or employment under any commission, committee, tribunal or inquiry set up by the government or a Minister, (section 2(1)).

Perhaps the most disturbing feature of the Act is the provision that a Minister can certify that any document is secret or confidential and that certificate shall be conclusive evidence of the fact that it is secret or confidential—not *prima facie* evidence, but 'conclusive' evidence (section 2(3)), thus precluding the courts from inquiring into the nature of the certified document.

The Act made it an offence to communicate such information unless authorised to do so or under a duty to do so as a holder of public office or in the interest of the State (section 4(1)). It applied to all civil servants, in fact to anybody, by making it a criminal offence to communicate any information, no matter how trivial and no matter to whom, unless there was authorisation to do so. Subsection 2 of section 4 requires that reasonable care be taken to avoid unlawful communication, which suggests a negligence standard rather than strict liability. The legislature may therefore have mitigated the rigours of the offence but not its scope, since Part II of the Act is not confined to state security and covers any information.

2. Official Secrets and the Media

Through the adoption of the Official Secrets Act the British obsession with secrecy and security was imported into Irish law.[81] The pertinent question for present purposes is how that climate of secrecy affects the media. In Britain there have been numerous cases of attempts to ban publications, such as the *Crossman Diaries*[82] and *Spycatcher*.[83] Criminal prosecutions have been taken against journalists like Duncan Campbell, for reporting, in his case, on a major surveillance project involving the interception and analysis of radio communications.[84] Newspapers have been ordered to return leaked documents, as was the case when the *Guardian* published a story about the delivery of cruise missiles to Greenham Common. In that case the civil servant who had leaked the information was prosecuted under section 2 of the Official Secrets Act 1911 and imprisoned.[85] In another case relating to Northern Ireland, a public interest immunity certificate was signed by the Secretary of State for Northern Ireland banning access to the Stalker report in the interests of national security. Mr John Stalker had been appointed to inquire into allegations of a shoot-to-kill policy in the North.[86]

Perhaps the most memorable case of all is the Clive Ponting case of 1984.[87] Ponting was the civil servant who gave information to his member of parliament about the sinking of the *Belgrano* during the Falklands War. He was duly prosecuted under section 2 of the Official Secrets Act but stated in evidence that he felt obliged to tell Parliament how it had been misled by ministers. The documents in question were not classified and no question of national security arose; instead the case was taken on the grounds of breach of confidence, the confidence that a civil servant owed by virtue of his employment contract. Channel Four Television was ordered by the trial judge, under section 4(2) of the Contempt of Court Act 1981, not to re-create each evening the day's proceedings. A Sunday newspaper also found itself in trouble for reporting details of what had happened during the *in camera* proceedings, even though no specific order had been made to prohibit it. The remarkable thing was that the jury found Ponting not guilty. Unfortunately that case was not the end of the road, however, as episodes like the Zircon affair[88] and *Spycatcher* have shown.

There is some protection for the British media under section 10 of the Contempt of Court Act 1981, in that journalists or those responsible for publication are not obliged, if called as witnesses in court, to reveal their sources unless it is established to the satisfaction of the court that disclosure is necessary in the interests of justice or national security or for the prevention of disorder or crime. In Britain the 1911 Act has been replaced by the Official Secrets Act 1989. The new legislation covers a narrower range of information but also applies to media disclosure of any information covered by the Act, the publication of which causes harm, however trivial.[89]

Official Secrets in Ireland

In Ireland the Official Secrets Act 1963 remains in operation, although the Dáil Committee on Legislation and Security has invited submissions from interested parties to its review of the Act.[90] There have been surprisingly few prosecutions under the Act, although its impact in creating and maintaining a culture of secrecy has been no less real as a result. Section 13 of the Act, which prohibits the possession of any document containing, or any record whatsoever of, information relating to the operations of the Garda Síochána, was invoked against a 'Today Tonight' current affairs television programme on the leaking of an official Garda memorandum on the security of the British Ambassador during his holiday in Sneem, Co. Kerry. The decision to invoke the Act was an attempt to prevent the media from detailing the precise nature of the leak. It appears that the document had been marked 'confidential' but did not carry a 'secret' or 'top secret' classification; that is it was sensitive but routine information.[91] However laudable its purpose, the wording of the section is unduly wide. Section 12 of the Act also allows the prosecution—not the court—to apply to have any part of a hearing under the Act held *in camera* on the grounds that it would be prejudicial to the safety or preservation of the State and 'the court shall make an order to that effect'. (For a discussion of *in camera* proceedings, see Chapter 7.)

The only successful prosecution of the media under the Act in recent years has been that of the *Irish Independent* and its editor in the *Shergar* case in 1984.[92] Shergar was a racehorse that had been kidnapped, and the newspaper and its editor were each fined £100 in the District Court on charges of breaching the Official Secrets Act by publishing Garda identikit pictures of two suspects in the case. They had obtained and communicated to the public confidential information (i.e. the pictures), reproduced from a Garda bulletin which was stamped 'confidential', although the pictures themselves were not. About fifteen hundred copies of the bulletin had been circulated to Garda stations throughout the State, to the Department of Justice, and to police forces abroad. Added to that was the fact that daily press conferences had been held during the Garda investigations. In those circumstances, counsel asked, how could the pictures be regarded as secret and confidential?[93] Could it not be argued also that the Official Secrets Act should be reserved for important matters of State, not for minor matters before the District Court? Because the ambit of Part II of the Act is extremely wide, it lacks a central focus and unity of purpose. The serious and the trivial are lumped together and given blanket protection at the expense of the rights of the individual and the public's right to disclosure. Even on its widest interpretation, the constitutional interest in the 'authority of the State' could not justify blanket protection of this kind. At a minimum, the scope of section 4 in particular needs to be precisely delimited.

Three years after *Shergar*, a more common-sense approach prevailed in AG *for England and Wales v Brandon Book Publishers*,[93] when Carroll J. in the High Court refused an injunction to prevent distribution of a book called *One Girl's War*, about the wartime exploits of the British Secret Service. The war had ended more than thirty years previously and the book posed no threat to the authority of this State, which would have been the only reason under our Constitution for granting the injunction as a restriction on freedom of expression. Because no considerations of public interest arose in this jurisdiction, the case was based solely on the principle of confidentiality, deriving from the employment of the author of the book. Importantly for the media, Carroll J. cited with approval the dicta of Mason J. in the Australian case of *Commonwealth of Australia v John Fairfax and Sons Ltd*[95] to the effect that:

> It is unacceptable in our democratic society that there should be a restraint on the publication of information relating to government when the only vice of that information is that it enables the public to discuss, review and criticise government action.

Accordingly, the Court will determine the government's claim to confidentiality by reference to the public interest. Unless disclosure is likely to injure the public interest, it will not be protected.

Carroll J. also recognised that:

> what was at stake was the very important right to communicate now and not when the case has worked its way through the courts.[96]

In another development in 1988 An Foras Forbartha was abolished and replaced by an Environmental Research Unit wholly within the Department of the Environment, with the result that staff had to abide by the Official Secrets Act.[97] The dangers that such a restriction poses for the public interest in information on such a sensitive issue as the environment is all too clear. In 1990 the Dáil Committee on Public Accounts was told that it could not see a consultancy report prepared for government prior to its sale of its share in Tara Mines. The reason given was that it contained confidential commercial information, which could not be disclosed under a clause inserted in the original agreement between the government and Tara Mines in 1975.[98] More recently it was reported that workers in a new State-sponsored body, Shannon Airport Marketing, were asked to sign the Act as part of their employment contract.[99] The Act was invoked against the media again in 1995 at the very time when it was under official review and when the government's plans to introduce freedom of information legislation were at an advanced stage. Journalist Liz Allen and Independent

Newspapers were prosecuted for publishing a confidential Garda document which purported to show that the force had prior knowledge of the multi-million pound Brinks-Allied robbery in January 1995. The case was heard in the District Court in March 1996 and fines imposed.[100]

The main difficulties with the Official Secrets Act, therefore, are its all-embracing scope, the fact that it is liable to be invoked to deal with the most trivial of situations as well as those of national importance and, most worrying of all, the culture of secrecy that it emanates from and has in turn engendered. The case for freedom of information legislation is all the more pressing as a result. A culture of secrecy pervades Irish society and the media have a role to play in breaking it down. The Greencore or Telecom scandals would not have become public if it had not been for the media, who persisted in their investigations despite threats from lawyers.[100] More is known about the activities of certain Irish companies from the information they have to reveal to the authorities in the US under legislation there than they have ever revealed here.[101] The Official Secrets Act is the epitome of a culture of secrecy, but it is not the only element contributing to that culture. For instance, the libel laws in Britain allowed Robert Maxwell to carry out frauds over decades with impunity. In the dawning of a new culture of openness that freedom of information legislation heralds, the whole machinery of censorship and secrecy needs to be reviewed and reformed.

Further Reading

Ewing, Keith, and Gearty, Conor, *Freedom under Thatcher: Civil Liberties in Modern Britain*, Oxford: Clarendon Press, 1990.

Hall, Eamonn G., 'The Majestic Guarantee — Freedom of Speech', (1995) Dlí — *the Western Law Gazette*, p. 79.

Index on Censorship, vol. 22, nos 8 & 9, 1993 (Re. Ireland).

Irish Council of Civil Liberties, *Submissions to the Ministerial Review of Section 31 of the Broadcasting Act 1960*, March 1993, November 1993; *Submission to the UN Human Rights Committee*, March 1993.

Notes

1 *Whitney v California* 274 US 357 375, (1927).
2 *Cohen v California* 403 US 15 23–5, (1971).

3 Anthony Lewis, John Foster Memorial Lecture 1987, 9 *London Review of Books* No. 21, 26 (November 1987); see also Anthony Lewis, *Make No Law*, New York: Vintage Books, 1992.

4 376 US 254 (1964).

5 283 US 697 (1931).

6 403 US 713 (1971).

7 *New York Times v US* 328 F. Supp. 324, (1971) *per* Gurfein J. at p. 331.

8 68 *Dáil Debates*, col. 425 (report stage).

9 67 *Dáil Debates*, col. 1634.

10 [1986] IR 597, [1987] ILRM 135.

11 [1982] IR 337, [1983] ILRM 89.

12 Ibid., at p. 94 *per* O'Higgins C.J. Reference was also made to the Constitution by O'Flaherty J. in *O'Toole v RTÉ* [1993] ILRM 458.

13 See Brian Inglis, *The Freedom of the Press in Ireland, 1784–1841*, London: Faber and Faber, 1954.

14 Peter F. Carter-Ruck, Richard Walker and Harvey Starte, *Carter-Ruck on Libel and Slander*, 3rd edn., London: Butterworths, 1985, p. 173.

15 John Horgan, 'State Policy and the Press', 8 *Media and Popular Culture, The Crane Bag*, vol. 8, no. 2, 1984, p. 51.

16 See also Law Reform Commission, *Report on the Crime of Libel* (LRC 41–1991), 1991, at p. 10.

17 The Act was short-lived. It was passed in response to the killing of the Minister for Justice and was repealed the following year.

18 S. 33. This Act, which established a military tribunal to try offences, totally undermined the 1922 Constitution then in force.

19 S. 6 of the 1931 Act and s. 21 of the 1939 Act, respectively.

20 S. 9 of the 1931 Act and s. 23(1) of the 1939 Act, respectively.

21 Official Notice of Military Censorship of Newspapers and Publications, 2 July 1922. See *Collected Orders*, Part 1, p. 67; 1 *Dáil Debates*, cols 797–8.

22 See n. 15, at p. 52.

23 See Kieran Woodman, *Media Control in Ireland, 1923–1983*, Galway: University Press, 1985, p. 75–6; Hugh Oram, *The Newspaper Book: A History of Newspapers in Ireland, 1649–1983*, Dublin: MO Books, 1983; n. 15, at p. 54, *The Irish Times*, 7–13 August 1983, a series of six articles by Joe Carroll.

24 89 *Dáil Debates*, cols 715–721.

25 24 *Seanad Debates*, col. 2573.

26 An 'incriminating document' is defined in the Act as one issued by, or emanating from, an unlawful organisation, or appearing to be so issued or so to emanate or purporting or appearing to aid and abet any such organisation or calculated to promote the formation of an unlawful organisation (s. 2).

27 The provision in the Offences against the State Act 1939 may have been taken over from the Newspapers, Printers and Reading Rooms Repeal Act 1869, which did not apply to Ireland. That provision was originally intended to suppress certain treasonable and seditious societies in existence during the Napoleonic Wars. See Colin Manchester, 'The Newspapers, Printers and Reading Rooms Repeal Act 1869: A Case for Repeal? (1982) LS, vol. 2, 180.

28 James P. Casey, *Constitutional Law in Ireland*, 2nd edn., London: Sweet and Maxwell, 1992, at p. 449, says that in the US such a sweeping statute would be unconstitutional.

29 UN Human Rights Committee, July 1993, paras 11, 19. Law Reform Commission, *Consultation Paper on the Crime of Libel*, 1991, rec. 25. The LRC took the view that the scheme of censorship, the Censorship Acts and the Offences against the State Act 1939 should be examined: 'Many of these provisions are outdated and may be inconsistent with modern views on what is required in the public interest. Others may be constitutionally suspect. Some are confusing and ambiguous'. See also n. 16, rec. 30.

30 448 *Dáil Debates*, cols 1538–1587.

31 Part V of the 1939 Act, which allows the government to pass a resolution establishing a special court when the ordinary courts are inadequate to handle a particular situation,

is part of the emergency legislation. The present Special Criminal Court dates from 1972.

32 Prohibition of Forcible Entry and Occupation Act 1971, s. 4(1).

33 Criminal Law Act 1976, s. 3, which was introduced in response to the violence in Northern Ireland and therefore is emergency in nature.

34 Prohibition of Incitement to Hatred Act 1989, s. 1. New race relations legislation is to be introduced in NI, The Irish Times, 28 April 1995.

35 See Lelia Doolan, Jack Dowling, and Bob Quinn, Sit Down and Be Counted: The Cultural Evolution of a Television Station Dublin: Wellington Publishers, 1969, at p. 55; 227 Dáil Debates, col. 1661; 228 Dáil Debates, cols 1002–3.

36 224 Dáil Debates, 1045–6.

37 See n. 11.

38 Ibid., at p. 94 per O'Higgins C.J.

39 Ibid., at p. 97.

40 See n. 12.

41 Sunday Tribune, 8 November 1987, 24 April 1988.

42 The Irish Times, 24 August 1984.

43 The Irish Times, 23 November 1987.

44 The Irish Times, 30 March 1988. One interview was reported to contain the statement 'I am committed to the use of the bullet and the bomb.'

45 Journalist Jenny McGeever's subsequent High Court action against RTÉ was settled; Sunday Tribune, 18 September 1988.

46 See Article 19, Censorship, Secrecy and the Irish Troubles, London 1989. In compliance with the terms of the Representation of the People Act, the ban was lifted during the run-up to local, general and European elections to allow candidates to be asked about election issues only; The Irish Times, 11 April 1989.

47 (1991) 12 HRLJ No. 6–7, 254.

48 Ibid., at 259.

49 Ibid., at 260.

50. Ibid.

51 Jersild v Denmark, Application No. 15890/89, decision of the Court, 23 September 1994: see also Castells v Spain (1992) 14 EHRR 445; Series A, no. 236.

52 Ibid at para.51.

53 R v Secretary of State for the Home Department, ex parte Brind [1991] 1 AC 696, [1991] 2 WLR 588 (HL). The British broadcasting ban was upheld by the High Court in Belfast in 1990, when an application for judicial review was refused. A Sinn Féin City Councillor had argued that the ban breached the NI Constitution Act 1973, which prevents government ministers from discriminating against groups or individuals on grounds of religious belief or political opinion (The Irish Times, 8 September 1990; ITLR 26 November 1990). Some months earlier, a song by the Pogues about the Guildford Four was banned from the airwaves under the British ban (Sunday Tribune, 22 October 1989). The British ban was extended in December 1990 to cover cable and nondomestic satellite television services (The Irish Times, 20 December 1990). In 1994 Bernadette McAliskey lost a High Court action, challenging the BBC's decision to use subtitles instead of her voice in broadcasting a studio debate on political violence. She had never been a member of any of the listed organisations. In the televised debate she said she understood why violence occurred (The Irish Times, 28 May 1994).

54 The Irish Times, 25 May 1994.

55 Kevin Boyle, lecture, Trinity College Dublin, 1992, edited version, 'Freedom of Expression and Democracy', in Liz Heffernan, ed., Human Rights, A European Perspective, Dublin: The Round Hall Press, 1994, p. 211, at p. 212 (footnote 4).

56 Unreported, High Court, 31 July 1992; O'Toole v RTÉ [1993] ILRM 454 (Sup Ct).

57 Ibid., High Court, at pp 7–8 of the typescript. O'Hanlon J. relied on the judgment of O'Higgins C.J. in State (Lynch) v Cooney [1982] IR 337, 364: '. . . the order is not directed against a broadcast by a particular person as an individual, or against any group of individuals, as such. It is directed against a broadcast on behalf of Sinn Féin or by any person or persons purporting to represent that organisation. . .'

58 Ibid., High Court, at p. 8 of the typescript. A ministerial order prohibiting all access to members of Sinn Féin would, in the judge's view, have been open to considerable doubt as a valid exercise of the powers conferred on the minister under s. 31, as amended.

59 See n. 55, High Court, at p. 9 of typescript.

60 See n. 55, Supreme Court, at p. 467 *per* O'Flaherty J.

61 *Brandon Book Publishers Ltd v RTÉ* [1993] ILRM 806; *Brandon Book Publishers Ltd v* IRTC, unreported, High Court, 29 October 1993: RTÉ has a copy clearance department that vets copy before broadcasting.

62 *The Irish Times*, 19 August 1992.

63 See n. 60, IRTC, at p. 17 of typescript.

64 Ibid., at p. 17 of the typescript. Carney J. relying on the principles of *State (Keegan) v Stardust Victims Compensation Tribunal* [1986] IR 642; [1987] ILRM 202.

65 *Council of Civil Service Union v Minister for the Civil Service* [1985] AC 375, 410.

66 *R v Secretary of State for the Home Department, ex parte Brind* [1991] 1 AC 696, [1990] 1 All ER 469, at p. 480.

67 [1991] 2 WLR 588, [1991] 1 All ER 720.

68 UN Human Rights Committee, Response to Irish Report, 28 July 1993, at para. 15.

69 Ibid., at para. 21.

70 The first televised party political broadcast on behalf of Sinn Féin, a one-minute video for the European elections, was transmitted on 26 May 1994, some few months after the decision not to renew the Ministerial order activating s. 31.

71 *The Irish Times*, 7 February 1994, 25 May 1994.

72 Series A, no. 236; (1992) 14 EHRR 445.

73 Ibid., at para. 46.

74 Series A, no. 239; (1992) 14 EHRR 843.

75 *The Observer and The Guardian v* UK, Series A, no. 216; (1992) 14 EHRR 153.

76 Ibid., at para. 11.

77 Ibid., at para. 56.

78 194 *Dáil Debates*, cols 599–600, 603.

79 The British Official Secrets Acts of 1911 and 1920 remained in force in Ireland in the form adopted in 1928 under the Adaptation of Enactments Act 1922 until repealed by s. 3 of the 1963 Act.

80 See 194 *Dáil Debates*, col. 603; 196 *Dáil Debates*, col. 668.

81 See, generally, Keith Ewing and Conor Gearty, *Freedom under Thatcher*, Oxford: Clarendon Press, 1990.

82 *AG v Jonathon Cape Ltd* [1976] QB 752.

83 *AG v Guardian Newspapers Ltd* [1987] 3 All ER 316.

84 The 'Zircon' affair, 1987; see Anthony Wilfred Bradley, 'Parliamentary Privilege, Zircon and National Security', (1987) *Public Law* 488; n. 80, at 147–52.

85 *Guardian Newspapers Ltd v Secretary of State for Defence* [1984] 3 All ER 601.

86 *The Irish Times*, 20 May 1994.

87 *R v Ponting* [1985] Crim LRev 318. See also, Rosamund M. Thomas, 'The British Official Secrets Acts 1911-1939 and the Ponting case' [1986] Crim LRev 491.

88 See n. 83.

89 On the implications of the Act for the media, see Stephanie Palmer, 'Tightening Secrecy Law: The Official Secrets Act 1989' (1990) *Public Law* 243.

90 Notices to this effect were published in the national newspapers during May 1995. See also *The Irish Times*, 22 November 1995 and 29 November 1995 on review of Act.

91 See *The Irish Times*, 15 August 1987, 17 August 1987, 20 August 1987; *Sunday Tribune*, 16 August 1987. The DPP decided not to bring charges against journalist Emily O'Reilly over the publication in November 1993 of the government's draft policy document on the North. A Garda investigation into the leak was ordered by the Tánaiste and Minister for Foreign Affairs, Mr Spring. *The Irish Times*, 28 April 1994.

92 DPP *v Independent Newspapers*, *The Irish Times*, 8 February 1984, 20 July 1984: *Irish Independent*, 31 July 1984; Casey, n. 28, at p. 455, mentions that *The Irish Times* was also threatened with prosecution in 1976 when it was about to publish details of a

proposed deal between the State and Bula Mining Ltd. but that no proceedings ensued.

93 The conviction was upheld on appeal.

94 [1986] IR 597, [1987] ILRM 135.

95 Ibid., at pp 136–7, citing (1980) 147 CLR 39, at p. 51. See also Gerard Hogan, 'Free Speech, Privacy and the Press in Ireland', (1987) *Public Law* 509.

96 See n. 94 at 138.

97 *The Irish Times*, 10 September 1988.

98 *The Irish Times*, 16 February 1990, 2 March 1990.

99 *The Irish Times*, 8 February 1995.

100 *The Irish Times*, 8 November 1995, 16 December 1995.

101 See Sam Smyth, in *Sunday Independent*, 15 September 1991.

102 See *The Irish Times*, 27 March 1992.

103 See Anthony Lewis, 'Mr Maxwell's Lesson—How British Libel Law Stifles Criticism', *New York Times*, 9 December 1991.

CHAPTER ELEVEN

Media Structures and Regulation — Present and Future

The regulation of broadcasting has always been considered necessary for two main reasons. Firstly, in the early days, access to the electromagnetic spectrum was limited. The allocation of frequencies was the subject of international negotiation between governments and was therefore seen as the preserve of governments. Technological developments have since opened up access. Secondly, broadcasting, particularly television broadcasting, which is still relatively new, has been regarded somewhat apprehensively as a powerful medium, especially because it is brought directly into people's homes. As a result, its impact is immediate. Governments therefore perceived the need to regulate.

Government Regulation of Broadcasting

The first manifestation of government intervention came in the form of a requirement to have a licence to broadcast and a licence to receive broadcasting. This was established by law in the Wireless Telegraphy Act 1926, followed by the Broadcasting Acts 1960–93, and applied to the commercial stations by the Radio and Television Act 1988.[1] Radio began as an arm of government, operated by the Department of Posts and Telegraphs and controlled by the Department of Finance who held the purse strings. It developed initially as a cultural and entertainment medium, with a diet of music, some language programmes and talks on farming and horticulture, but very little news.

In 1960 the RTÉ Authority was established under the Broadcasting Authority Act as a semi-state body to take control of television and sound broadcasting on behalf of the State. The Act gave RTÉ a monopoly over broadcasting, while finance was still largely controlled by government, which set the licence fee. However, RTÉ was permitted to carry advertising as a further source of revenue and was to engage in public service broadcasting. Since 1988, however, RTÉ's monopoly has been broken by the introduction of commercial broadcasting, followed by community broadcasting and special interest broadcasting.

The pattern in Ireland was not unlike that in a number of other Western European countries. RTÉ television was established at arm's length from government, under the control of a semi-state authority. Under the 1960 Act it had a monopoly but was saddled with considerations of public responsibility, national culture, fairness, impartiality, privacy, good taste, concern for the whole community and the need for understanding and peace. It was required to maintain balance, impartiality and fairness in its news and current affairs coverage. RTÉ was obliged to treat election candidates fairly, although that did not mean that it had to treat them equally.[2] It was prohibited also from broadcasting material likely to incite to crime or to undermine the authority of the State. The fact that certain powers were reserved to the government and minister, including the power to appoint and remove from office the members of the RTÉ Authority, proved problematic in practice and led to the introduction of amending legislation in 1976.

This 1976 Act also established the Broadcasting Complaints Commission (BCC) with power to investigate and adjudicate complaints within specified categories, including the operation of section 31 and the fairness and impartiality requirements; also advertisements and material published by RTÉ. The only sanction provided was that RTÉ must publish the particulars of any complaint when requested to do so by the BCC and in an agreed manner. Reports of decisions are published in the RTÉ *Guide* and usually in the national newspapers. The BCC produces annual reports which are laid before both Houses of the Oireachtas. One problem with the BCC is its low level of visibility: it is a part-time commission, meeting only when complaints arise and operating from a box number. Its role was expanded in 1988 to allow it to deal with complaints against the commercial stations also.[3] There is now an obligation on television broadcasters, though not radio broadcasters, under the EC Directive of 1989, to provide a right of reply to viewers.[4]

In regard to advertising, RTÉ has traditionally been in competition with the national newspapers and, to a lesser extent, with the provincial press. Now the local broadcasting stations are dependent on advertising too and stations broadcasting from Northern Ireland are attracting cross-border advertising. RTÉ has a decided advantage over the newcomers in that it has had a monopoly for so long and also has the safety-net of income from licence fees. The 1990 Broadcasting Act set about 'levelling the playing-pitch' by placing a 'cap', an upper limit, on the amount of advertising income RTÉ could accept (section 3). The section was repealed by the Broadcasting Authority (Amendment) Act

1993, which also obliged RTÉ to spend a percentage of its income in commissioning independent television programmes (section 4). RTÉ also operates a code of advertising to comport with restrictions and to take account of the responsibilities it has in respect to taste and decency.[5]

The constitutionality of the State broadcasting monopoly was challenged in *Nova Media Services Ltd v Minister for Posts and Telegraphs*[6] and *Sunshine Radio Productions Ltd v Minister for Posts and Telegraphs*.[7] The applicants in both cases were 'pirate' stations whose premises had been raided and equipment seized by employees of the Department of Posts and Telegraphs. They claimed that the Wireless Telegraphy Act 1926, which prohibits broadcasting or the possession of broadcasting equipment except under licence, was unconstitutional in that it infringed their freedom of expression guaranteed by Article 40.6.1.i. The High Court accepted that a stateable case had been made on the constitutional argument but refused the relief sought, namely an interlocutory injunction restraining further raids and seizures. The Court applied the balance of convenience test, a test which, arguably, is no longer acceptable in freedom of expression cases following the European Court of Human Rights decision in *Spycatcher*.[8]

By the time the *Nova* and *Sunshine Radio* cases were taken, the 1926 Act was hopelessly out of date and totally ineffective in curbing the pirate stations, which by then numbered eighty or ninety. The fines that could be imposed under the Act were ludicrously small. In one case a station with a turnover of several hundred thousand pounds was fined a paltry £20.[9] Pirate stations were able to operate, therefore, beyond the reach of the law, unencumbered by section 31 restrictions or worries about public responsibility, privacy or taste. For the most part, though, they were playing wall-to-wall music. Nonetheless, it was a major failing on the part of the legislators that no one in the state with the exception of RTÉ could broadcast lawfully within the State for a period of sixty years. The Act had made provision for licensing by the Minister but in all that time no licences were forthcoming. The 1988 legislation was therefore long overdue.

Introduction of Commercial Broadcasting

The Broadcasting and Wireless Telegraphy Act 1988 obliged pirate stations interested in acquiring a broadcasting licence to go off the air by midnight on 31 December 1987. The Radio and Television Act 1988 then provided for a system of licensing. It established the Independent

Radio and Television Commission (IRTC) (section 3), with powers to grant licences (section 4), initially for a period of seven years, and then subject to review. The Act set out the criteria to be applied by the IRTC in granting licences. For example, it had to have regard to the quality, range and type of programmes proposed, to what extent they would cater for the Irish language, culture and minority interests or provide opportunities for Irish talent in music, dance and entertainment (section 6).

The new stations would be required to include a minimum level of news and current affairs (20 per cent) in their daily programme schedule, and this would be monitored by the IRTC (section 9). This requirement was much criticised at the time because of the expense involved in terms of staff, planning and resources. It was also argued that such requirements belong to the realm of public service broadcasting not commercial broadcasting. However, experience has shown that for most stations it is feasible and that audiences have an insatiable appetite for local news, a fact already borne out by the thriving provincial press and by Raidió na Gaeltachta. However, some local stations have been experiencing teething troubles, while the national commercial radio station, Century Radio, collapsed altogether and TV3, the third national television station, did not get off the ground at all. However, TV3 and a new national radio station, as well as a new Irish language television station, Teilifís na Gaeilge, are expected to become operational in 1996. Meanwhile, the Irish licence for satellite channels was secured in 1986 by Atlantic, owned by the American Hughes Communications Corporation, and RTÉ now broadcasts across Europe and the United States on the Astra satellite, as well as selling programmes to cable channels.

The transition from a government-controlled monopoly has therefore been a difficult one. The strength of RTÉ's position in the market proved problematic for the new challengers. Advertising was limited, restrictions were imposed on content and on mode of transmission. The planned third national television station was initially to be carried on MMDS, the multi-point microwave distribution system, which had been tested in Canada and was thought suitable for rural Ireland, where cable was impractical. However, TV3 had difficulty meeting the IRTC's terms in order to take up their licence and the IRTC decided to withdraw it. In the case that followed, TV3 *v* IRTC,[10] an order of *certiorari* was granted quashing the decision of the IRTC to withdraw the licence from TV3. The order was granted on the grounds of natural justice, as the Commission had not given any notice of its intention to withdraw the licence or given TV3 an opportunity to be heard, that is, to make its case. An appeal to the Supreme Court by the IRTC was dismissed.[11] Discussions between the two parties continued through 1994 and the licence was eventually restored to the consortium, now strengthened by the inclusion of Ulster Television.

In addition to the requirement of a minimum amount of news and current affairs in the Radio and Television Act 1988, an upper limit was placed on the amount of advertising that could be carried (section 10): not more than 15 per cent of the total programming or ten minutes per hour.[12] The section 31 ban was also extended by the Radio and Television Act to the new commercial stations (section 12) and the IRTC had the task of preparing guidelines for the commercial stations on how the section was to be applied.[13] In 1993 Brandon Book Publishers sought judicial review of the IRTC's decision not to allow advertisements for Gerry Adams's book of short stories to be carried on the commercial stations (see Chapter 10 for discussion on this issue). In January 1994, after the government allowed the section 31 order to lapse, the IRTC drew up new guidelines, which were regarded as more flexible than those of RTÉ. They contain a strong endorsement of free speech and a strong presumption against prior restraint.[14] The local stations are also governed by section 9 of the 1988 Act, the equivalent of section 18 of the Broadcasting Authority Act, prohibiting the broadcasting of matter likely to promote or incite to crime or tending to undermine the authority of the State. The IRTC's guidelines offer an interpretation of section 9, which they say should be taken to relate to identifiable harm.[15]

In this and other matters the IRTC has a monitoring function to ensure that the local stations are complying with the terms of their licence. For instance, the IRTC can review the news content of a particular station's output and can, if satisfied that there is sufficient diversity of news and current affairs in the locality, reduce the 20 per cent figure. It can also order stations to change their schedule, where they are not providing sufficient local programming, for example.[16]

In terms of structures, the Act does not impose any ban on newspaper involvement in ownership of the new stations. As a result, newspapers became involved in many of the new stations and, indeed, with cable companies and the new distribution system, MMDS. Events since then in the newspaper industry, in particular the dominance of Independent Newspapers, have served to confirm misgivings about this involvement and its capacity to become a source of danger to pluralism and diversity.[17] Indeed, it may prove detrimental that for so long debate has centred mainly on questions of licences, personnel and advertising revenue, rather than on the complex practical and philosophical issues surrounding the whole future of broadcasting in general. The larger long-term questions of control, supervision and the implications of satellite broadcasting had not been addressed to any great extent until the publication of the government's Green Paper on Broadcasting in 1995.[18]

The Future of Broadcasting

In common with other European countries, Ireland has had a long commitment to public service broadcasting. That ethos is still important and has been brought into focus by the development of private commercial broadcasting. The maintenance of that ethos has justified a more interventionist role on the part of the regulators, while at the same time the possibilities offered by new technology and the growing internationalisation, indeed globalistation, of the media strengthen the argument for deregulation. The competition from American media, where deregulation has already occurred, conspires with the convergence of the various forms of media—audio-visual, satellite, electronic, multimedia—to add to the complexity of the problem. It may be argued that what needs to be safeguarded, from a national cultural point of view, are the *values* of public service broadcasting, not necessarily the particular means. Those values include independence from political and commercial pressures, wide access to news and views, and the social and cultural responsibilities that require the provision of a comprehensive service. Other European countries have shared those values but differed in the detailed approach to implementing them.[19] The European Community, now the European Union, and the Council of Europe have introduced measures aimed at dealing with the overspill of broadcasting across national boundaries and at promoting competition but maintaining minimum standards.

European Community Law and the Media

1. The European Court of Justice

The judgment of the European Court of Justice in *Italy v Sacchi*[20] in 1974 first established the relevance of The Treaty of Rome (the EEC Treaty) to the media. The case concerned the unauthorised broadcasting of foreign programmes into Italy via cable and the monopoly that existed in television programming in that country at the time. The transfer of television programmes transnationally was held to constitute a service and therefore to fall within the Treaty's concept of free movement of services. In the same way, trade in films, sound recordings, apparatus and products used for the transmission of television signals is subject to the rules relating to the free movement of goods. The distinction made in the early cases between goods and services in this field is, however, somewhat artificial given the developments that have taken place in technology and the arrival of multimedia technologies. The *Coditel*[21] and *Debauve*[22] cases in 1980 were found to involve the application of nondiscriminatory rules (i.e. they applied to domestic and foreign services alike), which were permissible 'in the absence of harmonisation'. *Coditel* concerned the application to foreign transmissions of Belgian copyright rules and *Debauve* the application of a ban on television advertising. The ban on advertising in the *Dutch Advertisers* case,[23] however, was found to be discriminatory, as it was aimed at the retransmission of foreign satellite programmes only. The Court held that it could not be justified on public policy grounds as its aim was to prevent advertising except through a public agency which had a monopoly.[24] These cases formed the background to and gave the impetus to the EC Directive of 1989, which sought to at least coordinate, if not actually to harmonise, national rules.[25]

2. The European Community Directive 1989

It has been recognised in the recitals to the Directive, however, that there is a much broader principle at stake than just freedom to provide goods and services. That freedom is also a 'specific manifestation in Community law of a more general principle, namely the freedom of expression as enshrined in Article 10(1) of the Convention for the Protection of Human Rights and Fundamental Freedoms'.[26] For that reason, freedom in relation to broadcasting and television programmes under the Directive must be in accordance with Article 10(1) and subject only to the limits set by Article 10(2) of the Convention and Article 56(1) of the Treaty. In a Greek case, *Elliniki Radiophonia Teleorassi-Anonimi Etairia v Dimotiki Etairia Plirioforissis*,[27] the Court of Justice examined exclusive rights to broadcasting in light of Article 10. The rights were within the Member State's own territory and were not based on economic grounds. The main problem to be addressed by the Directive was that satellites, in conjunction with cable delivery systems had the capacity to spill over national boundaries, with the result that Member States were not in a position to regulate them.

One of the main purposes of the Directive was the harmonising of television advertising. Copyright was omitted as no agreement could be reached, and a separate copyright directive was entered into, which came into force on July 1, 1995. However, Article 4 of the 1989 Television Directive places a duty on Member States to ensure that broadcasters reserve the majority of transmission time for European works,[28] the fear being that American programmes will swamp the European market. The types of programmes excluded from the Article 4 provision (news, sports events, games, advertising and teletext services) indicate that the concern is for the European film industry. The duty is somewhat watered down, however, by the use of such phrases as 'where practicable' and 'to be achieved progressively'.[29]

Article 6 sets out the meaning of 'European works' and how the origin of the works is to be established by reference to the residence of authors and workers. 'Authors' appears to include the director and writers of the screen play and music, and 'workers' would include actors and film crew. In this respect, the Directive is protectionist. It aims to:

> promote markets of sufficient size for television productions in the Member States to recover necessary investments, not only by establishing common rules opening up national markets but also by envisaging for European productions where practicable and by appropriate means, a majority proportion in television programmes in all Member States.[30]

Article 5 deals with quotas for independent works, the aim being to safeguard the smaller independent sector.

Article 8 of the Directive may have a relevance for Teilifís na Gaeilge:

> Where they consider it necessary for purposes of language policy, the Member States, while observing Community law, may as regards some or all programmes of television broadcasters under their jurisdiction, lay down more detailed or stricter rules in particular on the basis of language criteria.

The general requirement that there be no discrimination on the basis of national interests means that if a distinction is made, it must be on genuine grounds, like language. Thus the French could require that only French language programmes be shown, as long as that includes French language programmes from other countries.

Articles 10 to 19 lay down the rules relating to advertising. Television advertising must be readily recognised as such and kept separate from other parts of the programme service by optical and/or acoustic means. Subliminal techniques or surreptitious advertising are not to be used (Article 10). Advertisements may be inserted during programmes, provided the integrity and value of the programme is not prejudiced. Natural breaks, such as the interval in a sports event, should be used for advertising slots. Feature films are to be interrupted on the basis of duration, once for each complete period of 45 minutes. In other programmes, a period of at least twenty minutes, should elapse between advertising breaks. There should be no breaks in the broadcast of religious services, and none in news, current affairs, documentaries, religious or children's programmes, unless the programmes are of at least thirty minutes' duration (Article 11). Advertising must respect human dignity and must not discriminate, be offensive, be prejudicial to health, safety or the environment (Article 12). A number of prohibitions are also detailed.[31] Particular regard must be had for minors (Article 16), and special requirements are laid down for sponsored programmes (Article 17). Total amounts of advertising within the hourly and daily programming are fixed (Article 18), and Member States are free to lay down stricter periods if they wish (Article 19).

3. Human Rights Dimension

The place of advertising within the freedom of expression guarantee of Article 10 of the European Convention on Human Rights has been examined in a number of cases, a few of them involving the media. In *Markt Intern and Beermann v Germany*,[32] for example, the European Court of Human Rights found no breach of Article 10. Although Article 10 did apply to commercial speech, the publication in question, which reported the dissatisfaction of a consumer with a mail-order firm, was found to be premature, as the firm had agreed to investigate the matter. The premature publication would have had adverse effects on the firm's business. Then, in 1993 the European Commission on Human Rights declared inadmissible a complaint that a fine imposed in respect of indirect commercial publicity (pictures of Coca Cola bottles and other brand products in a children's news programme) constituted an unnecessary interference with the broadcaster's freedom of expression.[33]

The European Convention on Transfrontier Television 1989 contains provisions on advertising. All advertisements must be fair and honest, must not be misleading and, if addressed to children, must have regard to their interests and susceptibilities. Advertisers must not exercise any editorial influence over the content of programmes (Article 11).

Other measures, similar to those in the EC Directive relate to the duration, form and presentation of advertising, the insertion of advertisements between and within programmes. Both documents contain prohibitions on tobacco advertising and restrictions on advertisements for alcohol. Both regulate sponsorship.

Articles 11–16 of the Convention deal with advertising. Articles 17–18 deal with sponsorship. The Convention also provides for the setting up of a standing committee to deal with questions concerning the interpretation of the Convention, to suggest modifications, make recommendations and handle any difficulties that arise (Articles 20–21). Article 25 provides for conciliation, Article 26 for arbitration.

4. European Competition Law

The emergence of large media companies and economic pressures generally have led to a situation of concentration of ownership and cross-ownership, that is, the same person(s) owning or having a controlling interest in both newspapers and broadcasting stations, sometimes also in advertising, print and distribution companies.[34] In such a situation there is a greater opportunity for a company to cut its own costs or drive up competitors' costs. It also puts the company in a stronger position to outbid rivals in the pursuit of lucrative sports coverage or the rights to show top films and to take on the dominance of the American conglomerates. Some degree of strength over and above that wielded by smaller companies may well be desirable in some respects, but there is also a danger that over-concentration will force out competitors and lead to a lack of diversity in news and current affairs coverage. The key issue is not so much ownership as such but how to maintain a diversity of sources in the face of economic factors militating against it. The device used to try to counteract these forces is competition law.

European Community law, in particular Articles 85 and 86 of the Treaty of Rome, have provided a basis for Member States to take action to eliminate anticompetitive practices. Article 85 is concerned with agreements that would prevent, restrict or distort competition, while Article 86 prohibits abuse of a dominant position in the market. These articles have been given force in Irish law by the Competition Act 1991, section 4 and section 5. It was under these provisions that the Competition Authority in 1994 was asked by the Minister for Enterprise and Employment[35] to investigate the situation in the Irish newspaper industry following Independent Newspapers' acquisition of a 24.9 per cent shareholding in the Irish Press group. The Authority was concerned with two main issues: the question of transfrontier competition in the industry and the issue of dominance in the industry.[36] The situation as found by the Authority was one in which English newspapers formed only 7 per cent of overall sales in Ireland. However, the tabloid percentage of this market had been increasing, while the quality market had been falling.[37] The Authority concluded, however, that regardless of how the market is viewed, Independent Newspapers had a dominant position and was clearly capable of inflicting considerable harm on most of its rivals and could force them out of the market altogether.[38]

It is not, of course, the fact of a dominant position that is relevant but rather the abuse of a dominant position (Competition Act 1991, section 5). Predatory pricing, that is, below cost selling in order to weaken or eliminate competitors, can usually only be engaged in by a dominant firm and is indicative of abuse of that dominant position. The Authority concluded that English newspaper companies were not engaged in predatory pricing and that the fall-off in sales of Irish newspapers was attributable to other causes, such as the high cost structure and price gap.[39] The acquisition by Independent Newspapers of a stake in the Irish Press group, on the other hand, was found to be designed to prevent a rival acquiring control of the Press newspapers,[40] to have prevented the emergence of more intense competition in the various segments of the market and therefore to amount to abuse of a dominant position.[41] It was therefore adjudged to be both an abuse of a dominant position contrary to section 5 of the Competition Act 1991 and an anticompetitive agreement contrary to section 4 of the same Act. Although it was outside its remit to pronounce on it, the Authority expressed the view that if the provision of ongoing finance by Independent Newspapers to the *Sunday Tribune*, to enable it to continue operating, was designed to inflict damage on rival newspapers, then that too would amount to abuse of a dominant position.[42]

As a result of the Authority's findings, Independent Newspapers is expected to be asked to divest itself of its shares in the two newspaper groups. The long-term future for both looks bleak. If the newspapers do not survive, the use of competition law will have the effect of either encouraging new companies to come into the market or, failing that, will have brought about a situation where there are less newspapers operating than before. Had competition law not been invoked, the newspapers might have survived, at least for a time, but the position of Independent Newspapers would have been so strong as to be able to control the market and also, possibly, newspaper content. When Independent Newspapers' interests in private commercial broadcasting, cable systems and newspaper distribution are taken into account, the potential for conflict at a future date becomes apparent.

This kind of dilemma has led to a certain amount of questioning, on free speech grounds, of the legitimacy of imposing restrictions on media ownership at all. Restrictions have been upheld, however, even in the United States in situations where diversity required them; for example, where a community was serviced by only one newspaper or broadcasting station. The purpose of the restrictions was held not to limit the scope or content of speech but rather to facilitate it.[43] This form of regulation is structural rather than content-based, and it is therefore not as suspect on free speech grounds. In Britain the Broadcasting Act 1990 laid down maximum holdings for cross-ownership. The constitutional courts in several European countries have also upheld the legitimacy of restrictions on ownership in the interests of assuring a plurality of sources of information and opinions.[44] The difficulty of harmonising laws on media ownership has proven insurmountable as yet and plans by the European Commission to bring in a directive have been postponed. A Green Paper on pluralism was published in 1992 and consultative hearings were held in 1994. The European Parliament has demanded action and the Commission is now expected to finalise its position shortly.

In what must be one of the longest running battles on competition law, the European Court of Justice recently ruled that RTÉ and Independent Television Publications had abused a dominant position in not allowing other companies to publish full listings of television programmes. They had only allowed listings on a day-by-day basis and weekly highlights, which prevented *Magill* magazine from publishing its *Magill* TV *Guide*. Viewers who wanted to know the week's programming schedule had no alternative but to buy the weekly guides published by the television stations themselves. The Court ruled that *Magill* and other interested companies should be allowed to publish full listings subject to payment of a reasonable level of royalties.[45] In March 1985, when *Magill* first announced its intention to publish a weekly TV guide, RTÉ entered into negotiations with *Magill* and offered a very restrictive licence to which *Magill* reluctantly agreed.[46] Under the terms and conditions of that licence, *Magill* was to be entitled to publish RTÉ's programme schedules for the day of issue only, i.e. Thursday's programmes each week or Friday and Saturday's programmes or Saturday and Sunday's. In addition, it could refer briefly to not more than twelve programmes each from RTÉ 1 and RTÉ 2's programmes for the coming week. Some time later when the conditions of the licence were breached, Costello J. granted an interlocutory injunction restraining the defendants from publishing their TV *Guide*, pending the trial of the action.[47] The competition issue was investigated by the EC Commission, which found a breach of the Community's rules. The Commission's decision was upheld by the Court of First Instance in 1991, but that ruling was in turn appealed to the Court of Justice. A final decision was given in April 1995.

Copyright and Related Rights

The *Magill* case also raised issues of copyright in television listings. The law of copyright protects original or creative work from being unfairly exploited without the permission or authorisation of those who created it. Copyright means the exclusive right to use and authorise others to use, that is to reproduce, publish, perform in public, broadcast, cause to be transmitted or make an adaptation of the work in question. Key issues that arise include the nature and scope of creative work, who is entitled to the protection of the law in relation to the creative work and what is the extent of the protection.

The Copyright Act 1963 indicates the scope of various types of creative work. For example, literary work includes any written table or compilation. The Act also makes separate provision for authors' right (Part II) and neighbouring or derivative rights (Part III). Thus the authors of literary, dramatic, musical and artistic works have a proprietary interest in their work and under copyright law can authorise or license its use and take legal action if their rights are infringed. Neighbouring rights on the other hand belong to people involved in the production of sound recordings, films, broadcasts and publishing. It is the skill and investment involved in the production that are protected in those cases. The result is that in respect of broadcasting, for example, there may be multiple copyright owners: the author of the work on which the broadcast is based, that is the script and the screenplay, the composer of the theme music, the producer of the film and of the programme itself once it is broadcast. There is no copyright in news as such although there could be in the presentation or format. In fact any work that involves skill, labour and judgment whether in the research, writing or translation, or in the putting together and presentation of a film, video, broadcast or publication may attract copyright protection. The Act provides remedies for copyright infringement (Part IV) but also makes exception for research and private study and for criticism or review (section 12).

In the Magill case it was accepted that copyright exists in television listings, that they constitute an original work and therefore attract copyright protection. When the copyright issue in the case first came before the High Court, RTÉ claimed that Magill had infringed its copyright in its programme schedules.[48] Lardner J. in the High Court held that the term 'literary work' in sections 2 and 8 of the Copyright Act 1963 was not confined to work exhibiting literary art or style but had the broad sense of any written or printed composition. Furthermore, the requirement of originality related to the expression of matter in writing or print rather than the ideas expressed. A compilation for the purposes of section 2 would entitle its author to copyright under section 8 if the written or printed work was an original composition and involved labour, time and skill in its compilation. The television listings in this case were, therefore, 'literary works' within the sense of the Act and the television stations were entitled to copyright, which had been infringed by Magill.[49]

In a further series of cases involving copyright, Phonographic Performance (Ireland) Ltd (PPI), a copyright collection agency for recording companies, had complained of widespread copyright infringement by discotheques playing music recorded and released by its members. In one such case, PPI v Cody,[50] Keane J. held:

> The right of the creator of a literary, dramatic, musical or artistic work not to have his or her creation stolen or plagiarised is a right of private property within the meaning of Article 40.3.2 and 43.1 of the Constitution, as is the similar right of a person who has employed his or her technical skills and/or capital in the sound recording of a musical work . . . [It] is the duty of the organs of the State, including the courts, to ensure, as best they may, that these rights are protected from unjust attack and, in the case of injustice done, vindicated.

The 1963 Act provides that copyright subsists in 'sound recordings' as well as literary, dramatic, musical and artistic works. The composers of musical works are entitled to prohibit the performance of their work in public, regardless of royalties offered. The maker of the recording, on the other hand, cannot refuse permission for the recording to be played in public, provided 'equitable remuneration' is paid.[51]

Under sections 7 and 17(4)(b) of the 1963 Act, unless the copyright owner has given consent, it is an act of copyright infringement to cause a published sound recording to be heard in public without the payment of 'equitable remuneration' to the copyright owner. The problem that arises concerns determining what is 'equitable remuneration'. Disputes can be referred to the Controller of Industrial and Commercial Property, in accordance with sections 31 and 32 of the Act. The Controller's decision is binding. In the case of a collection agency like PPI, operating a licence system, the Controller's decision is binding on all those who come within the category covered by the licence. In a case taken against it by PPI, RTÉ claimed that it had followed the procedures prescribed by the Copyright Act 1963.[52] However, there was disagreement as to whether RTÉ could negotiate terms on a one-to-one basis or whether one tariff should apply to all, as PPI contended, in accordance with the licence scheme which it operated. RTÉ claimed that it had paid equitable remuneration as required by the Act for a number of years and then, when further agreement could not be reached with PPI, had referred the matter to the Controller of Industrial and Commercial Property for determination. The High Court held in favour of PPI, but on appeal to the Supreme Court RTÉ's right to offer royalty payments (equitable remuneration) and to refer any dispute to the Controller was upheld. RTÉ did not need a licence to play recordings in public, the Court said, and royalty payments did not need to be paid in advance. [53]

A new EC Directive on Copyright came into effect in 1995. The Directive was given effect in Irish law by the European Communities (Term of Protection of Copyright) Regulations 1995. It increases the period of protection from fifty years to seventy years. In the case of authors' rights protection will now run for the lifetime of the author plus seventy years. A similar period applies in the case of cinematograph films from the date of death of the last to survive among the principal director, author of the screenplay or dialogue or composer of music specifically created for the film. In the case of a sound recording the period of protection remains at fifty years from the date of first publication. A new Irish Copyright Act is also in preparation.

Irish operators of cable and MMDS networks, in addition to having to obtain the necessary licences from the Department of Communications, are required to obtain the permission of owners of copyright in any foreign broadcasts that are to be transmitted by cable or MMDS in Ireland. To transmit the British stations, therefore, they need the permission of the broadcasters and of the owners of the copyright in the contents of the broadcasts. It can be extremely difficult to acquire all these necessary authorisations. BBC Enterprises, on behalf of the licensors and owners of the copyright drew up a standard form copyright licensing agreement to represent the terms upon which licences would be granted to cable and MMDS operators in Ireland. The European Commission took a favourable view of the agreement.[54] The EC Directive on satellite broadcasting and cable retransmission, which requires certain minimum standards of protection, provides that the right of copyright owners to grant or refuse authorisation can be exercised only through a collecting agency.[55]

In relation to the acquisition of television rights to sports events, the EBU (European Broadcasting Union), an association of radio and television broadcasters, was exempted from the provisions of Article 85(1) of the EEC Treaty and allowed to collectively acquire rights, subject to granting access to third parties. The cost of acquiring rights to sports events has soared to such an extent that it would be very difficult for individual broadcasters to compete.[56]

Complaints Bodies

As media technology is developing so rapidly and the media are becoming so powerful in economic terms, as well as so pervasive in people's lives, attention has turned in recent years to questions of media accountability. This has resulted in a proliferation of complaints bodies, some statutory, some self-regulatory. In Britain, for example, the Press Council, established in 1953 to handle complaints in the print media and promote press freedom, was replaced in 1991 by the Press Complaints Commission, with the narrower role of implementing a code of conduct drawn up by newspaper editors. The British Broadcasting Complaints Commission is a statutory body which adjudicates on complaints of unjust or unfair treatment or unwarranted invasion of privacy in programmes. The Broadcasting Standards Council, a nonstatutory body set up in 1988, monitors sex and violence in broadcasting and carries out research.[57]

In Ireland, the two broadcasting bodies at present are the RTÉ Authority and the IRTC. Broadcasting complaints in both sectors are handled by the statutory Broadcasting Complaints Commission (BCC). The government's Green Paper on Broadcasting considers the case for merging the policy and regulatory functions of the RTÉ Authority and IRTC to form 'one over-arching Authority that would assume overall responsibility for broadcasting policy . . .', a 'Super Authority'.[58] It also questions whether the structures under which the BCC operates are adequate and the most effective and efficient for today's needs and to cater for broadcasting into the next century.[59] The Commission, established under the Broadcasting Authority (Amendment) Act 1976, has a minimum membership of three, is part-time, appointed by the government for a period of five years, operates from a box number and determines if there has been a breach of their statutory obligations by broadcasters. It cannot impose any sanctions, other than publication of its adjudications.

In addition, there are forms of self-regulation in both the print and broadcasting sectors and in the advertising industry.[60] The National Union of Journalists (NUJ), with members in both print and broadcast journalism, has a code of conduct which dates from 1936. It imposes duties of fairness and accuracy and the avoidance of distortion and misrepresentation. It supports the correction of inaccuracies, the provision of apologies and rights of reply and obliges journalists to use only straightforward means to obtain information and photographs, unless justified by the public interest. Confidential sources are to be protected; acceptance of bribes, inducements and advertising are prohibited; so too is the taking of private advantage of information obtained in the course of duty. Discriminatory descriptions of people on such grounds as race, colour, gender, sexual orientation are not to be originated or processed. The NUJ also has a disciplinary system which was used, for example, to fine a Northern Ireland newspaper for racist remarks about travellers (see Chapter 9) and in relation to the report in *The Phoenix* magazine which gave rise to the case of *Hilliard v Penfield Enterprises* (see Chapter 8).

Since 1989 all the national newspapers in Ireland have had in-house Readers' Representatives to deal with communications and complaints from readers. It is their job to act on the readers' behalf, to channel complaints to the appropriate person(s) within the organisation and, where necessary, to elicit a suitable remedy. The majority of complaints received since 1989 have concerned inaccurate or misleading reporting and, in the vast majority of those cases, corrections or clarifications were published, most in the next issue. Only a very small percentage of complaints was left unresolved. Like the Broadcasting Complaints Commission, the Readers' Representatives system needs to be highly visible, so that readers will know about it and be in a position to use it. It also needs to be effective, which requires the co-operation of management, editorial staff and particularly journalists, if greater accuracy is to be achieved and inaccuracies corrected in the paper.[61] In the provincial newspapers, which are smaller, mainly weekly publications that are closer to their own community, it is often possible for the editor to handle readers' complaints himself/herself. Corrections and clarifications are published where necessary or a voluntary right of reply is given to the aggrieved reader. The question of press standards and complaints systems are among the many issues referred to the government's commission on the newspaper industry, established in 1995 under the chairmanship of the former Chief Justice, Thomas Finlay.

Licensing Systems

Throughout its long history the press in Ireland has been free of any licensing requirement. Now that technology allows for broadcasting on a global basis the need or desirability for continuing to license it has also been questioned. In *Groppera Radio AG and others v Switzerland*,[62] the applicants complained that a ban on cable retransmissions in Switzerland of their broadcasts from Italy infringed their right to impart information and ideas regardless of frontiers. The European Court of Human Rights held that there had been no breach of Article 10. National licensing systems were necessary for the orderly regulation of broadcasting enterprises but were subject to the requirements of paragraph 2 of Article 10. In *Groppera* the ban was justified under Article 10.2 as it pursued the legitimate aims of prevention of disorder in telecommunications and protection of the rights of others by ensuring a fair allocation of frequencies internationally and nationally.[63] The measures taken by the Swiss authorities had not overstepped the margin of appreciation.[64] In *Autronic AG v Switzerland*,[65] the Court found that the Swiss authorities had breached Article 10 by preventing a private company from picking up signals from a Soviet satellite for rebroadcasting into Switzerland. Article 10 applied not only to the content of information, the Court said, but to the mode of transmission or reception as well. To restrict the mode of transmission or reception was to interfere with the right to receive and impart information in Article 10.[66]

In the Austrian radio cases,[67] the European Court of Human Rights found that Austria had breached Article 10 of the Convention by retaining a State monopoly over broadcasting and refusing to licence other stations. The Court again stressed the fundamental role of freedom of expression and of the press in a democratic society, which

> cannot be successfully accomplished unless it is grounded in the principle of pluralism, of which the State is the ultimate guarantor.[68]

As a result of the technical progress made over the last decades, the Court said, justification for not granting licences could no longer be found in considerations relating to the number of frequencies and channels available. Other countries had either granted licences subject to specified conditions or had made provision for forms of private participation in the activities of the national corporation.[69] Austria's refusal to do so was disproportionate to the aim pursued and, accordingly, was not necessary in a democratic society.[70]

In 1995 the Irish State was being sued by a County Cork community group which was refused a broadcasting licence in 1992.[71] The group had been using an unlicensed deflector system, which the State argued would cause too many problems by way of interference with other signals. The High Court held that the group was entitled to an injunction requiring the Minister to reconsider its application for a licence. The present period, therefore, is one of turmoil. It is technology-driven, and legislation is struggling to cope with the changing situation. As the opening sentence of the government's Green Paper on Broadcasting[72] says:

> The need to put the Irish broadcasting sector back on a sound legislative footing comes at a time of intense change in Europe, change that is happening at an accelerating pace in a vexed continent, flooded with virtually instantaneous information, circulated by even more sophisticated technologies.

Satellite and cable distribution systems mean that individual States are less able to regulate content. The commercial aspect has begun to dominate the cultural. The global trend is towards deregulation. Digital compression technology means that many channels will in future be fitted into the capacity formerly occupied by one. Developments in the last few years have been incredible. The possibility of intercepting satellite feed was evidenced by China's crackdown on student protesters in Beijing. Chinese State Television ran a long excerpt from an American ABC network interview which ABC had not actually broadcast. This means that the Chinese must have intercepted it as it reached the US. A man who said in the interview that he had witnessed the bloodshed was 'turned in' within an hour and later sentenced to ten years in a labour camp.[73] Technology now enables the *International Herald Tribune* to be published simultaneously, on a daily basis, in cities right across the world, from London to Singapore, Tokyo to New York. In 1990 a Japanese television reporter gave daily interviews from space aboard a Russian space station.[74] As the government's Green Paper on Broadcasting[75] puts it:

> The process of globalisation which information flows facilitate means that complex networks of power reside less and less in a unified territorial site or bloc and increasingly in decentralised companies and

institutions. . . . Cultural industries, including broadcasting, are undergoing deep change under the influence of forces that go beyond the policy-making of national governments.

The paper goes on to warn that broadcasting can be the motor of modernisation, cultural innovation, social transformation, even democratisation. It can cultivate a healthy public sphere in which national self-confidence flourishes and is orientated towards the future as a set of challenges to be met in a progressive way. It can critically interrogate a nation's history, culture and identify and offer a vantage point for the renewal of that heritage.

[Broadcasting] can also be a threat, pitting profit motive against collective rights, deterritorialised imperialism against minority cultural needs. It can disfigure us, politically, homogenise us linguistically, and depress our inclination for cultural expression. A primary objective of this Green Paper is to stimulate debate on ways in which, through legislation, we can maximise the promise and reduce the threat.[76]

Further Reading

Barendt, Eric, *Broadcasting Law*, Oxford: Clarendon Press, 1993.

Gibbons, Thomas, 'Freedom of the Press: Ownership and Editorial Values', *Public Law* 1992, 279.

Gibbons, Thomas, *Regulating the Media*, London: Sweet and Maxwell, 1991.

Hall, Eamon, *The Electronic Age: Telecommunication in Ireland*, Dublin: Oak Tree Press, 1993.

Skouris, Wassilios, ed., *Advertising and Constitutional Rights in Europe*, Baden-Baden: Nomos Verlagsgesellschaft, 1994.

Notes

1 There are various other wireless telegraphy acts and orders; see Eamonn Hall, *The Electronic Age: Telecommunication in Ireland*, Table of Statutes, at p. 526, Dublin: Oak Tree Press, 1993.
2 See *State (Lynch) v Cooney* [1982] IR 337, [1983] ILRM 89; *Madigan v RTÉ* [1994] ILRM 472, where the court accepted that past election performance could be *one* of the criteria used by RTÉ in allocating broadcasting time to candidates, but not the only one.
3 Radio and Television Act, s.11.
4 EC Directive 89/552/EEC 3 October 1989, Article 23. The obligation to provide a right of reply has been incorporated into the Broadcasting Act 1990, s. 8.
5 Section 18 of the Broadcasting Authority Act 1960, as amended. See also *Broadcasting Guidelines for RTÉ Personnel*, RTÉ 1989, p. 119. A new code of advertising standards to

replace the voluntary codes of RTÉ and the IRTC was issued recently by the Minister for Arts, Culture and the Gaeltacht under the Broadcasting Act 1990 following the EC Directive. *The Irish Times,* 23 September 1995. On the impact of equality legislation on newspaper advertising, see Leo Flynn, 'Discriminatory Newspaper Advertising' (1993) ILT 157, at p. 158. On the suitability or otherwise of the remedies recommended by Equality Officers, see *Cork Examiner v EEA* (EE 13/1990) *and Independent Newspapers v EEA* (EE 17/1991).

6 [1984] ILRM 161.
7 [1984] ILRM 170.
8 *The Observer and the Guardian v UK,* Series A, no. 216 (1992) 14 EHRR 153.
9 The penalties were increased by the Broadcasting and Wireless Telegraphy Act 1988.
10 Unreported, High Court, 4 May 1992.
11 Supreme Court, 26 October 1993; *The Irish Times,* 27 October 1993. On the whole saga of TV3, see Colum Kenny, 'TV3 and the Regulation of Competition in Broadcasting', in Marie McGonagle, ed., *Essays on Law and Media,* Dublin: The Round Hall Press, forthcoming.
12 The Broadcasting Act 1990, s. 3, imposed severe restrictions on the amount of advertising that RTÉ could carry (7.5 per cent of daily programming), but this has now been replaced by the Broadcasting Authority (Amendment) Act 1993, s. 2, which allows the RTÉ Authority to fix the total daily times for broadcasting advertisements and the maximum amount of advertising per hour 'subject to the approval of the Minister'. The EC Directive on transfrontier broadcasting also lays down detailed rules governing television advertising in Articles 10–21. Article 18 says that the amount of advertising shall not exceed 15 per cent of daily transmission time, or 20 per cent if it includes direct offers of products to the public; spot advertsing shall not exceed 20 per cent, or one hour per day.
13 There were instances of members of Sinn Féin being barred from the local stations; see *The Irish Times,* 16 December 1989.
14 IRTC Guidelines 17 January 1994. See *The Irish Times,* 18 January 1994, and Eamonn Hall, 'The Majestic Guarantee—Freedom of Speech', (1995) Dlí No. 9, 79. RTÉ also issued new guidelines in January 1994: *Broadcast Authority Acts 1960–93, Guidance for Staff on Observance of Section 18(1) of the Broadcasting Authority Act 1960.* Michael Foley, Media Correspondent of *The Irish Times,* points out that the RTÉ Guidelines 'are effectively instructions to its own staff', whereas the IRTC's are advisory. *The Irish Times,* 19 January 1994.
15 Ibid., Hall, at p. 83. See also, Colum Kenny, 'Section 31 and the Censorship of Programmes' (1994) 12 ILT 50. For a philosophical analysis of s. 31, see Desmond Clarke, 'Section 31 and Censorship: A Philosophical Perspective', (1994) 12 ILT 53.
16 This happened recently when two companies operating stations in the Cavan/Monaghan and Roscommon/Longford areas merged. They were ordered to retain separate stations and distinctly local programming. *The Irish Times,* 17 January 1995.
17 The demise of the Irish Press titles and findings of the Competition Authority, for example. In September 1993 the government established a commission to examine the Irish newspaper industry. It is due to report in 1996.
18 Green Paper on Broadcasting: *Active or Passive? Broadcasting in the Future Tense,* Dublin: Government Publications, 1995.
19 See generally Eric Barendt, *Broadcasting Law,* Oxford: Clarendon Press, 1993. Wolfgang Hoffmann-Riem, 'Trends in the development of broadcasting law in Western Europe' (1992) 7 Eurj Comm 147.
20 [1974] 1 ECR 409. Case 155/73.
21 *Coditel v Ciné* Vog Films [1980] 2 ECR 881. Case 62/79.
22 *Procureur du Roi v Debauve* [1980] 2 ECR 833. Case 52/79.
23 [1989] 3 CMLR 113. Case 352/85. *Bond Van Adverteerders (Dutch Advertisers' Association) and Others v The State (Netherlands).*
24 Ibid., at p. 155. See also TV 10 SA v *Commissariaat Voor de Media* (1994) ECJR 1–4795.
25 89/552/EEC 3–10–89, OJEC L 298/23 17–10–89.
26 Ibid.
27 Case No. C-260/89; judgment of 18 June 1991, unreported.

28 See, on quotas, Vincenzo Salvatore, 'Quotas on TV Programmes and EEC Law' (1992) CML Rev., 967.

29 The phrase 'where practicable' is to be removed from the Article in proposals put to the Council of Ministers by the European Commission in April 1995. A report on the application of the Directive and proposals to amend it were published on 31 May 1995. The requirement itself of a majority of European works will continue for another ten years.

30 See n. 25, text of Directive, introductory paragraphs (recitals).

31 The advertising of tobacco products (Article 13) and prescription medicines (Article 14) are prohibited. Advertisements for alcohol are restricted (Article 15).

32 (1990) 12 EHRR 161.

33 Nederlandes Omroepprogramma Stichting v the Netherlands Application No. 16844/90, decision of 13 October 1993. See generally Dirk Voorhoof, 'Restrictions on Television Advertising and Article 10 of the European Convention on Human Rights', (1993) 12 Intl Jl of Advertising, 189.

34 See n. 19, Barendt, at ch. VI for an analysis of concentration as horizontal, vertical, multimedia and multisectoral integration. See also E. Roof, J. Trauth, J. Huffman, 'Structural Regulation of Cable Television: A Formula for Diversity' (1993) 15 C&L 43.

35 In accordance with s.11 of the Competition Act 1991. The Competition Authority, established by the Competition Act 1991, also officially revoked the licence for the operation of the British Nett Book Agreement in June 1994. The agreement, which allowed price-fixing of books and protected smaller book sellers, was found to contravene the Act. It followed a ruling of the EC Court of First Instance in Luxembourg (Publishers Association v EC Commission, Case T-66/89, Court of First Instance, 9 July 1992, unreported) that the agreement contravened Article 85 of the EEC Treaty. See Ciaran Walker, 'Court of First Instance Judgment on the Net Book Agreement: Implications for the Irish Book Market' [1992] 6 ENT LR 215.

36 The Report of the Authority: Competition Authority, Interim Report of Study on the Newspaper Industry, 30 March 1995, is interesting also as a source of data and information on the industry.

37 Ibid., at para. 8.32.

38 Ibid., at para. 8.34.

39 Ibid., at para. 8.51.

40 Ibid., at para. 8.53.

41 Ibid., at para. 8.55.

42 Ibid., at para. 8.57.

43 FCC v NCCB 436 US 775 (1978).

44 See n. 19, Barendt, at pp 126-7.

45 Decision of the Court of Justice 6 April 1995; see The Irish Times, 7 April 1995.

46 RTÉ v Magill TV Guide Ltd [1988] IR 97. The Sun newspaper was also prevented by injunction from publishing RTÉ's listings for the ten days of Christmas. The Irish Times, 4 December 1992.

47 [1988] IR 97.

48 [1989] IR 554, [1990] ILRM 534, Lardner J. also considered the competition issue.

49 Ibid., at p. 563.

50 [1994] 2 ILRM 241.

51 The Irish Times, 20 October 1992, 24 January 1995.

52 [1994] 2 ILRM 241, 247. See also PPI v Controller of Industrial and Commercial Property [1993] 1 IR 267, appeal pending. The functions of the Controller include adjudicating on disputes regarding copyright in sound recordings and related matters referred to him under s. 31 or s. 32 of the Copyright Act 1963.

53 The Copyright (Foreign Countries) (No. 2) Order 1978 extended the protection of the 1963 Act to the makers of recordings in countries that were party to the Berne Convention, the Universal Copyright Convention and the Rome Convention. EC Directive 92/108/EEC OJ L346, 27 November 1992, p. 6 deals with rental and lending rights. A new EC Directive is expected to harmonise levies on the sale of blank audio cassettes and

video tapes and to compensate for the loss of royalties that results from home-taping. *The Irish Times*, 26 August 1994.

54 *Re BBC Enterprises Ltd* [1993] 5 CMLR 300.

55 Directive 93/83/EEC OJ L248 of 6 October 1993, p. 15.

56 See Commission decision of 11 June 1993, OJ L179 of 22 July 1993, p. 23, and John Enser, 'The Commission's Decision in the Eurovision Case: A Triumph of Pragmatism over Principle?' [1993] 6 ENT LR 193.

57 See Chapter 5. See also, Thomas Gibbons, *Regulating the Media*, London: Sweet and Maxwell, 1991, pp149–166; Boyle and McGonagle, *Media Accountability: The Readers' Representative in Irish Newspapers*, Dublin: NNI, 1995. Students will enjoy Geoffrey Robertson's amusing, indeed scathing, account of the various British complaints bodies in *Freedom, the Individual and the Law*, 7th edn., London: Penguin Books, 1993, ch. 6, p. 255.

58 See n. 18, at para. 5.10.

59 Ibid., at para. 5.3.

60 The Advertising Standards Authority of Ireland (ASAI) draws up and oversees a code of advertising, which is updated from time to time. Fines can be levied on member firms for breaches of the code. A voluntary self-regulatory system is in place on a European level, operated by the ASAI and similar bodies in other countries.

61 See n. 57, Boyle and McGonagle, at p. 12. See also Alastair Mowbray, 'Newspaper Ombudsmen: the British Experience', (1991) 12 JMLP 91.

62 Series A, no. 173; (1990) 12 EHRR 321.

63 Ibid., at para. 70.

64 Ibid., at para. 73.

65 Series A, no. 178; 12 EHRR 485.

66 Ibid., at para. 47.

67 *Informationsverein Lentia and Ors v Austria*, judgment of 24 November 1993

68 Ibid., at para. 38.

69 Ibid., at para. 39. See generally John O'Dowd, 'Broadcasting Policy and European Law' in McGonagle, n. 11.

70 Ibid., at para. 43. See also Vincent Porter, 'State Licensing and the Freedom of Expression in Broadcasting' (1994) 15(1) JMLP 23.

71 *Southcoast Community Television Broadcasting v Ireland*, *The Irish Times*, 3–4 May 1995, 11 November 1995. Another case involved 'smart cards' and encrypted signals: *News Datacom Ltd v Lyons* [1994] 1 ILRM 450 ('The mere fact that the conduct of the defendant is questionable as a matter of ethics or morality is not a reason . . . to grant an injunction . . .' p. 457 *per* Flood J.)

72 See n. 18, at ch. 1, para. 1.1.

73 Jay Peterjell, 'Betraying the Source', *Columbia Journalism Review*, March/April 1990, p. 6.

74 *The Irish Times*, 3 December 1990.

75 See n. 18, at para. 1.2.

76 Ibid., at para. 1.8.

Index

comparative contract law

cases, materials and exercises

thomas kadner graziano

Professor of Law, University of Geneva

translations by eleanor grant

palgrave
macmillan

First published in English 2009 by
PALGRAVE MACMILLAN

Palgrave Macmillan in the UK is an imprint of Macmillan Publishers Limited,
registered in England, company number 785998, of Houndmills, Basingstoke,
Hampshire RG21 6XS.

Palgrave Macmillan in the US is a division of St Martin's Press LLC,
175 Fifth Avenue, New York, NY 10010.

Palgrave Macmillan is the global academic imprint of the above companies
and has companies and representatives throughout the world.

Palgrave® and Macmillan® are registered trademarks in the United States,
the United Kingdom, Europe and other countries.

ISBN-13: 978–0–230–57979–8   paperback

This book is printed on paper suitable for recycling and made from fully
managed and sustained forest sources. Logging, pulping and manufacturing
processes are expected to conform to the environmental regulations of the
country of origin.

A catalogue record for this book is available from the British Library.

10 9 8 7 6 5 4 3 2 1
18 17 16 15 14 13 12 11 10 09

Printed and bound in Great Britain by CPI Antony Rowe, Chippenham and Eastbourne

Thomas Kadner Graziano studied law at the University of Frankfurt and the University of Geneva, and studied comparative law at the Universities of Salamanca, Strasbourg, London and Trento (Italy). He completed his doctoral thesis at the Goethe-University Frankfurt and obtained an LL.M. from Harvard Law School. After his studies in the US, he spent time as a research fellow at Université Jean Moulin, Lyon 3. He obtained his postdoctoral teaching qualification from Humboldt-Universitaet zu Berlin, teaching comparative law and conflict of laws there and at Universitaet Potsdam and the University of Florida. Since 2001, Professor Kadner Graziano has taught law at the University of Geneva and is Director of the Law Faculty's programme on transnational law. Visiting Professorships were held at the Université de Poitiers, the University of Florida, and the University of Exeter. He is also a Fellow of the European Centre of Tort and Insurance Law (ECTIL) in Vienna.

Foreword

"In order to achieve more convergence of national contract laws, one solution would be for the Commission to promote comparative law research and co-operation between – amongst others – academics and legal practitioners (including judges and experts). This co-operation could aim to find common principles in relevant areas of national contract law."[1]

The 10 case studies used in this book cover fundamental and highly topical issues of contract law and provide solutions to these issues in various national contract law systems, the Vienna Sales Convention (CISG), the UNIDROIT Principles of International Commercial Contracts, the Principles of European Contract Law and the European Draft Common Frame of Reference (DCFR).

The substantive issues covered include contract formation (offers and invitations to treat; the conditions for the formation of a contract; the obligation to maintain an offer and the freedom to revoke offers; the conditions for modification of contracts) as well as performance, breach and remedies (in particular the right to specific performance of a contract or the right to damages; the role of the fault of the seller in an action for damages in the event of delivery of goods not in conformity with the contract; change of circumstances; the transfer of ownership of property). The last two case studies deal with the law applicable to cross-border contracts and the harmonisation of contract law in Europe.

The book invites readers to study both contract law and comparative methodology using a *case-orientated and problem-based approach*.[2] In order to limit the amount of material in the book, difficult choices had to be made. The material (e.g. extracts from national civil codes, court decisions and extracts of academic literature from different countries) sets out the law as it applies in England and Wales, the United States, France, Germany, Italy, Switzerland, and a selection of other countries such as the Netherlands, Poland, Russia, and China. The laws of other countries are included where they provide innovative or different solutions to the issue being examined. The legal systems in each case study were chosen as they were considered to be representative; similar solutions may also be in force in other countries.

Choosing the materials for the book was a difficult task. The author is very grateful to *Andrew Tettenborn*, University of Exeter (UK), to *George Dawson* and *Jeffrey Harrison*, University of Florida (US), and to *Sylvain Marchand*, University of Geneva (Switzerland), for their valuable comments on the draft of this book, and to *Rong Yang*, University of Tianjin (China) and University of Poitiers (France) for her advice on Chinese contract law.

---

[1] Communication from the Commission to the Council and the European Parliament on European Contract Law, Brussels, 11.07.2001, COM(2001) 398 final, at no 52.

[2] For more information on the approach used, see the Introduction, below, **A.I.**, p. 3, and the Introduction to the Comparative Methodology, below, **A.II.**, p. 7.

The materials are provided in their original language version accompanied by an English translation.[3] In order for the publication of this book to succeed, it was essential to have precise translations of the foreign materials. Some of the materials (in particular extracts of civil codes and statutes) were already available in English.[4] Many other texts, in particular many court decisions, much of the academic literature and some of the code provisions and statutes, needed to be translated into English. These materials were translated by *Eleanor Grant* (LL.B., Research Assistant at the University of Geneva, 2007–08). Her work included the translation of court decisions of the French *Cour de cassation*. Due to the cryptic style the *Cour de cassation* uses when drafting its decisions, the translation of French case law requires a perfect understanding of both French and English law. In addition, as many terms and concepts do not have corresponding legal terms in the other language, it is necessary to transpose (often complicated) legal ideas to produce an accurate translation of the text. This is one of the most demanding aspects of legal translation. With a perfect understanding of the foreign materials, *Eleanor Grant* was able to achieve this highly demanding work brilliantly. Her contribution was absolutely fundamental to the success of this project.

I would also like to express my gratitude to my other research assistants at the University of Geneva, *Matthias Erhardt, Johannes Landbrecht, Maria Ludwiczak, Henry Matz*, and *Joya Raha* who each made valuable contributions to the book.

Many thanks to *Esther Pralong* and *Claudine Zbinden* for their help with the drafts of the book, and to *Claudine Zbinden* for her multilingual corrections of the text.

I would also like to thank Palgrave Macmillan, and in particular *Jasmin Naim, Rob Gibson* and *David Stott* for their professional management in preparing the book for publication.

Last but not least I would like to thank my students at the University of Geneva, the University of Exeter and the University of Florida for their comments and most stimulating discussions of the cases and their solutions under different legal orders.[5] I am indebted to *Annette Weber* (Zurich and Geneva) and *Michel Reymond* (Geneva) for their comments on the final draft.

The book proposes a new kind of pedagogic material and a new educational comparative strategy. I would be very grateful for any comments regarding your experience using the book and for any suggestions or criticisms you may have.[6]

The materials in this book were last updated in February 2009. A companion website featuring updates on latest developments can be found at www.palgrave.com/law/Kadner.

Thomas Kadner Graziano
Ivybridge and Geneva
June 2009

---

[3] With a view to concentrating on the main issues, some of the academic literature and case law has been reproduced without the original footnotes. Readers who want further information and references are invited to consult the books and case reports that are cited.

[4] For references, see below, translations, pp. xxiii–xxiv.

[5] The French version of this book is the course text book for the *"Certificat de droit transnational (CDT)"* programme offered at the law faculty of the University of Geneva. It is undertaken by students who have successfully completed at least two years studying law at a university in Switzerland or abroad. More information is available at www.unige.ch/droit/transnational/.

[6] The author can be contacted at thomas.kadner@unige.ch.

Acknowledgements

The author and the publisher wish to thank the following persons and institutions for permission to reproduce extracts of copyright material:

American Law Institute for:
Restatement of the Law Second – Contracts, Vol. 1 (§§ 1-177), 1981.

Verlag C.H. Beck for:
Münchener Kommentar zum Bürgerlichen Gesetzbuch, Vol. 3, Schuldrecht, Besonderer Teil I, §§ 433-610, 5th edn, 2008.

DIANA WALLIS and Verlag C.H. Beck for:
DIANA WALLIS, 'Is It A Code?', *ZEuP* 2006, 513–14.

Cambridge University Press for:
ARTHUR TAYLOR VON MEHREN and PETER L. MURRAY, *Law in the United States*, 2nd edn, 2007.

PHILIPPE MALAURIE and Dalloz for:
PHILIPPE MALAURIE, *D.* 1974, Jurisprudence, pp. 37 et seq.

PHILIPPE MALINVAUD and Dalloz for:
PHILIPPE MALINVAUD, 'Réponse – hors délai – à la Commission européenne: à propos d'un code européen des contrats', in: *Le Recueil Dalloz* 2002, n° 33, pp. 2542 et seq.

CLAUDE WITZ and Dalloz for:
CLAUDE WITZ, 'Plaidoyer pour un code européen des obligations', *Recueil Dalloz* 2000, Chroniques, p. 79 (81) (quotation).

Dalloz for:
- FRANÇOIS TERRÉ AND PHILIPPE SIMLER, *Droit civil: Les biens*, Collection Précis Dalloz, série droit privé, 7th edn, 2006.
- FRANÇOIS TERRÉ AND YVES LEQUETTE, *Les grands arrêts de la jurisprudence civile*, Henri Capitant, Tome 2, Collection Grands arrêts Dalloz, 12th edn, 2008.
- PHILIPPE LE TOURNEAU (avec la collaboration de CHRISTOPHE GUETTIER/ANDRÉ GUIDICELLI/ DIDIER KRAJESKI/JÉRÔME JULIEN/MICHEL LEROY/PHILIPPE STOFFEL-MUNCK), *Droit de la responsabilité et des contrats*, 7th edn, 2008.
- FRANÇOIS TERRÉ, PHILIPPE SIMLER AND YVES LEQUETTE, *Droit civil: Les obligations*, Collection Précis Dalloz, série droit privé, 9th edn, 2005.
- GEORGES HOLLEAUX, *D.* 1959, Jurisprudence, pp. 537 et seq.
- Cour de cassation, chambre sociale, 22 mars 1972, *D.* 1972, Jurisprudence, p. 468, note anonyme.

Thomson Reuters (Foundation Press) for:
E. ALLAN FARNSWORTH ET AL, *Cases and Materials on Contract*, 7th edn, 2008.

Giuffrè for:
PIETRO RESCIGNO, *Codice Civile*, 7th edn, 2008.
PIETRO TRIMARCHI, *Istituzioni di diritto privato*, 16th edn, 2005.

Hart Publishing for:
HUGH BEALE/ARTHUR HARTKAMP/HEIN KÖTZ/DENIS TALLON (eds), *Cases, Materials and Text on Contract Law*, Ius Commune Casebooks for the Common Law of Europe, 2002.

Helbing Lichtenhahn Verlag for:
LUC THÉVENOZ AND FRANZ WERRO (eds), *Commentaire Romand: Code des obligations*, Vol. I, 2003.

OLE LANDO AND HUGH BEALE and Kluwer Law International for:
Commission on European Contract Law: *Principles of European Contract Law*, Parts I and II, eds OLE LANDO AND HUGH BEALE, 2000.

Kluwer Law International for:
- DANNY BUSCH ET AL. (EDS), *The Principles of European Contract Law and Dutch Law: A Commentary*, 2002.
- HERBERT BERNSTEIN AND JOSEPH LOOKOVSKY, *Understanding the CISG in Europe*, 2nd edn, 2003.
- JEROEN M. J. CHORUS/PIET-HEIN M. GERVER/EWOUD H. HONDIUS/ALIS K. KOEKKOEK, *Introduction to Dutch Law*, 3rd edn, 1999.
- JOHN O. HONNOLD, *Uniform Law for International Sales under the 1980 United Nations Convention*, 3rd edn, 1999.
- JÜRGEN BASEDOW, 'Codification of Private Law in the European Union: the making of a Hybrid', 9 *ERPL* (2001) 35–49.
- STEPHEN WEATHERILL, 'Reflections on the EC's Competence to Develop a "European Contract Law"', *ERPL* 3 (2005) 405–18.

Nomos Verlag for:
MELVIN A. EISENBERG, 'Why is American Contract Law so Uniform? – National Law in the United States', in Hans-Leo Weyers (ed.), *Europäisches Vertragsrecht*, 1997, pp. 23–43.

Oxford University Press for:
KONRAD ZWEIGERT AND HEIN KÖTZ, *An Introduction to Comparative Law* (translated by TONY WEIR), 1998.
P.S. ATIYAH, *An Introduction to the Law of Contract*, 6th edn, 2005.
PETER SHEARS AND GRAHAM STEPHENSON, *James' Introduction to English Law*, 13th edn, 1996.
MICHAEL P. FURMSTON, *Cheshire, Fifoot & Furmston's Law of Contract*, 15th edn, 2007.
GUENTER TREITEL, *An Outline of The Law of Contract*, 6th edn, 2004.

Palgrave Macmillan for:
EWAN MCKENDRICK, *Contract Law*, 8th edn, 2009.

Sellier for:
STUDY GROUP ON A EUROPEAN CIVIL CODE AND RESEARCH GROUP ON EC PRIVATE LAW (ACQUIS GROUP), *Draft Common Frame of Reference*, 2009.

HERBERT SCHÖNLE and the Société genevoise de droit et de legislation for:
HERBERT SCHÖNLE, Remarques sur la responsabilité causale du vendeur selon les art. 195 al. 1 et 208 al. 2 CO, *Semaine Juridique* 1977, pp. 465 et seq.

Stämpfli for:
HEINZ REY, *Grundriss des schweizerischen Sachenrechts, Band I, Die Grundlagen des Sachenrechts und das Eigentum*, 3rd edn, 2007.

MICHAEL JOACHIM BONELL for:
MICHAEL JOACHIM BONELL, *An International Restatement of Contract Law – The UNIDROIT Principles of International Commercial Contracts*, 3rd edn, 2005.

UNIDROIT and CHRISTINE CHAPPUIS for:
CHRISTINE CHAPPUIS, Le renoncement à la cause et à la consideration dans l'avant-projet d'Acte uniforme OHADA sur le droit des contrats, *Revue de droit uniforme/Uniform Law Review* 2008, 253–91.

UNIDROIT for:
Principles of International Commercial Contracts, 2004

Thomson Reuters (West Publishing) for:
JAMES J. WHITE AND ROBERT S. SUMMERS, *Uniform Commercial Code*, 5th edn, 2000.

Contents

Bibliography

Academy of European Private Lawyers, Coordinator: Giuseppe Gandolfi, Pavia, *European Contract Code, Preliminary Draft*, Milano: Giuffrè, 2007.

Academy of European Private Lawyers (Academy Coordinator: Giuseppe Gandolfi, Pavia), *European Contract Code, Draft, Text in French, English, German, Spanish, and Italian*, www.accademiagiusprivatistieuropei.it.

American Law Institute, *Restatement of the Law Second – Contracts 2nd, Vol. 1 (§§ 1-177)*, St Paul/Minnesota: American Law Institute Publishers, 1981.

Atiyah, Patrick S. and Stephen A. Smith, *Atiyah's Introduction to the Law of Contract*, 6th edn, Oxford: Oxford University Press, 2005.

Beale, Hugh, Arthur Hartkamp, Hein Kötz and Denis Tallon (eds), *Cases, Materials and Text on Contract Law* (Ius Commune Casebooks for the Common Law of Europe), Oxford: Hart Publishing, 2002.

Bernstein, Herbert and Joseph Lookovsky, *Understanding the CISG in Europe – A Compact Guide to the 1980 United Nations Convention for the International Sale of Goods*, 2nd edn, The Hague/London/Boston: Kluwer Law International, 2003.

Bonell, Michael, *An International Restatement of Contract Law, The UNIDROIT Principles of International Commercial Contracts*, 3rd edn incorporating the UNIDROIT Principles 2004, Ardsley, New York: Transnational Publishers Inc., 2005.

Busch, Danny, Ewoud Hondius, Hugo van Kooten, Harriët Schelhaas and Wendy Schrama (eds), *The Principles of European Contract Law and Dutch Law – A Commentary*, Nijmegen & The Hague/London/New York: Kluwer Law International, 2002.

Busch, Danny, Ewoud Hondius, Hugo van Kooten, Harriët Schelhaas and Wendy Schrama (eds), *The Principles of European Contract Law (Part III) and Dutch Law – A Commentary II*, Nijmegen & The Hague/London/New York: Kluwer Law International, 2006.

Canivet, Guy, Mads Andenas and Duncan Fairgrieve (eds), *Comparative Law Before the Courts*, London: British Institute of International & Comparative Law, 2004.

Capitant, Henri, François Terré and Yves Lequette, *Les grands arrêts de la jurisprudence civile*, Tome 2: Obligations, contrats spéciaux, sûretés, 12th edn, Paris: Dalloz, 2008,

Chorus, Jeroen M. J., Piet-Hein M. Gerver, Ewoud H. Hondius and Alis K. Koekkoek, *Introduction to Dutch Law*, 4th rev. edn, Alphen aan den Rijn: Kluwer, 2006.

Commission on European Contract Law, *Principles of European Contract Law, Text in French, English, German, Spanish, Italian and Dutch*, http://frontpage.cbs.dk/law/commission_on_european_contract_law/index.html.

Commission on European Contract Law – *see* Lando, Ole/Hugh Beale.

Dicey, Morris and Collins, Conflict of Laws, 14th edn, vol. 2, London: Sweet & Maxwell, 2006.

Díez-Picazo, Luis and Antonio Gullón, *Sistema de Derecho Civil, Vol. III: Derecho de Cosas y Derecho Inmobiliario Registral*, 7th edn, Madrid: Tecnos Editorial, 2001.

Farnsworth, Allan, *Contracts*, 4th edn, New York: Aspen Publishers, 2004.

Farnsworth, Allan et al., *Contracts – Cases and Materials*, 7th edn, New York: Thomson Reuters/Foundation Press, 2008.

Furmston, Michael P., *Cheshire, Fifoot & Furmston's Law of Contract*, 15th edn, Oxford: Oxford University Press, 2007.

Goode, Roy, Herbert Kronke and Ewan McKendrick, *Transnational Commercial Law*, Oxford: Oxford University Press, 2007.

Gordley, James (ed.), *The Enforceability of Promises in European Contract Law*, Cambridge: Cambridge University Press, 2001.

Guest, A.G., *Benjamin on Sale of Goods*, 7th edn, London: Sweet & Maxwell, 2006.

Hartkamp, Arthur, Martijn Hesselink, Ewoud Hondius, Carla Joustra, Edgar du Perron and Muriel Veldman (eds), *Towards a European Civil Code*, 3rd edn, Nijmegen: Kluwer Law International, 2004.

Holmes, Oliver Wendell, *The Common Law*, Boston: Little Brown, 1881.

Honnold, John O., *Uniform Law for International Sales under the 1980 United Nations Convention*, 3rd edn, The Hague: Kluwer Law International, 1999.

Honsell, Heinrich, Nedim Peter Vogt, Wolfgang Wiegand (eds), *Kommentar zum Schweizerischen Privatrecht, Obligationenrecht I, Art. 1-529*, 3rd edn, Basel: Helbing & Lichtenhahn, 2003.

Kötz, Hein and Axel Flessner, *European Contract Law* (by Hein Kötz, English translation by Tony Weir), Oxford: Clarendon Press, 1997.

Lando, Ole and Hugh Beale (eds), *Principles of European Contract Law, Parts I and II*, 2nd edn, The Hague/London/Boston: Kluwer Law International, 2000. Text of the Principles also at http://frontpage.cbs.dk/law/commission_on_european_contract_law/index.html.

Le Tourneau, Philippe (avec la collaboration de Christophe Guettier, André Guidicelli, Didier Krajeski, Jérôme Julien, Michel Leroy andPhilippe Stoffel-Munck), *Droit de la responsabilité et des contrats*, 7th edn, Paris: Dalloz, 2008.

Levasseur, Alain, *Comparative Law of Contracts. Cases and Materials*, Durham/North Carolina: Carolina Academic Press, 2008.

Ling, Bing, *Contract Law in China*, Hong Kong/Singapore/Malaysia: Sweet & Maxwell, 2002.

Major, W.T. and Christine Taylor, *Law of Contract*, 9th edn, Harlow: Pitman Publishing, 1996.

McKendrick, Ewan, *Contract Law*, 8th edn, Basingstoke/New York: Palgrave Macmillan, 2009.

Von Mehren, Arthur Taylor and Peter L Murray, *Law in the United States*, 2nd edn, Cambridge: Cambridge University Press, 2007.

Mincke, Wolfgang, *Einführung in das niederländische Recht*, Munich: Beck, 2002.

Münchener Kommentar zum Bürgerlichen Gesetzbuch, Band 3, Schuldrecht, Besonderer Teil I, §§ 433-610, 5th edn, Munich: Beck, 2008.

Pasquau Liaño, Miguel (ed.), *Jurisprudencia Civil Comentada – Código Civil, Tomo I, Art. 1 a 1.087*, Granada: Comares, 2000.

Pothier, Robert-Joseph, "Traité des obligations, 1761, réimprimé avec des augmentations", in Jean-Joseph Bugnet, *Oeuvres de Pothier annotées et mises en corrélation avec le Code civil et la législation actuelle*, Tome 2, Paris: Cosse et N. Delamotte, 1848.

Pufendorf, Samuel von, *Le droit de la Nature et des Gens, ou Système Général des Principes les plus importants de la Morale, de la Jurisprudence et de la Politique*, traduit du latin par Jean Barbeyrac, Basel: E. & J.R. Thourneisen, Freres, 1771.

Ranieri, Filippo, *Europäisches Obligationenrecht*, 2nd edn, Wien/New York: Springer, 2003.

Rescigno, Pietro, *Codice Civile*, 7th edn, Milan: Giuffrè, 2008.

Rey, Heinz, *Grundriss des schweizerischen Sachenrechts – Band I, Die Grundlagen des Sachenrechts und das Eigentum*, 3rd edn, Bern: Stämpfli, 2007.

Schwenzer, Ingeborg and Markus Müller-Chen, *Rechtsvergleichung – Fälle und Materialien*, Tübingen: Mohr Siebeck, 1996.

Shears, Peter and Graham Stephenson, *James' Introduction to English Law*, 13th edn, London: Butterworths, 1996.

Smith, J.C. and J.A.C. Thomas, *A Casebook on Contract*, 11th edn, London: Sweet & Maxwell, 2000.

Smits, Jan M. (ed.), *Elgar Encyclopedia of Comparative Law*, Cheltenham (UK)/Northampton, Mass. (USA): Edward Elgar Publishing Ltd, 2006.

Study Group on a European Civil Code and Research Group on EC Private Law (Acquis Group), *Principles, Definitions and Model Rules of European Private Law – Draft Common Frame of Reference*, Munich: Sellier, 2009.

Terré, François and Yves Lequette, *Grands arrêts de la jurisprudence civile, Vol. II*, 11th edn, Paris: Dalloz, 2000.

Terré, François, Philippe Simler, Yves Lequette, *Droit civil. Les obligations*, 9th edn, Paris: Dalloz, 2005.

Terré, François and Philippe Simler, *Droit civil. Les biens*, 7th edn, Paris: Dalloz, 2006.

Thévenoz, Luc and Franz Werro (eds), *Commentaire Romand, Code des obligations, Vol. I*, Genève/Basel/Munich: Helbing & Lichtenhahn, 2003.

Treitel, Guenter, *The Law of Contract*, 12th edn, London: Sweet & Maxwell, 2007.

Treitel, Guenter, *An Outline of the Law of Contract*, 6th edn, Oxford: Oxford University Press, 2004.

Trimarchi, Pietro, *Istituzioni di diritto privato*, 17th edn, Milan: Giuffrè, 2007.

UNIDROIT, International Institute for the Unification of Private Law, *Principles of International Commercial Contracts 2004*, Rome: UNIDROIT, 2004.

UNIDROIT, *Principles of International Commercial Contracts* (Rome 2004), www.unilex.info.

Zimmermann, Reinhard, *The Law of Obligations – Roman Foundations of the Civilian Tradition*, Cape Town: Juta & Co., 1990; 1st edn, reprint, Cape Town: Juta & Co., 2006.

Zweigert, Konrad and Hein Kötz, *An Introduction to Comparative Law* (transl. by Tony Weir), 3rd edn, Oxford: Oxford University Press, 1998.

Table of abbreviations

ABGB	Allgemeines Bürgerliches Gesetzbuch (Austrian Civil code)
AcP	Archiv für die civilistische Praxis (German law journal)
al.	Alinéa (Section)
All ER	All England Law Reports
Am. Bus. L.J.	American Business Law Journal
Am. J. Comp. L.	American Journal of Comparative Law
Ann. Surv. Int'l & Comp. L.	Annual Survey of International & Comparative Law
Art.	Article
Arts	Articles
BB	Betriebs-Berater (German law journal)
BBl.	Bundesblatt (Swiss reporter of Federal law)
BG	Bundesgericht (Swiss Federal court)
BGB	Bürgerliches Gesetzbuch (German Civil code)
BGE	Entscheidungen des Schweizerischen Bundesgerichts, amtliche Sammlung (official collection of the case-law of the Swiss Federal court)
BGH	Bundesgerichtshof (German Federal court)
Build. L.M.	Building Law Monthly
Bull. Civ.	Bulletin des arrêts de la Cour de cassation, Chambres civiles (Official collection of the case-law of the French Cour de cassation)
C. cass.	Cour de cassation (French Court of cassation)
C. civ.	Code civil (civil code)
Chi. J. Int'l L.	Chicago Journal of International Law
CISG	United Nations Convention on Contracts for the International Sale of Goods
Const. L.J.	Construction Law Journal
Ct. Cl.	Court of Claims Reports (1863–1982) (USA)
C.T.L.R.	Computer and Telecommunications Law Review
D.	Recueil Dalloz de doctrine, de jurisprudence et de législation, 1945–1964 (French law journal)
D.S.	Recueil Dalloz Sirey de doctrine, de jurisprudence et de législation, since 1965 (French law journal)
ed.	editor
Edin. L.R.	Edinburgh Law Review
edn	edition
eds	editors

EG	Eleanor Grant, LL.B., Research Assistant to the author at the University of Geneva (2007–08)
EGBGB	Einführungsgesetz zum Bürgerlichen Gesetzbuch (German Civil code, introductory rules)
E.B.L.Rev.	European Business Law Review
ELJ	European Law Journal
E.L.Rev.	European Law Review
ERA	European Law Academy, Trier
ERPL	European Review of Private Law
EWS	Europäisches Wirtschafts- und Steuerrecht (Law Journal)
F. Supp.	Federal Supplement (USA)
I.B.L.J.	International Business Law Journal
Int.Enc.Comp.L.	International Encyclopedia of Comparative Law
JCP	Juris-Classeur périodique, La Semaine Juridique (French law journal)
JuS	Juristische Schulung (German law journal)
J.L. & Com.	Journal of Law and Commerce
JZ	Juristen-Zeitung (German law journal)
Kan. L. Rev.	University of Kansas Law Review
K.B.	King's Bench Division
LG	Landgericht (German court of 1st instance and court of appeal, depending of the value in dispute)
LJ	Lord Justice
Loy. L.A. Int'l & Comp. L. Rev.	Loyola of Los Angeles International & Comparative Law Review
LQR	Law Quarterly Review
Minn. J. Int'l. L.	Minnesota Journal of International Law
ML	Maria Ludwiczak, LL.M., Research Assistant to the author at the University of Geneva (since 2008)
NCPC	Nouveau Code de procédure civile (French Code of civil procedure)
NJW	Neue Juristische Wochenschrift (German law journal)
NJW-RR	Neue Juristische Wochenschrift – Rechtsprechungs-Report (German law journal)
N.W.2d	North Western Reporter, 2nd series (USA)
OHG	Oberster Gerichtshof (Austrian Supreme court)
OLG	Oberlandesgericht (German Court of appeal)
OR	Obligationenrecht (Swiss Code of Obligations)
para.	paragraph
Pas.	Pasicrisie belge (collection of Belgian case law)
PECL	Principles of European Contract Law
Q.B.	Queen's Bench Division
RabelsZ	Rabels Zeitschrift für ausländisches und internationales Privatrecht (German comparative law journal)
Regent U.L. Rev.	Regent University Law Review
Rev. int. dr. comp.	Revue internationale de droit comparé

RGZ	Sammlung der Reichsgerichtsrechtsprechung in Zivilsachen (Official collection of the case-law of the Supreme court of the ancient German empire)
RIS	(Austrian) Rechtsinformationssystem, www.ris.bka.gv.at
RIW	Recht der internationalen Wirtschaft (German law journal)
R.J.T.	Revue juridique Themis
RRa	ReiseRecht aktuell – Zeitschrift für das Tourismusrecht (German law journal)
RTD Civ.	Revue trimestrielle de droit civil
s.	section
SGA	Sale of Goods Act, England
SR	Systematische Sammlung des Bundesrechts (systematic collection of Swiss statutes)
StGB	Strafgesetzbuch (penal code)
SZIER	Schweizerische Zeitschrift für internationales und europäisches Recht (Swiss comparative law journal)
Tex. Rev. Law & Pol.	Texas Review of Law & Politics
Tul. L. Rev.	Tulane Law Review
UNIDROIT	International Institute for the Unification of Private Law (www.unidroit.org)
Unif. L. Rev.	Uniform Law Review / Revue de droit uniforme (UNIDROIT)
Vand. J. Transnat'l L.	Vanderbilt Journal of Transnational Law
VersR	Versicherungsrecht (German law journal)
Vol.	volume
Wis. L. Rev.	Wisconsin Law Review
Wm and Mary L. Rev.	William & Mary Law Review
W. Va L. Rev.	West Virginia Law Review
ZEuP	Zeitschrift für Europäisches Privatrecht (German comparative law journal)
ZfRV	Zeitschrift für Rechtsvergleichung (Austrian comparative law journal)
ZGB	Zivilgesetzbuch (civil code)
ZPO	Zivilprozessordnung (code of civil procedure)
ZRP	Zeitschrift für Rechtspolitik (German law journal)
ZVglRWiss	Zeitschrift für Vergleichende Rechtswissenschaft (German comparative law journal)

English translations of statutes, cases and legal doctrine by Eleanor Grant (LL.B., Research Assistant at the University of Geneva, 2007–08).

Translations of statutes of the following jurisdictions are taken from the sources below. Whilst all translations are believed to be correct and accurate, readers requiring a definitive interpretation should direct themselves to the original sources.

China

Contract Law of The People's Republic of China (1999), transl. and compiled by *John Jiang & Henry Liu*. At http://www.cclaw.net/download/contractlawPRC.asp.

Denmark

Danish Sales of Goods Act, http://www.forbrug.dk/english/laws/saleofgoods/.

Finland

Finnish Sale of Goods Act (355/1987), http://www.finlex.fi/en/laki/kaannokset/1987/en19870355.pdf.

France

www.legifrance.org/.

Germany

http://www.gesetze-im-internet.de/englisch_bgb/index.html (§§ 125, 145–148, 651e, 651i–651j, 516, 518, 534, 780, 929, 932 BGB).

http://www.iuscomp.org/gla/statutes/BGB.html (§§ 241, 280, 313, 433, 434, 437 BGB).

Greece

Greek Civil Code, Translation by *Constantin Taliadoros*, Athen/Komotini 2000.

Italy

The Italian civil code and complementary legislation, transl. by *Mario Beltramo, Giovanni E. Longo, John Henry Merryman*, Dobbs Ferry N.Y., 1991.

Lithuania

http://www3.lrs.lt/pls/inter3/dokpaieska.showdoc_l?p_id=245495.

Netherlands

Niederländisches Bürgerliches Gesetzbuch, *F. Nieper/A.S. Westerdijk* (Red.), Buch 3 Allgemeiner Teil des Vermögensrechts, bearbeitet von *Stefan Caspari/Franz Nieper*; Buch 4 Erbrecht, bearbeitet von *Claudia Hein*; Buch 5 Sachenrecht, bearbeitet von *Arjen S. Westerdijk*, München und The Hague/London/Boston 1996.

Niederländisches Bürgerliches Gesetzbuch, *F. Nieper/A.S. Westerdijk* (Red.), Buch 6
Allgemeiner Teil des Schuldrechts, bearbeitet von *Franz Nieper*; Bücher 7 und 7A
Besondere Verträge, bearbeitet von *Stefan Caspari, Claudia Hein, Arjen S. Westerdijk*.
München und The Hague/London/Boston 1995.

Serbia and Montenegro
The Law of Contract and Torts (*Zakon o obligacionim odnosima*), ed. by *Ile Kovačević*, Beograd
1997.

Spain
Civil Code of Spain, transl. by *Julio Romanach Jr*, Baton Rouge La 1994.

Switzerland
Swiss Code of Obligations, Arts 1–551, English translation of the official text, ed. by the
Swiss-American Chamber of Commerce, Zurich 2008.
Swiss Civil Code, law of persons (Arts 1–89*bis*), family law (Arts 90–456): English translation
of the official texts, ed. by the Swiss-American Chamber of Commerce, Zurich 2008.

Part A: Introduction

Chapter I

Contract Law in the 21st Century– the purpose of this book

"In a shrinking world [...] there must be some virtue of uniformity of outcome whatever the diversity of approach in reaching that outcome." Lord Bingham, *Fairchild v. Glenhaven* (House of Lords)[1]

In Europe and in many other parts of the world, the reform of contract law is very much on the agenda. Contract law as it currently stands is characterised, first, by the great diversity of the traditional national contract law systems and, secondly, by the coexistence of the national systems of contract law, uniform and harmonised law, and non-binding contract instruments (principles of contract law); these non-binding instruments are available for the international community to adopt in contracts, and are used by judges and legislators as a source of inspiration for law reform as well as for filling the gaps in national contract laws. This book provides an introduction to both comparative contract law and comparative methodology.

I. Contract law in the 21st Century – overview

National contract laws continue to play an important role in practice, particularly in purely domestic scenarios. However, nowadays they are far from being the only rules to be applied in the field of contract law. This is particularly true for transnational contracts.

For transnational sales contracts, the domestic systems coexist with uniform rules, in particular the *United Nations Convention on Contracts for the International Sale of Goods* (CISG or Vienna Sales Convention).[2] According to Article 1(1) of the Vienna Sales Convention, it is applicable to contracts for the sale of goods between parties whose places of business are in different Contracting States, or when the conflict of law rules of the country in which the court is located lead to the application of the law of a Contracting State. The Vienna Sales Convention has proved to be probably the most successful exercise in the global harmonisation of the law; it is in force in 73 States (*inter alia* the USA, Canada, China, Japan, Russia, Australia and the EU Member States with the exception of England, Ireland, Portugal and Malta).

---

[1] [2002] 3 All ER 305 at 334 (liability for damage due to exposure to asbestos; problem of proving the causal link between the negligent behaviour of several, subsequent employers and the damage suffered by their employee; the court took into consideration the laws of Germany, Austria, Switzerland, The Netherlands, Norway, France, Italy, Greece, California, Canada, Australia, South Africa, and the American Restatement Second on Torts, at 326–34).

[2] United Nations Convention on Contracts for the International Sale of Goods; Text, Contracting States, Cases and Bibliography available at: www.unilex.info.

In the mid-1990s, the International Institute for the Unification of Private Law (UNIDROIT[3]) presented its *Principles of International Commercial Contracts* (UNIDROIT Principles).[4] At the same time, the Commission on European Contract Law, a private group of researchers coordinated by the Danish law professor Ole Lando, presented its *Principles of European Contract Law*, modern rules of contract law that, like the UNIDROIT Principles, are the result of two decades of comparative research and, again like the UNIDROIT Principles, are perfectly adapted to the needs of transnational actors.[5] Today, parties to (transnational) contracts not only have a choice between the rules of different domestic contract laws and the CISG[6]; they can also choose to incorporate the UNIDROIT Principles or the Principles of European Contract Law into their contracts. In arbitration procedures they may even decide to submit their contract entirely and exclusively to these modern contract instruments and bind the arbitral tribunal accordingly.[7]

Over the last few decades, the European Community has enacted a series of Directives in the field of contract law, governing numerous specific aspects, namely those relating to specific marketing techniques, in particular with regard to consumer contracts. This selective and sectoral approach to harmonisation has, however, led to inconsistencies and has proved to have considerable limitations.[8] Therefore, the European Parliament has called for work to be started on the possibility of developing a more comprehensive European private law in several of its resolutions.[9] In 2001, in response to these resolutions, the European Commission launched a process of consultation and discussion about the way in which problems resulting from divergences between national contract laws in the EU should be dealt with on the European level.[10] This culminated in the publication of a first draft of a *Common Frame of Reference (CFR)* in January 2008 and, in 2009, in the publication of an improved version of the *Draft Common Frame of Reference*. The draft *CFR* was largely inspired by the Principles of European Contract Law and by the *Acquis Principles*. The *Acquis Principles* were presented in 2007 by the European Research Group on Existing EC Private Law (Acquis Group).[11] The *CFR* is intended to provide the European Commission with a "tool-box" and act as a guide for future Community legislation in the field of contract law and related areas.[12] Some observers consider the *CFR* to

---

[3] UNIDROIT is an independent intergovernmental organisation headquartered in Rome. Its purpose is to study needs and methods for modernising, harmonising and co-ordinating private and in particular commercial law between States and groups of States; see www.unidroit.org/dynasite.cfm?dsmid=84219.

[4] International Institute for the Unification of Private Law (UNIDROIT): Principles of International Commercial Contracts, Text, Official Comment, Cases and Bibliography available at: www.unilex.info.

[5] Commission on European Contract Law, *Principles of European Contract Law*, Text in French, English, German, Spanish, Italian and Dutch available at: http://frontpage.cbs.dk/law/commission_on_european_contract_law/index.html; Text, commentary and annotations in: Ole Lando and Hugh Beale (eds), Commission on European Contract Law: *Principles of European Contract Law*, Parts I and II, The Hague: Kluwer Law International, 2000.

[6] For the conditions of the application of the CISG, see below, **Part B, Case 9.**

[7] For more information, see below, **Part B, Case 9.**

[8] See **Part B, Case 10**, in particular **I., IV.1, 2.**

[9] See the case scenario below, **Part B, Case 10.**

[10] Communication from the Commission to the Council and the European Parliament on European Contract Law, Brussels, 11.07.2001, COM(2001) 398 final; extract below, **Part B, Case 10, I.**; see further the Communication from the Commission to the Council and the European Parliament, *A more coherent European contract law – an action plan*, Brussels, 12.2.2003, COM(2003) 68 final, extract below, **Part B, Case 10, IV.1.**

[11] European Research Group on Existing EC Private Law (Acquis Group), www.acquis-group.org.

[12] See the Communication from the Commission of 2003 (above, n 10) and Diana Wallis, "Is It A Code?", *ZEuP* 2006, 513–14, extract below, **Part B, Case 10, IV.3.**

be the first step towards a European contract code,[13] whilst others are firmly opposed to the creation of such a code.[14]

Numerous countries, for example the Netherlands and many countries in Central and Eastern Europe, have either recently modernized their civil codes, including the rules on contract law, or are about to do so. They have taken their inspiration from foreign sources and comparative law to such an extent that the comparative method has been described as the "main method used for private law in today's legislative drafting".[15]

In France, a project is currently underway to reform the law of obligations in the *Code civil*. It promises to be the most significant reform of the law since the Code's entry into force in 1804. Whereas other legislators have taken their inspiration from international principles of contract law, this reform will probably leave in place many special features of French contract law.

In 1999, a new Chinese contract code came into force, largely inspired by the UNIDROIT Principles.[16] This new code needs to be applied and its provisions need to be interpreted. It suggests itself that the interpretation of similar rules abroad should be taken into consideration when working with this new code. For foreign actors, it is interesting to note that the new Chinese contract law provides for many solutions that are well known in other regions of the world, in particular in Europe and in the CISG Contracting States.

The Organisation for the Harmonization of Business Law in Africa (*Organisation pour l'Harmonisation en Afrique du Droit des Affaires*, OHADA) is made up of 16 West African States. At OHADA's request, UNIDROIT has developed a preliminary draft of a Uniform Act on Contract Law, the aim being the unification of the contract law of the OHADA Member States.[17]

Most of the recent legislation on contract law, and most current projects on contract law, are thus based on comprehensive comparative analysis. For international actors, the diversity of the law makes it more and more important to compare different solutions to a given problem, to analyse the pros and cons of different approaches, to choose between different options and thus to benefit from a comparative perspective. In the field of contract law, a truly international legal discourse is developing.

II.   The purpose of this book

This book provides an introduction to contract law in all its diversity. It is an invitation to study both contract law and comparative methodology using a case-orientated and problem-based approach.

Part A introduces a modern approach to comparative law and comparative methodology,[18] and gives reasons for the choice of the legal orders that are found in Part B of the book. Chapter

---

[13]   See, on this issue, DIANA WALLIS (above, n. 12).

[14]   For more details, see the materials provided below, **Part B, Case 10**.

[15]   PAUL VARUL, "Legal Policy Decisions and Choices in the Creation of New Private Law in Estonia", *Juridica international* (Estonia) 2000, 104, at 107: "The main method used for private law in today's legislative drafting is the comparative method".

[16]   中华人民共和国合同法 (*Contract Law of the People's Republic of China, 1999*); for references see **Part B, Case 1, n. 17**.

[17]   For references, see **Part B, Case 2, XII. 5 and n. 13**.

[18]   Below, **II**.

III of Part A provides a brief introduction to the Principles of European Contract Law and to the UNIDROIT Principles of International Commercial Contracts, and sets out the needs to which these uniform rules respond, and the purposes for which they were designed.[19]

Each of the 10 case studies in Part B starts with a scenario taken from the case law of a European country which raises a highly topical issue of contract law. Targeted questions follow, serving to guide the reader through the materials, and encouraging reflection on the differences and similarities inherent in the contract law of the 21st century. In each of the first eight case studies, materials from different legal orders are provided. They allow the reader to solve the respective case scenario under different national laws, as well as under international law and the non-binding principles of contract law. The materials (e.g. extracts from national civil codes, court decisions and extracts from academic literature from different countries) are provided in the original version with English translations. They present the law as it currently stands in England and Wales, the United States, Germany, France, Italy, Switzerland, and a selection of other countries, such as the Netherlands, Poland, Russia and China.

Readers are given precise questions to guide them through their work with each case and the materials. The first step is to solve each case according to the different national laws. The second step is to analyse and compare the solutions found in the different national laws, and to discover if any common principles exist for the issue in question. The reader then looks at international legal materials such as the *CISG*, the *UNIDROIT Principles of International Commercial Contracts*, the *Principles of European Contract Law*, the *Draft European Contract Code* and the *Draft Common Frame of Reference*, and analyses and compares the solutions for each of the case scenarios. Where the solutions diverge, the reader is invited to analyse their respective pros and cons, and to discuss which of the solutions might be the most appropriate to resolve the problem at issue from a comparative and international perspective.

Case study 9 deals with the question of how the different national contract law systems are coordinated at present; it provides some basic information on conflict of law issues in contractual matters, and points to the strengths and weaknesses of dealing with legal diversity from the perspective of conflict of laws (or private international law). Lastly, case study 10 addresses the question of the role of contract law in common markets and in regional organizations of States and, in particular, the question of the future of European contract law.

Working with the book will help to familiarize the reader with foreign contract laws, the Vienna Sales Convention, and the modern contract instruments and rules on contract law. The book provides an invitation to work with legal materials from different countries such as continental civil codes and court decisions (e.g. decisions of the French or Belgian *Cour de Cassation*, the German and Swiss Federal Courts of Justice, and the English Court of Appeal and House of Lords). At the same time, and due to the format of the textbook, readers have the opportunity to explore the peculiarities of form and style in foreign legal materials first hand.

The comparative approach enables the reader to take inspiration from different legal orders, be it as a future solicitor, barrister, or judge, and prepares him or her for work in an increasingly international environment that will, for a long time to come, be characterized by legal diversity. The book is based on the firm conviction that comparative methodology cannot be taught using a purely theoretical approach; the reader is therefore invited to *learn by doing*.[20] Last but not least, working with this textbook should help readers to better understand their foreign colleagues with different legal backgrounds, and to feel at home in a world filled with very diverse legal thinkers.

---

[19] Below, **III.1. and 2.**
[20] For the suggested method to be applied, see below, **II.**

Restructuring the International Legal Landscape: a brief introduction to the comparative methodology used in this book*

Contents

The following chapter provides an introduction to the "international approach" to comparative

---

* For a previous version of this article in German, see THOMAS KADNER GRAZIANO, "Die Europäisierung der juristischen Perspektive und der vergleichenden Methode – Fallstudien", *Zeitschrift für vergleichende Rechtswissenschaft (ZVglRWiss)* 2007, 248–71; for a previous version in French with a different case study, see *id.*, "L'européanisation du droit privé et de la méthode comparative – Etude de cas", *Schweizerische Zeitschrift für internationales und europäisches Recht/Revue suisse de droit international et de droit européen (SZIER/RSDIE)* 2004, 233–54.

methodology that can be used when working with the cases in Part B of the book. This method widens the perspectives and the spectrum of possible solutions when dealing with legal issues, and should make it possible to have a discourse of legal issues among lawyers across national borders. This should contribute to creating a common European legal science and a common legal consciousness across national borders. It is further argued that in the 21st century the comparison in the field of private law can no longer be limited to the main representatives of the "legal families" (i.e. English or US law, German and French law), and it gives reasons for the choice of the countries included in the comparative analysis in Part B of the book.

I.   The role of comparative law: point of departure

Ever since the great civil law codifications of the 19th century and the first years of the 20th century[1] entered into force throughout continental Europe, lawyers on the Continent have used comparative law in order to find guidance for the interpretation of their respective national codes, to enhance their national laws, and to fill the gaps in their national codes, statutes or case law. English judges, just like their counterparts in other common law countries, have always taken inspiration from the comparison with the case law of other common law countries such as the US, Australia, or Canada, and have thus improved their domestic case law. Since the beginning of the 1990s, English judges have also been more and more willing to take into consideration not only other common law jurisdictions, but also the legislation and case law of countries on the Continent.[2] Comparative law was primarily used to improve one's own domestic law. The comparative method which was used for this purpose took the comparatist's own national legal system as the *starting point* and as the *sole point of reference* for research.[3]

Since the end of the 20th century, legal scholars have been talking more and more of the

---

[1]   I.e. the French *Code civil* of 1804, the Austrian Civil Code of 1811 (*ABGB*), the Italian *Codice civile* of 1865, the Portuguese *Código civil* of 1867, the Spanish *Código civil* of 1889 and – in a second wave of codifications – the Swiss Code of Obligations of 1881, the German Civil Code of 1896/1900 (*BGB*) and the Swiss Civil Code and the revised Code of Obligations of 1907/1911.

[2]   See, e.g., the English cases *James Buchanan & Co Ltd* v. *Babco Forwarding and Shipping (UK) Ltd* [1977] 1 All ER 518 (Court of Appeal) (comparison of the interpretation of an international convention by the courts in France, the Netherlands and Germany; *White and another* v. *Jones and others* [1995] 1 All ER 691 (House of Lords) (comparison with the laws of Germany, New Zealand, the USA – in particular California – France and the Netherlands); *Fairchild* v. *Glenhaven Funeral Services Ltd and others* [2002] 3 All ER 305 (House of Lords) (comparison with the laws, e.g., of Germany, Austria, Norway, Canada, Australia, Italy, South Africa and Switzerland); *Alfred McAlpine Construction Ltd* v. *Panatown Ltd* [2001] 1 AC 518 (HL) (German law); *Campbell* v. *Mirror Group Newspapers Ltd* [2003] 1 All ER 224 (Court of Appeal) (German and French law); *National Westminster Bank plc* v. *Spectrum Plus Ltd and others* [2005] UKHL 41 (HL) (laws of the USA, India, Ireland, Canada and decisions of the European Courts in Strasbourg and Luxemburg). See also GUY CANIVET, MADS ANDENAS, DUNCAN FAIRGRIEVE (eds), *Comparative Law Before the Courts*, London: BIICL, 2004.

[3]   See, e.g., ZWEIGERT AND KÖTZ, *An Introduction to Comparative Law*, 3rd edn (transl. TONY WEIR), Oxford: Clarendon Press, 1998 , p. 46.

Europeanisation or – on a wider level – about the internationalisation[4] of private law and of comparative method. The term "Europeanisation" refers, on the one hand, to the communitisation of the law by the institutions of the European Union. On the other hand, the term "Europeanisation of private law and of the comparative method" refers to a process that aims at establishing a discourse of legal issues among lawyers throughout Europe, at creating a common European legal science and consciousness and – in the medium or long term – at contributing to the so-called non-mandatory or soft harmonisation of private law. It is in this second sense that the terms "Europeanisation" and "internationalisation" are used in this book.

In order to meet these new aims, the comparative method needs to be further developed and to be adapted so as to attain an *international comparative method* which leaves the mere national approach behind in favour of a genuine international perspective of comparative law.[5]

In order to highlight these changes and in order to illustrate the comparative methodology that can be used when working with the cases in Part B of the book, two case studies (set out below under II.) drawn from Part B will be discussed from three different angles:

(a) *first of all* without having any regard whatsoever to comparative law (see III. below);
(b) *secondly* on the basis of the traditional method of comparative law (see IV. below); and
(c) *thirdly* on the basis of an approach which can be termed the *international approach* to comparative law (see V, below).

II. Case studies

1. Case scenario 1: Offer or invitation to treat?

The latest personal computers are displayed in a shop window at a very attractive price. A customer comes into the shop and says that he would like to buy one of the computers at the advertised price. Another customer has seen the computers advertised in promotional material that gives all the relevant information, including the price. He contacts the salesperson and tells

---

4   Or, more precisely, the "re-Europeanisation" or "re-Internationalisation", see, e.g., REINHARD ZIMMERMANN, "Civil Code and Civil Law – The 'Europeanization' of Private Law within the European Community and the Re-Emergence of a European Legal Science" (1994/95) 1 *Columbia Journal of European Law* 63; *id.*, "Ius Commune and the Principles of European Contract Law: Contemporary Renewal of an Old Idea", in Hector L. MacQueen and Reinhard Zimmermann (eds), *European Contract Law: Scots and South African Perspectives*, Edinburgh: Edinburgh University Press, 2006, 1; RENÉ DAVID, "The International Unification of Private Law", *Int. Enc. Comp. L.*, Vol. II, Ch. 5, Tübingen, Paris, New York (1969), 5-570 *et seq.* (pp. 209 *et seq.*); REINER SCHULZE, "European Legal History – A New Field of Research in Germany", *The Journal of Legal History* 13 (1992), pp. 270–95; THIJMEN KOOPMANS, "Towards a New Ius Commune", in Bruno de Witte and Caroline Forder (eds), *The Common Law of Europe and the Future of Legal Education*, Deventer: Kluwer, 1992, pp. 43–51.

5   ZWEIGERT AND KÖTZ, above n. 3, p. 46: "comparative law will itself begin to be truly international"; AXEL FLESSNER AND HEIN KÖTZ, *European Contract Law*, Vol. I, Clarendon Press: Oxford, 1997, p. V.

him that he would like to buy one of the computers. The salesperson no longer wants to sell the computer at the advertised price. Has a contract been formed?[6]

The outcome of the case depends on the question of whether displaying goods in shops and disseminating advertisements merely invites the potential client to make an offer, so that the salesperson could still refuse to enter into a contract, or if shop displays and advertisements are valid offers that the client may accept with the effect that a contract is formed.

Case scenario 2: Contracts and the requirements for the transfer of property

As part of a large-scale project, two businesses (herein referred to as "the seller" and "the purchaser") plan, *inter alia*, the sale of two machines. However, without the parties' knowledge, the contractual relationship, including the contract for the sale of the machines, is void. To fulfil his contractual obligation, the seller delivers the machines to the purchaser. The parties agree that the machines now belong to the purchaser. Has the purchaser acquired property in the machines?[7]

III. Outcome of the cases according to different national laws

How would a judge solve such a case if he or she considered only his or her own national legislation and case law, that is to say without any resort whatsoever to the insights of comparative law?

1. Case scenario 1

The first case, which concerns an everyday contract, is dealt with in many different ways under the private laws of the European countries:[8]

▶ English courts consider window displays and advertisements to be invitations to treat.
▶ Under *German* law, window displays and advertisements are traditionally not considered to

---

[6]   See below, **Part B, Case 1.**
[7]   See below, **Part B, Case 8.**
[8]   References for all below, **Part B, Case 1.**

be offers but rather as invitations to treat (invitatio ad offerendum). Recent case law has confirmed that this is also the case for advertisements on the Internet.

▶ With regard to both advertisements and window displays, if all the essential elements for the conclusion of a contract are present, *French* courts consider there to be an offer which binds the seller and can be accepted by an interested party. Only where the identity of the contracting party is important (in particular regarding contracts for credit where solvability *solvency* is an issue), is an advertisement or a window display considered an offer to treat.

▶ *Swiss* law differentiates between window displays and advertisements: whereas the former are considered offers, the latter are, according to the prevailing opinion, just invitations to treat.

▶ According to *Italian* law, window displays and displays in a shop are offers but advertisements are not; however, some judgments have decided to the contrary.

▶ *Dutch* case law differentiates between types of advertisement – between advertisements for specific goods and advertisements for unidentified goods. The former constitute invitations to treat, whereas the latter constitute offers "while stocks last".

▶ According to the Civil Code of *Lithuania*, as well as according to the Statute of Contract and Torts of *Serbia*, displays in a shop window generally constitute offers whereas advertisements are, in general, considered to be invitations to treat. Under the Serbian statute, if the person who produced the advertisement refuses to conclude a contract under the conditions stipulated without a valid reason, that person must, however, compensate the interested party.

▶ According to both the *Russian* Civil Code and the *American* Restatement of Laws on the subject, an advertisement addressed to the public constitutes, in principle, an invitation to treat.

▶ The Contract Law of the People's Republic of *China* considers an advertisement containing all the necessary information for the conclusion of a contract to be a valid offer.

Examining a multitude of legal orders shows that there is a series of different solutions for this fundamental question of contract law. Often, jurists in their respective countries are not aware that such different legal rules simultaneously exist in other countries. It is not unknown for them to assume the rule of law in force in their respective country to be the only reasonable rule to follow.

2. Case scenario 2

The second case, which involves a contract for the sale of two machines which is void, deals with a fundamental question of contract and property law: the link between the agreement to sell and the transfer of property.[9]

▶ According to *French*, *Italian* and *Polish* law, as well as, in principle, *English* law, property is transferred by the contract of sale. If the contract is – as is the case in our example – invalid, the property is not transferred to the purchaser and the seller remains the owner of the machines.

---

[9] References for all below, **Part B, Case 8.**

▷ On the other hand, according to *German* and *Greek* property law, acquisition of the property by the purchaser does *not* depend on the validity of the contract of sale. The transfer of the property is, on the contrary, dependent on whether the possession of the thing sold is transferred to the purchaser and whether the parties agree that the property passes from the seller to the purchaser (the so-called real contract, *dinglicher Vertrag*). Under these legal orders, the purchaser in the above scenario would therefore be the owner of the machines.

▷ Under *Swiss*, *Dutch* and *Spanish* law, the conditions for the transfer of property are the same as under Greek and German law. However, the agreement concerning the transfer of property is dependent on the validity of the contract of sale which forms the basis of the agreement. As in this case the contract is void, there is no "real contract" (*contrat réel*) for the transfer of property to the purchaser. The seller therefore remains the owner.[10]

As with the first case scenario, the observer is struck by the great variety of solutions. One cannot help but notice, as in many other areas of private law, that there is a significant amount of diversity in Europe. However, if we limit ourselves to the examination of our national rules, and if lawyers do not take into account the solutions and experiences of other European countries, then the same issues will be looked at in parallel, and legal orders will not mutually influence one another or benefit from the experiences of other countries. Consequently, a common discourse of legal problems and a common understanding of legal problems will not develop in Europe.

IV.   The traditional approach to comparative law

Comparative law allows a lawyer to discover a whole range of possible solutions for each legal problem, and it offers the opportunity to take advantage of the experience of other legal orders. Comparative law provides us with inspiration for new, more modern or "better" solutions; it widens our horizons and leads to new insights.

The comparative lawyer has always had and always will have to decide on which foreign legal orders to take into account for comparison. In this respect courts and academics in different countries have developped different preferences. Courts in common law countries, in particular English courts, usually take inspiration from the case law of other common law jurisdictions, such as the US, Canada or Australia. On the Continent, the Swiss Federal Court, which often adopts a comparative approach, usually takes into account the laws of neighbouring countries, i.e. the laws of Germany, France, Italy or Austria. For the Swiss Federal Court, just as for other courts on the Continent, the main criteria for choosing a foreign legal system for comparative purposes seem to have been accessibility, language and geographical proximity.

The comparative legal doctrine, on the contrary, traditionally focuses on the main representatives of the so-called legal families. Comparatists in the 20th century have

---

10   Next, the question is whether, and if so under what conditions, the purchaser can transfer the property to a third party, i.e. to subsequent bona fide purchasers; see, on this issue, **Case 8** below and the materials provided.

traditionally divided the vast number of legal orders into a few large groups, called the "legal families".[11] In Europe, a distinction is made between the Romanistic legal family, the Germanic legal family and the common law.[12] Often the discussion is confined to a comparison of the national law of the comparatist's country of origin and the laws of countries which represent a particular legal family, i.e. the law of France, Germany, England, and sometimes the law of a Scandinavian country. It is also common for a second member of the Germanic legal family, i.e. Swiss law, to be taken into account because of the high quality of Swiss codes and case law. For a long time, the provisions of legal systems which belong to one of these families resembled those of their main exponent and have for that reason been neglected in comparative exercises. This has been the case for Italian, Spanish, Belgian and Dutch law which, as they all belonged to the French legal family, have often been represented by French law. Limiting a comparison of laws to those legal systems which represent a legal family has, for a long time, been an efficient approach, as it reduces the number of national laws which have to be examined without having any considerable impact on the outcome.

In the above case scenarios, the legislator or the courts in those countries where the issue has not yet been resolved, ought, therefore, according to the traditional approach to comparative law, to look at French, German and English law, i.e. at the representatives of the main legal families, in order to find inspiration for the legal problem in question. Under this traditional approach, the comparative overviews given in Part B of this book could thus be limited to the laws of England, France and Germany.

However, the aim of the traditional method of comparative law is neither to create a common legal consciousness of lawyers throughout Europe, nor to contribute to the harmonisation of the law in Europe. Its harmonising effect remains minimal as the emphasis is put on national law and its improvement.

V.   The international approach to comparative law

1. Starting point: dissolution of the legal families

Today, the legal families are in a process of dissolution. Civil codes which were characteristic of entire legal families – like, for instance, the French *Code civil* – have grown old, and the differences between French law and the other members of the same legal family have become ever more apparent on numerous points. This is the case for Italian, Spanish and Portuguese law, and above all for Dutch civil law since the entry into force of the new Civil Code in 1992,

---

[11] See, e.g., ZWEIGERT AND KÖTZ, above n. 3, p. 63 *et seq.*; RENÉ DAVID AND CAMILLE JAUFFRET-SPINOSI, *Les grands systèmes de droit contemporains*, 11th edn, Paris: Dalloz, 2002, nos 16 *et seq.*

[12] However, according to the dominant opinion in France, the legal orders of the French and of the Germanic tradition belong to the same Romano-Germanic legal family, see DAVID AND JAUFFRET-SPINOSI, above n. 11, 25 *et seq.*, esp. n. 53; GILLES CUNIBERTI, *Grands systèmes de droit contemporains*, Paris: LGDJ, 2007, n. 5 *et seq.*

the *Burgerlijk Wetboek*. Today, in many areas, legal orders have different solutions from those provided for by the traditional representative of their legal family, sometimes to such an extent that for many legal issues it is no longer sensible to take the former "mother" law as the representative of the other legal orders. This evolution has made the criterion of a "legal family" obsolete with respect to many issues of private law. It is therefore no longer possible to confine comparative legal research simply to the representatives of the ancient legal families.

The above scenarios confirm this finding: in both cases, the solutions provided under Swiss and Dutch law, as well as Italian law (for the first scenario) and Spanish law (for the second scenario), diverge considerably from the solution provided for by the traditional representative of their legal families. They are often more distinct. These legal orders therefore cannot be represented by their legal family and its main representative, i.e. German or French law, in the real-life situations set out above, nor in many others.

For a long time the legal systems in Central and Eastern Europe were part of a particular legal family, the socialist legal family.[13] That family has ceased to exist. Many of its former members have recently joined the European Union (EU), others are knocking on the EU´s door. They all wish to be taken into account in the current comparative law debates and wish to contribute to these debates. There is no reason for excluding these systems from consideration; quite the contrary, there is every reason for including them, as they are adopting new acts which will be among the most recent – and on occasions amongst the most modern – in Europe.

2. Regrouping on the basis of solutions: change of perspective

One of the basic assumptions underlying the international approach towards comparative law is that the solutions used by different legal systems in order to cope with a problem have, as a matter of principle, the same value. As we have seen, the traditional objective of comparative law was to enhance national law. New aims are being added to that traditional objective: (i) the aim of initiating a discussion of private law issues in an international context and therefore creating a truly European or even worldwide legal discourse, and (ii) the aim of using comparative law to help in the process of harmonisation. To the extent that the latter objectives gain in importance, the legal system of a single country loses its role as the sole point of reference for the comparative research.

In a situation where a comparison cannot – or can no longer – be confined to representatives of legal families, one should, as a matter of principle, take all the different (European) legal systems into account.[14] Such an approach avoids comparing only some of the solutions and avoids the exclusion of the disregarded legal orders from the European debate and their fading away from both the European debate and from the European legal consciousness. Comparative law must address these dangers.

---

[13] ZWEIGERT AND KÖTZ, *An Introduction to Comparative Law*, Vol. I, 2nd edn, 1984, pp. 332 *et seq.*; DAVID AND JAUFFRET-SPINOSI, *Les grands systèmes de droit contemporains*, see, e.g., the 8th edn, 1982, pp. 155 *et seq.*

[14] This is indeed the approach of the European Commission when preparing legislation in the field of harmonisation of the laws in Europe.

It should, however, be emphasised that one will not always find a solution for a specific legal problem in each and every (European) legal order, which will in practice result in a significant reduction of the number of national legal systems to be examined. For the first scenario, for example (i.e. the scenario relating to contract law), many legal orders do not yet have any legislation or case law specifying whether the display of goods and advertisements are offers or invitations to treat, therefore leaving this question open for debate.

However, even if the number of systems to be taken into consideration has been reduced, it still remains considerable. The great diversity of the laws in force in the different countries forces us to face the question of how to cope with so many different legal orders. After the dissolution of the "legal families", other criteria for grouping legal orders together will have to be found. One possibility could be to arrange the European legal orders on the basis of their *solutions* to a specific legal question. Today, the great challenge for the comparative lawyer is thus to *regroup* and to *systematise* the solutions of European private law. Such systematisation can no longer start from the perspective of a national law. The starting point can no longer be the different legal systems and their gaps and faults; it must be the legal issue under examination. This systematisation may be explained as follows.

(a) Looking for fundamentally different solutions and systematising accordingly
The first task is to identify, among the numerous solutions of the different European legal orders, those which differ fundamentally. Experience has shown that for a given problem one will rarely discern more than *three or four* fundamentally different options. At that stage, and once the main principles behind the different solutions have become clear, it is rather easy to form new groups and to divide the legal orders accordingly. The great diversity which is presently governing European private law can hence be reduced to three or four solutions, which allows one to obtain, for each specific legal question, a clear overall view of private law in Europe or elsewhere.

The scenarios above illustrate this point. In the *first scenario*, which deals with contractual matters, the different solutions found in Europe can be grouped into three categories[15]:

- The first group consists of the legal systems that take a sceptical view with regard to qualifying a proposition made to the public as an offer. These legal systems do not view window displays or advertisements as contractually binding offers, but rather as invitations to treat (*invitatio ad offerendum*).[16]
- The second type of solution, unlike the first, generally takes advertisements and window displays to be offers.[17]
- Legal orders belonging to the third group make certain distinctions: some distinguish between the display of goods and advertisements,[18] occasionally with a variation providing that a person who sends out an advert and subsequently refuses to enter into a contract must

---

[15] See also below, **B., Case 1, XIII.**

[16] German, English and Russian law all belong to this group and – outside Europe – American law; for the exact references, see below, **B, Case 1**.

[17] This is the solution of French law. Outside Europe this solution is possible under the Contract Law of the People's Republic of China for cases in which the advertisement contains all relevant data for the conclusion of a contract; for exact references, see below, **B, Case 1**.

[18] This is the case under Swiss, Dutch and Italian law, as well as under the law of Serbia.

compensate the interested party;[19] other legal orders distinguish between specific goods (*corps certains*) and unidentified goods (*choses de genre*); in addition, with advertisements, the offer is often limited according to the available stock.[20]

The *second scenario*, relating to property law, deals with the conditions for the acquisition of property where the original contract (of sale) is void. We can distinguish *three solutions* to this question:

▶ According to the legal systems in the *first group*,[21] the transfer of property comes from the exchange of obligations (i.e. the contract of sale) and does not require a "real contract" or publicity (*principles of consent and causality*).

▶ According to the *second group* of legal orders,[22] the transfer of property depends on whether the owner and the first purchaser have agreed upon the transfer ("real contract") and the purchaser will be given possession of the property. If the contract of sale is void, this has, however, a knock-on effect on the real contract, which invalidates the acquisition of property by the first purchaser (*principles of separation and causality*).

▶ The legal orders in the *third group*[23] use the same conditions as the second group, i.e. the transfer of property depends on whether the owner and the first purchaser have agreed upon the transfer and the purchaser will be given possession of the property. However, the transfer of property is completely independent from the validity of the exchange of obligations, i.e. of the contract of sale (*principles of separation and abstraction*). In this third group of legal orders, in our scenario the purchaser therefore acquires property in the machines.

These differences between the legal orders also have important consequences for the question if, and under what conditions, the purchaser of the machines can subsequently transfer the property in the machines to third parties, and if these subsequent purchasers can acquire the property in the machines.[24]

(b) Comparing the solutions

Once the legal orders have been rearranged according to the solutions they provide for a given legal problem, it is possible and convenient to weigh up advantages and disadvantages of each solution. Instead of having a multitude of legal orders to compare, one is dealing with a much more manageable number of solutions.

As can be seen from the scenarios above, as well as from many other cases, the composition of the groups differs according to the problem being examined. The case scenarios also show that the traditional legal families no longer provide a useful criterion for systematising the law in many situations. In the first scenario, for example, the first group includes legal systems belonging to the Germanic legal family as well as the English common law and Russian law; the third group includes members of the Latin legal family, the former socialist family as well

---

19   This is the case under the law of Serbia.
20   This is the approach under Dutch law.
21   This group includes French, Italian and Polish law and, in principle, also English law; for the exact references, see below, **B, Case 8**.
22   Swiss, Dutch and Spanish law belong to this group.
23   For movable property, German and Greek laws belong to this group. For real property, Greek law provides, on the contrary, the principle of consensualism.
24   See below, **Part B, Case 8** and the materials provided there.

as a representative from the Germanic legal family. In the second scenario, the laws of France, Italy, Poland as well as English law are in the first group; in the third group we find the laws of Germany and Greece; the laws of Switzerland, the Netherlands and Spain make up the second, intermediate group. Here again, the composition of the groups does not correspond to the traditional legal families. So, in the current state of development of private law in Europe, one could talk of "variable groups". For many legal issues, "fixed groups", like the traditional legal families, no longer exist.

When performing such regrouping, it would be preferable for the comparative lawyer to disregard the legal order in which he or she is rooted, as this would enable research to be carried out with the minimum degree of prejudice. Experience shows that the better the lawyer is acquainted with foreign law, thanks to studying comparative law or studying or working abroad, the easier he or she will attain such objectivity.

VI. Added value of the internationalisation of the comparative method

It might be argued that the international approach to comparative law requires a lot of work and concentration; however, such an approach to comparative research is well worth the effort for at least *four reasons*.

1. Objectivity in the appreciation of solutions

First of all, this research, in taking an international perspective as its starting point, will lead to a more objective assessment of the solutions than an exercise which adopts a national perspective. It favours a critical view on arguments which are put forward to justify the solutions of national legal systems. Our two case scenarios illustrate this finding.

In the first case study, concerning contract law, one of the arguments put forward by the legal orders in the first group is that considering window and shop displays and advertisements to be offers would cause too many practical problems for businesses. It is mainly for this reason that window and shop displays as well as advertisements are generally not considered offers but rather invitations to treat (*invitatio ad offerendum*).

The legal systems that make up the second and third groups demonstrate that these worries relating to window displays seem not to be justified. In addition, French law shows that, in the interest of the protection of those to whom advertisements are addressed, advertisements can easily be considered offers if they contain all the information necessary for the conclusion of a contract.

In our second scenario (relating to property law), it could be argued that the solution advanced by the first group (*French, Italian, Polish* and in theory *English* law) endangers legal certainty as it allows for the acquisition of property without any act of publicity and could come into conflict with the interests of third parties. It can be argued that the solution advanced by the third group (that is to say the "abstraction principle" used in *German* and *Greek* law) is not only very complicated but also superfluous when dealing with the acquisition of a third party in good faith[25]; as shown in the materials provided in Case 8,[26] this solution protects a third party purchaser even if the latter does not merit such protection (i.e. a subsequent purchaser who acquires the property despite being aware of the flaw in the contract between the seller and first purchaser).

2. Discoveries to be made

Furthermore, the international method of comparative law allows certain "discoveries" to be made.

In the first case scenario, it can be seen that the traditional "all or nothing" solution, according to which displays in windows and shops and advertisements are either offers or invitations to treat, is in force only in the legal orders that used to represent the traditional legal families, i.e. in Germany, England and France. The solutions found in Italy and in many smaller countries, such as Switzerland, The Netherlands, Lithuania or Serbia, which are often more modern, distinguish either between window displays and advertisements or according to the product, which is the case under Dutch law, which differentiates between identified and unidentified goods.

The smaller legal orders that are traditionally overshadowed by their bigger neighbours may also set an example for the future. Indeed, the Principles of European Contract Law drawn up by the Commision on European Contract Law (or "Lando Commission"), as well as the Draft Common Frame of Reference, do not follow any of the traditional solutions advanced by the main legal systems but rather provide for a solution like those found in the smaller legal systems.[27]

In the second scenario, involving property law, it is once again the smaller legal orders that show a possible future line of development. Swiss and Dutch laws both require an act of publicity for the transfer of property. They thereby better protect the interests of third parties and guarantee a greater degree of legal certainty than is the case under the legal orders making up the *first group*, which simply require the agreement of the parties (French, Italian, Polish and English law). In comparison with German and Greek law (i.e. the representatives of the *second group*), Swiss and Dutch law have the advantage of being much simpler. Furthermore, Swiss and Dutch law only protect a third party purchaser (in our case the subsequent purchasers) who acts in good faith and thus merits this protection.[28]

It is for this reason that in Part B of this book, particular attention will be paid not only to the legal orders that have traditionally been at the centre of the comparatists' interest, but also to the legal orders of smaller countries which present interesting, inspiring and often persuasive solutions.

---

[25] That is why the Swiss Federal Court abandoned this approach in a famous decision of 1929, BG/TF 29.11.1929 (*Grimm c. Masse en faillite Näf-Ackermann*), BGE/ATF 55 II 302.

[26] Below, **Part B, Case 8**.

[27] For references, see below, **B, Case 1**.

[28] In the present context the analysis necessarily has to be brief. For more details, see the references below, **B, Case 8, X**.

3. Harmonising effect

The suggested approach brings about a significant harmonising effect on European private law. The findings which flow from observing the highest possible number of European legal systems sometimes allow the discovery of *common principles* which appear throughout Europe. In areas where different legal orders take different approaches, this method allows a lawyer to uncover a large number of possible solutions to a given problem, and invites him or her to weigh up the arguments for and against all possible solutions.

The criteria, solutions or principles identified through this comparative effort could, for instance, be adopted in a *uniform law* at an international level. This is currently envisaged, for example, by the European Parliament and, to some extent, also by the European Commission.[29] Another example is the Member States of the Organisation for the Harmonisation of Business Law in Africa (*Organisation pour l'Harmonisation en Afrique du Droit des Affaires*, OHADA).[30] The solution could also be used in *national codes* or *statutes*, something which has been seen in the last few years in relation to contract law mainly in Central and Eastern Europe and outside Europe, for example in China.[31]

In countries where the codes leave some margin of appreciation for the judiciary (which is the case for most of the highly controversial questions of private law), the criteria, principles and solutions identified could also be adopted by the courts without it being necessary to change legislation.[32] The outcome of this would be the soft harmonisation of European private law while at the same time preserving the existence of a variety of national laws which serve as a source of wealth and inspiration.[33] Such an approach would also allow the development and coexistence of different solutions in different countries. Some countries could hence serve as

---

[29]   See below, **Case 10**.

[30]   The project on the harmonisation of the law of contracts of the Member States of OHADA is largely based on the UNIDROIT Principles of International Commercial Contracts; cf the contributions in *Unif. L. Rev.* 2008-1/2: "The Harmonisation of Contract Law Within OHADA", in particular: MARCEL FONTAINE, "L'avant-projet d'Acte uniforme OHADA sur le droit des contrats: vue d'ensemble", *Unif. L. Rev.* 2008, 203; PIERRE MAYER, "The Harmonisation of Contract Law Within OHADA – General report", *Unif. L. Rev.* 2008, 393, at 400 *et seq.*

[31]   The Contract Law of the People's Republic of China of 1999 is also largely based on the UNIDROIT Principles; see, e.g., C STEPHEN HSU, "Contract Law of the People's Republic of China", 16 (2007) *Minn. J. Int'l L.* 115; DANHAN HUANG, "The UNIDROIT Principles and their Influence in the Modernization of Contract Law in the People's Republic of China", *Unif. L. Rev.* 2003, pp. 107–17; JOHN H. MATHESON, "Convergence, Culture and Contract Law in China", 15 (2006) *Minn. J. Int'l L.* 329; JING XI, "The Impact of the UNIDROIT Principles on Chinese Legislation", in Eleanor Cashin Ritaine and Eva Lein (eds), *The UNIDROIT Principles 2004*, Zürich: Schulthess, 2007, pp. 107 *seq.*, with further references; SHAOHUI ZHANG, "L'influence des Principes d'UNIDROIT sur la réforme du droit chinois des obligations", *Unif. L. Rev.* 2008, 153.

[32]   See, e.g., CANIVET *et al.* (eds), above n. 2; ESIN ÖRÜCÜ, "Comparative Law in Practice: The Courts and the Legislator", in Örücü and Nelken (eds), *Comparative Law – A handbook*, Oxford: Hart, 2007, Ch. 18 (pp. 411 *et seq.*).

[33]   On the benefits of diversity, see, e.g., ROGER COTTERRELL, "Is it so Bad to be Different?, Comparative Law and the Appreciation of Diversity", in Örücü and Nelken (eds), above n. 32, Ch. 6 (pp. 133 *et seq.*); see also KADNER GRAZIANO, "Does Europe need a contract code", below, **Case 10, IV. 4**.

laboratories, in the same manner as can, for instance, be observed in the area of private law in the United States.[34] If legal discussions are taken to a European level, "soft harmonisation" seems, at least for the time being, in many private law matters to be preferable over a mandatory unification of the law.

As long as the horizon of lawyers stops at national borders, neighbouring legal orders are ignored and, consequently, there are no discussions or common visions, diversity at the European level should be considered a weakness. However, once the international approach to comparative law is adopted, this weakness will become a strength and diversity will become an asset.

4. Establishing an authentic community of European lawyers

Lastly, an insight into the solutions used in as many countries as possible breaks down prejudices, increases understanding and favours discussion between lawyers of different legal orders. The international method of comparative law will thus enable the development of a *common legal science*, and it will contribute to the establishment of an *"authentique communauté européenne de juristes pouvant aisément dialoguer entre eux"*[35] (i.e. an authentic European community of lawyers who can easily consult with one another).

By including the law of the countries of Eastern Europe in the comparison, for example Polish, Hungarian, Romanian, Lithuanian, Serbian or Russian law, the common basis of arguments and solutions would also extend over those countries which, until now, have been taken into account only to a very limited extent by European comparative law.

VII. New challenges for comparative lawyers

A comparative method which adheres to an international approach requires intense research efforts and thorough analysis. Studying the different national legal orders, examining their approaches and solutions, and determining the similarities and differences is the current and future task of universities and comparative lawyers.

This approach could possibly, but not necessarily, lead to a common solution, as each lawyer may draw his or her own conclusions from his or her comparative research. Nevertheless, the

---

[34] See MELVIN EISENBERG, "Why is American Contract Law so Uniform", in Hans-Leo Weyers (ed.), *Europäisches Vertragsrecht*, Baden-Baden: Nomos, 1997, 23–43, excerpts below, **Case 4, III. 4**.

[35] CLAUDE WITZ, "Plaidoyer pour un code européen des contrats", *Recueil Dalloz et Sirey de doctrine, de jurisprudence et de législation (D.)* 2000 Chron., 79, at 81.

arguments and ideas will become familiar to lawyers all over Europe. It is not the uniformity of certain solutions that will lead to a truly European legal discourse and scholarship; just as in the private law of the US, diversity may subsist for many issues of law. It is, on the contrary, the fact that lawyers all over Europe are familiar with each other's approaches to legal problems that will lead to a truly international discourse of legal problems. Arguably, the international method of discourse will lead to the establishment of a common European legal science and a truly European legal consciousness.[36]

In order to attain such a Europeanisation of legal debates, it is necessary to establish a common European legal literature, i.e. to develop manuals, textbooks and casebooks of reference which facilitate access to the solutions in force in the different European countries and which allow one to work in an effective manner with the common basis of solutions. Over the last two decades, many institutes and groups of researchers have been established in order to research and formulate common principles of private law in Europe.[37] Treatises which adopt the international approach to comparative law, as well as casebooks and manuals that are aimed at students and practitioners throughout Europe, are presently being published.[38] An authentic European legal literature is thus emerging.

---

[36] For an example of the use of this method, see THOMAS KADNER GRAZIANO, "Loss of a Chance in European Private Law – 'All or nothing' or partial liability in cases of uncertain causation", *ERPL* 2008, 1009–42.

[37] See the brilliant overview by HANS-PETER MANSEL, at www.ipr.uni-koeln.de/eurprivr/ arbeitsgruppen.htm. He lists the following institutions and groups: UNIDROIT, www.unidroit.org; UNIDROIT has presented, eg, the *UNIDROIT Principles of International Commercial Contracts*, 2nd edn, 2004, and the *Principles and Rules of Transnational Civil Procedure*, 2004; COMMISSION ON EUROPEAN CONTRACT LAW (LANDO COMMISSION), www.cbs.dk/departments/law/staff/ol/ commission_on_ecl/ index.html; the group has presented the *Principles of European Contract Law I & II*, 1999, and the *Principles of European Contract Law III*, 2002; STUDY GROUP ON A EUROPEAN CIVIL CODE (i.e. the successor of the Commission on European Contract Law), www.sgecc.net/, with its working teams: The Hamburg Working Team on Credit Securities; The Working Team on Proprietary Securities; The Working Team on E-Commerce; The Salzburg Working Team on Transfer of Movable Property; The Working Team on Rental of Movable Property; The Osnabruck Working Team on Extra-Contractual Obligations; The Dutch Working Team on Sales, Services and Longterm Contracts; The Project Group on a Restatement of European Insurance Contract Law (Innsbruck Group) and The Working Team on Trusts; EUROPEAN GROUP ON TORT LAW, www.egtl.org and www.ectil.org, author of the *Principles of European Tort Law*; INTERNATIONAL WORKING GROUP ON EUROPEAN TRUST LAW, author of the *Principles on European Trust Law*; ACADEMY OF EUROPEAN PRIVATE LAWYERS (Gandolfi Group), author of the *Code Européen des Contracts – Avant-projet*, 2002/2004; EUROPEAN RESEARCH GROUP ON EXISTING EC PRIVATE LAW (ACQUIS GROUP), www.acquis-group.org, author of the *Acquis Principles* and co-author of the *Draft Common Frame of Reference*; THE COMMON CORE OF EUROPEAN PRIVATE LAW PROJECT (Trento Group), www.jus.unitn.it/dsg/common-core/home.html; COMMISSION ON EUROPEAN FAMILY LAW, www.law.uu.nl/priv/cefl; WORKING GROUP ON THE APPROXIMATION OF THE CIVIL PROCEDURE LAW (Storme Group); SOCIETY OF EUROPEAN CONTRACT LAW (SECOLA), www.secola.org/; CEP (Centrum für Europäisches Privatrecht), www.jura.uni-muenster.de/cep; WORKING GROUP ON UNIFORM TERMINOLOGY FOR EUROPEAN PRIVATE LAW, www.dsg.unito.it/ut/; JOINT NETWORK ON EUROPEAN PRIVATE LAW (CoPECL), www.copecl.org/; EUROPÄISCHES JUSTIZIELLES NETZ FÜR ZIVIL- UND HANDELSSACHEN, http://europa.eu.int/comm/justice_home/ejn/index_de.htm.

[38] FILIPPO RANIERI, *Europäisches Obligationenrecht*, 3rd edn, Wien: Springer, 2009; HEIN KÖTZ, *European Contract Law*, Vol. I (transl. by TONY WEIR), Oxford: Clarendon Press, 1997; HUGH BEALE, HEIN KÖTZ, ARTHUR HARTKAMP AND DENIS TALLON, *Cases, Materials and Text on Contract Law*, Oxford: Hart, 2002;

However, this body of literature will be consulted only by lawyers who have been introduced to an international comparative approach during their education. Only those who become accustomed to working with foreign legal orders during their education will be ready and will show a sufficient degree of openness to have recourse to these sources in their daily work, and to take into account the solutions and tendencies revealed in the area of European private law.

As it is difficult to imagine that judges will base decisions on this literature if they themselves have not been trained in this method, it must be at the educational level that openness towards foreign law is created. A truly European view should be embedded in legal education in order for the comparison of different European legal orders to become a matter of course.

In the medium or long term, it would be desirable to use an international comparative method not only in comparative law courses, but also when teaching private law in general,[39] following the example of private law teaching in the United States of America. In the US, the most important areas of private law, like contracts, torts, property law, family law or the law of succession, have not been unified. They are not part of the federal law, but belong to state law. Each state of the Federation thus has its own contract law or tort law, in the same way as each European State has its own contract law and its own rules governing extra-contractual liability, the law of property, family law or the law of successions. Nonetheless, American universities do not teach the private law of a single state, for instance the private law of the state where the university is located. On the contrary, what is being taught are common principles of private law, with the help of case law from different states. The laws of California and New York are obviously used more than the laws of smaller states (as is the case for European comparisons which take into account the laws of large countries like Germany, England, France and Italy more often than the laws of small countries). However, in the United States the choice of material presented and used is made according to its persuasiveness or originality. This could be an approach used in European legal education as well.

In the US, this is the result of a continuous and lasting comparative effort which takes into account the laws of all the states of the Federation.[40] Such a reorganisation of legal education has one important consequence: it brings about a discussion of legal problems and of their solutions at a common national level. This discussion at a national level in itself causes the creation of a common legal consciousness shared by lawyers of all 50 states – whereas in

---

THOMAS KADNER GRAZIANO, *Le contrat en droit privé européen*, Basel: Helbing Lichtenhahn, 2006; *id.*, *Europäisches Vertragsrecht*, Basel: Helbing Lichtenhahn 2008; WALTER VAN GERVEN, JEREMY LEVER AND PIERRE LAROUCHE, *Cases, Materials and Text on National, Supranational and International Tort Law*, Oxford: Hart, 2000; CEES VAN DAM, *European Tort Law*, Oxford: Oxford University Press, 2006; CHRISTIAN VON BAR, *The Common European Law of Torts*, Vols. 1 and 2, Oxford: Oxford University Press, 1998 and 2000; GERT BRÜGGEMEIER, *Common Principles of Tort Law*, London: BIICL 2006; JACK BEATSON AND ELTJO SCHRAGE, *Cases, Materials and Text on Unjustified Enrichment*, Oxford: Hart 2003; PETER SCHLECHTRIEM, *Restitution und Bereicherungsausgleich in Europa*, Vol. 1, Tübingen: Mohr Siebeck, 2000; Vol. 2, 2003; THOMAS KADNER GRAZIANO, *Europäisches Internationales Deliktsrecht*, Tübingen: Mohr Siebeck, 2003; *id.*, *La responsabilité délictuelle en droit international privé européen*, Basel: Helbing Lichtenhahn, 2004; INGEBORG SCHWENZER AND MARKUS MÜLLER-CHEN, *Rechtsvergleichung – Fälle und Materialien*, Tübingen: Mohr Siebeck, 1996.

39 WALTER VAN GERVEN, "A Common Framework of Reference and Teaching", in *European Journal of Legal Education*, Vol. 1, Issue 1, 1–15.

40 On this and the following, see EISENBERG, "Why is American Contract Law so Uniform", in Weyers (ed.), *Europäisches Vertragsrecht*, excerpts below, **Case 4, III. 4.**

Europe, in the absence of daily discussions of legal problems from a European perspective, such a consciousness which would be common to all European lawyers is still a distant prospect. Moreover, in the United States the common discourse has a harmonising effect in all of the 50 states. Foreign lawyers, who would expect American private law to be quite fragmented, are often surprised by its relative uniformity. On a practical level, this type of teaching implies that the American state in which a lawyer completed his or her legal education is irrelevant – whereas in Europe, working in a country other than the one in which one studied still causes lawyers enormous problems.

It has become automatic, in the United States, to take into account the law in force in other states of the Federation (with their value not as binding law but as *persuasive authority*). Quoting judgments or legislation from other states is daily business for American judges or attorneys, even though the judge is not bound by the judgments or legislation of other states. Conversely, in Europe, decisions in which judges admit openly to having drawn inspiration from solutions of neighbouring countries are still rare – this is at any rate the case in large countries, and remains so despite tendencies towards more openness which have developed in recent years.

In Europe, comparisons with the US immediately lead to comments that linguistic problems limit the possibility of looking across borders. The multiplicity of languages spoken in Europe indeed presents a challenge, but this can be remedied by translation. Authors of fundamental academic works should have their work translated into as many European languages as possible so that they can be used on a European scale. To achieve this goal successfully, a considerable investment (especially financial) needs to be made. Another remedy for the linguistic problem would be for the current generation of European lawyers to learn English, French and German, either at school or at university. Command of those three languages would allow them to unlock nine European legal systems, as well as the law of the United States, many other common law countries and many members of the French legal family.

As far as the legal orders of Central, Eastern and Northern European countries are concerned, it will, realistically, be the responsibility of these countries' lawyers to provide their European colleagues with English, French or German translations of their national codes and statutes, leading case law and the most fundamental developments of their legal doctrine. Certain groups of European scholars, such as, for example, the *European Group on Tort Law* in Vienna, count among their members researchers from all European countries, and represent the laws of all European countries in studies published by them. These groups hereby contribute substantially to the diffusion of knowledge of these legal orders.[41] This work should be continued.

In Europe, when one proposes to teach from a European perspective which no longer focuses on the solutions of a single country, one becomes the target of a tide of criticism: curricula of law schools are already crammed; hardly any time would be left to devote attention to foreign or European trends. However, such a comparative approach does not necessarily imply an increase in subject matter. At present, textbooks usually expound alternative solutions put forward by the domestic legal doctrine in the country in which the research is undertaken. Along with these, the solutions in force in other European countries could be presented, allowing students to understand that the rules in force in their country provide one solution, among many other possibilities, to a specific legal problem.

---

[41]   See the publications of the European Center for Tort and Insurance Law (ECTIL), to which the European Group on Tort Law is linked: www.ectil.org/.

VIII.   Outlook

The *international comparative method* and the truly international perspective in dealing with legal problems to which it leads will only have a chance in practice if an adequate number of European textbooks, manuals and casebooks are available, allowing this method and perspective to be taught. It is the enormous task of comparatists to develop such a legal literature.

The advantages will, however, be manifold, both for students and for legal practitioners. In the same way that it would be unthinkable in the United States not to take into account the law of other states of the Federation when it comes to resolving new legal problems, or when reconsidering the appropriateness of solutions that are already in force, it should be out of the question in Europe for the legal orders of neighbouring countries to be ignored when solving legal problems.

Chapter III

Principles of Contract Law: the needs to which they respond and the purposes for which they are designed*

The following chapter provides an introduction to the materials that will be used throughout the book. Most scholars are aware of the fact that individual nation States have their own bodies of (contract) law and are also aware of the United Nations Convention on Contracts for the International Sale of Goods (CISG). Perhaps not all scholars are familiar with the different sets of non-binding contract instruments (the "Principles of contract law") that have been presented since the mid-1990s of the last century. For this reason, the following chapter provides extracts from two leading treatises on the two most important sets of non-binding contract principles. The following extracts serve three purposes: (1) to present these principles to the reader; (2) to present the needs to which they respond; and (3) to present the purposes for which they are designed. (For the conditions under which parties can choose these Principles as the rules governing their contracts, see Part B, Case 9, IV.)

1. The Principles of European Contract Law

PRINCIPLES OF EUROPEAN CONTRACT LAW

PARTS I AND II

Combined and Revised

Prepared by
The Commission of European Contract Law
Chairman: Professor Ole Lando

Edited by

OLE LANDO AND HUGH BEALE

Preface

How it started

In 1974 a symposium was held at the Copenhagen Business School. The subject was the EEC Draft Convention on the Law Applicable to Contractual and Noncontractual

---

* For information on the Draft Common Frame of Reference, see **Case 10, IV., 1**. and **3**.

Obligations. At a dinner in Tivoli Gardens after the symposium I sat next to Dr Winfried Hauschild who was Head of Division in the Directorate General for the Internal Market of the Commission of the European Communities, and who assisted the working group of experts which prepared the Draft Convention. We agreed that the proposed choice of law rules would be insufficient. They would never establish the legal uniformity necessary for an integrated European market. Uniform substantive law rules were needed. Dr Hauschild said: "We need a European Code of Obligations".

In 1976 another symposium was held in the newly established European University Institute near Florence. Its subject was New Perspectives of a Common Law of Europe. I was asked to present a paper and found here an opportunity to argue for what I then called a European Uniform Commercial Code.

In the years that followed efforts were made to find qualified people from all the EC Member States who were interested in preparing what now became the Principles of European Contract Law and to get the necessary funds. This took some time.

Introduction

1. THE NEED FOR UNIFORM RULES

The Principles of European Contract are the product of work carried out by the Commission on European Contract Law, a body of lawyers drawn from all the member States of the European Union, under the chairmanship of Professor Ole Lando. They are a response to a need for a Union-wide infrastructure of contract law to consolidate the rapidly expanding volume of Community law regulating specific types of contract. There are many benefits to be derived from a formulation of principles of contract law within Europe.

A)   The Facilitation of Cross-Border Trade Within Europe

Both within and outside Europe there is a growing recognition of the need for measures of harmonisation to eliminate those differences in national laws which are inimical to the efficient conduct of cross-border business within Europe. Such harmonisation measures confer particular benefits on contracting parties carrying on business in different States, enabling them to contract with reference to a set of rules which apply uniformly over the territories of the various States, which are detached from any particular legal system, which are available in languages of which at least one is likely to be known to the parties, and which over time will become much more familiar to those who use them than the individual national laws of the various foreign countries in which they transact business.

B)   The Strengthening of the Single European Market

The harmonisation of principles of contract law is of special importance to the proper functioning of the Single European Market, the very essence of which is a broadly unitary approach to law and regulation that surmounts the obstacles to trade and the distortions of the market resulting from differences in the national laws of Member States affecting trade within Europe.

C)   The Creation of an Infrastructure for Community Laws Governing Contracts

The lawmakers of the European Community are increasingly active in the field of contracts. Directives have been issued affecting contracts relating to insurance, employment, commercial agency, consumer credit, consumer safety, doorstep sales and unfair terms in consumer contracts, to mention but a few, and the list is steadily growing. Yet there is no general contract law infrastructure to support these specific Community measures. There are at present considerable disparities between the laws of the Member States governing contracts, including such major matters as formation, formal and essential validity, substantive effects, remedies for non-performance and the conditions under which non-performance is excused. There is not even a common terminology. Hence the Principles are designed not merely to reduce the adverse effects of differences in national laws within the Single European Market but also to provide a foundation of contract law within the Community upon which more specific harmonisation measures can be constructed. Without such a body of Community-wide principles of contract law the effect of many of the measures being taken towards European legal integration in relation to consumer and commercial transactions is likely to be weakened significantly.

D) The Provision of Guidelines for National Courts and Legislatures

The Principles are intended to reflect the common core of solutions to problems of contract law. Some of these have proved increasingly troublesome for national courts and legislators. The Principles are also intended to be progressive. On many issues covered by national law they may be found to offer a more satisfactory answer than that which is reached by traditional legal thinking. For example, their provisions relating to the assurance of performance and to the grant of relief where a change of circumstances renders performance of the contract excessively onerous deal in a balanced way with recurrent difficulties on which most national laws are silent. The Principles are thus available for the assistance of European courts and legislatures concerned to ensure the fruitful development of contract law on a Union-wide basis. Even beyond the borders of the European Union, the Principles may serve as an inspiration for the Central and Eastern European legislators who are in the course of reforming their laws of contract to meet the needs of a market economy.

E) The Construction of a Bridge between the Civil Law and the Common Law

One of the most intractable problems of European legal integration is the reconciliation of the civil law and the common law families. It is, of course, true that there are significant differences even between one civil law system and another; it is also true that in many cases common problems will be solved in much the same way by the various legal systems, to whichever legal family they may belong. But there remain major differences between civil law and common law systems in relation to legal structure and reasoning, terminology, fundamental concepts and classifications and legal policy. Two examples from the field covered by the Principles suffice to make the point. The first is that in civil law systems there is a general and pervasive principle of good faith; in the European common law systems there is no such general principle. They have a requirement of good faith only in limited situations and have a series of specific rules achieving some of the same results as might be required by good faith but without referring to that concept. The second is that the civil law considers it legitimate for a contract to contain penalty clauses designed to deter a party from breaking the contract; the common law regards the imposition of penalties (as opposed to liquidated damages by way of compensation for anticipated loss) as improper and unenforceable. Differences of these kinds are inimical to the efficient functioning of the Single European Market. One of the major benefits offered by the Principles is to provide a bridge between the civil law and the common law by providing rules designed to reconcile their differing legal philosophies.

2. THE PURPOSES FOR WHICH THE PRINCIPLES ARE DESIGNED

It will be apparent from the foregoing that the Principles of European Contract Law are intended to be of service in a number of ways to a wide range on institutions, enterprises and individuals.

A) Foundation for European Legislation

The Principles provide a necessary legal foundation for measures taken and to be taken in the future by the organs of the European Union. The Principles will assist both the organs of the Community in drafting measures and courts, arbitrators and legal advisers in applying Community measures.

In 1989 the European Parliament passed a Resolution requesting that a start be made on the preparatory work for drawing up a European Code of Private Law. The preamble to the Resolution states that

> "... unification can be carried out in branches of private law which are highly important for the development of a Single Market, such as contract law ..."(Resolution of 26 May 1989, OJEC No. C 158/401 of 26 June 1989).

This request was repeated in 1994 (Resolution of 6 May 1994, OJEC No. C 205 (519) of 25 July 1994.)

One objective of the Principles of European Contract Law is to serve as a basis for any future European Code of Contracts. They could form the first step in the work.

B) Express Adoption by the Parties

The Principles will be useful for parties who are living or carrying on business in different States and who wish their contractual relations to be governed by a set of neutral rules not based on anyone national legal system but drawing on the best solutions offered by the laws of jurisdictions within (and sometimes outside) Europe. They can declare that the contract is to be governed by the Principles of European Contract Law.

C) A Modern Formulation of a Lex Mercatoria

Parties to international contracts who want their agreement to be governed by internationally accepted principles, or who are unable to agree on a reference to a national legal system, have the option to adopt the *lex mercatoria* to govern their contract. It not infrequently happens that they opt for arbitration according to, if not the *lex mercatoria* by name, "general principles of law", "internationally accepted principles" or some other such phrase. Where is the arbitrator who has to deal with such a contract to find those principles? He may feel that he knows what is customarily accepted, or he may feel able to make a common sense judgment, but neither is a reliable way of deciding the case. If there is a statement of internationally accepted principles, the arbitrator's life will be much easier and the uncertainty engendered by adopting such a phrase will be reduced. One of the immediate aims of the Principles is to provide such a statement that is acceptable within Europe and which can be applied directly by arbitrators in the type of case envisaged – in effect a modern European lex mercatoria.

D) A Model for Judicial and Legislative Development of Contract Law

The Principles offer help to courts and arbitrators called upon to decide issues which are not adequately governed by the national law or other system of rules applicable. The court or arbitrator may adopt the solution provided by the Principles knowing that it represents the common core of the European systems, or a progressive development from that common core. Equally the solutions of the Principles may be adopted by legislators reforming their contract law. The Commission hopes in particular that the Principles will be of service to those charged with reform of contract law in the newly-emerged democracies of Central Europe.

E) A Basis for Harmonisation

Ultimately the Member States of the European Union may wish to harmonise their contract law. The Principles can serve as a model on which harmonisation work may be based.

Thus the Principles have both immediate and longer-term objectives. They are available for immediate use by parties making contracts, by courts and arbitrators in deciding contract disputes and by legislators in drafting contract rules whether at the European or the national level. Their longer-term objective is to help bring about the harmonisation of general contract law within the European Union.

3. THE SUBJECTS COVERED

The law of contract is considered to be the part of the general law for which the international business community most urgently needs harmonisation. Those attempting to unify European contract law, particularly within the Community, need above all uniform principles and a uniform terminology.

The Principles are confined to the general law of contractual obligations. They do not deal with any specific types of contract, nor do they make special provision for consumer contracts, which raise policy issues more appropriately determined by Community law and national legislation. On the other hand, the Principles are not confined to commercial relationships but are intended to apply to contracts generally, including contracts between merchants and consumers.

The Commission has not hesitated to borrow from legislation and Conventions dealing with specific types of contract through provisions which are suitable for general application. Thus the United Nations Convention on Contracts for the International Sale of Goods of 1980 (CISG) has been a particularly fruitful source of ideas for the Principles. But while the Principles will be found particularly useful in international trade transactions within Europe, they are not confined to such transactions and may be applied equally to purely domestic contracts.

The Commission has taken a functional approach in deciding which topics to be included in the Principles. The Principles embrace rules which in some legal systems are considered to form part of the law of torts or the law of restitution when the rules in question are closely linked to issues in contract covered by the Principles. Thus, chapter 2 on the formation of contracts includes liability for negotiations (*culpa in contrahendo* etc.), although in some legal systems this liability is considered to form part of the law of torts. The Principles govern the restitutionary effects of the avoidance for invalidity of contracts; in chapter 4 on validity it is provided that on avoidance either party may claim restitution of whatever it has supplied under the contract provided it makes concurrent restitution of whatever it has received. If restitution cannot be made in kind for any reason, a reasonable sum must be paid for what has been received. In Chapter 9 Section 3 on Termination of the Contract for Non-performance, the Principles provide for the recovery of money paid or property transferred by a party for a performance which it did not receive, and recovery of a reasonable sum for a performance which was received and cannot be returned.

4. SOURCES

The Principles are designed primarily for use in the Member States of the European Union. They have regard to the economic and social conditions prevailing in the Member States. The Commission on European Contract Law has therefore drawn in some measure on the legal systems of every Member State. This does not, of course, imply that every legal system has had equal influence on every issue considered. In fact no single legal system has been made the starting point from which the Principles and the terminology which they employ are derived. Nor have the draftsmen of the Principles seen it as their task to make interpolations or compromises between the existing national laws, except as is necessary in order to weld the Principles into a workable system.

The Commission has not confined its sources to the national laws of Member States. It has drawn on a wide range of legal materials from both within and outside Europe, including the American *Uniform Commercial Code* and *Restatements* of contract and of restitution. Some of the provisions in the Principles reflect suggestions and ideas which have not yet materialised in the law of any State.

5. STRUCTURE AND METHOD

[...]

The method adopted may be compared with the American *Restatement of the Law of Contract*, the second edition of which was published in 1981. However, the task is different. The Restatement is broadly intended as a formulation of existing law, since in almost all States the law of contract is based on the common law. In the Union, which is characterised by the existence of a number of divergent legal systems, general principles applicable across the Union as a whole must be established by a more creative process whose purpose is to identify, so far as possible, the common core of the contract law of all the Member States of the Union and on the basis of this common core to create a workable system.

Every effort has been made to draft short and general rules which will be easily understood not only by lawyers but also by their clients. With a view to ensuring that the rules are readily comprehensible and are responsive to the needs of prospective users, earlier drafts of the Principles have been discussed with practising lawyers in six of the Member States (Belgium, France, Germany, Portugal, Spain and the United Kingdom) and appropriate additions and modifications made.

6. THE ACCOMMODATION OF FUTURE DEVELOPMENTS

The Principles of European Contract Law are a set of general rules which are designed to provide maximum flexibility and thus to accommodate future developments in legal thinking in the field of contract law. The Commission has therefore resisted the temptation to seek to cover every particular eventuality, which would lead to excessive detail and specificity and inhibit the future development of European contract law. [...]

2.   The UNIDROIT Principles of International Commercial Contracts

Michael Joachim Bonell

AN INTERNATIONAL RESTATEMENT OF CONTRACT LAW

The UNIDROIT Principles of International Commercial Contracts

Third Edition
Incorporating the UNIDROIT Principles 2004

CHAPTER 1

WHY AN INTERNATIONAL RESTATEMENT OF CONTRACT LAW?

When, in the early 1920s, the newly founded American Law Institute decided to embark upon the project of the Restatements, it was to remedy the deficiencies which in those days were becoming more and more apparent in the development of the law of the United States. As set out in a report submitted in 1923 to a meeting of representative judges, lawyers and law teachers,

> "[t]wo chief defects in American law are its uncertainty and its complexity. These defects cause useless litigation, prevent resort to the courts to enforce just rights, make it often impossible to advise persons of their rights and when litigation is begun, create delay and expense."[1]

According to the same report, one of the main causes of the defects was the presence of forty-eight states, each of which, as well as the Federal Government was an independent source of law, with the result that the law on any subject in any one jurisdiction might differ from the law of one or more or all of the other jurisdictions.

---

[1]   Report of the Committee on the Establishment of a Permanent Organization for the Improvement of the Law Proposing the Establishment of an American Law Institute (reproduced in The American Law Institute 50th Anniversary, Philadelphia 1973, p. 3 *et seq.* (p. 15)).

"[...] These variations in law are themselves a potent cause of uncertainty and complexity [...] not only where transactions are carried on in two or more states, but also where transactions are carried on wholly within one state."[2]

Hence the idea of the production of a "Restatement of the Law". Indeed, by restating in a systematic manner the law relating to a number of subjects, judges, academics and lawyers were called upon to make a substantial contribution to obviate the unsatisfactory situation. To quote the report again,

"[the restatement's] object should not only be to help make certain much that is now uncertain and to simplify unnecessary complexities, but also to promote those changes which will tend better to adapt the laws to the needs of life [...]."[3]

Furthermore,

"[t]he character of the restatement [...] can best be described by saying that it should be at once analytical, critical and constructive [...]."

In other words, while it is true that

"[...] the primary object of the restatement is to set forth the law",

on the other hand

"[...] it must be more than a collection and comparison of statutes and decisions [...] more than an exposition of the existing law [...] [it] should also take account of situations not yet discussed by courts or dealt with by the legislatures but which are likely to cause litigation in the future [...] [it] should make clear what is believed to be the proper rule of law [...] the changes proposed [should] be either in the direction of simplifying the law [...] or in the direction of better adaptation of the details of the law to the accomplishment of ends generally admitted to be desirable."[4]

UNIDROIT'S[5] initiative to prepare Principles of International Commercial Contracts originated, though in an entirely different context, from quite similar considerations and is directed towards much the same objectives.

---

2   Report of the Committee on the Establishment of a Permanent Organization, *cit.* (*supra* n. 1), p. 17.
3   Report of the Committee on the Establishment of a Permanent Organization, *cit.* (*supra* n. 1), p. 21.
4   Report of the Committee on the Establishment of a Permanent Organization, cit. (supra n. 1), pp. 22–23.
5   UNIDROIT, located in Rome (Italy), is an independent intergovernmental organisation founded in 1926 and presently composed of 59 Member States. Its main purpose is "to study the means for the harmonization and coordination of private law between States [...]" and to this effect it is called upon not only "to prepare draft laws or draft conventions intended to establish a uniform law," but also "to undertake studies of comparative private law" (*cf.* Art 1 of the Statute). On the role of UNIDROIT in the unification of law during the last decades *cf.* H. KRONKE, Ziele – Methoden – Kosten – Nutzen: Perspektiven der Privatrechtsharmonisierung nach 75 Jahren UNIDROIT, in Juristen Zeitung 2001, p. 1149 *et seq.* For further information see the UNIDROIT internet website http://www.UNIDROIT.org.

The present state of international trade law is far from satisfactory.[6] Despite the unprecedented growth in the volume of trade and the development, thanks also to the revolutionary changes in worldwide communication systems, of increasingly integrated markets, if not at the global, then at least at the regional level, cross-border transactions continue to a large extent to be subject to domestic laws.[7]

These domestic laws may not only vary considerably in content, but are often ill-suited for the special needs of international trade.[8] As pointed out by *Francesco Galgano*[9]

"[their] inadequacy [...] derives from two characteristics of contemporary economy. The first is the meta-national nature of the economy which is antithetical to the national character of the legal systems. The second is that the economy is in continuous change which demands flexible instruments of adaptation from the law to change, in antithesis to the rigidity of the laws."

With respect to some domestic laws it may even be almost impossible to find out what solution they provide for the issue at stake, because of the rudimentary character of the legal sources and the difficulty of access to them. Yet also highly developed legal systems often prove to be outdated. As *Sir Roy Goode* observed with respect to the highly praised English law[10]

"[w]hen I visit other common law countries, and in particular Canada and the United States, I am immensely impressed with their concern to keep their commercial law up to date [...] When I return to England I feel [...] depressed by [...] our inertia and complacent belief in the superiority of English commercial law [...] How is it that we feel able to embark on the 21st century with commercial law statutes passed in the 19th?"

Their intrinsic qualities apart, the very fact that different domestic laws governing international contracts do exist inevitably raises a problem of conflict of laws. In fact, in each case it is necessary to establish which of the various legal systems having contacts with the given contract will ultimately govern it. The uncertainties and inconveniences that derive from this are only too evident. Because of the different national rules of private international law, parties risk remaining uncertain as to the law applicable to their contract until the competent forum is established. Even then, depending on the conflict-of-laws-rules of the forum, the same contract may well be subject to the law of State X or

---

[6] See, among others, K.-P. BERGER, The Creeping Codification of the Lex Mercatoria, Kluwer Law International 1999, p. 9 *et seq.*

[7] As pointed out by J.M. PERILLO, UNIDROIT Principles of International Commercial Contracts: The Black Letter Text and a Review, in 43 Fordham Law Review (1994), p. 281 *et seq.* (p. 316), "[a]s the market changes from the gathering of merchants in a limited geographical spot to a global interchange of communications, the myriad local laws of the marketplace are no longer adequate to assure the commercial community that even-handed rules will govern their transactions."

[8] For some specific examples of such inadequacies, see K.-P. BERGER, The Creeping Codification of the *Lex Mercatoria, cit. (supra* n. 6), p. 14 *et seq.* F. VISCHER – L. HUBER – D. OSER, Internationales Vertragsrecht, 2nd ed. Bern 2000, p. 67.

[9] F. GALGANO, The New *Lex Mercatoria*, in 2 Annual Survey of International and Comparative Law (1995), p. 99 (p. 103).

[10] R. GOODE, Commercial Law in the Next Millennium, London 1998, pp. 100-101.

to the law of State Y.[11] Moreover, as rightly pointed out,[12] judges, while paying lip-service to the forum's conflict of law rules, in practice tend to favour in most cases the application of their own domestic substantive law. Last but not least, even if a judge was prepared to apply a foreign law, it is far from granted that he or she will be in a position to interpret it properly.

It is true that as of the beginning of the last century and above all in the second half of it States have been adopting an increasing number of international conventions in the fields of both private international law and substantive law, with a view to eliminating the uncertainties arising out of the coexistence of different national legal systems.[13] Yet, despite some undoubtable success, [...], the overall results of the unification process by legislative means are rather disappointing especially in the light of a cost/benefit analysis.[14]

To begin with, international treaties often risk remaining a dead letter, or nearly so.[15] As has been pointed out,[16]

"the treaty collections are littered with conventions that have never come into force, for want of the number of required ratifications, or have been eschewed by the major trading States. There are several reasons for this: failure to establish from potential interest groups at the outset that there is a serious problem which the proposed convention will help to resolve; hostility from powerful pressure groups; lack of sufficient interest of, or pressure on,

---

[11] L. OLAVO BAPTISTA, The UNIDROIT Principles for International Commercial Law Project: Aspects of International Private Law, in 69 Tulane Law Review (1995), p. 1209 *et seq.* (p. 1211) speaks of an authentic "mine field", which business people have to wade through.

[12] F.K. JUENGER, The *Lex Mercatoria* and Private International Law, in Uniform Law Review 2002, p. 171 (at p. 176).

[13] There is as yet no single source of information for all instruments of uniform law. For up-to-date information on the texts adopted by the various organisations active in the different fields (UNCITRAL, IMO, WIPO, ILO, UNIDO, *etc.*, within the United Nations family; UNIDROIT, the Hague Conference on Private International Law, the Council of Europe, the European Union, the Organization of American States, *etc.*) it is best to consult their respective Internet websites. Moreover, a periodical survey of the status of ratifications and of accessions to international conventions in published in the Uniform Law Review, published by UNIDROIT. For a compilation of primary materials relating to international trade law accompanied by commentary, see most recently R. GOODE – H. KRONKE – E. MCKENDRICK – J. WOOL (eds.), Transnational Commercial Law. International Instruments and Commentary, Oxford 2004.

[14] This also applies to technically extremely valid instruments, such as the 1975 U.N. Convention on the Limitation Period in the International Sale of Goods (as amended by the 1980 Protocol) which has been ratified by no more than one third of the Contracting States of CISG, among which only a few of the major trading nations, or the 1988 Ottawa Conventions on International Financial Leasing and on International Factoring, adopted by only nine and six States, respectively, let alone the 1980 Convention on International Multimodal Transport of Goods, the 1983 Geneva Convention on Agency in the International Sale of Goods, the 1991 Convention on the Liability of Operators of Transport Terminals in International Trade and the 2001 Convention on Assignement of Receivables in International Trade, non of which has up until now been ratified by a sufficient number of States to permit their entry into force.

[15] [...].

[16] R. GOODE, International Restatements of Contract and English Contract Law, in Uniform Law Review 1997, p. 231 *et seq.* (pp. 232–233).

government to induce them to burden still further an already over-crowded legislative timetable; mutual hold-backs, each State waiting to see what others will do, so that in the end none of them does anything."

Maybe an important factor explaining the decreasing willingness of national legislators to ratify international treaties is simply the change in atmosphere on the international scene. As noted by another expert of international uniform law[17]

"[t]he international treaty was conceived as a tool for the unification of the private law in the small and neatly ordered nineteenth century world consisting of a small number of so-called civilised nations. [...] Negotiations took place in a more private atmosphere, and the delegates of a few participating States were sufficiently motivated to push their respective Governments towards ratification once they had returned to their home countries. In a world of two hundred independent States, multilateral diplomatic Conferences have become mass events in which delegates no longer have the same personal commitment towards one another [...] National delegates will therefore hardly feel compelled to bring the Convention project to a successful close by urging ratification back at home."

Moreover, international conventions, even if they enter into force, are normally rather fragmentary in character.[18] Thus, most of them deal exclusively with the effects of the respective kinds of transactions covered (*e.g.* leasing, factoring, assignment, *etc.*), or even – as is the case of the different conventions in the field of transport law – only with the liability regime of one of the parties, i.e. the carrier, multimodal transport operator or terminal operator. Even a comprehensive instrument like the 1980 United Nations Convention on Contracts for the International Sale of Goods (CISG), just as the two 1964 Hague Uniform Laws on the International Sale of Goods (ULIS) and on the Formation of Contracts for the International Sale of Goods (ULF) on which it is based, suffers from a number of significant *lacunae*, such as questions concerning the validity of the contract, effects on property rights, questions arising from the use by one or both of the parties of standard forms, the impact of State control over the import/export of certain goods or over the exchange of currency on the contract of sale as such or on the performance of any of the parties' obligations, *etc.*

In addition, international conventions, once incorporated in the various national legal systems, are likely to be interpreted differently in different countries and, in the case of *lacunae*, will be supplemented by rules taken from non-unified domestic law. As pointed out by *Jürgen Basedow*[19]

"[i]n the practice of Contracting States, the rules of an international Convention are exposed to the centrifugal influences flowing from the respective national legal systems and resultant divergent interpretations, and there are no procedural safeguards against such decay of uniformity at the application stage."

---

[17]   J. BASEDOW, Uniform Law Conventions and the UNIDROIT Principles of International Commercial Contracts, in Uniform Law Review 2000, p. 129.

[18]   On the fragmentary character of existing international uniform law in general, see H. KÖTZ, Rechtsvereinheitlichung – Nutzen, Kosten, Methoden, Ziele, *cit.* (*supra*), p. 3 et seq.

[19]   J. BASEDOW, Uniform Law Conventions and the UNIDROIT Principles of International Commercial Contracts, *cit.* (*supra* n. 17), 129.

Finally, international conventions have by their very nature a very limited capacity, if any, for being adopted to subsequent changes in the technical or economic environment. As has been observed,[20]

> "[...] the drafters of these codifications tend to look on harmonization as an event that happens once and for all. They see their codes as monuments that will stand without change [...] this static, monumental quality is most mischievous. As times change and the law does not, codification becomes the enemy of substantive reform."

Or, to quote another expert of international uniform law,[21]

> "[t]he inflexibility of many international conventions may be too heavy a price to pay. The need to revise the law arises constantly, and international procedures sometimes slow the process of necessary law reform to an unacceptable extent."[22]

Nor can the different model clauses and standard contract terms which the interested business circles have been developing since the end of the 19th century in response to the inadequacies of the various domestic laws[23] provide a satisfactory alternative.

These instruments were predominantly issued by individual enterprises or by national trade associations and commodity exchanges operating in the most important commercial and financial centres.[24] Consequently, not only is their content likely to be one-sided, but they are inevitably influenced by legal concepts of their respective countries of origin and normally contain a provision for the application of the law of those countries and/or the settlement of possible disputes on their territory.[25] No wonder that such instruments are therefore often criticised for their "legitimacy deficit" [...].

---

[20]   A. ROSETT, Unification, Harmonization, Restatement, Codification and Reform in International Commercial Law, *cit.* (*supra*), p. 688.

[21]   A.L. DIAMOND, Conventions and Their Revision, in Unification and Comparative Law in Theory and Practice. Contribution in Honour of J.G. Sauveplanne, Deventer-Antwerp-Boston-London-Frankfurt, 1984, p. 45 *et seq.* (p. 60).

[22]   On the lack of flexibility of most international uniform law instruments and the way in which this may hamper the law reform process, see also P.H. NEUHAUS – J. KROPHOLLER, Rechtsvereinheitlichung - Rechtsverbesserung?, in RabelsZeitschrift, 1981, p. 73 *et seq.* (p. 80: "Uniform law carries within it the risk of rigidity" (translation from German original)); P. BEHRENS, Voraussetzungen und Grenzen der Rechtsfortbildung durch Rechtsvereinheitlichung, in RabelsZeitschrift 1986, p. 19 *et seq.* who points out that, in order to facilitate the necessary adaptation of uniform law to new developments, codification should not be too detailed, but rather be confined to the statement of general principles (p. 32: "To preserve a measure of flexibility in order to be able to adapt to future developments, it is not advisable to envisage a detailed codification. It would be more appropriate in many areas to focus on the unification of general principles of law, whose implementation leaves sufficient room for manoeuvre." (translation from German original)).

[23]   [Footnotes in the following text partially omitted].

[24]   Suffice it to mention the numerous standard commodity contracts issued by the long established and prestigious London-based Grain and Feed Trade Association, the Federation of Oil, Seed and Fats Associations, the London Metal Exchange and the Refined Sugar Associaton, *etc.*

[25]   Thus all standard contracts prepared by the above-mentioned London-based trade associations contain a reference to English law (to the exclusion of uniform law instruments) as the applicable law and to the English courts or arbitration to be held in London for settlement of disputes, regardless of where the parties have their places of business.

Yet even both in form and in substance truly supra-national or anational instruments, prepared by international non-governmental organisations offer only a partial solution. This is true in particular of INCOTERMS or the Uniform Customs and Practices for Documentary Credits (UCP) prepared by the International Chamber of Commerce (ICC) dealing only, though in great detail, with the most common delivery terms and letter of credit as a particular mode of payment, respectively. [...]. Indeed, these instruments, though on account of their origin more balanced in content, still presuppose a more general regulatory system to refer to for the purpose of settling the questions they do not expressly address and to establish the conditions and limits of their validity.

It is true that, at least according to most domestic laws, parties are free to lay down in their contract a detailed and possibly exhaustive regulation of their rights and obligations so as to avoid to the greatest possible extent any recourse to external sources. Yet – apart from the fact that in so doing the parties often encounter insurmountable difficulties arising from the language barriers between them and the absence of internationally uniform legal terminology on which they can rely – such supposedly self-regulatory contracts or "*contrats sans loi*" equally cannot do without a general legal framework within which to operate.[26]

Even the parties' exercise of their right, likewise nowadays generally admitted, to choose the law governing their contract does not always provide a satisfactory solution.

To begin with, the parties´ choice is quite often the result of a last minute decision, made without adequate legal assistance and thereby sometimes leading to rather awkward results. As vividly described by an experienced German attorney[27]

> "[P]articularly *nonchalant* are those frequently recurring cases where [...] the parties conduct their negotiations without legal assistance on the basis of an Anglo-Saxon contract form but then decide to subject their contract to the law of another legal system (*e.g.* a civil law jurisdiction)" (translation from German original).

Yet even where the issue of the applicable law is given sufficient attention, it is far from being taken for granted that the parties end up with a mutually satisfactory decision. This is especially true in cases where, for reasons of prestige or political imperative, a party is not willing to choose the law of a foreign country, although perfectly aware that its own national law is clearly inadequate to regulate the kind of transaction at hand.

A situation of this kind frequently occurs, for example, in the oil industry, with reference to which it has been observed[28]

---

26   As pointed out by K. HIGHET, The Enigma of the *Lex Mercatoria*, in 63 Tulane Law Review (1989), p. 613 *et seq.* (p. 614) "[t]he only way in which a contract can exist independently of a legal system is to consider it as a voluntary compact operating by virtue of the collective will of the parties. [...] To the extent that one can rely on an agreement's allocation of rights and obligations, one must logically look beyond the will of the parties to the legal framework within which that will may be expressed and possess content."

27   E. BRÖDERMANN, Die erweiterten UNIDROIT-Principles 2004, in Recht der Internationalen Wirtschaft 2004, p. 721 *et seq.* (note 122 at p. 730).

28   V. GAYMER, The UNIDROIT Principles as a Guide for the Drafting of Contracts: A View from an International Commercial Lawyer, in Institute of International Business Law and Practice (ed.), UNIDROIT Principles for International Commercial Contracts: A New *Lex Mercatoria*?, ICC Publication n° 490/1 (1995), p. 95 *et seq.* (p. 100).

"[o]ne sometimes encounters [...] a situation where one of the contracting parties is a government or state owned concern in a country which itself has inadequate commercial or petroleum laws [...]. That party, for political reasons, may be unable to agree to the adoption of another country's law as the law governing the contract and it will often recognise that its own country's laws are inappropriate [...]."

But also in the absence of obstacles of a political nature, problems still exist. Freedom of choice is – at least as far as the domestic courts are concerned – traditionally restricted to existing domestic laws, with the result that, in addition to the above-mentioned short-comings of domestic laws *per se*, one or even both of the parties will have to accept a law with which they are not familiar or, conversely, which they know only too well and do not like at all. The difficulties, at least in psychological terms, deriving from the former kind of situation for parties and indeed, at times, for arbitrators, have been vividly described by one of the most experienced international arbitrators:[29]

"Those who have participated in an international arbitration governed by foreign law have experienced the frustration of being told the law by a participant who is a 'native' of that legal system. If the native is not the sole arbitrator or the president of the tribunal, but one who is or may be suspected of being interested in the outcome of the dispute you may have reason to fear that you are not always told the whole truth about the law. Nevertheless, you remain the foreigner who speaks without authority, you are the dilettante where the other is the expert. If he is your co-arbitrator you have often very little to say."

As to the second kind of situation, it has been pointed out that[30]

"[...] as the twenty-first century moves inexorably on we American lawyers are likely to find ourselves dealing more and more with parties of roughly equal bargaining power, many of them from the third world and distrustful of Anglo-American or even European law, wanting a neutral system not tied to a particular country and one that will protect from harsh terms and bargains that have gone south."

Yet the same situation may well occur even when the legal system in question is highly developed and the foreign party is far from inexperienced. For instance,

"[...] there are Japanese companies that would be horrified if the applicable law were to be that of the United States. The reason is that they fear jury trials and punitive damages as well as discovery, especially when claims concern the quality of their merchandise. So in this case, they prefer arbitration, which is secret, usually final, and resolved by a specialist."[31]

---

[29] O. LANDO, Assessing the Role of the UNIDROIT Principles in the Harmonization of Arbitration Law, in 3 Tulane Journal of International and Comparative Law (1994), p. 129 *et seq.* (pp. 140-141).

[30] P. LINZER, The UNIDROIT Principles of International Commercial Contracts: Should American Lawyers Pull Their Hair Out Over Them, In 13 Texas Transnational Law Quarterly (1997) p. 1 *et seq.*

[31] H. HIROSE, The Place of the UNIDROIT Principles in Non-Western Legal Traditions (paper presented at the bi-annual 25th Conference of the International Bar Association, held in Melbourne, 9–14 October 1994).

Nor – as may be admitted before an arbitral tribunal – could a reference to the "general principles of law" or the "*lex mercatoria*" as the law governing the contract constitute a valid alternative. As will be shown in greater detail below, in the absence of a sufficiently precise definition of the nature and content of such general principles or of the supposed *lex mercatoria* such a choice risks producing even greater uncertainty and unpredictability.

At least some of these deficiencies currently encountered in international trade law are intended to be overcome by the UNIDROIT Principles.

The UNIDROIT Principles are, above all, drafted in clear and simple language so as to permit any educated person, even if not a trained lawyer, easily to understand them.

In setting forth the rules they also deliberately avoid using terminology peculiar to any given legal system, thereby creating a legal *lingua franca* to be used and uniformly understood throughout the world.

As to their content, the UNIDROIT Principles represent a mixture of both tradition and innovation. In other words, while reflecting concepts found in many, if not all, legal systems, they also – especially when irreconcilable differences between the various domestic laws render a choice inevitable – embody what in the light of the special needs of international trade are perceived to be the best solutions, even if these solutions still represent a minority view.

Finally, the fact that the UNIDROIT Principles are not intended to become a binding instrument permitted not only a wider discretion in their preparation, but also renders them more flexible and capable of rapid adaptation to the changing conditions in international trade practice.

These inherent characteristics of the UNIDROIT Principles should at the same time absolve those involved in their preparation from the accusation of being over-ambitious in engaging in such a vast project. Or, as one particularly authoritative participant in the project put it,[32]

> "[...] at the thought of drafting principles for the entire world [...] [w]e do not tremble for at least four reasons. One, we are drafting mere principles and not a uniform law, so that whatever rules we write are only likely to be applied if they find favour with someone concerned with a particular transaction or dispute [...] Two, most of our principles are unlikely to miscarry because they are framed with evident generality (*e.g.*, 'good faith and fair dealing') or they have built-in safety valves (*e.g.*, 'unless the circumstances indicate otherwise'), giving them enough flexibility to permit a judge or arbitrator to use common sense in applying them so as to avoid an arbitrary or unfair result. Three, in some instances we have declined to deal with tough questions, as in the area [...] of invalidity on a variety of grounds under the applicable domestic law. And four, [...] UNIDROIT is free to amend the Principles [...] from time to time to take care of problems that later surface."

Likewise, as to the supposed contradiction between, on the one hand, the purposes of the UNIDROIT Principles – above all that of serving as a model for national and international legislators, and that of being applied as the rules governing the contract – as indicated in the Preamble and, on the other hand, that they are not a binding

---

[32] E.A. FARNSWORTH, Closing Remarks, in 40 The American Journal of Comparative Law (1992), p. 699 *et seq.* (pp. 699–700).

instrument and consequently their acceptance will depend upon their persuasive authority only,[33] it has been pointed out that[34]

> "[...] the impact of the [P]rinciples may prove to be even greater than that of an international convention, for a convention has no force at the time it is concluded and represents at most a provisional indication of support by participating States which may or may not crystallise, whereas the Principles represent the unconditional commitment and consensus of scholars of international repute from all over the world."

CHAPTER 2

THE UNIDROIT PRINCIPLES OF INTERNATIONAL COMMERCIAL CONTRACTS: PREPARATION AND SOURCES OF INSPIRATION

---

1. The 1994 edition of the UNIDROIT Principles

The idea of preparing a kind of "restatement" of the law of international commercial contracts in general was first formulated by *Mario Matteucci* at an international colloquium held in Rome in 1968 to celebrate the 40th anniversary of the foundation of UNIDROIT. Recalling the experience of the "Restatements of the law" in the United States of America, the then Secretary-General and later President of UNIDROIT raised the question as to whether a similar initiative could be successfully undertaken at the international level as well:[35]

> "[...] Obviously the restatement will have no binding force *vis-à-vis* States, but it could represent a conceptual preparation for unification. If one could offer judges a body of rules reflecting the common principles that can be extracted from the case law of the various countries, in the different areas of international relations, this could represent the first step towards a uniform code. Judges and practitioners could gradually become familiar with these rules, and perhaps at a later stage one could consider converting these rules from simple statements to binding provisions by means of treaties or in other forms [...]." (translation from French original)

---

[33] For such criticism, see in particular H. RAESCHKE-KESSLER, Should an Arbitrator in an International Arbitration Procedure apply the UNIDROIT Principles?, in Institute of International Business Law and Practice (ed.), UNIDROIT Principles for International Commercial Contracts: A New *Lex Mercatoria?*, ICC Publication n° 490/1 (1995), p. 167 *et seq.* (pp. 171–173); C. KESSEDJIAN, Un exercice de rénovation des sources du droit des contrats du commerce international: Les Principes proposés par l'UNIDROIT, in Revue critique de droit international privé 1995, p. 641 *et seq.* (pp. 646–652).

[34] R. GOODE, Commercial Law in the Next Millennium, *cit.* (*supra*), p. 234.

[35] Cf. IVth Meeting of the Organizations concerned with Unification of Law, in UNIDROIT (ed.), Unification of Law – Yearbook 1967-1968, II, p. 267 *et seq.* (p. 268).

On the basis of preliminary studies carried out by the Secretariat, the UNIDROIT Governing Council – the Institute's highest scientific organ – decided in 1971 to include in the Work Programme of the Institute what in the original French version of the resolution was indicated as an "*essai d'unification portant sur la partie générale des contrats (en vue d'une Codification progressive du droit des obligations* 'ex contractu')".

After the new Work Programme was approved by the Member States of UNIDROIT, the President of the Institute set up a small Steering Committee, composed of Professors *René David* (University of Aix-en-Provence), *Clive M. Schmitthoff* (City University of London) and *Tudor Popescu* (University of Bucharest), in representation of the civil law, the common law and the former socialist systems, with the task of making preliminary inquiries on the feasibility of such a project. In a first report in 1974 the Steering Committee stressed the great importance of the project and laid down in broad terms the structure it should take for its realisation.

However, due to other commitments of the Institute, the project – initially given the somewhat misleading title of "Progressive Codification of International Trade Law" and only later renamed "Preparation of Principles for International Commercial Contracts" – did not for some years enjoy priority status.

Only in 1980 was a special Working Group set up with the task of preparing the various draft chapters of the Principles. The members of the Group [...] included representatives of all the major legal and socio-economic systems of the world [...] While most of the members – all leading experts in the field of contract law and international trade law – were academics, some [were] high ranking judges or civil servants; they all sat, however, in a personal capacity and did not express the views of their governments. Referring to this latter fact, one of the members of the Group observed:[36]

"[i]t made it strikingly more possible to conduct a realistic search for the 'best' solution. An automatic assumption that one's own domestic solution is always the 'best' would have been a very serious handicap to any member of the working group."

The working atmosphere within the Group was always excellent. In the words of one of its members,[37]

"[...] while our discussions [were] often lively they [were] rarely confrontational and every effort [was] made to find solutions that avoid[ed] or at least minimize[d] strongly held objections of individual members."

And with regard to the sorts of arguments – other than those based on legislative texts – which dominated the discussion, he went on to say,

"[s]ome arguments might be described as 'philosophical' in nature, as [was] the case for arguments based on the concepts of the autonomy of the parties and *pacta sunt servanda*. Proposals based [...] on the law-and-economics notion of efficient breach [were] not likely to

---

[36] M.P. FURMSTON, The UNIDROIT Principles and International Commercial Arbitration, in Institute of International Business Law and Practice (ed.), UNIDROIT Principles, *cit.* (*supra*), p. 199 *et seq.* (p. 201). [...]

[37] E.A. FARNSWORTH, Closing Remarks, *cit.* (*supra*) p. 701.

be warmly received. [...] Other arguments might be described as 'political', as [was] the case for 'north-south' disputes between developing and industrialized countries and 'east-west' disputes between countries on the two sides of what was once known as the Iron Curtain. [...] Other arguments [were] 'systematic' in nature, consisting of assertions that a group of countries, [such as] Latin American countries, holds a consistent view on some matter. (It [was] not usually considered appropriate to insist on a single country's idiosyncratic solution, although the argument that 'lawyers in my country will not understand that' – or '*ça ne se traduit pas en français*' – [was] not unknown.) Still other arguments [were] 'practical' in nature, turning on how well or how badly a proposed rule can be expected to work in a practical business context."

This positive view of the Group's working method is echoed by outside observers. To quote but one[38]:

"[p]rovisions within the *Principles* regarding issues on which the common law and the civil law systems have different conceptual frameworks (*e.g.*, specific performance and penalty clauses) show that the drafters were able to break out of their respective conceptual straitjackets to reach common ground. This only could have happened by a process of mutual education and the expansion of understanding."

Naturally, the Group never considered itself exclusive, but always welcomed outside assistance. However, individual experts were invariably contacted in their personal capacity, not as representatives of a particular interest group. As one of the participants pointed out,[39]

"the Principles were prepared without any political interference by particular lobbies. This is one of the advantages of a project on contracts in general, as opposed to negotiations concerning specific transactions (sales, transport, *etc.*), where the serenity of the atmosphere is often disturbed by the intervention of interested business circles. The experts preparing the Principles had in mind only two abstract categories, the 'obligor' and the 'obligee'; they attempted to find in an objective manner the best equilibrium between these two parties, with respect to formation as well as to performance and non-performance of the contract." (translation from French original)

[...]

From the outset the Working Group appointed from among its members Rapporteurs for each of the different chapters of the Principles.

[...]

The task of the Rapporteurs consisted in preparing, after the necessary comparative studies, a first draft together with comments.

These preliminary drafts were discussed by the Group as a whole at its working sessions which took place twice a year and lasted for one week. They were then revised

---

38   J.M. PERILLO, UNIDROIT Principles of International Commercial Contracts: The Black Letter Text and Review, *cit.* (*supra*), p. 284.

39   M. FONTAINE, Les Principes UNIDROIT comme guide dans la rédaction des contrats internationaux, in Institute of International Business Law and Practice (ed.), UNIDROIT Principles, *cit.* (*supra*), p. 73 *et seq.* (p. 77).

again by the Rapporteurs so as to include the changes decided upon by the Group. After their second reading the drafts were circulated, together with a list of the issues which had proved most controversial, among a wider group of experts, belonging to both academic and business circles throughout the world. These experts, which included the more than one hundred correspondents of the Institute, were asked to express their opinion on the drafts. The revised versions were also examined at the annual sessions of the UNIDROIT Governing Council which offered its advice on the policy to be followed, especially in those cases where the Working Group had found it difficult to reach a consensus. Moreover, the drafts were submitted to the Governments of the Member States of the Institute for information. All the observations and proposals for amendment received were submitted to the Working Group so as to enable it to take them into account when proceeding to the third and final reading of the drafts.

The Working Group concluded the last reading of the different draft chapters in February 1994, after which the text was submitted to a special Editorial Committee, chaired by *E. Allan Farnsworth* and composed of the Rapporteurs on the various chapters and the Secretary-General of UNIDROIT, *Malcolm Evans*. The latter undertook the arduous task of supervising the final editing of the UNIDROIT Principles.

In May 1994 the Governing Council gave its formal *imprimatur* to the UNIDROIT Principles and recommended their widest possible distribution in practice. [...]

The UNIDROIT Principles were originally drafted in English, which was the working language of the Working Group. However, in order to facilitate their use throughout the world, it was decided from the beginning that they should be made available in as many as possible other language versions, and that the respective member(s) of the Working Group should be responsible for their preparation. As a result, the integral version of the 1994 edition of the UNIDROIT Principles was published not only in all five official languages of UNIDROIT, *i.e.* English, French, German, Italian, and Spanish, but also in Arabic, Chinese, Czech, Dutch, Farsi, Hungarian, Japanese, Portuguese, Romanian, Russian, Slovak and Vietnamese. Moreover, the black letter rules have been translated into Bulgarian, Croatian, Hebrew, Korean and Serbian.

2. The 2004 edition of the UNIDROIT Principles

When deciding in 1994 to publish the UNIDROIT Principles, the Governing Council of UNIDROIT stressed the need to monitor their use "with a view to a possible reconsideration of them at some time in future."

The immediate success of the UNIDROIT Principles worldwide prompted UNIDROIT as early as 1997 to resume work "with a view to the publication of an enlarged second edition of the Principles". To this end, a new Working Group was set up, composed of some seventeen members again chosen with a view to ensuring, on the one side, the widest possible representation of all the major legal systems and/or geo-political regions of the world, and on the other hand, the highest professional qualification. [...]

It was clear from the outset that the focus of the new edition of the UNIDROIT Principles was on enlargement rather than revision of the 1994 edition. The Working Group chose the following new topics as priority items: authority of agents, third party rights, set-off, assignment of rights, transfer of obligations and assignment of contracts, limitation periods and waiver. [...]

The working method was basically the same as that adopted for the preparation of the 1994 edition of the UNIDROIT Principles. [...]

3. Sources of inspiration

(a) In general

Already during the preparation of the Restatements of the law in the United States the question was asked

> "[h]ow can a restatement of diverse and heterogeneous legal propositions become itself consistent and coherent."[40]

The answer given was that

> "[o]bviously some propositions of law must be rejected in favour of others with which they are inconsistent; the 'weight of authority' test can be applied [...] Yet this is no mere matter of counting cases; respect for the reasoning of an opinion or for the reputation of the court will be thrown into the scale [...];"

and where, as it is with respect to a number of questions, there is no such authority

> "[...] one chooses the law that one thinks ought to be."[41]

The method adopted in preparing the UNIDROIT Principles was very similar.

The UNIDROIT Principles, like the Restatements in the United States, are intended to enunciate rules which are common to (most) existing legal systems, even though this objective played a considerably less important role than in the Restatements. The reasons for this have been summarised by one of the Rapporteurs:[42]

> "[I]t is important to emphasise that the working group did not attempt to find a lowest common denominator of contract rules. This kind of enterprise makes good sense in a federal jurisdiction like the United States where the differences between individual States are relatively small; where the conceptual apparatus of all contract lawyers is common; and, where on many issues all States will apply the same rule. The working group tried to produce a set of principles which was internally coherent. Obviously, this objective could not be reached simply by taking a series of majority views on a whole range of contract problems."

To the extent that the UNIDROIT Principles do not reflect the common core of the various national systems, they aim at selecting the solutions which seem best adapted to the special requirements of international trade. As stated by another Rapporteur,[43]

---

[40] E.W. PATTERSON, The Restatement of the Law of Contracts, in 33 Columbia Law Review (1933), p. 397 *et seq.* (p. 399).

[41] E.W. PATTERSON, The Restatement of the Law of Contracts, *cit. (supra)*, pp. 399–400. [...].

[42] M.P. FURMSTON, The UNIDROIT Principles and International Commercial Arbitration, *cit. (supra)*, p. 205.

[43] M. FONTAINE, Les principes pour les contrats commerciaux internationaux élaborés par UNIDROIT, *cit. (supra)*, p. 30.

"The intention is to prepare Principles acceptable to business people engaged in international trade and coming from different legal systems from around the world. The proposed instrument must, on one hand, take into account the latest changes in the most recent codifications [...]. On the other hand, the Principles address themselves primarily to practitioners and should respond to the real needs of the protagonists of international commerce." (translation from French original).

Consequently, whenever it was necessary to choose between conflicting rules, the criterion used was not merely arithmetical. In other words, what was decisive was not just which rule was adopted by the majority of countries, but rather which of the rules under consideration had the most persuasive value and/or appeared to be particularly well suited for cross-border transactions. As stated in the Introduction to the 1994 edition of the UNIDROIT Principles

"[f]or the most part to the Unidroit Principles reflect concepts to be found in many, if not all, legal systems. Since however the Principles are intended to provide a system of rules especially tailored of the needs of international commercial transactions, they also embody what are perceived to be the best solutions, even if still not yet generally adopted."

For obvious reasons it was impossible to take into account the law of every single country of the world, nor could every legal system have an equal influence on each issue at stake.[44]

As far as international legislation is concerned, such an important and universally applied instrument as the 1980 United Nations Convention on Contracts for the International Sale of Goods was of course an obligatory point of reference. [...]

(b)   Tradition v. innovation

Although those involved in the preparation of the UNIDROIT Principles never considered their role to be that of legislators empowered to lay down entirely new rules, but understood their task to be essentially one of "re-stating" the existing international contract law, it cannot be denied that, especially within the Working Group, there were from the beginning two conflicting "souls" or schools of thought. On the one side were the "traditionalists", rather reluctant to depart from long-established principles, particularly if those principles formed part of their own legal system; on the other side were the "innovators", more open to recent developments, even when these developments belonged to a foreign legal system and were not yet generally accepted.

On the whole the two sides balanced each other out, so that it is rather difficult to ascertain the extent to which the UNIDROIT Principles are innovative rather than to be seen as reflecting traditional views.

In part the answer might be very similar to what was said in response to the same question in respect to the United States' Restatement (Second) of the Law of Contracts, namely that

---

[44]   From among the national codifications or compilations of law greater attention was naturally given to the most recent ones, such as the United States Uniform Commercial Code and the Restatement (Second) of the Law of Contracts, the Algerian Civil Code, the Dutch Civil Code, the Civil Code of Quebec and the law of obligations of the German Civil Code as amended in 2002.

"[s]ometimes innovation does not take the form of a new substantive rule but rather of a new perspective on the problem, reflected in the substitution of a new terminology or analysis for a traditional one [...]. Even where substantive rules are concerned, it is no easy task to assess the extent of innovation [...] often a paucity of cases or a confusion in the courts' analyses makes it impossible starkly to contrast innovation with tradition."[45]

There are, however, rules which are clearly innovative, at least for a number of domestic laws. The reason for this is to be found partly in the desire better to meet the special needs of international trade practice and partly in the necessity to take account of the different economic and political conditions existing in the world today.

[...]

---

[45] Cf. E.A. FARNSWORTH, Ingredients in the Redaction of the Restatement (Second) of Contracts, in 81 *Columbia Law Review* (1981), p. 1 *et seq.* (pp. 5–6).

Part B: Case Studies

Chapter I

Formation of contracts

"A contract is an agreement giving rise to obligations which are enforced or recognised by law. The factor which distinguishes contractual from other legal obligations is that they are based on an agreement of the parties."[1]

Case 1: Offer or invitation to treat (*invitatio ad offerendum*)?

Scenario 1

The latest computers are displayed in a shop window at a very attractive price. A customer comes into the shop and says that he would like to buy one of the computers at the advertised price.

Another customer has seen the computers advertised in promotional material that gives all the relevant information, including the price. He contacts the salesperson and tells him that he would like to buy one of the computers.

The salesperson no longer wants to sell the computer at the advertised price.

Scenario 2

In a newspaper advertisement, a job is offered. An interested party responds by declaring that he accepts the job offer. The employer does not want to employ this person.

---

1   GUENTER TRIETEL, *The Law of Contract*, 12th edn, London: Sweet & Maxwell, 2007, p. 1.

Questions[2]

(1) Did the salesperson make a valid offer by:
     (a) displaying the computer in the shop window;
     (b) advertising the computer in the promotional material;
     (c) advertising the job in the newspaper?
     Has a contract been formed? Or are these acts merely invitations to treat and any offer is therefore made subsequently by the customer?
        Use the extracts of laws, judicial decisions and academic literature below to answer the questions in relation to each legal order.
        You will see that the solutions differ from one country to another. How many different solutions can be identified? Present the solutions in a systematic manner.[3]

(2) What are the arguments for and against the different solutions found in the materials?

(3) How would the above scenarios be solved under:
     (a) the United Nations Convention on Contracts for the International Sale of Goods (CISG or Vienna Sales Convention);
     (b) the Principles of International Commercial Contracts (UNIDROIT Principles);
     (c) the Principles of European Contract Law (Lando Principles);
     (d) the Draft Common Frame of Reference;
     (e) the Draft European Contract Code presented by the Academy of European Private Lawyers?

(4) In your opinion, which solution best meets the interests of all of the parties involved? Could this solution also be used with regard to Internet sales?

---

[2] The present case deals exclusively with the impact that window displays and advertisements may have on the conclusion of contracts. It should be noted, however, that in the Member States of the European Union, as well as in most other European countries, misleading advertisements are, in certain circumstances, also considered as acts of unfair competition leading to actions for injunction, damages etc., or provoking sanctions under administrative or criminal law; see, e.g., Art. 6(1)(d) with Art. 5, Directive 2005/29/EC of the European Parliament and of the Council of 11 May 2005 concerning unfair business-to-consumer commercial practices in the internal market (Unfair Commercial Practices Directive), OJ L 149/22, 11.6.2005; Directive 98/6/EC of the European Parliament and of the Council of 16 February 1998 on consumer protection in the indication of the prices of products offered to consumers, OJ L 80/27; and the Acts of the Member States transposing these Directives; see also the Swiss Federal Law on Unfair Competition, Art. 18: "Misleading Announcement of Prices: It shall be prohibited (a) to announce prices, (b) to announce price reductions or (c) to mention other prices in addition to the price to be effectively paid, in a misleading manner."

[3] For the method to employ, see "II. Introduction to the Comparative Methodology: Case Studies", above, Part A, p. 7.

Table of contents

I.   England

1. *Fisher* v. *Bell* [1961] 1 QB 394, [1960] 3 All ER 731
(High Court, Queen's Bench Division)

FISHER *v.* BELL.

[QUEEN'S BENCH DIVISION (Lord Parker, C.J., Ashworth and Elwes, JJ.), November 10, 1960.]

Criminal Law – Dangerous weapons – Flick knife – Knife, displayed in shop window with price attached – Whether "offer for sale" – Restriction of Offensive Weapons Act, 1959 (7 & 8 Eliz. 2 c. 37), s. 1 (1).

A shopkeeper displayed in his shop window a knife with a price ticket behind it. He was charged with offering for sale a flick knife, contrary to s. 1 (1) of the Restriction of Offensive Weapons Act, 1959.

Held: the shopkeeper was not guilty of the offence with which he was charged because the displaying of the knife in the shop window was merely an invitation to treat and the shopkeeper had not thereby offered the knife for sale, within the meaning of s. 1 (1) of the Act of 1959.

Keating v. *Horwood* ([1926] All E.R. Rep. 88) and *Wiles* v. *Maddison* ([1943] 1 All E.R. 315) distinguished.

Appeal dismissed.

[...]

LORD PARKER, C.J.: This is an appeal by way of Case Stated by justices for the City and County of Bristol, before whom an information was preferred by the appellant, a chief inspector of police, against the respondent that he on a certain day in a shop unlawfully did offer for sale a knife which was, to use ordinary terms, a flick knife, contrary to s. 1 of the Restriction of Offensive Weapons Act, 1959. Section 1 (1) of the Act provides:

"Any person who manufactures, sells or hires or offers for sale or hire, or lends or gives to any other person – (a) any knife which has a blade which opens automatically by hand pressure applied to a button, spring or other device in or attached to the handle of the knife, sometimes known as a 'flick knife' … shall be guilty of an offence …"

The justices, without deciding whether the knife in question was a knife of the kind described in the statute, decided that the information must be dismissed on the ground that there had not been an offer for sale.

The short facts are these. The respondent keeps a retail shop in Bristol and, in October, 1959, a police constable, walking past the shop, saw in the window, amongst other articles, one of these knives. Behind the knife in the window was a ticket with the words· "Ejector knife–4s." The police officer went in and informed the respondent that he would be reported for offering for sale such knife, and the respondent replied: "Fair enough".

The sole question is whether the exhibition of that knife in the window with the ticket constituted an offer for sale within the statute. I think that most lay people would be inclined to the view (as, indeed, I was myself when I first read these papers), that if a knife were displayed in a window like that with a price attached to it, it was nonsense to say that that was not offering it for sale. The knife is there inviting people to buy it, and in ordinary language it is for sale; but any statute must be looked at in the light of the general law of the country, for Parliament must be taken to know the general law. It is clear that, according to the ordinary law of contract, the display of an article with a price on it in a shop window is merely an invitation to treat. It is in no sense an offer for sale the acceptance of which constitutes a contract. That is clearly the general law of the country. Not only is that so, but it is to be observed that, in many statutes and orders which prohibit selling and offering for sale of goods, it is very common, when it is so desired, to insert the words "offering or exposing for sale", "exposing for sale" being clearly words which would cover the display of goods in a shop window. Not only that, but it appears that under several statutes – we have been referred in particular to the Prices of Goods Act, 1939, and the Goods and Services (Price Control) Act, 1941 – Parliament, when it desires to enlarge the ordinary meaning of those words, has a definition section enlarging the ordinary meaning of "offer for sale" to cover other matters including, be it observed, exposure of goods for sale with the price attached.

In those circumstances, I, for my part, though I confess reluctantly, am driven to the conclusion that no offence was here committed. At first sight it appears absurd that knives of this sort may not be manufactured, they may not be sold, they may not be hired, they may not be lent, they may not be given, but apparently they may be displayed in shop windows; but even if this is a casus omissus – and I am by no means saying that it is – it is not for this court to supply the omission. I am mindful of the strong words of LORD SIMONDS in *Magor & St. Mellons Rural District Council* v. *Newport Corpn.* In that case one of the lords justices in the Court of Appeal had, in effect, said that the court, having discovered the supposed intention of Parliament, must proceed to fill in the gaps – what the legislature has not written, the court must write – and in answer to that contention LORD SIMONDS in his speech said:

> "It appears to me to be a naked usurpation of the legislative function under the thin disguise of interpretation …"

For my part, approaching this matter apart from authority, I find it quite impossible to say that an exhibition of goods in a shop window is itself an offer for sale. We were, however, referred to several cases, one of which is *Keating* v. *Horwood* (…), a decision of this court. There, a baker's van was being driven on its rounds. There was bread in it that had been ordered and bread in it that was for sale, and it was found that that bread was underweight, contrary to the Sale of Food Order, 1921. That order was an order of the sort to which I have referred already and which prohibited the offering or exposing for sale. In giving his judgment, LORD HEWART, C.J., said:

> "The question is whether, on the facts, there was (i) an offering, and (ii) an exposure, for sale. In my opinion, there were both."

AVORY, J., agreed. SHEARMAN, J., however, said:

"I am of the same opinion. I am quite clear that this bread was exposed for sale, but have had some doubt whether it can be said to have been offered for sale until a particular loaf was tendered to a particular customer."

There are [several] matters to observe on that case. The first is that the order plainly contained the words "expose for sale", and, on any view, there was in that case an exposing for sale. Therefore, the question whether there was an offer for sale was unnecessary for decision. Secondly, the principles of general contract law were never referred to; […] For my part, I cannot take that as an authority for the proposition that the display here in a shop window was an offer for sale.

The other case to which I should refer is *Wiles* v. *Maddison* (…). I find it unnecessary to go through the facts of that case, which was a very different case and where all that was proved was an intention to commit an offence the next day, but, in the course of his judgment, VISCOUNT CALDECOTE, C.J., said:

"A person might, for instance, be convicted of making an offer of an article of food at too high a price by putting it in his shop window to be sold at an excessive price, although there would be no evidence of anybody having passed the shop window or having seen the offer or the exposure of the article for sale at that price."

Again, be it observed, that was a case where, under the Meat (Maximum Retail Prices) Order, 1940, the words were: "No person shall sell or offer or expose for sale or buy or offer to buy …" Although LORD CALDECOTE, C.J., does refer to the making of an offer by putting an article in the shop window, before the sentence is closed he has, in fact, turned the phrase to one of exposing the article. I cannot get any assistance in favour of the appellant from that passage. Accordingly, I have come to the conclusion in this case that the justices were right, and this appeal must be dismissed.

ASHWORTH, J.: I agree.

ELWES, J.: I also agree.

Appeal dismissed

Solicitors: *Robins, Hay & Waters,* agents for *Town clerk,* Bristol (for the appellant); *Haslewoods,* agents for *Cooke, Painter, Spofforth & Co.,* Bristol (for the respondent).
[*Reported by* F. GUTTMANN, ESQ., *Barrister-at-Law.*]

2. *Pharmaceutical Society of GB* v. *Boots Cash Chemists (Southern) Ltd* [1953] 1 QB 401, [1952] 2 All ER 456

PHARMACEUTICAL SOCIETY OF GREAT BRITAIN *v.* BOOTS CASH CHEMISTS (SOUTHERN), LTD

[QUEEN'S BENCH DIVISION (Lord Goddard, C.J.), July 16, 1952.]

Poison – Sale by retail – Sale by or under supervision of registered pharmacist – Chemist's "self-service" shop – Pharmacist supervising transaction at time of payment – Pharmacy and Poisons Act, 1933 (c. 25), s. 18 (1) (a) (iii).

A chemist's "self-service" shop comprised a single room with shelves round the walls and on an "island" fixture on which were stocked drugs and proprietary medicines which were specified in Part I of the Poisons List compiled under s. 17 (1) of the Pharmacy and Poisons Act, 1933, in packages and other containers with the prices marked on them. A customer entering the shop took a wire basket, selected the articles he required from the shelves, put them in the basket, and carried them to the cashier at one of the two exits. The cashier scrutinised the articles, stated the total price, and accepted payment, a registered pharmacist employed by the chemist supervising the transaction at this stage and being authorised to prevent any customer from removing any article if he thought fit.

HELD: the taking of the articles from the shelves constituted an offer by the customer to buy and not the acceptance by him of an offer by the chemist to sell, and the sale was, therefore, completed on the acceptance of the price which took place "under the supervision of a registered pharmacist" as required by s. 18 (1) (*a*) (iii) of the Pharmacy and Poisons Act, 1933.

[…]

LORD GODDARD, C.J.: This is a Special Case stated under R.S.C., Ord. 34, r. 1, and agreed between the parties and it turns on s. 18 (1) of the Pharmacy and Poisons Act, 1933, which provides:

> "Subject to the provisions of this Part of this Act, it shall not be lawful – (a) for a person to sell any poison included in Part I of the Poisons List, unless […] the sale is effected by, or under the supervision of, a registered pharmacist."

The defendants have adopted what is called a "self-service" system in some of their shops – in particular, in a shop at 73, Burnt Oak Broadway, Edgware. The system of self-service consists in allowing persons who resort to the shop to go to shelves where goods are exposed for sale and marked with the price. They take the article required and go to the cash desk, where the cashier or assistant sees the article, states the price, and takes the money. In the part of the defendants' shop which is labelled "Chemist's dept." there are on certain shelves ointments and drugs, some of which contain poisonous substances but in such minute quantities that there is no acute danger. These substances come within Part I of the Poisons List, but the medicines in the ordinary way may be sold without a doctor's prescription and can be taken with safety by the purchaser. There is no suggestion that the defendants expose dangerous drugs for sale. Before any person can leave with what he has bought he has to pass the scrutiny and supervision of a qualified pharmacist.

The question for decision is whether the sale is completed before or after the intending purchaser has paid his money, passed the scrutiny of the pharmacist, and left the shop, or, in other words, whether the offer out of which the contract arises is an offer of the purchaser or an offer of the seller.

In *Carlill* v. *Carbolic Smoke Ball Co.* […] a company offered compensation to anybody who, having used the carbolic smoke ball for a certain length of time in a prescribed manner, contracted influenza. One of the inducements held out to people to buy the carbolic smoke ball was a representation that it was a specific against influenza. The plaintiff used it according to the prescription, but, nevertheless, contracted influenza. She sued the Carbolic Smoke Ball Co. for the compensation and was successful. In the Court of Appeal BOWEN, L.J., said ([1893] 1 Q.B. 269):

> "… there can be no doubt that where a person in an offer made by him to another person, expressly or impliedly intimates a particular mode of acceptance as sufficient to make the bargain binding, it is only necessary for the other person to whom such offer is made to follow the indicated method of acceptance; and if the person making the offer, expressly or impliedly intimates in his offer that it will be sufficient to act on the proposal without communicating acceptance of it to himself, performance of the condition is a sufficient acceptance without notification."

Counsel for the plaintiffs says that what the defendants did was to invite the public to come into their shop and to say to them: "Help yourself to any of these articles, all of which are priced", and that that was an offer by the defendants to sell to any person who came into the shop any of the articles so priced. Counsel for the defendants, on the other hand, contends that there is nothing revolutionary in this kind of trading, which, he says, is in no way different from the exposure of goods which a shop-keeper sometimes makes outside or inside his premises, at the same time leaving some goods behind the counter. It is a well-established principle that the mere fact that a shop-keeper exposes goods which indicate to the public that he is willing to treat does not amount to an offer to sell. I do not think I ought to hold that there has been here a complete reversal of that principle merely because a self-service scheme is in operation. In my opinion, what was done here came to no more than that the customer was informed that he could pick up an article and bring it to the shop-keeper, the contract for sale being completed if the shop-keeper accepted the customer's offer to buy. The offer is an offer to buy, not an offer to sell. The fact that the supervising pharmacist is at the place where the money has to be paid is an indication that the purchaser may or may not be informed that the shop-keeper is willing to complete the contract. One has to apply common sense and the ordinary principles of commerce in this matter. If one were to hold that in the case of self-service shops the contract was complete directly when the purchaser picked up the article, serious consequences might result. The property would pass to him at once and he would be able to insist on the shop-keeper allowing him to take it away, even where the shop-keeper might think it very undesirable. On the other hand, once a person had picked up an article he would never be able to put it back and say that he had changed his mind. The shop-keeper could say that the property had passed and he must buy.

It seems to me, therefore, that it makes no difference that a shop is a self-service shop and that the transaction is not different from the normal transaction in a shop. The shop-keeper is not making an offer to sell every article in the shop to any person who may come in, and such person cannot insist on buying by saying: "I accept your offer". Books are displayed in a bookshop and customers are invited to pick them up and look at them even if they do not actually buy them. There is no offer of the shop-keeper to sell before the customer has taken the book to the shop-keeper or his assistant and said that he wants to buy it and the shop-keeper has said: "Yes." That would not prevent the shop-keeper, seeing the book picked up from saying:

> "I am sorry I cannot let you have that book. It is the only copy I have got, and I have already promised it to another customer".

Therefore, in my opinion, the mere fact that a customer picks up a bottle of medicine from a shelf does not amount to an acceptance of an offer to sell, but is an offer by the customer to buy. I feel bound also to say that the sale here was made under the supervision of a pharmacist. There was no sale until the buyer's offer to buy was accepted by the acceptance of the purchase price, and that took place under the supervision of a pharmacist. Therefore, judgment is for the defendants.

Judgment for the defendants.

Solicitors: *A. C. Castle* (for the plaintiffs); *Masons* (for the defendants).

[*Reported by* F. A. AMIES, ESQ., *Barrister-at-Law.*]

3. EWAN McKENDRICK, *Contract Law*, 8th edn, n. 3.3

3.3 Advertisements

The general rule is that a newspaper advertisement is an invitation to treat rather than an offer. In *Partridge* v. *Crittenden* [1968] 1 WLR 1204, the appellant advertised Bramblefinch cocks and hens for sale at a stated price. He was charged with the offence of 'offering for sale' wild live birds contrary to the Protection of Birds Act 1954. It was held that the advertisement was an invitation to treat and not an offer and so the appellant was acquitted. Lord Parker CJ stated that there was 'business sense' in treating such advertisements as invitations to treat because if they were treated as offers the advertiser might find himself contractually obliged to sell more goods than he in fact owned. However, as we have seen, this argument is not conclusive because it could be implied that the offer is only capable of acceptance 'while stocks last'.

Nevertheless there are certain cases where an advertisement may be interpreted as an offer rather than an invitation to treat. The classic example is the case of *Carlill* v. *Carbolic Smoke Ball*[4] [...].

---

[4] See on this case the opinion of LORD GODDARD in *Pharmaceutical Society* v. *Boots*, above, **I.2** (note by the author).

II.   United States of America

1. American Law Institute, *Restatement of the Law Second: Contracts*[5]

§ 26. Preliminary Negotiations
A manifestation of willingness to enter into a bargain is not an offer if the person to whom it is addressed knows or has reason to know that the person making it does not intend to conclude a bargain until he has made a further manifestation of assent.

Comment:
[…]

b. Advertising. Business enterprises commonly secure general publicity for the goods or services they supply or purchase. Advertisements of goods by display, sign, handbill, newspaper, radio or television are not ordinarily intended or understood as offers to sell. The same is true of catalogues, price lists and circulars, even though the terms of suggested bargains may be stated in some detail. It is of course possible to make an offer by an advertisement directed to the general public (see § 29), but there must ordinarily be some language of commitment or some invitation to take action without further communication.

Illustrations:
1. A, a clothing merchant, advertises overcoats of a certain kind for sale at $50. This is not an offer, but an invitation to the public to come and purchase. The addition of the words "Out they go Saturday; First Come First Served" might make the advertisement an offer.
2. A advertises that he will pay $5 for every copy of a certain book that may be sent to him. This is an offer, and A is bound to pay $5 for every copy sent while the offer is unrevoked.
[…]

REPORTER'S NOTE

[…]
Comment b. Illustration 1 is […] supported by many cases […].

---

[5] For information on the "Restatements" see, e.g., E. ALLAN FARNSWORTH, *An Introduction to the Legal System of the United States*, 3rd edn, New York: Oceana, 1996, pp. 87–88; see also MELVIN EISENBERG, *Why Is American Contract Law So Uniform?*, extracts below, **Case 4, III.4.**

2. Farnsworth, Young, Sanger, Cohen, Brooks, *Contracts – Cases and Materials*, 7th edn, pp. 134–36, and Supreme Court of Minnesota, *Lefkowitz* v. *Great Minneapolis Surplus Store*, 86 N.W. 2d 689 (1957)

ADVERTISEMENTS AS OFFERS

[...] The general rule is that an advertisement is not an offer, but rather an invitation by the seller to the buyer to make an offer to purchase.

[...]

If advertisements were held to be offers, what would be a store's position if the demand for the advertised wares exceeded its supply? Might the problem of unexpected demand be solved if sellers were required to have on hand a reasonable supply of advertised merchandise? Another solution might require "first come, first served" to be read into every advertisement. [...].

Whether an advertisement can *ever* be an offer is considered in the next case.

LEFKOWITZ v. GREAT MINNEAPOLIS SURPLUS STORE, 86 N.W.2d 689 (Minn. 1957). [The Great Minneapolis Surplus Store published the following advertisement in a Minneapolis newspaper:

SATURDAY 9 A.M.

2 BRAND NEW PASTEL

MINK 3-SKIN SCARFS

Selling for $89.50

Out they go Saturday, Each $1.00

1 BLACK LAPIN STOLE

Beautiful, worth $139.50 ..... $1.00

FIRST COME

FIRST SERVED

Lefkowitz was the first to present himself on Saturday and demanded the Lapin stole for one dollar. The store refused to sell to him because of the "house rule" that the offer was intended for women only. Lefkowitz sued the store and was awarded $138.50 as damages. The store appealed.]

MURPHY, JUSTICE.... On the facts before us we are concerned with whether the advertisement constituted an offer, and, if so, whether the plaintiff's conduct constituted an acceptance. There are numerous authorities which hold that a particular advertisement in a newspaper or circular letter relating to a sale of articles may be construed by the court as constituting an offer, acceptance of which would complete a contract. [...] The test of whether a binding obligation may originate in advertisements addressed to the general public is "whether the facts show that some performance was promised in positive terms in return for something requested." 1 Williston, Contracts (rev. ed.) § 27. [...] [W]here the offer is clear, definite and explicit, and leaves nothing open for negotiation, it constitutes an offer, acceptance of which will complete the contract. [...] Whether in any individual instance a newspaper advertisement is an offer rather than an invitation to make an offer depends on the legal intention of the parties and the surrounding circumstances. [...] We are of the view on the facts before us that the offer by the defendant of the sale of the Lapin fur was clear, definite, and explicit, and left nothing open for negotiation. [...] The defendant contends that the offer was modified by a "house rule" to the effect that only women were qualified to receive the bargains advertised. The advertisement contained no such restriction. This objection may be disposed of briefly by stating that, while an advertiser has the right at any time before acceptance to modify his offer, he does not have the right, after acceptance, to impose new or arbitrary conditions not contained in the published offer.

Affirmed.

NOTES

[...]

(3) *Consumer Protection.* In GEISMAR v. ABRAHAM & STRAUSS, 439 N.Y.S.2d 1005 (Dist.Ct.1981), a disappointed shopper sued a department store that had advertised a set of china dishes regularly priced at $280 for only $39.95, but had refused to sell them at that price. The court held that since the advertisement was not an offer, there was no breach of contract. But it went on to hold that she could recover $50 under a New York statute providing that any person "injured" by advertising "which is misleading in a material respect" is entitled to recover actual damages or $50, whichever is greater. Many other states have enacted laws dealing with false advertising [...]. In addition, Section 5 of the Federal Trade Commissions Act declares "unfair or deceptive acts or practices" to be unlawful as a matter of federal law.

[...]

III. Switzerland[6]

1. Code des Obligations (*Swiss Code of Obligations*)

Art. 1. Conclusion du contrat. Accord des parties. Conditions générales[7]
(1) Le contrat est parfait lorsque les parties ont, réciproquement et d'une manière concordante, manifesté leur volonté.
(2) Cette manifestation peut être expresse ou tacite.

Art. 1. Conclusion of contract, manifestation of mutual assent, in general.
(1) For a contract to be concluded, a manifestation of the parties' mutual assent is required.
(2) Such manifestation may be either express or implied.

Art. 7. Offre sans engagement et offres publiques.
(1) L'auteur de l'offre n'est pas lié s'il a fait à cet égard des réserves expresses, ou si son intention de ne pas s'obliger résulte soit des circonstances, soit de la nature spéciale de l'affaire.
(2) L'envoi de tarifs, de prix courants, etc., ne constitue pas une offre de contracter.
(3) Le fait d'exposer des marchandises, avec indication du prix, est tenu dans la règle pour une offre.

Art. 7. Offer without obligation, notices, public display
(1) There is no obligation on the part of the offeror if he adds to his offer a declaration that he declines to be bound, or if such reservation arises from the nature of the transaction or the circumstances.
(2) The sending of tariffs, price lists, and the like does not itself constitute an offer.
(3) The display of goods with an indication of their price is, however, as a rule, considered to be an offer.

---

[6] For an introduction to Swiss law see, e.g., Zweigert and Kötz, *An Introduction to Comparative Law*, 3rd edn, Oxford: Oxford University Press, 1998, pp. 167–79; Pascal Pichonnaz, "Switzerland", in Jan M. Smits (ed.), *Elgar Encyclopedia of Comparative Law*, Cheltenham: Edward Elgar Publishing, 2006, pp. 702–8; F. Dessemontet and T. Ansay, *Introduction to Swiss Law*, 3rd edn, The Hague *et al*: Kluwer Law International, 2004.

[7] Switzerland has four national languages: German, French, Italian and Romansh (German being the most widely spoken as a first language, followed by French, Italian and then Romansh). We have chosen to provide the reader with the text in French with an English translation. The texts are also available in German (*Obligationenrecht*) and Italian (*Codice delle obbligazion*).

2. Tribunal fédéral[8] (*Swiss Federal Court*) 20.2.1979 (Nussberger c. K.), ATF 105 II 23

TRIBUNAL FÉDÉRAL[9]
Droit civil

VENTE. CONCLUSION DU CONTRAT. OFFRE PUBLIQUE. ERREUR ESSENTIELLE COMMISE PAR NÉGLIGENCE [...]

Nussberger c. K., 20 février 1979

A.   Werner Nussberger est bijoutier-joaillier à Baden. En automne 1974, il a exposé dans une vitrine proche de son magasin, sis à l'Obere Gasse à Baden, une bague ornée d'une opale bleue et de 25 brillants. Il en avait fixé le prix à 13 800 fr.; mais, par inadvertance, son employée Silvia Meier a mis à la bague une étiquette indiquant un prix de 1380 fr. Le 15 octobre 1974, K. est entré dans la boutique de Nussberger, afin d'acheter la bague en question. Jürg Jauslin l'a servi; il a établi le «certificat de garantie» relatif à la bague, puis l'a remise à K. pour le prix mentionné sur l'étiquette, à savoir 1380 fr. Nussberger a découvert l'erreur le lendemain. Il a déclaré à K. qu'il se départait du contrat et lui a demandé de restituer la bague contre remboursement du prix d'achat de 1380 fr. Aucun accord n'est intervenu.

B.   En janvier 1975, Nussberger a actionné K. devant le Tribunal du district de Baden et a conclu à la restitution de la bague contre paiement simultané du prix de 1380 fr.; subsidiairement, il a demandé que le défendeur soit condamné à lui verser 12 420 fr. Celui-ci a conclu au rejet de l'action; reconventionnellement, il s'est déclaré prêt à rendre la bague au demandeur contre restitution du prix de vente, paiement de 2120 fr. à titre de dommages-intérêts et remboursement des frais de l'expertise qu'il avait requise.
Par jugement du 29 juin 1977, le Tribunal du district de Baden a rejeté l'action; sur appel du demandeur, la 2e Cour civile du Tribunal supérieur du canton d'Argovie a confirmé la décision de première instance le 29 juin 1978.

C.   Le demandeur a recouru en réforme contre l'arrêt du Tribunal supérieur; il a conclu à l'admission de sa demande et au rejet de l'action reconventionnelle. Le défendeur n'a pas déposé de réponse.
Le TF a admis le recours, annulé l'arrêt attaqué et renvoyé la cause à la juridiction cantonale pour nouvelle décision dans le sens des considérants.

---

[8]   *Bundesgericht* (German), *Tribunale Federale* (Italian).

[9]   With regard to the languages used in the decisions of the Federal Tribunal see: La Loi sur le Tribunal fédérale (LTF) 17 June 2005, *Translation*: Art. 54 (1) (Language of the proceedings): "Proceedings are conducted in one of the official languages (German, French, Italian, Romansh), as a general rule in the language of the disputed decision. If the parties use a different official language, this language may be used." See also, the Federal Constitution of Switzerland 18 April 1999 (Current as of 31 January 2006), *Translation*: Art. 70 (1) (Languages): "The official languages of the Confederation are German, French and Italian. Romansh shall be an official language for communicating with persons of Romansh language. [...]".

Motifs:

1.　Selon l'art. 7 al. 3 CO, le fait d'exposer des marchandises, avec indication du prix, est tenu dans la règle pour une offre. C'est aussi le cas, notamment, lorsque la chose à vendre est exposée non dans le magasin, mais, comme en l'espèce, hors de ce dernier, dans une vitrine (*Schönenberger/Jäggi*, n. 28 ad art. 7 CO). L'arrêt attaqué ne renferme aucun indice suivant lequel le défendeur savait ou aurait dû savoir que le demandeur voulait vendre la bague à un prix supérieur à celui qui figurait sur l'étiquette. Le contrat a donc été parfait sitôt que le défendeur a déclaré son acceptation à Jauslin, employé du demandeur (art. 1er al. 1er CO). La juridiction précédente ne constate pas que Jauslin ait fait une nouvelle offre ni que le défendeur l'ait acceptée. Dans ces circonstances, l'attitude de Jauslin importe peu. En revanche, l'indication erronée du prix, due à l'employée Meier, auxiliaire du demandeur, est imputable à celui-ci comme s'il avait lui-même commis la faute; il peut cependant se prévaloir de l'erreur de cette auxiliaire.

2.　a)　Le demandeur invoque l'erreur. […]

Translation

Nussberger v. K., 20 February 1979

A.　Werner Nussberger is a jeweller in Baden. In the autumn of 1974, he put a ring set with a blue opal and 25 diamonds in a window close to his shop located at Obere Gasse in Baden. He had priced the ring at 13 800 Swiss Franks (Fr); but, his employee Silvia Meier inadvertently put a price tag of 1380 Fr on the ring. On 15 October 1974, K. entered Nussberger's shop to buy the ring in question. Jürg Jauslin served him; he established the certificate of guarantee for the ring, then handed it over to K. for the ticket price, *i.e.* 1380 Fr. Nussberger found out about the mistake the next day. He told K. that he was withdrawing from the contract and asked him to return the ring in exchange for a refund of the purchase price of 1380 Fr. No agreement was reached.

B.　In January 1975, Nussberger sued K. before the district court of Baden, claiming restitution of the ring in exchange for payment of the purchase price of 1380 Fr; in addition he asked that the defendant be compelled to pay him 12 420 Fr. The defendant moved for the case to be dismissed and by way of counter claim, K. declared himself ready to give the ring back to the claimant in return for repayment of the purchase price, a payment of 2120 Fr by way of damages and the reimbursement of legal costs.

In its judgment of 29 June 1977, the district court of Baden rejected the claim; on appeal by the claimant, the 2nd Civil Court of the High Court of the Canton of Aargau upheld the decision of the court of first instance on 29 June 1978.

C.　The claimant lodged an appeal against the High Court's decision; petitioning for the admission of his claim and the dismissal of the counterclaim. The defendant did not submit a response. The Federal Court accepted the appeal, annulled the disputed decision and sent the case back to the canton for a new decision.

Decision:

1.　According to Art. 7(3) CO, the display of goods with an indication of their price is, as a rule, considered to be an offer. This is also the case where goods are not exposed in a shop but, as in this instance, outside of the latter, in a window (*Schönenberger/Jäggi*, n. 28 and Art. 7 CO). The decision in question does not contain any indication by which the defendant knew or ought to have known that the applicant wanted to sell the ring at a higher price than shown on the tag. The contract was therefore perfect as soon as the defendant communicated his acceptance to Jauslin, the claimant's employee (Art. 1(1) CO). The previous court is not of the opinion that Jauslin made a new offer nor that the defendant accepted such an offer. In these circumstances, the attitude of Jauslin is of little importance. On the other hand, the incorrect labelling of the price, by employee Ms Meier, auxilliary of the claimant, is attributable to the latter as if he had made the error himself; he may however claim the mistake of his auxilliary.

2. a) The claimant invokes the mistake. […]

3. Luc Thévenoz and Franz Werro (eds), *Commentaire Romand: Code des obligations*, Vol. I (comment by François Dessemontet) (translation of the French original)

Art. 7

[…]

II. Individual, non-binding offer […] (Art. 7(1))

[…]

B. Implied reservation in non-binding offers

5   This reservation [i.e. the rule in Art. 7(1)[10]] results from the circumstances of the case. The first situation that may be envisaged is an advertisement in a newspaper or on a poster. In general, advertisements are not considered to be offers. Excessive advertising may prompt sanctions of a different kind […]. However, one may wonder whether rendering retailers contractually bound to the letter of their advertisements, as is the case abroad, would not also be likely to prevent misleading and false advertising and to compensate their harmful consequences for buyers.

[…]

III. Price lists, current prices, catalogues, etc. (Art. 7(2))

9   In Swiss law, when one sends tariffs, price lists, catalogues, etc., one does not make an offer. The reason for this being quantitative restrictions. Moreover, the solution in the Code of Obligations can possibly be explained by the fact that it is not an offer addressed to anyone in particular. […] Some authors nevertheless consider that there could be an offer if the validity period of the catalogue is specified.

---

[10]   Added by the author.

10   Consequently, price lists, catalogues, etc. are not considered binding unless accompanied by an offer relating to them.

IV.   Display of goods (Art. 7(3))

11   Art. 7(3) of the Code of Obligations establishes the opposite rule to Art. 7(2): goods displayed are **offered** for sale in the legal sense of the word.

12   This rule is only applicable to **merchandise**. Owing to its clear text, the Federal Court does not apply it by analogy to services, e.g. entry to the cinema. One may wonder whether this point of view is justified in a society in which services and intangible goods or services play a much more significant role than in the past.

13   **When the price is indicated** on displayed goods, the action of the shopkeeper displaying the merchandise is considered to be an offer. [...]

14   [...] An offer through the intermediary of a television channel or the Internet is often an offer by way of displaying the merchandise; it all depends on the programme or the website: if it allows you to place a firm order, the virtual window can contain offers ("add to basket") and invitations to tender ("to obtain further information"), or just advertisements ("car X from £ [...]").

[...]

IV. Germany[11]

1. Bürgerliches Gesetzbuch (BGB) (*German Civil Code*)

§ 145. **Bindung an den Antrag.**
Wer einem anderen die Schließung eines Vertrags anträgt, ist an den Antrag gebunden, es sei denn, dass er die Gebundenheit ausgeschlossen hat.

§ 145. *Binding effect of an offer*
Any person who proposes to enter into a contract with another is bound by the offer, unless he has excluded the possibility of being bound by it.

2. Reichsgericht (*Supreme Court of the former German Empire*) 7.11.1931, RGZ 133, 388

V. Zivilsenat, Urteil vom 7. November 1931 in Sachen D (Kl.) w. Stadtgemeinde B (Bekl.)

Der Kläger schrieb in großen Tageszeitungen und in einer von ihm herausgegebenen Wochenschrift über die Aufführungen des städtischen Theaters in B. Da seine Kritiken der Stadtverwaltung missfielen, beschloss sie, ihm den Zutritt zum Theater zu untersagen. Dies teilte sie ihm […] fernmündlich mit. Trotzdem besuchte der Kläger die am Abend dieses Tages veranstaltete Aufführung von „Faust, Erster Teil" mit einer Eintrittskarte, die er sich nach Empfang jener Mitteilung für 6 Reichsmark hatte besorgen lassen. Vor Schluss der Vorstellung wurde er durch ein Mitglied der Theaterleitung, das einen Polizeioffizier zuzog, aus dem Theater gewiesen. Das wiederholte sich bei der Aufführung von „Faust, Zweiter Teil" […], zu der sich der Kläger ebenfalls mittels einer durch einen anderen für 6 Reichsmark besorgten Karte Eintritt verschafft hatte.

Mit der Klage begehrt der Kläger […] Feststellung, dass die Beklagte verpflichtet sei, ihm auf gültige Eintrittskarten hin Einlass in die Vorstellungen zu gewähren […].

Gründe:

[E]ine […] Bindung des Theaterunternehmers wird im Schrifttum auf der Grundlage bejaht, dass die Ankündigung einer Theatervorstellung ein bindendes Vertragsangebot an das Publikum sei, welches jedermann durch das Verlangen nach Aushändigung einer Eintrittskarte annehmen könne […]. Aber der bloßen Ankündigung ist keine solche Bedeutung beizumessen. Sie ist nach dem erkennbaren Willen des Unternehmers und nach der dem Wesen der Sache entsprechenden allgemeinen Auffassung – ebenso wie

---

[11]   See on German contract law from a comparative perspective, ULRICH MAGNUS, "German Contract Law in the International Arena: A Review of The German Law of Contract: A Comparative Treatise", 81 (2006) *Tul. L. Rev.* 565.

sonstige an die Allgemeinheit ergehende Ankündigungen und Zusendungen von Preislisten – lediglich eine unverbindliche Bereiterklärung, Theaterbesuchsverträge abzuschließen, aber nicht schon Teil des demnächst zu schließenden Vertrags. [...]

Translation[12]

The plaintiff was a theatre critic who wrote reviews of performances in the city theatre in B. His articles appeared in the major daily papers and in a weekly magazine which he himself publishes. Disgruntled by his criticisms, the defendant city authorities decided to deny him access to their theatre, and communicated this decision to him by telephone [...] Despite this communication, the plaintiff attended a performance of Faust, Part I that very evening, having had a ticket purchased for him for 6RM. During the performance one of the theatre staff, accompanied by a police officer, required him to leave the theatre. The same thing occurred at a performance of Faust, Part II [...], the plaintiff having again procured an entrance ticket through an intermediary for 6RM.

The plaintiff [...] sought a declaration that the defendant was bound to admit him to performances for which he held a valid ticket [...].

Reasons

[...] While recognising that theatre operators are under no duty to contract, some writers put them under a rather similar obligation by arguing that when they advertise a forthcoming theatrical event they are making a binding offer to the public which anyone can accept by asking for and obtaining a ticket [...]. But it is wrong to attribute such force to a mere announcement. It is obviously the intention of the entrepreneur, and it is obvious to the public in this situation that this is simply a non-binding declaration of readiness to contract such as one finds in other public announcements or in the circulation of price lists. While the announcement betokens readiness to sell tickets, it does not form part of any contract subsequently concluded. [...]

3. Bundesgerichtshof (*German Federal Court*) 16.1.1980, NJW 1980, 1388

BGH, Urt. v. 16.1.1980

Aus den Gründen: [...] Nach herrschender Meinung ist aber das Ausstellen von Schaufensterware, auch wenn sie mit Preisangaben versehen ist, keine Vertragsofferte im Sinne des § 145 BGB, vielmehr wird der Kunde durch die ausgestellte Ware erst aufgefordert, ein verbindliches Vertragsangebot abzugeben (vgl. *Palandt-Heinrichs*, BGB, 39. Aufl., § 145 Anm. 1). [...]. [Der BGH schliesst sich im Folgenden dieser Auffassung an, der Verf.]

---

12 Source of the translation: www.utexas.edu/law/academics/centers/transnational/ work/german-cases/cases_reich.shtml?07nov1931.

Translation

[…] The prevailing view in case law and academic writing is that the display of goods in a window is not an offer within the meaning of § 145 BGB even if the price is indicated. On the contrary, the display of goods invites the customer to make an offer […]. [The Federal Court shares this opinion.]

4. Bundesgerichtshof (*German Federal Court*) 26.1.2005, NJW 2005, 976

BGH, Urt. v. 26.1.2005 – VIII ZR 79/04

Zum Sachverhalt: Die Klägerin (Kl.) veräussert Computer nebst Zubehör über eine Website im Internet. Im Januar 2003 legte der zuständige Mitarbeiter der Kl. für das Notebook der Firma S, Typ V.S., einen Verkaufspreis von 2650 € fest und gab diesen in das EDV-gesteuerte Warenwirtschaftssystem der Kl. ein. […] Als Ergebnis dieses Vorgangs enthielt die Datenbank jedoch nicht den eingegebenen Betrag von 2650 €, sondern einen Verkaufspreis von 245 €. […] Der Beklagte bestellte […] ein Notebook […] zu dem auf der Internetseite angegebenen Verkaufspreis von 245 €.

Aus den Gründen: […] II. […] 1. […] Das Berufungsgericht ist davon ausgegangen, dass die Kl. nicht bereits mit der Präsentation des Notebooks auf ihrer Internetseite ein gemäss § 145 BGB verbindliches Angebot abgegeben hat, sondern dass sie insoweit lediglich zur Abgabe von Angeboten aufgefordert hat (invitatio ad offerendum). Daraus folgt, dass ein Angebot erst in der Bestellung der Beklagten […] zu dem auf der Internetseite der Kl. angegebenen Verkaufspreis von 245 € zu sehen ist. […]

Translation

Facts: The claimant company sells computers as well as computer accessories on a website. In January 2003, the claimant company's employee responsible for such matters, set the price of a laptop, model VS made by company S, at €2650 and entered this into the computer program that manages the merchandise […] The computer program did not register the entered amount of €2650 in the database, but rather a selling price of €245. […] The defendant ordered […] a laptop […] at the price of €245 as shown on the website.

Decision: […] II. […] 1. […] The Court of Appeal is of the opinion that the presentation, by the claimant company, of the laptop computer on its website did not constitute an offer within the meaning of § 145 BGB, but simply an invitation to treat (*invitatio ad offerendum*). Consequently, it is only the defendant's order that is considered to be an offer […] for the price of €245 which appears on the website. […]

V. France

1. Code civil français (*French Civil Code*)

DES CONTRATS OU DES OBLIGATIONS CONVENTIONNELLES EN GÉNÉRAL

OF CONTRACTS AND OF CONVENTIONAL OBLIGATIONS IN GENERAL

Art. 1101
Le contrat est une convention par laquelle une ou plusieurs personnes s'obligent, envers une ou plusieurs autres, à donner, à faire ou à ne pas faire quelque chose.

Art. 1101
A contract is an agreement by which one or several persons bind themselves, towards one or several others, to transfer, to do or not to do something.

Art. 1582
(1)   La vente est une convention par laquelle l'un s'oblige à livrer une chose, et l'autre à la payer.
[…]

Art. 1582
(1)   A sale is an agreement by which one person binds himself to deliver a thing, and another to pay for it. […]

Art. 1589
(1)   La promesse de vente vaut vente, lorsqu'il y a consentement réciproque des deux parties sur la chose et sur le prix.
[…]

Art. 1589
(1)   A promise of sale is the same as a sale, where there is reciprocal consent of both parties as to the thing and the price. […]

2. Cour de cassation[13] (civ. 3e) (*Court of Cassation, 3rd Civil Law Chamber*) 28.11.1968 (*Maltzkorn c. Braquet*), JCP 1969.II.15797

15797   CONTRATS ET OBLIGATIONS. – Offre de contracter. Offre au public. Obligation du pollicitant. Vente d'immeuble (Cass. civ. 3e, 28 novembre 1968; Maltzkorn c. Braquet) […].

LA COUR; – *Sur le moyen unique:* – Vu l'article 1589 du Code civil; – Attendu que l'offre faite au public lie le pollicitant à l'égard du premier acceptant dans les mêmes conditions que l'offre faite à personne déterminée; – Attendu qu'il résulte des énonciations de l'arrêt partiellement confirmatif que Maltzkorn, ayant pris connaissance d'une annonce parue dans le journal *L'Ardennais* du 23 mai 1961, proposant la vente d'un terrain déterminé au prix de 25'000 F, fit connaître à Braquet, propriétaire, qu'il acceptait son offre; que cependant Braquet prétendit n'être pas engagé par cette offre; – Attendu que pour écarter la demande de Maltzkorn, tendant à la régularisation de la vente, l'arrêt relève que «l'offre faite par la voie de la presse, d'un bien ne pouvant être acquis que par une seule personne, ne saurait être assimilée à l'offre faite à une personne déterminée; qu'elle constitue seulement un appel à des amateurs éventuels et ne peut, en conséquence lier son auteur à l'égard d'un acceptant»; qu'en statuant par ce motif d'ordre général, alors qu'elle constatait que Braquet avait déclaré que «la ferme n'était toujours pas vendue» lorsqu'il avait reçu notification de l'acceptation, et sans relever aucune circonstance d'où elle ait pu déduire que l'annonce constituait seulement une invitation à engager des pourparlers ou que l'offre de Braquet comportait des réserves, la Cour d'appel n'a pas donné de base légale à sa décision;

Par ces motifs: – Casse et annule l'arrêt rendu entre les parties par la Cour d'appel de Nancy, le 24 novembre 1966, et renvoie devant la Cour d'appel de Reims.

MM. de Montéra, prés.; Cornuey, rapp.; Paucot, av. gén.; Me Coulet, av.

Translation

The Court; – […] Under article 1589 of the Civil Code; – Whereas an offer made to the public at large binds the offeror *vis-à-vis* the first person who accepts it, in the same way as an offer made to a specific person; – Whereas it results from the partially confirmative decision that Maltzkorn, having become aware of an advertisement proposing the sale of a given piece of land for 25 000 F in the newspaper *Ardennais* on 23 May 1961, made known to Braquet, the owner, that he accepted the latter's offer; that, however, Braquet claimed not to be bound by the offer; – Whereas the grounds for dismissal of Maltzkorn's claim for an order requiring the sale to be completed, as set out in the contested judgment, state that "an offer made in a newspaper for the sale of an asset which can only be

---

[13]   In private law matters, the *Cour de cassation* is the highest court in France. It has the power to confirm a judgment or to quash and annul it. If quashed and annulled, the case is sent before another court of first instance or a court of appeal in order to deliver a decision respecting the ruling of the *Cour de cassation*. This process is called the renvoi. The *Cour de cassation* rules on points of law, not on the facts. The facts of the case are re-examined by the court of first instance or a court of appeal.

purchased by one person cannot be equated with an offer made to a specific person; it constitutes merely an invitation to treat addressed to potential purchasers, and cannot therefore bind the person by whom it is made *vis-à-vis* a person who accepts it"; – Whereas in making that general ruling, despite its finding that Braquet, upon receiving notice of the acceptance, had stated that "the farm has not yet been sold", and without mentioning any factor which could have prompted it to infer that the advertisement constituted merely an invitation to enter into negotiations or that Braquet's offer was subject to any qualification, the Court of Appeal failed to establish any legal basis for its decision;

Decides: – To quash and annul the decision of the Court of Appeal in Nancy given on 24 November 1966 and hereby sends the case before the Court of Appeal in Reims for a decision.

Messrs. de Montéra, President; Cornuey, Reporter; Paucot, Advocate General; Ms Coulet, Counsel.

3. FRANÇOIS TERRÉ, PHILIPPE SIMLER, YVES LEQUETTE, *Droit civil: Les obligations* (9th edn) (translation of the French original)

109 *The precision of the offer* ◊ An expression of willingness only constitutes an offer if it is sufficiently *precise*. In order for the simple acceptance of an offer to be adequate to form a contract, the offer must clearly specify the conditions of the potential contract by setting out, at the very least, its essential elements.

[...]

110 *The firmness of the offer* ◊ In order for a proposal to enter into a contract to qualify as an offer, its acceptance alone must suffice to form a contract. Consequently, a proposal would not constitute an offer, even if it contained the essential elements of the proposed contract, if the person who made it had signalled his desire not to be bound if it were accepted. This is also the case where the person proposing to enter into a contract reserves the possibility to choose the other contracting party.

Such a reservation could be expressly stipulated: a manufacturer or retailer draws up a detailed draft contract for use with potential customers stipulating all the while that the offer is "subject to confirmation". As a result the person who initiates the contract has the intention of reserving the final say in the conclusion of the contract for himself; he remains free to accept or not to accept orders made on the strength of his proposal to enter into a contract. The reservation causes a role reversal: the addressee of the proposal to contract becomes the offeror even though he has adhered to the conditions set out by the person proposing to contract.

A reservation may also be *implied,* resulting from the nature of the proposed agreement. This is the case where the proposal to enter into a contract is addressed to the public and is of an *intuitu personae* character, that is to say that the identity of the contracting party is a decisive factor. By publishing an advert to rent out a building or to fill a job opening, the author obviously does not intend to be bound to accept the first person who presents himself and this is so even if this person were to accept all the terms of the lease or employment contract that would be put to him. The author of the advertisement remains free to choose to contract with the party who appears the most suitable from amongst those who respond to his proposal, or indeed to choose not to contract with any of them. The same is true for an offer to give someone credit because the person who proposes the contract must be able to assess the solvency of the person who accepts. Here again, the offeror will not be the person who initiated the contractual process but the person who responded to this first move.

One cannot however consider an offer to be disqualified from being an invitation to enter into negotiations just because it is accompanied by a reservation. It all depends on the nature of the reservation.

[…] An offer made "while stocks last" remains a valid offer. As long as there is still stock remaining, the offeror must honour all the orders that he receives. Far from depending on the will of the person who commits himself, the validity of the offer depends on whether the terms are sufficiently objective to make judicial control possible […]

111 Consumer Protection ◊ Certain rules on consumer protection stipulate that the offer to contract must necessarily come from a professional, even if he did not take the first step in the contractual process. These texts also regulate the form of the contract, the content of the offer as well as the period during which it must remain open. These measures are in line with a group of measures that aim to put the consumer in such a position so as he is well informed and thus able to give his consent after careful consideration […]

4. Philippe Le Tourneau *et al.*, *Droit de la responsabilité et des contrats*, n° 3713 (translation of the French original)

B. Special obligations arising expressly or implicitly from contracts concluded by a professional

[…]

2° Loyalty of the contracting party

[…]

g. Moral duties

[…]

3713 Application: taking into account the advertising material of professionals. Principle. A strong trend is emerging – one which seems to us to be excellent – to take into account a professional's *advertising material*, or at least those materials that are given to the client (catalogues, brochures, pamphlets, leaflets, but not posters or advertisements in the media – […]), when analysing contractual obligations. In other words, the message in the advertisement would engage the responsibility of the retailer who disseminates it: its content would be integrated into the contract as if it were, no more or less than an annex to it, on the condition that the contract does not include a provision stating otherwise [...]. Basically, a sufficiently precise and definite advertisement constitutes an *offer to contract* which, when its terms are accepted by the customer, binds the advertiser, as the content is integrated into the contract [...]. It is a way of ensuring truthfulness: in this instance, truthfulness to oneself, to one's word and writings, in a word, requiring that all professionals *act consistently* [...].

VI.   Italy[14]

1. Codice civile italiano (*Italian Civil Code*)

Art. 1336.   Offerta al pubblico.
(1) L'offerta al pubblico, quando contiene gli estremi essenziali del contratto alla cui conclusione è diretta, vale come proposta, salvo che risulti diversamente dalle circonstanze o dagli usi.
[...]

Art. 1336.   *Offer to the public.*
(1)   An offer to the public, when it contains the essential terms of the contract toward whose formation it is directed, is effective as an offer, unless it appears otherwise from the circumstances or usage [...].

2. Pietro Rescigno, *Codice Civile* (7th edn), comment on Art. 1336 (translation of the Italian original)

1 *Conditions of the offer.*   An offer to the public may be individual or multiple according to whether the proposed contract concerns one or many objects; in the first case, the offer expires with the first acceptance, in the second case, all acceptances that correspond to available goods are effective. [...].

2 *Offer to the public and invitation to treat.*   An offer to the public can be distinguished from a simple invitation to make an offer and/or a proposal that, even if it is addressed to a circle of persons, aims to attract an individual offer which must then in turn be accepted by the person who initiated the proposal [...] Advertisement of a product normally constitutes an invitation to purchase [...]; however, according to the decision of the Tribunal of Milan on 3 August 1949, advertisements in newspapers can constitute valid offers when the essential elements of the contract are present, T Milano 3.8.1948, GI, 1949, I, 2, 154. [...]

5 *Multiple acceptances.*   Where there are multiple, simultaneous acceptances of an offer (that is to say where there is no determinable order of preference), the offeror must be given the power to choose [...].

---

[14]   For a brief introduction to Italian law, see Zweigert and Kötz, above n. 6, pp. 104–7; Barbara Pozzo, 'Italy', in Jan M. Smits (ed.), *Elgar Encyclopedia of Comparative Law*, Cheltenham: Edward Elgar Publishing Ltd, 2006, pp. 352–56. On the Codice civile, see, e.g., Giorgio Cian, "Fünfzig Jahre italienischer Codice civile:, *ZEuP* 1993, pp. 120–31.

6   Casuistry.   [...]
6.4.   According to BIANCA, the display of goods for sale in shops or in supermarkets is the equivalent of an offer made to the public. In such a case, the conclusion of the contract would occur at the moment when the goods that one wishes to buy in exchange for payment of a price are presented at the cash desk. [...]

VII.   The Netherlands[15]

1. Burgerlijk Wetboek (*Dutch Civil Code*)

Art. 3:37
(1)   Tenzij anders is bepaald, kunnen verklaringen, met inbegrip van mededelingen, in iedere vorm geschieden, en kunnen zij in een of meer gedragingen besloten liggen.
[...]

Art. 3:37
(1)   Unless otherwise provided, declarations, including communications, can be made in any form; declarations may be inferred from conduct.
[...]

Art. 6:217
(1)   Een overeenkomst komt tot stand door een aanbod en de aanvaarding daarvan.
[...]

Art. 6:217
(1) A contract is formed by an offer and its acceptance.
[...]

Art. 6:227
De verbintenissen die partijen op zich nemen, moeten bepaalbaar zijn.

Art. 6:227
The obligations which parties assume must be determinable.

2. DANNY BUSCH *et al.* (eds), *The Principles of European Contract Law and Dutch Law: A Commentary,* Arts 2:201–2:208 (pp. 105 ff.) (comment by T. HARTLIEF)

[...]

1. General. *a) The offer and acceptance model.* A contract comes into being by the mutual consent of the parties. In general the mutual consent is brought about when an offer is accepted. Offer and acceptance are both juridical acts and as such are not only governed by Art. 6:217 BW ff. but also by the general provisions on juridical acts in Book 3, Title 2. [...]

---

[15]   For a brief introduction to Dutch law, see ZWEIGERT AND KÖTZ, above n. 6, pp. 101–3; J. SMITS, "The Netherlands", in Smits, (ed.), above n. 14, pp. 493–96; J.M.J. CHORUS, P.-H. M. GERVIER, E.H. HONDIUS AND A.K. KOEKKOEK, *Introduction to Dutch Law*, 3rd edn, Deventer/Boston: Kluwer, 1999.

2. Existence of the contract. *a) Requirements for an offer to become effective.* Being a proposal to make a contract, an offer becomes a contract when it is accepted. A proposal amounts to an offer if that proposal is defined in such a manner that by its acceptance a contract is immediately formed. That means that the requirements of Art. 6:227 BW have to be met. [...] An acceptance is the expression of consenting to the terms of an offer. Both the offer and acceptance are the expression of intention which can be expressed by words (spoken or written), conduct and even by not acting (see Art. 3:37 (1) BW [...]). *b) Proposals to the public.* Proposals to the public may take many forms: advertisements, posters, circulars, window displays, invitations to tender, auctions etc. [...] *c) An offer or simply an invitation to make an offer?* An offer has to be distinguished from an invitation to negotiate or to make an offer. Interpreting the expressions and conduct of the parties is decisive. [...] In general advertising a specific good for sale, like a house or a car, is an invitation to negotiate or to make an offer. See Hoge Raad 10 April 1981, NJ 1981, 532 (Hofland v. Hennis) [...]

3. Goods and services offered at stated prices. The Dutch Code does not contain a provision like Art. 2:201 paragraph (3) PECL, even though, in general, a public proposal to supply goods or services at stated prices is presumed to be an offer to sell or supply at that price until the stock of goods, or the supplier's capacity to supply the service, becomes exhausted. [...]

VIII.   Serbia

Zakon o obligacionim odnosima
(*The Law of Contract and Torts*)

Član 32.   Ponuda.
(1)   Ponuda je predlog za zaključenje ugovora učinjen određenom licu, koji sadrži sve bitne sastojke ugovora tako da bi se njegovim prihvatanjem mogao zaključiti ugovor. [...]

Art. 32.   Offer.
(1)   An offer shall be a proposal for entering into a contract made to a specific person and containing all essential constitutive elements of the contract, so that its acceptance would amount to entering into the contract.
[...]

Član 33.   Opšta ponuda.
Predlog za zaključenje ugovora učinjen neodređenom broju lica, koji sadrži bitne sastojke ugovora čijem je zaključenju namenjen, važi kao ponuda, ukoliko drukčije ne proizlazi iz okolnosti slučaja ili običaja.

Art. 33.   General Offer.
A proposal to conclude a contract made to an unspecified number of persons and containing the essential constitutive elements of the contract envisaged by the proposal shall be valid as an offer, unless something else follows from the circumstances of the case or the usage.

Član 34.   Izlaganje robe.
Izlaganje robe sa označenjem cene smatra se kao ponuda, ukoliko drukčije ne proizlazi iz okolnosti slučaja ili običaja.

Art. 34.   Display of Merchandise.
Display of merchandise with a price indicated shall be considered to be an offer, unless something else follows from the circumstances of the case or from the usage.

Član 35.   Slanje kataloga i oglasa.
(1)   Slanje kataloga, cenovnika, tarifa i drugih obaveštenja, kao i oglasi učinjeni putem štampe, letaka, radija, televizije ili na koji drugi način, ne predstavljaju ponudu za zaključenje ugovora, nego samo poziv da se učini ponuda pod objavljenim uslovima.
(2)   Ali če pošiljalac takvih poziva odgovarati za štetu, koju bi pretrpeo ponudilac, ako bez osnovanog razloga nije prihvatio njegovu ponudu.

Art. 35.   Sending Catalogues and Advertisements.
(1) Sending catalogues, price-lists, tariffs and other information, as well as advertisements published in the press, presented by way of leaflets, by radio, television or in some other way, shall not be considered as an offer to enter into contract, but only as an invitation to treat under the terms announced.
(2) However, the sender of such an invitation shall be liable for damage caused to the offeror, after failing, without a justified reason, to accept the offer.

IX. Lithuania

Lietuvos Respublikos Civilinis kodeksas
(*Civil Code of the Republic of Lithuania*)

6.171 straipsnis. Viešoji oferta.
1.   Viešąja oferta laikomas visiems skirtas pasiūlymas sudaryti sutartį, taip pat prekių pažymėtomis kainomis išdėstymas parduotuvės vitrinoje ar lentynoje arba atlyginimo pažadėjimas už tam tikrų veiksmų atlikimą.
2.   Viešoji oferta, atšaukta tokia pat forma, kaip buvo pareikšta, tampa negaliojanti, nors apie jos atšaukimą sužinojo ne visi asmenys, kuriems oferta buvo žinoma.
3.   Viešąja oferta nelaikomi kainoraščiai, prospektai, katalogai, tarifai ir kita informacinė medžiaga, išskyrus įstatymų nustatytas išimtis.

Art. 6.171.   Offer to the public.
1.   An offer to the public is a proposal for concluding a contract where such proposal is addressed to everyone, also the display of goods with the indicated prices on the shelves in a shop or in the shop window, or a promise to pay for the performance of certain actions.
2.   Revocation of an offer to the public, if made in the same form as the offer, shall extinguish the offer even though not all persons who are aware of the offer have received the notice on the revocation.
3.   Price-lists, prospectuses with prices, priced catalogues, tariffs and other information materials shall not be considered an offer to the public unless there are exceptions established by law.

X. Russia[16]

Гражданский кодекс Российской Федерации
(*Civil Code of the Russian Federation*)

Статья 435. Оферта.
(1) Офертой признается адресованное одному или нескольким конкретным лицам предложение, которое достаточно определенно и выражает намерение лица, сделавшего предложение, считать себя заключившим договор с адресатом, которым будет принято предложение. Оферта должна содержать существенные условия договора.

[…]

Art. 435. Offer.
(1) *A proposal addressed to one or several concrete persons shall be recognised as an offer if it is sufficiently precise and expresses the intention of the person who made it, to be bound by the contract with the addressee who accepts it. The offer shall contain the essential terms of the contract. […]*

Статья 437. Приглашение делать оферты. Публичная оферта.
(1) Реклама и иные предложения, адресованные неопределенному кругу лиц, рассматриваются как приглашение делать оферты, если иное прямо не указано в предложении.
(2) Содержащее все существенные условия договора предложение, из которого усматривается воля лица, делающего предложение, заключить договор на указанных в предложении условиях с любым, кто отзовется, признается офертой (публичная оферта).

Art. 437. Invitation to Make an Offer. Public Offer.
(1) *Advertisements and other proposals, addressed to an indefinite circle of persons, shall be regarded as an invitation to make an offer, unless the contrary is expressly indicated in the proposal.*
(2) *A proposal containing all the essential terms of the contract and expressing the willingness of the person who is making the proposal, to conclude the contract on the terms indicated in the proposal, with any person responding to it, shall be recognized as a public offer.*

---

[16] For a brief introduction to Russian contract law, see CHRISTOPHER OSAKWE, "Modern Russian Law of Contracts: A Functional Analysis", 24 (2002) *Loy. L.A. Int'l & Comp. L. Rev.* 113. On Russian law in general, see WILLIAM BUTLER, 'Russia', in Smits (ed.), above n. 14, pp. 630–41. For a detailed account, see WILLIAM BUTLER, *Russian Law*, 2nd edn, Oxford: Oxford University Press, 2006.

XI. China[17]

1. 中华人民共和国合同法 *(Contract Law of the People's Republic of China)*

第 13 条

当事人订立合同，采取要约、承诺方式。

Art. 13. *Offer–Acceptance.*
A contract is concluded by the exchange of an offer and an acceptance.

第 14 条 要约是希望和他人订立合同的意思表示，该意思表示应当符合下列规定：

（一）内容具体确定；

（二）表明经受要约人承诺，要约人即受该意思表示约束。

Art. 14. *Definition of Offer.*
An offer is a party's manifestation of intention to enter into a contract with the other party, which shall comply with the following:
(i) Its terms are specific and definite;
(ii) It indicates that upon acceptance by the offeree, the offeror will be bound thereby.

第 15 条

要约邀请是希望他人向自己发出要约的意思表示。寄送的价目表、拍卖公告、招标公告、招股说明书、商业广告等为要约邀请。

商业广告的内容符合要约规定的，视为要约。

Art. 15. *Invitation to Offer.*
An invitation to offer is a party's manifestation of intention to invite the other party to make an offer thereto. A delivered price list, announcement of auction, call for tender, prospectus, or commercial advertisement, etc. is an invitation to offer.

A commercial advertisement is deemed an offer if its contents meets the requirements of an offer.

---

[17] For an account of Chinese contract law and its sources of inspiration, see C. STEPHEN HSU, "Contract Law of the People's Republic of China", 16 (2007) *Minn. J. Int'l L.* 115; DANHAN HUANG, "The UNIDROIT Principles and their Influence in the Modernization of Contract Law in the People's Republic of China", *Unif. L. Rev.* 2003, pp. 107–17; JOHN H. MATHESON, "Convergence, Culture and Contract Law in China", 15 (2006) *Minn. J. Int'l. L.* 329; PATRICIA PATTISON AND DANIEL HERRON, "The Mountains Are High and the Emperor is Far Away: Sanctity of Contract in China", 40 (2003) *Am. Bus. L.J.* 459; JING XI, "The Impact of the UNIDROIT-Principles on Chinese Legislation", in Eleanor Cashin Ritaine and Eva Lein (eds), *The UNIDROIT Principles 2004 – Their Impact on Contractual Practice, Jurisprudence and Codification*, Zurich/Basel/Geneva: Schulthess, 2007, pp. 107–18; YUQUING ZHANG AND DANHAN HUANG, "The New Contract Law in the People's Republic of China and the UNIDROIT Principles of International Commercial Contracts: A Brief Comparison", *Unif. L. Rev.* 2000, pp. 429–41. For a brief overview on Chinese law, see, e.g., ZWEIGERT AND KÖTZ, above n. 6, pp. 286–94.

2. BING LING, *Contract Law in China*

3.2.2   *Offer as Distinguished from Invitation to Offer*

[...]

3.2.2.2   Display of merchandise in shops

3.015   This is not expressly dealt with in the Contract Law. The Consumer Rights and Interests Protection Law requires all merchandise supplied by shops to be marked with the price. Most commentators follow the prevailing position in civil law jurisdictions [Footnote with references to the Swiss Code of Obligations, Art. 7(3) and to the Civil Code of the Republic of China (Taiwan)] and consider the display of merchandise with the selling price marked as an offer. The display of merchandise with the selling price marked usually indicated more of an intention to sell the merchandise upon acceptance by the customer than an intention to bargain with the customer, but the customary practice in a particular place or trade must be taken into account. Price lists that are not sent to customers but are displayed in a shop should presumably also be treated as offers, for they seem to indicate a higher degree of readiness on the merchant's part to sell the listed merchandise upon acceptance by the customer than delivered price lists.

XII. The Vienna Sales Convention and the Principles of Contract Law[18]

1. United Nations Convention on Contracts for the International Sale of Goods (CISG)[19]

Art. 8

(1) For the purposes of this Convention statements made by and other conduct of a party are to be interpreted according to his intent where the other party knew or could not have been unaware what that intent was.

(2) If the preceding paragraph is not applicable, statements made by and other conduct of a party are to be interpreted according to the understanding that a reasonable person of the same kind as the other party would have had in the same circumstances.

[...]

Art. 14

(1) A proposal for concluding a contract addressed to one or more specific persons constitutes an offer if it is sufficiently definite and indicates the intention of the offeror to be bound in case of acceptance. A proposal is sufficiently definite if it indicates the goods and expressly or implicitly fixes or makes provision for determining the quantity and the price.

(2) A proposal other than one addressed to one or more specific persons is to be considered merely as an invitation to make offers, unless the contrary is clearly indicated by the person making the proposal.

2. JOHN O. HONNOLD, *Uniform Law for International Sales under the 1980 United Nations Convention*, 3rd edn

Article 14.
Criteria for an Offer

133 The basic criterion for an offer, under prevailing law and the Convention, is whether one party has indicated to another "the intention ... to be bound in case of acceptance". In applying this standard, two subsidiary factors need to be taken into account – the number of people addressed and the definiteness of the proposal. These standards are set forth in [Art. 14 of the Convention].

---

[18] For an overview of the Vienna Sales Convention, see, e.g., GOODE, KRONKE AND MCKENDRICK, *Transnational Commercial Law*, Oxford: Oxford University Press, 2007, 7.01 ff.

[19] On the conditions of application of the Vienna Sales Convention, see below, **Case 9**.

134 **A. Indication of Intent to be Bound**

When one party is in doubt over whether the other intends to be bound or merely to open negotiations the question can usually be resolved quickly by phone or wire. Moreover, doubts suggested by the bare text of the parties' statements will often be dissipated when (as Art. 8 requires) those statements are interpreted in their full context, including "the negotiations, any practices which the parties have established between themselves, usages and any subsequent conduct of the parties." In short, the parties' understanding is a question of fact that is individual to each transaction; the general guides in Article 14 for interpreting the parties' intent, to which we now turn, play subordinate and supporting roles.

135 **(1) Communications to an Indefinite Group: "Public Offers"**

Article 14 incorporates the generally accepted premise that a party may make an offer to as large a group as it wishes. However, a communication addressed to a large group, if construed as an offer, can involve practical difficulties and hazards. For example, sellers often give wide distribution to catalogues describing a line of goods and indicating prices. Some months may be required for the preparation, printing, and distribution of the catalogue. During this period some of the goods may become unavailable because of heavy demand, shortage of materials, or other production difficulties, and cost increases may call for readjustment of prices. If supply or production difficulties are widespread, or if the general price level rises sharply, the seller may face a flood of orders. If these orders should be "acceptances" of an "offer," the result could be ruin for the seller and a windfall for the buyers. In these settings a "reasonable person" (Art. 8(2)) would not think that the catalogue "indicates an intention … to be bound" (Art. 14(1)) and courts have been reluctant to construe communications to create such hazards.

These practical considerations are reflected in Article 14(2): If a proposal is not "addressed to *one or more specific persons,*" it is not an offer "unless the contrary is *clearly indicated* by the person making the proposal."

136 **(a) "Specific Persons".** Even if a proposal is addressed to "one or more specific persons" it is not an offer unless under the basic test of paragraph (1) it "indicates the intention of the offeror to be bound in case of acceptance." This test may be decisive when the line between paragraph (1) and paragraph (2) is difficult to draw.

To take a common case: Supplier mails a catalogue to 500 prospective buyers; each envelope is addressed to a specific person. Is this a proposal "addressed to one or more specific persons" and therefore governed by paragraph (1)? The answer should be No. The purpose underlying the dividing line between paragraphs (1) and (2) is to avoid the hazards latent in widespread communications mentioned at §135. To this end, the phrase "addressed to one or more specific persons" should refer to communications that are *restricted to* the addressees; a seller who mails out a catalogue normally intends as wide a distribution as possible and would be glad for the addressee to pass the catalogue on to others. Thus, such a mailing to named addressees should be governed by paragraph (2): the intent "to be bound in case of acceptance" must be "clearly indicated."

3. International Institute for the Unification of Private Law (UNIDROIT): *Principles of International Commercial Contracts*[20]

Art. 2.1.2.   Definition of offer.
A proposal for concluding a contract constitutes an offer if it is sufficiently definite and indicates the intention of the offeror to be bound in case of acceptance.

OFFICIAL COMMENT

In defining an offer as distinguished from other communications which a party may make in the course of negotiations initiated with a view to concluding a contract, this article lays down two requirements: the proposal must (i) be sufficiently definite to permit the conclusion of the contract by mere acceptance and (ii) indicate the intention of the offeror to be bound in case of acceptance.

1.   Definiteness of an offer

Since a contract is concluded by the mere acceptance of an offer, the terms of the future agreement must already be indicated with sufficient definiteness in the offer itself. Whether a given offer meets this requirement cannot be established in general terms. Even essential terms, such as the precise description of the goods or the services to be delivered or rendered, the price to be paid for them, the time or place of performance, etc., may be left undetermined in the offer without necessarily rendering it insufficiently definite: all depends on whether or not the offeror by making the offer, and the offeree by accepting it, intends to enter into a binding agreement, and whether or not the missing terms can be determined by interpreting the language of the agreement in accordance with Arts. 4.1 et seq., or supplied in accordance with Arts. 4.8 or 5.1.2. Indefiniteness may moreover be overcome by reference to practices established between the parties or to usages (see Art. 1.9), as well as by reference to specific provisions to be found elsewhere in the Principles (e.g. Arts. 5.1.6 (Determination of quality of performance), 5.1.7 (Price determination), 6.1.1 (Time of performance), 6.1.6 (Place of performance), and 6.1.10 (Currency not expressed)).

Illustration

1. A has for a number of years annually renewed a contract with B for technical assistance for A's computers. A opens a second office with the same type of computers and asks B to provide assistance also for the new computers. B accepts and, despite the fact that A's offer does not specify all the terms of the agreement, a contract has been concluded since the missing terms can be taken from the previous contracts as constituting a practice established between the parties.

---

[20]   On the aims, origins and drafting of the Principles of International Commercial Contracts see MICHAEL JOACHIM BONELL, *An International Restatement of Contract Law, The UNIDROIT Principles of International Commercial Contracts*, 3rd edn, incorporating the UNIDROIT Principles 2004, Ardsley/New York: Transnational Publishers, 2005, pp. 9 ff., see the extract above, **A, III., 2**, p. 31; GOODE *et al.*, above n. 18, Ch. 14.01 ff.

2. Intention to be bound

The second criterion for determining whether a party makes an offer for the conclusion of a contract, or merely opens negotiations, is that party's intention to be bound in the event of acceptance. Since such an intention will rarely be declared expressly, it often has to be inferred from the circumstances of each individual case. The way in which the proponent presents the proposal (e.g. by expressly defining it as an "offer" or as a mere "declaration of intent") provides a first, although not a decisive, indication of possible intention. Of even greater importance are the content and the addressees of the proposal. Generally speaking, the more detailed and definite the proposal, the more likely it is to be construed as an offer. A proposal addressed to one or more specific persons is more likely to be intended as an offer than is one made to the public at large.

> Illustrations
> [...]
>
> 3. A, a government agency, advertises for bids for the setting up of a new telephone network. Such an advertisement is merely an invitation to submit offers, which may or may not be accepted by A. If, however, the advertisement indicates in detail the technical specifications of the project and states that the contract will be awarded to the lowest bid conforming to the specifications, it may amount to an offer with the consequence that the contract will be concluded once the lowest bid has been identified.

[...]

4. Commission on European Contract Law: *Principles of European Contract Law*[21]

Offer and Acceptance

Article 2:201: Offer
(1) A proposal amounts to an offer if:
    (a) it is intended to result in a contract if the other party accepts it, and
    (b) it contains sufficiently definite terms to form a contract.
(2) An offer may be made to one or more specific persons or to the public.
(3) A proposal to supply goods or services at stated prices made by a professional supplier in a public advertisement or a catalogue, or by a display of goods, is presumed to be an offer to sell or supply at that price until the stock of goods, or the supplier's capacity to supply the service, is exhausted.

---

[21] On the origins and the aims of the Principles of European Contract Law, see OLE LANDO AND HUGH BEALE (eds), *Principles of European Contract Law, Parts I and II, Combined and Revised*, 2nd edn, The Hague/London/Boston: Kluwer, 2000, Preface and Introduction, see the extracts above, **Part A III., 1**, pp. 25–30; GOODE *et al.*, above n. 18, Ch. 14.01 ff.

Commentary

[…]

C.   *Proposals to the Public*

Proposals which are not made to one or more specific persons (proposals to the public) may take many shapes: advertisements, posters, circulars, window displays, invitations of tenders, auctions etc. These proposals are generally to be treated as offers if they show an intention to be legally bound. However, proposals made "with an eye to the person" are generally presumed to be invitations to make offers only. This applies to an advertisement of a house for rent at a certain price. Further, an advertisement for a job-opening for persons who meet certain requirements does not oblige the advertiser to employ the one offering his or her services and meeting the requirements. Construction contracts are often made on the basis of public bidding. Owners generally only invite tenders, which are the offers.

[…] [P]ersons who make advertisements etc. may wish prospective suppliers or purchasers to know that they will be able to deliver or acquire the goods or services by accepting the proposal, and that they do not risk refusal of their "acceptance" and the consequent waste of their efforts and reliance costs. Therefore, proposals which are sufficiently definite and which can be accepted by anybody without respect of person are to be treated as offers. This consideration has led to the provision in paragraph (3) and will also result in a proposal being an offer in other cases.

> *Illustration 1*: Merchant A advertises in a trade paper that he will buy "all fresh eggs delivered to him before 22 February" and pay a certain price. A's advertisement is to be considered an offer which may be accepted by bringing the eggs to his premises.

> *Illustration 2*: In the local paper Bell advertises a plot of land for sale to the first purchaser to tender 25.000 Euros in cash. This constitutes an offer and when Mart tenders 25.000 Euros there is a contract.

D.   *Goods and Services Offered at Stated Prices*

Article 2:201(3) provides that a proposal to supply goods and services at stated prices made by a professional supplier in a public advertisement or a catalogue or by display of goods is presumed to be an offer to sell or supply at that price until the stock of goods or the supplier's capacity to supply the service, is exhausted.

The professional supplier which advertises goods in the way described is, unless it indicates otherwise, taken to have a reasonable capacity to provide services.

The rule states a presumption. A different intention may appear from the advertisement, etc. and may follow from the circumstances. Thus, if the goods or services are offered on credit terms the supplier may refuse to deal with persons of poor credit-worthiness.

5. Study Group on a European Civil Code and Research Group on EC Private Law (Acquis Group): *Draft Common Frame of Reference*[22]

Section 2:
Offer and acceptance

II. – 4:201: Offer
(1)   A proposal amounts to an offer if:
    (a)   it is intended to result in a contract if the other party accepts it; and
    (b)   it contains sufficiently definite terms to form a contract.
(2)   An offer may be made to one or more specific persons or to the public.
(3)   A proposal to supply goods from stock, or service, at a stated price made by a business in a public advertisement or a catalogue, or by a display of goods, is treated, unless the circumstances indicate otherwise, as an offer to supply at that price until the stock of goods, or the business's capacity to supply the service, is exhausted.

6. Academy of European Private Lawyers, Pavia: *European Contract Code (Draft)*[23]

Art. 13.   Offer and invitation to make an offer
1.   A statement aiming to form a contract amounts to an offer if it contains all terms of the said contract or sufficient information concerning its content that such statement can be the object of an acceptance pure and simple, and if it states or at least implies the offeror's intention to be bound in case of acceptance.

2.   A statement not fulfilling the conditions of the preceding paragraph or which, being addressed to no specific persons, is an advertising communication does not constitute an offer and cannot be accepted. It is an invitation to make an offer, unless it contains a promise in favour of a person carrying out a certain action or revealing the existence of a given situation; in such case it is a promise to the public according to Art. 23.

---

[22]   On the Common Frame of Reference, see below, **Case 10, IV. 1**: Communication from the Commission to the Council and the European Parliament: A more coherent European contract law – an action plan, Brussels, 12.2.2003, COM(2003) 68 final; DIANA WALLIS, 'Is It A Code', *ZEuP* 2006, 513–14 (see below, **Case 10, IV. 4**).

[23]   For information on this project, see, e.g., GIUSEPPE GANDOLFI, "Le Code européen des contrats", in Jean-Philippe Dunand and Bénédict Winiger (eds), *Le Code civil français dans le droit européen*, Brussels: Bruylant, 2005, pp. 275–85.

XII. Summary

1. Overview of the solutions according to the different legal orders and the principles of contract law

	Goods displayed in a shop window or inside shops	Advertisements	Job Advertisement
England	**Invitation to treat** *Fisher v. Bell*, the customer makes an offer at the cash desk, *Pharmaceutical Society v. Boots*.	A matter of fact, *i.e.* the intention of the parties; principle: **Invitation to treat**, MC KENDRICK, p. 37; exception: *Carlill v. Carbolic Smoke Ball*: an advert may be a universal offer that requires only acceptance to form a contract. In *Carlill* the advert was an offer to the whole world and a contract was made with those persons who performed the conditions of the advert ' on the faith of the advertisement'.	**No Offer** Same as the rule regarding advertisements.
USA	**Invitation to treat** Restatement Contracts 2nd § 26 and Commentary.	Principle: **Invitation to treat** Exception: – as in English law (see above), Restatement Contracts 2nd § 26 and Commentary – advertisement contains words of limitation such as "first come, first served" , see *Lefkowitz v. Great Minneapolis Surplus Store*	**No Offer** Same as the rule regarding advertisements.
Switzerland	**Offer** Art. 7(3) Swiss Code of Obligations; *Nussberger c. K* (BGE 105 II 23); F. DESSEMONTET, Commentary, section 11.	**Invitation to treat** Art. 7(2) Swiss Code of Obligations; F. DESSEMONTET, Commentary, section 5.	**No Offer** Same as the rule regarding advertisements.

	Invitation to treat	Invitation to treat	No Offer
Germany	Invitation to treat § 145 German Civil Code; German Federal Court, NJW 1980, 1388.	Invitation to treat § 145 BGB; Supreme Court of the former German Empire, RGZ 133, 388.	Same as the rule regarding advertisements.
France	**Offer**, as long as the declaration contains all of the necessary elements, an offer made to the public binds the person who makes it to the first person who accepts. Cour de Cassation, JCP 1969.II.15797.	**Offer**, when it contains all the elements necessary to form a contract and no reservation can be identified; an offer "while stocks last" is an offer that binds its author to those who accept it while stock remains. TERRÉ/SIMLER/LEQUETTE, section 110ff; LE TOURNEAU, section 3713.	**Invitation to treat** when dealing with an *intuitu personae* proposal, as the author reserves the right to choose whether or not to accept, TERRÉ/SIMLER/LEQUETTE, section 110.
Italy	**Offer**, provided the proposal contains all the essential elements of the contract; the conclusion of the contract occurs at the cash desk, Art. 1336 Italian Civil Code; RESCIGNO, section 6.4.	Principle: **Invitation to treat** In certain circumstances there will be a binding offer where all the essential elements of the contract are present, RESCIGNO, section 2.	
The Netherlands	**Offer**, while stock remains, HARTLIEF, section 3.	The object of the advertisement is the decisive factor. An advertisement offering a specific good for sale is an **invitation to treat**, HARTLIEF, section 2; An advertisement for goods or services is an **offer** for as long as stock remains, HARTLIEF, section 3.	
Serbia	**Offer**, Art. 34 Law of Contracts and Torts.	Principle: **Invitation to treat**, Art. 35(1) Law of Contracts and Torts; Obligation to pay damages when there is a refusal to enter into a contract without a justified reason, Art. 35(2).[24]	

---

24 In other legal orders, an action for damages may be based on the rules on unfair competition, see above n. 2

	Goods displayed in a shop window or inside shops	Advertisements	Job Advertisement
Lithuania	**Offer**, Art. 6.171(1)	**Invitation to treat**, Art. 6.171(3)	
Russia	Principle: **Invitation to treat**, Art. 437 Civil Code of the Russian Federation; Exception: according to the conditions set out in Art. 437(2) Civil Code of the Russian Federation.		Same as the rule regarding advertisements
China	**Offer**, BING LING, Section 3.015	Principle: **Invitation to treat** , Art. 15 Contract Law of the People's Republic of China; Exception: **Offer**, when the advertisement contains all the necessary element of an offer, Art. 15(2) and Art. 14 Contract Law of the People's Republic of China.	
CISG	**Invitation to treat** Art. 14(2); J.O. HONNOLD, Section 135.	**Invitation to treat**	**Invitation to treat**
UNIDROIT Principles	**Offer**, when proposal contains all the necessary information for the conclusion of a contract and indicates the intention to be bound in case of acceptance, Art. 2.1.2.		
PECL and DCFR	**Offer** — Offer made by a professional supplier until the stock of goods is exhausted., Art. 201:2(3) PECL and Art. II.4:201(3) DCFR	**Invitation to treat**	**Invitation to treat** PECL, Commentary, Art. 201, C.
Gandolfi Code	**Offer**, when proposal contains all necessary information for the conclusion of a contract and indicates the intention to be bound in case of acceptance, Art. 13(1).	**Invitation to treat** Art. 13(2).	

2. Systematic overview

Solution 1	Solution 2 (with variant)	Solution 3
Offer Display of merchandise and Advertising	**Offer or invitation to treat** Display of merchandise: Offer Advertising: Invitation to treat	**Invitation to treat** Display of merchandise and Advertising
– French law – PECL and DCFR (displays and advertisements by professional retailers are considered offers for as long as stock remains)	– Swiss law – Italian law – Law of Serbia (special feature: damages can be claimed in the event of an unjustified refusal to enter into a contract) – Dutch law (special feature: advertisements for fungibles are, in principle, considered offers as long as stock remains) – Lithuanian law – Chinese law – "Gandolfi Code"	– German law – English law – US law (except if advertisement contains words of limitation such as "first come, first served") – Russian law – Vienna Convention (CISG)

3. Further Reading

HUGH BEALE *et al.* (eds), *Cases, Materials and Text on Contract Law* (Ius Commune Casebooks for the Common Law of Europe), Oxford: Hart Publishing, 2002, Chapter 2.1, Offer and acceptance, 177–95.

PATRICK BLANCHARD, "Offer and acceptance in international contract negotiation: a comparative study", *I.B.L.J.* 2008, 1, 3–27.

HASAN A. DEVECI, "Consent in online contracts: old wine in new bottles", *C.T.L.R.* 2007, 13(4), 223–31.

ALLAN FARNSWORTH, *Contracts*, 3rd edn, New York: Aspen Publishers, 2004, 129–36 (USA).

ROY GOODE, HERBERT KRONKE AND EWAN MCKENDRICK, *Transnational Commercial Law*, Oxford: Oxford University Press, 2007, Chapter 7 (Vienna Sales Convention), Chapter 14 (Restatements of Contract Law).

HEIN KÖTZ AND AXEL FLESSNER, *European Contract Law*, Vol. I (by Hein Kötz), Oxford: Clarendon Press, 1997, 18–20.

ROBERTO ROSAS, "Comparative study of the formation of electronic contracts in American law with references to international law", *C.T.L.R.* 2007, 13(1), 4–26.

In-depth analysis:

ARTHUR TAYLOR VON MEHREN, "The Formation of Contracts", *Int. Enc. Com. L.*, Vol. VII/1, Tübingen: Mohr Siebeck, 2008, Chapter 9.

Case 2: Conditions for the formation of a contract – agreement or more? (*cause and consideration*)

> "Consideration stands, doctrinally speaking, at the centre of the Common Law's approach to contract"[1]

> "Tout engagement doit avoir une cause honnête."[2]

"Beati possidentes"[3]

Scenario 1
Mr Caillet, the caretaker of an apartment building (the "concierge"), is planning to retire shortly. Before Mr Caillet leaves his position, Ms Nivesse, who is interested in the job, promises to pay him a sum of money if he introduces her to the owner of the building. Mr Caillet introduces Ms Nivesse and she is hired as the new concierge. However, she refuses to pay Mr Caillet the promised sum because the owner of the building was in no way compelled to hire her following Mr Caillet's introduction and was free to hire whoever he chose to replace the old concierge.

Is Ms Nivesse right, or should she pay?

Scenario 2
Mr Eastwood brings up Sarah, the infant daughter of one of his friends who has died leaving Sarah as the sole heir to his fortune. Mr Eastwood is not a wealthy man so has to borrow a large sum of money to raise Sarah. When Sarah reaches 18, she promises in writing to reimburse Mr Eastwood. She marries Mr Kenyon and he also promises in writing to pay back Mr Eastwood. Mr Eastwood asks Sarah and her husband to make good their promise but they refuse.

Who is in the right?

---

[1] ARTHUR TAYLOR VON MEHREN and PETER L MURRAY, *Law in the United States*, 2nd edn, Cambridge: Cambridge University Press, 2007, p. 83.

[2] "Every agreement must have an honest *cause*", ROBERT-JOSEPH POTHIER, "Traité des obligations, 1761, réimprimé avec des augmentations: 1764", no. 42, in: Jean-Joseph Bugnet, *Oeuvres de Pothier annotées et mises en corrélation avec le Code civil et la législation actuelle*, Tome 2, Paris: Cosse & Marchal, 1848, p. 24.

[3] "Blessed are those who are in possession."

Questions

(1) What are the conditions for the formation of a valid contract under *Swiss* and *Austrian* law? What outcome would you suggest for Mr Caillet´s claim in applying the rules of *Swiss* and *Austrian* law?

(2) What are the conditions for the formation of a valid contract under the *French* Civil Code? Is Mr Caillet entitled to the promised amount? What does the *Cour de cassation* decide on the matter? What reasons are given for this approach? What does Philippe Malaurie believe is the real reasoning behind the decision? What is the aim and the function of the *cause*? Is there a *cause* in Scenario 2?

(3) What are the conditions for the formation of a valid contract under *English* law? Is there *consideration* in the above scenarios? What is the aim and function of *consideration* in English law?

(4) What outcome of the *Eastwood* case would you suggest under § 86 of the Restatement (Second) according to which some promises are enforceable without consideration? How would you solve this case under § 5-1105 of the General Obligations Law of New York?

(5) What issues would the facts of *Eastwood* v. *Kenyon* raise, e.g., in *German* law? Upon what would the success of Mr Eastwood's demand for payment of the promised sum be dependent? What outcome would you suggest under German law? What outcome would you suggest under *Swiss* law?

(6) What are the conditions for the formation of a valid contract under:
   (a) the Principles of European Contract Law;
   (b) the Draft Common Frame of Reference;
   (c) the UNIDROIT Principles;
   (d) the draft Gandolfi Code?
   What is your opinion on these solutions?

(7) How are the aims and functions of the *cause* and *consideration* achieved in legal orders that do not impose such requirements? In your answer, consider the tests for the validity (or avoidability) of contracts provided for in the Principles of European Contract Law and in the UNIDROIT Principles. These Principles were elaborated after extensive comparative research in this area.

Table of contents

I. Switzerland

Obligationenrecht (*Swiss Code of Obligations*)[4]

Art. 1. Abschluss des Vertrages. Übereinstimmende Willensäusserung. Im Allgemeinen.

(1) Zum Abschlusse eines Vertrages ist die übereinstimmende gegenseitige Willensäusserung der Parteien erforderlich.

(2) Sie kann eine ausdrückliche oder stillschweigende sein.

Art. 1.   Conclusion of contract, manifestation of mutual assent, in general.

(1)   For a contract to be concluded, a manifestation of the parties' mutual assent is required.

(2)   Such manifestation may be either express or implied.

---

[4]   Under Swiss law, the contract in scenario 1 would be regarded as a contract of brokerage: Art. 412 ff. of the Swiss Code of Obligations. Art. 417 of the Swiss Code of Obligations stipulates that the debtor may ask the court to reduce a broker's fee if an *excessive* fee was promised for procuring the opportunity to conclude an employment contract; see on Swiss law also below, **XI.4.**, and CHRISTINE CHAPPUIS, below, **XI.5.**

II.   Austria

Österreichisches Allgemeines Bürgerliches Gesetzbuch, ABGB (*Austrian Civil Code*)[5]

Abschließung des Vertrages

§ 861
Wer sich erklärt, dass er jemandem sein Recht übertragen, das heißt, dass er ihm etwas gestatten, etwas geben, dass er für ihn etwas tun, oder seinetwegen etwas unterlassen wolle, macht ein Versprechen; nimmt aber der andere das Versprechen gültig an, so kommt durch den übereinstimmenden Willen beider Teile ein Vertrag zu Stande. So lange die Unterhandlungen dauern, und das Versprechen noch nicht gemacht, oder weder zum voraus, noch nachher angenommen ist, entsteht kein Vertrag.

Conclusion of contracts

§ 861
He who declares that he transfers his right to another, that is to say declares that he wants to permit him to do something, give him something, do something for him or refrain from doing something makes a promise; but if the other person validly accepts the promise, a contract is formed by the unanimous agreement of the parties. As long as negotiations are ongoing and the promise has not yet been accepted there is no contract.

---

5   For a brief introduction to the Austrian ABGB see ZWEIGERT AND KÖTZ, *An Introduction to Comparative Law*, 3rd edn, Oxford: Oxford University Press, 1998, pp. 157–66; and also FRANZ-STEFAN MEISSEL, "Le Code civil autrichien, contre-partie du Code civil français?", in Jean-Philippe Dunand and Bénédict Winiger (eds), *Le Code civil français dans le droit européen*, Brussells: Bruylant, 2005, pp. 119–39.

III.   The Netherlands

Burgerlijk Wetboek (*Dutch Civil Code*)

Art. 6:217
(1)   Een overeenkomst komt tot stand door een aanbod en de aanvaarding daarvan.
[...]

Art. 6:217
(1)   A contract is formed by an offer and its acceptance.
[...]

IV.   France

1. Code civil (*French Civil Code*)

DES CONDITIONS ESSENTIELLES POUR LA VALIDITE DES CONVENTIONS
OF THE ESSENTIAL REQUISITES FOR THE VALIDITY OF AGREEMENTS[6]

Art. 1108
Quatre conditions sont essentielles pour la validité d'une convention:
Le consentement de la partie qui s'oblige;
Sa capacité de contracter;
Un objet certain qui forme la matière de l'engagement;
Une cause licite dans l'obligation.

Art. 1108
Four requisites are essential for the validity of an agreement:
The consent of the party who binds himself;
His capacity to contract;
A definite object which forms the subject-matter of the undertaking;
A lawful cause in the obligation.

DE LA CAUSE
OF CAUSE

Art. 1131
L'obligation sans cause, ou sur une fausse cause, ou sur une cause illicite, ne peut avoir aucun effet.

Art 1131
An obligation without a cause or with a false or unlawful cause has no effect.[7]

Art. 1132
La convention n'est pas moins valable, quoique la cause n'en soit pas exprimée.

Art. 1132
An agreement is nevertheless valid, although its cause is not expressed.

Art. 1133
La cause est illicite, quand elle est prohibée par la loi, quand elle est contraire aux bonnes mœurs ou à l'ordre public.

Art. 1133
A cause is unlawful where it is prohibited by legislation, where it is contrary to public morals or to public policy.

---

[6]   Official translation of the French Civil Code, available at www.legifrance.gouv.fr.
[7]   Translation by EG.

2. Cour de cassation (civ. 1re) 20.2.1973 (*Caillet c. Dame Nivesse*), D.S. 1974, 37, with a note by PHILIPPE MALAURIE

COUR DE CASSATION
(1re CH. CIV.)
20 février 1973

CONTRATS ET OBLIGATIONS, Reconnaissance de dette, Cause, Détermination, Concierge, Convention de "bons offices", Successeur, Présentation au propriétaire, Validité (non).

(Caillet C. Dame Nivesse.) – ARRÊT

LA COUR: – Sur le moyen unique, pris en ses deux branches; – Attendu que, selon les énonciations de l'arrêt attaqué (Paris, 27 avr. 1971), la dame Nivesse, désireuse de succéder à Caillet comme gardienne d'immeuble, a signé à son bénéfice une reconnaissance de dette dont la cause n'était pas exprimée, que le montant de cette reconnaissance correspondait, selon la dame […] Nivesse […] pour l'essentiel à la rémunération de Caillet pour la présentation de dame Nivesse au propriétaire de l'immeuble comme successeur au poste de gardien; que la cour d'appel, statuant sur la demande en paiement de Caillet […], a déclaré sans cause la reconnaissance en ce qu'elle rémunérait l'exercice par Caillet d'un droit qu'il ne possédait pas; – Attendu qu'il est fait grief à la cour d'appel d'avoir ainsi statué alors que, selon les conclusions de la dame Nivesse et les constatations de l'arrêt attaqué, la contrepartie de la reconnaissance consistait non dans la cession d'un droit au poste de gardien, mais dans l'engagement du gardien démissionnaire de présenter son successeur; qu'il s'agissait d'un contrat aléatoire, dûment causé; qu'un tel engagement de bons offices, que l'arrêt aurait dénaturé, était valable ainsi que l'avaient décidé les premiers juges en des motifs auxquels la cour d'appel aurait dû répondre dès lors que les époux Caillet avaient demandé la confirmation du jugement; – Mais attendu que les juges du second degré, en énonçant que la reconnaissance de dette était […] "causée par le prix de l'intervention de Caillet représentée comme déterminante et susceptible de fonder un droit au profit de dame Nivesse à occuper le poste que Caillet quittait" et que ce dernier ne détenait aucun droit qu'il puisse céder à l'obtention dudit poste, ont souverainement apprécié les éléments de fait établissant la cause véritable de l'acte et ainsi, sans dénaturer celui-ci, répondu implicitement mais nécessairement aux motifs que les premiers juges avaient retenus dans le jugement infirmé; que le moyen n'est pas fondé;

Par ces motifs, rejette.

Du 20 févr. 1973. – 1re Ch. civ. – MM. Bellet, pr. – Pauthe, rap. – Schmelck, av. gén. – Nicolas et Ryziger, av.

NOTE

(1)   Dans l'arrêt rapporté, la Cour de cassation approuve les juges du fond d'avoir annulé pour absence de cause une promesse de paiement […] Il s'agissait en l'espèce d'un billet sans cause exprimée que, peu avant sa nomination, avait souscrit le gardien d'un immeuble, au profit de son prédécesseur; le débat portait sur l'existence de la cause.

Avant de discuter la solution (II), j'exposerai comment le problème a été présenté, posé et résolu (I).

I. – A. – Dans leur conflit, les deux parties s'accordaient au moins sur un point: la somme promise avait [comme] raison (c'est à dessein que je prends en ce moment ce mot vague, et non celui de cause, pour n'en préjuger ni l'existence, ni l'absence) [...] la rémunération d'une "présentation": le gardien démissionnaire avait présenté son successeur au propriétaire. La contestation portait uniquement sur la légitimité de cette rémunération.

Le débiteur – c'est-à-dire le nouveau gardien, celui qui avait souscrit la promesse – soutenait que ce billet manquait [...] de cause, parce qu'il avait pour objet essentiel de rémunérer une prestation ne correspondant à aucun droit. [...] [D]ans la mesure où le billet rémunérait la "présentation", il était sans cause, car il rémunérait un droit inexistant – c'est-à-dire rien du tout – , puisque le propriétaire n'était aucunement lié par la présentation, en pouvant engager librement le gardien de son choix pour remplacer le démissionnaire.

Le créancier – c'est-à-dire l'ancien gardien – soutenait que ce billet avait une cause, résidant [...] dans la présentation. Sans doute, cette dernière ne liait-elle pas le propriétaire qui avait bien la liberté de remplacer son employé comme il l'entendait. Mais pour aléatoire qu'il fût, un service n'en avait pas moins été rendu: il justifiait donc l'engagement librement et volontairement pris par le souscripteur de la promesse de payer.

[...]

C. – La Cour de cassation, en l'espèce, approuve les juges du fond d'avoir accueilli le raisonnement du débiteur: le billet qui a pour objet de rémunérer la présentation d'un concierge au propriétaire manque de cause, parce que ce propriétaire était libre de choisir le concierge qui lui convenait. En d'autres termes, *une présentation qui ne correspond à aucun droit ne peut conférer aucun droit.* Ou encore, en d'autres termes, l'absence de cause est découverte "au deuxième degré": le billet a bien, en un certain sens, une cause, la "présentation", mais cette présentation ne correspond elle-même à aucun droit, le billet n'a donc, en réalité, aucune cause.

II. – Pour discuter la solution, j'en apprécierai d'abord les fondements (A), avant, plus techniquement, d'en faire l'analyse juridique (B) et de l'apprécier dans ses résultats (C).

A. – Dans sa signification théorique, l'arrêt de la Cour de cassation n'est que l'application d'un principe fondamental de notre Droit: il ne suffit pas qu'une obligation soit voulue pour être valable; il faut aussi qu'elle soit causée. En d'autres termes, l'obligation contractuelle n'est valable que si elle remplit deux conditions: l'une toute subjective – il faut qu'elle ait été voulue – , l'autre, plus objective – il faut qu'elle ait une cause.

C'est donc souligner très nettement le rôle de la cause dans les contrats. Pas de la cause illicite, car rien dans cet acte ne porte directement atteinte à l'intérêt général ou à des principes fondamentaux de la vie en société. En quoi est-il immoral de rémunérer le service que l'on rend à autrui en le présentant à un tiers qui peut lui être utile? C'est uniquement une question d'absence de cause qui peut être discutée. La volonté n'est donc pas le seul élément générateur de l'obligation: elle n'engage que parce que et dans la mesure où elle a été causée. La cause est la justification, la limite et la garantie du pouvoir autonome de la volonté: mode de contrôle de la valeur du contrat, elle n'est pas simplement une exigence technique, mais permet d'imposer au contrat le respect d'une politique économique et sociale.

B. – Techniquement, l'analyse est plus difficile à faire: elle porte sur la raison d'être de cette promesse de paiement: la présentation de son successeur effectivement faite par le concierge démissionnaire au propriétaire peut-elle, juridiquement, être la cause d'une rémunération?

Il n'est pas douteux qu'en fait la faculté de présenter une personne à un emploi confère un pouvoir, le patronage, qui est lui-même une source de clientèle: c'est une réalité politique très ancienne, qui s'est développée dans le commerce et qui, aujourd'hui, tend à gagner d'autres terrains. Imaginez qu'elle existe maintenant dans le domaine universitaire, qu'un professeur ait le droit de présenter son successeur ou son assistant: gageons qu'il se constituera une clientèle de disciples fervents et admiratifs, prêts à toutes les servilités. La faculté de "présenter" à un emploi donne donc toujours à celui qui l'exerce un *pouvoir de fait*, le pouvoir du seigneur sur ses vassaux, une résurgence de la féodalité.

Ce pouvoir est un *pouvoir de droit*, source par conséquent d'effets juridiques, dans la profession libérale. Il a été même un des mécanismes fondamentaux de la capitalisation de la profession; il permet à celui qui est présenté de profiter des droits de son auteur (profession et clientèle); réciproquement, il permet à celui qui en est l'auteur actif d'obtenir, en contrepartie, un capital. [...]

La question n'intéresse ici que les professions salariées: on exposera d'abord le raisonnement de la Cour de cassation (1), avant de lui faire des objections (2).

1) Dans les professions salariées, ce pouvoir de présentation paraît inexistant, tout au moins, selon un auteur, chaque fois que l'employeur garde les mains libres pour designer son successeur, ce qui est le cas de beaucoup le plus habituel (Catala, "La transformation du patrimoine", *Rev. trim. dr. civ.* 1966, 185, n° 16 et 28); ce pouvoir ne peut donc être la source d'aucun droit. C'est ce raisonnement qu'en l'espèce ont suivi les juges du fond approuvés par la Cour de cassation, en relevant que le créancier "ne détenait aucun droit qu'il puisse céder", qui puisse donc servir de cause à la promesse de paiement. [...] La solution [...] repose [...] sur l'idée qu'il est, en principe, impossible ou interdit de capitaliser volontairement la fonction de salarié; celui qui met fin volontairement à ses fonctions d'employé ne peut aucunement monnayer sa "resignatio in favorem", quel qu'en soit l'effet: il ne peut obtenir aucune somme d'argent de son successeur même si ce dernier a été agréé par l'employeur et réciproquement, il ne peut réclamer aucune indemnité à l'employeur qui refuse d'une manière quelconque d'accueillir sa présentation.

Dans quelques cas limités, jusqu'ici exceptionnels, les employeurs se sont pourtant vu limiter leur liberté de ne pas agréer le successeur que leur propose le salarié: dès lors, ils ne peuvent refuser la présentation, qu'en versant une indemnité. A la cessation de ses fonctions, le salarié est indemnisé, *ou* par son successeur s'il est agréé par l'employeur, *ou* par ce dernier s'il refuse la présentation. En pouvant ainsi monnayer sa succession, le salarié parvient à capitaliser sa profession [...]

Un bon exemple peut en être trouvé dans la situation des agents d'assurance. L'agent qui cesse volontairement ses fonctions, *ou bien* reçoit un prix de cession du successeur agréé par la compagnie d'assurances [...]; *ou bien*, en cas de refus de l'assureur, reçoit de ce dernier une indemnité compensatrice; réciproquement, le nouvel agent paiera le droit d'exercer sa profession *soit* à son prédécesseur – si c'est par lui qu'il est présenté – , *soit* directement à la compagnie d'assurances, si c'est elle qui le choisit [...] Il faut bien remarquer que l'indemnité compensatrice et le prix de cession sont les deux faces du même phénomène, que l'une ne peut exister que si l'autre existe: chacune se sert mutuellement de cause. Il faut aussi remarquer que l'agent d'assurances n'est pas un salarié comme les autres, puisque sociologiquement il a certains traits de la profession libérale dans son activité comme dans sa profession: il a, en effet, une sorte de clientèle (on dit un portefeuille).

Rien de tel dans le gardien d'immeuble: il ne peut obtenir de l'argent pour sa présentation, parce qu'au cas où elle serait refusée, il ne saurait exiger du propriétaire une indemnité compensatrice. C'est en ce sens que le paiement de la présentation manque de cause.

Cependant, sur le terrain purement technique où nous sommes encore, le raisonnement n'est peut-être pas irréfutable.

2) Non pas tellement pour une raison sociologique. Les revenus des gardiens d'immeubles ne proviennent pas exclusivement des salaires que leur versent leurs employeurs: de leurs relations avec les habitants de l'immeuble gardé, ils peuvent trouver des ressources complémentaires (étrennes, denier à Dieu, etc.); parfois même, paraît-il, ils participent à la négociation de la vente ou de la location des appartements gardés. Ils ne sont donc pas, en fait, uniquement des salariés. C'est une condition qu'ils partagent avec d'autres employés (coiffeur, chauffeur de taxi, garçon de café, etc.): il n'est pas dit qu'en fait certains d'entre eux, le chasseur de chez Maxim's par exemple, ne bénéficient pas d'un pouvoir de présentation contre capital. Il demeure que ce n'est pas eux qui prospectent et se constituent la clientèle – elle appartient à l'employeur – , et surtout, l'employeur garde un pouvoir pleinement libre de choisir leur successeur: cette situation sociologique n'est pas une situation juridique. Lorsqu'ils sont salariés, le gardien d'immeuble, le garçon de café, le chauffeur de taxi n'ont donc pas une clientèle qu'ils puissent céder.

Plus juridiquement, le pourvoi soulevait une autre objection, à laquelle la Cour de cassation ne répond pas explicitement. Elle est tirée de la notion d'aléa, ou plus précisément de forfait. Les parties auraient entendu faire un contrat à forfait, en stipulant que le prix de la présentation devrait être payé, quel que fût son effet, que le propriétaire l'accueille ou ne l'accueille pas. [...]

L'interprétation de volonté est plausible, mais elle doit être complétée. Où est donc la cause de ce forfait? Pas dans la volonté, mais dans un élément objectif qui lui est extérieur: le service rendu. En accomplissant une mission de bons offices (comme le dit joliment le pourvoi), le gardien démissionnaire a rendu un service à son successeur: or, dans notre société, tout service rendu justifie une rémunération, sauf s'il l'a été à titre libéral. En d'autres termes, le gardien a été un intermédiaire entre les parties; il s'est entremis, il a donc droit à un salaire, comme tout courtier. Sans doute, la jurisprudence admet-elle la réductibilité de ce genre de rémunération [...], à la mesure de l'utilité du service rendu (cause vue du côté du débiteur) et du travail fourni (cause vue du côté du créancier); or, un service a été rendu, un travail a été effectué. Pour réductible qu'il soit, ce salaire n'en est pas moins dû: aussi l'obligation du débiteur avait donc bien une cause.

En réalité, la pure technique juridique est impuissante à justifier la solution. Le salarié ne peut, nous dit la Cour de cassation, rémunérer sa succession parce que l'employeur est libre dans son choix. C'est cette solution qui doit être justifiée directement, sous peine de tomber dans un cercle vicieux: la présentation est faite sans droit, parce que le propriétaire n'a pas à la respecter: c'est précisément ce qu'il faut démontrer, par une politique juridique.

C. – Du point de vue de la politique juridique, une autre solution eût été inopportune: il eût été consternant qu'un salarié, tel le concierge ou le gardien d'un immeuble, pût monnayer sa succession et ainsi accroître le capitalisme de rentiers qui pullule dans notre société. Sans doute, tous ceux qui exercent une profession essaient aujourd'hui de valoriser leur situation pour en faire un capital, qu'ils négocient précisément par la présentation de leur successeur. On ne peut aujourd'hui être officier ministériel, commerçant ou chauffeur de taxi artisan sans avoir acheté le droit de le devenir. "Beati possidentes", comme l'avait prophétisé M. Savatier (*Métamorphoses*, t. 1, p. 368 s.). S'il continue à s'étendre, le mouvement aurait pour effet de généraliser le principe de la vénalité des fonctions, avec ses conséquences morales – la sélection par l'argent – , économiques – la charge parasitaire d'un service inutile – , politiques – le privilège des possédants – . Capitalisme de rentiers qui peut être rapproché du socialisme de souris, vers lequel la jurisprudence semble parfois s'orienter […] Cette troisième voie entre le capitalisme et le socialisme serait la pire de toutes.

Philippe MALAURIE,
*Professeur à l'Université de droit, d'économie
et de sciences sociales de Paris (Paris II).*

Translation

THE COURT: – As to the sole ground of appeal taken in its two parts – Whereas according to the contested judgment ([Court of Appeal of] Paris 27 April 1971) Ms Nivesse, who wanted to succeed Mr Caillet as caretaker (*concierge*) of the building, signed an acknowledgment of debt in Mr Caillet's favour which did not express the *cause*, that the amount of this acknowledgment corresponded, according to Ms […] Nivesse […] mainly to the payment of Caillet for introducing Ms Nivesse to the owner of the building as the replacement for the position of *concierge*; that the court of appeal, ruling on Caillet's claim for payment […] declared the acknowledgment to be without a *cause* as it paid Caillet for transferring a right he did not have; – Whereas [Caillet] challenges the court of appeal for having decided in such a way when, according to the submissions of Ms Nivesse and the findings of the challenged decision, the counterpart of the acknowledgment of debt was not the transfer of a right to the position of *concierge*, but the undertaking by the resigning *concierge* to introduce his successor; that this was an aleatory contract with a valid *cause*; that such an agreement to act as an intermediary, that the ruling distorted, was valid as had been decided on the facts by the judges at first instance which the court of appeal ought to have responded to as soon as Mr and Mrs Caillet had asked for confirmation of the judgment; – However, whereas the judges at second instance, by pronouncing that the *cause* for […] the acknowledgment of debt was "the price of the intervention of Caillet seen as decisive and likely to bestow upon Ms Nivesse the right to take up the position left by Caillet" and that Caillet did not dispose of any right to the position which he could transfer, assessed the facts without the possibility of appeal as establishing the true *cause* of the act and thus, without distorting this assessment, responded implicitly but necessarily to the reasons upheld in the invalidated decision by the judges at first instance; therefore that the ground for appeal was ill-founded.

For these reasons the Court rejects the appeal.

20 February 1973 – 1st Civil Law Chamber – Mssrs. Bellet, President – Pauthe, Reporter – Schmelck, Advocate General – Nicolas and Ryziger, Counsel.

Comment

(1) In the reported judgment, the *Cour de cassation* approved the decision of the trial judges (*juges du fond*) to declare void a promise of payment for absence of a *cause* [...] The instant case concerned a promissory note signed by the concierge of a building just before her appointment, in favour of her predecessor; the debate surrounded the existence of a *cause*.

Before discussing the solution (II), I will explain how the problem was presented, dealt with and resolved (I).

I. – A. – In their dispute, the parties were in agreement about at least one thing: the reason (I am intentionally using this vague term, and not the term *cause*, so as not to prejudge whether or not a *cause* exists) for the promised sum was payment for an "introduction": the resigning concierge introduced his successor to the owner of the building. The dispute exclusively concerned the legitimacy of this payment.

The debtor – that is to say the new concierge, the person who signed the promissory note – maintained that this note did not have [...] a *cause*, because its essential object was to pay for a service which did not correspond to a right [he was able to transfer]. [...] [I]nsofar as the note paid for the "introduction [of Mme Nivesse to the owner of the property]", it did not have a *cause*, because it paid for a non-existent right – that is to say for nothing at all –, since the owner was in no way bound by the introduction, he could hire the concierge of his choice to replace the person who had resigned.

The creditor – that is to say the former concierge – maintained that the note had a *cause*, lying [...] in the introduction. Without a doubt, the introduction did not bind the owner who was free to replace his employee however he so chose. However, no matter how uncertain it was, a service was nonetheless given: this therefore justified the free and voluntary agreement undertaken by the person who made the promise to pay.

[...]

C. – In the instant case, the *Cour de cassation* approved the decision of the trial judges (*juges du fond*) to accept the reasoning of the debtor: the promissory note, the object of which was the introduction of the concierge to the owner lacked a *cause*, because the owner was free to choose the concierge he wanted. In other words, *an introduction that does not correspond to a right cannot confer a right.* Or else, in other words, the absence of a *cause* is discovered in the "second stage": the note, in a sense, has a *cause*, the "introduction", but this introduction does not correspond to any right, the note, in reality, therefore has no *cause*.

II. – In the discussion of the solution, I will first assess the facts (A), then undertake a legal analysis (B) and assess the result (C).

A. – Theoretically speaking, the decision of the *Cour de cassation* is simply the application of a fundamental principle of our law: for an obligation to be valid, it is not sufficient that it is merely desired; it must also have a *cause*. In other words, a contractual obligation is valid only if it satisfies two conditions: the first completely subjective – the obligation must have been wanted –, the second more objective – the obligation must have a *cause*.

The importance of the *cause* in contract law is clearly emphasised. This is not a case of an illicit *cause* because nothing in the transaction endangers the general interest or the fundamental principles of society. What is immoral about paying for the service someone receives when they are introduced to a third party who may be useful to them? It is just the issue of the absence of a *cause* that can be discussed. A person's will is therefore not the only constitutive element of the obligation: the obligation is binding only when and to the extent that it has a *cause*. The *cause* is the justification for, the limit and the guarantee on the free will of the parties: a way of controlling the value of contracts, the *cause* is not just a technical requirement, it is a way of forcing contracts to respect economic and social policy.

B. – Technically speaking, the analysis is more difficult: it concerns the *raison d'être* of the promise to pay: legally speaking, can the introduction of his successor to the owner of the building by the concierge who is leaving be the *cause* of payment?

No doubt the ability to put someone forward for a job confers a power, patronage, that is in itself a source of clientele: it is an ancient political reality that developed in business and is now striving to enter into other domains. Imagine if, in the academic field, there were a professor who had the right to put forward his successor or assistant: it is a safe bet that he would build up a clientele of ardent, admiring followers at his service. The ability to "put someone forward" for a job therefore always gives the person disposing of it the *de facto* power, the power of a lord over his vassals, a resurgence of the feudal system.

This power is a *de facto* power and it is the source of legal consequences for those exercising a *profession libérale*.[8] It was even one of the fundamental mechanisms of the capitalisation of such professions; it allows the person being introduced to benefit from the rights of the person leaving his or her position (job and clients); on the other hand, it allows the person upon leaving to receive, as a counter-performance, payment [for the transfer of his job and clients]. […]

Here, the question relates only to salaried employment: first of all, the reasoning of the *Cour de cassation* will be outlined (1), then it will be critically examined (2).

1) With regard to salaried employment, the power of introduction seems non-existent, at the very least, according to one author, every time the employer is free to choose the successor, which is most frequently the case (Catala, "La transformation du patrimoine", *Rev. trim. Dr. civ.* 1966, 185, nos 16 and 28); therefore this power cannot be the source of any right. This is the reasoning the *juges du fond* followed and the *Cour de cassation* approved in the instant case, noting that the creditor "did not dispose of any right that

---

8   The term *profession libérale* includes architects, doctors, lawyers, accountants, etc. People exercising such professions must be chartered by a central body to be able to practise. They have a certain personal responsibility for their work (note by EG).

he could transfer" and that could therefore act as the *cause* of the promise of payment. […] The solution […] is based on the idea that it is, in principle, impossible or prohibited deliberately to make money from one's position as a salaried worker; someone who chooses to end his employment can in no way profit from this: he cannot receive any money from his successor even if his successor is taken on by the employer and he cannot claim any compensation from an employer who refuses, in whatever way, to welcome an introduction.

In a limited number of exceptional cases, the employers are however taken to have limited their freedom to refuse the successor put forward by the employee: consequently they cannot refuse the proposed candidate without paying compensation to the employee. At the end of his employment, the employee is compensated either by his successor if he is taken on by the employer or by his employer if he refuses the proposed successor. By being allowed to profit from his succession, the employee manages to make money from his profession, like an *officier ministériel*.[9]

Insurance brokers are a good example. An insurance broker who voluntarily leaves his job, *either* receives payment from his successor (*un prix de cession*) who was approved by the insurance company […] *or*, where the company refused the candidate, receives compensation (*une indemnité compensatrice*) from the company; and vice versa, the new broker pays *either* his predecessor – if he introduced him – *or* the insurance company directly, if they chose him, for the right to exercise his profession […] The *prix de cession* and the *indemnité compensatrice* are two aspects of the same phenomenon, they cannot exist without one another: each acts as the *cause* for the other. It must be pointed out that an insurance broker is not an employee like other employees, as sociologically there are certain aspects of the profession which are also aspects of the *profession libérale*: an insurance broker has clients (he has what is referred to as a portfolio).

There is nothing of the sort for a concierge: he cannot obtain money for putting someone forward because if the person were to be refused he would not be able to demand compensation from the owner. It is because of this that payment for an introduction lacks a *cause*.

However, in a purely technical respect, as is being discussed here, the reasoning is perhaps not irrefutable.

2) The reason for this is not really sociological. The income of a concierge does not come exclusively from the salary paid by his employer: he can supplement his income thanks to his relationship with the residents of the building (New Year bonuses, tips, etc.); sometimes, it seems, the concierge even participates in the negotiation process for the sale or renting out of the apartments he looks after. Concierges are therefore not just employees. It is a status they share with other workers (hairdressers, taxi drivers, waiters, etc.): some of them, for example the bellboy at Maxim's, probably enjoy the power to propose someone for their job in return for money. The fact remains that they do not seek and build up a clientele – the clientele belongs to the employer – , and above all, the employer retains the power to freely choose the successor of his employees: this is a sociological, not a legal, situation. When they are employees, concierges, waiters, taxi drivers do not have a clientele that they can transfer.

---

9 The holder of an office conferred for life by a public authority.

Legally speaking, the appeal raises another objection which the *Cour de cassation* does not respond to explicitly. The objection is based on the concept of chance, or more precisely the concept of buying a chance.The parties would have intended to conclude a contract with a fixed price, stipulating that the price of the introduction must be paid, no matter what the outcome, no matter whether the employer welcomes it or not. [...]

Such an interpretation of the intention is plausible, but it must be completed. What is the *cause* of this fixed price? It is not the intention, but rather an objective fact which is separate to the intention: the service performed. By accomplishing a mission of *bons office*[10] (as the decision so nicely puts it) the concierge who was leaving the position performed a service for his successor: and in our society, every service performed merits payment, except if it was done on a voluntary basis. In other words, the concierge acted as intermediary between the parties; he acted as the mediator and therefore has the right to payment, like any broker. Without a doubt, the case law permits the reduction of this type of payment in line with the utility of the service provided (the *cause* from the side of the debtor) and of the work done (the *cause* from the side of the creditor); and yet a service has been provided, work has been done. Regardless of the fact that the payment can be reduced, it is due nonetheless: so the debtor's obligation has a *cause*.

In reality, the solution cannot be justified by legal technicalities alone. The *Cour de cassation* tells us that an employee cannot be paid for his succession because his employer is free to choose the successor. It is this solution that must be justified at the risk of being caught in a vicious circle: the introduction is made without a right to transfer the position and thus does not warrant payment because the owner is not bound by it: it is precisely this that must be dealt with by legal policy.

C. – From a legal policy point of view, a different solution would have been inappropriate: it would have been alarming for an employee, such as a concierge or caretaker, to have the ability to profit from his succession and thus gain the benefits of a person of independent means. Without a doubt, everyone exercising a profession today wants to use their profession to their advantage by making money from introducing their sucessor. Today, one cannot be an *officier ministériel*, retailer or taxi driver without having bought the right to become one. "Beati possidentes", as prophesied by Savatier (*Métamorphoses*, t.1, p. 368ff). If this movement continues to grow, then the result will be that the principle that jobs are for sale, with all its moral consequences – selection by money – , economic consequences – the parasitic costs of a useless service – , political consequences – the privilege of the wealthy – , will become more generalised. [...]

Philippe MALAURIE,
Professeur à l'Université de droit, d'économie
et de sciences sociales de Paris (Paris II).

---

[10]   That is to say, by acting as intermediary.

3. François Terré, Philippe Simler and Yves Lequette, *Droit civil: Les obligations*, 9th edn (translation of the French original)

SECTION 2. THE *CAUSE*

331 *Introduction* ◊ Article 1108 of the civil code makes the validity of an agreement subject to the existence of a "lawful reason for the obligation" (a lawful *cause*) and Article 1131 continues by clarifying the requirement: "an obligation without a *cause* or with a false or unlawful *cause* has no effect". From simply reading these provisions, it is clear that a contract can be validly concluded only if, firstly, the obligation or obligations that it produces have a *cause* and secondly, this *cause* complies with the law. In other words, the requirement is two-fold: a *cause* must *exist* and be *lawful.*

To satisfy this two-fold requirement, it is necessary to understand what is meant by *cause*. And yet, the civil code does not define this difficult to grasp concept anywhere. This silence has led to a wide variety of opinions. As for the *notion* itself: without a doubt, no other legal concept has had such different meanings throughout the course of history. As for its *function*: this has been the subject of famous disputes between those who are against (*anti-causalistes*) and those who are for (*causalistes*) the *cause*, the former claiming the concept is useless, the latter glorifying its role.

[…]

§ 2. The existence of the *cause*

336 *Issues* ◊ In pursuance of Article 1131 of the civil code "an obligation without a *cause* … has no effect". Why have this rule?

Unless suffering from an impairment of his mental faculties, every person entering into a contract does so to achieve a certain aim. By asserting that an obligation without a *cause* is without effect, Article 1131 clearly indicates that for an obligation to be validly formed, there must not only be a willingness on the part of the person who is to be bound but also this willingness must have a *cause*. In other words, Article 1131 allows someone who has entered into an obligation to be released from it if it appears that the aim he was pursuing cannot be realized. In a way, judges make sure that every obligation undertaken is sufficiently justified. It is said that the requirement that a *cause* must exist is insisted upon with a view to assuring *protection of the individual.*

In order to avoid such a rule destroying *legal certainty*, the concept must be strictly interpreted. Otherwise, it would be possible for the person who had undertaken the obligation to claim afterwards that he was pursuing such and such an aim which turned out to be impossible to achieve, to get out of the agreement. To avoid abuse, the tendency in case law when looking at the *cause* is to look at the obvious reason behind the *cause*, the immediate aim driving each contracting party. Given that this aim is always the same for a specific type of contract, the advantage is that it is known by both parties. Nevertheless, as we will see in the following sections, the most recent case law on the matter sees subjectivisation of the *cause* […].

We will now look at absence of a *cause* (A), proof (B) and sanctions (C).

A. **Absence of a** *cause*

337   *Division* ◊ In order to define this rather complex notion we will continue in two stages. First, the main features of the criteria which define the concept of the *cause* will be examined (1°). Next, the concept will be looked at in more detail (2°).

338   **1° *Criteria*** ◊ Understood as the immediate aim, the reason which motivates each contracting party, the *cause* is always the same for a given type of contract. Following Domat's interpretation, the *summa divisio* is onerous contracts and gratuitous contracts. On the one hand, the idea of the *cause* is not understood in the same way in each case. Whereas, with onerous contracts, the *cause* of the obligation of one of the parties is always the benefit received or expected by the other, with gratuitous contracts the agreement of the person who commits himself is based on "some reasonable, fair reason, like the service provided or some other quality of the beneficiary or just the pleasure of doing some good (DOMAT, *Les lois civiles dans leur ordre naturel*, livre II, titre I, sect. I, n° 5.). On the other hand, the need for legal certainty, respect for the expectations of the other contracting party which as we have seen is the determining factor is not as important in the one case as in the other. It is very important for onerous contracts, less so for gratuitous contracts, where the donee seeks to retain a benefit obtained without counter-performance.

339   **a) *Onerous contracts*** ◊ With regard to onerous contracts, which are, by definition, reciprocal, the counter-performance received or expected is the raison d'être for the undertaking of each party. It is inconceivable that someone not acting out of generosity should find himself bound without receiving something in return. Such an arrangement would underestimate the economic and social purpose of onerous contracts which is to act as an instrument of exchange. [...]

340   **1) *Bilateral contracts*** ◊ For bilateral contracts, the *cause* of the obligation of each of the parties lies in the obligation of the other. In other words, the benefit offered by each of the contracting parties serves as the *cause* of the obligation of the other party. So, with a contract for sale, the purchaser promises to pay the price because the seller commits to giving him the item for sale, and conversely, the seller promises to deliver the item because the purchaser promises to pay him the price.

The *cause* of one obligation being the object of the other obligation, *the obligation loses its cause when the counter-performance is non-existent*. So the obligation of the seller has no *cause* if the price is derisory; the obligation of the purchaser has no *cause* if the thing does not exist. On the other hand, the personal motivation of each party is of little importance; it is of little importance, for example, why the seller decided to sell the item rather than keep it. These are motives, different in each case, and which if taken into account risk undermining legal certainty.

It has been maintained by *anti-causaliste* doctrine that the *cause* as understood is a useless notion. The absence of a *cause* in the obligation of one party always coincides with the absence of an object in the obligation of the other, the requirement that a *cause* must exist does the same job as the requirement that there must be an object. However appealing at first sight, the argument does not stand up upon closer analysis: if the *cause* was not included in the conditions for the formation of a contract, only obligations without an object would be annulled. Consequently, the other obligation would need to be executed by the other party even though he would receive nothing in return. For example, suppose there were a sale for something that does not exist, the seller's obligation would be void for lack of object, but not that of the purchaser, the price having been determined in the contract. The concept of the *cause* avoids this unfair result by creating an interdependence of the obligations: if one of the obligations is void through lack of object, the other is void due to lack of a *cause*. The contract is entirely null and void.

Further proof of the usefulness of the *cause* is provided by the legal systems that – like German and Swiss law – do not have this concept as a condition of validity for legal transactions. The obligation is valid because of the consent of the debtor, but these legal systems could not possibly permit one party to remain bound when that party will not receive a counter-performance. These legal orders thus recognise an action based on unjust enrichment (*enrichissement sans cause*). That is to say that the exclusion of the *cause* from contractual obligations requires it to be found instead in extra-contractual obligations.

[…]

346 *Promise to pay a pre-existing debt* ◊ A person commits himself to pay a certain sum of money to someone else on a certain date without the other person making any reciprocal commitment. The promisor may do so of his own free will, in which case the promise is a gratuitous promise. However, he may also make such a commitment in order to extinguish a pre-existing debt to the beneficiary. The promise therefore has as its *cause* the debt to be settled. The commitment is made, in such a case, not with a counter-performance stipulated in the contract in mind, but with something outside of the contract in mind. If this external element does not exist, the promise is void for lack of a *cause*. This is the case, for example, for the commitment of a cinema owner to compensate for damage he wrongly believed himself to have caused to an artist. It is also the case for a man who commits to provide for a child of whom he wrongly believed himself to be the biological father because of things the mother had said. […]

349 **b) *Gratuitous contracts*** ◊ Gratuitous contracts are characterised by the deliberate lack of counter-performance. It is, for the author, an intentional impoverishment. The abstract *cause*, that is found in all gifts, lies in the *intent to give*. For example, the *cause* of the obligation to transfer the property assumed by the donor is embodied in his desire to give to the donee.

So understood, the *cause* turns out to be an irreplacable qualifying instrument; where there is no intent to give, there is no gift. On the other hand, with regard to protection of the individual, the *cause* only fulfils its role imperfectly. To ensure that the will of the donor has a valid *cause*, it seems useful to look further than the abstract *cause*, to the reality of the motives that led him to give the gift. Only looking at the intention to give would be carrying out a purely formal check, since the intention to give is the consent. Domat, often said to be the inventor of the abstract *cause*, was not maintaining otherwise when he wrote that "with gifts and other contracts where one person does or gives something … the undertaking of the person who gives is founded on some reasonable and just reason, like a service performed, or some other merit of the beneficiary or solely the pleasure of doing good." Without a doubt, such a shifting of the concept of the *cause* towards the motives is likely to somewhat alter legal certainty. However this turns out to be less important for gratuitous acts than for onerous acts. By definition, the beneficiary is fighting to keep a benefit which was promised without him sacrificing anything in return.

What little case law there is on the subject clearly takes this direction. In fact, there is no hesitation in the case law to consider the motive to be the *cause* where it relates to a quality of the beneficiary or the behaviour of the beneficiary and is decisive. [...] Testamentary gifts have also been annulled where the author believed the legatee to be his natural son or that he had no heir. Were similarly annulled: [certain testamentary gifts] agreed upon in the light of tax laws that were subsequently abolished with retroactive effect as well as a gift given to a couple motivated by their love for one another which rapidly turned out not to be so strong when shortly afterwards one filed for divorce. A gift to pay for something already done was also annulled when the reason why the donor consented turned out not to exist.

[...]

V. Spain

Código civil (*Spanish Civil Code*)[11]

Art. 1254

El contrato existe desde que una o varias personas consienten en obligarse, respecto de otra u otras, a dar alguna cosa o prestar algún servicio.

Art. 1254

A contract exists from the time one or several persons consent to obligate themselves with respect to another, or others, to give a thing or to perform a service.

Art. 1261

No hay contrato sino cuando concurren los requisitos siguientes:
1. Consentimiento de los contratantes.
2. Objeto cierto que sea materia del contrato.
3. Causa de la obligación que se establezca.

Art. 1261

There is no contract unless the following requirements are met:
1. *Consent of the contracting parties.*
2. *A certain object that is the subject matter of the contract.*
3. *A cause of the obligation that is established.*

Art. 1262

(1) El consentimiento se manifiesta por el concurso de la oferta y de la aceptación sobre la cosa y la causa que han de constituir el contrato.
[...]

Art. 1262

(1) Consent is manifested by the concurrence of the offer and the acceptance on the thing and the cause that will constitute the contract.
[...]

Art. 1274

En los contratos onerosos se entiende por causa, para cada parte contratante, la prestación o promesa de una cosa o servicio por la otra parte; en los remuneratorios, el servicio o beneficio que se remunera, y en los de pura beneficencia, la mera liberalidad del bienhechor.

---

[11] For a brief introduction to Spanish law see, e.g., ZWEIGERT AND KÖTZ, above n. 5, pp. 107–08; ANTONI VAQUER, 'Spain' in Jan M. Smits (ed.), *Elgar Encyclopedia of Comparative Law*, Cheltenham: Edward Elgar Publishing Ltd, 2006, pp. 672–76; CHARLOTTE VILLIERS, *The Spanish legal tradition: An introduction to the Spanish law and legal system*, Aldershot: Dartmouth Publishing, 1999; ELENA MERINO-BLANCO, *The Spanish Legal System*, London: Sweet & Maxwell, 1996.

Art. 1274
In onerous contracts, the performance or promise by the other party of a thing or a service shall be considered as the cause for each contracting party; in remunerative contracts, the service or benefit being remunerated; and in those of pure charity, the mere liberality of the benefactor shall be the cause.

Art. 1275
Los contratos sin causa, o con causa ilícita, no producen efecto alguno. Es ilícita la causa cuando se opone a las leyes o a la moral.

Art. 1275
Contracts without a cause, or with an unlawful cause, produce no effect. A cause is unlawful when it is contrary to law or good morals.

Art. 1276
La expresión de una causa falsa en los contratos dará lugar a la nulidad, si no se probase que estaban fundados en otra verdadera y lícita.

Art. 1276
The expression of a false cause in a contract shall be grounds for its nullity unless it is proven that it was founded on another cause that was true and lawful.

Art. 1277
Aunque la causa no se exprese en el contrato, se presume que existe y que es lícita mientras el deudor no pruebe lo contrario.

Art. 1277
Cause is presumed to exist and to be lawful, even though it is not expressed in the contract, as long as the debtor does not prove the contrary.

VI. Italy

Codice civile (*Italian Civil Code*)

Dei requisiti del contratto
Requisites of Contracts

Art. 1325. Indicazione dei requisiti.
I requisiti del contratto sono:
1) l'accordo delle parti;
2) la causa;
3) l'oggetto;
4) la forma, quando risulta che è prescritta dalla legge sotto pena di nullità.

Art. 1325 Indication of requisites.
The requisites of the contract are:
1) *agreement of the parties;*
2) *cause;*
3) *object;*
4) *form, when prescribed by law, under penalty of nullity.*

Della causa del contratto
Causa of Contracts

Art. 1343. Causa illecita.
La causa è illecita quando è contraria a norme imperative, all'ordine pubblico o al buon costume.

Art. 1343. Unlawful causa.
The cause is unlawful when it is contrary to mandatory rules, public policy, or morals.

Art. 1344. Contratto in frode alla legge.
Si reputa altresì illecita la causa quando il contratto costituisce il mezzo per eludere l'applicazione di una imperativa.

Art. 1344. Contract in fraud of law.
The cause is also considered unlawful when the contract constitutes the means for evading the application of a mandatory rule.

Art. 1345. Motivo illecito.
Il contratto è illecito quando le parti si sono determinate a concluderlo esclusivamente per un motivo illecito cumune ad entrambe.

Art. 1345. Unlawful motive.
A contract is unlawful when the parties are led to conclude it solely for an unlawful motive, common to both.

Della nullità del contratto
Nullity of Contract

Art. 1418. Cause di nullità del contratto.
(1) Il contratto è nullo quando è contrario a norme imperative, salvo che la legge disponga diversamente.
(2) Producono nullità del contratto la mancanza di uno dei requisiti indicati dall'art. 1325, l'illiceità della causa, l'illiceità dei motivi nel caso indicato dall'art. 1345 [...]

Art. 1418. *Causes of nullity of contract.*
(1) A contract that is contrary to mandatory rules is void, unless the law provides otherwise.
(2) A contract is rendered void by the lack of one of the requisites indicated in Article 1325, unlawfulness of cause, unlawfulness of the motives in the case indicated in Article 1345 [...]

VII.   Quebec, Canada

Civil Code of Quebec[12]

§ 1. – Conditions of formation of contracts.
I – General provision

Art. 1385
(1)   A contract is formed by the sole exchange of consents between persons having capacity to contract, unless, in addition, the law requires a particular form to be respected as a necessary condition of its formation, or unless the parties require the contract to take the form of a solemn agreement.
(2)   It is also the essence of a contract that it have a cause and an object.

IV – Cause of contracts

Art. 1410
(1)   The cause of a contract is the reason that determines each of the parties to enter into the contract.
(2)   The cause need not be expressed.

Art. 1411
A contract whose cause is prohibited by law or contrary to public policy is null.

---

12   For a brief introduction to Canadian law, see: ZWEIGERT AND KÖTZ, above n. 5, pp. 115–18; MICHAEL DETURBIDE, 'Canada', in Smits (ed.), above n. 11, pp. 116–19.

VIII.   Louisiana, USA

Civil Code

Art. 1927

(1)   A contract is formed by the consent of the parties established through offer and acceptance.

(2)   Unless the law prescribes a certain formality for the intended contract, offer and acceptance may be made orally, in writing, or by action or inaction that under the circumstances is clearly indicative of consent.

(3)   [...]

IX. England

1. W.T. MAJOR AND CHRISTINE TAYLOR, *Law of Contract,* 9th edn, pp. 1, 47–64

1
INTRODUCTION

[...]

2. Essential elements

There are three fundamental elements in any simple contract. They are:

(a) Agreement. The parties must have reached, or be deemed to have reached, agreement. This is usually established by identifying a clear offer from the offeror which has been unconditionally accepted by the offeree.

(b) Intention. The parties must have intended, or be deemed to have intended, to create legal relations.

(c) Consideration. According to the terms of the agreement, some advantage moves from each party to the other. The giving of mutual advantages by the parties is the essence of a bargain. Any advantage or benefit moving from one party to another is known as consideration.
In any transaction where one of these elements is missing there is no contract.

[...]

4
CONSIDERATION

THE NATURE OF CONSIDERATION

1. The nature and definition of consideration

Consideration is the principal essential ingredient of enforceability of agreements. The classic nineteenth-century definition of consideration, found in the case of *Currie* v. *Misa* (1875), is that a valuable consideration 'may consist either in some right, interest, profit, or benefit accruing to the one party, or some forbearance, detriment, loss, or responsibility given, suffered, or undertaken by the other'. A more concise definition is given by Pollock, namely that 'an act or forbearance of one party, or the promise thereof, is the price for which the promise of the other is bought, and the promise thus given for value is enforceable.' Pollock's definition was adopted by the House of Lords in *Dunlop* v. *Selfridge* (1915), the leading case on consideration.

2. Executory and executed consideration

Valuable consideration may be something promised or something done. Regarding a simple contract as a transaction which is essentially a bargain, consideration may be a price promised, or a price paid. 'Price' is used here in the broadest sense and is not confined to money alone.

[…]

RULES GOVERNING CONSIDERATION

3. Consideration must not be past

Where it is alleged that a contract exists on the basis of an act followed by a promise, the courts will not enforce such a promise. In such cases the consideration is described as 'past'. The rule is well illustrated by a number of classic cases.

> *Eastwood* v. *Kenyon* (1840): The plaintiff was the executor of John Sutcliffe, who had died intestate as to his real property leaving as his heir-in-law his only child, Sarah, an infant at the time of his death. The plaintiff spent his own money on the improvement of the realty. To reimburse himself, the plaintiff borrowed £140 from one Blackburn, giving a promissory note. When Sarah reached full age she promised the plaintiff that she would pay to the plaintiff the amount of the note. After Sarah's marriage, her husband promised the plaintiff that he would pay to the plaintiff the amount of the note. The plaintiff sued Sarah's husband on this promise and was met by the defence that no consideration was given for the promise. HELD: the benefit conferred on the defendant (through his wife) by the plaintiff was not consideration to support the defendant's subsequent promise to pay the plaintiff.

It was said by Lord Denman in that case: 'Taking then the promise of the defendant, as stated on this record, to have been an express promise, we find that the consideration for it was past and executed long before; and yet it is not laid to have been at the request of the defendant nor even of his wife when sole … and the declaration really discloses nothing but a benefit voluntarily conferred by the plaintiff and received by the defendant with an express promise by the defendant to pay money. … In holding this declaration bad because it states no consideration but a past benefit not conferred at the request of the defendant, we conceive that we are justified by the old common law of England.'

> *Roscorla* v. *Thomas* (1842): At T's request, R bought T's horse for £30. After the sale, T promised R that the horse was sound and free from vice. The horse proved to be vicious. HELD: There was no consideration to support T's promise and he was not bound. The sale itself could not be valuable consideration, for it was completed at the time the promise was given.

> *Re McArdle* (1951): M and his wife lived in a house which was part of the estate of M's father, in which M and his brothers and sister were beneficially interested expectant on the death of their mother, who was tenant for life. In 1943 and 1944, Mrs M paid £488 for improvements and decorations to the house. In 1945, the beneficiaries all signed a document addressed to Mrs M which provided: 'In consideration of your carrying out certain alterations and improvements to the house, we the beneficiaries under the will (of their father) hereby agree that the executors shall repay you from the said estate when so distributed the sum of £488 in settlement of the amount spent on such improvements.' In 1945, the tenant for life died and Mrs M claimed payment of £488. HELD, by the Court of Appeal: As the work had been done and paid for before the beneficiaries made their promise to repay Mrs M, the consideration was past and the promise contained in the document was not binding.

4. Exceptions to the past consideration rule

An apparent exception to the past consideration rule may be found where services are rendered upon request raising the implication of a promise to pay.

[...]

[I]n some circumstances, particularly where the transaction is of a commercial nature, an implied promise to pay may arise despite the apparent lack of a previous request by the promisor.

> *Re Casey's Patents* (1892): The owners of patent rights promised their manager a share in those rights in consideration for his previous services for them. HELD: The promise was enforceable and not merely supported by past consideration. Bowen LJ said, 'The fact of a past service raises an implication that at the time it was rendered it was to be paid for, and, if it was a service which was to be paid for, when you get in a subsequent document a promise to pay, that promise may be treated as an admission which evidences or as a positive bargain which fixes the amount of that reasonable remuneration on the faith of which the service was originally rendered.'

This dictum of Bowen LJ was applied by the Privy Council in *Pao On* v. *Lau Yiu Long* (1980). In that case Lord Scarman stated the principle as follows: 'An act done before the giving of a promise to make a payment or to confer some other benefit can sometimes be consideration for the promise. The act must have been done at the promisor's request, the parties must have understood that the act was to be remunerated either by a payment, or the conferment of some other benefit and payment, or the conferment of a benefit, must have been legally enforceable had it been promised in advance'.

These cases are conventionally cited as being exceptions to the rule of past consideration but the exception may be more apparent than real. If the subsequent promise to pay is no more than a quantification and evidence of an obligation to pay which had already arisen by virtue of a simple contract between the parties then the consideration should not be deemed to be past at all. [...]

5. Statutory exceptions to the past consideration rule

[...]

Further, where a right of action to recover a debt or other liquidated claim is barred by the Limitation Act 1980, and the person liable acknowledges the claim or makes any payment in respect thereof, the right shall be deemed to have accrued on and not before the date of the acknowledge or the last payment; Limitation Act 1980, s. 29(5). This means that a promise by a debtor to pay a statute-barred debt is actionable. Notice that s. 29 provides for a fresh accrual of a *right of action*: the section concerns procedural rights and not the accrual of substantive contractual rights. The acknowledgment does not create a fresh course of action. Thus the section provides only an apparent exception to the rule that past consideration is no consideration.

6. Consideration must move from the promisee

[...]

7. Joint promisees

[...]

8. Consideration need not be adequate

According to the doctrine of freedom of contract, the courts will not interfere with a bargain freely reached by the parties. It is not part of the court's duty to assess the relative value of each party's contribution to the bargain. Once it is established that a bargain was freely reached, it will be presumed that each party stipulated according to his wishes and intentions at the time. There is no reason, for example, why a party should not be bound by a promise to sell a new Rolls Royce car for one penny. If the agreement is freely reached, the inadequacy of the price is immaterial to the existence of a binding contract.

[...]

Chappell & Co. v. *Nestlé Co.* (1960): The Nestlé company offered to the public gramophone records of a certain dance tune for 1s 6d each together with three chocolate bar wrappers. The wrappers were thrown away on receipt by the company. On the question whether the wrappers were part of the consideration given for each record it was held by the House of Lords that the wrappers were part of the consideration even though they were of no further value once received by the company.

[...]

9. Consideration must be sufficient

Consideration must have some value, usually expressed as being something of 'value in the eyes of the law'. It matters not how small that value is, so long as it is worth something; indeed, the word 'value' is sometimes used to mean consideration. If a thing of value can be identified, then there will be sufficiency of consideration and, as seen, the court will not enquire as to its adequacy. However, the consideration provided must be capable of expression in economic terms.

[...]

Hamer v. *Sidway* (1891): An uncle promised his nephew $5,000 if the nephew would refrain from 'drinking liquor, using tobacco, swearing and playing cards or billiards for money until he should become 21 years of age'. The nephew complied but the defendant, the uncle's executor, refused to make the payment. One argument put forward by the defence was that giving up tobacco and drinking would actually benefit the nephew rather than the uncle. HELD: The argument regarding the benefit to the nephew was not substantiated. The promise was enforceable because the nephew had provided consideration by restricting his lawful freedom of action and there was no information as to how arduous that would have been for him.

[...]

11. Promise not to sue

If an individual agrees to compromise a valid claim for an uncertain amount, or even a genuinely dubious claim, there is no doubt that the promise to drop the claim is consideration for the promise to pay the sum offered in settlement.

[...]

WAIVER MUST BE SUPPORTED BY CONSIDERATION

12. Part payment of a debt

Where a debtor pays a lesser sum to his creditor than that which is due, the debtor is not discharged from his obligation to pay the balance. At common law the debtor remains liable even where the creditor has agreed to release him from further liability, for the creditor's promise is not supported by any consideration moving from the debtor. [...]

13. Where payment of a lesser sum discharges an obligation to pay a greater sum

The rule as stated above is only applicable if the promise of the creditor to accept a lesser sum is unsupported by fresh consideration from the promisee. However, if, at the creditor's request, some new element is introduced, such as payment at a different place, or at a different time, compliance with this request will amount to consideration for the waiver. This concept was acknowledged in *Pinnel's Case* itself.

> *Pinnel's Case* (1602): Here Pinnel sued Cole in debt for £8 10s due on [...] 11 November 1600. Cole's defence was that, at Pinnel's request, he had paid £5 2s 6d on 1 October and that Pinnel had accepted this payment in full satisfaction of the original debt. Judgment was given for the plaintiff on a point of pleading but the court made it clear that, had it not been for a technical flaw, they would have found for the defendant on the ground that the part payment had been made on an earlier day than that stipulated in the bond. Early payment was a 'new element' which clearly would benefit the creditor and would therefore amount to consideration for the promise to accept a lesser sum.

[...]

PROMISSORY ESTOPPEL

15. The doctrine as a defence

Where a party has waived his contractual rights against another, and that other party has changed his position in reliance on the waiver, it may be unjust to allow an action against him on the original contract to succeed. In equity, the party who waived his rights may be estopped from denying that he intended the waiver to be binding.

The modern law of promissory estoppel stems from the decision of the House of Lords in *Hughes* v. *Metropolitan Rail Co.* (1877). [...]

Drawing on the doctrine enunciated in *Hughes* v. *Metropolitan Rail Co.*, Denning J. (as he then was), in the case of *Central London Property Trust* v. *High Trees House* (1947), gave a definition of what would amount to promissory estoppel in relation to waiver of a contractual right. [...] [A]ccording to Denning J., 'if one party promises to forego or not to rely upon his strict legal rights and the other party, in reliance on that promise, acts upon it, then the promisor is estopped from asserting his full legal rights until he has given reasonable notice of his intention to do so'.

[...]

Nevertheless [...] the House of Lords has not yet given its blessing to the doctrine of promissory estoppel and has expressly reserved the question of the existence or at least the extent of the doctrine.

[...]

18. The other party must have altered his position

It is essential to the doctrine of promissory estoppel that the debtor should have acted on the promise. [...]

2. Michael P. Furmston, *Cheshire, Fifoot and Furmston's Law of Contract*, 15th edn, pp. 93–97

Chapter 4
CONSIDERATION

1 FUNCTION AND DEFINITION

[...]

In developed English law, that is since the sixteenth century, the crucial factor is the presence or absence of 'consideration'. [...] [I]t has [...] been persuasively argued that the doctrine of consideration represents the adoption by English law of the notion that only bargains should be enforced.

This view has not gone unchallenged. The history of consideration is still not completely clear but it seems inherently unlikely that sixteenth century English judges would ever have asked themselves a highly abstract question such as 'Should we enforce bargains or promises?' The pragmatic habits of the English and the absence of institutional writing make it probable that in the sixteenth and seventeenth centuries there was no single *doctrine* of consideration, but a number of considerations which were recognised as adequate to support an action for breach of a promise. So consideration probably meant at this stage the reason for the promise being binding, fulfilling something like the role of *causa* or *cause* in continental systems.

Lord Mansfield's attack on consideration

The doctrine of consideration was accepted throughout the seventeenth and in the first half of the eighteenth century as an integral part of the new law of contract. But when Lord Mansfield became Chief Justice of the King's Bench in 1756 its pride of place was challenged. At first Lord Mansfield refused to recognise it as the vital criterion of a contract and treated it merely as evidence of the parties' intention to be bound. If such an intention could be ascertained by other means, such as the presence of writing, consideration was unnecessary. This direct assault was repelled with ease. In *Rann v Hughes* in 1778 it was proclaimed that:

> ... all contracts are, by the laws of England, distinguished into agreements by specialty, and agreements by parol; nor is there any such third class ... as contracts in writing. If they be merely written and not specialties, they are parol, and a consideration must be proved.

Lord Mansfield's second approach was more insinuating. Accepting the concept of consideration as essential to English contract, he defined it in terms of moral obligation.

> Where a man is under a moral obligation, which no Court of law or equity can enforce, and promises, the honesty and rectitude of the thing is a consideration ... The ties of conscience upon an upright mind are a sufficient consideration.

According to this view, whenever a man is under a moral duty to pay money and subsequently promises to pay, the pre-existing moral duty furnishes consideration for the promise. The equation of consideration and moral obligation was accepted, though with increasing distrust, for nearly sixty years, and was finally repudiated only in 1840. In *Eastwood* v. *Kenyon*:

> On the death of John Sutcliffe, his infant daughter, Sarah, was left as his sole heiress. The plaintiff, as the girl's guardian, spent money on her education and for the benefit of the estate, and the girl, when she came of age, promised to reimburse him. She then married the defendant, who also promised to pay. The plaintiff sued the defendant on this promise.

Lord Denman dismissed the action and condemned the whole principle of moral obligation upon which it was founded. Such a principle was an innovation of Lord Mansfield, and to extirpate it would be to restore the pure and original doctrine of the common law. Moreover, as he pointed out, the logical inference from the acceptance of moral duty as the sole test of an actionable promise was the virtual annihilation of consideration. The law required some factor additional to the defendant's promise, whereby the promise became legally binding; but, if no more was needed than the pressure of conscience, this would operate as soon as the defendant voluntarily assumed an undertaking. To give a promise was to accept a moral obligation to perform it.

Attempts to define consideration

As a result of *Eastwood* v. *Kenyon* it was clear that consideration was neither a mere rule of evidence nor a synonym for moral obligation. How then was it to be defined? In the course of the nineteenth century it was frequently said that a plaintiff could establish the presence of consideration in one of two ways. He might prove either that he had conferred a benefit upon the defendant in return for which the defendant's promise was given or that he himself had incurred a detriment for which the promise was to compensate.

The antithesis of benefit and detriment, though reiterated in the courts, is not altogether happy. [...] The typical modern contract is the bargain struck by the exchange of promises. [...] A further disadvantage to the use of the word 'detriment' is that it has to be understood in a highly technical sense. So a promise to give up smoking is capable of being a detriment in the law of consideration even though smoking is bad for the promisor. This is technically sound but likely to confuse.

A different approach to the problem of consideration may be made through the language of purchase and sale. The plaintiff must show that he has bought the defendant's promise either by doing some act in return for it or by offering a counter-promise. Sir Frederick Pollock summarised the position in words adopted by the House of Lords in 1915:

> An act or forbearance of one party, or the promise thereof, is the price for which the promise of the other is bought, and the promise thus given for value is enforceable.

This definition of consideration as the price paid by the plaintiff for the defendant's promise is preferable to the nineteenth-century terminology of benefit and detriment. It is easier to understand, it corresponds more happily to the normal exchange of promises and it emphasises the commercial character of the English contract.

[...]

3. P. S. ATIYAH, *An Introduction to the Law of Contract,* 6th edn, pp. 93, 128–29

Beyond Offer and Acceptance:
Formalities, Intent to Create Legal
Relations, and Consideration

[93]   […] [M]aking a promise or agreement […] is not generally sufficient to create a contract under English law. According to the orthodox understanding, three further requirements must be satisfied: (1) the parties must intend to create legal relations, (2) the arrangement must be supported by consideration, and (3) any stipulated formalities must be fulfilled.

[…] [I]t is not easy to explain why these requirements (in particular the "intent" and "consideration" requirements) are a part of English law. On the one hand, none of the requirements are practically very important. Particularly in commercial contexts, the intent, consideration, and formal requirements are typically satisfied automatically, as a natural consequence of the ordinary features of the parties' arrangements. On the other hand, in those rare cases where these requirements are significant, the decision not to enforce the arrangement often appears unjust. The decision often appears, at first sight anyway, to be based on a mere technicality – a rule with no apparent connection to whatever substantive issue may be at stake. […] The rules in question are presented as positive requirements that any binding contract must fulfill, not as tools for identifying particular arrangements that should *not* be enforced. In short, the requirements […] appear to conflict with the ideal of freedom of contract. They appear, in other words, to be paternalistic limits on an individual's ability to make binding contracts. […]

Conclusion: the future of consideration

[128]   The doctrine of consideration has served and continues to serve many useful functions, but a strong argument can be made that most, if not all, of these functions would be served by other legal doctrines. That has already happened in significant measure with the doctrine's traditional function of *denying* contractual enforcement to certain kinds of promises and agreements: the doctrine is now rarely used to invalidate agreements made under duress in a domestic setting, or to contravene public policy objectives […] The few situations where the consideration doctrine is still used for this purpose could be taken over, it would seem, by other doctrines, including those of "unconscionability" and "public policy". This approach would have the advantage that cases raising such issues would be treated alongside others involving similar problems. In particular, reclassifying certain consideration cases as cases raising questions of unconscionability or public policy would force lawyers to address the real issues in these cases more directly, for example, by discussing more openly which kinds of pressure *should* be regarded as unfair and unacceptable.

It also seems clear that the doctrine's other main function – that of imposing formal requirements of validity on donative promises – could be fulfilled more effectively by a legislated solution. A simple rule to the effect [129] that donative promises must be in writing to be binding or in a deed would be more transparent than the current rule and, importantly, would apply only to those promises for which formalities are really needed. […]

X.   United States of America

1. American Law Institute, *Restatement of the Law Second: Contracts*

§ 71.   Requirement of Exchange. Types of Exchange
(1)   To constitute consideration, a performance or a return promise must be bargained for.
(2)   A performance or return promise is bargained for if it is sought by the promisor in exchange for his promise and is given by the promisee in exchange for that promise.
[...]

§ 86.   Promise for benefit received.
(1)   A promise made in recognition of a benefit previously received by the promisor from the promisee is binding to the extent necessary to prevent injustice.
(2)   A promise is not binding under Subsection (1)
(a)   if the promise conferred the benefit as a gift or for other reasons the promisor has not been unjustly enriched; or
(b)   to the extent that its value is disproportionate to the benefit.

Comment:
[...]
   a. "Past consideration"; "moral obligation". [...] The mere fact of promise has been thought to create a moral obligation, but it is clear that not all promises are enforced. Nor are moral obligations based solely on gratitude or sentiment sufficient to themselves support a subsequent promise.

Illustrations:
   1.   A gives emergency care to B's adult son while the son is sick and without funds far from home. B subsequently promises to reimburse A for his expenses. The promise is not binding under this Section [since the promisor has not been unjustly enriched].
      [...]
   6.   A finds B's escaped bull and feeds and cares for it. B's subsequent promise to pay reasonable compensation to A is binding.
   7.   A saves B's life in an emergency and is totally and permanently disabled in so doing. One month later B promises to pay A $15 every two weeks for the rest of A's life, and B makes the payments until he dies. The promise is binding.

REPORTER'S NOTE

[...]
Comment d. Illustration 6 is based on Boothe v. Fitzpatrick, 36 Vermont 681 (1864). Illustration 7 is based on Webb v. McGowin, 232 Alabama 374, 168 So. 199 (1936) [...]

2. New York: General Obligations Law

§ 5-1105

A promise in writing and signed by the promisor [...] shall not be denied effect as a valid contractual obligation on the ground that consideration for the promise was passed or executed, if the consideration is expressed in the writing and is proved to have been given or performed and would be a valid consideration but for the time when it was given or performed.

XI.　Germany and Switzerland (2)

1. Bürgerliches Gesetzbuch (BGB) (*German Civil Code*)

§ 780.　Schuldversprechen.
Zur Gültigkeit eines Vertrags, durch den eine Leistung in der Weise versprochen wird, dass das Versprechen die Verpflichtung selbständig begründen soll (Schuldversprechen), ist, soweit nicht eine andere Form vorgeschrieben ist, schriftliche Erteilung des Versprechens erforderlich. Die Erteilung des Versprechens in elektronischer Form ist ausgeschlossen.

§ 780.　*Debt commitment*
For the validity of a contract by means of which performance is promised such that the promise is supposed to establish the duty by itself (debt commitment) and to the extent that no other form is specified, providing the commitment in written form is required. Providing the commitment in electronic form is excluded.

§ 516.　Begriff der Schenkung.
(1) Eine Zuwendung, durch die jemand aus seinem Vermögen einen anderen bereichert, ist Schenkung, wenn beide Teile darüber einig sind, dass die Zuwendung unentgeltlich erfolgt.
[...]

§ 516.　*Concept of donation*
(1) A bestowal by means of which someone enriches another person from his own assets, is a donation if both parties are in agreement that the bestowal occurs without remuneration.
[...]

§ 518.　Form des Schenkungsversprechens.
(1) Zur Gültigkeit eines Vertrags, durch den eine Leistung schenkweise versprochen wird, ist die notarielle Beurkundung des Versprechens erforderlich. Das Gleiche gilt, wenn ein Schuldversprechen oder ein Schuldanerkenntnis der in den §§ 780, 781 bezeichneten Art schenkweise erteilt wird, von dem Versprechen oder der Anerkennungserklärung.
(2) Der Mangel der Form wird durch die Bewirkung der versprochenen Leistung geheilt.

§518.　*Form for promise of a donation*
(1) For the validity of a contract by which performance is promised as a donation notarial recording of the promise is required. The same applies to the promise or the declaration of acknowledgement if the promise or acknowledgement of a debt is granted as a donation in the manner cited in sections 780 and 781.
(2) Want of form is cured by effecting the performance promised.

§ 534. Pflicht- und Anstandsschenkungen.
Schenkungen, durch die einer sittlichen Pflicht oder einer auf den Anstand zu nehmenden Rücksicht entsprochen wird, unterliegen nicht der Rückforderung und dem Widerruf.

§ 534. *Donations of duty and decency*
Donations to meet a moral duty or made out of considerations of decency are not subject to recovery and revocation.

§ 125. Nichtigkeit wegen Formmangels.
Ein Rechtsgeschäft, welches der durch Gesetz vorgeschriebenen Form ermangelt, ist nichtig. [...]

§ 125. *Voidness due to a defect of form*
A legal transaction lacking the form prescribed by law is void.
[...]

2. Reichsgericht (*Supreme Court of the former German Empire*) 23.2.1920, RGZ 98, 176

VI. Zivilsenat, Urt. v. 23. Februar 1920 I.S. Ku. (Bekl.) w. Ke. (Kl.) VI 387/19

Der Beklagte hatte von 1898 an mit der Klägerin etwa zehn Jahre lang ein Verhältnis, dem drei Kinder, darunter ein noch lebendes, entsprossen sind. [...] [Er hat] ihr am 1. März 1904 folgenden Schein ausgestellt: "Gebe hiermit schriftlich, dass ich für Jossi [...] stets gesorgt habe und auch weiter sorgen werde. [...] Sollte es der Fall sein, dass ich heiraten würde, was ziemlich ausgeschlossen ist, so verpflichte ich mich, in diesem Falle Jossi eine Summe von mindestens 15.000 Mark zu geben." Der Beklagte hat sich im Jahre 1911 verheiratet. Die Klägerin fordert von ihm die Zahlung von 15.000 Mark.

Der Beklagte hat die Gültigkeit seiner Verpflichtung bestritten, weil sie [...] als Schenkungsversprechen der gesetzlichen Form entbehre.

Die beiden Vordergerichte haben ihn klaggemäß verurteilt. Auch seine Revision hatte keinen Erfolg.

Gründe:

Unter den Parteien ist unstreitig, dass das Zahlungsversprechen des Beklagten seine Verpflichtung losgelöst von ihrem Rechtsgrund, also selbständig begründen sollte. Der Schein enthält mithin ein Schuldversprechen im Sinne des § 780 BGB, das den Beklagten so lange bindet, als er nicht dartut, dass es, wie er behauptet, [...] unwirksam sei. Ein Schuldversprechen hat Vertragscharakter. [...] [D]as Berufungsgericht [gibt] von den "Verhältnissen" der Parteien folgendes Bild. Sie hätten während ihrer zehnjährigen Beziehung [...] wie Mann und Frau zusammengelebt. Zu den Kosten des gemeinschaftlichen Haushalts habe Klägerin nach Kräften beigetragen [...] Sie habe ihre Ersparnisse als Kellnerin dafür ausgegeben und durch Vermieten von Zimmern für Mittel gesorgt. [...] [Die Klägerin] habe ihren Beruf aufgegeben und sich ausschließlich dem Beklagten gewidmet. Sie habe ihm ihre Jugend und die Aussicht auf ein besseres Fortkommen geopfert. [...] Hiernach nimmt das Berufungsgericht zutreffend an, dass [...] sittliche Pflicht und anständige Denkungsweise dem Beklagten geboten hätten, die Klägerin für die Opfer, die sie ihm gebracht, für die Dienste und Leistungen zu entschädigen und ihre Zukunft sicherzustellen, wenn er dazu in die Lage komme.

Sollte aber das Schuldversprechen die Klägerin für das, was sie für den Beklagten getan, schadlos halten und die Nachteile ausgleichen, die sie durch das Verhältnis getroffen hatten, so verneint das Berufungsgericht mit Recht, dass es sich um ein Schenkungsversprechen handele. Denn es fehlt an der Voraussetzung der Schenkung, dass die Parteien über die Unentgeltlichkeit einig waren. [...]

Translation

From 1898 the defendant had a relationship with the plaintiff for about ten years, during which three children were born, one of whom is still alive. [...] On the 1st March 1904, [he had] declared in writing: "I have always taken care of Jossi [...] and I commit myself in writing that I will continue to take care of her. [...] Should I marry, which seems to be out of the question, I commit myself that, in such a case, I will pay Jossi the sum of at least 15 000 Marks." In 1911, the defendant got married. The plaintiff asked him to pay her 15 000 Marks.

The defendant contests the validity of his commitment, because [...] it was not made in the form prescribed by law for donations to be valid.

The court of first instance as well as the court of appeal ordered him to pay the amount claimed by the plaintiff. His appeal failed.

Reasons:

The parties do not dispute the fact that the defendant's promise of payment should engage his responsibility, independent of any other legal basis. The paper signed by the defendant constitutes therefore a debt commitment in the sense of § 780 BGB, by which the defendant is bound as long as he has not established that the obligation is, as he claims, [...] void. A debt commitment is a contractual agreement. [...] [T]he court of appeal paints the following picture of the "relationship" between the parties. During the 10 years of their relationship [...], they had lived together like husband and wife. The plaintiff had contributed to the costs of their household to the best of her abilities. [...] She had contributed her earnings as a waitress and gained further income by renting out rooms [...] [The plaintiff] had given up her job and dedicated herself to taking care of the defendant on a full-time basis. She sacrificed her youth for him and her prospects of earning a better living. [...] On the basis of these findings, the court of appeal is right to conclude that [...] moral duties and considerations of decency impose on the defendant a duty to compensate the plaintiff for the sacrifices she made for him as well as for the services rendered and the performances made and to provide her with a secure future, as soon as he was able to do so.

If the purpose of the debt commitment was to compensate the plaintiff for all she had done for the defendant, and to make good all the sacrifices she had to make in the course of the relationship, the court of appeal was right to deny that the commitment was made as a gift. The reason being that the precondition for a gift, requiring that the parties must agree on the gratuitous character of the promise, was not fulfilled. [...]

3. *Münchener Kommentar zum Bürgerlichen Gesetzbuch, Band 3, Schuldrecht, Besonderer Teil I, §§ 433–610, 5th edn (comment by J. Koch) (translation of the German original)*

§ 516

24 **2. Gratuitous promises. a) General principles.** [...] [A promise is gratuitous] if, according to the agreement, it does not depend on a benefit moving from the party receiving the advantage to the party providing it and if it is not meant to extinguish a debt [...] It is not sufficient for a promise to be gratuitious if, according to an objective view, it does not depend on a benefit moving from the party receiving the advantage to the party providing it; in addition, the parties must **intend the promise to be gratuitous.** [...]

30 **cc) Retrospective payment.** The link between an advantage promised and a performance by the party receiving the advantage can also be established *ex post*, i.e. if the advantage is promised in order to remunerate for a performance that was initially carried out without asking for payment. [...] It is controversial if it is possible to agree *ex post* that a donation be **changed** retrospectively into a contract against payment. Some authors are of the opinion that, if initially a donation was made, it is excluded to transform the agreement *ex post* into a contract against payment [...] However, there is no reason in private law for not accepting that the parties use their freedom of contract in order to change the initial agreement about the cause of an advantage given and to **turn** the gift **retrospectively into a contract against payment** as long as this does not violate mandatory provisions or the rights of third parties (footnote 133: This is the largely dominant opinion [with many cites to case law and legal doctrine]).

31 **dd) Donation meant to be a reward.** If a donation can be **changed** retrospectively into a contract against payment, it is necessary to draw a line between such agreements and donations that are meant to be a "reward", i.e. where the advantage is not promised as a counter-performance for the benefit received but as a reward given gratuitously, such rewards being considered donations in the sense of §§ 516 BGB ff. The answer to the question how to draw this line depends on the intentions of the parties to the agreement, in particular the intention of the person giving the advantage. In order for the agreement to be a contract against payment, the person promising the benefit must be of the opinion that a benefit received deserves a (higher) remuneration. That is why he offers to **modify the contract** and to provide a remuneration (instead of a donation) [...] If the advantage is meant to be a "reward", the person promising the advantage does not intend to modify the previous agreement but wants to reciprocate for a benefit reveived gratuitiously. [...]

4. Obligationenrecht (*Swiss Code of Obligations*)

Donation
Art. 243.   Promesse de donner
[1] La promesse de donner n'est valable que si elle est faite par écrit.
[...]

Donation
Art. 243.   *Promise to make a donation*
[1]*A promise to donate is valid only if made in writing.*
[...]

XII. The Principles of Contract Law

1. Commission on European Contract Law: *Principles of European Contract Law*

Art. 1:102: Freedom of Contract

(1) Parties are free to enter into a contract and to determine its contents, subject to the requirements of good faith and fair dealing, and the mandatory rules established by these Principles.

(2) The parties may exclude the application of any of the Principles or derogate from or vary their effects, except as otherwise provided by these Principles.

Art. 2:101. Conditions for the Conclusion of a Contract

(1) A contract is concluded if:

    (a) the parties intend to be legally bound, and

    (b) they reach a sufficient agreement

without any further requirement.

(2) A contract need not be concluded or evidenced in writing nor is it subject to any other requirement as to form. The contract may be proved by any means, including witnesses.

[...]

Art. 2:101 – COMMENTS

A. *Contract*

In these Principles the notion contract covers:

– agreements under which two or more parties have undertaken an obligation to make a performance,

– agreements where the offeree accepts the offer by doing the act or suffering the forbearance which the offeror asks of it,

– agreements where only one party has obligations and where its promise needs acceptance by the offeree,

– promises to which one party is bound without acceptance by the other, as provided in Article 2:107 below.

The rules on contract also govern agreements to modify or end existing contracts, see Article 1:107.

B. *Intention*

In order to be bound by a contract a party must have an intention to be legally bound. Whether in fact it has such intention is immaterial if the other party has reason to infer from the first party's statement or other conduct that it intends to be bound, see Article 2:102.

C. *Agreement*

Where more than one party is to be bound the parties must agree. Their agreement may be reached by one party's acceptance of the other's offer, see Section 2, by agreeing to a contract which has been drafted by a third party, or in other ways. What constitutes sufficient agreement is spelled out in Article 2:103.

In some cases where only one party is to be bound an expression of agreement by the other party is not needed. Promises which are intended to become binding without acceptance are to be treated as contracts, see Article 2:107.

D. *No Further Requirement*

Whether or not agreement is needed there are no further requirements. No form is required, see Comment F. Nor is it necessary that a promisee undertakes to furnish or furnishes something of value in exchange for the promise (consideration). Even an undertaking to lend money and a promise to receive a deposit are effective before they have been performed. A contract is not invalid because at the time of its conclusion it was impossible to perform the obligation assumed, see Article 4:102.

E. *Binding Character of a "Gratuitous" Promise*

Some legal systems do not enforce a party's "gratuitous" promise. Some do so but only if it is couched in a solemn form or is found to serve a socially desirable purpose which cannot be achieved by other means.

The fear that the enforcement of such "gratuitous" promises, even though no formality has been observed, will lead to socially undesirable results is not well founded. In fact many of these promises serve legitimate commercial purposes.

Nor is it necessary to inquire into the social desirability of the promise if it is sincerely made. Experience shows that the legal systems which enforce gratuitous promises do not encounter problems. "Crazy" promises made by persons of a sound mind are so rare that they may be disregarded, while even the presence of a formality or of an exchange does not guarantee that the contract is a sensible one. On the other hand, those legal systems which do not enforce "gratuitous" promises have faced problems when such promises sincerely made have since been revoked. These problems do not only arise when the promisee has acted in reliance on the promise, and injustice can be avoided only by enforcing the promise, but also in other situations. For this reason these promises should be enforced.

F. *No Formal Requirement*

Article 2:10 1(2) lays down the principle that, unless the parties otherwise agree, the conclusion as well as the modification and the termination by agreement of a contract are valid without any form, be it writing, sealing, authentication by a notary, filing in a public registry etc. This principle is widely accepted among the legal systems at least as far as commercial contracts are concerned. For international contracts it is particularly important since many such contracts have to be concluded or modified without the delays which the observance of formalities will cause.

This provision also applies to unilateral promises, see Article 2:107.

[Comparative] NOTES
[...]

Art. 4:103. Fundamental Mistake as to Facts or Law

(1) A party may avoid a contract for mistake of fact or law existing when the contract was concluded if:

    (a) (i)   the mistake was caused by information given by the other party; or

        (ii) the other party knew or ought to have known of the mistake and it was contrary to good faith and fair dealing to leave the mistaken party in error; or

        (iii) the other party made the same mistake,

and

    (b) the other party knew or ought to have known that the mistaken party, had it known the truth, would not have entered the contract or would have done so only on fundamentally different terms.

(2) However a party may not avoid the contract if:

    (a) in the circumstances its mistake was inexcusable, or

    (b) the risk of the mistake was assumed, or in the circumstances should be borne, by it.

Article 4:106. Incorrect Information

A party who has concluded a contract relying on incorrect information given it by the other party may recover damages in accordance with Article 4:117(2) and (3) even if the information does not give rise to a fundamental mistake under Article 4:103, unless the party who gave the information had reason to believe that the information was correct.

Art. 4:107. Fraud

(1) A party may avoid a contract when it has been led to conclude it by the other party's fraudulent representation, whether by words or conduct, or fraudulent non-disclosure of any information which in accordance with good faith and fair dealing it should have disclosed.

(2) A party's representation or non-disclosure is fraudulent if it was intended to deceive.

(3) In determining whether good faith and fair dealing required that a party disclose particular information, regard should be had to all the circumstances, including:

    (a) whether the party had special expertise;

    (b) the cost to it of acquiring the relevant information;

    (c) whether the other party could reasonably acquire the information for itself; and

    (d) the apparent importance of the information to the other party.

Art. 4:108. Threats

A party may avoid a contract when it has been led to conclude it by the other party's imminent and serious threat of an act:

    (a) which is wrongful in itself, or

    (b) which it is wrongful to use as a means to obtain the conclusion of the contract, unless in the circumstances the first party had a reasonable alternative.

Art. 4:109. Excessive Benefit or Unfair Advantage

(1) A party may avoid a contract if, at the time of the conclusion of the contract:

    (a) it was dependent on or had a relationship of trust with the other party, was in economic distress or had urgent needs, was improvident, ignorant, inexperienced or lacking in bargaining skill, and

(b) the other party knew or ought to have known of this and, given the circumstances and purpose of the contract, took advantage of the first party's situation in a way which was grossly unfair or took an excessive benefit.

(2)   Upon the request of the party entitled to avoidance, a court may if it is appropriate adapt the contract in order to bring it into accordance with what might have been agreed had the requirements of good faith and fair dealing been followed.

(3)   A court may similarly adapt the contract upon the request of a party receiving notice of avoidance for excessive benefit or unfair advantage, provided that this party informs the party who gave the notice promptly after receiving it and before that party has acted in reliance on it.

2. Study Group on a European Civil Code and Research Group on EC Private Law (Acquis Group): *Draft Common Frame of Reference*

Book II
Contracts and other juridical acts

Chapter I:
General provisions

II. – 1:102: Party autonomy
(1)   Parties are free to make a contract or other juridical act and to determine its contents, subject to any applicable mandatory rules.

[...]

II. – 1:106: Form
(1)   A contract or other juridical act need not be concluded, made or evidenced in writing nor is it subject to any other requirement as to form.
[...]

Chapter 4:
Formation
Section 1:
General provisions

II. – 4:101: Requirements for the conclusion of a contract
A contract is concluded, without any further requirement, if the parties:
(a)   intend to enter into a binding legal relationship or bring about some other legal effect; and
(b)   reach a sufficient agreement.

II. – 4:102: How intention is determined

The intention of a party to enter into a binding legal relationship or bring about some other legal effect is to be determined from the party's statements or conduct as they were reasonably understood by the other party.

[...]

Chapter 7:
Grounds of invalidity

Section 1:
General provisions

II. – 7:101: Scope

(1) This Chapter deals with the effects of:
    (a) mistake, fraud, threats, or unfair exploitation; and
    (b) infringement of fundamental principles or mandatory rules.

[...]

Section 2:
Vitiated consent or intention

II. – 7:201: Mistake

(1) A party may avoid a contract for mistake of fact or law existing when the contract was concluded if:
    (a) the party, but for the mistake, would not have concluded the contract or would have done so only on fundamentally different terms and the other party knew or could reasonably be expected to have known this; and
    (b) the other party;
        (i) caused the mistake;
        (ii) caused the contract to be concluded in mistake by leaving the mistaken party in error, contrary to good faith and fair dealing, when the other party knew or could reasonably be expected to have known of the mistake;
        (iii) caused the contract to be concluded in mistake by failing to comply with a pre-contractual information duty or a duty to make available a means of correcting input errors; or
        (iv) made the same mistake.

[...]

II. – 7:204: Liability for loss caused by reliance on incorrect information

(1) A party who has concluded a contract in reasonable reliance on incorrect information given by the other party in the course of negotiations has a right to damages for loss suffered as a result if the provider of the information:
    (a) believed the information to be incorrect or had no reasonable grounds for believing it to be correct; and
    (b) knew or could reasonably be expected to have known that the recipient would rely on the information in deciding whether or not to conclude the contract on the agreed terms.

[...]

II. – 7:205: Fraud

(1) A party may avoid a contract when the other party has induced the conclusion of the contract by fraudulent misrepresentation, whether by words or conduct, or fraudulent non-disclosure of any information which good faith and fair dealing, or any pre-contractual information duty, required that party to disclose.

[...]

II. – 7:206: Coercion or threats

(1) A party may avoid a contract when the other party has induced the conclusion of the contract by coercion or by the threat of an imminent and serious harm which it is wrongful to inflict, or wrongful to use as a means to obtain the conclusion of the contract.

(2) A threat is not regarded as inducing the contract if in the circumstances the threatened party had a reasonable alternative.

II. – 7:207: Unfair exploitation

(1) A party may avoid a contract if, at the time of the conclusion of the contract:

    (a) the party was dependent on or had a relationship of trust with the other party, was in economic distress or had urgent needs, was improvident, ignorant, inexperienced or lacking in bargaining skill;

  and

    (b) the other party knew or could reasonably be expected to have known this and, given the circumstances and purpose of the contract, exploited the first party's situation by taking an excessive benefit or grossly unfair advantage.

[...]

II. – 7:301: Contracts infringing fundamental principles

A contract is void to the extent that:

    (a) it infringes a principle recognised as fundamental in the laws of the Member States of the European Union; and

    (b) nullity is required to give effect to that principle.

II. – 7:302: Contracts infringing mandatory rules

(1) Where a contract is not void under the preceding Article but infringes a mandatory rule of law, the effects of that infringement on the validity of the contract are the effects, if any, expressly prescribed by that mandatory rule.

(2) Where the mandatory rule does not expressly prescribe the effects of an infringement on the validity of a contract, a court may;

    (a) declare the contract to be valid;

    (b) avoid the contract, with retrospective effect, in whole or in part; or

    (c) modify the contract or its effects.

[...]

3. Academy of European Private Lawyers, Coordinator: GUISEPPE GANDOLFI, Pavia: *European Contract Code, Draft*

PRELIMINARY PROVISIONS

Art. 1.   Notion.

1.   A contract is the agreement of two or more parties to establish, regulate, alter or extinguish a legal relationship between said parties. It can also produce obligations or other effects on only one of the parties.

2.   Except as provided for in the following provisions, a contract can also be created by conclusive behaviours, following a previous statement of intent or according to usage or good faith.

Art. 2.   Contractual autonomy.

1.   The parties can freely determine the contents of the contract, within the limits imposed by mandatory rules, morals and public policy, as established in the present code, Community law or national laws of the Member States of the European Union, provided always that the parties thereby do not solely aim to harm others.

[...]

4. UNIDROIT: *Principles of International Commercial Contracts*

Art. 3.2.   Validity of mere agreement.

A contract is concluded, modified or terminated by the mere agreement of the parties, without any further requirement.

OFFICIAL COMMENT

The purpose of this article is to make it clear that the mere agreement of the parties is sufficient for the valid conclusion, modification or termination by agreement of a contract, without any of the further requirements which are to be found in some domestic laws.

1.   No need for consideration

In common law systems, consideration is traditionally seen as a prerequisite for the validity or enforceability of a contract as well as for its modification or termination by the parties. However, in commercial dealings this requirement is of minimal practical importance since in that context obligations are almost always undertaken by both parties. It is for this reason that Art. 29(1) CISG dispenses with the requirement of consideration in relation to the modification and termination by the parties of contracts for the international sale of goods. The fact that the present article extends this approach to the conclusion, modification and termination by the parties of international commercial contracts in general can only bring about greater certainty and reduce litigation.

2.   No need for cause

This article also excludes the requirement of cause which exists in some civil law systems and is in certain respects functionally similar to the common law "consideration".

Illustration

1.   At the request of its French customer A, bank B in Paris issues a guarantee on first demand in favour of C, a business partner of A in England. Neither B nor A can invoke the possible absence of consideration or cause for the guarantee.

It should be noted however that this article is not concerned with the effects which may derive from other aspects of cause, such as its illegality. See comment 2 on Art. 3.3.

Article 3.4.   Definition of mistake.
Mistake is an erroneous assumption relating to facts or to law existing when the contract was concluded.

Art. 3.5.   Relevant mistake.
(1)   A party may only avoid the contract for mistake if, when the contract was concluded, the mistake was of such importance that a reasonable person in the same situation as the party in error would only have concluded the contract on materially different terms or would not have concluded it at all if the true state of affairs had been known, and
     (a) the other party made the same mistake, or caused the mistake, or knew or ought to have known of the mistake and it was contrary to reasonable commercial standards of fair dealing to leave the mistaken party in error; or
     (b) the other party had not at the time of avoidance reasonably acted in reliance on the contract.
(2)   However, a party may not avoid the contract if
     (a) it was grossly negligent in committing the mistake; or
     (b) the mistake relates to a matter in regard to which the risk of mistake was assumed or, having regard to the circumstances, should be borne by the mistaken party.

Art. 3.8.   Fraud.
A party may avoid the contract when it has been led to conclude the contract by the other party's fraudulent representation, including language or practices, or fraudulent non-disclosure of circumstances which, according to reasonable commercial standards of fair dealing, the latter party should have disclosed.

Art. 3.9.   Threat.

A party may avoid the contract when it has been led to conclude the contract by the other party's unjustified threat which, having regard to the circumstances, is so imminent and serious as to leave the first party no reasonable alternative. In particular, a threat is unjustified if the act or omission with which a party has been threatened is wrongful in itself, or it is wrongful to use it as a means to obtain the conclusion of the contract.

Art. 3.10.   Gross disparity.

(1)   A party may avoid the contract or an individual term of it if, at the time of the conclusion of the contract, the contract or term unjustifiably gave the other party an excessive advantage. Regard is to be had, among other factors, to

(a)   the fact that the other party has taken unfair advantage of the first party's dependence, economic distress or urgent needs, or of its improvidence, ignorance, inexperience or lack of bargaining skill, and

(b)   the nature and purpose of the contract.

(2)   Upon the request of the party entitled to avoidance, a court may adapt the contract or term in order to make it accord with reasonable commercial standards of fair dealing.

(3)   A court may also adapt the contract or term upon the request of the party receiving notice of avoidance, provided that that party informs the other party of its request promptly after receiving such notice and before the other party has reasonably acted in reliance on it. The provisions of Article 3.13(2) apply accordingly.

5. CHRISTINE CHAPPUIS, "Le renoncement à la cause et à la consideration dans l'avant-projet d'Acte uniforme OHADA sur le droit des contrats", *Revue de droit uniforme* 2008, 253–91[13]

The preliminary draft OHADA Uniform Act on Contract Law (hereafter: Preliminary Draft) sanctions a double renunciation. The Preliminary Draft does not count *la cause* or consideration amongst the requirements for a valid contract [...] Like its model, the UNIDROIT *Principles of International Commercial Contracts*, the Preliminary Draft is centred on the parties' agreement. The [parties'] mutual willingness [to contract], a result of the exchange of an offer and an acceptance, is enough to validly bind the parties. [...]

I. –*LA CAUSE* OR CONSIDERATION: AN IMPOSSIBLE CHOICE

The doctrines of *la cause* and consideration share the questionable privilege of not being understood by lawyers who were not trained in French law or in the Common law [respectively]. [...] Doing without both of them, the modern trend is to deal with the problems raised using other legal institutions. The Preliminary Draft follows the modern trend [...]

1. The foreign lawyer's incomprehension

[...] The two doctrines will firstly be examined from the point of view of a Swiss lawyer, as a foreign lawyer.

2. Validity of contracts, consideration and *la cause* in Swiss law

When asked about the validity of a contract, a Swiss lawyer is in the habit of checking, in this order: 1. the existence of an agreement between the parties (Articles 1 to 10 of the Swiss Code of obligations, hereafter: CO); 2. the respect of any rules as to form, bearing in mind that the general principle is that no particular form is required (Articles 11 to 16 CO); 3. the respect of the limitations provided for by law on the subject-matter of the contract (Articles 19 to 20 CO); 4. the absence of a defect in consent (Articles 21, 23 to 31 CO); and 5. the parties' capacity to conclude the contract as well as, if appropriate, the rules on agency (Articles 32 to 40 CO).

---

[13] [Comment added by the author] At the request of the Organisation for the Harmonization of Business Law in Africa (*Organisation pour l'Harmonisation en Afrique du Droit des Affaires, OHADA*), the International Institute for the Unification of Private Law (UNIDROIT) has developed a preliminary draft of an OHADA Uniform Act on Contract Law, the aim being the unification of the contract law of the OHADA Member States. Text and Explanatory Note by MARCEL FONTAINE available online at: «www.unidroit.org»; The Member States of OHADA are: Benin, Burkina Faso, Cameroon, Chad, Central African Republic, Comoros, Congo, Equatorial Guinea, Ivory Coast, Gabon, Guinea, Guinea-Bissau, Mali, Niger, Senegal, and Togo. The Democratic Republic of Congo is soon to join. Like the UNIDROIT Principles, the OHADA draft also abandons the doctrines of *la cause* and consideration. The proposal has sparked lively debate in OHADA, see the contributions in the special issue of the *Uniform Law Review* 2008-1/2, pp. 1 ff.

Notwithstanding the slightly different terminology and structure, a Swiss lawyer would find corresponding sections in the Preliminary Draft [...]

On the other hand, faced with the requirement of consideration for the contract, the necessary counterpart without which a promise is not binding on its maker, the Swiss lawyer is lost. [...] A unilateral contract comprising of an obligation to be acquitted by one party only, is a type of contract that is recognised in Swiss law. It allows, for example, one party to bind himself on the basis of a donation contract (*contrat de donation*) (Article 239 ff. CO), admittedly only valid if done in writing (Article 243(1) CO), or a contract of guarantee binding only the party who guarantees the debt of a third party. [...]

As for the notion of *la cause*, it is not totally unfamiliar to a Swiss lawyer who will, for a start, think of unjust enrichment or enrichment "without cause" [*enrichissement sans cause*, enrichment without any valid reason] (Article 62 ff. CO). However, here, Swiss law is aiming at the *cause* of a transfer of property, not the *cause* of a contract or an obligation. It requires anyone who has been unjustly enriched out of another person's property to make restitution [...] This is why payment of a sum of money taken on the basis of a contract that was not concluded, is null and void, or has been annulled, must be restituted on the basis of the rules of unjust enrichment. [...]

When searching for corresponding features of Swiss and French law, you will [...] end up at Article 17 CO [...]: "Cause of obligation". However, this provision deals with a very special issue relating to the acknowledgement of debt. Such an acknowledgement "is valid whether or not a cause of obligation is mentioned". [...] As such, the declaration made by X to Y: "I owe you 100 000", produces legal effects even if it does not indicate the *cause* of the debt, *i.e.* the reasons for which X owes 100 000 to Y (payment, reimbursement of an overpayment, damages following an accident, *etc.*). The resulting legal effects are, however, limited to the matter of proof of the existence of the debt by the creditor and of the protection of third parties in good faith (Articles 18(2) and 164(2) CO). [...]

La cause, as understood in Swiss law, is but a false friend of French law's *cause*, the visible proximity of the terms making it dangerous for the comparatist.

3. An outside look at the problems dealt with by *la cause*

[...] [F]oreign lawyers attempt to understand the concrete problems that are solved in French law by checking the existence, and then the lawfulness of the *cause*.

[...] An obligation loses its *cause* when the counterpart is lacking, as such, when the price is derisory or, for bilateral contracts, when the absence of an obligation leads to the other disappearing. It seems very tempting to make *la cause* into an instrument of contractual fairness and balance. This explains why a certain subjectivisation of the *cause* of the obligation, going as far as checking the economic purpose of the contract, can be observed. Consequently, the question has to be asked, whether the *cause* is not a measure necessary only because the French Civil Code is lacking a legal mechanism that is suitable for achieving contractual fairness and balance [with regard to the reciprocity of obligations]. The possibility, provided for in Article 3/10 of the Preliminary Draft [as well as in the UNIDROIT Principles] not to give legal effect to a contract that gives an excessive advantage to one party, at the request of the disadvantaged party, adequately responds to the need to ensure a minimum amount of contractual fairness.

[...]

It may be remembered that the specific problems solved by verifying the existence of the *cause* are close to the prohibition on *lésion* [unfairness in the provisions of a contract] or mistake; problems relating to the lawfulness and the morality of the *cause* correspond to the limits imposed on the parties' agreement by the legal system. As for the Preliminary Draft, it treats factual situations linked to the absence of *cause* with the provisions on initial impossibility of performance, defects in consent, excessive advantage, omissions, determination or non-performance of the obligation. Situations where the *cause* is illegal or immoral are dealt with like cases of invalidity for illegality [...]

III. – GENERAL CONCLUSIONS

[...]

Every legal system has to come to a compromise with the insufficiencies, often of historical origin, of its laws and the limitations linked to the power of examination of its high courts. The courts do their best to find equitable solutions that are reasonably founded in law. They must occasionally reach these solutions in a roundabout way. Admittedly, these detours have their own national justifications, but they provide bad models for new, easily applicable and predictable rules. *La cause* and consideration are such detours. They both developed like a gas, the expansion of which could not be contained. The heterogeneous nature of the situations targeted explains the complexity of the notions and their nature of being difficult to access for foreign lawyers. [...] There is no choice but to admit that a body of rules, wanting to be attractive to parties and offering legal certainty necessarily cannot keep doctrines [...] that operate in such a delicate way.

The Preliminary Draft is intended to apply to Member States with different legal orders and different, or even, incompatible concepts. Also intended to reassure parties coming from outside legal systems, the Draft must avoid using notions that are difficult to understand. [...]

XIII.   Further reading

Hugh Beale *et al.* (eds), *Cases, Materials and Text on Contract Law* (Ius Commune Casebooks for the Common Law of Europe), Oxford: Hart Publishing, 2002, Ch.1.3.3, Cause [...] and consideration, 127–154.

Patrick Blanchard, "Offer and acceptance in international contract negotiation: a comparative study", *I.B.L.J.* 2008, 1, 3–27.

Nicholas C. Dranias, "Consideration as Contract: A Secular Natural Law of Contracts", 12 (2008) *Tex. Rev. Law & Pol.* 267–327.

Allan Farnsworth, *Contracts*, 3rd edn, New York: Aspen Publishers, 2004, 45–99 (USA).

James Gordley, "Consideration", in Jan M. Smits (ed.), *Elgar Encyclopedia of Comparative Law*, Cheltenham: Elgar Publishing, 2006, 180–86.

James Gordley (ed.), *The Enforceability of Promises in European Contract Law*, Cambridge: Cambridge University Press, 2001.

HEIN KÖTZ AND AXEL FLESSNER, *European Contract Law*, Vol. I (by HEIN KÖTZ), Oxford: Clarendon Press, 1997, 52–77.

PABLO LERNER, "Promises of Rewards in a Comparative Perspective", 10 (2004) *Ann. Surv. Int'l & Comp. L.* 53–101.

RICHARD A. LORD, "The At-Will Relationship in the 21st Century: A Consideration of Consideration", 58 (2006) *Baylor L. Rev.* 707–77.

BASIL S. MARKESINIS, "Cause and Consideration: a Study in Parallel", *Cambridge Law Journal* 1978, 53–75.

MALCOLM S. MASON, "The Utility of Consideration – A Comparative View", *Columbia Law Review* 1941, 825–48.

MICHAEL J.T. MCMILLEN, "Symposium: Islamic Business And Commercial Law: Contractual Enforceability Issues: Sukuk and Capital Markets Development", 7 (2007) *Chi. J. Int'l L.* 427–67.

ARTHUR T. VON MEHREN, "Civil-Law Analogues to Consideration: An Exercise in Comparative Analysis", *Harv. L. Rev.* 1959, 1009–78.

C. SCOTT PRYOR, "Consideration in the Common Law of Contracts: A Biblical-Theological Critique", 18 (2005/2006) *Regent U.L. Rev.* 1–51.

LAWRENCE M. SOLAN, "Contract as Agreement", 83 (2007) *Notre Dame L. Rev.* 353–408.

MATTHIAS STORME, "The Binding Character of Contracts – Causa and Consideration", in Arthur Hartkamp *et al.* (eds), *Towards a European Civil Code*, 2nd edn, Nijmegen: Kluwer, 1998, Ch. 15, 239–54.

REINHARD ZIMMERMANN, *The Law of Obligations – Roman Foundations of the Civilian Tradition*, Cape Town: Juta & Co., 1990, 549–76.

Case 3: Obligation to maintain an offer or freedom to revoke an offer?

"The problem of whether an offer is or is not revocable is traditionally one of the most controversial issues in the context of the formation of contracts."[1]

Scenario[2]

A wine cooperative participates in a trade fair for the wine industry, offering, among others, a red wine not previously marketed in the country. Following the trade fair, on 10 June a supermarket sends the wine cooperative an order for 20,000 cases of this wine at a price of US $68.00 per case, for a total contract price of US $1,360,000.

When the order arrives on 11 June, the wine cooperative's sales manager is absent from the office on a business trip. Since the order as placed by the supermarket is slightly different from the wine cooperative's price quotation, it is necessary to await the return of the cooperative's sales manager to authorise its acceptance.

On 13 June, the wine cooperative receives an e-mail message sent by the supermarket purporting to withdraw the offer. The cooperative's sales manager returns on 14 June. Unaware of the e-mail purporting to withdraw the offer, he signs the contract and sends it to the supermarket. The signed contract is received at the supermarket on 15 June.

Variation

In the letter accompanying the order, the supermarket's wine buyer stipulated that he needed an acceptance of the order by 16 June, since it was important for him to be able to plan for the wine promotion; if there were no acceptance of the order by then, the supermarket would turn to another wine distributor.

---

[1] UNIDROIT: Principles of International Commercial Contracts, Comment on Art. 2.1.4.

[2] Inspired by the case scenario of the Fifteenth Annual Willem C. Vis International Commercial Arbitration Moot, Vienna 2008, and the Fifth Annual Willem C. Vis (East) International Commercial Arbitration Moot, Hong Kong 2008.

Questions

(1) Whether there is a contract depends largely on the question whether the supermarket could revoke its offer. What would be the response to this question under the different *Continental* legal orders and the *Civil Code of Quebec*, when applying the rules on contract law that you will find in the material below?

   Does the response differ where the offeror stipulates a time limit for acceptance in his offer?

   Present the solutions found in the different countries systematically.

(2) What would be the outcome under *English* law? Why is it the case under English law that "one party cannot be bound without the other"? What is the significance of the *postal rule* for the revocation of offers?

   How would the case be solved under the *American Restatement of Law Second, Contracts*?

   How does the *Uniform Commercial Code* deal with the problem of whether or not an offer should be revocable?

   What is the answer given in the *Civil Code of Louisiana*?

   In which respect does the solution in the US case *Rhode Island Tool Company* v. *United States* differ from the "English approach" to the revocability of offers?

(3) How would you solve the above case scenario and its variation under:
   (a) the *United Nations Convention on Contracts for the International Sale of Goods* (CISG or Vienna Sales Convention);
   (b) the *UNIDROIT Principles of International Commercial Contracts*;
   (c) the *Principles of European Contract Law* (Lando Principles);
   (d) the *Draft Common Frame of Reference*.

   How is an offer that includes a time limit for acceptance dealt with under the CISG and the UNIDROIT Principles on the one hand, and under the Principles of European Contract Law and the Draft Common Frame of Reference on the other?

(4) Which rules may have been used as a source of inspiration for the articles on the revocation of offers in the *Dutch, Polish* and *Lithuanian* civil codes?

   Which regulation(s) may have served as the model for Articles 18 and 19 of the *Contract Law of the People's Republic of China*?

(5) What are the arguments for and against the different solutions found in the materials? In your opinion, which solution relating to the revocability of offers best meets the interests of all of the parties involved?

Table of contents

VIII. United States of America

IX. The Vienna Sales Convention and the Principles of Contract Law

X. China

XI. Summary

I.   Various Continental Legal Systems

1. Schweizerisches Obligationenrecht
(*Swiss Code of Obligations*)

Art. 3.   Antrag und Annahme. Antrag mit Annahmefrist.
(1)   Wer einem andern den Antrag zum Abschlusse eines Vertrages stellt und für die Annahme eine Frist setzt, bleibt bis zu deren Ablauf an den Antrag gebunden.
(2)   Er wird wieder frei, wenn eine Annahmeerklärung nicht vor Ablauf dieser Frist bei ihm eingetroffen ist.

Art. 3.   Offer and acceptance. Offer with time limit for acceptance.
(1)   Whoever extends an offer to another person to enter into a contract, and fixes a time limit for acceptance thereof, shall remain bound by the terms of his offer until the expiration of such time limit.
(2)   The offeror shall be released therefrom if a declaration of acceptance has not reached him prior to the expiration of the time limit.

Art. 4.   Antrag ohne Annahmefrist. Unter Anwesenden.
(1)   Wird der Antrag ohne Bestimmung einer Frist an einen Anwesenden gestellt und nicht sogleich angenommen, so ist der Antragsteller nicht weiter gebunden.
(2)   Wenn die Vertragschliessenden oder ihre Bevollmächtigten sich persönlich des Telefons bedienen, so gilt der Vertrag als unter Anwesenden abgeschlossen.

Art. 4.   Offer without time limit for acceptance. Among persons present.
(1)   If an offer is made to a person present without the setting of a time limit, the offeror shall be deemed no longer to be bound if the offer is not accepted forthwith.
(2)   If the contracting parties, or persons authorized by them, personally use the telephone, the contract is deemed to be concluded between persons present.

Art. 5.   Unter Abwesenden.
(1)   Wird der Antrag ohne Bestimmung einer Frist an einen Abwesenden gestellt, so bleibt der Antragsteller bis zu dem Zeitpunkte gebunden, wo er den Eingang der Antwort bei ihrer ordnungsmässigen und rechtzeitigen Absendung erwarten darf.
(2)   Er darf dabei voraussetzen, dass sein Antrag rechtzeitig angekommen sei.
(3)   Trifft die rechtzeitig abgesandte Annahmeerklärung erst nach jenem Zeitpunkte bei dem Antragsteller ein, so ist dieser, wenn er nicht gebunden sein will, verpflichtet, ohne Verzug hievon Anzeige zu machen.

Art. 5.   Among persons not present.
(1)   If the offer is made to a person not present without setting a time limit, the offeror shall remain bound until such time as he should reasonably expect receipt of a reply dispatched properly and in due time.
(2)   The offeror may thereby presume that his offer arrived in due time.
(3)   If the declaration of acceptance was dispatched in due time, but arrived with the offeror only after expiration of that time, the offeror is bound unless he gives notice, without delay, of his intent not to be bound.

Art. 9. Widerruf des Antrages und der Annahme.

(1) Trifft der Widerruf bei dem anderen Teile vor oder mit dem Antrage ein, oder wird er bei späterem Eintreffen dem andern zur Kenntnis gebracht, bevor dieser vom Antrag Kenntnis genommen hat, so ist der Antrag als nicht geschehen zu betrachten.

(2) Dasselbe gilt für den Widerruf der Annahme.

Art. 9. *Revocation of the offer and the acceptance.*

(1) If the offeror revokes his offer, and such revocation reaches the other party prior to, or at the same time as, the offer, or if, in the case of a later arrival, the other party has knowledge of the revocation before he has knowledge of the offer, the offer shall be deemed not to have been made.

(2) The same applies to the revocation of an acceptance.

Art. 10. Beginn der Wirkungen eines unter Abwesenden geschlossenen Vertrages.

(1) Ist ein Vertrag unter Abwesenden zustande gekommen, so beginnen seine Wirkungen mit dem Zeitpunkte, wo die Erklärung der Annahme zur Absendung abgegeben wurde.

(2) Wenn eine ausdrückliche Annahme nicht erforderlich ist, so beginnen die Wirkungen des Vertrages mit dem Empfange des Antrages.

Art. 10. *Coming into effect of an contract concluded between persons not present.*

(1) A contract concluded among persons not present shall take effect at the time when the declaration of acceptance is given for dispatch.

(2) If an express acceptance is not required, the contract shall begin to take effect when the offer is received.

2. Bürgerliches Gesetzbuch (BGB)
(*German Civil Code*)

Vertrag

§ 145. Bindung an den Antrag.

Wer einem anderen die Schließung eines Vertrags anträgt, ist an den Antrag gebunden, es sei denn, dass er die Gebundenheit ausgeschlossen hat.

§ 145. *Binding effect of an offer.*

Any person who offers to another to enter into a contract is bound by the offer, unless he has excluded being bound by it.

§ 146. Erlöschen des Antrags.

Der Antrag erlischt, wenn er dem Antragenden gegenüber abgelehnt oder wenn er nicht diesem gegenüber nach den §§ 147 bis 149 rechtzeitig angenommen wird.

§ 146. *Expiry of an offer.*

An offer expires if a refusal is made to the offeror, or if no acceptance is made to this person in good time in accordance with sections 147 to 149.

§ 147. Annahmefrist.

(1) Der einem Anwesenden gemachte Antrag kann nur sofort angenommen werden. Dies gilt auch von einem mittels Fernsprechers von Person zu Person gemachten Antrage.

(2) Der einem Abwesenden gemachte Antrag kann nur bis zu dem Zeitpunkt angenommen werden, in welchem der Antragende den Eingang der Antwort unter regelmäßigen Umständen erwarten darf.

§ 147. *Period for acceptance.*

(1)   An offer made to a person who is present may only be accepted immediately. This also applies to an offer made by one person to another using a telephone or another technical facility.

(2)   An offer made to a person who is absent may be accepted only until the time when the offeror may expect to receive the answer under ordinary circumstances.

§ 148. Bestimmung einer Annahmefrist.

Hat der Antragende für die Annahme des Antrags eine Frist bestimmt, so kann die Annahme nur innerhalb der Frist erfolgen.

§ 148. *Fixing a period for acceptance.*

If the offeror has determined a period of time for the acceptance of an offer, the acceptance may only take place within this period.

3. Österreichisches Allgemeines Bürgerliches Gesetzbuch (ABGB) (*Austrian Civil Code*)

§ 862.

Das Versprechen (Antrag) muss innerhalb der vom Antragsteller bestimmten Frist angenommen werden. In Ermanglung einer solchen muss der einem Anwesenden oder mittels Fernsprechers von Person zu Person gemachte Antrag sogleich, der sonst einem Abwesenden gemachte Antrag längstens bis zu dem Zeitpunkt angenommen werden, in welchem der Antragsteller unter der Voraussetzung, dass sein Antrag rechtzeitig angekommen sei, bei rechtzeitiger und ordnungsmäßiger Absendung der Antwort deren Eintreffen erwarten darf; widrigenfalls ist der Antrag erloschen. Vor Ablauf der Annahmefrist kann der Antrag nicht zurückgenommen werden. [...]

§ 862.

An offer must be accepted within the time limit fixed by the offeror. In the absence of such a time limit, a promise made to a person present or a promise made by telephone from person to person, must be accepted immediately, and a promise made to an absent person must be accepted at the latest at the moment where the offeror, presuming his offer arrived on time, could expect the response if it was sent properly and on time; if not, the offer is void. An offer cannot be revoked before the end of the period of time for acceptance. [...]

4. Αστικός Κώδικας (*Greek Civil Code*)[3]

'Αρθρο 185. Προταση για σψμβαση.
'Οποιος προτείνει τη σύναψη σύμβασης δεσμεύεται όλο το χπονικο διάστημα μέσα οτο οποίπ μποπεί να την αποδεχτεί εκείνος στον οποίο έγινε η πρόταση.

Art. 185.   Offer to enter into a contract.
A person offering to conclude a contract is bound thereby during the whole time period in which the addressee of the offer can proceed with its acceptance.

'Αρθρο 186.   Ανάκληση πρότασης.
'Οποιος πρότεινε τη σύναψη μιας σύμβασης έχει το δικαίωμα να ανακαλέσει την πρόταση, αν απέκλεισε τη δέσμευσή του από την πρόραση ή αν από τη φύση της σύμβασης ή από τις ειδικές περιστάσεις συνάγεται ότι αποκλείεται η δέσμευση.

Art. 186.   Withdrawal of offer.
A person who offered to conclude a contract shall have the right to withdraw his offer if he had excluded the binding effect thereof or if by the nature of the contract or by reason of special circumstances it can be deduced that the binding effect is excluded.

5. Código civil português (*Portuguese Civil Code*)[4]

Art. 230.   Irrevogabilidade da proposta.
(1)   Salvo declaração em contrário, a proposta do contrato é irrevogável depois de ser recebida pelo destinatário ou de ser dele conhecida.
(2)   Se, porém, ao mesmo tempo que a proposta, ou antes dela, o destinatário receber a retractação do proponente ou tiver por outro meio conhecimento dela, fica a proposta sem efeito.
(3)   A revogação da proposta, quando dirigida ao público, é eficaz, desde que seja feita na forma da oferta ou em forma equivalente.

Art. 230.   Irrevocability of offers.
(1)   Except where the contrary is stated, an offer to enter into a contract is irrevocable once it has been received by the offeree or has come to his attention.
(2)   Nevertheless, if, at the same time as receiving the offer or before, the offeree receives or becomes aware by other means of a revocation by the offeror, the offer is no longer effective.
(3)   The revocation of an offer, when it is addressed to the public, is effective from the moment when it is made in the same or an equivalent form as the offer.

---

[3]   Translation adapted by EG. On Greek law see, e.g., Zweigert and Kötz, *An Introduction to Comparative Law*, 3rd edn, Oxford: Oxford University Press, 1998, pp. 155–6; Eugenia Dacoronia, "Greece", in Jan M. Smits (ed.), *Elgar Encyclopedia of Comparative Law*, Cheltenham: Edward Elgar Publishing Ltd, 2006, pp. 289–93; K. Kerameus and P. Kozyris, *Introduction to Greek Law*, 2nd rev. edn, Deventer: Kluwer Law and Taxation Publishers, 1993.

[4]   For a brief information on Portuguese law, see Zweigert and Kötz, above n. 3, pp. 108–9.

6. Zakon o obligacionim odnosima
(*The Law of Contract and Torts, Serbia*)

Član 37.   Do kada ponuda obavezuje.
(1)   Ponuda u kojoj je određen rok za njeno prihvatanje obavezuje ponudioca do isteka tog roka.

[...]

(4)   Ponuda učinjena odsutnom licu, u kojoj nije određen rok za prihvatanje, vezuje ponudioca za vreme koje je redovno potrebno da ponuda stigne ponuđenome, da je ovaj razmotri, o njoj odluči i da odgovor o prihvatanju stigne ponudiocu.

Art. 37.   How Long an Offer is Binding.
(1)   An offer with an indication of the time limit for its acceptance shall be binding on the offeror until the expiration of that time limit.

[...]

(4)   An offer made to an absent person, without indication of the acceptance time limit, shall be binding for the offeror in the course of a period usually needed for the offer to reach the offeree, for his considering it, for making his decision, and for the answer confirming the acceptance to reach the offeror.

II. France

1. Cour de cassation (Ch. Soc.) 22.3.1972 (Société salaisonnière du Centre «Les Tourettes» c. Vandendriesche), D.S. 1972, 468 with Note

COUR DE CASSATION

(CH. SOC.)

22 mars 1972

CONTRAT DE TRAVAIL, Formation, Offre, Employeur, Révocation avant essai, Faute, Délai, Préjudice, Réparation, Cadre.

(Soc. salaisonnière du Centre «Les Tourettes»

c. Vandendriesche.) – ARRET

LA COUR; – Sur le moyen unique, pris de la violation des art. 1101, 1108, 1109 et s., 1134, 1315, 1349, 1353, 1382 et s., 1179, 1780 c. civ. [etc.] – Attendu qu'il ressort de la procédure et des constatations des juges du fond qu'à la suite d'une offre d'emploi, publiée par la Société salaisonnière du Centre et à la demande de cette dernière, Vandendriesche s'est rendu de Brest à Saint-Mathieu (Haute-Vienne), pour discuter au siège de la société de la conclusion éventuelle d'un contrat de travail de chef de fabrication; que par lettre datée du 3 mars 1970, la société lui a «confirmé» sa «décision» de l'engager aux conditions précisées par ailleurs, lui demandant, si ses propositions lui agréaient, de l'informer de la date à laquelle il envisageait de prendre ses fonctions et de lui faire parvenir des certificats de travail, que sous la date du 14 mars, elle lui a écrit pour annuler son «offre d'emploi» au motif qu'elle n'avait pas, à ce jour, reçu son accord, que le conseil d'administration venait de décider de ne créer aucun emploi dans l'immédiat; qu'elle fait grief à la sentence prud'hommale qu'elle attaque, (Cons. Prud'h. Brest, 22 juill. 1970) d'avoir, tout en constatant qu'elle avait réfuté la réclamation de Vandendriesche, accueilli la demande de dommages et intérêts formée par celui-ci aux motifs que la rupture n'était pas intervenue pendant la période d'essai, que toute offre comporte, avant acceptation, un délai de réflexion raisonnable, que si le véritable motif du retrait de la pollicitation avait été le défaut d'acceptation du destinataire, la société avait, en l'espèce, agi précipitamment, le silence gardé par celui-ci pendant neuf jours ne pouvant être assimilé à un refus et qu'en n'embauchant pas le salarié, bien qu'elle s'y fut obligée, en raison de sa décision de ne plus créer d'emploi nouveau, compte tenu de la situation économique, la société avait engagé sa responsabilité, alors que ces motifs contradictoires, dubitatifs et hypothétiques ne confèrent pas de base légale à la décision, que tant que la convention n'est pas formée par l'échange des consentements, la volonté unilatérale et spécialement l'offre de l'une des parties peut être rétractée, seul, le contrat, liant définitivement celle-ci, alors que l'employeur, responsable de la bonne marche de son entreprise est juge de l'organisation de son exploitation et peut aménager ses services comme il l'entend et alors, qu'il n'est dû aucune indemnité quand la rupture de la convention intervient, sans intention de nuire, avant l'achèvement de la période d'essai;

Mais attendu que la sentence attaquée, loin de constater dans ses motifs ou son dispositif que la société résistait victorieusement à la réclamation du demandeur, relève que si Vandendriesche ne pouvait établir qu'il avait, ainsi qu'il l'affirmait, avisé par simple lettre du 11 mars 1970 son futur employeur de son intention de prendre ses fonctions le 23, un délai de neuf jours, seulement, s'était écoulé entre la réception par le salarié de son engagement et celle de sa révocation par l'employeur; qu'ayant estimé, d'une part, que ce délai n'excédait pas le temps de réflexion et de réponse, qu'à défaut de l'avoir préalablement fixé, la société était tenue d'accorder à Vandendriesche, d'autre part, que la décision qu'aurait prise, durant ce laps de temps, le conseil d'administration, de ne procéder, en raison de la situation économique, à aucune création d'emploi et de rétracter son offre, ne pouvait être opposée à un salarié que la société venait de s'obliger à embaucher en l'incitant à donner sa démission de son précédant emploi et à exposer des frais de voyages; que ladite société était mal venue, pour tenter de se dégager de ses obligations, à faire état de ce qu'une période d'essai avait été prévue dès lors que leurs relations avaient été rompues avant tout essai et qu'elle avait, à la légère, fait une offre ayant entraîné un préjudice pour l'intéressé, les juges du fond qui en ont déduit que la société n'avait pu, sans faute, révoquer dans de telles conditions l'engagement d'emploi qu'elle avait adressé à Vandendriesche, ont, sans encourir les reproches du moyen, légalement justifié leur décision;

Par ces motifs, rejette.

Du 22 mars 1972. – Ch. soc. – MM. Laroque, pr. – Vayssettes, rap. – Mellottée, av. gén. – Galland, av.

NOTE. – (1 et 2) La rupture avant exécution de l'essai doit être distinguée de celle survenue au cours de celui-ci. Le retrait d'une offre de travail est considéré comme fautif par l'arrêt rapporté. Bien que le contrat n'ait pas été, semble-t-il, effectivement conclu. C'est donc d'un retrait de pollicitation qu'il s'agit, avant signature d'un engagement et non pas de l'inexécution du contrat signé avant exécution de l'essai. [...]

L'offre, en droit civil classique, peut, en principe, être retirée tant que la convention n'est pas signée. Une jurisprudence ancienne et nombreuse le confirme [...]

Toutefois, l'offre ne doit pas être rétractée quand celui de qui elle émane s'est expressément ou implicitement obligé à ne pas la retirer avant une époque déterminée [...] Si la solution est admise, la doctrine s'interroge sur son fondement: avant-contrat, volonté unilatérale, abus de droit, faute délictuelle?

En droit du travail, cette jurisprudence est transposable, comme le démontre l'arrêt ci-dessus rapporté. Faute et préjudice sont constatés: l'employeur s'était obligé à embaucher le salarié en l'incitant à démissionner d'un précédent emploi et à exposer des frais de voyages; la rétractation de l'offre causait donc par là même un préjudice au candidat [...]

Déjà, dans cette affaire, avait été présenté et condamné, un argument qui est également repoussé aujourd'hui par la Cour suprême: A savoir que si l'essai avait eu lieu, l'employeur aurait pu à tout moment y mettre fin sans être tenu de motiver sa conduite […]

Se pose alors la question de savoir si ce principe de liberté de rupture ne reçoit pas d'exceptions […].

Translation

THE COURT; – On the sole grounds of appeal, based upon the violation of Arts 1101, 1108, 1109 ff., 1134, 1315, 1349, 1353, 1382 ff. 1179, 1780 of the *Code Civil* [Civil Code], 19, 23, 29 of Book I of the *Code de travail* [Employment Code] [etc.]; Whereas it emerges from the proceedings and the findings of the trial judges that following the advertisement of a job vacancy, published by the "Société salaisonnière du Centre" and at the request of said company, Vandendriesche went to Brest in Saint-Mathieu (Haute-Vienne) to discuss the eventual conclusion of an employment contract for the position of production manager at the head office of the company; that by letter dated 3 March 1970, the company gave Vandendriesche "confirmation" of their "decision" to take him on subject to the conditions agreed upon, asking him, if he accepted, to inform them of the date he was planning to take up his position and provide them with *certificats de travail* [documents from a previous employer giving dates and nature of employment], that on 14 March the company wrote to him to revoke the "offer of employment" because they had not received his agreement by that day, and because the board of directors had just decided not to create a job for the time being; that the company contests the decision of the industrial tribunal which is subject to this appeal (Labour Court of Brest, 22 July 1970) for having allowed Vandendriesche's claim for damages, while establishing that the company had rebutted the former's claim, on the grounds that the breach had not occurred during the acceptance period, that every offer includes a reasonable period of reflection before acceptance, that if the real reason for retracting the offer had been the lack of acceptance by the offeree, the company had, in this instance, acted hurriedly, the nine days of silence of Vandendrische could not be taken as a refusal and that by not employing him, although obliged to do so, because of the decision not to create a new position, taking into account the economic situation, the company's liability was engaged, while, according to the company´s reasoning, these contradictory, doubtful and hypothetical reasons do not give a legal basis to the decision, that so long as the agreement was not formed by the exchange of consent, the unilateral statement of intention and in particular the offer of one of the parties can be retracted as long as the contract has not been concluded, whereas the employer, responsible for the smooth operation of his business, is the judge of the organisation of how to achieve this and can arrange his services as he sees fit, and so he is not due any compensation when the contract is breached, without malice, before the completion of the acceptance period;

But whereas the contested judgment, far from establishing in its reasoning or judgment that the company was successfully resisting the claims of the defendant, points out that if Vandendriesche could not establish that he had, as he claimed, notified his future employer by letter on 11 March 1970 of his intention to take up his position on the 23rd, a period of only nine days having run from the reception by the employee of his offer of employment and its revocation by the employer; that having estimated, on the one hand, that the period did not exceed the period of time for reflection and response, that having not fixed one beforehand, the company was obligated to grant Vandendriesche; on the other hand, that the decision that was taken, during this period, by the board of directors not to undertake the creation of any jobs and to retract their offer, could not be used against an employee that the company had just bound itself to employ by encouraging him to resign from his previous employment and incur travel expenses; that the aforementioned company was in no position, in order to attempt to get out of its obligations, to point to the fact that a trial period had been agreed upon since the relationship was ended before the trial period had even begun, the company had, without thinking, made an offer which caused damage to the interested party, the trial judges who inferred from that that the company could not have revoked its offer in such conditions without committing a civil wrong […] legally substantiated their decision

For these reasons the Court rejects the appeal.

NOTE. – (1 and 2) The termination [of employment] before the execution of the trial period must be distinguished from that which occurs during the trial period. The revocation of an offer of employment was considered wrongful in the reported judgment. Although it seems that the contract had not actually been concluded. This is therefore a revocation of an offer before the signing of the contract and not non-performance of a signed contract before the execution of the trial period.
[…]

An offer, in classic civil law, can, in theory, be revoked as long as the contract is not signed. This is confirmed by numerous previous cases.

However, an offer cannot be revoked when the person making it expressly or implicitly bound himself not to revoke it before a specified date […] Even though the solution is widely accepted, academic writing still questions its foundation: preliminary contract, unilateral undertaking, abuse of rights, extra-contractual liability?

In employment law, this case law may be transposed, as shown by the judgment cited above. Fault and damage are established: the employer bound himself to hire the employee by encouraging him to resign from his previous job and incur travel expenses; therefore the retraction of the offer caused damage to the candidate […]

In this case, an argument that is today rejected by the Supreme Court was put forward and dismissed: that is to say that if the trial period had taken place, the employer would have been able to terminate it [the trial period] at any moment without having to give reasons for his conduct […]

Therefore, the question of whether this freedom to break off [pre-contractual arrangements] is subject to exceptions arises […]

2. Code civil français (*French Civil Code*)

Art. 1382
Tout fait quelconque de l'homme, qui cause à autrui un dommage, oblige celui par la faute duquel il est arrivé, à le réparer.

Art. 1382[5]

Anything whatsoever done by someone, which causes damage to another, requires the person at fault to compensate it.

Art. 1383

Chacun est responsable du dommage qu'il a causé non seulement par son fait, mais encore par sa négligence ou par son imprudence.

Art. 1383

Everyone is liable for the damage he causes not only by his intentional act, but also by his negligent conduct or by his imprudence.

3. François Terré, Philippe Simler, Yves Lequette, *Droit civil: Les obligations* (translation of the French original)

115 *The duration of an offer: offers with and without time limits* ◊ An offer can include a time limit. Sometimes this time limit is imposed by the law.

This is the case for certain consumer protection measures that not only stipulate that the offer must come from a professional but also that it must be kept open for a certain time period so that the customer can examine it at his leisure. So, Article L. 311-8 of the Consumer Code relating to consumer *credit contracts*, states that "submission of the offer obliges the lender to maintain the terms indicated therein for a minimum period of fifteen days from issue". The time limit is set at 30 days from reception when one is dealing with a credit contract for the purchase of land (Article L. 312-10 (1) Consumer Code; see also Article 23 of the Law of 12 July 1984 on hire purchase). This is sometimes also the case between professionals. [...] There is therefore a minimum time period decreed by the legislator in the interest of the addressee, but that does not prevent the contracting parties from stipulating a longer time limit. With regard to electronic contracts, Article 1369-4 of the Civil Code [...] specifies that the author of an offer "shall remain bound by it so long as it is available by electronic means of his own accord".

It is more frequently the offeror himself that stipulates the time period. It may be numerically fixed or result from the specific wording of the offer itself. The reasons guiding the offeror may vary: giving the offeree sufficient thinking time, but also avoiding offers formulated for advertising purposes in particularly favourable terms (e.g. low price, big discount, free credit, notary fees paid by the seller ...) remaining open for too long and saddling the offeror with an excessive financial burden. Once the time period has run out, the offer is null. A subsequent acceptance therefore cannot form a contract.

---

5 Translation by EG.

Even though the author of the offer did not stipulate a time limit, the courts may estimate that it is only valid for a reasonable period. Assessed without appeal by the trial judges, the length of such a period varies according to the circumstances: the tacit intention of the offeror, the nature of the planned contract, custom, the distance between the parties, fluctuation in exchange rates.

[…]

116 *b) Legal system. The issues* ◊ Acceptance of the offer leads to the formation of the contract, the offeror loses all possibility of revoking it at that moment. […]

But what happens when the acceptance does not immediately follow the offer? Does the offer have to be kept open by its author or can he revoke it? […]

117 *1) Principles* ◊ In the French legal tradition these questions receive a response based on the defence of individual freedom. An offer only exists if it reflects the real will of its author. As a result, if this will changes or if the person dies, there are no longer any grounds for the offer. It is inferred from that:

1. that an offer can be revoked by the person who made it as long as it has not been accepted. […]

2. […]

In this model only the conclusion of the contract can protect the offeree from revocation of the offer by the offeror […]

This model is often compared with that of the German Civil Code which establishes a diametrically opposed principle: "Any person who offers to another to enter into a contract is bound by the offer, unless he has excluded being bound by it." (§ 145) It follows:

1. that the offeror must maintain the offer for a certain period of time which varies according to the circumstances;

[…]

With this model, the offer is detached from the personality of the offeror; it has an independent legal existence.

French academic writing often explains this difference in solutions by the difference in attitudes of the two systems with regard to the theory of unilateral undertakings: whereas an offer is considered to be a binding unilateral legal undertaking that creates a real obligation on the offeror in German law, in French law, which is traditionally reserved when it comes to the power that one's will should have to be binding, does not accord an offer any binding character. The analysis has been challenged for the reason that in German law an offer is not an independent legal transaction but simply a declaration of will to which the law attributes a legal value.

118 *2) Limitations* ◊ As is often the case in law, it was necessary to come to a compromise with the strictness of the principles, in such a way that the opposition between these two systems is more apparent than real. The necessity for limitations is, in fact, particularly sensitive in French law. The principle of free revocability of offers indeed does not come without disadvantages, especially with regard to legal certainty. Giving the offeror the freedom to revoke the offer at any moment gives the offer a certain insecurity that risks depriving the offeree of desirable thinking time:

to protect himself from such a revocation, he might be tempted to accept the offer hastily. Granting the offeror this freedom also permits him to cause damage to the offeree with impunity: travel and other expenses that he will have taken on to examine the offer are therefore lost; anticipating the conclusion of a contract, the offeree might well have missed out on advantageous deals or even have changed his own legal position irreversibly.

Also, the rule that an offer can be feely revoked is only fully operatioal in French law while the offer has not yet reached the offeree or offerees. Therefore there is no damage to fear. This is why it is always possible to revoke an offer made by post, by using a quicker mode of communication, telegram, telex … On the other hand, once the offer comes to the attention of the offeree the rule is limited in a number of ways.

1. Legal limitations Offers for loans and various credit transactions (Art. L. 311-8 Consumer Code), offers for loans for the purchase of land (Art. L. 312-10 (1) Consumer Code) offers for hire purchase (Art. 23 of the Law of 12 July 1984) must be maintained for a limit between 15 and 30 days according to the particular scenario […] An early revocation of the offer does not obstruct the conclusion of a contract so long as the acceptance occurs after this revocation but within the specified time period. […]

2. Limitations established in case law. Where there is no legal text, the courts, anxious to preserve legal certainty, sometimes impose on the offeror an obligation to maintain the offer. Both the existence and the extent of this obligation are essentially dependent upon the terms used by the offeror.

– When the offeror fixes a precise time limit, the courts require him to maintain his offer open until the end of this period: "if an offer to sell could, in theory, be retracted so long as it had not been accepted, it is quite different where the person making the offer expressly committed himself not to retract it before a certain time".

– When the offeror has not fixed a time limit, the offer can, in theory, be freely revoked. However, the *Cour de cassation* invites courts to look at whether the offer did not "implicitly include a reasonable limit for acceptance". It is sometimes said that the stipulation of such a time limit would more particularly accompany offers addressed to a specific person. Be that as it may, the length of this period is, in general, brief, especially in commercial matters in order to respect the speed of transactions. Decided by the trial judges without the possibility to appeal, it all depends on the circumstances.

The withdrawal of an offer made in violation of the fixed or designated time limit is punished by the granting of damages. Law courses usually teach that where there is an offer to a specific person with a time limit fixed by the offeror, acceptance being made after revocation but before the expiration of the time limit, this would lead to the conclusion of a contract. Although perfectly acceptable in law, such a solution has never been explicitly recognised by the courts. The cited decisions are actually cases where the revocation occurred after the acceptance, that is to say at a time when the contract was already concluded.

119   **3) *Foundation of the solution*** ◊ Whereas the need for these limitations is unanimously accepted, divergences appear once one tries to discover the reasons underlying them. […]

While reaffirming the rule that an offer can be freely revoked, a significant portion of academic writing has justified the limitations on the rule while remaining loyal to the tradition of French law that sees contracts and liability [in tort] as the two main sources of obligations. An offer must be kept open because of the existence of a preliminary contract, or else because its withdrawal would be the source of [tortious] liability.

The so-called *preliminary contract* theory was advanced by Demolombe. When an offeror makes an offer stating that he will maintain it open for a specified time period, a second offer is added to the first. This accessory offer contains only benefits for the offeree, it can be presumed that they have tacitly accepted it. A preliminary contract, binding the offeree to maintain his offer open for the length of time indicated, is thus formed. According to this theory, where no time limit is stipulated, it should nevertheless always be assumed that the offeror intended to give his partner in business time for reflection. Hence there is an implicit offer of a time limit that, like the first, would be tacitly accepted.

This explanation has been criticised for its artifice. Indeed, if the silence of the offeree can amount to acceptance of the offer when it is made for his sole advantage […], it is still necessary that the resulting contract is not a mere fiction. The explanation advanced by Demolombe is also a wonderful illustration of the excessive extension of the theory of the autonomy of the parties.

Other authors look to the principles of *tort law*. Withdrawal of an offer would amount to a civil wrong that would cause damage to the addressee. The offeror would remedy this either by way of paying damages or possibly by way of reparation in kind, consisting in granting the addressee the advantage of the transaction by deciding that the contract was formed despite the withdrawal of the offer. This explanation is objected to as it is based on a vicious circle: there is only a tort if there is an obligation which is precisely what is trying to be proved! The response to this may be that it is the conditions in which the offer was withdrawn that lead to liability. It has also been suggested to look to the theory of abuse of rights to solve this problem. An offer, especially when it is addressed to a specific person and includes a time limit, gives rise to a legitimate expectation in the mind of the addressee, the hope of a contract, which would be dashed by a premature withdrawal. The need for security inherent in all business relations requires one not to betray the trust of a partner in business.

Breaking tradition, some authors have put forward a third explanation based on the theory of *unilateral undertakings*. The need for certainty of legal relations, as identified above, led the courts to consider that a unilateral undertaking can create obligations. Obviously, there must also be a real undertaking by the offeror so that the explanation is not just an artifice. Yet, this can only be the case when the offeror has included a time limit in his offer and not where the courts infer a reasonable time limit for acceptance from the circumstances. Hence the dualist analysis maintained by certain authors: the offeror shall be bound by a unilateral declaration of will when he undertakes to maintain an offer for a certain time limit. Otherwise, the tort law theory shall come into play.

The controversy is of limited practical importance with regard to the revocation of offers. Whether one thinks in terms of tort law or unilateral undertakings, the acceptance of a withdrawn offer could lead to the conclusion of a contract as long as it occurred before the expiration of the time limit stipulated by the offeror, in the first instance by way of reparation in kind, in the second by way of the meeting of wills, the revocation being ineffective in cancelling the offer. However, as has been shown, the French courts have never taken the plunge […].

[…]

III.   Belgium

Cour de cassation belge (1ʳᵉ ch.), 9.5.1980, Pas. 1980 I 1127 (Principle decided in the case)[6]

COUR DE CASSATION

1ʳᵉ CH. – **9 mai 1980.**

[...]

1° Le caractère obligatoire d'une offre faite en vue de conclure une convention trouve son fondement dans un engagement résultant de la manifestation de la volonté unilatérale de celui qui fait cette offre, de sorte qu'il suffit que l'autre partie accepte l'offre pour que la convention soit conclue [...]

Translation

[...]

1° The binding character of an offer made with a view to forming a contract is founded upon an undertaking resulting from the unilateral will of the person making the offer, with the result that it is sufficient that the other party accepts the offer in order for the contract to be formed [...]

---

[6]   On Belgian law, see NATHALIE VAN LEUVEN, "Belgium", in Smits (ed.), above n. 3, pp. 110–15; H. BOCKEN AND W. DE BONDT, *Introduction to Belgian Law*, Brussels: Bruylant, 2001.

IV. Italy

Codice civile (*Italian Civil Code*)

Art. 1328. Revoca della proposta e dell'accettazione.
(1) La proposta può essere revocata finché il contratto non sia concluso. Tuttavia, se l'accentante ne ha intrapreso in buona fede l'esecuzione prima di avere notizia della revoca, il proponente è tenuto a indennizzarlo delle spese e delle perdite subite per l'iniziata esecuzione del contratto.
(2) L'accettazione può essere revocata, purché la revoca giunga a conoscenza del proponente prima dell'accettazione.

Art. 1328. Revocation of offer and acceptance.
(1) An offer can be revoked until the contract is concluded. However, if the acceptor has begun performance in good faith before having notice of the revocation, the offeror is bound to indemnify him for the expenses and losses sustained in beginning performance of the contract.
(2) The acceptance can be revoked, provided that the revocation comes to the knowledge of the offeror before the acceptance.

Art. 1329. Proposta irrevocabile.
(1) Se il proponente si è obbligato a mantenere ferma la proposta per un certo tempo, la revoca è senza effetto.
[...]

Art. 1329. Irrevocable Offer.
If the offeror has bound himself to keep the offer open for a certain time, the revocation is without effect.
[...]

V. The Netherlands, Poland, Lithuania

1. Burgerlijk Wetboek (*Dutch Civil Code*)

Art. 6:219

(1) Een aanbod kan worden herroepen, tenzij het een termijn voor de aanvaarding inhoudt of de onherroepelijkheid ervan op andere wijze uit het aanbod volgt.

(2) De herroeping kan slechts geschieden, zolang het aanbod niet is aanvaard en evenmin een mededeling, houdende de aanvaarding is verzonden. Bevat het aanbod de mededeling dat het vrijblijvend wordt gedaan, dan kan de herroeping nog onverwijld na de aanvaarding geschieden.

(3) Een beding waarbij één der partijen zich verbindt om, indien de wederpartij dit wenst, met haar een bepaalde overeenkomst te sluiten, geldt als een onherroepelijk aanbod.

Art. 6:219

(1) An offer may be revoked, unless it includes a term for acceptance, or irrevocability results otherwise from the offer.

(2) Revocation may only take place as long as the offer has not been accepted and a communication accepting the offer has not been expedited. Where the offer states that it is without commitment, revocation can take place even after acceptance, if it is done without delay.

(3) A stipulation whereby one party binds himself to enter into a certain contract with another party at the latter's option is deemed to be an irrevocable offer.

2. Kodeks cywilny (Polish Civil Code)[7]

Art. 66[2] §1. W stosunkach między przedsiębiorcami oferta może być odwolana przed zawarciem umowy, jeżeli oświadczenie o odwolaniu zostało zlożone drugiej stronie przed wyslaniem przez nią oświadczenia o przyjęciu oferty.

§2. Jednakże oferty nie można odwolać, jeżeli wynika to z jej treś ci lub określono w niej termin przyjęcia.

Art. 66[2] §1. In relations between entrepreneurs an offer may be revoked before the contract is concluded if the declaration of revocation was submitted to the other party before his sending a declaration of acceptance of the offer.

§2. However, the offer may not be revoked if irrevocability results from its contents or a time limit has been fixed therein.

---

7 The Polish Civil Code was enacted in 1964. Article 66[2] in its current version dates from 14 February 2003. On Polish law see, e.g., MICHAŁ GONDEK, "Poland", in Smits (ed.), above n. 3, pp. 548–53.

3. Lietuvos Respublikos Civilinis kodeksas
(*Civil Code of the Republic of Lithuania*)

6.169 straipsnis. Ofertos atšaukimas

1. Kol sutartis nesudaryta, ofertą galima atšaukti, jeigu pranešimą apie jos atšaukimą akceptantas gauna prieš išsiųsdamas akceptą.
2. Tačiau oferta negali būti atšaukta, jeigu:
   1) ofertoje nurodant tam tikrą terminą jai akceptuoti ar kitokiu būdu nustatyta, kad ji neatšaukiama;
   2) akceptantas turėjo protingą pagrindą manyti, kad oferta yra neatšaukiama ir, remdamasis ja, atitinkamai veikė.

Article 6.169. Revocation of an offer

1. *Until a contract is concluded, an offer may be revoked if the revocation reaches the offeree before he has dispatched the acceptance.*
2. *Nevertheless, an offer cannot be revoked if:*
   1) *it is indicated therein, whether by stating a fixed time-limit for acceptance or otherwise, that it is irrevocable;*
   2) *there were reasonable grounds for the offeree to rely on the offer as being irrevocable, and he acted accordingly.*

VI.   Quebec, Canada

Civil Code of Quebec

Art. 1390

(1)   An offer to contract may be made to a determinate or an indeterminate person, and a term for acceptance may or may not be attached to it.

(2)   Where a term is attached, the offer may not be revoked before the term expires; if none is attached, the offer may be revoked at any time before acceptance is received by the offeror.

VII.   England

1. J. C. Smith and J. A. C. Thomas, *A Casebook on Contract*, pp. 79–82

ROUTLEDGE v. GRANT

Common Pleas (1828) 4 Bing. 653; 1 M. & P. 717; 3 C. & P. 267; 6 L.J.C.P.166;
29 R.R. 672; 130 E.R. 920

The defendant offered to take a lease of the plaintiff's premises, "a definitive answer to be given within six weeks from March 18, 1825". On April 9 the defendant withdrew his offer, and on April 29 the plaintiff purported to accept it. The Court of Common Pleas held that there was no contract.

Best C.J.: Here is a proposal by the defendant to take property on certain terms; namely, that he should be let into possession in July. In that proposal he gives the plaintiff six weeks to consider; but if six weeks are given on one side to accept an offer, the other has six weeks to put an end to it. One party cannot be bound without the other. This was expressly decided in *Cooke* v. *Oxley* [...] [The Chief Justice then considered *Payne* v. *Cave* (...) and *Adams* v. *Lindsell* (...).] ... As the defendant repudiated the contract on April 9, before the expiration of the six weeks, he had a right to say that the plaintiff should not enforce it afterwards.

Notes:
1. In *Mountford* v. *Scott* [1975] 1 All E.R. 198 (C.A.) V, in consideration of the payment of £l, granted in writing an option to P to purchase V's house for £10,000, exercisable within six months. Before the option was exercised, V purported to withdraw his offer. P exercised the option and it was held that he was entitled to specific performance of the contract to sell the house. The offer was irrevocable even though the consideration for it might be described as a token payment; and it was the contract for sale which was specifically enforced. [...]
[...]

Law Revision Committee, 6th Interim Report (Statute of Frauds and the Doctrine of Consideration), Cmd. 5449, 1937, para. 38, p. 22

It appears to us to be undesirable and contrary to business practice that a man who has been promised a period, either expressly defined or until the happening of a certain event, in which to decide whether to accept or to decline an offer cannot rely upon being able to accept it at any time within that period. If the offeror wants a consideration for keeping it open, he can stipulate for it and his offer is then usually called an "option". Merely because he does not so stipulate, he ought not to be allowed to revoke his offer with impunity. We consider that the fixing of a definite period should be regarded as evidence of his intention to make a binding promise to keep his offer open, and that his promise should be enforceable. If no period of time is fixed, we think it may be assumed that no contractual obligation was intended.

It may be noted here that according to the law of most foreign countries a promisor is bound by such a promise. It is particularly undesirable that on such a point the English law should accept a lower moral standard.

Notes:

1. "A builder may submit a tender in reliance on offers from suppliers of materials expressed to remain 'firm' for a fixed period. If those offers are withdrawn within that period and after his tender has been accepted, he may be gravely prejudiced": [...]

2. The proposals of the Law Revision Committee have been reconsidered by the Law Commission in their Working Paper No. 60, "Firm Offers". The principal provisional recommendation made is that "An offeror who has promised that he will not revoke his offer for a definite time should be bound by the terms of that promise for a period not exceeding six years, *provided that* the promise has been made in the course of a business ..."; and that an offeror who breaks such a promise should be liable to damages.

2. MICHAEL P. FURMSTON, *Cheshire, Fifoot and Furmston's Law of Contract*, 15th edn, pp. 72–73

4   TERMINATION OF OFFER

[...]

A   Revocation

It has been established ever since the case of *Payne v Cave* in 1789 that revocation is possible and effective at any time before acceptance: up to this moment *ex hypothesi* no legal obligation exists. Nor, as the law stands, is it relevant that the offeror has declared himself ready to keep the offer open for a given period. Such an intimation is but part and parcel of the original offer, which must stand or fall as a whole. The offeror may, of course, bind himself, by a separate and specific contract, to keep the offer open; but the offeree, if such is his allegation, must provide all the elements of a valid contract, including assent and consideration. In *Routledge v Grant* the defendant offered on 18 March to buy [*sic*] the plaintiff's house for a certain sum, 'a definite answer to be given within six weeks from the date'. Best CJ held that the defendant could withdraw at any moment before acceptance, even though the time limit had not expired. The plaintiff could only have held the defendant to his offer throughout the period, if he had bought the option by a separate and binding contract.

3. Guenter Treitel, *The Law of Contract,* 12th edn by Edwin Peel (ed.), 2-023–2-034

(b) Communication of Acceptance

(i) General rule

The general rule is that an acceptance has no effect until it is communicated to the offeror. One reason for this rule is the difficulty of proving an uncommunicated decision to accept "for the Devil himself knows not the intent of a man". But this is not the sole reason for the rule, which applies even where the fact of acceptance could be proved with perfect certainty, *e.g.* where a person writes his acceptance on a piece of paper which he simply keeps; where a company resolves to accept an application for shares, records the resolution, but does not communicate it to the applicant [...] The main reason for the rule is that it could cause hardship to an offeror if he were bound without knowing that his offer had been accepted. [...]

For an acceptance to be "communicated" it must normally be brought to the notice of the offeror. [...]

(ii) Exceptional cases

In a number of cases, an acceptance is, or may be, effective although it is not communicated to the offeror.

Communication to offeror's agent. [...]

Conduct of offeror. [...]

Terms of offer. An offer may expressly or impliedly waive the requirement that acceptance must be communicated. This is often the case where an offer invites acceptance by conduct. Thus where an offer to sell goods is made by sending them to the offeree, it may be accepted by simply using them without communicating this fact to the offeror. Similarly, it seems that, where an offer to buy goods is made by asking the seller to supply them, it may be accepted by simply despatching the goods to the buyer. [...]

(iii) Acceptance by post

There are many possible solutions to the problem: when does a posted acceptance take effect? Such an acceptance could take effect when it is actually communicated to the offeror, when it arrives at his address, when it should, in the ordinary course of post, have reached him, or when it is posted. As the following discussion will show, each of these solutions is open to objections on the grounds of convenience or justice. This is particularly true where the acceptance is lost or delayed in the post.

The posting rule. What is usually called the general rule is that a postal acceptance takes effect when the letter of acceptance is posted. For this purpose a letter is posted when it is in the control of the Post Office, or of one of its employees authorised to receive letters: handing a letter to a postman authorised to *deliver* letters is not posting.

Reasons for the rule. Various reasons for the rule have been suggested. One is that the offeror must be considered as making the offer all the time that his offer is in the post, and that therefore the agreement between the parties is complete as soon as the acceptance is posted. But this does not explain why posting has any significance at all: any other proof of intention to accept would equally well show that the parties were in agreement. Another suggested reason for the rule is that, if it did not exist

> "no contract could ever be completed by the post. For if the [offerors] were not bound by their offer when accepted by the [offerees] till the answer was received, then the [offerees] ought not to be bound till after they had received the notification that the [offerors] had received their answer and assented to it. And so it might go on ad *infinitum*" (*Adams v Lindsell* (1818) 1 B. & Ald. 681 at 683).

But it would be perfectly possible to hold that the acceptance took effect when it came to the notice of the offeror, whether the offeree knew of this or not. Such a rule would not result in an infinity of letters. Yet another suggested reason for the rule is that the Post Office is the common agent of both parties, and that communication to this agent immediately completes the contract. But the contents of a sealed letter cannot realistically be said to have been communicated to the Post Office, which in any case is at most an agent to *transmit* the acceptance, and not *to receive* it. A mere delivery of the acceptance to such an agent does not of itself complete a contract. Finally, it has been suggested that the rule minimises difficulties of proof: it is said to be easier to prove that a letter has been posted than that it has been received. But this depends in each case on the efficiency with which the parties keep records of incoming and outgoing letters.

The rule is in truth an arbitrary one, little better or worse than its competitors. When negotiations are conducted by post, one of the parties may be prejudiced if a posted acceptance is lost or delayed; for the offeree may believe that there is a contract and the offeror that there is none, and each may act in reliance on his belief. The posting rule favours the offeree, and is sometimes justified on the ground that an offeror who chooses to start negotiations by post takes the risk of delay and accidents in the post; or on the ground that the offeror can protect himself by expressly stipulating that he is not to be bound until actual receipt of the acceptance. Neither justification is wholly satisfactory, for the negotiations may have been started by the offeree; and the offer may be made on a form provided by the offeree, in which case he, and not the offeror, will for practical purposes be in control of its terms. The rule does, however, serve a possibly useful function in limiting the offeror's power to withdraw his offer at will: it makes a posted acceptance binding although that acceptance only reaches the offeror after a previously posted withdrawal reaches the offeree.

Must be reasonable to use post. The posting rule only applies when it is reasonable to use the post as a means of communicating acceptance. Generally an offer made in a letter sent by post may be so accepted; but it may be reasonable to accept by post even though the offer was not sent in this way. In *Henthorn v Fraser* the mere fact that the parties lived at a distance justified acceptance by post of an oral offer. It would not normally be reasonable to reply by a posted letter to an offer made by telex, e-mail or telephone. Nor would it be reasonable to accept by post if the acceptor knew that the postal service was disrupted.

Instantaneous and electronic communications. The posting rule does not apply to acceptances made by some instantaneous mode of communication, *e.g.* by telephone or by telex. Such acceptances are therefore governed by the general rule that they must have been communicated to the offeror. The reason why the rule does not apply in such cases is that the acceptor will often know at once that his attempt to communicate was unsuccessful, so that it is up to him to make a proper communication. But a person who accepts by letter which goes astray may not know of the loss or delay until it is too late to make another communication. Fax messages seem to occupy an intermediate position. The sender will know at once if his message has not been received at all, and where this is the position the message should not amount to an effective acceptance. But if the message is received in such a form that it is wholly or partly illegible, the sender is unlikely to know this at once, and it is suggested an acceptance sent by fax might well be effective in such circumstances. The same principle should apply to other forms of electronic communication such as e-mail or web-site trading: here again the effects of unsuccessful attempts to communicate should depend on whether the sender of the message knows (or has the means of knowing) at once of any failure in communication.

Applications of the posting rule. [...] The English cases in fact only support three "consequences" of the posting rule. The first (and probably the most important) is that a posted acceptance prevails over a previously posted withdrawal of the offer which had not yet reached the offeree when the acceptance was posted. A second, and more controversial, application of the rule is that an acceptance takes effect on posting even though it never reaches the offeror because it is lost through an accident in the post, and the same rule probably applies where the acceptance is merely delayed through such an accident. Thirdly, the contract is taken to have been made at the *time* of posting so as to take priority over another contract affecting the subject-matter made after the original acceptance had been posted but before it had reached the offeror. [...]

Misdirected acceptance. A letter of acceptance may be lost or delayed because it bears a wrong, or an incomplete, address. Normally, such misdirection will be due to the carelessness of the offeree and the posting rule should not apply to such cases. Even if an offeror can be said to take the risk of accidents in the post, it would be unreasonable to impose on him the further risk of the offeree's carelessness.
   [...]

VIII.   United States of America

1. American Law Institute, Restatement of the Law Second, Contracts

§ 42.   Revocation by Communication from Offeror Received by Offeree.
An offeree's power of acceptance is terminated when the offeree receives from the offeror a manifestation of an intention not to enter into the proposed contract.

Comment:
  a.   Revocability of offers. Most offers are revocable. […] [T]he ordinary offer is revocable even though it expressly states the contrary, because of the doctrine that an informal agreement is binding as a bargain only if supported by consideration. […]

Illustration:
  1.   A makes a written offer to B to sell him a piece of land. The offer states that it will remain open for thirty days and is not subject to countermand. The next day A orally informs B that the offer is terminated. B's power of acceptance is terminated unless the offer is a contract under § 25.

[…]

§ 63.   Time When Acceptance Takes Effect
Unless the offer provides otherwise,

  (a)   an acceptance made in a manner and by a medium invited by the offer is operative and completes the manifestation of mutual assent as soon as put out of the offeree's possession, without regard to whether it ever reaches the offeror […]

Comment:
  a.   Rationale. […] [An] explanation of the rule that the acceptance takes effect on dispatch is that the offeree needs a dependable basis for his decision whether to accept. In many legal systems such a basis is provided by a general rule that an offer is irrevocable unless it provides otherwise. The common law provides such a basis through the rule that a revocation of an offer is ineffective if received after an acceptance has been properly dispatched. […]

§ 25.   Option Contracts.
An option contract is a promise which meets the requirements for the formation of a contract and limits the promisor's power to revoke an offer.

2. Uniform Commercial Code (USA)

§ 2-205. Firm Offers.
An offer by a merchant to buy or sell goods in a signed writing which by its terms gives assurance that it will be held open is not revocable, for lack of consideration, during the time stated or if no time is stated for a reasonable time, but in no event may such period of irrevocability exceed three months; but any such term of assurance on a form supplied by the offeree must be separately signed by the offeror.

3. Civil Code of Louisiana

Art. 1928
An offer that specifies a period of time for acceptance is irrevocable during that time.

4. United States Court of Claims, *Rhode Island Tool Company* v. *United States*, 130 Court of Claims Reports 698[8]

United States Court of Claims.
RHODE ISLAND TOOL COMPANY
v.
The UNITED STATES.
No. 49913.
Feb. 8, 1955.

130 Ct. Cl. 698, 1128 F. Supp. 417 (1955)

[…] Before JONES, Chief Justice, and LITTLETON, WHITAKER, MADDEN, and LARAMORE, Judges.

JONES, C. J.:
    […]
On September 10, 1948, in response to an invitation to bid, plaintiff submitted a bid on a number of items contained in the invitation […]

---

[8] The US Court of Federal Claims has nationwide jurisdiction over most suits for monetary claims against the Government and sits, without a jury, to determine issues of law and fact. The general jurisdiction of the Court, described in 28 U.S.C. § 1491, is, among others, over claims for damages for breaches of contracts with the Government.

The sales manager of the plaintiff who prepared the bid failed to notice a change in the description of the bolt from stud to machine [...] The machine bolts were a more expensive type of bolt.

[...] Notice of award to plaintiff was mailed on October 4, 1948. [...]

The plaintiff discovered its error late on Friday afternoon, October 1, and on [...] Monday, October 4, 1948, plaintiff's sales manager [...] immediately telephoned [the defendant] notifying [the defendant] that it desired to withdraw its bid [...] The record does not show whether the notice of award was mailed before or after the telephone conversation in which plaintiff advised the defendant of its mistake and asked to withdraw its bid. It was received by plaintiff after the telegram of withdrawal had been sent. [...]

The question is whether, in all the circumstances of this case, the depositing of the notice of award in the mail constitutes a binding contract from which plaintiff cannot escape, notwithstanding the mistake was brought to the attention of the contracting officials before the notice of award was received.

We believe that when the record is considered as a whole in the light of modern authorities, there was no binding contract, since plaintiff withdrew its bid before the acceptance became effective.

Under the old post office regulations when a letter was deposited in the mail the sender lost all control of it. It was irrevocably on its way. After its deposit in the mail the post office became, in effect, the agent of the addressee. Naturally the authorities held that the acceptance in any contract became final when it was deposited in the post office, since the sender had lost control of the letter at that time. That was the final act consummating the agreement.

But some years ago the United States Postal authorities completely changed the regulation. [...] When this new regulation became effective, the entire picture was changed. The sender now does not lose control of the letter the moment it is deposited in the post office, but retains the right of control up to the time of delivery. The acceptance, therefore, is not final until the letter reaches destination, since the sender has the absolute right of withdrawal from the post office, and even the right to have the postmaster at the delivery point return the letter at any time before actual delivery. [...]

IX.　The Vienna Sales Convention and the Principles of Contract Law

1. United Nations Convention on Contracts for the International Sale of Goods (CISG)

Art. 16

(1)　Until a contract is concluded an offer may be revoked if the revocation reaches the offeree before he has dispatched an acceptance.

(2)　However, an offer cannot be revoked:

    (a)　if it indicates, whether by stating a fixed time for acceptance or otherwise, that it is irrevocable; or

    (b)　if it was reasonable for the offeree to rely on the offer as being irrevocable and the offeree has acted in reliance on the offer.

2. UNIDROIT: Principles of International Commercial Contracts

Art. 2.1.4.　Revocation of offer

(1)　Until a contract is concluded an offer may be revoked if the revocation reaches the offeree before it has dispatched an acceptance.

(2)　However, an offer cannot be revoked

    (a)　if it indicates, whether by stating a fixed time for acceptance or otherwise, that it is irrevocable; or

    (b)　if it was reasonable for the offeree to rely on the offer as being irrevocable and the offeree has acted in reliance on the offer.

OFFICIAL COMMENT

The problem of whether an offer is or is not revocable is traditionally one of the most controversial issues in the context of the formation of contracts. Since there is no prospect of reconciling the two basic approaches followed in this respect by the different legal systems, i.e. the common law approach according to which an offer is as a rule revocable, and the opposite approach followed by the majority of civil law systems, the only remaining possibility is that of selecting one approach as the main rule, and the other as the exception.

1. Offers as a rule revocable

Para. (1) of this article, which is taken literally from Art. 16 CISG, states that until the contract is concluded offers are as a rule revocable. The same paragraph, however, subjects the revocation of an offer to the condition that it reaches the offeree before the offeree has dispatched an acceptance. It is thus only when the offeree orally accepts the offer, or when the offeree may indicate assent by performing an act without giving notice to the offeror (see Art. 2.1.6(3)), that the offeror's right to revoke the offer continues to exist until such time as the contract is concluded. Where, however, the offer is accepted by a written indication of assent, so that the contract is concluded when the acceptance reaches the offeror (see Art. 2.1.6(2)), the offeror's right to revoke the offer terminates earlier, i.e. when the offeree dispatches the acceptance. Such a solution may cause some inconvenience to the offeror who will not always know whether or not it is still possible to revoke the offer. It is, however, justified in view of the legitimate interest of the offeree in the time available for revocation being shortened. As to determination of the time of dispatch, see Art. 2.1.8 and the comment thereto.

2. Irrevocable offers

Para. (2) provides for two important exceptions to the general rule as to the revocability of offers: (i) where the offer contains an indication that it is irrevocable and (ii) where the offeree, having other good reasons to treat the offer as being irrevocable, has acted in reliance on that offer.

a. Indication of irrevocability contained in the offer

The indication that the offer is irrevocable may be made in different ways, the most direct and clear of which is an express statement to that effect by the offeror (e.g. "This is a firm offer"; "We shall stand by our offer until we receive your answer"). It may, however, simply be inferred from other statements by, or conduct of, the offeror. The indication of a fixed time for acceptance may, but need not necessarily, amount by itself to an implicit indication of an irrevocable offer. The answer must be found in each case through a proper interpretation of the terms of the offer in accordance with the various criteria laid down in the general rules on interpretation in Chapter 4. In general, if the offeror operates within a legal system where the fixing of a time for acceptance is considered to indicate irrevocability, it may be assumed that by specifying such a fixed time the offeror intends to make an irrevocable offer. If, on the other hand, the offeror operates in a legal system where the fixing of a time for acceptance is not sufficient to indicate irrevocability, the offeror will not normally have had such an intention.

Illustrations

1. A, a travel agency, informs a client of a cruise in its brochure for the coming New Year holidays. It urges the client to book within the next three days, adding that after that date there will probably be no more places left. This statement by itself will not be considered to indicate that the offer is irrevocable during the first three days.

2. A invites B to submit a written offer of the terms on which B is prepared to construct a building. B presents a detailed offer containing the statement "Price and other conditions are not good after 1 September". If A and B operate within a legal system where such a statement is considered to be an indication that the offer is irrevocable until the specified date, B can expect the offer to be understood as being irrevocable. The same may not necessarily be the

case if the offeree operates in a legal system where such a statement is not considered as being sufficient to indicate that the offer is irrevocable.

b.   Reliance by offeree on irrevocability of offer

The second exception to the general rule regarding the revocability of offers, i.e. where "it was reasonable for the offeree to rely on the offer as being irrevocable", and "the offeree has acted in reliance on the offer", is an application of the general principle prohibiting inconsistent behaviour laid down in Art. 1.8. The reasonable reliance of the offeree may have been induced either by the conduct of the offeror, or by the nature of the offer itself (e.g. an offer whose acceptance requires extensive and costly investigation on the part of the offeree or an offer made with a view to permitting the offeree in turn to make an offer to a third party). The acts which the offeree must have performed in reliance on the offer may consist in making preparations for production, buying or hiring of materials or equipment, incurring expenses etc., provided that such acts could have been regarded as normal in the trade concerned, or should otherwise have been foreseen by, or known to, the offeror.

Illustrations

3.   A, an antique dealer, asks B to restore ten paintings on condition that the work is completed within three months and that the price does not exceed a specific amount. B informs A that, so as to know whether or not to accept the offer, B finds it necessary to begin work on one painting and will then give a definite answer within five days. A agrees, and B, relying on A's offer, begins work immediately. A may not revoke the offer during those five days.

4.   A seeks an offer from B for incorporation in a bid on a project to be assigned within a stated time. B submits an offer on which A relies when calculating the price of the bid. Before the expiry of the date, but after A has made the bid, B informs A that it is no longer willing to stand by its offer. B's offer is irrevocable until the stated date since in making its bid A relied on B's offer.

3. Commission on European Contract Law:
Principles of European Contract Law

Article 2:202: Revocation of an Offer

(1)   An offer may be revoked if the revocation reaches the offeree before it has dispatched its acceptance or, in cases of acceptance by conduct, before the contract has been concluded under Article 2:205(2) or (3).

(2)   An offer made to the public can be revoked by the same means as were used to make the offer.

(3)   However, a revocation of an offer is ineffective if:

(a)   the offer indicates that it is irrevocable; or

(b)   it states a fixed time for its acceptance; or

(c)   it was reasonable for the offeree to rely on the offer as being irrevocable and the offeree has acted in reliance on the offer.

COMMENTS

A.   *Revocation and Withdrawal Distinguished*

An offer becomes effective when it reaches the offeree, see Article 1:303(2) and (6). However, before it reaches the offeree the offer may be countermanded or withdrawn and it will not become effective, see Article 1:303(5). It cannot then be accepted by the offeree. […]

B.   *Acceptance by Conduct*

[…]

C.   *Offers to the Public*

Revocation of offers to the public which are not irrevocable under Article 2:202(2) can be made by the same means as the offer. The revocation must then be as conspicuous as the offer. If the offer appeared as an advertisement in a newspaper the revocation must appear at least as visibly in the paper as the advertisement.

The revocation of an offer made in an advertisement which was mailed to the offeree must reach it before it dispatches its acceptance. If the offer has been published in a newspaper the paper bringing the revocation must be in the offeree's mail box or available in the news-stands before the offeree dispatches its acceptance.

D.   *Irrevocable Offer*

Under paragraph 2 there are three exceptions to the general rule in paragraph I:

(a)   if the offer indicates that it is irrevocable;
(b)   if it states a fixed time for its acceptance;
(c)   if the offeree had reason to rely on the offer as being irrevocable, and has acted in reliance on the offer.

In these cases the offer if accepted becomes binding even though it was purportedly revoked before it was accepted. If the offeror does not perform the contract it may become liable for non-performance, and will have to pay damages under the rules of chapter 9, section 5.

E.   *Irrevocability Stated*

The indication that the offer is irrevocable must be clear. It may be made by declaring that the offer is a "firm offer" or by other similar expressions. It may also be inferred from the conduct of the offeror.

F.   *Fixed Time for Acceptance*

Another way of making the offer irrevocable is to state a fixed time for its acceptance. This statement must also be clear. If the offeror states that its offer "is good till January 1" the offer is irrevocable. The same applies if it states that the offer "lapses on September 1". If on the other hand the offeror only advises the offeree to accept quickly, its offer will be revocable.

G. *Reliance*

The third exception to the rule in paragraph 1 concerns cases where "it was reasonable for the offeree to rely on the offer as being irrevocable" and the "offeree has acted in reliance on the offer". Reliance may have been induced by the behaviour of the offeror. It may also be induced by the nature of the offer.

> *Illustration 1:* Contractor A solicits an offer from sub-contractor B to form part of A's bid on a construction to be assigned within a stated time. B submits its offer and A relies on it when calculating the bid. Before the expiry of the date of award, but after A has made its bid, B revokes its offer. B is bound by its offer until the date of assignment.

An offer of a reward may be irrevocable with regard to persons who have acted in reliance on the offer.

> *Illustration 2:* In an advertisement A promises a "reward" of £1.000 in addition to damages to purchasers of its "high pressure" cooker, which will be on the market the following day, if the cooker explodes. A month later it revokes the promise in another advertisement. Customers who before the offer was revoked have bought a cooker which eventually explodes can claim the "reward".
>   See also comment C to Article 1:201.

[...]

NOTES

1. Are offers revocable? Effects of wrongful revocation.
In this matter the laws of the Union differ on various questions. [...]

2. Offers are revocable but may be made irrevocable
Like art. 2:202, some laws provide that an offer is revocable, but that it may follow from the offer or from the circumstances that it is irrevocable. If in spite of its revocation the offeree accepts an irrevocable offer in due time, there is a contract.

Art. 1328 of the ITALIAN CC provides that the offeror may revoke the offer until he learns of the offeree's acceptance. However, the offeror's revocation is without effect if he has made the offer irrevocable or has undertaken to keep the promise open for a certain time, see CC art 1329. It the offer is accepted within the time originally envisaged by the offer, there is a contract in spite of the revocation. [...] The rules in the DUTCH BW art. 2:119 come close to those of the Italian CC with the exception that an offer can be revoked until the offeree has dispatched his acceptance. [...]

[...] The wording of art. 16 para 2 (a) CISG reflects a disagreement among the delegates of the Diplomatic Conference which in 1980 adopted CISG. The common lawyers wished the offeror's fixing of a period for acceptance to be a time limit after which the offer could no longer be accepted but before which it could still be revoked. The civil lawyers saw the fixing of a time limit for acceptance as a promise by the offeror not to revoke the offer within that time limit [...].The wording of art. 2 (a) was a compromise. The offer can be made irrevocable, but the provision has not cleared the controversy as to whether the mere fixing of a time for acceptance makes the offer irrevocable. Common lawyers believe that it does not *per se* make the offer irrevocable, there must he additional grounds for assuming that, see v. *Caemrnerer Schlechtriem* art. 16 note 10 and *Honnold* no 141 ff. The question is to be solved by the rules in CISG art. 8 on interpretation of statements.

Article 2:202 of the Principles obviates this doubt. The fixing of a time for acceptance will make the offer irrevocable for that period.

3. *Tort liability for improper revocation*
The FRENCH courts have held that the offeror can revoke his offer until it has been accepted. The offeror may, however, expressly or by implication, for instance by fixing a time limit for acceptance, promise not to revoke his offer; and even if no such promise is made it may follow from the circumstances of the case or from usage that the offeror cannot revoke it without incurring liability. If the offeror nevertheless revokes his offer there will generally be no contract but the offeror will incur liability in damages if he revokes the offer before a reasonable time has lapsed […]. The rules are reported to be the same in LUXEMBOURG.

4. *Even offer stated to be irrevocable may be revoked*
In the COMMON LAW the offer is revocable even if it is stated to be irrevocable. By giving a notice to the offeree the offeror may revoke his offer before acceptance. The offeree can make the offer irrevocable with the offeror's consent by furnishing a consideration for holding the offer open, for instance by paying the offeror £1, or by using a deed. […]

5. *Offers are generally irrevocable*
Under some laws the offer is binding and remains so until it lapses, either because it has not been accepted within the time limit set for its acceptance, which is either the time fixed by the offeror or a reasonable time, or because it has been rejected. An acceptance of the offer in due time makes it into a contract even though it has been revoked. The offeror may, however, in his offer state that it is revocable.

These rules apply in GERMANY, see BGB § 145, AUSTRIA, see ABGB § 862, GREECE see CC art. 185, PORTUGAL see CC art. 230. BELGIUM, see *Dirix & van Oevelen, "Kroniek verbintenissensrecht 1985–1992" Rechtskundig Weekblad* 1992–93, 1210 and in the NORDIC LAW, see Contracts Act §§ 1, 3, 7, and 9. § 9 of the DANISH and SWEDISH Contract Acts provide that where a person has stated in his proposal that it is made "without obligation", or has used similar expressions, his statement shall be regarded as an invitation to make an offer. In FINLAND, which has not adopted § 9, the same rule applies.

[…]

4. Study Group on a European Civil Code and Research Group on EC Private Law (Acquis Group): *Draft Common Frame of Reference*

II. – 4:202: Revocation of offer
(1)   An offer may be revoked if the revocation reaches the offeree before the offeree has dispatched an acceptance or, in cases of acceptance by conduct, before the contract has been concluded.

(2) An offer made to the public can be revoked by the same means as were used to make the offer.

(3) However, a revocation of an offer is ineffective if:

    (a) the offer indicates that it is irrevocable;

    (b) the offer states a fixed time for its acceptance; or

    (c) it was reasonable for the offeree to rely on the offer as being irrevocable and the offeree has acted in reliance on the offer.

X. China

中华人民共和国合同法
(Contract Law of the People's Republic of China)

第 18 条

要约可以撤销。撤销要约的通知应当在受要约人发出承诺通知之前到达受要约人。

Art. 18   Revocation of Offer
An offer may be revoked. The notice of revocation shall reach the offeree before it has dispatched a notice of acceptance.

第 19 条

有下列情形之一的，要约不得撤销：

（一）要约人确定了承诺期限或者以其他形式明示要约不可撤销；

（二）受要约人有理由认为要约是不可撤销的，并已经为履行合同作了准备工作。

Art. 19   Irrevocable Offer
An offer may not be revoked:
(i)   if it expressly indicates, whether by stating a fixed time for acceptance or otherwise, that it is irrevocable;
(ii)   if the offeree has reason to regard the offer as irrevocable, and has undertaken preparation for performance.

XI. Summary

1. Overview of the solutions according to the different legal orders and the principles of contract law

Solution 1	Solution 2 (with variant)	Solution 3
Offer binds its author, no revocation.	Intermediate solution: **Principle**: Offer can be revoked **Exception**: Offer is irrevocable when it includes an express time limit for acceptance or when the irrevocability is implied from the circumstances.	Offer is revocable.
– Swiss law (Art. 3(1), 5(1) OR) – German law (§ 145 BGB) – Austrian law (Art. 862 S. 3 ABGB) – Greek law (Art. 185, 186 ZGB) – Portuguese law (Art. 230 Código civil) – Serbian law (Art. 37(1), (4) Law of Contract and Torts) – Belgian law (Cour de cass. 1980) **Exception**: Offer may be revoked when its binding effect has been excluded in the offer, or if it can be shown from the nature of the contract or the circumstances that the offer is revocable (Art. 7(1) CO, § 145 BGB, Art. 186 Greek Civil Code)	– French law (Cour de cass. 1972; TERRÉ, SIMLER, LEQUETTE no. 115 ff.) – Italian law (Art. 1328, 1329 CC includes special features, compensation awarded in certain circumstances) – Dutch law (limitation: postal rule, Art. 219(1), (2) BW) – Polish law (limitation: postal rule, Art. 66[2] CC) – Lithuanian law, limitation: postal rule (Art. 6.169 CC) – Civil Code of Quebec (Art. 1390(2)) – Chinese contract code, Arts 18, 19 – CISG (limitation: postal rule, Art. 16(1); Special feature: the time limit is just one indication that the offer may be irrevocable) – UNIDROIT Principles (Art. 2.4, like CISG)	– English law (*Routledge* v. *Grant*), limitation where acceptance has been posted, see: TREITEL, 2.(2)(d) – USA: Restatement Contracts 2nd, § 42, limitation: postal rule, see Restatement 2nd, § 63; see however *Rhode Island Tool Company* v. *United States* **Exception**: UCC, § 2-205, when: – it is an offer to buy or sell goods; – it was made by a merchant; – it is in written form and is signed; – assurance was given that it will be held open.

Solution 1	Solution 2 (with variant)	Solution 3
	– Principles of European Contract Law (Art. 2:202(1) and (3); limitation: postal rule) **Consequences of an ineffective revocation of an offer** – Obligation to pay compensation (French law, Cour de Cass. 1972; TERRÉ, SIMLER, LEQUETTE no. 119 in *fine*) – Inadvertent revocation of an offer, contract is concluded by acceptance (e.g. Italian law, Art. 1329 CC; PECL)	

2. Further reading

HUGH BEALE, ARTHUR HARTKAMP, HEIN KÖTZ AND DENIS TALLON (eds), *Cases, Materials and Text on Contract Law* (Ius Commune Casebooks for the Common Law of Europe), Oxford: Hart Publishing, 2002, Ch. 2.1.2.C. Revocability of an offer, 194–206.

MELVIN A. EISENBERG, "The Revocation Of Offers", 2004 *Wis. L. Rev.* 271–308.

ALLAN FARNSWORTH, *Contracts*, 3rd edn, New York: Aspen Publishers, 2004, 152–55 (USA).

HEIN KÖTZ AND AXEL FLESSNER, *European Contract Law*, Vol. I (by Hein Kötz), Tübingen: Mohr Siebeck, 21–25.

CHARLES L. KNAPP, "An Offer You Can't Revoke", 2004 *Wis. L. Rev.* 309–22.

FILIPPO RANIERI, *Europäisches Obligationenrecht*, Wien/New York: Springer, 173 et seq.

VALERIE WATNICK, "The Electronic Formation of Contracts and the Common Law 'Mailbox Rule'", 56 (2004) *Baylor L. Rev.* 175–203.

Case 4: Modification of contracts – the free will of the parties or limits on the freedom to contract? (*"consideration"* revisited)

> *"It is not [...] surprising that a principle enunciated in relation to the rigours of seafaring life during the Napoleonic wars should be subjected during the succeeding 180 years to a process of refinement and limitation in its application in the present day."*[1]

Scenario

Roffey Brothers, a construction company, enters into a contract to renovate 27 flats. The contract includes a penalty clause under which Roffey Brothers would incur liability to the other party if it was late in finishing the work.

Roffey Brothers sub-contracts to Williams, a carpenter, who committs to undertaking the carpentry work in the flats for £20,000. After completing some of the work, Williams runs into financial difficulties. He tells Roffey Brothers that the amount calculated for the carpentry work is too low and that it will not be possible for him to finish the work under such terms. In fact, the market price for such work is about £24,000.

At Roffey Brothers' request, the parties renegotiate the terms of the contract and provide for an increase in payment of £10,300, to be paid in instalments while the work is completed. Roffey Brothers has numerous aims in modifying the contract in such a way: (i) to get Williams to finish his work within the deadline; (ii) to avoid the application of the penalty clause in the contract[2]; and (iii) to avoid the problem and costs of finding and hiring a new carpenter.

Williams works again, but Roffey Brothers refuses to pay the extra money. Is the modification of the contract valid?

---

[1] *Glidewell*, L.J., in *Williams* v. *Roffey Bros and Nicholls (Contractors) Ltd.*, [1991] 1 QB 1, [1990] 1 All ER 512, at 522 (CA).

[2] *Penalty clauses*, as opposed to *liquidated damages* clauses, are unenforceable under English law. A penalty clause serves to punish the party in breach and is unenforceable as such an aim is considered impermissible. A clause that stipulates an *excessive amount* of money to be paid in the event of a breach would be classified as a penalty clause. Even though they are unenforceable in English law, such a clause is not struck out of the contract, it is just not enforced by the courts beyond the actual loss of the party invoking it (*Jobson* v. *Johnson* [1989] 1 All ER 621). The party thus cannot recover the excessive amount but just the amount he lost. Liquidated damages clauses, on the other hand, are a *genuine* pre-estimate of the loss that would be suffered by the innocent party in the event of a breach of contract. Such a clause is enforceable. The *label* used by the parties *is not determinative*, and so courts may find that a clause labelled as a "penalty clause" in the contract is, in actual fact, not punitive and therefore a liquidated damages clause. For further information, see Ewan McKendrick, *Contract Law*, Basingstoke/New York: Palgrave Macmillan, 2007, pp. 438-45.

Questions

(1) The majority of European civil codes have the same conditions for the modification as for the conclusion of contracts, so do not expressly mention the modification of contracts in the code.[3] Other codes and regulations, such as the *Russian* Civil Code, the *Chinese* Civil Code, the Civil Code of *Louisiana*, the Vienna Convention and the UNIDROIT Principles,[4] on the contrary, expressly mention the modification of contracts. In the light of the materials given in Case 2, why is it a good idea that the Vienna Convention expressly mentions that "[a] contract may be modified or terminated by the mere agreement of the parties", and why is such a statement not necessary for the conclusion of a contract under this Convention?

(2) In *American* and *English* law, the modification of contracts, like the conclusion of contracts,[5] raises particular issues. What issue is raised by the above scenario in *English* law, and how was the problem resolved by the Court of Appeal? According to the materials that follow, how could the case be solved under *US* law? What role does *consideration* play in the modification of contracts according to:
   (a) the English decision in *Williams* v. *Roffey Bros*;
   (b) the Uniform Commercial Code (UCC);
   (c) the Restatement of Law Second; and
   (d) the US decision in *Angel* v. *Murray*?

(3) How would the validity of the modification of the contract in the above scenario be analysed according to the Principles of European Contract Law and the UNIDROIT Principles? How would you resolve the above scenario under these Principles?[6]

(4) How are the Uniform Commercial Code and the Restatement on Contracts used in the reasoning of the Supreme Court of Rhode Island in *Angel* v. *Murray*? Could the Principles of European Contract Law and the UNIDROIT Principles play the same role in European courts as the Restatement does in American law? Give reasons for your answer.

   In the US, contract law is generally governed not by federal law but by State law. Why is US contract law nevertheless so remarkably uniform, particularly when compared to contract law in Europe?

---

[3] See the Code provisions cited above, **Case 2**.
[4] Art. 3.2, see above, **Case 2**.
[5] See above, **Case 2**.
[6] See the materials provided above, **Case 2**.

Table of contents

I. Different civil codes and the CISG

1. Гражданский кодекс Российской Федерации
(*Civil Code of the Russian Federation*)

Статья 420. Понятие договора.
(1) Договором признается соглашение двух или нескольких лиц об установлении, изменении или прекращении гражданских прав и обязанностей.
[...]

Art. 420. The Concept of the Contract.
(1) The contract shall be recognized as the agreement, concluded by two or by several persons on the institution, modification or termination of the civil rights and duties.
[...]

Статья 432. Основные положения о заключении договора.
(1) Договор считается заключенным, если между сторонами, в требуемой в подлежащих случаях форме, достигнуто соглашение по всем существенным условиям договора. Существенными являются условия о предмете договора, условия, которые названы в законе или иных правовых актах как существенные или необходимые для договоров данного вида, а также все те условия, относительно которых по заявлению одной из сторон должно быть достигнуто соглашение.
(2) Договор заключается посредством направления оферты (предложения заключить договор) одной из сторон и ее акцепта (принятия предложения) другой стороной.

Art. 432. The Basic Provisions on the Conclusion of a Contract.
(1) The contract shall be regarded as concluded, if an agreement has been achieved between the parties on all its essential terms, in the form proper for the similar kind of contracts.
As essential shall be recognized the terms, dealing with the object of the contract, the terms, defined as essential or indispensable for the given kind of contracts in the law or in the other legal acts, and also all the terms, about which, by the statement of one of the parties, an accord shall be reached.
(2) The contract shall be concluded by way of forwarding the offer (the proposal to conclude the contract) by one of the parties and of its acceptance (the acceptance of the offer) by the other party.

2. 中华人民共和国合同法
(*Contract Law of the People's Republic of China*)

第一章　一般规定

Chapter One: General Provisions

第 1 条

为了保护合同当事人的合法权益，维护社会经济秩序，促进社会主义现代化建设，制定本法。

Art. 1. Purpose.
This Law is formulated in order to protect the lawful rights and interests of contract parties, to safeguard social and economic order, and to promote socialist modernization.

第 2 条
本法所称合同是平等主体的自然人、法人、其他组织之间设立、变更、终止民事权利义务关系的协议。

[...]

Art. 2. Definition of Contract; Exclusions.
For purposes of this Law, a contract is an agreement between natural persons, legal persons or other organizations with equal standing, for the purpose of establishing, altering, or discharging a relationship of civil rights and obligations.
[...]

3. Civil Code of Louisiana

Art. 1906
A contract is an agreement by two or more parties whereby obligations are created, modified or extinguished.

4. United Nations Convention on Contracts for the International Sale of Goods (CISG)

Art. 29
(1) A contract may be modified or terminated by the mere agreement of the parties.
(2) A contract in writing which contains a provision requiring any modification or termination by agreement to be in writing may not be otherwise modified or terminated by agreement. However, a party may be precluded by his conduct from asserting such a provision to the extent that the other party has relied on that conduct.

II. England

1. Court of Appeal, *Williams* v. *Roffey* [1991] 1 QB 1, [1990] 1 All ER 512

Williams v Roffey Bros and Nicholls (Contractors) Ltd

COURT OF APPEAL, CIVIL DIVISION

[1991] 1 QB 1, [1990] 1 All ER 512, [1990] 2 WLR 1153, 48 Build LR 69, 10 Tr Law 12

HEARING-DATES: 2, 3, 23 NOVEMBER 1989

23 November 1989

[…]
GLIDEWELL LJ […]

The facts

The plaintiff is a carpenter. The defendants are building contractors who in September 1985 had entered into a contract with Shepherd's Bush Housing Association Ltd to refurbish a block of flats called Twynholm Mansions, Lillie Road, London SW6. The defendants were the main contractors for the works. [T]he work of refurbishment was to be carried out in 27 of the flats.

The defendants engaged the plaintiff to carry out the carpentry work in the refurbishment of the 27 flats, including work to the structure of the roof. [T]he plaintiff was engaged […] by a sub-contract in writing made on 21 January 1986 by which the plaintiff undertook to provide the labour for the carpentry work to the roof of the block and for the first and second fix carpentry work required in each of the 27 flats for a total price of £20,000. […]

The plaintiff and his men began work on 10 October 1985. The judge found that by 9 April 1986 the plaintiff had completed the work to the roof, had carried out the first fix to all 27 flats and had substantially completed the second fix to 9 flats. By this date the defendants had made interim payments totalling £16,200.

It is common ground that by the end of March 1986 the plaintiff was in financial difficulty. The judge found that there were two reasons for this, namely: (i) that the agreed price of £20,000 was too low to enable the plaintiff to operate satisfactorily and at a profit. Mr Cottrell, a surveyor employed by the defendants, said in evidence that a reasonable price for the works would have been £23,783 (ii) […]

The defendants, as they made clear, were concerned lest the plaintiff did not complete the carpentry work on time. The main contract contained a penalty clause. The judge found that on 9 April 1986 the defendants promised to pay the plaintiff the further sum of £10,300, in addition to the £20,000, to be paid at the rate of £575 for each flat in which the carpentry work was completed.

The plaintiff and his men continued work on the flats until the end of May 1986. By that date the defendants, after their promise on 9 April 1986, had made only one further payment of £1,500. At the end of May the plaintiff ceased work on the flats. [T]he defendants engaged other carpenters to complete the work, but in the result incurred one week's time penalty in their contract with the building owners.

The action

The plaintiff [...] claimed the sum of £10,847. [...]

The issues

Before us counsel for the defendants advances two arguments. His principal submission is that the defendants' admitted promise to pay an additional £10,300, at the rate of £575 per completed flat, is unenforceable since there was no consideration for it. [...]

Was there consideration for the defendants' promise made on 9 April 1986 to pay an additional price at the rate of £575 per completed flat?

The judge made the following findings of fact which are relevant on this issue. (i) The sub-contract price agreed was too low to enable the plaintiff to operate satisfactorily and at a profit. Mr Cottrell, the defendants' surveyor, agreed that this was so. (ii) Mr Roffey, the managing director of the defendants, was persuaded by Mr Cottrell that the defendants should pay a bonus to the plaintiff. The figure agreed at the meeting on 9 April 1986 was £10,300.

The judge quoted and accepted the evidence of Mr Cottrell to the effect that a main contractor who agrees too low a price with a sub-contractor is acting contrary to his own interests. He will never get the job finished without paying more money.

The judge therefore concluded:

> "In my view where the original sub-contract price is too low, and the parties subsequently agree that the additional moneys shall be paid to the sub-contractor, this agreement is in the interests of both parties. This is what happened in the present case, and in my opinion the agreement of 9 April 1986 does not fail for lack of consideration."

In his address to us counsel for the defendants outlined the benefits to the defendants which arose from their agreement to pay the additional £10,300 as (i) seeking to ensure that the plaintiff continued work and did not stop in breach of the sub-contract, (ii) avoiding the penalty for delay and (iii) avoiding the trouble and expense of engaging other people to complete the carpentry work.

However, counsel submits that, though the defendants may have derived, or hoped to derive, practical benefits from their agreement to pay the "bonus", they derived no benefit in law, since the plaintiff was promising to do no more than he was already bound to do by his sub-contract, *i.e.* continue with the carpentry work and complete it on time. Thus there was no consideration for the agreement.

Counsel for the defendants relies on the principle of law which, traditionally, is based on the decision in *Stilk* v. *Myrick* (1809) 2 Camp 317, 170 ER 1168. That was a decision at first instance of Lord Ellenborough CJ. On a voyage to the Baltic, two seamen deserted. The captain agreed with the rest of the crew that if they worked the ship back to London without the two seamen being replaced, he would divide between them the pay which would have been due to the two deserters. On arrival at London this extra pay was refused, and the plaintiff's action to recover his extra pay was dismissed. Counsel for the defendant argued that such an agreement was contrary to public policy, but Lord Ellenborough CJ's judgment (as reported in Campbell's Reports) was based on lack of consideration. It reads (2 Camp 317 at 318 - 319, 170 ER 1168 at 1169):

> "I think *Harris* v. *Watson* ((1791) Peake 102, [1775–1802] All ER Rep 493) was rightly decided but I doubt whether the ground of public policy, upon which Lord Kenyon is stated to have proceeded, be the true principle on which the decision is to be supported. Here, I say the agreement is void for want of consideration. There was no consideration for the ulterior pay promised to the mariners who remained with the ship. Before they sailed from London they had undertaken to do all they could under the emergencies of the voyage. They had sold all their services till the voyage should be completed. [...] [T]he desertion of a part of the crew is to be considered an emergency of the voyage as much as their death and those who remain are bound by the terms of their original contract to exert themselves to the utmost to bring the ship in safety to her destined port. Therefore, without looking to the policy of this agreement, I think it is void for want of consideration [...]."

[...]

In *Ward* v. *Byham* [1956] 2 All ER 318, [1956] 1 WLR 496 the plaintiff and the defendant lived together unmarried for five years, during which time the plaintiff bore their child. After the parties ended their relationship, the defendant promised to pay the plaintiff £1 per week to maintain the child, provided that she was well looked after and happy. The defendant paid this sum for some months, but ceased to pay when the plaintiff married another man. On her suing for the amount due at £1 per week, he pleaded that there was no consideration for his agreement to pay for the plaintiff to maintain her child, since she was obliged by law to do so: see s 42 of the National Assistance Act 1948. The county court judge upheld the plaintiff mother's claim, and this court dismissed the defendant's appeal.

Denning LJ said ([1956] 2 All ER 318 at 319, [1956] 1 WLR 496 at 498):

> "I approach the case, therefore, on the footing that, in looking after the child, the mother is only doing what she is legally bound to do. Even so, I think that there was sufficient consideration to support the promise. I have always thought that a promise to perform an existing duty, or the performance of it, should be regarded as good consideration, because it is a benefit to the person to whom it is given. Take this very case. It is as much a benefit for the father to have the child looked after by the mother as by a neighbour. If he gets the benefit for which he stipulated, he ought to honour his promise, and he ought not to avoid it by saying that the mother was herself under a duty to maintain the child. I regard the father's promise in this case as what is sometimes called a unilateral contract, a promise in return for an act, a promise by the father to pay £1 a week in return for the mother's looking after the child. Once the mother embarked on the task of looking after the child, there was a binding contract. So long as she looked after the child, she would be entitled to £1 a week. The case seems to me to be within the decision of *Hicks* v. *Gregory* (8 CB 378, 137 ER 556) on which the judge relied. I would dismiss the appeal."

However, Morris LJ put it rather differently. He said ([1956] 2 All ER 318 at 320, [1956] 1 WLR 496 at 498 499):

> "[...] It seems to me [...] that the father was saying, in effect: Irrespective of what may be the strict legal position, what I am asking is that you shall prove that the child will be well looked

after and happy, and also that you must agree that the child is to be allowed to decide for herself whether or not she wishes to come and live with you. If those conditions were fulfilled the father was agreeable to pay. On those terms, which in fact became operative, the father agreed to pay £1 a week. In my judgment, there was ample consideration there to be found for his promise, which I think was binding."

Parker LJ agreed. As I read the judgment of Morris LJ, he and Parker LJ held that, though in maintaining the child the plaintiff was doing no more than she was obliged to do by law, nevertheless her promise that the child would be well looked after and happy was a practical benefit to the father, which amounted to consideration for his promise.

[...]

There is, however, another legal concept of relatively recent development which is relevant, namely that of economic duress. Clearly, if a sub-contractor has agreed to undertake work at a fixed price, and before he has completed the work declines to continue with it unless the contractor agrees to pay an increased price, the sub-contractor may be held guilty of securing the contractor's promise by taking unfair advantage of the difficulties he will cause if he does not complete the work. In such a case an agreement to pay an increased price may well be voidable because it was entered into under duress. Thus this concept may provide another answer in law to the question of policy which has troubled the courts since before *Stilk* v. *Myrick* (1809) 2 Camp 317, 170 ER 1168, and no doubt led at the date of that decision to a rigid adherence to the doctrine of consideration.
[...]

[T]he present state of the law on this subject can be expressed in the following proposition: (i) if A has entered into a contract with B to do work for, or to supply goods or services to, B in return for payment by B and (ii) at some stage before A has completely performed his obligations under the contract B has reason to doubt whether A will, or will be able to, complete his side of the bargain and (iii) B thereupon promises A an additional payment in return for A's promise to perform his contractual obligations on time and (iv) as a result of giving his promise B obtains in practice a benefit, or obviates a disbenefit, and (v) B's promise is not given as a result of economic duress or fraud on the part of A, then (vi) the benefit to B is capable of being consideration for B's promise, so that the promise will be legally binding.

As I have said, counsel for the defendants accepts that in the present case by promising to pay the extra £10,300 the defendants secured benefits. There is no finding, and no suggestion, that in this case the promise was given as a result of fraud or duress.

If it be objected that the propositions above contravene the principle in *Stilk* v. *Myrick*, I answer that in my view they do not: they refine and limit the application of that principle, but they leave the principle unscathed, e.g. where B secures no benefit by his promise. It is not in my view surprising that a principle enunciated in relation to the rigours of seafaring life during the Napoleonic wars should be subjected during the succeeding 180 years to a process of refinement and limitation in its application in the present day.

It is therefore my opinion that on his findings of fact in the present case, the judge was entitled to hold, as he did, that the defendants' promise to pay the extra £10,300 was supported by valuable consideration, and thus constituted an enforceable agreement. [...]

For these reasons I would dismiss this appeal.

[...]

PURCHAS LJ. [...]

In my judgment [...] the rule in *Stilk* v. *Myrick* remains valid as a matter of principle, namely that a contract not under seal must be supported by consideration. Thus, where the agreement on which reliance is placed provides that an extra payment is to be made for work to be done by the payee which he is already obliged to perform, then unless some other consideration is detected to support the agreement to pay the extra sum that agreement will not be enforceable. *Harris* v. *Watson* and *Stilk* v. *Myrick* involved circumstances of a very special nature, namely the extraordinary conditions existing at the turn of the eighteenth century under which seamen had to serve their contracts of employment on the high seas. There were strong public policy grounds at that time to protect the master and owners of a ship from being held to ransom by disaffected crews. Thus, the decision that the promise to pay extra wages even in the circumstances established in those cases was not supported by consideration is readily understandable. Of course, conditions today on the high seas have changed dramatically and it is at least questionable, counsel for the plaintiff submitted, whether these cases might not well have been decided differently if they were tried today. The modern cases tend to depend more on the defence of duress in a commercial context rather than lack of consideration for the second agreement. In the present case, the question of duress does not arise. The initiative in coming to the agreement of 9 April came from Mr Cottrell and not from the plaintiff. It would not, therefore, lie in the defendants' mouth to assert a defence of duress. [...]

The question must be posed: what consideration has moved from the plaintiff to support the promise to pay the extra £10,300 added to the lump sum provision? In the particular circumstances which I have outlined above, there was clearly a commercial advantage to both sides from a pragmatic point of view in reaching the agreement of 9 April. The defendants were on risk that as a result of the bargain they had struck the plaintiff would not or indeed possibly could not comply with his existing obligations without further finance. As a result of the agreement the defendants secured their position commercially. There was, however, no obligation added to the contractual duties imposed on the plaintiff under the original contract. Prima facie this would appear to be a classic *Stilk* v. *Myrick* case. It was, however, open to the plaintiff to be in deliberate breach of the contract in order to "cut his losses" commercially. In normal circumstances the suggestion that a contracting party can rely on his own breach to establish consideration is distinctly unattractive. In many cases it obviously would be and if there was any element of duress brought on the other contracting party under the modern development of this branch of the law the proposed breaker of the contract would not benefit. With some hesitation [...] I consider that the modern approach to the question of consideration would be that where there were benefits derived by each party to a contract of variation even though one party did not suffer a detriment this would not be fatal to the establishing of sufficient consideration to support the agreement. If both parties benefit from an agreement it is not necessary that each also suffers a detriment. [...] For these reasons and for the reasons which have already been given by Glidewell LJ, I would dismiss this appeal.

Appeal dismissed. Leave to appeal to the House of Lords granted.

Solicitors: John Pearson, New Malden (for the defendants); Terence W. Lynch & Co. (for the plaintiff).

2. ROGER HALSON, "Sailors, Sub-Contractors and Consideration" (1990) 106 *LQR* 183–85

Notes

SAILORS, SUB-CONTRACTORS AND CONSIDERATION

EVERYONE will remember *Stilk* v. *Myrick* (1809) 2 Camp. 317 from their student days. The luckless sailors' claim for extra wages foundered on the rocks of the pre-existing duty doctrine of consideration; they did not furnish any additional consideration for the promise of more pay. However it seems that times have changed (a little anyway) with the Court of Appeal's decision in *Williams* v. *Roffey Bros & Nicholls (Contractors) Ltd* [1990] 1 All E.R. 512.

[…]

A distinction is often drawn between two different definitions of consideration; factual and legal. The factual definition emphasises the *fact* of benefit or detriment; the legal definition, for which *Stilk* v. *Myrick* is often cited, recognises as consideration only those acts which the promisor was not already under a *legal* obligation to perform (see further Treitel, *Law of Contract* (7th ed.), p. 54).

The consideration identified by GIidewell L.J. [in *Williams* v. *Roffey Bros & Nicholls*] comprised: the assurance that the plaintiff would continue working and not halt work in breach of contract, the avoidance of the penalty clause operating, and the avoidance of the expense of engaging different carpenters to complete the work. It is respectfully submitted that these benefits to the defendant can only amount to factual consideration and only then if they represent losses which would not be recoverable as damages in the event of breach (perhaps any penalty payment would be too remote?). The judgments of Russell and Purchas L.JJ. also appear to proceed upon a factual definition of consideration.

[…]

The adoption in *Williams* v. *Roffey Bros.* of a factual, rather than a legal definition of consideration effects a subtle but significant change in the law relating to modification of contract. In so far as a test of factual consideration is more easily satisfied than one requiring legal consideration, it is the presence or absence of duress which will ultimately determine the enforceability of a modification. Thus, the principles of economic duress are pushed to the fore. This shift of emphasis is to be welcomed. When premised upon a legal definition of consideration the pre-existing duty doctrine was too blunt and indiscriminate. If strictly applied it would deny legal force to many freely negotiated modifications like that in *Williams* v. *Roffey Bros.* The principles of economic duress offer a more sophisticated means of distinguishing extorted and non-extorted modifications.

However, the lack of unanimity in the court's application of the factual definition of consideration may suggest that a bolder approach should have been taken. Perhaps a proper opportunity will arise to take the route of the Uniform Commercial Code, s. 2-209(1) and dispense completely with the requirement of consideration in the case of agreements modifying existing contracts. Such an approach would relieve the courts of the need to search for a scintilla of factual consideration before they can give effect to an uncoerced modification.

[...]

III. USA

1. American Law Institute: Restatement of the Law Second, Contracts

FORMATION OF CONTRACTS – MUTUAL ASSENT

IN GENERAL

§ 17. Requirement of a Bargain.
(1) Except as stated in Subsection (2), the formation of a contract requires a bargain in which there is a manifestation of mutual assent to the exchange and a consideration. [...]

FORMATION OF CONTRACTS – CONSIDERATION

THE REQUIREMENT OF CONSIDERATION

§ 71. Requirement of Exchange. Types of Exchange
(1) To constitute consideration, a performance or a return promise must be bargained for.
(2) A performance or return promise is bargained for if it is sought by the promisor in exchange for his promise and is given by the promisee in exchange for that promise.
(3) The performance may consist of
    (a) an act other than a promise, or
    (b) a forbearance, or
    (c) the creation, modification, or destruction of a legal relation.
(4) The performance or return promise may be given to the promisor or to some other person. It may be given by the promisee or by some other person.

[...]

Illustrations:
    1. [...]
    2. A receives a gift from B of a book worth $10. Subsequently, A promises to pay B the value of the book. There is no consideration for A's promise. This is so even though B, at the time he makes the gift, secretly hopes that A will pay him for it. [...]
    3. A promises to make a gift of $10 to B. In reliance on the promise B buys a book from C and promises to pay C $10 for it. There is no consideration for A's promise. [...]
    4. A desires to make a binding promise to give $1000 to his son B. Being advised that a gratuitous promise is not binding, A writes out and signs a false recital that B has sold him a car for $1000 and a promise to pay that amount. There is no consideration for A's promise.

5. A desires to make a binding promise to give $1000 to his son B. Being advised that a gratuitous promise is not binding, A offers to buy from B for $1000 a book worth less than $1. B accepts the offer knowing that the purchase of the book is a mere pretence. There is no consideration for A's promise to pay $1000.

[…]

§ 73. Performance of Legal Duty.

Performance of a legal duty owed to a promisor which is neither doubtful nor the subject of honest dispute is not consideration; but a similar performance is consideration if it differs from what was required by the duty in a way which reflects more than a pretence of bargain.

§ 79. Adequacy of Consideration; Mutuality of Obligation.

If the requirement of consideration is met, there is no additional requirement of
  (a) a gain, advantage, or benefit to the promisor or a loss, disadvantage, or detriment to the promisee; or
  (b) equivalence in the values exchanged; or
  (c) "mutuality of obligation."

Comment:
  […]
c. *Exchange of unequal values.* To the extent that the apportionment of productive energy and product in the economy are left to private action, the parties to transactions are free to fix their own valuations. […] Valuation is left to private action in part because the parties are thought to be better able than others to evaluate the circumstances of particular transactions. […] Ordinarily, therefore, courts do not inquire into the adequacy of consideration. […] Gross inadequacy of consideration may be relevant to issues of capacity, fraud and the like, but the requirement of consideration is not a safeguard against imprudent and improvident contracts except in cases where it appears that there is no bargain in fact.

CONTRACTS WITHOUT CONSIDERATION

§ 89. Modification of Executory Contract.

A promise modifying a duty under a contract not fully performed on either side is binding
  (a) if the modification is fair and equitable in view of circumstances not anticipated by the parties when the contract was made;

[…]

Comment:
a) *Rationale.* This Section relates primarily to adjustments in on-going business transactions.

[…]

b) *Performance of legal duty.* The rule of § 73 finds its modern justification in cases of promises made by mistake or induced by unfair pressure. Its application to cases where those elements are absent has been much criticized and is avoided if paragraph (a) of this

Section is applicable. The limitation to a modification which is "fair and equitable" goes beyond absence of coercion and requires an objectively demonstrable reason for seeking a modification. Compare Uniform Commercial Code § 2-209 Comment. [...]

Illustrations:

1.   By a written contract A agrees to excavate a cellar for B for a stated price. Solid rock is unexpectedly encountered and A so notifies B. A and B then orally agree that A will remove the rock at a unit price which is reasonable but nine times that used in computing the original price, and A completes the job. B is bound to pay the increased amount.

2.   A contracts with B to supply for $300 a laundry chute for a building B has contracted to build for the government for $150,000. Later, A discovers that he made an error as to the type of material to be used and should have bid $1,200. A offers to supply the chute for $1,000, eliminating overhead and profit. After ascertaining that other suppliers would charge more, B agrees. The new agreement is binding.

3.   A is employed by B as a designer of coats at $90 a week for a year beginning November 1 under a written contract executed September 1. A is offered $115 a week by another employer and so informs B. A and B then agree that A will be paid $100 a week and in October execute a new written contract to that effect, simultaneously tearing up the prior contract. The new contract is binding.

[...]

2. Uniform Commercial Code

§ 2-209.   Modification, Rescission and Waiver.
(1)   An agreement modifying a contract within this Article[7] needs no consideration to be binding.
(2)   [...]
(3)   The requirement of the statute of fraud section of this Article (Section 2-201) must be satisfied if the contract as modified is within its provisions.
[...]

Official Comment

[...]

Purposes of Changes and New Matter:

1.   This section seeks to protect and make effective all necessary and desirable modifications of sales contracts without regard to the technicalities which at present hamper such adjustments.

2.   Subsection (1) provides that an agreement modifying a sales contract needs no consideration to be binding.

---

[7]   *I.e.* a contract for the sale of goods (*note by the author*).

However, modifications made hereunder must meet the test of good faith imposed by this Act. The effective use of bad faith to escape performance on the original contract terms is barred, and the extortion of a "modification" without legitimate commercial reasons is ineffective as a violation of the duty of good faith. Nor can a mere technical consideration support a modification made in bad faith.

The test of "good faith" between merchants or as against merchants includes "observance of reasonable commercial standards of fair dealing in the trade" (Section 2-103), and may in some situations require an objectively demonstrable reason for seeking a modification. But such matters as a market shift which makes performance come to involve a loss may provide such a reason even though there is no such unforeseen difficulty as would make out a legal excuse from performance under Sections 2-615 and 2-616.

[...]

3. Supreme Court of Rhode Island, *Alfred L. Angel et al.* v. *John E. Murray, Jr, Director of Finance of the City of Newport et al.*, 113 R.I. 482

Alfred L. Angel et al. v. John E. Murray, Jr., Director of Finance of the City of Newport, et al.

Supreme Court of Rhode Island

113 R.I. 482; 322 A.2d 630; 1974 R.I. LEXIS 1202; 85 A.L.R.3d 248

July 22, 1974

[...]

ROBERTS C. J.:

This is a civil action brought by Alfred L. Angel and others against John E. Murray, Jr, Director of Finance of the City of Newport, the city of Newport, and James L. Maher, alleging that Maher had illegally been paid the sum of $20,000 by the Director of Finance and praying that the defendant Maher be ordered to repay the city such sum. [...]

The record discloses that Maher has provided the city of Newport with a refuse-collection service under a series of five-year contracts beginning in 1946. On March 12, 1964, Maher and the city entered into another such contract for a period of five years commencing on July 1, 1964, and terminating on June 30, 1969. The contract provided, among other things, that Maher would receive $137,000 per year in return for collecting and removing all combustible and noncombustible waste materials generated within the city.

In June of 1967 Maher requested an additional $10,000 per year from the city council because there had been a substantial increase in the cost of collection due to an unexpected and unanticipated increase of 400 new dwelling units. Maher's testimony, which is uncontradicted, indicates the 1964 contract had been predicated on the fact that since 1946 there had been an average increase of 20 to 25 new dwelling units per year.

After a public meeting of the city council where Maher explained in detail the reasons for his request and was questioned by members of the city council, the city council agreed to pay him an additional $10,000 for the year ending on June 30, 1968. Maher made a similar request again in June of 1968 for the same reasons, and the city council again agreed to pay an additional $10,000 for the year ending on June 30, 1969.

[…]

[W]e are […] confronted with the question of whether the additional payments were illegal because they were not supported by consideration.

- A -

As previously stated, the city council made two $10,000 payments. The first was made in June of 1967 for the year beginning on July 1, 1967, and ending on June 30, 1968. Thus, by the time this action was commenced in October of 1968, the modification was completely executed. That is, the money had been paid by the city council, and Maher had collected all of the refuse. Since consideration is only a test of the enforceability of executory promises, the presence or absence of consideration for the first payment is unimportant because the city council's agreement to make the first payment was fully executed at the time of the commencement of this action. […] However, since both payments were made under similar circumstances, our decision regarding the second payment (Part B, infra) is fully applicable to the first payment.

- B -

It is generally held that a modification of a contract is itself a contract, which is unenforceable unless supported by consideration. See Simpson, *Contracts* § 93. In *Rose* v. *Daniels, 8 R. I. 381 (1866)*, this court held that an agreement by a debtor with a creditor to discharge a debt for a sum of money less than the amount due is unenforceable because it was not supported by consideration.

   Rose is a perfect example of the pre-existing duty rule. Under this rule an agreement modifying a contract is not supported by consideration if one of the parties to the agreement does or promises to do something that he is legally obligated to do or refrains or promises to refrain from doing something he is not legally privileged to do. *See* Calamari & Perillo, *Contracts* § 60 (1970); 1A Corbin, *Contracts* §§ 171–72 (1963); 1 Williston, *Contracts* § 130 Annot; *12 A.L.R. 2d 78* (1950). In *Rose* there was no consideration for the new agreement because the debtor was already legally obligated to repay the full amount of the debt.

   Although the pre-existing duty rule is followed by most jurisdictions, a small minority of jurisdictions, Massachusetts, for example, find that there is consideration for a promise to perform what one is already legally obligated to do because the new promise is given in place of an action for damages to secure performance. *See Swartz v. Lieberman, 323 Mass. 109, 80 N.E.2d 5 (1948); Munroe v. Perkins, 26 Mass. (9 Pick.) 298 (1830). Swartz* is premised on the theory that a promisor's forbearance of the power to breach his original agreement and be sued in an action for damages is consideration for a subsequent agreement by the promisee to pay extra compensation. This rule, however, has been widely criticized as an anomaly. *See* Calamari & Perillo, *supra*, § 61; Annot., *12 A.L.R.2d 78, 85–90 (1950)*.

   The primary purpose of the pre-existing duty rule is to prevent what has been referred to as the "hold-up game." *See* 1A Corbin, *supra*, § 171. A classic example of the "hold-up game" is found in *Alaska Packers' Ass'n* v. *Domenico, 117 F. 99 (9th Cir. 1902)*. There 21 seamen entered into a written contract with Domenico to sail from San Francisco to Pyramid Harbor, Alaska. They were to work as sailors and fishermen out of Pyramid Harbor during the fishing season of 1900. The contract specified that each man would be paid $50 plus two cents for each red salmon he caught. Subsequent to their arrival at Pyramid Harbor, the men stopped work and demanded an additional $50. They threatened to return to San Francisco if Domenico did not agree to their demand. Since it was impossible for Domenico to find other men, he agreed to pay the men an additional $50. After they returned to San Francisco, Domenico refused to pay the men an additional $50. The court found that the subsequent agreement to pay the men an additional $50 was not supported by consideration because the men had a pre-existing duty to work on the ship under the original contract, and thus the subsequent agreement was unenforceable.

Another example of the "hold-up game" is found in the area of construction contracts. Frequently, a contractor will refuse to complete work under an unprofitable contract unless he is awarded additional compensation. The courts have generally held that a subsequent agreement to award additional compensation is unenforceable if the contractor is only performing work which would have been required of him under the original contract. *See, e.g., Lingenfelder* v. *Wainwright Brewing Co., 103 Mo. 578, 15 S.W. 844 (1891)*, which is a leading case in this area. *See also* cases collected in Annot., *25 A.L.R. 1450 (1923)*, supplemented by Annot., *55 A.L.R. 1333 (1928)*, and Annot., *138 A.L.R. 136 (1942)*; *cf. Ford & Denning* v. *Shepard Co., 36 R. I. 497, 90 A. 805 (1914)*.

These examples clearly illustrate that the courts will not enforce an agreement that has been procured by coercion or duress and will hold the parties to their original contract regardless of whether it is profitable or unprofitable. However, the courts have been reluctant to apply the pre-existing duty rule when a party to a contract encounters unanticipated difficulties and the other party, not influenced by coercion or duress, voluntarily agrees to pay additional compensation for work already required to be performed under the contract. For example, the courts have found that the original contract was rescinded, *Linz* v. *Schuck, 106 Md. 220, 67 A. 286 (1907)*; abandoned, *Connelly* v. *Devoe, 37 Conn. 570 (1871)*, or waived, *Michaud* v. *MacGregor, 61 Minn. 198, 63 N.W. 479 (1895)*.

Although the pre-existing duty rule has served a useful purpose insofar as it deters parties from using coercion and duress to obtain additional compensation, it has been widely criticized as a general rule of law. With regard to the pre-existing duty rule, one legal scholar has stated: "There has been a growing doubt as to the soundness of this doctrine as a matter of social policy. In certain classes of cases, this doubt has influenced courts to refuse to apply the rule, or to ignore it, in their actual decisions. Like other legal rules, this rule is in process of growth and change, the process being more active here than in most instances. The result of this is that a court should no longer accept this rule as fully established. It should never use it as the major premise of a decision, at least without giving careful thought to the circumstances of the particular case, to the moral deserts of the parties, and to the social feelings and interests that are involved. It is certain that the rule, stated in general and all-inclusive terms, is no longer so well-settled that a court must apply it though the heavens fall." 1A Corbin, *supra*, § 171; *see also* Calamari & Perillo, *supra*, § 61.

The modern trend appears to recognize the necessity that courts should enforce agreements modifying contracts when unexpected or unanticipated difficulties arise during the course of the performance of a contract, even though there is no consideration for the modification, as long as the parties agree voluntarily.

Under the Uniform Commercial Code, § 2-209(1), which has been adopted by 49 states, "[an] agreement modifying a contract [for the sale of goods] needs no consideration to be binding." [...] Although at first blush this section appears to validate modifications obtained by coercion and duress, the comments to this section indicate that a modification under this section must meet the test of good faith imposed by the Code, and a modification obtained by extortion without a legitimate commercial reason is unenforceable.

The modern trend away from a rigid application of the pre-existing duty rule is reflected by § 89 of the American Law Institute's Restatement Second of the Law of Contracts which provides: "A promise modifying a duty under a contract not fully performed on either side is binding (a) if the modification is fair and equitable in view of circumstances not anticipated by the parties when the contract was made."

We believe that § 89 is the proper rule of law and find it applicable to the facts of this case. It not only prohibits modifications obtained by coercion, duress, or extortion but also fulfils society's expectation that agreements entered into voluntarily will be enforced by the courts [...] *See generally* Horwitz, *The Historical Foundations of Modern Contract Law*, 87 Harv. L. Rev. 917 (1974). Section 89, of course, does not compel a modification of an unprofitable or unfair contract; it only enforces a modification if the parties voluntarily agree and if (1) the promise modifying the original contract was made before the contract was fully performed on either side, (2) the underlying circumstances which prompted the modification were unanticipated by the parties, and (3) the modification is fair and equitable.

The evidence, which is uncontradicted, reveals that in June of 1968 Maher requested the city council to pay him an additional $10,000 for the year beginning on July 1, 1968, and ending on June 30, 1969. This request was made at a public meeting of the city council, where Maher explained in detail his reasons for making the request. Thereafter, the city council voted to authorize the Mayor to sign an amendment to the 1954 contract which provided that Maher would receive an additional $10,000 per year for the duration of the contract. Under such circumstances we have no doubt that the city voluntarily agreed to modify the 1964 contract.

Having determined the voluntariness of this agreement, we turn our attention to the three criteria delineated above. First, the modification was made in June of 1968 at a time when the five-year contract which was made in 1964 had not been fully performed by either party. Second, although the 1964 contract provided that Maher collect all refuse generated within the city, it appears this contract was premised on Maher's past experience that the number of refuse-generating units would increase at a rate of 20 to 25 per year. Furthermore, the evidence is uncontradicted that the 1967–1968 increase of 400 units "went beyond any previous expectation." Clearly, the circumstances which prompted the city council to modify the 1964 contract were unanticipated. Third, although evidence does not indicate what proportion of the total this increase comprised, the evidence does indicate that it was a "substantial" increase. In light of this, we cannot say that the council's agreement to pay Maher the $10,000 increase was not fair and equitable in the circumstances.

The judgment appealed from is reversed, and the cause is remanded to the Superior Court for entry of judgment for the defendants.

4. MELVIN A. EISENBERG,[8] "Why is American Contract Law So Uniform? National Law in the United States", in Hans-Leo Weyers (ed.), *Europäisches Vertragsrecht*, 1997, pp. 23–43

I.　*Introduction*

Contract law in the United States is generally governed by state law. Since there are fifty states, and the District of Columbia is like a state for these purposes, as a matter of legal theory there are fifty-one bodies of American contract law. Furthermore, American contract law is in large part governed by the common law, that is, by judge-made law. [...]

Given fifty-one bodies of law and a lack of official canonically stated rules, it might be expected that American contract law would be highly fractured. However, that is not the case. Rather, contract law in the United States is remarkably uniform, with one pointed exception: Louisiana, which was founded by France, and governed for a long time by Spain, retains a civil-law tradition. The question, how has the United States managed to achieve this relatively uniform body of contract law despite the presence of so many jurisdictions and the absence of official canonical rules, is important both in its own right and because it may bear on the unification of European contract law. The purpose of this paper is to consider that question.

Contract law is not the only body of American state law that is relatively uniform. Therefore, although contract law may be affected by some special elements, the question why contract law is relatively uniform must be considered as part of a wider inquiry into why various bodies of American state law are relatively uniform. I will begin that inquiry by defining terms and by drawing some preliminary distinctions. I will then develop a concept that I will call American national law, and examine the general forces that have produced that law. I will next consider certain special forces that have operated on contract law as a branch of American national law. Finally, I will consider some implications of the American experience for a harmonization of European law.

II.　*Preliminary Distinctions*

[...] [T]he uniformity of contract law in the United States has been achieved by nonmandatory unification: Contract law is essentially state law, and only a few bits and pieces of contract law have been federalized [footnote 4: Among the areas of contract law that have been partly federalized are consumer warranties [...]; door-to-door sales contracts [...]; and unsolicited offers in the mail [...]). Thus the question addressed in this paper can be recast as: What nonmandatory elements have led to the uniformity of contract law in the United States?
[...]

8　MELVIN A. EISENBERG is a Professor at the University of California at Berkeley.

III. *Federal, Local, and National Law*

American law is conventionally divided into federal law and state law. I will refer to discourse about those two bodies of law as statements of federal law and statements of local law.

By *statements of federal law*, I mean statements that take the express or implied form "Based on official sources, it is a rule of federal law that R", where R is the stated rule. For example, the statements "Federal law prohibits certain kinds of labeling on alcoholic beverages" or "Free speech is guaranteed under the U.S. Constitution" are statements of federal law. [...]

By *statements of local law*, I mean statements that expressly or impliedly take the express or implied form "Based on official sources, it is a rule of State S that R", where State S is a designated state. (Of course, such rules may also be stated in the form "It is a rule of States S, T, and U that R"). For example, the statements, "Under New York law, contracts require consideration" and "In Pennsylvania and Ohio, an acceptance is effective on dispatch" are statements of local law.

Federal and local law might seem to exhaust the categories of law in the United States, because conventional jurisprudence normally conceives of law as the law of some jurisdiction. However, if you walk into almost any law school in America, or read almost any leading American legal treatise, you will find that many or most of the propositions that you hear or read are neither statements of federal law nor statements of local law. Rather, these propositions are statements of law in general terms, divorced from particular jurisdictions. Practicing lawyers will often talk in the same way.

A striking aspect of this method of discourse about law in America is that it is so fundamental and so ingrained that those who use this kind of discourse are scarcely conscious, if they are conscious at all, that what they are doing might seem relatively unusual from a jurisprudential point of view. Like Molière's bourgeois gentleman, who did not realize that he was speaking "prose", the American legal community does not realize, or realizes in only a limited way, that its everyday discourse reflects an unspoken fundamental premise about the nature of law that is in need of both explanation and examination.

To begin with, then, it is necessary to name this form of legal discourse, and the name I will give it is statements of American national law or, more simply, national law. By *statements of American national law* I mean statements, made in the context of the American legal system, that expressly or impliedly take the form "Rule R is law" and that are not expressly or impliedly statements of federal or local law – that is, are not expressly or impliedly statements that Rule R is established by official authorities as the law of the federal government or the law of one or more designated states. For example, the statements "Contracts require consideration" and "An acceptance is effective on dispatch", unaccompanied by supporting citations, are statements of national law. Correspondingly, by *American national law* I mean the body of legal rules that discourse of this kind describes.

Often, as in the examples just given, statements of American national law are unaccompanied by supporting citations to the law of particular jurisdictions. However, even statements of legal rules that are accompanied by such citations can be deemed statements of national law where the claim of the statement outruns the citations. On the one hand, the claim in the statement is categorical, like "Contracts require consideration".

On the other hand, the citations will typically be limited to cases from two or three states, and even when there are citations to more than two or three states, it is seldom if ever implied that the author of the statement warrants that every state has adopted the rule.

Indeed, it is not unusual for a rule to be described as law in the United States even though it has been adopted only by the courts of two or three states, or even though it has not been adopted by any court. For example, there is a well-accepted rule of American contract law that where an offer is made in a face-to-face or telephonic conversation, the offer lapses at the end of the conversation unless a contrary intention is indicated. This rule was stated, for example, in Williston's leading treatise, first published in the 1920s, and in Corbin's leading treatise, first published in the 1950s, and is stated as well in the *Restatement of Contracts* and in various modern treatises, including the current versions of Williston and Corbin. As originally published, the Williston treatise cited only two cases in support of the rule. The Corbin treatise cited no cases at all. Today, the two treatises cite only three additional cases. Even of these few cases, some are really not on point although they contain stray dicta that support the rule, and those that are on point are ambiguous. Many other well-established rules of "contract law" – that is, national contract law – also have extremely limited support in official sources.

Statements of American national law differ from statements of local or federal law in a fundamental respect: by their nature they purport to state the law, yet they do not purport to state the law of a jurisdiction. Of course, there are parallels to American national law elsewhere. The *Unidroit Principles of International Commercial Contracts* and the *Principles of European Contract Law* are prominent examples. Like statements of American national law, the *Unidroit Principles* and the *European Principles* purport to state law but do not purport to state the law of a particular jurisdiction. Other examples include the law merchant; the "general principles of law" sometimes specified by contract; and international law.

In general, however, these bodies of rules are parallels to, rather than exact counterparts of, American national law. The *Unidroit Principles* and the *European Principles* are very new and their legal authority remains to be determined by the test of time. Furthermore, the Preamble to the *Unidroit Principles* strongly emphasizes contractual adoption, either directly or by reference to "general principles of law" or the like, although the Preamble does also contemplate judicial application even in the absence of contractual adoption.

The Preamble and Article 1:101 of the *Principles of European Contract Law* take a similar approach.

The legal status of the law merchant as a freestanding body of law is unclear. Certainly, in the United States it is not today recognized as a body of independent law. The legal status of "general principles of law" adopted by agreement is also unclear. [...] Moreover, neither the law merchant nor general principles of law have been highly elaborated, indeed, one stated reason for the Unidroit and European *Principles* is to supply clear rules where the parties agree that their contract will be governed by general principles of law. Perhaps the closest historical parallel to American national law was Digest-based law in Europe in the Middle Ages. [...]

IV. *Elements of Nonmandatory Harmonization in the United States*

I turn now to the issue, what nonmandatory elements have led to the harmonization of law in the United States through the development of American national law.

A. *The Economic Element*

One obvious answer is that it is economically advantageous to have uniform law throughout the country, particularly in the areas of commercial law. There is no doubt that this economic element is important, and I will return later to ways in which this element has been doctrinally played out, but nevertheless this answer is insufficient. It would also be economically advantageous to have uniform law throughout North America, but that has not occurred. It would be economically advantageous to have uniform law throughout Europe, but even today the realization of that objective is in a stage of infancy. It would be economically advantageous to have a uniform international commercial law, but the Convention for the International Sale of Goods has come into being only recently, and a number of national states have yet to adopt it. As important as the economic element is, other kinds of social and doctrinal elements must also be at play to explain the existence of American national law.

B. *Legal Scholarship*

One of these elements is the nature of legal scholarship in the United States. It is only a slight oversimplification to say that most prestigious American legal scholars cast most of their legal work in terms of either pure-theory, federal law, or national law. As a corollary, virtually all the non-federal, non-pure-theory legal scholarship that is widely admired in the United States, and widely familiar to scholars, judges, and practitioners, takes the form of national law.

Why should this be so? One reason is that the American scholarly community tends to award recognition and prestige for theoretical and normative work, as opposed to descriptive and positive work. In principle, it may be as easy to do theoretical and normative analysis of local law as of national law. In practice, however, this tends not to be the case. Generally speaking, consumers of work on local law are interested primarily, and often almost exclusively, in descriptive and positive analysis. Scholars who work on local law must therefore pitch their scholarship in those terms if they are to have an audience. Furthermore, as a practical matter it is often easier to analyze national law in theoretical and normative terms than to analyze local law in this manner. The spread of legal data-points on the national landscape invites a creative integration of the points into a clear line. The process of creative integration, in turn, invites a theoretical and normative enterprise. The lesser number of data-points in local law works in the opposite direction. Furthermore, once the prestige system starts it is self-perpetuating. Because recognition and prestige goes to scholars who work on pure theory, federal law, and national law, scholars who seek recognition and prestige will gravitate toward these fields, not to local law.

Other factors, perhaps more important, are also at work. For one thing, there is an issue of audience. The audience for pure theory, federal law, and national law is nationwide, because an article or book cast in pure, federal, or national terms is potentially of interest to everyone in the American legal community with an interest in the subject-matter. In contrast, the audience for local law is normally confined to the members of the legal community of a single state and those practicing lawyers outside the state who happen to have an interest in the law of the state.

[…] A scholar who believes he has something important to say, as most good scholars do, will prefer national law to local law because national law will give him the widest possible audience. A scholar who wants to generalize and theorize, as most good scholars do, will prefer national law over local law because national-law data is a better source for generalization and the construction of theories.

C.   *Legal Education*

Perhaps even more important than legal scholarship, as a harmonizing force in the United States, is legal education. All the leading law schools in the United States – and probably the bulk of all law schools – teach exclusively, or almost exclusively, pure theory, federal law, and national law. Every leading casebook in the United States is either a federal-law casebook or a national-law casebook.

These elements are related both to each other and to the elements that influence legal scholarship. Casebooks are a form of scholarship, and the factors that apply to traditional scholarship apply to casebooks as well. For example, writing a casebook in local-law terms would severely restrict the audience for the casebook, and most law-school teachers aspire to be analytical in their teaching and to teach analytical skills, not merely to describe the law. Furthermore, because many points in every body of state law are unsettled by the courts of a given state, it would often be difficult to find sufficient materials to write a local-law casebook, except perhaps in the very largest states.

In addition, the leading law schools in the United States have long aspired to be, and held themselves out to be, national schools, with national student bodies. Teaching local law, which might be useful only in the state in which the school was located, would be inconsistent with this aspiration. What is true of the leading law schools is true of virtually all law schools, because virtually all law schools consider themselves to be, aspire to be, or emulate leading law schools. (An illuminating aspect of the national character of American legal education is the irrelevance of the state in which an academic received his legal education and passed the bar. If an American legal educator in, say, Iowa was asked whether it mattered that an applicant for a faculty position had been educated in a New York law school, he would think that the person who posed the question must be from another planet.)

D.   *Bar Examinations*

Just as legal scholarship and legal education focus on national law, so too do most bar examinations, even though these examinations are administered separately by each state, and passage of any single examination confers admission only to the bar of the relevant state. In part, the focus of state bar examinations on national rather than local law is due to the fact that the bar examiners themselves reflect the American legal culture. In addition, a focus on local law would be out of synchronization with the education given to students who take the bar.

The national-law orientation of state bar examinations reinforces the importance of national law. It also provides support to teaching national law, because it relieves the law schools from the pressure to teach local law that might exist if the bar examinations were oriented to local law.

E.   *Legal History*

Another critical element in the development of American national law lies in American legal history. Although the precise details varied from state to state, generally speaking

English common law was officially or unofficially made the law of the original thirteen and other early states. […]

With the exception of Louisiana, the newer states, one way or another, followed the original thirteen states. […]

This common origin of American state law had three kinds of effects. First, even where state-law doctrines developed differently, they developed from the same conceptual basis, and to the extent different states developed different doctrines, the doctrines would be more likely to look like fraternal twins than members of different species. Second, Americans were trained from the beginning to think they had a national law, that is, English law. Third, as a result of this history, together with their subsequent legal education, American lawyers have a common vocabulary and a common doctrinal base. The significance of this history is brought home by the experience in Louisiana, whose early law was based on the civil law, and which has on the whole continued to go its own doctrinal way in Code areas like contracts and property.

F.　*The Methodology of American Common Law*

Contract law is in large part a matter of common law, that is, judge-made law. Although it might seem that this condition would lead to a fracturing of contract law, in fact it has contributed to the uniformity of contract law. To see why this is so, it is necessary to begin with the methodology of the common law, and more particularly, American common law.

[…]

The most basic method of reasoning in the common law is reasoning from precedent.

[…]

Reasoning from precedent normally begins with precedents that were handed down in the deciding court's jurisdiction and are binding on the deciding court. Call these local precedents. Two other methods of reasoning in the common law, reasoning by analogy and reasoning from principle, also normally or frequently begin with local precedents. Often, however, the courts reason from doctrines found in texts that are not binding on the deciding court, but that are nevertheless generally recognized by the profession as authoritative legal sources. These texts include sources that are official in the deciding court's jurisdiction but are not binding on the deciding court, such as cases decided by lower courts; sources that are official only in other jurisdictions, such as cases decided by courts outside the deciding court's jurisdiction; and secondary sources authored by members or students of the profession, such as *Restatements*, treatises, and law review articles. I shall refer to these nonbinding texts individually as *professional sources* and collectively as the *professional literature*. The significance of this literature is suggested by a study of opinions in sixteen American state supreme courts during 1940–1970, which found that citations to out-of-state cases accounted for about one-fourth of all citations to state cases, and that secondary sources were cited in almost half the opinions. Anecdotally, a Justice of the United States Supreme Court, Stephen Breyer, was recently quoted as having said that "most lawyers would rather have the support of two paragraphs of Areeda on antitrust [a leading American treatise] than four courts of appeals and three Supreme Court Justices."

[…]

If, in a common-law area, a doctrine is supported in the professional literature, the courts are likely at least to take the doctrine seriously. If a doctrine is *established* in the professional literature, and there is no applicable local precedent, the doctrine will normally be treated as law in virtually the same way as local precedents would be. [...]

Indeed, doctrines established in the professional literature will often be treated as law even if they lead to a result different from that suggested by local precedent, as long as local precedent is not squarely contradictory. For example, if local precedent establishes the rule that a donative promise is unenforceable, courts will nevertheless characteristically employ the rule, established in the professional literature, that a donative promise is enforceable if relied upon.

The practice of treating doctrines established in the professional literature as law also both nourishes and draws on the concept of national law. It nourishes the concept, because it is partly due to the practice that American legal scholars can write about and teach national law with confidence that it is a meaningful body of law. It draws on the concept, because it is in the professional literature that national law is to be found, and because when law students who have been educated in national law become practicing lawyers and judges, they will have internalized both the national doctrines they have learned in law school and the institutional principle that doctrines established in the professional literature can, should, and typically will be treated as law.

G. A Look Back

I started this paper by observing that it might be expected that American contract law would be highly fractured [...] It can now be seen that the opposite is true. [...] The common law methodology gives heavy weight to the standard of social congruence. Doctrines that are determined to be socially congruent by the courts of one state are likely to be found socially congruent by other courts. Doctrines that are determined to be socially incongruent by the courts of one state are likely to be found socially incongruent by other courts. Such convergence will occur not just spontaneously, but because under the practice of reasoning from the professional literature, what courts do in one state becomes relevant to determining the law of other states. In contrast, American state legislatures, although also affected by social propositions, may be somewhat more likely than American state courts to shape local legislation partly on the basis of local political pressures.

V. Special Elements in the Harmonization of Contract Law

[...] The central position of national law in American contract law [...] was [...] reinforced by four great works of scholarship: a treatise on contract law by Samuel Williston, one of the leading figures in classical contract law, first published in 1921; a treatise on contract law by Arthur Corbin, a founder of modern American contract law, first published in 1951; the *Restatement of Contracts*, of which Williston was the Chief Reporter, published in 1932; and Article 2 of the Uniform Commercial Code ("UCC"), of which Karl Llewellyn, another leading contracts scholar, was Chief Reporter, published in 1952.

Influential treatises are not unique to the United States, but the influence of the Williston and Corbin treatises is nevertheless striking. For a long time, it was virtually de rigueur to cite one or both treatises in any opinion on an issue of contract law that was not firmly settled by local binding precedents. Because both treatises – like virtually every leading American treatise – were written in sweeping national-law terms, the enormous authority of these treatises gave a further push to national contract law.

The *Restatement of Contracts* is a more indigenous American product. The Restatement was a product of the American Law Institute ("ALI"). The ALI is an organization composed of lawyers, judges, and legal academics. The ALI's objective is to promote the clarification and simplification of the law, and its better adaptation to social needs. The ALI has sought to achieve this objective in part by preparing Restatements of various branches of the common law, including [...] Contracts.

The theory of the Restatements has changed somewhat over time. The introduction to the original *Restatement of Contracts* stated that "The function of the Institute is to state clearly and precisely in the light of the [courts'] decisions the principles and rules of the common law". The present theory is that the ALI "should feel obligated in [its] deliberations to give weight to all of the considerations that the courts, under a proper view of the judicial function, deem it right to weigh in theirs". Many of the original Restatements, including the *Restatement of Contracts*, were eventually superseded by revisions known as *Restatement Seconds*. The *Restatement Second of Contracts* was published in 1981. To a significant extent, the differences in approach between Williston and Corbin are paralleled by differences in approach between *Restatement First* and *Restatement Second*, and *Restatement Second* marks a considerable advance over *Restatement First*.

It sometimes seems to be thought that the uniformity of certain bodies of American law, such as contracts, is a result of the Restatements. However, although the Restatements have contributed to the harmonization process in the United States, they are more effect than cause. The underlying concept of a Restatement reflects, rather than generates, the concept of American national law. It is only because there was already a culture of American national law that the Restatements were conceived, and were so successful.

Uniform Acts are somewhat less indigenous to the United States than Restatements. However, it seems likely that few if any countries have carried out the concept of such acts as systematically as American states. Most Uniform Acts are the product of the National Conference of Commissioners on Uniform State Laws ("NCCUSL"), which consists of commissioners appointed by each state. NCCUSL has the power to recommend legislation to the states on subjects in which uniformity of law among the states is thought to be desirable, but has no power to require the adoption of such legislation. A few Uniform Acts, including the UCC, are the joint products of NCCUSL and the ALI.

Uniform Acts do not involve mandatory harmonization, like EC Regulations or Directives. Each state has a free choice whether to adopt a proposed Uniform Act and, for that matter, whether to adopt a Uniform Act in its pristine form or with local amendments. Some Uniform Acts have been adopted by less than substantially all the states – indeed, some have been adopted by only a handful of states. Other Uniform Acts have been adopted by all or substantially all the states. The UCC, which has been adopted by every state except Louisiana is an example.

Many provisions of the UCC are of major importance in contracts. Most of these provisions are in Article 2 (Sales). The direct applicability of that Article is set out in UCC § 2-102, which provides that "Unless the context otherwise requires, this Article applies to transactions in goods".

Because Article 2 in terms governs only contracts for the sale of goods, it might be thought that Article 2 would have served to fracture American contract law, by breaking out an important part of contracts for special treatment. In fact, however, Article 2 has generally had a unifying influence on American contract law. It was drafted under the leadership of a great contract law scholar. It reflected many advanced contract-law ideas. Many of its provisions are set out in very general terms. It builds on rather than replaces general contract law; for example, Article 2 does not define offers. Finally, reasoning from statutes (including the UCC) by analogy is a long-standing practice in common-law methodology. The unifying effect of Article 2 on contract law is reflected in the fact that a major reason for the promulgation of the *Restatement Second of Contracts* was to incorporate UCC concepts in the *Restatement.* And, of course, Article 2 fully harmonizes the contract law of every state in regard to an extremely important part of contract law.

VI. *Implications for the Integration of European Law*

In this Part, I will touch briefly on the implications of the American experience for European contract law. In one sense these implications are limited. There are many ways to harmonize law, and the elements of harmonization in American contract law are not exclusive. Accordingly, European contract law may be successfully integrated without regard to those elements. Nevertheless, the American experience suggests the importance of sociological elements in the harmonization of law. Indeed, the significance of such elements is reflected in the timing of the *Unidroit Principles* and the *European Principles.* Surely it is no accident that lawyers are beginning to work on unifying European contract law just when, for the first time in history, many people are beginning to think that they can be not only English or German, but European.

Given the importance of sociological elements, it may be desirable, for those interested in the harmonization of European law, to focus not only on doctrinal unification but on institutional design. At least four institutional measures could be taken to facilitate that harmonization.

One measure would be to partly denationalize law-school curricula. Under one model, the teaching of law-school subjects would be *Europeanized.* In a Europeanized model, each subject would be taught with the comparative law of other European nations in mind. Under an alternative model, legal education would be *generalized.* In a generalized model, as each new issue arose in a course the initial focus would be the problems raised by that issue – the problems raised, for example, by mistake, interpretation, or remedies – and only then would attention be turned to the particular solution of the local national system. The solutions of other national systems, whether European or not, would be considered, not necessarily or not only for their own sake, but to instantiate the general problems raised by the relevant issue and the possible lines of solution.

A second measure would be the Europeanization or generalization of bar examinations. Indeed, without this element a change in legal education might not be feasible.

A third measure would be the Europeanization, or the further Europeanization, of legal scholarship.

A fourth measure would be the Europeanization or generalization of judicial citation practices, so that European courts could and would make use of extranational material in the same way that American courts make use of the professional literature.

[...]

IV. Further reading

Case comment: Consideration and modification of contracts, *Build. L.M.* 2005, Jun, 11–12.

ALLAN FARNSWORTH, *Contracts*, 3rd edn, New York: Aspen Publishers, 2004, 267–85 (USA).

MURIEL FABRE-MAGNAN AND RUTH SEFTON-GREEN, "Defects of Consent in Contract Law", in Arthur Hartkamp *et al.* (eds), *Towards a European Civil Code*, 3rd edn, Nijmegen: Kluwer Law International, 2004, Ch. 22, 399–413.

GRACE M. GIESEL, "A Realistic Proposal for the Contract Duress Doctrine", 107 (2005) *W. Va L. Rev.* 443–98.

JAMES GORDLEY, "Consideration", in Jan M. Smits (ed.), E*lgar Encyclopedia of Comparative Law*, Cheltenham: Elgar Publishing, 2006, 180–86.

ROGER HALSON, "The Modification of Contractual Obligation", 44 *Current Legal Problems* [1991] 111–33.

RICHARD HYLAND, "The American Restatements and the Uniform Commercial Code", in Arthur Hartkamp *et al.* (eds), *Towards a European Civil Code*, 3rd edn, Nijmegen: Kluwer Law International, 2004, Ch. 4, 59–75.

HEIN KÖTZ AND AXEL FLESSNER, *European Contract Law*, Vol. I (by HEIN KÖTZ), Oxford: Clarendon Press, 1997, 68–74.

HECTOR MACQUEEN, "Illegality and Immorality in Contracts: Towards European Principles", in Arthur Hartkamp *et al.* (eds), *Towards a European Civil Code*, 3rd edn, Nijmegen: Kluwer Law International, 2004, Ch. 23, 415–27.

A. J. PHIPPS, "Resurrecting the doctrine of common law forbearance", (2007) 123 *LQR*, 286–313.

M. DEL PILAR PERALES VISCASILLAS, "Modification and Termination of the Contract (Art. 29 CISG)", 25 (2005) *J.L. & Com.* 167.

Chapter II

Performance of contracts

"[T]he only universal consequence of a legally binding promise is that the law makes the promisor pay damages if the promised act does not come to pass"[1]

"Le droit d'agir en justice pour exiger la condamnation du débiteur à fournir la prestation due est conçu par l'ordre juridique suisse comme une composante inhérente à tout droit subjectif privé [...]"[2]

Case 5: Right to receive performance of a contract or just a right to receive damages?

Case scenarios

(1) The owner of a painting by the very famous 19th-century English artist J. M. W. Turner, enters into a contract to sell the painting to an interested party. Before the execution of the contract, the seller changes his mind and decides to keep the painting for his family. He is prepared to compensate the purchaser. However, the purchaser demands performance of the contract.

(2) Two businessmen enter into a contract for the sale of 10 standard packaging machines for the price of € 600,000. Subsequently, the market price of such machines increases and the seller regrets having entered into the contract. The purchaser insists on the delivery of the machines. Similar machines are readily available on the market for a higher price.

(3) A well-known German opera singer, the niece of a famous composer, is hired by Her Majesty's Theatre in London for a period of three months. The contract stipulates that she may not sing in other establishments for the duration of the contract. Nevertheless, she signs a contract with the Royal Opera House in Covent Garden for the same period for a higher salary. The directors of Her Majesty's Theatre want performance of the contract, or at the very least they want the singer to be prohibited from singing in another establishment for the duration of the contract.

---

[1] OLIVER WENDELL HOLMES, *The Common Law*, Boston: Little Brown, 1881, p. 301.

[2] "The right to initiate legal proceedings demanding that a debtor be compelled to provide the service due is seen by the Swiss legal order as an inherent component of all individual private rights [...]". LUC THEVENOZ AND FRANZ WERRO (eds), *Commentaire Romand: Code des obligations*, Vol. I, Basel: Helbing Lichtenhahn, 2003, Art. 97, n° 1.

Questions

(1) In each of the three case scenarios above, a contract has been concluded. One of the parties refuses to perform the agreed contract but the other party insists that the contract be performed.

How does the Vienna Sales Convention deal with such a situation?

(2) How is the question of whether there is a right to receive performance of a contract dealt with in the civil codes of *Quebec, Austria, Italy* and *The Netherlands,* and in the *Finnish* and *Danish* laws on the sale of goods according to the rules cited below?

(3) How would the three case scenarios above be treated under *German* and *French* law?

(4) What is the function of the *astreinte* in *French* law and of fines in *German* law? What are the fundamental differences between these two coercive measures?

Should any future European legislation in the field of contract law include the *astreinte* as a means of putting pressure on the debtor?

(5) What is the general rule in *English* law? Under what conditions might *specific performance* be granted?

How would the above case scenarios be treated under *English* law? How would they be treated under the *American* Uniform Commercial Code and under the Restatement Second, Contracts 2nd?

(6) In each of the different legal systems, when does a creditor have a right to receive performance of a contract? When is there no such right? How many different approaches can be identified? Present the solutions in a systematic manner.

In what circumstances would a creditor prefer to claim for performance of a contract rather than for damages?

(7) What solution is adopted by the UNIDROIT Principles, the Principles of European Contract Law, and the Draft Common Frame of Reference? The rules in the principles are inspired by the solutions found in which countries? Do the principles take the interests of the creditor sufficiently into account?

What is your opinion of Article 7.2.4 of the UNIDROIT Principles?

Table of contents

I.   Vienna Sales Convention

United Nations Convention on Contracts for the International Sale of Goods (CISG)

Art. 45
(1)   If the seller fails to perform any of his obligations under the contract or this Convention, the buyer may:
   (a)   exercise the rights provided in articles 46 to 52;
   (b)   claim damages as provided in articles 74 to 77.

[...]

Art. 46
(1)   The buyer may require performance by the seller of his obligations unless the buyer has resorted to a remedy which is inconsistent with this requirement.
(2)   If the goods do not conform with the contract, the buyer may require delivery of substitute goods only if the lack of conformity constitutes a fundamental breach of contract and a request for substitute goods is made either in conjunction with notice given under article 39 or within a reasonable time thereafter.
(3)   If the goods do not conform with the contract, the buyer may require the seller to remedy the lack of conformity by repair, unless this is unreasonable having regard to all the circumstances. A request for repair must be made either in conjunction with notice given under article 39 or within a reasonable time thereafter.

Art. 28
If, in accordance with the provisions of this Convention, one party is entitled to require performance of any obligation by the other party, a court is not bound to enter a judgment for specific performance unless the court would do so under its own law in respect of similar contracts of sale not governed by this Convention.

II. Various Legal Orders

1. Civil Code of Quebec

Art. 1590
(1)   An obligation confers on the creditor the right to demand that the obligation be performed in full, properly and without delay.
(2)   Where the debtor fails to perform his obligation without justification on his part and he is in default, the creditor may, without prejudice to his right to the performance of the obligation in whole or in part by equivalence,
  1.   force specific performance of the obligation;

  [...]

  3.   take any other measure provided by law to enforce his right to the performance of the obligation.

2. Burgerlijk Wetboek (*Dutch Civil Code*)

Art. 3:296
(1)   Tenzij uit de wet, uit de aard der verplichting of uit een rechtshandeling anders volgt, wordt hij die jegens een ander verplicht is iets te geven, te doen of na te laten, daartoe door de rechter, op vordering van de gerechtigde, veroordeeld.

[...]

Art. 3:296
(1)   Unless the law, the nature of the obligation or a juridical act produce a different result, the person who is obliged to give, to do or not to do something vis-à-vis another is ordered to do so by the judge upon the demand of the person to whom the obligation is owed.

[...]

3. Kauppalaki (*Finnish Law on the Sale of Goods*)[3]

§ 23
(1)   Ostajalla on oikeus pysyä sopimuksessa ja vaatia sen täyttämistä. Myyjä ei kuitenkaan ole velvollinen täyttämään sopimusta, jos sille on olemassa este, jota myyjä

---

[3]   For an overview on the Scandinavian legal orders, see ZWEIGERT AND KÖTZ, *An Introduction to Comparative Law*, 3rd edn, Oxford: Oxford University Press, 1998, pp. 276–85.

ei voi voittaa, tai jos sopimuksen täyttäminen edellyttäisi uhrauksia, jotka ovat kohtuuttomia verrattuna ostajalle siitä koituvaan etuun, että myyjä täyttää sopimuksen.
(2) Jos este tai epäsuhde lakkaa kohtuullisessa ajassa, ostaja saa kuitenkin vaatia, että myyjä täyttää sopimuksen.
(3) Ostaja menettää oikeuden vaatia sopimuksen täyttämistä, jos hän viivyttelee kohtuuttoman kauan vaatimuksen esittämisessä.

§ 23
(1) The buyer is entitled to enforce the contract and to require its performance. The seller is, nevertheless, not obliged to perform the contract if there is an impediment that he cannot overcome or if the performance would require sacrifices that are disproportionate to the buyer's interest in performance by the seller.
(2) If the impediment or disproportion ceases to exist within a reasonable time, the buyer may, nevertheless, require performance of the contract.
(3) The buyer loses his right to require performance of the contract if he defers his claim for an unreasonably long time.

4. Købeloven (*Danish Law on the Sale of Goods*)[4]

§ 21
(1) Leveres salgsgenstanden ikke i rette tid og skyldes dette ikke køberens forhold eller en hændelig begivenhed, for hvilken han bærer faren, har køberen valget mellem at forlange genstanden leveret og at hæve købet.

[...]

§ 21
(1) If the goods are not delivered by the agreed time and this is not due to circumstances attributable to the buyer or an accidental event for which the buyer bears the risk, the buyer may demand performance or declare the contract avoided.

[...]

5. Codice civile (*Italian Civil Code*)

Art. 1453. Risolubilità del contratto per inadempimento.
Nei contratti con prestazioni corrispettive, quando uno dei contraenti non adempie le sue obbligazioni, l'altro può a sua scelta chiedere l'adempimento o la risoluzione del contratto, salvo, in ogni caso, il risarcimento del danno.

---

[4] For a brief introduction to Danish law see ULLA ROSENKJAER, ANNE GLEERUP AND LEIF RØRBAEK, *An Introduction to Danish Law*, 2nd edn, Drammelstrupgaard, 2008; BØRGE DAHL, TORBEN MELCHIOR AND DITLEV TAMM (eds), *Danish Law in a European Perspective*, 2nd edn, Copenhagen: Thomson, 2002.

Art. 1453. *Dissolution of contract for non-performance.*
In contracts providing for mutual counterperformance, when one of the parties fails to perform his obligations, the other party can choose to demand either performance or dissolution of the contract, saving, in any case, compensation for damages.

6. Österreichisches Allgemeines Bürgerliches Gesetzbuch (ABGB) *(Austrian Civil Code)*

§ 918.
(1)   Wenn ein entgeltlicher Vertrag von einem Teil entweder nicht zur gehörigen Zeit, am gehörigen Ort oder auf die bedungene Weise erfüllt wird, kann der andere entweder Erfüllung und Schadenersatz wegen der Verspätung begehren oder unter Festsetzung einer angemessenen Frist zur Nachholung den Rücktritt vom Vertrag erklären.

[...]

§ 918.
(1)   When one party to a nongratuitous contract does not perform it at the time, the place or in the way agreed, the other party can either require performance as well as damages for delay or after having fixed an appropriate time period for performance, terminate the contract.

§ 919
Ist die Erfüllung zu einer festbestimmten Zeit oder binnen einer festbestimmten Frist bei sonstigem Rücktritt bedungen, so muss der Rücktrittberechtigte, wenn er auf der Erfüllung bestehen will, das nach Ablauf der Zeit dem anderen ohne Verzug anzeigen;
[...]

§ 919
If performance is to be completed within a fixed time period or by a specified date or else risk termination, the party who has the right to terminate the contract must, if they still insist on requiring performance, make this known to the other party without delay after the expiration of the time period or passing of the deadline.

III. Germany

1. Bürgerliches Gesetzbuch, BGB
(*German Civil Code*)

§ 241. Pflichten aus dem Schuldverhältnis
(1) Kraft des Schuldverhältnisses ist der Gläubiger berechtigt, von dem Schuldner eine Leistung zu fordern. Die Leistung kann auch in einem Unterlassen bestehen.

[...]

§ 241. Duties arising from an obligation
(1) By virtue of an obligation a creditor is entitled to claim performance from the debtor. The performance may also consist in forbearance.

[...]

§ 433. Vertragstypische Pflichten beim Kaufvertrag.
(1) Durch den Kaufvertrag wird der Verkäufer einer Sache verpflichtet, dem Käufer die Sache zu übergeben und das Eigentum an der Sache zu verschaffen. Der Verkäufer hat dem Käufer die Sache frei von Sach- und Rechtsmängeln zu verschaffen.
(2) Der Käufer ist verpflichtet, dem Verkäufer den vereinbarten Kaufpreis zu zahlen und die gekaufte Sache abzunehmen.

§ 433. Typical duties in a contract of sale.
(1) By a contract of sale, the seller of a thing is bound to deliver the thing to the buyer and to transfer ownership of the thing to the buyer. The seller must procure the thing for the buyer free from material and legal defects.
(2) The buyer is bound to pay the seller the agreed purchase price and to take delivery of the thing.

§ 611. Vertragstypische Pflichten beim Dienstvertrag.
(1) Durch den Dienstvertrag wird derjenige, welcher Dienste zusagt, zur Leistung der versprochenen Dienste, der andere Teil zur Gewährung der vereinbarten Vergütung verpflichtet.
(2) Gegenstand des Dienstvertrages können Dienste jeder Art sein.

§ 611. Typical contractual duties in a service contract
(1) By means of a service contract, a person who promises to perform a service is bound to perform the services promised, and the other party is bound to pay the agreed remuneration.
(2) Services of any type may be the subject matter of service contracts.

2. Zivilprozessordnung, ZPO
(*German Code of Civil Procedure*)

Zwangsvollstreckung zur Erwirkung der Herausgabe von Sachen
und zur Erwirkung von Handlungen und Unterlassungen

*Execution of judgments to obtain the return of goods and the
performance of an obligation to do something or refrain from doing something*

§ 883. Herausgabe bestimmter beweglicher Sachen.

(1) Hat der Schuldner eine bewegliche Sache oder eine Menge bestimmter beweglicher Sachen herauszugeben, so sind sie von dem Gerichtsvollzieher ihm wegzunehmen und dem Gläubiger zu übergeben.

[...]

§ 883. *Return of specific personal property*

(1) If a debtor is obliged to deliver a specific item of personal property (chattel) or a specified number of items of personal property (chattels), these items must be taken from him by the bailiff and returned to the creditor.

§ 884. Leistung einer bestimmten Menge vertretbarer Sachen.

Hat der Schuldner eine bestimmte Menge vertretbarer Sachen oder Wertpapiere zu leisten, so gilt die Vorschrift des § 883 Abs. 1 entsprechend.

§ 884. *Delivery of a specified quantity of identified goods.*

If the debtor must provide a specified quantity of identified goods or documents, § 883(1) is applicable.

§ 887. Vertretbare Handlungen.

(1) Erfüllt der Schuldner die Verpflichtung nicht, eine Handlung vorzunehmen, deren Vornahme durch einen Dritten erfolgen kann, so ist der Gläubiger von dem Prozessgericht des ersten Rechtszuges auf Antrag zu ermächtigen, auf Kosten des Schuldners die Handlung vornehmen zu lassen.

(2) Der Gläubiger kann zugleich beantragen, den Schuldner zur Vorauszahlung der Kosten zu verurteilen, die durch die Vornahme der Handlung entstehen werden, unbeschadet des Rechts auf eine Nachforderung, wenn die Vornahme der Handlung einen größeren Kostenaufwand verursacht.

(3) Auf die Zwangsvollstreckung zur Erwirkung der Herausgabe oder Leistung von Sachen sind die vorstehenden Vorschriften nicht anzuwenden.

§ 887. *Obligation to do something that may be done by a third party.*

(1) If the debtor does not fulfil an obligation to do something that could be performed by a third party, the creditor can, on the authority of the court of first instance, granted at his request, have the obligation performed at the expense of the debtor.

(2) At the same time, the creditor can request that the debtor be ordered to pay the expected cost of the performance of the obligation, which does not affect his right to claim extra payment if the performance of the obligation costs more.

(3) These paragraphs are not applicable to the execution of judgments on claims for the return or the delivery of property.

§ 888. Nicht vertretbare Handlungen.

(1) Kann eine Handlung durch einen Dritten nicht vorgenommen werden, so ist, wenn sie ausschließlich von dem Willen des Schuldners abhängt, auf Antrag von dem Prozessgericht des ersten Rechtszuges zu erkennen, dass der Schuldner zur Vornahme der Handlung durch Zwangsgeld und für den Fall, dass dieses nicht beigetrieben werden kann, durch Zwangshaft oder durch Zwangshaft anzuhalten sei. Das einzelne Zwangsgeld darf den Betrag von fünfundzwanzigtausend Euro nicht übersteigen. [...]

(2) Eine Androhung der Zwangsmittel findet nicht statt.

(3) Diese Vorschriften kommen im Falle der Verurteilung zur Eingehung einer Ehe, im Falle der Verurteilung zur Herstellung des ehelichen Lebens und im Falle der Verurteilung zur Leistung von Diensten aus einem Dienstvertrag nicht zur Anwendung.

§ 888. *Acts which cannot be performed by a third party.*

(1) If an act cannot be performed by a third party, that is to say that it depends exclusively on the will of the debtor, the debtor may be ordered, on the basis of a request to the court of first instance, to perform the act or pay a fine and, where the fine cannot be recovered, face imprisonment or simply face imprisonment alone. Each fine must not exceed an amount of €25.000. [...]

(2) The debtor need not be forewarned of the sanctions.

(3) These paragraphs are not applicable to judgments relating to marriage, judgments relating to the restitution of conjugal rights and judgments for the performance of services under an employment contract.

§ 890. Erzwingung von Unterlassungen und Duldungen.

(1) Handelt der Schuldner der Verpflichtung zuwider, eine Handlung zu unterlassen oder die Vornahme einer Handlung zu dulden, so ist er wegen einer jeden Zuwiderhandlung auf Antrag des Gläubigers von dem Prozessgericht des ersten Rechtszuges zu einem Ordnungsgeld und für den Fall, dass dieses nicht beigetrieben werden kann, zur Ordnungshaft oder Ordnungshaft bis zu sechs Monaten zu verurteilen. Das einzelne Ordnungsgeld darf den Betrag von zweihundertfünfzigtausend Euro, die Ordnungshaft insgesamt zwei Jahre nicht übersteigen.

(2) Der Verurteilung muss eine entsprechende Androhung vorausgehen, die, wenn sie in dem die Verpflichtung aussprechenden Urteil nicht enthalten ist, auf Antrag von dem Prozessgericht des ersten Rechtszuges erlassen wird.

(3) Auch kann der Schuldner auf Antrag des Gläubigers zur Bestellung einer Sicherheit für den durch fernere Zuwiderhandlungen entstehenden Schaden auf bestimmte Zeit verurteilt werden.

§ 890. *Performance of obligations to refrain from doing something or to tolerate something.*

(1) If the debtor contravenes his obligation to refrain from doing something or to tolerate an act, the court of first instance may, on the application of the creditor, impose a fine and if this cannot be recovered, impose a prison sentence, or just impose a prison sentence of up to six months. Each fine must not exceed the amount of €250.000, the prison sentences may not exceed 2 years in total.

> (2)   *The sentence must be preceded by a forewarning that, if not contained in the pronounced judgment, is given by the trial judge at first instance upon request.*
> (3)   *The debtor may also, upon the request of the creditor, be ordered to provide security for a certain period of time, for damage caused by future violations.*

3. Konrad Zweigert and Hein Kötz, *An Introduction to Comparative Law*, 3rd edn (transl. Tony Weir), pp. 470–74

VIII.   The Performance of Contracts

35

Claims to Performance and Their Enforcement

I

A PERSON who enters a contract expects the other party to do as he promised. He may be disappointed. The *goods* may not be delivered, the purchased premises may not be vacated, the tenant may stay on after the end of the lease, the singer may not give the covenanted recital, or the ex-employee may set himself up in competition contrary to his promise. The question then arises what forms of relief the legal system will offer the innocent contractor who has been deceived in his expectation that the contract will be performed. One point is agreed in all modern legal systems: the creditor must not simply proceed to help himself and snatch the goods from the vendor, thrust the tenant into the street, or use similar private and forcible methods to compel the other contracting party to perform his promise. The innocent party must go to court and establish the claims which accrue to him on non-performance of the contract before he takes any further steps against the debtor, and those steps too must proceed under the supervision of the state.

The contractor who has suffered a loss because he has not got what he was promised may be content with monetary compensation. This will normally be the case if something as good as what was promised can he procured elsewhere, even at a higher price, for the innocent party will be content to sue the defaulter for damages for the extra he has to pay. But what is to be done when it is difficult or even impossible to calculate the harm, or when no calculation one can do will reflect any special interest the creditor may have in having the contract performed? If a man buys a picture which has a 'sentimental value' for him, inestimable in money, perhaps because it is a portrait of a noted ancestor, is he only to claim damages if the picture is not delivered or can he ask a court to order the auctioneer to deliver the picture to him? Under what circumstances – and this is our first question – may a court, at the instance of the plaintiff, order the defendant to perform his contract *in natura*, that is, order the auctioneer to deliver the picture, the tenant to vacate the dwelling, the singer to give the concert as promised, and the employee to cease from competition?

Even if the court grants the creditor's claim for performance, he still does not have what he really wants, for many debtors do not satisfy a claim even if it has been established in court, either because they cannot do so or think they cannot, or because they do not want to. Here the state helps the creditor by set procedures for using its coercive powers to satisfy his claim against the debtor's will, unless the debtor's co-operation is required, when it will influence his will with forceful sanctions, threatened or applied.

We shall devote no further attention to the execution of money claims such as judgments for the price of goods. This is done in all countries by having state execution officials seize and sell the property of the debtor and then hand the proceeds of the sale to the creditor.

Two questions therefore remain for discussion. Under what circumstances may a contractor ask a court to issue judgment ordering the other party to perform the contract? How is such a judgment, not being simply a money judgment, actually executed?

II

In *German* law and in related systems it is axiomatic that a creditor has the right to bring a claim for performance of a contract and to obtain a judgment ordering the debtor to fulfill it. For this purpose it is immaterial whether the debtor's obligation is to deliver goods pursuant to a sale, to vacate a dwelling house, or to produce a work of art. The view that it is of the very essence of an obligation that it be actionable in this sense is so fundamental that it is not expressly stated in any legislative text, but the words of §241 of the Civil Code, that the creditor is entitled, on the grounds of the creditor–debtor relationship, to demand performance from the debtor, imply that actual performance may be demanded before a court and that a judgment ordering performance in kind may be issued by it.

However, a judgment ordering the debtor to perform is not of much use to the creditor unless the legal system provides the means to make it effective. Accordingly one must turn to the question whether and how such a judgment can be enforced. The way in which the question is dealt with in German law is quite characteristic. The Code of Civil Procedure carefully distinguishes all the various types of claim which might underlie a judgment for performance, and provides quite distinct forms of execution for each of them. Thus §883–6 of the Code deal with the execution of judgments on claims for the delivery of property. The method provided – the only method – is for the bailiff (*Gerichtsvollzieher*) to take the chattel from the debtor or to require him to leave the premises, with the help of the police, if necessary, and then to hand over the chattel or premises to the creditor. If the claim on which the creditor has obtained judgment is that the debtor should take some positive action other than handing over the property, a distinction is made, if the act in question is one which could he equally well performed by someone else, that is, it need not he performed by the debtor personally but is, as the Code of Civil Procedure puts it, *vertretbar*, then the method of execution – the only method – is for the creditor, on the authority of the court granted at his request, to have the act performed by a third party at the expense of the debtor (*Ersatzvornahme*, §887 Code of Civil Procedure).

As examples of acts which are *vertretbar,* or capable of substitute performance, one may cite manual tasks which call for no especial talent and can therefore be carried out by third parties – the execution of building operations (LG Hagen JR 1948, 314), the installation of a lift in an apartment block (KG JW 1927, 1945), the printing of a manuscript (OLG Munich MDR 1955, 682). The making of an extract from the books of a business or the production of its accounts may also be 'vertretbar' if an expert could do it after inspecting the debtor's records (OLG Hamburg MDR 1955, 43).

If the act to which the creditor lays claim is one which can be performed only by the debtor himself, it is said to be *unvertretbar.* In such a case the method of execution provided by the Code of Civil Procedure (§888) is to threaten the unwilling debtor with a fine or imprisonment.

This is possible only when the act in question 'depends exclusively on the will of the debtor', in the words of §888 Code of Civil Procedure. It is therefore not possible where, for example, the debtor's obligation is to do something which calls for special artistic or scientific talent, for the performance of such acts does not depend exclusively on the debtor's will. However good his intentions may be, a composer cannot compose his sonata nor a law professor write his commentary without the right inspiration, mood, energy, and other preconditions of great spiritual creativity (see OLG Frankfurt OLGE 29, 251). Finally the Code of Civil Procedure lists in §888 several more specific cases where these methods of penal pressure are unavailable. Thus one may not execute a judgment obtained by one spouse requiring the other to reconstitute the conditions of married life, and one may not execute a judgment which orders the defendant to perform services under a contract of employment. The employer may certainly obtain a judgment which imposes on the employee the duty to perform his obligations under the contract of service (so, in terms, RGZ 72, 393, 394), but this judgment cannot be enforced, because the employee must at all times remain free to decide how to dispose of his labour, even if this involves a breach of contract; in such a case the employer must content himself with a claim for damages.

There is a special regulation for the case where the positive act required of the debtor by the judgment is a declaration of intention or consent (Willenserklärung); the effect of §894 Code of Civil Procedure is that as soon as the judgment is final the declaration is deemed to have been made.

If, instead of requiring the debtor to take positive action, the judgment orders him to abstain from action or to permit someone else to take action, §890 Code of Civil Procedure applies: should the debtor act in breach of such a duty, the court may, on the application of the creditor, imprison him or fine him, the fine going once again to the Treasury. The debtor must have notice that such sanctions are to be invoked: this notice is normally contained in the original judgment.

IV.   France

1. Code civil français (*French Civil Code*)

Art. 1142

Toute obligation de faire ou de ne pas faire se résout en dommages et intérêts, en cas d'inexécution de la part du débiteur.

Art. 1142

An obligation to do something or to refrain from doing something ends in damages in the event of non-performance on the part of the debtor.[5]

Art. 1143

Néanmoins, le créancier a le droit de demander que ce qui aurait été fait par contravention à l'engagement, soit détruit; et il peut se faire autoriser à le détruire aux dépens du débiteur, sans préjudice des dommages et intérêts, s'il y a lieu.

Art. 1143

Nevertheless, a creditor is entitled to request that what has been done through breach of the undertaking be destroyed; and he may have himself authorised to destroy it at the expense of the debtor, without prejudice to damages, if there is an entitlement to them.[6]

Art. 1144

Le créancier peut aussi en cas d'inexécution, être autorisé à faire exécuter lui-même l'obligation aux dépens du débiteur. [...] Celui-ci peut être condamné à faire l'avance des sommes nécessaires à cette exécution.

Art. 1144

A creditor may also, in the event of non-performance, obtain authorisation to have the obligation performed himself, at the debtor's expense. [...] The latter may be ordered to advance the sums necessary for that performance.

Art. 1184

(1) La condition résolutoire est toujours sous-entendue dans les contrats synallagmatiques, pour le cas où l'une des deux parties ne satisfera point à son engagement.

(2) Dans ce cas, le contrat n'est point résolu de plein droit. La partie envers laquelle l'engagement n'a point été exécuté, a le choix ou de forcer l'autre à l'exécution de la convention lorsqu'elle est possible, ou d'en demander la résolution avec dommages et intérêts.

(3) La résolution doit être demandée en justice, et il peut être accordé au défendeur un délai selon les circonstances.

---

5   Translation by EG.
6   Translation by EG.

> **Art. 1184**
> *(1)   A resolutive condition is always implied in synallagmatic contracts, covering the event in which one of the two parties does not carry out his undertaking.*
> *(2)   In such a case, the contract is not automatically terminated. The party towards whom the undertaking has not been fulfilled has the choice either to compel the other party to fulfil the agreement where this is possible, or to request termination of the contract and damages.*
> *(3)   An application for termination must be made before the courts, and the defendant may be granted time according to circumstances.*[7]
>
> **Art. 1610**
> Si le vendeur manque à faire la délivrance dans le temps convenu entre les parties, l'acquéreur pourra, à son choix, demander la résolution de la vente, ou sa mise en possession, si le retard ne vient que du fait du vendeur.
>
> **Art. 1610**
> *If the seller fails to make delivery within the time agreed upon by the parties, the purchaser may choose to apply for avoidance of the sale, or for his being vested with possession, if the delay results only from an act of the seller.*

2. Cour de cassation française, 3ᵉ ch. civ. (*French Cour de cassation*) 11 mai 2005, Belhadj c/ SA Les Bâtisseurs du Grand delta, Bull. civ. 2005 III, n° 103, p. 96 = D. 2005. IR. 1504

LA COUR [...]

Sur le moyen unique:

Vu l'article 1184 du Code civil;

Attendu que la partie envers laquelle l'engagement n'a point été exécuté peut forcer l'autre à l'exécution de la convention lorsqu'elle est possible;

Attendu, selon l'arrêt attaqué (CA Aix-en-Provence, 23 sept. 2003), que M. et Mme Tahar Belhadj ont signé avec la société Les Bâtisseurs du Grand Delta un contrat de construction de maison individuelle dont ils ont réglé la totalité du prix tout en refusant de signer le procès-verbal de réception en raison d'une non-conformité aux stipulations contractuelles relatives au niveau de la construction; qu'ils ont assigné la société de construction afin d'obtenir sa condamnation à démolir puis reconstruire la maison, ou, à défaut, sa condamnation au paiement d'une somme équivalente au coût des opérations de démolition et de reconstruction;

Attendu que pour débouter M. et Mme Tahar Belhadj de leur demande, l'arrêt retient que la non-conformité aux stipulations contractuelles ne rend pas l'immeuble impropre à sa destination et à son usage et ne porte pas sur des éléments essentiels et déterminants du contrat; Qu'en statuant ainsi, alors qu' elle avait constaté que le niveau de la construction présentait une insuffisance de 0,33 mètre par rapport aux stipulations contractuelles, la

---

[7]   Translation by EG.

cour d'appel qui n'a pas tiré les conséquences légales de ses propres constatations, a violé le texte susvisé;

Par ces motifs:

Casse et annule […] l'arrêt rendu le 23 septembre 2003, entre les parties, par la cour d'appel d'Aix-en-Provence […] et […] les renvoie devant la cour d'appel de Grenoble;

Translation

THE COURT […]

On the only ground for appeal:

In view of Article 1184 of the Civil Code;

Whereas the party towards whom the obligation has not been performed can compel the other to perform the agreement where this is possible;

Given that, according to the contested decision (Court of Appeal, Aix-en-Provence, 23 September 2003), Mr and Mrs Tahar Belhadj signed a construction contract for a detached house with the company *Les Bâtisseurs du Grand Delta* for which they paid the whole of the price and refused to sign the acceptance report because of non-compliance with the provisions of the contact in relation to the height of the construction; that they have brought proceedings against the construction company in order to obtain an order against the company to demolish and then reconstruct the house, or, in the absence of this, an order to pay the sum equivalent to the cost of demolition and reconstruction;

Given that in order to dismiss Mr and Mrs Tahar Belhadj's claim, the decision holds that the non-compliance with the provisions of the contract does not render the building unfit for purpose and use and does not affect the essential and decisive elements of the contract; that by ruling in this way, when it had established that the height of the construction fell short of the height in the contractual provisions by 0.33 metres, the court of appeal did not draw the legal consequences from its own observations, infringed the aforementioned text;

For these reasons:

Quashes […] the decision given on 23 September 2003, between the parties, by the court of appeal in Aix-en-Provence […] and […] sends the parties before the court of appeal in Grenoble;

Case note, Sabine Bernheim-Desvaux, Sanction du défaut de conformité aux stipulations contractuelles de construction [*Remedy for lack of conformity with the contractual provisions on construction*] JCP 2005. II. 10152 (Translation from the French original)

[…]

Right to performance strictly in conformity with the contract

By virtue of Article 1184 of the Civil Code, the creditor [the person to whom the obligation is owed] can compel the other party to perform the agreement where this is possible. This right to performance in conformity with the contract, although in contrast with Article 1142 of the Civil Code, is the result of the combined efforts of academic writing and case law. In fact, the largely majority academic opinion [...] considers that compulsory performance is part of the essence of the obligation as only this remedy is capable of ensuring that the rights of the parties as well as the law are entirely respected. This ideal remedy is legitimately founded in the binding force of contracts and in the respect of someone's word. Demolombe wrote, on this matter in *Traité des contrats* (*vol. 24, 2ᵉ éd., 1870, n° 488*): "the fundamental principle of our matter is that agreements lawfully entered into take the place of law for those who have made them (*Civil Code, Art. 1134*); and as a result, it is the creditor's right to request, from the debtor [the person who owes performance of the obligation], effective performance of the same obligation as contracted for". This academic opinion has strongly influenced substantive law [...] and the courts order performance of a contract unless physically or morally impossible because it infringes one of the debtor's essential freedoms (*Cass. 1ʳᵉ civ., 20 janv. 1953: JCP G 1953, II, 7677*). Compulsory performance is mandatory for the court as it is bound by the contract which is the law between the parties. It is irrelevant whether the creditor has suffered harm [...] Equally, it does not matter that performance of the obligation be financially or socially disastrous and that the debtor loses everything [...]

The binding nature of this measure thus encourages virtuous behaviour and reinforces legal certainty, while at the same time avoiding judicial activism often considered to be suspicious. And yet ...

Appropriateness of judicial discretion to grant remedies

When compulsory performance is possible, the question of its economic efficiency is raised in practice before for the courts [...] Particularly in the field of construction, it would be beneficial to give the courts the discretionary power to grant remedies, mainly in order for them to calculate the proportionality of the cost of repairs (or of the demolition and reconstruction) compared to the creditor's interest. [...] Even though this [proposal] was favourably received by the Cour de cassation until the 1960s [...] the tendency has completely reversed today [...]

3. Cour de cassation (civ. 1ʳᵉ) 20.10.1959 (*Soc. X... c. P...*), D. 1959, 537, with case note by G. HOLLEAUX

COUR DE CASSATION
(CH. CIV., 1ʳᵉ SECT. CIV.)
20 octobre 1959

ASTREINTE, ASTREINTE PROVISOIRE, NATURE JURIDIQUE, DOMMAGES-INTÉRÊTS, DISTINCTION, LIQUIDATION, GRAVITÉ DE LA FAUTE, FACULTÉS DU DEBITEUR.

Est légalement justifié l'arrêt décidant que l'astreinte provisoire, mesure de contrainte entièrement distincte des dommages-intérêts, et qui n'est en définitive qu'un moyen de vaincre la résistance opposée à l'exécution d'une condamnation, n'a pas pour objet de compenser le dommage né du retard et est normalement liquidée en fonction de la gravité de la faute du débiteur récalcitrant et de ses facultés [...]

(Soc. X… C. P…) – ARRET

LA COUR; – Sur le moyen unique, en ses deux branches: – Attendu qu'il est reproché à l'arrêt attaqué (Riom, 10 déc. 1956, D. 1956. 101) d'avoir, lors de la liquidation d'une astreinte précédemment ordonnée pour assurer l'exécution d'une obligation de faire, pris en considération la résistance fautive du débiteur, sans s'attacher à mesurer l'importance du préjudice causé au créancier par le retard de l'exécution, alors que selon le pourvoi, le juge qui liquide une astreinte est tenu de ne pas dépasser le montant du dommage dont la constatation est indispensable pour justifier la condamnation; – Mais attendu qu'en décidant que l'astreinte provisoire, mesure de contrainte entièrement distincte des dommages-intérêts, et qui n'est en définitive qu'un moyen de vaincre la résistance opposée à l'exécution d'une condamnation, n'a pas pour objet de compenser le dommage né du retard et est normalement liquidée en fonction de la gravité de la faute du débiteur récalcitrant et de ses facultés, la cour d'appel, dont l'arrêt est motivé, a légalement justifié sa décision;

Par ces motifs, rejette.

Du 20 oct. 1959. – Ch. civ., 1re sect. civ. – MM. Battestini, 1er pr. – Holleaux, rap. – Jodelet, av. gén. – Goutet et Cail, av.

Translation

A judgment is legally justified in deciding that a provisional astreinte, *which is a measure of compulsion completely distinct from damages, and which is after all only a means of overcoming resistance to performance of a judicial order, does not have the object of compensating for harm resulting from delay and is normally fixed in terms of the seriousness of the debtor's fault and the extent of his means.* […][8]

(Soc. X… v. P…) – DECISION

THE COURT; – On the sole grounds for appeal, taken in its two parts: – Given that the decision under attack (Riom, 10 December 1956, D. 1956, 101) is criticised for fixing the amount payable under an *astreinte* previously granted in order to enforce the execution of an obligation to perform a service in relation to the debtor's culpable recalcitrance rather than the harm caused to the creditor by the delay in performance, whereas, according to the applicant, in fixing the amount of an *astreinte* the judge must determine the amount of harm caused and may not order the payment of any higher sum; – But given that in deciding that the provisional *astreinte*, a remedy quite distinct from that of damages and really only a means of overcoming a refusal to obey a judicial order, is not designed to compensate for damage caused by the delay but is normally fixed in relation to the seriousness of the debtor's fault and the extent of his means, the decision of the Court of Appeal is properly reasoned and justified.

For these reasons dismisses the application for review.[9]

---

[8] Translated by TONY WEIR, http://www.utexas.edu/law/academics/centers/transnational/work_new/french/case.php?id=1194.

[9] Translated by TONY WEIR, http://www.utexas.edu/law/academics/centers/transnational/work_new/french/case.php?id=1194.

CASE NOTE[10]

(1)   The circumstances of the instant case make clear the pressing importance of the legal question submitted to the *Cour de cassation*: the legal nature of the *astreinte*.

A manufacturing company is ordered to change a piece of work done in violation of the rights of an individual. With a view to ensuring the execution of the decision, the court of appeal accompanied the order with an *astreinte*, calculated for every day of the delay. Nevertheless, the company did not execute the decision. The final amount of the *astreinte* was fixed by the judge and a new *astreinte* was ordered. The company continued to refuse to execute the decision. Once again the final amount of the *astreinte* was fixed by the judge, followed by the ordering of a new *astreinte*. In vain. Finally, by a new decision (the fourth), a new *astreinte*, this time for 10.000 Francs per day, was ordered for a three month period. Performance still not having been made, the beneficiaries requested payment of the *astreinte* in its full amount (900 000 Francs) and the fixing of a new more severe *astreinte*.

It was only then that the company, which up to that point seemed indifferent to the moderate payments to cover the previous, modest *astreintes*, finally became concerned. The company argued that the *astreinte* is nothing but damages and that its payment should therefore equal the damage actually suffered due to non-performance or delay in the performance of the order. And the company requested a provisional court order for an expert report to evaluate the damage.

On that note, the court of appeal clearly committed itself on the nature of the *astreinte* (Riom, 10 December 1956, D. 1956. 101; S. 1957. 112) which it considers to be a *measure of compulsion* completely unrelated to the concept of damages. And in the light of the company's stubbornness not to carry out a decision of the courts, the court of appeal complied with a request for payment of the *astreinte* in full, without making any reference to the damage.

The issue to be decided in the above case was extremely serious. The fate of the entire institution of *astreintes* was dependent upon it. After all is said and done, if the *astreinte* were to be considered only as just damages for delay in fulfilling a legal obligation, the courts would, in matters relating to decisions, the object of which is an obligation to do or to refrain from doing something, more often than not, be completely unequipped to deal with a recalcitrant litigant. Only the possibility and the threat of financial penalties of an increasing amount which can rise to a high amount, is capable of making a litigant of bad faith rethink his position.

I. – The *astreinte*, – of which one must bear in mind the specific character and field of application, which is to be a technique for assuring execution of a judicial decision and only a judicial decision – , is an institution that was created – invented, so to speak – for that purpose, by the practice of the courts at the beginning of the 19th century.

Without going further back, we find an already fully formed *astreinte* in a remarkable judgment of the *chambre civile* from 29 January 1834 (S. 34 1. 129). This judgment is of capital importance. The judgment was about an order to give back a room of which a person had unduly taken possession. This person, says the judgment, "can be ordered,

---

[10]   Translation of French original.

in addition to the restitution of the room, to pay damages for every day of the delay, even though no harm could result from the delay in the return of the room".

The *astreinte*, used from the beginning of the 19th century, in a way, finds its legitimacy and precise definition in this judgment. Despite maintaining the name "damages", the judgment proclaims that this is actually completely different to real damages, since it is – it says – independent of the consideration of damage, independent of the *mere existence* of damage.

The nature of the *astreinte* as an "order given as a means of coercion" was confirmed a few years later by the *chambre des requêtes* (22 November 1841, S. 42. 1. 170). It was to be present in the case-law throughout the 19th century. In addition, the use of the term "damages", which the courts found hard not to employ, introduced a certain ambiguity in the idea of the *astreinte*, which is actually more apparent than real. This was already seen in the decision of 1834, on which the academic writing, however, is very clear.

This decision from 1834 is mirrored a century later by the leading case of the *chambre des requêtes* of 7 February 1922 *(Gaz. Trib.* 1922. 1. 214) that, reaffirming the nature of the *astreinte* as purely coercive, which, the decision says, "has as its sole object to put [the debtor] under a stringent obligation" to execute the decision pronounced against him, decided that the amount of the *astreinte* can accrue concurrently with damages for delay in fulfilling a legal obligation proper.

II. – This necessitates clarification of the distinction between the two categories of *astreinte*. They are: 1°*definitive astreintes* that orders – at the rate of every day of the delay in the execution of the decision, or at the rate of every breach of a decision ordered either for the accomplishment of an act or more frequently for an abstention – , payment of an amount of money already fixed as definitive by the judge and 2° *provisional astreintes* that entail at the end of the time period for which they are ordered, the revision of the amount of the *astreinte*, […][its final amount being fixed by the judge].

[…]

IV. – According to modern academic writing, the idea of the *astreinte* as a private punishment is generally recognised. Some authors recognise the *astreinte* with regret without necessarily denying the indisputable practical utility of an institution which they consider to be an irreplaceable judicial creation […] As for the majority of modern authors, they are totally in favour of the notion of the *astreinte* as a sanction, entirely independent from the notion of damages from which it is different because of its raison d'être and function.

[…]

V. – That is exactly what the discussion was all about. The theory behind the decision by the court in Riom – the same as is professed by the majority of the courts that rule on the facts, aware of the essential character of the institution that is the *astreinte* functioning as a sanction for a recalcitrant attitude, and not to be mixed up with damages – could not be condemned without bringing down the entire institution at the same time.

No serious legal objection to this concept can be cited. This judicial invention under pressure from practical demands has its legitimacy in more than a century of practice. In particular, the *astreinte* is not contradictory to the old rule *nemo praecise potest cogi ad factum*[11] (used in Art. 1142 of the Civil Code) because this rule only ever banned the use of coercion on a person which is contrary to personal freedom; the use of coercive measures on property has always been admissible without restrictions.

[...] In the decision reported above – which is obviously a leading authority – the civil chamber, in rejecting the application for review of the decision of the court in Riom, shows itself to be faithful to the traditional and only reasonable view of the *astreinte* in no uncertain terms. It does not consider the *astreinte* to be a method of compensation but one of compulsion and execution. Neither is it according to the harm caused or the harm that could be caused to the beneficiary of the order by the late execution by the other party that the amount of the *astreinte* should be fixed [...] Rather it should be fixed in relation to the power of resistance of the person under the order, which, as indicated in the decision, is assessed notably – however this is just one point of view – with reference to the extent of their financial resources (see Josserand, *op. cit.*, t. 2, n° 597-3; H. et L. Mazeaud, *op. cit.*, 4e éd., t. 3, n° 2499), and in a more general way by considering how culpable his refusal – always reprehensible in itself – to obey a court order was.

G. Holleaux.

4. Loi n° 91-650 du 9 juillet 1991 portant réforme des procédures civiles d'exécution (*Law n° 91–650 of 9 July 1991 reforming the civil procedures for execution of judgments*), consolidated version of 22 April 2006

Art. 1er
Tout créancier peut, dans les conditions prévues par la loi, contraindre son débiteur défaillant à exécuter ses obligations à son égard.

Art. 1
Any obligee may, under the conditions laid down by legislation, compel his defaulting obligor to perform his obligations.

L'astreinte[12]

Art. 33
(1) Tout juge peut, même d'office, ordonner une astreinte pour assurer l'exécution de sa décision.
(2) Le juge de l'exécution peut assortir d'une astreinte une décision rendue par un autre juge si les circonstances en font apparaître la nécessité.

Art. 33
(1) Any judge can, even without consultation, order an astreinte to ensure the execution of his decision.

---

[11] "No one can be compelled to do something."
[12] Translation by EG.

(2)   *The judge responsible for the execution of the judgment can order an* astreinte *for a decision given by a different judge if it appears necessary in the circumstances.*

Art. 34

(1)   L'astreinte est indépendante des dommages-intérêts.

(2)   L'astreinte est provisoire ou définitive. L'astreinte doit être considérée comme provisoire, à moins que le juge n'ait précisé son caractère définitif.

(3)   Une astreinte définitive ne peut être ordonnée qu'après le prononcé d'une astreinte provisoire et pour une durée que le juge détermine. Si l'une de ces conditions n'a pas été respectée, l'astreinte est liquidée comme une astreinte provisoire.

Art. 34

(1)   *An* astreinte *is independent of damages.*

(2)   *An* astreinte *is either provisional or definitive. An* astreinte *is to be considered as provisional unless the judge specifies it is definitive in nature.*

(3)   *A definitive* astreinte *can only be ordered after the pronouncement of a provisional* astreinte *and only for a period of time determined by a judge. If one of these conditions has not been respected the* astreinte *is to be considered as provisional.*

Art. 36

(1)   Le montant de l'astreinte provisoire est liquidé en tenant compte du comportement de celui à qui l'injonction a été adressée et des difficultés qu'il a rencontrées pour l'exécuter.

(2)   Le taux de l'astreinte définitive ne peut jamais être modifié lors de sa liquidation.

(3)   L'astreinte provisoire ou définitive est supprimée en tout ou partie s'il est établi que l'inexécution ou le retard dans l'exécution de l'injonction du juge provient, en tout ou partie, d'une cause étrangère.

Art. 36

(1)   *The amount of a provisional* astreinte *is set taking into account the behaviour of the person to whom the court order is addressed and the difficulties he encountered executing the court order.*

(2)   *The rate of a definitive* astreinte *cannot be modified during its payment.*

(3)   *A provisional or definitive* astreinte *is cancelled, in whole or in part, if it is established that the inexecution or the delay in the execution of the court order results from an unrelated cause.*

Art. 56

(1)   L'huissier de justice chargé de l'exécution fait appréhender les meubles que le débiteur est tenu de livrer ou de restituer au créancier en vertu d'un titre exécutoire, sauf si le débiteur s'offre à en effectuer le transport à ses frais.

(2)   Lorsque le meuble se trouve entre les mains d'un tiers et dans les locaux d'habitation de ce dernier, il ne peut être appréhendé que sur autorisation du juge de l'exécution.

Art. 56

(1)   *The bailiff responsible for the execution of the judgment will seize the property that the debtor is bound to deliver or give back to the creditor except if the debtor offers to undertake transportation at his own expense.*

(2)   *When the property is in the possession of a third party and in the latter's home, it can only be seized with the authorisation of the judge responsible for execution of the judgment.*

5. KONRAD ZWEIGERT AND HEIN KÖTZ, *An Introduction to Comparative Law*, 3rd edn (transl. TONY WEIR), pp. 475–79

III.

[...] [T]he French courts have, since the beginning of the nineteenth century, developed a special coercive technique called the 'astreinte' (for full details see REMIEN, Rechtsverwirklichung durch Zwangsgeld , p. 33 ff.). On issuing a judgment requiring a debtor to perform *in natura* a court may order that for every day he remains in default the debtor must pay a specified sum of money to the plaintiff as 'astreinte'. [...]

It must not be supposed that an astreinte is available only where the statutory methods of execution are inapplicable or impractical. An astreinte may be issued to promote the delivery of a specified motor vehicle [...] or the conveyance and delivery of landed property [...], although in such cases direct execution through the huissier is perfectly possible. [...]

Nor do the courts hesitate to impose astreintes in cases where the creditor might have used the method of 'surrogate performance' offered by art. 1144 Code civil, as where a neighbour was ordered to remove a boundary wall [...] or a vendor to dismantle faulty machinery he had delivered [...]

[...]

The *astreinte* really comes into its own when there is no statutory means for executing judgments, for example, where the debtor has been ordered to do something other than pay money or deliver things, such as issue a certificate of employment (Soc. 29 June 1966, Bull. civ. 1966, IV. 534), or move his business (Com. 6 Oct. 1966, Bull. civ. 1966, III. 424). The *astreinte* is also used where the plaintiff wants to prevent the defendant from doing something, the difference here being that the amount of the *astreinte* depends on how often the debtor contravened his duty to desist rather than on how long he remained in breach. Thus, when a soft drink manufacturer was enjoined from using bottles so like those of the plaintiff as to constitute unfair competition, the *astreinte* was in the form that the defendant should pay 10 francs 'par infraction constaté' (Com. 31 March 1965, Bull. civ. 1965 III. 219).

Superficially it might seem that the *astreinte* is like the money penalties which may be imposed *in terrorem* under §§ 888 and 890 of the German Code of Civil Procedure in judgments which order the debtor to cease and desist or to co-operate in doing the requisite act. There is an important distinction, however, since the *astreintes* go into the pocket of the creditor while the monetary penalties go to the state treasury.

This significant difference becomes comprehensible if we remember that in France it was the courts which invented the *astreinte* and had to do it extra legem, 'en marge des textes', for they realized that in view of the inadequacy of the statutory methods of execution the only way of ensuring that judgments were satisfied was by threatening defaulting debtors with monetary penalties. Even if the idea that such payments might be made to the state had occurred to the French courts, they could hardly have acted on it in the absence of any statutory basis.

[...]

Although the *astreinte* is an entrenched institution of French court practice, it has constantly been criticized in legal writings, and these criticisms gain in force as its coercive and penal character is increasingly admitted by the courts. Indeed, it is not at all clear why the creditor, in addition to receiving compensation for the harm he has suffered, should also obtain the amount of the *astreinte* which is designed to overcome the debtor's reluctance to honour the judgment, especially if the *astreinte* is fixed in relation to the culpability of the debtor's behaviour and to the extent of his financial resources. [...] The actual law provides that the *astreinte* goes in full to the creditor, and also makes clear that the purpose of the *astreinte* is to put pressure on the debtor rather than to compensate the creditor (art. 33 ff. Law no. 91-650 of 9 July 1991, from Law of 5 July 1972).

> [...] The astreinte has been adopted by several other European countries, such as Greece (art. 946 f. Code of Civil Procedure), Poland (art. 1050 f. Code of Civil Procedure), and Portugal (art. 829-A Civil Code), the latter with the remarkable feature that the monetary penalty is to be split equally between the state and the creditor. The UNIDROIT Principles for International Commercial Contracts allow for the sanction of an *astreinte*, payable to the creditor, if not inconsistent with mandatory rules of the *lex fori* (art 7.2.4).

V.   England

1. PETER SHEARS AND GRAHAM STEPHENSON, *James' Introduction to English Law*, 13th edn, pp. 23–28

Chapter 2

The administration of the law

[...]

1   The background

A   THE COMMON LAW

Our 'common law' was originally derived from the judicial precedents of the old courts of common law and it now consists of the whole body of judicial precedents. The old common law courts consisted of the Court of Exchequer, the Court of Common Pleas (or 'Common Bench') – both dating from the twelfth century – and the Court of King's (or as appropriate Queen's) Bench were royal courts set up by the Crown and they superseded a network of local courts which had existed since Anglo-Saxon times. The law which these latter courts administered was local customary law which varied in content in different parts of the country.

Naturally, when the Royal Courts, which were centralized and assumed jurisdiction over all of the country, came into being they evolved and applied a uniform system of law, common throughout the land: hence this law came to be called '*common*' in contradistinction to the older local laws.

The term 'common law' is, however, now used in several different senses as marking special contrasts. For instance, we say that England, the United States (with the exception of Louisiana) and most of the Commonwealth countries are 'common law' countries when we wish to contrast the Anglo-American systems as a whole with those of countries like France whose law ultimately derives from the Roman law: and we call these '*civil* law' countries. The expression 'common law' can also be used to denote our own 'case' law as a whole contrasted with our statute law. And within our own system 'common law', as will appear, is also contrasted with 'equity'.

Having thus explained the primary meaning of 'common law', as that system of principles which was built up by the common law courts we must now consider the basis upon which those principles were evolved. This requires a brief description of the 'Forms of Action' or the 'Writ System' as they, or it, were called.

In these days a civil action starts with the serving of a *writ of summons*: this is a formal document and the purpose of serving it is to give notice to the *defendant* (person sued) upon whom it is served that the *plaintiff* (complainant) intends to bring proceedings against him, and to warn him to defend the action. The formulation of the grounds of the plaintiff's case comes substantially, through the pleadings, at a later stage.

Under the old law the system was different. The standard machinery for starting an action at common law in any of the three common law courts was the *original writ* ('original' because it originated, or started, the action). There was nothing mysterious about a '*writ*': writs were simply concise written orders emanating from high authority – in the case of a royal writ from the King, through the Chancery, the secretarial department of State. The use of writs for administrative purposes goes back to Anglo-Saxon times and was probably a borrowing from Frankish court practice. It echoes the 'mandates' of ancient Rome.

The 'original writs' with which we are here concerned were documents obtained (for a fee) from the administrative offices of the Chancery. There were many variations in form according to what sort of matter was involved, but the general purpose for which most of them were designed was to secure the presence of the defendant before the royal courts, usually through the agency of the sheriff (as the principal royal official) of the county in which the dispute arose. Further, and this is a vital point, each writ contained a brief statement of the plaintiff's ground of claim. If the position had invariably been for the chancery clerks or for the judge at the trial to decide whether these facts (if proved) disclosed a cause of action against the defendant the content of the writs would have been of no *general* importance. We shall see that writs could be of such a nature and that the fact was fundamental in the development of the law, but the first thing to stress is that – as is natural in any administrative system – writs rapidly became stylised. Claims concerning certain types of misconduct came to be recognized and each type of misconduct came to have its own appropriate writ.

Bringing an action at common law thus came generally to consist in selecting the writ appropriate (as he hoped to prove in court) to the facts of a plaintiff's case. For instance, there was the ancient writ of Right by which the 'demandant' (plaintiff) claimed from the 'tenant' (defendant) that the latter 'unjustly' and without a 'claim of right' deprived him of his land. There was the ancient writ of Debt, alleging that the defendant owed (*debet*) him so much money, and the writ of Detinue stating that the defendant detained (*detinet*) from the plaintiff something which was his. Into one or other of the accepted forms, such as these, the facts of the case had to fit; if they did not fit, however just the claim, the plaintiff must fail.

But though writs thus became stereotyped there had to be a means of creating new ones, otherwise the law could not have developed. The agencies of evolution varied. Sometimes Parliament would recognise a new form of action (writ), sometimes the creation would be administrative – as by the Chancery clerks – sometimes, as in the case of the all-important writ of Trespass, we think we can trace it to an innovator – in that case said to be William Raleigh, a thirteenth-century judge, and the teacher of Bracton. However, by the fourteenth century, after much hesitation and political obstruction, a practice emerged by which the *courts* upon the *facts stated*, and upon proof by the plaintiff of actual loss inflicted on him by the defendant, allowed actions '*on the case*' to succeed: in other words the courts were authorized in such circumstances to grant *new* writs. It must not be thought that this task was lightly undertaken, for the mediaeval judges never forgot that in Francis Bacon's words, they were 'lions' *under* 'the throne' and that innovation might displease the Crown. Indeed, cautiously and lawyer-like, the development of new writs through actions on the case was, at first, at least, slow and a matter of development by strict *analogy* from pre-existing writs. Yet, in this way our common law grew. The Register of Writs expanded in the course of time; and at any given time the Register, recording the sum total of available writs, *contained* the *common law.* Within the ambit of the writs lay people's rights: no writ, no right – unless the court *would* grant a new writ.

Thus the stream of the evolution of the common law can be traced in the proliferation of the Forms of Action (writs). This evolution is a long one, extending over more than seven hundred years […]

The modern procedure based upon the Judicature Acts now prevails and the ancient system has gone. Legal innovation (especially legislative) during the past hundred years has been prolific, so that we have cut away from the roots created by the writs; yet the framework of our civil actions is still based upon them. And it is unwise to forget Maitland's warning that 'the Forms of Action we have buried, but they rule us from their graves'. The common law, as opposed to statute law with its fits and starts, is still an evolutionary creation from its ancient fountain-heads.

It may, perhaps, be added that the principal defect of the writ system was its formalism – a besetting sin of early law paralleled by the *legis actiones* of ancient Rome. While the Forms of Action ruled it was not only true that the plaintiff had normally to find a writ to suit his case but also that if he chose the *wrong* writ his claim must fail. There was no changing of horses in mid-stream (no 'amendment' as we now know it): one rode one's writ to judgment, and if it then turned out to be the wrong writ one could only go back and try another 'horse' – assuming that one had the time, the money and the patience. Finally, it is worth remarking that the evolution of the writ system provides a stock example of the fact that law evolves by granting remedies for grievances rather than by formulating abstract 'rights'. The 'right' acquired is the result of the remedy given. […]

B EQUITY

Before the Royal Courts of Justice were housed at their present place (in the Strand) they used to sit in Westminster Hall. The three common law courts were on one side of the Hall and the Court of Chancery was on the other. In this court *equity* was administered, and litigants who could not obtain justice in the common law courts would cross the Hall to seek the Chancellor's aid.

The office of Chancellor (more recently 'Lord Chancellor') has an ancient history. Originally the *'cancellarius'* (from Latin *'cancellus'*: a bar or lattice) was an usher who served at the bar of a Roman court. In its more illustrious form the office goes back to the court of Charlemagne and had been translated to England by the time of Edward the Confessor. In this form the Chancellor became the King's right-hand man ('Secretary of State for all Departments', as the historian, Bishop Stubbs, put it) and the most powerful official in the realm. He headed the 'Chancery', the royal secretariat, and he was responsible for the use and custody of the Great Seal of the Realm. He was, moreover, closely associated with the administration of justice, for, as has been remarked, the original writs were issued from the Chancery. Further, he was an important member of the *King's Council* whose duty it became to consider and adjudicate upon petitions addressed to the Council by subjects who sought justice from it as the body most close to the king himself. Petitions might be presented for various reasons. In particular, they were often presented by people who had, in one way or another, failed to obtain justice in the common law courts. This failure was usually due to one of three causes. First, the common law was in some ways *defective*: for example, the early common law remedies for breaches of contract were grossly inadequate. And secondly, the only *remedy* which the common law courts would usually supply was the award of damages, and damages are by no means always a satisfactory form of relief. Third, although the law was adequate to meet the case, *justice might not always be obtainable* in the common law courts because of the greatness of one of the parties, who might, in mediaeval times, often be in a position to over-awe the court itself. The Chancellor could remedy these defects; he was one of the chief royal officials, and being closely associated with the King, he was bound by neither the rules nor the procedure of the common law courts; nor was he likely to be over-awed by any man.

In hearing these petitions (or 'bills' as they came later to be called when the Chancery had become a court) the Chancellors slowly began to evolve a set of rules which remedied the defects in the common law, and to grant new remedies different from, and more effective than, the common law remedies. Thus they redressed breaches of contract, for they regarded them as morally reprehensible breaches of faith; and it must be remembered that the early Chancellors were ecclesiastics. They also decreed *specific performance* and granted *injunctions*. Moreover, in the course of time, they made use of a special writ of *subpoena*, by which they could compel the attendance of parties or witnesses under threat of fine or imprisonment, should they fail to attend.

The Chancellors, therefore, came to administer justice, but at first they had no independent court; and usually acted in consultation with the Council and even with the judges themselves. By the close of the fifteenth century the Chancellor was acting in a judicial capacity upon his own initiative; so that the history of the *Court of Chancery*, as opposed to the more ancient Chancery (*ie* secretariat of State) itself, really begins then. This court continued to exist until the Judicature Acts abolished it, retaining the memory of its name in the 'Chancery' Division of the High Court of Justice.

The new rules which were thus administered in the Court of Chancery came to be known as the rules of '*Equity*' (derived from the Latin *aequitas=levelling*). [Three] points need be noted.

First, it was only gradually that equity developed into a systematic body of rules; indeed, it was not fully developed until systematised under the chancellorship of Lord Eldon (Lord Chancellor 1801–1806; 1807–1827). The early Chancellors administered it according to discretion (Cardinal Wolsey's administration seems to have been conspicuously fair); so much so that John Selden (1548–1554: lawyer, populist and antiquarian) once remarked that early equity varied 'according to the length of the Chancellor's foot'. From the chancellorship of Sir Thomas More (1529–1532), however, it became usual to appoint *legally* trained Chancellors and this, by the nineteenth century, had led the Court of Chancery to rely upon precedent almost as much as the common law. But even today the administration of equity rests upon discretion; and specific performance of a contract, for example, will not be decreed in a case in which it would be unfair to do so.

In the second place, and conversely, before Sir Thomas More's chancellorship, the Chancellors were usually not only administrative officials but also ecclesiastics and chief of the royal chaplains: it followed that in exercising their discretion, and laying the foundation of the rules of equity, they borrowed from the canon (church) and civil (Roman) law from which the former was to a large extent derived.

In the third place, by the very nature of its origin, equity *assumes the law*: it did not come to defeat the common law but to supplement it and to '*fulfil*' it. It is not a rival, but an ancillary system of rules: as Maitland put it, it is a 'gloss or appendix' to the law. Moreover, as another maxim of equity has it, 'Equity *follows* the law', and yet another, that it 'acts *in personam*', upon the conscience (not surprisingly in view of its ecclesiastical origin) of a defendant. These considerations lead to the result that a person who has an *equitable right* to property has something of less validity than one who acquires a *legal right* to the same property ie a right protected by the common law. […]

2. W. T. MAJOR AND CHRISTINE TAYLOR, *Law of Contract,* 9th edn, pp. 288 ff

SPECIFIC PERFORMANCE

22. An equitable remedy

A decree of specific performance is issued by the court to the defendant, requiring him to carry out his undertaking exactly according to the terms of the contract. Specific performance is an equitable remedy and is available only where there is no adequate remedy at common law or under a statute. Generally, this means that specific performance is available only where the payment of a sum of money would not be an adequate remedy. Specific performance is, therefore, an appropriate remedy in cases of breach of a contract for the sale or lease of land, or of breach of contract for the sale of something which is not readily available on the market, e.g. a rare book.

23. A discretionary remedy

The granting or withholding of a decree of specific performance is in the discretion of the court. The discretion is, however, exercised on certain well-established principles:

(a) Specific performance will never be granted where damages or a liquidated demand is appropriate and adequate.

(b) The court will take into account the conduct of the plaintiff, for he who comes to equity must come with clean hands.

(c) The action must be brought with reasonable promptness, for delay defeats the equities. Undue delay sufficient to cause the court to withhold an equitable remedy is known as laches.

(d) Specific performance will not be awarded where it would cause undue hardship on the defendant.

(e) A promise given for no consideration is not specifically enforceable, even if made under seal.

(f) Specific performance will not be awarded for breach of a contract of personal services.

(g) Specific performance will not be awarded for breach of an obligation to perform a series of acts which would need the constant supervision of the court.

Thus building contracts are specifically enforceable only in certain special circumstances.

(h) Specific performance will not be awarded for breach of a contract wanting in mutuality, i.e. a contract which is not binding on both parties. Thus where a contract is voidable at the option of one party, he will not get specific performance against the other. This rule is of particular importance in connection with minors' voidable contracts.

[...]

3. GUENTER TREITEL, *An Outline of the Law of Contract,* 6th edn, pp. 408–16

4 SPECIFIC ENFORCEMENT IN EQUITY

A contract is specifically enforced when the court orders the defendant actually to perform his undertaking. Such an order may be positive or negative according to the nature of the undertaking. The court may (positively) order the defendant to do something, for example to convey a house, or to deliver a picture. Such an order is known as one of specific performance. Alternatively, the court may (negatively) order the defendant to forbear from doing something which he has promised not to do, for example it may restrain him from competing with the claimant. Such an order is known as an injunction.

Disobedience of an order of specific performance or of an injunction is contempt of court, and can be punished in the last resort by imprisonment of the defendant. [...]

a Specific performance
The common law did not specifically enforce obligations except those to pay money. With this exception, there was, and is, no *right* to specific performance: the remedy is equitable and (like most such remedies) discretionary. Its scope is limited in a number of ways, of which the following are the most important.

i Damages must be 'inadequate'
Specific performance will not be ordered where the claimant can be adequately protected by an award of damages. This will generally be the case where he has bought shares or generic goods which are available in the market. On the seller's default, the buyer can go into the market, get a substitute, and recover any extra cost by way of damages. Specific performance will, on the other hand, be ordered where no satisfactory substitute can be obtained: for example where the sale is of land or of a house (however ordinary), or of 'unique' goods such as an heirloom or a great work of art. Cases which formerly took a narrow view of this category are open to the question now that the courts tend to ask, not whether damages are 'adequate', but whether specific performance is the more appropriate remedy. The category of 'unique' goods has been expanded to include such 'commercially unique' things as ships or machinery for which no satisfactory substitute is available to the claimant; and specific relief has been ordered even of a contract to supply generic goods needed by the buyer for his business and not available from another source because of temporary shortage of supply. Damages may also be regarded as the less appropriate remedy for other reasons, such as the difficulty of assessing them. [...]

ii Discretion of the court

The court has a discretion to refuse specific performance even where this remedy would be a more appropriate one than damages. This discretion (which cannot be excluded by the terms of the contract) is, however, 'to be governed as far as possible by fixed rules and principles'. In particular, there are three grounds on which the remedy may be refused.

The first is undue hardship to the defendant. On this ground specific performance may be refused where the cost of performance to the defendant is wholly out of proportion to the benefit which performance will confer on the claimant; or where, as a result of severe financial misfortune and incapacitating illness, specific performance would cause exceptional personal distress to the defendant. But specific performance would not be refused merely because the vendor of a house was caught on a rising market and so had difficulty in buying another house with the proceeds of sale.

Secondly, specific performance may be refused because the contract itself was grossly unfair. For this purpose it is not enough for a seller to show simply that the price was too low; but the remedy will be refused if, in addition, the buyer took unfair advantage of his superior knowledge or if he exploited his superior bargaining strength by rushing the other party into the transaction. Thus where an antique dealer bought valuable china jars from a widow for a fifth of their real value it was said that he could not specifically enforce the contract. […]

Thirdly, specific performance may be refused if the court in some other way disapproves of the claimant's conduct: […]

iii Personal service

The court will not specifically enforce a contract of personal service. One reason for this rule was that to order the employee to work would unduly interfere with his personal liberty; and it is now provided by statute that no court shall compel an employee to do any work by ordering specific performance of a contract of employment or by restraining the breach of such a contract by injunction. [Trade Union and Labour Relations (Consolidation) Act 1992, s. 236.] […]

iv Other contracts

Specific performance will not be ordered of a promise without consideration, even though it is binding at law because it is made by deed. The reason for the rule is that equity will not aid a 'volunteer' (ie a person who has given no consideration). […]

v Difficulty of supervision

Specific performance is sometimes refused on the ground that the defendant has undertaken continuous duties, the performance of which the court cannot, or is unwilling to, supervise. On this ground, specific performance has been refused of a landlord's undertaking to have a porter 'constantly in attendance'; of a contract to deliver goods by instalments; and of a contract to do building work. […]

[…]

b Injunction

Where a contract contains a negative promise (such as a promise not to build, or not to compete), the breach of that promise may be restrained by injunction. Such an order is known as a prohibitory injunction where it directs the defendant not to break the promise in the future; and as a mandatory injunction where it directs the defendant to undo a breach committed in the past [...]

The principles governing injunctions to some extent resemble those governing specific performance. An injunction may, for example, be refused where its grant would be oppressive to the defendant and where damages could readily be assessed and would adequately compensate the claimant. An injunction will also be refused if its practical effect would be to compel the performance of a contract which is not specifically enforceable. For example an injunction will not be granted to restrain an employee from breaking his obligation to work or (normally) to restrain an employer from dismissing the employee. This would be so even if the contract contained a provision which was negative in form, such as a promise 'not to resign' or 'not to dismiss' for a given period.

A contract which is not specifically enforceable may, however, contain a narrower negative promise. In the leading case of *Lumley* v. *Wagner* the defendant agreed to sing at the claimant's theatre twice a week for three months, and she also promised not to use her talents at any other theatre during that period. She was restrained by injunction from breaking this negative promise. In such cases the effect of the injunction may be to put some pressure on the defendant to perform the positive obligation. But that is no objection to the granting of the injunction unless the pressure is so severe as to be, for practical purposes, irresistible. In one case a film actress was restrained from breaking a promise not to act for third parties: it was said that she could still earn her living by doing other work. But in a contrasting case a pop group had appointed the claimant as their manager for five years and promised not to make recordings for anyone else. An injunction to restrain the group from breaking this promise was refused as it would 'as a practical matter' force them to continue to employ the claimant. Where an employee promises not to work *in any capacity* except for the employer, an injunction to restrain the breach of that promise will normally be refused; for were it granted the only 'choice' left to the employee would be one between remaining idle and performing his positive obligation to work. The employer can, however, obtain an injunction if he undertakes that, while the injunction is in force, he will go on paying the employee and give him the opportunity of continuing to work for the employer where this is necessary to maintain the employee's skill and reputation.

[...]

4. Lord Chancellor's Court: *Lumley* v. *Wagner* (1852) De GM&G 604, [1843–60] All ER 368

LUMLEY *v.* WAGNER

[LORD CHANCELLOR'S COURT (Lord St. Leonards, L.C.), May 22, 26, 1852]
[Reported 1 De G.M. & G. 604; 21 L.J.Ch. 898; 19 L.T.O.S. 264;
16 Jur. 871; 42 E.R. 687]

Injunction – Contract for personal service – Undertaking not to serve any third person – Jurisdiction to grant injunction to restrain breach of undertaking – Effect to compel specific performance of contract.

The court will grant an injunction to restrain the breach of the negative part of a contract even though it cannot specifically enforce the performance of the positive part of the contract, e.g., where the positive part is an undertaking to render personal services, and the effect of the injunction is to compel the specific performance of the contract as a whole.

By a contract in writing W. bound herself to sing for three months at the plaintiff's theatre and "not to use her talents" at any other theatre.

Held: the court had jurisdiction to grant an injunction to restrain W. from appearing at a theatre other than that of the plaintiff.

Injunction – Damages – Plaintiff's right to recover damages – Jurisdiction to grant injunction.

Per LORD ST. LEONARDS, L.C. – It is no objection to the exercise of the jurisdiction by injunction that the plaintiff may have a legal remedy [i.e., a right to recover damages].

[…]

Bill filed on April 22, 1852, by the plaintiff, Benjamin Lumley, lessee of Her Majesty's Theatre, London, praying that the defendants, Johanna Wagner, Albert Wagner, her father, and Frederick Gye, lessee of Covent Garden Theatre, might be restrained from committing any breach of an agreement dated Nov. 9, 1851.

The agreement provided:

"The undersigned Mr. Benjamin Lumley, possessor of Her Majesty's Theatre at London, and of the Italian Opera at Paris, of the one part, and Mademoiselle Johanna Wagner, cantatrice of the court of His Majesty the King of Prussia, with the consent of her father, Mr. A. Wagner, residing at Berlin, of the other part, have concerted and concluded the following contract. – First, Mademoiselle Johanna Wagner binds herself to sing for three months at the theatre of Mr. Lumley, Her Majesty's, London, to date from April 1, 1852 (the time necessary for the journey comprised therein) and to give the parts following, 1st, Romeo, Montecchi; 2nd, Fides, Prophète; 3rd Valentine, Huguenots; 4th, Anna, Don Juan; 5th, Alice, Robert le Diable; 6th, an opera chosen by common accord. […]

(Signed) JOHANNA WAGNER,
ALBERT WAGNER."

The bill stated, that in November, 1851, Joseph Bacher met the plaintiff in Paris, when the plaintiff objected to the agreement as not containing a usual and necessary clause preventing the defendant Johanna Wagner from exercising her professional abilities in England without the consent of the plaintiff, whereupon Joseph Bacher, as the agent of the defendants Johanna Wagner and Albert Wagner, and being fully authorised by them for the purpose, added an article in writing which was as follows:

> "Mademoiselle Wagner engages herself not to use her talents at any other theatre, nor in any concert or re-union, public or private, without the written authorisation of Mr. Lumley.
>
> Dr. Joseph Bacher,
>
> For Mademoiselle Johanna Wagner,
>
> and authorised by her."

The bill then stated that the defendants J. and A. Wagner subsequently made another engagement with the defendant Gye, by which it was agreed that the defendant J. Wagner should, for a larger sum than that stipulated by the agreement with the plaintiff, sing at the Royal Italian Opera, Covent Garden, and abandon the agreement with the plaintiff. [...]

The bill prayed that the defendants Johanna Wagner and Albert Wagner might be restrained from violating or committing any breach of the last article of the agreement; that the defendant Johanna Wagner might be restrained from singing and performing or singing at the Royal Italian Opera, Covent Garden, or at any other theatre or place without the sanction or permission in writing of the plaintiff during the existence of the agreement with the plaintiff; [...] The plaintiff having obtained an injunction from Parker, V.C., on May 9, 1852, the defendants now moved by way of appeal before the Lord Chancellor to discharge his Honour's order.

Bethell, Malins, and *Martindale* for the defendants.
Bacon and *H. Clarke* for the plaintiff.

LORD ST. LEONARDS, L.C. – The question which I have to decide in the present case arises out of a very simple contract, the effect of which is, that the defendant Johanna Wagner should sing at Her Majesty's Theatre for a certain number of nights, and that she should not sing elsewhere (for that is the true construction) during that period. As I understand the points taken by the defendants' counsel in support of this appeal they in effect come to this, namely, that a court of equity ought not to grant an injunction except in cases connected with specific performance, or where the injunction, being to compel a party to forbear from committing an act (and not to perform an act), that injunction will complete the whole of the agreement remaining unexecuted.

[...]

The present is a mixed case, consisting [...] of an act to be done by Johanna Wagner alone, to which is superadded a negative stipulation on her part to abstain from the commission of any act which will break in upon her affirmative covenant – the one being ancillary to, and concurrent and operating together with the other. The agreement to sing for the plaintiff during three months at his theatre, and during that time not to sing for anybody else, is [...], in effect, one contract, and though beyond all doubt this court could not interfere to enforce the specific performance of the whole of this contract, yet in all sound construction and according to the true spirit of the agreement, the engagement to perform for three months at one theatre must necessarily exclude the right to perform at the same time at another theatre. [...] Wherever this court has not proper jurisdiction to enforce specific performance, it operates to bind men's consciences, as far as they can be bound, to a true and literal performance of their agreements, and it will not suffer them to depart from their contracts at their pleasure, leaving the party with whom they have contracted to the mere chance of any damages which a jury may give. [...]

It was objected that the operation of the injunction in the present case was mischievous, excluding the defendant Johanna Wagner from performing at any other theatre while this court had no power to compel her to perform at Her Majesty's Theatre. It is true that I have not the means of compelling her to sing, but she has no cause of complaint if I compel her to abstain from the commission of an act which she has bound herself not to do, and thus possibly cause her to fulfil her engagement. The jurisdiction which I now exercise is wholly within the power of the court, and, being of opinion that it is a proper case for interfering, I shall leave nothing unsatisfied by the judgment I pronounce. [...] The injunction may also, as I have said, tend to the fulfilment of her engagement, though, in continuing the injunction, I disclaim doing indirectly what I cannot do directly.

Referring again to the authorities, I am well aware that they have not been uniform, and that there undoubtedly has been a difference of decision on the question now revived before me, but, after the best consideration which I have been enabled to give to the subject, the conclusion at which I have arrived is, I conceive, supported by the greatest weight of authority. [...]

[...]

Motion refused.

5. Sale of Goods Act 1979

52. (1) In any action for breach of contract to deliver specific or ascertained goods the court may, if it thinks fit, on the plaintiff's application, by its judgment or decree direct that the contract shall be performed specifically, without giving the defendant the option of retaining the goods on payment of damages.

(2) The plaintiff's application may be made at any time before judgment or decree.

(3) The judgment or decree may be unconditional, or on such terms and conditions as to damages, payment of the price and otherwise as seem just to the court.

(4) The provisions of this section shall be deemed to be supplementary to, and not in derogation of, the right of specific implement in Scotland.

VI. United States of America

1. Uniform Commercial Code

§ 2-716. Buyer's Right to Specific Performance [...]
(1). Specific performance may be decreed where the goods are unique or in other proper circumstances.
[...]

2. American Law Institute, *Restatement of the Law Second, Contracts*

§ 357. Availability of Specific Performance and Injunction.
(1) Subject to the rules stated in §§ 359-69, specific performance of a contract duty will be granted in the discretion of the court against a party who has committed or is threatening to commit a breach of the duty.
[...]

§ 359. Effect of Adequacy of Damages.
(1) Specific performance or an injunction will not be ordered if damages would be adequate to protect the expectation interest of the injured party.
[...]

§ 360. Factors Affecting Adequacy of Damages
In determining whether the remedy in damages would be adequate, the following circumstances are significant:
  (a) the difficulty of proving damages with reasonable certainty,
  (b) the difficulty of procuring a suitable substitute performance by means of money awarded as damages, and
  (c) the likelihood that an award of damages could not be collected.

§ 366. Effect of Difficulty in Enforcement or Supervision
A promise will not be specifically enforced if the character and magnitude of the performance would impose on the court burdens in enforcement or supervision that are disproportionate to the advantages to be gained from enforcement and to the harm to be suffered from its denial.

§ 367. Contracts for Personal Service or Supervision
(1) A promise to render personal service will not be specifically enforced.
(2) A promise to render personal service exclusively for one employer will not be enforced by an injunction against serving another if its probable result will be to compel a performance involving personal relations the enforced continuance of which is undesirable or will be to leave the employee without other reasonable means of making a living.

VII.   Principles of Contract Law

1. UNIDROIT: Principles of International Commercial Contracts

Art. 7.2.2.   Performance of non-monetary obligation.
Where a party who owes an obligation other than one to pay money does not perform, the other party may require performance, unless
  (a)   performance is impossible in law or in fact;
  (b)   performance or, where relevant, enforcement is unreasonably burdensome or expensive;
  (c)   the party entitled to performance may reasonably obtain performance from another source;
  (d)   performance is of an exclusively personal character; or
  (e)   the party entitled to performance does not require performance within a reasonable time after it has, or ought to have, become aware of the non-performance.

OFFICIAL COMMENT

1.   Right to require performance of non-monetary obligations
In accordance with the general principle of the binding character of the contract (see Art. 1.3), each party should as a rule be entitled to require performance by the other party not only of monetary, but also of non-monetary obligations, assumed by that party. While this is not controversial in civil law countries, common law systems allow enforcement of non-monetary obligations only in special circumstances.

Following the basic approach of CISG (Art. 46) this article adopts the principle of specific performance, subject to certain qualifications.

The principle is particularly important with respect to contracts other than sales contracts. Unlike the obligation to deliver something, contractual obligations to do something or to abstain from doing something can often be performed only by the other contracting party itself. In such cases the only way of obtaining performance from a party who is unwilling to perform is by enforcement.

2.   Remedy not discretionary
While CISG provides that "a court is not bound to enter a judgement for specific performance unless the court would do so under its own law in respect of similar contracts of sale not governed by [the] Convention" (Art. 28), under the Principles specific performance is not a discretionary remedy, i.e. a court must order performance, unless one of the exceptions laid down in the present article applies.

3. Exceptions to the right to require performance

a. *Impossibility*

A performance which is impossible in law or in fact, cannot be required (sub-para. (a)). However, impossibility does not nullify a contract: other remedies may be available to the aggrieved party. See Arts. 3.3 and 7.1.7(4).

[...]

b. *Unreasonable burden*

In exceptional cases, particularly when there has been a drastic change of circumstances after the conclusion of a contract, performance, although still possible, may have become so onerous that it would run counter to the general principle of good faith and fair dealing (Art. 1.7) to require it.

> Illustration
>
> 1. An oil tanker has sunk in coastal waters in a heavy storm. Although it would be possible to lift the ship from the bottom of the sea, the shipper may not require performance of the contract of carriage if this would involve the ship-owner in expense vastly exceeding the value of the oil. See Art. 7.2.2(b).

The words "where relevant, enforcement" take account of the fact that in common law systems it is the courts and not the obligees who supervise the execution of orders for specific performance. As a consequence, in certain cases, especially those involving performances extended in time, courts in those countries refuse specific performance if supervision would impose undue burdens upon courts.

As to other possible consequences arising from drastic changes of circumstances amounting to a case of hardship, see Arts. 6.2.1 et seq.[13]

c. *Replacement transaction*

Many goods and services are of a standard kind, i.e. the same goods or services are offered by many suppliers. If a contract for such staple goods or standard services is not performed, most customers will not wish to waste time and effort extracting the contractual performance from the other party. Instead, they will go into the market, obtain substitute goods or services and claim damages for non-performance.

In view of this economic reality sub-para. (c) excludes specific performance whenever the party entitled to performance may reasonably obtain performance from another source. That party may terminate the contract and conclude a replacement transaction. See Art. 7.4.5.

The word "reasonably" indicates that the mere fact that the same performance can be obtained from another source is not in itself sufficient, since the aggrieved party could not in certain circumstances reasonably be expected to have recourse to an alternative supplier.

---

[13] See below, **Case 7.**

Illustration

2. A, situated in a developing country where foreign exchange is scarce, buys a machine of a standard type from B in Tokyo. In compliance with the contract, A pays the price of US $100.000 before delivery. B does not deliver. Although A could obtain the machine from another source in Japan, it would be unreasonable, in view of the scarcity and high price of foreign exchange in its home country, to require A to take this course. A is therefore entitled to require delivery of the machine from B.

d. *Performance of an exclusively personal character*

Where a performance has an exclusively personal character, enforcement would interfere with the personal freedom of the obligor. Moreover, enforcement of a performance often impairs its quality. The supervision of a very personal performance may also give rise to insuperable practical difficulties, as is shown by the experience of countries which have saddled their courts with this kind of responsibility. For all these reasons, sub-para. (d) excludes enforcement of performance of an exclusively personal character.

The precise scope of this exception depends essentially upon the meaning of the phrase "exclusively personal character". The modern tendency is to confine this concept to performances of a unique character. The exception does not apply to obligations undertaken by a company. Nor are ordinary activities of a lawyer, a surgeon or an engineer covered by the phrase for they can be performed by other persons with the same training and experience. A performance is of an exclusively personal character if it is not delegable and requires individual skills of an artistic or scientific nature or if it involves a confidential and personal relationship.

Illustrations

3. An undertaking by a firm of architects to design a row of 10 private homes can be specifically enforced as the firm can delegate the task to one of the partners or employ an outside architect to perform it.

4. By contrast, an undertaking by a world-famous architect to design a new city hall embodying the idea of a city of the 21st century cannot be enforced because it is highly unique and calls for the exercise of very special skills.

The performance of obligations to abstain from doing something does not fall under sub-para. (d).

e. *Request within reasonable time*

Performance of a contract often requires special preparation and efforts by the obligor. If the time for performance has passed but the obligee has failed to demand performance within a reasonable time, the obligor may be entitled to assume that the obligee will not insist upon performance. If the obligee were to be allowed to leave the obligor in a state of uncertainty as to whether performance will be required, the risk might arise of the obligee's speculating unfairly, to the detriment of the obligor, upon a favourable development of the market.

For these reasons sub-para. (e) excludes the right to performance if it is not required within a reasonable time after the obligee has become, or ought to have become, aware of the non-performance.

[...]

Art. 7.2.4.   Judicial penalty.
(1)   Where the court orders a party to perform, it may also direct that this party pay a penalty if it does not comply with the order.
(2)   The penalty shall be paid to the aggrieved party unless mandatory provisions of the law of the forum provide otherwise. Payment of the penalty to the aggrieved party does not exclude any claim for damages.

OFFICIAL COMMENT

1.   Judicially imposed penalty
Experience in some legal systems has shown that the threat of a judicially imposed penalty for disobedience is a most effective means of ensuring compliance with judgments ordering the performance of contractual obligations. Other systems, on the contrary, do not provide for such sanctions because they are considered to constitute an inadmissible encroachment upon personal freedom.

The present article takes a middle course by providing for monetary but not for other forms of penalties, applicable to all kinds of orders for performance including those for payment of money.

2.   Imposition of penalty at discretion of the court
The use of the word "may" in para. (1) of this article makes it clear that the imposition of a penalty is a matter of discretion for the court. Its exercise depends upon the kind of obligation to be performed. In the case of money judgments, a penalty should be imposed only in exceptional situations, especially where speedy payment is essential for the aggrieved party. The same is true for obligations to deliver goods. Obligations to pay money or to deliver goods can normally be easily enforced by ordinary means of execution. By contrast, in the case of obligations to do or to abstain from doing something, which moreover cannot easily be performed by a third person, enforcement by means of judicial penalties is often the most appropriate solution.

3.   Beneficiary
Legal systems differ as to the question of whether judicial penalties should be paid to the aggrieved party, to the State, or to both. Some systems regard payment to the aggrieved party as constituting an unjustified windfall benefit which is contrary to public policy.

While rejecting this latter view and indicating the aggrieved party as the beneficiary of the penalty, the first sentence of para. (2) of this article expressly mentions the possibility of mandatory provisions of the law of the forum not permitting such a solution and indicating other possible beneficiaries of judicial penalties.

4.   Judicial penalties distinguished from damages and from agreed payment for non-performance
The second sentence of para. (2) makes it clear that a judicial penalty paid to the aggrieved party does not affect its claim for damages. Payment of the penalty is regarded as compensating the aggrieved party for those disadvantages which cannot be taken into account under the ordinary rules for the recovery of damages. Moreover, since payment of damages will usually occur substantially later than payment of a judicial penalty, courts may to some degree be able, in measuring the damages, to take the payment of the penalty into account.

Judicial penalties are moreover to be distinguished from agreed payments for non-performance which are dealt with in Art. 7.4.13, although the latter fulfil a function similar to that of the former. If the court considers that the contractual stipulation of the payment of a sum in case of non-performance already provides a sufficient incentive for performance, it may refuse to impose a judicial penalty.

5. Form and procedure
A judicial penalty may be imposed in the form of a lump sum payment or of a payment by instalments. The procedure relating to the imposition of a judicial penalty is governed by the lex fori.

6. Penalties imposed by arbitrators
Since according to Art. 1.11 "court" includes an arbitral tribunal, the question arises of whether arbitrators might also be allowed to impose a penalty.

While a majority of legal systems seems to deny such a power to arbitrators, some modern legislation and recent court practice have recognised it. This solution, which is in keeping with the increasingly important role of arbitration as an alternative means of dispute resolution, especially in international commerce, is endorsed by the Principles. Since the execution of a penalty imposed by arbitrators can only be effected by, or with the assistance of, a court, appropriate supervision is available to prevent any possible abuse of the arbitrators' power.

7. Recognition and enforcement of decisions imposing penalties
Attention must be drawn to the problems of recognition and enforcement, in countries other than the forum State, of judicial decisions and of arbitral awards imposing penalties. Special rules on this matter are sometimes to be found in national law and to some extent in international treaties.

2. Commission on European Contract Law:
Principles of European Contract Law

Art. 9:102.   Non-monetary Obligations.
(1)   The aggrieved party is entitled to specific performance of an obligation other than one to pay money, including the remedying of a defective performance.
(2)   Specific performance cannot, however, be obtained where:
    (a)   performance would be unlawful or impossible; or
    (b)   performance would cause the debtor unreasonable effort or expense; or
    (c)   the performance consists in the provision of services or work of a personal character or depends upon a personal relationship, or
    (d)   the aggrieved party may reasonably obtain performance from another source.
(3)   The aggrieved party will lose the right to specific performance if it fails to seek it within a reasonable time after it has or ought to have become aware of the non-performance.

3. Study Group on a European Civil Code and Research Group on EC Private Law (Acquis Group): *Draft Common Frame of Reference*

III. – 3:302: Enforcement of non-monetary obligations

(1)   The creditor is entitled to enforce specific performance of an obligation other than one to pay money.

(2)   Specific performance includes the remedying free of charge of a performance which is not in conformity with the terms regulating the obligation.

(3)   Specific performance cannot, however, be enforced where:
(a)   performance would be unlawful or impossible;
(b)   performance would be unreasonably burdensome or expensive; or
(c)   performance would be of such a personal character that it would be unreasonable to enforce it.

(4)   The creditor loses the right to enforce specific performance if performance is not requested within a reasonable time after the creditor has become, or could reasonably be expected to have become, aware of the non-performance.

(5)   The creditor cannot recover damages for loss or a stipulated payment for non-performance to the extent that the creditor has increased the loss or the amount of the payment by insisting unreasonably on specific performance in circumstances where the creditor could have made a reasonable substitute transaction without significant effort or expense.

VIII.　China

1.　中华人民共和国合同法 *Contract Law of the People's Republic of China*, 1999), Arts 107, 110

第七章　违约责任

Chapter Seven: Liabilities for Breach of Contracts

第 107 条

当事人一方不履行合同义务或者履行合同义务不符合约定的，应当承担继续履行、采取补救措施或者赔偿损失等违约责任。

Art. 107　*Types of Liabilities for Breach*
If a party fails to perform its obligations under a contract, or rendered non-conforming performance, it shall bear the liabilities for breach of contract by specific performance, cure of non-conforming performance or payment of damages, etc.

第 110 条

当事人一方不履行非金钱债务或者履行非金钱债务不符合约定的，对方可以要求履行，但有下列情形之一的除外：

（一）法律上或者事实上不能履行；

（二）债务的标的不适于强制履行或者履行费用过高；

（三）债权人在合理期限内未要求履行。

Art. 110　*Non-monetary Specific Performance; Exceptions*
Where a party fails to perform, or rendered non-conforming performance of, a non-monetary obligation, the other party may require performance, except where:
- *(i)　performance is impossible in law or in fact;*
- *(ii)　the subject matter of the obligation does not lend itself to enforcement by specific performance or the cost of performance is excessive;*
- *(iii)　the obligee does not require performance within a reasonable time.*

2. BING LING, *Contract Law in China*

8.071　The provision is substantially based on the UNIDROIT-Principles, article 7.2.2. The imposition of the several limitations on the right to specific performance is a significant change in the law. [...]

[...]

8.073 Secondly, the obligation is unsuitable for enforced performance. The concept of "unsuitability" is not clearly defined and leaves room for controversy. It is generally accepted that specific performance cannot be required in regard to performance of an exclusively personal character, for otherwise the personal freedom and dignity of the defaulting party may be unduly compromised. Performance that is inseparable from the distinctive skills or status of the debtor (such as performance requiring the use of individual artistic or intellectual skills) falls within this category. But obligations of forbearance and obligations undertaken by a legal person or another organisation do not involve the personal liberty concerns and are suitable for specific performance. Performance that involves routine professional or personal service (such as the service of a lawyer […]) is delegable and is thus suitable for specific enforcement. [Footnotes with references to Chinese doctrine, to Chinese court decisions and to the UNIDROIT-Principles and their comments]

[…]

8.078 Commentators […] state another exception to the right of specific performance. Specific performance is barred if substitute performance from another source may be reasonably obtained. The final version of the Contract Law does not include this exception, and it seems difficult to try to read it into article 110. […] [I]t would seem unduly punitive to the defaulting party and might cause needless transaction cost if the defaulting party should be forced to perform the contract where substitute performance is reasonably available elsewhere. It would be desirable if this exception is adopted in future judicial interpretation of the Contract Law.

IX.   Summary

1. Overview of the solutions according to the different legal orders and the principles of contract law

Principle: Right to receive performance in case of non-performance of contractual obligations	Principle: Right to receive damages for non-performance of contractual obligations
– Civil Code of **Quebec** (Art. 1590) – **Dutch Law** (Art. 3:296 I BW) – **Finnish Law** (§ 23 Kauppalaki) – **Danish Law** (§ 21 Købeloven) – **Italian Law** (Art. 1453 Codice civile) – **Austrian Law** (§ 918, 919 ABGB) – **German Law** (§ 241 BGB, §§ 883-890 ZPO) – **French Law** (Arts 1184(2), 1610 Code Civil, Act reforming the civil procedures for execution of judgments, Case law (see Cour de cass. and case note) – **CISG** (rule: Art. 46, limitation: Art. 28) – **UNIDROIT Principles** (Art. 7.2.2) – **PECL** (Art. 9:102) – **DCFR** (III. – 3:302) **Coercive measures for execution of claims for performance** – Fine to be paid to the state (e.g. § 888(1) German Code of Civil Procedure) – *Astreinte*/Judicial penalty to be paid to the creditor (Art. 33 ff. of the French Law reforming the civil procedures for execution of judgments; Art. 7.2.4 UNIDROIT Principles)	– **England** (case law, e.g. *Lumley* v. *Wagner*; see explanations in TREITEL; MAJOR and TAYLOR), – **USA** (Restatement Contracts 2nd, § 359(1))

Exceptions:	Exception:
– No right to receive performance for obligations to perform services under an employment contract (e.g. § 888(3) German Code of Civil Procedure)	– Specific performance is (at the discretion of the court) available where damages are inadequate (England: see explanations in TREITEL; MAJOR and TAYLOR, USA: UCC, § 2-716(1);
– No right to receive performance in case of breach of contract where the service is of an exclusively personal character or where the party entitled to performance may reasonably obtain performance from another source (Art. 7.2.2(c), (d) UNIDROIT Principles; Art. 9:102 (2) (c), (d) Principles of European Contract Law)	Restatement Contracts 2nd, §§ 359 ff.)
	Counter-exception:
	– No right to receive performance of personal services under an employment contract or where the service is of an exclusively personal matter (*Lumley* v. *Wagner*; Restatement Contracts § 367(1))

2. Further reading

HUGH BEALE *et al.* (eds), *Cases, Materials and Text on Contract Law* (Ius Commune Casebooks for the Common Law of Europe), Oxford: Hart Publishing, 2002, Ch. 6.2, Enforcement *in natura*, 674–722.

ALLAN FARNSWORTH, *Contracts*, 3rd edn, New York: Aspen Publishers, 2004, 734–57 (USA).

JUAN CARLOS LANDROVE AND JAMES JOHN GREUTER, "The Civil *Astreinte* as an Incentive Measure in Litigation and International Arbitration Practice in Switzerland: Is There a Need for Incorporation?", in Christine Chappuis, Bénédict Foëx and Thomas Kadner Graziano (eds), *L'harmonisation internationale du droit*, Zurich: Schulthess, 2007, 523–552.

RONALD J. SCALISE JR, "Why No 'Efficient Breach' in the Civil Law?: A Comparative Assessment of the Doctrine of Efficient Breach of Contract", 55 (2007) *Am. J. Comp. L.* 721–66.

KONRAD ZWEIGERT AND HEIN KÖTZ, *An Introduction to Comparative Law*, 3rd edn, Oxford: Oxford University Press, 1998, 470–85.

Case 6: Damages and the role of fault in the event of delivery of goods not in conformity with the contract

"[I]t does not matter whether the failure to fulfil a contract by the seller is because he is indifferent or wilfully negligent or just unfortunate. [...] What matters is the fact of performance. Has he performed it or not?"[1]

"Whether fault should be adopted as an essential element of liability for breach of contract was one of the most controversial issues during the drafting of the Contract Law."[2]

Scenario

Company B is a wholesaler of wine-producing material. The company sells, *inter alia*, corks that it buys from its supplier, a cork-manufacturing company, A. Company A has always made and delivered corks of a high quality.

B sells 50,000 corks made by A to C, a wine-grower. Before delivering them to C, B does not check them. C uses the corks for the bottles of wine he produces. When going to sell the bottles, C discovers there is mould in them. The mould has formed due to a defect in the corks. C claims the value of the 50,000 bottles of ruined wine as compensation from B.

B invokes, as a defence, that Company A had always delivered products of high quality, that there was no reason to believe that the corks from this delivery were substandard, and that the damage is not due to B's fault. Suppose that:

(a) B could not have discovered this defect even if he had examined the corks before delivering them to C; or
(b) B could have discovered the defect if he had carefully examined the corks.

Will B have to pay damages to C?

---

1   Per Sellers J, in *Nicolene Ltd v. Simmonds* [1952] 2 Lloyd's Rep 419 (QB).
2   BING LING, *Contract Law in China*, Hong Kong: Sweet & Maxwell, 2002, s. 8.031.

Questions

(1) According to the information below, can C obtain damages from B under:
    (a) *Belgian,*
    (b) *French,*
    (c) *German,*
    (d) *Swiss,* and
    (e) *English* law?
    How would the situation be dealt with according to the information on *US* law?

(2) Systematically present the different approaches regarding fault in the event of delivery of goods not in conformity with the contract. Compare these differing approaches.

(3) How is Article 79 of the Vienna Convention interpreted by the different courts? Which interpretation should be kept? How would the above case be solved using this interpretation of Article 79?

(4) How would the above case scenario be solved under the Principles of European Contract Law, under the Draft Common Frame of Reference, and under the UNIDROIT Principles?

(5) In your opinion, which solution best meets the interests of the economy and of the parties involved? Give reasons for your answer.

Table of contents

I.   France and Belgium

1. Code civil français et Code civil belge
(*French and Belgian Civil Code*)[3]

Art. 1641
Le vendeur est tenu de la garantie à raison des défauts cachés de la chose vendue qui la rendent impropre à l'usage auquel on la destine, ou qui diminuent tellement cet usage, que l'acheteur ne l'aurait pas acquise, ou n'en aurait donné qu'un moindre prix, s'il les avait connus.

Art. 1641
A seller is bound by a guarantee against any hidden defect in a thing sold which renders it unfit for the intended purpose, or of less use for that purpose such that, had the buyer known of the defect, he would not have bought the thing or would only have bought it at a reduced price.

Art. 1642
Le vendeur n'est pas tenu des vices apparents et dont l'acheteur a pu se convaincre lui-même.

Art. 1642
A seller is not liable for defects which are apparent and which the buyer could have seen for himself.

Art. 1645
Si le vendeur connaissait les vices de la chose, il est tenu, outre la restitution du prix qu'il en a reçu, de tous les dommages et intérêts envers l'acheteur.

Art. 1645
If the seller knew of the defect in the thing, he is liable for damages to the buyer in addition to returning the price he received from the buyer.

Art. 1646
Si le vendeur ignorait les vices de la chose, il ne sera tenu qu'à la restitution du prix, et à rembourser à l'acquéreur les frais occasionnés par la vente.

Art. 1646
Where the seller did not know of the defects of the thing, he is only liable for restitution of the price and for reimbursing the buyer for the costs occasioned by the sale.

The French and Belgian courts have consistently treated a professional seller-manufacturer or a trader of a defective thing as a seller in bad faith according to Article 1645 of the Civil code.

---

[3]   Translation by EG, based on the translation provided in Hugh Beale *et al.*, *Cases, Materials and Text on Contract Law* (Ius Commune Casebooks for the Common Law of Europe), Oxford: Hart Publishing, 2002, p. 664.

The seller is consequently held liable to pay all damages to the buyer. With regard to the extent of this responsibility and the limits on it, the Belgian *Cour de cassation* and the French *Cour de cassation* have decided as shown in the extract below.

2. Cour de cassation belge/Hof van Cassatie, section française, 1ère ch., 19.9.1997, Pas. 1997, I, 362

"VENTE. – Vendeur. – Fabricant. – Vendeur spécialisé. – Chose vendue. – Défaut. – Vice caché. – Garantie. – Vice indécelable. – Conséquence. – Art. 1641, 1643, 1645 et 1646 C. civ. "

La demanderesse vend des bouteilles à la défenderesse, la Sté Distrinet, qui les mets en vente dans son magasin; lors d'un simple déplacement d'une bouteille par une cliente de la Sté Distrinet, la bouteille explose et blesse l'enfant de la cliente. La Cour d'appel de Liège condamne la demanderesse à payer des dommages-intéréts à la Sté Distrinet. Pourvoi en cassation par la demanderesse.

"LA COUR,

Vu l'arrêt attaqué, rendu le 7 juin 1995 par la cour d'appel de Liège;

Sur le deuxième moyen, pris de la violation des articles 1641, 1643, 1645 et 1646 du Code civil, en ce que l'arrêt confirme le jugement du 19 décembre 1990 retenant la responsabilité de la demanderesse en sa qualité de vendeur fabricant, ou à tout le moins, de vendeur spécialisé de choses pareilles à celle vendue [...]

Quant à la première branche:

Attendu qu'un vendeur, lorsqu'il est fabricant ou vendeur spécialisé, a l'obligation de fournir la chose sans vice et doit à cette fin prendre toutes les mesures nécessaires pour déceler tous les vices possibles; si l'existence d'un vice est démontrée, il est tenu à la réparation du dommage subi par l'acheteur, à moins d'établir le caractère indécelable du vice;

Attendu que si l'arrêt considère que la bouteille litigieuse livrée par la demanderesse à la défenderesse était bien affectée d'un vice, il relève que "toutes les mesures (étaient exécutées) lors de la fabrication des bouteilles et de leur mise en service, afin de satisfaire aux normes imposées et qu'il (était) procédé à des essais de résistance excédant la ligne de sécurité, notamment lors de la mise sous pression des bouteilles";

Qu'il considère également que "la bouteille litigieuse était affectée dès sa fabrication d'un vice intrinsèque, occulte, indécelable, lequel existait nécessairement lorsque (la demanderesse) en fit vente à (la défenderesse)";

Qu'en décidant, nonobstant ces considérations, de condamner la demanderesse, outre la restitution du prix, à tous les dommages et intérêts envers la défenderesse, l'arrêt viole les dispositions légales citées par la demanderesse;

Qu'en cette branche, le moyen est fondé;

[...]

PAR CES MOTIFS,
[…] Casse l'arrêt attaqué en tant qu'il statue sur l'action en garantie dirigée par la société anonyme Distrinet contre la demanderesse; […] Renvoie la cause […] devant la cour d'appel de Bruxelles."

Translation

"SALE. – Seller. – Manufacturer. – Specialist seller. – Thing sold. – Defect. – Hidden defect. – Guarantee. – Undetectable defect. – Consequence.
– Arts 1641, 1643, 1645 and 1646 Civil Code."

The applicant sells bottles to the respondent, the company Distrinet, which then sells them in its shop; while the bottle was simply being moved by one of Distrinet's customers, it exploded and injured the customer's child. The Court of Appeal in Liège ordered the applicant to pay damages to Distrinet. Appeal by the [applicant].

THE COURT,
Given the contested decision handed down on 7 June 1995 by the Court of Appeal in Liège;
On the second ground for appeal, based on the violation of Articles 1641, 1643 and 1646 of the Civil Code, insofar as the decision confirms the judgment of 19 December 1990 upholding the applicant's liability in his capacity as seller-manufacturer, or at the very least, as a specialised seller of things like the one sold […];
As for the first part:
Whereas a seller, who is also the manufacturer or who is a specialist seller, must provide the thing free from defects and must, to this end, take all necessary measures for the detection of all possible defects; if a defect is shown to exist, the seller must compensate for the damage suffered by the buyer, unless he establishes that the defect was undetectable;
Whereas even though the decision considers that the bottle in question delivered by the applicant to the respondent was indeed defective, it nevertheless emphasises that "all measures were taken during the manufacture of the bottles and their putting into circulation in order to satisfy the required standards and that resistance, and in particular pressurisation, tests more rigorous than the required minimum standard were undertaken";
That the decision also considers that "the bottle in question was marred with an intrinsic, hidden, undetectable defect from the moment it was made which necessarily existed when (the applicant) sold it to (the respondent)";
That by deciding, notwithstanding these considerations, to order the applicant, in addition to the restitution of the price, to pay damages to the respondent, the decision breached the legal provisions cited by the claimant;
On this ground, the appeal is well-founded;
[…]

FOR THESE REASONS,

[…] Quashes the contested decision as far as it relates to the Distrinet Corporation's action against the applicant for breach of a contractual warranty; […] Case sent […] before the Court of Appeal in Brussels.

3. Cour de cassation française, Chambre commerciale, 27.11.1973, Bulletin des arrêts Cour de cassation, Chambre commerciale n° 345 p. 308, pourvoi 71-12364

LA COUR; – *Sur le premier moyen:* – attendu que, selon les énonciations de l'arrêt attaqué (Paris, 24 avril 1971), la société Valcke Frères vendit en 1958 à Noël, armateur, propriétaire du chalutier "Cap Juby", un réducteur de vitesse destiné a équiper ce navire, mis en service en 1948; que, le 29 avril 1965, alors que le "Cap Juby" se trouvait en mer, le réducteur subit une avarie; qu'un premier examen permit de constater que la jante de la roue de sortie était fendue; que le Service technique des constructions et armes navales (Stcan) appelé par les parties à examiner l'organe mécanique endommagé, établit un rapport selon lequel la rupture de la jante trouvait son origine dans l'existence de craquelures longitudinales de la couche cémentée dans quatre fonds de denture; que, se fondant sur l'existence d'un vice caché, Noël et la société d'assurance mutuelle des bateaux de pêche de l'ouest, assureur du navire, assignèrent la société Valcke en paiement des frais d'assistance, de remorquage et de remise en état, ainsi que d'une indemnité pour immobilisation, Noël demandant en outre que le coût de la réparation du réducteur soit laissé à la charge de la société Valcke; attendu qu'il est fait grief à l'arrêt d'avoir fait droit à ces demandes […];

Mais attendu que […] la cour d'appel a souverainement estimé qu'antérieurement à la vente, le réducteur litigieux était atteint d'un vice caché en rendant impropre à l'usage auquel il était destiné; d'ou il suit que le moyen n'est pas fondé;

Sur le deuxième moyen […]: attendu que l'arrêt est encore critiqué pour avoir, infirmant partiellement la décision des premiers juges, mis à la charge de la société Valcke la réparation de l'entier préjudice résultant du vice, alors que […] si, dans certaines circonstances, le vendeur professionnel est tenu de connaître les vices cachés de la chose qu'il vend, tel n'est pas le cas lorsque, comme en l'espèce, le vice ne se révèle qu'après un long usage (32.000 heures) et ne peut être décelé qu'à la suite d'examens minutieux aboutissant pratiquement à la destruction de la pièce étudiée;

Mais attendu […] que la cour d'appel déclare justement qu'en sa qualité de vendeur professionnel, la société Valcke était tenue de connaître les vices affectant la chose vendue;

Par ces motifs: rejette le pourvoi formé contre l'arrêt rendu le 24 avril 1971 par la cour d'appel de Paris.

Translation

THE COURT; – *On the first ground for appeal:* – whereas, according to the contested decision (Paris, 24 April 1971), in 1958, the company Valcke Frères sold to Noël, a ship-owner and owner of the trawler "Cap Juby", a speed reducer meant for this ship, which went into service in 1948; that on 29 April 1965, whilst "Cap Juby" was at sea, the reducer had a problem; that a first examination was enough to show that the rim of the output gear had cracked; that the technical service of naval buildings and arms (Stcan) called by the parties to examine the damaged mechanical system issued a report according to which the breaking of the rim was due to the existence of longitudinal cracks in the case-hardened layer at the bottom land of four gear teeth; that, based on the existence of a hidden defect, Noël and the mutual insurance company for fishing boats in the West, the ship's insurance company, brought a claim for payment of the costs of assistance, towing and repair as well as compensation for immobilisation against the company Valcke, Noël also claiming that the cost of repairing the reducer be payable by the company Valcke; whereas a complaint was lodged against the decision which granted these claims [...];

However, whereas [...] the Court of Appeal considered, without the possibility to appeal, that before the sale, the reducer in question was affected by a hidden defect rendering it unfit for the use it was destined for; from which it follows that the ground for appeal is not justified.

On the second ground for appeal [...]: whereas the decision is still criticised for having made compensation for all harm resulting from the defect payable by company Valcke, partially confirming the decision of the judges at first instance, whereas [...] even though, in certain circumstances, a professional seller is required to know the hidden defects of the thing he sells, such is not the case when, as in this case, the defect does not become apparent until after a long period of use (32 000 hours) and can only be detected after meticulous examinations practically destroying the thing studied;

However, whereas [...] the Court of Appeal rightly declared that in its capacity of professional seller, the company Valcke was required to know of the defects affecting the thing sold;

For these reasons: rejects the appeal against the decision given on 24 April 1971 by the Court of Appeal in Paris.

II. Germany

1. Bürgerliches Gesetzbuch, BGB
(*German Civil Code*)

§ 433 Vertragstypische Pflichten beim Kaufvertrag.
(1) Durch den Kaufvertrag wird der Verkäufer einer Sache verpflichtet, dem Käufer die Sache zu übergeben und das Eigentum an der Sache zu verschaffen. [...]

§ 433 *Standard obligations in contracts of sale*
(1) By a contract of sale the seller of a thing is bound to hand over the thing to the buyer and to transfer to him ownership of the thing. [...]

§ 434 Sachmangel.
(1) Die Sache ist frei von Sachmängeln, wenn sie bei Gefahrübergang die vereinbarte Beschaffenheit hat. Soweit die Beschaffenheit nicht vereinbart ist, ist die Sache frei von Sachmängeln,
1. wenn sie sich für die nach dem Vertrag vorausgesetzte Verwendung eignet, sonst
2. wenn sie sich für die gewöhnliche Verwendung eignet und eine Beschaffenheit aufweist, die bei Sachen der gleichen Art üblich ist und die der Käufer nach der Art der Sache erwarten kann.

[...]

§ 434 *Defects as to quality*
(1) The thing is free from defects as to quality if, upon the passing of the risk, the thing is in the agreed quality. If the quality has not been agreed, the thing is free from defects as to quality,
1. *if it is fit for the use specified in the contract, and otherwise*
2. *if it is fit for the normal use and its quality is such as is usual in things of the same kind and can be expected by the buyer by virtue of its nature.*

[...]

§ 437 Rechte des Käufers bei Mängeln.
Ist die Sache mangelhaft, kann der Käufer, wenn die Voraussetzungen der folgenden Vorschriften vorliegen und soweit nichts anderes bestimmt ist,
1. nach § 439 Nacherfüllung verlangen,
2. nach den §§ 440, 323 und 326 Abs. 5 von dem Vertrag zurücktreten oder nach § 441 den Kaufpreis mindern und
3. nach den §§ 440, 280, 281, 283 und 311a Schadensersatz oder nach § 284 Ersatz vergeblicher Aufwendungen verlangen.

§ 437 *Buyer's rights in the event of defects*
If the thing is defective, then, if the requirements of the following provisions are satisfied and save as otherwise provided, the buyer may
1. *demand supplementary performance under § 439;*
2. *terminate the contract under §§ 440, 323, and 326(5), or reduce the purchase price under § 441; and*

3. *claim compensation under §§ 440, 280, 281, 283 and 311a, or reimbursement for wasted expenditure under § 284.*

§ 280 Schadensersatz wegen Pflichtverletzung

(1) Verletzt der Schuldner eine Pflicht aus dem Schuldverhältnis, so kann der Gläubiger Ersatz des hierdurch entstehenden Schadens verlangen. Dies gilt nicht, wenn der Schuldner die Pflichtverletzung nicht zu vertreten hat.

[...]

§ 280 *Compensation for breach of duty*

(1) If the obligor fails to comply with a duty arising under the obligation, the obligee may claim compensation for the loss resulting from this breach. This does not apply if the obligor is not liable for the failure.

[...]

§ 276 Verantwortlichkeit des Schuldners

(1) Der Schuldner hat Vorsatz und Fahrlässigkeit zu vertreten, wenn eine strengere oder mildere Haftung weder bestimmt noch aus dem sonstigen Inhalt des Schuldverhältnisses, insbesondere aus der Übernahme einer Garantie oder eines Beschaffungsrisikos zu entnehmen ist. [...]

(2) Fahrlässig handelt, wer die im Verkehr erforderliche Sorgfalt außer Acht lässt.

[...]

§ 276 *Liability of the obligor*

(1) The obligor is liable for deliberate and negligent acts or omissions, unless the existence of a stricter or more lenient degree of liability is specified or to be inferred from the other subject matter of the obligation, in particular the assumption of a guarantee or the acquisition risk. [...]

(2) A person acts negligently if he fails to observe the relevant accepted standards of care.

[...]

2. Bundesgerichtshof, BGH (*Federal Supreme Court of Germany*) 25.09.1968, NJW 1968, 2238

Zur Frage der Haftung des Zwischenhändlers für Folgeschäden bei Lieferung fehlerhaften Treibstoffs. BGH, Urt. v. 25.9.1968 – VIII ZR 108/66

Der Kläger bezog von der Beklagten [...] für die in seinem [...] [U]nternehmen verwendeten mit Diesel-Motoren ausgestatteten Kraftfahrzeuge 15.000 l Diesel-Kraftstoff. Die Beklagte hatte das Öl von ihrem Lieferanten unmittelbar im Streckengeschäft nach K. zum Kläger befördern lassen, ohne es vorher auf Lager zu nehmen.

Nachdem der Kläger den Kaufpreis von 6.452,50 DM bezahlt hatte, stellte er Schäden an den Motoren fest, die er auf schädliche Eigenschaften des Diesel-Öls der Beklagten zurückführte und die er mit einem Kostenaufwand von 18.253 DM beheben ließ [...]

Der Kläger nimmt die Beklagte auf Zahlung der aufgewendeten 18.253 DM und auf Erstattung weiterer Unkosten sowie des Verdienstausfalls in Anspruch. Insgesamt hat er einen Betrag von 26.678 DM nebst Zinsen eingeklagt. Beide Vorinstanzen haben die Klage abgewiesen. Die Revision des Klägers hatte keinen Erfolg.

Aus den Gründen: […]

II. 1. […] b) […] Die Beklagte betätigte sich als Zwischenhändlerin. Als solche war sie für den Regelfall, d.h. wenn nicht besondere Umstände vorlagen […] nicht zur Untersuchung der an die Verbraucher weiterveräußerten Ware verpflichtet. Dieser vom Berufungsgericht vertretene Standpunkt entspricht einer gefestigten Meinung in Rechtsprechung und Schrifttum […] Dieser Grundsatz gilt in erster Linie für den Kauf einer Speziessache […] Er ist aber auch auf Gattungskäufe anzuwenden, wenn nichts anderes sich aus den Umständen ergibt (SOERGEL-SIEBERT, BGB, 10. Aufl., § 433 Anm. 70; Brüggemann in HGB-RGRK, 2. Aufl., § 377 Anm. 101; Reichsgericht, RGZ 125, 78). Das Reichsgericht hat allerdings in der soeben angeführten Entscheidung eine solche Prüfungspflicht aus den Umständen geschlossen. Die Beklagte hatte dort den an das klagende Stahlwerk [Schrott geliefert], obwohl sie wissen musste, dass damals viel chromhaltiger Schrott im Handel war (die starke Chromhaltigkeit hatte an den Martinsöfen des Stahlwerks Schäden verursacht). Dieser Fall war also besonders gelagert. Er zeigt, dass im Regelfalle eine Untersuchungspflicht des Verkäufers von Gattungsware nicht anzunehmen ist.

Hat sich bereits eine entsprechende Verkehrsübung gebildet, so findet die Pflicht zur Untersuchung der Ware auf etwa schädliche Eigenschaften hierin ihre Grundlage. Ist mit der Lieferung eine Ratserteilung verbunden, so setzt, soweit erforderlich, die mit dieser besonderen Verpflichtung verbundene Sorgfaltspflicht eine vorherige Untersuchung der Ware voraus, auf die sich die Beratung erstreckt (Senatsurteil v. 25.3.1958 – VIII ZR 48/57 = NJW 58, 866 L = BB 58, 426 = MDR 58, 422). Die angeführte Entscheidung behandelt den Fall, dass der Verkäufer (von Leim) dem Abnehmer fahrlässig falsche Angaben über die Brauchbarkeit für einen gewissen Zweck gemacht hatte, so dass eine Haftung zwar nicht aus […] Vertragsverletzung [des Kaufvertrages], aber aus Verletzung eines Beratungsvertrags in Betracht kam. Der Senat ging dabei grundsätzlich davon aus, dass auch den Verkäufer einer Gattungssache hinsichtlich der Brauchbarkeit der Ware zu einem bestimmten Zweck selbst dann keine Untersuchungspflicht treffe, wenn dieser Zweck vorher zur Sprache gekommen ist. An dieser Ansicht ist festzuhalten. Da im vorliegenden Falle eine besondere Beratungsverpflichtung nicht übernommen war, wäre die Beklagte nur dann zur Untersuchung des Dieselkraftstoffs verpflichtet gewesen, wenn sich das aus einer Verkehrsübung oder aus den besonderen Umständen des Falles ergeben hätte.

Ein entsprechender Handelsbrauch wird vom Kläger nicht behauptet. Dieser Gesichtspunkt scheidet daher aus.

[…]

Etwas anderes wäre nur dann anzunehmen, wenn die Beklagte Veranlassung gehabt hätte, der Güte der Ware zu misstrauen. Nach den rechtlich einwandfreien Feststellungen des Berufungsgerichts ist das indes nicht der Fall

[…]

d) Rechtlich nicht zu beanstanden ist es weiterhin, wenn das Berufungsgericht die Beklagte auch nicht für ein etwaiges schuldhaftes Verhalten der Vorlieferantin haften lässt. [...]

Translation

On the question of the liability of intermediaries for the damaging effects subsequent to the delivery of defective fuel. BGH, Urt. v. 25.9.1968 – VIII ZR 108/66

The claimant had 15,000 litres of diesel delivered for his business by the defendant for use in motor vehicles equipped with diesel engines. The defendant had the oil transported from his supplier directly to the claimant at K. without taking it to his own storage facility first.

After the claimant had paid the purchase price of 6,452.50 DM, he noticed permanent damage to the engines that he attributed to the poor quality of the defendant's diesel and which cost 18,253 DM to have repaired. [...]

In his claim, the claimant requests payment of the 18,253 DM spent and reimbursement of other expenses and of lost earnings. Altogether he claims a sum of 26,678 DM with interest. The claim was dismissed in the lower courts. The claimant's appeal was unsuccessful.

On the reasons: [...]

II. 1. [...] b) [...] The defendant acted as an intermediary. As such, he was, as a rule, that is to say, providing there were no special circumstances, [...] not obliged to examine goods sold on to a consumer. This view taken by the Court of Appeal is in accordance with the established opinion in case law and academic writing. [...] This rule is above all applicable to the purchase of identified goods [...] It is however also applicable to the purchase of unidentified goods if nothing else is applicable in the circumstances (SOERGEL-SIEBERT, BGB, 10. Aufl., § 433 Anm. 70; Brüggemann in HGB-RGRK, 2. Aufl., § 377 Anm. 101; Reichsgericht, RGZ 125, 78). However, in the aforementioned decision, the *Reichsgericht*[4] found such a duty of examination to exist in the particular circumstances. In that case, the defendant had [delivered scrap metal] to the claimant steel works although he must have known that there was a lot of scrap metal containing chrome in circulation at the time (high levels of chrome had caused damage to the furnaces at the steel works). This case was therefore very particular in nature. It shows that, as a rule, there is no presumption that a seller of unidentified goods is under a duty of examination.

If it is already a market practice, the duty to examine the goods for harmful properties is based on this reason. If advice was given upon delivery, there is a presumed duty of diligence linked to particular obligations that there was, as far as possible, a preliminary examination of the merchandise which served as the basis for the advice (Senatsurteil v. 25.3.1958 – VIII ZR 48/57 = NJW 58, 866 L = BB 58, 426 = MDR 58, 422). The aforementioned decision dealt with a case in which the seller (of glue) had, through negligence, given the buyer false information on the suitability of the product for a given purpose in such a way so as that there was no liability for [...] [breach of the sales contract] but there was liability for breach of a consultation contract. The Supreme Court took as its fundamental starting point that a seller of unidentified goods is under no obligation

---

4   Supreme Court of the former German Empire

of examination with regard to the usefulness of the good for a specific purpose even if this purpose was brought up beforehand. This point of view is to be followed. As in the present case there was no particular consultation obligation, the defendant would only have been under an obligation to examine the diesel if that was the market practice or if the particular circumstances of the case required it.

The existence of such a commercial practice was not asserted by the claimant. This point of view was therefore excluded.

[…]

It would only be different where the claimant had reason to doubt the quality of the goods. However, according to the uncontestable appreciation of the facts by the Court of Appeal, that is not the case.

[…]

d)   There is nothing to object to if the Court of Appeal does not make the defendant legally responsible for the deliverer's possibly culpable conduct. […]

3. BGH 18.2.1981, NJW 1981, 1269

BGH, Urt. V. 18.2.1981 – VIII ZR 14/80 (Düsseldorf)

Zum Sachverhalt: Die Klägerin, die unter anderem Großanstriche ausführt, bestellte bei dem Beklagten, der einen Großhandel mit Tapeten, Bodenbelägen, Farben usw. betreibt, 20 Rollen Klebeband der Marke *M*. Dieses Klebeband […] war von einer Firma *D*. hergestellt und von einer Firma *A*. dem Beklagten geliefert worden. […] In der Gebrauchsanweisung befindet sich folgender Hinweis: „*M* lässt sich immer leicht entfernen, selbst wenn Sie am Montag abdecken, am Mittwoch streichen und am Freitag wieder entfernen." Die Kl. verwendete das Klebeband […] Als sie nach 7–9 Tagen das Klebeband abnehmen wollte, […] konnte [es] nur unter Schwierigkeiten entfernt werden. Mit der Behauptung, sie habe durch die Entfernung des Klebebandes Aufwendungen gehabt, macht die Kl. Ansprüche gegen den Bekl. geltend, die sie auf 13.000 DM bezifferte.

[…]

Aus den Gründen: […].
II. […] 3. Die Kl. hat auch keinen Schadensersatzanspruch […]
a) Nach gefestigter Meinung in Rechtsprechung und Schrifttum ist ein Zwischenhändler grundsätzlich nicht zur Untersuchung der die Verbraucher weiterveräußerten Ware verpflichtet. Das gilt nicht nur bei Speziessachen, sondern in der Regel auch bei Gattungskäufen (*BGH*, NJW 1968, 2238 […]). Hatte der Bekl. aber keine Untersuchungspflicht und hatte er, wie er unwidersprochen behauptet hat, zuvor keine Beanstandungen des Klebebandes *M* erhalten, so konnte er nicht wissen, dass das Klebeband mit dem Material, auf dem es von der Kl. verwendet wurde, nicht „kompatibel" war. Dann ist aber nicht einzusehen, inwiefern dem Bekl. eine schuldhafte […] Vertragsverletzung zur Last fallen sollte. […]

Translation

Federal Supreme Court of Germany,
BGH, Urt. v. 18.2.1981 – VIII ZR 14/80 (Düsseldorf)

On the facts: The claimant, who, amongst other things, paints large surfaces, ordered 20 rolls of brand M. adhesive tape from the defendant who is a wholesale trader of wallpaper, flooring, paint etc. This adhesive tape [...] was manufactured by company D. and was delivered to the defendant's company, company A. [...] In the instructions for use, there is the following tip: "M. can always be removed even if it is opened on Monday, painted on Wednesday and removed again on Friday". The claimant used the adhesive tape [...]. When she wanted to remove the adhesive tape after 7–9 days, [...] this could only be done with great difficulty. With her claim, she asserts against the defendant that the removal of the adhesive tape caused her damage of an estimated 13,000 DM.

[...]

On the reasons: [...]
II. [...] 3. The claimant has no claim for damages [...]
a)   According to established opinion in case law and academic writing, an intermediary is, in principle, not required to examine goods sold on to a consumer. That is the case not only for identified goods but, as a rule also for unidentified goods (*BGH*, NJW 1968, 2283 [...]). Since the defendant had no duty of examination and had received no complaints about the adhesive tape M., he could not know that the adhesive tape would not be "compatible" with the material that the claimant used. In these circumstances it is excluded that the defendant should be held responsible for a negligent breach of contract.
[...]

III. Switzerland

1. Schweizerisches Obligationenrecht
(*Swiss Code of Obligations*)

Art. 97. Ausbleiben der Erfüllung. Ersatzpflicht des Schuldners. Im Allgemeinen.
(1) Kann die Erfüllung der Verbindlichkeit überhaupt nicht oder nicht gehörig bewirkt werden, so hat der Schuldner für den daraus entstehenden Schaden Ersatz zu leisten, sofern er nicht beweist, dass ihm keinerlei Verschulden zur Last falle.
(2) [...]

Art. 97. Non-performance. Obligation to compensate by the obligor. In general.
(1) If the performance of an obligation can not at all or not duly be effected, the obligor shall compensate for the damage arising therefrom, unless he proves that no fault at all is attributable to him.
(2) [...]

Art. 197. Gewährleistung wegen Mängel der Kaufsache. Gegenstand der Gewährleistung. Im Allgemeinen.
(1) Der Verkäufer haftet dem Käufer sowohl für die zugesicherten Eigenschaften als auch dafür, dass die Sache nicht körperliche oder rechtliche Mängel habe, die ihren Wert oder ihre Tauglichkeit zu dem vorausgesetzten Gebrauche aufheben oder erheblich mindern.
(2) Er haftet auch dann, wenn er die Mängel nicht gekannt hat.

Art. 197. Warranty against defects in the object of the purchase. Object of Warranty. In general.
(1) The seller is liable to the buyer both for express warranties made and that the object of the purchase has no physical or legal defects which eliminate or substantially reduce its value or its fitness for the intended use.
(2) The seller is liable even if he did not know of the defects.

Art. 205. Inhalt der Klage des Käufers. Wandelung oder Minderung.
(1) Liegt ein Fall der Gewährleistung wegen Mängel der Sache vor, so hat der Käufer die Wahl, mit der Wandelungsklage den Kauf rückgängig zu machen oder mit der Minderungsklage Ersatz des Minderwertes der Sache zu fordern.
(2) Auch wenn die Wandelungsklage angestellt worden ist, steht es dem Richter frei, bloss Ersatz des Minderwertes zuzusprechen, sofern die Umstände es nicht rechtfertigen, den Kauf rückgängig zu machen.
(3) Erreicht der geforderte Minderwert den Betrag des Kaufpreises, so kann der Käufer nur die Wandelung verlangen.

Art. 205. Content of buyer's action. Action for rescission or reduction of purchase price.
(1) In the case of warranty against defects in the object of the purchase, the buyer may either elect to sue for rescission of the purchase contract, or to sue for a reduction of the purchase price, in order to be compensated for the reduction in value of the object of the purchase.

(2) Even if an action for rescission has been initiated, the judge is free to adjudge compensation for the reduction in value only provided that the circumstances do not justify a rescission of the purchase contract.

(3) If the reduction in value claimed equals the purchase price, then the buyer can only demand rescission.

Art. 208. Durchführung der Wandelung. Im Allgemeinen.

(1) Wird der Kauf rückgängig gemacht, so muss der Käufer die Sache nebst dem inzwischen bezogenen Nutzen dem Verkäufer zurückgeben.

(2) Der Verkäufer hat den gezahlten Verkaufspreis samt Zinsen zurückzuerstatten und überdies, entsprechend den Vorschriften über die vollständige Entwehrung, die Prozesskosten, die Verwendungen und den Schaden zu ersetzen, der dem Käufer durch die Lieferung fehlerhafter Ware unmittelbar verursacht worden ist.

(3) Der Verkäufer ist verpflichtet, den weitern Schaden zu ersetzen, sofern er nicht beweist, dass ihm keinerlei Verschulden zur Last falle.

Art. 208. Execution of rescission. In general.

(1) In the case of rescission of a purchase, the buyer must return to the seller the object of the purchase, together with any benefits collected in the meantime.

(2) The seller must repay the purchase price paid, including interest (Art. 73), and, in addition, in compliance with the rules relating to complete deprivation, compensate the buyer for costs of litigation, disbursements, as well as for such damage as has been directly caused to the buyer as a result of the delivery of the defective goods.

(3) The seller is obligated to compensate for further damage unless he proves that no fault at all is attributable to him.

2. Tribunal fédéral suisse/Schweizerisches Bundesgericht (*Swiss Federal Court*) 17.11.1953, *Cofrumi S.A. c. Transatlanta S.A.*, ATF 79 II 376

3. – […] Le débiteur répond de toute faute et doit réparer tout dommage qui est dans un rapport de causalité adéquate avec elle (art. 97 et suiv. CO). […]

Si l'on compare les dispositions [de l'art.] 208 CO aux règles générales des art. 97 et suiv. CO, elles apparaissent comme des prescriptions exceptionnelles. Alors qu'en général le débiteur qui n'exécute pas son obligation ou qui l'exécute mal n'est tenu du dommage qu'en cas de faute, [l'art.] 208 CO institue une responsabilité causale: le vendeur, qu'il ait commis une faute ou non, doit réparer le préjudice direct qu'il cause à l'acheteur. Dérogeant aux principes généraux du CO, ces règles doivent être interprétées restrictivement et il convient d'en limiter l'application au dommage qu'il est justifié de faire supporter par le vendeur même quand on ne peut lui reprocher aucune faute.

Or, le vendeur doit savoir ce qu'il vend. S'il livre une chose qui ne lui appartient pas ou qui est entachée de vices rédhibitoires, il est équitable qu'il réponde, même s'il n'a pas commis de faute, des dépenses que l'acheteur a faites et du dommage positif qu'il a subi à cause du contrat de vente. Mais l'acheteur ne saurait demander plus que d'être replacé dans la situation qu'il aurait si le contrat n'avait pas été conclu. Il serait exagéré de lui donner le droit de réclamer son gain manqué et de lui permettre ainsi de réaliser un bénéfice à la charge d'un vendeur qui, n'étaient les règles exceptionnelles [de l'art.] 208 CO, pourrait se dégager de toute responsabilité en établissant l'absence de faute de sa part. On doit donc admettre qu'en vertu [de l'art.] 208 al. 2 CO, l'acheteur peut seulement exiger la réparation de son dommage positif (*damnum emergens*). Il ne saurait en revanche réclamer des dommages-intérêts pour sa perte de gain qu'en se fondant sur [l'art.] 208 al. 3 CO, c'est-à-dire si le vendeur ne prouve pas n'avoir commis aucune faute […].

Translation

3. – […] The obligor is liable for all faults and must compensate for all damage that has an adequate causal link with such faults (Art. 97 CO ff.). […]

Compared with the general rules in Article 97 ff. of the Code of Obligations (CO), the provisions [of Article] 208 CO seem like exceptional measures. Whereas, in general, an obligor who does not fulfill his obligation or who fulfills it incompletely is only liable for damages where he is at fault, [Article] 208 CO introduces a causal liability: a seller, whether he is at fault or not, must compensate for the direct damage that he causes the buyer. Departing from the general principles of the CO, these rules must be interpreted restrictively and it is appropriate to limit their application to damage that can justifiably be attributed to the seller even when he is not at fault.

However, a seller ought to know what he is selling. If he delivers something that does not belong to him or that is marred by hidden faults, it is fair that he pays the buyer's costs and the positive damage caused by the sales contract even if he has not committed a fault. However, the buyer would not be able to ask for more than to be placed back in the situation that he would have been in if the contract had not been concluded. It would be excessive to give him the right to claim for his loss of profit and also to allow him to make a profit from a seller who, were it not for the exceptional rules [of Article] 208 CO, would be able to clear himself of any liability by establishing that he was not at fault. It must therefore be the case that, by virtue [of Article] 208(2) CO, a buyer can only claim compensation for his positive damage (*damnum emergens*). On the other hand, he would not be able to claim compensation for his loss of profit by relying on [Article] 208(3) CO, that is to say if the seller proves that he did not commit a fault […]

3. HERBERT SCHÖNLE, "Remarques sur la responsabilité causale du vendeur selon les art. 195 al. 1 et 208 al. 2 CO", *SJ* 1977, p. 465 ff.[5] (translation)

III. – A SELLER'S CAUSAL LIABILITY FOR DEFECTIVE GOODS

[…]

3. – Direct damage in Article 208(2) CO
Let us suppose that both the seller's contractual liability is not excluded or limited by the

---

[5]   Footnotes omitted.

general conditions of sale and that the rights set out in Art. 208(2) CO have not yet lapsed. At the end of the day, who is liable for the damage? This question raises the extremely controversial issue of how Art. 208(2) CO should be interpreted because, very often, in the distribution chain of mass-produced products, the last seller (the garage-owner who sells dangerous tyres, the person who sells defective cars) will be able to provide exonerative proof that he was not at fault within the meaning of Art. 97(1) and 208(3) CO. Three (controversial!) observations can be made when trying to interpret Art. 208(2) CO whilst taking into account the general system of contractual liability:

a) Art. 208(2) CO only requires damages to be paid for the buyer's "negative interest"[6];
b) Art. 208(2) CO only requires damages to be paid for the part of the "negative interest" that "has been directly caused [...] as a result of the delivery of the defective goods";
c) Art. 208(2) CO does not require damages to be paid for the loss of profit on the thing sold. [...]

a) The obligation to pay damages for a part of the "negative interest"

The judgment of the Federal Court in *Cofrumi S.A. contre Transatlanta S.A.* in 1953 confirms the dominant opinion that Art. 208(2) CO can only be intended to cover the buyer's "negative interest" to be put in the position that he would have been in if he had never made the sales contract. [...]

b) The obligation to pay damages for the part of the "negative interest" that comprises direct damage.

Direct damage as in Art. 208(2) CO is not the same as the "negative interest" in its entirety [...] The question of whether the damage "has been directly caused as a result of the delivery of the defective goods" (Art. 208(2) CO) is a question relating to the intensity of the causal relationship between the act that caused the damage (*i.e.* the defect of the thing sold) and the damage that occurred. Putting limits on this is difficult. [...] Direct damage as in Art. 208(2) CO is the part of the "negative interest" that is exclusively caused by the defect in the thing sold and normal use of it by the buyer as part of its agreed or customary use. Indirect damage as in Art. 208(3) CO is therefore the other part of the "negative interest" that finds itself at the end of the causal chain which contains, apart from the defect and normal use of the thing sold, other events causing damage, intermediate causes without which the damage would not have occurred or would not have reached the total amount of the "negative interest". [...] Example: by virtue of Art. 208(2) CO, a seller who is not at fault must pay damages for

---

[6] Damage can be viewed in one of the two following ways: by reference to the "positive interest" or "negative interest" of the innocent party. Evaluating the "positive interest" would mean considering the position a contracting party would be in had the contract been fulfilled in full and compensating him accordingly. Evaluating the "negative interest" would mean considering the position a contracting party would be in if he had never made the contract and calcaluting the compensation on that basis. Alternative terminology would be to use "expectation interest" and "reliance interest" repectively (*explanation added by the author*).

all harm caused to persons and property suffered by the buyer exclusively due to an accident resulting from the normal use of a defective car as "unmittelbar verursachter Mängelfolgeschaden" (direct and consequential damage flowing from the defect). If, however, the buyer is injured or his property is damaged subsequently because he slips when he is trying to walk into a hospital and breaks his leg and if this damage has an adequate causal link with the car accident, the seller will only compensate him if he was at fault under the conditions set out in Art. 208(3) CO because this is only indirect damage. [...]

IV.   England

1. Sale of Goods Act 1979

Section 14.   Implied terms about quality or fitness
(1)   [...]
(2)   Where the seller sells goods in the course of a business, there is an implied term that the goods supplied under the contract are of satisfactory quality.
(2A)   For the purposes of this Act, goods are of satisfactory quality if they meet the standard that a reasonable person would regard as satisfactory, taking account of any description of the goods, the price (if relevant) and all the other relevant circumstances.
(2B)   For the purposes of this Act, the quality of goods includes their state and condition and the following (among others) are in appropriate cases aspects of the quality of goods –
 (a)   fitness for all the purposes for which goods of the kind in question are commonly supplied,

[...]

Section 53.   Remedy for breach of warranty[7]
(1)   Where there is a breach of warranty by the seller [...] the buyer [...] may –
 (a)   [...]
 (b)   maintain an action against the seller for damages for the breach of warranty.
(2)   [...]

2. High Court, Queen's Bench Division: *Nicolene Ltd* v. *Simmonds* [1952] 2 Lloyd's Rep 419

NICOLENE LTD *v* SIMMONDS

Mr. Justice SELLERS: In this case, the plaintiffs claim against the defendant damages for breach of contract in respect of the non-delivery of 3,000 tons of Thomas quality reinforcing bars which they claim should have been delivered to them under a contract which was entered into between the parties.

The business of this matter is very simple. The defendant undertook personally to deliver to the plaintiffs, according to certain terms which had been agreed, these steel bars, and he undertook this obligation when he understood that he had contracted with some suppliers to fulfil his obligation. Some difficulty arose either because he had not entered into a firm contract or because the people with whom he thought he had

---

[7]   A warranty is a term in a contract, such as the implied term under s. 14 of the Sale of Goods Act 1979, the breach of which does not entitle the other party to treat the contract as terminated but does entitle him to compensation.

contracted failed in their obligation, and he then tried to get the material elsewhere. He went to the Continent and tried to get it from there, including some potential suppliers in Switzerland, but in the result he could not get the commodity to fulfil his obligation to the plaintiffs. On Nov. 28, 1951, he wrote in the ordinary course of business to the plaintiffs saying that he was very sorry to have to say that he had not been successful in obtaining a definite promise of delivery of reinforcing rods for Pakistan against sterling payment, and he added: "Should my efforts be fruitful, I will immediately let you know."

The time for the performance of the plaintiffs' contract to supply this material to Pakistan expired two days afterwards at the end of November, and, so far as the matter rested between business men, it would appear then that the seller had been unable to fulfil his bargain and was liable for the consequences.

But when the plaintiffs put the matter into the hands of their solicitors […] every ingenuity and subtlety has been employed, first of all to delay this case coming to trial, and then to find some defence to the claim which has been made; and for two days this Court has had to inquire into a variety of defences […]. In my view, each one of those ingenious efforts fails […]

[…] It was in [the defendant's] interest to fulfil this contract and it was said that he was unable to fulfil his contract by reason of the failure of other people. In the ordinary way, of course, it does not matter whether the failure to fulfil a contract by the seller is because he is indifferent or wilfully negligent or just unfortunate. It does not matter what the reason is. What matters is the fact of performance. Has he performed it or not? […]

3. GUENTER TREITEL, *An Outline of The Law of Contract,* 6th edn, pp. 312–14, 389–90

Chapter 16
Performance and breach

Every contract imposes obligations on at least one of the parties. […]

A party who fails to perform his obligations under the contract will generally be in breach, so that performance and breach can be regarded as the two sides of the same coin. […]

1 THE DUTY TO PERFORM

a Terms of the contract
It goes almost without saying that the extent of the duty to perform depends primarily on the terms of the contract. Performance must be exactly in accordance with these terms. […] [F]ailure to perform exactly in accordance with the contract is prima facie a breach.

[…]

b Standard of the duty
Once it has been determined *what* each contracting party must do, the next question is this: is a party liable for *any* failure in performance, or only for a failure which can, in some sense, be said to be due to his fault? Contractual liability is in many cases strict: that is, it

arises quite independent of fault. The point is most clearly illustrated by the case of a buyer who cannot pay the agreed price for goods simply because his bank has failed: there is no doubt that he is in breach of contract. Similarly, a seller of goods may be unable to deliver because he is let down by his suppliers or because he is unable to find shipping space to get the goods to their agreed destination: again he is in breach even though his inability to deliver was not due to any failure on his part to take reasonable steps to secure performance. The same principle can apply to defects of quality. In one case it was held that a seller of contaminated milk was in breach of contract even though he had taken all reasonable precautions to ensure that the milk was pure. Perhaps the most striking case of all was one in which a bottle of lemonade was supplied by manufacturers to a shopkeeper who sold it to a customer. The lemonade contained carbolic acid and it was held that the shopkeeper (though in no moral sense at "fault") was liable to customers for breach of contract. [...][8]

[...]

d   Methods of limiting damages

A breach of contract may be a starting point of a series of events which cause loss to the claimant; but the law does not hold the defendant liable for all such loss. Our concern in this section is with rules by which the law limits such liability.

[...]

i   *Remoteness*

The first of these rules is that damages will not be awarded for loss that is 'too remote'. This principle is illustrated by the leading case of *Hadley* v. *Baxendale*, where a shaft in a mill at Gloucester broke and had to be sent to the makers at Greenwich to serve as a pattern for a new one. The defendants undertook to carry the shaft to Greenwich, but in breach of contract delayed its delivery for a few days, during which the mill was kept idle. The millers claimed damages for the resulting loss of profits but the court regarded this loss as too remote a consequence of the breach. The underlying idea is that it is undesirable to make a defendant pay for such remote loss, for to hold him so liable might either deter him from entering into contracts at all, or lead him unduly to raise his charges to meet such liability. He will be liable only if one of two rules laid down in *Hadley* v. *Baxendale* is satisfied.

First, the loss must arise 'naturally, ie, according to the usual course of things, from such breach of contract itself'. This test was not satisfied in *Hadley* v. *Baxendale* because 'in the great multitude of cases' a carrier's delay in delivering a broken mill shaft would not keep the mill idle: the millers might have had, or been able to get, a spare shaft. In the contrasting *Victoria Laundry* case, a large boiler had been sold to a laundry and was, in breach of contract, delivered 22 weeks late, so that the buyers could not use it (as they had intended to do) to expand their business. It was held that the sellers were liable for the general loss of profits suffered by the buyers. Having regard to the subject-matter, the likelihood of such loss was obviously very much greater in the *Victoria Laundry* case than in *Hadley* v. *Baxendale*.

---

[8]   On the limits of contractual responsibility in English law, see below, **Case 7**.

Secondly, the defendant may be liable if the loss was such 'as may reasonably be supposed to have been in the minds of both parties at the time they made the contract as the probable result of the breach'. Liability under this rule depends in the first place on what the defendant knew of the claimant's circumstances; and in *Hadley v Baxendale* the defendants did not know enough to make them liable under this rule. It seems that they knew that the mill was stopped, but not that it would remain idle until the new shaft arrived from Greenwich. In the *Victoria Laundry* case the defendants knew that the buyers were in the laundry business; but not that the buyers wanted the boiler for the purpose of some exceptionally lucrative government contracts. Hence the defendants were not liable for the actual loss suffered because the buyers could not perform *those contracts*, but only for loss of ordinary profits.

Under the second rule in *Hadley v Baxendale* the defendant is not liable if he is unaware of the special circumstances; but it does not follow that he will be liable *merely* because he knows of them. To impose this degree of liability there must be 'some knowledge *and acceptance* by one party of the purpose and intention of the other in entering into the contract'. […]

V.   USA

1. Uniform Commercial Code

§ 2-313.   Express Warranties by Affirmation, Promise, Description, Sample.
(1)   Express warranties by the seller are created as follows:
  (a)   Any affirmation of fact or promise made by the seller to the buyer which relates to the goods and becomes part of the basis of the bargain creates an express warranty that the goods shall conform to the affirmation or promise.
  (b)   Any description of the goods which is made part of the basis of the bargain creates an express warranty that the goods shall conform to the description.
  (c)   Any sample or model which is made part of the basis of the bargain creates an express warranty that the whole of the goods shall conform to the sample or model.
(2)   It is not necessary to the creation of an express warranty that the seller use formal words such as "warrant" or "guarantee" or that he have a specific intention to make a warranty, but an affirmation merely of the value of the goods or a statement purporting to be merely the seller's opinion or commendation of the goods does not create a warranty.

§ 2-314   Implied Warranty: Merchantability; Usage of Trade.
(1)   Unless excluded or modified [...], a warranty that the goods shall be merchantable is implied in a contract for their sale if the seller is a merchant with respect to goods of that kind. [...]
(2)   Goods to be merchantable must be at least such as:
  (a)   pass without objection in the trade under the contract description; and
  (b)   in the case of fungible goods, are of fair average quality within the description; and
  (c)   are fit for the ordinary purposes for which such goods are used; [...]

§ 2-315.   Implied Warranty: Fitness for Particular Purpose.
Where the seller at the time of contracting has reason to know any particular purpose for which the goods are required and that the buyer is relying on the seller's skill or judgment to select or furnish suitable goods, there is [...] an implied warranty that the goods shall be fit for such purpose.

§ 2-714.   Buyer's Damages for Breach in Regard to Accepted Goods.
(1)   Where the buyer has accepted goods [...] he may recover as damages for any non-conformity of tender the loss resulting in the ordinary course of events from the seller's breach as determined in any manner which is reasonable.
(2)   The measure of damages for breach of warranty is the difference at the time and place of acceptance between the value of the goods accepted and the value they would have had if they had been as warranted, unless special circumstances show proximate damages of a different amount.

(3)   In a proper case any incidental and consequential damages under the next section may also be recovered.

§ 2-715.   Buyer's Incidental and Consequential Damages.

(1)   Incidental damages resulting from the seller's breach include expenses reasonably incurred in inspection, receipt, transportation and care and custody of goods rightfully rejected, any commercially reasonable charges, expenses or commissions in connection with effecting cover and any other reasonable expense incident to the delay or other breach.

(2)   Consequential damages resulting from the seller's breach include:

   (a)   any loss resulting from general or particular requirements and needs of which the seller at the time of contracting had reason to know and which could not reasonably be prevented by cover or otherwise; and

   (b)   injury to person or property proximately resulting from any breach of warranty.

2. JAMES J. WHITE AND ROBERT S. SUMMERS, *Uniform Commercial Code*, 5th edn

Chapter 9

WARRANTY

§ 9–1   Introduction

[…] [W]e will focus primarily on the meaning of four warranty sections: 2-313, 2-314, 2-315, and 2-312. […] Most important is the implied warranty or merchantability (§ 2-314); next in importance are express warranties, (§ 2-313).

At the outset, one should understand how a warranty lawsuit looks to a plaintiff's lawyer. […] First [the claimant] must prove that the defendant made a warranty, express or implied, under 2-313, 2-314, or 2-315. Second, he must prove that the goods did not comply with the warranty, that is, that they were defective at the time of the sale. Third, he must prove that his injury was caused, proximately and in fact, by the defective nature of the goods. […] Fifth, he must prove his damages. […] [T]he warranty plaintiff need not prove negligence […]

§ 9–7   The Implied Warranty of Merchantability, Section 2-314 – Introduction

The implied warranty of merchantability in 2-314 is an important warranty. It is a first cousin to strict tort liability, and "products liability" cases are often tried under the merchantability banner. […] In a merchantability lawsuit a plaintiff must prove that the defendant deviated from the standard of merchantability and that this deviation caused the plaintiff's injury both proximately and in fact. […] Under 2-314, a plaintiff must prove that (1) a merchant sold goods, (2) which were not "merchantable" at the time of sale, (3) injury and damages to the plaintiff or its property, (4) which were caused proximately and in fact by the defective nature of the goods, and (5) notice to the seller of injury. […]

[...] Elsewhere we deal with the question of whether a buyer must rely on certain representations made by the seller in order for an express warranty to arise. No such reliance is required under 2-314; [...] the implied warranty [...] attaches to the goods at the time of the "sale". [...] [T]he New Mexico Supreme Court noted that "[t]he warranty is implied because the manufacturer holds himself out as being skilled in the construction of his products and as being able to manufacture them without latent defects in materials or workmanship". We think that the same logic applies equally as well to all other "merchants" under 2-314.

§ 9–8 The Implied Warranty of Merchantability, Section 2-314 – Merchantability Defined

[...] [T]he plaintiff's lawyer has to convince the jury or a judge that the goods his client purchased were not merchantable, not "fit for the ordinary purpose" for which such goods are purchased. [...] The buyer may be called on to convince the jury, for example, that merchantable wine must be of a certain color, that merchantable cherries must be of a certain diameter, or that a merchantable logging chain must be able to pull a certain weight without breaking. [...]

§ 9–10 Fitness for a Particular Purpose, Section 2–315

[...]

The most common circumstance in which one meets the warranty of fitness for a particular purpose is where a business buys goods that have to be specially selected or particularly manufactured and assembled for its business. [...] In these cases, the "particular purpose" of the buyer is communicated to the seller in the course of negotiations and occasionally through the contract itself. The buyer's reliance is disclosed by its request for assistance. [...]

Chapter 10

DAMAGES FOR BREACH OF WARRANTY

[...]

§ 10–2 Damaged for Breach of Warranty – The Basic Formula, Section 2-714(1) and (2)
Section 2-714(1) states the general rule for recovery of direct damages – the buyer may recover any damages "resulting in the ordinary course of events from the seller's breach as determined in any manner which is reasonable." [...]

§ 10–3 Damaged for Breach of Warranty – Incidental Damages, Section 2-715(1)
[...] The Code does not define incidental damages; rather 2-715(1) lists many expenses that are included as incidental damages. However, Comment 1 to 2-715 stresses that those listed "are not intended to be exhaustive" but are merely illustrative of the typical kinds of incidental expenses that can be recovered under 2-715 [...]
[...] An example of an award of incidental damages in a breach-of-warranty case is Lewis v. Mobil Oil Corp., in which the seller supplied unsuitable oil to the buyer's hydraulic sawmill system. The oil caused the system to work improperly for two and one-half years. The court found that the seller had breached its warranty of fitness for a

particular purpose, and it held that the buyer was entitled to incidental damages for amounts spent on excessive quantities of oil used and on repairs and replacement of mechanical parts damaged by the failure of the oil to function as warranted.

§ 10–4 Damaged for Breach of Warranty – Consequential Damages

a. Hadley v. Baxendale

Most of the law regarding consequential damages can be traced back to the classic English case, Hadley v. Baxendale.[9] [...]

An aggrieved buyer will often seek general or direct damages for seller's breach of warranty under 2-714(1) and (2). [...] At the same time the buyer may seek consequential damages under 2-714(3) and 2-715(2). [...]

To recover consequential damages under 2-715(2), what must the buyer prove? Some but not all of what the buyer must show is set forth in 2-715(2). [...] [T]he concept of consequential damages is "not defined in terms in the Code" but is used "in the sense given by the leading cases on the subject. [...] In Russo v. Hilltop Lincoln-Mercury, Inc., defective wiring caused a fire which destroyed the buyer's new automobile. [...] Only the difference between the automobile's warranted and actual value at the time of acceptance could be recovered as general damages under 2-714(2). The defective wiring system reduced the actual value of the automobile at the time of acceptance below the purchase price, but did not render the auto worthless as of acceptance date. A large part of the fire damage was therefore consequential. [...]

---

[9] See above, **IV.3**.

VI. Vienna Sales Convention

1. United Nations Convention on Contracts for the International Sale of Goods (CISG)

Art. 35

(1) The seller must deliver goods which are of the quantity, quality and description required by the contract and which are contained or packaged in the manner required by the contract.

(2) Except where the parties have agreed otherwise, the goods do not conform with the contract unless they:

    (a) are fit for the purposes for which goods of the same description would ordinarily be used;

    (b) are fit for any particular purpose expressly or impliedly made known to the seller at the time of the conclusion of the contract, except where the circumstances show that the buyer did not rely, or that it was unreasonable for him to rely, on the seller's skill and judgement;

    (c) possess the qualities of goods which the seller has held out to the buyer as a sample or model;

    (d) are contained or packaged in the manner usual for such goods or, where there is no such manner, in a manner adequate to preserve and protect the goods.

(3) The seller is not liable under subparagraphs (a) to (d) of the preceding paragraph for any lack of conformity of the goods if at the time of the conclusion of the contract the buyer knew or could not have been unaware of such lack of conformity.

Art. 36

(1) The seller is liable in accordance with the contract and this Convention for any lack of conformity which exists at the time when the risk passes to the buyer, even though the lack of conformity becomes apparent only after that time.

(2) The seller is also liable for any lack of conformity which occurs after the time indicated in the preceding paragraph and which is due to a breach of any of his obligations, including a breach of any guarantee that for a period of time the goods will remain fit for their ordinary purpose or for some particular purpose or will retain specified qualities or characteristics.

Art. 45

(1) If the seller fails to perform any of his obligations under the contract or this Convention, the buyer may:

    (a) exercise the rights provided in articles 46 to 52;

    (b) claim damages as provided in articles 74 to 77.

(2) The buyer is not deprived of any right he may have to claim damages by exercising his right to other remedies.

[...]

Art. 74

Damages for breach of contract by one party consist of a sum equal to the loss, including loss of profit, suffered by the other party as a consequence of the breach. Such damages may not exceed the loss which the party in breach foresaw or ought to have foreseen at the time of the conclusion of the contract, in the light of the facts and matters of which he then knew or ought to have known, as a possible consequence of the breach of contract.

Art. 79

(1)   A party is not liable for a failure to perform any of his obligations if he proves that the failure was due to an impediment beyond his control and that he could not reasonably be expected to have taken the impediment into account at the time of the conclusion of the contract or to have avoided or overcome it or its consequences.

(2)   If the party's failure is due to the failure by a third person whom he has engaged to perform the whole or a part of the contract, that party is exempt from liability only if:

    (a)   he is exempt under the preceding paragraph; and

    (b)   the person whom he has so engaged would be so exempt if the provisions of that paragraph were applied to him.

(3)   The exemption provided by this article has effect for the period during which the impediment exists.

(4)   The party who fails to perform must give notice to the other party of the impediment and its effect on his ability to perform. If the notice is not received by the other party within a reasonable time after the party who fails to perform knew or ought to have known of the impediment, he is liable for damages resulting from such nonreceipt.

(5)   Nothing in this article prevents either party from exercising any right other than to claim damages under this Convention.

2. Tribunal de Commerce de Besançon (*Commercial Court in Besançon*) 19.01.1998 (*Christian Flippe c. Sarl Douet Sport Collections*), n° 97 009265, http://www.unilex.info/

Le demandeur, Monsieur Christian FLIPPE, animateur d'un club de JUDO en Suisse, a fait l'acquisition auprès de la SARL DOUET SPORTS COLLECTIONS de 69 sweats enfants pour 16.008 francs hors taxes et 29 sweats adultes pour 7.395 francs hors taxes, marchandise facturée le 31 juillet 1995 [...] pour un montant total hors taxes de 23.403 francs, facture acquittée par Monsieur FLIPPE.

Ces sweats étaient destinés à la revente aux membres d'un club de Judo.

[...] La revente de ces articles ayant débuté à la mi-septembre, Monsieur FLIPPE reçut à compter du 15 décembre 1995 une dizaine de lettres de réclamation de la part des acquéreurs, relatives à un fort rétrécissement, de l'ordre de 6 à 8 centimètres, des articles au lavage.

[...]

Sur quoi le Tribunal: Attendu [...] qu'il existe un réel problème de conformité sur les articles vendus à Monsieur FLIPPE par la SARL DOUET SPORTS COLLECTIONS,

Attendu que Monsieur FLIPPE est de nationalité suisse et que la marchandise vendue a bien été facturée à son lieu de résidence dans ce même pays, la Convention de Vienne s'applique entre les deux parties,

Attendu que conformément aux articles 35, 36, 39 et 49 de ladite Convention, Monsieur FLIPPE ayant fait part à la SARL DOUET SPORTS COLLECTIONS du problème de conformité rencontré à l'usage de la marchandise livrée dans le délai de deux années, il convient d'admettre qu'il serait en droit d'obtenir la résolution de la vente,

Attendu néanmoins que [...] la SARL DOUET se trouvant en position de vendeur d'un produit dont la fabrication et notamment l'élaboration des tissus échappent à son contrôle, il convient, à défaut de manifestation de mauvaise foi de sa part, de lui accorder le bénéfice de l'article 79 de la Convention de Vienne.

Le tribunal opérera donc réfaction du prix dans la proportion de 35 % de la valeur facturée et condamnera la SARL DOUET SPORTS COLLECTIONS à rembourser à Monsieur FLIPPE la somme de 8.191,05 francs, [...] le versement des dommages et intérêts au taux légal étant exclus.

Concernant la demande de dommages et intérêts pour résistance abusive et préjudice commercial, il conviendra de ne pas y faire droit.

[...]

PAR CES MOTIFS

Le Tribunal, statuant contradictoirement, en premier ressort, après en avoir délibéré conformément à la loi,

Déclare partiellement recevable la demande de Monsieur Christian FLIPPE.

Translation[10]

The claimant, Mr Christian FLIPPE, the organiser of a judo club in Switzerland, purchased 69 child's sweatshirts for 16,008 Francs exclusive of tax and 29 adult's sweatshirts for 7,395 Francs exclusive of tax from the company SARL DOUET SPORTS COLLECTIONS for a total of 23,403 Francs exclusive of tax, invoiced on 31 July 1995, invoice paid by Mr FLIPPE.

These sweatshirts were to be sold on to the members of a judo club.

[...] Resale of these articles began in mid-September. From 15 December 1995, Mr FLIPPE received about ten letters of complaint from the purchasers concerning significant shrinkage of the articles after washing, in the order of 6 to 8 centimetres.

[...]

The Court: Whereas [...] there is a real problem with the conformity of the articles sold to Mr FLIPPE by SARL DOUET SPORTS COLLECTIONS,

Whereas Mr FLIPPE is of Swiss nationality and the merchandise sold was invoiced to his place of residence in the same country, the Vienna Convention applies to the two parties,

Whereas, in acordance with Articles 35, 36, 39 and 49 of the aforementioned Convention, Mr FLIPPE having informed SARL DOUET SPORTS COLLECTIONS of the problem with conformity met upon use of the delivered goods within the time limit of two years, it should be accepted that he would have the right to avoid the sale,

---

[10]   Translation by EG

Whereas, nevertheless, [...] SARL DOUET SPORTS COLLECTIONS is in the position of a seller of a product, the manufacturing of which and in part the development of the fabrics for which, is out of its control, it should, where there is no bad faith, be given the benefit of Article 79 of the Vienna Convention.

The court will therefore reduce the price charged by 35% for the shrinkage and order SARL DOUET SPORTS COLLECTIONS to reimburse Mr. FLIPPE the sum of 8191.05 Francs [...] payment of damages at the legal rate being excluded.

[...]

FOR THESE REASONS

The court, deciding at first instance in contentious proceeding after having discussed the matter in accordance with the law, declares Mr Christian FLIPPE's claim partially admissable.

3. Bundesgerichtshof (*Federal Supreme Court of Germany*) 24.03.1999, JZ 1999, 791

Tatbestand:

Die Klägerin betreibt in Österreich eine Rebschule, die sich unter anderem mit der Aufzucht und Veredelung von Schnittreben sowie dem Handel mit diesen befasst. Bei der Veredelung verwendet sie ein spezielles Wachs, um das Austrocknen der Reben zu verhindern und die Infektionsgefahr zu verringern. Das Wachs, das die Klägerin zum Teil auch weiterverkaufte, bezog sie seit mehreren Jahren von der Beklagten, deren Inhaber auch eine Rebschule betreibt. Die Beklagte ihrerseits bezog das Wachs von der Firma F.W., Herstellerin des Wachses war die Firma S.-Werke GmbH.

Mit Schreiben vom 18. Januar 1994 bat die Klägerin die Beklagte wie in den Vorjahren um Unterbreitung eines Angebotes für "ca. 5000 kg Rebwachs schwarz". Bezugnehmend auf dieses Schreiben bot die Beklagte der Klägerin mit Schreiben vom 21. Januar 1994 5000 kg "Rebwachs schwarz" zu einem Preis von 5,43 DM je Kilogramm an. Die Klägerin gab am 31. Januar 1994 eine entsprechende Bestellung auf.

Bei dem daraufhin an die Klägerin gelieferten Wachs handelte es sich um eine Neuentwicklung der Firma S.-Werke, die von der Beklagten in Auftrag gegeben war. Die Beklagte hatte die Ware vor der Belieferung der Klägerin weder tatsächlich übernommen noch geprüft. Die Lieferung erfolgte in der Originalverpackung direkt von der Herstellerin, der Firma S.-Werke, die hiermit von der Beklagten über die Firma F.W. be auftragt worden war.

Die Klägerin verwendete das Wachs teilweise zur Behandlung ihrer eigenen Reben. Daneben veräußerte sie sowohl Wachs als auch Reben, die in ihrem Betrieb mit dem Wachs behandelt worden waren, an andere Rebschulen weiter, die wiederum ihrerseits eigene Reben mit dem Wachs behandelten und auch Kunden mit Reben belieferten, die mit Hilfe des Wachses zuvor veredelt worden waren.

Mit Schreiben vom 16. Juni 1994 rügte die Klägerin gegenüber der Beklagten die Mangelhaftigkeit des Wachses und machte massive Ausfälle der mit dem Wachs behandelten Reben geltend. Im vorliegenden Rechtsstreit begehrt sie von der Beklagten

Schadensersatz in Höhe des Gegenwertes von 14.146.348,40 öS. Die Beklagte lehnt einen Ersatz ab. Sie führt die behaupteten Schäden auf Erfrierung zurück und ist der Auffassung, sie sei nach Art. 79 CISG von einer Haftung als Zwischenhändlerin befreit, da die Schadensursache außerhalb ihres Einflussbereiches liege. […]

Das Landgericht hat die Klage abgewiesen. Auf die dagegen gerichtete Berufung der Klägerin hat das Oberlandesgericht die Klage dem Grunde nach für gerechtfertigt erklärt und den Rechtsstreit zur Entscheidung über die Höhe des Anspruchs an das Landgericht zurückverwiesen. Dagegen wendet sich die Beklagte mit ihrer Revision, mit der sie eine Wiederherstellung des landgerichtlichen Urteils erstrebt.

Entscheidungsgründe:

[…]

II.

[…]

1.

Ohne Erfolg wendet sich die Revision […] gegen die Feststellung der Mangelhaftigkeit des von der Beklagten der Klägerin 1994 gelieferten schwarzen Rebwachses.

Zu Recht begründet das Berufungsgericht seine Entscheidung damit, der Sachverständige habe ohne jede Einschränkung festgestellt, dass aufgrund der dargestellten Versuche und Analysen kein Zweifel an dem ursächlichen Zusammenhang zwischen dem verwendeten Rebwachs und den aufgetretenen Schäden im Jungfeld der Rebschule bestehe. […] Zu Recht stellt […] das Berufungsgericht darauf ab, dass die Beklagte gemäß Art. 35 Abs. 2 Buchst. a CISG Wachs zu liefern hatte, das sich für die Behandlung von Reben eignet, dass das von der Beklagten 1994 gelieferte schwarze Rebwachs aber den – beiden Parteien bekannten und von ihnen auch vorausgesetzten – Anforderungen in der Praxis nicht gerecht wurde und deshalb nicht vertragsgemäß im Sinne des Art. 35 CISG war.

2.

Die Revision macht weiter geltend, die Beklagte habe für den durch die Verwendung des Rebwachses hervorgerufenen Schaden jedenfalls deswegen nicht einzustehen, weil sie bloße Zwischenhändlerin gewesen sei und die nicht vertragsgerechte Beschaffenheit des Rebwachses daher außerhalb ihres Einflussbereichs gelegen habe (Art. 79 CISG). Auch dieser Angriff bleibt ohne Erfolg.

a)

Es kann dabei dahingestellt bleiben, ob Art. 79 CISG alle denkbaren Fälle und Formen einer haftungsbegründenden Nichterfüllung von Vertragspflichten umfasst und nicht auf bestimmte Formen der Vertragsverletzung beschränkt ist und deshalb die Lieferung einer wegen eines Mangels vertragswidrigen Sache einschließt (vgl. Schlechtriem/Stoll, Kommentar zum einheitlichen UN-Kaufrecht, 2. Aufl. 1995, Art. 79 Rdnr. 45–47; Staudinger/Magnus, Wiener UN-Kaufrecht, 1994, Art. 79 Rdnr. 25–26; Piltz, Internationales Kaufrecht, München 1993, § 4 Rdnr. 217 f.; Herber/Czerwenka, Internationales Kaufrecht, München 1991, Art. 79 Rdnr. 8; Schlechtriem, Internationales UN-Kaufrecht, Tübingen 1996, S. 164 f.) oder ob ein Verkäufer, der fehlerhafte Ware geliefert hat, sich überhaupt nicht auf Art. 79 CISG berufen kann (vgl. Nicholas,

Impracticability and Impossibility in the UN Convention on Contracts for the International Sale of Goods, in: Galston/Smith, International Sales, New York, Matthew Bender, 1984, Chapter 5, § 5.10 bis 5.14; Tallon, in, Bianca/Bonell, Commentary on the International Sales Law, Milan 1987, Art. 79 Arm. 2.6.2.; Honnold, Uniform Law for International Sales Under the United Nations Convention, December 1982, Art. 79 N. 427; vgl. auch Lautenbach, Die Haftungsbefreiung im internationalen Warenkauf nach dem UN Kaufrecht und dem schweizerischen Kaufrecht, Dissertation der Universität Zürich, 1990, S. 33 f.; Keil, Die Haftungsbefreiung des Schuldners im UN-Kaufrecht, Dissertation der rechtswissenschaftlichen Fakultät der Ruhr Universität Bochum, Frankfurt am Main 1993, S. 18 f.).

Eine Befreiung gemäß Art. 79 CISG kommt, wovon das Berufungsgericht im Ergebnis zu Recht ausgegangen ist, nicht in Betracht, weil jedenfalls die Mangelhaftigkeit des Rebwachses nicht außerhalb des Einflussbereiches der Beklagten liegt. Sie hat deshalb für die Folgen der nicht vertragsgemäßen Lieferung einzustehen.

Die Entlastungsmöglichkeit des Art. 79 CISG führt nicht zu einer Veränderung der vertraglichen Risikoverteilung. Nach dem Einheitskaufrecht liegt der Grund für die Haftung des Verkäufers darin, dass er sich verpflichtet hat, dem Käufer vertragsgemäße Ware zu verschaffen. Wenn das vertragswidrige Verhalten des oder der Vorlieferanten überhaupt ein Hinderungsgrund im Sinne des Art. 79 CISG ist, so doch grundsätzlich ein solcher, den der Verkäufer nach dem Inhalt des Kaufvertrags vermeiden oder überwinden muss. Dies entspricht dem typischen Sinn eines solchen Vertrages (Magnus in: Honsell [Hrsg.], Kommentar zum UN-Kaufrecht, 1997, Art. 79 Rdnr. 10; a.A. wohl Schlechtriem/Stoll aaO Art. 79 Rdnr. 47 ff. jew. m.w.Nachw.). Aus der Sicht des Käufers macht es keinen Unterschied, ob der Verkäufer die Ware selbst herstellt mit der Folge, dass die Nichterfüllung grundsätzlich in seinem tatsächlichen Einflussbereich liegt, so dass eine Befreiung gemäß Art. 79 Abs. 1 CISG im Regelfall ausscheidet oder ob er sich diese von Vorlieferanten verschafft. So wie der Verkäufer bei Gattungsschulden dafür haftet, dass sein Vorlieferant ihn pünktlich beliefert (vgl. z.B. Staudinger/Magnus aaO Art. 79 Rdnr. 22; Schlechtriem/Stoll aaO Art. 79 Rdnr. 30 f.), haftet er auch dafür, dass ihn sein Vorlieferant fehlerfrei beliefert. Das Einheitskaufrecht unterscheidet insoweit nicht zwischen einer nicht rechtzeitigen Lieferung und der Lieferung einer nicht vertragsgemäßen Ware. Für beide Vertragsverletzungen gilt derselbe Haftungsmaßstab. Dass die Parteien bei Vertragsschluss eine andere Risikoverteilung vereinbart haben, zeigt die Revision nicht auf und ist auch sonst nicht ersichtlich.

Nach Art. 79 CISG kommt eine Entlastung des Verkäufers von den Folgen nicht vertragsgerechter Beschaffenheit der Ware – soweit überhaupt (s.o.) – nur in Betracht, wenn diese seinem Einflussbereich nicht mehr zugeordnet werden kann. Da der Verkäufer, wie gezeigt, das Beschaffungsrisiko trägt, kann er sich auch dann, wenn die Ursachen für die Mangelhaftigkeit der Ware – wie hier – im Vor- oder Zuliefererbereich liegen, nach Art. 79 Abs. 1 oder 2 CISG nur entlasten, wenn die Mangelhaftigkeit auf Umständen beruht, die außerhalb seines eigenen und des Einflussbereichs jedes seiner Vorlieferanten liegen. Dass dies der Fall ist, vermag die Revision nicht aufzuzeigen. Soweit sie darauf verweist, dass die Herstellerfirma im Jahr 1994 bei der Produktion des gelieferten Rebwachses eine möglicherweise aus Ungarn bezogene ungeeignete Grundsubstanz verwendet habe, ist dies mit Blick auf Art. 79 CISG nicht erheblich, denn für einen derartigen in ihrem Einflussbereich liegenden Produktionsfehler hätte die Herstellerfirma – und damit im Verhältnis zur Klägerin auch die Beklagte – einzustehen.

b)

[...] Die Haftung nach dem einheitlichen Kaufrecht beruht, entgegen der Ansicht der Vorinstanz, nicht darauf, dass der Zwischenhändler verpflichtet ist, die Ware vor der Lieferung an seinen Käufer zu untersuchen, was, wie die Revision meint, in diesem Fall nicht erforderlich gewesen wäre, da das bisher bezogene Rebwachs immer mangelfrei gewesen sei. Denn auf ein Verschulden des Verkäufers kommt es wegen der gesetzlichen und mangels anderer Vereinbarung zwischen den Parteien in den Vertrag einbezogenen Risikoverteilung mit der Folge einer Garantiehaftung des Verkäufers nicht an. [...]

Translation[11]

Facts

The plaintiff runs a vine nursery in Austria dealing, inter alia, with the breeding and refinement of vines as well as the sale of these vines. In the grafting process, the [plaintiff] uses a special wax in order to protect the vines from drying out and in order to reduce the risk of infection. The wax, which the plaintiff also in part resold, was purchased by [the plaintiff] for many years from the defendant company, whose owner also runs a vine nursery. The defendant in turn obtained the wax from the F.W. company. The manufacturer of the wax was the company S. Werke GmbH.

In a letter dated January 18, 1994, the plaintiff asked the defendant, as in previous years, to submit an offer for "about 5,000 kg black vine wax." With reference to this letter, the defendant offered the plaintiff, in a letter dated January 21, 1994, 5,000 kg of "black vine wax" at the price of DM [Deutsche Mark] 5.43 per kilogram. On January 31, 1994, the plaintiff placed such an order.

The wax which was thereupon delivered to the plaintiff was a type of wax newly developed by S. Werke, as requested by the defendant. The defendant had neither actually received, accepted nor inspected the goods prior to delivery to the plaintiff. The delivery took place in the original packaging directly from the manufacturer, S. Werke, as requested by the defendant via the F.W. Company.

The plaintiff partially used the wax for the treatment of its own vines. In addition, the plaintiff also sold the wax and vines which had been treated in its nursery with the wax to other nurseries which, in turn, treated their vines with the wax and also delivered vines that had been treated with the help of the wax to other customers.

In a letter dated June 16, 1994, the plaintiff gave notice of the defective wax to the defendant and complained of major damage to vines treated with the wax. In the lawsuit at issue, the plaintiff demands the value of sA [Austrian Schillings] 14,146,348.40 in damages from the defendant. The defendant refuses to compensate [the buyer]. [The defendant] attributes the alleged damages to frost and argues that it is exempt from any liability as an intermediary pursuant to Art. 79 CISG because the reasons for the damage are out of its control.

[...]

---

11   http://www.iuscomp.org/gla/judgments/cisg/z990324.htm. This case is published in the German Law Archive courtesy of Pace Law School Institute of International Commercial Law. Translation by *Alston & Bird LL.P.* Editors: William M. Barron, Esq.; Birgit Kurtz, Esq. Very slight modifications made.

The *Landgericht* [Court of First Instance] dismissed the complaint. Upon the appeal of the plaintiff, the *Oberlandesgericht* [Regional Appellate Court] held that the complaint presented a valid cause of action and remanded the case to the *Landgericht* for further hearings on the amount of damages. The appeal of the defendant argues against this and requests the reinstatement of the *Landgericht* judgment.

The Reasons for the Decision
[…]

II.

[…]

1.
The appeal tries unsuccessfully to overturn the decision of the Lower Court with respect to the defectiveness of the black vine wax delivered to the plaintiff by the defendant in 1994.

The Court of Appeals correctly justifies its decision by the fact that the expert determined, without any reservations, that pursuant to his experiments and analyses there is no doubt that a causal connection existed between the vine wax used and the damage to the vine nursery's field. […] The Court of Appeals correctly relies on the fact that the defendant was obligated, pursuant to CISG Art. 35(2)(a), to deliver wax that is suitable for the treatment of vines, but that the black vine wax delivered by the defendant in 1994 did not meet the industry standards – of which both parties were aware and which both parties applied – and that therefore the wax was not in conformity with the contract within the meaning of CISG Art. 35.

2. The appeal further asserts that the defendant is, in any event, not liable for the damages caused by the use of the vine wax because it was only the intermediary and, therefore, the vine wax's non-conformity with the contract was beyond its control (CISG Art. 79). This attack is also unsuccessful.

a) It may remain undecided whether CISG Art. 79 encompasses all conceivable cases and forms of non-performance of contractual obligations creating a liability and is not limited to certain types of contractual violations and, therefore, includes the delivery of goods not in conformity with the contract because of their defectiveness (*compare* Schlechtriem/Stoll, Kommentar zum einheitlichen UN-Kaufrecht, 2d ed. 1995, Art. 79 n. 45–47; Staudinger/Magnus, Wiener UN-Kaufrecht, 1994, Art. 79 n. 25-26; Piltz, Internationales Kaufrecht, Munich 1993, § 4 n. 217 *et seq.*; Herber/Czerwenka, Internationales Kaufrecht, Munich 1991, Art. 79 n. 8; Schlechtriem, Internationales UN-Kaufrecht, Tübingen 1996, p. 164 *et seq.*), or whether a seller who has delivered defective goods cannot rely on Art. 79 CISG at all (*compare* Nicholas, Impracticability and Impossibility in the UN Convention on Contracts for the International Sale of Goods, in: Galston N.M./Smit H., International Sales, New York, Matthew Bender, 1984, Chapter 5 § 5.10 to 5.14; Tallon, in Bianca/Bonell, Commentary on the International Sales Law, Milan 1987 Art. 79 cmt. 2.6.2.; Honnold, J.O., Uniform Law for International Sales under the United Nations Convention, December 1982, Art. 79 N. 427; *compare also* Lautenbach, Die Haftungsbefreiung im internationalen Warenkauf nach dem UN-Kaufrecht und dem schweizerischen Kaufrecht, Doctor's Thesis of the University of Zurich, 1990 p. 33 *et seq.*; Keil, Die Haftungsbefreiung des Schuldners im UN-Kaufrecht, Doctor's Thesis of the law faculty of the Ruhr-University Bochum, Frankfurt am Main 1993, p. 18 *et seq.*). An exemption pursuant to Art. 79 CISG, upon which the Court of Appeals correctly based its decision, is not applicable because, in any case, the defectiveness of the vine wax was not outside the defendant's control. It is, therefore, responsible for the consequences of a delivery of goods not in conformity with the contract.

The possibility of exemption under CISG Art. 79 does not change the allocation of the contractual risk. According to the [CISG], the reason for the seller's liability is that he has agreed to provide the purchaser with goods that are in conformity with the contract. If the supplier's (or suppliers') breach of the contract is a general impediment within the meaning of CISG Art. 79 at all, it is generally an impediment that the seller must avoid or overcome according to the content of the contract of sale. This follows the typical meaning of such a contract (Magnus in: Honsell [publisher], Kommentar zum UN-Kaufrecht, 1997, Art. 79 n. 10; *but see* Schlechtriem/Stoll, *supra*, Art.79 n. 47 *et seq.* with further citations). From the buyer's point of view, it makes no difference whether the seller produces the goods himself – with the consequence that the non-performance is generally in his actual control so that, as a rule, a dispensation pursuant to CISG Art. 79(1) is generally excluded – or whether the seller obtains the goods from suppliers. Just as in the case of unspecified obligations, where the seller is liable for the timely delivery by his supplier (compare, e.g., Staudinger/Magnus, *supra*, Art. 79 n. 22; Schlechtriem/Stoll, *supra*, Art.79 n. 30 et seq.), he is also responsible to see that his supplier delivers defect-free goods. In this respect, the [CISG] does not distinguish between an untimely delivery and a delivery of goods not in conformity with the contract. For both breaches of contract the same standard of liability applies. The appeal does not indicate that the parties agreed to a different allocation of risk at the formation of the contract, nor is this otherwise apparent.

Pursuant to CISG Art. 79, the seller's exemption from consequences of goods not in conformity with the contract can only be considered – if at all (see above) – when the non-conformity cannot be deemed to be within the seller's control. Because the seller has the risk of acquisition (as shown), he can only be exempted under CISG Art. 79 (1) or (2) (even when the reasons for the defectiveness of the goods are – as here – within the control of his supplier or his sub-supplier) if the defectiveness is due to circumstances out of his own control and out of each of his suppliers' control. The appeal cannot show this. Insofar as the appeal points out that the manufacturer, in 1994, used an inappropriate raw material possibly imported from Hungary during the production of the delivered vine wax, this is not relevant with respect to CISG Art. 79 because the manufacturer would be liable – and thus also the plaintiff vis-à-vis the defendant – for those product defects within its control.

b)
[…] The liability under the [CISG] is, contrary to the Lower Court 's opinion, not based on the supplier's obligation to inspect the goods before delivery to its purchaser, which – according to the appeal – was not necessary in this case because the vine wax previously purchased had always been free of defects. That is so because the seller's culpability is not important due to the statutory allocation of risk and the lack of a different agreement between the parties concerning the allocation of risk, resulting in a guarantee [warranty] liability of the seller. […]

4. ICC Court of Arbitration, Basel 1995, Arbitral Award n° 8128, http://www.unilex.info/

In order to perform a contract with a third party, a Swiss buyer entered into a contract with an Austrian seller for the supply of chemical fertilizer. The seller in turn applied to a Ukrainian supplier to obtain part of the fertilizer. The buyer sent to the Ukrainian supplier the packaging to be used for delivery (sacks manufactured by the buyer under the seller's instructions). As the sacks sent by the buyer did not conform to the technical rules of the Ukrainian chemical industry, the supplier could not make use of them. Consequently, the goods were not delivered within the period of time fixed in the contract. The buyer asked the seller in writing when the goods would be delivered, expressly adding that, in the absence of a clear commitment by the seller, it would avoid the contract with respect to the part of the goods not yet delivered. Since the seller's reply was generic, the buyer had to make a substitute purchase at a higher price in order to be able to perform the contract already concluded with the third party. The buyer commenced arbitral proceedings demanding damages, including the cost of the sacks it had supplied as well as the loss deriving from the substitute purchase. The buyer also asked for interest, at the London International Bank Offered Rate (LIBOR) plus 2%.

The Arbitral Tribunal found that the seller had fundamentally breached the contract (Art. 25 CISG) as it had breached its duty to give the buyer the necessary instructions for the correct manufacture of the packaging.

Moreover, the seller was not exempted from performance pursuant to Art. 79 CISG, since the seller is responsible for non delivery caused by its supplier, as part of the seller's risk (Art. 79(2) CISG).

5. Tribunal of International Commercial Arbitration at the Russian Federation Chamber of Commerce 16.03.1995, n° 155/94 (Abstract), http://www.unilex.info/

A contract was concluded between a Russian seller and a German buyer for the supply of a specific quantity of chemical products within a period of time specified in the contract (fourth quarter of 1992). The goods were not delivered to the buyer within the specified period. From January to May 1993, the buyer repeatedly informed the seller that it insisted on the goods being delivered in accordance with the contract concluded and was ready to extend the time-limit for delivery. In May 1993, the buyer informed the seller that, as a result of the latter's breach of its contractual obligations, the buyer had purchased the goods specified in the contract from a third party. In May 1994, the buyer sued the seller for breach of contract, claiming compensation for damages suffered as a result of the seller's failure to honour the contract, such damages consisting in the difference between the price of the goods established in the contract and the price at which the buyer was obliged to purchase the goods from the third party.

In its reply to the claim, the seller maintained that it should be discharged from liability on the grounds that it had been unable to deliver the goods for reasons beyond its control, namely because of an emergency production stoppage at the plant manufacturing the goods specified in the contract.

Referring to Art. 79 CISG, the tribunal decided that the seller (respondent) was unable to prove the facts that would have discharged it from its liability for non-performance of its obligations since refusal on the part of the manufacturer of the goods to supply them to the respondent could not be deemed sufficient grounds for such discharge from liability. The respondent should bear liability for failure to fulfil its obligations on the additional grounds that it was unable to establish that it could not reasonably be expected to take account, in concluding the contract, of the obstacle preventing its compliance with the contract or to avoid or surmount that obstacle or its consequences. [...]

VII.   Principles of Contract Law

1. Commission on European Contract Law:
Principles of European Contract Law

NON-PERFORMANCE AND REMEDIES IN GENERAL

Art. 8:101.   Remedies Available.
(1)   Whenever a party does not perform an obligation under the contract and the non-performance is not excused under Article 8:108, the aggrieved party may resort to any of the remedies set out in Chapter 9.
(2)   Where a party's non-performance is excused under Article 8:108, the aggrieved party may resort to any of the remedies set out in Chapter 9 except claiming performance and damages.
(3)   A party may not resort to any of the remedies set out in Chapter 9 to the extent that its own act caused the other party's non-performance.

Art. 8:102.   Cumulation of Remedies.
Remedies which are not incompatible may be cumulated. In particular, a party is not deprived of its right to damages by exercising its right to any other remedy.

Art. 8:108.   Excuse due to an Impediment.
(1)   A party's non-performance is excused if it proves that it is due to an impediment beyond its control and that it could not reasonably have been expected to take the impediment into account at the time of the conclusion of the contract, or to have avoided or overcome the impediment or its consequences.
(2)   Where the impediment is only temporary the excuse provided by this Article has effect for the period during which the impediment exists. However, if the delay amounts to a fundamental non-performance, the creditor may treat it as such.
(3)   The non-performing party must ensure that notice of the impediment and of its effect on its ability to perform is received by the other party within a reasonable time after the non-performing party knew or ought to have known of these circumstances. The other party is entitled to damages for any loss resulting from the non-receipt of such notice.

PARTICULAR REMEDIES FOR NON-PERFORMANCE

Damages and Interest

Art. 9:501.   Right to Damages.
(1)   The aggrieved party is entitled to damages for loss caused by the other party's non-performance which is not excused under Article 8:108.
(2)   The loss for which damages are recoverable includes:
  (a)   non-pecuniary loss; and
  (b)   future loss which is reasonably likely to occur.

> **Art. 9:502.   General Measure of Damages.**
> The general measure of damages is such sum as will put the aggrieved party as nearly as possible into the position in which it would have been if the contract had been duly performed. Such damages cover the loss which the aggrieved party has suffered and the gain of which it has been deprived.
>
> **Art. 9:503.   Foreseeability.**
> The non-performing party is liable only for loss which it foresaw or could reasonably have foreseen at the time of conclusion of the contract as a likely result of its non-performance, unless the non-performance was intentional or grossly negligent.

Art. 8:108:   Excuse due to an Impediment

Commentary

A.   *General*

Article 8:108 governs the consequences when an event which is not the fault or responsibility of a party prevents it from performing. The Principles also contain a provision for revision of the contract if unforeseen circumstances supervene and make performance excessively onerous (Article 6:111). Thus, unlike the equivalent article of CISG (see Notes below), Article 8:108 has to apply only in cases where an impediment prevents performance.

The rules in Article 8:108 are not mandatory. The parties may modify the allocation of the risk of impossibility of performance, either in general or in relation to a particular impediment; usages (especially in carriage by sea) may have the same effect.

B.   *Scope*

The excuse may apply to any obligation arising out of the contract, including obligations to pay money. While insolvency would not normally be an impediment within the meaning of the text, as it is not "beyond the control" of the debtor, a government ban on transferring the sum due might be.

The term "impediment" covers every sort of event (natural occurrences, restraints of princes, acts of third parties).

It is conceivable that an impediment at the time the contract was made existed without the parties knowing it. For example, the parties might sign a charter of a ship which, unknown to them, has just sunk. This situation is not covered by Article 8:108 but the contract might be avoidable under Article 4:103, Mistake as to Facts or Law.

C.   *The Circumstances of the impediment*

The conditions laid down for the operation of the Article are analogous to the conditions traditionally required for *force majeure*. They are necessarily in general terms, given the great variety of fact situations to which they must apply. It is for the party which invokes it to show that the conditions are fulfilled.

(i)   *outside the debtor's control*

First, the obstacle must be something outside the debtor's sphere of control. The risk of its own activities it must bear itself. Thus the breakdown of a machine, even if unforeseeable and unpreventable, cannot be an impediment within the Article and this avoids investigation of whether the breakdown was really unforeseeable and the consequences unpreventable. The same is true of the actions of persons for whom the debtor is responsible and particularly the acts of the people it puts in charge of the performance. The debtor cannot invoke the default of a subcontractor unless it was outside its control – for instance because there was no other subcontractor which could have been employed to do the work; and the impediment must also be outside the subcontractor's sphere of control.

> *Illustration 1:* In consequence of an unexpected strike in the nationalized company which distributes natural gas, a chinaware manufacturer which heats its furnaces only with gas is obliged to interrupt its production. The manufacturer is not liable toward its own clients, if the other conditions of excuse are fulfilled. The cause of non-performance is external.

> *Illustration 2:* The employees of a company unforeeably go on strike in order to force the management to buy foreign machines which will improve the working conditions. For the time being it is actually not possible to obtain these machines. The company cannot claim as against its customers that the strike is an excuse, as the event is not beyond its control.

[...]

(ii)   *could not have been taken into account*

[...]

(iii)   *insurmountable impediments*

[...]

D.   *Effects*

An impediment to performance which fulfils the conditions just set out relieves the party which has not performed from liability. But again it is necessary to define just what is meant by this rather general expression, which may be ambiguous. Here the approach is a pragmatic one: one must start with the remedies that are available to the aggrieved party (as does Article 8:101, which in paragraph (2) sets out the remedies which do not apply when a non-performance is excused, namely specific performance and damages).

First, any form of specific performance (Article 9:101 and 9:102) is by definition impossible. Nor do damages of any kind, including "liquidated damages" and penalties, apply unless the parties have agreed otherwise.

The question of the ending of the contract, on the other hand, is more complex. [...]

E.   *Temporary impediment*

It is commonly agreed that a temporary impediment in principle results in only a temporary excuse. This is what is provided by paragraph (2).

It may be, however, that late performance will be of no use to the aggrieved party. Therefore it is given the right to terminate the contract provided that the delay is itself fundamental (see Article 8: 103).

Illustration 6: An impresario in Hamburg has engaged a famous English tenor to sing at the Hamburg Opera from 1 to 31 October. The singer catches Asian flu and has to retire to bed (this would constitute an impediment within paragraph (1)): he tells the impresario that he will be unable to come to Hamburg before 10 October. Assuming that the tenor's presence for the whole month is an essential part of the contract, the impresario may terminate. If he chooses not to do so, the contract remains in force for the remaining period but the tenor's fees will be reduced proportionately. [...]

F. *Notice*
Paragraph (3) of Article 8:108 is an application of the obligation of good faith which governs the whole of the Principles.

[...]

The sanction for failing to give this notice is liability for the extra loss suffered by the aggrieved party as the result of not being informed: normally the aggrieved party will recover damages.

Illustration 8: In the example given in Illustration 6, if the tenor does not warn the impresario immediately of his unavailability, the latter may recover compensation for being deprived of the chance to obtain a replacement, so reducing his loss.

Notes

1. *Force majeure and impossibility*
    Article 8:108 (1) is modelled on CISG art. 79 (1), which has been followed in the FINNISH and SWEDISH Sale of Goods Acts, §§ 27 and 40. See also *Unidroit* art. 7.1.7.

(a) Civil law systems
Even if all legal systems now admit that impossibility of performance should be excused, the way the excuse is given effect varies considerably.

[...]

(b) Common Law
ENGLISH and IRISH law take a different route. A party is normally obliged to fulfil his promise and will be liable in damages for failure to perform. However, he is sometimes excused where performance has become impossible without his fault, e.g because the subject matter of the contract has been destroyed. If the impossibility occurred after the contract was made, and it is impossible to perform the contract as a whole, the non-performing party may be excused under the doctrine of frustration, see *Taylor* v. *Caldwell* (1863) 3 B. & S. 828, Q. B.. The results of frustration are similar to those under Article 8.108, in that both parties are discharged automatically. SCOTTISH law broadly follows the Common law.
    [...]

2. Study Group on a European Civil Code and Research Group on EC Private Law (Acquis Group): *Draft Common Frame of Reference*

Chapter 3:
Remedies for Non-Performance
Section 1:
General

III. – 3:101: Remedies available
(1) If an obligation is not performed by the debtor and the non-performance is not excused, the creditor may resort to any of the remedies set out in this Chapter.
(2) If the debtor's non-performance is excused, the creditor may resort to any of those remedies except enforcing specific performance and damages.
(3) The creditor may not resort to any of those remedies to the extent that the creditor caused the debtor's non-performance.

III. – 3:102: Cumulation of remedies
Remedies which are not incompatible may be cumulated. In particular, a creditor is not deprived of the right to damages by resorting to any other remedy.

[...]

III. – 3:104: Excuse due to an impediment
(1) A debtor's non-performance of an obligation is excused if it is due to an impediment beyond the debtor's control and if the debtor could not reasonably be expected to have avoided or overcome the impediment or its consequences.
(2) Where the obligation arose out of a contract or other juridical act, non-performance is not excused if the debtor could reasonably be expected to have taken the impediment into account at the time when the obligation was incurred.
(3) Where the excusing impediment is only temporary the excuse has effect for the period during which the impediment exists. However, if the delay amounts to a fundamental non-performance, the creditor may treat it as such.
(4) Where the excusing impediment is permanent the obligation is extinguished. Any reciprocal obligation is also extinguished. [...]

[...]

Section 7:
Damages and interest

III. – 3:701: Right to damages
(1) The creditor is entitled to damages for loss caused by the debtor's non-performance of an obligation, unless the non-performance is excused.
(2) The loss for which damages are recoverable includes future loss which is reasonably likely to occur.

(3) "Loss" includes economic and non-economic loss. "Economic loss" includes loss of income or profit, burdens incurred and a reduction in the value of property. "Non-economic loss" includes pain and suffering and impairment of the quality of life.

III. – 3:702: General measure of damages

The general measure of damages for loss caused by non-performance of an obligation is such sum as will put the creditor as nearly as possible into the position in which the creditor would have been if the obligation had been duly performed. Such damages cover loss which the creditor has suffered and gain of which the creditor has been deprived.

III. – 3:703: Foreseeability

The debtor in an obligation which arises from a contract or other juridical act is liable only for loss which the debtor foresaw or could reasonably be expected to have foreseen at the time when the obligation was incurred as a likely result of the non-performance, unless the non-performance was intentional, reckless or grossly negligent.

3. UNIDROIT: *Principles of International Commercial Contracts*

Art. 7.1.1. Non-performance defined.

Non-performance is failure by a party to perform any of its obligations under the contract, including defective performance or late performance.

Art. 7.4.1. Right to damages

Any non-performance gives the aggrieved party a right to damages either exclusively or in conjunction with any other remedies except where the non-performance is excused under these Principles.

Art. 7.4.2. Full compensation

(1) The aggrieved party is entitled to full compensation for harm sustained as a result of the non-performance. Such harm includes both any loss which it suffered and any gain of which it was deprived, taking into account any gain to the aggrieved party resulting from its avoidance of cost or harm.

(2) Such harm may be non-pecuniary and includes, for instance, physical suffering or emotional distress.

Art. 7.4.4. Foreseeability of harm

The non-performing party is liable only for harm which it foresaw or could reasonably have foreseen at the time of the conclusion of the contract as being likely to result from its non-performance.

Art. 7.1.7. Force majeure

(1) Non-performance by a party is excused if that party proves that the non-performance was due to an impediment beyond its control and that it could not reasonably be expected to have taken the impediment into account at the time of the conclusion of the contract or to have avoided or overcome it or its consequences.

(2)   When the impediment is only temporary, the excuse shall have effect for such period as is reasonable having regard to the effect of the impediment on the performance of the contract.

(3)   The party who fails to perform must give notice to the other party of the impediment and its effect on its ability to perform. If the notice is not received by the other party within a reasonable time after the party who fails to perform knew or ought to have known of the impediment, it is liable for damages resulting from such non-receipt.

(4)   Nothing in this article prevents a party from exercising a right to terminate the contract or to withhold performance or request interest on money due.

Official Comment [to Art. 7.1.7]

1.   The notion of force majeure

This article covers the ground covered in common law systems by the doctrines of frustration and impossibility of performance and in civil law systems by doctrines such as force majeure, Unmöglichkeit, etc. but it is identical with none of these doctrines. The term "force majeure" was chosen because it is widely known in international trade practice, as confirmed by the inclusion in many international contracts of so-called "force majeure" clauses.

[…]

2.   Effects of force majeure on the rights and duties of the parties

The article does not restrict the rights of the party who has not received performance to terminate if the non-performance is fundamental. What it does do, where it applies, is to excuse the non-performing party from liability in damages.

[…]

3.   Force majeure and hardship

The article must be read together with Chapter 6, section 2 of the Principles dealing with hardship. […]

4.   Force majeure and contract practice

The definition of force majeure in para. (1) of this article is necessarily of a rather general character. International commercial contracts often contain much more precise and elaborate provisions in this regard. The parties may therefore find it appropriate to adapt the content of this article so as to take account of the particular features of the specific transaction.

VIII. China

1. 中华人民共和国合同法 *(Contract Law of the People's Republic of China)*

第七章 违约责任

Chapter Seven: Liabilities for Breach of Contracts

第 107 条

当事人一方不履行合同义务或者履行合同义务不符合约定的，应当承担继续履行、采取补救措施或者赔偿损失等违约责任。

Art. 107. *Types of Liabilities for Breach.*

If a party fails to perform its obligations under a contract, or rendered non-conforming performance, it shall bear the liabilities for breach of contract by specific performance, cure of non-conforming performance or payment of damages, etc.

第 117 条

因不可抗力不能履行合同的，根据不可抗力的影响，部分或者全部免除责任，但法律另有规定的除外。当事人迟延履行后发生不可抗力的，不能免除责任。

本法所称不可抗力，是指不能预见、不能避免并不能克服的客观情况。

Art. 117. *Force Majeure.*

(1)   A party who was unable to perform a contract due to force majeure is exempted from liability in part or in whole in light of the impact of the event of force majeure, except otherwise provided by law. Where an event of force majeure occurred after the party's delay in performance, it is not exempted from liability.

(2)   For purposes of this Law, force majeure means any objective circumstance which is unforeseeable, unavoidable and insurmountable.

第 118 条

当事人一方因不可抗力不能履行合同的，应当及时通知对方，以减轻可能给对方造成的

Art. 118. *Duty to Notify in Case of Force Majeure*

If a party is unable to perform a contract due to force majeure, it shall timely notify the other party so as to mitigate the loss that may be caused to the other party, and shall provide proof of force majeure within a reasonable time.

第 121 条

当事人一方因第三人的原因造成违约的，应当向对方承担违约责任。当事人一方和第三

Art. 121. *Breach Due to Act of Third Person*

Where a party's breach was attributable to a third person, it shall nevertheless be liable to the other party for breach. Any dispute between the party and such third person shall be resolved in accordance with the law or the agreement between the parties.

2. BING LING, *Contract Law in China*

CHAPTER 8

LIABILITY FOR BREACH OF CONTRACT

[...]

8.1.3   *Fault*

8.030   Liability flows not from injury but from fault which is as plain as the law of chemistry whereby what makes candles burn is not light but oxygen. The above statement by Rudolf von Jhering has often been repeated by Chinese jurists in support of the view that contractual liability should be fault-based. In civil law tradition, fault is an essential element of civil liability for tort and non-performance of obligations [Footnote with references to the German Civil Code, the Swiss Code of Obligations, and the Civil Code of the Republic of China (Taiwan)]. [...] A party is at fault in its non-performance if it intends to effect the non-performance or if it fails to exercise due care in its non-performance. Before 1999, the Economic Contract Law of the People's Republic of China of 1981 (ECL) expressly specified fault of the breaching party as the basis of liability for breach of contract. The Supreme People's Court (SPC) confirmed in its interpretation of the ECL that fault is an essential element for contractual liability. The reference to fault was deleted in the Foreign Economic Contract Law of the People's Republic of China of 1985 (FECL) and the Technology Contract Law of the People's Republic of China of 1987 (TCL). Article 106 of the General Principles of Civil Law of 1986 (GPCL) expressly refers to fault in the second paragraph as a constituent element for tortuous liability, but omits any reference to fault in the first paragraph dealing with contractual liability. Commentators differ as to whether the GPCL, the FECL and the TCL have thus adopted the principle of strict liability whereby fault is not a necessary element of contractual liability. Those scholars who advocated the fault-based liability mostly agreed that in an action for breach of contract the aggrieved party does not have to prove the existence of fault, but the breaching party is exonerated from liability if it disproves its fault. This position is consistent with other civil law jurisdictions adopting the fault-based approach [Footnote with references to the German Civil Code, the Swiss Code of Obligations, and the Civil Code of the Republic of China (Taiwan)] and has some support in judicial practice [in China].

8.031   Whether fault should be adopted as an essential element of liability for breach of contract was one of the most controversial issues during the drafting of the Contract Law. It was argued, on the one hand, that (a) the fault-based approach emphasises the moral underpinnings of contracts and serves to promote public morals in the market economy; (b) contract law should not only promote commercial efficiency and expediency, but should also cater to concerns for social justice and ethics; (c) the requirement of fault allows reasonable leeway for people to conduct their affairs without having to worry about legal liability; (d) the fault liability principle has been well accepted by the courts and the general public and has formed part of the popular legal consciousness; and (e) the strict liability principle is incompatible with the civil law tradition that Chinese law is based on.

8.032   On the other hand, it was argued that: (a) the strict liability approach would enhance the sense of responsibility of the parties and ensure better performance of contracts in society; (b) dispensing with the fault requirement saves the difficult task of determining and assessing fault for the courts and the parties and serves to enhance the efficiency of civil litigation; (c) strict liability for breach of contract is derived from contractual obligations that are voluntarily undertaken by the parties and reflects ultimately the autonomy of the will of the parties; (d) the strict liability approach had already been accepted by existing law (GPCL, FECL and TCL); and (e) the strict liability principle is now accepted by the international uniform contract law endorsed by both civil law and common law countries such as the CISG, the UNIDROIT-Principles and Principles of European Contract Law.

   [...] In the end, the strict liability approach prevailed. Article 107 of the Contract Law imposes contractual liability on a party who has committed an act of breach and makes no reference to the fault of the breaching party. [...] [I]t is generally recognized that article 107 enunciates the strict liability principle for breach of contract. The act of non-performance is the only essential element for contractual liability. Where there is an act of breach, the breaching party is liable regardless of whether the aggrieved party may prove the breaching party's fault or whether the breaching party may disprove its fault.

8.033   An important corollary of the strict liability principle is that a party is liable for breach of contract even though the breach is caused by a third person. [...]

8.039   Under the strict liability principle, a party is liable for breach of contract even if the breach or the impossibility of performance is caused by an event not attributable to it. But the standard of care I regard to the performance is not absolute. A party is not liable for non-performance that is caused by *force majeure*.[12]
   [...]

---

[12]   See **Case 7** below.

IX. Summary

1. Overview of the solutions according to the different legal orders and principles of contract law

Scenario a)   *The defect in the goods could not have been discovered by carrying out an examination (i.e. the seller was not at fault)*

Seller liable (contractual liability is independent of whether the seller is at fault, strict liability)	Seller not liable (contractual liability is dependent on the existence of a fault on the seller's part)
– **French law**: There is an irrebuttable presumption that a professional seller is aware of defects in the thing sold, see: Art. 1645 C. civ. and Cour de cass. 1973. – **Swiss law**: Distinctive feature: a seller is only obliged to compensate for the direct damage caused to the buyer, see Art. 280(2) Code of obligations; BG 1953; SCHÖNLE. – **English law**: SGA 1979, s. 14, s. 53(1)(b); Case law e.g. *Nicolene* v. *Simmonds*; see also TREITEL. – **USA**: UCC, § 2-714(1), (3), § 2-715. – **Chinese law**: Arts 107, 121 of the Chinese Contract Law; see BING LING, n. 8.031 *et seq.* – **CISG**: Art. 45(1) (b), Art. 74, does not fall within the scope of Art. 79, see BGH 1999; ICC Court of Arbitration, Basel 1995; Russian Arbitral Tribunal, 1995, *contra*: Trib. com. Besançon 1998. – **PECL**: Art. 8:101(1), Art. 9:501 ff., does not fall within the scope of Art. 8:108. – **DCFR**: Art. III. 3:101(1), does not fall within the scope of Art. III. 3:701. – **UNIDROIT Principles**: Art. 7.1.1, Art. 7.4.1, does not fall within the scope of Art. 7.1.7.	– **Belgian law**: There is a rebuttable presumption that a professional seller is aware of defects in the thing sold, see Art. 1645 C. civ. and Hof van Cassatie 1997. – **German law**: Rebuttable presumption that the seller is at fault, § 437 n. 3, § 280(1) BGB; in practice there is no fault because the seller is under no duty to examine the thing sold, BGH 1968, 1981. – **Swiss law**: Distinctive feature: compensation for indirect damage is due only where the seller is at fault, see Art. 208(3) Code of obligations; BG 1953; SCHÖNLE; in practice: no fault as the seller is under no obligation to examine the thing sold, see SCHÖNLE. However, the damage in the case scenario is direct damage.

Scenario b) The seller would have discovered the defect in the goods had he carried out an examination

Seller liable	Seller not liable
– **French law** – **Belgian law** – **Swiss law** (for direct damage) – **English law** – **USA** – **Chinese law** – **CISG** – **PECL** – **UNIDROIT Principles**	– **German law**: no fault here either (§ 280(1) BGB) as, in general, the seller is not under a duty to examine the thing sold, see BGH 1968. – **Swiss law**: for indirect damage: liability for fault under Art. 208(3) Code of obligations; no fault as an intermediary is, as a rule, under no obligation to examine the thing sold, see SCHÖNLE; the damage in the scenario is, however, direct damage.

2. Systematic overview

Solution 1: Claim for damages independent of whether the seller is at fault.	*Solution 2*: Differentation according to the type of damage.	*Solution 3*: Claim for damages dependent on the seller being at fault (in relation to knowledge of the defect). There is a rebuttable presumption of fault.
– **French law** – **English law** – **USA** – **CISG** – **PECL and DCFR** – **UNIDROIT Principles**	Swiss law: – Seller's liability is independent of whether he is at fault with regard to direct damage, Art. 208(2) CO. – Liability for indirect damage where seller is at fault. Fault is presumed, Art. 208(3) CO.	– **German law** – **Belgian law**

3. Further reading

HUGH BEALE *et al.* (eds), *Cases, Materials and Text on Contract Law* (Ius Commune Casebooks for the Common Law of Europe), Oxford: Hart Publishing, 2002, Ch. 6.1, 659–74.

ALLAN FARNSWORTH, *Contracts*, 3rd edn, New York: Aspen Publishers, 2004, 534–35, 757–820.

JAMES GORDLEY, "The Foreseeability Limitation on Liability in Contract", in Arthur Hartkamp *et al.* (eds), *Towards a European Civil Code*, 3rd edn, Nijmegen: Kluwer, 2004, Ch. 12, 215–28.

OLE LANDO, "Non-Performance (Breach) of Contracts", in Arthur Hartkamp *et al.* (eds), *Towards a European Civil Code*, 3rd edn, Nijmegen: Kluwer, 2004, Ch. 28, 505–15.

KONRAD ZWEIGERT AND HEIN KÖTZ, *An Introduction to Comparative Law*, Oxford: Oxford University Press, 1998, 486–88 and 496–515.

For a detailed analysis, refer to GARETH JONES and PETER SCHLECHTRIEM, Breach of Contract, *Int.Enc.Com.L.*, Vol. VII/1, Tübingen: Mohr Siebeck, 2008, Chapter IV: Breach of Contract and Relevance of Fault.

Case 7: Termination or alteration of a contract in the event of a fundamental change of circumstances?

"Pacta sunt servanda"?

"A contract validly entered into is binding upon the parties. […]"[1]

Scenario

Jane, John and their son George book a two-week family holiday to Thailand for the following February. Three weeks before their trip, South-East Asia is devastated by a tsunami of unprecedented magnitude. Thailand is one of the worst affected countries. The family is informed by the travel agency that the city in Thailand the family is due to visit is only slightly affected. The hotel and beach resort remain intact. However, many of the inhabitants of the region, as well as many employees of the hotel, have lost family members who worked in the most devastated regions. The risk of there being another tsunami in the coming months is low.

The family is shaken by the devastation that took place in South-East Asia. The family no longer wants to take the trip as the inhabitants of the region are in shock and are mourning the deaths of thousands of their countrymen, and perhaps even family members who were in the worst affected areas when the disaster occurred. Under such circumstances, the family considers it inappropriate to take a vacation in one of the countries most heavily affected by the tsunami, and would find it impossible to relax and enjoy the stay.

The tour operator believes the family is bound by its travel contract given that neither the hotel nor the beach resort is affected by the tsunami and that there is no particular danger in the area. Also, following this catastrophe, Thailand will be in particular need of the income from the tourist industry to pay for its reconstruction. In any event, the tour operator thinks that he is entitled to compensation if the family does not go on holiday.

Is the family still bound by the contract? If so, can the family cancel its trip? In the event of a cancellation, will the family have to compensate the tour operator?

---

[1] International Institute for the Unification of Private Law (UNIDROIT): *Principles of International Commercial Contracts*, Art. 1.3 (Binding character of contract).

Questions

(1) What is the legal problem raised in this scenario? What are the interests involved? What principles are in conflict?

(2) Do the EU Directive on package travel, package holidays and package tours and the UNIDROIT International Convention on Travel Contracts provide a solution for such a case? What would be the legal position under the Directive if the tour operator had substituted Sri Lanka with another destination?

(3) What are the approaches to this problem taken in:
  (a) *Swiss* law,
  (b) *German* law,
  (c) *Austrian* law,
  (d) *Dutch* law, and,
  (e) the law of *Serbia*,
according to the special rules on travel contracts, and according to the general rules and the case law applicable in case of change of circumstances cited in the materials? What rules found in the legislation or case law of these legal orders offer a solution to this legal problem?

What arguments would you put forward if you were representing:
  (a) the tour operator
  (b) the family?

(4) In the materials below, you will find Article 388 of the *Greek* Civil Code and Article 1467 of the *Italian* Civil Code. Is the approach taken in these provisions limited in a situation such as the case scenario above? Compare these articles with Article 6:258 of the *Dutch* Civil Code, § 313 of the *German* Civil Code and Articles 133 ff. of the Law of Contract and Torts from *Serbia*.
  How has the issue been dealt with in the Italian case law and academic literature?

(5) The *French* Civil Code has its own particular approach to change of circumstances. What is different about French law? What is the reasoning behind the French approach, and what are its weaknesses? Under what conditions would a contracting party be freed from its contractual obligations under French law?

(6) What is *English* law's approach to changes of circumstances? (*Krell* v. *Henry* is one of the leading cases in England in this area.) What are the special features of this approach? How would the *Canal de Craponne* case be resolved under English law?

(7) What is the approach adopted in the Principles of European Contract Law, the UNIDROIT Principles, and the Draft Common Frame of Reference? Can the case scenario be resolved adequately through the application of Article 6:111 PECL, Articles 6.2.1 to 6.2.3 UNIDROIT Principles or Article III–1:110 of the Draft Common Frame of Reference?
  Compare these articles with the general provisions relating to change of circumstances in the national legal orders.

(8) Which rule would you suggest for responding to the problem of a fundamental change of circumstances?

Table of contents

I. EU Directive and UNIDROIT Principles

1. Council Directive of 13 June 1990 on package travel, package holidays and package tours (90/314/EEC), OJ L 158, 23/06/1990, pp. 59–64[2]

Art. 2

For the purposes of this Directive:

(1) 'package' means the pre-arranged combination of not fewer than two of the following when sold or offered for sale at an inclusive price and when the service covers a period of more than twenty-four hours or includes overnight accommodation:

    (a) transport;

    (b) accommodation;

    (c) other tourist services not ancillary to transport or accommodation and accounting for a

      significant proportion of the package.

    [...]

(2) 'organizer' means the person who, other than occasionally, organizes packages and sells or offers them for sale, whether directly or through a retailer;

(3) 'retailer' means the person who sells or offers for sale the package put together by the organizer;

(4) 'consumer' means the person who takes or agrees to take the package [...]

[...]

Art. 4

[...]

(3) Where the consumer is prevented from proceeding with the package, he may transfer his booking, having first given the organizer or the retailer reasonable notice of his intention before departure, to a person who satisfies all the conditions applicable to the package. The transferor of the package and the transferee shall be jointly and severally liable to the organizer or retailer party to the contract for payment of the balance due and for any additional costs arising from such transfer.

[...]

(5) If the organizer finds that before the departure he is constrained to alter significantly any of the essential terms, such as the price, he shall notify the consumer as quickly as possible in order to enable him to take appropriate decisions and in particular:

– either to withdraw from the contract without penalty,

---

[2] It should be noted that, in order to be applicable to a specific case, the Directive needs to be transposed into the national laws of the EU Member States.

– or to accept a rider to the contract specifying the alterations made and their impact on the price.

[...]

6.   If the consumer withdraws from the contract pursuant to paragraph 5, or if, for whatever cause, other than the fault of the consumer, the organizer cancels the package before the agreed date of departure, the consumer shall be entitled:

(a)   either to take a substitute package of equivalent or higher quality where the organizer and/or retailer is able to offer him such a substitute. If the replacement package offered is of lower quality, the organizer shall refund the difference in price to the consumer;

(b)   or to be repaid as soon as possible all sums paid by him under the contract.

In such a case, he shall be entitled, if appropriate, to be compensated by either the organizer or the retailer, whichever the relevant Member State's law requires, for non-performance of the contract, except where:

[...]

(ii)   cancellation, excluding overbooking, is for reasons of force majeure, i.e. unusual and unforeseeable circumstances beyond the control of the party by whom it is pleaded, the consequences of which could not have been avoided even if all due care had been exercised.

[...]

2. UNIDROIT: International Convention on Travel Contracts (CCV), Brussels, April 23, 1970[3]

SCOPE OF APPLICATION

Art. 2

(1)   This Convention shall apply to any travel contract concluded by a travel organizer or intermediary, where his principal place of business or, failing any such place of business, his habitual residence, or the place of business through which the travel contract has been concluded, is located in a Contracting State.

(2)   This Convention shall apply without prejudice to any special law establishing preferential treatment for certain categories of travellers.

---

[3]   Entry into force: 21.2.1976; in force in Argentina, Benin, Cameroon, Italy and Togo.

GENERAL OBLIGATIONS OF TRAVEL ORGANIZERS AND INTERMEDIARIES AND OF TRAVELLERS

Art. 3

In the performance of the obligations resulting from contracts defined in Article 1, the travel organizer and intermediary shall safeguard the rights and interests of the traveller according to general principles of law and good usages in this field.

Art. 8

Unless the parties agree otherwise, the traveller may substitute another person for the purpose of carrying out the contract provided that such person satisfies the specific requirements relating to the journey or sojourn, and that the traveller compensates the travel organizer for any expenditure caused by such substitution, including non-reimbursable sums payable to third parties.

Art. 9

The traveller may at any time cancel the contract in whole or in part, provided he compensates the organising travel agent in accordance with domestic law or the provisions of the contract.

Art. 10

(1) The travel organizer may, without indemnity, cancel the contract, in whole or in part, if before the contract or during its performance, circumstances of an exceptional character manifest themselves of which he could not have known at the time of conclusion of the contract, and which, had they been known to him at that time, would have given him valid reason not to conclude the contract.

[...]

(3)   In event of cancellation of the contract before its performance, the travel organizer shall refund in full any payments received from the traveller. [...]

Art. 16

The traveller shall be liable for any loss or damage caused by his wrongful acts or default to the travel organizer [...] as a consequence of non-compliance with the obligations incumbent upon him under this Convention or under contracts subject thereto, wrongful acts or default being assessed having regard to a traveller's normal behaviour.

II. Switzerland

1. Schweizerisches Bundesgesetz über Pauschalreisen vom 18. Juni 1993 (*Swiss Federal Act on Package Holidays, 18 June 1993*)

1. Abschnitt: Begriffe

Art. 1. Pauschalreise.
(1) Als Pauschalreise gilt die im voraus festgelegte Verbindung von mindestens zwei der folgenden Dienstleistungen, wenn diese Verbindung zu einem Gesamtpreis angeboten wird und länger als 24 Stunden dauert oder eine Übernachtung einschliesst:
   (a) Beförderung;
   (b) Unterbringung;
   (c) andere touristische Dienstleistungen, die nicht Nebenleistungen von Beförderung oder Unterbringung sind und einen beträchtlichen Teil der Gesamtleistung ausmachen.

[...]

Section 1: Definitions

Art. 1. *Package holidays.*
(1) Package holiday means the pre-arranged combination of at least two of the following services when sold at a total price and when the service covers a period of more than twenty-four hours or includes overnight accommodation:
   (a) transport;
   (b) accommodation;
   (c) other tourist services not ancillary to transport or accommodation and accounting for a significant proportion of the package.

[...]

6. Abschnitt: Wesentliche Vertragsänderungen

Art. 8. Begriff.
(1) Als wesentliche Vertragsänderung gilt jede erhebliche Änderung eines wesentlichen Vertragspunktes, welche der Veranstalter vor dem Abreisetermin vornimmt.
(2) Eine Preiserhöhung von mehr als zehn Prozent gilt als wesentliche Vertragsänderung.

Section 6: Material change of the contract

Art. 8. *Definition.*
(1) Material change of the contract means all significant changes to an essential element of the contract made by the tour operator before the departure date.
(2) An increase in price of more than 10 percent is considered to be a material change of the contract.

Art. 10. Konsumentenrechte.

(1) Der Konsument kann eine wesentliche Vertragsänderung annehmen oder ohne Entschädigung vom Vertrag zurücktreten.

(2) Er teilt den Rücktritt vom Vertrag dem Veranstalter oder dem Vermittler so bald wie möglich mit.

(3) Tritt der Konsument vom Vertrag zurück, so hat er Anspruch:

    (a) auf Teilnahme an einer anderen gleichwertigen oder höherwertigen Pauschalreise, wenn der Veranstalter oder der Vermittler ihm eine solche anbieten kann;

    (b) auf Teilnahme an einer anderen minderwertigen Pauschalreise sowie auf Rückerstattung des Preisunterschieds; oder

    (c) auf schnellstmögliche Rückerstattung aller von ihm bezahlten Beträge.

(4) Vorbehalten bleibt der Anspruch auf Schadenersatz wegen Nichterfüllung des Vertrages.

Art. 10. Consumers' rights

(1) A consumer can accept a material change to the contract or withdraw from the contract without compensation.

(2) The consumer shall inform the tour operator or the retailer as soon as possible.

(3) Where the consumer withdraws from the contract, he is entitled to:

    (a) a substitute package holiday of equivalent or higher quality if the organiser or retailer can offer him one;

    (b) a substitute package holiday of lower quality as well as a refund of the difference in price; or

    (c) a refund of all sums paid as soon as possible.

(4) The consumer reserves the right to claim damages for breach of contract.

9. Abschnitt: Abtretung der Buchung der Pauschalreise

Art. 17

(1) Ist der Konsument daran gehindert, die Pauschalreise anzutreten, so kann er die Buchung an eine Person abtreten, die alle an die Teilnahme geknüpften Bedingungen erfüllt, wenn er zuvor den Veranstalter oder den Vermittler innert angemessener Frist vor dem Abreisetermin darüber informiert.

(2) Diese Person und der Konsument haften dem Veranstalter oder dem Vermittler, der Vertragspartei ist, solidarisch für die Zahlung des Preises sowie für die gegebenenfalls durch diese Abtretung entstehenden Mehrkosten.

Section 9: Transfer of the booking of the package holiday

Art. 17

(1) If the consumer is prevented from taking the package holiday, he may transfer his booking, having first given the organiser or the retailer reasonable notice of his intention before the departure date, to a person who satisfies all the conditions applicable to the package holiday.

(2) This person and the consumer shall be jointly and severally liable to the organiser or retailer party to the contract for the payment of the price as well as for any additional costs arising from such transfer.

2. Luc Thévenoz and Franz Werro (eds), Commentaire Romand, *Code des obligations*, Vol. I (comment by Bernd Stauder) (translation of the French original)

Art. 17 of the Swiss Federal Act on Package Holidays

[...]

III.   Requirements

[…]

6   The law requires that the consumer be **prevented** from taking the holiday. This requirement is supposed to limit the consumer's right to cases where he would be unable to go (sickness, accident, professional obligations, etc.) and exclude the right where the consumer simply changes his mind. If the unforeseen difficulty has to be interpreted objectively (impossibility to go), a consumer who does not want to travel would not have the right to transfer the holiday to someone else. In such an event, the general rule of Art. 377 of the Code of obligations would be applicable and the consumer would have to compensate the tour operator. […]

3. Schweizerisches Obligationenrecht (*Swiss Code of Obligations*)[4]

Der Werkvertrag

The Work Contract

Art. 373.   Höhe der Vergütung. Feste Übernahme.
(1)   Wurde die Vergütung zum voraus genau bestimmt, so ist der Unternehmer verpflichtet, das Werk um diese Summe fertigzustellen, und darf keine Erhöhung fordern, selbst wenn er mehr Arbeit oder grössere Auslagen gehabt hat, als vorgesehen war.
(2)   Falls jedoch ausserordentliche Umstände, die nicht vorausgesehen werden konnten oder die nach den von beiden Beteiligten angenommenen Voraussetzungen ausgeschlossen waren, die Fertigstellung hindern oder übermässig erschweren, so kann der Richter nach seinem Ermessen eine Erhöhung des Preises oder die Auflösung des Vertrages bewilligen.
(3)   Der Besteller hat auch dann den vollen Preis zu bezahlen, wenn die Fertigstellung des Werkes weniger Arbeit verursacht, als vorgesehen war.

---

[4]   Translation by Swiss-American Chamber of Commerce.

Art. 373.   Amount of Compensation. Fixed Price.
(1)   If the compensation has been precisely stipulated in advance, the contractor is obligated to complete the work for this sum and may not claim an increase even if he had more labour or larger expenditures than had been foreseen.
(2)   If, however, extraordinary circumstances which could not have been foreseen or which were excluded from the assumptions made by the parties, impede the completion or render it exceedingly difficult, the judge may, at his discretion, authorise an increase of the price or dissolution of the contract.
(3)   The principal shall also pay the full price if the completion of the work has caused less labour than had been foreseen.

Art. 377.   Rücktritt des Bestellers gegen Schadloshaltung.
Solange das Werk unvollendet ist, kann der Besteller gegen Vergütung der bereits geleisteten Arbeit und gegen volle Schadloshaltung des Unternehmers jederzeit vom Vertrag zurücktreten.

Art. 377.   Withdrawal of the principal against indemnification.
As long as the work is incomplete, the principal may withdraw at any time from the contract against compensation for the labour already performed and against full indemnification of the contractor.

4. Schweizerisches Zivilgesetzbuch (*Swiss Civil Code*)

Art. 2.   Inhalt der Rechtsverhältnisse. Handeln nach Treu und Glauben.
(1)   Jedermann hat in der Ausübung seiner Rechte und in der Erfüllung seiner Pflichten nach Treu und Glauben zu handeln.
[...]

Art. 2.   Content of relationships. Acting in good faith
(1)   Each person shall be required to exercise his rights and fulfil his duties in good faith.
[...]

5. Tribunal fédéral suisse (*Swiss Federal Court*) 4.5.1922, ATF 48 II 242

Arrêt de la 1ʳᵉ Section civile du 4 mai 1922
dans la cause
Segessemann & Cie contre **Dreyfus Frères & Cie.**

4. — [...] Bien que le droit suisse positif ne connaisse pas, comme cause générale d'extinction des obligations contractuelles, la *clausula rebus sic stantibus*, le législateur ne

s'est pas dissimulé cependant qu'il existe des cas où les changements qui se sont produits depuis que l'engagement a été contracté doivent avoir pour effet de rendre caduc cet engagement, quand bien même aucune des causes reconnues d'extinction des obligations ne se trouvent réalisées (cf. 373, 352, 545 CO) et la jurisprudence du Tribunal fédéral (RO **45** 2 N° 60 cons. 5; **46** 2 N° 75; **47** 2 N° 54) comme aussi la jurisprudence allemande (Entscheidungen des Reichsgerichts vol. 100, N^OS 38 et 39) a admis que si dans la règle celui qui a conclu un contrat assume les risques d'une transformation préjudiciable des conditions d'exécution, il peut en être autrement lorsque des événements exceptionnels, et qui ne pouvaient être prévus, ont pour conséquence de rendre l'exécution du contrat si onéreuse pour le débiteur que le maintien de l'obligation conduirait à sa ruine. Dans ce dernier cas, il est non seulement conforme à l'équité de le libérer d'un engagement contracté dans des conditions toutes différentes, mais même au point de vue juridique cela se justifie, soit qu'on fasse appel aux règles de la bonne foi, soit qu'on admette une impossibilité relative d'exécution non imputable au débiteur, soit enfin qu'on applique par analogie les dispositions légales relatives au droit de se départir de certains contrats. Mais [...] ce n'est qu'à titre tout à fait exceptionnel que la *clausula rebus sic stantibus* peut être appliquée en droit suisse. Il est dans l'esprit général du CO de s'en tenir à l'adage *pacta sunt servanda* et une application par analogie de l'article 373, al. 2 CO à d'autres contrats doit se faire avec une extrême prudence si l'on ne veut porter une sérieuse atteinte à la sécurité des transactions.

Translation

Decision of the 1st Civil Section, 4 May 1922
in the case
Segessemann & Cie v. *Dreyfus Frères & Cie.*

4. — [...] Although substantive Swiss law does not recognise the *clausula rebus sic stantibus* as a general basis for the termination of contractual obligations, the legislator has not however closed its eyes to the fact that there are cases in which changes that have occurred since the agreement was made should make the agreement void, even when none of the recognised reasons for termination are fulfilled (cf. 373, 352, 545 CO) and the Federal Court's case law [...] like German case law [...] accepted that even though, in general, the person who made the contract takes on the risk of any detrimental change of the conditions of performance, the situation is different when exceptional and unforeseeable circumstances make performance of the contract so onerous for the debtor that maintaining the obligation would lead to his financial ruin. In such a case, it is not only in keeping with equity to free him from an agreement concluded under completely different circumstances, but also, from a legal point of view, it is justified by either appealing to the rules of good faith, or admitting the relative impossibility of performance not attributable to the debtor, or lastly by admitting that the provisions on the right to withdraw from certain contracts apply by analogy. However [...] it is only in very exceptional circumstances that the *clausula rebus sic stantibus* can be used in Swiss law. The general spirit of the Code of obligations is to stick to the adage *pacta sunt servanda* and the application by analogy of Article 373 (2) CO to other contracts must be done with extreme care to avoid a serious attack on the security of transactions.

III.   Germany

1. Bürgerliches Gesetzbuch, BGB
(*German Civil Code*)

Reisevertrag

Travel contracts

§ 651 e.   Kündigung wegen Mangels.

[...]

(3)   Wird der Vertrag gekündigt, so verliert der Reiseveranstalter den Anspruch auf den vereinbarten Reisepreis. Er kann jedoch für die bereits erbrachten [...] Reiseleistungen eine [...] Entschädigung verlangen. [...]

§ 651 e.   Termination for defect.

[...]

(3)   If the contract is terminated, the tour operator loses the right to be paid the agreed package price. The tour operator can, however, claim damages [...] for services already provided. [...]

§ 651 i.   Rücktritt vor Reisebeginn.
(1)   Vor Reisebeginn kann der Reisende jederzeit vom Vertrag zurücktreten.
(2)   Tritt der Reisende vom Vertrag zurück, so verliert der Reiseveranstalter den Anspruch auf den vereinbarten Reisepreis. Er kann jedoch eine angemessene Entschädigung verlangen. Die Höhe der Entschädigung bestimmt sich nach dem Reisepreis unter Abzug des Wertes der vom Reiseveranstalter ersparten Aufwendungen sowie dessen, was er durch anderweitige Verwendung der Reiseleistung erwerben kann.
(3)   Im Vertrag kann für jede Reiseart unter Berücksichtigung der gewöhnlich ersparten Aufwendungen und des durch anderweitige Verwendung der Reiseleistungen gewöhnlich möglichen Erwerbs ein Vomhundertsatz des Reisepreises als Entschädigung festgesetzt werden.

§ 651 i.   Withdrawal prior to the commencement of travel.
(1)   Prior to the commencement of travel, the traveller can, at any time, withdraw from the contract.
(2)   If the traveller withdraws from the contract, the tour operator therefore loses the right to payment of the agreed price of the package. However, the tour operator can demand some compensation. The amount of compensation is determined by the price of the travel package minus the value of the expenditure saved by the tour operator and what he can earn from the alternative deployment of the travel services.
(3)   The contract may, for each type of trip, taking into account the usual expenditure saved and the profit that can usually be made from an alternative deployment of the travel services, specify a percentage of the package price as compensation.

§ 651 j. Kündigung wegen höherer Gewalt.
(1) Wird die Reise infolge bei Vertragsabschluss nicht voraussehbarer höherer Gewalt erheblich erschwert, gefährdet oder beeinträchtigt, so können sowohl der Reiseveranstalter als auch der Reisende den Vertrag allein nach Maßgabe dieser Vorschrift kündigen.
(2) Wird der Vertrag nach Absatz 1 gekündigt, so findet die Vorschrift des § 651 e Abs. 3 Satz 1 und 2 […] Anwendung. Die Mehrkosten für die Rückbeförderung sind von den Parteien je zur Hälfte zu tragen. Im Übrigen fallen die Mehrkosten dem Reisenden zur Last.

§ 651 j. Termination for force majeure.
(1) If, through force majeure, the travel package is substantially obstructed, jeopardised or impaired, the tour operator or traveller can terminate the contract by the simple application of this provision.
(2) If the contract is terminated pursuant to paragraph 1, the provisions of § 651 e(3) sentences 1 and 2 […] apply. The parties each bear half of the additional costs of return transport. Other additional costs are payable by the traveller.

2. Landgericht Köln (*Cologne Court*) 28.3.2001 ("Earthquake in Mexico" case), NJW-RR 2001, 1064

LG Köln, Urt. v. 28. 3. 2001 – 10 S 395/00

Zum Sachverhalt: Die Kläger, die bei der Beklagten eine am 9.10.1999 beginnende Rundreise durch Mexiko gebucht hatten, haben mit Schreiben vom 8.10.1999 ihren Rücktritt von der Reise unter Hinweis auf die Regenfälle, Überschwemmungen und Erdbeben in Mexiko erklärt. Die Beklagte hat bei der Rückerstattung des Reisepreises 90% des Preises als Stornokosten einbehalten. […]

Aus den Gründen: […] Die Kläger waren zwar auf Grund des § 651 i I BGB berechtigt, jederzeit vor Reisebeginn vom Vertrag zurückzutreten, jedoch hat dies gemäß § 651 i II 2, III BGB grundsätzlich zur Folge, dass der Reiseveranstalter eine angemessene Entschädigung in Höhe der […] vereinbarten Stornogebühren verlangen kann. Einen derartigen Anspruch hat die Beklagte auch geltend gemacht und lediglich einen geringen Teil des bereits vollständig entrichteten Reisepreises zurückgezahlt. Eine grundsätzlich vollständige Befreiung von der Verpflichtung zur Entrichtung einer Entschädigung kommt hingegen nur in Betracht, falls den Klägern gemäß § 651 j BGB ein Kündigungsrecht wegen höherer Gewalt zustand, denn einen Entschädigungsanspruch im Sinne der §§ 651 j II, 651 e III 2 BGB hat die Beklagte jedenfalls nicht substantiiert dargetan.
  Ein Kündigungsrecht gemäß § 651 j BGB bestand jedoch nicht, denn es fehlt zumindest an der erforderlichen konkreten Gefahr für die Durchführbarkeit der Reise im Zeitpunkt der Kündigungserklärung.

Ein Fall höherer Gewalt in dem von § 651 j BGB vorausgesetzten Sinne liegt […] in einem von außen kommenden, unabwendbaren und unverschuldeten Ereignis […]. Heftige Regenfälle, Überschwemmungen und Erdbeben – wie sie circa eine Woche vor dem geplanten Reiseantritt in Mexiko aufgetreten waren – sind auch grundsätzlich als Fälle höherer Gewalt in diesem Sinne einzustufen. Erforderlich ist jedoch ferner, dass durch die höhere Gewalt eine *konkrete* Gefahr für die Durchführbarkeit der Reise entstand; subjektive Befürchtungen einzelner Reisender reichen insoweit nicht aus.

Abflugtermin sollte erst der 9.10.1999 sein. Zu diesem Zeitpunkt kam es jedenfalls nicht mehr zu weiteren heftigen Regenfällen; auch ein weiteres Erdbeben wurde nicht gemeldet. Dafür, dass weitere Unwetter bzw. Erdbeben unmittelbar bevorstanden, ist auch nichts dargetan. Im Zeitpunkt des Antritts der Reise lagen auch keine fortwirkenden erheblichen Gefährdungen bzw. Erschwerungen infolge der vorausgegangenen Naturereignisse – beispielsweise in Form von Überschwemmungen – vor. Zumindest objektiv gab es bei der Durchführung der Reise – wie auch der tatsächliche Ablauf der Ereignisse zeigt – keinerlei Schwierigkeiten. Die durch vorhergehende äußere Ereignisse und Pressemeldungen veranlassten Befürchtungen der Kläger reichten jedoch nicht aus, um gleichwohl ein Kündigungsrecht im Sinne des § 651 j BGB zu begründen.

[…] Da die Kläger als Pauschalreisende in Hotels untergebracht worden wären, dürfte sie die beklagenswerte Obdachlosigkeit von Teilen der Bevölkerung ebenso wenig tangiert haben wie eine mögliche Seuchengefahr. […]

[…]

Die Kläger können sich damit lediglich auf ihr allgemeines Kündigungsrecht gemäß § 651 i BGB berufen. Dies hat zur Folge, dass die Beklagte gemäß § 651 i III BGB für die bereits erbrachten Leistungen eine angemessene Entschädigung verlangen kann. Dies hat die Beklagte […] getan und unter Berufung auf die Allgemeinen Geschäftsbedingungen 90% des Reisepreises als Entschädigung einbehalten.

[…] Je kürzer die Zeit zwischen der Rücktrittserklärung des Kunden und dem geplanten Reiseantritt ist, desto geringer sind die wirtschaftlichen Dispositionsmöglichkeiten des Reiseveranstalters für eine anderweitige Verwendung der für den Kunden vorgesehenen Reiseplätze […]

[D]ie Vereinbarung einer Pauschale von 90% für den Fall des Rücktritts innerhalb von zwei Wochen vor Reisebeginn [ist] nicht zu beanstanden.

Translation

Facts: The claimants, who had booked a tour of Mexico beginning 9.10.1999 with the defendant on 8.10.1999, informed the defendant in writing of their withdrawal from the travel package with reference to the rain, flooding and earthquake in Mexico. Upon reimbursement, the defendant retained 90% of the price of the trip as a cancellation fee. […]

Reasons: […] Although the claimants are, pursuant to § 651 i (1) BGB, authorised to withdraw from the contract at any time prior to the commencement of travel, this means, in general, according to § 651 i (2) sentence 2, (3) BGB, that the tour operator can claim compensation up to […] the sum agreed upon as a cancellation fee. The defendant asserted such a claim and only reimbursed a minimal part of the price of the trip already paid in its entirety. Release, generally complete, from the obligation to pay compensation only becomes a possibility if the claimant has the right to terminate the contract for force majeure pursuant to § 651 j BGB as the defendant has, in any case, not substantially presented a claim for compensation in the sense of § 651 j (2) and 651 e (3) sentence 2 BGB.

There was, however, no right to terminate the contract by virtue of § 651 j BGB as there was no concrete danger to the performance of the travel package at the moment termination was declared.

There is force majeure in the sense of § 651 j BGB […] where there is an external, unavoidable event attributable to no-one […] Heavy rain, floods and an earthquake, like those that occurred in Mexico approximately one week before the planned commencement of travel, are events which should generally be considered to be cases of force majeure in this way. However, it is also necessary for a *concrete* danger to the performance of the travel package to result from the force majeure. The subjective fears of an isolated traveller are not enough.

Departure should only have been on 9.10.1999. However, at that time, the heavy rain had stopped and no other earthquake had been reported. Furthermore, there was no immediate indication that more bad weather or another earthquake were going to recur.

At the commencement of travel, there were no more threats of natural disaster nor was there any significant worsening of the situation following the natural disasters that had occurred, such as, for example, the floods. From an objective point of view at least, as can be seen by the actual course of events, there was no difficulty for the trip to take place. The claimant's fears caused by the previous events and by the information disseminated by the press are not, however, enough upon which to base a right to withdraw from the contract in the sense of § 651 j BGB.

[…] As the claimant was in hotel accommodation as part of a package holiday, the fact that a part of the population is homeless should not affect him, particularly with regards to the possible danger of an epidemic […]

[…] The claimants can thus only base their claim on the general right to withdraw in § 651 i (3) BGB. The consequence of this is that the defendant can, by virtue of § 651 i (3) BGB, demand compensation for the service already provided. That is what the defendant […] did and, by referring to the general terms of business, he retained 90% of the sale price as compensation.

[…] The shorter the time between the client's withdrawal and the commencement of travel, the less chance the tour operator has to deploy the travel services alternatively […].

[The] agreement stipulating a fixed rate of 90% in cases of withdrawal in the two weeks preceding the commencement of travel [is] not open to criticism.

3. Amtsgericht Dachau (*Dachau Court of First Instance*), 22.11.2005 ("Tsunami" case), RRa 2006, 78

AG Dachau, Urt. v. 22.11.2005 – 3 C 687/05

Entscheidungsgründe

Die Klägerin hat Anspruch auf die geltend gemachte Entschädigung in Höhe der in

Ziffer 5) ihrer Allgemeinen Geschäftsbedingungen geregelten Stornogebühren, nämlich 15% des ursprünglichen Reisepreises von 3.300.- EUR, somit in Höhe von 495.- EUR.

[...] Dem Klageanspruch kann nicht mit Erfolg entgegen gehalten werden, dass der Beklagte den Vertrag mit Schreiben vom 3.1.2005 stornierte.

Zwar kann der Beklagte gemäss § 651i BGB berechtigt, jederzeit vor Reiseantritt vom Vertrag zurücktreten, jedoch hat dies gemäss § 651i Abs. 2 Satz 2, Abs. 3 BGB zur Folge, dass der Reiseveranstalter eine angemessene Entschädigung in Höhe der durch Allgemeine Geschäftsbedingungen vereinbarten Stornogebühren verlangen kann. Einen derartigen Anspruch macht die Klägerin im vorliegenden Fall geltend.

Auf ein Kündigungsrecht gemäss § 651j BGB wegen höherer Gewalt kann sich der Beklagte nicht berufen, denn es fehlt an der erforderlichen konkreten Gefahr für die Durchführbarkeit der Reise im Zeitpunkt der Kündigungserklärung.

Die zu Weihnachten 2004 eingetretene Flutkatastrophe, die auch das vom Beklagten gebuchte Reiseziel betraf, ist als Fall höherer Gewalt in dem von § 651j BGB vorausgesetzten Sinne eines von aussen kommenden, unabwendbaren und unverschuldeten Ereignisses einzustufen; erforderlich ist jedoch ferner, dass durch die höhere Gewalt eine konkrete Gefahr für die Durchführbarkeit der Reise bestand. Die blossen subjektiven Befürchtungen des Beklagten und seiner Reisebegleiter reichen insoweit nicht aus.

Es kann letztlich dahingestellt bleiben, ob eine konkrete Gefahr für die Durchführbarkeit der Reise zum Zeitpunkt des Eintritts der Flutkatastrophe bestand, ob also das vom Beklagten gebuchte Hotel und die Region von der Flutkatastrophe betroffen waren, denn darauf kommt es letztlich nicht an. Massgeblich ist vielmehr der Zeitpunkt des Beginns der geplanten Reise und zu dem Zeitpunkt bestand eine derartige konkrete Gefahr jedenfalls nicht mehr.

Abflugtermin sollte der 20.2.2005 sein. Bis zu diesem Zeitpunkt kam es nicht zu weiteren Überflutungen und der Beklagte hat auch nicht dargetan, dass zu diesem Zeitpunkt noch fortwirkende erhebliche Gefährdungen, bzw. Erschwerungen in Folge der vorausgegangenen Naturkatastrophe vorgelegen hätten.

Die Klägerin trug vielmehr vor, dass die vom Beklagten gebuchte Rundreise im Land durchgeführt werden konnte und weder das Hotel noch die Infrastruktur der Region durch die Flutwelle beeinträchtigt worden seien. Gegenteiliges wurde vom insoweit beweisbelasteten Beklagten nicht substantiiert vorgetragen und nicht nachgewiesen.

Die durch die vorhergehenden äusseren Ereignisse und Pressemeldungen zwar nachvollziehbaren Befürchtungen des Beklagten reichen nicht aus, ein Kündigungsrecht im Sinne von § 651j BGB zu begründen, denn es kommt auf den Zeitablauf an, der zwischen dem Ereignis und dem Reisebeginn liegt. Je länger ein Naturereignis zurückliegt, desto mehr müssen derartige Befürchtungen zurücktreten. Ferner muss sich der Reisende gegebenenfalls auf Informationen des Reiseveranstalters dazu verweisen lassen, inwieweit bei Reisebeginn noch mit Beeinträchtigungen zu rechnen sein mag und damit korrespondierend besteht die Verpflichtung des Reiseveranstalters, sich über die Lage vor Ort zu informieren. Grundsätzlich ist bei Naturkatastrophen jedenfalls davon auszugehen, dass deren Folgen schneller abklingen als etwa politische Gefahrenlagen.

Nachdem seit der Naturkatastrophe bis zum Reiseantritt mehr als sieben Wochen verstrichen waren, konnte damit gerechnet werden, dass – selbst wenn im Reisegebiet Beeinträchtigungen bestanden – diese beseitigt waren bis zum Reiseantritt. Dem

Beklagten war es zuzumuten, auf die Informationen des Reiseveranstalters über die Durchführbarkeit der geplanten Reise zu vertrauen.

Der Beklagte kann sich daher lediglich auf sein allgemeines Kündigungsrecht gemäss § 651i BGB berufen und schuldet deshalb die geltend gemachte Entschädigung in Höhe der durch wirksame Einbeziehung der Allgemeinen Geschäftsbedingungen der Klägerin vereinbarten Stornogebühren.

[...]

Translation

The claimant has a right to compensation of the amount specified in subsection (5) of their general business conditions for the regular cancellation fee, namely 15% of the initial package price of 3300 euros, consequently the amount of 495 euros.

[...] The defendant cannot successfully counter the claim by advancing that he terminated the contract in writing on 3.1.2005.

Admittedly, the defendant can, at any time before the commencement of travel, legitimately, in accordance with § 651i BGB, withdraw from the contract; however this has the result that the tour operator can demand reasonable compensation of the amount agreed upon as the cancellation fee in the general business conditions. The claimant makes such a demand in the present case.

The claimant cannot refer to a right to terminate the contract in accordance with § 651j BGB because of the lack of the requisite concrete danger to the practicability of the trip at the time of the notice to terminate being given.

At Christmas 2004, the destination booked by the defendant was affected by a flood disaster, an act of god as in § 651j BGB, which is classified as an outside event for which no-one is to blame; [in order for § 651j BGB to apply,] it is however necessary for there to be a concrete danger to the practicability of the trip. The merely subjective fears of the defendant and his travelling companion are not sufficient in this respect.

Ultimately, it is unimportant to assess whether there was a concrete danger to the practicability of the trip at the time of the flood disaster and also, whether the hotel booked and the region were affected because, in the end, it does not depend on this. What is decisive is rather the time of the beginning of the planned trip and at the time there was certainly no longer such a concrete danger.

The departure date should have been 20.2.2005. There was no further flooding before this date and the defendant has not demonstrated that, at this time, there continued to be a considerable threat, that is, an impediment [to the trip] as a consequence of the preceding natural disaster.

The claimant, on the contrary, expressed that the tour booked for the defendant was possible and that neither the hotel nor the region's infrastructure had been damaged by the tidal wave. In this respect, evidence to the contrary has not been substantially demonstrated or proven by the defendant.

The defendant's fears, though admittedly comprehensible due to the prior events and press reports, are not sufficient upon which to base a right of termination under § 651j BGB, because this depends on the lapse of time between the event and the commencement of travel. The further back in time a natural event occurred, the more such fears subside. Furthermore, the traveller would be required, if applicable, to ask the tour operator if there were still any adverse effects and the tour operator would be under the corresponding obligation to find out about the situation in the place of destination. In principle, the effects of a natural disaster subside quicker than a political situation.

More than seven weeks passed between the natural disaster and the beginning of the trip, it can therefore be estimated, that – except if there are adverse effects in the area in which the trip is to take place – there would be no problem preventing the trip from going ahead. The defendant was expected to trust the tour operator's information on the feasibility of the planned trip.

The defendant is therefore referred to the general right to withdraw from the contract in accordance with § 651i BGB and for that reason owes the requested compensation of the amount that was effectively included in the claimant's general terms of business as the agreed cancellation fee.

[...]

4. Bürgerliches Gesetzbuch, BGB
(*German Civil Code*)

Anpassung und Beendigung von Verträgen

Adaptation and termination of contracts

§ 313. Störung der Geschäftsgrundlage[5]

(1) Haben sich Umstände, die zur Grundlage des Vertrags geworden sind, nach Vertragsschluss schwerwiegend verändert und hätten die Parteien den Vertrag nicht oder mit anderem Inhalt geschlossen, wenn sie diese Veränderung vorausgesehen hätten, so kann Anpassung des Vertrags verlangt werden, soweit einem Teil unter Berücksichtigung aller Umstände des Einzelfalls, insbesondere der vertraglichen oder gesetzlichen Risikoverteilung, das Festhalten am unveränderten Vertrag nicht zugemutet werden kann.

(2) Einer Veränderung der Umstände steht es gleich, wenn wesentliche Vorstellungen, die zur Grundlage des Vertrags geworden sind, sich als falsch herausstellen.

(3) Ist eine Anpassung des Vertrags nicht möglich oder einem Teil nicht zumutbar, so kann der benachteiligte Teil vom Vertrag zurücktreten. An die Stelle des Rücktrittsrechts tritt für Dauerschuldverhältnisse das Recht zur Kündigung.

§ 313. *Interference with the basis of the contract*

(1) If circumstances upon which a contract was based have materially changed after conclusion of the contract and if the parties would not have concluded the contract or would have done so upon different terms if they had foreseen that change, adaptation of the contract may be claimed in so far as, having regard to all the circumstances of the specific case, in particular the contractual or statutory allocation of risk, it cannot reasonably be expected that a party should continue to be bound by the contract in its unaltered form.

---

[5] In cases not falling within the scope of § 651j BGB, recourse can be had to the general rule of § 313 BGB.

(2)   *If material assumptions that have become the basis of the contract subsequently turn out to be incorrect, they are treated in the same way as a change in circumstances.*

(3)   *If adaptation of the contract is not possible or cannot reasonably be imposed on one party, the disadvantaged party may terminate the contract. In the case of a contract for the performance of a recurring obligation, the right to terminate is replaced by the right to terminate on notice.*

IV.   Austria

The Austrian legislator transposed Directive 90/314/CEE into Austrian law in a law on consumer protection (*Konsumentenschutzgesetz*). The legislator did not introduce a consumer right to withdraw from a travel contract which would go further than what is provided for in the Directive. The doctrine of "variation of contract in case of change of circumstances" is recognised by the Austrian Supreme Court of Justice in a constant line of case law. After the September 11 terrorist attacks, the court decided as shown in the following extract.

Österreichischer Oberster Gerichtshof (*Austrian Supreme Court of Justice*) 26.8.2004 ("11. September 2001"), 6Ob145/04y, RIS-Justiz, RS 0111961

OGH 26. August 2004, 6 Ob 145/04 y

Mag. Rupert L***** hatte bei der Beklagten über ein Reisebüro für die Zeit vom 2. bis 11.10.2001 eine Reise von Salzburg nach New York und Chicago gebucht. Aufgrund der durch die Terroranschläge vom 11.9.2001 in den USA veränderten Lage stornierte er am 15.9.2001 diese Privatreise. Die Beklagte zahlte einen Teil des Entgelts zurück, behielt aber eine "Stornogebühr" [in Höhe von 487 Euro] zurück. Mag. Rupert L. trat seinen Rückforderungsanspruch an den klagenden Verband ab. Dieser stützt das Zahlungsbegehren seiner Klage vom 21.8.2002 im Wesentlichen darauf, dass wegen der Terroranschläge in den USA die Geschäftsgrundlage für die Reise weggefallen sei. Die Kriegserklärung einer islamistischen Terrororganisation habe sich gegen das ganze Land gerichtet. Über die Ereignisse und die künftigen Sicherheitsrisiken sei in den Medien breit berichtet worden. Der Antritt der Reise sei für den Kunden der Beklagten unzumutbar geworden.

Die Beklagte beantragte die Abweisung des Klagebegehrens. [...] Die Terroranschläge hätten sich nicht gegen touristische Ziele gerichtet. Ab dem 26.9.2001 habe es für Reisende in die USA keine unzumutbaren Beeinträchtigungen gegeben. Es habe regulärer Flugbetrieb geherrscht.

Das **Erstgericht** wies das Klagebegehren ab. [...] Das **Berufungsgericht** gab der Berufung des Klägers nicht Folge. [...] Die Terroranschläge vom 11.9.2001 hätten sich an einem einzigen Tag ereignet, woran sich massive Sicherheitsvorkehrungen angeschlossen hätten, sodass eine ernsthafte Bedrohungslage nicht mehr gegeben gewesen sei. Reisen nach dem 26.9.2001 seien ohne Behinderungen möglich gewesen [...]

Aus der Begründung:

Die Revision ist zulässig und berechtigt.

[...] Zum Wegfall der Geschäftsgrundlage als Anspruchsbasis für einen kostenlosen Rücktritt vom Reisevertrag wurde in den beiden einschlägigen Vorentscheidungen 8 Ob

99/99p = SZ 72/95 und 1 Ob 257/01b = ZVR 2003, 58/19, in denen es ebenfalls um Terroranschläge ging, anerkannt, dass das nur als subsidiäres und letztes Mittel aufzufassende Institut des Wegfalls der Geschäftsgrundlage unter gewissen Voraussetzungen einer Partei es ermöglicht, sich von rechtsgeschäftlichen Bindungen zu lösen. Von den Parteien des Reisevertrags nicht voraussehbare Erschwerungen, Gefährdungen oder Beeinträchtigungen der Reise können zum Rücktritt berechtigen, wenn die Reise für den Kunden unzumutbar geworden ist. Wann dies der Fall ist, hängt grundsätzlich von den Umständen des Einzelfalls ab. Wenn es sich nur um vereinzelte Anschläge handelt, mögen sie auch terroristischer Natur sein, steht kein Rücktrittsrecht zu. Die Anschläge müssen eine Intensität erreichen, die unter Anlegung eines durchschnittlichen Maßstabes als Konkretisierung einer unzumutbaren Gefahr derartiger künftiger Anschläge erscheint. Nur dann berechtigen sie zur Auflösung des Vertrages wegen Wegfalls der Geschäftsgrundlage. [...] Es ist zu fragen, wie ein durchschnittlicher, also weder ein besonders mutiger, noch ein besonders ängstlicher Reisender die künftige Entwicklung an dem in Aussicht genommenen Urlaubsziel beurteilt hätte. [...]

Die Intensität der Terroranschläge hatten eine historische Dimension, die selbst bei mutigen, jedenfalls aber bei sogenannten "Durchschnittsreisenden" Angstgefühle auslösten. Vor der Gefahr weiterer Anschläge wurde nahezu in allen Medien mit plausiblen Gründen [...] gewarnt. Die Urheberschaft der Anschläge war nicht näher geklärt. Zum Zeitpunkt der Rücktrittserklärung am 15.9.2001 war nicht damit zu rechnen, in absehbarer Zeit ein verlässliches Bild über die Gefährdungslage zu erhalten. Die Rücktrittserklärung des Kunden war nicht diejenige einer besonders ängstlichen Person. [...] An dieser Beurteilung vermögen auch die vom Berufungsgericht hervorgehobenen Umstände, dass massive Sicherheitsvorkehrungen in den USA getroffen wurden und dass sich dadurch das Sicherheitsrisiko verringert habe, nichts zu ändern. Dem ist entgegen zu halten, dass nach erfolgten Terroranschlägen im betroffenen Land jeweils die Sicherheitsmaßnahmen verstärkt werden, dass dadurch aber weitere Anschläge nicht verhindert werden können. Insbesondere der Flugverkehr kann nicht vollständig gesichert werden; es ist unmöglich, alle sogenannten "weichen Ziele" in Großstädten zu bewachen und vor Terror zu schützen. Es ist gerade die neue Dimension der Anschläge vom 11.9.2001, dass es trotz der weltweiten Sicherheitskontrollen auf Flughäfen gelungen ist, vier Flugzeuge im amerikanischen Luftraum gleichzeitig zu entführen und die Selbstmordanschläge auszuführen. Da die Reise des zurücktretenden Kunden der Beklagten gerade in das Zielgebiet New York erfolgen sollte, und gerade diese Großstadt in der Berichterstattung von Anfang an immer wieder wegen ihrer politischen Bedeutung und Symbolkraft als Ziel möglicher Großanschläge genannt wurde, ist der hier strittige kostenlose Rücktritt vom Reisevertrag aus den angeführten Gründen als gerechtfertigt zu qualifizieren. [...]

Translation

Mr Rupert L. had booked a trip from Salzburg to New York and Chicago for the period 2 to 11.10.2001 with the defendant company, through the intermediary of a travel agency. Owing to the change of circumstances caused by the terrorist attacks of 11.9.2001, he cancelled this trip on the 15.9.2001. The defendant company refunded part of the sum already paid but withheld a "cancellation fee" [of 487 Euros]. Mr Rupert L. transferred his claim for restitution to the claimant association. The association essentially bases its claim for payment dated 21.8.2002 on the fact that, because of the terrorist attacks in the USA, the foundation of the contract would have disappeared. An Islamic terrorist organisation's declaration of war would have been directed at the whole country. The media had widely reported the events and security threats to come. It would not have been reasonable for the defendant's customer to go on the trip.

The defendant demanded the claim be rejected. [...] The terrorist attacks had not been directed towards tourist locations. From 26.9.2001, there would no longer have been any unreasonable prejudice for travellers to the USA and normal air traffic would have prevailed.

The **Court of first instance** rejected the complaint. [...] The **Court of appeal** did not follow up the claimant's appeal. [...] The September 11 attacks had only occurred on one day and had been followed by massive security measures, so that there was no longer a serious threat. Trips after 26.9.2001 would have been possible without any difficulties [...]

Reasons:

The appeal is admissible and well founded.

[...] On a change of circumstances as the basis for a claim for termination of a travel contract without charge, it was recognised in two previous analogous decisions (8 Ob 99/99p = SZ 72/95 und 1 Ob 257/01b = ZVR 2003, 58/19), in which there were also attacks, that the doctrine of change of circumstances is to be considered as a means of last resort authorising one party to sever contractual obligations under certain conditions. Parties are entitled to terminate the travel contract where unforeseeable worsening of the situation, threats and interferences with the trip make it unreasonable for the customer to take the trip. As a rule, it depends on the individual circumstances of the case as to whether this is the case. When there are only isolated attacks, which can also be terrorist in nature, there is no right to withdraw. The attacks must have reached an intensity which, on an ordinary scale, appears to be the concretisation of an unreasonable threat of a future attack. It is therefore only in such cases that contracts can be terminated for change of circumstances because of attacks. [...] The question is how an ordinary traveller, *i.e.* not particularly brave or particularly fearful, would have assessed the future development of the situation in the planned holiday destination. [...]

The intensity of the terrorist attacks was on a historic scale which sparked fear even amongst the brave but certainly amongst "ordinary travellers". Nearly all the media warned against the risk of further attacks, citing plausible reasons [...] The origin of the attacks was not clear. At the moment termination was declared, on 15.9.2001, it was estimated not to be possible to obtain a reliable assessment of the security situation in the foreseeable future. The customer's declaration of termination was not that of a particularly anxious person.[...] The circumstances stressed by the court of appeal, that is to say the massive security measures taken in the USA and through this the decrease in the security risk, do not change anything for this judgment. On the contrary, it must be remembered that following the occurrence of terrorist attacks, security measures are always reinforced in the country concerned without other attacks necessarily being avoided. Air traffic, in particular, cannot be completely secured; it is impossible to watch over all the "weak points" in cities and protect them from terror. It is precisely the new dimension of the September 11 attacks that succeeded, despite worldwide security checks in airports, in simultaneously hijacking four aeroplanes in American airspace and carrying out suicide attacks. The customer who terminated the contract was due to take a trip precisely in the New York region. From the beginning, this city was always, and rightly, classed as the possible target for a large-scale attack due to its political significance and symbolic stature. For these reasons, the termination of the travel contract without charge, which is in question here, is assessed as being justified. […]

V. The Netherlands

Burgerlijk Wetboek (*Dutch Civil Code*)

Art. 7:503

(1) De reiziger kan de reisovereenkomst te allen tijde met onmiddellijke ingang opzeggen.

(2) Indien de reiziger opzegt wegens een aan hem toe te rekenen omstandigheid, vergoedt de reiziger de reisorganisator de schade die deze tengevolge van de opzegging lijdt. De schadevergoeding bedraagt ten hoogste eenmaal de reissom.

(3) Indien de reiziger opzegt wegens een niet aan hem toe te rekenen omstandigheid, he eft hij recht op teruggave of kwijtschelding van de reissom of, indien de reis reeds ten dele is genoten, een evenredig deel daarvan.

Art. 7:503

(1) The traveller may, at any time, terminate the travel contract with immediate effect.

(2) If the traveller terminates the contract for a reason attributable to himself, he must compensate the tour operator for the damage resulting from this termination. Compensation cannot exceed the total value of the trip.

(3) If the traveller cancels his trip because of circumstances not attributable to himself, he is entitled to a refund of the package price or to be exempt from paying it; if he has already used part of the travel package, he is only entitled to part of the price calculated accordingly.

Art. 6:258

(1) De rechter kan op verlangen van een der partijen de gevolgen van een overeenkomst wijzigen of deze geheel of gedeeltelijk ontbinden op grond van onvoorziene omstandigheden welke van dien aard zijn dat de wederpartij naar maatstaven van redelijkheid en billijkheid ongewijzigde instandhouding van de overeenkomst niet mag verwachten. Aan de wijziging of ontbinding kan terugwerkende kracht worden verleend.

(2) Een wijziging of ontbinding wordt niet uitgesproken, voor zover de omstandigheden krachtens de aarde van de overeenkomst of de in het verkeer geldende opvattingen voor rekening komen van degene die zich erop beroept.

[...]

Art. 6:258

(1) Upon the demand of one of the parties, the judge may modify the effects of a contract, or he may set it aside in whole or in part on the basis of unforeseen circumstances which are of such a nature that the co-contracting party, according to criteria of reasonableness and equity, may not expect that the contract be maintained in an unmodified form The modification or the setting aside of the contract may be given retroactive force.

(2) The modification or the setting aside of the contract is not pronounced to the extent that the person invoking the circumstances should be accountable for them according to the nature of the contract or common opinion.

[...]

VI.   Serbia

Zakon o obligacionim odnosima
(*The Law of Contract and Torts*)

Raskidanje ili izmena ugovora zbog promenjenih okolnosti

Repudiation or alteration of contract due to changed circumstances (hardship)

Član 133.   Pretpostavke za raskidanje.
(1)   Ako posle zaključenja ugovora nastupe okolnosti koje otežavaju ispunjenje obaveze jedne strane, ili ako se zbog njih ne može ostvariti svrha ugovora, a u jednom i u drugom slučaju u toj meri da je očigledno da ugovor više ne odgovara očekivanjima ugovornih strana i da bi po opštem mišljenju bilo nepravično održati ga na snazi takav kakav je, strana kojoj je otežano ispunjenje obaveze, odnosno strana koja zbog promenjenih okolnosti ne može ostvariti svrhu ugovora može zahtevati da se ugovor raskine.
(2)   Raskid ugovora ne može se zahtevati ako je strana koja se poziva na promenjene okolnosti bila dužna da u vreme zaključenja ugovora uzme u obzir te okolnosti ili ih je mogla izbeći ili savladati.
(3)   [...]
(4)   Ugovor se neće raskinuti ako druga strana ponudi ili pristane da se odgovarajući uslovi ugovora pravično izmene.
(5)   Ako izrekne raskid ugovora, sud će na zahtev druge strane obavezati stranu koja ga je zahtevala da naknadi drugoj strani pravičan deo štete koju trpi zbog toga.

Art. 133.   *Prerequisites for Repudiation.*
(1)   Should, after concluding the contract, circumstances emerge which hinder the performance of the obligation of one party, or if, due to them, the purpose of the contract cannot be realized, while in both cases this is expressed to such a degree that it becomes evident that the contract no longer meets the expectations of the contracting parties, and that, generally speaking, it would be unjust to maintain its validity as it stands, the party having difficulties in performing the obligation, namely the party being unable, due to the changed circumstances, to realize the purpose of the contract, may request its repudiation.
(2)   Repudiation of the contract may not be requested if the party claiming the changed circumstances had a duty, at the time of entering into contract, to take into account such circumstances, or if he could have avoided or surmounted them.
(3)   [...]
(4)   A contract shall not be repudiated should the other party offer or accept that the relevant terms of contract be altered in an equitable way.
(5)   After pronouncing repudiation of the contract, the court shall, at the request of the other party, impose a duty against the party requesting it, to compensate the other party for equitable part of the loss sustained due to repudiation.

Član 134. Dužnost obaveštavanja.

Strana koja je ovlašćena da zbog promenjenih okolnosti zahteva raskid ugovora dužna je da o svojoj nameri da traži raskid ugovora obavesti drugu stranu čim je saznala da su takve okolnosti nastupile, a ako to nije učinila, odgovara za štetu koju je druga strana pretrpela zbog toga što joj zahtev nije bio na vreme saopšten.

Art. 134. Duty of Notification.

A party authorized due to changed circumstances to request repudiation of the contract shall have a duty to notify the other party of his intention to request repudiation immediately after becoming aware of the emergence of such circumstances, and in case of not acting accordingly, the first party shall be liable for loss sustained by the other party because of the failure to be notified of the request on time.

Član 135. Okolnosti od značaja za odluku suda.

Pri odlučivanju o raskidanju ugovora, odnosno o njegovoj izmeni, sud se rukovodi načelima poštenog prometa, vodeći računa naročito o cilju ugovora, o normalnom riziku kod ugovora odnosne vrste, o opštem interesu, kao i o interesima obeju strana.

Art. 135. Circumstances Relevant for Court Decision.

While deciding on repudiation of the contract or on its alteration, the court shall be directed by the principles of fair dealing, while especially taking into consideration the purpose of the contract, the normal risk involved with such contracts, the general interest, as well as the interests of both parties.

Član 136. Odricanje od pozivanja na promenjene okolnosti.

Strane se mogu ugovorom unapred odreći pozivanja na određene promenjene okolnosti, osim ako je to u suprotnosti sa načelom savesnosti i poštenja.

Art. 136. Disclaim by Reason of Hardship.

The parties may, in their contract, exclude in advance the right to claim changed circumstances, unless that is contrary to the principles of good faith and fair dealing.

VII.   Greece

Αστικος Κωδικας (*Greek Civil Code*)

'Αρθρο 388.   Απροοπρη

(1)   Αν τα περιστατικά στα οποία κυρίως, ενόψει της καλής πίοτης και των συναλλακρικών ηθών τα μέρη στήριζαν τη σύναψη αμφοτεροβαρούς σύμβασδης, μεταβλήθηκαν ύστερα από λόγους που ήραν έκτακτοι και δεν μπορούσαν να προβλεφθούν, και από τη μεταβολή αυτή η παροχή του οφειλέτη, ενόψει και τφς αντιπαροχής, έγινε υπέρμετρα επαχθής, το δικαστήριο μπορεί κατά την κρίση τον με αίτηση του οφειλέτη να την αναγάηει στο μέτρο που αρμόζει και να αποφασίσει τη λύση της σύμβασης εζολοκλήρου ή κατά το μέρος που δεν εκτελέστηκε ακόμη.

(2)   Αν αποφασιστεί η λύση της σύμβασης, επέρχεται απόσβεση των υποχρεώσεων παροχής που πηγάζουν απ΄ αυτήν και οι συμβαλλόμενοι έχουν αμοιβαία υποχρέωση να αποδώσουν τις παροχές που έλαβαν κατά ρις διατάζεις για τον αδικαιολόγφτο πλουτισμό

Art. 388.   Unforeseeable change of circumstances.

(1)   If, having regard to the requirements of good faith and business usages, the circumstances on which the parties had based the conclusion of a bilateral agreement have subsequently changed on exceptional grounds that could not have been foreseen and the performance due by the debtor, taking the counter-performance into consideration too, has as a result of the change become excessively onerous, the Court may, at the request of the debtor and according to its appreciation, reduce the debtor's performance to the appropriate extent or decide on the dissolution of the contract in whole or with regard to its non performed part.

(2)   If the dissolution of the contract has been decided upon, the obligations to perform arising therefrom shall be extinguished and the contracting parties shall be reciprocally obligated to restitute the performances by which each benefited pursuant to the provisions governing enrichment without just cause.

VIII.   Italy

1. Codice civile italiano (*Italian Civil Code*)

Art. 1467.   Contratto con prestazioni corrispettive.
(1)   Nei contratti a esecuzione continuata o periodica ovvero a esecuzione differita, se la prestazione di una delle parti è divenuta eccesivamente onerosa per il verificarsi di avvenimenti straordinari e imprevidibili, la parte che deve tale prestazione può domandare la risoluzione del contratto, con gli effetti stabiliti dall'articolo 1458.
(2)   La risoluzione non può essere domandata se la sopravvenuta onerosità rientra nell'alea normale del contratto.
(3)   La parte contro la quale è domandata la risoluzione può evitarla offrendo di modificare equamente le condizioni del contratto.

Art. 1467.   Contract for mutual counterperformances.
(1)   In contracts for continuous or periodic performance or for deferred performance, if extraordinary and unforeseeable events make the performance of one of the parties excessively onerous, the party who owes such performance can demand dissolution of the contract, with the effects set forth in Article 1458.
(2)   Dissolution cannot be demanded if the supervening onerousness is part of the normal risk of the contract.
(3)   A party against whom dissolution is demanded can avoid it by offering to equitably modify the conditions of the contract.

2. Pietro Trimarchi, *Istituzioni di diritto privato*, 16th edn (translation of the Italian original)

NON-PERFORMANCE OF A CONTRACT AND ALTERATION OF THE CONTRACTUAL BALANCE

[...]

256.   Outline of the issues.

[…]

There are circumstances in which a contract's content, although not expressly stated, has been determined in such a way that there would be no economic justification if it were not accepted that one party's reason [for entering into the contract] was not only known by the other party but set as the foundation of the contract. In such a case, the reason becomes part of the structure of the contract: one talks of "presupposition" (*presupposizione*).

A classic example is the renting of a balcony at an elevated price for the day set for the queen's coronation procession. If the route of the procession is altered or if the ceremony is postponed, the necessary precondition of the contract is lacking.

[...]

If the plan for the procession is altered after the contract is entered into, [...], one finds oneself [...] within the limits of [...] "unexpected circumstances" (*sopravvenienza*). The theory is very similar to the theory [...] according to which the law grants remedies where obligations subsequently become excessively onerous. In fact, from the moment it was decided that the procession would not pass beneath the balcony, the value of granting the use of the balcony reduced significantly and the counter-performance became disproportionate. There is, however, a difference: where an obligation subsequently becomes excessively onerous, there is still a sense to the contract if it is altered in such a way as that the balance between the service and the counter-performance is re-established (and, in fact, [...] termination can be avoided by way of an offer to restore the balance of the contract); here, on the other hand, the contract is, for the renter, devoid of any utility as well as all justification.

Although there is no express legal provision, constant case law considers that the absence (initial or subsequent) of a necessary precondition justifies the resolution of a contract (Cass. Civ., 28 agosto 1993, n. 9125; [...]). This solution results from either the application by analogy of the provisions on subsequent excessive onerousness, or from the principles of [...] cause and motives, or finally, from the fundamental idea of implicit conditions.

IX.　France

1. Code civil français (*French Civil Code*)[6]

Art. 1134
(1)　Les conventions légalement formées tiennent lieu de loi à ceux qui les ont faites.
(2)　Elles ne peuvent être révoquées que de leur consentement mutuel, ou pour les causes que la loi autorise.
(3)　Elles doivent être exécutées de bonne foi.

Art. 1134
(1)　Legally formed agreements shall act as law for those who have made them.
(2)　They may only be revoked by mutual consent, or for reasons permitted by law.
(3)　They must be performed in good faith.

Art. 1147
Le débiteur est condamné, s'il y a lieu, au paiement de dommages et intérêts, soit à raison de l'inexécution de l'obligation, soit à raison du retard dans l'exécution, toutes les fois qu'il ne justifie pas que l'inexécution provient d'une cause étrangère qui ne peut lui être imputée, encore qu'il n'y ait aucune mauvaise foi de sa part.

Art. 1147
A debtor shall be ordered to pay damages, if appropriate, for either the non-performance of the obligation, or for delay in performance, whenever he cannot prove that the non-performance is due to an external cause which cannot be attributed to him, even when there is no bad faith on his part.

Art. 1148
Il n'y a lieu à aucun dommages et intérêts lorsque, par suite d'une force majeure ou d'un cas fortuit, le débiteur a été empêché de donner ou de faire ce à quoi il était obligé, ou a fait ce qui lui était interdit.

Art. 1148
Damages are not appropriate where a debtor was prevented from transferring or from doing that which he was bound to do, or did what he was forbidden from doing, because of force majeure or of an unexpected event.

---

[6]　Translation by EG.

2. Cour de cassation (ch. civ.) 6.3.1876 (*De Galliffet c. Commune de Pélissanne*), in HENRI CAPITANT *et al.*, *Les grands arrêts de la jurisprudence civile*, Tome 2, 12th edn, n° 165

IMPRÉVISION. CONTRAT À EXÉCUTION SUCCESSIVE. CHANGEMENT DES CIRCONSTANCES. DÉSÉQUILIBRE DES PRESTATIONS. ABSENCE DE RÉVISION

Civ. 6 mars 1876

(D. 76. 1. 193, note Giboulot)

De Galliffet C. Commune de Pélissanne

La règle que consacre l'article 1134 du Code civil étant générale et absolue et régissant notamment les contrats à exécution successive, il n'appartient pas aux tribunaux, quelque équitable que puisse leur paraître leur décision, de prendre en considération le temps et les circonstances pour modifier les conventions des parties et substituer des clauses nouvelles à celles qu'elles ont librement acceptées.

Faits. — Ils sont complètement rapportés dans le jugement du tribunal civil d'Aix, du 18 mars 1841, dont les passages essentiels sont reproduits ci-dessous:

«Attendu que, par l'acte du 22 juin 1567, Adam de Craponne s'oblige à faire et construire un canal destiné à arroser les vergers, vignes, prés et autres propriétés des habitants de la commune de Pélissanne sous diverses clauses et conditions qui sont, entre autres, que: [...] pour chaque fois que lesdits particuliers arroseront leurs propriétés, ils payeront audit Adam de Craponne ou à ses hoirs: 3 sols pour chaque carteirade, payables à chaque arrosage, incontinent et ainsi perpétuellement [...];

— Attendu qu'il est évident que le prix de 15 centimes payés aujourd'hui, comme il y a trois siècles, pour chaque arrosage d'une carteirade, qui contient environ 190 ares, est insuffisant et hors de toute proportion avec le prix des eaux que le marquis de Galliffet paye lui-même à l'œuvre générale de Craponne, pour les fournir ensuite aux arrosants de Pélissanne [...], tous prix, dépenses et salaires augmentés considérablement; — Attendu que l'insuffisance du produit des arrosages a été reconnue [...] puisqu'on lit dans un rapport officiel transmis au Gouvernement en 1778 que le canal de Craponne ne pourrait exister longtemps si on n'augmentait pas le prix de ces arrosages; [...]

Attendu qu'il serait injuste de soumettre le marquis de Galliffet à continuer de supporter une charge augmentée par l'état actuel des choses, et cela sans augmenter le droit d'arrosage, qui n'est plus une indemnité proportionnée à cette charge, avec laquelle ce droit a cessé d'être en rapport; [...] — Attendu qu'en demandant dans ses conclusions [...], que le droit d'arrosage fût à l'avenir payé 60 centimes au lieu de 15 centimes, le marquis de Galliffet a entendu nécessairement que cette augmentation ait son effet à partir de la demande judiciaire, et que c'est ainsi qu'elle doit être ordonnée, etc.»

[L]e 31 décembre 1873, un arrêt de la cour d'Aix statua en ces termes sur l'augmentation de la redevance d'arrosage:

«Attendu que si les conventions légalement formées tiennent lieu de loi aux parties et si elles ne peuvent être modifiées que du consentement commun, il n'en est pas de même pour les contrats qui ont un caractère successif; — Qu'il est reconnu, en droit, que ces contrats, qui reposent sur une redevance périodique, peuvent être modifiés par la justice, lorsqu'il n'existe plus une corrélation équitable entre les redevances d'une part et les charges de l'autre; [...]

Attendu, en fait, que les conventions de 1560 et 1567 présentent ce caractère successif; que l'œuvre de Craponne, en prenant l'engagement de fournir de l'eau aux arrosants de Pélissanne, a stipulé, comme compensation, une redevance déterminée; que cette redevance de 3 sols par carteirade, qui pouvait être suffisante à cette époque, cesse de l'être aujourd'hui que les dépenses pour l'entretien du canal ont considérablement augmenté; [...] — Attendu que les premiers juges, en fixant cette augmentation à 60 centimes par carteirade, ont sagement apprécié les faits du procès; [...] que c'est là le chiffre, en moyenne, que coûte l'arrosage d'un hectare; qu'il y a donc lieu d'adopter les motifs des premiers juges et de confirmer, sur ce chef, leur décision; [...]»

Pourvoi [en Cassation] par la commune de Pélissanne et par les syndics des arrosants.

Moyens. — 1° Excès de pouvoir et violation de l'article 1134 du Code civil, en ce que, sous le prétexte qu'il s'agissait d'un contrat successif, l'arrêt attaqué a substitué un prix nouveau à celui qui résultait de la convention des parties. [...]

ARRÊT

LA COUR; — [...] *sur le premier moyen du pourvoi*: — Vu l'article 1134 du Code civil; — Attendu que la disposition de cet article n'étant que la reproduction des anciens principes constamment suivis en matière d'obligations conventionnelles, la circonstance que les contrats dont l'exécution donne lieu au litige sont antérieurs à la promulgation du Code civil ne saurait être, dans l'espèce, un obstacle à l'application dudit article; — Attendu que la règle qu'il consacre est générale, absolue, et régit les contrats dont l'exécution s'étend à des époques successives de même qu'à ceux de toute autre nature; — Que, dans aucun cas, il n'appartient aux tribunaux, quelque équitable que puisse leur paraître leur décision, de prendre en considération le temps et les circonstances pour modifier les conventions des parties et substituer des clauses nouvelles à celles qui ont été librement acceptées par les contractants; — Qu'en décidant le contraire et en élevant à 30 centimes de 1834 à 1874, puis à 60 centimes à partir de 1874, la redevance d'arrosage, fixée à 3 sols par les conventions de 1560 et 1567, sous prétexte que cette redevance n'était plus en rapport avec les frais d'entretien du canal de Craponne, l'arrêt attaqué a formellement violé l'article 1134 ci-dessus visé; — *Par ces motifs*, casse...

Translation

UNFORSEEABILITY. CONTRACT INVOLVING SUCCESSIVE PERFORMANCES. CHANGE OF CIRCUMSTANCES. IMBALANCE OF OBLIGATIONS. ABSENCE OF REVISION

Civ. 6 March 1876

(D. 76. 1. 193, note Giboulot)

De Galliffet v. Commune de Pélissanne

The rule laid down in Article 1134 of the Civil code being general and absolute and governing, in particular, contracts involving successive performances, it is not for the courts, however equitable their decision may seem, to take into account the times and the circumstances in order to modify the parties' agreements and substitute new clauses for those that were freely accepted.

Facts. — They are fully reported in the Civil Court of Aix's ruling of 18 March 1841, the essential passages of which are reproduced below:

"Given that, by an act of 22 June 1567, Adam de Craponne bound himself to construct a canal to irrigate the orchards, vineyards, meadows and other properties belonging to the inhabitants of the commune of Pélissance under various clauses and conditions which are, *inter alia*, that: […] each time the aforementioned individuals irrigate their land, they shall pay the aforementioned Adam de Craponne or his heirs: 3 sols[7] for every carteirade,[8] payable upon each irrigation, forthwith and in perpetuity […];

— Whereas it is clear that the price of 15 centimes paid today, as it was three centuries ago, for each irrigation of a carteirade, which contains about 190 ares,[9] is insufficient and out of all proportion with the price of water that the marquis of Galliffet himself pays to l'Œuvre Générale de Craponne,[10] to then provide irrigation for the people of Pélissanne […], all prices, expenses and salaries having increased considerably; — Whereas the insufficiency of the income from the irrigations had been recognised […] since it states in an official report sent to the government in 1778 that the de Craponne canal could not exist for much longer if the price of irrigation was not increased; […]

Whereas it would be unfair to subject the marquis de Galliffet to continuing to bear a charge increased by the current state of affairs, and this without increasing the right to irrigation, which is no longer compensation in proportion with this charge, with which this right ceased to be in line; […] — Whereas by asking in his submissions that the right to irrigation be paid for at a rate of 60 centimes instead of 15 centimes, the marquis of Galliffet necessarily meant this increase to take effect from the time the legal claim was made and so this is how it should be ordered, etc."

[On t]he 31 December 1873, the court of Aix gave a decision ruling on the increase in the irrigation charge in the following terms:

---

[7] Old French money, equivalent to 15 centimes.
[8] Old unit of measurement, equal to approximately 19 000 square metres.
[9] Old unit of measurement, equivalent to 100 square metres.
[10] Association of mill owners and users of the canal water.

"Whereas even though legally formed agreements shall act as law for the parties and can only be modified by mutual consent, this is nevertheless not the case for contracts that are successive in nature; — That it is recognised, in law, that these contracts, which are based on a periodic charge, can be modified by the courts, when there is no longer a fair correlation between the charge on the one hand and the burden of the other;

Whereas, in fact, the 1560 and 1567 agreements are indeed successive in nature; that l'Œuvre Générale de Craponne, when taking on the commitment to provide water to the people irrigating their land in Pélissanne, stipulated as compensation, a given charge; that this charge of 3 sols per carteirade, which would have been sufficient at this time, ceases to be sufficient today now that the expense of maintaining the canal has increased considerably; [...] — Whereas the judges at first instance, by fixing this increase at 60 centimes per carteirade, wisely considered the facts of the case; [...] that that is the average cost of irrigating one hectare; that it is therefore necessary to adopt the reasoning of the judges at first instance and to confirm, on this count, their decision; [...]"

Appeal [to the *Cour de cassation*] by the commune of Pélissanne and by the irrigation managers.

Grounds for the appeal. — 1° Abuse of power and violation of Article 1134 of the Civil code that, on the pretext of it being a contract involving successive performances, the contested decision substituted a new price for the price that resulted from the parties' agreement. [...]

DECISION

THE COURT; — [...] *on the first ground for appeal*: — In view of Article 1134 Civil code; — Whereas the provision of this article simply repeats established principles constantly followed in relation to contractual obligations, the fact that the contracts, the performance of which gives rise to these proceedings, were made prior to the promulgation of the Civil code shall not, in this instance, stand in the way of the application of the aforementioned article; — Whereas the rule that it enshrines is general, absolute, and governs contracts for which the performance extends over successive periods as well as those of any other nature; — That, in no case is it for the courts, however equitable their decision may seem, to take into account the times and the circumstances in order to modify the parties' agreements and substitute new clauses for those that were freely accepted; — That by deciding to the contrary and raising the irrigation fee, fixed at 3 sols by the 1560 and 1567 agreements, to 30 centimes for 1834 to 1874 and to 60 centimes from 1874, on the pretext that the fee was no longer in proportion with the maintenance costs of de Craponne's canal, the contested decision manifestly violated Article 1134 above; — *For these reasons*, quashes ..."

OBSERVATIONS[11]

[...]

I. — Refusal of revision for unforseeability

2 No case, in this area, is more significant than that of *Canal de Craponne*. The purpose of the agreements in question made in 1560 and 1567 was to provide water to feed the

---

[11] Translation of the French original.

irrigation canals in the Arles plain, for a charge of 3 sols per carteirade (190 ares). During the 19th century, the company that used the canal, citing the fall in the value of money and the rise in the cost of labour, requested an increase in the tax which was no longer in proportion with the maintenance costs. The court in Aix having increased this charge to 60 centimes, its decision was quashed. No consideration of the times or of equity can, in actual fact, according to the *Cour de cassation*, allow the courts to change the parties' agreement; Article 1134 of the Civil code, a general and absolute text, lays this down. The law of the contract is an "iron law" which imposes itself on the courts like it does on the parties.

The solution was not without precedent. [...] The period of inflation following the First World War was the occasion for the *Cour de cassation* to reaffirm the solution in the most diverse domains [...] Despite its age and steadfastness, this case law should not have been followed by the administrative courts. In the *Gaz de Bordeaux* case, the *Conseil d'Etat*, on the contrary, actually accepted the theory of unforseeability. Noting that an unforeseen increase of coal had shaken up the economics of a concession contract, the court recognised the concessionaire's right to compensation from the authority granting the concession [...] Again the disruption of the contract must be due to an unforeseeable event, unrelated to the contracting parties and must only be temporary in nature; if the imbalance is permanent, it is possible to terminate the contract [...]

3 The diversity of points of view proves, if this was indeed necessary, the difficulty of the problem to be solved.

In favour of the solution maintained by the *Cour de cassation*, it has been pointed out that the situation cannot simply be seen as one of the hypothetical cases in which the parties would have been allowed not to execute the contract or possibly to readjust it. Indeed, there is not force majeure, as the performance of the obligations has admittedly become difficult but not impossible; nor is there overcharging, as the imbalance does not come from an initial inequality of the obligations, but from an external upheaval which occurred after the conclusion of the contract. Nevertheless, the technical means likely to form the basis of a revision of a contract are not totally lacking. The idea that the *cause* should not only play a role at the moment a contract is formed but also during its performance may also be put forward. Consequently, a certain equivalence ought to be maintained between the contracting parties' obligations. Recourse could also be had to the rule which requires agreements to be performed in good faith (Article 1134(3)); is it not flouting this principle to demand the strict performance of a contract when the change of circumstance makes the burden of one party overwhelming and the obligation of the other derisory? (see, for the position of the German courts, Rieg, *Le rôle de la volonté dans l'acte juridique en droit civil français et allemand*, 1961, [...]).

Similarly, the possibility for revision could also have been inferred from Article 1135 of the Civil code which stipulates that "agreements are binding not only as to what is expressed therein, but also as to all the consequences which equity, usage or statute give to the obligation according to its nature." However, as has been seen, the court challenges all references to equity in the decision reproduced above. Lastly, it would always have been possible to imply a specific clause, a *rebus sic stantibus* clause, into all contracts of long duration, pursuant to which consent is dependent on the continuation of the state of affairs that existed on the day on which it was expressed. [...]

4 Consequently, it can be claimed that, the courts made a deliberate choice to refuse to take up revision for unforeseeability [...] This can be explained by mainly legal as well as economic reasons. *Legal* reasons: the courts were afraid, on the one hand, that contracting parties in bad faith were trying to get out of their commitments and, on the other hand, that judges' arbitrary power which favours contractual instability, were going against legal certainty. *Economic* reasons: the revision of the contract is admittedly often the only way to avoid the financial ruin of one of the parties and from that the non-performance of the contract. [...] However, allowing revision in one case risks making it impossible for the other party to perform obligations taken on by him under other contracts and from this even to cause a generalised unbalance "by a game of chain reactions which is impossible to limit or even plan for" [...] Yet, the court is not in the position to assess whether its decision, by definition individual, will be good or bad for the national economy. Hence their refusal to carry out a revision. It is for the legislator, better equipped to assess the economic consequences of whatever choice, to intervene promptly, where the contractual injustice is particularly blatant and where a significant category of people risk financial ruin. Such was the case notably after the two world wars. [...]

II. — Criticism of the solution

5 Accepted by nearly all civil [law] academic opinion, this argument is not however totally convincing. In fact, the comparative law example shows that, whereas it was very widely accepted in the 19th century in other European countries, this position has been abandoned since then, sometimes following an evolution in the case law (Great Britain, Germany, Spain, Switzerland), sometimes due to legislative intervention (Italy, Greece, Portugal) [...] Yet, it seems that in none of these countries has the acceptance of revision for unforeseeability led to the feared uncertainty [...]

6 [...] Putting forward an obligation of good faith reactivated by a solidarist conception of contracts, an active trend in academic opinion argues in favour of the acceptance of judicial revision of contracts from the moment that their execution, because of their imbalance, risks to cause the financial ruin of one of the contracting parties [...] Certain recent decisions can be seen as a first step in this direction. In the famous decision in *Huard*, the *Cour de cassation* agreed with the court of Paris which considered that where there is a change of circumstances exposing a distributor to strengthened competition, the supplier is compelled by the requirement of good faith, to negotiate a commercial cooperation agreement with the distributor in order to allow him to align himself with his competitors [...] And more recently, the *Cour de cassation* condemned the courts of first instance which had refused the revision of a contract of a commercial agent who complained of the competition he found himself confronted with from buying syndicates who got supplies from his principals [...] Admittedly, in both cases, the problem was not, strictly speaking, one of unforeseeability, since far from being due to unexpected events, the situations justifying the adjustment of the price had been the situation of one of the contracting parties. The fact remains that these decisions "directly lead to the requirement to renegotiate the price" [...]

   The Principles of European Contract Law (Art. 6-111) and the Unidroit Principles (Art. 6.2.1–2.3) give the courts the power to either terminate or modify the contract. However, they emphasise the exceptional nature of the action which is only available if performance is excessively onerous for one of the parties. The texts insist upon the parties' primary obligation which is to reach an amicable agreement. [...]

3. Cour de Cassation (civ. 1re) 8.12.1998 (*Sté Castorama c. Sté ICEV Lid'air voyages*), Bull. Civ. 1998 I n° 346 p. 238

La Cour: — *Sur le moyen unique, pris en ses deux branches:* — Attendu que, suivant contrat du 29 mai 1990, la société Castorama a confié à la société ICEV Lid'air voyages le transport et l'hébergement de cinq cents membres de son personnel, du 21 au 24 janvier 1991, à Marrakech, au prix de 2 848 000 francs; qu'après avoir envisagé de renoncer au voyage en raison des tensions au Moyen-Orient et dans les pays arabes, la société Castorama a déclaré, le 21 décembre 1990, en maintenir la réalisation; que, le 14 janvier 1991, veille de la guerre en Irak, elle a annulé le voyage «en raison de l'aggravation de la crise du Golfe»; qu'elle a demandé le remboursement de la totalité des sommes versées à l'organisateur du voyage en invoquant, pour justifier la rupture unilatérale du contrat, la force majeure résultant de la guerre du Golfe; — Attendu que la société Castorama fait grief à l'arrêt attaqué (Paris, 12 avril 1996 […]) d'avoir [… rejeté la demande][12]; — Mais attendu, d'une part, que la cour d'appel, ayant retenu que les circonstances invoquées comme constitutives de la force majeure n'étaient pas insurmontables, a, par ce seul motif, légalement justifié sa décision, sur ce point; — Attendu, d'autre part, que la cour d'appel a relevé que la ville de Marrakech et le Royaume du Maroc n'étaient pas, en janvier 1991, des lieux à haut risque d'attentats et que le ministre des Affaires étrangères, dans sa circulaire du 17 janvier 1991, n'avait pas cité le Maroc parmi les pays dans lesquels il dissuadait les ressortissants français de se rendre, mais seulement parmi ceux pour lesquels des conseils de prudence étaient prodigués aux touristes; qu'elle a ainsi répondu, en les écartant, aux conclusions invoquées; — D'où il suit que le moyen ne peut être accueilli en aucune de ses branches;

Par ces motifs: — rejette le pourvoi.

Translation

The Court: – *on the sole ground for appeal taken in its two parts:* — Whereas, according to the contract of 29 May 1990, the Castorama company entrusted the transport and accommodation of five hundred of its members of staff, from 21 to 24 January 1991, in Marrakech for the price of 2 848 000 Francs, to the company ICEV Lid'air voyages; that after having considered cancelling the trip because of tensions in the Middle East and in Arabic countries, the Castorama company, on 21 December 1990, stated that it was to stand by the trip; that, on 14 January 1991, the eve of the Iraq war, it cancelled the trip "because of the worsening of the crisis in the Gulf"; that it requested reimbursement of the totality of the sums paid to the tour operator, citing force majeure resulting from the Gulf war as justification for the unilateral breach of the contract; — Whereas Castorama challenged the decision under review (Paris, 12 April 1996 […]) for having [… rejected the request]; — However, whereas, on the one hand, the Court of appeal, having held that the circumstances cited as constituting the force majeure were not insurmountable, by this sole reason, legally justified its decision on this point; — Whereas, on the other hand, the Court of appeal noted that the city of Marrakech and the kingdom of Morocco were not,

---

[12]   Added by the author.

in January 1991, areas at high risk of attacks and that the foreign minister, in his circular on 17 January 1991, had not cited Morocco amongst the countries that he was dissuading French citizens from going to, but only amongst those for which safety advice was being given to tourists; that the court thus responded, by dismissing them, the cited conclusions; — It therefore follows that the ground for appeal cannot be upheld in either of its parts;

   For these reasons: — rejects the appeal.

X. England

1. W. T. MAJOR AND CHRISTINE TAYLOR, *Law of Contract*, 9th edn, pp. 255–65

DISCHARGE BY FRUSTRATION

16. Absolute contracts

The general rule is that a contractual obligation is absolute, and if a party undertakes to contract to do something he is absolutely bound to do it. If subsequent events make it impossible for him to comply with his obligations then he will be in breach of contract and liable in damages to the other party. This view of contractual obligations being 'absolute' can be seen in the early case of *Paradine* v. *Jane* (1648) where the plaintiff brought an action to recover rent due under a lease and was met with the defence that the defendant has been deprived of possession of the land by the action of an enemy army of a German prince, Prince Rupert. The court held that if the defendant sought to be excused from his contractual obligations in particular circumstances, then he should have made provision for such eventualities in his contract.

17. The doctrine of frustration

Obviously, the stipulation that the contract should cover every eventuality is somewhat unrealistic. Consequently, over a period of time, the doctrine of frustration has developed a number of exceptions to this general rule of absolute contractual liability. These exceptions allow the parties to be discharged from further performance of their obligations if, without fault on the part of either party, some unforeseeable event occurs after the formation of the contract which makes further performance impossible or illegal so that any attempted performance would amount to something quite different from what must have been contemplated by the parties when they made their contract.

18. The basis of the doctrine of frustration

The strict rule in *Paradine* v. *Jane* was first relaxed so as to allow the development of the doctrine of frustration in the case of *Taylor* v. *Caldwell*.

> *Taylor* v. *Caldwell* (1863): The defendants agreed to let the plaintiff have the use of the Surrey Gardens and Music Hall on four specific days for the purpose of giving a series of four concerts and day and night fetes. After the making of this agreement and before the date fixed for the first concert, the Hall was destroyed by fire. The contract contained no express stipulation with reference to fire. The plaintiffs, who had spent money on advertisements and otherwise in preparing for the concerts, brought this action to recover damages. It was contended that, according to the rule in *Paradine* v. *Jane*, the destruction of the premises by fire did not exonerate the defendants from performing their part of the agreement. HELD: The continuation of the contract was subject to an implied condition that the parties would be excused if the subject matter was destroyed. Both parties were excused from the performance of the contract as the contract was discharged by frustration.

In reaching this decision the court stipulated that the principle in *Paradine* v. *Jane* was confined to 'positive and absolute' contracts, in other words contracts in which performance had been guaranteed, irrespective of all risks. [...]

[...] In the *Joseph Constantine* case, Viscount Simon said: "The doctrine of discharge from liability by frustration has been explained in various ways, sometimes by speaking of the disappearance of a foundation which the parties assumed to be the basis of their contract, sometimes as deduced from a rule arising from impossibility of performance, and sometimes as flowing from the inference of an implied term. Whichever way it is put, the legal consequence is the same". [...]

[...] Lord Radcliffe [said] that "frustration occurs whenever the law recognizes that, without default of either party, a contractual obligation has become incapable of being performed because the circumstances in which performance is called for would render it a thing radically different from that which was undertaken by the contract. [...] There must be as well such a change in the significance of the obligation that the thing undertaken would, if performed, be a different thing from that contracted for".

FACTUAL CIRCUMSTANCES IN WHICH A CONTRACT MAY BE FRUSTRATED

19. Impossibility

Decisions show that the doctrine of frustration may be invoked in circumstances where the contract becomes impossible to perform due to the total or partial destruction of some object necessary to the performance of the contract. This is obviously the basis on which the case of *Taylor* v. *Caldwell* proceeded. [...]

20. Supervening illegality

Frustration may also occur where a change in the law or state intervention renders any attempted performance illegal. [...]

21. Non-occurrence of an event

Where an event which is fundamental to the contract does not occur then the contract may be frustrated despite the fact that it is still physically possible to carry out the contract. This is demonstrated by the [...] case *Krell* v. *Henry* (1903) [...]

22. Frustration of purpose

It is very rare for a contract to be held to have been frustrated by an event which leaves it possible to perform but which makes it much more onerous to one party. [...]

[I]t is accepted that it is unlikely that a contract will be frustrated merely because an event has occurred which renders that contracted for by one party worth less than he anticipated or where an unexpected event merely makes the contract more expensive to perform. [...]

> *Tsakiroglou & Co. Ltd* v. *Noblee Thorl GmbH* (1962): Here the contract was to sell groundnuts c.i.f. Hamburg. HELD: The contract was not frustrated by the blockage of the Suez canal, even though the nuts were to be loaded at Port Sudan and would normally have been carried through the canal. The seller could have performed by shipping them via the Cape of Good Hope even though that would have taken longer and been more expensive.

2. Court of Appeal: *Krell* v. *Henry* [1903] 2 KB 740; [1900–03] All ER Rep 20

Historical Context

Very particular facts gave rise to this leading case in English law. Queen Victoria had just died after reigning for 64 years. The coronation of the new king, Edward VII, was therefore being planned. Such an occasion involves great celebrations, including a procession through the streets of London. Members of the public rented windows and balconies from which they could watch the royal procession going past. The London ceremonies were planned for 26 and 27 June 1902.

Mr Henry rented Mr Krell's London flat for 26 and 27 June. There was no reference to the procession in the contract, but it was due to pass in front of the flat and there would be a good view of it from the flat's window. The rent and the short rental period were only justified in those very special circumstances.

At the last minute, the King became ill and the ceremonies were cancelled. Mr Krell demanded payment of the rent from Mr Henry.

KRELL *v.* HENRY

[COURT OF APPEAL (Vaughan Williams, Romer and Stirling, L.J.J.), July 13, 14, 15, August 11, 1903]

[Reported [1903] 2 K.B. 740; 72 L.J.K.B. 794; 89 L.T. 328; 52 W.R. 246; 19 T.L.R. 711]

Contract — Frustration — State of things foundation of contract — Destruction by event not in contemplation of parties — Extrinsic evidence as to surrounding facts and knowledge of parties when making contract — Contract for hire of seats to view coronation processions — Cancellation of processions.

Aug. 11, 1903. **VAUGHAN WILLIAMS, L.J.**, read the following judgment.— [...]

"where, from the nature of the contract, it appears that the parties must from the beginning have known that it could not be fulfilled unless, when the time for the fulfilment of the contract arrived, some particular specified thing continued to exist, so that when entering into the contract they must have contemplated such continued existence as the foundation of what was to be done; there, in the absence of any express or implied warranty that the thing shall exist, the contract is not to be construed as a positive contract, but as subject to an implied condition that the parties shall be excused in case, before breach, performance becomes impossible from the perishing of the thing without default of the contractor."

[...] The doubt in the present case arises as to how far this principle extends. [...] The English law applies the principle not only to cases where the performance of the contract becomes impossible by the cessation of existence of the thing which is the subject-matter of the contract, but also to cases where the event which renders the contract incapable of performance is the cessation or non-existence of an express condition or state of things, going to the root of the contract, and essential to its performance. [...]

[…] I think that you first have to ascertain, not necessarily from the terms of the contract, but, if necessary, from necessary inferences, drawn from surrounding circumstances recognised by both contracting parties, what is the substance of the contract, and then to ask the question whether that substantial contract needs for its foundation the assumption of the existence of a particular state of things. If it does, this will limit the operation of the general words, and in such case if the contract becomes impossible of performance by reason of the non-existence of the state of things assumed by both contracting parties, as the foundation of the contract, there will be no breach of the contract thus limited.

What are the facts of the present case? […] In my judgment, the use of the rooms was let and taken for the purpose of seeing the royal processions. It was not a demise of the rooms or even an agreement to let and take the rooms. It is a licence to use rooms for a particular purpose and none other. And in my judgment the taking place of those processions on the days proclaimed along the proclaimed route, which passed 56A, Pall Mall, was regarded by both contracting parties as the foundation of the contract. […]

It was suggested in the course of the argument that if the occurrence, on the proclaimed days, of the coronation and the processions in this case were the foundation of the contract, and if the general words are thereby limited or qualified, so that in the event of the non-occurrence of the coronation and processions along the proclaimed route they would discharge both parties from further performance of the contract, it would follow that if a cabman was engaged to take someone to Epsom on Derby-day at a suitable enhanced price for such a journey, both parties to the contract would be discharged in the contingency of the race at Epsom for some reason becoming impossible, but I do not think this follows, for I do not think that in the cab case the happening of the race would be the foundation of the contract. No doubt the purpose of the engager would be to go to see the Derby, and the price would be proportionately high; but the cab had no special qualifications for the purpose which led to the selection of the cab for this particular occasion. Any other cab would have done as well. Moreover, I think that, under the cab contract, the hirer, even if the race went off, could have said: "Drive me to Epsom, I will pay you the agreed sum, you have nothing to do with the purpose for which I hired the cab"— and that if the cabman refused he would have been guilty of a breach of contract, there being nothing to qualify his promise to drive the hirer to Epsom on a particular day, whereas in the case of the coronation, there is not merely the purpose of the hirer to see the coronation processions, but it is the coronation processions and the relative position of the rooms which is the basis of the contract as much for the lessor as the hirer"; […]

Each case must be judged by its own circumstances. In each case one must ask oneself, first: What, having regard to all the circumstances, was the foundation of the contract?; secondly: Was the performance of the contract prevented?; and thirdly: Was the event which prevented the performance of the contract of such a character that it cannot reasonably be said to have been in the contemplation of the parties at the date of the contract? If all these questions are answered in the affirmative (as I think they should be in this case), I think both parties are discharged from further performance of the contract. I think that the coronation processions were the foundation of this contract, and that the non-happening of them prevented the performance of the contract; and, secondly, I think that the non-happening of the processions, to use the words of Sir James Hannen in *Baily v. De Crespigny* […], was an event

"of such a character that it cannot reasonably be supposed to have been in the contemplation of the contracting parties when the contract was made, and that they are not to be held bound by general words which, though large enough to include, were not used with reference to the possibility of the particular contingency which afterwards happened."

The test seems to be, whether the event which causes the impossibility was or might have been anticipated and guarded against. […]

[…] I think for the reasons which I have given that the principle of *Taylor* v. *Caldwell* ought to be applied. […]

ROMER L.J [and] **STIRLING L.J** [concurred].

Appeal dismissed.

Solicitors: *Cecil Bisgood; M. Grunebaum.*

[*Reported by* E. A. SCRATCHLEY, ESQ., *Barrister-at-Law.*]

3. Court of Appeal, *Staffordshire Area Health Authority v. South Staffordshire Waterworks Co.* [1978] 1 WLR 1387

Staffordshire Area Health Authority v South Staffordshire Waterworks Co

COURT OF APPEAL, CIVIL DIVISION

[1978] 3 All ER 769, [1978] 1 WLR 1387, 77 LGR 17, (101 LQR 102)

HEARING-DATES: 21, 24, 25, 26, 27 APRIL, 2 MAY 1978

2 MAY 1978

Contract – Time – Duration of contract – Determinable by reasonable notice – Contract by water company to supply water at set rate to hospital – Contract expressed to continue 'at all times hereafter' – Inflation increasing normal water charges twentyfold since contract made – Whether water company entitled to terminate contract by reasonable notice – Whether contract to be construed in context of circumstances in which made.

LORD DENNING MR. Four simple words "at all times hereafter" have given rise to this important case. […]

Contracts which contain no provisions for determination […]

[…] The cost of supply of goods and services goes up with inflation through the rooftops and the fixed payments goes down to the bottom of the well so that it worth little or nothing. Rather than tolerate such inequality, the courts will construe the contracts so as to hold that it is determinable by reasonable notice. […] They say that in the circumstances as they have developed – which the parties never had in mind – the contract ceases to bind the parties forever. It can be determined on reasonable notice. […]

Inflation

[…] We have […] had mountainous inflation and the pound dropping to cavernous depths. […] Here we have in the present case a striking instance of a long term obligation entered into 50 years ago. […] In these 50 years, and especially in the last 10 years, the cost of supplying the water has increased twentyfold. […] It seems to me that we have reached the point which Viscount Simon contemplated in *British Movietone Ltd* v. *London and District Cinemas Ltd* [1952] A.C. 166, 185. Speaking à propos of the depreciation of currency, he envisaged a situation where "a consideration of the terms of the contract, in the light of circumstances existing when it was made, shows that they never agreed to be bound in a fundamentally different situation which has now unexpectedly emerged, [and he went on to say that when such a situation emerges] the contract ceases to bind at that point – not because the courts in its discretions thinks it just and reasonable to qualify the terms of the contract, but because on its true construction it does not apply to the situation." […]

So here the situation has changed so radically since the contract was made 50 years ago that the term of the contract "at all times hereafter" ceases to bind: and it is open to the court to hold that the contract is determined by reasonable notice.

Conclusion

I do not think that the water company could have determined the agreement immediately after it was made. […] But, in the past 50 years, the whole situation has changed so radically that one can say with confidence: "The parties never intended that the supply should be continued in these days at that price." Rather than force such unequal terms on the parties, the courts should hold that the agreement could be and was properly determined in 1975 by the reasonable notice of six months. […]

4. *Guenter Treitel, The Law of Contract*, 12th edn, ed. by EDWIN PEEL

19-037   **Contracts of indefinite duration.** […] In *Staffordshire Area Health Authority* v. *South Staffordshire Waterworks Co.* a hospital had in 1919 contracted to give up to a waterworks company its right to take water from a well, and the company had in return promised "at all times hereafter" to supply water to the hospital at a fixed price specified in the contract. In 1975, the cost to the company of making the supply had risen to over 18 times that fixed price and the company gave seven months' notice to terminate the agreement. It was held that this notice was effective. Lord Denning M.R. regarded the contract as frustrated by the change of circumstances which had occurred between 1919 and 1975. But this view is, with respect, open to question, as it was based on the very passage of his own judgment in the *British Movietonews* case which had there been disapproved by the House of Lords. The preferable reason for the decision in the *Staffordshire* case is, therefore, that of the majority, who held that the agreement was, on its true construction, intended to be of indefinite (and not of perpetual) duration: hence the case fell within the general principle under which, in commercial agreements of indefinite duration, a term is often implied entitling either party to terminate by reasonable notice. It follows from this reasoning that the decision would have gone the other way if the agreement had been for a fixed term, e.g. for 10 years. The agreement could then not have been terminated by notice before the end of the 10 years, nor would an increase in the suppliers' costs during that period have been a ground of frustration. This view is supported by later authority and seems also to be correct in principle: if parties enter into a fixed term fixed price contract they must be taken thereby to have allocated the risks of market fluctuations. [...]

XI.   Principles of Contract Law

1. Commission on European Contract Law:
Principles of European Contract Law

Art. 6:111.   Change of Circumstances.

(1) A party is bound to fulfil its obligations even if performance has become more onerous, whether because the cost of performance has increased or because the value of the performance it receives has diminished.

(2) If, however, performance of the contract becomes excessively onerous because of a change of circumstances, the parties are bound to enter into negotiations with a view to adapting the contract or terminating it, provided that:

    (a)   the change of circumstances occurred after the time of conclusion of the contract,

    (b)   the possibility of a change of circumstances was not one which could reasonably have been taken into account at the time of conclusion of the contract, and

    (c)   the risk of the change of circumstances is not one which, according to the contract, the party affected should be required to bear.

(3) If the parties fail to reach agreement within a reasonable period, the court may:

    (a)   end the contract at a date and on terms to be determined by the court; or

    (b)   adapt the contract in order to distribute between the parties in a just and equitable manner the losses and gains resulting from the change of circumstances.

In either case, the court may award damages for the loss suffered through a party refusing to negotiate or breaking off negotiations contrary to good faith and fair dealing.

Comment

A.   *General*

The majority of countries in the European Community have introduced into their law some mechanism intended to correct any injustice which results from an imbalance in the contract caused by supervening events which the parties could not reasonably have foreseen when they made the contract. In practice, contracting parties adopt the same idea, supplementing the general rules of law with a variety of clauses, such as "hardship" clauses.

The Principles adopt such a mechanism, taking a broad and flexible approach, as befits the pursuit of contractual justice which runs through them: they prevent the cost caused by some unforeseen event from falling wholly on one of the parties. The same idea may be expressed in different terms: the risk of a change of circumstances which was unforeseen may not have been allocated by the original contract and the parties or, if they cannot agree, the court must now decide how the cost should be borne. The mechanism reflects the modern trend towards giving the court some power to moderate the rigours of freedom and sanctity of contract.

[...]

On the other hand, this concept of *"imprévision"* (it is convenient to borrow this term from French administrative case law) is distinct from "impossibility", which is covered by Article 8:108. Although in either case an unforeseen event has occurred, impossibility presupposes that the event has caused an insurmountable obstacle to performance, whereas in *"imprévision"* performance may still be possible for the debtor but will be ruinous for it. Of course there is sometimes a very fine line between a performance which is only possible by totally unreasonable efforts, and a performance which is only very difficult even if it may drive the debtor into bankruptcy. It is up to the court to decide which situation is before it (see also the comment to Article 8:108).

"Imprévision" is also differentiated from impossibility by its consequences. The latter, if it is total, can only lead to the end of the contract (see Article 9:301 and comment). *"Imprévision"* gives the court the choice of declaring the contract terminated or revising its terms.

However, the court's decision to terminate or to modify the contract is very much a last resort. The whole procedure is devised to encourage the parties to reach an amicable settlement: hence the obligation to enter negotiations. The court may also remit the matter to the parties for a last effort of negotiation. In the absence of an agreement, it is up to the court to decide. [...]

B. *Conditions for the procedure to apply*
Strict conditions must be fulfilled for the renegotiation mechanism to be triggered. These are set out in Article 6:111(2).

(i) Performance Excessively Onerous
The first condition follows directly from the first subsection: the change in circumstances must have brought about a major imbalance in the contract. Any contract, especially one of a long duration, is made in a particular economic context which may not last – it is this notion which underlies the ancient *"clausula rebus sic stantibus"*. A subsequent change in the economic context is not enough to give rise to the right to have the contract revised. The *"imprévision"* mechanism only comes into play if the contract is completely overturned by events, so that although it still can be performed, this will involve completely exorbitant costs for one of the parties. The terms of the paragraph show clearly that the court should not interfere merely because of some disequilibrium.

The "excessive onerosity" may be the direct result of increased cost in performance – for example, the increased cost of transport if the Suez Canal is closed and ships have to be sent round the Cape of Good Hope. Or, as the paragraph states, it may be the result of the expected counter-performance becoming valueless; for example, if the cost of building work which has already been executed is to be determined by reference to some index of a price which collapses in a quite unforeseeable way.

[...]

Illustration 1: A canning business buys the whole of a producer's future crop of tomatoes at 10 pence per kilo. It cannot demand renegotiation when by harvest time the market price has fallen to 5 pence per kilo because of an unexpected flood of imported tomatoes.

Illustration 2: A contract is made to supply for irrigation for fifty years at a fixed price but the price becomes derisory through inflation. The supplier may be able to demand renegotiation.

(ii)   Time Factor

The second condition is that the change of circumstances must have occurred after the contract was made. If, unknown to either party, circumstances which make the contract excessively onerous for one of them already existed at that date, the rules on mistake will apply, see Articles 4:103 and 4:105.

(iii)   Circumstances could not have been taken into account

Thirdly, the change of circumstances should not have reasonably been taken into account by the parties. This condition is parallel to that applicable to impossibility of performance and should be interpreted in the same way. Hardship cannot be invoked if the matter would have been foreseen and taken into account by a reasonable man in the same situation, by a person who is neither unduly optimistic or pessimistic, nor careless of his own interests.

> *Illustration 3*: During a period when the traffic in a particular region is periodically interrupted by lorry drivers' blockades, the reasonable man would not choose a route through that region in the hope that on the day in question the road will be clear; he would choose another route.

(iv)   Risk

Lastly it must be decided whether the party affected by a change in circumstances should be required to bear the risk of the change, either because it expressly undertook to do so (for instance by taking the risk of a shift in exchange rates) or because the contract is a speculative one (for instance a sale on the futures market). If so, the party cannot make use of this section.

C.   *The obligation to renegotiate*

Like many expressly agreed clauses, Article 6:111 envisages at the outset a process of negotiation to reach an amicable agreement varying the contract. [...]

The obligation to renegotiate is independent and carries its own sanction in paragraph (3)(c). The compensation provided by (3)(c) will normally consist of damages for the harm caused by a refusal to negotiate or a breaking off of negotiations in bad faith (for instance, the expenses of bringing the action insofar as these have not been recouped by an award of costs). It may be awarded against either party.

D.   *The court's powers*

If the parties' negotiations do not succeed, either of the parties may bring the matter before the court.

The court will intervene only in the last resort, but it is given wide powers. The court may, in effect, either terminate the contract or modify its terms. In accordance with the purpose of the provision, its first aim should be to preserve the contract. The court could even require the parties to make a last effort at renegotiation if it believes that there is still a chance of saving the contract. It may employ any means that are permitted under its national law, such as appointing a mediator to assist the parties. If the negotiations are unsuccessful it will have to make a decision on the merits in accordance with paragraph (3).

The modification of the clauses of the contract must be aimed at re-establishing the balance within the contract by ensuring that the extra cost imposed by the unforeseen circumstances are borne equitably by the parties. They may not be placed solely on one of them.

Illustration 4: A town council has arranged for the supply of electricity by a private company at a fixed tariff. If the price of the coal used to produce the electricity increases dramatically because of shortages, the additional payment which the town should be required to make should not cover the whole of the additional cost of the coal. Part of the extra cost should fall on the company. Unlike the risks which result from total impossibility, the risks of unforeseen events are to be shared.

[…]

2. Study Group on a European Civil Code and Research Group on EC Private Law (Acquis Group): *Draft Common Frame of Reference*

III. – 1:110: Variation or termination by court on a change of circumstances

(1) An obligation must be performed even if performance has become more onerous, whether because the cost of performance has increased or because the value of what is to be received in return has diminished.

(2) If, however, performance of a contractual obligation or of an obligation arising from a unilateral juridical act becomes so onerous because of an exceptional change of circumstances that it would be manifestly unjust to hold the debtor to the obligation a court may:

(a) vary the obligation in order to make it reasonable and equitable in the new circumstances; or

(b) terminate the obligation at a date and on terms to be determined by the court.

(3) Paragraph (2) applies only if:

(a) the change of circumstances occurred after the time when the obligation was incurred,

(b) the debtor did not at that time take into account, and could not reasonably be expected to have taken into account, the possibility or scale of that change of circumstances;

(c) the debtor did not assume, and cannot reasonably be regarded as having assumed, the risk of that change of circumstances; and

(d) the debtor has attempted, reasonably and in good faith, to achieve by negotiation a reasonable and equitable adjustment of the terms regulating the obligation.

3. UNIDROIT: *Principles of International Commercial Contracts*

HARDSHIP

Art. 6.2.1. Contract to be observed.

Where the performance of a contract becomes more onerous for one of the parties, that party is nevertheless bound to perform its obligations subject to the following provisions on hardship.

Art. 6.2.2. Definition of hardship.

There is hardship where the occurrence of events fundamentally alters the equilibrium of the contract either because the cost of a party's performance has increased or because the value of the performance a party receives has diminished, and

    (a) the events occur or become known to the disadvantaged party after the conclusion of the contract;

    (b) the events could not reasonably have been taken into account by the disadvantaged party at the time of the conclusion of the contract;

    (c) the events are beyond the control of the disadvantaged party; and

    (d) the risk of the events was not assumed by the disadvantaged party.

Art. 6.2.3. Effects of hardship.

(1) In case of hardship, the disadvantaged party is entitled to request renegotiations. The request shall be made without undue delay and shall indicate the grounds on which it is based.

(2) The request for renegotiation does not in itself entitle the disadvantaged party to withhold performance.

(3) Upon failure to reach agreement within a reasonable time either party may resort to the court.

(4) If the court finds hardship it may, if reasonable,

    (a) terminate the contract at a date and on terms to be fixed, or

    (b) adapt the contract with a view to restoring its equilibrium.

XII. Further reading

HUGH BEALE *et al.* (eds), *Cases, Materials and Text on Contract Law* (Ius Commune Casebooks for the Common Law of Europe), Oxford: Hart Publishing, 2002, Ch. 5, 592–657.

ALLAN FARNSWORTH, *Contracts*, 3rd edn, New York: Aspen Publishers, 2004, 619–47 (USA).

NANCY KIM, "Mistakes, Changed Circumstances and Intent", 56 (2008) *Kan. L. Rev.* 473–516.

MARTIN SCHMIDT-KESSEL AND KATRIN MAYER, "Supervening events and force majeure", in Jan M. Smits (ed.), *Elgar Encyclopedia of Comparative Law*, Cheltenham: Elgar Publishing, 2006, 689–98.

RUTH SEFTON-GREEN, "The DCFR, the Avant-projet Catala and French legal scholars: a story of cat and mouse?", *Edin. L.R.* 2008, 12(3), 351–73.

DENNIS TALLON, "Hardship", in Arthur Hartkamp *et al.* (eds), *Towards a European Civil Code*, 3rd edn, Nijmegen: Kluwer, 2004, Ch. 27, 499–504.

GUENTER TREITEL, *Frustration and Force Majeure*, London: Sweet & Maxwell, 1994.

REINHARD ZIMMERMANN, *The Law of Obligations – Roman Foundations of the Civilian Tradition*, Cape Town: Juta & Co., 1990, 579–82.

KONRAD ZWEIGERT AND HEIN KÖTZ, *An Introduction to Comparative Law*, 3rd edn, Oxford: Oxford University Press, 1998, 516–36.

Case 8:   Contracts and the transfer of ownership of property in European private law

> "§V. [...] *Grotius soutient, que, selon le Droit Naturel, les Conventions toutes seules suffisent pour transférer la Propriété [...], & que la Délivrance de la chose n'est nécessaire qu'en vertu du Droit Civil purement Positif [...] Les Interprètes du Droit Romain prétendent, au contraire, que la Délivrance est absolument nécessaire & que, sans cela, les Conventions les plus expresses ne font pas changer de maître à une chose.*"[1]

> "*Nemo plus iuris ad alium transferre potest, quam ipse haberet*"?[2]

Scenario

As part of a large-scale project, two businesses (hereafter: the seller and the first purchaser) plan, *inter alia*, the sale of two machines. However, without the parties' knowledge, the contractual relationship, including the contract for the sale of the machines, is void.[3] Unaware of the fact that the contract is void, the seller delivers the machines to the first purchaser in order to fulfil his contractual obligation. The parties believe that there is a binding contract and agree that the machines now belong to the purchaser.

The first purchaser then sells and transfers the machines to two subsequent purchasers. One of these subsequent purchasers is not aware that the contract between the seller and the first purchaser is void (the *bona fide* purchaser). The other subsequent purchaser, on the other hand, knows that the contract between the seller and first purchaser is void (the purchaser in bad faith[4]).

When the seller realises that his contract with the first purchaser is void, he demands the return of the machines from the subsequent purchasers. They refuse to give the machines back.

---

[1]   Translation: §V. [...] Grotius maintains that, according to natural law, agreements alone are sufficient for the transfer of ownership of property [...] & that the delivery of the thing is only necessary by virtue of purely statutory civil law [...] Scholars of Roman law claim, however, that delivery is absolutely necessary & that, without that, the clearest of agreements do not change who has control of a thing. SAMUEL VON PUFENDORF, *Le droit de la Nature et des Gens, ou Système Général des Principes les plus importants de la Morale, de la Jurisprudence, et de la Politique*, 1706, with a Latin to French translation by Jean Barbeyrac, Basle: E. & J. R. Thourneisen, Freres, 1732, livre IV, chapitre IX, p. 559.

[2]   ULPIANUS, *Digesta* 50, 17, 54, translation: No person can transfer a better title than he has.

[3]   For the purposes of this case it is presumed that the contract is *void*. The case does *not* deal with the issue of whether a contract is void or merely *voidable*. On this issue in English law, see, EWAN MCKENDRICK, *Contract Law*, 7th edn, Basingstoke: Palgrave Macmillan, 2007, paras 4.6, 14.3 ff., 17.2.

[4]   This purchaser is hereafter referred to as the "purchaser in bad faith" even though knowledge of the invalidity of the contract between the seller and first purchaser on the part of the subsequent purchaser renders the purchaser a bad faith purchaser in some legal orders but not in others.

Questions

(1) The question of the effect of a contract on the transfer of ownership is entirely left to the different national legal orders. This is the case even in situations in which the contract is governed by the Vienna Convention on the International Sale of Goods (or CISG) (see Art. 4(b) of the Vienna Convention).

   What are the conditions for the valid transfer of ownership of property from an owner to a purchaser under the different legal orders below? Did the first purchaser acquire ownership of the machine in the case scenario above? Did the two subsequent purchasers acquire ownership of the property? If so, by virtue of which legal rules?

(2) Systemise and compare the different solutions concerning:
   (a) the transfer of ownership of property;
   (b) acquisition of property in good faith.
   How many different groups of solutions are there?

(3) What rules governing the transfer of ownership of property and acquisition of property in good faith do you find the most convincing? Give reasons for your answer.

Table of contents

I. Vienna Sales Convention

United Nations Convention on Contracts for the International Sale of Goods (CISG)

Art. 30

The seller must deliver the goods, hand over any documents relating to them and transfer the property in the goods, as required by the contract and this Convention.

Art. 4

This Convention governs only the formation of the contract of sale and the rights and obligations of the seller and the buyer arising from such a contract. In particular, except as otherwise expressly provided in this Convention, it is not concerned with:

(a)   the validity of the contract or of any of its provisions or of any usage;

(b)   the effect which the contract may have on the property in the goods sold.

II. England

1. Sale of Goods Act 1979

2. Contract of sale.
(1)   A contract of sale of goods is a contract by which the seller transfers or agrees to transfer the property in goods to the buyer for a money consideration, called the price.

[...]

(4)   Where under a contract of sale the property in the goods is transferred from the seller to the buyer the contract is called a sale.
(5)   Where under a contract of sale the transfer of the property in the goods is to take place at a future time or subject to some condition later to be fulfilled the contract is called an agreement to sell.
(6)   An agreement to sell becomes a sale when the time elapses or the conditions are fulfilled subject to which the property in the goods is to be transferred.

27.   Duties of seller and buyer.
It is the duty of the seller to deliver the goods, and of the buyer to accept and pay for them in accordance with the terms of the contract for sale.

17.   Property passes when intended to pass.
(1)   Where there is a contract for the sale of specific or ascertained goods the property in them is transferred to the buyer at such time as the parties to the contract intend it to be transferred.
(2)   For the purpose of ascertaining the intention of the parties regard shall be had to the terms of the contract, the conduct of the parties and the circumstances of the case.

18.   Rules for ascertaining intention.
Unless a different intention appears, the following are rules for ascertaining the intention of the parties as to the time at which the property in the goods is to pass to the buyer.
  Rule 1.—Where there is an unconditional contract for the sale of specific goods in a deliverable state the property in the goods passes to the buyer when the contract is made, and it is immaterial whether the time of payment or the time of delivery, or both, be postponed.

  [...]

21.   Sale by person not the owner.
(1)   Subject to this Act, where goods are sold by a person who is not their owner, and who does not sell them under the authority or with the consent of the owner, the buyer acquires no better title to the goods than the seller had [...]

[...]

23. Sale under voidable title.
When the seller of goods has a voidable title to them, but his title has not been avoided at the time of the sale, the buyer acquires a good title to the goods, provided he buys them in good faith and without notice of the seller's defect of title.

25. Buyer in possession after sale.
(1) Where a person *having bought or agreed to buy*[5] goods obtains, with the consent of the seller, possession of the goods [...], the delivery or transfer by that person [...], of the goods [...], under any sale [...], to any person receiving the same in good faith and without notice of any [...] right of the original seller in respect of the goods, has the same effect as if the person making the delivery or transfer were a mercantile agent[6] in possession of the goods [...] with the consent of the owner.

[...]

2. High Court (QB): *Feuer Leather Corporation* v. *Frank Johnston & Sons Ltd* [1981] Com LR 251

NEILL J: [...] The burden of proving a bona fide purchase for value without notice rests on the person who asserts it. Such a rule seems to me to be logical [...]

3. A. G. GUEST, *Benjamin's Sale of Goods*, 7th edn

1. IN GENERAL

7-001   *Nemo dat quod non habet.* The general rule in English law is that no one can transfer a better title to goods than he himself possesses. This rule is often expressed in terms of the Latin maxim *nemo dat quod non habet.* It is partially set out in section 21(1) of the Sale of Goods Act 1979 [...] At one time, the only effective exception to this rule was that of a sale in market overt. But, in response to commercial and social demands, further exceptions to the rule have been progressively introduced both by the common law and by statute. As Denning L.J. has remarked: "In the development of our law, two principles have striven for mastery. The first is for the protection of property: no one can give a better title than he himself possesses. The second is for the protection of commercial transactions: the person who takes in good faith and for value without notice should get a good title. The first principle has held sway for a long time, but it has been modified by the common law itself and by statute so as to meet the needs of

---

5   Emphasis added.
6   In such a situation, the agent can validly transfer ownership of the goods.

our own times." The second principle is fairly precisely delineated by a finite number of exceptions to the *nemo dat* rule. These are discussed in the sections which follow.

[...]

7. BUYER IN POSSESSION

7-069 **Buyer in possession.** [...] [S]ection 25(1) of the Sale of Goods Act 1979 [...] re-enacts in substance section 9 of the Factors Act 1889, to which Act reference may be made for the interpretation of its wording. At common law, a disposition by a buyer in possession was subject to the ordinary rule that *nemo dat quod non habet*. A limited exception was established by section 4 of the Factors Act 1877 and this was extended and reformulated in the Act of 1889.

7-070 **"Bought or agreed to buy."** In order to claim the protection of this subsection the person to whom the buyer has delivered or transferred the goods [...] must show that the buyer has "bought or agreed to buy" the goods. In most cases, the subsection will be invoked where there has been merely an agreement to sell, that is to say, where there is a contract of sale, but the transfer of the property in the goods to the buyer is to take place at a future time or subject to some condition later to be fulfilled. The buyer must, however, be contractually bound to purchase the goods under a contract of sale. [...] It has been held to be immaterial that the agreement is unenforceable [...] or that it is voidable at the election of the seller on the ground of fraud. But if the agreement is absolutely void, *e.g.* for mistake as to the person or even possibly for illegality, there will have been no agreement to buy the goods.

7-071 At first sight it seems curious that a disposition by a person who has *bought* the goods should also have been included, since, as a normal rule, a buyer to whom the property in goods has passed under a contract of sale will be able to confer a good title by virtue of his property in them. In such a case no question will arise as to the good faith of the person receiving them, nor will the other limitations imposed by this subsection be of any relevance. But there may be some situations where the property in the goods sold will have passed to the buyer, and he will have obtained possession of them, but subject to some right or interest still vested in the seller. For example, it seems that an unpaid seller might still retain his lien over the goods notwithstanding that they are in the buyer's possession if such possession has been given to the buyer temporarily and for a limited purpose; or special rights may have been reserved by agreement to the seller under which he retains an interest in the goods. In these situations, a disponee of the goods from the buyer might not obtain a good title except by relying on section 25(1) of the Act. However, the most important application of the word "bought" in this subsection is where the buyer has obtained both property in and possession of the goods under the contract of sale, but his title has subsequently been avoided by the seller. In this case, it would seem that, having obtained possession of the goods with the consent of the seller, the buyer may be able to pass a good title to a disponee.

4. Ewan McKendrick, *Contract Law*, 8th edn, pp. 53–55

4.6 Mistake negativing consent

[…]

[…] The identity of the person with whom one is contracting or proposing to contract is often immaterial. A simple example is provided by the sale of goods in a shop. The owner of the shop will often be indifferent as to the identity of the person purchasing the goods. What matters is not the identity of the customer as such, but his willingness and ability to pay for the goods. But let us suppose that the customer wishes to pay for the goods by cheque or by credit card. This may change matters because, if the customer is not who he says he is, the shop may find that its demand for payment on the cheque or its demand for payment from the credit card company will be rejected and it must then look to the defaulting customer for redress. Even here, however, the identity of the customer does not generally give rise to legal difficulties as between the shop and the customer […] The customer, whoever he is, is liable to pay for the goods he has acquired. The legal difficulties tend to arise in the case where the customer sells the goods which he has purchased to a third party who pays for the goods in all good faith (that is to say, he is unaware of the circumstances which surround the earlier transaction).

In such cases the defaulting customer is usually a rogue […]: he had no intention of paying for the goods at the time of their acquisition from the original owner and sold them on to an innocent third party almost immediately after acquiring them. In the typical case, by the time that the owner discovers the true situation (that is, he will not be paid by his customer), the goods have already been transferred by the rogue into the possession of the third party. Given that a claim against the rogue is unlikely to be fruitful (either because he cannot be found or because he has been found and is not worth suing), the original seller is likely to wish to bring a claim against the third party in possession of the goods. In essence, the claim of the original seller is that he remains the owner of the goods and is entitled to have them back (or their financial value). The innocent third party purchaser will generally respond to the effect that he is the owner of the goods, having bought them in all good faith. Thus the core of the dispute relates to the location of the ownership of the goods. English law, rather unusually, does not deal with such claims through the law of property. Rather, it employs the law of tort in order to protect property rights. The original seller will therefore typically bring a claim in tort (usually a claim in the tort of conversion) against the innocent third party purchaser in which he will assert that the purchaser is dealing with the goods in such a way as to interfere with his rights as owner of the goods. The third party purchaser will deny the claim on the ground that he is the owner of the goods and so it cannot be said that he has in any way interfered with the claimant's rights. How does this dispute relate to the law of contract? The answer is that the rogue can only pass on to the purchaser such rights as he himself possesses. English law recognises a general principle entitled *nemo dat quod non habet* (you cannot give what you do not have). The effect of the rule is to require an examination of the rights acquired by the rogue under the initial transaction with the original seller and this is where the law of contract has a vital role to play. If the contract validly transfers ownership in the goods to the rogue then the rogue can in turn confer rights of ownership on the third party purchaser: conversely, if the initial contract is ineffective to confer rights of ownership on the third party then the rogue will not be able to confer rights of ownership on the rogue purchaser (unless one of the exceptions to the *nemo dat* rule is found to be applicable). In this way the rights as between the original owner and the rogue will determine whether the claim of the original owner or the third party purchaser will prevail.

Turning to the contract between the original seller and the rogue, there is clearly something wrong with it. The rogue has assumed a false identity and will generally be guilty of fraud: in many cases he will have induced the seller to enter into the contract by a fraudulent misrepresentation as to his identity. The important point to note here is that fraudulent misrepresentation renders a contract voidable; that is to say, the contract remains valid and can operate to transfer ownership in the goods until such time as the contract has been set aside. This does not present an attractive option for a seller because the rogue will, in all probability, have transferred the goods to an innocent third party purchaser before he has had the opportunity to discover the truth and set aside the transaction with the rogue. On this basis the innocent third party purchaser will win because he will acquire ownership of the goods from the rogue. A more attractive option from the perspective of the seller is to assert that the contract with the rogue was void on the ground that it had been entered into under a mistake. Mistake can operate to render a contract void and a contract which is void is set aside for all purposes and generally produces no legal effects whatsoever. So, if the contract was void for mistake, the rogue could not have obtained property in the goods from the original seller and therefore has no property rights to pass on to the innocent third party purchaser. On this basis the original seller will win and will be entitled to recover the goods (or, more likely, their financial value) from the third party purchaser.

Two further […] points ought to be made […] The first is that there are policy issues at stake here in determining the outcome of the competition between the original owner and the third party purchaser. […] The point to be made here is that the judges do not have a free hand to decide these policy issues. In the case of contracts for the sale of goods Parliament has enshrined the *nemo dat* rule in legislation (see section 21(1) of the Sale of Goods Act 1979) and so it is not open to the courts to question the appropriateness of that general rule. The court can obviously consider whether or not the case falls within one of the existing exceptions to the *nemo dat* rule but it cannot seek to displace the general rule in favour of a principle which favours the protection of the innocent third party purchaser. The second point is that it might seem odd that the original seller can improve his position by relying on mistake rather than fraud. Fraud appears to be the more serious vitiating factor […] Yet it only renders a contract voidable. Mistake, by contrast, […] can and does render a contract void. Some judges have recoiled from the proposition that a claimant can improve his position by relying on mistake rather than fraud (see, for example, the speech of Lord Nicholls in *Shogun Finance Ltd* v. *Hudson* [2003] UKHL 62; [2004] 1 AC 919) but the proposition that mistake can render a contract void, whereas fraud only renders a contract voidable, is probably too firmly entrenched in the law to be uprooted judicially. […]

III. France

1. Code civil français (*French Civil Code*)

Art. 711
La propriété des biens s'acquiert et se transmet par succession, par donation entre vifs ou testamentaire, et par l'effet des obligations.

Art. 711
Ownership of property is acquired and transmitted by succession, by gift inter vivos or will, and by the effect of obligations.

Art. 1138
(1)   L'obligation de livrer la chose est parfaite par le seul consentement des parties contractantes.
(2)   Elle rend le créancier propriétaire et met la chose à ses risques dès l'instant où elle a dû être livrée, encore que la tradition n'en ait point été faite, à moins que le débiteur ne soit en demeure de la livrer; auquel cas la chose reste aux risques de ce dernier.

Art. 1138
(1)   An obligation to deliver a thing is completed by the sole consent of the contracting parties.
(2)   [The obligation] makes the creditor the owner and places the thing at his own risk from the moment when it should have been delivered, even if the delivery has not been made, unless the debtor is in default of delivery; in which case, the thing remains at the risk of the latter.

Art. 1141
Si la chose qu'on s'est obligé de donner ou de livrer à deux personnes successivement, est purement mobilière, celle des deux qui en a été mise en possession réelle est préférée et en demeure propriétaire, encore que son titre soit postérieure en date pourvu toutefois que la possession soit de bonne foi.

Art. 1141
Where a thing which one is bound to deliver to two persons successively is a chattel, the one of the two who has been put in actual possession is preferred and remains owner of it, even though his title is subsequent as to date, provided however that the possession is in good faith.

Art. 1582
(1)   La vente est une convention par laquelle l'un s'oblige à livrer une chose, et l'autre à la payer.
[...]

Art. 1582
(1)   A sale is an agreement by which one person binds himself to deliver a thing, and another to pay for it.
[...]

Art. 1583

Elle est parfaite entre les parties, et la propriété est acquise de droit à l'acheteur à l'égard du vendeur, dès qu'on est convenu de la chose et du prix, quoique la chose n'ait pas encore été livrée ni le prix payé.

Art. 1583

[The sale] is completed between the parties, and ownership of the property passes from the seller to the buyer, as soon as the thing and the price have been agreed upon, even though the thing has not yet been delivered nor the price paid.

Art. 2276

(1)   En fait de meubles, la possession vaut titre.

(2)   Néanmoins, celui qui a perdu ou auquel il a été volé une chose peut la revendiquer pendant trois ans à compter du jour de la perte ou du vol, contre celui dans les mains duquel il la trouve; sauf à celui-ci son recours contre celui duquel il la tient.

Art. 2276

(1)   With regard to chattels, possession is equivalent to a title.

(2)   Nevertheless, someone who has lost something or had something stolen can claim it back from the person who has it for the three years from the day of the loss or theft; subject to the remedy of the latter against the person he obtained it from.

2. Cour de cassation, 20 février 1996, Bull. civ. 1996 I n° 96 p. 66

«[L]'art. [2276] du Code civil [...] suppose que le propriétaire véritable revendique le meuble dont il a perdu possession entre les mains *d'un tiers*,[7] défendeur au procès en revendication [...] »

Translation

"Art. [2276] of the French Civil code [...] presumes that the true owner is claiming the chattel of which he lost possession to a *third party*,[8] the defendant in the claim [...]"

3.   Cour d'appel de Paris, 15 février 1961 (*Dame Morel d'Arleux* c. *Desourtheau et autres*), D. 1961, sommaires p. 43

«Pour pouvoir invoquer l'art. [2276] c. civ., [l'acquéreur] doit être de bonne foi, c'est-à-dire avoir pu croire que l'objet lui a été remis par son légitime propriétaire, de sorte que la possession ne puisse être considérée d'origine obscure.»

---

[7]   Emphasis added by the author.

[8]   Emphasis added by the author. I.e. the owner is claiming it from a third party other than the party with whom he contracted.

Translation

"To be able to invoke Art. [2276] of the *Code civil*, [the acquirer] must have acted in good faith, that is to say believed that the object was transferred to him by its legitimate owner, so that the possession cannot be considered as being from an unknown origin."

4. Code civil français (*French Civil Code*)

Art. 2274
La bonne foi est toujours présumée, et c'est à celui qui allègue la mauvaise foi à la prouver.

Art. 2274
Good faith is always presumed, and it is for the person who alleges bad faith to prove it.

5. FRANÇOIS TERRÉ AND PHILIPPE SIMLER, *Droit civil: Les biens,* 7th edn (translation of the French original)

§ 2 Possession of movable property in good faith

[…]

426 *The two meanings of the rule: method of acquisition and presumption of title.* ◊ The rule set out in Article [2276] has two meanings, two functions: depending on the case, possession constitutes a method of acquisition or fulfils an evidentiary function.

1) A person who acquires a chattel *a non domino* in good faith, that is to say from someone who is not the owner, does not acquire the property by the effect of the contract, because the alienator cannot transfer a right that does not belong to him. However, if the acquirer is put in possession, this fact makes him the owner. From which it results that the owner to which the chattel previously belonged can no longer claim it back from the possessor (unless the chattel was lost or stolen). And, in addition, if the right transferred to the acquirer is terminable or voidable, these defects are wiped out by the fact of the vesting in possession. It can therefore be said that a claim for recovery is excluded when the chattel has been acquired by a possessor in good faith, possession creating a new abstract title in favour of the possessor, that is to say independent of his transferred title.

As such, the rule is justified by commercial needs. Chattels are destined to circulate between people; for the most part, it is impossible for an acquirer to verify the rights of the seller and to reconstruct the chain of previous owners, transactions involving movable property not normally being evidenced in writing and chattels being transferred, very simply, from person to person. The acquirer would have no security if he could be subject to a claim for recovery or an action for annulment because of previous transactions. Justice demands protection of someone who came into possession of a chattel under normal conditions and who has done nothing wrong […]

2)   Secondly, the rule set out in Article [2276] has an *evidentiary function*: possession presupposes, in the absence of proof to the contrary, that the possessor gained title to the property legitimately. It is presumed that a possessor who claims to have acquired a chattel did so by a contract made with the true owner. […] Article [2276] […] grants [the possessor an exemption from proving that he acquired the chattel by a contract made with the true owner], and that is the second meaning of the rule: possession is equivalent to title; the law assumes therefore that the possessor was vested in possession by virtue of a valid transfer of title […], and it is for the claimant to rebut this presumption. […]

IV. Italy and Poland

1. Codice civile (*Italian Civil Code*)

Art. 922. Modi di acquisto [della proprietà].
La proprietà si acquista per occupazione, per invenzione, per accessione, per specificazione, per unione o commistione, per usucapione, per effetto di contratti, per successione a causa di morte e negli altri modi stabiliti dalla legge.

Art. 922. Modes of acquisition [of property].
Ownership is acquired by occupation, invention, accession, specification, union or commixtion, usucaption, as a result of contract, by succession at death, and in the other ways established by law.

Art. 1376. Contratto con effetti reali.
Nei contratti che hanno per oggetto il trasferimento della proprietà di una cosa determinata, la costituzione o il trasferimento di un diritto reale ovvero il trasferimento di un altro diritto, la proprietà o il diritto si trasmettono e si acquistano per effetto del consenso delle parti legittimamente manifestato.

Art. 1376. Contracts with real effects.
In contracts having as their object the transfer of ownership of a specific thing, the constitution or transfer of a real right or the transfer of another right, such as ownership or right is transferred and acquired by virtue of the lawfully expressed agreement of the parties.

Art. 1378. Trasferimento di cosa determinata solo nel genere.
Nei contratti che hanno per oggetto il trasferimento di cosa determinata solo nel genere, la proprietà si trasmette con l'individuazione fatto d'accordo tra le parti o nei modi da esse stabiliti. Trattandosi di cose che devono essere trasportate da un luogo a un altro, l'individuazione avviene anche mediante la consegna al vettore o allo spedizioniere.

Art. 1378. Transfer of thing specified only as to its kind [i.e. unidentified goods].
In contracts having as their object the transfer of things specified only as to their kind, ownership passes on specification of the goods by the parties or in the manner established by them. In the case of things which must be carried from one place to another, specification also takes place by delivery to the carrier or to the forwarding agent.

Art. 1153. Effetti dell'acquisto del possesso.
(1) Colui al quale sono alienati beni mobili da parte di chi non è proprietario, ne acquista la proprietà mediante il possesso, purché sia in buona fede al momento della consegna e sussista un titolo idoneo al trasferimento della proprietà.

[...]

Art. 1153. Effects of acquisition of possession.
(1) He to whom movable property is conveyed by one who is not the owner acquires ownership of it through possession, provided that he be in good faith at the moment of consignment and there be an instrument or transaction capable of transferring ownership [e.g. a contract of sale].

[...]

Art. 1154.   Conoscenza dell'illegittima provenienza della cosa.
A colui che ha acquistato conoscendo l'illegittima provenienza della cosa non giova l'erronea credenza che il suo autore o un precedente possessore ne sia divenuto proprietario.

Art. 1154.   Knowledge of illegitimate provenance of thing.
The erroneous belief that his transferor or a prior possessor had become owner does not justify one who acquires knowing the illegitimate provenance of the thing.

Art. 1147.   Possesso di buona fede.
(1)   È possessore di buona fede chi possiede ignorando di ledere l'altrui diritto.
(2)   La buona fede non giova se l'ignoranza dipende da colpa grave.
(3)   La buona fede è presunta e basta che che vi sia stato al tempo dell'acqisito.

Art. 1147.   Possession in good faith.
(1)   One who possesses without knowledge that he prejudices another's right is a possessor in good faith.
(2)   Good faith does not apply if the ignorance is the result of gross negligence.
(3)   Good faith is presumed and it is sufficient that it existed at the time of acquisition.

2. Kodeks cywilny (*Polish Civil Code*)[9]

Art. 535
(1)   Przez umowę sprzedaży sprzedawca zobowiązuje się przenieść na kupującego wlasność rzeczy i wydać mu rzecz, a kupujący zobowiązuje sić rzecz odebrać i zaplacić sprzedawcy cenę.

[...]

Art. 535.   [Definition].
(1)   Under a contract of sale the seller binds himself to transfer ownership of the thing to the buyer and to deliver it to him, and the buyer binds himself to take delivery of the thing and pay the seller the purchase price.

[...]

Art. 155
(1)   Umowa sprzedaży, zamiany, darowizny lub inna umowa zobowiązująca do przeniesienia wlasności rzeczy co do tożsamości oznaczonej przenosi wlasność na nabywcę, chyba że przepis szczególny stanowi inaczej albo że strony inaczej postanowiły.

[...]

---

[9]   For a brief introduction to Polish law, see, e.g., MICHAL GONDEK, "Poland"', in Jan M. Smits (ed.), *Elgar Encyclopedia of Comparative Law*, Cheltenham: Edward Elgar Publishing, 2006, pp. 548–53.

Art. 155. *[Transfer of title by contract].*
(1) A contract of sale, of exchange, of donation or any other contract that obliges one party to transfer ownership of specified goods, transfers ownership to the acquirer unless a special rule stipulates otherwise or the parties have agreed to something else.

[...]

Art. 169
(1) Jeżeli osoba nie uprawniona do rozporządzania rzeczą ruchomą zbywa rzecz i wydaje ją nabywcy, nabywca uzyskuje wlasność z chwilą objęcia rzeczy w posiadanie, chyba że działa w zlej wierze.

[...]

Art. 169. *[Acquisition from an unauthorised person].*
(1) If a person not entitled to dispose of a thing sells and delivers it to the acquirer, ownership passes to the acquirer when he gets possession unless he was acting in bad faith.

[...]

V. Germany

1. Bürgerliches Gesetzbuch (BGB)
(*German Civil Code*)

§ 433. Vertragstypische Pflichten beim Kaufvertrag .

(1)   Durch den Kaufvertrag wird der Verkäufer einer Sache verpflichtet, dem Käufer die Sache zu übergeben und das Eigentum an der Sache zu verschaffen. Der Verkäufer hat dem Käufer die Sache frei von Sach- und Rechtsmängeln zu verschaffen.

(2)   Der Käufer ist verpflichtet, dem Verkäufer den vereinbarten Kaufpreis zu zahlen und die gekaufte Sache abzunehmen.

§ 433. *Typical duties in a contract of sale.*

(1)   By a contract of sale, the seller of a thing is bound to deliver the thing to the buyer and to transfer ownership of the thing to the buyer. The seller must procure the thing for the buyer free from material and legal defects.

(2)   The buyer is bound to pay the seller the agreed purchase price and to take delivery of the thing.

§ 929. Einigung und Übergabe.

Zur Übertragung des Eigentums an einer beweglichen Sache ist erforderlich, dass der Eigentümer die Sache dem Erwerber übergibt und beide darüber einig sind, dass das Eigentum übergehen soll. Ist der Erwerber im Besitz der Sache, so genügt die Einigung über den Übergang des Eigentums.

§ 929. *Agreement and Transfer.*

For the transfer of ownership of a chattel it is necessary for the owner to deliver the thing to the acquirer and that both agree that the ownership be transferred ["real" contract]. If the acquirer is already in possession of the thing, the agreement on transfer of ownership is sufficient.

2. Reichsgericht (*Supreme Court of the Former German Empire*), 21.4.1906, RGZ 63, 179

"Die sachenrechtlichen Erfüllungsgeschäfte (z.B. Übergabe, [...]) sind nach dem Systeme des Bürgerlichen Gesetzbuches als Rechtsgeschäfte konstruiert, die die Macht, eine sachenrechtliche Wirkung hervorzubringen (z.B. Eigentum zu übertragen), in sich selbst tragen. [...] Man nennt die sachenrechtlichen Erfüllungsgeschäfte daher auch abstrakte Rechtsgeschäfte, abstrakt insofern, als sie auf sich selbst gestellt sind, und in dem Kausalgeschäfte, das ihnen zugrunde liegt, [...] keinen ihre Wirksamkeit bedingenden Faktor herübernehmen."

Translation

"Acts directed to fulfil the obligation to transfer title (e.g. the delivery of goods [...]) are, according to the German Civil Code, considered to be legal transactions which are empowered to have the effect of transferring title (e.g. the transfer of property) *in their own right*.[10] [...] These acts are therefore also referred to as abstract legal acts. Abstract in the sense that they are independent of the validity of the obligation they intend to fulfil [i.e. they are valid even if a contract creating the obligation to transfer the title, e.g. a sales contract, is void]."

3. Hugh Beale *et al.* (eds), *Cases, Materials and Text on Contract Law*, pp. 20–21, 28–29 (text by Denis Tallon)

1.1.3.C. CONTRACTS GIVING RISE TO OBLIGATIONS AND CONTRACTS TRANSFERRING OR CREATING PROPERTY RIGHTS

[...]

[...] [U]nder German law and the systems which follow that model, the contract merely creates the obligation [e.g. to transfer property]. Property is transferred or rights *in rem* created by means of another act, separate from the contract, pursuant to the principle of separability (*Abstraktionsprinzip*). Under that principle the former [e.g. the contract of sale] may be null and void without affecting the validity of the latter [i.e. the act transferring property]. [...]

[...]

1.1.4. A GERMAN LAW: THE PRINCIPLE OF SEPARABILITY (*ABSTRAKTIONSPRINZIP*)

[...] [German law makes a] distinction between contracts transferring property and contracts creating obligations [...] The principle of separability proclaimed by German law, and by certain other systems of law, asserts that the transfer of property is effected by [...] [a transaction] completely separate [from the contract creating the obligation to transfer the property] [...] This is how Zweigert and Kötz expound this principle:

Zweigert and Kötz[11]

Now if a legal system not only makes this distinction between the contract of sale and the real contract [...], but also makes the validity of each independent of the validity of the other, it accepts the doctrine of the "abstract real contract". By virtue of this doctrine, once a purchaser has made a "real" contract with his vendor and has received delivery of the purchased property from him, in principle he obtains ownership in the thing even if the contract of sale was void from the beginning, or is subsequently rescinded or is invalid in any other way: the "real" agreement [i.e. the agreement under § 929 BGB that the

---

10 Emphasis added.
11 K. Zweigert and H. Kötz, *Introduction to Comparative Law*, 2nd edn, Oxford: Clarendon Press, 1987, at 178–79.

property shall be transferred] is thus "abstract" because, given delivery [...], it transfers the property even if no valid contract of sale [between the seller and the acquirer] was concluded or if the contract of sale was originally valid but has subsequently lapsed. Of course in such a case the purchaser[12] is not entitled to retain the property; he has become owner, but has done so in the absence of a valid contract of sale, that is, "without legal cause", and is therefore bound to retransfer the property to the vendor as an "unjust enrichment" pursuant to § 812 BGB.

These rules apply in German law not only when property is sold but also when it is donated or given in exchange, or when it is transferred to a creditor as security for a loan [...]: in all these cases a distinction is drawn between the "basic transaction" or "causal transaction" (namely the contract of sale [§ 433 BGB], or the declaration of gift or security [...]) and the "completion transaction" or "performance transaction", namely the transfer of property [§ 929 BGB]; the abstract completion agreement may be valid notwithstanding the invalidity of the basic transaction and thus the purchaser, the donee, the creditor [...] will have become owner.

4. Bürgerliches Gesetzbuch (BGB) (*German Civil Code*)

§ 932. Gutgläubiger Erwerb vom Nichtberechtigten.
(1) Durch eine nach § 929 erfolgte Veräußerung wird der Erwerber auch dann Eigentümer, wenn die Sache nicht dem Veräußerer gehört, es sei denn, dass er zu der Zeit, zu der er nach diesen Vorschriften das Eigentum erwerben würde, nicht in gutem Glauben ist. [...]
(2) Der Erwerber ist nicht in gutem Glauben, wenn ihm bekannt oder infolge grober Fahrlässigkeit unbekannt ist, dass die Sache nicht dem Veräußerer gehört.

§ 932. *Acquisition in good faith from an unauthorised person*
(1) A disposal made in accordance with § 929 makes the acquirer the owner even if the thing does not belong to the seller, unless he is in bad faith at the time at which, according to these provisions, he would acquire ownership. [...]
(2) An acquirer acts in bad faith if it is known to him, or unknown to him because of gross negligence, that the thing does not belong to the seller.

---

[12] I.e. the person to whom the property was transferred by the owner although the contract of sale the parties intended to conclude was void or avoided (note by the author).

VI.   Greece

Αστικός Κώδικας (*Greek Civil Code*)

´Αρθρο 513.   Εννοια της πώλησης.

Με τη σύμβαση της πώλησης ο πωλητής έχει την υποχρέωση να πεταβιβάσει την κυριότητα του πράγματος ή το δικαίωμα, που αποτελούν το αντικείμενο της πώλησης και να παραδώσει το πράγμα και ι αγοραστής έχει την υποχρέωση να πληρώσει το τίμημα που συμφωνήθηκε

Art. 513.   Meaning of sale.

By a contract of sale the seller binds himself to transfer the ownership of the thing or the right that constitute the subject-matter of the sale and the purchaser binds himself to pay the price agreed.

´Αρθρο 1034.   Κτήση κινητού με σύπβαση.

Για τη πεταβίβαση τφς κυριότητας κινητού απαιτείται παράδιση της νοπής του από τον κυ΄ριο σ΄ αυτόν που την αποκτά και συμφωνία των δύο ότι μετατίθεται η κυριότητα.

Art. 1034.   Acquisition of movable by contract.

The transfer of ownership of a movable requires that possession thereof shall be passed from the owner to the acquirer and that both agree to the effect that ownership be transmitted.

´Αρθρο 1036.   Κτήση κινητού από μη κύριο.

(1)   Με την εκποίηση κινητού κατά το άρθρο 1034 εκείνος που αποκτά γίνεται κύριος και αν ακόμη η κυριότηρα του πράγματος δεν ανήκει σ΄ αυτόν που εκποιεί, εκτός αν κατά το χρόνο της παράδοσης της νοπής εκείνος που αποκτά βρίσκεται σε κακή πίστν.

[...]

Art. 1036.   Acquisition of movable from a person who is not the owner.

(1)   Following the alienation of a movable pursuant to the provisions of Article 1034 the acquirer shall become the owner thereof even if the ownership of the thing did not belong to the alienator except if at the time of the delivery of possession the acquirer acted in bad faith.

[...]

´Αρθρο 1037

Στην περίπτωση του προηγούπενου άρθρου εκείνος που αποκτά βρίσκεται σε κακή πίστν, αν γνωρίζει ή αγνοεί από βαριά αμέλεια ότι το κινητό πρα΄γμα δεν ανη΄κει κατα΄ κυριο΄τητα σ΄ αυτο΄υ που εκποιει΄.

Art. 1037

An acquirer acted in bad faith in the case provided for in the preceding article if he knew or ignored due to gross negligence imputable to him that the alienator did not have ownership of the movable thing alienated.

VII. Switzerland

1. Schweizerisches Obligationenrecht
(*Swiss Code of Obligations*)

Art. 184. Rechte und Pflichten im Allgemeinen.
(1) Durch den Kaufvertrag verpflichten sich der Verkäufer, dem Käufer den Kaufgegenstand zu übergeben und ihm das Eigentum daran zu verschaffen, und der Käufer, dem Verkäufer den Kaufpreis zu bezahlen.

[...]

Art. 184. Rights and obligations in general.
(1) A contract of purchase is a contract whereby the seller binds himself to deliver to the buyer the object of the purchase and to transfer title thereto to the buyer and the buyer binds himself to pay the purchase price to the seller.

[...]

2. Schweizerisches Zivilgesetzbuch
(*Swiss Civil Code*)

Art. 714. Erwerbsarten. Übertragung. Besitzübergang.
(1) Zur Übertragung des Fahrniseigentums bedarf es des Überganges des Besitzes auf den Erwerber.
(2) Wer in gutem Glauben eine bewegliche Sache zu Eigentum übertragen erhält, wird, auch wenn der Veräußerer zur Eigentumsübertragung nicht befugt ist, deren Eigentümer, sobald er nach den Besitzesregeln im Besitze der Sache geschützt ist.

Art. 714. Methods of acquisition. Transfer. Transfer of possession.
(1) Transfer of ownership in chattels requires transfer of possession to the acquirer.
(2) Whoever, in good faith, obtains a chattel for the purpose of acquiring ownership becomes the owner as soon as he is protected under the rules of possession, even if the alienator was not entitled to transfer the ownership[13].

Art. 933. Verfügungs- und Rückforderungsrecht. Bei anvertrauten Sachen.
Wer eine bewegliche Sache in gutem Glauben zu Eigentum [...] übertragen erhält, ist in seinem Erwerbe auch dann zu schützen, wenn sie dem Veräußerer ohne jede Ermächtigung zur Übertragung anvertraut worden war.

---

[13] Art. 714 refers to *inter alia* Art. 933 (author's note).

Art. 933.   *Right to dispose and right to restitution. Things entrusted.*
Whoever acquires a chattel in good faith in order to become its owner [...] is protected in his acquisition, provided the thing was entrusted to the transferor even if he had no authority to make such transfer.

Art. 3.   Guter Glaube.
(1) Wo das Gesetz eine Rechtswirkung an den guten Glauben einer Person geknüpft hat, ist dessen Dasein zu vermuten.

[...]

Art. 3.   *Good faith.*
(1) If the law makes the existence or effect of a right conditional on good faith, such good faith will be presumed.

[...]

3. Schweizerisches Bundesgericht (*Swiss Federal Court*), 29.11.1929 i.S. Grimm gegen Konkursmasse Näf, BGE 55 II 302

Das Bundesgericht zieht in Erwägung:

[...] 2. Allein selbst wenn die Kontrahenten im massgeblichen Zeitpunkt über den Eigentumsübergang einig gewesen wären, so könnte doch wegen Fehlens eines gültigen Rechtsgrundgeschäfts dem Kläger nicht zugestanden werden, dass er Eigentümer der streitigen Sachen geworden sei. Freilich hat sich das Bundesgericht unter der Herrschaft des [alten Obligationenrechts] im Anschluss an das Gemeine Recht gegen die Abhängigkeit der Gültigkeit der Übertragung des Eigentums an Mobilien von der Gültigkeit des Kausalgeschäftes ausgesprochen. [...] Nachdem nun aber das ZGB durch Art. 974 die Frage für Grundstücke positiv anders geordnet, dagegen für bewegliche Sachen neuerdings offen gelassen hat, drängt sich eine neue Prüfung auf, und diese muss zur Aufgabe der früheren Rechtsprechung führen. Grundlage der früheren Rechtsprechung war ein Dogma des Gemeinen Rechts, das sich zwar in seiner Allgemeinheit nicht auf eindeutige Quellen zu stützen vermochte, aber jedenfalls den Bedürfnissen des Rechtsverkehres Rechnung trug, namentlich nach der Richtung, dass es auf den Schutz des gutgläubigen Dritterwerbers hinauslief, der dem Gemeinen Rechte sonst fremd war (vgl. hierüber IHERING, Geist des römischen Rechtes (2. Auflage) III 1 S. 207; GIRARD-SENN, Droit romain S. 318; KRIEGSMANN, Rechtsgrund der Eigentumsübertragung S. 117). Die Übernahme dieses "großen Grundsatzes" der Unabhängigkeit des sog. dinglichen Rechtsgeschäftes von der obligatorischen causa in das deutsche BGB – das doch den Schutz des gutgläubigen Dritterwerbers in weitem Umfang einführte –, wofür in erster Linie doktrinäre Gründe und nicht etwa die Einsicht in dessen Zweckmäßigkeit im Rechtsverkehr angeführt wurden (Motive zum Entwurf des BGB II S. 3, III S. 6 ff.), wurde denn auch scharf bekämpft [...]. Indessen konnte an dem ursprünglichen (in den Motiven zum BGB) ausgesprochenen Satz, der dingliche Vertrag sei notwendig dem Begriffe nach abstrakt, nicht festgehalten werden. Im Gegenteil wird in Theorie und Praxis, wenn irgendwie möglich, die Abhängigkeit des dinglichen Geschäfts vom obligatorischen dadurch zu erzielen gesucht, dass den Parteien eine diesbezügliche Bedingung untergeschoben wird, auch wenn sie sich darüber ausgeschwiegen haben; ja diese Bedingung wird geradezu als verkehrsüblich bezeichnet [...] Vielfach wird denn überhaupt die Abstraktion des dinglichen Geschäfts von der Kausalvereinbarung als eine künstliche Konstruktion bezeichnet [...] Und das österreichische Recht, das den Eigentumswechsel bei beweglichen Sachen ebenfalls von der Tradition abhängig macht, vermag ohne jene Konstruktion auszukommen [...] Nichts zwingt dazu, ihr auf das schweizerische Mobiliarsachenrecht noch einen Einfluss zuzugestehen, zumal nachdem das Immobiliarsachenrecht sich ihr entzogen hat. [...] Endlich wird die Annahme der Konstruktion von der abstrakten Natur des dinglichen Vertrages über bewegliche Sachen auch nicht durch dringende Bedürfnisse des Rechtsverkehrs gefordert [...] Ob diesem Ziel nach der Einführung weitgehenden Schutzes des gutgläubigen Dritterwerbers und der Rechtsvermutungen zugunsten des Besitzers noch weitergehend nachzustreben sei, ist übrigens eine Frage. Wieso aber der Erwerber selbst, dessen bösgläubige Rechtsnachfolger – bösgläubig in dem Sinne, dass ihnen die Ungültigkeit des Kausalgeschäftes nicht verborgen geblieben sein kann – und schließlich im Konkurs des Erwerbers dessen Konkursgläubiger vor dem Veräußerer Schutz verdienen sollten, ist nicht einzusehen. [...]

Translation (extracts)

"4th operative part of the judgment: the transfer of ownership of property is not an abstract act.[14] Consequently, the validity of the transfer of property depends on the validity of the legal transaction generating the obligations which are the reason for the transfer [e.g. a sales contract][15] (change to the previous case-law)."

"Under the old Code of obligations – and in conformity with the Germanic interpretation of the continental common law of Roman origin – the Federal Tribunal ruled that the validity of a transfer of property is not dependent on the act which is the reason for the transfer [e.g. the underlying contract of sale] [...] However the Swiss Civil code now sets out, in Art. 974, an opposing solution, but only for land, leaving the question of chattels open. In these circumstances, it is important to re-examine this question, which should lead to a reversal of former case-law. This case-law was based on a dogma traditionally adopted in Germanic law that [...] contributed notably to the protection of a third party purchaser in good faith, which was something that was, in principle, not of much concern in the continental common law of Roman origin (v. Ihering, *Geist des römischen Rechts*, 2nd ed., III 1 p. 207; Girard-Senn, *Droit romain*, p. 318

---

14 In German law (see **V.2** above), the transfer of property is an abstract act in the sense that it is independent of an agreement to transfer property, e.g. a sales contract. This is no longer the case in Switzerland.

15 This is known as the *causa*. The *principle of causality* (as opposed to the principle of abstraction) requires every conveyance of a property right to have a valid *causa* which serves as the basis for the conveyance (e.g. acquisition, transfer). This means that disposal of property alone is not sufficient to establish ownership, there must also be such an underlying *causa*.

2^ei Kriegsmann, *Rechtsgrund der Eigentumsübertragung*, p. 117). This "important principle" of the independence of the [validity of the] legal transaction referred to as "real" ("dinglich", [i.e. the transaction concerning exclusively the transfer of property and not the underlying obligation it is meant to fulfil] from any underlying personal link between the parties [such as a contract of sale], was taken up by the BGB which however established protection of the bona fide third party on a large scale. [...] [However, the] adoption of a system based on an abstract nature of the transfer with regard to chattels does not meet pressing practical needs. [...] [Th]e aim of the system was to simplify and facilitate property transactions [...] One might [...] wonder if there is still any reason to strive for this goal since the Swiss civil code introduced [...] an extensive system of protection with regard to bona fide purchasers. In other words, why should we show more concern for a [subsequent] purchaser in bad faith, i.e. a purchaser who was aware that the personal link between the parties to a prior contract [e.g. a contract of sale between the owner/seller and a first purchaser] was void, than for the owner/seller?

4. HEINZ REY, *Grundriss des schweizerischen Sachenrecht, Band I. Die Grundlagen des Sachenrechts und das Eigentum,* 3rd rev. edn (translation of the German original)

Chapter 7: Movable property

§ 23 Acquisition of movable property from the owner

[...]

I. Conditions

1688   For a valid transfer of movable property, two *cumulative* conditions must be fulfilled: the conclusion of a valid underlying transaction [e.g. a sales contract] and the transfer of possession of the property from the alienator to the acquirer.

1688a   The third condition, required by some authors [SCHWANDER, TUOR/SCHNYDER/ SCHMID, STEINAUER], of a "real" contract is discussed below [1705, 1707].

1. A valid underlying transaction

1689   For a valid transfer of movable property (in addition to the transfer of possession [...]) a valid legal transaction creating an obligation [...], also referred to as the underlying transaction [e.g. a sales contract], is required.

1690   This condition results from the principle of causality[16] that governs Swiss property law [...] [since the Swiss Federal Tribunal's decision of 1929 (*supra*)].

1691   The underlying transaction is an obligations-contract.[17] Ownership is not

---

[16]   The *principle of causality* requires every conveyance of a property right to have a valid *causa* (e.g. a sales contract) which serves as the basis for the conveyance. This means that disposal of property alone is not sufficient to establish ownership, there must also be such an underlying *causa* (note by the author).

[17]   That is to say, a contract that creates an obligation, such as a sales contract, and not a "real" contract as discussed below (note by the author).

transferred to the acquirer upon the valid formation of the obligations-contract; this contract only creates an obligation on the alienator to transfer ownership to the acquirer. Accordingly, the acquirer does not gain ownership from the alienator through the valid conclusion of such an underlying transaction but only the right to demand the transfer of property.
[...]

2. *"Die Tradition"*

a) The importance of *Tradition* in the transfer of movable property

1693   In relation to the valid transfer of movable property, *Tradition* undertaken by the alienator is a disposal [...], by which the ownership of the movable property is transferred to the acquirer. By transferring possession, the alienator fulfils his obligation, arising from the underlying transaction, to transfer ownership to the acquirer [...]

1694   In respect to third parties, *Tradition* is a *means of public disclosure* used to publicise the transfer of ownership vis-à-vis these third parties[18] [...]

[...]

cc)   Excursus: *Tradition* as a "contract"

[...]

bbb)   Tradition as a "real" contract

1705   In Swiss academic writing, *tradition* is occasionally referred to as a "real" contract – that is to say, a performance-contract [LIVER, SCHWANDER, MERZ]. These authors say that during the transfer, a certain state of mind must be present: At the moment of the actual handing over of the thing, there must be an intention to transfer and acquire property respectively.

[...]

1707   There is, however, no need for a real contract under the Swiss concept of the transfer of property by authorised persons, as, according to § 929 of the BGB, such contracts consist solely of the mutual consent as to the transfer of property (strongly rejected by PIOTET, Transferts, Nr. 42 ff.). The agreement on the transfer of property is already included in the underlying transaction (see HAAB/SIMONIUS, ZGB 714 N 40). So, for example, in the law governing the sale of goods it is "essential" that contracts include the necessary agreement on the object and at the same time, an agreement that the goods must be transferred from one party to the other (KELLER/SIEHR, p. 8); [...]

---

[18]   Under Swiss law, the transfer of property needs, in principle, a certain act of publicity vis-à-vis third parties in order to take effect. With respect to land, publicity is done by way of registration. However, as there is no register for personal property, possession fulfils the requirement of publicity. Therefore, with regard to movable property, the transfer of possession is a condition for the transfer of ownership (note added by the author).

VIII.   The Netherlands

1. Burgerlijk Wetboek (*Dutch Civil Code*)

Art. 3:84
(1)   Voor overdracht van een goed wordt vereist een levering krachtens geldige titel, verricht door hem die bevoegd is over het goed te beschikken.

[...]

Art. 3:84
(1)   Transfer of property requires delivery pursuant to a valid title by the person who has the right to dispose of the property.

[...]

Art. 3:90
(1)   De levering vereist voor de overdracht van roerende zaken, niet-registergoederen, die in de macht van de vervreemder zijn, geschiedt door aan de verkrijger het bezit der zaak te verschaffen.

[...]

Art. 3:90
(1)   Delivery, required for the transfer of movables which are unregistered property and which are under the control of the alienator, is made by giving possession of the thing to the acquirer.

[...]

Art. 3:86
(1)   Ondanks onbevoegdheid van de vervreemder is een overdracht overeenkomstig artikel 90 [...] van een roerende zaak, niet-registergoed, [...] geldig, indien de overdracht anders dan om niet geschiedt en de verkrijger te goeder trouw is.

[...]

Art. 3:86
(1)   Even if an alienator is not entitled to dispose of property, a transfer made in accordance with article 90 [...] of unregistered movable property [...] is valid, if the transfer is not gratuitous and the acquirer is acting in good faith.

[...]

Art. 3:118
(1)   Een bezitter is te goeder trouw, wanneer hij zich als rechthebbende beschouwt en zich ook redelijkerwijze als zodanig mocht beschouwen.
(2)   Is een bezitter eenmaal te goeder trouw, dan wordt hij geacht dit te blijven.
(3)   Goede trouw wordt vermoed aanwezig te zijn; het ontbreken van goede trouw moet worden bewezen.

Art. 3:118
(1)   A possessor who believes himself to be the title-holder and is reasonably justified in that belief, is a possessor in good faith.
(2)   Once a possessor is in good faith, he is considered to remain so.
(3)   Good faith is presumed; absence of good faith must be proven.

Art. 3:119
(1)   De bezitter van een goed wordt vermoed rechthebbende te zijn.

[…]

Art. 3:119
(1)   The possessor of property is presumed to be the title-holder.

[…]

2. Jeroen M. J. Chorus *et al.*, *Introduction to Dutch Law*, 4th rev. edn, pp. 114–116

§ 3.   Acquisition of Ownership and of Other Property

[…]

17.   Requirements for the transfer of title

In order to achieve *overdracht* (transfer of title), *levering* (*traditio*, delivery, conveyance) must be effected by a person who has the right to dispose of the property and it must be effected by virtue of a valid *titel van eigendomsverkrijging; (causa)* (*BW* 3:84 para. 1).

18.   Titel van eigendomsverkrijging (causa)

By the expression 'a valid *titel* (*causa*)' in this context a legal relationship intended to transfer a title, and justifying such transfer, is meant; in most cases it is an obligation entailing the transfer of title. This legal relationship may ensue from statute, as in the case of tort, from contracts, like sale […] It has been much debated, especially during the first half of the 20th century, whether […] the requirement of a valid *causa* should indeed be imposed. The adherents of the so-called '*causa* doctrine' answered this question affirmatively, the champions of the 'abstract doctrine' negatively. The *Hoge Raad* in 1950 preferred the views of the causa doctrine supporters [HR 5 May 1950, NJ 1951 1]. This *causa* doctrine was adopted by the *BW*[19] of 1992.

According to the *causa* doctrine a transfer of title is void if the *traditio* lacks a valid *causa*. The *causa* is invalid *e.g.* if it arises from a contract which is null *ab initio*, such as a sale which by its content is contrary to public order. A *causa* which was valid at the time of the transfer of title, may retroactively cease to exist and thereby annul the transfer, *e.g.* if a sale is annulled on account of a vice of consent.

---

[19]   Burgerlijk Wetboek, i.e. the Dutch Civil Code (note by the author).

The disadvantage inherent in this system is, of course, that it may affect the position of third parties who become successors in title. If A sells and transfers without valid *causa* to B and B sells and transfers again, to C, then C has become successor in title to someone who could not lawfully dispose of the property since B had not become the owner. 'Third party successors', such as C in this example, are protected in certain situations. In order to be protected the third party successor, at any rate, must have acted in good faith, which means that he did not know the *causa* was defective nor ought to have known that it was. The *BW* of 1992 has considerably expanded the protection granted to third party successors in good faith.

[...]

19.   Beschikkingsbevoegdheid *(right to dispose of property)*

The main rule concerning the right to dispose of property is laid down is the maxim *nemo plus iuris transferre potest quam ipse habet*, nobody is able to transfer more right than he himself has. Among those having the right to dispose of property are the owner [...]. [I]mportant exceptions are made to the requirement that the transferor has a right to dispose. They are meant to protect third parties relying on an apparent right to dispose.

[...]
    2.   In respect of movables [...] the third party may usually rely on possession in order to ascertain who has the right to dispose, the 'procedural function' of possession (*BW* 3:119).

20.   Levering (traditio, *delivery, conveyancing*)

Dutch law differs from French law in that it requires *levering* (*traditio*, delivery, conveyancing), a special juridical act of conveyancing, for an effective transfer of title to be achieved. This *traditio* is realized [...] in respect of non-registered movable property [...] by providing the acquirer with possession of the movable [...]

IX. Systematic Overviews

1. Transfer of property by the owner to the first purchaser

Group 1	Group 2	Group 3
The principle of consent and causality = the contract transfers ownership directly	**The principle of separation and causality** = the transfer of property requires the acquisition of actual possession, agreement on the transfer of ownership and a valid underlying obligations contract	**The principle of separation and abstraction** = the transfer of property requires the acquisition of actual possession and agreement on the transfer of ownership (the validity of the underlying obligations contract is not important)
– **French Law** (Arts 711, 1138(2), 1583 Code civil) – **Italian Law** (Arts 922, 1376 Codice civile) – **Polish Law** (Arts 155(1) Polish Civil Code) – **English Law** (Sale of Goods Act 1979, s. 17, s. 18 Rule 1)	– **Swiss Law** (Art. 714(1) Swiss Civil Code; Swiss Federal Court decision of 1929; Rey) – **Dutch Law** (Arts 3:84, 3:90 BW; Chorus et al. n° 15 ff.; Mincke, n° 139 ff.)	– **German Law** (§ 929 BGB, 1st sentence) – **Greek Law** (Art. 1034 Greek Civil Code)
Solution of Case 8: The seller remains the owner, the first purchaser does not acquire ownership.	**Solution of Case 8:** The seller remains the owner, the first purchaser does not acquire ownership.	**Solution of Case 8:** The first purchaser becomes the owner

2. Acquisition of property in good faith from an unauthorised person

Group 1	Group 2	Group 3
For the subsequent purchaser to acquire ownership, the following conditions must be fulfilled: – The subsequent purchaser must have obtained possession from the alienator. – He must be acting in good faith (with regard to the property). Good faith is presumed.	For the subsequent purchaser to acquire ownership, the following conditions must be fulfilled: – The subsequent purchaser must have obtained possession from the alienator. – He must be acting in good faith (with regard to the property) – He must establish that he was acting in good faith (it is not presumed). – The contract between the seller and the first purchaser must, in principle, be valid (it cannot be void, but it may be voidable).	No good faith acquisition
– **French law** (Arts 2276, 2274 Code civil; TERRÉ AND SIMLER, n° 426) – **Italian law** (Arts 1153(1), 1147(3)) – **Polish law** (Art. 169 § 1 Polish Civil Code) – **Swiss law** (Art. 714 II, 933, 3 I Swiss Civil code) – **Dutch law** (Art. 3:86, 3:90 and 3:118 of the Dutch Civil code) – **German law** (§ 932 BGB) – **Greek law** (Arts 1036, 1037 Greek Civil Code) In German and Greek law, the rules on acquisition in good faith are, however, not applicable in Case 8 since the first purcher acquired ownership (see overview no. 1) and could transfer property to the subsequent purchaser.	**English law** (Sale of Goods Act 1979, ss. 21, 23 and especially 25(1); BENJAMIN'S SALE OF GOODS n° 7-069 ff.; MCKENDRICK 4.6; High Court 1981)	**Roman law** (Dig. 50, 17, 54: *nemo potest*) **English law** (if the contract between the seller and the first purchaser was void, second purchasers cannot acquire ownership in good faith, Sale of Goods Act 1979, s. 25; BENJAMIN'S SALE OF GOODS n° 7-068

Group 1	Group 2	Group 3
Solution of Case 8: Under French, Italian, Polish, Swiss, and Dutch Law, the subsequent bona fide purchaser acquires ownership, the subsequent purchaser in bad faith does not. Under German and Greek law, the subsequent purchasers gain ownership from the title-holder, so both the bona fide purchaser and the purchaser in "bad faith" become the owner.	**Solution of Case 8:** As the contract between the seller and first purchaser is void, none of the subsequent purchasers can acquire ownership.	**Solution of Case 8:** The seller remains the owner.

X.   Further reading

1. Books and articles written in English

Hugh Beale, Arthur Hartkamp, Hein Kötz and Denis Tallon (eds), *Cases, Materials and Text on Contract Law*, Oxford: Hart Publishing, 2002, Ch. 1.1.3.C, 20–21; Ch. 1.1.4., Ch. 1.1.4.A. 28–31.

Peter Benson, "Law and Morality: Contract Law: Contract as a Transfer of Ownership", 48 (2007) *Wm and Mary L. Rev.* 1673–1731.

Ulrich Drobnig, "Transfer of property", in Arthur Hartkamp *et al.* (eds), *Towards a European Civil Code*, 3rd edn, Nijmegen: Kluwer Law International, 2004, Ch. 40, 725–40.

Lars van Vliet, "Transfer of movable property", in Jan M. Smits (ed.), *Elgar Encyclopedia of Comparative Law*, Cheltenham: Edward Elgar Publishing Ltd, 2006, 730–37.

Lars van Vliet, "Iusta causa traditionis and its history in European private law", *ERPL* 2003, 342–78.

Lars van Vliet, *Transfer of movables in German, French, English and Dutch law*, Nijmegen: Ars Aequi Libri, 2000.

2. Books and articles written in German

Ulrich Eisenhardt, "Die Entwicklung des Abstraktionsprinzips im 20. Jahrhundert", in Gerhard Köbler and Hermann Nehlsen, *Wirkungen europäischer Rechtskultur, Festschrift für Karl Kroeschell zum 70. Geburtstag*, München: Beck, 1997, 215–32.

Franco Ferrari, "Vom Abstraktionsprinzip zum Konsensualprinzip zum Traditionsprinzip – Zu den Möglichkeiten der Rechtsangleichung im Mobiliarsachenrecht", *ZEuP* 1993, 52–78.

Filippo Ranieri, *Europäisches Obligationenrecht*, Wien / New York: Springer, 379–431.

Andreas Roth, "Abstraktions- und Konsensprinzip und ihre Auswirkungen auf die Rechtsstellung der Kaufvertragsparteien", *ZVglRWiss* 92 (1993), 371–94.

Kurt Siehr, "Der gutgläubige Erwerb beweglicher Sachen – Neue Entwicklungen zu einem alten Problem", *ZVglRWiss* 80 (1981), 273–92.

Karsten Thorn, "Mobiliarerwerb vom Nichtberechtigten, Neue Entwicklungen in rechtsvergleichender Perspektive", *ZEuP* 1997, 442–74.

Andreas Wacke, "Eigentumserwerb des Käufers durch schlichten Konsens oder erst mit Übergabe? Unterschiede im Rezeptionsprozess und ihre mögliche Überwindung", *ZEuP* 2000, 254–62.

Hans Wieling, "Das Abstraktionsprinzip für Europe!", *ZEuP* 2001, 301–07.

Chapter III

The law applicable to cross-border contracts and the future of European contract law

Case 9: The law applicable to cross-border contracts (introduction)

"Si l'Europe doit être un vrai marché unique, ne faudrait-il pas qu'une opération contractuelle entre deux entreprises de part et d'autre de la frontière soit aussi bien balisée qu'un contrat conclu entre deux entreprises au sein d'un même Etat?"[1]

Scenario

An English car dealer sends an order for 15 sports cars to a German manufacturer. The German manufacturer receives the order and makes a note of it. Before he is able to send an acceptance, the English car dealer revokes his order by fax.

Nevertheless, the German manufacturer sends a message accepting the order, relying on § 145 of the German Civil Code (BGB), according to which an offeror is bound by his offer. The English car dealer relies on the general rule that offers are revocable, which is set out in English case law, and also on the "postal rule", according to which an offer can be revoked at any time up until the acceptance is dispatched.[2]

A variation on the above

An English jeweller orders a batch of watch mechanisms from a Swiss manufacturer. The Swiss manufacturer receives the order. Before he can send his acceptance, the English jeweller cancels his order. The manufacturer nevertheless gives the jeweller notice that he accepts the order, relying on Article 5 of the Swiss Code of Obligations, according to which an offeror is bound by his offer up until the moment that he could expect to receive a reply dispatched properly and in a timely fashion.[3]

---

[1] CLAUDE WITZ, "Plaidoyer pour un code européen des obligations", *Recueil Dalloz* 2000, Chroniques, p. 79 (81). Translation: If Europe is to be a real single market, should it not be the case that a contractual transaction between two companies on different sides of a border be as well marked out as a contract concluded between two companies in the same State?

[2] For further discussion of § 145 BGB and the "postal rule", see above **Case 3**.

[3] On Art. 5 of the Swiss Code of Obligations, see above, **Case 3**.

Questions

(1) Under what conditions is the United Nations Convention on Contracts for the International Sale of Goods (CISG or Vienna Sales Convention) applicable? The CISG is in force in all the Member States of the European Union except the UK, Ireland, Malta and Portugal. Would the Vienna Convention be applicable if the facts of the scenario were litigated before:
(a) the German courts;
(b) the English courts? [4]

Where appropriate, refer to the Rome I Regulation as applicable for contracts concluded after 17 December 2009.

(2) In the above scenario, which of the parties is right?

(3) Would the CISG be applicable in the *variation* if the case were brought before the Swiss courts? [5]

(4) Would a contract of sale concluded between a seller with its place of business in the USA (e.g. in New York) and a buyer with its place of business in:
(a) Switzerland
(b) England
be governed by the CISG, the Uniform Commercial Code or by English law if brought before a court in the USA? (See Articles 1 and 95 of the CISG.)

(5) What law would apply to the Anglo-German contract in the *scenario* if the parties had agreed on the application of "Swiss law" (i.e. they chose the law of a third State) when the contract was concluded?

Would your answer be different if the parties had expressly referred in their contract to the relevant articles in the Swiss Code of Obligations?

(6) (a) What would the applicable law be in the *scenario* if the parties, when contracting, had stipulated that the contract should be governed by:
  – the Principles of European Contract Law (PECL);
  – the UNIDROIT Principles; or
  – the *lex mercatoria*? [6]
(b) What would the applicable law be if the parties had, at the same time as choosing the PECL, the UNIDROIT Principles, or the *lex mercatoria*, also agreed to submit their case to arbitration?

---

[4]　It is presumed that the courts have jurisdiction.
[5]　Switzerland is not a Member State of the European Union. It is a Contracting State of the CISG.
[6]　The *lex mercatoria* is "that part of transnational commercial law which consists of the unwritten customs and usages of merchants, so far as these satisfy certain externally set criteria for validation", Roy Goode, Herbert Kronke and Ewan McKendrick, *Transnational Commercial Law*, Oxford: Oxford University Press, 2007, at 1.04 and 1.60.

Table of contents

V. Summary

I.

1. United Nations Convention on Contracts for the International Sale of Goods 1980 (CISG)[7]

Art. 1

(1)   This Convention applies to contracts of sale of goods between parties whose places of business are in different States:

(a)   when the States are Contracting States; or

(b)   when the rules of private international law lead to the application of the law of a Contracting State.

[...]

Art. 2

This Convention does not apply to sales:

(a)   of goods bought for personal, family or household use, unless the seller, at any time before or at the conclusion of the contract, neither knew nor ought to have known that the goods were bought for any such use;

[...]

Art. 3

(1)   Contracts for the supply of goods to be manufactured or produced are to be considered sales unless the party who orders the goods undertakes to supply a substantial part of the materials necessary for such manufacture or production.

(2)   This Convention does not apply to contracts in which the preponderant part of the obligations of the party who furnishes the goods consists in the supply of labour or other services.

Art. 6

The parties may exclude the application of this Convention or, subject to article 12, derogate from or vary the effect of any of its provisions.

Art. 16

(1)   Until a contract is concluded an offer may be revoked if the revocation reaches the offeree before he has dispatched an acceptance.

(2)   However, an offer cannot be revoked:

(a)   if it indicates, whether by stating a fixed time for acceptance or otherwise, that it is irrevocable; or

(b)   if it was reasonable for the offeree to rely on the offer as being irrevocable and the offeree has acted in reliance on the offer.

---

[7]   A list of the Contracting States is available at: http://www.unilex.info.

Art. 95
Any State may declare at the time of the deposit of its instrument of ratification, acceptance, approval or accession that it will not be bound by subparagraph (1)(b) of article 1 of this Convention.[8]

2. Regulation (EC) No 593/2008 of the European Parliament and of the Council of 17 June 2008 on the law applicable to contractual obligations (Rome I)[9]

Article 1
Material scope
1.　This Regulation shall apply, in situations involving a conflict of laws, to contractual obligations in civil and commercial matters. [...]

Article 2
Universal application
Any law specified by this Regulation shall be applied whether or not it is the law of a Member State.

Article 3
Freedom of choice
1.　A contract shall be governed by the law chosen by the parties. The choice shall be made expressly or clearly demonstrated by the terms of the contract or the circumstances of the case. By their choice the parties can select the law applicable to the whole or to part only of the contract.

[...]

Article 4
Applicable law in the absence of choice
1.　To the extent that the law applicable to the contract has not been chosen in accordance with Article 3 and without prejudice to Articles 5 to 8, the law governing the contract shall be determined as follows:
　　(a)　a contract for the sale of goods shall be governed by the law of the country where the seller has his habitual residence;
　　(b)　a contract for the provision of services shall be governed by the law of the country where the service provider has his habitual residence;
[...]

8　This reservation was declared, e.g., by the USA, Canada (with respect to British Columbia), and China.
9　OJ L 177, 4.7.2008, pp. 6–16.

2.   Where the contract is not covered by paragraph 1 or where the elements of the contract would be covered by more than one of points (a) to (h) of paragraph 1, the contract shall be governed by the law of the country where the party required to effect the characteristic performance of the contract has his habitual residence.

3.   Where it is clear from all the circumstances of the case that the contract is manifestly more closely connected with a country other than that indicated in paragraphs 1 or 2, the law of that other country shall apply.

4.   Where the law applicable cannot be determined pursuant to paragraphs 1 or 2, the contract shall be governed by the law of the country with which it is most closely connected.

Article 10
Consent and material validity
1.   The existence and validity of a contract, or of any term of a contract, shall be determined by the law which would govern it under this Regulation if the contract or term were valid.

2.   Nevertheless, a party, in order to establish that he did not consent, may rely upon the law of the country in which he has his habitual residence if it appears from the circumstances that it would not be reasonable to determine the effect of his conduct in accordance with the law specified in paragraph 1.

Article 11
Formal validity
1.   A contract concluded between persons who, or whose agents, are in the same country at the time of its conclusion is formally valid if it satisfies the formal requirements of the law which governs it in substance under this Regulation or of the law of the country where it is concluded.

2.   A contract concluded between persons who, or whose agents, are in different countries at the time of its conclusion is formally valid if it satisfies the formal requirements of the law which governs it in substance under this Regulation, or of the law of either of the countries where either of the parties or their agent is present at the time of conclusion, or of the law of the country where either of the parties had his habitual residence at that time.

[...]

Article 19
Habitual residence
1.   For the purposes of this Regulation, the habitual residence of companies and other bodies, corporate or unincorporated, shall be the place of central administration. The habitual residence of a natural person acting in the course of his business activity shall be his principal place of business.

2.   Where the contract is concluded in the course of the operations of a branch, agency or any other establishment, or if, under the contract, performance is the responsibility of such a branch, agency or establishment, the place where the branch, agency or any other establishment is located shall be treated as the place of habitual residence.

3.   For the purposes of determining the habitual residence, the relevant point in time shall be the time of the conclusion of the contract.

Article 20

Exclusion of *renvoi*

The application of the law of any country specified by this Regulation means the application of the rules of law in force in that country other than its rules of private international law, unless provided otherwise in this Regulation.

Article 24

Relationship with the Rome Convention

1.   This Regulation shall replace the Rome Convention in the Member States, except as regards the territories of the Member States which fall within the territorial scope of that Convention and to which this Regulation does not apply pursuant to Article 299 of the Treaty.

2.   In so far as this Regulation replaces the provisions of the Rome Convention, any reference to that Convention shall be understood as a reference to this Regulation.

Article 25

Relationship with existing international conventions

1.   This Regulation shall not prejudice the application of international conventions to which one or more Member States are parties at the time when this Regulation is adopted and which lay down conflict-of-law rules relating to contractual obligations.
[...]

Article 28

Application in time

This Regulation shall apply to contracts concluded after 17 December 2009.

3. Herbert Bernstein and Joseph Lookovsky,
Understanding the CISG in Europe,
2nd edn, pp. 14–16[10]

§ 2-4.   Article 1 (1) (b) and Article 95 Declarations

[...]

> *Illustration 2a*: Merchant-buyer B in England mails an order for 10 dozen designer dresses (FOB Le Havre) to seller-manufacturer S in France. S purports to accept the order by posting a brief confirmation letter to B. Later, claiming non-conformity of the goods, B refuses to accept them, and S demands to be paid.

A *French* court asked to decide the ensuing dispute between S and B could not apply the CISG by virtue of Article 1(1) (a) because the United Kingdom is not [...] a Contracting State. But in this situation, the court would be bound to apply the CISG nonetheless,

---

[10]   Some footnotes omitted.

because the relevant French private international law rule calls for the application of the "seller's law"[18].

In all likelihood, the result would be the same if the dispute were brought before an *English* court, in that the private international law of England would presumably point to French law[19], which in this case should lead to the application of the CISG[20]. Thus a *non*-Contracting State, such as presently […] the United Kingdom, may end up applying the CISG because of an interaction of the forum's private international law and Art. 1(1)(b) of CISG[21].

[…]

---

[18]   Re, the 1955 Hague Convention […]

[19]   In the absence of a choice by the parties, under [Art. 4(1)(a) of the Rome I Regulation, a contract for the sale of goods is governed by the law of the country where the seller has his habitual residence].

[20]   When English private international law rules refer to French law, this includes a reference to Art. 1(1)(b) CISG which, under French private international law [1955 Hague] rules, points to the seller's law, i.e. the CISG. […]

[21]   When a court in a *non*-Contracting State applies the rule in Article 1(1)(b), it is obviously not acting in performance of the (public international law) obligation based on the CISG treaty. Rather, such a court applies this rule as a provision of the *internal law of the Contracting State* whose application is *prescribed by the forum's conflicts rule.* […]

4. Dicey, Morris & Collins on The Conflict of Law, 14th edn, Vol. 2

33-123   There is one possible circumstance in which an English court might be required to apply the United Nations Convention[11] despite the fact that the United Kingdom has not ratified the Convention. This is where the law applicable to the contract of sale under the Rome [I Regulation] is found to be the law of a country which is a party to the United Nations Convention and that country would regard the Convention as applicable. This conclusion cannot be stated with any certainty, however, since it is possible to construe Article 21 of the Rome Convention [Article 25(1) of the Rome I Regulation] as rendering international conventions applicable, even in this circumstance, only as between Contracting States which are parties thereto. If this latter view is correct, then since the United Kingdom is not a party to the United Nations Convention, the law applicable to a contract of sale, if that of a foreign country which is a party to the United Nations Convention, will be the contract law of this country, excluding the rules of that latter Convention.

---

[11]   The United Nations Convention on Contracts for the International Sale of Goods (CISG).

II.

1. Schweizerisches Bundesgesetz über das Internationale Privatrecht (*Swiss Federal Act on Private International Law*)

Art. 116
(1) Der Vertrag untersteht dem von den Parteien gewählten Recht.
(2) Die Rechtswahl muss ausdrücklich sein oder sich eindeutig aus dem Vertrag oder aus den Umständen des Falles ergeben. Im übrigen untersteht sie dem gewählten Recht.

Art. 116
(1) The contract is governed by the law chosen by the parties.
(2) The choice shall be made expressly or clearly demonstrated by the terms of the contract or the circumstances of the case. It is governed by the law chosen.

Art. 118
(1) Für den Kauf beweglicher körperlicher Sachen gilt das Haager Übereinkommen vom 15. Juni 1955 betreffend das auf internationale Kaufverträge über bewegliche körperliche Sachen anzuwendende Recht.

[...]

Art. 118
(1) The sale of movables is governed by the Hague Convention of 15 June 1955 on the Law Applicable to International Sales of Goods.

[...]

2. Convention on the Law Applicable to International Sales of Goods (Hague Sales Convention 1955)[12]

Art. 1
(1) This Convention shall apply to international sales of goods.
(2) It shall not apply to sales of securities, to sales of ships and of registered boats or aircraft, or to sales upon judicial order or by way of execution. It shall apply to sales based on documents.
(3) For the purposes of this Convention, contracts to deliver goods to be manufactured or produced shall be placed on the same footing as sales provided the party who assumes delivery is to furnish the necessary raw materials for their manufacture or production.

---

[12] The Convention is in force in Denmark, Finland, France, Italy, Norway, Sweden, and Switzerland.

(4) The mere declaration of the parties, relative to the application of a law or the competence of a judge or arbitrator, shall not be sufficient to confer upon a sale the international character provided for in the first paragraph of this Article.

Art. 2

(1) A sale shall be governed by the domestic law of the country designated by the Contracting Parties.

(2) Such designation must be contained in an express clause, or unambiguously result from the provisions of the contract.

(3) Conditions affecting the consent of the parties to the law declared applicable shall be determined by such law.

Art. 3

(1) In default of a law declared applicable by the parties under the conditions provided in the preceding Article, a sale shall be governed by the domestic law of the country in which the vendor has his habitual residence at the time when he receives the order. If the order is received by an establishment of the vendor, the sale shall be governed by the domestic law of the country in which the establishment is situated.

(2) Nevertheless, a sale shall be governed by the domestic law of the country in which the purchaser has his habitual residence, or in which he has the establishment that has given the order, if the order has been received in such country, whether by the vendor or by his representative, agent or commercial traveller.

(3) In case of a sale at an exchange or at a public auction, the sale shall be governed by the domestic law of the country in which the exchange is situated or the auction takes place.

III.

1. Österreichischer Oberster Gerichtshof (*Austrian Supreme Court of Justice*), 22.10.2001, 1 Ob 77/01g, http://www.unilex.info/

[...]

Entscheidungsgründe:

Die klagende ungarische Aktiengesellschaft als Verkäuferin schloss am 4. Februar 1994 mit der beklagten österreichischen Aktiengesellschaft als Käuferin einen Liefervertrag über die Lieferung von Gasölen und Benzinen für den Zeitraum 1. Februar 1994 bis 31. Jänner 1995; vereinbart wurde darin die Anwendung österreichischen Rechts. [...]

[...]

b) Die Vorinstanzen setzten sich mit der Frage nach dem anzuwendenden Recht eingehend auseinander, bejahten das Zustandekommen einer Rechtswahlvereinbarung der Streitteile und unterstellen die Rechtsbeziehung der Streitteile ex contractu nach §§ 11 und 35 Abs 1 [des österreichischen IPR-Gesetzes] [...] zutreffend dem österreichischen Sachrecht. [...]

Die beklagte Partei zieht die von den Vorinstanzen [...] vorgenommene Einbeziehung des UN-K in den Kreis des anzuwendenden Rechts zu Unrecht in Zweifel: Bei Vertragsabschluss stand das UN-K sowohl in Ungarn [...] als auch in Österreich [...] in Geltung: Die Parteien, die ihre Niederlassung in verschiedenen Staaten haben, schlossen einen (Rahmen-)Liefervertrag über Waren ab (Art. 1 Abs 1 lit a UN-K). Grundsätzlich ist daher das UN-K – als Teil der österreichischen Rechtsordnung - von der Rechtswahl mitumfasst. Ist das UN-K anwendbar, so müssen die Parteien, die seine Anwendung nicht wollen, eine entsprechende Ausschlussvereinbarung treffen; der Ausschluss kann ausdrücklich oder stillschweigend erfolgen [...] Den ausdrücklichen Anwendungsausschluß behauptet die beklagte Partei nicht einmal; zur Annahme eines stillschweigenden Ausschlusses besteht entgegen dem Rechtsmittelvortrag kein Anlass, darf dieser doch nur dann angenommen werden, wenn ihn ein hinreichend deutlicher Parteiwille nahelegt. Ergibt sich [...] nicht mit hinreichender Deutlichkeit, dass ein Ausschluss gewollt ist, so bleibt es bei der Anwendung des UN-K [...] Die pauschale Wahl des Rechts eines Ratifizierungsstaats des UN-K kann nach ganz herrschender Ansicht für sich mangels zusätzlicher – hier aber fehlender – Anhaltspunkte nicht den Ausschluss des UN-K bedeuten [...] In der Entscheidung 2 Ob 328/97t [...] wurde ausgesprochen, hätten die Vertragsparteien eines Sukzessivlieferungsvertrags ihre Niederlassungen in verschiedenen Staaten und wählten sie das Recht eines UN-K Mitgliedstaats, so sei das UN-K auch ohne ausdrückliche Erwähnung, dass sie dessen Anwendung wünschten, anzuwenden. Die Rechtswahl ohne Kundgabe eines dahingehenden Abwahlwillens ist nicht als konkludenter Ausschluss des UN-K zu werten, weil dieses als Bestandteil des vereinbarten Rechts auch von dieser Verweisung erfasst wird und im Rahmen seines Anwendungsbereichs dem sonst zur Anwendung kommenden unvereinheitlichten Recht vorgeht [...]

Auch die Vereinbarung von INCOTERMS – wie hier – deutet nicht notwendigerweise auf die Abbedingung des UN-K hin, weil diese nur einzelne Aspekte des Kaufvertrags regeln und deshalb nicht die Anwendung eines bestimmten, vom UN-K abweichenden Kaufrechts als Basis voraussetzen [...] Das Rechtsmittel vermag auch nicht aufzuzeigen, in welchem Punkt die INCOTERMS dem UN-K vorgehen sollten. Die Anwendung des UN-K wurde somit nicht gemäß Art. 6 wirksam ausgeschlossen [...], ist doch nach dem vorliegenden Sachstand die österreichische Rechtsordnung als Ganzes und nicht bloß in Teilbereichen Gegenstand der Rechtswahlvereinbarung.

[...]

Translation[13]

[...]

On 4 February 1994, the Hungarian Plaintiff [Seller] and the Austrian Defendant [Buyer] concluded a supply contract over the delivery of gasoline and gas oil for the period of 1 February 1994 to 31 January 1995. The contract contained a choice of law clause in favor of Austrian law. [...]

[...]

b) The previous instances considered the question of the applicable law, affirmed the valid agreement of a choice of law clause between the parties, and correctly applied Austrian domestic law to the parties' contractual relationship following IPRG §§ 11 and 35(1) [Austrian Code on Private International Law]. [...]

[Buyer]'s appeal wrongly doubts the finding of the previous instances [...] that the CISG is to be included in the law governing the contract. At the time of the conclusion of the contract, the CISG had entered into force both in Hungary [...] and in Austria [...] The parties, who have their places of business in different Contracting States, concluded a (framework) contract for the delivery of goods (Art. 1(1)(a) CISG). Therefore, the choice of Austrian law generally includes the CISG, which forms part of the Austrian legal system. If the CISG is applicable, parties who do not wish to have the Convention govern their contract need to reach a corresponding agreement to exclude its application; the exclusion may be made expressly or impliedly [Art. 6 CISG]. [...] [A]n implicit exclusion may only be assumed if the corresponding intent of the parties is sufficiently clear. If it cannot be established with sufficient clarity that an exclusion of the Convention was intended [...], then the CISG is to be applied [...]

According to the prevailing opinion, the general choice of law of a Contracting State to the Convention does not lead to its exclusion, unless there are further indications to the contrary – which is not the case in the present dispute [...] In decision 2 Ob 328/97t, [...], the Supreme Court held that the CISG applies if two parties to an installment contract have their places of business in different States and choose the law of a CISG member State, even if they do not explicitly agree on its application. The choice of law without an explicit declaration that the Convention be excluded does not constitute an implicit exclusion, because the CISG is a part of the chosen law, it is therefore included in the

---

[13] Translation by Ruth M. Janal, ed. by Jan Henning Berg, at http://cisgw3.law.pace.edu/cases/011022a3.html.

referral, and takes precedence over the non-unified law which would otherwise be applicable […]

The agreement to apply Incoterms – as in the present case – also does not necessarily indicate an agreement to exclude the CISG, because they provide only for singular aspects of the sales contract and do not require the basis of a certain sales law that diverges from the CISG […] The [Buyer]'s appeal further fails to show in which point Incoterms are supposed to take priority over the CISG. The application of the CISG was consequently not validly excluded under its Art. 6 […], because the facts reveal that the choice of law clause referred to the Austrian legal system as a whole and not to only parts of it.

2. Tribunale Civile di Monza (*Civil Court of Monza, Italy*), 14.01.1993 (Nuova Fucinati S.p.A. ./. Fondmetal International A.B.), http://www.unilex.info/

Su ricorso della Fondmetall International AB con sede in Kyrgogatan 44-S-411 15 Goteborg (Svezia) il Presidente del Tribunale di Monza ingiungeva in data 20.7.88 alla s.p.a. Nuova Fucinati con sede in Monza di consegnare alla ricorrente mille tonnellate metriche di ferrocromo 'Lumpy' così come ordinate con scrittura del 3.2.88 [...]

[...]

MOTIVI DELLA DECISIONE

[...]

Poichè si discute di una vendita internazionale di cose mobili intervenuta tra un'impresa italiana (venditrice) ed un'impresa svedese (acquirente), la prima questione da risolvere è se il contratto sia o meno soggetto alla Convenzione di Vienna 11.4.1980, resa esecutiva in Italia con legge dell'11.2.1985, n. 765 ed ivi entrata in vigore l'1.1.1988. [...]

[...]

Ora, è vero che la legge convenzionalmente applicabile al contratto è quella italiana, in virtù della esplicita clausola inserita nella conferma d'ordine ('law: italian law to apply'); ed è anche vero che, essendo la Convenzione di Vienna ormai vigente nell'ordinamento interno, deve essere valutata alla stregua di qualsiasi altra legge di questo Stato.

[...]

Translation[14]

On the appeal of Fondmetal International AB with its headquarters in Kyrgogatan 44-S-411 15 Gothenburg (Sweden) the President of the Court of Monza orders on 20 July 1988 Nuova Fucinati S.p.A. with its headquarters in Monza to deliver to the appellant one thousand metric tons of ferrochrome "Lumpy" as ordered in the written document dated 3 February 1988 […]

---

[14] Translation by ML.

[...]

GROUNDS FOR THE DECISION

[...]

As this is a case involving the international sale of goods between an Italian company (the seller) and a Swedish company (the purchaser), the first question to be answered is whether the contract is or is not governed by the Vienna Convention of 11 April 1980, which was implemented in Italy by the law of 11 February 1985, n. 765 and which entered into force on 1 January 1988. [...]

[...]

It is true that the law applicable to the contract by agreement is the Italian law in accordance with the express clause contained in the order confirmation ("law: Italian law to apply"); and it is also true that, the Vienna Convention, as it is, from now on, part of the internal legal system, must be considered to be like any other law of that State.

[...]

3. Tribunal cantonal (*Cantonal court, Canton of Vaud, Switzerland*), 8.12.2000, G. & L. C. I.), SZIER/RSDIE 2002, pp. 147–50

[...] Lorsque les parties sont convenues d'une clause d'élection de droit en faveur d'un Etat contractant, il faut déterminer si elles ont voulu désigner le droit interne national de ce pays ou le droit spécial régissant la vente internationale, puisqu'il fait aussi partie du droit interne. [...] La doctrine est partagée sur la portée à attribuer, dans ce cadre, à une clause d'élection de droit. [...] Au niveau jurisprudentiel, une certaine tendance se dessine en faveur d'une application restrictive de l'article 6 de la Convention de Vienne. Les tribunaux refusent, en principe, de voir dans une clause d'élection de droit une mise à l'écart de la Convention de Vienne (Arrêt du Tribunal cantonal lucernois du 6 octobre 1995, rapporté in RSDIE 4/96 p. 132; Arrêt de la Cour de cassation française du 17 décembre 1996, rapportée in RSDIE 1/98 p. 89; Arrêt de la Cour d'arbitrage de la Chambre du commerce et de l'industrie de Budapest du 8 mai 1997 dans la cause Vb 96038; Witz, L'application de la Convention de Vienne en France, in: Les ventes internationales, pp. 1 ss, p. 12; contra: jugement du Tribunal de district de Weinfelden du 23 novembre 1998, rapporté in RSDIE 2/99 p. 198).

[...] [L]es termes utilisés par l'article 6 CV ("les parties peuvent exclure") doivent être compris dans le sens d'une présomption d'applicabilité de la Convention. Force est donc d'admettre que le simple renvoi au droit d'un Etat contractant (élection de droit) n'est pas encore suffisant pour écarter la Convention de Vienne, puisque celle-ci est devenue partie intégrante de ce droit [...]

Translation

[…] When the parties have agreed on a choice of law clause stipulating the law of a Contracting State, it is necessary to decide whether they wanted to designate the domestic law of that country or the special regime governing international sales, as this also forms part of internal law. […] Academic opinion is divided on the scope that should be given to a choice of law clause in this context. […] Case-law seems to tend towards a restrictive application of Art. 6 of the Vienna Convention. In general, courts refuse to interpret a choice of law clause as excluding the Vienna Convention (see the decision of the Cantonal Court of Lucerne, 6 October 1995, reported in RSDIE 4/96 p. 132; Decision of the French *Cour de Cassation*, 17 December 1996, reported in RSDIE 1/98 p. 89; Decision of the Arbitral Court of the Chamber of Commerce and Industry of Budapest, 8 May 1997 in the case Vb 96038; Witz, "L'application de la Convention de Vienne en France", in: *Les ventes internationales*, pp. 1 ff., p. 12; *contra*: Judgement of the District Court of Weinfelden, 23 November 1998, reported in RSDIE 2/99 p. 198)

[…]

[T]he terms used in Art. 6 of the Vienna Convention ("the parties may exclude") should be understood as a presumption in favour of the applicability of the Convention. One is thus driven to the conclusion that a simple reference to the law of a Contracting State (choice of law) is not enough to exclude the Vienna Convention as the Convention has become an integral part of this law […]

4. Oberlandesgericht Rostock (*Appellate Court of Rostock, Germany*), Urt. v. 10.10.2001, Az. 6 U 126/00, http://www.unilex.info/

Zwischen den Parteien ist ein Kaufvertrag über die Lieferung von 240 halben Langusten zu einem Preis von 8,60 DM/Stück zustande gekommen. […]
[…] Auf den vorliegenden Rechtsstreit finden die Vorschriften des UN-Übereinkommens über den internationalen Warenkauf (CISG) Anwendung, da die Vertragsparteien ihre Niederlassung in verschiedenen Vertragsstaaten haben und Kaufverträge über bewegliche Sachen abgeschlossen haben […] Zwar haben die Parteien durch die Benennung der Normen des HGB eine Rechtswahl dahingehend getroffen, dass deutsches Vertragsrecht Anwendung findet und damit die Vorschriften des Code civil ausgeschlossen; auch bei Geltung deutschen Vertragsrechts ist das CISG als unmittelbar geltendes deutsches Recht anzuwenden. Es ist in Deutschland nach seiner Ratifikation am 26.05.1981 am 01.01.1991 in Kraft getreten, Frankreich hat die Normen am 27.08.1981 ratifiziert und am 01.01.1988 in Kraft gesetzt […] Die Parteien haben auch im Laufe des Rechtsstreits keine ausdrückliche Rechtswahl hinsichtlich des unvereinheitlichten deutschen Rechts nach Art. 27 EGBGB (HGB und BGB) getroffen. Zwar kann eine stillschweigende Vereinbarung deutschen Rechts angenommen werden, wenn beide Parteien während der gesamten Dauer des zivilrechtlichen Verfahrens, ohne Zweifel zu äußern, von der Geltung deutschen Rechts ausgingen (BGHZ 53, 189, 191 f.);

OLG Düsseldorf, NJW-RR 1987, 483 m. w. N.); dies kann sich insbesondere durch Anführung der Vorschriften dieser Rechtsordnung äußern oder durch übereinstimmende und rügelose Hinnahme der Anwendung durch die Vorinstanz [...] Da das CISG jedoch ebenfalls deutsches geltendes Recht ist, kann ein Ausschluß dieser Normen nur dann angenommen werden, wenn die Parteien dies deutlich zum Ausdruck gebracht haben, etwa durch eine eindeutige Bezugnahme auf das unvereinheitlichte Recht, die ein Erklärungsbewusstsein und einen Erklärungswillen erkennen läßt (Beispiel: "Es gilt Kaufrecht des BGB"; [...]). Eine solche Erklärung haben die Parteien trotz Hinweises des Senats nicht vorgenommen. Das bloße Verhandeln unter Bezugnahme auf die Regeln der § 377 ff. HGB genügt insofern nicht, weil es ebenso in der Meinung erfolgen kann, die Regeln seien ohnehin anwendbar [...]

Translation[15]

The parties have concluded a sales contract for 240 half crawfish at a price of 8.60 DM each. [...]

[...] The CISG is applicable to the dispute because the parties have their permanent establishments in different countries which have both adopted the CISG and because the contract concerns moveable goods [...] By naming provisions of the German Commercial Code (HGB) in their contract, the parties have impliedly agreed on the law applicable to the contract. This choice of law can, however, only be understood as an exclusion of the French Code Civil and a choice of German contractual law in general. The CISG is therefore applicable as a part of the German contractual law. It came into force in Germany on 1 September 1991, after its ratification on 26 May 1981. France ratified the CISG on 27 August 1981. The CISG entered into force in France on 1 January 1988 [...] The parties have not made a choice of the non-unified German law (HGB and BGB) according to Art. 27 EGBGB.

A silent choice of German law can be assumed if both parties assumed the applicability of German law without any doubt through the entire proceeding (BGHZ 53, p. 189, 191 et seq.; OLG Düsseldorf, NJW-RR 1987, p. 483 with further references). Such an assumption by the parties can especially be inferred from the citing of provisions of that law or by both parties not criticizing the application of that law by a court of first instance [...] However, as the CISG is German law, an exclusion of that law would need to be expressed clearly enough, for example, by a reference to non-unified law which shows the parties knew to make a legally relevant declaration and had the will to do so (e.g., "The law applicable is the sales law of the BGB", [...]). The parties have not made such a declaration even though they had been informed of its necessity by this Chamber. Merely referring to § 377 HGB is insufficient, because such reference might also be made because the parties think that that law was applicable anyway [...]

---

[15] http://cisgw3.law.pace.edu/cases/011010g1.html. Translation by LINUS MEYER; ed. by the Institut für ausländisches und Internationales Privat- und Wirtschaftsrecht der Universität Heidelberg, Daniel Nagel, editor.

IV.

1. Commission on European Contract Law:
Principles of European Contract Law

Scope of the Principles

Art. 1:101.   Application of the Principles.
(1)   These Principles are intended to be applied as general rules of contract law in the European Union.
(2)   These Principles will apply when the parties have agreed to incorporate them into their contract or that their contract is to be governed by them.
(3)   These Principles may be applied when the parties:
    (a)   have agreed that their contract is to be governed by "general principles of law", the "lex mercatoria" or the like; or
    (b)   have not chosen any system or rules of law to govern their contract.
(4)   These Principles may provide a solution to the issue raised where the system or rules of law applicable do not do so.

2. UNIDROIT: *Principles of International Commercial Contracts*

PREAMBLE
(Purpose of the Principles)

These Principles set forth general rules for international commercial contracts.
They shall be applied when the parties have agreed that their contract be governed by them.(*)
They may be applied when the parties have agreed that their contract be governed by general principles of law, the *lex mercatoria* or the like.
They may be applied when the parties have not chosen any law to govern their contract.
They may be used to interpret or supplement international uniform law instruments.
They may be used to interpret or supplement domestic law.
They may serve as a model for national and international legislators.

(*) Parties wishing to provide that their agreement be governed by the Principles might use the following words, adding any desired exceptions or modifications:
"This contract shall be governed by the UNIDROIT Principles (2004) [except as to Articles ...]".
Parties wishing to provide in addition for the application of the law of a particular jurisdiction might use the following words:
"This contract shall be governed by the UNIDROIT Principles (2004) [except as to Articles ...], supplemented when necessary by the law of [jurisdiction X]".

3. Regulation (EC) No 593/2008 of the European Parliament and of the Council of 17 June 2008 on the law applicable to contractual obligations (Rome I)

Recitals

(13) Regulation does not preclude parties from incorporating by reference into their contract a non-State body of law or an international convention.

(14) Should the Community adopt, in an appropriate legal instrument, rules of substantive contract law, including standard terms and conditions, such instrument may provide that the parties may choose to apply those rules.

4. *Dicey, Morris & Collins on The Conflict of Laws,* 14th edn

32-081 **General principles of law.** [...] Article 1(1) of the Rome Convention [now: Rome I Regulation] makes it clear that the reference to the parties' choice of "the law" to govern a contract is a reference to the law of a country. It does not sanction the choice or application of a non-national system of law, such as the *lex mercatoria* or general principles of law. [...] [I]t had been said in England that "contracts are incapable of existing in a legal vacuum. They are mere pieces of paper devoid of all legal effect unless they were made by reference to some system of private law which defines the obligations assumed by the parties to the contract by their use of particular forms of words ..." It is suggested that a choice of *lex mercatoria* or general principles of law is not an express choice of law under the Rome Convention. So also in *Shamil Bank of Bahrain EC* v. *Beximco Pharmaceuticals Ltd* the Court of Appeal held that a choice of the principles of Sharia law was not a choice of law of a country for the purposes of the Rome Convention.

5. Schweizerisches Bundesgericht (*Swiss Federal Court*) 20.12.2005, BGE 132 III 285

A.   Die X. AG mit Sitz in St. Gallen (Klägerin), vertreten durch einen FIFA-Agenten, schloss am 16. August 1999 mit der Y. mit Sitz in A. (Beklagte), einer griechischen Aktiengesellschaft, einen Vertrag über den Transfer eines von der Klägerin vertretenen Spielers. Gemäss dieser Vereinbarung sollte die Klägerin [mehrere Vermittlungsgebühren] erhalten [...]

B.
[...]

1.   In Art. 3 des Vertrages vom 16. August 1999, auf welchen die Klägerin ihre Forderung stützt, haben die Parteien bestimmt, ihre Vereinbarung solle den FIFA-Regeln und dem Schweizer Recht unterstehen ("This agreement is governed by FIFA rules and Swiss law").

Die Vorinstanz hat diese Vertragsklausel als kumulative Rechtswahl in dem Sinne interpretiert, dass die FIFA-Regeln dem nationalen schweizerischen Recht als lex specialis vorgehen sollten. Sie hat das Reglement angewendet, das die FIFA speziell für Spielervermittlungen am 10. Dezember 2000 erlassen hat und das ein Verfahren für Streitigkeiten vorsieht. Danach sind unter anderem Rechtsvorkehren spätestens zwei Jahre nach den zugrunde liegenden Vorfällen den zuständigen Organen einzureichen. Die Vorinstanz hat diese Bestimmung als Verwirkungsfrist interpretiert und die Klage mit der Begründung abgewiesen, im Zeitpunkt der Klageeinreichung sei die zweijährige Verwirkungsfrist bereits abgelaufen gewesen.

Die Klägerin rügt, die Vorinstanz habe Art. 116 Abs. 1 IPRG verletzt, denn das FIFA-Reglement könne nicht Gegenstand einer Rechtswahl sein.

1.1   Nach Art. 116 Abs. 1 IPRG untersteht der Vertrag dem gewählten Recht. Die Rechtswahl als kollisionsrechtliche Verweisung hat zur Folge, dass sowohl die dispositiven als auch die zwingenden Normen der gewählten Rechtsordnung zur Anwendung gelangen und die Bestimmungen des ohne Rechtswahl (im Rahmen einer "objektiven" Anknüpfung nach Art. 117 IPRG) anwendbaren Vertragsstatuts ersetzen [...] Dagegen lässt die materiellrechtliche Verweisung die gewählten Normen zum Vertragsinhalt werden. Sie ermöglicht den Parteien, ihre Rechtsbeziehung in den Schranken des anwendbaren Sachrechts frei zu gestalten [...]

1.2   Ob die Parteien im Rahmen von Art. 116 Abs. 1 IPRG nur staatliche Rechtsordnungen wählen können oder ob auch die Wahl anationaler Normen zulässig ist, geht aus dem Wortlaut der Bestimmung nicht eindeutig hervor [...]
In der Lehre ist die Frage umstritten [...]

1.3   Nach der Praxis des Bundesgerichts kommt Regelwerken privater Organisationen auch dann nicht die Qualität von Rechtsnormen zu, wenn sie sehr detailliert und ausführlich sind wie beispielsweise die SIA-Normen (BGE 126 III 388 E. 9d S. 391 mit Hinweisen) oder die Verhaltensregeln des internationalen Skiverbandes (BGE 122 IV 17 E. 2b/aa S. 20; BGE 106 IV 350 E. 3a S. 352, je mit Hinweisen). Von privaten Verbänden aufgestellte Bestimmungen stehen vielmehr grundsätzlich zu den staatlichen Gesetzen in einem Subordinationsverhältnis und können nur Beachtung finden, so weit das staatliche Recht für eine autonome Regelung Raum lässt [...] Sie bilden kein "Recht" im Sinne von Art. 116 Abs. 1 IPRG und können auch nicht als "lex sportiva transnationalis" anerkannt werden [...] Die Regeln der (internationalen) Sportverbände können nur im Rahmen einer materiellrechtlichen Verweisung Anwendung finden und daher nur als Parteiabreden anerkannt werden, denen zwingende nationalrechtliche Bestimmungen vorgehen [...]

1.4   [...] Dem Verweis auf das FIFA-Reglement kann nur die Bedeutung einer materiellrechtlichen Verweisung, d.h. einer (globalen) Übernahme in den Vertrag der Parteien zukommen. [...] Die Bestimmung in Ziffer 3 des Vertrages der Parteien ist als materiellrechtliche Verweisung zu verstehen, während die Rechtswahl sich allein auf die schweizerische Rechtsordnung bezieht, deren zwingende Normen somit Anwendung finden.

2.   Nach herrschender Meinung verbietet Art. 129 OR eine vertragliche Verkürzung der Verjährungsfrist [...] [E]ine Bedingung, wonach die Forderung binnen bestimmter Frist irgendwie gerichtlich einzuklagen sei, [ist] der Abkürzung der Verjährungsfrist gleichzustellen. Indem die Vorinstanz Art. 22 Abs. 3 des FIFA-Reglements im Ergebnis als Abkürzung der gesetzlichen Verjährungsfrist (Art. 127 OR) ausgelegt hat, hat sie die zwingende Norm von Art. 129 OR des schweizerischen Rechts missachtet, das die Parteien in Ziffer 3 des Vertrages gewählt haben. Der angefochtene Entscheid ist aus diesem Grund aufzuheben. [...]

Translation[16]

The following decision of the Swiss Federal Court illustrates the predominant international opinion on the issue of the choice of non-State rules by the parties to a contract and on the scope of such a choice (note by the author):

SUMMARY

PRIVATE INTERNATIONAL LAW. CHOICE OF LAW. SCOPE OF THE FIFA REGULATIONS IN COMPARISON WITH STATE LAW. – PRIVATE INTERNATIONAL LAW ACT, ART 116(1), CODE OF OBLIGATIONS, ART 129.

Facts:
A contract concluded by Company X-AG, with its headquarters in St.-Gall, and Y., a company under Greek law, with its headquarters in A., provided in Art. 3 for the application of the FIFA Regulations, as well as the rules of Swiss law.

When dealing with a claim made by Company X-AG, the Commercial Court in St. Gall rejected the claim, considering it to be time-barred, the FIFA Regulations providing for a limitation period of two years from the events in question.

On appeal, allowed by the Federal Court, the applicant cited a breach of Art. 116(1) [Swiss] Private International Law Act [LDIP] on the grounds that the FIFA Regulations could not be the object of a choice of law.

Law:
1.1 – According to Art. 116(1) LDIP, a contract is governed by the law chosen by the parties. A choice of law, as a subjective conflict-of-law rule, leads to the application of both the mandatory and optional provisions of the chosen legal order. These rules, chosen by the parties, replace those applicable in the absence of a choice of law (Art. 117 LDIP). On the other hand, a choice made on the level of the substantive law [instead of at the private international law level] incorporates the rules referred to in the contract. It allows the

---

[16]   Translation of a case summary published in French in *Semaine Judiciaire* (*SJ*) 2006, 390–91.

parties to freely regulate their legal relationships within the framework of the applicable law (*Amstutz/Vogt/Wang*, Commentaire bâlois, N. 11 ad art. 116 LDIP; *Keller/Kren Kostkiewicz*, Commentaire zurichois, N. 8 et 83 ss ad art. 116 LDIP).

1.2 – Art. 166(1) LDIP does not clearly say whether the parties can only choose a national law or whether they have the option to choose non-State rules.

1.3 – Whilst academic opinion is divided, the Federal Court has already had the chance to clarify, in its case law, that the autonomous rules of private organisations do not have the status of legal rules, even if they are very detailed [...] (like, for example, the SIA [Swiss Association of Engineers and Architects] rules: ATF 126 III 388 c. 9d p.391, with reference; or the International Ski Federation's rules of conduct for skiers: ATF 122 IV 17 c. 2b/aa p. 6, 106 IV 350 c. 3a p. 352, with reference). Provisions drawn up by private organisations find themselves in a subordinate role to State laws; they can only be taken into consideration when permitted by the State law (*Jérôme Jaquier*, La qualification juridique des règles autonomes des organisations sportives, thèse Neuchâtel 2004, N. 212).

They do not constitute a "law" in the sense of Art. 116(1) LDIP and cannot even be recognised as "lex sportiva transnationalis", as recommended by *Jaquier* (op. Cit., N. 293 ff.). The autonomous rules of international sporting organisations can only be chosen at the substantive law level [as opposed to the private international law level] *i.e.* they can only replace those rules of the applicable State law that are non-mandatory; insofar as the rules of the national law are mandatory, these rules must prevail (*Keller/Kren Kostkiewicz*, Commentaire zurichois, N. 84 ad art. 116 LDIP).

2. – According to the predominant opinion, Art. 129 of the Code of obligations [CO] prohibits a contractual agreement reducing the limitation period. [...] [A clause] according to which the claim must be legally made within a certain period, [is] assimilated to a reduction of the limitation period.

When the cantonal court interpreted the FIFA Regulations as reducing the legal limitation period (Art. 127 CO), it failed to recognise the mandatory rule of Swiss law in Art. 129 CO, to which the parties declared to submit themselves (Art. 3 of the contract). Consequently, the appeal must be allowed and the case sent back to the cantonal court for a new decision.

(Federal Court, 1st Civil Court. 20 December 2005. X. AG v. Y. 4C.1/2005).

6. UNIDROIT: *Principles of International Commercial Contracts*

4. The Principles as rules of law governing the contract

a. Express choice by the parties

Parties who wish to choose the Principles as the rules of law governing their contract are well advised to combine such a choice of law clause with an arbitration agreement. The reason for this is that the freedom of choice of the parties in designating the law governing their contract is traditionally limited to national laws. Therefore, a reference by the parties to the Principles will normally be considered to be a mere agreement to incorporate them in the contract, while the law governing the contract will still have to be determined on the basis of the private international law rules of the forum. As a result, the Principles will bind the parties only to the extent that they do not affect the rules of the applicable law from which the parties may not derogate. […]

The situation is different if the parties agree to submit disputes arising from their contract to arbitration. Arbitrators are not necessarily bound by a particular domestic law. This is self-evident if they are authorised by the parties to act as *amiable compositeurs or ex aequo et bono*. But even in the absence of such an authorisation parties are generally permitted to choose "rules of law" other than national laws on which the arbitrators are to base their decisions. See in particular Art. 28(1) of the 1985 UNCITRAL Model Law on International Commercial Arbitration; see also Art. 42(1) of the 1965 Convention on the Settlement of Investment Disputes between States and Nationals of other States (ICSID Convention).

In line with this approach, the parties would be free to choose the Principles as the "rules of law" according to which the arbitrators would decide the dispute, with the result that the Principles would apply to the exclusion of any particular national law, subject only to the application of those rules of domestic law which are mandatory irrespective of which law governs the contract.

V. Summary

Overview of the answers to questions 1–6[17]

Questions 1(a) and 2: The law applicable before the German courts[18]

I. Uniform substantive law in this field?
To find out which law is applicable, the first question to ask is whether there is a *uniform substantive law* governing this area.

The uniform substantive law governing the international sale of goods is the UN Convention on Contracts for the International Sale of Goods (CISG). Germany is a Contracting State. The CISG must therefore be applied by the German courts if the conditions for the application of the CISG are met.[19]

II. Conditions for the application of the CISG
1. According to Article 1(1), for the CISG to be applicable there must be (i) a contract (ii) for the sale of goods (iii) between parties whose places of business are in different States.

    This dispute relates to the conclusion of a contract for the sale of 15 sports cars. The parties' places of business are in Germany and England. The three conditions for the applicability of the CISG set down in Article 1(1) are therefore fulfilled.
2. Article 1(1)(a) goes on to stipulate that the States in which the parties have their places of business must be Contracting States.

    Germany is a Contracting State but England is not, so the requirement set down in Article 1(1)(a) is *not* fulfilled.
3. Where the requirement in Article 1(1)(a) is not fulfilled, the CISG may still be applicable if the Private International Law (PIL) of the forum leads to the application of the law of a Contracting State of CISG, Article 1(1)(b).

    The PIL relating to contractual obligations is governed by the Rome I Regulation in all EU Member States:
    (a) According to Article 1 of the Rome I Regulation, it shall apply, in situations involving a conflict of laws, to contractual obligations in civil and commercial matters. According to Article 10, the existence and validity of a contract are determined by the law that would govern it if the contract were valid. In our scenario these conditions are met.

---

[17] This overview is aimed at helping students who are not familiar with Private International Law/Conflicts of Law to answer the questions. The overview should be used in conjunction with the materials. For suggestions for further reading on this topic see **V.2.** below.

[18] It is presumed that the German courts have jurisdiction; for issues of jurisdiction, see Council Regulation (EC) No 44/2001 of 22 December 2000 on jurisdiction and the recognition and enforcement of judgments in civil and commercial matters (Brussels I), OJ L 12, 16.1.2001, p. 1. Regulation as last amended by Regulation (EC) No 1791/2006 (OJ L 363, 20.12.2006, p. 1).

[19] Finding the CISG applicable means that there will be no national laws conflicting with each other. In this case, it is not necessary to coordinate national laws using Private International Law (PIL) rules.

Article 3 of the Rome I Regulation states that the parties are *free to decide* upon the applicable law.

In our case scenario, the parties have not made an express choice of the applicable law, neither have they clearly demonstrated by the terms of the contract or the circumstances of the case that they wished a certain law to apply. As the parties have not jointly agreed on the law applicable to the contract, it must be determined by way of reference to objective criteria.

(b) Where parties have not chosen the applicable law, Article 4(1) of the Rome I Regulation stipulates that "a contract for the sale of goods shall be governed by the *law of the country where the seller has his habitual residence*" (emphasis added). According to Article 19, "the habitual residence of companies and other bodies, corporate or unincorporated, shall be the *place of central administration*" (emphasis added).

In our case scenario, the seller's central administration is in Germany. Article 4(1) of the Rome I Regulation therefore leads to the application of German law. According to Article 20 of the Rome I Regulation, the substantive rules of German law are applicable.

4. The PIL of the forum thus leads to German law, i.e. the law of a Contracting State of the CISG. The conditions of Article 1(1)(b) of the CISG are therefore fulfilled and the CISG is applicable to the contract.

III. Solution on the substantive law under the CISG

Under Article 16(1) of the CISG, an offer may be revoked if the revocation reaches the offeree before he has dispatched an acceptance. According to the general rule laid down in Article 16(1), up until the moment the German manufacturer sent an acceptance, the English car dealer was free to revoke his offer (as none of the exceptions provided for in Article 16(2) was applicable).

Questions 1(b) and 2: The law applicable before the English courts[20]

I. Uniform law in this field?

The CISG is not in force in England so the English courts are, at this point, not bound to apply it.

II. Applicable law under the PIL of the forum

The PIL relating to contractual obligations is governed by the Rome I Regulation in all EU Member States:

1. According to Article 3 of the Rome I Regulation, the parties are free to decide upon the applicable law.

   In this case scenario, the parties have not agreed upon the applicable law as allowed under Article 3 of Rome I so it must be determined using objective criteria.

2. In accordance with Article 4(1) of the Rome I Regulation, where parties have not chosen the applicable law, "a contract for the sale of goods shall be governed by the law of the country where the seller has his habitual residence". According to Article 19, "the habitual residence of companies and other bodies, corporate or unincorporated, shall be the place of central administration".

---

[20] It is presumed that the courts have jurisdiction.

In our case scenario, the seller has his central administration in Germany so Article 4(1) of the Rome I Regulation leads to the application of German law. According to the dominant opinion in Europe, this reference to a law of a *Contracting State* of CISG (here, German law) also includes the CISG which is an integral part of this law (see e.g. Bernstein and Lookovsky, at **I.3.** above; Dicey, Morris & Collins, at **I.4.** above, citing also a minority opinion). The English courts will therefore most probably solve the case under the CISG (even though England is not a Contracting State of the CISG).

III.   Solution on the substantive law under the CISG

As a result of Article 16(1) of the CISG, the English car dealer is able to revoke the offer at any point until an acceptance has been sent.

However, if the English court were to disregard the dominant opinion mentioned above and apply German law excluding the CISG, § 145 of the German Civil Code (*BGB*) would be applicable and the offer would not be revocable. The English car dealer would then be bound by his offer.

Question 3: The law applicable before the Swiss courts (Variation)[21]

1.   Switzerland is a Contracting State of the CISG, so Swiss judges, like German judges, are bound to examine the case and see whether the CISG applies.

     According to Article 1(1)(a) of the CISG, in order for CISG to apply the parties must have their central administration in a Contracting State (see above).

     The Swiss party has its central administration in a Contracting State but the English party does not, so the conditions set down in Article 1(1)(a) of the CISG are, as in the first scenario, not fulfilled.

2.   The CISG can nevertheless be applicable if Article 1(1)(b) applies. This article states that the CISG is applicable if the PIL of the *lex fori*, in the variation the Swiss Federal Act on Private International Law, leads to the application of the law of a Contracting State.

     Under Article 118 of the Swiss Federal Act on Private International Law, the sale of movables is governed by the Hague Convention of 15 June 1955 on the Law Applicable to International Sales of Goods. Where the parties have not decided on the applicable law (by choosing the applicable law under Article 2 of the Hague Convention), it is determined under Article 3(1) of the Hague Convention, according to which a sale is governed by the domestic law of the country in which the vendor's establishment is situated at the time when he receives the order.

     The seller's establishment is in Switzerland. This leads to the application of Swiss law. Switzerland is a Contracting State of the CISG, so Article 1(1)(b) of the CISG is fulfilled. The contract is therefore covered by the CISG.

3.   Article 16(1) of the CISG allows an offeror to revoke his offer up until the moment an acceptance is sent.

     The Swiss manufacturer sent his acceptance after having received the revocation of the offer from the English company. The English company thus successfully revoked its offer under Article 16(1) of the CISG.

---

[21]   It is presumed that the courts have jurisdiction.

Question 4(a): Seller's place of business in the USA and buyer's place of business in Switzerland, case brought before US courts

I. Uniform substantive law in this field?
To find out which law is applicable, the first question to ask is, once again, whether there is a uniform substantive law governing this area.

The uniform substantive law governing the international sale of goods is the UN Convention on Contracts for the International Sale of Goods (CISG). The USA is a Contracting State, so the CISG must be applied by the courts in the USA if the conditions for its application are met.

II. Conditions for the application of the CISG
1. According to Article 1(1), for the CISG to be applicable there must be (i) a contract (ii) for the sale of goods (iii) between parties whose places of business are in different States.

   The dispute relates to a contract for the sale of watch mechanisms. The parties' places of business are in the US and Switzerland. The three conditions for the applicability of the CISG set down in Article 1(1) are therefore fulfilled.
2. Article 1(1)(a) goes on to stipulate that the States in which the parties have their places of business must be Contracting States.

   The US and Switzerland are Contracting States of the CISG. The case is thus governed by the CISG.

Question 4(b): Seller's place of business in the US and buyer's place of business in England, case brought before US courts

I. Uniform substantive law in this field?
The USA is a Contracting State, so the CISG must be applied by the courts in the US if the conditions for the application of the CISG are met.

II. Conditions for the application of the CISG
1. According to Article 1(1), for the CISG to be applicable there must be (i) a contract (ii) for the sale of goods (iii) between parties whose places of business are in different States.

   The three conditions set down in Article 1(1) are fulfilled.
2. Article 1(1)(a) stipulates that the States in which the parties have their places of business must be Contracting States.

   The US is a Contracting State of the CISG but England is not. The requirement set down in Article 1(1)(a) is therefore *not* fulfilled.
3. US courts would *not* apply Article 1(1)(b) of the CISG as the US has declared that it will not be bound by subparagraph (1)(b) of Article 1 of the CISG (see above, note 8).

   Before US courts, a sales contract between a seller in the US and a buyer in England would therefore not be governed by the CISG. The courts would instead apply their own choice of law rules which would, depending on the US state in which the claim is brought, lead to the application of the UCC (or of English law).

Question 5: What law would apply to the Anglo-German contract in the scenario if the parties had agreed on the application of 'Swiss law'?

1. Before German and English courts, the contract between the English dealer and the German manufacturer would be governed by the CISG (see above, **Question (1)(a)**).

However, Article 6 of the CISG provides the possibility for the parties to opt out of the Convention and to exclude the application of the CISG if they wish to do so.

According to the dominant opinion of the courts and the dominant international academic opinion, the choice of the law of a Contracting State of CISG is, in principle, *not* regarded as an exclusion of the CISG. On the contrary, the law of the Contracting State chosen includes the international conventions that are in force in that State and that are an integral part of the legal order chosen (see the extracts above, III). The contract would therefore be governed by Swiss law, including the CISG.

2. An exclusion of the CISG would need to be expressed clearly enough (for example, by a statement such as "The law applicable is the sales law of the Swiss Code of Obligations"). Arguably, merely referring to the rules of the relevant articles in the Swiss Code of Obligations is insufficient, because such a reference might also be made because the parties think that that law was applicable anyway (see, e.g. the decision of the Rostock court at **III. 4** above).

Question 6(a): What would the applicable law be in the scenario if the parties, when contracting, had stipulated that the contract should be governed by (i) the Principles of European Contract Law, (ii) the UNIDROIT Principles, or (iii) the lex mercatoria?

As we have seen above, **Question (1)(a)**, before German and English courts, the contract between the English dealer and the German manufacturer would, in principle, be governed by the CISG.

Article 6 of the CISG provides the possibility for the parties to opt out of the Convention and to exclude the application of the CISG. If the parties expressly choose other rules of law, as they did in the present scenario, in doing so they implicitly exclude the CISG (Article 6 CISG).

The next step is to determine the law applicable to the contract according to the PIL rules of the forum, i.e. the rules of the Rome I Regulation. According to Article 3, the parties are free to decide upon the applicable "law".

According to the dominant case law and legal literature, "law" refers to the law of a State. The autonomous rules of private organisations do not have the status of legal rules, even if they are very detailed. In a proposal submitted in 2003, the European Commission suggested extending party autonomy to the choice of "principles of law", such as the Principles of European Contract Law and the UNIDROIT Principles, which would, if chosen by the parties have entirely replaced State laws.[22] However, this proposal was eventually rejected in the legislative process. Therefore, arguably, "law", in the sense of Article 3 of the Rome I Regulation, comprises only State laws. A reference made by the parties to the principles will therefore be considered to be a mere agreement to incorporate them in the contract, while the law governing the contract will still have to be determined on the basis of the PIL rules of the forum. In the scenario of Question 6(a), the parties have therefore not chosen a *law* in the sense of Article 3 of the Rome I Regulation.

---

[22] The proposal provided: "The parties may also choose as the applicable law the principles or rules of the substantive law of contract recognized internationally or in the Community. However, questions relating to matters governed by such principles or rules which are not expressly settled by them shall be governed by the general principles underlying them or, failing such principles, in accordance with the law applicable in the absence of a choice under this Regulation."

Where parties have not chosen the applicable law, Article 4(1) of the Rome I Regulation stipulates that "a contract for the sale of goods shall be governed by the *law of the country where the seller has his habitual residence"*, i.e. the country in which he has his *"place of central administration"* (Article 19).

In our case scenario, the seller's central administration is in Germany, so Article 4(1) of the Rome I Regulation leads to the application of German law, i.e. to the application of the BGB, as in this scenario the parties have, arguably, excluded the CISG by choosing a different set of rules to govern their contract.

Where parties refer to the Principles of European Contract Law or the UNIDROIT Principles, they incorporate them into their contract where the relevant rules of German law are not mandatory. The contract is thus governed by the chosen principles.

Question 6 (b): What would be the answer if the parties had also agreed to submit their case to arbitration?

Arbitrators are not bound by a particular domestic law so, in arbitration procedures, the parties are free to choose principles as the "rules of law". The chosen principles would apply to the exclusion of any particular national law, subject only to the application of those (very few) rules of domestic law that are mandatory irrespective of which law governs the contract (see **IV.6.** above: UNIDROIT: *Principles of International Commercial Contracts*, Preamble, Official Comment).

2. Further reading

On the applicability of the Vienna Sales Convention/CISG

CHRISTOPHE BERNASCONI, "The Personal and Territorial Scope of the Vienna Convention on Contracts for the International Sale of Goods (Article 1)", *Netherlands International Law Review* 1999, 137–72.
PETER HUBER AND ALASTAIR MULLIS, *The CISG: A New Textbook for Students and Practitioners*, Munich: Sellier, 2007.

Casebooks on the CISG

INGEBORG SCHWENZER AND CHRISTIANA FOUNALAKIS, *International Sales Law*, London: Routledge Cavendish, 2007.
See also: www.unilex.info

On the law applicable to contractual obligations in Europe

Dicey, Morris & Collins on the Conflict of Laws, 14th edn, London: Sweet & Maxwell, 2006, Vol. 2, Ch. 32.
MATTHIAS LEHMANN, "Liberating the Individual from Battles between States: Justifying Party Autonomy in Conflict of Laws", 41 (2008) *Vand. J. Transnat'l L.* 381–434.

On the choice of non-State rules

LAURO DA GAMA E SOUZA JR, "The Unidroit Principles of International Commercial Contracts and their Applicability in the Mercosur Countries", 36 (2002) *R.J.T.* 375–419.

EMMANUEL S. DARANKOUM, "L'application des Principes d'Unidroit par les arbitres internationaux et par les juges etatiques", 36 (2002) *R.J.T.* 421–79.

CATHERINE KESSEDJIAN, "Party Autonomy and Caracteristic Performance in the Rome Convention and the Rome I Proposal", in Jürgen Basedow, Harald Baum and Yuko Nishitani (eds), *Japanese and European Private International Law in Comparative Perspective*, Tübingen: Mohr Siebeck, 2008, 105–25 (at 114–17).

RALF MICHAELS, "Privatautonomie und Privatkodifikation – Zu Anwendbarkeit und Geltung allgemeiner Vertragsrechtsprinzipien", *RabelsZ* 62 (1998), 580–626.

GIAN PAOLO ROMANO, "Le choix des Principes UNIDROIT par les contractants à l'épreuve des dispositions impératives", in Eleanor Cashin Ritaine and Eva Lein (eds), *The UNIDROIT Principles 2004 – Their Impact on Contractual Practice, Jurisprudence and Codification*, Zürich: Schulthess, 2007, 35–54.

WULF-HENNING ROTH, "Zur Wählbarkeit nichtstaatlichen Rechts", in H.-P. Mansel, Thomas Pfeiffer, Herbert Kronke, Christian Kohler and Rainer Hausmann (eds), *Festschrift für Erik Jayme*, Vol. I, München: C.H. Beck, 757–72.

FRIEDERIKE SCHÄFER, "Die Wahl nichtstaatlichen Rechts nach Art. 3 Abs. 2 des Entwurfs einer Rom I VO – Auswirkungen auf das optionale Intrument des europäischen Vertragsrechts", *GPR* 2006, 54–59.

On non-State rules in general

MICHAEL BONELL, *An International Restatement of Contract Law, The UNIDROIT Principles of International Commercial Contracts*, 3rd edn incorporating the UNIDROIT Principles 2004, Ardsley, New York: Transnational Publishers Inc., 2005.

MICHAEL BONELL, "The New Edition of the Principles of International Commercial Contracts adopted by the International Institute for the Unification of Private Law", *Uniform Law Review* 2004, 5–40.

MICHAEL JOACHIM BONELL, "The CISG, European Contract Law and the Development of a World Contract Law", 56 (2008) *Am. J. Comp. L.* 1–28.

ELEANOR CASHIN RITAINE AND EVA LEIN (eds), *The UNIDROIT Principles 2004 – Their Impact on Contractual Practice, Jurisprudence and Codification*, Zurich: Schulthess, 2007.

ARTHUR HARTKAMP, "Principles of Contract Law", in Hartkamp *et al.* (eds), *Towards a European Civil Code*, 3rd edn, Nijmegen, 2004, Ch. 7, 125–43.

OLE LANDO, "CISG and Its Followers: A Proposal to Adopt Some International Principles of Contract Law", 53 (2005) *Am. J. Comp. L.* 379–401.

VERNON VALENTINE PALMER, "From Lerotholi to Lando: Some Examples of Comparative Law Methodology", 53 (2005) *Am. J. Comp. L.* 261–90.

GRACE XAVIER, "Global harmonisation of contract laws fact – or fiction?", *Const. L.J.* 2004, 20(1), 3–18.

Case 10:   The future of European contract law

> *"On peut être bon Européen et considérer avec réticence l'unification des droits européens; on ne peut être bon Européen et vouloir maintenir, sans effort d'harmonisation, la situation actuelle, c'est-à-dire la complète insularité de chaque système juridique européen."*[1]

Scenario

The European Parliament, in two resolutions of 1989 and 1994, called for work to be started on the possibility of developing a European Code of Private Law. The Parliament was of the opinion that harmonisation of certain sectors of private law would be essential to the completion of the internal market and that the unification of major branches of private law in the form of a European Civil Code would be the most effective way of meeting the Community's legal requirements in order to achieve a single market without frontiers. In a third resolution in 2000, the European Parliament once again declared that greater harmonisation of civil law would be essential in the internal market.

In response to these resolutions, the European Commission published a communication on European contract law in 2001. The Commission made a public request seeking information as to whether divergences in contract law between Member States cause problems. The Commission also wanted to receive information on the need for a more comprehensive European legislation on contract law or even a European contract code.

Following these initiatives, the debate on the eventual harmonisation of European contract law has intensified.

---

[1]   Translation: One can be pro-European and be reluctant with regard to the unification of European laws; one cannot be pro-European and want to maintain, without any attempt at harmonisation, the status quo, that is to say the total insularity of each European legal system. RENÉ DAVID, "L'avenir des droits européens: unification ou harmonisation" (1955), reproduced in David René, *Le droit comparé – Droits d'hier, droits de demain*, Paris: Economica, 1982, p. 295 (at 296).

Questions

(1) Over the years, what role have the EU institutions played in the harmonisation or unification of European contract law? To what extent is European contract law unified, and to what extent does diversity prevail?

(2) Does the EU currently have the legislative competence to adopt a European contract code?

(3) To what extent is contract law in the United States of America uniform; to what extent is it diverse? How is the fragmentation avoided of the contract laws of the different states in the USA? With regard to the uniformity and diversity of contract law, can the situation in the USA be used as an example for European private law? What are the similarities and differences between the situations in the USA and Europe?

(4) In your opinion, should a European contract code be enacted modelled on, for example, the Principles of European Contract Law, the UNIDROIT Principles, the Gandolfi Draft Code or the Draft Common Frame of Reference? What conclusions would you draw, in this respect, from working with the cases in this book? Which of the European Commission's four proposed courses of action presented in its 2001 Communication do you favour? Why?

(5) If a new EU instrument were to be adopted (i.e. if the Commission's fourth proposed solution were adopted), should national contract laws be replaced by a European contract code, or should national contract laws and a European contract code coexist, each having its own field of application? Give reasons for your answer.

Table of contents

I.   The European Union's role in the harmonisation of contract law

Communication from the Commission on European Contract Law, Brussels, 11.07.2001, COM(2001) 398 final

COMMISSION OF THE EUROPEAN COMMUNITIES

Brussels, 11.07.2001
COM(2001) 398 final

COMMUNICATION FROM THE COMMISSION
TO THE COUNCIL AND THE EUROPEAN PARLIAMENT
ON EUROPEAN CONTRACT LAW

Executive Summary[2]

This Communication is intended to broaden the debate on European Contract law involving the European Parliament, Council and stakeholders, including businesses, legal practitioners, academics and consumer groups.

The approximation of certain specific areas of contract law at EC level has covered an increasing number of issues. The EC legislator has followed a selective approach adopting directives on specific contracts or specific marketing techniques where a particular need for harmonisation was identified. The European Commission is interested at this stage in gathering information on the need for farther-reaching EC action in the area of contract law, in particular to the extent that the case-by-case approach might not be able to solve all the problems which might arise. The Commission is seeking information as to whether problems result from divergences in contract law between Member States and if so, what. In particular, the Communication asks whether the proper functioning of the Internal Market may be hindered by problems in relation to the conclusion, interpretation and application of cross-border contracts. Also the Commission is interested in whether different national contract laws discourage or increase the costs of cross-border transactions. The Communication also seeks views on whether the existing approach of sectoral harmonisation of contract law could lead to possible inconsistencies at EC level, or to problems of non-uniform implementation of EC law and application of national transposition measures.

If concrete problems are identified, the Commission would also like to receive views on what form solutions should or could take. In order to assist in defining possible solutions, the Communication includes a non-exhaustive list of possible solutions. Other solutions may be suggested by any interested party, however.

---

[2]   Footnotes partly omitted. The numbering of the footnotes differs from the original text.

- To leave the solution of any identified problems to the market.
- To promote the development of non-binding common contract law principles, useful for contracting parties in drafting their contracts, national courts and arbitrators in their decisions and national legislators when drawing up legislative initiatives.
- To review and improve existing EC legislation in the area of contract law to make it more coherent or to adapt it to cover situations not foreseen at the time of adoption.
- To adopt a new instrument at EC level. Different elements could be combined: the nature of the act to be adopted (regulation, directive or recommendation), the relationship with national law (which could be replaced or co-exist), the question of mandatory rules within the set of applicable provisions and whether the contracting parties would choose to apply the EC instrument or whether the European rules apply automatically as a safety net of fallback provisions if the contracting parties have not agreed to a specific solution.

[...]

1.   INTRODUCTION

1. Over recent years, discussion has intensified on possible harmonisation of substantive private law, in particular contract law.[3]
2. The European Parliament has adopted a number of resolutions on the possible harmonisation of substantive private law. In 1989 and 1994 the European Parliament called for work to be started on the possibility of drawing up a common European Code of Private Law.[4] The Parliament stated that harmonisation of certain sectors of private law was essential to the completion of the internal market. The Parliament further stated that unification of major branches of private law in the form of a European Civil Code would be the most effective way of carrying out harmonisation with a view to meeting the Community's legal requirements in order to achieve a single market without frontiers.
3. Furthermore, in its resolution of 16 March 2000 concerning the Commission's work program 2000, the European Parliament stated "that greater harmonisation of civil law has become essential in the internal market" and called on the Commission to draw up a study in this area.[5] In its reply of 25 July 2000 to the European Parliament, the Commission stated that it would "present a communication to the other Community institutions and the general public with the aim of launching a detailed and wide-ranging discussion, without losing sight of the date of 2001 set by the European Council" at Tampere. The Commission also stated that "in view of the importance of secondary legislation for the development of the internal market and future commercial and technological trends, this communication will analyse this

---

[3]   Cf. Ole Lando and Hugh Beale (eds.), *Principles of European Contract Law Parts I and II*, (Kluwer Law International, 2000); Academy of European Private Lawyers, *European Contract Code – Preliminary draft*, (Universita Di Pavia, 2001) hereafter referred to as "the Pavia Group"; the 'Study Group for a European Civil Code'. A comprehensive discussion, including a detailed bibliography, of the issues concerning civil law in Europe can be found in Hartkamp, Hesselink, Hondius, Joustra, Perron (eds.), *Towards a European Civil Code* (Kluwer Law International, 1998).

[4]   OJ C 158, 26.6.1989, p. 400 (Resolution A2-157/89); OJ C 205, 25.7.1994, p. 518 (Resolution A3-0329/94).

[5]   OJ C 377, 29.12.2000, p. 323 (Resolution B5-0228, 0229 – 0230 / 2000, p. 326 at point 28).

legislation – in force or in preparation – at Community level in the relevant areas of civil law in order to identify and assess any gaps, as well as the academic work which has been or is being carried out".

4. Indeed the conclusions of the European Council held in Tampere requested, in paragraph 39, 'as regards substantive law, an overall study on the need to approximate Member State's legislation in civil matters in order to eliminate obstacles to the good functioning of civil proceedings'.[6] A consultative document has been announced in the Commission's "scoreboard for the evaluation of progress in the establishment of an area of freedom, security and justice".[7] The Tampere European Council dealt with issues concerning judicial civil cooperation on the basis of title IV of the EC Treaty. In this regard, this Communication can be considered as a first step towards the implementation of the Tampere conclusions.

5. Finally, this Communication was also included in the Commission communication on E-Commerce and Financial Services[8] within the policy area of ensuring coherence in the legislative framework for financial services.

6. Leading representatives of the academic world have had detailed discussions on harmonising certain sectors of contract law. Two drafts of a contract code[9] and of general principles of contract law[10] have recently been published. This academic work continues, and includes work on other issues not included in the two published drafts, such as contracts in the specific areas of financial services, insurance contracts, building contracts, factoring and leasing as well as some areas of the law of property. In particular, the academic work is focusing on areas that have a particular significance for securing rights across the European borders.[11]

7. The aim of the academic work carried out varies from the establishment of a binding code to principles similar to `restatements´ that can be used to provide reliable comparative information on the European legal situation in these areas.

---

[6] Presidency Conclusions, Tampere European Council 15 and 16 October 1999, SI (1999) 800.

[7] COM(2000) 167, 24.3.2000, last updated in May 2001, see COM(2001) 278 final, 23.5.2001

[8] COM(2001) 66 final, 7.2.2001, p. 11.

[9] The "Pavia Group" has recently published its *"European Contract Code – Preliminary draft"*, (Universita Di Pavia, 2001) based on the work of the Academy of European Private Lawyers. This code contains a body of rules and solutions based on the laws of members of the European Union and Switzerland and covers the areas of contractual formation, content and form, contractual interpretation and effect, execution and non-execution of a contract, cessation and extinction, other contractual anomalies and remedies.

[10] The "Commission on European Contract Law" (which has received a major part of its subsidies from the Commission of the EC) has published *Principles of European Contract Law Parts I and II*, edited by Ole Lando and Hugh Beale (Kluwer Law International, 2000). These common principles for the countries of the European Community concern the issues of formation, validity, interpretation and contents of contracts, the authority of an agent to bind his principal, performance, non-performance and remedies. The book provides text proposals for common rules and includes commentary and comparative analysis for each rule.

[11] Another important ongoing academic exercise in this area is the «Study Group on a European Civil Code» consisting of academic experts of the 15 Member States and some candidate countries. Their work concerns areas like «Sales/Services/Long Term Contracts», «Securities», «Extracontractual Obligations» or «Transfer of property on movable Goods» and includes a comparative research with the final objective of a fully formulated and commented draft on the areas concerned.

8. The approximation of certain specific areas of contract law at EC level has covered an increasing number of issues. In the area of consumer law, no fewer than seven Directives dealing with contractual issues have been adopted in the period from 1985 to 1999.[12] Other areas also show increased harmonisation.[13]

9. This sectoral harmonisation has concerned specific contracts or specific marketing techniques. Directives have been adopted where a particular need for harmonisation was identified.

2.　PURPOSE OF THE COMMUNICATION

10. The European Commission is interested at this stage of the discussion in gathering information on the need for farther-reaching EC action in the area of contract law, in particular to the extent that the case-by-case approach might not be able to solve all the problems which might arise. This does not preclude the right of initiative of the Commission in the future to make proposals for specific actions on contract law aspects if a specific need for this exists, in particular on-going initiatives launched or to be launched in the framework of the Internal Market policy.

11. The purpose of this Communication is, therefore, to broaden the debate by encouraging contributions from consumers, businesses, professional organisations, public administrations and institutions, the academic world and all interested parties. Part C examines the current situation of contract law, the reasons for its importance in cross-border negotiations and problems of uniform application of EC law. Part D presents a general framework for future EC policy in the area of contract law.

---

[12]　Directive 1999/44/EC of the European Parliament and of the Council of 25 May 1999 on certain aspects of the sale of consumer goods and associated guarantees (OJ L 171, 7.7.1999, p.12). Council Directive 93/13/EEC of 5 April 1993 on unfair terms in consumer contracts (OJ L 95, 21.4.1993, p. 29). Council Directive 90/314/EEC of 13 June 1990 on package travel, package holidays and package tours (OJ L 158, 23.6.1990, p. 59). Council Directive 85/577/EEC of 20 December 1985 to protect the consumer in respect of contracts negotiated away from business premises (OJ L 372, 31.12.1985, p. 31). Council Directive 87/102/EEC of 22 December 1986 for the approximation of the laws, regulations and administrative provisions of the Member States concerning consumer credit (OJ L 42, 12.2.1987, p. 48) as modified by Directive 90/88 (OJ L 61, 10.3.1990, p. 14) and Directive 98/7 (OJ L 101, 1.4.198, p. 17). Directive 97/7/EC of the European Parliament and of the Council of 20 May 1997 on the protection of consumers in respect of distance contracts (OJ L 144, 4.6.1997, p. 19). Directive 94/47/EC of the European Parliament and the Council of 26 October 1994 on the protection of purchasers in respect of certain aspects of contracts relating to the purchase of the right to use immovable properties on a timeshare basis (OJ L 280, 29.10.1994, p. 83).

[13]　Council Directive 86/653/EEC of 18 December 1986 on the co-ordination of the laws of the Member States relating to self-employed commercial agents (OJ L 382, 31.12.1986, p. 17), Directive 2000/31/EC of the European Parliament and of the Council of 8 June 2000 on certain legal aspects of information society services, in particular electronic commerce, in the Internal Market (OJ L 171, 17.7.2000, p. 1), Directive 2000/35/EC of the European Parliament and of the Council of 29 June 2000 on combating late payment in commercial transactions (OJ L 200, 8.8.2000, p. 35), Council Directive 85/374/EEC of 25 of July 1985 on the approximation of the laws, regulations and administrative provisions of the Member States concerning liability for defective products (OJ L 210, 7.8.1985, p. 29) as modified by the Directive 99/34/EC (OJ L 141, 4.6.1999, p. 20), Directive 97/5/EC of the European Parliament and the Council of 27 January1997 on cross-border credit transfers (OJ L 43, 14.2.1997, p. 25) should be noted as examples.

12. Contract law encompasses several areas of law. These are linked to Member States' different cultural and legal traditions, but most Member States' legal regimes for contract law have similar concepts and rules. Contract law constitutes the principal body of law regulating cross-border transactions and some Community legislation regulating contract law already exists, although this legislation has taken a sector-by-sector approach.

13. The areas concerned by this Communication include contracts of sale and all kind of service contracts, including financial services.[14] General rules on performance, non-performance and remedies are an indispensable basis for these contracts and are therefore also covered. Additionally, rules on general issues such as the formation of a contract and its validity and interpretation are also essential. Furthermore, because of the economic context, rules on credit securities regarding movable goods as well as the law of unjust enrichment may also be relevant. Finally, the aspects of tort law linked to contracts and to its other features relevant to internal market should also be taken into consideration insofar as they are already part of existing EC law.

14. [...]

15. The Commission intends to focus the attention of this Communication on two areas: firstly on possible problems resulting from divergences of national contract law, and secondly on options for the future of contract law in the EC. This will enable the Commission to define its future policy in this area and to propose any necessary measures.

3. PRESENT SITUATION OF CONTRACT LAW

3.1. Existing legislation

3.1.1. *International Instruments*

16. International remedies offer solutions to certain potential problems related to differences in national contract law. The first remedy is the application of uniform private international rules to determine which law is applicable to the contract. The most important of these rules is the 1980 Rome Convention,[15] ratified by all Member States.

17. The rules of the Rome Convention apply to contractual obligations in any situation involving a choice between the laws of different countries[16]. Under the Rome Convention parties may agree on which national law to apply. However, the Convention places limits on this choice of applicable law and determines which law is applicable if no choice is made. [...]

18. The second remedy is the establishment of harmonisation of substantive law rules on an international level. Here the most relevant instrument is the 1980 United Nations Convention on contracts for the international sale of goods (the CISG), adopted by all Member States except the United Kingdom, Portugal and Ireland [and Malta].

---

[14] COM (2001) 66 final, 7.2.2001, p. 11.

[15] 1980 Rome Convention on the law applicable to contractual obligations [replaced by the Rome I Regulation, see **Case 9, I.2.**].

[16] Alongside the convention there is also the the the Council Regulation (EC) No 44/2001 of 22 December 2000 on jurisdiction and the recognition and enforcement of judgments in civil and commercial matters (OJ L12,16.1.2001, p. 1) [Brussels Regulation, that determines which forum is competent to deal with a case].

19. The CISG establishes uniform rules for the international sale of goods, which apply to sales contracts unless the parties state otherwise. Some areas are excluded from the scope of the Convention, such as the sale of goods bought for personal, family or household use and the sale of stocks, shares, investment securities or negotiable instruments.

20. The Convention includes provisions dealing with the formation of a contract (offer and acceptance of offer), and the rights and obligations of the seller and the buyer. The Convention does not govern the validity of the contract or of its provisions, nor does it cover the effect which the contract may have on the property in the goods sold. The Convention also does not address the seller's liability beyond the contract.

3.1.2.   Description of the Community acquis

21. Several Community acts include provisions harmonising private law. Certain Directives specify rules on the conclusion of a contract, on the form and the content of an offer and its acceptance and on the performance of a contract, i.e. the obligations of the contractual parties. Several Directives also specify in detail the content of the information to be provided by the parties at different stages, in particular before concluding a contract. Certain Directives cover rights and obligations of the contracting parties regarding the execution of a contract, including poor execution and non-execution.

22. [...]

3.2.   Implications for the Internal market

23. The Commission would like to find out if the co-existence of national contract laws in the Member states directly or indirectly obstructs to the functioning of the internal market, and if so to what extent. If such obstacles do exist, the European Institutions may be called upon to take appropriate action.

24. The EC Treaty has given the European Institutions powers to facilitate the establishment and functioning of the internal market, in particular the free movement of goods, persons, services and capital. This has allowed the European Community to significantly reduce impediments for economic actors, including manufacturers, service providers, intermediaries and consumers, to operate throughout the EC and beyond.

25. Technical developments, such as the possibilities offered by the Internet for electronic commerce, have made it easier for economic actors to conclude transactions over long distances. The introduction of the Euro as the common currency of twelve of the Member States is also an important factor in facilitating cross-border trade. However, in spite of the major successes achieved thus far, certain problems still remain. Markets are not as efficient as they could and indeed should be, to the detriment of all parties involved.

26. The exchange of goods and services, be it through sales, leasing or barter is governed by a contract. Problems in relation to agreeing, interpreting and applying contracts in cross-border trade may therefore affect the functioning of the internal market. Do existing contract law rules meet the current and future needs of businesses and consumers in the internal market, or is EC action required?

27. Generally, national contract law regimes lay down the principle of contractual freedom. Accordingly, contracting parties are free to agree their own contract terms.

However, each contract is governed by the laws and court decisions of a particular state. Some of these national rules are not mandatory and contracting parties may decide either to apply these rules or to agree different terms instead. Other national rules, however, are mandatory, in particular where there is an important disparity between the positions of the contracting parties, such as contracts with tenants or consumers.

28. Normally, these different national regimes do not create any problems for cross border transactions, as parties can decide which law will govern their contract. By choosing one national law, they accept all the mandatory rules of that law, as well as those non-mandatory rules which they do not replace by different terms. However, conflicts may arise between mandatory rules of the laws in one country with contradictory mandatory rules of another national law. These conflicts between different mandatory rules may have a negative impact upon cross-border transactions.

29. Although not required by national laws, certain clauses in contracts may result from common practice in a given member state, especially if such practice has been formalised in standard contracts. It may be hard to agree a contract containing terms and conditions different from those generally applied in a particular member state. There may be important economic or even legal reasons why it is hard or even impossible for a party to agree to the terms and conditions in a standard contract that is generally used in the other party's member state. Yet, for similar reasons, it may be hard for the latter party to accept the type of terms which are common practice in the first party's member state.

30. For consumers and SMEs [small and medium enterprises] in particular, not knowing other contract law regimes may be a disincentive against undertaking cross-border transactions. This has been part of the rationale for some existing Community acts aimed at improving the functioning of the internal market. Suppliers of goods and services may even therefore regard offering their goods and services to consumers in other countries as economically unviable and refrain from doing so. In the field of subcontracting, the provisions covering subcontracting and supply contracts are quite different in the different Member States.[17] These differences may make it difficult for subcontractors – mostly SMEs – to make cross-border agreements.

31. Moreover, disparate national law rules may lead to higher transaction costs, especially information and possible litigation costs for enterprises in general and SMEs and consumers in particular. Contractual parties could be forced to obtain information and legal advice on the interpretation and application of an unfamiliar foreign law. If the applicable law has been chosen in the contract, this applies to the contractual party whose law has not been chosen. It applies to a minor extent also to contracts where the parties have agreed standard contract terms in the cases where these terms do not cover all possible problems.

---

[17] Provisions range from a specific subcontracting law in Italy and a law on payment conditions to subcontractors in France, to civil code provisions on contractual relations in most Member States (e.g. in Germany subcontracting falls under a 1976 law on the general terms of business and under a few articles of the civil code).

32. These higher transaction costs may, furthermore, be a competitive disadvantage, for example in a situation where a foreign supplier is competing with a supplier established in the same country as the potential client.

33. The Commission is seeking contributions on how far issues described above create problems for the internal market, and what other issues relating to contract law also obstruct the functioning of the internal market.

3.3. Uniform application of Community law

34. The European Community legislator must ensure consistency in the drafting of EC legislation as well as in its implementation and application in the Member States. The measures adopted by the European Community must be consistent with each other, interpreted in the same manner and produce the same effects in all Member States. The European Court of Justice (the ECJ) has stated that "the need for uniform application of Community law and the principle of equality require that the terms of a provision of Community law which makes no express reference to the law of the Member States for the purpose of determining its meaning and scope must normally be given an autonomous and uniform interpretation throughout the Community".[18]

35. In the area of contract law the European legislator has taken a 'piecemeal' approach to harmonisation. This approach combined with unforeseen market developments, could lead to inconsistencies in the application of EC law. For example, under certain circumstances[19] it is possible to apply both the Doorstep Selling Directive and the Timeshare Directive. Both Directives give the consumer a right of withdrawal; however, the time period during which the consumer can exercise this right is different. Although such cases of conflicts between rules are exceptional, the Commission would welcome information on problems resulting from possible inconsistencies between EC rules.

36. Using abstract terms in EC law can also cause problems for implementing and applying EC law and national measures in a non-uniform way. Abstract terms may represent a legal concept for which there are different rules in each national body of law.[20]

---

[18] Case C-357/98 *The Queen* v. *Secretary of State for the Home Department ex parte: Nana Yaa Konadu Yiadom* [2000] ECR-9265, at para. 26. Cf. also Case C-287/98 *Luxemburg* v. *Linster* [2000] ECR-6917, at para. 43; Case C-387/97 *Commission* v. *Greece* [2000] ECR-5047; Case C-327/82 *Ekro* v. *Produktschap voor Vee en Vlees* [1984] ECR I – 107, at para. 11. The principle of uniform application also applies in the area of private law cf. Case C-373/97 *Dionisios Diamantis* v. *Elliniko Dimosio (Greek State), Organismos Ikonomikis Anasinkrotisis Epikhiriseon AE (OAE)* [2000] ECR I-1705, at para. 34; Case C-441/93 *Pafitis and Others* v. *TKE and Others* [1996] ECR I-1347, at para. 68 to 70.

[19] Cf. Case C–423/97, *Travel-Vac S.L. and Manuel José Antelm Sanchís* [1999] ECR I–2195.

[20] These matters have recently been examined by a EP study, drafted by a team of high ranking independent legal experts. It states with regard to the example of the term "damage" that: 'The European laws governing liability do not yet have even a reasonably uniform idea of what damage is or how it can be defined, which naturally threatens to frustrate any efforts to develop European directives in this field'; European Parliament, DG for Research: *'Study of the systems of private law in the EU with regard to discrimination and the creation of a European Civil Code'* (PE 168.511, p. 56). Some Directives (Art. 9 of Directive 85/374/EEC, Art. 17 of Directive 86/653/EEC) contain differing definitions of the term «damage». Each definition, however, is intended solely for the purpose of each respective Directive. Other Directives (Art. 5 of Directive 90/314/EEC) use the term without defining it.

37. In general, differences between provisions in directives can be explained by differences in the problems which those directives seek to solve. One cannot, therefore, require that a term used to solve one problem is interpreted and applied in precisely the same manner in a different context. However, differences in terms and concepts that cannot be explained by differences in the problems being addressed should be eliminated.

38. In addition, domestic legislation adopted by Member States to implement EC directives refers to domestic concepts of these abstract terms. These concepts vary significantly from one Member State to another[21]. The absence of a uniform understanding in EC law of general terms and concepts at least in specific or linked areas) may lead to different results in commercial and legal practice in different Member States.[22]

39. This kind of problem does not only apply to horizontal questions concerning general terms of contract law as mentioned above. It is also relevant to specific economic sectors.[23]

40. The Commission is reflecting whether – in order to avoid the kind of problems described above – the necessary consistency could be ensured through the continuation of the existing approach or should be improved through other means. The Commission is therefore interested in receiving information on practical problems relating to contract law resulting from the way that EC rules are applied and implemented in the Member States.

4. OPTIONS FOR FUTURE EC INITIATIVES IN CONTRACT LAW

41. Responses to this document may show that there are impediments to the functioning of the internal market for cross border transactions. If these problems cannot be solved satisfactorily through a case-by-case approach, a horizontal measure providing for comprehensive harmonisation of contract law rules could be envisaged at EC level. However, there are of course limits on the power of the Commission and the other EC institutions to intervene in this area.

---

[21] This problem is highlighted by a case pending with the ECJ (C–168/00, *Simone Leitner/TUI Deutschland GmbH & Co KG*). On the basis of a package travel contract concluded under Austrian law with a German tour operator, the complainant seeks compensation for 'moral damages' (unrecoverable holiday spent in hospital). Austrian law does not grant compensation for this kind of damage, but the laws of Germany and some other Member States do. The complainant points at Article 5 of the Package Travel Directive, saying that this Article establishes a specific concept of 'damage' that includes 'moral damage'.

[22] The Commission has emphasised, for example, in its report on the application of the Commercial Agents Directive (COM (1996) 364 final, 23.7.1996) that the application of the system of compensation for damage foreseen in the Directive concerning the same factual situation produces completely different practical results in France and the UK due to different methods of calculation for the quantum of compensation.

[23] The problem referred to here also exists outside the contract law area. Thus, in its report on the Regulation of European Securities Markets, the Committee of Wise Men led by Alexandre Lamfalussy pointed to problems resulting from the use in certain directives in the financial area of ambiguous notions, which allowed member states to apply these directives in a disparate manner. Final Report, Brussels, 15.2.2001, Annex 5 (Initial Report of 9. 11.2000).

42. Any measure must be in accordance with the principles of subsidiarity and proportionality, as described in Article 5 of the EC Treaty and the protocol on subsidiarity and proportionality. As the European Parliament pointed out in its resolutions on the Better Lawmaking reports,[24] the subsidiarity principle is a binding legal standard that does not rule out the legitimate exercise of the EU's competencies. The need to achieve balanced application of this principle has been highlighted by a number of Member States[25] and the European institutions.

43. The principle of subsidiarity serves as a guide as to how the Community powers are to be exercised at Community level. Subsidiarity is a dynamic concept and should be applied in the light of the objectives set out in the Treaty. It allows Community action within the limits of its powers to be expanded where circumstances so require, and conversely, to be restricted or discontinued where it is no longer justified.[26] There should be clear benefits to taking action at Community level instead of national level. Where the intention is to have an impact throughout the EC, Community-level action is undoubtedly the best way of ensuring homogeneous treatment within national systems and stimulating effective co-operation between the Member States.

44. Moreover, legislation should be effective and should not impose any excessive constraints on national, regional or local authorities or on the private sector, including civil society. The principle of proportionality, which is one of the general principles of Community law, requires that measures adopted by Community institutions do not exceed the limits of what is appropriate and necessary in order to attain the objectives legitimately pursued by the legislation in question; when there is a choice between several appropriate measures, recourse must be had to the least onerous, and the disadvantages caused must not be disproportionate to the aims pursued […]

45. Preparing legislative proposals by way of communications and green and white papers is one way of consulting the private sector, civil society and institutions at all levels on the expediency, level and content of legislative instruments in order to achieve these objectives. Additionally, the Commission will seek to identify areas of intervention by involving both civil society and business with a view to producing legislative instruments geared to users' real needs. This Communication and possible further documents are intended to determine whether EC action is needed and if so in which areas.

46. There are a number of options that can be considered should the case-by case approach not fully solve the problem. This Communication briefly examines four possible scenarios:
    I. no EC action;
    II. promote the development of common contract law principles leading to more convergence of national laws;
    III. improve the quality of legislation already in place;
    IV. adopt new comprehensive legislation at EC level.

---

24 COM (2000) 772 final, 30.11.2000, p. 3.
25 COM (2000) 772 final, 30.11.2000, p. 3.
26 See Protocol on the application of the principles of subsidiarity and proportionality (OJ C 340, 10.11.1997, p.105).

47. [...]
48. Another approach, which is not discussed here as it goes beyond the level of a European initiative, could be the negotiation of an international treaty in the area of contract law. This would be comparable to the CISG but with a broader scope than purely the sale of goods. However, the provisions of the CISG could also be integrated into options II and IV which would increase their acceptance in commercial and legal practice.

4.1. Option I: No EC action

49. In many cases the market creates problems of public concern, but it also develops its own solutions. The effectiveness of the market in responding to different social values and to public opinion should not be underestimated. As a result of competitive behaviour, many of the problems created by the market may be solved automatically by the pressure exercised by the interest groups involved (consumers, NGOs, enterprises). Public authorities can enhance this coincidence of self-interest and public interest.
50. Different incentives by Member States and trade associations e.g. offering assistance and advice on cross-border transactions can efficiently channel the market in a specific direction (for example speed up the use of new technologies or encourage new types of commercial practices). These could compensate for economic and psychological risks of cross-border trade activity, whether these risks are perceived or real. Different services from economic operators can efficiently overcome problems of cross border transactions that have been identified. For example, trade associations could offer assistance or advice to SMEs.[27]
51. Economic developments, in particular the increasing integration of markets into a genuine internal market, also create incentives for national policymakers and legislators to look for solutions to problems with contracts involving parties in other Member States. This could result in a certain degree of "soft harmonisation" – not driven by binding EC rules, but coming about as a result of economic developments. This could solve some of the problems for intra-community trade, provided that there is a genuine and fair free choice of law for contracting parties, full, correct and freely available information about the existing rules and practices and fair and affordable alternative dispute resolution mechanisms.

---

[27] Below are two examples of national/industry associations' initiatives that aim at providing a solution for cross-border contractual problems through voluntary agreements on cross-border model contracts:
  – In 1999, a group of six German industry federations, the so-called working group of the components supply industry, agreed on a set of minimum clauses for cross-border contracts. However, this model applies to cross-border contracts ruled exclusively by German law (the contractual parties must agree to rule the cross-border contract in question under German law) and includes provisions on prices, confidentiality, moulds, equipment, industrial property rights, guarantee, liability, product damage, etc.
  – Also ORGALIME (European group of the mechanical, electrical, electronic and metalworking industries) issued a model for international "consortium agreement" to foster cross-border inter-enterprise co-operation.

4.2. Option II: Promote the development of common contract law principles leading to more convergence of national laws

52. In order to achieve more convergence of national contract laws, one solution would be for the Commission to promote comparative law research and co-operation between – amongst others – academics and legal practitioners (including judges and experts). This co-operation could aim to find common principles in relevant areas of national contract law. The existing work in this area could be used and developed, including the results of academic studies and conclusions drawn in international academic forums. The framework for this research and co-operation could be a kind of partnership, in which the EC institutions – and more particularly the Commission – could play a co-ordination role. In the field of trans-national contracts, some common solutions, principles or even sets of rules could be defined.

53. The outcome of these discussions could vary from common principles to the drafting of guidelines or specific codes of conduct for certain types of contracts. The common principles could be useful for contractual parties at the drafting stage of new contracts, as well as for the execution of contracts. They could also be useful for national courts and arbitrators who have to decide legal issues – especially concerning cross-border cases – which are not fully covered by binding national rules or where no legislative rules exist at all. The courts or arbitrators would know that the principles they were applying represented the solution common to all the national contract law systems in the EU. At the same time common principles could help national courts which have to apply foreign law to have a basic understanding of the underlying general principles of law. The guidelines could be followed as much as possible by Member States or the EC when issuing new legislation or adapting old legislation in the area of national contract law.

54. The application of common principles could even lead to the creation of customary law, provided that there is a long and continued application and a commonly shared conviction. This might influence or even change existing commercial practice in the Member States that could create impediments to the full functioning of the internal market.

55. Once those common principles or guidelines were established and agreed upon by all interested parties in the Member States, broad dissemination should be ensured amongst those who would be supposed to apply them. This would ensure coherent and uniform application of the common principles or guidelines. These common principles or guidelines could however only be applied on a voluntary basis. If this were indeed done continuously by a sufficiently large number of legal practitioners as well as EC and national legislators, this would bring about greater convergence in the area of European contract law. However, for this option to be meaningful, it is clear that the common principles should be defined in such a way as to meet all legitimate requirements.

56. Another solution could concern standard contracts. In order to facilitate economic transactions, a large number of standard contracts are in use in all Member States. Such standard contracts spare parties the need to negotiate the contract-terms for every single transaction. They also provide a degree of certainty to parties and obtain almost semi-regulatory status. It is precisely for this reason that it is often difficult to agree to a contract with a party in another Member State which does not comply with

the standard contract terms that the other party is used to. Parties from different Member States may indeed be used to different terms which are in standard use in their respective states. These problems could be solved, in conformity with Community law, if standard contracts were developed for use throughout the EC. The Commission could promote the development of such standard contracts by interested parties.

4.3. Option III: Improve the quality of legislation already in place

57. The Lisbon European Council has asked the Commission, the Council and the Member States "to set out by 2001 a strategy for further co-ordinated action to simplify the regulatory environment". Answering to this request, the Commission has given an initial response through an Interim Report to the Stockholm European Council which takes stock of the situation and sets out the Commission's initial thoughts on putting the Lisbon mandate into practice.

58. Improving the quality of legislation already in place implies first modernising existing instruments. The Commission intends to build on action already undertaken on consolidating, codifying and recasting existing instruments centred on transparency and clarity. Quality of drafting could also be reviewed; presentation and terminology could become more coherent. Apart from those changes regarding the presentation of legal texts, efforts should moreover be systematically focused on simplifying and clarifying the content of existing legislation. Finally, the Commission will evaluate the effects of Community legislation and will amend existing acts if necessary.

59. Where appropriate, directives could be subject to simplification of their provisions. In fact, for several years now, the EC has been pursuing a policy of simplifying Community legislation. The SLIM initiative (simpler legislation for the internal market) remains one of the most ambitious examples of the ongoing simplification work. Simplification exercises could be used to improve the quality, reduce the volume of existing regulatory instruments, and, at the same time remedy possible inconsistencies or even contradictions between legal instruments.

60. Moreover, a further improvement would be to adapt the substance of existing legal instruments where necessary before adopting new ones. For instance, the scope of application of various directives should be extended if necessary and if appropriate to those contracts or transactions which have many similar features with those covered by the directive but, for various reasons, were in not included in the scope of application of the directive at the moment of its adoption. This would ensure greater coherence within a well-defined sector of activities or type of transactions. Along the same lines, reasons why different solutions are given to similar problems in the context of different directives should be re-examined.

4.4. Option IV: Adopt new comprehensive legislation at EC level

61. Another option would be an overall text comprising provisions on general questions of contract law as well as specific contracts. For this option, the choice of instrument and the binding nature of the measures need to be discussed.

62. The choice of instrument depends on a number of factors, including the degree of harmonisation envisaged.

63. A Directive would, on one hand, give Member States a certain degree of flexibility to adapt the respective provisions of the implementation law to their specific national economic and legal situation. On the other hand, it may allow differences in implementation which could constitute obstacles to the functioning of the internal market.

64. A Regulation would give the Member States less flexibility for its integration into the national legal systems, but on the other hand it would ensure more transparent and uniform conditions for economic operators in the internal market.

65. A Recommendation could only be envisaged if a purely optional model is chosen.

66. Concerning the binding nature of the measures to be proposed, the following approaches, which can also be combined, are:

a)   A purely optional model which has to be chosen by the parties. An example would be a Recommendation or a Regulation which applied when the parties agree that their contract was to be governed by it.

b)   A set of rules which would apply unless their application were excluded within the contract. This kind of legislation already exists in the context of the late payments directive or in the CISG. This approach would create fall-back provisions where the contracting parties are free to agree on other solutions by way of contract, i.e. the application of a co-existing national law or contract-specific solutions. It would ensure that contractual parties keep complete contractual freedom to define the content of the contract. At the same time, it would represent a "safety net" which would only apply if no specific contractual provisions were in place.

c)   A set of rules whose application cannot be excluded by the contract.

67. The third approach would replace existing national law, while the first would coexist with national law. The second approach could co-exist with national law or replace it.

68. Each applicable set of rules could distinguish between mandatory and non-mandatory rules.

69. A combination of the above-mentioned second and third option could, for instance, be envisaged in areas of law like consumer protection where, besides a general and automatically applicable set of fall-back provisions, some mandatory provisions which cannot be waived by the contracting parties still apply.

4.5.   Any other option

70. As indicated above, the list of options is not exhaustive but only indicative. Therefore, the Commission welcomes any other suggestions for efficient and effective solutions to the problems identified.

5.   CONCLUSIONS

71. The purpose of this Communication is to initiate an open, wide-ranging and detailed debate with the participation of the institutions of the European Community as well as of the general public, including businesses, consumer associations, academics and legal practitioners. In the light of the feedback received, the Commission will, within its right of initiative, decide on further measures.

72. In particular, the Commission would like to have views on problems for the functioning of the internal market resulting from the co-existence of different national contract laws. To be the most useful, such information should be as specific

as possible. Ideally, it should include concrete examples of cases in which differences between the contract laws of the Member States have made intra-community trade more onerous or even impossible for manufacturers, service providers, traders or consumers. This may include cases in which sellers, businesses or consumers have incurred substantial additional costs as a result of differing legal requirements in Member States.

73. Moreover, the Commission is keen to receive feedback on which of the possible options explained in part D (or other possible solutions) would be the most appropriate in order to solve the problems identified in the present Communication. [...]

II. Legislative competence of the EU to develop a European contract code

1. Consolidated version of the Treaty Establishing the European Community, OJ C 321E, 29.12.2006, p. 37

Article 5
1. The Community shall act within the limits of the powers conferred upon it by this Treaty and of the objectives assigned to it therein.
2. In areas which do not fall within its exclusive competence, the Community shall take action, in accordance with the principle of subsidiarity, only if and in so far as the objectives of the proposed action cannot be sufficiently achieved by the Member States and can therefore, by reason of the scale or effects of the proposed action, be better achieved by the Community.
3. Any action by the Community shall not go beyond what is necessary to achieve the objectives of this Treaty.

Article 14
1. The Community shall adopt measures with the aim of progressively establishing the internal market over a period expiring on 31 December 1992, in accordance with the provisions of this Article and of Articles 15, 26, 47(2), 49, 80, 93 and 95 and without prejudice to the other provisions of this Treaty.
2. The internal market shall comprise an area without internal frontiers in which the free movement of goods, persons, services and capital is ensured in accordance with the provisions of this Treaty.

Article 61
In order to establish progressively an area of freedom, security and justice, the Council shall adopt:
   [...]
   (c) measures in the field of judicial cooperation in civil matters as provided for in Article 65;
   [...]

Article 65
Measures in the field of judicial cooperation in civil matters having cross-border implications, [...] in so far as necessary for the proper functioning of the internal market, shall include:
   (a) improving and simplifying:
      – the system for cross-border service of judicial and extrajudicial documents,
      – cooperation in the taking of evidence,
      – the recognition and enforcement of decisions in civil and commercial cases, including decisions in extrajudicial cases;
   (b) promoting the compatibility of the rules applicable in the Member States concerning the conflict of laws and of jurisdiction;

(c) eliminating obstacles to the good functioning of civil proceedings, if necessary by promoting the compatibility of the rules on civil procedure applicable in the Member States.

Article 94

The Council shall, acting unanimously on a proposal from the Commission and after consulting the European Parliament and the Economic and Social Committee, issue directives for the approximation of such laws, regulations or administrative provisions of the Member States as directly affect the establishment or functioning of the common market.

Article 95

(1) By way of derogation from Article 94 and save where otherwise provided in this Treaty, the following provisions shall apply for the achievement of the objectives set out in Article 14. The Council shall, acting in accordance with the procedure referred to in Article 251 and after consulting the Economic and Social Committee, adopt the measures for the approximation of the provisions laid down by law, regulation or administrative action in Member States which have as their object the establishment and functioning of the internal market.

[…]

(3) The Commission, in its proposals envisaged in paragraph 1 concerning health, safety, environmental protection and consumer protection, will take as a base a high level of protection, taking account in particular of any new development based on scientific facts. Within their respective powers, the European Parliament and the Council will also seek to achieve this objective.

[…]

Article 308

If action by the Community should prove necessary to attain, in the course of the operation of the common market, one of the objectives of the Community, and this Treaty has not provided the necessary powers, the Council shall, acting unanimously on a proposal from the Commission and after consulting the European Parliament, take the appropriate measures.

2. European Court of Justice, Case C-376/98 *Germany* v. *Parliament and Council* [2000] ECR I-8419 (*Tobacco Advertising*)

JUDGMENT OF THE COURT

5 October 2000

(Directive 98/43/EC – Advertising and sponsorship of tobacco products – Legal basis – Article 100a of the EC Treaty (now, after amendment, Article 95 EC))

In Case C-376/98,

Federal Republic of Germany, [...]

applicant,

v

European Parliament, [...]

and

Council of the European Union, [...]

defendants,

supported by

French Republic, [...] by **Republic of Finland,** [...] by **United Kingdom of Great Britain and Northern Ireland**, [...] and by **Commission of the European Communities,** [...]

interveners,

APPLICATION for the annulment of Directive 98/43/EC of the European Parliament and of the Council of 6 July 1998 on the approximation of the laws, regulations and administrative provisions of the Member States relating to the advertising and sponsorship of tobacco products (OJ 1998 L 213, p. 9),

THE COURT,

composed of: G.C. Rodríguez Iglesias, President, J.C. Moitinho de Almeida (Rapporteur), D.A.O. Edward, L. Sevón and R. Schintgen (Presidents of Chambers), P.J.G. Kapteyn, C. Gulmann, A. La Pergola, J.-P. Puissochet, P. Jann, H. Ragnemalm, M. Wathelet and F. Macken, Judges,

Advocate General: N. Fennelly,

[...]

gives the following

Judgment

1. By application lodged at the Registry of the Court on 19 October 1998, the Federal Republic of Germany brought an action under Article [230] of the EC Treaty [...] for

the annulment of Directive 98/43/EC of the European Parliament and of the Council of 6 July 1998 on the approximation of the laws, regulations and administrative provisions of the Member States relating to the advertising and sponsorship of tobacco products (OJ 1992 L 213, p. 9, hereinafter 'the Directive).

[...]

3. The Directive was adopted on the basis of Article [47(2)] of the EC Treaty [...], Article [55] of the EC Treaty [...] and Article [95] of the EC Treaty [...]

[...]

5. According to Article 3 of the Directive:
'1. Without prejudice to Directive 89/552/EEC, all forms of advertising and sponsorship shall be banned in the Community.

[...]

9. In support of its application, the Federal Republic of Germany puts forward seven pleas in law alleging, respectively, that Article [95] of the Treaty is not an appropriate legal basis for the Directive [...]

[...]

The pleas alleging that the legal basis is incorrect

Arguments of the parties

12. The applicant, relying both on the characteristics of the tobacco products advertising market and on its analysis of Article [95], considers that Article [95] of the Treaty is not the proper legal basis for the Directive.

13. As regards, first, the characteristics of the market, the applicant submits that tobacco products advertising is essentially an activity whose effects do not extend beyond the borders of individual Member States.

14. Whilst tobacco products advertising is often conceived by the manufacturer, the specific presentation of advertising media to consumers is the result of a strategy based on the particular features of each market. The decision regarding the specific form of the advertising, musical background, colours and other features of advertising products is taken at national level so that they conform with the cultural idiosyncracies of each Member State.

15. Trade in so-called 'static advertising media (such as posters, cinema advertising and advertising for the hotel and catering sector, for example, via parasols and ash-trays) between Member States is practically non-existent and has to date not been subject to any restrictions. For tax reasons, advertising involving free distribution is also limited to national markets.

16. The applicant submits that the press is the only significant form of 'non-static advertising media in economic terms. Admittedly, advertising magazines and daily papers serve as media for tobacco products, but intra-Community trade in such products is very limited. Considerably less than 5% of magazines are exported to other Member States and daily newspapers are used to a much lesser extent than magazines for carrying tobacco advertising. In Germany, in 1997, the share of total advertising revenue of daily papers accounted for by tobacco products advertising was 0.04%.

17. The limited extent of cross-frontier trade in newspapers accounts for the fact that they are not subject to restrictions by Member States which prohibit their national press from accepting advertisements for tobacco products. Belgian and Irish law expressly authorise imported press carrying such advertising and actions before French courts seeking to prohibit such imports have been unsuccessful.

[…]

23. With respect, second, to its analysis of Article [95] of the Treaty, the applicant submits, first, that Article [95] grants the Community legislature competence to harmonise national legislation to the extent to which harmonisation is necessary in order to promote the internal market. A mere reference to that article in the preamble to the measure adopted is not sufficient, otherwise judicial review of the selection of Article [95] as a legal basis would be rendered impossible. The measure must actually contribute to the improvement of the internal market.

24. That, the applicant submits, is not the case here. […]

[…]

32. Finally, the applicant submits that recourse to Article [95] is not possible where the 'centre of gravity of a measure is focused not on promoting the internal market but on protecting public health.

33. According to settled case-law, the Community may not rely on Article [95] when the measure to be adopted only incidentally harmonises market conditions within the Community […]

[…]

The Court's analysis

[…]

80. In this case, the approximation of national laws on the advertising and sponsorship of tobacco products provided for by the Directive was based on Articles [95], […] of the Treaty.

[…]

82. Under Article [3(1)(c)] of the EC Treaty […], the internal market is characterised by the abolition, as between Member States, of all obstacles to the free movement of goods, persons, services and capital. Article [14] of the EC Treaty […], which provides for the measures to be taken with a view to establishing the internal market, states in paragraph 2 that that market is to comprise an area without internal frontiers in which the free movement of goods, persons, services and capital is ensured in accordance with the provisions of the Treaty.

83. Those provisions, read together, make it clear that the measures referred to in Article [95] of the Treaty are intended to improve the conditions for the establishment and functioning of the internal market. To construe that article as meaning that it vests in the Community legislature a general power to regulate the internal market would not only be contrary to the express wording of the provisions cited above but would also be incompatible with the principle embodied in Article [5] of the EC Treaty […] that the powers of the Community are limited to those specifically conferred on it.

84. Moreover, a measure adopted on the basis of Article [95] of the Treaty must genuinely have as its object the improvement of the conditions for the establishment and functioning of the internal market. If a mere finding of disparities between national rules and of the abstract risk of obstacles to the exercise of fundamental freedoms or of distortions of competition liable to result therefrom were sufficient to justify the choice of Article [95] as a legal basis, judicial review of compliance with the proper legal basis might be rendered nugatory. The Court would then be prevented from discharging the function entrusted to it by Article [220] of the EC Treaty […] of ensuring that the law is observed in the interpretation and application of the Treaty.

85. So, in considering whether Article [95] was the proper legal basis, the Court must verify whether the measure whose validity is at issue in fact pursues the objectives stated by the Community legislature […]

[…]

Elimination of obstacles to the free movement of goods and the freedom to provide services

96. It is clear that, as a result of disparities between national laws on the advertising of tobacco products, obstacles to the free movement of goods or the freedom to provide services exist or may well arise.

97. In the case, for example, of periodicals, magazines and newspapers which contain advertising for tobacco products, it is true, as the applicant has demonstrated, that no obstacle exists at present to their importation into Member States which prohibit such advertising. However, in view of the trend in national legislation towards ever greater restrictions on advertising of tobacco products, reflecting the belief that such advertising gives rise to an appreciable increase in tobacco consumption, it is probable that obstacles to the free movement of press products will arise in the future.

98. In principle, therefore, a Directive prohibiting the advertising of tobacco products in periodicals, magazines and newspapers could be adopted on the basis of Article [95] of the Treaty with a view to ensuring the free movement of press products, on the lines of Directive 89/552, Article 13 of which prohibits television advertising of tobacco products in order to promote the free broadcasting of television programmes.

99. However, for numerous types of advertising of tobacco products, the prohibition under Article 3(1) of the Directive cannot be justified by the need to eliminate obstacles to the free movement of advertising media or the freedom to provide services in the field of advertising. That applies, in particular, to the prohibition of advertising on posters, parasols, ashtrays and other articles used in hotels, restaurants and cafés, and the prohibition of advertising spots in cinemas, prohibitions which in no way help to facilitate trade in the products concerned.

[…]

105. In those circumstances, it must be held that the Community legislature cannot rely on the need to eliminate obstacles to the free movement of advertising media and the freedom to provide services in order to adopt the Directive on the basis of Articles [95], […] of the Treaty.

[...]

117. [...] [A] directive prohibiting certain forms of advertising and sponsorship of tobacco products could have been adopted on the basis of Article [95] of the Treaty. However, given the general nature of the prohibition of advertising and sponsorship of tobacco products laid down by the Directive, partial annulment of the Directive would entail amendment by the Court of provisions of the Directive. Such amendments are a matter for the Community legislature. It is not therefore possible for the Court to annul the Directive partially.

[...]

On those grounds,

THE COURT

hereby:

1. Annuls Directive 98/43/EC of the European Parliament and of the Council of 6 July 1998 on the approximation of the laws, regulations and administrative provisions of the Member States relating to the advertising and sponsorship of tobacco products;
2. [...]

Delivered in open court in Luxembourg on 5 October 2000.

3. Jürgen Basedow, "Codification of Private Law in the European Union: the making of a Hybrid" (2001) 9 *ERPL* 35–49

[...]

3. The Powers of the Community to Codify Private Law

Desirable as it appears a European code can only be adopted if the Community is empowered to do so. [...] The bases of competence which the Treaty offers for such [...] legislation are articles 61 and 65 relating to the judicial co-operation in civil matters, articles 94 and 95 dealing with the approximation of laws for the purposes of the common or internal market, and article 308.

The latter competence can be excluded right away. As it is clearly stated in article 308, that provision confers only a subsidiary, although comprehensive competence upon the Community. It has been used a couple of times for legislation creating additional models of private law institutions such as the Community trade mark i.e. legislation which did not purport to approximate national laws but created something new which private business can choose as an alternative to internal institutions. In the field of general private law this idea of the "[twenty-eighth] model" is not viable except perhaps for a transition period. Thirty years of experience with the Hague Sales Conventions and the Vienna Sales

Convention demonstrate that legal practitioners tend to avoid such additional instruments by appropriate contract clauses. They prefer the well-known framework of domestic law. While the Vienna Sales Convention is applicable in the absence of a contractual *abrogation* the "[twenty-eighth] model" would require a *prorogation*, i.e. a positive agreement of the parties on the application of that additional set of rules. How can legal practitioners be expected to make such an explicit choice if their preference for legal continuity even makes them avoid the Vienna Sales Convention? A civil code adopted as the "[twenty-eighth] model" would be doomed to insignificance. All the other concepts of a civil code would, however, require changes of national legislation and would therefore be covered by bases of competence other than article 308.

Another possible basis for European codification of civil law might be the authority of the Community under articles 61 and 65 to adopt measures in the field of judicial co-operation in civil matters. These powers were transferred from the third pillar of the European Union to its first pillar by the Treaty of Amsterdam. Their bearing upon substantive private law is still uncertain. [...] [I]t appears very doubtful whether the new provisions allow for a comprehensive Community legislation in this field. "Measures in the field of judicial co-operation in civil matters" is a generic term which relates to legal rules concerning fact situations that somehow involve at least two different Member States. That description fits provisions in the areas of international civil litigation and of the conflict of laws. It even includes the adoption of substantive rules for international fact situations as are laid down in various uniform law conventions, e.g. the Vienna Sales Convention or the international transport conventions. But the substantive private law contained in the national codes is conceived for domestic fact situations of the respective country. There are "cross border implications" as required by article 65 only by virtue of the rules on private international law. Although the list of possible measures in article 65 only has an exemplary significance it equally suggests that those measures must be related to transboundary fact situations. An additional limitation imposed upon the Community policy in this field can be inferred from the scope of Title IV: measures in this field must relate to the free movement of persons, i.e. the freedom of establishment or the free movement of workers. It is difficult to see how uniform rules on the sale of goods, on lease or loan contracts can fulfil that condition.

A European civil code would amount to a comprehensive approximation of national laws. The appropriate basis therefore would either be article 94 or article 95. [...] Both provisions presuppose that the Community measures are closely related to the establishment and functioning of the internal or common market. While this condition usually is identified with the absence of state restrictions of the basic freedoms time has come to acknowledge that traders do not engage in transboundary commerce merely because they are allowed to do so. In addition to the barriers imposed by national laws there are also psychological barriers resulting from the various uncertainties of international trade relations: differences in languages and commercial practices, uncertainties concerning private international law and the foreign substantive law, and the risk of unenforceability of judgements in foreign countries. While some of these barriers cannot be overcome by Community measures, others can. Without a closer discussion the traditional opinion refuses to accept the aforementioned legal risks and the psychological barriers caused by them as a sufficient basis for Community legislation under article 95.

It is submitted that this restrictive view can no longer be maintained after the Treaty of Amsterdam has taken effect. It has inserted into the EC Treaty the new article 65 which allows, inter alia, for the harmonization of private international law. Since article 65 requires that Community measures taken under that provision are "necessary for the proper functioning of the internal market", it presupposes that differences existing between the national legislations in the field of conflict of laws may effectively curtail the proper functioning of the internal market; if not the explicit reference to measures "promoting the compatibility of the rules applicable in the member states concerning the conflict of laws" would be meaningless. Bearing in mind that conflict rules merely refer a case to a competent national legal system without providing for a substantive solution, we must conclude that differences between the substantive private laws of the Member States are even more liable to impede the proper functioning of the internal market. If that is true in the context of article 65, it cannot be denied when it comes to the application of article 95. Thus, while article 65 has a very limited bearing upon the harmonisation or unification of substantive private law for other reasons it suggests a new reading of article 95 which allows for the adoption of a comprehensive private law legislation on that basis.

However, the impact of private law upon the functioning of the internal market cannot be ascertained in the same way for all parts of private law. Such an assessment can be made with regard to the law of contracts and to ancillary aspects relating non-contractual obligations, in particular to the law of torts and restitution. But it is doubtful whether the internal market actually depends upon a uniform law relating to chattel and real property. A collateral in movables is needed as a security in intra-community export operations, and a European mortgage might help to further integrate the capital markets. But these targets can perhaps be achieved by measures presenting a "[twenty-eighth] model" under article 308, i.e. without a comprehensive harmonisation of the laws of chattel and real property. As far as the laws of domestic relations and succession are concerned, it will also be difficult to establish the required market relation. In these areas the needs of European integration can be fulfilled by two ways: measures to be adopted under articles 61 and 65 can provide for the recognition of court decisions in other Member States, and Community legislation adopted under article 308 could provide for a "[twenty-eighth] model" concerning a European will and a European contract on matrimonial property regimes.

4. Outline of a European Civil Code

The preceding discussion shows that the Treaty in its present form does not allow for a comprehensive codification of private law. What can be conceived is a European law of obligations while the other parts of private law would essentially continue to be regulated by national laws.

The form of such a European act would by necessity be a regulation, the adoption of a directive must be excluded. […] It […] must be directly applicable and is incompatible with the peculiar characteristics of the directive which allows each Member State to implement its content in the form which best can be reconciled with the systematic structures of its own legal order. A European code is not meant to fit into a national system but to shape a European system. This requirement excludes article 94 as the proper basis of legislation, for this provision does not enable the Community to make regulations. This is different in case of article 95 although the diplomatic conference of 1986 adopted a declaration under which the Commission is to couch its proposals based upon article 95 in the form of a directive by preference. But the choice of the appropriate legal form of an act has to be made in the light of the purposes of article 95 in the first place. Where requirements of the internal market cannot be coped with by the adoption of directives the enactment of a regulation may be necessary and will be lawful under article 95. It would appear, moreover, that the Member States at present are less determined then they were to insist upon that declaration of 1986. [...]

The resulting situation will be characterised by the co-existence of a European Code of obligations and national sets of rules mostly contained in the codes of the Member States dealing with the law of movables, real property, family law and succession. As a consequence, the national parts of private law would have to be adjusted to the terminology and the system imposed by the European Code of Obligations. Member States might also wish to maintain the unity of their codes by including a declaratory copy of the European provisions on obligations into the national code. While such manoeuvres have been criticised by the Court of Justice for dissimulating the European nature of the respective provisions they appear unobjectionable if their European nature and their correspondence to particular articles of the European code is clearly indicated in the single rules. In that case, a national copy of the European Code would not hamper access to the European court system.

[...]

4. PHILIPPE MALINVAUD, "Réponse – hors délai – à la Commission européenne: à propos d'un code européen des contrats, *Recueil Dalloz* 2002, n° 33, p. 2542 (translation of the French original)

[...]

B – Legal basis in the text

Unlike national legislators, the Community legislator only enjoys conferred powers. The legislator can therefore only act within the framework of the provisions set out in the European treaties, in this instance in the Treaty establishing the European Community (EC Treaty). There is no legal basis to justify a massive undertaking to unify European civil law and furthermore the principles of subsidiarity and proportionality even seem to prohibit such an undertaking.

1 – Lack of legal basis in the text

Article 95 [...] of the EC Treaty is generally invoked by those in favour of a European contract code, or even a European civil code. This text allows the Council to decide on "measures for the approximation of the provisions laid down by law, regulation or administrative action in Member States which have as their object the establishment and functioning of the internal market" by qualified majority. It is the pivotal text for the creation of an internal market, upon which various directives on the protection of consumers are based, and possibly, in the future, upon which the future European Consumer Code will be based (Article 153 of the Treaty, which refers to Article 95, could therefore provide the necessary legal basis for the development of a European Consumer Code). However, in reality, the internal market already exists and copes outstandingly well with the diversity of laws. In addition, the matter of a European contract law, and *a fortiori* the matter of a European civil law, due to its size, goes well beyond the scope of Article 95. This is why Article 95 cannot be used as the basis for Union action in this domain. What is more, recent case-law from the Court of Justice of the European Communities has condemned every use of this text which was too extensive.

Article 308 of the EC Treaty […] allows the Council, when the treaty does not provide for any specific competence, acting unanimously and after consulting the Parliament, to take the appropriate measures "if action by the Community should prove necessary to attain, in the course of the operation of the common market, one of the objectives of the Community". This text significantly extends the Community's powers, but use of it must remain exceptional so as to avoid upsetting the balance upon which the separation of powers between the European Union and the Member States is founded. Moreover, the Commission has just reiterated, in its communication on the future of Europe, that Article 308 does not permit the creation of new powers and that "the normal and democratic way of adapting the Union's powers is to amend the Treaty".

In the same vein, one might invoke the theory of implicit powers, recognised by the ECJ since 1956 (29 November 1956, Fédéchar). By virtue of this theory, the Union must be recognised as having, as well as its express powers, the powers necessary to realise these [express powers]. However, it is hard to see how a European contract code could be founded on such a fragile basis, easily bypassed by the principles of subsidiarity and proportionality which play a regulatory role in the exercise of powers.

2 – Absolute character of the principles of subsidiarity and proportionality

The principle of subsidiarity was introduced by the Treaty of Maastricht. It is confirmed in several texts including Article 5(2) of the EC Treaty by virtue of which "the Community shall act within the limits of the powers conferred upon it by this Treaty and of the objectives assigned to it therein". Once the decision to exercise a power has been taken, it is the principle of proportionality that determines the scope of the legislation: in accordance with Article 5(3), "any action by the Community shall not go beyond what is necessary to achieve the objectives of this Treaty". These principles are increasingly important because they act as a counterbalance to the almost inevitable extension of the powers of Europe. They need to be reinforced by specific measures of control.

Given the current legal situation, Europe does not have the power to impose a European contract code on the Member States. Only a European Consumer Code could, at a push, be founded on Article 95 EC Treaty without violating the principles of proportionality and subsidiarity. It remains to be seen if, with a view to the future of the Union, the treaties should be modified in order to allow for the development of a common European private law.

[…]

5. STEPHEN WEATHERILL, "Reflections on the EC's Competence to Develop a 'European Contract Law'" (2005) 3 *ERPL* 405–18

[...]

Reflections on the Issue of Competence

3.1 Principle and Practice in EC Constitutional Law

Article 5(1) EC asserts the constitutionally fundamental principle that the EC can do no more than its Treaty permits. It has only the competence conferred on it by its Member States. It enjoys no explicit competence to legislate in the field of contract law.

But this, of course is not the end of the story. It is the EC's harmonization programme that supplies the key to understanding the basis for intervention into contract law. In so far as national laws vary, the argument has typically proceeded that the construction of a unified trading space within the EU was hindered. Therefore harmonisation of laws at EC level was required – 'common rules for a common market'. [...]

So Article 94 or Article 95 [...] provided a basis for harmonizing laws in pursuit of market integration which extended into the field of contract law. The list includes Directive 90/314 on package travel, Directive 93/13 on unfair terms in consumer contracts, Directive 85/577 to protect the consumer in respect of contracts negotiated away from business premises, Directive 87/102 concerning consumer credit, as amended by Directive 90/88 and Directive 98/7, Directive 94/47 on timeshare basis, Directive 97/7 on the protection of consumers in respect of distance contracts, Directive 99/44 on certain aspects of the sale of consumer goods and associated guarantees, and Directive 2002/65 concerning the distance marketing of consumer financial services. This is EC contract law, and it is predominantly EC consumer contract law, though there are modest interventions to be found outside the consumer sphere, such as Directive 2000/35 on late payments in commercial transactions and Directive 86/653 on commercial agents.

In some circumstances the perception that diversity among national contract laws hindered the establishment of a single market may have been genuinely held and justified. In some cases, however, the political reality was that the Member States were committed to the development of an EC consumer policy and, in the absence of any more appropriate legal basis in the Treaty, chose to 'borrow' the competence to harmonise laws to put it in place. So Directive 85/577 states in its Preamble that the practice of doorstep selling is the subject of different rules in different Member States, and that 'any disparity between such legislation may directly affect the functioning of the common market'. This is hard to believe. The Directive was largely motivated by the prevailing political consensus in favour of EC consumer protection [...]. In truth the Member States, acting unanimously in Council, had 'borrowed' the competence to harmonise in the Treaty and the question of whether such consumer contract law making dressed up in the clothes of harmonisation was truly constitutionally valid was not addressed in any practically significant manner. [...]

3.2 'Tobacco Advertising'

Legislative practice is troublingly inconsistent with the assertion found in Article 5(1) that the EC possesses only the competences attributed to it by its Treaty. This is the point at which the European Court's deservedly famous *Tobacco Advertising* ruling injects doubt about the constitutional validity of some of the legislative *acquis*. The Court annulled Directive 98/43 on the advertising of tobacco products on the application of Germany [...] The measure had been adopted as part of the harmonisation programme. The Court was unimpressed. It insisted that harmonisation measures 'are intended to improve the conditions for the establishment and functioning of the internal market'. The Community legislature enjoys no general power to regulate the internal market. Accordingly, 'curing' legal diversity *per se* will evidently not do as an adequate basis for legislative intervention founded on Article 95 EC. The EC measure must work harder in the service of market integration. The Directive in question did not cross the required threshold. It prohibited the advertising of tobacco products in circumstances remote from the imperatives of market-making – for example, on ashtrays and parasols used on streets cafés. The implication of the Court's judgment is that this was, in effect, public health policy, for which the Community possesses a competence, but the relevant provision, Article 152, expressly forbids harmonisation. In declaring that the Community legislature does not enjoy 'a general power to regulate the internal market' the Court accordingly gave practical force to the constitutionally fundamental principle of attributed competence found in Article 5(1) EC in the particular context of delivering an interpretation of the limits on the use of Article 95.

Tobacco Advertising injects 'competence anxiety' into a number of sectors remote from the judgment's particular concern and it has already become a rich source of speculation about the constitutional validity of existing rules and proposed initiatives. [...] Some Directives are today revealed as vulnerable to challenge because they make little visible contribution to market-making. Directive 85/577 on Doorstep Selling would be high on any list of candidates!

3.3 Competence and the Commission's Three Documents on Contract Law

[...] [T]he 'competence sensitivity' injected by *Tobacco Advertising* now pervades the Commission's thinking about the future of European Contract law. In the documents issued in 2001, 2003 and 2004 the debate is not simply about what *should* be done by the EC in the field of contract law. It is also about what – constitutionally – *can* be done. [...]

[...] [I]t is plain that the shadow of the *Tobacco Advertising* ruling has been cast over the Commission's thinking. The Communication calls explicitly for information on whether diversity between national contract laws 'directly or indirectly obstructs the functioning of the internal market, and if so to what extent', with a view to considering appropriate action by the EC's institutions. The Commission is actively seeking to uncover areas in which the internal market is malfunctioning because of deficiencies in the existing bloc of harmonised contract law. The Commission wants hard – Court-proof – data to underpin any claim to competence under the Treaty to shape an EC contract law. [...] The mood is different from the relatively carefree attitude to competence taken in the consumer contract law Directives adopted in the 1980s. In part this is because prior to the entry into force of the Single European Act in 1987 the voting rule in Council was unanimity, which meant that the presence of political consensus was the practical be all and end all of the decision whether to legislate. Today the rise of qualified majority voting in Council throws up the possibility of outvoted minorities converting political defeat in Council into a constitutional challenge before the Court – precisely as occurred in *Tobacco Advertising* itself. [...]

5 Conclusion

[...] Without a reliable pattern of legal rights 'on paper' the consumer will simply not treat the internal market as trustworthy or viable. He or she will retreat to the relative security of local purchasing. [...] [I]t would be argued that breeding confidence among consumers is essential to the establishment and functioning of the internal market. This can be done by the creation of harmonised legal protection, albeit that inquiry into the genuine contribution of such legal rules to promoting confidence must be conducted by the legislature. The 'consumer confidence' argument should not simply be the new motor of 'competence creep' applied to the harmonisation programme.

In conclusion, the Commission's development of European contract law raises some intriguing and, as yet, cautiously addressed questions about constitutional propriety. The issue will continue to bubble close to the surface. What is needed to make a market? Given ambiguities rooted in Articles 14 and 95 EC which preclude an easy answer to this question, the Commission's preference not to adopt an over-confident view of what competence the EC Treaty grants in these realms is understandable.

III. Do common markets need a uniform contract law? – The example of the US

MELVIN EISENBERG, "Why is American Contract Law so Uniform? – National Law in the United States", in Hans-Leo Weyers (ed.), *Europäisches Vertragsrecht,* **1997, pp. 23–43**

See above, **Case 4**, at **III.4**.

IV. Do common markets need a uniform contract law? – Europe

1. Communication from the Commission to the Council and the European Parliament: A more coherent European contract law – an action plan, Brussels, 12.2.2003, COM(2003) 68 final

COMMISSION OF THE EUROPEAN COMMUNITIES

Brussels, 12.2.2003
COM(2003) 68 final

COMMUNICATION FROM THE COMMISSION TO THE EUROPEAN
PARLIAMENT AND THE COUNCIL

A MORE COHERENT EUROPEAN CONTRACT LAW

AN ACTION PLAN[28]

Executive summary

The Commission Communication on European contract law of July 2001 launched a process of consultation and discussion about the way in which problems resulting from divergences between national contract laws in the EU should be dealt with at the European level. The present Action Plan maintains the consultative character of this process and presents the Commission's conclusions. It confirms the outcome of that process, i.e. that there is no need to abandon the current sector-specific approach. It also summarises the problems identified during the consultation process, which concern the need for uniform application of EC contract law as well as the smooth functioning of the internal market. This Action Plan suggests a mix of non-regulatory and regulatory measures in order to solve those problems. In addition to appropriate sector-specific interventions, this includes measures:

– to increase the coherence of the EC *acquis* in the area of contract law,
– to promote the elaboration of EU-wide general contract terms, and
– to examine further whether problems in the European contract law area may require non-sector-specific solutions such as an optional instrument.

In addition to continuing to put forward sector-specific proposals where these are required, the Commission will seek to increase, where necessary and possible, coherence between instruments, which are part of the EC contract law *acquis*, both in their drafting

---

[28] http://eurlex.europa.eu/LexUriServ/LexUriServ.do?uri=COM:2003:0068:FIN:EN:PDF.

and in their implementation and application. Proposals will, where appropriate, take into account a common frame of reference, which the Commission intends to elaborate via research and with the help of all interested parties. This common frame of reference should provide for best solutions in terms of common terminology and rules, i.e. the definition of fundamental concepts and abstract terms like "contract" or "damage" and of the rules that apply for example in the case of non-performance of contracts. A review of the current European contract law *acquis* could remedy identified inconsistencies, increase the quality of drafting, simplify and clarify existing provisions, adapt existing legislation to economic and commercial developments which were not foreseen at the time of adoption and fill gaps in EC legislation which have led to problems in its application. The second objective of the common frame of reference is to form the basis for further reflection on an optional instrument in the area of European contract law.

In order to promote the elaboration by interested parties of EU-wide general contract terms, the Commission intends to facilitate the exchange of information on existing and planned initiatives both at a European level and within the Member States. Furthermore, the Commission intends to publish guidelines, which will clarify to interested parties the limits which apply.

Finally, the Commission expects comments as to whether some problems may require non-sector-specific solutions, such as an optional instrument in the area of European contract law. The Commission intends to launch a reflection on the opportuneness, the possible legal form, the contents and the legal basis for possible solutions.

[…]

1.   INTRODUCTION

1.   In July 2001, the Commission published its Communication on European Contract Law.[29] The Communication was the first consultation document issued by the European Commission that envisaged a more fundamental discussion about the way in which problems resulting from divergences between contract laws in the EU should be dealt with at European level. Its follow-up is the subject of this Action Plan.

2.   The Communication launched a process of consultation and discussion. The Commission is aware of its long-term nature and intends to maintain its consultative character. Only through continuous involvement of all Community institutions and all stakeholders can it be ensured that the final outcome of this process will meet the practical needs of all economic operators involved and finally be accepted by all concerned. For this reason, the Commission has decided to submit the present Action Plan as a basis for further consultation.

3.   In particular, this Action Plan seeks to obtain feedback on a suggested mix of non-regulatory and regulatory measures, i.e. to increase coherence of the EC *acquis* in the area of contract law, to promote the elaboration of EU-wide standard contract terms and to examine whether non-sector specific measures such as an optional instrument may be required to solve problems in the area of European contract law. As such, it constitutes a further step in the ongoing process of discussion on the developments in European contract law.

---

[29]   Footnotes omitted.

2. DESCRIPTION OF THE PRESENT PROCESS

4. The Communication on European contract law launched a consultation procedure that yielded numerous contributions from governments and stakeholders, including businesses, legal practitioners, academics and consumer organisations. The flow of incoming mail has continued since the process was started. Up to now, the Commission has received 181 responses to the Communication.

[...]

7. None of the contributions indicated that the sectoral approach as such leads to problems or that it should be abandoned. All contributors nevertheless reacted to the various options. Only a small minority favoured Option I which suggested leaving the solution of identified problems to the market. There was considerable support for Option II, i.e. to develop – via joint research – common principles of European contract law. An overwhelming majority supported Option III, which proposed the improvement of existing EC law in the area of contract law. A majority was, at least at this stage, against Option IV, which aimed at a new instrument on European contract law. However, an important number of contributors suggested that further thought might be given to this in the light of future developments in pursuance of Options II and III.

[...]

9. The European Parliament adopted the "Resolution on the approximation of the civil and commercial law of the Member States" on 15 November 2001. The Resolution, addressed to the Commission, requests a detailed action plan with short-term, medium-term and long-term measures within a fixed timetable.

[...]

3. IDENTIFIED PROBLEM AREAS

14. Many of the contributions to the consultation launched by the Commission Communication on European contract law point to concrete and practical problems. Others observe, in a more general manner, that divergences between national contract laws do indeed create problems both for the uniform application of EC law and for the smooth functioning of the internal market. Inconsistency within EC legislation itself was also criticised by many contributors, some of them giving concrete examples. However, none of the contributions indicated that the sectoral approach as such leads to problems or that it should be abandoned.

[...]

3.1. Uniform application of Community law

16. Different types of problems have been mentioned. As a category of inconsistencies that is intrinsic to EC legislation in the field of contracts, it was mentioned that similar situations are treated differently without relevant justification for such different treatment. The problem of divergent requirements and consequences in some of the directives applying to the same commercial situation was emphasised.

[...]

20. In other cases abstract terms are defined in some Directives, while they are not defined in others. For example the term "damage" is defined in the Product Liability Directive for the purposes of this Directive, while it is not defined in either the Commercial Agents Directive or the Package Travel Directive. The term "durable medium" is defined in the Directive on Distance Selling of Financial Services, but not in the general Distance Selling Directive.

21. One problem, which was raised in the consultation, is whether in such a case the given definition in one directive can also be used for the interpretation of other directives, i.e. whether the relevant abstract term can be interpreted in the light of the whole *acquis communautaire* or at least of the part, which is more broadly concerned. This methodological approach was also used by the Advocate General in Simone Leitner/TUI Deutschland GmbH & Co KG. However in this specific case, the ECJ interpreted the general term "damage" only in the light of the Package Travel Directive and did not follow its Advocate General. It is true that this decision cannot necessarily be generalised. However, if the interpretation of an abstract term in the light of the specific Directive is the guiding principle, then such an interpretation can lead to fragmentation of national legislation. For example, Member States which have referred to an existing national legal concept with a general definition in their implementation laws might have to adapt this existing definition in order to implement the specific meaning of this abstract term in the light of the relevant Directive.

22. A general observation concerning fragmentation of national contract laws, which was made by several contributions, was that the national legislator is faced with a dilemma. Either the implementation of directives with a limited scope entails a much larger adaptation of the national legal system than what is actually foreseen by the Community measure in question, or the implementation is restricted to the pure transposition of the directive in question. In some cases this might create inconsistencies in the national legal system.

23. Another category of problems concerned inconsistencies in the application of national implementations as a consequence of the introduction, by directives, of concepts, which are alien to the existing national legislation. It was mentioned that when implementing a directive, some national legislators maintain the existing national legislation in parallel, thereby creating a situation which leads to legal uncertainty, for example the coexistence of two laws on Unfair Contract Terms in one Member State. [...]

[...]

3.2. Implications for the internal market

25. The barriers described in the present chapter cover obstacles and disincentives to cross-border transactions deriving directly or indirectly from divergent national contract laws or from the legal complexity of these divergences, which are liable to prohibit, impede or otherwise render less advantageous such transactions.

[...]

27. It has already been pointed out that a large number of problems for cross-border contracts could be avoided, at least for one party to the contract, by choosing the appropriate applicable law. [...]

28. However, it has also been underlined in a number of contributions, especially by export-oriented industries, that the choice of applicable law is not always commercially realistic or desirable.

29. Firstly, it does not help the contracting party, which does not have sufficient economic bargaining power to impose its choice of law in the negotiations. It has also been pointed out that taking advice on the unknown applicable law will involve considerable legal costs and commercial risks for this party to the contract without necessarily giving the most economically favourable solution.

30. This is particularly important for SMEs since the legal assistance costs are proportionately higher for them. As a result, SMEs will either be dissuaded from cross-border activities altogether or will be put at a clear competitive disadvantage compared to domestic operators.

31. Secondly, it has been highlighted in the consultation that this situation is even more dissuasive for consumers. Their national laws are in most cases not the laws applicable to the contract. This may be because the law of the trader is chosen as the applicable law under standard terms or because it is objectively determined as the applicable law under Article 4 of the Rome [I Regulation]. [...]

[...]

34. [...] Many contributions criticised the divergence of rules on fundamental issues of contract law which create problems and entail higher transaction costs. [...]

35. Other examples concern divergent requirements for the formation of contracts which create obstacles. This concerns special requirements of form, such as the requirement for certain contracts to be concluded before a notary or the necessity of authentication of documents which is mandatory for certain contracts and necessitates higher costs for businesses and consumers. This concerns also the requirement for certain contracts to be in writing or in a certain language.

36. Another category of problems mentioned by many contributions concerned the divergence of rules on the inclusion and application of standard contract terms. In some jurisdictions, it is sufficient merely to make reference to standard terms, whereas in others they must be attached to the contract or signed separately. In some Member States such as Italy (Article 1341 *codice civile*), certain clauses must be individually initialled to become valid. Such rules may apply independently of the choice of law made by the contracting parties.

37. Between Member States, there are considerable differences as to which contract terms are considered inadmissible (and therefore invalid) by the courts. In some Member States such as Germany or the nordic countries, courts exert strict control over the fairness of contractual terms even in business-to-business contracts. Other Member States provide for a limited control by way of interpretation or only allow specific contract clauses to be struck down in commercial contracts.

38. This creates uncertainty for businesses that use standard terms; it also hampers the use of ready made standard contracts that were actually created to facilitate cross-border transactions and intended for use in any legal system. It is indeed necessary to use different standard contracts in different Member States, which in

turn makes it impossible to use the same business model for the whole European market.

39. This leads to another category of frequently mentioned problems concerning the divergence of national rules as regards clauses excluding or limiting contractual liability in specific contracts or standard contract terms and their recognition by the law courts in another Member State. Examples mention the full responsibility of suppliers for hidden defects (*vices cachés*) under French case law, and the mandatory impossibility, under Czech law, of restricting contractual liability for future damages. In this context, contributions mention also different national mandatory rules on limitation periods. Export-oriented industries indicated that the resulting unrestricted liability for suppliers could lead to very high commercial risks, which discourage or impede the conclusion of cross-border transactions.

40. In the context of contractual liability, contributions highlighted also that being unaware of the specific requirements of the relevant applicable contract law often leads to unanticipated costs. Examples include the obligation for merchants to serve a prompt notice of default in respect of defective goods under the German Commercial Code (§ 377) in order to preserve their right of redress and the *bref délai* under Art. 1648 of the French Civil Code.

41. Numerous contributions concerned problems as regards to the divergent national rules on contract law on the one hand and on the rules on transfer of property and securities concerning movable goods on the other hand. The national rules on the transition of property differ and therefore the moment of transition of property is different. Furthermore, this can also depend on the nature of the contract which, again, is different in national legal systems. It must be borne in mind that the possibility of a choice of law only concerns contractual rules, and not rules applicable to rights in rem, e.g. transition of property, where the applicable law is the *lex rei sitae*. Many businesses are not aware of this limitation. It has been pointed out that EC law addresses part of the problem by providing for the validity of retention of title clauses, but it does not go beyond this.

42. Reservation of title is regulated differently from jurisdiction to jurisdiction and the effectiveness of relevant contract clauses varies accordingly. This applies even more to possible extensions where the reservation of title also covers, for example, a claim for the purchase price which arises upon a resale of the sold goods by the buyer or over products made from the sold goods. These extensions can also cover future claims or not only the purchase price of the specific goods delivered under a particular contract of sale, but all the buyer's outstanding indebtedness.

43. The divergence of rules often entails that, in the case of the sale of goods with reservation of title, the "security" foreseen in the contract disappears at the moment when the good in question is brought across the border. It is generally observed that divergence of rules on securities creates a great risk for operators on the market. As a consequence for the supply side, the seller is forced to look to other forms of securities which are, such as bank guarantees, substantially more expensive and realistically speaking, unobtainable from the outset for SMEs. The result for the demand side is that trade credit provided by the seller to the buyer will be higher priced since the seller's risk is to a considerable degree increased or decreased depending upon the availability of proprietary security and its legal effectiveness. This risk can only be partially alleviated by costly legal opinions.

44. Similar problems have been mentioned in the financial services sector for granting trans-border credit, which is only possible if the corresponding securities are guaranteed. It has been pointed out that the analysis of the validity of the cross-border transfer of securities necessitates costly in-depth legal expertise, which discourages from or impedes such cross-border transactions. In addition, it was mentioned that such analysis is rather time-consuming which, in cases of cross-border transactions to provide finance for re-capitalisation in order to prevent insolvency, might be a critical factor which prevents the whole operation.

45. Above all, some security instruments for movable goods are simply not known in other Member States and vanish if the secured goods are transferred across borders. An example given concerns the transfer of movable goods under the contractual agreement of a so-called "*Sicherungsübereignung*" from Germany to Austria. These differences also adversely affect the possibility of entering into cross-border leasing contracts.

46. Contributions also indicated differences in national contract laws concerning credit assignments. [...]

47. In the area of financial services, contributions stated that firms are unable to offer, or are deterred from offering, financial services across borders because products are designed in accordance with local legal requirements, or because the imposition of differing requirements under other jurisdictions would give rise to excessive costs or unacceptable legal uncertainty. [...]

48. The same problems occur particularly with insurance contracts. [...] The wording of a single policy that could be marketed on the same terms in different European markets has proved impossible in practice.

[...]

50. In the field of consumer protection, many businesses complain about the great diversity in national regimes, which creates obstacles for cross-border business to consumer transactions. This is mainly imputed to the fact that EC directives in that field are based on the principle of minimum harmonisation, so as to allow Member States to maintain rules that are more favourable to consumers than those foreseen in Community law. [...]

51. [...] The Commission sets out, in the following section, suggestions for a mix of non regulatory and regulatory approaches in order to tackle some of these problems. [...]

4. SUGGESTED APPROACH: A MIX OF NON-REGULATORY AND REGULATORY MEASURES

[...]

4.1. To improve the quality of the EC *acquis* in the area of contract law

55. As indicated above, one of the conclusions drawn from the consultation thus far is that it is possible for the EU to continue a sector-specific approach. However, the consultations have also emphasised the need to increase coherence of the existing *acquis* in the contract law area and avoid unnecessary inconsistencies in new *acquis*. This is why the Commission intends to take a number of measures aimed at increasing coherence of the EC *acquis* in the contract law area, notably by improving the quality of the legislation.

[...]

4.1.1. A common frame of reference

59. A common frame of reference, establishing common principles and terminology in the area of European contract law is seen by the Commission as an important step towards the improvement of the contract law *acquis*. This common frame of reference will be a publicly accessible document which should help the Community institutions in ensuring greater coherence of existing and future *acquis* in the area of European contract law. [...]

60. If the common frame of reference is widely accepted as the model in European contract law which best corresponds to the needs of the economic operators, it can be expected also to be taken as a point of reference by national legislatures inside the EU and possibly in appropriate third countries whenever they seek to lay down new contract law rules or amend existing ones. Thus the frame of reference might diminish divergences between contract laws in the EU.

[...]

Although the details of the common frame of reference will be decided on the basis of the research and input from economic operators, it can be expected to contain the following elements:

- It should deal essentially with contract law, above all the relevant cross-border types of contract such as contracts of sale and service contracts.
- General rules on the conclusion, validity and interpretation of contracts as well as performance, non-performance and remedies should be covered as well as rules on credit securities on movable goods and the law of unjust enrichment.

Several basic sources should principally be considered:

Advantage should be taken of existing national legal orders in order to find possible common denominators, to develop common principles and, where appropriate, to identify best solutions.

- It is particularly important to take into account the case law of national courts, especially the highest courts, and established contractual practice.
- The existing EC *acquis* and relevant binding international instruments, above all the UN Convention on the International Sale of Goods (CISG), should be analysed.

[...]

4.2. To promote the elaboration of EU - wide standard contract terms

81. The principle of contractual freedom, which is the centrepiece of contract law in all Member States, enables contracting parties to conclude the contract which most suits their particular needs. This freedom is restricted by certain compulsory contract law provisions or requirements resulting from other laws. However, compulsory provisions are limited and parties to a contract do enjoy a significant degree of freedom in negotiating the contract terms and conditions they want. [...]

82.   Nevertheless, in a large majority of cases, and in particular for fairly straightforward and often repeated transactions, parties often are interested in using standard contract terms. The use of standard contract terms spares the parties the costs of negotiating a contract.

83.   Such standard terms are often formulated by one of the contracting parties, in particular, where a single contracting party possesses sufficient bargaining power to impose its contract terms, either as a seller or a service provider or as a purchaser of goods or services. [...]

84.   Although standard contract terms and conditions are used very broadly, most of them have been developed by parties from a single Member State. Such contract terms may therefore be less adapted to the particular needs of cross-border transactions. The Commission is aware, however, of initiatives in which standard contract terms have been developed specifically for international transactions. These contract terms are increasingly being used also for contracts concluded inside single Member States.

85.   This demonstrates the usefulness of standard terms developed for use in various Member States and, in particular, in cross-border transactions. The Commission believes that if such general terms and conditions were developed more widely, they could solve some of the alleged problems and disincentives reported. This is why the Commission intends to promote the establishment of such terms and conditions in the following ways:

a)   Facilitating the exchange of information on initiatives.

86.   As a first step in promoting the development of EU-wide standard terms and conditions, it is important to establish a list of existing initiatives both at a European level and within the Member States. Once such a list is made available, parties interested in developing standard terms and conditions could obtain information on similar initiatives in other sectors or in the same sectors in other Member States. Thus they could learn from the mistakes of others and benefit from their successes ("best practices"), while they could also obtain names and addresses of their counterparts in other Member States who could be interested in a joint effort to create EU wide standard terms and conditions.

[...]

4.3.   Further reflection on the opportuneness of non-sector specific measures such as an optional instrument in the area of European contract law

89.   During the consultation, there were calls to continue reflections on the opportuneness of non-sector-specific measures in the area of European contract law.

90.   Some arguments have been made in favour of an optional instrument, which would provide parties to a contract with a modern body of rules particularly adapted to cross-border contracts in the internal market. Consequently, parties would not need to cover every detail in contracts specifically drafted or negotiated for this purpose, but could simply refer to this instrument as the applicable law. It would provide both parties, the economically stronger and weaker, with an acceptable and adequate solution without insisting on the necessity to apply one party's national law, thereby also facilitating negotiations.

91. Over time, economic operators would become familiar with these rules in the same way they may be familiar with their national contract laws existing at this moment. This would be important for all parties to a contract, including in particular SMEs and consumers, and in facilitating their active participation in the internal market. Thus, such an instrument would facilitate considerably the cross-border exchange of goods and services.

92. The Commission will examine whether non-sector-specific-measures such as an optional instrument may be required to solve problems in the area of European contract law. It intends to launch a reflection on the opportuneness, the possible form, the contents and the legal basis for possible action of such measures. As to its form one could think of EU wide contract law rules in the form of a regulation or a recommendation, which would exist in parallel with, rather than instead of national contract laws. This new instrument would exist in all Community languages. It could either apply to all contracts, which concern cross-border transactions or only to those which parties decide to subject to it through a choice of law clause. The latter would give parties the greatest degree of contractual freedom. They would only choose the new instrument if it suited their economic or legal needs better than the national law which would have been determined by private international law rules as the law applicable to the contract.

[...]

95. It is clear that in reflecting on a non-sector-specific instrument, the Commission will take into account the common frame of reference. The content of the common frame of reference should then normally serve as a basis for the development of the new optional instrument. [...]

96. The Commission would welcome comments on the scope of an optional instrument in relation to the CISG. The optional instrument could be comprehensive, i.e. covering also cross-border contracts of sale between businesses, and thereby include the area covered by the CISG. It could also exclude this area and leave it to the application of the CISG.

97. As with all measures mentioned in this Action Plan it is the purpose of this Action Plan to invite comments from EC institutions and stakeholders on the suggestions.

5. CONCLUSION

98. The purpose of this Action Plan is to receive feedback on the suggested mix of non-regulatory and regulatory measures as well as input for the further reflection on an optional instrument in the area of European Contract Law. It also intends to continue the open, wide-ranging and detailed debate, launched by the Communication on European contract law with the participation of the institutions of the European Community as well as the general public, including businesses, consumer associations, academics and legal practitioners.

[...]

2. STEFAN VOGENAUER AND STEPHEN WEATHERILL, "The European Community's competence for a comprehensive harmonisation of contract law – an empirical analysis" [2005] E. L. Rev. 821–37

[...]

The views of European business

The Commission is [...] particularly aware of the need to establish competence under the EC Treaty. The most convincing basis for a Community competence to enact a comprehensive European contract law going beyond the current, fragmentary approach to legislation would seem to be Art.95 EC. In order to establish this, two requirements would have to be met. First [...], the Commission would be required to show that further steps in the area of contract law must actually contribute to eliminating obstacles to the free movement of goods or the freedom to provide services or to removing appreciable distortions of competition. Secondly, the enactment of a comprehensive Community contract law would have to be proportionate, Art. 5(3) EC, i.e. it would have to be appropriate for attaining the removal of such obstacles and distortions, it must not go beyond what is necessary to achieve these objectives, and the disadvantages caused must not be disproportionate to the aims pursued—in particular when there is a choice between several appropriate measures recourse must be had to the least onerous.

This is why the consultation exercise set in motion by the Commission's 2001 Communication can essentially be narrowed down to three questions: First, do the divergences in contract laws across the Member States result in obstacles to trade in goods and services, such as increasing the costs of cross-border transactions or creating other barriers? Secondly, is the existing piecemeal approach to European legislation in contract law sufficient to remove such obstacles, or does it rather create further difficulties, for instance an inconsistent application of European law in the various Member States? Thirdly, are there any options for legislative activities by the Community which are more appropriate for eliminating any existing trade obstacles?

[...]

[...] If we want to know whether the diverging contract laws in Europe really form a barrier to cross-border trade and impede on the proper functioning of the internal market, we might as well ask the main users of contract law: businesses and consumers. Perhaps surprisingly, this has hardly been done on a large scale. [...] As far as cross-border transactions are concerned, data has, so far, only been collected in the wake of the Commission's Green Paper on European Union Consumer Protection and thus in the context of business-to-consumer ("B2C") transactions.

Thus, a survey conducted on behalf of the Commission amongst 15,043 European consumers from the then 15 Member States in January 2002 revealed that, on average, consumers perceive the level of protection to be higher in their country than abroad: Only 32 per cent of consumers consider their rights to be well protected in a potential dispute with a seller or manufacturer in another Member State, whereas 56 per cent have this confidence with regard to their own country. A comparable survey on crossborder shopping, conducted a couple of months later, found that only 13 per cent of European consumers had bought or ordered products or services for private use from shops or sellers located in another Member State during the preceding 12 months. A quarter of all respondents stated that they felt less confident buying abroad than in their country of residence. The main reasons they gave for this were difficulties with the resolution of after sales problems, such as complaints, returns, refunds, guarantees (88 per cent), and the difficulty of taking legal action through the courts (83 per cent). These findings are supported by a survey amongst 12 of the then 14 European Consumer Centres on consumer advice conducted in May 2002. When asked what, according to their experience, the main obstacles to cross-border trade were from the consumer point of view, the consumer advisers ranked the same two reasons on top. Both of them are certainly related to problems of language and non-familiarity with business practices elsewhere, but obviously they depend on the different legislative frameworks as well. It is therefore not surprising that, when asked about suitable measures to increase confidence in cross-border purchases, almost 8 in 10 consumers lacking such confidence mentioned full harmonisation of consumer rights and protection or the possibility of suing foreign sellers in the courts of the consumer's Member State and under his or her national laws. […]

[…]

The business survey conducted in early 2005: respondents and methodology

[…] [I]n our view, in early 2005, three-and-a-half years after the Commission had started its consultation exercise, it could hardly be said that the three questions raised at the outset of this section had received a conclusive answer. The case for further Community intervention in the area of contract law had simply not been made. This is why, in the run-up to a conference on the harmonisation of European contract law to be held at the Oxford Institute of European and Comparative Law on March 18 and 19, 2005, we embarked on a fresh start. In doing so we acted as academic advisors to Clifford Chance, the world's biggest law firm and the co-organisers of the conference. Clifford Chance had written a fairly critical response to the Commission's 2003 Action Plan, followed by an equally disapproving article by one of their partners who reached the conclusion that "before too many moves are made, serious research needs to be undertaken to establish whether or not [users of contract law] really do find different legal systems an obstacle to trade and do want a uniform law to solve this".

Since the bulk of previous research had been directed to consumers' affairs it seemed appropriate to focus on the experiences, perceptions and expectations of businesses. Thus the survey was conducted amongst 175 firms. They were based in eight Member States. The countries chosen seemed to offer a fairly representative mix of larger and smaller economies, old and new Member States and more "europhile" and more "eurosceptic" traditions. Two of them, Germany and the Netherlands, had recently undergone major revisions of their domestic contract laws. The companies surveyed belonged to a wide range of industries. Most of them were major businesses (at least 250 employees), some of them national, European or even global players. However, care was taken that almost a fifth (19.4 per cent) were small (10–49 employees) or medium sized (50–249 employees) enterprises ("SMEs"), conventional wisdom being that SMEs suffer most under the existing divergences between national contract laws. Two-thirds of the individuals responding worked in the legal departments of their firms; the others were directors, vice presidents, company secretaries or served in similar functions. [...]

Results of the survey

[...]

With regard to current practices of trans-border trade, participants were asked about their attitudes when choosing the law to govern a contract. The ability to choose from different contract laws across Europe was seen as an advantage by almost two-thirds of the businesses, with strong national variations and major enterprises expressing a much stronger preference for the possibility of choice of law than SMEs. [...]

As it happens, more than 4 out of 10 companies at least occasionally choose a foreign contract law because their local law is not suitable to achieve their aims. When asked what is the most used law when conducting cross-border transactions, "UK law" (for these purposes probably taken to mean English law) was mentioned by roughly a quarter of the respondents. It is chosen approximately two-and-a-half times more frequently than any other law, no other country scoring more than 11 per cent (France). Perhaps remarkably New York law was only said to be used in 1 per cent of cross-border transactions; 2 per cent referred to "American law". However, 41 per cent of the respondents declared a willingness to choose a suitable non-European law if no European law was suitable for their purpose. When asked which characteristics of contract law influenced their choice, most answered that a suitable contract law has to enable trade, be predictable and fair. A smaller number thought that it was important that the governing contract law be flexible, short and concise or prescriptive.

On the other hand, 42 per cent of European businesses tend to avoid certain European jurisdictions because of their legal system. The countries named most frequently by those who occasionally avoid other contract laws were Italy (32 per cent), France (23 per cent), the UK (23 per cent), Germany (16 per cent), Spain (16 per cent) and Greece (15 per cent). The reasons given for this varied hugely. Some were very specific, such as "the way in which liberation is handled in Germany", but most were extremely vague, for instance the propositions that Belgian judges were "too arbitrary", that transactions and proceedings in Italy and Spain were "too lengthy" or that French law was "too protectionist" and "too focussed on the interest of their citizens". Often the reasons given were coloured with a certain lack of knowledge, for example when a UK company declared that it avoided French and Italian law because "they don't have a developed commercial law". Quite revealingly, the reasons most frequently given for the avoidance of another jurisdiction's law were the extent to which it was "different" from own contract law and a business's unfamiliarity with the respective jurisdiction.

Given that businesses enjoy rather broad freedom to choose or to avoid particular domestic contract laws and that they frequently do so, does the existing divergence in national legal systems present an obstacle to cross-border trade at all? To start with, almost two-thirds of European businesses experience "some" (51 per cent) or even "large" (14 per cent) obstacles to cross-border trade between Member States. But are these due to legal issues? We asked our respondents to rank seven factors which might impede on their ability to conduct cross-border transactions. The list comprised both policy and non-policy induced obstacles, i.e. factors that can or cannot, in principle, be addressed by legislation. Five factors belonged to the first group: tax, variations between legal systems, the cost of obtaining foreign legal advice, the differences in implementation of European Directives and bureaucracy/corruption. They were seen as slightly more significant than the non-policy induced obstacles listed, namely cultural differences and language. Thus it is clear that legal divergences have a comparably strong adverse impact on crossborder trade. However, these obstacles are generally not perceived to be insurmountable. As one respondent observed, in "fringe areas, it might make a difference between whether a deal is viable or not, but it wouldn't get into the way of a lucrative deal". Still, 10 per cent of those who felt there were obstacles considered them to have a "large" financial impact, 52 per cent thought they had "some" and 27 per cent believed they had a "minimal" financial impact on their organisation. And more than a quarter of the companies perceiving such obstacles were "often" (7 per cent) or "sometimes" (21 per cent) deterred from conducting cross-border transactions. More than 4 out of 10 (43 per cent) were "not very often" deterred.

[...]

Given that the existing state of European contract law does not seem to provide an adequate solution, are there any options for legislative activities by the Community which are more appropriate for eliminating any existing trade obstacles? The answer was an unequivocal "Yes". Eighty-three per cent of all businesses and even 88 per cent of all SMEs surveyed approved of the concept of a harmonised European contract law. In some countries the figures were significantly higher, reaching 95 per cent in Italy and 100 per cent in Hungary. By far the least enthusiastic responses came from the UK where 20 per cent viewed the concept "not at all favourably", but even there 64 per cent of the businesses were positively predisposed towards the idea. Amongst industries, the services sector was markedly more sceptical than other areas, with only 67 per cent being favourably disposed.

The question then arises as to how best to achieve a harmonised European contract law. When offered three choices, 38 per cent opted for improvements on the basis of the status quo, namely for a more uniform implementation and interpretation of Directives. This somewhat more conservative route was especially popular amongst French (50 per cent) and UK (43 per cent) businesses. Twenty-eight per cent of all respondents favoured the option of having a European contract law in addition to the existing national contract laws. Finally, 30 per cent advocated the bold step of introducing a European contract law that would replace national laws. This was, overall, the most favoured option amongst SMEs (38 per cent as opposed to 28 per cent amongst majors), but it was the most unpopular route in the UK where it was only favoured by 13 per cent.

Clearly, as has been shown above, the introduction of a European contract law that replaces national contract laws is presently not on the Commission's agenda. However, in view of the Commission's thoughts on an "optional instrument" the establishment of a European contract law in addition to existing national contract laws does not seem to be entirely unrealistic. If such a contract law were to be established, we asked, should it be mandatory or optional? Only a fifth of the respondents thought that it should be mandatory for all cross-border transactions. As opposed to this, 74 per cent wanted some form of optionality. They were fairly evenly spread out amongst those who favoured an additional regime for all cross-border transactions, be it with a possibility to opt in (21 per cent) or to opt out (21 per cent), and those who supported an additional regime for all contracts, cross-border and national, be it with a possibility to opt in (19 per cent) or to opt out (13 per cent). These findings correspond with the general importance attached to the ability to choose the governing law of contract reported above.

Assuming an optional European contract law were to be established, how likely would European businesses be to use it in connection with cross-border transactions? Overall, 82 per cent of the respondents would be "likely" or "very likely" to use it. Again, UK businesses were decidedly less enthusiastic (54 per cent) than their counterparts on the continent, notably in Poland (100 per cent), Hungary (95 per cent) and Italy (95 per cent). Incidentally, there is, despite the widespread approval of an optional contract law in principle, strong scepticism as to whether it can be achieved in practice. Only 54 per cent of the respondents thought that further harmonisation of contract law is achievable.

[...]

Conclusions: where to go next

To summarise our findings: European businesses enjoy far-reaching possibilities to choose the contract law applicable to a particular cross-border transaction, and they make ample opportunity of this. It is certainly not impossible or even unduly burdensome to engage in cross-border trade in the internal market. However, two-thirds of companies face costly obstacles to trading with others in a different jurisdiction. A major reason for this is the existence of different legal systems. As a result, roughly a quarter of all businesses are effectively deterred from cross-border trade. The piecemeal approach hitherto adopted towards harmonisation in the area of contract law is not perceived to be an effective remedy. Almost two-thirds of European businesses have experienced divergences amongst various Member States in the implementation and interpretation of Directives, and a third of them felt that these impinged on their ability or desire to conduct cross-border trade. Thus, we would submit, a case can be made for further Community action in the field of European contract law on the basis of Art. 95 EC.

As to the way ahead, a surprising 83 per cent of businesses view the concept of a harmonised contract law favourably. In order to achieve this the solution favoured by a small margin is an improvement in the implementation and interpretation of existing Directives. However, taken together, almost 6 out of 10 respondents would like to see a more comprehensive European contract law, either substituting existing national contract laws or in addition to them. But businesses would like to retain the freedom to choose another, more suitable law. So, if a European contract law were to be established alongside national contract regimes, only 20 per cent would like it to be mandatory for all cross-border transactions. If they were offered the choice of an optional European contract law, 82 per cent of European companies believe they would be likely to use it at some stage. Thus it seems inevitable to conclude that the "way forward" proposed by the Commission in 2004 is, in principle, met with approval by the business community: European business wants an improvement in the implementation and interpretation of the existing Directives, and the suggested qualitative improvement of the acquis would certainly help to this effect. Furthermore, European business has a strong interest in having an optional instrument at its disposal, it would be highly likely to use it and the elaboration of a common frame of reference is certainly a useful step in this direction (albeit not a cogent one; other possibilities might well be imagined).

So far, the Commission has justified the elaboration of the Common Frame of Reference as a necessary condition for the improvement of the acquis. [...] In the future, on the basis of our survey's findings it will be possible to justify the project as a useful step towards a possible optional instrument which in turn can be presented as one possibility to overcome obstacles to cross-border trade. Thus the Commission, moving on its "way forward" announced in 2004, seems to be on the right track.

Accordingly our survey lends a degree of support to the Commission's initiatives. [...]

[...] It should [...] have now become clear that it is impossible to deny this process any constitutional legitimacy from the outset.

3. DIANA WALLIS, "Is It a Code?" (2006) *ZEuP* 513–14

Is it a Code?

[...] [T]here has been much speculation, debate, accusation and even alarm that the European Commission's European Contract Law Initiative and the accompanying Acquis Review are a cover, or Trojan horse, for the development of a full blown European contract code. It may be that this has to some extent distracted attention from the more laudable and stated aims of the project as a mammoth exercise in better law-making, which was how the UK presidency presented it at their conference at London's Guildhall European Contract Law conference: *Better Lawmaking through the Common Frame of Reference*, held on 26th September 2005. In his opening address, the Lord Chancellor sounded the note of alarm and made it clear in no uncertain terms that as far as he was concerned English contract law was not up for amendment or discussion through this process; it was a definite hands-off warning to the Commission. The point is: was it necessary? Is the whole debate about "is it a code or not" a distraction? What should be the real concerns or preoccupations in this process?

[...]

Looking at the genesis of the Contract Law Initiative it appears in some earlier resolutions of the European Parliament stretching back to 1989 which have continuously pointed out the savings to be made in transactional terms across the Internal Market for business and consumers if there were further harmonisation. The theory being that differing laws can in themselves form a barrier to the good functioning of the market a perception endorsed by the more recent independent survey carried out by Clifford Chance. This conclusion or perception may well be correct but what is also clear is that now is not the political moment, coming at a time when the voters of Europe have just rejected a constitution, to hit them with a code! Rather there is a need to approach it from the other way about and show what can be achieved by better legislation that has a beneficial effect on transactions undertaken in people's daily lives.

So, in this situation, the European Parliament and even the British Lord Chancellor have no difficulty in signing up for a project based on the concept of better legislation. There should be no mistake; this is the biggest project of its kind that the EU has yet seen and certainly the biggest news in the whole area of European civil law for the coming years. The centrepiece of the project is the creation of the Common Frame of Reference (CFR). This has variously been defined as a 'tool- kit' for the legislator, a sort of dictionary or encyclopaedia of terms and comparative law. It will be a huge opus, hence the concern that it looks like a code. It may look like a code in terms of its chapters or headings, but of course what will make it a code or not will be its actual content and the way it is to be used. [...]

This difference is paramount to the European Parliament. Any review of existing legislation, for instance of the existing consumer directives that cover contract law, will need the involvement of the Parliament as a co-legislator. By comparison, the creation of any ,soft' instrument would leave the Parliament as a mere ,consultee', arguably with no more influence than the army of stakeholders and researchers who are already engaged by the Commission in the process. [...] Contract law might seem like a technical area for experts and working groups but it is of course full of ,political' choices; most especially, but not exclusively, where consumers are involved and mandatory rules may be needed. Hence the Parliament is currently engaged in finding a method whereby it can continuously engage in this ongoing process [...] and retain a guiding hand direction and development of the CFR instrument.

[...] [T]he European Parliament [does not think] that it is dealing with a code, it [...] thinks [however] it is shaping something very important that has to be right for future generations, who might just, in a different political context, use it as the basis for a code. Timing and presentation can make all the difference!

4. THOMAS KADNER GRAZIANO, "Does Europe Need A Contract Code?"[1]

Does Europe Need a Contract Code?

The future of private law is on the European agenda. The European Parliament has repeatedly asked for work to be started on a European Civil Code. Since 2001 and following several Communications of the European Commission, the debate has focused on the field of contract law. In January 2009, the development entered a new stage with the publication of a draft Common Frame of Reference (CFR). Development in the field of European contract law is currently proceeding with breathtaking speed and the CFR may be the first step towards a European contract code.

Using three case scenarios, the following article balances the arguments for and against a European contract code. It focuses on the question of whether a European contract code could, or should, replace existing national contract laws or if the national laws of contract and a new European contract code could coexist, with the scope of the European contract code being, in principle, limited to cross-border situations.

---

[1]   Updated version of an article previously published in French: "Le futur de la Codification du droit civil en Europe: harmonisation des anciens Codes ou création d'un nouveau Code?", in Jean-Philippe Dunand and Bénédict Winiger (eds), *Le Code civil français dans le droit européen*, Bruxelles: Bruylant, 2005, 257–74; and in German: "Die Zukunft der Zivilrechtskodifikation in Europa – Harmonisierung der alten Gesetzbücher oder Schaffung eines neuen?" in *ZEuP* 2005, 523–40.

INTRODUCTION

The European Parliament, in three resolutions of 1989, 1994, and 2001, called for work to be started on the possibility of developing a European code of private law.[2] The Parliament is of the opinion that harmonisation of certain areas of private law is essential to attain an internal market and that the unification of major branches of private law in the form of a European civil code would be the most effective way of meeting the Community's legal requirements in order to achieve a single market without frontiers.

In response to these resolutions, in 2001 the European Commission 'launched a process of consultation and discussion about the way in which problems resulting from divergences between national contract laws in the EU should be dealt with at the European level.'[3]

In 2003, the European Commission published an 'Action Plan' and announced the idea to elaborate a 'Common Frame of Reference' (CFR) which should help to improve existing and future Community legislation in the field of contract law. The second objective of the Common Frame of Reference is 'to form the basis for further reflection on an optional instrument in the area of European contract law'.[4]

In January 2009, the Draft Common Frame of Reference was published.[5] It is intended to provide the Commission with a 'tool-box' and act as a guide for future Community legislation in the field of contract law and related issues.[6] Some observers consider the CFR to be the first step towards a European contract code.[7]

---

[2] Resolution on action to bring into line the private law of the Member States of 26 May 1989, OJ C 158 1989, p. 400; Resolution on the harmonisation of certain sectors of the private law of the Member States of 6 May 1994, OJ C 205 1994, p. 518; Resolution of 15 November 2001 OJ C 140E 2002, p. 538.

[3] Communication from the Commission to the Council and the European Parliament on European Contract Law, 11.07.2001, COM (2001) 398 final, Executive Summary.

[4] Communication from the Commission to the European Parliament and the Council: A More Coherent European Contract Law – An Action Plan, 12.02.2003 COM (2003) 68 final; see also the third document in this series: Communication from the Commission to the European Parliament and the Council: European Contract Law and the revision of the acquis: the way forward COM (2004) 651. On the objectives of the CFR, see, e.g, D. STAUDENMAYER, 'The Way Forward in European Contract Law', (2005) *ERPL* 95 at 96 ff; M. W. HESSELINK, 'The European Commission's Action Plan: Towards a More Coherent European Contract Law?', (2004) *ERPL* 397 at 401 ff; M. RÖTTINGER, 'Towards a European Code Napoléon/ABGB/BGB? – Recent EC Activities for a European Contract Law', (2006) *EJL* 807 at 818 ff.

[5] Study Group on a European Civil Code/Research Group on EC Private Law (Acquis Group), *Principles, Definitions and Model Rules of European Private Law: Draft Common Frame of Reference (DCFR)*, Munich: Sellier, 2009.

[6] See, e.g., RÖTTINGER, above n. 4, at 809 ff.

[7] See, e.g., House of Lords (European Union Committee), *12ᵗʰ Report of Session 2004–05, European Contract Law – the way forward? – Report with evidence* (HL Paper 95) (London: The Stationery Office, 2005), no. 7: "A CFR would facilitate the preparation of the so-called 'optional instrument' which would supplement, and could even displace, national contract law. The optional instrument would be capable of evolving in time into a European Civil Code on Contract."; no. 62 ff, 115, 141: "Once the CFR has been agreed it would not be a major task to convert or adapt it into an optional instrument. The CFR may turn out to be something of a Trojan Horse"; H. COLLINS, "The 'Common Frame of Reference" for EC Contract Law: a Common Lawyer's Perspective", in M. Meili and M. R. Mugeri (eds), *L'armonizzazione del diritto private europeo*, Milan: Giuffrè, 2004, 107: "Let's just call it a Code"; HESSELINK, above n. 4, at 401: "A

When considering the future of contract law in Europe, three fundamental questions must be addressed:

1) Does Europe need a contract code, modelled on, for example, the Principles of European Contract Law, and – once a final version has been presented – on the Common Frame of Reference (CFR)? [8]

2) Should the contract laws set out in the national Civil codes or in the national case law be replaced by a European contract code *or* should we foresee their *coexistence* with a European code, with each contract law system having its own sphere of application?

3) What are the *next steps* on the way towards a more harmonised or more homogeneous contract law in Europe?

1. DOES EUROPE NEED A CONTRACT CODE? – THE EFFECT OF SURPRISE

The question of whether a European contract code is needed raises numerous issues. This contribution will concentrate on one central issue which will be referred to as the *effect of surprise*.

In a strictly national context, the existing systems of contract law in Europe, such as the English law of contract, the rules on contracts in the French *Code civil*, the German *Bürgerliches Gesetzbuch (BGB)*, the Italian *Codice civile*, the Swiss Code of Obligations, etc. have proved themselves. Regularly confronted with new challenges, the national contract laws have demonstrated their great flexibility and, where necessary, they have been adapted by national legislation and by numerous measures at European level to meet new needs and conditions. When it comes to domestic use, the existing systems work well in Europe.[9]

European Civil Code in Disguise?", at 402: "the concept of a CFR makes it possible for the Commission to quietly prepare […] a draft European Code without saying so; E. H. HONDIUS, "Towards a European Civil Code" in A. S. Hartkamp *et al.* (eds), *Towards a European Civil Code*, The Hague: Kluwer Law International, 2nd edn, 2004, 13: "a 'pre-code'". Contrast with D. WALLIS, 'Is It a Code?', (2006) ZEuP 513–14 (excerpt above, at **IV.3**).

[8] In the current discussion, the questions if and to what extent a European contract code is really needed are often dealt with only briefly, see, e.g., House of Lords *European Contract Law – the way forward?*, above n. 7, nos 67 and 129: "The case for harmonisation of contract law across Europe has yet to be made. It is something that would have to be considered on its merits", nos 114 and 140: "We believe, and the Commission accepts, that an extensive impact assessment needs to be undertaken before any further work is undertaken on the optional instrument. As the Law Society said, that assessment should seek to determine whether an optional instrument would have a real effect on reducing cross-border transaction costs."; RÖTTINGER, above n. 4, at 824: "[N]o impact assessment has ever has ever been undertaken with regard to the real need of a CFR, an optional instrument, or STC. Nor has the potential impact of these instruments on the economy, on the level of consumer protection, or on the Internal Market, been analysed. Do we really need them? What will the added value be?"; HESSELINK, above n. 4, at 418: "it is absolutely indispensable that the Commission immediately instigates a true debate on the advantages and disadvantages of such a code"; N. KORNET, "Is there a Need for a Uniform Contract Law in Europe? Empirical Perspectives", (2005) ZEuP 677, at 677 and at 679. See, however, H. COLLINS, "The Freedom to Circulate Documents: Regulating Contracts in Europe", (2004) EJL 787–803, at 790 ff.

[9] See, however, SIR ROY GOODE, in R. Goode, *Commercial Law in the Next Millennium*, London: Sweet & Maxwell, 1998, pp 100–101, who observed with respect to the English law of contracts: "[w]hen I visit

The situation is different when talking about transnational cases. When it comes to such cross-border cases, the diversity of the solutions of the existing codes and case law is often the source of legal uncertainty and of unpleasant surprises.[10] Examining three case scenarios extracted from decisions of courts in Europe helps to illustrate the *surprises* that can be encountered in European contract law at present.

(a)   Three Illustrations

A number of the responses to the Commission's Communications describing the particular difficulties encountered in transboundary situations concerned the *conclusion of contracts*. It is therefore this phase that the following examples relate to.

In the *first scenario* (taken from Case 2 above[11]) someone decides to leave their job. Another person, who is interested in the job, promises to pay the person who is leaving a significant sum of money in return for being introduced to his employer as a potential replacement. Both parties are aware that the employer is in no way bound by this introduction. The potential replacement is introduced to the employer and is hired. However, he refuses to pay the promised sum to his predecessor, arguing that the employer was not bound to employ him because of the introduction as he was free to employ whoever he wanted to employ.

In the vast majority of European legal systems, for a contract to be concluded the parties need only to be in agreement.[12] Therefore, in this case the contract would be valid and the promised sum would be due. However, Article 1108 of the French Civil Code requires there to be a *cause* in addition to an agreement of the parties for a valid contract to be concluded. In a similar case, the French *Cour de cassation* decided that there was no *cause*.[13] Therefore, under French law, it follows that there would be no contract in the above case and the party leaving the job would not be entitled to the promised sum.[14]

---

other common law countries, and in particular Canada and the United States, I am immensely impressed with their concern to keep their commercial law up to date [...] When I return to England I feel [...] depressed by [...] our inertia and complacent belief in the superiority of English commercial law [...] How is it that we feel able to embark on the 21st century with commercial law statutes passed in the 19th?" See, for French law, B. FAUVARQUE-COSSON, "Faut-il un Code civil européen?", (2002) *Revue trimestrielle de droit civil* 463 at 464, n. 2: "Si le Code civil a prouvé ses capacités de résistance en perdurant malgré les changements incessants du droit, il a vieilli. Ses parties les plus anciennes ont été, soit négligées, soit revues par la jurisprudence qui les a tout à la fois faites et défaites. Par ailleurs, une succession de réformes législatives partielles a fragilisé le monument" ("Whereas the Civil Code has proved its resistance by enduring despite constant changes to the law, it has nevertheless aged. The oldest parts of it have been either neglected or revised by case-law which has modified them. In addition, a succession of partial legislative reforms has weakened the monumental law").

10   See also W. BLAIR and R. BRENT, "A Single European Law of Contract?", (2004) *E.B.L.Rev.* 5 at 13: "businesses may enter into legal relationships on the basis of a deficient understanding of the legal rules applicable to their commercial relationship. Businesses do not always reckon on many peculiarities of foreign contract law ... [T]here is plenty of scope for businesses to be taken by surprise".

11   At p. 94.

12   See, e.g., Art. 1 of the Swiss Code of Obligations; § 861 of the Austrian Civil Code; this is also the case for German law, see, e.g., DÖRNER, "Vorbemerkung zu §§ 145–57, n. 1", in *Bürgerliches Gesetzbuch, Handkommentar*, 4th edn, Baden-Baden: Nomos.

13   Cour de Cassation 20 février 1973 (*Caillet c. Dame Nivesse*), [1974] *D. S.* 37 (excerpts above, **Case 2, IV.2.**).

14   The French courts thus used the *cause* as a device, unknown in many other legal orders, to strike out

In a *second scenario* (the scenario of Case 4 above[15]), a sales contract is concluded. During the execution of the contract, difficulties arise and delivery becomes more onerous. Following fresh negotiations, one party gives the other more time to complete their obligation, agrees to pay a higher price or agrees to something similar which renders the other party's obligation easier to fulfil. According to the agreement, the party advantaged by the change is not to pay a price for the modification.[16]

The majority of Continental legal systems would consider such a modification valid. For an English lawyer, however, a contract is not simply an agreement but an exchange of promises.[17] If the party advantaged by the modification does not give or promise to give something in return, the modification is not supported by what English lawyers refer to as *consideration*, a key element in the English and American laws of contract. Since in our example no consideration was given or promised, the modification of the contract does not create new binding obligations and is unenforceable.

In an exclusively English case, the contracting parties (or rather their lawyers) know (or ought to know) that *consideration*, a feature which is unknown in Continental legal orders, is a prerequisite for a valid contract. In an exclusively French case, the contracting parties (or rather their lawyers) know (or ought to know) their domestic law, that is to say, know that the existence of a licit *cause* is necessary for a contract to be valid.[18] In cross-border relations, on the other hand, a foreign party will most probably not be aware of these conditions. For this party, the notion of the *cause* as well as that of *consideration*, as conditions for the formation of a valid contract, could be the source of unpleasant surprises. A party who is not aware of such a condition cannot take the precautions necessary to avoid the inconveniences that special features of foreign laws may cause, for example, in the *second scenario*, promising to do something in return for the modification of a contract, even if it is not proportionate to the benefit received,[19] to ensure the validity of the modification.

The same phenomenon can be observed in relation to the *third scenario* (drawn from Case 3, above[20]): A makes an offer to B. The offer stipulates a three week period for acceptance. Within this period and while B is still contemplating the offer, A revokes it.

---

an agreement the courts judged to be socially undesirable although the agreement was neither illegal nor in violation of public order or public morals; see case-note by P. MALAURIE, (1974) *D. S.* 37 (excerpts above, **Case 2, IV.2.**).

[15] At p. 191.

[16] See, e.g., the English case *Williams* v. *Roffey Bros and Nicholls (Contractors) Ltd* [1990] 1 All ER 512 (Court of Appeal), and the American case *Alfred L. Angel et al.* v. *John E. Murray, Jr, Director of Finance of the City of Newport et al.*, 113 R.I. 482 (Supreme Court of Rhode Island) (excerpts of both cases above, **Case 4, II.1. and III.3.**).

[17] See, e.g., M. FURMSTON, *Cheshire, Fifoot & Furmston's Law of Contract*, Oxford: Oxford University Press, 15th edn, 2007, Ch. 4, p. 93 ff; P. S. ATIYAH, *An Introduction to the Law of Contract*, Oxford: Oxford University Press, 6th edn, 2005, pp. 93 ff.

[18] The *cause* is a special feature of French law which can also be found in the legal systems of the other members of the French legal family (albeit sometimes with very different interpretations), see, e.g., the Spanish Civil Code (*Código civil*), Arts 1254, 1261, 1262, 1274–1277, the Italian *Codice civile*, Arts 1325, 1343–1345, 1418 and the Civil Code of Quebec, Arts 1385, 1410, 1411.

[19] Consideration must be sufficient, it need not be adequate; it must have some value, see, e.g., G. H. TREITEL, *The Law of Contract*, 11th edn, London: Sweet & Maxwell, 2003, pp. 73–77; W. T. MAJOR and C. TAYLOR, *Law of Contract*, Harlow: Pitman Publishing, 9th edn, 1996, p. 47 ff, Ch. 4, rules 8 and 9.

[20] At p. 150.

In the majority of European countries, an offeror is bound by his offer for a certain amount of time; either for the period set out in the offer or, in the absence of a set period, for a reasonable length of time. This gives the other party time to consider and evaluate the offer.[21]

However, in certain countries, the offeror can freely revoke his offer up until the moment an acceptance has reached him or has been dispatched. This is the famous *postal rule* of English law in action.[22] Such a rule has also been introduced, with modifications, into the Dutch *Burgerlijk Wetboek* and, more recently, also into the Polish and Lithuanian Civil Codes.[23] Under English law, an offer can be revoked even if the offer sets out a period for acceptance, or if the offeror expressly states that the offer shall be irrevocable. It is clear that the issue of whether an offer can or cannot be revoked is fundamental in pre-contractual relationships. The revocation of an offer under foreign law, applicable to the contract, could considerably surprise and hereby disadvantage a party from a country where offerors are bound by their offers.

The *cause, consideration* and the *postal rule* are prominent examples of the particularities of national laws. They are special features that are deeply entrenched in these laws and have survived numerous attempts to reform them at national level. Another example of a peculiarity of French law that could surprise foreign actors is the refusal by the French courts to adapt or annul contracts where there has been a fundamental and unforeseeable change of circumstances.[24] This case law makes it indispensable to take precautions for such a change of circumstances in the contract itself. However, these examples are just the *tip of the iceberg*; there are innumerable features and particularities of national laws that could surprise foreign actors. Further examples of variations between national laws and therefore potential surprises include: different conditions as to the form of contracts; different conditions as to the validity of standard forms; different duties to examine goods received and different consequences when this duty is not respected; different limitation periods in the event of non-performance of contractual obligations; different conditions for the validity of terms providing for the retention of title to goods, etc. The comparative commentaries that relate to the articles of the Principles of European Contract Law, as well as the responses that the European Commission received following its Communication of 2001[25] show many more examples of such differences.

Many particularities of national laws cannot be explained by logic. The reasons for them are purely historic in nature. While these reasons are deeply-rooted at the national level, they are the cause of many surprises and legal insecurity at international level. They

---

[21] See, e.g., Arts 3 and 5 of the Swiss Code of Obligations, §§ 145 to 147 of the German Civil Code, § 862 of the Austrian Civil Code, Arts 185 and 186 of the Greek Civil Code, Art. 230 of the Portuguese Civil Code.

[22] For further explanation of the postal rule, see, for example, TREITEL, above n. 19, pp. 24–30.

[23] Art. 6:219 (1) and (2) of the new Dutch Civil Code; Polish Civil Code (*Kodeks cywilny*), Art. 66[2]; Art. 6.169 of the Civil Code of the Republic of Lithuania (*Lietuvos Respublikos Civilinis kodeksas*).

[24] Cour de Cass. civ. 6 mars 1876 (*De Galliffet c. Commune de Pélisanne ou 'Canal de Craponne'*), in H. CAPITANT, *Les grands arrêts de la jurisprudence civile*, Tome 2, Paris: Dalloz, 12th edn, 2008, n. 165 and F. TERRÉ et al., *Droit civil: Les obligations*, Paris: Dalloz, 9 th edn, 2005, n. 462 and n. 465 ff (excerpts above, **Case 7, IX.2.**).

[25] See above n. 3.

may therefore act as a disincentive to cross-border trade[26] and disadvantage foreign actors. "[T]he closer one is to the actual [...] prospect of cross-border trade, the more likely it is that diversity of contract law will be perceived to be a hindrance to trade."[27]

(b)   The Principles of European Contract Law

Peculiarities of national legal orders that do not have a logical (or fair) basis, but are essentially just historical throw-backs, have been left out of the Principles of European Contract Law (the Lando Principles) and of the UNIDROIT Principles of International Commercial Contracts.[28] The Lando Principles, like the UNIDROIT Principles, are adapted for international use. The rules are clear and simple and allow contracting parties to avoid unpleasant surprises.

Returning to the above examples, Article 2:101(1) of the Lando Principles sets out that "[a] contract is concluded if: (a) the parties intend to be legally bound, and (b) they reach a sufficient agreement, *without any further requirement*" (emphasis added). The last part of the article relates to the notion of the *cause*, present in French law, and the English notion of *consideration*, making clear that neither is required under the Principles.[29]

Article 2:202(1) of the Lando Principles adopts the English approach to the revocability of offers (the famous postal rule), but it does so in a very moderate way, introducing, in Article 2:202(3), exceptions inspired by Continental contract laws.[30] Under the Principles, an offer stating a fixed time period for acceptance or otherwise indicating that it is irrevocable cannot be revoked before the fixed time limit has expired.

Article 6:111 of the Lando Principles sets out a clear rule relating to a change of circumstances which rejects the extreme position taken under French law.

(c)   Existing remedies?

Neither European Directives in the field of contract law nor rules on private international law (or conflicts of law) can solve the problem of surprise effectively.

Directives have been criticised, and rightly so, for taking a patchwork approach and being sectoral and pointillist.[31] The transposition of directives varies from country to

---

[26]   Compare, e.g., BLAIR and BRENT, above n. 10, at 14; RÖTTINGER, above n. 4, at 812; C. WITZ, "Plaidoyer pour un code européen des obligations", (2000) *Recueil Dalloz (D.), Chroniques, Doctrine*, p. 79 at 81; J. BASEDOW, "Un droit commun des contrats pour le marché européen", (1998) *Rev. int. dr. comp.* 7 at 24: "en l'état actuel du droit, la conclusion des contrats transfrontaliers équivaut souvent, pour les parties et leurs conseillers juridiques, à un vol sans visibilité" ("With the law as it currently stands, cross-border contracts are often the equivalent of the parties and their legal advisers being robbed blind").

[27]   BLAIR and BRENT, above n. 10, at 12: "Thus, a retailer in Luxembourg is more likely to perceive hindrance than a retailer in Manchester".

[28]   UNIDROIT, International Institute for the Unification of Private Law: Principles of International Commercial Contracts. English version with commentary is available at: http://www.unidroit.org/english/principles/contracts/main.htm.

[29]   See O. Lando and H. Beale (eds), *Principles of European Contract Law*, Parts I and II, The Hague: Kluwer Law International, 2nd edn, 2000, Art. 2:101, Notes 3 (a) and (b).

[30]   *Ibid.*, Art. 2:102, Notes 1 ff.

[31]   H. KÖTZ, "Gemeineuropäisches Zivilrecht", in *Liber Amicorum Zweigert* (1981) 481; H. KÖTZ, "Rechtsvereinheitlichung – Nutzen, Kosten, Methoden, Ziele", (1986) *RabelsZ* 1; see also J. BASEDOW, "Codification of Private Law in the European Union: the making of a Hybrid", (2001) *ERPL* 35 at 37;

country, which sometimes adds to the problem of the lack of transparency in the European system, leads to "community-created inconsistencies"[32] and creates new surprises for international actors.[33] This observation has been confirmed by the responses to the European Commission's Communication of 2001 as well as by the business survey conducted in 2005.[33a]

European private international law, in particular the 'Rome I Regulation', cannot solve the problem of surprise, or of the unknown and therefore of legal uncertainty either. Uniform private international law (PIL) makes it possible to foresee the law applicable to a contract, and as such helps to avoid certain surprises. However, that said, PIL designates a *national* law which is not adapted to meet the needs of a cross-border situation. It cannot avoid the surprises relating to the *contents* of the foreign law applicable to the contract, and therefore cannot avoid the effect of surprise mentioned above.[34]

It goes without saying that the choice of the law of a neutral third country (traditionally English or Swiss law) – another compromise contracting parties might consider – does not resolve the problem of surprise either. In fact, instead of surprising just one of the actors, the risk here is that the peculiarities of the law of a third country will be imposed on both parties, with neither of the parties being familiar with the special features of this law.[35]

Could law reforms at the national level create the necessary legal certainty and avoid unpleasant surprises? The doctrines of the *cause* and *consideration* and the *postal rule*, as well as other special characteristics of national laws, have already resisted numerous attempts at reform on the national level.[36] Recent experiences of reform, notably the reform of the law of obligations in Germany[37] and a current reform bill in France, do not offer too much hope either.

Although the German reform was initiated by a European directive and although the preparatory works were largely inspired by the Vienna Sales Convention (or CISG), the UNIDROIT Principles, the Lando Principles and foreign law, the new German law of obligations is – according to Ole Lando – still too complicated to be understood by a foreigner who has not undertaken in-depth research into German law.[38]

RÖTTINGER, above n. 4, at 816. For the deficiencies of the current approach, see House of Lords *European Contract Law – the way forward?*, above n. 4, nos 3 ff, 40 ff.

[32] BLAIR and BRENT, above n. 10, at 7, 9 ff.

[33] WITZ, above n. 26, at 80, points out the harmful effects of directives and the de-harmonisation of European contract law caused by a sectoral approach to harmonisation. For the limitations of a sectoral approach to harmonisation, see also BASEDOW, above n. 26, at 24.

[33a] See VOGENAUER and WEATHERILL, above **IV.2.**

[34] See, e.g., FAUVARQUE-COSSON, above n. 9, at 473 no. 25; O. LANDO, "Optional or Mandatory Europeanisation of Contract Law", (2002) *ERPL* 59–70 at 62.

[35] See the example given by LANDO, above n. 34, at 62. For a more optimistic account of the possibility of PIL offering a solution to the problem, see Y. LEQUETTE, "Quelques remarques à propos du projet du code civil européen de M. von Bar" (2002), *D. S.*, Chroniques, p. 2202 at 2204.

[36] See, e.g., the attempts of the Law Revision Committee to remedy some of the problems linked with the doctrine of consideration and the revocation of offers, 6th Interim Report (Statute of Frauds and the Doctrine of Consideration) Cmd. 5449, 1937, para. 38, p. 22, reproduced in J. C. SMITH and J. A. C. THOMAS, *A Casebook on Contract*, 7th edn, London: Sweet & Maxwell, 1982, p. 65 (excerpts above, **Case 2, VIII.1.**).

[37] *Gesetz zur Modernisierung des Schuldrechts* (Act on the reform of the German law of obligations), *Bundesgesetzblatt* 2001, I, 3138.

[38] O. LANDO, "Das neue Schuldrecht des Bürgerlichen Gesetzbuches und die Grundregeln des

In France, a project is currently underway to reform the law of obligations in the *Code civil*.[39] It proves to be the most significant reform of the law since the Code's entry into force in 1804. However, the reform would leave in place many special features of French contract law, including the *cause*. This is the case even though many of these features are unknown in the rest of Europe and are the source of considerable inconvenience for foreign parties in transnational cases.

The special features of English contract law have endured despite numerous calls for reform. As early as in 1937, the English Law Revision Committee declared that it 'appears to be undesirable and contrary to business practice that a man who has been promised a period […] in which to decide whether to accept or to decline an offer cannot rely upon being able to accept it at any time within that period.' The Law Revision Committee drew attention to the fact that 'according to the law of most foreign countries a promisor is bound by such a promise'. The Committee concluded that it 'is particularly undesirable that on such a point the English law should accept a lower moral standard'. However, in the 70 years since this critique was made, English contract law has proved to be very resistant to proposals for reform in this area.

(d) Summary

So, could law reform at the national level remedy the problem of unpleasant surprises and of legal uncertainty? It appears, from the examples above and many more similar case scenarios, that the problem of encountering unpleasant surprises in cross-border situations can only be efficiently remedied by the creation of a European contract code. Neither the choice between national laws by way of (harmonised) conflicts-of-laws rules nor law reforms at a national level can solve the problems of surprise and of legal uncertainty in transboundary cases.

The Principles of European Contract Law, the UNIDROIT Principles and the Draft Common Frame of Reference are adapted to meet the needs of transnational actors. If a European contract code was modelled on these rules, the surprises which are caused by the peculiarities of national laws and which lead to uncertainty, risks and costs, would be avoided. With the increase in cross-border trade, the need for a law of contract that is adapted accordingly is becoming, and will become, more and more pressing.[40]

---

europäischen Vertragsrechts", (2003) *RabelsZ* 231 speaks of a "Irrgarten des neuen Rechts" (maze of new laws) (p. 234), and a "Labyrinth, in dem sich nur der Eingeweihte zu Hause fühlt" (Labyrinth in which only the specialists feels at home) (p. 238); the new law would be "für Laien und Ausländer unverständlich" (incomprehensible for laymen and foreigners) (p. 244), it would be a "Irrgarten von Regeln" (maze of rules) (p. 244).

[39] PIERRE CATALA (dir), *Avant-projet de réforme du droit des obligations et de la prescription*, Paris: La Documentation Française, 2006. For an English translation, see J. CARTWRIGHT and S. WHITTAKER (transl.), *Proposals for Reform of the Law of Obligations and the Law of Prescription*, Oxford, 2007, available at: http://www.justice.gouv.fr/art_pix/rapportcatatla0905-anglais.pdf. See also the translation by the Association Henri Capitant, A. LEVASSEUR (transl.), *Traduction anglaise de l'avant-projet*, available at: http://www.henricapitant.org/IMG/pdf/Traduction_definitive_Alain_Levasseur.pdf.

[40] See the results of the business survey conducted in 2005, VOGENAUER and WEATHERILL, excerpts above, **IV.2.**; and LANDO, above n. 34, at 69: "the more trade and communication continue to grow, the more urgent the unification of the law of contract will become". Contrast with P. LEGRAND, "Sens et non-sens d'un Code civil européen", (1996) *Rev. int. dr. comp.* 779 at 808: "il est illusoire de penser qu'un code

2. NATIONAL CONTRACT LAWS AND A EUROPEAN CONTRACT CODE – CAN THEY COEXIST?

Would a European contract code be an *alternative* to the existing national contract laws, replacing them completely, *or* could the national laws of contract and a new European code *coexist*, with the scope of the European contract code being limited to cross-border situations?

(a)   Arguments for the replacement of national contract laws by a European contract code[41]

Several arguments support the replacement of existing contract laws by a new European contract code.

First of all, there is obviously the argument in favour of simplicity and efficiency. The coexistence of several systems is regarded as being complicated and hard to manage.[42] Teaching, studying and applying a single system would be simpler and more efficient than teaching, studying and applying:

- the existing codes for purely internal relations;
- the European code for cross-border, European contracts;
- the system provided for by the CISG for relations with countries outside Europe (for countries where the CISG is in force);
- a fourth system, this time one of private international law (based on the Rome I Regulation), for cases which are not covered by the three previous systems.

In addition, the possibility to withdraw from a European contract code (the possibility to *opt out*) and choose a national law instead, would decrease the importance of the new code right from the start.[43] Experiences with the CISG in certain countries, like Germany and Switzerland, have shown that parties systematically opt out of uniform law and choose a national law instead.[44]

---

civil assure la sécurité juridique' (it is an illusion to think that a civil code can assure legal certainty"); P. MALAURIE, *Le code civil européen des obligations et des contrats – Une question toujours ouverte*, Colloque de Leuven (Belgique), [2002] *JCP, Doctrine*, p. 281 n°15.

[41]   In favour of such a replacement, see, e.g., LANDO, above n. 34, at 69; WITZ, above n. 26, at 82; BASEDOW, above n. 31, at 35 ff; BASEDOW, above n. 26, at 7 ff; C. VON BAR, "Le groupe d´études sur un Code civil européen", (2001) *Rev. int. dr. comp.* 127 at 132 ff; F. STURM, "Der Entwurf eines Europäischen Vertragsgesetzbuches", (2001) *JZ* 1097 at 1097 ff; B. LURGER, *Grundfragen der Vereinheitlichung des Vertragsrechts in der Europäischen Union*, Vienna: Springer, 2002, pp. 158 ff.
     Contrast with, e.g., COLLINS, above n. 7, at 796: "Talk about a European civil code is both irrelevant and dangerous"; LEQUETTE, above n. 35, at 2202 ff; LEGRAND, above n. 40, at 780 ff; G. CORNU, "Un code civil n'est pas un instrument communautaire" (2002), *D. S.*, Chroniques, p. 351 ff; P. MALINVAUD, "Réponse – hors délai – à la Commission européenne : à propos d'un code européen des contrats" (2002), *D. S.*, Chroniques, p. 2542 at 2549 ff, 2551.

[42]   WITZ, above n. 26, at 82; H. SONNENBERGER, "Der Ruf unserer Zeit nach einer europäischen Ordnung des Zivilrechts" (1998) 53(20) *JZ* 982 at 986; LURGER, above n. 41, p. 159.

[43]   See, e.g., LURGER, above n. 41, p. 159.

[44]   See, e.g., BASEDOW, above n. 31, at 44, who concludes: "A civil code adopted as a [28 th] model would be doomed to insignificance".

What is more, limiting the scope of application of a European contract code to cross-border contracts would have the curious effect of reserving the most modern system of private law in Europe to international situations.[45]

Another argument is that only the replacement of the existing contract laws by a European contract code would be compatible with the aim of an internal market. Such an internal market would require rules to be the same whether dealing with a purely domestic relationship or a cross-border one. According to this argument, the rules governing contracts should thus be completely independent of the habitual residence or place of business of the actors.[46]

Last but not least, another argument in favour of the replacement of the existing contract laws with a new European contract code is that it would be difficult and complicated to define their respective scopes of application if the two were to coexist.[47]

(b)   Arguments for having a system of coexistence[48]

Assuming that there is indeed a need for a European contract code, many arguments seem to favour such a European contract code completely replacing the existing national

---

[45]   VON BAR, above n. 41, at 133.

[46]   WITZ, above n. 26, at 82; VON BAR, above n. 41, at 132; J. BASEDOW, "Ein optionales Europäisches Vertragsgesetz – opt-in, opt-out, wozu überhaupt?", (2004) ZEuP 2004, 1 at 3 ff.

[47]   U. DROBNIG, "Europäisches Zivilgesetzbuch – Gründe und Grundgedanken", in D. Martiny and N. Witzleb (eds), *Auf dem Weg zu einem Europäischen Zivilgesetzbuch*, Berlin: Springer, 1999, p. 123; VON BAR, above n. 41, at 132; LURGER, above n. 41, p. 158 ff.

[48]   In response to the reactions, the Commission received following its Communication in 2001 (above n. 3), it seems that the Commission now expresses a preference for a system of coexistence (see, e.g., the 2003 action plan, above n. 4). For thoughts on such an optional instrument, see BLAIR and BRENT, above n. 9, at 19 ff; D. STAUDENMAYER, "Ein optionelles Instrument im Europäischen Vertragsrecht" (2003), ZEuP 828 at 831 ff.

For a discussion of duality and coexistence, see DROBNIG, above n. 47, at 123; U. DROBNIG, "A Subsidiary Plea: A European Contract Law for Intra-European Border-Crossing Contracts", in S. Grundmann and J. Stuyck (eds), *An Academic Green Paper on European Contract Law*, The Hague: Kluwer Law International, 2002, 343; S. LEIBLE, "Die Mitteilung der Kommission zum Europäischen Vertragsrecht – Startschuss für ein Europäisches Vertragsgesetzbuch?", (2001) EWS 471 at 480 ff. Coexistence is also proposed by FAUVARQUE-COSSON, above n. 9, at 480 n. 40, who considers it to be the second of three steps to a European contract law. See also BLAIR and BRENT, above n. 10, at 21; W. TILMAN, "Zweiter Kodifikationsbeschluss des Europäischen Parlaments", (1995) ZEuP 534 at 537 ff, option (c)(1). For arguments for coexistence during a transitional phase, see WITZ, above n. 26, at 82: "la mise à l'écart des droits nationaux pourrait ainsi se faire de manière progressive" ("the replacement of national laws may also be done progressively").

For arguments against coexistence, see, e.g., MALAURIE, above n. 40, at 281 n. 15: "le droit interne national des contrats ne pourra pas longtemps être différent du droit européen des contrats transfrontières; le marché interne des nations européennes doit avoir les mêmes règles que le marché européen" ("It will not be possible for domestic laws of contract to be different from the European law on cross-border contracts for very long; the domestic markets of European nations must have the same rules as the European market"); BASEDOW, above n. 46, at 3: "Diese Lösung ist […] integrationspolitisch verfehlt. Sie liefe auf die Perpetuierung der rechtlichen Binnengrenzen hinaus [...]", "würde […] verhängnisvolles Signal für Angleichungsbestrebungen in anderen Politikbereichen aussenden" ("This solution is […] a failed policy of integration. It amounts to the perpetuation of the internal legal boundaries […]", "would […] send a disastrous signal for attempts at harmonisation in other political

contract law systems. *However,* despite all these arguments, it seems that the best solution, for the moment and even in the long term, would be the *coexistence* of a new European code and national laws.

This solution would see the existing codes continuing to apply at national level to purely internal situations. The aim of having a European code would be to tackle the unsatisfactory treatment of cross-border operations. In a system of coexistence, the parties would be able to subject a cross-border contract to the rules of a national law (*opt out* of the European contract code)[49] or choose to subject their purely internal transaction to the rules of the European contract code (*opt in*).

The contractual law governing internal relations and cross-border relations does not necessarily need to be the same. The CISG, which is in force in almost 70 countries, shows that the contrary can work perfectly well.

As for the delimitation of the scopes of application of the national contract law systems on the one hand and the European code on the other, inspiration can be taken from the first article of the CISG, which clearly demonstrates that the setting out of the scope of uniform law and domestic contract law is indeed possible without any major complications.[50] One could, for example, imagine that the European contract code would apply to contracts between parties whose habitual residence or place of business is in different States when these States are Member States of the EU. One could further imagine the application of the European contract code when the forum's rules of private international law lead to the application of the law of an EU Member State.[51]

Whereas it has, for a long time, been true that parties with their place of business in exporting countries have systematically opted out of uniform law (in particular the CISG) and have chosen a national law instead, recent studies show that this is no longer the case.[52]

The prospect of having coexisting systems appears to be, a priori, the most *realistic* solution.[53] National legislators would be more willing to relinquish their powers in a key area of private law if this was limited to cross-border matters. The success of the CISG is a particularly good example of this approach working well.

---

fields"); and for a more optimistic view of the possibility of success of coexistence, see J. BASEDOW, "Insurance contract law as part of an optional European Contract Act", (2003) *Lloyd's Maritime and Commercial Law Quarterly* 498 (in relation to insurance contracts).

[49] On the possibility of opting-in and opting-out, see, e.g., Communication from the Commission to the Council and the European Parliament on European Contract Law, above n. 3, no. 66; see also Staudenmayer, above n. 48, at 835 ff; BASEDOW, above n. 46, at 1 ff.

[50] See the United Nations Convention on Contracts for the International Sale of Goods (CISG or Vienna Sales Convention), Art. 1(1): "This Convention applies to contracts of sale of goods between parties whose places of business are in different States: (*a*) when the States are Contracting States; or (*b*) when the rules of private international law lead to the application of the law of a Contracting State".

[51] If this (second) rule were adopted, a sales contract between, e.g., an English seller and American buyer would, before English courts, under the Rome I Regulation, *in the absence of a choice of law clause*, be governed by the European contract code; a contract between an American seller and an English buyer would be subject to the respective US law.

[52] See the data provided by J. MEYER, "UN-Kaufrecht in der deutschen Anwaltspraxis", (2005) *RabelsZ* 457-86; E HONDIUS, "CISG and a European Civil Code", (2007) *RabelsZ* 99–114 at 112.

[53] See DROBNIG, above n. 47, at 123.

The issue of whether the European Union has the competence to legislate in the field of contract law is highly controversial.[54] Recent case law of the European Court of Justice has emphasised that diversity of law per se will not be sufficient as an adequate basis for intervention of the EU, and has insisted that harmonisation measures "are to improve the conditions for the establishing and functioning of the internal market".[55] Showing an impact on the internal market and establishing a competence of the European Union on the basis of Article 95 of the EC Treaty is obviously much easier for rules applying to cross-border situations than for measures aiming at full unification of contract law.

Another advantage of adopting a system of coexistence is that it avoids the possibility of a *culture shock*[56] being caused by abandoning the existing national contract law systems which, in some countries, are highly praised and even considered to be a part of the cultural heritage. According to Jean Carbonnier and a number of other French authors,[57] *"la véritable constitution [de la France], c'est le Code civil"* ("The very essence of the French legal system, or even of France itself, is its Civil Code").[58] According to these authors, the Civil Code sets out the terminology and the grammar of French law.[59] In England, the link between law and cultural identity has repeatedly been emphasised. In a recent paper, Hugh Collins compared the idea to replace the national contract laws by a European contract code 'to a kind of mass destruction, that is destruction of the national private law traditions of every Member State and their replacement with uniform laws'.[60]

---

[54] On the EU's legislative competence to enact a European code of contract law, see – with different opinions on this issue – S. WEATHERILL, "Reflections on the EC's Competence to Develop a 'European Contract Law' ", (2005) *ERPL* 405–18; MALINVAUD, above n. 41, at n° 31; BASEDOW, above n. 30, 35–49.

[55] Beginning with *'Tobacco Advertising'*, Case C-376/98 *Germany* v. *Parliament and Council* [2000] ECR I-8419. See, e.g., J. USHER, "Annotation", (2001) *Common Market Law Review* 1519. See also the subsequent case law: Case C-491/01 *R* v. *Secretary of State for Health ex parte British American Tobacco (Investments) Ltd and Imperial Tobacco Ltd* [2002] ECR I-11543; Cases C-465/00 et al *Rechnungshof* v. *Osterreichischer Rundfunk et al* [2003] ECR I-4989.

[56] See, e.g., FAUVARQUE-COSSON, above n. 9, at 464 no. 2; E. JAYME, *Ein Internationales Privatrecht für Europa*, Heidelberg: Decker & Müller, 1991, p. 8 ff. For an opposing view, see, e.g., DROBNIG, above n. 47, at 123.

[57] Notably by LEQUETTE, above n. 35, at 2206; LEGRAND, above n. 40, at 780 ff; CORNU, above n. 41, at 351 ff; MALINVAUD, above n. 41, at 2547 ff.

[58] J. CARBONNIER, "Le Code civil", in P. Nora, *Les lieux de mémoire, t. 1: La Nation*, Paris: Gallimard, 1997, p. 1345; see also J. CARBONNIER, *Droit civil: Introduction*, Paris: Presses Universitaires de France, 26th edn, 1999, no. 82: "dans une société dont le droit public avait changé de constitution dix fois en cent cinquante ans, il était bon de maintenir à la constitution civile – la véritable – cette légitimité qu'assure, *more britannico*, la continuité des formes" ("In a society where public law had changed form ten times in one hundred and fifty years, it was good to maintain the legitimacy of the civil constitution – the real constitution – as it ensured the continuity of form").

[59] LEQUETTE, above n. 35, at 2206; MALINVAUD, above n. 41, at 2547.

[60] H. COLLINS, "Editorial: The Future of European Private Law: An Introduction", (2004) *E.L.Rev.* 649: "What is being considered is a code of contract law, broadly conceived, perhaps as a first step to a wider codification of private law. [...] This proposal is contemplating what would amount to a kind of mass destruction, that is destruction of the national private law traditions of every Member State and their replacement with uniform laws"; *id.*, "European Private Law and Cultural Identity of States" (1995) *ERPL* 353–65, see, e.g., p. 362: "[I]t is a mistake to regard the law as an autonomous institution, which can be reformed and reconstructed merely by reference to rational choice. It is connected inextricably both to moral values in the community and to economic institutional arrangements". On "Cultural

The key to a future European solution is to take into account these cultural aspects and concerns, as well as the fact that some of the national contract law systems are held in such high esteem in their countries. A system of coexistence avoids the possibility of losing rules of national law, such as English contract law or the contract rules of the French *Code civil* that have influenced entire legal families.[61] It is clear that the traditional legal families do not play the same role today as they did in the 19th and 20th centuries. However, English contract law and the contract law of the French *Code civil* have always had a strong influence outside of Europe. The civil law of these countries remains an important link, bringing together the legal orders that make up the legal families.[62] Completely replacing an essential part of the law with a European contract code runs the risk of severing the ties between the 'mother' legal system and the other members of the legal family. Responses to the Commission's Communication of 2001 from English lawyers show their reluctance to adopting a mandatory EU instrument and demonstrate fears that such a move would decrease the importance of the common law in the world.[63] Adopting a system where the codes coexist takes into account these concerns, whilst at the same time encouraging the search for modern solutions by pursuing the European contract code which will most probably increase the influence of Europe outside its borders once again.[64]

The very character of European law – and of Europe itself – serves as another argument in favour of coexistence. It is diversity that makes Europe what it is; it is the differences, the tolerance and the appreciation of Europe's diversity that brings the citizens of Europe together.[65] If a European contract code were to replace the existing case law and codes for cross-border contracts *and* for purely internal contracts, the diversity and plurality of legal discourse in Europe would be lost.[66] This could have an ossifying effect and would risk leading to rigidity, a lack of choice and even a lack of inspiration.[67] Like in other domains, when it comes to law, diversity is a source of wealth, of inspiration. Preserving this richness is yet another argument in favour of a system of coexistence and diversity.

Diversity" see also S. WEATHERILL, "Why Object to the Harmonization of Private Law by the EC?", (2004) *ERPL* 633 at 647 ff and at 658 ff.

[61] In relation to the influence of the French *Code civil* in the world, see, e.g., R. DAVID and C. JAUFFRET-SPINOSI, *Les grands systèmes de droit contemporains*, Paris: Dalloz, 11th edn, 2002, nos 55 ff.

[62] On this point, see, e.g., MALINVAUD, above n. 41, at 2548.

[63] Society of Public Teachers of Law in Great Britain and Northern Ireland, *Response to Communication from the European Commission on European Contract Law* Com (2001) 398 final; SIR ROY GOODE, *Communication on European Contract Law*; Law Society of England and Wales, *Communication on European Contract Law: A position paper on behalf of the Law Reform Committee of the General Bar Council of England & Wales*. All responses are available on the European Commission's website, at: http://ec.europa.eu/consumers/cons_int/safe_shop/ fair_bus_pract/cont_law/comments/index_en.htm (last consulted 1 February 2008). The last response raises concerns about a mandatory scheme of harmonisation having a detrimental effect on the "export" of English law, i.e. the choice of English law by contracting parties world-wide, and the economic ramifications.

[64] On this point, see, e.g., WITZ, above n. 26, at 82.

[65] MALAURIE, above n. 40, at 283 ff, no 12.

[66] LEGRAND, above n. 40, at 779, eg 807, 812: "Pluralisme ou monotonie? Différence ou ennui? Europe authentique ou synthétique?".

[67] LEQUETTE, above n. 35, at 2204 ff no 5; MALAURIE, above n. 40, at 281 ff, e.g., nos 9, 11, 16, 17; see also FAUVARQUE-COSSON, above n. 9, at 472.

Philippe Malaurie wrote, and rightly so, that *"l'Europe [...] uniforme [...] aurait perdu son âme"* ("a uniform Europe would be a soulless Europe").[68]

The effect of surprise that served to support arguments in favour of introducing a European contract code applies only when dealing with cross-border contracts.[69] On a national level, the existing codes have proved themselves, and it seems difficult to justify subjecting purely internal cases to a European regime.

If diversity of private law is not efficiently coordinated in transboundary situations, it is conducive to division, complications and, on a European scale, constitutes a weakness. The challenge today is thus to rationalise the diversity of European private law. Having national contract laws coexisting with a European contract code would be a way of achieving this aim. This solution would let the diversity of laws live on whilst resolving the problem of surprise and of legal uncertainty in cross-border relations.[70]

Coexisting systems would also allow for continued development of the law and the "testing" of or experimentation with new solutions in different countries, and would foster the famous "laboratory effect" that is so frequently and quite rightly described as a great strength of private law in the United States of America.[71]

A European contract code, coexisting with national contract laws, would only have a chance of success if it was held in the same regard as the respective national systems in the system of legal education. It can be envisaged that national contract law and the European code would be taught in the same course, a course that would not concentrate solely on a national law but instead look at several systems.[72] Teaching young lawyers both systems of contract law at the same time and in the same core module on contracts would not be a weakness, it would be an advantage of having a dualist system: from the outset, lawyers would learn that there is rarely only one possible solution to a legal problem. They would learn that several solutions can exist or coexist and that, where appropriate, a choice between them is made. Young lawyers would thus be introduced to the comparative method early on in their legal training. Just as being bilingual can sometimes lead to a better understanding of cultural differences, being conversant with two legal systems can lead to a better understanding of the law.[73] *"La différence [...] contribue à un meilleur entendement du droit"* ("Difference [...] contributes to a better understanding of the law").[74]

---

[68] MALAURIE, above n. 40, at 284 no 12; see, for "pluralisme culturel" as well as for pluralism in the "culture juridique européenne": FAUVARQUE-COSSON, above n. 9, at 473 ff.

[69] In purely internal cases, parties are taken to know their national law.

[70] For the relationship of an optional instrument with private international law, see STAUDENMAYER's inspiring article, above n. 4, at 101 ff.

[71] MALAURIE, above n. 40, at 285, no 15; LEQUETTE, above n. 35, at 2204; MALINVAUD, above n. 41, at 2549; on contract law in the USA see the excellent article of M. EISENBERG, "Why is American Contract Law so Uniform – National Law in the United States", in H. Weyers (ed.), *Europäisches Vertragsrecht*, Baden-Baden: Nomos, 1997, 23–43 (excerpts above, **Case 4, III.4.**).

[72] A European contract code should therefore occupy a very different place in the curriculum at European universities than that of the CISG today. One of the main reasons for which parties exclude the CISG and do not choose the UNIDROIT or Lando Principles to be applicable to their contract is ignorance. Contrast with, e.g., FAUVARQUE-COSSON, above n. 9, at 479 no 39.

[73] LEGRAND, above n. 40, at 805.

[74] *Ibid.*, at 806.

The coexistence of the systems would have a constructive effect on the existing national laws as they would be in competition with the new European contract code.[75] Their legitimacy would be regularly called into question, which could serve to motivate lawyers to find even better solutions.[76]

The price to be paid for having a system of coexistence would, it seems, be easily outweighed by the enormous benefits such a system would bring.

(c)   What might the next steps be in the development of a European contract law?

(i)   The Principles of European Contract Law, like the UNIDROIT Principles of International Commercial Contracts, present convincing proposals for a general part of a common European law of contract. The high quality of these Principles is still undisputed today, over a decade after they were first presented. The European Principles and the UNIDROIT Principles have become a source of inspiration and a point of reference for many national legislators; the UNIDROIT Principles have also become a source of inspiration for an increasing amount of international case law.

Proposals for common European rules for specific contracts are included in the Draft Common Frame of Reference. These proposals need to be discussed throughout Europe. They need to be critically analysed and, where necessary, improved. The development in the field of European contract law is currently proceeding with breathtaking speed. One of the tasks now is to make sure that the high quality which is one of the key features of the Principles of European Contract Law and of the UNIDROIT Principles is maintained.

(ii) For the European contract code to be applicable to consumer contracts, it must include rules relating to consumer law corresponding to the current European and national protection level.[77] Principles of an *acquis* of European consumer contract law have recently been published by the Research Group on EC Private Law ('Acquis Group') and are also part of the Draft Common Frame of Reference, published by the Study Group on a European Civil Code and the 'Acquis Group' in 2009. Comments prepared by these groups will follow in 2009. These proposals also need to be carefully analysed, discussed throughout Europe and, where necessary, improved.

---

[75] See Kornet, above n. 8, at 679: "One virtue of legal diversity that was highlighted by a number of speakers throughout the seminar, was that it stimulates innovation, and facilitates a learning process for lawmakers"; Fauvarque-Cosson, above n. 9, at 472, no 24 : "La compétition entre les lois incite, mieux que l'unité, à la modernité" ("Competition between laws, more so than unity, prompts modernity").

[76] E.g. at the Law School of the University of Geneva, students are taught the Swiss law of obligations and introduced to the CISG in the same (core) module of their degree. Young lawyers benefit from this approach, developing an open mind and quickly begin to compare the two systems, taking full advantage of the possibility to comment critically on the national system.

[77] See Staudenmayer, above n. 4, at 103–04: "The inclusion of mandatory consumer protection provisions into the optional instrument would mean that [businesses] have only to respect these provisions, but not any more 25 different sets of national mandatory provisions. [...] Businesses could therefore use one single contract in order to market their goods or services, which would no longer have to be adapted to different national mandatory provisions. This would mean a considerable reduction of transaction costs for retail business and industry".

(iii) Law schools could support this process by teaching in the same core module on contract law not only the law of obligations in force in the country in which the university is located but also the CISG, the Principles of European Contract Law or – once a final version has been presented by the Commission – the CFR.

CONCLUSION

In purely domestic cases, the national contract law systems have proved their worth. For cases that involve more than one country, there is, however, an increasing need for a European contract code.

The *coexistence* of national contract law systems and a European contract code would solve the problem of unpleasant surprises arising in transboundary situations; it would significantly enrich the European legal landscape and it would lead to a situation of healthy competition between the national systems and the European code.

Consequently, Europe does not have to make a choice between the traditional domestic contract law systems and a new contract code. Europe is in the fortunate position to be able to have both: the existing national codes and case law systems for internal cases *and* a European code, the product of an exercise in comparative law, for cross-border situations and for internal situations where the parties have chosen it as the applicable law.

V.   Further reading

For a favourable account of the possibility of adopting a more comprehensive European legislation in the field of contract law, see for example:

In English

CHRISTIAN VON BAR, "From Principles to Codification: Prospects for European Private Law", 8 *Columbia Journal of European Law* (2002), 379–88.

STEFAN GRUNDMANN AND JULES STUYCK (eds), *An Academic Green Paper on European Contract Law* (The Hague: Kluwer Law International, 2002) (with 26 contributions on issues of European contract law and its harmonisation).

OLE LANDO, "Optional or Mandatory Europeanisation of Contract Law", 8 *ERPL* (2000), 59–69.

OLE LANDO, "Does the European Union need a Civil Code", *RIW* 2003, 1–2.

In French

BÉNÉDICTE FAUVARQUE-COSSON, "Faut-il un Code civil européen?", *Revue trimestrielle de droit civil* 2002, 463–80.

CLAUDE WITZ, "Plaidoyer pour un code européen des obligations", *Recueil Dalloz* 2000, Chroniques, Doctrine, pp. 79–83.

In German

CHRISTIAN VON BAR, "Die Study Group on a European Civil Code", in: P. Gottwald *et al.* (eds), *Festschrift für Dieter Henrich zum 70. Geburtstag*, Bielefeld: Gieseking 2000, 1–11.

JÜRGEN BASEDOW, "Das BGB im künftigen europäischen Privatrecht: Der hybride Kodex", *AcP* 200 (2000), 445–92.

JÜRGEN BASEDOW, "Ein optionales Europäisches Vertragsgesetz – opt-in, opt-out, wozu überhaupt?", 1 *ZEuP* 2004, 1–4.

ULRICH DROBNIG, "Europäisches Zivilgesetzbuch – Gründe und Grundgedanken", in Dieter Martiny and Normann Witzleb (eds), *Auf dem Weg zu einem Europäischen Zivilgesetzbuch*, Berlin: Springer, 1999, 109–23.

STEFAN GRUNDMANN, "Der optionale Europäische Kodex auf der Grundlage des Acquis Communautaire – Eckpunkte und Tendenzen", in Heinz-Peter Mansel *et al.* (eds), *Festschrift für Erik Jayme: Band I*, München: Sellier 2004, 125–75.

HANS-JÜRGEN SONNENBERGER, "Der Ruf unserer Zeit nach einer europäischen Ordnung des Zivilrechts", *Juristen-Zeitung (JZ)* 1998, 982–91.

DIRK STAUDENMAYER, "Ein optionelles Instrument im Europäischen Vertragsrecht", *ZEuP* 2003, 828–46.

For a critical account of the possibility of adopting comprehensive European private law, see for example:

In English

PIERRE LEGRAND, "A Diabolical Idea", in Arthur Hartkamp *et al.* (eds), *Towards a European Civil Code*, 3rd edn, Nijmegen: Kluwer Law International, 2004, Ch. 14, 245–72.
PIERRE LEGRAND, "Against a European Civil Code", (1997) 60 *Modern Law Review* (1997), 44–63.
BASIL MARKESINIS, "Why a Code is not the best way to advance the cause of European legal unity", 5 *ERPL* 1997, 519–24.

In French

GÉRARD CORNU, "Un code civil n'est pas un instrument communautaire", *Recueil Dalloz (D.)* 2002, Chroniques, Doctrine, 351–52.
PIERRE LEGRAND, "Sens et non-sens d'un Code civil européen", *Revue internationale de droit comparé* 1996, 779–812.
YVES LEQUETTE, "Quelques remarques à propos du projet du code civil européen de M. von Bar", *Recueil Dalloz (D.)* 2002, Chroniques, Doctrine, 2202–14.
PHILIPPE MALAURIE, "Le code civil européen des obligations et des contrats – Une question toujours ouverte." Colloque de Leuven (Belgique), *Juris-Classeur Périodique (JCP) La Semaine Juridique* 2002, Doctrine, 281–85.

On the Common Frame of Reference (CFR):

CHRISTIAN VON BAR, "Coverage and Structure of the Academic Common Frame of Reference", 3 *ERCL* (2007) 350–61.
HUGH BEALE, "The Future of the Common Frame of Reference", 3 *ERCL* (2007) 257–76.
ANGELIKA FUCHS (ed.), "A Common Frame of Reference – How should it be filled?", *ERA-Forum* 2003, 99–145.
WALTER VAN GERVEN, "A Common Framework of Reverence and Teaching", *European Journal of Legal Education* (2004), 1–15.
MEGLENA KUNEVA, "Introduction [to the project of a Common Frame of Reference]", 3 *ERCL* (2007) 239–44.
OLE LANDO, "The Structure and the Legal Values of the Common Frame of Reference (CFR)", 3 *ERCL* (2007) 245–56.
EWA LETOWSKA and ANETA WIEWIOROWSKA-DOMAGALSKA, "The Common Frame of Reference – The Perspective of a new Member State", 3 *ERCL* (2007) 277–94.
UGO MATTEI, "Basics First Please! A Critique of Some Recent Priorities shown by the Commission's Action Plan", in Arthur Hartkamp *et al.* (eds), *Towards a European Civil Code*, 3rd edn, Nijmegen: Kluwer Law International, 2004, Ch. 16, 297–304.
MARIEKE ODERKERK, "The CFR and the Method(s) of Comparative Legal Research", 3 *ERCL* (2007) 315–31.
HANS SCHULTE-NÖLKE, "EC Law and the Formation of Contract – from the Common Frame of Reference to the 'Blue Button'", 3 *ERCL* (2007) 332–49.

Index of provisions of codes and principles cited

Art. 3.10   145
Art. 6.2.1   370
Art. 6.2.2   370
Art. 6.2.3   370
Art. 7.1.1   312
Art. 7.1.7   312
Art. 7.2.2   258
Art. 7.2.4   261
Art. 7.4.1   312
Art. 7.4.2   312
Art. 7.4.4   312
*Study Group on a European Civil Code
and Research Group on EC Private Law
(Acquis Group): Draft Common Frame of
Reference*
  II, Art. 1:102(1)   140
  II, Art. 1:106   140
  II, Art. 4:101   140
  II, Art. 4:102   141
  II, Art. 4:201   89
  II, Art. 4:202   186

II, Art. 7:101(1)   141
II, Art. 7:201   141
II, Art. 7:204   141
II, Art. 7:205   142
II, Art. 7:206   142
II, Art. 7:207   142
II, Art. 7:301   142
II, Art. 7:302   142
III, Art. 1:110   369
III, Art. 3:101   311
III, Art. 3:102   311
III, Art. 3:104   311
III, Art. 3:302   263
III, Art. 3:701   311
III, Art. 3:702   312
III, Art. 3:703   312
*Academy of European Private Lawyers,
European Contract Code, Draft*
  Art. 1   143
  Art. 2(1)   143
  Art. 13   89

Subject index